D1526149

T.E. LAWRENCE:
A BIBLIOGRAPHY

T.E. LAWRENCE: A BIBLIOGRAPHY

Philip M. O'Brien

G.K. HALL & CO.
70 LINCOLN STREET, BOSTON, MASS.

First published by St. Paul's Bibliographies,
West End House, 1 Step Terrace, Winchester, UK,
in 1988;
published in the United States of America and Canada
by G.K. Hall & Co.,
70 Lincoln Street, Boston, Massachusetts 02111,
in 1988

for
AE

Library of Congress Cataloging in Publication Data

O'Brien, Philip M., 1940–
T.E. Lawrence: a bibliography
Includes index.
1. Lawrence, T.E. (Thomas Edward), 1888–1935
– Bibliography
I. Title
Z8491.5.027   1987
016.9404'15'0924   87–11993 [D568.4.L45]

ISBN 0-8161-8945-5

© Philip M. O'Brien 1988

Publication of this comprehensive bibliography
was facilitated by the generosity of Mr Edwards Metcalf.
He was motivated by the desire for as complete a record of
T.E. Lawrence as possible to be assembled and made available
for scholars. This has been a seven-year joint project
by Mr Metcalf and the compiler.

Prepared for press by Celliwic Maid/Ivory Head Press,
Sturminster Newton, Dorset,
and printed in Great Britain
at the University Printing House, Oxford

CONTENTS

Illustrations   *vi*

Foreword   *vii*

Preface   *ix*

Author's note   *xiii*

Abbreviations   *xiv*

PART 1   THE LAWRENCE CANON

A   Books by T.E. Lawrence, Prefaces, Introductions, Translations, etc.   3

B   Periodical articles by T.E. Lawrence   220

C   Newspaper articles by T.E. Lawrence   224

D   Incidental works containing writings of T.E. Lawrence   226

PART 2   BIOGRAPHY AND CRITICISM

E   Books about T.E. Lawrence   231

F   Incidental books containing chapters and references to
    T.E. Lawrence   471

G   Periodical articles about T.E. Lawrence   548

H   Newspaper articles about T.E. Lawrence   614

Index   *661*

ILLUSTRATIONS

Plate 1 *Carchemish:* the report of the archaeological work in which T.E. Lawrence was involved, 1911–1914 *(by kind permission of Maggs Brothers).*

Plate 2 *Arab Bulletin* of 1916–18 issued by the Intelligence Bureau in Cairo.

Plate 3 *Catalogue of an Exhibition of Arab Portraits by Kennington (by kind permission of the Bodleian Library).*

Plate 4 *Seven Pillars,* 1919–20: Title page of the 1922 'Oxford' edition.

Plate 5 Four Corvinus Press books written by T.E. Lawrence.

Plate 6 *The Odyssey:* 1932 edition of Lawrence's translation.

Plate 7 *The Mint:* Title page of 1936 U.S. edition.

Plate 8 Two of the five Golden Cockerel books by T.E. Lawrence *(by kind permission of Maggs Brothers).*

Plate 9 *Steel Chariots:* war memoirs involving the Arab campaign in August 1917) *by kind permission of Maggs Brothers); First 5 Years:* Right: leaflet by 18th Finchley Scout Group.

Plate 10 Publication of an address by Lord Halifax at Lawrence's memorial service.

Plate 11 *Emir Dynamit:* a German boys' work about Lawrence published in 1931.

Plate 12 *Lawrence av Arabien* and *Glaube der Wüste;* two European works on Lawrence.

Plate 13 *Lawrence Il Re Senza Corona;* an original Italian work on Lawrence *(by kind permission of the Houghton Library, Harvard University).*

Plate 14 One of two original works on Lawrence published in Japanese.

Plate 15 *Casus Lavrens:* a vehemently anti-Lawrence work published in Turkey in 1950.

Plate 16 *Lawrence ve Arap Isyani* another Turkish work, published in 1965, denouncing T.E. Lawrence.

FOREWORD

The Study of T.E. Lawrence, the man, is only now beginning because his attributes, versatility and contributions to society are at last being fully appreciated. For too long he has been presented in the media as just a dashing soldier of fortune.

A closer look at T.E. Lawrence reveals a fascinating man, a polymath; he was an acknowledged authority on the history of the Crusades, military history and archaeology, and an expert in guerilla warfare who was well-versed in intelligence operations. He wrote poetry and essays; he translated from Greek and French; and for a time he reviewed books regularly for a weekly journal. He had a great love of books and fine printing and at one time hoped to have his own press. He could consort happily with people in all walks of life and was much respected by those who knew him.

As a lifelong collector of T.E. Lawrence's work – and frustrated by the lack of information about him – I was for ever seeking a scholar who was well informed about him and who appreciated the need for a bibliography. It took me some time before I was able to convince Dr Philip O'Brien that he should undertake this.

I hope the reader will enjoy these pages and will find them as interesting and rewarding as I did when helping Dr O'Brien to prepare them. We both hope that readers will inform us of material we have inadvertently omitted so that we may include it in the next edition.

EDWARDS H. METCALF
San Marino, California

PREFACE

'I hate bibliophiles, and did my best to throw them off the track with The S.P.; so I did not number my copies, or declare how large the edition was (the published guesses are wide of the truth) or have a standard binding, or signatures, or index, or anything posh.' (*Letters*, 328). Thus Lawrence wrote in 1927 to Edward Garnett. Submission to the bibliographer's attention has, however, become the penalty of the fame he attained.

There is no current, full-dress Lawrence bibliography, especially of the material published since the Duval bibliography, or even of some items published before its appearance. The present work is an attempt to give, in as complete a fashion as is possible, full reference to all works by and about T.E. Lawrence. The main objective is to help readers and researchers attain a better understanding and appreciation of the man who has remained a viable object of biography since the first one was published by Lowell Thomas in 1924. I have stated elsewhere that we know far more about the details of his life than of many others, but still know less of the man. His achievements on varying fronts – warfare, archaeology, authorship, translation, letter-writing, speedboat design, military reform, statesmanship – have been examined closely and have withstood scrutiny. He has been classed as the twentieth-century anti-hero, but fits that stereotype uneasily, if for no other reason than his success at most of the things to which he turned his attention.

The following bibliography is the result of six years' work. I consider myself very lucky to have had available for this project one of the finest of Lawrence collections, supplemented by my own and other collections. I also have been fortunate to have been able to visit the Kilgour collection at the Houghton Library and the collection in the Ransom Humanities Research Center at the University of Texas, Austin, and two other private collections, each of which contained unique items. I wish to state at the outset that, in spite of the material available through all these sources, the bibliography is not definitive. I expect to discover many more items in the years ahead that belong here – and this does not include those few items for which I now have references, but for which I have been unable to locate copies. In this latter category the greatest number are foreign language works. In addition there are some single sheets which might be thought by some to belong in the bibliography, and there are no doubt many periodical and newspaper articles not mentioned. Periodicals and newspapers are close to impossible to bring entirely into focus. Some critics will no doubt even be so uncharitable as to feel that listing them should not have been attempted. Yet in the interest of comprehensiveness I have included them. Only printed material has been included; films, recordings, sheet music and holograph material have been excluded. There is no doubt in my mind that a supplement will be called for in the future.

Published works about Lawrence show clearly the fascination with which he has been regarded, not only in his lifetime but in the fifty years since his untimely death. The bibliographer can aid this serious study by helping create a correct, orderly, comprehensive and thoroughly documented listing of his work. This bibliography is a response to a demonstrated need. It is intended to be of catalytic value to the meeting of that need and to nurture continued interest in the growth of that listing. It is hoped that anyone interested in T.E. Lawrence will find here the means to a more informed and selective interpretation of materials concerning his life.

It is my aim to present precise information about Lawrence's printed writings, helping eradicate the frustrations often faced by researchers through the lack of such bibliographical offering. This bibliographic effort supplements the story of Lawrence's own literary labours and of the biographical studies, and provides a work of reference for those who read and study him, and for those who gather the books, pamphlets, leaflets, journal and newspaper articles, in which material by and about him was given to the public. Considerable effort has been given to tracing the progress of Lawrence's writings through printings, and in establishing their positions in the chronology.

Aside from foreign titles not presently locatable, there is a poorly defined group of publications bearing Canadian imprints which appear in the publication records. Letters to three of the most commonly cited of these publishers brought disclaimers that the books in question were ever theirs. The conclusion that the references to Canadian imprints in CBI and BIP are merely notices of Canadian distribution of the British editions cannot be accepted completely, as at least two titles described here bear Canadian imprints. There is presently an interest in Canada to identify Canadian imprints which may reveal others, if they exist.

The locations of the major repositories of Lawrence materials are given in the *New Cambridge Bibliography* (Volume 4). One additional repository that should be noted is the Huntington Library, San Marino, California.

Content of the book

To respond to the demands of the student and collector, full bibliographical descriptions are given here of the impressions and editions of Lawrence's printed works. Some of the items are listed for the first time. Annotations have intentionally been severely curtailed. The bibliography is an attempt to give basic information to help researchers, book collectors, librarians and scholars identify the materials of the canon as well as the critical and biographical works on Lawrence. This is a guide to the literature not a substitute for it. I have sought to establish the outline of what exists up to the present. Part 1 is Lawrence's canon, including periodical and newspaper articles in a chronological arrangement for each type of material. Reprinted sections of his works follow the newspaper section. All editions of a given work stand together after the first appearance arranged, in alphabetical order of the country of origin. Part 2 is individual works about Lawrence. The two Parts are divided as follows:

Part 1

Section A The T.E. Lawrence canon: all prefaces, introductions, forewords, contributions to others' works, book reviews, blurbs for dust wrappers, prospectuses and translations, in one chronology.

Section B Contributions to periodicals, including letters published posthumously.

Section C Newspaper articles as above.

Section D Books containing reprinted sections of Lawrence's work.

Part 2

Section E Full descriptions of books about Lawrence arranged chronologically. Includes bibliographies and material related to the film *Lawrence of Arabia*.

Section F Incidental books containing references to Lawrence, alphabetical by author's name and unclassed.

Section G Periodical articles about Lawrence, including both biography and book reviews.

Section H Newspaper articles as above.

Index *Authors, titles, periodicals, newspapers, and publishers.*

Contents of the entries

The full descriptions are composed of the following elements:

Author Basic author, title, publisher, date information.

Edition Designation of edition. National origin of publication is given. No attempt has been made to report English-language editions in one sequence. American and English editions are given separate sequences. First American, First English, First German, etc., is used rather than the designation 'only edition'.

Title page description Full transcription of title page. Rules are generally not measured.

Collation Leaf measurement , followed by collation formula, number of leaves and pagination sequences. π = unsigned preliminary. x = extra unsigned gathering even where reasonable inference could be assumed.

Contents   Listing of contents with page designations. Matter on verso of title page is not transcribed; information of importance is mentioned in 'Notes'.

RT   Running titles, verso followed by recto.

Plates   Plates, maps, etc., beginning with frontispiece, indicating which pages plates follow.

Typography and paper   Signature patterns.

Text   Measurement of given number of lines of type,including ascenders and descenders,followed in parentheses by same number of lines including RT, followed by length of line on page. All given in centimetres.

Paper   Description of paper, its treatment in the edition and measurement of leaves' bulk.

Binding   Colour name followed by ISCC–NBS colour name designation, followed by transcription of binding lettering, front cover, spine, back cover; description of edges, bands, end papers.

Published at   Publisher's price, and date of publication if known.

Notes   Annotations as needed, number of copies in edition, notes on text, variants, impressions, series.

Copies   Location of copies examined are for North American locations only. This is done in order to aid the reader in America, often a difficult task in this large country. Those readers in the British Isles should expect to locate copies of most items in one of the major repositories of Lawrence material.

   Abbreviations not self-explanatory have generally been avoided. No items are included that have not been seen by the compiler except for some of the journals and newspapers. Any item given full description was examined in as many copies as possible. Square brackets are used throughout to enclose words, phrases, titles, page numbers and the like, not quoted from the book, pamphlets or paper being described.

AUTHOR'S NOTE

I assume complete responsibility for all errors and omissions, with recognition of the able work of my predecessors in the field of Lawrence bibliography. Where so many friends and institutions have given their assistance, it is impossible to give proper acknowledgements. But there are a few that must be recognised. At the head of the list, and without whose encouragement, verging on insistence, this bibliography would not exist, stands Mr Edwards Metcalf. Among the staff of the Huntington Library who were always courteous and pleasant, special thanks go to Mary Wright and Gene Garcia. President Mills and Dean Richard Wood of Whittier College deserve thanks for allowing me the time to pursue my research. Steve Tabachnick, Charles Grosvenor, Christopher Matheson, Adugnaw Worku and Joe Dmhowski all shared my interest and gave time, support and encouragement. They also showed me that the work was of interest to others. Dr Bruce Tovee served as a silent and gracious host while turning me loose among his books. Edward Carpenter has most kindly read the manuscript, not once but three times, combing it with diligence for my many and repeated typos. And to the many collectors to whom scholarship owes a debt and to those among them who are also scholars, much gratitude is owed. In many libraries single copies of lesser works reside and these have been made available and loaned without hesitation, helping make available this or that detail when it was found necessary to ask for verification and checking.

The bibliographical work of Maurice Larés and Jeremy Wilson on Lawrence, which was underway during the time this work was compiled, served as a valuable stimulus. Both were diligent in their pursuit of the rare and unknown. They have contributed much to the present work. In addition, Helen Lefroy's editorial assistance has been invaluable in seeing the work through to the end.

This list of acknowledgements cannot be closed without reference to my wife Christina and daughters Tara and Kirsten. Many hours spent on the work might have been otherwise unavailable except through their understanding and patience.

PHILIP M. O'BRIEN
Whittier Library, California
October 1987

ABBREVIATIONS

AC	Author's collection
ACC	Austin Community College
Bod	Bodleian Library, Oxford
BL	British Library
BPL	Boston Public Library
Cal	Private Collection in California
Can	Private Collection in Canada
CCM	Calvin College, Michigan
CPL	Cleveland Public Library
CSUS	California State University, Sacramento
DPL	Detroit Public Library
H	Harvard University
HL	Huntington Library
Ho	Honnold Library Claremont Colleges
INL	*see* NLI
LAPL	Los Angeles Public Library
LC	Library of Congress
M	University of Missouri St. Louis
NLI	National Library Iceland
NYPL	New York Public Library
PPL	Pasadena Public Library
Prl.	Preliminary leaf (leaves)
Prp.	Preliminary page(s)
SJSU	San Jose State University
SUA	SUNY at Albany
UCB	University of California, Berkeley
UCLA	University of California, Los Angeles
UCI	University of California, Irvine
UCSB	University of California, Santa Barbara
UoC	University of Chicago
UT	University of Texas, Austin
UW	University of Washington

PART 1
THE LAWRENCE CANON

SECTION A

BOOKS BY T.E. LAWRENCE, PREFACES, INTRODUCTIONS, TRANSLATIONS, ETC.

Lawrence's works

This section is devoted to editions of Lawrence's writings and to books and pamphlets which he edited or compiled; also books with introductions and prefatory letters by him. Included are leaflets, even when such printings are not first separate printings; also programmes, menus and the like, and a few items of such importance as to merit inclusion, because they require detailed description or are so commonly listed as Lawrence items that they would be missed by those who may consult this book. Complete consistency is not attempted. Numerous items, even of minor importance, are included for the sake of the record. Items falling in this category are most commonly prospectuses of the works included.

The arrangement of entries in this section is chronological under the year of first publication. No attempt has been made to determine in every case the exact date of publication, although where this is known it is given. Prospectuses follow the entry for the book they advertise, as do all subsequent editions. Following the English and/or American editions, other-language editions are arranged in alphabetical order of the country of origin. For all full descriptive entries, line endings are indicated by a vertical slash, | ; title page and binding lettering are transcribed in the same manner. No attempt has been made to distinguish between large and small capitals. Collation description is standard. When the verso of the last leaf and subsequent blank leaves are blank, these have been indicated as a separate paging sequence in square brackets. The peculiarities of signatures have been described, although rarely has any suggestion been offered to explain these irregularities.

The writings of T.E. Lawrence fall into four chronological segments. While these groupings are not without some minor problems they are:

1 A period in which his 'professional' work was written: archaeology and military science, 1914–1919.

2 The literary period in which he published his best known work including *Seven Pillars of Wisdom* and *The Mint*, 1921–1935.

3 The 'literary remains' era, 1936–1954, during which his literary executors published much of his writing posthumously.

4 A period of assessment which began in 1955 and continues to the present.

List of Lawrence's works

1914 *Carchemish*
       The Wilderness of Zin
       Military Report on the Sinai Peninsula, 1914
1915 *Handbook of the Turkish Army*
1916–1918 *Arab Bulletin*
1919 *A Brief Record of the Advance of the Egyptian Expeditionary Force*
1921 *Travels in Arabia Deserta*
       Catalogue of An Exhibition
       Report on Middle East Conference
1922 *Seven Pillars of Wisdom*
1924 *The Twilight of the Gods*
       The Forest Giant
1927 *An Album of Illustrations to Colonel T.E. Lawrence's Seven
             Pillars of Wisdom*
       Catalogue of an Exhibition
       Revolt in the Desert
1928 *The Imperial Camel Corps With Colonel Lawrence*
1930 Prospectus for *Her Privates We*
1932 *The Odyssey*
       Arabia Felix
       The Two Hundred Class Royal Air Force Seaplane Tender
       No Decency Left
1933 *Letters From T.E. Shaw to Bruce Rogers*
1935 *Announcement Card to Correspondents*
       Then and Now
       River Niger
1936 *More Letters From T.E. Shaw to Bruce Rogers*
       The Mint
       Crusader Castles
       A Letter From T.E. Lawrence to His Mother
       Letters From T.E. Shaw to Viscount Carlow
1937 *Diary of T.E. Lawrence MCMXI*
       Two Arabic Folk Tales
       An Essay on Flecker
       Faisals Aufgebot
1938 *The Letters of T.E. Lawrence*
       T.E. Lawrence to His Biographers
1939 *Eight Letters From T.E. Lawrence*
       Oriental Assembly

1939   *Secret Despatches From Arabia*
1940   *Men in Print*
       Selections From Seven Pillars of Wisdom
1941   *Selected Letters of T.E. Lawrence*
1942   *Shaw-Ede*
       T.E. Lawrence av Arabien
1951   *The Essential T.E. Lawrence*
       Der Glaube der Wüste
1954   *The Home Letters of T.E. Lawrence and His Brothers*
1955   *Leben Ohne Legende*
1959   *From a Letter of T.E. Lawrence*
1960   Stéphane *T.E. Lawrence*
1965   *To S.A.*
       The Voyages of Ulysses
1968   *Evolution of a Revolt*
1971   *Minorities*
1975   *Five Hitherto Unpublished Letters*
1977   *The Suppressed Introductory Chapter*

1914

Carchemish

From 1911 to 1914 Lawrence was employed by the British Museum at an archaeological dig in northern Syria. The site, on the Tigris, was known as Carchemish, a major Hittite centre. D.G. Hogarth, Lawrence's mentor, was instrumental in obtaining the position for Lawrence who worked along with C. Leonard Woolley and P.L.O. Guy. The results of the work done at this site were reported in this three-volume work. Lawrence wrote text only for the first volume (1914), but his photos and notes are included in all three volumes (1921, 1952).

The three summers Lawrence spent here were very influential in his later activities in the Near East. During this time he met Dahoum, the 'S.A.' of the *Seven Pillars of Wisdom* dedicatory poem, the person Lawrence claimed to be the well-spring for his efforts on behalf of Arab liberation from the rule of Turkey.

A001 D.G. HOGARTH, Carchemish, British Museum, 1914

First English Edition

CARCHEMISH | REPORT ON THE EXCAVATIONS AT DJERABIS | ON BEHALF OF THE BRITISH MUSEUM | CONDUCTED BY | C. LEONARD WOOLLEY, M.A. | AND | T.E. LAWRENCE, B.A. | PART I | INTRODUCTORY | BY | D.G. HOGARTH, M.A., F.B.A. | PRINTED BY ORDER OF THE TRUSTEES | *SOLD AT THE BRITISH MUSEUM* | AND BY MESSRS. LONGMANS AND CO., 39 PATERNOSTER ROW | MR. BERNARD QUARITCH, 11 GRAFTON STREET, NEW BOND STREET, W. | MESSRS. ASHER AND CO., 14 BEDFORD STREET, COVENT GARDEN | AND MR. HUMPHREY MILFORD, OXFORD UNIVERSITY PRESS, AMEN CORNER, LONDON | 1914

Collation 32 × 25.5 cm: [A]^2 B–E^4, 18 leaves plus 27 plates, pp.[i]–iv, [1]–29, [1–3], plate A 1–11, B 1–16.

Contents Prp.[i] title page, [ii] printer's credit, [iii]–iv preface, pp.[1]–25 text, [26] blank, [27]–29 list of plates, [1–2] maps, [3] blank, plate A 1–11, B 1–16.

RT On both verso and recto [according to chapter].

Plates see Collation.

Typography and paper $ 1 signed B.

Text 20 lines, 10.4 (10.8) × 17.4 cm.

Paper White, wove, unwatermarked, all edges trimmed, sheets bulk 8 mm.

Binding Grey paper covered boards 109 l.g. OL. On front cover: [same as title page]. On spine: [running up] BRITISH MUSEUM, CARCHEMISH; PART I – HOGARTH.

Notes Another issue, second impression 1969, same as above with following differences: [below author line on title page] PUBLISHED BY | THE TRUSTEES OF THE BRITISH MUSEUM; [Collation]: 31 × 25 cm, [A]^4 B–E^4 [F–M]^4, 48 leaves, pp.[i–vii], viii, [1], 2–29, [1–3], 27 plates; [Contents]: Prp.[i] bastard title, [ii–iii] blank, [iv] frontis., [v] title page, [vi] copyright statement, SBN, issue statement, printer's credit, [vii]–viii preface, 27 plates, A 1–11, B 1–16 [these are printed on recto of leaves, verso blank]; [Paper]: heavier, smooth; [Binding]: dark blue buckram 183 d. Blue. On spine only [running down, gilt] CARCHEMISH PART I BY D.G. HOGARTH [across at foot] 1969.
Lawrence's notes and photos used in all three volumes.

Copies AC, Cal, H, UT.

A002   C. LEONARD WOOLLEY, Carchemish, British Museum, 1921

First English Edition

CARCHEMISH | REPORT ON THE EXCAVATION AT JERABLUS | ON BEHALF OF THE BRITISH MUSEUM | CONDUCTED BY | C. LEONARD WOOLLEY, M.A. | WITH | T.E. LAWRENCE, B.A., AND P.L.O. GUY | PART II | THE TOWN DEFENCES | BY | C.L. WOOLLEY | PRINTED BY ORDER OF THE TRUSTEES | *SOLD AT THE BRITISH MUSEUM* | AND BY MESSRS. LONGMANS & CO., 39 PATERNOSTER ROW | MR. BERNARD QUARITCH, 11 GRAFTON STREET, NEW BOND STREET, W. | AND MR. HUMPHREY MILFORD, OXFORD UNIVERSITY PRESS, AMEN CORNER, LONDON | 1921

Collation   32 × 25 cm: $[A]^6 F-U^4 X^2$, 68 leaves, 57 plates, pp.[i–iii], iv–xii, [33]–156, [57 leaves of plates].

Contents   Fold-out frontis., [plate 2], Prp.[i] title page, [ii] printer's credit, [iii]–iv preface, [v] contents, [vi]–xii list of plates, pp.[1]–156 text, 57 plates, some with printed leaves before plates, some fold-out, all b/w photos.

RT   On verso CARCHEMISH. On recto [according to chapter].

Plates   See Collation.

Typography and paper $ 1, 2 signed F, F2.

Text   20 lines, 10.5 (10.8) × 17.3 cm.

Paper   White, wove, unwatermarked, all edges trimmed, sheets bulk 1.5 cm.

Binding   Grey paper covered boards 109 l. g. Ol. On front cover: [same as title page]. On spine: [running up] BRITISH MUSEUM. CARCHEMISH: PART II WOOLLEY.

Notes   Second impression 1969 as above with following differences: [below author line on title page] PUBLISHED BY | THE TRUSTEES OF THE BRITISH MUSEUM; [Collation]: 31 × 25 cm, $[A]-S^4$, [plates in fours with many fold-out plates tipped in], [i–v], vi–xvi, [33]–156, plates 3–28, A 12–18, B 18–32; [Contents]: Prp.[i] bastard title, [ii] blank, [iii] title page, [iv] copyright statement, SBN, issue statement, printer's credit, [v]–vi preface, [vii] reprint preface, [viii] blank, [ix] contents, [x]–xvi list of plates, pp.[33]–156 text, plates 3–28, A 12–18, B 18–32; [Binding]: dark blue buckram 183 d. Blue. On spine only [running down, gilt] CARCHEMISH PART II BY C.L. WOOLLEY [across at foot] 1969.
   Many of the photos were taken by Lawrence.

Copies   AC, Cal, H.

A003 C. LEONARD WOOLLEY, Carchemish, British Museum, 1952

First English Edition

CARCHEMISH | REPORT ON THE EXCAVATIONS AT JERABLUS | ON BEHALF OF THE BRITISH MUSEUM | CONDUCTED BY | D.G. HOGARTH, R. CAMPBELL THOMPSON | AND C. LEONARD WOOLLEY | WITH | T.E. LAWRENCE, P.L.O. GUY, AND H. REITLINGER | PART III | THE EXCAVATIONS IN THE INNER TOWN | BY | SIR LEONARD WOOLLEY | AND | THE HITTITE INSCRIPTIONS | BY | R.D. BARNETT | PUBLISHED BY | THE TRUSTEES OF THE BRITISH MUSEUM | LONDON | 1952

Collation 31.5 × 25 cm: [A–S]^4, [1]^5 [1^4 + 1] [2–5]^4, [6]^2 [7–9]^8 [10]^6 [10^8 – 2], 131 leaves, pp.[1–8], [157]–290, plates 29–71, AA–AC A.19–A.33 B.33–B.70 [1–2].

Contents Prp.[1–2] blank, [3] title page, [4] *'Sold at* | THE BRITISH MUSEUM | *and by* | H.M. STATIONERY OFFICE, *York House, Kingsway, London, W.C.2* | CAMBRIDGE UNIVERSITY PRESS, *200 Euston Road, London, N.W. I* | BERNARD QUARITCH, LTD., II *Grafton Street, London, W. I* | KEGAN PAUL, TRENCH, TRUBNER AND CO. | *43 Great Russell Street, London, W.C. I* | PRINTED IN GREAT BRITAIN | AT THE UNIVERSITY PRESS, OXFORD | BY CHARLES BATEY, PRINTER TO THE UNIVERSITY'*, [5] preface, [6] blank, [7] contents, [8] blank, [157]–268 text, [269]–285 list of plates, [286] blank, [287]–290 index, plates 29–71 on coated paper, plates AA–B.70 on uncoated paper, [1–2] blank.

RT On verso CARCHEMISH. On recto [according to chapter].

Plates See Collation.

Typography and paper $ 1 signed D.

Text 20 lines, 10.3 (10.6) × 17.3 cm.

Paper White, wove, unwatermarked, all edges trimmed, sheets bulk 1.8 cm.

Binding Grey paper covered boards 109 l. g. Ol. On front cover: [same as title page]. On spine: [running up] BRITISH MUSEUM : CARCHEMISH : PART III – WOOLLEY.

Notes T.E. Lawrence's notes and plates used in this volume as well as in two previous volumes.

Copies AC, Cal.

The Wilderness of Zin

During January and February 1914, Lawrence and Woolley, in the company of a British Army surveying detachment led by Capt. Newcombe, under the guise of an archaeological survey, mapped the Negev region of the Sinai Peninsula, then under Turkish suzerainty. The British sought updated maps for the war they felt was coming. To complete the fiction of the archaeological work, Woolley and Lawrence wrote *The Wilderness of Zin*. This is the first of Lawrence's works to appear in book form. "K. [Kitchener] (the only begetter of the survey) insisted on the Palestine Exploration Fund's bringing out its record of our archeological researching, p.d.q. as whitewash. Woolley and I had instructions to get it done instanter." (*Letters*, p.181.)

Part of the original printing was left in sheets and bound for sale at a later date, probably upon Lawrence's death. Cape in England and Scribner's in America published the book in 1936 when many of Lawrence's publications were published or reissued. This reprint contains three additional plates. Lawrence's specific contributions are identified in a preliminary note.

A004 C.LEONARD WOOLLEY & T.E. LAWRENCE, The Wilderness of Zin, Palestine Exploration Fund, 1914

First English Edition

PALESTINE EXPLORATION FUND | 1914. | [short rule] | THE WILDERNESS OF ZIN | (ARCHAEOLOGICAL REPORT) | *By* | *C. LEONARD WOOLLEY* | *and* | *T.E. LAWRENCE* | *With a Chapter on the Greek Inscriptions by M.N. Tod.* | [short rule] | PUBLISHED BY ORDER OF THE COMMITTEE | AND SOLD AT | THE OFFICES OF THE FUND, 2, HINDE STREET, MANCHESTER SQUARE, W.

Collation 27.8 × 21.3 cm: π^1 [a]–b^4 B–T^4 U^2 X ^{6} [1], 88 leaves, pp.[1–2], i–xvi, 1–158.

Contents Prp.[1] series title, [2] blank, [i] title page, [ii] printer's credit, [iii] list of members of Palestine Exploration Fund, [iv] blank, [v] dedication, [vi] prefatory note, [vii]–viii contents, [ix]–xii illustrations, [xiii]–xvi introduction, pp.[1] blank, [2] map, [3]–147 text, [148] blank, [149]–154 index, [155–158] list of Fund publications.

RT On verso THE WILDERNESS OF ZIN. On recto [according to chapter].

Plates Fold-out plan facing p.95, 37 plates on coated paper printed on one side only following p.148, numbered I–XXXVII.

Typography and paper $ 1,2 signed B b2, X x2 x3.

Text 20 lines, 10.6 (10.8) × 14.1 cm.

Paper   White, wove, unwatermarked, all edges trimmed, sheets bulk 1.5 cm.

Binding   Dark blue cloth spine 188 blackish B, grey paper covered boards 285 med Gy. On front cover: PALESTINE EXPLORATION FUND | [short rule] | ANNUAL | 1914–1915. | DOUBLE VOLUME. | [short rule] | PUBLISHED BY ORDER OF THE COMMITTEE, | AND SOLD AT | THE OFFICES OF THE FUND, 2, HINDE STREET, MANCHESTER SQUARE, W. On spine: [gilt] PALESTINE | EXPLORATION | FUND | ANNUAL | 1914–1915 | III. | [pub. device].

Published at   45s.

Notes   Lawrence's contribution cited in prefatory note, p.iii. Reissued in 1935 in variant binding: spine title lacks full stop after 1914–1915. First of Lawrence's work published in book form.

Copies   AC, Cal, UT.

A005   C.LEONARD WOOLLEY & T.E. LAWRENCE, The Wilderness of Zin, Cape, 1935

Proof copy of Second English Edition

[Outline letter, first three lines] THE | WILDERNESS | OF ZIN | *by* | C.LEONARD WOOLLEY | *and* | T.E. LAWRENCE | [pub. device] | *With a chapter on the Greek Inscriptions by* | M.N. TOD | JONATHAN CAPE | THIRTY BEDFORD SQUARE | LONDON

Collation   25.2 × 18.9 cm: [A]⁴ [A¹]⁴ [B]⁴ [B¹]⁴ C⁴ [C¹]⁴ D⁴ [D¹]⁴ E⁴ [E¹]⁴ F⁴ [F¹]⁴ G⁴ [G¹]⁴ H⁴ [H¹]⁴ I⁴ [I¹]⁴ K⁴ [K¹]⁴ L¹, plates 1–5⁸; 81 leaves, pp.1–162, 40 plates.

Contents   Pp.[1] bastard title, [2] blank, [3] title page, [4] issue statement, printer's credit, 5–6 contents, 7–10 illustrations, [11] dedication, [12] blank, 13–16 introduction, 17–20 preface, [21] blank, [22] map, 23–161 text, [162] blank, 1–40 plates.

RT   On verso THE WILDERNESS OF ZIN. On recto [according to chapter].

Plates   Forty b/w plates printed on one side only following last page of text.

Typography and paper $ 1 signed B.

Text   20 lines, 9.8 (10) × 13.6 cm.

Paper   White, wove, unwatermarked, all edges trimmed, sheets bulk 1.1 cm.

Binding   Light yellow brown paper 76 l. y Br. On front cover: THE WILDERNESS | OF ZIN | C.LEONARD WOOLLEY | T.E. LAWRENCE |

[pub. device] | Duplicate Proof for Retention | Does not contain Proof Reader's Marks. On spine [running up] THE WILDERNESS OF ZIN. On back cover: The Alden Press (Oxford) Ltd | Oxford.

Copies Cal, H.

A006   C.LEONARD WOOLLEY and T.E. LAWRENCE, The Wilderness of Zin, Cape, 1936

Second English Edition

[First three lines outline letters] THE | WILDERNESS | OF ZIN | *by* | C. LEONARD WOOLLEY | *and* | T.E. LAWRENCE | *With a chapter on the Greek Inscriptions by* | M.N. TOD | [pub. device] | *Introduction by* | SIR FREDERICK KENYON | JONATHAN CAPE | THIRTY BEDFORD SQUARE | LONDON

Collation   25 × 18.5 cm: [A] –I^8 K^{10} L–P^8 x^2, 124 leaves, pp.[1–2], [1–2], 3–161, [162], 40 plates, 163–166.

Contents   Prp.[1] bastard title, [2] blank, pp.[1] title page, [2] issue statement, printer's, papermaker's, binder's credits, 3–4 contents, 5–8 illustrations, [9] dedication, [10] blank, 11–14 introduction, 15 note, [16] blank, 17–20 T.E. Lawrence preface, [21] blank, [22] map, 23–161 text, [162] blank, 40 plates, 163–166 index.

RT   On verso THE WILDERNESS OF ZIN. On recto [according to chapter].

Plates   On coated paper, printed on one side only.

Typography and paper $ 1 signed B, K, K* [1,2].

Text   20 lines, 9.8 (9.9) × 13.6 cm.

Paper   Buff, wove, unwatermarked, top and fore edges trimmed, sheets bulk 1.8 cm.

Binding   Red brown buckram 40 s. r Br. On front cover: [gilt] THE WILDERNESS OF ZIN. On spine: [gilt] THE | WILDER- | NESS | OF ZIN | C. | LEONARD | WOOLLEY | & | T.E. | LAWRENCE | [pub. device]. T.e. brown.

Published at   18s.

Notes   Another state as above except that plates precede index and cloth is pale 13 deep Red. Contains three additional photos not present in first edition.

Copies   AC, Cal, H, UT, Ho.

A007   C. LEONARD WOOLLEY and T.E. LAWRENCE, The Wilderness of Zin, Scribner's, 1936

First American Edition

[Title outline lettering] THE | WILDERNESS | OF | ZIN | *by* | C. LEONARD WOOLLEY | *and* | T.E. LAWRENCE | *With an Introduction by* | SIR FREDERICK KENYON | *and a chapter on the Greek Inscriptions by* | M.N. TOD | NEW YORK | CHARLES SCRIBNER'S SONS | 1936

Collation   25 × 18.5 cm: [A]^8 B–I^8 K^{10} x^2, 84 leaves, pp.[1–2], [1–2], 3–166.

Contents   Prp.[1] bastard title, [2] blank, pp.[1] title page, [2] 'Printed in Great Britain', 3–4 contents, 5–8 illustrations, [9] dedication, [10] blank, 11–14 introduction, 15 note, [16] blank, 17–20 preface, [21] blank, [22] map. 23–161 text, [162] blank, 163–166 index.

RT   On verso THE WILDERNESS OF ZIN. On recto [according to chapter].

Plates   Fold-out plan facing p.111, 40 plates following p.162, L–P^8 numbered I–XL. Plates XXXVIII–XL were originally printed in text.

Typography and paper $ 1 signed H, K,K*.

Text   20 lines, 9.8 (9.9) × 13.1 cm.

Paper   White, wove, unwatermarked, all edges trimmed, sheets bulk 1.8 cm.

Binding   Red buckram 40 s. r Br. On front cover: [gilt] THE WILDERNESS OF ZIN. On spine: [gilt] THE | WILDER- | NESS | OF ZIN | C. | LEONARD | WOOLLEY | & | T.E. | LAWRENCE | SCRIBNER'S.

Published at $7.50.

Notes   As with British edition, copies are found with plates both before and after the index. Sheets printed in England. Some copies have 'Cape' at foot of spine.

Copies   AC, Cal, H.

A008   C.LEONARD WOOLLEY and T.E. LAWRENCE, Le Désert de Sin, Payot, 1937

First French Edition

BIBLIOTHÈQUE HISTORIQUE | [long rule] | C. LEONARD WOOLLEY & T.E. LAWRENCE | [short rule] | LE DÉSERT DE SIN | *INTRODUCTION DE SIR FREDERIC KENYON* | [short rule] | TRADUIT DE L'ANGLAIS PAR CHARLES MAURON | [short rule] | *Avec 59 figures, 2 cartes, 33 inscriptions grecques* | *dans le texte et 8 planches hors texte* | [pub. device] | PAYOT, PARIS |

106, BOULEVARD ST-GERMAIN | [short rule] | 1937 | *Tous droits de traduction, de reproduction et d'adaption* | *réservés pour tous pays.*

Collation   22 × 14 cm: [1]–13⁸, 104 leaves, pp.[1–7], 8–206, [2].

Contents   Pp.[1–2] blurb, [3] bastard title, [4] pub. ed, [5] title page, [6] dedication, [7]–10 introduction, [11] advertisement, [12]–16 preface, [17]–199 text, [200–204] plates, [205]–206 contents, [207] illustrations, [208] blank.

RT   On both verso and recto [according to chapter].

Plates   Four b/w plates on coated paper printed on both sides following pp.64, 96, 128, 160.

Typography and paper $ 1 signed 2.

Text   20 lines, 9.6 (10) × 10 cm.

Paper   White, wove, unwatermarked, all edges trimmed, sheets bulk 1.8 cm.

Binding   Yellow paper 89 p. Y. On front cover [within frame of single rules]: *BIBLIOTHÈQUE HISTORIQUE* | [long rule] | C.L. WOOLLEY et T.E. LAWRENCE | [short rule] | [maroon title] LE DÉSERT | DE SIN | [short rule] | *INTRODUCTION DE SIR FREDERIC KENYON* | [short rule] | [cut] | TRADUIT DE L'ANGLAIS PAR CHARLES MAURON | PAYOT, PARIS. On spine: [rule] | C.L. WOOLLEY | et T.E. LAWRENCE | [rule] | Le | Désert de Sin| 42fr. | sans majoration | [rule] | PAYOT, | PARIS | [rule] | 1937 | [rule]. On back cover [within rule frame], ads.

Published at   42 francs.

Copies   AC, H.

Military Report on the Sinai Peninsula, 1914

At the outbreak of war Lawrence tried to enlist, but was rejected because of his failure to reach the height requirement. He was able to obtain a commission with the General Staff Geographical Section. While there he worked on the production of new 1/250,000 scale maps of the Sinai Peninsula, based on material drawn largely from the *The Wilderness of Zin* survey, and compiled this report which also contains route guides. No author is named and it is not found in many collections.

A009   GREAT BRITAIN. General Staff, Geographical Section, War Office, Military Report on the Sinai Peninsula, 1914

First English Edition

[Within single rule frame] FOR OFFICIAL USE ONLY | [rule] | THIS

DOCUMENT IS THE PROPERTY | OF H.B.M. GOVERNMENT. | NOTE. | The information given in this document is | not to be communicated, either directly or | indirectly, to the Press or to any person not | holding an official position in His Majesty's | Service | [blue frame] MILITARY REPORT | ON | THE SINAI PENINSULA. | (With Notes on The Turkish Frontier Districts | and The Wadi Araba.) | [rule] | ROUTE REPORTS, WATER, &c. | [rule] | PREPARED BY THE GENERAL STAFF, WAR OFFICE. | [rule] | 1914. | [rule] | (B627) 1700 12/14 HQS 1533wo

Collation   19 × 12 cm: [1]^2 A–F^{16}, 98 leaves, prp.[1–4], pp.[1–2], 3–191, [1].

Contents   Prp.[1–2] blank, pp.[1] title page, [2] contents, 3–191 text, [1] LONDON: | PRINTED FOR HIS MAJESTY'S STATIONERY OFFICE, | BY HARRISON AND SONS, | PRINTERS IN ORDINARY TO HIS MAJESTY. | (B627) 1700 12/14 1533wo, [1–2] blank.

Typography and paper $ 1–4 signed B–1, B–2, B–3, B–4.

Text   Varies.

Paper   White, wove, unwatermarked, all edges trimmed, sheets bulk 8 mm.

Binding   Tan paper covers 76 l. y Br. On front cover [same as title page]. Fold map in cloth-reinforced pocket inside rear cover [map 34.5 × 42.5 cm].

Copies   Cal.

1915

Handbook of the Turkish Army

As part of his responsibilities as an intelligence officer Lawrence worked closely with Philip Graves in repeatedly updating the *Handbook of the Turkish Army*, sixth edition, the first having been published in 1892. It provides, in brief, a description of the Turkish military as it then existed.

There is no indication of Lawrence's contribution to the work. In *The Letters of T.E. Lawrence*, p.203n, Liddell Hart states: "Philip Graves and L. got out Handbook of Turkish Army; may have been a dozen editions; L. supervised the printing of them. L. and Graves spent most of their time among the Turkish prisoners and came to know more about the Turkish Army than the Turks themselves."

No copies of the 'First Provisional Edition' have been located; it may vary in some details.

A009a   GREAT BRITAIN. War Office, Intelligence Division. Handbook of the Turkish Army, Government Press, 1915

Second Provisional Edition

This Document is the property of H.B.M. Government. | [within single rule frame] FOR OFFICIAL USE ONLY. | [rule] | NOTE. | [short rule] | The information given in this book | is not to be communicated, either | directly or indirectly, to the Press, or | to any person not holding an official | position in His Majesty's Service. | [below frame] HANDBOOK | OF THE | TURKISH ARMY. | Second Provisional Edition. | MARCH 1, 1915. | [double rule] | PREPARED BY THE INTELLIGENCE DEPARTMENT, CAIRO. | *The greater part of the fresh information contained* | *in this provisional edition has been supplied by* MR. P.P. GRAVES. | [rule] | CAIRO. | GOVERNMENT PRESS. | 1915.

Collation   16.1 × 10.8 cm: π⁴ [1] – 10⁸, 84 leaves, pp.[i–iii], iv–viii, [1] – 134.

Contents   Prp.[I] title page, [II] IN 7150–1914–500, [III–VIII] contents, pp.[1] – 104 text, [105] blank, 106–134 appendices, printed on rectos only.

Plates   Following text; two coloured folded plates (25.1 × 33.8 cm and 29.6 × 24.9 cm), 12 leaves of photographs on art paper, 1 coloured drawing of an officer.

Typography and paper $ 1 signed 2.

Text   20 lines, 5.1 × 8.1 cm.

Paper   White, wove, unwatermarked, all edges trimmed with rounded fore-edges, sheets bulk 1.1 cm.

Binding   Cream-coloured paper covered boards, cream-coloured cloth spine. On front cover (printed in dark brown exactly as title page including statement within single rule frame).

Copies   National Army Museum, London.

1916

Arab Bulletin (1916–1918)

Thanks to his knowledge both of the Arabic language and of the Turkish areas of the Near East, Lawrence was soon transferred to Cairo in December 1914 , where he was attached to the Department of Intelligence. Lawrence was the first editor of the Arab Bureau's top-secret publication, the *Arab Bulletin,* and later became a contributor from the field during the Arab campaign. This irregular serial publication thus contains the first published records by Lawrence of the Arab campaign. His contributions were gathered and published later in *Secret Despatches* (1939). Copies of the *Arab Bulletin* are rare.

A010   Arab Bureau, Cairo, Arab Bulletin 1916–1918

First Edition

SECRET. | ARAB BULLETIN. | No. 1.

Collation   26.8 × 17.8 cm, nos. 1–107.

Contents   Vol. 1, 1916, parts 1–36; Vol. 2, 1917, parts 37–74; Vol. 3, 1918, parts 75–107.

Text   20 lines, 8.2 × 11.3 cm.

Paper   White, wove, unwatermarked, all edges trimmed, sheets bulk 2.8 cm (Vol. 1), 2.5 cm (Vol. 2), 1.8 cm (Vol. 3).

Binding   Binding varies.

Notes   Secret periodical on Arab affairs edited by Lawrence during much of its run. Lawrence's own contributions are as follows: Vol. 2, pp.2, 57, 74, 121, 122, 226, 240, 260, 300, 303, 307, 308, 336, 346, 397, 399, 401, 407, 415–417, 421, 473, 490; Vol.3, pp.35, 41, 49, 179, 208, 245, 263, 275, 307.
   Distribution was limited to 26 copies at first, later increased. A number of Lawrence's contributions were later published in *Secret Despatches*.

Copies   Cal, H.

A010a   Arab Bureau, Cairo, The Arab Bulletin, 1916–1918, Archive Editions, 1986

Second English Edition

THE | ARAB | BULLETIN OF THE ARAB BUREAU IN CAIRO, 1916–1918 | [rule] | *including* | Indexes for 1916, 1917 and 1918 | *and the supplementary* | Notes on the Middle East nos. 1–4, 1919–1920 | [rule] | With a new Introduction and explanatory note | by Dr. Robin Bidwell | [rule] | Volume I [II–IV] | 1916 [1917–1918] |Bulletin 1–36 [36–74] | [rule] | ARCHIVE EDITIONS | 1986

Collation   24.5 × 16 cm: Vol. 1, [1–19]^{16} [20]^8, 312 leaves, pp.[i–vi], vii–xxviii, pp.[1–4], 5–560, [1–2], [1]–23, [1] 001–009, [1]; Vol. 2, [1–18]^{16}, 280 leaves, prp.[1–4], pp.[1–2], 3–517, [1], [1–2], [1]–27, [1], 001–004, [1–2]; Vol. 3, [1–13]^{16}, 203 leaves, prp.[1–6], pp.519–526, [1–2], 9–372,

[1]−24, [1−2]; Vol. 4, [1−4]¹⁶, 69 leaves, prp.[1−6], pp.1−127, [1], 001, [1−3].

Contents Vol. 1: prp.[i] bastard title, [ii] blank, [iii] title page, [iv] issue, copyright, CIP, ISBN statements, [v] contents guide, [vi] blank, vii−xxiv introduction, xxv−xxviii brief biog. of contributors, pp.[1] half-title, [2−3] summary pages, [4] blank, 5−559 text, 560 note page, [1] section title, [2] blank, [1]−23 index, [1] blank, 001−009 explanatory notes, [1] blank. Vol.2: [1] bastard title, [2] blank, [3] title page, [4] issue, copyright, CIP, ISBN statements, pp.[1] half-title, [2] summary sheet, 3−517 text, [1] blank, [1] section title, [2] blank, [1]−27 index, [1] blank, 001−004 explanatory notes, [1−4] blank. Vol.3: prp.[1] bastard title, [2] blank, [1] title page, [2] issue, copyright, CIP, ISBN statements, pp.[1] blank, [2] summary sheet, 519−526 text, [1] section title, [2] summary sheet, 9−372 text, [1]−24 index, [1−3] explantory notes. Vol.4: prp.[1] bastard title, [2] blank, [3] title page, [4] issue, copyright, CIP, ISBN statements, [1] half-title, [2] summary sheet, pp.1−147 [1] blank, [1] section title, [2] summary sheet, [1]−127 text, [1] blank, 001 explanatory notes, [1] blank.

Text 20 lines, 8.2 × 11.3 cm.

Paper White, wove, unwatermarked, all edges trimmed, sheets bulk 3.1 cm (Vol. 1), 2.5 cm (Vol. 2), 2 cm (Vol. 3), 1.4 cm (Vol. 4).

Binding Black leather simulated cloth. On spine: [gilt] [double rule] | THE | ARAB | BULLETIN | [Double rule] | I [II] | [double rule] 1916− [1917] | [double rule] | ARCHIVE | EDITIONS | [double rule]. Red and silver head and tail bands.

Published at £595, October 1986, Collector's limited issue £1395.

Notes Lawrence contributions: Vol. 2, pp.4, 57, 74, 121−2, 161, 226, 240, 260, 300, 303, 307−8, 336, 346, 397, 399, 401, 407, 415−7, 421, 473, 490; Vol. 3, pp.35, 41, 49, 179, 208, 245, 263, 275, 307. Collector's Edition limited to 25 numbered sets.

Copies Cal.

1919

A Brief Record of the Advance of the Egyptian Expeditionary Force (1919)

This book contains the order of battle and the campaign maps for the Near Eastern front of which Lawrence's Arab campaign was a part. There are two pieces of the text written by Lawrence. This book is not always recognised as containing Lawrence's work, as the pieces are unsigned. The two pieces in question appear to have been extracted from official reports. These, along with the reports in the *Arab Bulletin* and in *The Times*, are his first published accounts of the Arab campaign.

The publisher, *The Palestine News*, was the official newspaper of the Egyptian Expeditionary Force and was edited by H. Pirie-Gordon.

A011   A Brief Record of the Advance of the Egyptian Expeditionary Force, Government Press and Survey of Egypt, 1919

First English Edition

[Royal coat of arms] | A BRIEF RECORD OF | THE ADVANCE OF THE | EGYPTIAN EXPEDITIONARY FORCE | UNDER THE COMMAND OF | GENERAL SIR EDMUND H.H. ALLENBY, G.C.B., G.C.M.G. | [short rule] | JULY 1917 TO OCTOBER 1918. | [short rule] | Compiled from Official Sources and Published by | [old English type] The Palestine News. | CAIRO | PRODUCED BY THE | GOVERNMENT PRESS AND SURVEY OF EGYPT. | 1919

Collation   29.4 × 22 cm: π^4 [1] −6^8, 60 leaves, pp.[1–6], [1]−114.

Contents   Prp.[1] title page, [2] errata list and glossary, [3–4] preface, [5– 6] contents, [1]−114 text.

RT   On verso THE ADVANCE OF THE. On recto EGYPTIAN EXPEDITIONARY FORCE.

Plates   Fifty-six plates, maps in black, blue-green and red, frontispiece. Plates have description of action for next plate on verso.

Typography and paper $ 1 signed 3.

Text   20 lines, 8.1 (8.8) × 16 cm.

Paper   White, wove, unwatermarked, all edges trimmed, sheets bulk 2.3 cm.

Binding   Buff paper covers 76 l.y Br, red cloth spine 44 d. r Br. On front cover: [same as title page]. On spine: [running up] THE ADVANCE OF THE E.E.F.

Published at   Published for Official Use, December 1918.

Notes   Sections on verso of plates facing pp.49–50, 'Sherifian Co-operation in September', and pp.51–53, 'Story of the Arab Movement', are compiled from Lawrence's notes written originally for the Arab Bureau.
   Copies printed, 16,000.
   One copy bound in sand-coloured cloth 90 gy. Y. as above with following differences: [Collation]: preface and contents leaves conjugate, half-title,

frontis., title pages single leaves. [Binding]: front cover as above. On spine: [triple rules] | [geometric cut] | [triple rules] | THE | ADVANCE | OF THE | E.E.F. | [triple rules] | [elongated geometrical cut] | [triple rules]. Frontis. has slight registration differences as Allenby's signature and the caption were a separate impression of the sheets.

Two presentation copies in red morocco with a gilt crest and ornate gilt lettering on front cover. Spine gilt with geometrical design incorporating spine lettering. All edges gilt, black watered silk end papers and blind tooled inner dentelles. One copy Allenby's, the other Pirie-Gordon's.

Copies   AC, Cal, UT.

A012   A Brief Record of the Advance of the Egyptian Expeditionary Force, HMSO, 1919

Second English Edition

[Royal coat of arms] A BRIEF RECORD OF | THE ADVANCE OF THE | EGYPTIAN EXPEDITIONARY FORCE UNDER THE COMMAND OF | GENERAL SIR EDMUND H.H. ALLENBY, G.C.B., G.C.M.G. | [short rule] | JULY 1917 TO OCTOBER 1918. | [short rule] | Compiled from Official Sources. | [short rule] | SECOND EDITION. | (THE FIRST EDITION WAS PUBLISHED BY "THE PALESTINE NEWS.") | [short rule] | LONDON: | PUBLISHED BY HIS MAJESTY'S STATIONERY OFFICE. | [rule] | To be purchased through any Bookseller or directly from | H.M. STATIONERY OFFICE at the following addresses: | IMPERIAL HOUSE, KINGSWAY, LONDON, W.C.2, AND | 28 ABINGDON STREET, LONDON, S.W.1; | 37 PETER STREET, MANCHESTER; | 1 ST. ANDREW'S CRESCENT, CARDIFF; | 23 FORTH STREET, EDINBURGH; | or from E. PONSONBY, Ltd., 116 GRAFTON STREET, DUBLIN. | [short rule] | 1919. | *Price 6/- Net.*

Collation   27.8 × 21.5 cm, [A]^8 B–G^8 H^4 [I–P]^8, 116 leaves, pp.[1–6], [1]–[114], leaves 1–56 [each with printing on verso except last].

Contents   Prp.[1] title page, [2] glossary, [3–4] preface, [5–6] contents, pp.[1]–113 text, [114] note on maps, [1–111] plates 1–56, [112] blank (plates have maps on recto and explanatory text on verso).

RT   On verso THE ADVANCE OF THE MARCH 21–22, 1918. On recto MARCH 22–29, 1918. EGYPTIAN EXPEDITIONARY FORCE.

Plates   Frontispiece of Allenby preceding prp.[1].

Typography and paper $ 1 signed, F.

Text   20 lines, 8.1 (8.5) × 15.7 cm.

Paper   White, wove, unwatermarked, all edges trimmed, sheets bulk 1.3 cm.

Binding   Grey paper covered boards 265 med. Gy, grey linen spine 266 d

Gray. On front cover [within double rule frame with rounded corners]: A Brief Record of | the Advance of the | Egyptian Expeditionary Force | July 1917 to | October 1918 | [royal coat of arms] | Compiled from Official Sources. On back cover: [lengthy colophon with addresses for places to purchase copies and prices].

Published at   6s.

Notes   Date on back cover is misprinted '1918'. Lawrence's contributions are opposite plates 49–50, 51–53. He is mentioned in text opposite plates 48 and 50.

Copies   AC, Cal.

1921

Travels in Arabia Deserta

Lawrence had long admired Charles M. Doughty's classic *Travels in Arabia Deserta*. He was instrumental in getting the second English edition published by the fledgling firm of Jonathan Cape in conjunction with the Medici Society.

Lawrence's notoriety was desired for the expensive two-volume set and he was persuaded to write his first introduction. This introduction was withdrawn in the third edition of 1923 and restored in the 1926 thin-paper edition and retained ever since both in England and the USA. It is not included in most of the abridgements with the exception of the editions of the Limited Editions Club and its affiliate, The Heritage Press. All of the non-English-language editions are either abridgements or selections.

Lawrence's wish to make *Travels in Arabia Deserta* available to a wider public at affordable prices was realised through re-publication followed by many subsequent editions. The Cape 'Definitive' edition of 1936 was published in a format matching that of 1935 *Seven Pillars of Wisdom*.

There are six large paper copies of the second English edition.

A013   CHARLES M. DOUGHTY, Travels in Arabia Deserta, Warner, Medici Society, Cape, 1921

Second English Edition

TRAVELS IN | ARABIA DESERTA | BY CHARLES M. DOUGHTY, WITH A NEW PREFACE BY THE AUTHOR, INTRODUCTION | BY T.E. LAWRENCE, FELLOW OF ALL SOULS | AND ALL ORIGINAL MAPS,

PLANS AND CUTS | [Medici Society Seal] | VOLUME I [II] | PHILIP LEE WARNER, PUBLISHER TO THE | MEDICI SOCIETY, LTD., AND JONATHAN | CAPE, LONDON: AND AT BOSTON, U.S.A. 1921

Collation 22 × 14.5 cm: Vol.I, [a]^2 b–c^8 1–39^8, 330 leaves, prp.[i–iv], v–xxxvi, pp.1–624; Vol.II, [a]^8 1–42^8 43^{10}, 354 leaves, pp.[1–2], [i–iv], v–xiv, pp.1–690 [1–2].

Contents Vol. I: prp.[i] bastard title, [ii] blank, [iii] title page, [iv] issue statement, printer's credit,[v]–xi prefaces of first two editions, [xii] correction note, [xiii]–xxxv introduction by Lawrence, [xxxvi] blank, pp.[1]–619 text, [620]–623 appendix to Vol.I, [624] blank. Vol. II: prp.[1–2] blank, [i] bastard title, [ii] blank, [iii] title page, [iv] issue statement, printer's credit, [v]–xiv contents, pp.[1]–539 text, 540–542 appendix to Vol. II, [543]–690 index and glossary of Arabic words, [1–2] blank.

Plates Vol. I, following pp.[ii], 106, 108, 112, 176, 384, 400, 404, 416, fold. maps 106, 110; Vol. II, fold. map in pocket inside rear cover.

Typography and paper $ 1,2 signed D.T. 2, 2–2.

Text 20 lines, 7.3 (7.9) × 10.1 cm.

Paper White, wove, unwatermarked, top edge trimmed, sheets bulk 3.3cm (Vol. I), 3.2 cm (Vol. II).

Binding Green cloth 151 d. gy G. On front cover: [blind stamped rules along outer edges, gilt cuts]. On spine: [double rules] | ARABIA | DESERTA | VOL. I [II] | *C.M.* | *DOUGHTY* | LEE WARNER & | JONATHAN CAPE | [double rules]. T.e. gilt. Black end papers.

Published at 9 gns, January 1921.

Notes Cape's first book, 500 copies.
   Six large paper copies of this second edition were printed in January 1921. These differ from the above in the following: [Collation]: 26.5 × 20 cm; [Plates]: 8 plates following pp.106, 108, 112, 176 fold., 384, 402, 404, 416 fold.; [Paper]: white, laid, watermarked, top edges trimmed, sheets bulk 6.5 cm (Vol. I), 7.5 cm (Vol. II); [Binding]: Tan buckram 76 l y Br., red and gold head and tail bands. Linen-backed coloured map in pocket inside rear cover of Vol. II. These six copies were distributed as follows: 1 Doughty, 2 Lawrence, 3 Medici Society, 4 Jonathan Cape, 5 Emir Feisal, 6 William H. Lee Warner.
   Reprinted September 1921 (trade issue).

Copies HL, UTA.

A014   CHARLES M. DOUGHTY, Travels In Arabia Deserta, Cape, 1921

Publisher's Prospectus

'*A great travel book* | *Surely the greatest in the English language*' | TRAVELS IN | ARABIA DESERTA | by | CHARLES M. DOUGHTY | [three leaf cuts]

Collation   22.5 × 14.5 cm: single leaf printed on both sides.

Contents   Pp.[1] title, beginning of text, [2] rest of text, quotes from reviews, order form.

Paper   White, wove, unwatermarked, all edges trimmed.

Published at   Free advertising flyer.

Copies   H.

A015   CHARLES M. DOUGHTY, Travels in Arabia Deserta, Cape & Medici, 1926

Fourth English Edition

TRAVELS IN | ARABIA DESERTA | BY CHARLES M. DOUGHTY, WITH | A NEW PREFACE BY THE AUTHOR, | INTRODUCTION BY T.E. LAWRENCE, | AND ALL ORIGINAL MAPS, PLANS | & ILLUSTRATIONS | THIN-PAPER EDITION IN ONE VOLUME | COMPLETE AND UNABRIDGED | JONATHAN CAPE LTD. & | THE MEDICI SOCIETY LIMITED | LONDON

Collation   22 × 14 cm: [a]^{10} b^{16} 1–40^{16} 41^{18}, (b and 40 are two gatherings of eights, one inserted within the other, the second gathering is signed b* etc., 41 is composed of 41^2 41**^{8}, each inserted within the other), pp.[i–vii], viii–lii, [1], 2–623, [3], [1], 2–690.

Contents   Prp.[i] half-title, [ii] blank, [iii] title page, [iv] issue statement, printer's credit [v] pub. note, [vi] blank, [vii]–xvi prefaces, [xvii–xxviii] introduction by T.E.Lawrence [xxix] blank, [xxx]–xl contents to Vol. I, [xli]–l contents to Vol.II, [li] section title, [lii] blank, pp.[1]–623 text, [1] blank, [2] section title, [3] blank, 1–539 text, 540–542 appendix, 543–690 index and glossary of Arabic words.

RT   On recto TRAVELS IN ARABIA DESERTA. On verso [according to page contents].

Plates   Nine line drawings by author, of varying sizes tipped in. Frontis. on coated paper, following pp.ii, 106, 108, 112, 176, 384, 402, 404, 416.

Typography and paper $ 1,5 signed 4,4*, 41 41* 41** (1,2,5).

Text   20 lines, 7.8 (8.2) × 10.1 cm.

Paper   Thin, white, wove, unwatermarked, all edges trimmed, sheets bulk 4 cm.

Binding   Black cloth. On spine: [gilt] [triple rule] | ARABIA | DESERTA | C.M. | DOUGHTY | JONATHAN CAPE & | THE MEDICI SOCIETY Ltd | [triple rule].

Published at   30s, March 1926.

Notes   Reprinted July 1926, identical to above.
   Reprinted September 1926, identical to above.
   Reprinted October 1927, identical to above.
   Reprinted May 1928.

Copies   AC.

A016   CHARLES M. DOUGHTY, Travels in Arabia Deserta, Cape, 1930

Fifth English Edition

TRAVELS IN | ARABIA DESERTA | BY CHARLES M. DOUGHTY, WITH | A NEW PREFACE BY THE AUTHOR, | INTRODUCTION BY T.E. LAWRENCE, | AND ALL ORIGINAL MAPS, PLANS | & ILLUSTRATIONS | THIN-PAPER EDITION IN ONE VOLUME | COMPLETE AND UNABRIDGED | JONATHAN CAPE LTD. | THIRTY BEDFORD SQUARE LONDON | AND AT TORONTO

Collation   22 × 14 cm: [a]^{10} b^{16} 1–40^{16} 41^{18} (b and 40 are two gatherings of eights, one inserted within the other, the second gathering is signed b* etc., 41 is composed of 41^2 41* and 41**^{8}, each inserted within the other), pp.[i –vii], viii–lii, [1], 2–623, [3], [1], 2–690.

Contents   Prp.[i] half-title, [ii] blank, [iii] title page, [iv] issue statement, publisher's address, printer's credit, [v] pub. note, [vi] blank, [vii] –viii preface, [xvii] –xxvii introduction by T.E. Lawrence, [xxix] blank, [xx] –xl contents to Vol. I, [xli] –l contents to Vol. II, [li] section title, [lii] blank, pp. [1] –623 text, [1] blank, [2] section title, [3] blank, 1–539 text, 540–542 appendix, 543–690 index and glossary of Arabic words.

RT   On recto TRAVELS IN ARABIA DESERTA. On verso [according to subject of opening].

Plates   Nine plates, of varying sizes, tipped in. Frontis. on coated paper, following pp.[ii], 106, 108, 112, 176, 384, 402, 404, 416.

Typography and paper $ 1,5 signed 4,4*, 41 41* 41** (1,2,5).

Text   20 lines, 7.8 (8.2) × 10.1 cm.

Paper   Thin , white, wove, unwatermarked, all edges trimmed, sheets bulk 4 cm.

Binding   Black cloth. On spine: [gilt] ARABIA | DESERTA | *C.M.* | DOUGHTY | JONATHAN CAPE. Top and fore edge trimmed. Boxed as issued.

Notes   October 1930. This is a reprint of the previous edition with a new title page and spine imprint.
Reprinted September 1933.

Copies   HL.

A017   CHARLES M. DOUGHTY, Travels in Arabia Deserta, Cape, 1936

Sixth English Edition

TRAVELS IN | [in red] ARABIA DESERTA | By | CHARLES M. DOUGHTY | [pub. device] | With an Introduction by | T.E. LAWRENCE | New and | definitive edition | VOLUME I [II]. | LONDON | JONATHAN CAPE 30 BEDFORD SQUARE | 1936

Collation   25.3 × 19.3 cm: Vol. I, [a] –TT^8, 336 leaves, pp.[1–6] 7–674; Vol. II, [A]^8 B*^{8} C2–NN2^8 OO*–UU*^{8} XX*^{4}, 348 leaves, pp.[1–4] 5–696.

Contents   Vol. I: pp.[1] bastard title, [2] list of author's works, [3] blank, [4] frontispiece, [5] title page, [6] issue statement, printer's, papermaker's credit, 7–16 contents, 17–28 introduction by T.E. Lawrence, 29–35 prefaces to first three editions, [36] blank, [37] section title, [38] blank, 39–672 text, 673–674 appendix to Vol. I. Vol. II: pp.[1] bastard title, [2] list of author's works, [3] title page, [4] issue statement, credits, 5–11 contents, [12] blank, 13 section title, [14] blank, 15–574 text, 575–576 appendix Vol. II, 577 section title, 578 blank, 579–696 index and glossary of Arabic words.

RT   On verso TRAVELS IN ARABIA DESERTA. On recto [according to subject of page].

Plates   Vol. I: 9 plates, frontis. pp.[3–4], others following pp.148, [149], [152], 218 fold., 430, 448, 452, 462 fold. Fold maps inside both rear covers.

Typography and paper $ 1 signed TT.

Text   20 lines, 9.8 (9.9) × 13.1 cm.

Paper   Buff, wove, unwatermarked, top edges trimmed, unopened, sheets bulk 3.8 cm (Vol. I), 3.8 cm (Vol. II).

Binding   Brown buckram 46 gy r Br. On spine: [gilt] ARABIA | DESERTA | [cut] | C.M. | DOUGHTY | VOLUME I [II] | JONATHAN CAPE. T.e. brown, end papers white. Each volume has fold. map pasted inside back cover.

Published at £3 15s.

Notes December 1943 reprint as above with following differences:[Plates]: poorer quality paper; [Paper]: poorer quality, sheets bulk 3.5 cm both volumes.

January 1944 reprint as above.

January, March 1949 reprints as above with following differences: [Contents]: papermaker's credit replaced by illustrator's credit; [Paper]:poorer quality.

Copies AC, HL.

A018 CHARLES M. DOUGHTY, Travels in Arabia Deserta, Cape, 1964

Sixth English Edition (smaller format)

CHARLES M. DOUGHTY | Travels in | Arabia Deserta | With an Introduction by | T.E. LAWRENCE | VOLUME I [II] | JONATHAN CAPE | THIRTY BEDFORD SQUARE LONDON

Collation 19.7 × 12.2 cm: guillotined sheets; Vol. I, 339; Vol. II, 348 leaves. Vol. I, pp.[4], 7–674, [4]; Vol. II, 696, [4].

Contents Vol. I: pp.[1] series and bastard titles, [2] blank, [3] title page, [4] issue, condition of sale statements, printer's, binder's credits 7–16 contents, 17–28 introduction by T.E.Lawrence, 29–35 prefaces to first three editions, [36] blank, [37] section title, [38] blank, 39–672 text, 673–674 appendix to Vol. I, [1–4] ads. Vol. II: pp.[1] series and bastard titles, [2] blank, [3] title page, [4] issue and copyright statements, printer's credit, 5–11 contents, [12] blank, [13] section title, [14] blank, 15–574 text, 575–576 appendix to Vol. II, [577] section title, [578] text, 579–696 glossary and index to Arabic words, [1–4] ads.

RT On verso TRAVELS IN ARABIA DESERTA. On recto [according to page].

Plates Vol. I: following pp.218, 448, 462.

Text 20 lines, 7.3 (7.5) × 10.1 cm.

Paper White, wove, unwatermarked, all edges trimmed, sheets bulk 3 cm (each volume).

Binding Pictorial paper covers. On front cover: CHARLES M. DOUGHTY 25s | Travels in [in pink] JONATHAN CAPE | Arabia Deserta [in pink] PAPERBACK | INTRODUCTION BY T.E. LAWRENCE | ILLUSTRATED | VOL. II. On spine: JCP 20 | [running down] CHARLES M. DOUGHTY | Travels in Arabia Deserta | [across at bottom] Jonathan | CAPE | PAPERBACK. On back cover: [front cover repeated and two excerpts from reviews].

Published at   25s.

Notes   Hardbound issue: Brown buckram 57 l. Br. On spine: ARABIA |
DESERTA | [cut] | C.M. | DOUGHTY | VOLUME I [II] | [pub. device]. T.e.
tan. Gold and brown striped head bands. [Pub. at]: 50s.

Copies   HL, M.

A019   CHARLES M. DOUGHTY, Travels in Arabia Deserta, Boni & Liveright, 1923

First American Edition

TRAVELS IN | ARABIA DESERTA | BY CHARLES M. DOUGHTY, | WITH
A NEW | PREFACE BY THE AUTHOR, AN INTRO- | DUCTION BY T.E.
LAWRENCE, AND ALL | ORIGINAL MAPS, PLANS AND CUTS |
VOLUME ONE [TWO] | BONI & LIVERIGHT, Inc., NEW YORK |
JONATHAN CAPE & THE MEDICI | SOCIETY LTD. :: :: LONDON | 1923

Collation   23 × 14.2 cm: Vol. I, π^8 [a]^6 b^4 c^2 1–39^8, 332 leaves, pp.[2], [i–v],
vi–xxvi, 1–624; Vol. II, π^8 1–43^8 44^1, 352 leaves, pp.[2], [i–v], vi–xiv,
1–690.

Contents   Vol. I: prp.[1–2] blank, [i] half-title, [ii] blank, [iii] title page, [iv]
'All Rights Reserved | by | BONI AND LIVERIGHT, INC. | NEW YORK |
PRINTED IN ENGLAND', [v] –xiv prefaces, xv–xxv introduction by T.E.
Lawrence, [xxvi] blank, [xv] –xxvi (sic) contents, pp.1–623 text, [624] blank.
Vol. II: prp.[1–2] blank, [i] half-title, [ii] blank, [iii] title page, [iv] copyright
statement, [v–xiv] contents, pp.1–542 text, 543–690 index and glossary of
Arabic words.

RT   On verso TRAVELS IN ARABIA DESERTA. On recto [according to
subject of page].

Plates   Vol. I: following pp.107, 108, 112, 176, 385, 402, 405, 416, fold-out
linen-backed map (55.9 × 73.4 cm) loosely inserted in pocket inside rear
cover.

Typography and paper $ 1,2 D.T. 7, D.T.II 7.

Text   20 lines, 7.4 (7.7) × 10.2 cm.

Paper   White, wove, unwatermarked, all edges trimmed, sheets bulk 4.5
cm (Vol. I), 4 cm (Vol. II).

Binding   Black linen. On spines: [all gilt] [Oxford rule] | ARABIA |
DESERTA | I [II] | C.M. | *DOUGHTY* | [cut] | BONI & LIVERIGHT |
[Oxford rule]. Yellow head and tail bands. Black end papers. Boxed as
issued.

Published at $17.50

Notes May 1924 identical to above with following differences: title page date change; [Contents]: prp.[iv] issue statement, printer's credits added. May 1925 identical to immediately above.

Copies AC.

A020 CHARLES M. DOUGHTY, Travels in Arabia Deserta, Boni & Liveright, 1926

First American Edition (thin paper edition)

TRAVELS IN | ARABIA DESERTA | BY CHARLES M. DOUGHTY, WITH | A NEW PREFACE BY THE AUTHOR, | INTRODUCTION BY T.E. LAWRENCE, | AND ALL ORIGINAL MAPS, PLANS | & ILLUSTRATIONS | THIN-PAPER EDITION IN ONE VOLUME | COMPLETE AND UNABRIDGED | NEW YORK | BONI & LIVERIGHT

Collation 21.7 × 14 cm: a^{10} b^{16} $1-40^{16}$ 41^{18}, b–40 are made up of two gatherings one inserted inside the other, 41 is made up as follows: 41^2 42^* 42^{**} [8] each inserted within the other, 684 leaves, pp.[i–vii], viii–lii, [1], 2–623, [3], [1], 2–690.

Contents Prp.[i] half-title, [ii] blank, [iii] title page, [iv] printer's credit, [v] pub. note, [vi] blank, [vii]–xvi prefaces, [xvii]–xxvii introduction by T.E.Lawrence, [xxix] blank, [xxx]–l contents, [li] section title, [lii] blank, pp. 1–623 text, [1] blank, [2] section title, [3] blank, 1–539 text, 540–542 appendix to Vol. II, 543–690 index and glossary of Arabic words.

RT On recto TRAVELS IN ARABIA DESERTA. On verso [according to contents of page].

Plates Nine line drawings by author on paper same weight as sheets, except for frontis., varying sizes, all in Vol. I following pp.106, 110, 112, 176, 384, 402, 416, foldout map inside rear cover.

Typography and paper $ signed 1,2 b,b* 1,1* 41, 41*,41**.

Text 20 lines, 7.3 (7.8) × 10.2 cm.

Paper Thin, white, wove, unwatermarked, all edges trimmed, sheets bulk 3.8 cm.

Binding Dark blue cloth 187 d. gy. B. On front cover: [gilt cut]. On spine: [gilt] [Oxford rule] | ARABIA | DESERTA | *C.M.* | *DOUGHTY* | BONI & LIVERIGHT | [Oxford rule]. Dark blue end papers.

Published at $10.00.

Copies AC.

A021   CHARLES M. DOUGHTY, Travels in Arabia Deserta, Random House, 1934

Second American Edition (thin paper edition)

TRAVELS IN | ARABIA DESERTA | BY CHARLES M. DOUGHTY, WITH | A NEW PREFACE BY THE AUTHOR, |INTRODUCTION BY T.E. LAWRENCE, | AND ALL ORIGINAL MAPS, PLANS,| & ILLUSTRATIONS | THIN-PAPER EDITION IN ONE VOLUME | COMPLETE AND UNABRIDGED | [pub. device] | RANDOM HOUSE | NEW YORK

Collation   21.7 × 14 cm: a^{10} b^{16} $1-40^{16}$ 41^{18}, b–40 are made up of two gatherings one inserted inside the other, 41 is made up as follows: 41^2 42^{*8} and 41^{**8}, each inserted within the other, 684 leaves, pp.[i–vii], viii–lii, [1], 2–623, [3], [1], 2–690.

Contents   Prp.[i] half-title, [ii] blank, [iii] title page, [iv] 'PRINTED IN GREAT BRITAIN', [v] pub. note, [vi] blank, [vii]–xvi prefaces, [xvii]–xxvii introduction by T.E. Lawrence, [xxviii] blank, [xxix]–l contents, [li] section title, [lii] blank, 1–623 text, [1] blank, [2] section title, [3] blank, 1–539 text, 540–542 appendix to Vol. II, 543–690 index and glossary of Arabic words.

RT   On recto TRAVELS IN ARABIA DESERTA. On verso [according to contents of page].

Plates   Nine drawings by author on paper same as sheets, except for frontis., varying sizes, all in Vol. I following pp.106, 110, 112, 176, 384, 402, 416, fold-out map inside rear cover.

Typography and paper $ signed 1,2 b,b* 1,1* 41,41*,41**.

Text   20 lines, 7.3 (7.8) × 10.2 cm.

Paper   Thin, white, wove, unwatermarked, all edges trimmed, sheets bulk 3.8 cm.

Binding   Dark blue cloth 187 d. gy. B. On front cover: [gilt cut]. On spine: [gilt] [Oxford rule] | ARABIA | DESERTA | *C.M.* | *DOUGHTY* | RANDOM HOUSE | [Oxford rule]. White end papers. Blue head and tail bands.

Published at $7.00.

Notes   Sheets are those of Boni & Liveright 1926 edition and identical to that edition except that spine imprint is RANDOM HOUSE at foot instead of BONI & LIVERIGHT. White end papers.

Copies   AC.

A022   CHARLES M. DOUGHTY, Travels in Arabia Deserta, Random House, 1937

Third American Edition

TRAVELS IN |[in red] ARABIA DESERTA | BY | CHARLES M. DOUGHTY | With an introduction by | T.E.LAWRENCE | New and | definitive edition | VOLUME I [II] | [pub. device] | NEW YORK · RANDOM HOUSE · MCMXXXVII

Collation   25.3 × 10.5 cm: Vol. I, [A] –TT⁸, 336 leaves, pp.1–674; Vol. II, A–UU*⁸, 348 leaves, pp.1–696. Frontispiece counted in pagination.

Contents   Vol. I: pp.[1] bastard title, [2] list of author's works, [3] blank, [4] frontis. [5] title page, [6] 'PRINTED IN GREAT BRITAIN', 7–16 contents, 17– 28 introduction by T.E. Lawrence, 29–35 prefaces to first three editions, [36] blank, [37] section title, [38] blank, 39–672 text, 673–674 appendix. Vol. II: pp.[1] bastard title, [2] list of author's works, [3] title page, [4] 'PRINTED IN GREAT BRITAIN', 5–11 contents, [12] blank, [13] section title, [14] blank, 15–574 text, 575–576 appendix, [577] section title, [578] blank, 579–696 index and glossary of Arabic words.

RT   On verso TRAVELS IN ARABIA DESERTA. On recto [according to chapter].

Plates   Only in Vol. I following pp.148, 150, 152, 218, 430, 448, 452, 462.

Typography and paper $ 1 signed C (Vol. I); C2 (Vol. II).

Text   20 lines, 9.8 (10) × 13.3 cm.

Paper   Buff, laid, unwatermarked, top edge trimmed, sheets bulk 4 cm (each volume).

Binding   Tan oatmeal cloth. On front cover: [in blue] [rule] | [Doughty's facs. signature] | [rule]. On spine: [within rectangle of blue edged in gilt] TRAVELS IN | ARABIA | DESERTA | [cut] | C.M. DOUGHTY | I [II] [within blue rectangle] | [at foot, within blue rectangle edged in gilt] Random House. Boxed as issued. T.e. blue, white end papers.

Published at $15.00.

Copies   HL.

A023   CHARLES M. DOUGHTY, Travels in Arabia Deserta, Random House, 1937

Fourth American Edition (one volume edition)

TRAVELS IN | [in red] ARABIA DESERTA | BY | CHARLES M. DOUGHTY | With an Introduction by | T.E. LAWRENCE | New and | definitive edition | in one volume | [pub. device] | RANDOM HOUSE· PUBLISHERS · NEW YORK

Collation   23.2 × 16.4 cm: [1–43]¹⁶, 688 leaves, pp.[1–24], 17–674, 13–696.

Contents   Prp.[1] bastard title, [2] list of author's works, [3] blank, [4] frontispiece, [5] title page, [6] 'MANUFACTURED IN UNITED STATES OF AMERICA', [7–16] contents of Vol. I, [17–23] contents of Vol. II, [24] blank, pp.[17]–28 introduction by T.E. Lawrence, 29–35 various prefaces, [36] blank, [37] section title, [38] blank, 39–674 text of Vol. I, [13] section title, [14] blank, 15–574 text of Vol. II, 575–576 appendix to Vol.II, [577] section title, [578] blank, 579–696 index and glossary of Arabic words.

RT   On verso TRAVELS IN ARABIA DESERTA. On recto [according to contents of page].

Plates   On sheets as part of gatherings in Vol. I only, following pp.3, 148, 150, 152, 430, 448, 451, 462, printed on one side only.

Typography and paper $ 1 signed C (Vol. I); C2 (Vol. II) [not for this edition].

Text   20 lines, 9.7 (9.9) × 13.3 cm.

Paper   White, wove, unwatermarked, all edges trimmed, sheets bulk 4.7 cm.

Binding   Tan oatmeal cloth. On front cover: [blue rule] | [Doughty's signature in facsimile] | [blue rule]. On spine: [within blue rectangle with gilt border] TRAVELS IN | ARABIA | DESERTA | [cut] | C.M. Doughty | [at foot, within blue rectangle with gilt border] Random House. T.e. blue.

Notes   Another state with altered title page: same as above except that title page has been reset as below: TRAVELS IN | ARABIA DESERTA | BY | CHARLES M. DOUGHTY | With an Introduction by | T.E. LAWRENCE | [within rectangle of single rules with rows of decorated cuts outside left and right sides] [swash] Season's Greetings | A.C. VROMAN, INCORPORATED | [below rectangle] New and | definitive edition | in one volume | RANDOM HOUSE PUBLISHERS NEW YORK.
Reprinted 1946 identical to above.
Reprinted 1947 identical to above, $7.50.
Reprinted 1949, as above, but title page all in black.

Copies   AC.

A024 CHARLES M. DOUGHTY, Travels in Arabia Deserta, Limited Editions Club, 1953

Fourth American Edition

[Double page spread, within double rule frame, multicoloured map of North Western Arabia showing Doughty's route, handlettered all in red] Travels in | Arabia Deserta | BY Charles M. Doughty | THE TEXT AS ABRIDGED AND ARRANGED BY EDWARD GARNETT, WITH | A PREFATORY NOTE BY MR. GARNETT, A GENERAL INTRODUCTION BY | T.E. LAWRENCE, AND ILLUSTRATIONS BY EDY LEGRAND | NEW YORK The Limited Editions Club 1953

Collation 26.6 × 19.1 cm: [1]^6 [2]^8 [3–4]^{10} [5]^{12} [6]^{10} [7]^{12} [8]^{10} [9]^{12} [10]^{10} [11]^{12} [12]^{10} [13]^{12} [14]^8 [15–18]^{10} [19]^{12} [20]^{10} [21]^{12} [22]^{10} [23]^{12}, 240 leaves, pp.[i–viii], ix–xvi, [xvii–xviii], xix–xxi, [xxii], [1–2], 3–455, [1–3].

Contents Prp.[i] cut, [ii] blank, [iii] cut, [iv] blank, [v] bastard title, within arabesque frame, [vi–vii] title pages, [viii] copyright statement,ix–xvi introduction by T.E. Lawrence, [xvii] illus., [xviii] contents, xix–xxi editor's preface, [xxii] blank, pp. [1] half-title, [2] illus., 3–451 text, 452–455 glossary, [1] colophon, [2–3] blank.

RT On both verso and recto [according to chapter].

Plates Illustrations are full page, printed in gatherings and counted in pagination.

Text 20 lines, 8.5 (9) × 6.5 cm, double column.

Paper White, wove, unwatermarked, all edges trimmed, sheets bulk 3 cm.

Binding Rough natural linen of natural tone. On front cover: [all in brown, arabesque frame, with drawing of rider on camel superimposed over Doughty's route in Arabia]. On back cover: [Arabesque design over whole cover in brown]. Binding has fore-edge flap that covers fore edge and extends back over part of front cover. On fore edge: [swash, running down] Travels in Arabia Deserta. Illustrated end papers.

Notes Copies printed, 1500.

Copies AC, HL.

A025 CHARLES M. DOUGHTY, Travels in Arabia Deserta, Heritage Press, 1953

Fourth American Edition (second issue)

[Double spread, all within double rule frame, all swash hand-lettered]

Travels in | Arabia Deserta | By Charles M. Doughty | THE TEXT AS ABRIDGED BY EDWARD GARNETT, WITH | A PREFATORY NOTE BY MR. GARNETT, A GENERAL INTRODUCTION BY | T.E. LAWRENCE, AND ILLUSTRATIONS BY EDY LEGRAND | NEW YORK: [swash] The Heritage Press

Collation   26.7 × 19 cm: π^4 [1]^{10} [2]^{12} [3]^{10} [4]^{12} [5]^{10} [6]^{12} [7]^{10} [8]^{12} [9]^{10} [10]^{12} [11]^{10} [12]^{12} [13]^8 [14]^{10} [15]^{10} [16]^{10} [17]^{10} [18]^{12} [19]^{10} [20]^{12} [21]^{10} [22]^{10} [23]^{12}, 240 leaves, pp.[i–ix], x–xxi, [xxii], [1–2], 3–453, [5], includes pastedown end papers.

Contents   Prp. [i–ii] pastedown end paper, [iii–iv] free end paper, [v] bastard title within arabesque frame, [vi–vii] title pages [viii] copyright statement, [ix] contents, x–xii editor's preface, [xiii] illus., xiv–xxi introduction by T.E.Lawrence, [xxii] blank, pp.[1] half-title, [2] illus., 3–449 text,450–453 glossary, [1] blank, [2–3] free end paper, [4–5] pastedown end paper.

RT   On both verso and recto [according to chapter] set in Civilite.

Plates   Illustrations are full page, printed in gatherings and counted in pagination.

Text   20 lines, 8.5 (9.3) × 6.5 cm, double column. Set in Cloister Old Style.

Paper   White, wove, unwatermarked,all edges trimmed, sheets bulk 2.7 cm.

Binding   Rough natural linen of natural tone. On front cover: [all in brown, arabesque frame, with drawing of rider on camel superimposed on Doughty's route in Arabia]. On spine: [swash, in brown running down] Travels in Arabia Deserta. On back cover: [in brown, same arabesque frame enclosing drawing of points of the compass]. All edges brown. Head and tail bands red and gold. Illustrated end papers.

Published at $6.00.

Notes   Printed by offset lithography from Limited Editions Club issue of same book.

Copies   AC, HL.

A027   CHARLES M. DOUGHTY, Travels in Arabia Deserta, Dover, 1979

Fifth American Edition

TRAVELS IN | ARABIA DESERTA | BY | CHARLES M. DOUGHTY | With an Introduction by | T.E. Lawrence | IN TWO VOLUMES | VOLUME I [II] | DOVER PUBLICATIONS, INC. | NEW YORK

Collation   23.3 × 16.5 cm: Vol. I [1–22]^{16}, Vol. II [1–22]^{16}, 352 leaves in each volume. Vol. I, pp.[1–6], 7–674, [10]; Vol. II, pp.[2], [1–4], 5–696, [6].

Contents Vol. I: pp.[1–2] blank, [3] bastard title, [4] frontis., [5] title page, [6] [Canadian and Great Britain pub. credits], issue statement, ISBN, LC numbers, USA pub. credit, 7–16 contents, illustrations, 17–28 introduction by T.E.Lawrence, 29–35 prefaces to first three editions, [36] blank, [37] VOLUME I, [38] blank, 39–672 text, 673–674 appendix, [1–10] ads. Vol.II: prp.[1–2] blank, pp.[1] bastard title, [2] blank, [3] title page, [4] issue statement, printer's credit, 5–11 contents, [12] blank, [13] VOLUME II, [14] blank, 15–574 text, 575–576 appendix, [577] section title, [578] blank, 579–696 index and glossary, [1–6] pub. ads.

RT On verso TRAVELS IN ARABIA DESERTA. On recto [according to chapter].

Text 20 lines, 9.7 (10.5) × 13.1 cm.

Paper White, wove, unwatermarked, all edges trimmed, sheets bulk 3.1 cm.

Binding Pictorial paper covers, Vol. I: brown, Vol. II: blue. On front cover: [all in white] Charles M. Doughty | TRAVELS IN | ARABIA DESERTA | With an Introduction by T.E.Lawrence | In Two Volumes | Volume I [II]. On spine: [all in white] Doughty | [running down] TRAVELS IN | ARABIA DESERTA | [across] Volume I [II] | Dover | [running down, ISBN number] | [across, pub. device]. On back cover: [blurb].

Published at $8.95 per volume.

Copies AC.

A028   CHARLES M. DOUGHTY, Arabia Deserta, Payot, 1949

First French Edition

BIBLIOTHÈQUE HISTORIQUE | [long rule] | CHARLES M. DOUGHTY | [short rule] | ARABIA DESERTA | TEXTES CHOISIS PAR EDWARD GARNETT | ET TRADUITS PAR JACQUES MARTY | [short rule] | *PRÉFACE DE T.E. LAWRENCE* | AUTEUR DES ((SEPT PILIERS DE LA SAGESSE)) | [short rule] | [pub. device] | PAYOT PARIS | 106, BOULEVARD SAINT-GERMAIN | [short rule] | 1949 | Tout droits de traduction de reproduction et d'adaption resérvés pour tous pays. | *Passages from Arabia Deserta, selected by E. Garnett, Jonathan Cape, 30, Bedford Square, London*

Collation 22.3 × 14.3 cm: [1]-21⁸, 168 leaves, pp.[1–6], 7–334, [335–336].

Contents Pp.[1] blank, [2] list of series titles, [3] title page, [4] quotes from reviews, [5–6] 7–18 preface by T.E. Lawrence, [19]–21 avertissement by Garnett, [22] blank, [23]–327 text, [328]–334 glossary, [335] contents, [336] blank.

RT   On both verso and recto [according to section].

Typography and paper $ 1 signed 3.

Text   20 lines, 8.2 (8.3) × 10.4 cm.

Paper   White, wove, unwatermarked, untrimmed, sheets bulk 2.5 cm.

Binding   Tan paper covers 73 p. OY. On front cover: [within rule frame] *BIBLIOTHÈQUE HISTORIQUE* | [long rule] | Charles M. Doughty | [short rule] | [in red] ARABIA | [in red] DESERTA | *PRÉFACE DE T.E. LAWRENCE* | [cut] | Textes choisis par Edward Garnett | et traduits par Jacques Marty | PAYOT, PARIS. On spine: [rule] | CHARLES | M. DOUGHTY | [rule] | Arabia | Deserta | [rule] | 780fr. | [rule] | PAYOT | PARIS | [rule]. On back cover [list of works by publisher, within single rule frame].

Published at   780 fr.

Copies   AC, HL.

A029   CHARLES M. DOUGHTY, Die Offenbarung Arabiens, List, 1937

First German Edition

CHARLES M. DOUGHTY | DIE OFFENBARUNG | ARABIENS | *(ARABIA DESERTA)* | [pub. device] | PAUL LIST VERLAG LEIPZIG

Collation   21.2 × 13 cm: [1] -38^8 39^4, 308 leaves, pp.[1–5], 6–612, [1–4].

Contents   Pp.[1] bastard title, [2] blank, [3] title page, [4] translator's credit, original title, typographer's credit, copyright statement, printer's credit, [5]–9 translator's foreword, [10]–16 prefaces, [17]–32 introduction by T.E.Lawrence, [33]–594 text, [595] translator's postscript, [596]–598 chronology and English measures, [599]–612 name and place index, [1] contents, [2–4] ads.

RT   On both verso and recto [according to chapter]

Plates   Frontispiece on coated paper, printed on one side only, following pp.[2]. Fold-out map inside rear cover.

Typography and paper $ 1,2 signed Doughty, Die Offenbarung Arabiens 2,2*.

Text   20 lines, 8.2 (8.5) × 10 cm.

Paper   White, wove, unwatermarked, all edges trimmed, sheets bulk 3.8 cm.

Binding   Green cloth 164 m. b. G. On front cover: [gilt] [swash] DIE OFFENBARUNG | ARABIENS. On spine: [gilt] [within gilt rectangle, lettering green] CHARLES | M. DOUGHTY | [below rectangle] [swash]

DIE | OFFEN / | BARUNG | ARABIENS | [gilt sword] | [pub. device]. T.e. green. Gold and white head and tail bands.

Notes Selected chapters.

Copies AC.

A030 CHARLES M. DOUGHTY, Reisen in Arabia Deserta, DuMont, 1979

First German Edition

Charles M. Doughty | Reisen in Arabia Deserta | Wanderungen in der Arabischen Wüste 1876–1878 | Mit einer Einleitung von Lawrence von Arabien | [in white] DuMont Buchverlag Köln

Collation 20.5 × 15 cm: guillotined sheets glued to paper covers, 128 leaves, pp.[1–6], 7–250, [6].

Contents Pp.[1] series title, [2–3] double spread title page, all lettering on recto, [4] translator's credit, copyright statement, CIP, ISBN, printer's, binder's statements, [5–6] contents, 7–9 pub. notes, 10–16 introduction by T.E.Lawrence, [17] section title, [18] synopsis, 19–249 text, 250 postscript, [1–6] ads.

RT On verso only [according to contents of page].

Text 20 lines, 8.1 (8.7) × 12.1 cm.

Paper White, wove, unwatermarked, all edges trimmed, sheets bulk 1.7 cm.

Binding Pictorial paper covers. On front cover: DuMont-Reiseberichte Charles M. Doughty | *Wanderungen in der* | *Arabischen Wüste 1876–1878* | *Mit einem Vorwort von* | *Lawrence von Arabien* | Reisen in | Arabia Deserta. On spine: [running up] Charles M. Doughty Arabia Deserta | [across at top in blue] ai | id. On back cover: [illus].

Published at DM28.

Notes Abridgement.

Copies AC.

A031 CHARLES M. DOUGHTY, Arabia Resa, Berghs, 1959

First Swedish Edition

CHARLES M. DOUGHTY | Arebisk resa | ÖVERSÄTTNING FRÅN ENGELSKAN | AV H.S. NYBERG | SVEN-ERIK BERGHS FÖRLAG | STOCKHOLM LONDON NEW YORK

Collation   22.1 × 14.2 cm: [1] – 22⁸, 176 leaves, pp.[1–4], 5–352.

Contents   Pp.[1] pub. device, [2] blank, [3] title page, [4] original title, copyright statement, printer's credit, 5–10 prefaces, 11–23 introduction by T.E.Lawrence, 24 map, 25–337 text, 338–352 glossary and index.

Typography and paper $ 1 signed 2,2- Arabisk resa.

Text   20 lines, 9 × 10.4 cm.

Paper   White, wove, unwatermarked, untrimmed, sheets bulk 2 cm.

Binding   Orange 50 s.O paper covers. On front cover: [swash] Arabisk | resa | av Charles M. Doughty | *In ledning av* T.E. LAWRENCE | BERGHS. [all in white printed over line drawing of figure riding camel]. On spine: [running up] *Charles M. Doughty* ARABISK RESA | [at foot, pub. device] | BERGHS. On back cover: [blurbs and pub. note].

Published at   26:50 SKR paper bound; 29:50 SKR hardbound.

Notes   Hardbound issue: [Binding]: Brown cloth 61 gy. Br. On front cover: [gilt cut]. On spine: [gilt, running up, *Charles M. Doughty* – ARABISK RESA. White head and tail bands.

Copies   AC.

Leicester Galleries 1921

Kennington had been commissioned by Lawrence to travel to the Near East to make portraits of many of the Arab personalities who had been participants in the Arab campaign. The entire series of pastels were displayed by Leicester Galleries in 1921. These were to be used to illustrate *Seven Pillars of Wisdom*. For the exhibition catalogue Lawrence contributed a preface. This catalogue is extremely rare. Often copies of the later exhibition catalogue of the illustrations for *Seven Pillars of Wisdom* (1927) (A099) are mistakenly identified as this one. The later exhibition catalogue contains the Lawrence preface with the first three paragraphs of the 1921 version omitted.

Reprinted in *T.E. Lawrence, Fifty Letters 1930–1935*, p.6, and in Oliver Brown, *Exhibitions*.

A032   LEICESTER GALLERIES, London, Catalogue of An Exhibition, 1921

First English Edition

CATALOGUE OF AN EXHIBITION | OF ARAB PORTRAITS BY | ERIC H. KENNINGTON | With a Prefatory Note by | T.E. LAWRENCE | ERNEST BROWN & PHILLIPS | THE LEICESTER GALLERIES | LEICESTER SQUARE, LONDON | OCTOBER, 1921

Collation   14.3 × 11.1 cm: [1]⁴, 8 leaves, pp.1–16.

Contents   Pp.[1–2] ads, [3] title page, [4] ad, 5–11 preface by T.E. Lawrence, 12–14 text, [15–16] ads.

Text   20 lines, 6.7 × 7.6 cm.

Paper   White, laid, unwatermarked, untrimmed, sheets bulk 3 mm.

Binding   Brown paper covers 76 l. y. Br. On front cover: [most of text within single rule frame] [above frame] REYNOLDS ROOM | [within frame] CATALOGUE OF AN EXHIBITION | OF ARAB PORTRAITS BY | ERIC H. KENNINGTON | With a Prefatory Note by| T.E. LAWRENCE | ERNEST BROWN & PHILLIPS | (W.L. PHILLIPS, C.L. PHILLIPS, O.F. BROWN) | THE LEICESTER GALLERIES | LEICESTER SQUARE LONDON | [below frame] EXHIBITION No. 323 OCTOBER, 1921. On back cover: [list of other exhibits]. Ads inside both covers.

Published at   3d.

Notes   Contains one paragraph, p.3, omitted from second publication of Lawrence's essay in 1927 (A099).
    Reprinted in *FIFTY LETTERS*, University of Texas, 1962, p.6, and in Brown, EXHIBITIONS, E255, pp.176–179.

Copies   H, UT.

Report on Middle East Conference

T.E. Lawrence contributed much to the deliberations behind this document. It is included in the canon as it contains much of his contribution in the settlement of Near Eastern affairs, even though his specific portion(s) cannot be clearly identified. A detailed discussion of some of these contributions can be found in: King, *The British Successor States in the Post-War Middle East*, Claremont Graduate School, 1978, Chapters 8–9.

A033   Great Britain. Colonial Office, Report on Middle East Conference, 1921

First English Edition

[Within single rule frame] COPYRIGHT – NOT TO BE REPRODUCED WITHOUT PERMISSION | [This Document is the Property of His Britannic Majesty's Government] | *Printed for the Colonial Office, June 1921.* | [rule, underlined] SECRET. | REPORT | ON | MIDDLE EAST CONFERENCE | HELD IN | CAIRO AND JERUSALEM. | [rule] | MARCH 12TH TO 30TH, 1921 | [rule] | WITH APPENDICES

Collation   35.5 × 21.5 cm: [1–3], 4–211 leaves.

Contents   Prl.[1] title page, [1–2] document sheets, [3]–12 text, 13–15 index of appendixes, 16–211 text of appendixes 1–32.

Text   20 lines, 8.4 × 15.8 cm.

Paper   White, wove, all edges trimmed, sheets bulk 2 cm.

Binding   Only copy seen was unbound.

Published at   Secret Government document.

Copies   Cal.

1922

Seven Pillars of Wisdom

In 1913 Lawrence wrote a book entitled *Seven Pillars of Wisdom*. It was designed to cover seven Middle Eastern cities: Cairo, C.P., Smyrna, Aleppo, Jerusalem, Urfa and Damascus (*Letters*, p.431). The manuscript of this book was burned in 1914. The description of six Syrian cities in Chapter 59 of *Seven Pillars of Wisdom* may give some indication of the contents and perhaps style of this early work.

The title which he was to use for his major work is from the Book of Proverbs. He appears to have had the intention of using a building metaphor. Remnants of this metaphor remain in the introduction: 'Foundations of Revolt' and Book 10: 'The House is Perfected'.

Previous published versions of portions of the *Arab Bulletin*, the passages in the *Advance of the EEF* and articles in *The Arab Bulletin*, as well as skeleton diaries he had kept during the campaign, serve as the basis for writing the record of the war years.

Lawrence began writing his version of the desert war in 1919 while attending the Paris Peace Conference. A major portion, if not all, of this first effort was lost at Reading Station in late 1919. A second version was written in London 1919–1920 in a period of three months. Lawrence burned this in 1922 in Chingford. The third manuscript was written in London, Jeddah and Amman, 1921, and in London, 1922. This third manuscript, some 330,000 words long, was donated to the Bodleian Library.

Sometime in 1921 Lawrence gave Robert Graves, then in desperate straits, three chapters of version two. Graves was able to sell these for publication (for £200) to *The World's Work*.

Between January and June 1922 Lawrence had eight copies of text three printed by the *Oxford Times*. Six copies still exist and fragments of one of the other two are extant. The text was printed in double-column format.

Lawrence reworked the text from 1923–1926 while in the RAF and Tank Corps. The 1922 'Oxford' version was loaned to various people for critical comments as follows: G.B. Shaw, E.M. Forster, Thomas Hardy, Rudyard Kipling, Siegfried Sassoon, Edward Garnett, D. G. Hogarth, Gertrude Bell, Gen. Wavell, Alan & G. Dawney, Robin Buxton, and W.H. Bartholomew.

In 1926 he published the elaborate 'Cranwell' or 'Subscriber's' edition in an edition of 217 copies. A text of 170,000 words was considered by Lawrence to be 'the final corrected text' (TQ Aut 1962 pp.48–9). The title page bears no author's name, no publisher's name or place of publication. The book was the product of a slow process of extensive rewriting during printing to achieve a number of ends. Lawrence hoped to have no line end less than half way across the page and to have as many pages as possible begin with decorative capitals or 'bloomers' and to have no words divided at the ends of lines. It was printed by Manning Pike and C.J. Hodgson and bound by a number of Britain's leading binders, The term 'Cranwell' is applied due to the fact that it was composed and rewritten during Lawrence's tour of duty while at the RAF College, Cranwell. The term 'subscriber's' derives from the sale of the book by subscription only.

In spite of the statement made by Lawrence, quoted at the beginning of the preface of this work, the number of copies is known thanks to a private record he compiled and which is now in the Humanities Research Center, University of Texas, Austin. To secure American copyright as well as to prevent general publication of the book in the USA, Lawrence authorised an American edition published by Doran in an edition of 22 copies at a price of $20,000 each. The text was set from proofs of the 'Cranwell' edition. It was to contain no introductory matter, no appendices and no illustrative material. The latter condition was not strictly met as there are a few line cuts in this American 'copyright' edition.

With the exception of the American copyright edition no other printings of the *Seven Pillars of Wisdom* were permitted until after his death in 1935. Jonathan Cape had authorised republication of the 1927 abridgment *Revolt in the Desert* very soon after news of Lawrence's death was announced but A.W. Lawrence was influential in halting republication of that work in favour of a general publication of the unabridged text of the 1926 edition. Within two months of Lawrence's death a first publication for the general public in an edition of 60,000 copies was achieved with many reprints to follow. This 1935 edition was made available in limited issues in addition to the trade issue both in Great Britain and the USA. There were also 60 special copies produced by the publisher to be given to members of the staff involved in its production. All but six of the 40 plus plates in the book were pasted in by hand and 100,000 copies were in print by the end of September 1935. In addition to two printers producing the book at one time, there were three binders at work at the height of demand. The story of its success is to be found in Howard, *Jonathan Cape, Publisher,* Cape, 1971. *Seven Pillars* is still in print today. Churchill said of it: "It ranks with the greatest books written in the English language' (*TEL by His Friends,* p.194). G.B. Shaw : "It is one of the great books of our time".

Seven Pillars of Wisdom has been published in many languages; sixteen such editions are described here. Editions in Chinese and Arabic are rumoured to exist, but no copies were located.

A034   T.E. LAWRENCE, Seven Pillars of Wisdom, privately printed, 1922

First English Edition (Oxford edition)

[All hand lettered] SEVEN PILLARS | OF | WISDOM | [rule] | a triumph | [rule] 1919–1920

Collation   27.9 × 21 cm: [1]⁴ [2]⁷ [fifth leaf removed] [3]⁶ [4]⁶ + 320 leaves = 343 leaves, prp.[1–20], leaves 1–6, 1, 7–9, 9, 10, [1], 26–46, [1], 47–69, [1], 70–75, [1], 76–94, [95], 96–132, [1], 133–164, [1], 165–195, [1], 196–222, [1], 223–244, [1], 245–269, [1], 270–307, [1], 308, [4].

Contents   Prl.[1–9] blank, [10] hand lettered title page, pp.[1] acknowledgments, [2] blank, 3 dedication, 4 blank, 5–6 [1] 7–9 9 10 contents, synopsis, [1] section title, [11] synopsis, 12–308 text, includes unpaged section titles as reflected in collation.

RT   On recto CHAPTER 52 [53 etc.].

Text   20 lines, 5.1 (5.5) × 6.6 (13.7) double column, sheets are page proofs printed on one side only, 6pt type, chapter numbers, page numbers, preliminary material and section titles all in Lawrence's hand.

Paper   Leaves 1–5 laid paper, 6–10 and section titles, rag parchment paper, sheets of text wove paper, unwatermarked, all edges trimmed, sheets bulk 2.8 cm.

Binding   Each copy bound differently.

Published at   Not for sale.

Notes   Corrections throughout in Lawrence's hand in the three copies examined. Eight copies printed, six remain, six copies bound. One was used in revision for 1926 edition and destroyed, the other was broken up with chapters sent to subscribers of the 1926 edition along with the 1925 prospectus of eight chapter proofs and apology for the delay in publication.
    In another copy leaves 1–3, 5–11 title page, dedication, contents are all typed, leaf 4 in manuscript, section titles typed.
    Locations of copies as follows:
      1 Houghton Library
      2 British Library
      3 Bodleian Library (also has original ms.)
      4 Private collection in USA
      5 Private collection in California
      6 Kennington copy
      7 Parts in collections in USA and Canada and as sold recently in Payne collection at auction, and 1986 by Maggs Bros. of London (catalogue 1070).

Copies   Cal, H, Bod, BL.

A035   T.E. LAWRENCE, The Foundations of Arab Revolt, privately printed, 1924

First state of prospectus for Second English Edition

THE FOUNDATIONS | OF ARAB REVOLT | Some Englishmen, of whom Kitchener was chief, | [etc., 14 additional lines of text]

Collation   25.2 × 19.5 cm: [1–3]⁸, 24 leaves, pp.[1–2], 3–43, [44], [1–4].

Contents   Pp.[1] blank, [2] title page and opening paragraph, 3–44 text, [1–4] blank.

Text   20 lines, 9.8 × 12.7 cm.

Paper   White, mould-made, top and bottom edges trimmed, unwatermarked, sheets bulk 4 mm.

Binding   Off-white plain paper wrappers 73 p. OY, glued to sheets.

Notes   Contains eight chapters including the first chapter later suppressed on the recommendation of G.B. Shaw.

About 100 copies were circulated to friends and prospective purchasers of *Seven Pillars* in 1924. It served as an elaborate prospectus for the 1926 edition, showing format, paper and type.

Chapters as follows: I pp.3–6, II 7–10, III 11–15, IV 16–21, V 22–27, VI 28–33, VII 34–40, VIII 41–[44].

Copies   H, UT.

A036   T.E. LAWRENCE, The Foundations of Arab Revolt, privately printed, 1925

Second state of prospectus for 1926 *Seven Pillars of Wisdom*

THE FOUNDATIONS OF ARAB REVOLT | [text begins immediately, 17 lines follow on this page]

Collation   25 × 19.3 cm: [1]² plate [1] –2⁸ 3⁴ 4², prp.[1–4] blank, 24 leaves, [1–2], 3–[40], [1–4].

Contents   Prp.[1–2] front cover, within paper wrappers, [3–4] front fly leaf, colour plate of Galil Bey Chal'lan, pp.[1] blank, [2] title, and opening paragraphs, 3–[40] text, chapters I–VII, [1–4] blank.

Plates   Colour collotype of Galil Bey Chal'lan before p.[1], Kennington line cut on p.40.

Text   20 lines, 9.7 × 12.6 cm.

Paper White, laid, unwatermarked, t.e. trimmed, sheets bulk 3 mm.

Binding White paper wrappers 73 pOY glued to covers.

Published at Sent to subscribers May 1925.

Notes Approximately 100 copies. This state lacks the introductory chapter included in state number one, the colour plate present here not included in first state. Accompanied by printed letter (26.2 × 19 cm) single sheet, printed both sides, laid paper, dated June 1, 1925. This second state is entirely reset.
   Pagination of chapters: I pp.3–6, II 7–11, III 12–17, IV 18–23, V 24–29, VI 30–36, VII 37–[40].

Copies H, Cal, UT.

A037   T.E. LAWRENCE, Notice to Subscribers, 1925

Printed letter

My estimate of the time required to provide an adequate edition | [etc]

Collation 25.5 × 19 cm: single sheet printed on both sides.

Contents Text of letter only.

Text 20 lines, 9.6 × 12.5 cm.

Paper White, laid, unwatermarked, all edges trimmed.

Published at June 1, 1925.

Notes Printed letter sent to subscribers re delay in printing of *Seven Pillars*.

Copies UT, Cal.

A038   T.E. LAWRENCE, Note From T.E. Shaw to His Subscribers, privately printed, 1926

First English Edition

Note from T.E.SHAW *to his subscribers*

Collation 20.3 × 13.1 cm: single sheet printed on one side only.

Contents Heading and 33 lines announcing that *Seven Pillars* is now ready and asking for balance of payment due on subscriptions.

Text 20 lines, 9.2 × 8 cm.

Paper White, wove, unwatermarked, all edges trimmed.

Notes Aprroximately 150 copies. Announcement of publication.

Copies H, UT.

A039   T.E. LAWRENCE, Some Notes on the Writing of the Seven Pillars of Wisdom, 1927

First English Edition

SOME NOTES ON THE WRITING OF THE | SEVEN PILLARS OF WISDOM BY T.E. SHAW

Collation   24.8 × 18.7 cm: single-fold leaflet, pp.[1–4].

Contents   Pp.[1] title, [2–4] text.

Text   10 lines, 5 × 12.5 cm.

Paper   White, laid, watermarked, all edges trimmed.

Notes   About 200 copies for distribution to subscribers of *Seven Pillars of Wisdom*.
  Reprinted in 1935 edition of *Seven Pillars of Wisdom* p.22.
  Served as an explanation of writing of book up to time of issue.
  Error on p.3 should read 'compliment' for 'complaint'; the latter included uncorrected in many subsequent issues.

Copies   Cal, H, BPL, UT.

A040   T.E. LAWRENCE, Seven Pillars of Wisdom, 1926

Second English Edition

SEVEN PILLARS | OF | WISDOM | *a triumph* | 1926

Collation   25 × 19 cm: [1]^2 [2]^6 [3]^2 [4–5]^8 [6]^4 [7–9]^8 [10]^2 [11–13]^8 [14]^2 [15–22]^8 [23]^{12} [24–27]^8 [28]^4 [29–32]^8 [33]^4 [34–36]^8 [37]^4 [38–46]^8 [47]^{16} [48]^4 60 plates x^2, 364 leaves + 60 plates, pp.[1–6], [I–VI], VII–XXII, [2], 1–42, [2], 41–91, [92], [2], 93–144, [2], 145–207, [208], [2], 209–293, [204], [4], 295–363, [364], 365–435, [2], 437–489, [490], [4], 491–521, [522], [2], 523–569, [570], [2], 571–653, [654], 655–660, [1–2], includes paste down end papers.

Contents   Prp.[1–6] blank, [I] title page, [III] blank, [IIII] frontispiece, [IV] blank, [V] dedicatory poem, [VI] acknowledgments, VII–XIV VIII [sic] XVI–XVIII synposis, XIX–XXII illustrations, pp.[1] blank, [2] section title, synopsis, 3–40 introduction, [1] blank, [2] section title, synopsis, 41–91 text Book I, [1] blank, [2] section title, synopsis, 93–144 text Book II, [1] blank, [2] section title, synopsis, 145-207 text Book III, [208] blank, [1] blank, [2] section title, synopsis, 209–293 text Book IV, [294] blank, [1–2] stub for plate CAMEL MARCH, [1] blank, [2] section title, synopsis, 295–363 text Book V, [364] blank, [1–2] stub for plate AT A WELL, [1] blank, [2] section title, synopsis, 365–435 text Book VI, [1] blank, [2] section title, synopsis, 437–489 text Book VII, [490] blank, [1–2] stub for plate IRISH TROOPS, [1] blank, [2] section title, synopsis, 491–521 text Book VIII, [522] Kennington plate tipped in, [1] blank, [2] section title, synopsis, 523-569 text Book IX, [570] blank, [1] blank, [2] section title, synopsis, 571–52 text Book X, 653 postscript, [654] blank, 655–656 nominal roll, 657–659 campaign chronology, 660 colophon: 'Text and decorations printed by Manning Pike with the assistance of H.J. Hodgson at 25 Charles Street, Plates by Charles, Whittingham and Griggs, London WII', [1–2] blank.

Plates   3 fold maps (36.5 × 19.5 cm, 36.5 × 19.5 cm, 25.5 × 37.5 cm): and 60 plates tipped in following last page. Others follow pp.[1], 294, 364, 490, 522. Two other plates listed are not present: PROPHET'S TOMB p.92, and A GARDEN p.208. PRICKLY PEAR is not in the illustrations list. Plates following pp.[1], 294, 364, 490, 522 are tipped in on stubs of excised leaves.

Text   20 lines, 9.8 × 12.7 cm.

Paper   White, mould-made, top edges trimmed, unwatermarked, sheets bulk 6.5 cm.

Binding   Each copy bound differently. Of those examined: On spine: [gilt] THE | SEVEN | PILLARS. T.e. gilt. Head and tail bands in red and gold. End papers illustrated by Kennington. copies both in full leather and three-quarter leather have been examined. Twenty copies were bound by Bumpus, other copies were bound by Best (two were seen), Sangorski & Sutcliffe, Harrison, Macleish, Roger de Coverly & Sons, Wood.

Published at   £31 10s, December 1925–January 1926.

Notes   Complete copies have notation at bottom of page XIX: Complete | Tes | [or] Complete Copy | i.xii.26 T.E.S.
    Privately printed for subscribers. Limited to 211 copies as follows: Complete 170 copies, incomplete (see below) 32, 9 spoils (*Texas Quarterly* p.56, Autumn 1962 v.5 no. 3).
    Cuts printed with text are on following pages: XVIII colour, 6, 23, 29, 36, 40, 47, 59, 65, 75, 91, 110, 115, 119, 161, 176, 192, 201, 207, 229, 280, 284–5, 301, 308, 321, 339, 347, 372, 395, 400, 411, 416, 443, 460, 465, 476, 482, 489, 509, 515, 521, 522, 536, 539, 554, 558, 564, 569, 591 (same as 460), 595, 599, 607, 616, 639, 644, 649, 652.
    Set in Monotype, approximately two-thirds of the pages start with paragraph and engraved capitals.
    No words are divided at end of line.
    No paragraph ends less than half way across page.
    Collation may vary.
    There is no Chapter XI in chapter numbering.
    'Cranwell' or Subscriber's Edition (incomplete) same as complete issue described above with following differences: plates listed in text are either not present or at end with other plates, order of plates varies. The copies examined had plates IRISH TROOPS and MUDDOWRA following pp.490 and 522 in complete copies are included with other plates at the back of the book. On page XIX is notation INCOMPLETE. These 32 incomplete copies 'were presented to the men who had served with him in Arabia and who

were not able to pay the high price asked for the complete issue' (German Reed, p.1, E043-E046).

One copy (23.3 × 18.8 cm) bound in black pigskin, all edges black, with no plates thought to be Lawrence's proof copy.

On same page as TEL signature he has corrected errors in the list of illustrations using a K to show that Kennington drew THE GADFLY. Often in copies which are otherwise certified as being complete two line drawings by Paul Nash are lacking, THE PROPHETS TOMB and THE GARDEN.

Lawrence's inventory lists: 127 copies sold to subscribers at 30 gns each, 19 incomplete copies given to 'architects' of the revolt, 17 complete copies given to friends, 26 incomplete copies given to people mentioned in book (= 211 full texts).

Some copies contain the Hughes-Stanton line cut THE POEM.

For detailed examination of typographical errors see: V.M. Thompson, *Not a Suitable Hobby For an Airman* (1986).

Copies   CA, Cal, H, UT.

A041   T.E. LAWRENCE, Seven Pillars of Wisdom, Cape, 1935

Third English Edition (Limited issue)

SEVEN PILLARS | OF WISDOM | a triumph | T.E. LAWRENCE | LONDON | JONATHAN CAPE 30 BEDFORD SQUARE | and at Toronto

Collation   25.5 × 19.3 cm: [A]⁸ B–TT⁸, 336 leaves, pp.[1–6], 7–672.

Contents   Pp.[1] 'SEVEN PILLARS OF WISDOM | THIS EDITION IS | LIMITED TO SEVEN | HUNDRED AND FIFTY | COPIES FOR SALE | COPY NUMBER | [pub. device]', [2] blank, [3]title page, [4] issue statement, printer's credit, [5] dedicatory poem, [6] letter by Lawrence, 7–18 synopsis, 19–20 list of illustrations, 21–26 preface, 27 half-title, 28 section synopsis, 29–660 text, 661 post note, 662–666 appendixes, 667–669 place name index, 670–672 personal name index.

RT   On both verso and recto [according to subject of page].

Plates   Facsimiles following pp.20, 22, 25, 47 plates (4 in colour) following pp.50, 60, 62, 66, 68 colour, 72, 84, 98, 108, 110, 114, 126, 150, 166, 174, 178, 198, 222 color, 230, 260, 292, 300, 308, 322, 360, 378, 384, 392, 432 colour, 436, 444, 484, 504, 520, 526, 534, 544, 558, 582, 596, 610, 618, 644, 654 colour, 658. Four maps following pp.33, 65, 73, 227. Guard tissues before facsimiles and colour plates.

Typography and paper $ 1 signed BB.

Text   20 lines, 9.7 (9.9) × 13 cm.

Paper   White, wove, unwatermarked, top edge trimmed, sheets bulk 4.8 cm.

Binding   Pigskin spine 79 l. gy. y Br. brown buckram boards 55 s. Br. Single gilt rule along inner edge of leather spine. On front cover: [gilt, within crossed swords, in script] the | sword | also means | cleanness | & | death. On spine: SEVEN | PILLARS | OF | WISDOM | T.E. | LAWRENCE | JONATHAN CAPE. On back cover: blind rule along edge of spine leather. Red and yellow head band. Marbled end papers. Boxed as issued. T.e. gilt. Plain brown paper dust wrapper (rarely present).

Published at   July 29, 1935.

Notes   Drawings on pp.304–305 are incorrectly listed as being on pp.302–303 in another issue, identical to above except bound in full brown buckram.

Binding of first trade edition (see following item) has white end papers and lacks the limitation statement on p.[1]. This issue is reported to have been so bound and issued in a small number (approximately 60) to members of the firm May 1935. Not for sale. Sheets bulk 4.3 cm. Letter to this effect September 17, 1935 by G. Wren Howard.

Limited to 730 copies.

Copies   AC, Cal, H, UT.

A042   T.E. LAWRENCE, Seven Pillars of Wisdom, Cape, 1935

Third English Edition

SEVEN PILLARS | OF WISDOM | a triumph | T.E. LAWRENCE | LONDON | JONATHAN CAPE 30 BEDFORD SQUARE | and at Toronto

Collation   25.5 × 19.3 cm: [A]^8 B–TT^8, 336 leaves, pp.[1–6], 7–672.

Contents   Pp.[1] SEVEN PILLARS OF WISDOM | [pub. device], [2] blank, [3] title page, [4] issue statement, printer's credit, [5] dedicatory poem, [6] letter by Lawrence, 7–18 synopsis, 19–20 list of illustrations, 21–26 preface, 27 half title, 28 section synopsis, 29–660 text, 661 post note, 662–666 appendixes, 667–669 place name index, 670–672 personal name index.

RT   On both recto and verso [according to subject of page].

Plates   47 plates following pp.2, 50, 60, 62, 66, 68, 72, 84, 98, 108, 110, 114, 126, 150, 166, 174, 198, 222, 230, 260, 292, 300, 308, 322, 360, 378, 384, 392, 432, 436, 444, 464, 484, 504, 520, 526, 534, 544, 558, 582, 596, 610, 618, 644, 650, 658; four maps following pp.33, 65, 73, 227.

Typography and paper $ 1 signed BB.

Text   20 lines, 9.7 (9.9) × 13 cm.

Paper   White, wove, unwatermarked, top edge trimmed, sheets bulk 4.5 cm.

Binding Dark red buckram, 44 d. r Br and 55 s. Br. or 46 gy. r Br. On front cover: [crossed sword device] [within sword in script] the | sword | also means | clean-ness | & | death. On spine: SEVEN | PILLARS | OF | WISDOM | T.E. | LAWRENCE | JONATHAN CAPE. T. e. light brown. White end papers.

Published at 30s, July 1935.

Notes Fourteen impressions 1–14 printed at Alden Press, Oxford, 5–6 also printed by Lewis, Cambridge. Incorrect listing of illustration on pp.304–305 is corrected in second impression.

A variant issue of the fifth impression of September 1935 is bound in full blue crushed morocco 201 d. p B, has marbled end papers same design as those of Cape limited issue but of darker hues, gilt top edge with blue & white head and tail bands. At foot of spine [pub. device] replaces the words Jonathan Cape.

Another issue same as above with following differences: [Binding]: Full maroon leather 14 v. deep Red. On front cover: two squares, one within the other with stars in corners of inner square. Crossed sword emblem on front cover. Spine plain. T.e. gilt. Red & yellow head & tail bands. Marbled end papers. One of six copies given to Lawrence's pall bearers, specially bound.

List of impressions:
2nd, August 1935
3rd, August 1935
4th, August 1935
5th, September 1935, dark brown copies printed both in Oxford & Cambridge
6th, October 1935, copies printed both in Oxford & Cambridge
7th, August 1936
8th, December 1936
9th, July 1937
10th, December 1937 46 gy. r
11th, July 1938
12th, November 1938
13th, February 1939
14th, April 1939: sheets bulk 4.5 cm.
First printing 60,000 copies.
Preface incorporates 'Some Notes on the Writing of the Seven Pillars of Wisdom'.
A part of 'Publisher's Note' is from 'Revolt in the Desert'.
Kennington line cut 'A Forced Landing' is incorrectly listed in first impression as being on pp.302–304. This error is corrected to pp.304–305 in second and subsequent impressions.

Copies AC, Cal, H, UT, Ho.

A043   T.E. LAWRENCE, Seven Pillars of Wisdom, Cape, 1935

Publisher's Prospectus of Third English Edition

PROSPECTUS | *Crown quarto, fully illustrated and unabridged, 30s. net* | Seven Pillars of Wisdom

Collation   25 × 19 cm: single fold , 2 leaves, pp.[1–4].

Contents   Pp.[1] title, text of description and start of text of press opinions, [2–4] continuation of text of press opinions, at foot of p.[4] order form.

Text   20 lines, 9.5 × 16.7 cm (double column).

Paper   Buff, wove, unwatermarked, all edges trimmed.

Published at   Free advertising flyer.

Copies   AC.

A044   T.E. LAWRENCE, Seven Pillars of Wisdom, Cape, 1935

Publisher's Prospectus of Third English Edition

Crown quarto, fully illustrated and unabridged 30s. net | In August 1935, Jonathan Cape will publish a complete, | unabridged, illustrated edition of | Seven Pillars of Wisdom

Collation   24.8 × 18.5 cm: single leaf, printed on both sides.

Contents   [Recto] title and blurb, [verso] blurb continued and order form.

Paper   Buff, wove, unwatermarked, all edges trimmed.

Published at   Free advertising flyer.

Copies   AC, Cal.

A045   T.E. LAWRENCE, Seven Pillars of Wisdom, Cape, 1935

Book Club Prospectus of Third English Edition

Crown quarto, Fully illustrated and unabridged 30s net | In August, 1935, Jonathan Cape will publish a complete, | unabridged, illustrated edition of | Seven Pillars of Wisdom

Collation   24.8 × 18.4 cm: single sheet printed on both sides, pp.[1–2].

Contents Pp.[1] title, blurb, [2] blurb continued, order form, Book Society address.

Paper White, wove, unwatermarked, all edges trimmed.

Published at Free advertising flyer.

Copies Cal.

A046 T.E. LAWRENCE, Seven Pillars of Wisdom, World Books, 1939

Fourth English Edition (Book Club)

SEVEN PILLARS | OF WISDOM | a triumph | T.E. LAWRENCE | VOLUME I [II] | WORLD BOOKS | 20 HEADFORT PLACE SW 1 | LONDON | *facing:* AUTHOR

Collation 19.7 × 13.7 cm: Vol. I, [A]^{16} B–L^{16}, 176 leaves, pp.[1–6], 7–352; Vol. II [M]^{16} N–U^{16} Y^{16}, 176 leaves, pp.[1–4], 353–700.

Contents Vol. I: pp.[1] bastard title, [2] blank, [3] title page, [4] issue statement, printer's, papermaker's credits, [5] dedicatory poem, [6] author's note, 7–18 synopsis, 19–24 preface, [25] half-title, 26–352 text. Vol. II prp.[1] bastard title, [2] illustrations, [3] title page, [4] issue statement, printer's, papermaker's credits, pp.353–684 text, 685–689 appendixes, [690] blank, 691–695 index to place names, 696–700 personal name index.

RT On both verso and recto [according to subject of page].

Plates Vol. I: five plates tipped in, printed on one side only following pp.[1], 64, 92, 224, 256. Vol. II: five plates following pp.[2], [4], 464, 637, 668.

Typography and paper $ 1,5 signed B,B*.

Text 20 lines 8.4 (8.5) × 10.2 cm.

Paper White, wove, unwatermarked, all edges trimmed, sheets bulk 2.5 cm.

Binding Brown buckram 77 m. y Br. On spine: [on black leather patch, within gilt frame of double rules, gilt] SEVEN | PILLARS | OF | WISDOM | I [II] | T.E. | LAWRENCE. T.e. brown.

Published at 2s 6d cloth, 3s 6d buckram.

Notes Another issue same as above with following differences: [Binding]: light brown oatmeal cloth. On front cover: [crossed sword design, in brown]. On spine: [in brown] SEVEN | PILLARS | OF | WISDOM | T.E. | LAWRENCE | [crossed swords with vol. number between swords].
Another issue as above t.e. unstained.
Another issue as above binding is 37 m. r O.
Another issue as above sheets bulk 2 cm.

Another issue as above with following differences: [Title page imprint]: 13 GROSVENOR PLACE SW1; [Contents]: [4] binder's credits added both volumes.

Another issue as immediately above but title page imprint reads: THE REPRINT SOCIETY | LONDON. Pub. device of World Books replaces crossed swords device at foot of spine. Both oatmeal cloth and brown buckram states exist. The Reprint Society was an associated club of World Books.

This title was the first published by World Books.

Copies AC, Cal.

A047   T.E. LAWRENCE, Seven Pillars of Wisdom, Cape, 1940

Fourth English Edition

SEVEN PILLARS | OF WISDOM | a triumph | T.E. LAWRENCE | JONATHAN CAPE | THIRTY BEDFORD SQUARE | LONDON | *facing:* AUTHOR

Collation   20 × 13.5 cm: [A]^{16} B–Y^{16}, 352 leaves, pp.[1–10], 11–700, [4].

Contents   Pp.[1–2] blank, [3] bastard title, [4] blank, [5] title page, [6] issue statement, printer's, papermaker's, binder's credits, [7] dedicatory poem, [8] blank, [9] letter by author, [10] blank, 11 list of contents, [12] blank, [13] illustrations, [14] blank, 15–20 preface by A.W. Lawrence, 21–684 text, 685–689 appendixes, [690] blank, 691–695 index of place names, 696–700 personal index, [1–4] blank.

RT   On both verso and recto [according to subject of page].

Plates   Eight on coated paper following pp.[4], 92, 224, 256, 384, 416, 636, 668. Maps following pp.31, 65, 73, 235.

Typography and paper $ 1,5 signed B,B* 0*.

Text   20 lines, 8.4 (8.5) × 10.2 cm.

Paper   Thin, white, wove, unwatermarked, all edges trimmed, sheets bulk 2.8 cm.

Binding   Blue cloth 173 m.g. B. On front cover: [blind stamped, crossed sword device]. On spine: [gilt] SEVEN | PILLARS | OF | WISDOM | [cut] | T.E. | LAWRENCE | [pub. device]. T.e. grey.

Published at   10s 6d.

Notes   List of Impressions:
   2nd, 1941 February, printing as above: 187 d. gy B
   3rd, 1941 September, as immediately above
   4th, 1941 December
   5th, 1942 April

6th, 1942 August, as 1941 February

7th, 1946 January, as above with following differences: [Typography and paper]: $ 1 signed 20 Lawrence; [Binding]: 182 m.B; printed in Sweden by Bonniers

8th, 1946 June, as 1941 February, T.e grey

9th, 1949, as 1941 February, with following differences: [Paper]: sheets bulk 3 cm; [Binding]: 182 m.B

10th, 1950 June

11th, 1951 December

12th, 1953 April

Various colours of cloth are reported; red, green, various blues.

Contains suppressed introductory chapter; first printing thus. This chapter was dropped from 1926 ed. on advice of G.B. Shaw. The suppressed chapter was reprinted in *Oriental Assembly* and *Men in Print*.

First edition in smaller format.

A.W. Lawrence preface has added postscript p.20.

Copies   AC, Cal, UT.

A048   T.E. LAWRENCE, Seven Pillars of Wisdom, Cape, 1954

Fifth English Edition

SEVEN PILLARS | OF WISDOM | a triumph | T.E. LAWRENCE | JONATHAN CAPE | THIRTY BEDFORD SQUARE | LONDON | *facing:* AUTHOR

Collation   20 × 13.5 cm: [A] –Y^{16}, 352 leaves, pp.[1–10], 11–700, [4].

Contents   Pp.[1–2] blank, [3] bastard title, [4] blank, [5] title page, [6] issue statement, printer's credit, [7] dedicatory poem, [8] blank, [9] letter by author, [10] blank, 11 contents, [12] blank, 13 illustrations, [14] blank, 15–20 preface by A.W. Lawrence, 21–684 text, 685–689 appendixes, [690] blank, 691–700 indexes, [1–4] blank.

RT   On both verso and recto [according to subject of page].

Plates   Eight b/w plates on coated paper printed on one side only following pp.[4], 92, 224, 256, 384, 416, 636, 668; maps pp.31, 65, 73, 235.

Typography and paper $ 1 signed B.

Text   20 lines, 8.3 (8.4) × 10 cm.

Paper   Thin, white, wove, unwatermarked, all edges trimmed, sheets bulk 2.8 cm.

Binding   Blue cloth 182 m. Blue. On front cover: [blind stamped crossed sword device]. On spine: [gilt] SEVEN | PILLARS | OF | WISDOM | [cut] | T.E. | LAWRENCE | [pub. device . T.e. grey.

Published at 18s.

Notes Text reset. List of impressions:
2nd, February 1955, same as above: [Binding]: 173 m. g B
3rd, 1963, [Pub at]: 25s
4th, January 1964
5th, 1965, same as above with following differences: [Pub. at]: 30s.

Copies AC, CA, Cal, H.

A049 T.E. LAWRENCE, Seven Pillars of Wisdom, Penguin, 1962

Sixth English Edition

T.E. LAWRENCE | [outline letters] SEVEN PILLARS | [outline letters] OF WISDOM | A TRIUMPH | PENGUIN BOOKS | IN ASSOCIATION WITH | JONATHAN CAPE

Collation 19.7 × 13 cm: guillotined sheets glued to covers, 352 leaves, pp.[1–14], 15–700, [4].

Contents Pp.[1] biographical paragraph on TEL, [2–5] maps, [6] blank, [7] title page, [8] issue, copyright statements, printer's, map credits, [9] dedicatory poem, [10] letter by author, [11] contents, [12] blank, [13] list of plates, [14] list of drawings, 15–20 introduction, 21–24 introductory chapter, [25] half-title, [26] synopsis, 27–683 text, [684] postscript, 685–689 appendixes, [690] blank, 691–700 indexes, [1–4] blank.

RT On both verso and recto [according to subject of page].

Plates Four plates on uncoated paper following p.352.

Text 20 lines 8.3 (8.4) × 10.1 cm.

Paper Thin, white, wove, unwatermarked, all edges trimmed, sheets bulk 2.5 cm.

Binding White paper covers. On front cover: [within grey panel] Lawrence of Arabia | Seven Pillars of Wisdom | [drawing of Lawrence by John] | [within grey panel] PENGUIN MODERN CLASSICS [within orange square, pub. device] 10/6. On spine: [within grey panel, pub. device] | [running down] T.E. Lawrence Seven Pillars of Wisdom | [within grey panel, across] 1696. On back cover: [within grey panel] Lawrence of Arabia | [quotes from reviews] | [within grey panel, within orange square, pub. device] PENGUIN MODERN CLASSICS.

Published at 10s 6d.

Notes List of impressions:
2nd, 1963
3rd, 1964, identical to above
4th, 1964, identical to above with following differences: [Binding]: On front cover: [within grey panel, at top] [pub. device] Penguin Modern Classics 10/6 | [white rule] | Lawrence of Arabia | [in white panel] Seven Pillars of Wisdom | [drawing of Lawrence by John]. On spine: [within grey panel at top] [pub. device] | [running down] T.E. Lawrence Seven Pillars of Wisdom | [across at bottom] 1696. On back cover: [within grey panel] Penguin Modern Classics [pub. device] | [white rule] | Lawrence of Arabia | [in white section, blurbs from reviews].
5th, 1966
6th, 1969
7th, 1971, as above with following differences: [Contents]: last four pages as follows: [1] general information about Penguin books, [2] blank, [3-4] ads; [Paper]: sheets bulk 2.8 cm; [Plates]: On front cover: [olive green] [pub. device] Penguin Modern Classics | [olive green] T.E. Lawrence | [long rule in olive green] | [in white] Seven Pillars | [in white] of Wisdom | [colour painting of Arab horsemen and Handley Page bomber]. On spine: [pub. device] | [running down, author's name in white] T.E. Lawrence. Seven Pillars of Wisdom | ISBN 0 14 | 00.1696 1. On back cover: [in white] Penguin Modern Classics [pub. device] | [in white] T.E. Lawrence | [long rule] | Seven Pillars | of Wisdom | [in blue, quotes from reviews, blurbs, cover design credit] | $4.95 | Biography/ | Literature | ISBN 0 14 | 00.1696 1; [Published at]: $4.95
8th, 1973, as immediately above
9th, 1975
10th, 1976, as immediately above.

Copies AC, Cal.

A050 T.E. LAWRENCE, Seven Pillars of Wisdom, Cape, 1973

Seventh English Edition

T.E. LAWRENCE | SEVEN PILLARS | OF WISDOM | a triumph | [pub. device] | JONATHAN CAPE | THIRTY BEDFORD SQUARE LONDON

Collation 21.5 × 13.5 cm: [A]–X^{16}, 352 leaves, pp.[1–10], 11–700, [701–704].

Contents Pp.[1–2] blank, [3] bastard title, [4] blank, [5] title page, [6] issue statement,ISBN, printer's, binder's, papermaker's credits,[7] dedicatory poem, [8] blank, [9] author's letter,[10] blank, 11 contents, [12] blank, 13 illustrations, [14] blank, 15–20 preface by A.W. Lawrence, 21–24 introduction, [25] half-title, [26] synposis of chapters I–VIII, 27–684 text, 685–689 appendixes, [690] blank, 691–700 indexes, [701–704] blank.

RT   On both verso and recto [according to contents of page].

Plates   Eight plates on coated paper. Printed on one side only, following pp.[4], 92, 224, 256, 384, 416, 636, 668; four maps on coated paper following pp.30, 64, 72, 234.

Typography and paper $ 1,5 signed c, c*.

Text   20 lines, 8.3 (8.5) × 10 cm.

Paper   White, wove, thin, unwatermarked, all edges trimmed, sheets bulk 3 cm.

Binding   Medium yellow brown 77 m. y Br. buckram. On spine: [gilt] [Oxford rule] | T.E. | LAWRENCE | [cut] | SEVEN PILLARS | OF | WISDOM | [Oxford rule] | [at foot] [pub. device]. T.e. black, yellow end papers.

Published at   £3.95.

Notes   Reset restoring cuts made by A.W. Lawrence in 1935 edition.

   Another issue, Book Club Associates 1974, identical to above with following differences: in place of Cape imprint on title page BOOK CLUB ASSOCIATES | LONDON; [Binding]: Brown paper covered boards 51 deep O. On spine: [club device replaces Cape device at foot of spine].

Copies   H.

A051   T.E. LAWRENCE, Seven Pillars of Wisdom, Cape, 1976

Eighth English Edition

T.E. LAWRENCE | SEVEN PILLARS OF WISDOM | A TRIUMPH | JONATHAN CAPE | THIRTY BEDFORD SQUARE | LONDON

Collation   21.6 × 13.5 cm: [1–16]^{16} [17]^{8} [18]^{16}, 280 leaves, pp.[i–viii], ix–xiii, [xiv], [1–2], 3–546.

Contents   Prp.[i] bastard title, [ii] blank, [iii] title page, [iv] issue statement, printer's credit, [v] dedicatory poem, [vi] author's preface, [vii] contents, [viii] illustrations, ix–xiii preface by A.W. Lawrence, [xiv] pub. note, pp.[1] half-title, [2] blank, 3–530 text, [531] postscript, 532–536 appendixes, 537–545 indexes, [546] blank.

RT   On verso SEVEN PILLARS OF WISDOM. On recto [according to chapter].

Plates   Eight b/w plates on coated paper, printed on one side only, following pp.[2], 26, 50, 178, 210, 274, 306, 520; maps following pp.11, 39, 47, 174.

Text   20 lines, 8.6 (8.7) × 10.3 cm.

Paper   Buff, wove, unwatermarked, all edges trimmed, sheets bulk 3 cm.

Binding   Brown buckram 54 br. O. On spine: [gilt] T.E. | LAWRENCE | [cut] | SEVEN | PILLARS | OF | WISDOM | [pub. device].

Published at   £10.95, December 1976.

Notes   Offset from 1935 edition with type reduced and lines added to each page to make fewer pages. Some text lines reset. Selection of illustrations are new photos of original artwork.

Another issue, Book Club Associates 1976, as above with following differences: in place of Cape imprint on title page BOOK CLUB ASSOCIATES | LONDON; [Binding]: Brown orange paper covered boards 54 b. O. On spine: Cape device replaced by Book Club device.

Another issue of Book Club Associates 1979 identical to immediately above.

Copies   AC, Cal.

A051a   T.E. LAWRENCE, Seven Pillars of Wisdom, Orchard, 1986

Ninth English Edition

SEVEN PILLARS | OF WISDOM | a triumph | T.E. LAWRENCE | NEW ORCHARD EDITIONS

Collation   24.8 × 19.1 cm: [1–42]¹⁶ [43]⁴, 340 leaves, pp.[1–4], 7–32, [1], 33–60, [1], 61–64, [1], 65–72, [1], 73–226, [1], 227–672.

Contents   Pp.[1] bastard title, [2] frontispiece 'Camel March', [3] title page, [4] issue copyright statements, printer's and binder's credits, 7–18 contents, [19] dedicatory poem, [20] author's letter, 21–26 preface, [27] half title, [28] synopsis, 29–661 text, [662]–666 appendixes, 667–672 indexes. Single leaves following pp.32, 60, 64, 72, 226 are illustrations.

RT   On both verso and recto according to text of page.

Text   20 lines, 10.8 (10) × 13.1 cm.

Paper   White, wove, unwatermarked, all edges trimmed, sheets bulk 3.3 cm.

Binding   Dark red 16 d. red cloth covered boards. On spine: [gilt, running down] THE SEVEN PILLARS | T.E. LAWRENCE | OF WISDOM a triumph | [across at foot, pub. device]. Red and gold head and tail bands.

Published at   £15.00.

Notes   Reprint of Cape 1935 edition; some plates are reduced and placed on page with text.

Copies   AC, Cal.

A052 T.E. Lawrence, Seven Pillars of Wisdom, Doran, 1926

First American Edition

THE SEVEN | PILLARS OF WISDOM | NEW YORK: | George H. Doran Company | MCMXXVI

Collation 28 × 20 cm: π² π² [1–14]⁸ [15]², 334 leaves, pp.[1–8], [1–2], 3–652, [1–8].

Contents Prp.[1–6] blank, [7] title page, [8] copyright statement, pp.[1] blank, [2] section summary, 3–652 text, [1] Of this book there | have been printed | and bound twenty- | two copies, each one of | which, is numbered and | signed by the publisher and | only ten of which are for sale. | *This is copy number* ____, [2] blank, [3–8] blank.

Text 20 lines, 9.7 × 12.7 cm.

Paper White, wove, watermarked, top edge trimmed, sheets bulk 5.3 cm, 44 lb white parchment substitute.

Binding Blue paper covered boards 186 gy. Blue vellum spine and corners. On spine: [on black leather label within gilt frame] THE | SEVEN | PILLARS | OF | WISDOM. T.e. gilt. Red and gold head and tail bands. Endpapers blue, same paper as covers. Duval describes a copy in brown buckram. Out of series copies, perhaps three thus, are bound in blue buckram spine and blue paper covered boards.

Published at $20,000, April 1926.

Notes Limited to 22 copies signed by George Doran. Doran collected specimen sheets for two additional copies. One of these was examined. Lacks final leaf [41⁸ −8 = 41⁷], bound in blue paper covered boards 185 p. Blue, blue buckram spine 186 gy Blue, maroon leather patch on spine, colophon page bears Doran's note 'Specimen sheets'. Loosely inserted letter from Doran stating that the book is in 16-page gatherings and this copy is one of two issued out of series from specimen sheets. Copies: 6 TEL, 2 Library of Congress, 10 for sale at $20,000 each, 4 Doran's (2 out of series by Doran). Even though TEL in a letter of 5 May 1927 instructed that all cuts be left out of the American edition, some were retained. This edition has a different cut on p.339 to the Cranwell edition; in the American edition the drawing is of the old man in Rumm, in the Cranwell edition two Syrians before high rocks are depicted. Cuts appear on pp.40, 284–285, 301, 339, 476, 480, 521, 550, 649.

Lawrence comments on this edition: '...the American thing, whose only merit is its rarity. All the text is there. Only it is ugly.' No illustrations other than the few cuts in text. Minor differences of text as compared to Cranwell edition, with two variant passages.

Copies Cal, H.

A053 T.E. LAWRENCE, Seven Pillars of Wisdom, Doubleday, Doran, 1935

Second American Edition [Limited Issue]

SEVEN PILLARS | OF WISDOM | a triumph | T.E. LAWRENCE | Garden City, New York | DOUBLEDAY, DORAN & COMPANY, INC. | MCMXXXV

Collation 25 × 19.5 cm: π^1 [1–42]^8, 337 leaves, pp.[2], [1–6], 7–672.

Contents Prp.[1] 'THIS EDITION IS LIMITED TO | SEVEN HUNDRED AND FIFTY COPIES | OF WHICH THIS IS | NO. .... ', [2] blank, pp.[1] bastard title, [2] blank, [3] title page, [4] printer's credit, issue, copyright statements, [5] dedicatory poem, [6] letter by author, 7–18 synopsis, contents, 19–20 illustrations, 21–26 preface, [27] half-title, [28] section introduction, 29–660 text, 661–666 appendixes, 667–672 indexes.

RT On both verso and recto [according to subject of page].

Plates Forty-eight plates following pp.48, 56 double, 64, 80 colour, 88 double, 96, 104 double, 112, 128, 144, 160, 176, 192, 208, 224 colour, 240, 256, 272, 288, 304, 320, 352, 368, 384, 400, 416 colour, 432, 448, 464, 480, 496, 512, 528 double, 544, 560, 576, 592, 608 double, 624, 640, 656 colour, 658. Fold maps following pp.33, 65, 73, 227 in red and black.

Text 20 lines, 9.3 (9.7) × 13.2 cm.

Paper White, wove, unwatermarked, top edge trimmed, sheets bulk 4.5 cm.

Binding Maroon buckram boards 16 d. Red, dark brown pigskin spine. On front cover: [gilt rule along inner edge of leather spine]. On spine: SEVEN | PILLARS | OF | WISDOM | T.E. | LAWRENCE | DOUBLEDAY | DORAN. On back cover: [gilt rule along inner edge of leather spine]. T.e. maroon. Red and yellow head and tail bands. White end papers. Boxed as issued.

Published at $25.00, 18 September 1935.

Notes Limited to 750 copies. Last line on verso of title page, FIRST EDITION., designates first printing.

Copies AC, Cal, H, UT.

A054 T.E. LAWRENCE, Seven Pillars of Wisdom, Doubleday, Doran, 1935

Second American Edition

SEVEN PILLARS | OF WISDOM | a triumph | T.E. LAWRENCE | Garden City, New York | DOUBLEDAY, DORAN & COMPANY, INC. | MCMXXXV

Collation 25 × 19.5 cm: [1–42]⁸, 336 leaves, pp.[1–6], 7–672.

Contents Pp.[1] bastard title, [2] blank, [3] title page, [4] printer's credit, issue, copyright statements, [5] dedicatory poem, [6] letter by author, 7–18 synopsis and contents, 19–20 illustrations, 21–26 preface, [27] half-title, [28] section introduction, 29–660 text, 661–666 appendixes, 667–672 indexes.

RT On both recto and verso [according to subject of page].

Plates Forty-eight plates following pp.48, 56 double, 64, 80, 88 double, 96, 104 double, 112, 128, 144, 160, 176, 192, 208, 224, 240, 256, 272, 288, 304, 320, 352, 368, 384, 400, 416, 432, 448, 464, 480, 496, 512, 528 double, 544, 560, 576, 592, 608 double, 624, 640, 656, 658. Maps following pp.33, 65, 73, 227 in red and black.

Text 20 lines, 9.3 (9.7) × 13.2 cm.

Paper White, wove, unwatermarked, all edges trimmed, sheets bulk 4 cm.

Binding Grey brown buckram 80 gy y Br. On front cover: [crossed swords device]. On spine: [gilt] SEVEN | PILLARS | OF | WISDOM | T.E. | LAWRENCE | DOUBLEDAY | DORAN. T.e. brown. Red and yellow head and tail bands. Boxed as issued.

Published at $5.00, 27 September 1935.

Notes First impression bears under the copyright statement on verso of title page: FIRST EDITION AFTER THE PRINTING OF A LIMITED EDITION | OF SEVEN HUNDRED AND FIFTY COPIES. Later impressions lack this statement. There are three states of the dust wrapper. The first is blank on back. Second has the type overlapping the drawing of Lawrence by John. The third state has the text of the blurb framing the drawing along one side and under the drawing.

Another issue bears an imprint date of 1936 on title page.

Copies AC, Cal, H, UT, Ho.

A055 T.E. LAWRENCE, Seven Pillars of Wisdom, Doubleday, Doran, 1935

Publisher's Prospectus of Second American Edition

ANNOUNCING THE PUBLICATION | OF | [title in red] Seven | Pillars | of | Wisdom | *By* T.E. LAWRENCE | [in red] COMPLETE AND UNABRIDGED | REGULAR EDITION priced at five dollars the | copy. *Ready September 27th.* | DE LUXE EDITION, limited to 750 numbered | copies, $25.00 the copy. *Ready September 18th.*

Collation 21.6 × 14 cm: single-fold leaflet.

Contents Pp.[1] title page, [2–3] blurb, [4] one line excerpts from reviews, order form.

Text 5 lines, 2 × 10.2 cm.

Paper Buff laid, watermarked, all edges trimmed.

Published at Free advertising flyer.

Copies AC, Cal.

A056 T.E. LAWRENCE, Seven Pillars of Wisdom, Doubleday, Doran, 1935

Publisher's Prospectus for Second American Edition

[No title]

Collation 26 × 19 cm: single-fold leaflet, 2 leaves, pp.[1–4].

Contents Pp.[1] colour reproduction of Kennington pastel of TEL, [2–3] The Story of "The Seven Pillars of Wisdom", lengthy blurb, [4] colour reproduction of Kennington plate of MATAR.

Text 20 lines, 8 × 7 cm (double column 14.6 cm).

Paper Tan, wove, simulated laid, unwatermarked, all edges trimmed.

Published at Free advertising flyer.

Copies AC, Cal.

A057 T.E. LAWRENCE, Seven Pillars of Wisdom, Doubleday, Doran, 1935

Book Club Prospectus of Second American Edition

[within ornate two-colour frame] *The Book-of-the-Month-Club* | *offers you* | [in red] FREE ... for your library | – a book which until last year was available | only in privately printed copies valued at $20,000 each. Unexpurgated, identical with | the original text is this special edition of | [title in red] SEVEN PILLARS | OF WISDOM | By T.E. LAWRENCE | [five-line blurb by Churchill].

Collation 23 × 17 cm: double-fold leaflet, pp.[1–6].

Contents Pp.[1] title page, [2–4] full-colour blurb on book with illustrations, three inside pages one spread, [5–6] blurb and explanation of Book of Month Club with likenesses of editorial board.

Text Varies.

Paper Tan, laid, unwatermarked, all edges trimmed.

Published at   Free advertising flyer.

Copies   AC.

A058   T.E. LAWRENCE, Seven Pillars of Wisdom, Doubleday, Doran, 1935

Publisher's promotional leaflet

How to Sell | SEVEN PILLARS OF WISDOM | BY T.E. LAWRENCE | TO BE PUBLISHED SEPTEMBER 27* | AN INFORMAL DIALOGUE | COMPILED IN CONNECTION WITH | THE NATIONWIDE PRIZE CONTEST | SPONSORED BY | DOUBLEDAY, DORAN & CO., INC. | *the contest closes midnight, Saturday, September 21st these dates | are final*

Collation   21.7 × 14 cm: [1]⁴, [1], 1–6, [1].

Contents   Pp.[1] cover title, [1] scene, time, personae, 2–4 text, 5–6 form for list of name and addresses of purchasers of book, 7 quotes from reviews.

Paper   White, wove, unwatermarked, all edges trimmed.

Binding   Yellow paper covers 86 l. Y. Stapled to sheets.

Published at   Free advertising flyer.

Copies   H.

A059   T.E. LAWRENCE, Seven Pillars of Wisdom, Doubleday, Doran, 1936

Second American Edition [small format]

SEVEN PILLARS | OF WISDOM | a triumph | T.E. LAWRENCE | Garden City, New York | DOUBLEDAY, DORAN & COMPANY, INC. | MCMXXXVI

Collation   23.3 × 17 cm: [1–20] ¹⁶ [21]⁴ [22]¹⁶, 340 leaves, pp.[1–6], 7–32, [2], 33–64, [2], 65–72, [2], 73–226, [2], 227–672, maps included in black only.

Contents   Pp.[1] bastard title, [2] blank, [3] title page, [4] printer's credit, issue, copyright statements, [5] dedicatory poem, [6] letter by author, 7–18 synopsis and contents, 19–20 illustrations, 21–26 preface, [27] half-title, [28] introduction of chapters I to VII, 29–[661] text and maps, [662]–666 appendixes, 667–669 index of place names, 670–672 index of personal names.

RT   On both verso and recto [according to subject of page].

Plates   Forty-eight plates following pp.2, 38, 54, 62, 68, 82, 90, 98, 114, 122,

130, 146, 154, 162, 178, 186, 218, 226, 240, 248, 280, 288, 304, 312, 320, 352, 368, 384, 400, 416, 432, 448, 464, 480, 496, 512, 528, 536, 544, 560, 568, 600, 608, 624 double, 640, 648.

Text   20 lines, 9.3 (9.7) × 13.2 cm.

Paper   White, wove, unwatermarked, top edges trimmed, sheets bulk 3.5 cm.

Binding   Oatmeal buckram. On front cover: [blind stamped crossed swords]. On spine: [gilt] SEVEN | PILLARS | OF | WISDOM | T.E. | LAWRENCE | DOUBLEDAY | DORAN. T.e. maroon.

Published at $3.00.

Notes   Another issue same as above, with following differences: [Binding]: Maroon linen 16 d. Red.

Another issue, same as above, with following differences: title page bears date: MCMXXXVII; [Binding]: maroon linen 16 d. Red; [Paper]: sheets bulk 3.8 cm.

Another issue same as above with following differences: [Binding]: oatmeal cloth; [Title page]: MCMXXXVII.

Copies   AC, Cal, UT.

A060   T.E. LAWRENCE, Seven Pillars of Wisdom, Garden City, 1938

Second American Edition (De Luxe Edition)

[within double rule frame which has swords, rifles and flags] SEVEN PILLARS | OF WISDOM | A Triumph | T.E. LAWRENCE | *De Luxe Edition* | [rule] | GARDEN CITY | PUBLISHING CO. | INCORPORATED | Garden City, N.Y.

Collation   23.3 × 17 cm: [1–20]^{16} [21]^4 [22]^{16}, 340 leaves, pp.[1–6], 7–32, [2], 33–64, [2], 65–72, [2], 73–226, [2], 227–672.

Contents   Pp.[1] bastard title, [2] blank, [3] title page, [4] printer's credit, issue, copyright statements, [5] dedicatory poem, [6] letter by author, 7–18 synopsis & contents, 19–20 illustrations, 21–26 preface, [27] half-title, [28] section introduction, 29–660 text, 661–666 appendixes, 667–672 indexes.

RT   On both recto and verso [according to subject of page].

Plates   Forty-seven plates, lacks Junor plate, following pp.[2], 32, 62, 90, 122, 154, 162, 178, 186, 218, 248, 280, 312, 344, 376, 408, 429, 440, 472, 504, 536, 568, 600, 632, 640. Maps following pp.33, 65, 73, 227.

Text   20 lines, 9.3 (9.7) × 13.2 cm.

Paper　White, wove, unwatermarked, top edge trimmed, sheets bulk 4.5 cm.

Binding　Brown buckram 57 l. Br. On front cover: [blind stamped crossed swords]. On spine: [gilt, four ornamental rules] | [within dark brown rectangle] SEVEN | PILLARS | OF | WISDOM | [rule] T.E. LAWRENCE | [three ornamental rules] | [large cut] | [four decorative rules] | [within brown rectangle] GARDEN CITY PUBLISHING CO. | [three ornamental rules]. On back cover: [blind stamped hand press], lower right corner]. T.e. brown.

Published at　$1.98.

Notes　Another issue, same as above, with following differences: [Contents]: CL added as last line on verso of title page; [Binding]: Maroon 13 deep Red. On front cover: [gilt double rule frame, within which are four corner decorations and oval in centre]. On spine: [triple decorative rules] | [rectangular decorative device] | [single rule] | [within black rectangle] SEVEN | PILLARS | OF | WISDOM | T.E. LAWRENCE | [double rule] | [three decorative rectangles] | [triple rules]. Red and yellow head and tail bands.
　　Another issue, as above, with following differences: [Binding]: black cloth. T.e. mauve. Sheets bulk 3.5 cm (1940?). Has Doubleday on title page, spine and dust wrapper.
　　Another issue, as above, with following differences: [Binding]: black cloth. T.e. not stained. red and white head and tail bands. Doubleday, 1953. Sheets bulk 4.2 cm. [Published at]: $6.95.
　　Another issue, as above, with following differences: CL added as last line of type on verso of title page; [Binding]: 76 l. y Br. On back cover: no blind stamping.
　　Another issue (1942?), as above, with following difference: [Binding]: 39 gy r O.

Copies　AC, Cal, UT.

A061　T.E. LAWRENCE, Seven Pillars of Wisdom, Dell, 1962

Third American Edition

[Double page spread] On verso: [pub. device] | T.E. LAWRENCE | A LAUREL EDITION. On recto: [running down] a Triumph | [across] SEVEN | PILLARS | OF WISDOM

Collation　18 × 10.6 cm: guillotined sheets glued to covers, 328 leaves, pp.[1–7], 8–655, [1].

Contents　Pp.[1] blurb, [2–3] title page, [4] copyright, issue statements, [5]

dedicatory poem, [6] author's note, [7]–20 synopsis, 21–26 preface, 27 introduction, 28–655 text, [1] epliogue.

RT On verso: *T.E. Lawrence.* On recto: *Seven Pillars of Wisdom.*

Text 20 lines, 7 (7.1) × 8.9 cm.

Paper White, newsprint, wove, unwatermarked, all edges trimmed, sheets bulk 2.5 cm.

Binding Pictorial paper covers. On front cover: [hand holding rifle and mounted horsemen in background] [in upper left corner, within double panelled rectangle, in purple] [top panel] DELL | [lower panel] LAUREL | EDITION | [running up beside rectangle] LY111 | [across] The legendary Lawrence of Arabia | [in upper right corner] *complete* | 95c | [in purple] T.E. LAWRENCE | tells the amazing story of how he lived, loved | and fought among the Arabs. "Superb . . . | Thrilling . . . Immortal." – NEW YORK HERALD TRIBUNE | [decorative purple rule] | SEVEN PILLARS | OF WISDOM | [decorative purple rule] | *soon to be a magnificent motion picture* | *"LAWRENCE OF ARABIA".* On spine: LYIII | [running down, purple] *SEVEN PILLARS OF WISDOM* | T.E. LAWRENCE | [across in purple, pub. device] | Dell. On back cover: [painting of Lawrence, colour] | [next four lines purple] THE GREATEST MILITARY ADVENTURE | STORY OF MODERN TIMES ORIGINALLY | PUBLISHED AT $150 A COPY NOW COM- | PLETE, UNEXPUR-GATED AND UNABRIDGED | [three quotes from reviews]. [upper right corner, running up] *cover printed in U.S.A. color illustration by PUCCI.* All edges green.

Published at 95c, March 1962.

Notes List of impressions:
  2nd, December 1962, same as above, with following differences: [Binding]: white paper covers. On front cover: [in upper left corner, within brown rectangle, in white] DELL | 7744 | LAUREL | EDITION | [in red] *This and Only This* | [in red] *is the Incredible Story of* | LAWRENCE OF ARABIA | [coloured drawing] | *exactly as told by T.E. LAWRENCE* | *in his thrilling masterpiece* | [in red] SEVEN PILLARS | OF WISDOM. On spine: [as above except 7744 substituted for LYIII], red replaces purple lettering. On back cover: [upper right corner, running up] cover printed in USA.
  3rd, May 1963
  4th, July 1963
  5th, February 1964
  6th, May 1954
  7th, January 1965
  8th, January 1966
  9th, June 1967.

Copies AC, Cal.

A062   T.E. LAWRENCE, Seven Pillars of Wisdom, Doubleday, 1966

Fourth American Edition

SEVEN PILLARS | OF | WISDOM | [rule] | *A Triumph* | T.E. LAWRENCE | *Doubleday & Company, Inc.* | GARDEN CITY, NEW YORK | 1966

Collation   20.8 × 14.3 cm: guillotined sheets, 315 leaves, pp.[i–vii], viii–xiv, [1–3], 4–622, [4].

Contents   Prp.[i] bastard title, [ii] blank, [iii] title page, [iv] issue, copyright statements, [v] dedicatory poem, [vi] letter by author, [vii] –viii contents, [ix] –xiv preface, pp.[1] introduction and synopsis, [2] blank, [3] – 606 text, [607] –612 appendixes, [613] –622 indexes, [1–4] blank.

RT   On verso SEVEN PILLARS OF WISDOM. On recto [according to book].

Text   20 lines, 8.4 (8.6) × 10.4 cm.

Paper   White, wove, unwatermarked, top and bottom edges trimmed, sheets bulk 4 cm.

Binding   Brown cloth 40. s.r Br. On spine: [gilt, within rectangle of single rules] SEVEN | PILLARS | OF | WISDOM | [rule] | T.E. | LAWRENCE | [at foot below rectangle] DOUBLEDAY. Yellow head and tail bands. Sand-coloured end papers.

Published at $5.95.

Notes   Lacks suppressed introductory chapter.

Copies   AC, Cal.

A063   T.E. LAWRENCE, Seven Pillars of Wisdom, International Collectors Library, 1966

Fourth American Edition (Book Club)

SEVEN PILLARS | OF | WISDOM | [rule] | *A Triumph* | T.E. LAWRENCE | INTERNATIONAL   COLLECTORS   LIBRARY | AMERICAN HEADQUARTERS | *Garden City, New York*

Collation   20.8 × 14 cm: [1–27]¹², 324 leaves, pp.[i–ix], x–xvi, [xvii–xviii], [1–3], 4–622, [8].

Contents   Prp.[i] bastard title, [ii] blank, [iii] title page, [iv] issue, copyright statements, [v] dedicatory poem, [vi] blank, [vii] letter by author, [viii] blank, [ix] –x contents, [xi] –xvi preface, [xvii] half-title, [xviii] blank, pp.[1]

introduction, [2] blank, [3] – [606] text, [607] –612 appendixes, [613] –622 indexes, [1–8] blank.

RT On verso SEVEN PILLARS OF WISDOM. On recto [according to book].

Text 20 lines, 8.5 (8.6) × 10.4 cm.

Paper White, wove, unwatermarked, top and bottom edges trimmed, sheets bulk 4 cm.

Binding Green simulated leather cloth 138 v.d.y G. On front cover: [gilt, within single rule frame, ships and seabirds design]. On spine: [seven gilt rectangles running horizontally, borders of wavy rules] [within top panel, birds and sea] | [within second] SEVEN PILLARS | OF WISDOM | T.E. LAWRENCE | [within third-fifth repeated ship design] | [within sixth] INTERNATIONAL | COLLECTORS | LIBRARY | [within seventh, birds and ripples]. T.e. gilt. Silk place markers in brown. Green and yellow head and tail bands. White end papers with ship designs.

Published at $3.65, February 1966.

Notes Another issue identical to above with following differences: [Binding]: spine designs are stretched out and lettering sizes are different [titles are larger and imprint smaller]. End papers plain dark green.

Copies AC, Cal.

A064   T.E. LAWRENCE, Seven Pillars of Wisdom, International Collectors Library, 1966

Book Club Prospectus of Fourth American Edition

INTERNATIONAL | COLLECTORS | LIBRARY Presents | [brown] Seven Pillars | [brown] of Wisdom | by T.E. Lawrence

Collation 20.5 × 13.5 cm: single fold leaflet printed on both sides.

Contents Pp.[1] title page, beginning of blurb, [2] blurb continued, brief biography of Lawrence, [3] blurb on binding, [4] quote from Joseph Butler, blurb on publisher.

Text 20 lines, 7.8 × 10 cm.

Paper Buff, watermarked, laid, all edges trimmed.

Published at Free advertising flyer.

Notes Another state, as follows: [title same]; [Collation]: 20.5 × 13.5 cm: single leaf printed on both sides; [Contents]: [recto] title, blurb, [verso] blurb on binding, information on publisher.
    Another state, as follows: [Title page]: [within frame of decorative rule and salmon square] *INTERNATIONAL | COLLECTORS LIBRARY | Presents*

as the February 1966 selection: | Seven Pillars of Wisdom | by T.E. Lawrence |
Classic saga of exciting adventure in the desert... | narrated by the fabulous
Lawrence of Arabia; [Collation]: 13.7 × 20.4 cm: single-fold leaflet printed
on both sides; [Contents]: pp.[1] title, start of blurb, [2–3] blurb continued,
on left side at foot picture and short biography of Lawrence, on right side at
foot blurb on binding, [4] list of other titles in series.

Copies   AC.

A065   T.E. LAWRENCE, Seven Pillars of Wisdom, Communications and Studies, 1966

Fourth American Edition (Book Club)

SEVEN PILLARS | OF | WISDOM | [tapered rule] | *A Triumph* | T.E.
LAWRENCE | *FIRST EDITION* | *of* | The PROGRAMMED CLASSICS |
Published by | Communication & Studies Inc. | Atlanta, Georgia

Collation   20.8 × 14 cm: [1–27]¹², 324 leaves, pp.[i–ix], x–xvi, [xvii–xviii],
[1–3], 4–622, [8].

Contents   Prp.[i] bastard title, [ii] blank, [iii] title page, [iv] issue copyright
statements, [v]–xvi preface, [xvii] half-title, [xviii] blank, pp.[1]
introduction, [2] blank, [3]–[606] text, [607]–612 appendixes, [613]–622
indexes, [1–8] blank.

RT   On verso SEVEN PILLARS OF WISDOM. On recto [according to
book].

Text   20 lines, 8.5 (8.6) × 10.4 cm.

Paper   White, wove, unwatermarked, top and bottom edges trimmed,
sheets bulk 4 cm.

Binding   Green simulated leather cloth 126 d. Ol G. On front cover: [gilt]
[double rule frame, small circles in the inner corners]. On spine: [six
rectangles interspaced with dotted rule, from top] [rectangles 1, 3, 5 have
decorative cut in centre and the frame is double rules,][second rectangle]
SEVEN | PILLARS OF | WISDOM [circles in inner corners] | [fourth
rectangle] T. E. LAWRENCE [circles in inner corners] | [sixth rectangle]
THE | PROGRAMMED | CLASSICS [circles in inner corners]. Green and
yellow head and tail bands. Dark green end papers.

Copies   AC.

A066   T.E. LAWRENCE, Los Siete Pilares de la Sabiduría, Sur, 1965

Second Argentine Edition

T.E. LAWRENCE | [in red] LOS SIETE PILARES | [in red] DE LA | [in red] SABIDUŔIA | UN TRIUNFO | [pub. device] | BUENOS AIRES

Collation   22 × 15.8 cm: [1–34]⁸, 272 leaves, pp.[1–6], 7–544.

Contents   Pp.[1–2] blank, [3] bastard title, [4] blank, [5] title page, [6] original title, issue, copyright statements, 7 editor's note, [8] blank, 9 dedicatory poem, [10] blank, 11 acknowledgments, [12] blank, 13–17 preface by A.W. Lawrence, [18] blank, 19–21 introduction, [22] blank, [23] half-title, [24] section title, 25–534 text, 535 postscript, [536] blank, 537–542 appendixes, [543] colophon, [July 1965], [544] blank.

Text   20 lines, 6.2 × 11.8 cm.

Paper   White, wove, unwatermarked, all edges trimmed, sheets bulk 3 cm.

Binding   Pictorial paper. On front cover: [in red] T.E. Lawrence | [title in red] LOS SIETE | PILARES | DE LA | SABIDUŔIA | [pub. device]. On spine: [running up] T[sic] E. Lawrence | [in red] Los Siete Pilares de la Sabiduría | [across at bottom] SUR.

Published at   July 1965.

Notes   Errata slip tipped inside front cover.

Copies   Cal.

A067   T.E. LAWRENCE, Seven Pillars of Wisdom, World Books Society, 1939

First Canadian Edition

SEVEN PILLARS | OF WISDOM | a triumph | T.E. LAWRENCE | WORLD BOOKS SOCIETY | TORONTO CANADA | *facing:* AUTHOR

Collation   19.8 × 13.3 cm: [A]¹⁶ B–Y¹⁶, 352 leaves, pp.[1–12], 13–700, [701–704].

Contents   Pp.[1]–2 blank, [3] bastard title, [4] blank, [5] title page, [6] original publisher credit, Printed in Great Britain, [7] dedicatory poem, [8] blank, [9] prefatory letter by author, [10] blank, [11] contents, [12] blank, 13 illustrations, [14] blank, [15–20] preface by A.W. Lawrence, 21–24 introductory chapter, [25] half title, [26] synopsis of Chapters i–vii, 27–683 text, [684] postscript, 685–689 appendixes, [690] blank, 691–700 indexes, [701–704] blank.

RT   On both verso and recto [according to contents of page].

Plates Ten plates on stock heavier than sheets following pp.4, 30, 64, 72, 92, 224, 234, 256, 384, 416.

Typography and paper $ 1 signed B.

Text 20 lines, 8.4 (8.5) × 10.2 cm.

Paper Buff, wove, unwatermarked, all edges trimmed, sheets bulk 3.8 cm.

Binding Yellow buckram 77 m. y Br. On spine: [on black leather patch, within gilt double rule frame, gilt] SEVEN | PILLARS | OF | WISDOM | T.E. | LAWRENCE. T.e. stained brown.

Copies Cal, UT.

A068   T.E. LAWRENCE, Visdommens Syv Søjler, Gyldendalske, 1936

First Danish Edition

T.E. LAWRENCE | [in red] VISDOMMENS SYV | [in red] SØJLER | EN TRIUMF | PAA DANSK VED | PETER DE HEMMER GUDME | [double rule] | GYLDENDALSKE BOGHENDEL – NORDISK | FORLAG – KOBENHAVN – MCMXXXVI

Collation 25.5 × 19.5 cm: [1]^8 2–41^8 42^6, 334 leaves, pp.[1–4], 5–667, [668].

Contents Pp.[1] bastard title,[2] blank,[3] title page, [4] issue statement, printer's credit, 5 dedicatory poem, 6 author's note, 7–18 contents, 19–20 illustrations, 21–26 foreword by A.W. Lawrence, [27] half title, [28] synopsis of books I–VII, [29]–655 text, 656–660 appendix, 661–667 index, [668] blank.

RT On both verso and recto [according to subject of page].

Plates Forty-eight plates, paper coated on one side only following pp.2, 48, 58, 60, 62, 64, 68, 80, 92, 104, 106, 108, 120, 144, 160, 168, 172, 192, 216, 224, 254, 286, 294, 302, 316, 352, 370, 376, 384, 424, 428, 434, 454, 474, 496, 512, 520, 524, 536, 550, 576, 590, 602, 608, 636, 644, 648, 652. Four fold maps at rear.

Typography and paper $ 1 signed 1,2 Visdommens Syv Søjler 4,4*.

Text 20 lines, 9.0 (9.2) × 13.5 cm.

Paper White, wove, unwatermarked, top edges trimmed, sheets bulk 5.3 cm.

Binding Deep 16 d. Red. On front cover: [crossed swords stamped in gilt, within in script] Svoerdet | betyder ogsaa | Renhedog | Dod. On spine: [gilt] VISDOM- | MENS | SYV | SØJLER | T.E. | LAWRENCE | GYLDENDAL. Cream end papers. T.e. maroon. Pale green and gold head and tail bands.

Published at   Paper Kr.22.50, Hardbound Kr.29.50.

Notes   Another issue in paper wrappers, identical to above, with following differences: [Paper]: top edge is not trimmed; [Binding]: Buff, heavy paper. On front cover: T.E. LAWRENCE | [in brown] VISDOMMENS | [in brown] SYV | [in brown] SØJLER | GYLDENDAL. On spine: T.E. LAWRENCE | [in brown] VISDOMMENS | [in brown] SYV | SØJLER | GYLDENDAL. On back cover: [pub. device].
   First printing, 3000 copies.
   Second printing, 1936, 1000 copies same as above.

Copies   AC, Cal.

A069   T.E. LAWRENCE, Visdommens Syv Søjler, Gyldendal, 1962

Second Danish Edition

T.E. LAWRENCE | VISDOMMENS | SYV SØJLER | *En Triumf* | PÅ DANSK VED PETER DE HEMMER GUDME | GYLDENDAL | 1962

Collation   24 × 16 cm: [1]^8 2–43^8 44^4, 348 leaves, pp.[1–9], 10–689, [7].

Contents   Pp.[1] bastard title, [2] blank, [3] title page, [4] issue statement, printer's credit, [5] dedicatory poem, [6] letter by author, [7] contents, [8] blank, [9]–15 foreword by A.W. Lawrence, [16]–19 introduction, [20] blank, [21] synopsis of books 1–7, [22] blank, [23]–671 text, [672]–678 appendixes, [679]–689 index, [1] blank, [2–5] maps, [6–7] blank.

RT   On verso *Visdommens syv Søjler.* On recto: [according to chapter, italics]

Typography and paper $ signed 1,2 11 Visdommen syv Søjler, 11*.

Text   20 lines, 9 (9.3) × 11.8 cm, set in Linotype Granjon.

Paper   White, wove, unwatermarked, untrimmed, sheets bulk 3.3 cm.

Binding   White paper wrappers. On front cover: T.E. LAWRENCE | VISDOMMENS | SYV SØJLER | GYLDENDAL. On spine: T.E. LAWRENCE | [running down] Visdommens syv Søjler | [across at foot] GYLDENDAL.

Published at   Kr.49,50 paperbound, Kr.65,00 hardbound.

Notes   Another issue, same as above, with following differences: [Collation]: 23 × 15.5 cm; [Paper]: buff; [Binding]: Deep red 14v. deep Red simulated leather cloth. On spine: [gilt, within top square of long rectangle made from single rule] T.E. LAWRENCE | VISDOMMENS | SYV | SØJLER. T.e. gray. Black and white head and tail bands.

Copies   AC, H.

A070   T.E. LAWRENCE, Les Sept Piliers de la Sagesse, Payot, 1936

First French Edition

T.E. LAWRENCE | [short rule] | LES SEPT PILIERS | DE LA SAGESSE | *SEVEN PILLARS OF WISDOM* | UN TRIOMPHE | [short rule] | TRADUCTION INTÉGRALE | PAR CHARLES MAURON | [short rule] | [pub. device] | PAYOT, PARIS | 106, Boulevard St-Germain | [short rule] | 1936 | *Tous droits réservés.*

Collation   22.7 × 14 cm: [1]^8 2–51^8 52^6, 414 leaves, pp.[1–9], 10–826, [2].

Contents   [1–2] blank, [3] bastard title, [4] blank, [5] title page, [6] issue, copyright statements, [7] dedicatory poem, [8] prefatory letter by author, [9–25] TABLEAU SYNOPTIQUE and INTRODUCTION [26] blank, 27–33 preface, [34] blank, [35] half-title, 36–821 text, [822] blank, 823–826 appendix, [1–2] blank.

RT   On both verso and recto [according to subject of page].

Typography and paper $ 1 signed LES SEPT PILIERS DE LA SAGESSE 14.

Text   20 lines, 9 (9.1) × 10 cm.

Paper   White, wove, unwatermarked, untrimmed, sheets bulk 5 cm.

Binding   Tan paper covers 93 y Grey. On front cover: [within blue rule frame] T.E. LAWRENCE | [short rule] | [in blue, with first and last letters interrupting frame] LES SEPT PILIERS | [in blue] DE LA SAGESSE | *SEVEN PILLARS OF WISDOM* | [short rule] | [pub. device] | PAYOT, PARIS. On spine: [rule] | T.E. LAWRENCE | [rule] | [in blue] Les Sept Piliers | [in blue] de la | [in blue] Sagesse | [rule] | 50fr. | [rule] | PAYOT, | PARIS | [short rule] | 1936 | [rule].

Published at   50 fr.

Notes   Another issue, 'Troisième tirage', 1937, same as above, with following differences: [Binding]: On spine: [rule] | T.E. LAWRENCE | [rule] |[in blue] Les Sept Piliers | [in blue] de la | [in blue] Sagesse | [rule] | 55 francs | sans | majoratium | [rule] | PAYOT | PARIS | [rule].
Another issue, 1949, same as above, with following differences: [Title page]: 1949 in place of 1936: [Collation]: 22.7 × 14 cm: [1]^8 2–52^8, 416 leaves, pp.[1–9], 10–826, [4]; [Contents]: same except pp.[4] opinions of reviewers, [6] copyright statement only, [1–4] pub. ads, [5–6] blank; [Paper]: sheets bulk 4 cm; [Binding]: white paper covers. On front cover: [within single rule frame] T.E. LAWRENCE | [short rule] | [in blue] LES SEPT PILIERS [1st and last words break frame] | DE LA SAGESSE | *SEVEN PILLARS OF WISDOM* | [drawing of T.E. Lawrence by John] | TRADUCTION INTÉGRALE PAR CHARLES MAURON | [interrupting frame] PAYOT, PARIS. On spine: [rule] T.E. LAWRENCE | [rule] Les Sept Piliers | de la | Sagesse | [rules] 1200 fr. | [rule] |PAYOT| PARIS | [rule]. On

back: [within single rule frame, list of pub. titles] | [below frame, printer's statement].

Another issue, 1965, Onzième édition, as above, with following differences: [Title page]: adds ONZIÈME ÉDITION above pub. device, substitutes 1965 for 1936; [Collation]: 22.5 × 14 cm: [1]^8 2–52^8, 416 leaves, pp.[1–9], 10–826, [6]; [Contents]: [1–6] at end are blank; [Paper]: better quality, sheets bulk 3.5 cm; [Binding]: [white paper with green rule] | T.E. LAWRENCE | [in green] LES SEPT PILIERS | [in green] DE LA SAGESSE | *SEVEN PILLARS OF WISDOM* | [drawing of T.E. Lawrence by John] | [in white on green band at foot] PAYOT, PARIS. On spine: T.E.LAWRENCE | [next four lines in green] LES | SEPT PILIERS | DE LA | SAGESSE | [pub. device] | PAYOT | PARIS. On back cover: [six quotes, pub. address, printer's statement, price]; [Published at]: 25,00 F (+T.L.)

Another printing, 1950, same as 1949, with following differences: [Collation]: 23 × 14.5 cm: pp.[1–9], 10–825, [1–7]; appendix ends on 825, [1] blank, [2–7] ads; [Published at]: 1,200 fr.

Copies AC, Cal, H.

A071 T.E. LAWRENCE, Les Sept Piliers de la Sagesse, Payot, 1969

Second French Edition

T.E. LAWRENCE | LES SEPT PILIERS | DE LA SAGESSE | (Seven Pillars of Wisdom) | TOME PREMIER [DEUXIÈME] | LIVRES I–IV [V–X] | 36 | PETITE BIBLIOTHEQUE PAYOT | 106, Boulevard Saint-Germain, Paris 6^e

Collation 18 × 11 cm: Vol. I, [1]^{16} 2–12^{16}, 192 leaves, pp.[1–4], 5–384; Vol. II, [1]^{16} 2–14^{16}, 224 leaves, pp.[1–14], 15–448.

Contents Vol. I: pp.[1] pub. device, [2] note on text, [3] title page, [4] copyright notice, 5 dedicatory poem, [6] blank, 7 author's preface, [8] blank, 9–16 synopsis of books, 17–23 preface by A.W. Lawrence, [24] blank, 25 section title, synopsis, [26] blank, 27–366 text, [367–368] blank, 369 contents, [370] blank, [371–372] quotes from reviews, [373] ads, [374] blank, [375–381] ads, [382] blank, [383] ads, [384] printer's colophon. Vol. II: pp.[1] pub. device, [2] notes on text, [3] title page, [4] notices of vol. I, copyright notice, [5– 14] synopsis of contents, 15 synopsis & section title, [16] blank, 17–430 text, 431 epilogue, [432] blank, 433–436 appendixes, 437 contents, [438] ad for Armitage book, [439–440] quotes from reviews, [441–447] ads, [448] printer's colophon.

Typography and paper $ 1 signed 2 LAWRENCE I, 2 LAWRENCE II.

Text 20 lines, 6.8 × 8.5 cm.

Paper White, wove, unwatermarked, all edges trimmed, sheets bulk 3.3 cm each volume.

Binding   Pictorial paper covers. On front cover: [within black band, across at top, in white] PETITE BIBLIOTHÈQUE PAYOT | [in orange] T.E. LAWRENCE | LES | SEPT PILIERS | DE LA SAGESSE | Tome I [II] | [within yellow [vol. I] & orange [vol. II] rectangle at bottom, drawing of T.E.L. in Abba] | LAWRENCE D'ARABIE. On spine: [within black band at top, in white] 37 | [running up in orange] T.E. LAWRENCE LES SEPTS PILIERS DE LA SAGESSE I [II] | [at bottom] ... On back cover: [photo stills from movie, quotes from three French critics, series notice].

Copies   AC, Cal.

A072   T. E. LAWRENCE, Die sieben Säulen der Weisheit, List, 1936

First German Edition

T E LAWRENCE | DIE | SIEBEN | SÄULEN | DER | WEISHEIT | [pub. device] | PAUL LIST VERLAG LEIPZIG

Collation   23.8 × 16.5 cm: π^4 1–53^8, 428 leaves, pp.[I–V], VI–VIII, [1]–, 848.

Contents   Prp.[I] bastard title, [II] blank, [III] title page, [IV] translator's, designer's credits, copyright notice, [V]–VIII foreword, [1]–834 text, 835–837 place name index, 838–842 name index, 843–844 illustration, 845–848 contents.

RT   On verso ERSTES BUCH [ZWEITES...]. On recto SECHSZEHNTES KAPITEL [SIEBZEHNTES..].

Plates   Thirty-eight b/w plates printed on on one side only following pp.[II], 32, 48, 56, 65, 72, 80, 96, 104, 128, 176, 184, 192, 224, 256, 264, 320, 352, 368, 392, 432, 464, 472, 528, 544, 552, 568, 608, 640, 656, 704, 752, 768, 776, 792, 816, 824, 832; four fold maps following pp.16, 40, 88, 272.

Typography and paper $ 1,2 signed 1,1*.

Text   20 lines, 9.8 (10.1) × 11 cm.

Paper   Off-white, wove, unwatermarked, all edges trimmed, sheets bulk 5 cm.

Binding   Rough woven Edelbast 76 l. y Br. (Edelbast is a quality plant fibre). On front cover: [within black leather rectangle, gilt] T·E·LAWRENCE. On spine: [within black leather rectangle] T·E | LAWRENCE | [within red leather rectangle immediately below black one] *Die Sieben* | *Säulen* | *der Weisheit*. T.e. maroon. White silk head and tail bands. Cream end papers.

Published at   21 RM, 25 RM.

Notes   Another issue, 'dreizehnte' and 'vierzehnte Auflage' (1300–1400

copies), same as above, with following difference: [Paper]: sheets bulk 5.5 cm.

Another issue, 'sechszehntes' and 'neunzehntes Auflage' (1600–1900 copies), same as above.

Copies   AC, Cal, UT.

A073   T.E. LAWRENCE, Die sieben Säulen der Weisheit, List, 1936

Publisher's Prospectus for First German Edition

[Within red double rule frame] Subskriptions- Einladung | [Oxford rule] | [John drawing of T.E.L.] | T.E. Lawrence

Collation   29.2 × 21 cm: [1]⁴, 4 leaves, unpaged [1–8].

Contents   Pp.[1] title page, 1–8 blurbs [each page has double rule frame in red] order form on pp.[8].

Text   5 lines, 2 cm.

Paper   Buff, laid, unwatermarked, sheets sewn.

Published at   Free advertising leaflet.

Copies   Cal.

A074   T.E. LAWRENCE, Die sieben Säulen der Weisheit, Bertelsmann, 1958

Second German Edition

T.E. LAWRENCE | DIE SIEBEN SÄULEN DER WEISHEIT | MIT 6 | GANZSEITIGEN BILDTAFLEN | 1958 | IM BERTELSMANN LESERING

Collation   20.5 × 12.5 cm: [1–23]¹⁶, 368 leaves, pp.[1–4], 5–732, [733], [3].

Contents   Pp.[1] pub. device], [2] blank, [3] title page, [4] original title, binder's, designer's, printer's credits, copyright statement, 5–8 foreword by A.W. Lawrence, [9] photo of TEL bust, [10] blank, 11–[721] text, [722–725] maps. [726]–728 place name index, 729–[733] personal name index, [1] illustrations, [2] contents, [3] blank, illustrations included in pagination.

Text   20 lines, 7.5 × 9 cm.

Paper   White, wove, unwatermarked, all edges trimmed, sheets bulk 4 cm.

Binding   Patterned paper covered boards, green leather spine 137 d. y G. On spine: [gilt] [fancy rule] | [five rows of equally spaced dots] | [fancy rule] | T·E· | LAWRENCE | DIE | SIEBEN | SÄULEN | DER | WEISHEIT |

[fancy rule] | [five rows of equally spaced dots] | [fancy rule] . Black and yellow head and tail bands. T.e. pale yellow.

Copies AC, Cal, H.

A075 T.E. LAWRENCE, Die sieben Säulen der Weisheit, List 1963

Third German Edition

T.E. LAWRENCE | DIE | SIEBEN | SÄULEN | DER | WEISHEIT | [pub. device] | PAUL LIST VERLAG | MÜNCHEN

Collation 21.2 × 12.8 cm: π^4 1–3^8 [4]^8 5–44^8 45^4, 362 leaves, pp.[i–iv], v–viii, 1–[712].

Contents Prp.[i] bastard title, [ii] blank, [iii] title page, [iv] translator's credit, issue statement, designer's credit, copyright statement, printer's, binder's credits, v–viii foreword, pp.1–699 text, 700–706 index, 707–[710] maps, [711] contents, [712] ads.

Plates Frontispiece on coated paper following p.[ii].

Typography and paper $ 1 signed 3.

Text 20 lines, 7.5 × 9 cm.

Paper White, wove, unwatermarked, all edges trimmed, sheets bulk 4 cm.

Binding Orange yellow linen 71 m. OY. On front cover: [in brown] T·E·LAWRENCE | [gilt] DIE SIEBEN | [gilt] SÄULEN | [gilt] DER WEISHEIT. On spine: [within brown rectangle, gilt] [rule] T·E·LAWRENCE | DIE | SIEBEN | SÄULEN | DER | WEISHEIT| [rule] | [within brown pyramid, gilt rectangle, within which pub. device]. T.e. pale yellow. Russet head and tail bands. White silk place marker.

Published at 17.80 DM.

Notes This issue 102–112 Auflage.
   Another issue, 113–120 auflage 1965, same as above, with following differences: [Binding]: brown head and tail bands. No silk place marker.

Copies AC, Cal.

A076 T.E. LAWRENCE, Die sieben Säulen der Weisheit, Europäischer Buchklub, 1964?

Fourth German Edition

T.E. LAWRENCE | DIE SIEBEN SÄULEN | DER WEISHEIT | EUROPÄISCHER BUCHKLUB | STUTTGART-SALZBURG

Collation 20.6 × 13 cm: [1]^8 2–4^8 x^4 5–42^8 x^4, 344 leaves, pp.[I–IV], V–VIII, 1–672, [8].

Contents Prp.[I] bastard title, [II] blank, [III] title page, [IV] original title, list of portraits on end papers, issue statement, binding credit, copyright statement, V–VIII foreword, pp.1–672 text, [1] map. [2] blank, [3] map, [4] blank, [5] map. [6] blank, [7] map, [8] blank.

Typography and paper $ 1 signed 2.

Text 20 lines, 7.4 × 9.4 cm.

Paper White, wove, unwatermarked, all edges trimmed, sheets bulk 3.3 cm.

Binding Yellow paper covered boards 94 l. Ol Br., brown leather spine 78 d. y Br. On front cover: [gilt cut, half moon and sword]. On spine: [blind stamped cut] | [within gilt ovoid rule, blue oval lettered in gilt] LAWRENCE | [short rule] | DIE | SIEBEN | SÄULEN | DER | WEISHEIT | [blind stamped cut] | [gilt book club device]. T.e. grey. Red and yellow striped head and tail bands. End papers portraits of [front] Lawrence and Auda, [back] Feisal and Allenby.

Copies AC, Cal.

A077   T.E. LAWRENCE, Die sieben Säulen der Weisheit, List, 1978

Fifth German Edition

T.E. LAWRENCE | Die sieben Säulen | der Weisheit | LIST VERLAG

Collation 21.5 × 13.3 cm: guillotined, 432 leaves, pp.[1–6], [1]–857, [1].

Contents Prp.[1] pub. device, [2] blank, [3] title page, [4] translator's, designer's credits, copyright statements, [5]–6 contents, pp.[1]–847 text, [848] blank, 849–851 place name index, [852] blank, 853–857 name index [1] blank.

RT On verso ZWEITES BUCH [DRITTES...]. On recto FÜNFTES KAPITEL [SECHSTES...].

Text 20 lines, 8.8 (9.6) × 10 cm.

Paper White, wove, unwatermarked, all edges trimmed, sheets bulk 3.5 cm.

Binding Brown linen 59 d. Br. On spine: [in white] T.E. Lawrence | [thick rule] | Die sieben | Säulen | der | Weisheit | List.

Published at 28 DM.

Copies AC, Cal.

A078 T.E. LAWRENCE, Die Sieben Säulen der Weisheit, List, 1979.

Sixth German Edition

T.E. Lawrence: | Die sieben Säulen der Weisheit | Deutsch von Dagobert von Mikusch | Deutscher | Taschenbuch | Verlag | [pub. device]

Collation 18 × 11 cm: guillotined sheets glued to covers, 432 leaves, pp.[1–6], 7–862, [2].

Contents Pp.[1] notes on author and book, [2] note on series, [3] title page, [4] cover photo credit, issue, copyright statements, ISBN, original title, credits, [5–6] contents, 7–853 text, 854 blank, 855–[863] indexes, [864] ads.

Text 20 lines, 9 × 9 cm.

Paper White, wove, unwatermarked, all edges trimmed, sheets bulk 2.5 cm.

Binding White paper covers. On front cover: >Lawrence von Arabien< | T.E. Lawrence: | Die sieben Säulen | der Weisheit | [brown and black photo from film] | dtv/List. On spine: [running up] [pub. device] Lawrence: Die sieben Säulen der Weisheit 1456. On back cover: [quote from G.B. Shaw] | DM 14.80 | [pub. device] | Deutscher | Taschenbuch | Verlag.

Published at DM 14.80.

Copies AC.

A079 T.E. LAWRENCE, A Bölcseség Hét Pillére, Révai, 1935

First Hungarian Edition

T.E. LAWRENCE | A BÖLCSESÉG HÉT PILLÉRE | I [II] | RÉVAI KIADAS

Collation 18.4 × 12 cm: Vol.I, π^8 1–25^8 24^2, 210 leaves, pp.[I–IV], V–XVI, [1–3], 4–403, [404]; Vol. II, π^2 1–26^8 27^2, 229 leaves, pp.[4], [1–3], 4–410, [2].

Contents Vol. I: prp.[I] bastard title, pub. device, [II] copyright statement, [III] title page, [IV] issue statement, credits, V–VI contents, VII illustrations, VIII introductory letter, IX–XII introduction by A.W. Lawrence, XIII–XVI chronology, pp.[1] half title, [2] synopsis of book, [3]–403 text, [404] blank. Vol. II: prp.[I] bastard title, pub. device, [II] copyright statement, [III] title page, [IV] issue statements, credits, V–VI contents, VII illustrations, VIII introductory letter by TEL, IX–XII A.W. Lawrence preface, XIII–XVI chronology, pp.[1] half title, [2] synopsis, [3]–403 text, [404] blank.

RT On both verso and recto [according to subject of page].

Plates Vol. I: four b/w plates on coated paper following pp.48, 128, 240. Vol.

II: pp.64, 128, 192, 256, 320, 384. Maps, Vol. I, following pp.16, 160, 352; Vol. II, pp.160.

Typography and paper $ 2 signed 1,1*.

Text 20 lines, 7.5 (8) × 9 cm.

Paper White, wove, unwatermarked, all edges trimmed, sheets bulk 3 cm, each volume.

Binding Black cloth. On front cover: [photo of Kennington bust inset]. On spine: [gilt] T.E. | LAWRENCE | [running up] A BÖLCSESÉG HÉT PILLÉRE | [across] I[II] | RÉVAI. Red head and tail bands.

Published at October 1935.

Notes Second printing, November 1935, same as above.

Copies AC, H.

A080 T.E. LAWRENCE, I Sette Pilastri della Saggezza, Bompiani, 1949

First Italian Edition

THOMAS EDWARD LAWRENCE | [next four lines in brown] I SETTE | PILASTRI | DELLA | SAGGEZZA| [cut, head Lawrence] | [brown rule] | BOMPIANI

Collation 23.5 × 16.6 cm: [1–2]⁸ 3–44⁸, 352 leaves, pp.[1–8], 9–704.

Contents Pp.[1] bastard title, [2] blank, [3] title page, [4] original title, printer's credit, copyright statement, [5] dedicatory poem, [6] blank, [7] prefatory letter, [8] blank, 9–12 introduction, [13] section title, [14] blank, 15–696 text, [697] section title, [698] blank, 699–702 contents, [703] printer's colophon, [704] blank.

RT On verso THOMAS EDWARD LAWRENCE. On recto I SETTE PILASTRI DELLA SAGGEZZA.

Plates Twenty-four plates on coated paper following pp.[4], 12, 48, 64, 112, 128, 176, 192, 224, 240, 288, 304, 352, 368, 416, 432, 480, 496, 544, 560, 608, 624, 672, 688.

Typography and paper $ 1 signed 3.

Text 20 lines, 7.5 (7.7) × 11.2 cm.

Paper White, wove, unwatermarked, all edges trimmed, sheets bulk 4 cm.

Binding Yellow brown cloth 79 l. gy y Br. On front cover: [gilt, head of TEL by John]. On spine: [gilt rule] | [within dark leather rectangle] [gilt rule] | THOMAS | EDWARD | LAWRENCE | [gilt rule] | [within second brown rectangle] | [gilt rule] | I SETTE | PILASTRI | DELLA | SAGGEZZA. Red and white head and tail bands.

Notes Another issue, 1949, Grey-green cloth 109 l. gy Ol.

Second edition, 1957, same as above, with following differences: [Collation]: 23.4 × 16 cm: [1] –41^8, 328 leaves, [1–8], 9–654, [2]; [Plates]: 23 b/w plates on coated paper following pp.[2], 48, 64, 96, 112, 144, 160, 192, 208, 256, 272, 320, 336, 384, 400, 448, 464, 512, 528, 576, 592, 624, 640; [Paper]: sheets bulk 3 cm; [Binding]:white cloth. On front cover: [gilt head]. On spine: [red leather patch] I SETTE | PILASTRI | DELLA | SAGGEZZA | [green patch] THOMAS | EDWARD | LAWRENCE| [at foot] BOMPIANI | [gilt rule]. Yellow and white head and tail bands.

Copies Cal.

A081 T.E. LAWRENCE, I Sette Pilastri della Saggezza, Bompiani, 1966

Second Italian Edition

I SETTE PILASTRI | DELLA SAGGEZZA | [rule] | *di* | THOMAS EDWARD LAWRENCE | VOLUME I [II] | BOMPIANI | [rule] | 1966

Collation 20.7 × 11.7 cm: Vol. I, [1]^8 2–26^8 [27]^4, 212 leaves, pp.[1–5], 6–419, [5]; Vol. II, [1]^8 2–30^8 31^4, 244 leaves, pp.[1–6], 7–481, [7].

Contents Vol. I: pp.[1] bastard title, [2] blank, [3] title page, [4] issue, copyright statements, [5] dedicatory poem, 6 prefatory letter by author, 7–8 biographical note, 9–14 introduction by E.M. Forster, 15–416 text, 417–419 contents, [1–5] list of titles in series. Vol. II: [1] bastard title, [2] blank, [3] title page, [4] issue, copyright statements, [5] –478 text, 479–481 index, [1] blank, 2–6 list of titles in series, [7] blank.

Typography and paper $ 1 signed vol. I 2* I sette pilastri della saggezza; vol. II 2** I sette pilastri della saggezza.

Text 20 lines, 7.5 × 8.6 cm.

Paper White, wove, unwatermarked, all edges trimmed, sheets bulk 2 cm (Vol. I), 2.5 cm (Vol. II).

Binding White and brown 53 m O paper covers. On front cover: I SETTE PILASTRI | DELLA SAGGEZZA | *Romanzo di* | Th. E. Lawrence | Vol. I [II] | [pub. device] | BOMPIANI. On spine: [running down] Th. E. LAWRENCE – I SETTE PILASTRI DELLA SAGGEZZA – I [II] | [rule running across] | BOMPIANI. On back cover: L. 1,250.

Published at Lire 2,500 for two volumes.

Notes Boxed as issued.

Copies AC.

A082   T.E. LAWRENCE, Seven Pillars of Wisdom, Heibon-sha, 1969

First Japanese Edition

[Running down] Toyo Bunko [across] 152 [running down] Heibonsha | [long rule] | Chie no Shichichu 1 | T.E. Lawrensu | Kashiwagura Toshizoo yaku | [long rule]

Collation   Vol. I, [1–24]⁸ [25]⁴ [26]², 198 leaves, pp.[1–2], [1]–28, [1–4], 5–364, [1–2]; Vol. II, [1–26]⁸, 208 leaves, pp.[1–2], 1–[10], [1–4], 5–397 [1–7]; Vol. III, [1–2], 1–2, 1–9, [1–4], 5–785, 18–2, [1], [1–14].

Contents   Vol. I: prp.[1] title page, [2] printer's credit, pp.[1] frontis. 2 preface, 3 contents, 4–5 dedicatory poem in Japanese, [6] dedicatory poem in English, 7–8 introductory letter by Lawrence, 9–16 synopsis, 17–18 illustrations, 19–28 preface by A.W. Lawrence, pp.[1] half-title, [2] map. [3] section title, [4] synopsis, 5–364 text, [1] colophon, [2] blank. Vol. II : prp.[1] title page, [2] printer's credit, pp. 1 preface, [2] contents, 3–8 synopsis, 8–9 illustrations, [10] blank, [1] half-title, [2] map, [3] section title, [4] synopsis, 5–389 text, 390–397 Lawrence chronology,[1] blank, [2] colophon, [2–7] blank. Vol. III: prp.[1] title page, [2] printer's credit, 1 preface, 2 contents, 1–7 synopsis, 7–9 illustrations, [10] blank, pp. [1] half-title, [2] map, [3] section title, [4] synopsis, 5–362 text, 363–364 postscript, 365–385 appendixes, [folded map], 18–1 indexes, [1] colophon, [2–11] pub. ads, [1–3] blank.

RT   On verso only [according to book].

Plates   Vol. I: frontis. before prp.[1], fold map after pp.354. Vol. II: fold map following pp.388. Vol. III: fold map following pp.[386].

Text   20 lines, 5.7 × 7.9 cm.

Paper   White, wove, unwatermarked, all edges trimmed, sheets bulk 1.8 cm (Vol. I), 2 cm (Vol. II), 2 cm (Vol. III).

Binding   Green cloth 125 m. Ol G. On spine: [running down] Chie no Shichichu 1 [2–3] | T.E. Lawrensu | Kashiwagura Toshizoo yaku | Toyo Bunko | [across] 152 [181–200] | Heibonsha. On back cover: [pub. device blind stamped]. Green silk place markers. Boxed as issued.

Published at   Vol. I, 500 Yen; Vol. II, 650 Yen; Vol. III, 650 Yen.

Copies   AC.

A083   T.E. LAWRENCE, Seitse Tarkuse Sammast, Noor-Eesti Kirjastus Tartus, 1939

First Lettish Edition

T.E. LAWRENCE | SEITSE | TARKUSE SAMMAST | TÔLKINUD | A.H. TAMMSAARE | II | [pub. device] | NOOR-EESTI KIRJASTUS TARTUS

Collation   Vol. II, 19.3 × 13 cm: [1] −21⁸, 168 leaves, pp.[1−4], 5−334, [2].

Contents   Vol. II: pp.[1] bastard title, [2] blank, [3] title page, [4] copyright statement, [5]−[335] text, [1−2] blank.

Plates   Vol. II: 8 b/w plates printed on one side only following pp.[2], 6, 16, 174, 186, 276, 284, 332.

Typography and paper $ 1 signed 4 Seitse tarkuse sammast I [II], vol.II 10,10*.

Text   20 lines, 7.7 × 9 cm.

Paper   White, wove, unwatermarked, all edges trimmed, sheets bulk 2.5 cm.

Binding   Only copy seen rebound. Vol. I not seen.

Copies   NYPL.

A084   T.E. LAWRENCE, Visdommens Syv Søyler, Gyldendal Norsk, 1970

First Norwegian Edition

T.E. LAWRENCE | VISDOMMENS | SYV SØYLER | *En Triunf* | OVERSATT AV OLAV ANGELL | GYLDENDAL NORSK FORLAG | OSLO 1970

Collation   23.8 × 16 cm: [1] −18¹⁶ 19⁸ 20² 21⁴, 302 leaves, pp.[1−10], 11−604.

Contents   Pp.[1] bastard title, [2] blank, [3] title page, [4] issue statement, [5] dedicatory poem, [6] blank, [7] prefatory letter, [8] blank, [9] contents, [10] blank, 11−15 foreword by A.W. Lawrence, [16] blank, [17] note by A.W. Lawrence [18] blank, 19−595 text, [596] postscript, 597−601 appendix [602−604] blank.

Typography and paper $ 1 signed 2 T.E. Lawrence.

Text   20 lines, 8.2 × 11.8 cm.

Paper   White, wove, unwatermarked, untrimmed, sheets bulk 3 cm.

Binding   White paper wrappers. On front cover: T.E. LAWRENCE | [long rule] | Visdommens syv | søyler | GYLDENDAL | NORSK FORLAG | [two-colour drawing of T.E. Lawrence, desert scene in background]. On spine:

[running down] [long rule] | [in purple] T.E. LAWRENCE | [purple] GYLDENDAL | [purple] Norsk Forlag | [long rule] | [in red] visdommens syv søyler | [long rule]. On back cover: [long blurb].

Copies Cal.

A086 T.E. LAWRENCE, Siedem filarów mądrości, Państwowy Instytut Wydawnczy, 1971

Second Polish Edition

T.E. LAWRENCE | Siedem filarów mądrości | TOM DRUGY | Przelożyt | Jerzy Schwakopf | PAŃSTWOWY INSTYTUT WYDAWNCZY

Collation 19.2 × 12.5 cm: Vol. I, $[1]^8$ $2-5^8$ $[6]^8$ $7(7-8)^{16}$ 8 $(9-10)^{16}$ 9 $(11-12)^{16}$ 10 $(13-14)^{16}$ 11 $(15-16)^{16}$ 12 $(17-18)^{16}$ 13 $(19-20)^{16}$ 14 $(21-22)^{16}$ 15 $(23-24)^{16}$ 16 $(25-26)^{16}$ $27-31^8$, 248 leaves, pp.[1–6], 7–492, [4]; Vol. II, $[1]-6^8$ 7 $(7-8)^{16}$ 9^8 10 $(10-11)^{16}$ $12-13^8$ 14 $(14-15)^{16}$ $16-24^8$ 25^4, 196 leaves, pp.[1–5], 6–388, [4]. Gatherings in parentheses are 16-page gatherings with two signatures, i.e. 7 $(7-8)^{16}$ is one gathering with signature 7 on first leaf and 8 leaf and 8 on ninth.

Contents Vol. I: pp.[1] bastard title, [2] series title, [3] title page, [4] original title, [5] dedicatory poem, [6] blank, [7]–8 preface, [9]–15 preface by A.W. Lawrence, [16] map. [17]–492 text, [1] contents, [2] blank, [3] printer's statement, [4] blank. Vol. II: pp.[1] bastard title, [2] series title, [3] title page, [4] original title, [5]–372 text, [373] note on text, 374–379 appendix, 380–385 translator's note and Polish transliteration, 386–388 postscript, [1] table of contents, [2–3] list of titles in series, [4] printer's colophon.

RT On both verso and recto [according to chapter].

Typography and paper $ 1 signed 17– Siedem filarow t. I signatures 11–26 have two signatures each gathering. See collation.

Text 20 lines, 8.2 (8.8) × 9.5 cm.

Paper White, wove, unwatermarked, all edges trimmed, sheets bulk 2 cm.

Binding Grey cloth 154 1. g Gray. On front cover: [pub. device] | [in brown] 17-Siedem filarów mądrości | T.E. LAWRENCE. On spine: [in brown, running up] Siedem filarooac]w mądrości | [across] LAWRENCE | [star] | [rectangle]. (Vol. 2 has two stars). On back cover: Cena zi I/II 60,-. Grey and white head and tail bands. End papers yellow with XX on each.

Copies AC.

A087   T.E. LAWRENCE, Cei Sapte Stâlpi, Fundaţia Pentru Literatură, 1937

First Romanian Edition

COLONEL T.E. LAWRENCE | ÇEI SAPTE STÂLPI | AI ÎNŢELEPCIUNI | Traducere din limba engleză de Petru COMARNESCU | *Cu 44 de planşe şi 4 hărţi afară din text.* | [pub. device] | BUCURESTI | FUNDAŢIA PENTRU LITERATURĂ ŞI ARTĂ „REGELE CAROL II" | 39, BULEVARDU | LASCAR CATARGI, 39 | 1937

Collation   23.5 × 15.5 cm: [1]-4^8 5^{10} [1]-44^8, 394 leaves, pp.[I–IX], X–LXXXII, [LXXXIII–IV], [1–2], 3–700, [4].

Contents   Prp.[I] bastard title, [II] issue, copyright statements, [III] title page, [IV] blank, [V] half title, [VI] blank, [VII] dedicatory poem, [VIII] letter by T.E. Lawrence, [IX]–XIV synopsis and contents, [XV] illustrations, [XVI]–XXII preface by A.W. Lawrence, [XXIII]–LXXXII introduction by translator, [LXXXIII] half-title, [LXXXIV] blank, pp.[1] synopsis of chapters I–VIII, [2]–[683] text, 684–688 appendixes, [689] section title, [690] blank, [691]–692 note on index by translator, [693]–700 index, [701] contents, [702] blank, [703] colophon, [704] blank.

RT   On both recto and verso [according to subject of page].

Plates   Twenty-one b/w plates on coated paper following pp.LXXXII, 28, 48, 60, 92, 204, 272, 310, 350, 374, 402, 440, 480, 506, 526, 576, 590, 600, 632, 636, 680; fold map inside rear cover.

Typography and paper $ 2 signed 6,6*.

Text   20 lines, 8.9 (9.7) × 11 cm.

Paper   White, wove, unwatermarked, all edges trimmed, sheets bulk 5.5 cm.

Binding   Pictorial paper covers. On front cover: SCRIITORII STREINI CONTEMPORANI | [in red] COLONEL T.E. LAWRENCE | [in red] CEI ŞAPTE STÄLPI | [in red] AI INTELEPCUNII | FUNDAŢIA PEŢRU LITERATURÄ ŞI ARTA "REGELE CAROL II". On spine: [double rule] | [lettering all in white] COLONEL T.E. LAWRENCE | CEI ŞAPTE | STÄLPI AI | INŢELEPCIUNII | [pub. device] | FUNDAŢIA PENTRU | LITERATÜRA SI ARTÄ | „REGELE CAROL II" | [double rule]. On back cover: b/w photo of Arabs in Damascus | Lei 240.

Published at   Lei 240.

Copies   H.

A088   T.E. LAWRENCE, Vishetens Sju Pelare, Stockholm, Natur Och Kultur, 1939

First Swedish Edition

T.E. LAWRENCE | VISHETENS SJU | PELARE | *en triumf* | STOCKHOLM | [rule] | BOKFÖRLAGET NATUR OCH KULTUR

Collation   25.7 × 18.5 cm; [1] –43⁸, 344 leaves, pp.[1–7], 8–688.

Contents   Pp.[1] bastard title, [2] blank, [3] title page, [4] copyright statement, original title, printer's credit, issue statement, [5] dedicatory poem [6] letter by author, [7] –18 contents, [19] –20 illustrations, [21] –26 foreword by A.W. Lawrence, [27] half-title, [28] synopsis of section, 29–671 text, [672] postscript, [673] –677 appendixes, [678] –683 index, [684] –685 translator's notes, [686–688] blank.

RT   On both verso and recto [according to contents of page].

Plates   On coated paper, printed on one side only, following pp.2, 52, 56, 60, 70, 72, 88, 96, 108, 112, 116, 128, 152, 172, 176, 184, 208, 228, 232, 264, 296, 304, 312, 326, 366, 384, 388, 396, 456, 444, 448, 472, 488, 512, 528, 536, 542, 552, 568, 592, 604, 624, 628, 656, 660, 670; fold maps following pp.33, 65, 73, 233.

Typography and paper $ 1 signed 2.- Vishetens sju pelare. 43.

Text   20 lines, 9.1 (9.3) × 12.8 cm.

Paper   Light buff, wove, unwatermarked, all edges trimmed, sheets bulk 4.3 cm.

Binding   Pale yellow 73 p. OY cloth. On front cover: [gilt] [decorative rule] | *T.E. LAWRENCE* | [short Oxford rule] | VISHETENS | SJU PELARE | [decorative rule]. On spine: [decorative rule] | [within dark green rectangle] *T.E. LAWRENCE* | [short rule] | VISHETENS | SJU PELARE. Brown marbled end papers. T.e. light green. Green and white head and tail bands.

Published at   Kr 22 paper, Kr 27 bound, Kr 32 half-leather.

Copies   AC, Cal, UT.

A089   T.E. LAWRENCE, Ustanak U Pustinji, Kosmos, 1938

First Yugoslav Edition

USTANAK | U PUSTINJI | SEDAM STUBOVA MUDROSTI | SVESKA PRVA | NAPISAO | T.E. LORENS | [pub device] | KOSMOS

Collation   21.8 × 14.5 cm: Vol. I, [1] –26⁸, 208 leaves, pp.[1–4], 5– [408], [1–8]; Vol. II, [1] –32⁸, 256 leaves, pp.[1–4], 5–501, [1–11].

Contents Vol. I: pp.[1] pub. device, [2]–3 title pages, [4] credits, original title, copyright, issue statements, 5–[10] preface, 11–[13] contents, [14] illustrations, [15] half-title, [16] dedicatory poem, [17] section title, [18] synopsis of chapters I–VIII, 19–[408] text, [1–8] ads. Vol. II: pp.[1] pub. device, [2–3] title page, [4] credits, original title, copyright,issue statements, 5–[8] contents, [9] illustrations, [10] blank, [11] half-title, [12] blank, [13] section title, [14] synopsis of chapters 55–58, 15–[503] text, [504] blank, [1–8] ads.

RT On verso LORENS USTANAK U PUSTINJI. On recto [according to subject of page].

Plates Vol.I: 25 b/w plates on coated paper following pp.[5], 33, 49, 65, 97, 113, 129, 145, 161, 177, 193, 209, 225, 241, 257, 273, 289, 305, 321, 337, 353, 369, 385, 398, 401; maps 25, 73, 81, 295. Vol. II: 29 plates on coated paper following pp.[5], 24, 33, 65, 97, 129, 145, 161, 176, 193, 219, 241, 257, 273, 305, 324, 337, 353, 369, 385, 401, 417, 433, 449, 465, 481, 497, 501.

Typography and paper $ 1,2 signed 10,10*.

Text 20 lines, 9 (9.1) × 10.8 cm.

Paper White, wove, unwatermarked, all edges trimmed, sheets bulk 2.8 cm (Vol. I), 3 cm (Vol. II).

Binding Orange cloth 68 s OY. On front cover: [within brown band, in orange] PUKOVNIK LORENS | [brown band] | [within brown band, in orange] USTANAK | U PUSTINJI | [two blue bands] | [within brown band, in orange] KOSMOS | [blue band]. On spine: [within blue band, in orange] LORENS | [brown band] | [blue rectangle] USTA- | NAK | U PU- | STINJI | I [II] | [blue pub. device] | [blue band] | [within brown band] KOSMOS | [blue band]. Gold head and tail bands.

Copies PL, H.

1924

The Twilight of the Gods

One of Lawrence's first purely 'literary' efforts was the introduction to the third edition of Richard Garnett's *The Twilight of the Gods*. Richard Garnett was the father of Edward Garnett, a reader and literary adviser for Jonathan Cape and John Lane. Both Lawrence and Edward admired Charles M. Doughty. Edward was also the person to whom Lawrence entrusted the first attempt to abridge the *Seven Pillars of Wisdom*. Lawrence's introduction is the tangible result of the mutual esteem these two men had for one another. This introduction is one work of Lawrence's not reprinted in collections of his minor writings.

A090 RICHARD GARNETT, The Twilight of the Gods, Bodley Head, 1924

Third English Edition (First Illustrated)

THE TWILIGHT | OF THE GODS | AND OTHER TALES | BY RICHARD GARNETT WITH | AN INTRODUCTION BY T.E. LAWRENCE | ILLUSTRATED BY HENRY KEEN | :: :: | [cut within triple rules] | LONDON: JOHN LANE THE BODLEY HEAD LIMITED | NEW YORK: DODD, MEAD AND COMPANY

Collation 23.8 × 15.5 cm: [A]^8 b^2 B–S^8 T^4 x ^{1}, 151 leaves, pp.[i–vi], vii–xviii, [xix–xx], [1]–279, [3].

Contents Prp.[i] bastard title, [ii] blank, [iii] title page, [iv] printer's credit, issue statement, [v] dedication, [vi] blank, vii–xiv introduction, xv–xvi contents, xvii–xviii illustrations, [xix] half-title, [xx] blank, [1]–279 text, [280] blank, [1] advertisement, [2] blank.

RT On verso THE TWILIGHT OF THE GODS. On recto [according to title of section].

Plates Twenty-eight plates tipped in following pp.ii, 32, 40, 50, 66, 82, 94, 102, 112, 122, 130, 148, 154, 162, 166, 172, 180, 200, 202, 208, 216, 228, 236, 244, 246, 252, 266, 272.

Typography and paper $ 1 signed b B.

Text 20 lines, 8.4 (8.8) × 9.8 cm.

Paper White, laid, unwatermarked, top edges trimmed, sheets bulk 2.5 cm.

Binding Black cloth. On front cover: [gilt and red stamped elaborate border encompassing bearded contorted face. Within this frame at bottom] THE TWILIGHT OF THE GODS. On spine: [gilt] THE | TWILIGHT | OF THE | GODS | RICHARD | GARNETT | [in red] | ILLVSTRATED BY | HENRY | [in red] KEEN | [cut] | [triple rule] | [floral cut] | [triple rule] | THE BODLEY HEAD |[triple rule] | [floral cut] | [triple rule]. T.e. red. Illus. end papers.

Published at 21s.

Notes 2nd impression 1924, 3rd 1926, 1928 illus tipped in, 5 pages ads, t.e. unstained, slightly smaller format, orange rules and decorations on front cover and spine.

1926 reprint has ad printed on p.280; lacks final leaf as above.

Illustrations mounted on guards; has only one page ad. T.e. cut unstained.

First English edition 1888, Second 1903 [three impressions].

Copies   AC, Cal, UT.

A091   RICHARD GARNETT, The Twilight of the Gods, Bodley Head, 1927

Fourth English Edition (Weekend Edition)

[Within frame of rules and small squares] THE TWILIGHT | OF THE GODS | *by* | RICHARD GARNETT | *With an Introduction by* | T.E. LAWRENCE | JOHN LANE | THE BODLEY HEAD LTD.

Collation   17.2 × 11.2 cm: [A]¹⁶ B–L¹⁶ *x*⁶, 182 leaves, pp.[i–vi], vii–xvi, 1–328, [1–8], [1–12].

Contents   Prp.[i] series and bastard titles, [ii] blank, [iii] title page, [iv] issue statement, printer's credit, [v] dedication, [vi] blank, vii–xiv introduction by T.E. Lawrence, xv–xvi contents, 1–323 text, [324] blank, 325–[328] notes, [1–8] ads, [1–12] series list.

RT   On verso *The Twilight of the Gods*. On recto [according to chapter].

Typography and paper $ 1 signed 1,5 C,C*.

Text   20 lines, 7.2 (7.8) × 8 cm.

Paper   White, laid, unwatermarked, all edges trimmed, sheets bulk 1.5 cm.

Binding   Red buckram 13 deep Red. On front cover: [gilt, stamped fac. sign. of author]. On spine: [decorative rule] | THE | TWILIGHT | OF THE | GODS | RICHARD | GARNETT | [decorative initials] | [decorative rule] | THE BODLEY | HEAD | [decorative rule].

Published at   29 October 1927.

Notes   Another issue, same as above, with following differences: [Binding]: Green linen 146 d. G. On spine: *THE | TWILIGHT | OF THE | GODS | RICHARD | GARNETT | THE | BODLEY | HEAD.*

Copies   AC, Cal.

A092   RICHARD GARNETT, The Twilight of the Gods, Dodd, Mead, 1924

First American Illustrated Edition

THE TWILIGHT | OF THE GODS | AND OTHER TALES | BY RICHARD GARNETT WITH | AN INTRODUCTION BY T.E. LAWRENCE |

ILLUSTRATED BY HENRY KEEN | :: :: | [cut within triple rules] |
LONDON: JOHN LANE THE BODLEY HEAD LIMITED | NEW YORK:
DODD, MEAD AMD COMPANY

Collation 23.8 × 15.5 cm: [A]^8 b^2 B–S^8 T^4 x^1, 151 leaves, pp.[i–vi],
vii–xviii, [xix–xx], [1]–[280], [1–2].

Contents Prp.[i] bastard title, [ii] blank, [iii] title page, [iv] printer's credit,
issue statement, [v] dedication, [vi] blank, vii–xiv introduction, xv–xvi
contents, xvii xviii illustrations, [xix] half-title, [xx] blank, pp.[1]–279 text,
[280] blank, [1] ad. [2] blank.

RT On verso THE TWILIGHT OF THE GODS. On recto [according to
section title].

Plates Twenty-eight plates tipped in following pp.ii, 32, 40, 50, 66, 82, 94,
102, 112, 122, 130, 148, 154, 162, 166, 172, 180, 200, 202, 208, 216, 228, 236,
244, 246, 252, 266, 272.

Typography and paper $ 1 signed b B.

Text 20 lines, 8.4 (8.8) × 9.8 cm.

Paper White, laid, unwatermarked, top edges trimmed, sheets bulk 2.5
cm.

Binding Black cloth. On front cover: [gilt and red stamped elaborate
border encompassing bearded contorted face. Within this frame at bottom]
THE TWILIGHT OF THE GODS. On spine: [gilt] THE | TWILIGHT | OF
THE | GODS | RICHARD | GARNETT | [in red] | ILLVSTRATED BY |
HENRY | [in red] KEEN | [cut] | [triple rule] | [floral cut] | [triple rule] |
DODD, MEAD | & COMPANY | [triple rule] | [floral cut] | [triple rule]. T.e.
red. Illus. end papers.

Copies AC, Cal, H.

A093 RICHARD GARNETT, The Twilight of the Gods, Knopf, 1926

Second American Edition

[Within frame of decorative cuts, swash] RICHARD GARNETT | [in pale
green] THE TWILIGHT | [green] OF THE GODS | AND OTHER TALES |
With an introduction by | T.E. LAWRENCE | [pub. device] | [swash] NEW
YORK | ALFRED A. KNOPF | 1926

Collation 21 × 14 cm: [1–20]^8, 160 leaves, pp.xvi, 304.

Contents Prp.[i] bastard title, [ii] item in series, [iii] title page, [iv] issue
statement, credits, [v] dedication, [vi] blank, vii–xiii introduction by T.E.
Lawrence, [xiv] blank, xv contents, [xvi] blank, pp.[1] half title, [2] blank,
3–300 text, 301–304 notes.

RT   On verso THE TWILIGHT OF THE GODS. On recto [according to chapter].

Text   20 lines, 9.9 (9.9) × 10.1 cm.

Paper   White, wove, unwatermarked, top edge trimmed, sheets bulk 2.5 cm.

Binding   Yellow-green cloth 136 m. y G, black linen spine. On front cover: [series logo blind stamped]. On spine: [gilt, decorative cut] | THE | TWILIGHT | OF THE GODS | [rule] | GARNETT | [rule] | [decorative cut] | ALFRED A. KNOPF | [decorative cut]. T. e. green.

Published at $3.00.

Notes   Another issue in full blue decorated cloth.

Copies   Cal.

The Forest Giant

By his own request Lawrence was given the French work, *Le Gigantesque*, to translate soon after his expulsion from the RAF and re-enlistment in the Tank Corps in 1923. He appears to have been motivated both by a need for funds and by the wish to fill his free time. He used much freedom in the translation and it can best be described as a 'loose' translation. He was asked to translate two other works from French: Custot's *Sturly* and Flaubert's *Salammbo*. He attempted the first and gave it up as a 'bad job'; by an ironic twist of fate it was then translated by Richard Aldington who later wrote a venomous biography of Lawrence (1955). *The Forest Giant* appeared in 1924, with an American edition published by Harper the same year, and reprinted by Cape and Doran in 1936.

A094   ADRIEN LE CORBEAU, The Forest Giant, Cape, 1924

First English Edition

[Within frame of decorative cuts] *The Forest Giant* | *by* | ADRIEN LE CORBEAU | [pub. device] | [double rule with dec. cuts at ends] | *Translated from the French by* | J.H. ROSS | [cut] | *Jonathan Cape* | ELEVEN GOWER STREET LONDON

Collation   18.8 × 12.7 cm: [A]–K⁸, 80 leaves, pp.[1–6], 7–158, [2].

Contents   Pp.[1–2] blank, [3] bastard title, [4] frontispiece, [5] title page, [6] issue statement, printer's credit, 7 contents, [8] blank, 9–158 text, [2] blank.

RT   On verso *The Forest Giant*. On recto [in italics, according to section].

Typography and paper $ 1 signed C.

Text 20 lines, 9.7 (10) × 8 cm.

Paper Thick, white, wove, unwatermarked, top edge trimmed, sheets bulk 1.5 cm.

Binding Yellow linen spine 86 l. Y., light grey olive paper covered boards 109 l. gy Ol. On spine: [paper patch same colour as boards] [decorative rule] | *The FOREST* | *GIANT* | *by* | ADRIEN | LE CORBEAU | [decorative rule].

Published at 6s, March 1924.

Copies AC, Cal, H, UT.

A095   ADRIEN LE CORBEAU, The Forest Giant, Cape, 1935

Second English Edition

THE FOREST GIANT | *by* | ADRIEN LE CORBEAU | [pub. device] | *Translated from the French by* | J.H. ROSS | *Illustrated with Woodcuts by* | AGNES MILLER PARKER | JONATHAN CAPE | THIRTY BEDFORD SQUARE LONDON

Collation 19 × 13.5 cm: [A]⁸ B−K⁸, 80 leaves, pp.[1−4], 5−160.

Contents Pp.[1] bastard title, [2] frontispiece, [3] title page, [4] issue statement, printer's, papermaker's, binder's credits, 5 contents, 6 illustrations, 7−8 publisher's note, 9 dedication, [10] blank, [11] half title, [12] blank, 13−159 text, [160] blank.

RT On verso THE FOREST GIANT. On recto [in italics, according to chapter].

Typography and paper $ 1 signed G.

Text 20 lines, 11.1 (11.1) × 8.9 cm.

Paper White, wove, watermarked, top edge trimmed, sheets bulk 1 cm.

Binding Leaf green linen 135 l y Gr. On spine: [gilt, running up] THE FOREST GIANT − ADRIEN LE CORBEAU, [across at bottom, pub. device].

Published at 5s.

Notes Contains new pub. note and dedication omitted from first edition.

Copies AC, Cal, H, UT.

A096 ADRIEN LE CORBEAU, The Forest Giant, Harper, 1924

First American Edition

[Double rule] | THE | FOREST GIANT | The Romance | of a Tree | [rule] | *Translated from the French of* | ADRIEN LECORBEAU | *by* L.H. ROSS | [rule] | [pub. device] | [two line quote from Pascal in italics] | [double rule] | Harper & Brothers | New York and London | MCMXXIV

Collation   19.1 × 11.5 cm: [1–8]⁸ [9]⁴ [10]⁸, 76 leaves, pp.[1–10], 1–139, [3].

Contents   Prp.[1–2] blank, [3] bastard title, [4] blank, [5] title page, [6] copyright, issue statements, [7] contents, [8] blank, [9] half title, [10] blank, pp.1–139 text, [1–3] blank.

RT   On both recto and verso *The Forest Giant.*

Text   20 lines, 8.5 (9.0) × 10.2 cm.

Paper   White, wove, unwatermarked, all edges trimmed, sheets bulk 1.3 cm.

Binding   Tan 76 l. y Br paper covered boards, olive brown buckram spine 96 d. Ol Br. On front cover: [all in red, except cut] *The* | FOREST | GIANT | [line cut] | *by* ADRIEN | LE CORBEAU. On spine [gilt] *The* | FOR- | EST | GI-| ANT | [decorative cut] | LE | CORBEAU | [thick rule] | HARPERS | [thick rule]. T.e. red.

Published at $2.00, December 1924.

Notes   Copies are reported with the translator's name corrected to read J.H. Ross, T.E. Lawrence's pseudonym. No copies with this correction have been seen.

Copies   AC, Cal, H, Ho.

A097 ADRIEN LE CORBEAU, The Forest Giant, Doubleday, Doran, 1936

Second American Edition

THE FOREST GIANT | *by* | ADRIEN LE CORBEAU | *Translated from the French by* | J.H. ROSS | *Illustrated with Woodcuts by* | AGNES MILLER PARKER | GARDEN CITY, NEW YORK | DOUBLEDAY, DORAN & COMPANY INC. | 1936

Collation   19 × 13.5 cm: [A]⁸ B–K⁸, 80 leaves, pp.[1–4], 5–160.

Contents   Pp.[1] bastard title, [2] frontispiece, [3] title page, [4] printer's credit, 5 contents, 6 illustrations, 7–8 publisher's note, 9 dedication, [10] blank, [11] half title, [12] blank, 13–159 text, [160] blank.

RT On verso *THE FOREST GIANT.* On recto [in italics, according to chapter].

Typography and paper $ 1 signed G.

Text 11.1 (11.1) × 8.9 cm.

Paper White, wove, watermarked, top edge trimmed, sheets bulk 1 cm.

Binding Green linen 126 d. Ol. G. On spine: [gilt, running down] THE FOREST GIANT. ADRIEN LE CORBEAU DOUBLEDAY, DORAN. T.e. green.

Published at $2.00

Notes Sheets printed in England.

Copies AC, Cal, H, UT.

1927

An Album of Illustrations to Colonel T.E. Lawrence's Seven Pillars of Wisdom

Leicester Galleries, exhibitors of Kennington's Arab portraits in 1921 and later the illustrations for the *Seven Pillars of Wisdom* in 1927, sold twelve sets of the colour plates included in the 'Cranwell' edition remaining after the complete copies of the 1926 edition were finished. There are, in addition, a few sets of proofs of the plates gathered up and bound. These lack a printed title page and are approximately 5 mm larger in size (Maggs Cat. 1055, item 28).

A098   T.E. LAWRENCE, An Album of Illustrations to Colonel T.E. Lawrence's Seven Pillars of Wisdom, Feb. 1927

First English Edition

[No title page]

Collation 25.5 × 22 cm: four folded plates attached to stubs, 53 plates pasted to leaves of heavy stock pierced by three metal rods. Blank leaves, two in front and three at back.

Binding Batik patterned paper covered boards.

Published at February 1927.

Notes One of twelve copies. The plates remaining from the 1927 *Seven Pillars* were collected in these sets and placed in covers, others were used in the limited edition of *Revolt In the Desert* (1927).

Copies Cal, H, Ca, UT.

Catalogue of an Exhibition, 1927

In 1927 there was an exhibition of the illustrations to *Seven Pillars of Wisdom*. The preface written for the 1921 (A032) exhibition of Kennington illustrations, with the first three paragraphs omitted, was used for this catalogue for the second exhibition. George Bernard Shaw also contributed a preface saying more about Lawrence than the exhibition.

A099 LEICESTER GALLERIES, LONDON, Catalogue of An Exhibition, 1927

First English Edition

CATALOGUE OF AN EXHIBITION | OF PAINTINGS, PASTELS, DRAWINGS | AND WOODCUTS | Illustrating Col.T.E. LAWRENCE'S | Book "Seven Pillars of Wisdom" | WITH PREFACES BY BERNARD SHAW | and T.E. LAWRENCE. | ERNEST BROWN & PHILLIPS | THE LEICESTER GALLERIES | LEICESTER SQUARE, LONDON | FEBRUARY 5th–21st, 1927 | EXHIBITION No. 427

Collation 14.5 × 11 cm: [1]^{14}, pp.1–28.

Contents Pp.1–4 ads, 5 title page, 6 ad for *Revolt in the Desert*, 7–13 preface by G.B. Shaw, 14–18 extract from T.E. Lawrence note written on Mr. Kennington's Arab portraits written in 1921, 19–26 text, 27–28 ads.

Plates Two photos on coated paper, wrapped around gathering, printed on one side only, following pp.4, 24.

Text 20 lines, 7.8 × 7.6 cm.

Paper White, laid, watermarked, untrimmed, sheets bulk 3 mm.

Binding Brown paper wrappers, stapled to sheets with one metal staple, 76 l. y Br. On front cover: REYNOLDS ROOM | [within single rule frame] CATALOGUE OF AN EXHIBITION | OF PAINTINGS, PASTELS, DRAWINGS | AND WOODCUTS | Illustrating T.E. LAWRENCE'S Book "Seven Pillars of Wisdom"| With Prefaces by BERNARD SHAW | and T.E. LAWRENCE | ERNEST BROWN & PHILLIPS | (Cecil L. Phillips Oliver F. Brown) | THE LEICESTER GALLERIES | LEICESTER SQUARE, LONDON. |[below frame] EXHIBITION No. 427 FEBRUARY 5th–21st, 1927. On back cover: [within frame] [list of other exhibitions], below frame, printer's credit.

Notes   Another issue, same as above, except that first line on front cover reads: REYNOLDS ROOM *2nd Edition (sic,* printing).

The first three paragraphs of Lawrence's introduction in the 1921 edition are not reprinted here (A032).

Another issue, 3rd Edition (sic), as above, except inclusion of added exhibit of Lawrence's gold Arab dagger and abba, No. 82.

Reprinted in *Oriental Assembly,* pp.151–157, and *The Essential T.E. Lawrence,* pp.228–231.

Copies   AC, Cal, H, UT.

Revolt in the Desert

Lawrence had lavished the finest materials and spared no expense in publication of the 1926 *Seven Pillars of Wisdom*. In doing so, costs for production of the book ballooned from his first estimate of £3000 to £13,000. In a letter of 26 March 1925 we find him contemplating selling first his library and then perhaps some of his property at Chingford Hill. He finally settled on an abridgement of *Seven Pillars of Wisdom*. This was undertaken in 1926 by Lawrence himself with the help of some of his fellow servicemen, the earlier attempt by Edward Garnett having been set aside.

Taking a set of proofs of the Cranwell edition and using a brush and purple ink, Lawrence marked out sections of the text. Whole chapters and large portions of others were dropped. Chapters 1–7 were dropped completely and, of 652 pages, 211 were omitted entirely (Howard, p.90). A sample page thus treated can be found in the 1935 limited issue of *Seven Pillars of Wisdom*.

Published in March 1927 in Great Britain and America, in both limited and general issues, with instalments appearing in the *Daily Telegraph*, three impressions were soon sold out and two more quickly followed in a period of four months. The number of copies in print exceeded 90,000. The fifth impression contains an added paragraph to the preface. This fifth impression was the last as Lawrence exercised his right to stop publication at any time. Once his debt had been cleared he ordered that no more copies were to be printed. The profits from this publication made the fortunes of the Cape publishing house, enabling them to set aside a large reserve (Howard, p.81). Wren Howard, one of the two principal directors of the firm said: 'The man, above all others, whose mark on Cape's history is indelibly printed. Always, from the very beginning, Lawrence was the key to our success.' (Howard, p.81).

In America the instalments appeared in *World's Work*. A 'gift' edition for the Christmas season of 1927 is often mistaken as the first American printing. It is by far the best-looking of all the American impressions and contains end papers by Kennington and an occasional line drawing in the text which appear elsewhere only in the 'Cranwell' edition of *Seven Pillars of Wisdom*. The merger of Doubleday and Doran soon after publication led to an imprint change. The subsequent 'Star Series' reprints appeared for many years using the same stereo plates as there were no contractual agreements to stop publication. Deterioration of type can be used to create a sequence for some of the impressions.

Like the 1935 edition of *Seven Pillars of Wisdom*, *Revolt in the Desert* was translated into many languages.

A100   T.E. LAWRENCE, Revolt in the Desert, Cape, 1927

Uncorrected Proofs of First English Edition

[Outline lettering] REVOLT IN THE | DESERT | [long Oxford rule] | *By* | [pub. device] | [Oxford rule] | LONDON: JONATHAN CAPE LTD.

Collation   23.5 × 15.5 cm: [A]^8 B–DD^8 EE^2, 218 leaves, pp.[1–4], 5–436.

Contents   Pp.[1] bastard title, [2] blank, [3] title page, [4] issue statement, printer's credit, 5–6 contents, 7 [title only] LIST OF ILLUSTRATIONS, [8] blank, 9 foreword,[10] blank, 11–435 text, [1] blank.

RT   [No RT, in margin recto] Revolt in | the Desert. In margin verso [according to chapter].

Typography and paper $ 1 signed AA.

Text   20 lines, 9.7 × 11 cm.

Paper   White, wove, unwatermarked, all edges trimmed, sheets bulk 1.5 cm.

Binding   Brown paper wrappers 601 l. gy. Br.

Copies   Cal, UT.

A101   T.E. LAWRENCE, Revolt in the Desert, Cape, 1927

First English Edition (Large paper, limited)

[In red] REVOLT IN THE DESERT | By | T.E. LAWRENCE | [pub. device] | LONDON | JONATHAN CAPE 30 BEDFORD SQUARE | 1927

Collation   26 × 20 cm: [A]^8 B–Z^8 AA–EE^8, 224 leaves, pp.[1–2], [1–2], 3–448.

Contents   Prp.[1] bastard title, [2] 'Of this large paper edition of *Revolt* | *in the Desert* have been printed 315 | copies, of which 300 only are for sale | Copy number ', pp.[1] title page, [2] 'PRINTED IN GREAT BRITAIN', 3–4 contents, 5–6 illustrations, 7–8 pub. note, 9 foreword, [10] blank, 11–435 text, [436] blank, 437–446 index.

RT   On verso REVOLT IN THE DESERT. On recto [according to chapter].

Plates   Nineteen plates printed on one side only following prp.2 colour, 12, 16 colour, 32 colour, 48 colour, 64 colour, 82, 88 colour, 106, 170, 180, 220 colour, 264 colour, 288 colour, 304 colour, 326 colour, 356, 393, 416. Tissue guards before each coloured plate. Captions printed on verso of plates. Fold map tipped in before free end paper in back.

Typography and paper $ 1 signed AA.

Text 20 lines, 9.9 (10) × 11 cm. Set in Caslon.

Paper White, wove, watermarked, top edge trimmed, sheets bulk 3.3 cm.

Binding Brown buckram boards 54 br. O, dark brown pigskin spine. On front cover: [single gilt rule along leather where it meets cloth]. On spine: [gilt] REVOLT | IN THE | DESERT | [cut] | T.E. | LAWRENCE. Back cover [single gilt rule along leather where it meets cloth]. T.e. gilt. Green and yellow head and tail bands.

Published at £5 5s, 10 March 1927.

Notes Limited to 315 copies of which 300 were for sale. Size of volume dictated by inclusion of coloured plates from 1926 *Seven Pillars*. In order to justify the inclusion of some of the persons represented in the plates and not otherwise mentioned in the text, a few extra paragraphs were added to the abridged text. Plates of line cuts are bound in.

Copies AC, Cal, H, UT.

A102   T.E. LAWRENCE, Revolt in the Desert, Cape, 1927

First English Edition

[In red] REVOLT IN THE DESERT | By | T.E. LAWRENCE | [pub. device] | LONDON | JONATHAN CAPE 30 BEDFORD SQUARE | 1927

Collation   23.3 × 16 cm: [A]^8 B–Z^8 AA–EE^8, 224 leaves, pp.[1–2], [1–2], 3–448.

Contents   Prp.[1] bastard title, [2] blank, pp. [1] title page, [2] 'PRINTED IN GREAT BRITAIN', 3–4 contents, 5–6 illustrations, 7–8 pub. note, 9 foreword, [10] blank, 11–435 text, [436] blank, 437–446 index.

RT   On verso REVOLT IN THE DESERT. On recto [according to chapter].

Plates   Sixteen plates, none in colour, following pp.2, 12, 16, 48, 64, 106, 170, 180, 220, 264, 288, 326, 356, 392; fold map before rear free end paper; tissues before plates.

Typography and paper $ 1 signed AA.

Text 20 lines, 9.9 (10) × 11 cm.

Paper White, wove, unwatermarked, top edge trimmed, sheets bulk 2.9 cm.

Binding Brown buckram 74 s. y Br. On spine: [gilt] REVOLT | IN THE |

DESERT | [cut] | T.E. | LAWRENCE | JONATHAN CAPE. On back cover: [pub. device blind stamped]. T.e. brown.

Published at   30s, 10 March 1927.

Notes   Following p.434, prospectus for *Arabia Deserta* tipped in, 20.8 × 13 cm.

A review copy, first impression March 1927, t.e. unstained, binding 43 m. r Br.

List of impressions:

2nd, March 1927; on this and all subsequent impressions issue statement added to verso of title page; 2nd–4th impressions have larger prospectus after p.434, 22.8 × 14.6 cm.

3rd, March 1927, as above.

4th, March 1927, as above.

5th, March 1927, as above with following differences: foreword has added paragraph which extends foreword text over to p.10 which is now numbered. Fifth impression copies exist with dust wrapper bearing 'Sixth impression' on spine with first word overprinted and 'fifth' printed above it.

Copies   AC, Cal, H, UT, Ho.

A102a   T.E. Lawrence, Revolt in the Desert, Cape, 1927

Prospectus for First English Edition

Colonel Lawrence's long-expected book | REVOLT IN THE DESERT | *by* | T.E. LAWRENCE | [John drawing of Lawrence] | *from a drawing of the Author by* | AUGUSTUS JOHN | One volume, short royal 8vo (9¼ × 6¼ inches) with | about 450 pages of text and sixteen illustrations | 30s net | *There is also a large paper edition limited to* | 300 *numbered copies, printed on hand-made* | *paper, crown 4to, with eleven illustrations* | in full colour and eight in monochrome at | *five guineas net* | LONDON | JONATHAN CAPE 30 BEDFORD SQUARE

Collation   23.2 × 16.3 cm: single-fold leaflet.

Contents   Pp.[1] title page, [2–3] blurb, [4] contents and order form.

Text   Varied.

Paper   Buff, wove, unwatermarked, all edges trimmed.

Published at   Free advertising flyer.

Copies   AC.

A103 T.E. Lawrence, The Seven Pillars of Wisdom and Revolt in the Desert, 1927

Prospectus for First English Edition

[All in red] THE | SEVEN PILLARS OF WISDOM | AND | REVOLT IN THE DESERT | BY | COLONEL T.E. LAWRENCE

Collation   20.3 × 12.7 cm: single-fold leaflet, pp.[1–4].

Contents   Pp.[1] title page, [2] note on work done for T.E.L. by Raymond Savage, [3] text, 'A Letter from Colonel T.E. Lawrence | TO | Raymond Savage', [4] blank.

Paper   White, wove, unwatermarked, all edges trimmed.

Published at   Free advertising flyer.

Notes   Concerns withdrawal of *Revolt in the Desert* from sale in England. Used as an advertising leaflet.

Copies   Cal.

A104 T.E. Lawrence, Revolt in the Desert, Folio Society, 1986

Second English Edition

Revolt in the Desert | *by* | 'T.E. LAWRENCE' | [cut] | *Introduction by* | RALEIGH TREVELYAN | *Photographs by* | T.E. LAWRENCE | AND OTHERS | *Sketches by* | EDWARD BAWDEN | [cut] | LONDON | *The Folio Society* | 1986

Collation   23.5 × 15.5 cm: [1–22]⁸, 176 leaves, pp.[i–iv], v–viii, 1–326.

Contents   Prp.[i] bastard title, [ii] frontis., [iii] title page, [iv] copyright statement, printer's, binder's, typesetter's credits, [v–vi] contents, [vii–viii] illus., pp.1–9 introduction, 10–12 publisher's note to first edition, 13 foreword, [14] blank, 15–318 text, 319–326 index.

RT   On verso *Revolt in the Desert*. On recto [according to chapter].

Typography and paper   11 pt. set in Bembo spaced one point.

Text   20 lines, 8.5 (8.8) × 11 cm.

Paper   White, wove, unwatermarked, all edges trimmed, sheets bulk 2 cm Wentworth Opaque paper.

Binding   Brown 85 d. yellow pictorial cloth. On spine: [within brown rectangle, gilt | REVOLT | IN THE | DESERT | [decorative cut] | T.E. | LAWRENCE | [at foot pub. device] Gold and brown head band. T.e. brown.

Published at $25.00.

Copies   AC, Cal.

A105   T.E. LAWRENCE, Revolt in the Desert, Doran, 1927

First American Edition (large paper, limited issue)

REVOLT IN THE DESERT | By | 'T.E. LAWRENCE' | [cut] | GEORGE H. DORAN COMPANY | NEW YORK MCMXXVII

Collation   26.3 × 20 cm: [1–22]⁸ [23]², 178 leaves, pp.[i–iv], v–xx, 1–336.

Contents   Prp.[i] bastard title, [ii] 'Of this large paper edition of *Revolt* | *in the Desert* 250 copies have been | printed: | Copy number', [iii] title page, [iv] copyright statement, Doran's colophon, issue statement, v–x introduction, xi–xii contents, xiii–xiv illustrations, xv–xvi pub. note, xvii foreword, [xviii] blank, xix half-title, [xx] blank, pp. 1–328 text, 329–335 index, [336] blank.

RT   On verso REVOLT IN THE DESERT. On recto [according to chapter].

Plates   Eighteen plates, (11 in colour, 7 b/w), fold map at rear before free end paper. Plates following [ii] colour, 2, 8 colour, 16 colour, 38 colour, 52 colour, 60, 70, 84, 98, 124, 158 colour, 182 colour, 204 colour, 234 colour, 242 colour, 260, 308, 322. Tissue guards bearing captions before each plate, captions are also printed on verso of plates; plate following p.16 is mounted upside down as shown by caption on verso. B/w plates pasted onto grey paper.

Text   20 lines, 9.1 (9.8) × 11 cm.

Paper   White, laid, watermarked, top edge trimmed, sheets bulk 3.5 cm.

Binding   Blue buckram 187 d. gy. B. On spine: [within brown leather rectangle, within gilt rule frame] REVOLT | IN THE | DESERT | [short rule] | 'T.E. | LAWRENCE'. T.e. gilt. Blue and yellow head and tail bands. Dark blue end papers. Boxed as issued.

Published at $30.00, March 1927.

Notes   Limited to 250 copies.

Copies   AC, Cal, H, UT.

A106   T.E. LAWRENCE, Revolt in the Desert, Doran, 1927

Publisher's Prospectus for large paper limited edition

REVOLT IN THE DESERT | By | T.E. LAWRENCE | [cut] | AN ANNOUNCEMENT | OF AN EDITION DE LUXE | LIMITED TO 250 COPIES | GEORGE H. DORAN COMPANY | NEW YORK MCMXXVII

Collation   26 × 19.2 cm: double-fold leaflet, pp.[1–8].

Contents   Pp.[1] title page, [2–3] blank, [4–5] text, [6–7] blank, [8] order form.

Paper   White, laid, watermarked, untrimmed.

Copies   H.

A107   T.E. LAWRENCE, Revolt in the Desert, Doran, 1927

First American Edition

REVOLT IN THE DESERT | By | 'T.E. LAWRENCE' | [cut] | GEORGE H. DORAN COMPANY | NEW YORK MCMXXVII

Collation   23 × 15.8 cm: [1–21]^8 [22]^{10}, 178 leaves, pp.[i–iv], v–xx, 1–336.

Contents   Prp.[i] bastard title, [ii] blank, [iii] title page, [iv] copyright statement, Doran's colophon, issue statement, v–x introduction, xi–xii contents, xiii–xiv illustrations, xv–xvi publisher's note, xvii foreword, [xviii] blank, xix half-title, [xx] blank, pp. 1–328 text, 329–335 index, [336] blank.

Plates   Sixteen b/w plates on coated paper, following pp.[ii], 12, 28, 44, 76, 92, 108, 124, 156, 172, 204, 220, 252, 268, 300, 316.

Text   20 lines, 9.1 (8.8) × 11 cm.

Paper   White, wove, unwatermarked, all edges trimmed, sheets bulk 3 cm.

Binding   Grey red buckram 19 gy. Red. On front cover: REVOLT IN | THE DESERT | 'T·E· LAWRENCE' | | [cut]. On spine: REVOLT | ·IN ·THE | DESERT | · | 'T·E | LAWRENCE' | · | [cut] | DORAN. T.e. brown. Pictorial end papers in pink and blue.

Published at $3.00, March 1927.

Notes   First impression is indicated by Doran's colophon (a black 'lozenge' with white GHD within) on the verso of title page between the copyright and printing statement. Later impressions do not bear this colophon. In 1927 Doran merged with Doubleday and one impression of this book appeared under the new imprint. At least two copies of this latter impression exist which have dust wrapper with George J. Hicks imprint on spine. Pub. at 15s, sheets bulk 3.7 cm, American impression sheets bulk 3.3 cm. Title page transcription: REVOLT IN THE DESERT | By | 'T.E. LAWRENCE' | [cut] | GARDEN CITY NEW YORK | DOUBLEDAY, DORAN & COMPANY, Inc. Spine imprint reads DOUBLEDAY | DORAN.

Copies   AC, Cal, H, UT, Ho.

A108   T.E. LAWRENCE, Revolt in the Desert, Doran, 1927

Second American Edition (gift edition)

REVOLT | IN THE DESERT | BY | 'T.E. LAWRENCE' | NEW YORK | George H. Doran Company | 1927

Collation   24 × 16 cm: [1–21]⁸ [22] 10s, 178 leaves, pp.[i–iv], v–[xx], 1–336.

Contents   Prp.[i] bastard title, [ii] blank, [iii] title page, [iv] copyright statement, issue statement, v–x introduction, xi–xii contents, xiii–xiv illustrations, xv–xvi publisher's note, xvii foreword, [xviii] blank, xix half-title, [xx] blank, pp. 1–328 text, 329–335 index, [336] blank.

Plates   Twenty-four b/w plates on coated paper following pp.[ii], 12, 28, 44, 58, 76, 92, 108, 114, 124, 148, 156, 172, 184, 204, 220, 238, 252, 268, 280, 292, 300, 308, 316; fold map inside rear cover.

Text   20 lines, 9.1 (8.8) × 11 cm.

Paper   White, wove, unwatermarked, top edges trimmed, sheets bulk 3 cm.

Binding   Brown buckram 54 br. O. On spine: [gilt] REVOLT | IN THE | DESERT | [cut] | T.E. | LAWRENCE | DORAN. T.e. brown. Black and white illustrated end papers designed by Kennington for 1926 *Seven Pillars*.

Published at $5.00.

Notes   This impression contains 18 b/w line cuts in the text from 1926 *Seven Pillars of Wisdom* not present in any other edition of *Revolt*. This format was a 'gift' issue for the 1927 Christmas season. It resembles in format, binding and dust wrapper the First English Edition and although it fails to achieve that stature, is certainly better for it. It contains Kennington end papers and some line cuts in the text found elsewhere only in the 1926 *Seven Pillars of Wisdom*.

Copies   AC, Cal, UT.

A109   T.E. LAWRENCE, Revolt in the Desert, Garden City, n.d.

Third American Edition

'T.E. LAWRENCE' | [decorative rule] | REVOLT | IN THE DESERT | [pub. device combined with series title] | GARDEN CITY, NEW YORK | GARDEN CITY PUBLISHING COMPANY, INC.

Collation   20.4 × 13.5 cm: [1–22]⁸, 176 leaves, pp.[i–iv], v–xii, [xiii–xvi], 1–335, [1].

Contents   Prp.[i] bastard title, [ii] blank, [iii] title page, [iv] copyright statement, v–x introduction, xi–xii contents, [xiii–xiv] pub. note, [xv] foreword, [xvi] blank, pp.1–328 text, 329–335 index, [1] blank.

RT   On verso REVOLT IN THE DESERT. On recto [according to chapter].

Plates   Frontispiece on coated paper tipped in following prp.[ii]; fold-out map inside rear cover.

Text   20 lines, 8.7 (8.9) × 11.1 cm.

Paper   White, wove, unwatermarked, all edges trimmed, sheets bulk 2.8 cm.

Binding   Rough brown cloth 54 br. O. On front cover: [all in dark brown] REVOLT IN | THE DESERT | 'T·E·LAWRENCE', [cut within blind stamped rectangle]. On spine: [all in brown] REVOLT | ·IN·THE· | DESERT[· | 'T·E | LAWRENCE' | [cut] | GARDEN CITY | PUBLISHING CO. | INC. T.e. light brown.

Published at $1.00.

Notes   There are many printings of this edition and no effective means of determining priority of issue. The following are points that can be used to roughly group issues. The earliest issues are slightly shorter (21 cm) and have a rough cloth binding, a blind stamped rectangle for the front cover cut and INC. as part of the spine imprint. A second group, while the same height, have a smooth cloth binding, lack the blind stamped rectangle and after one (or more) issues drop the INC. from the spine imprint. Varying cloth colours are used and the colours for the t.e. stain vary. The third group is 21.5 cm in height and all lack the INC. on the spine imprint, all have smooth cloth and lack the blind stamped rectangle. Greater contrast in the cloth colour is found and there is some variation in sheet bulk measurement. Throughout all these groups the deterioration in type can be traced. It appears that the same plates were used in all printings and careful collation of the cumulative type damage can prove profitable in determining the precise order of precedence among copies if one were sure of having copies of most issues. This edition began the 'Star Series' reprints.

Copies   AC, Cal.

A110   T.E. LAWRENCE, Bouře nad Asií, Orbis, 1932

First Czechoslovak Edition

T.E. LAWRENCE | BOUŘE NAD ASIÍ | POVSTÁNI NA POUŠTI | SPŘEDMLUVOU | G.B. ŚHAWA | PŘELOŽIL | ALOYS A HANA SKOUMALOVI | [short rule] | 4 OBRÁZKOVÉ PŘÍLOHY | A MAPA | 1932 | NAKLADATELSTVÍ „ORBIS" V PRAZE XII | FOCHOVA 62

Collation   22.5 × 14.5 cm: [1]−24⁸ [25]⁴, 196 leaves, pp.[1−4], 5−[383], [1−9].

Contents   Pp.[1] list of titles in series, [2] series title page, [3] title page, [4] contents, 5−7 G.B. Shaw preface, [8] blank, 9 introductory letter by T.E. Lawrence, [10] blank, 11−369 text, 370−373 postscript by translator, FNOSKA, 374 POZNÁMKA PŘEKLADATELÚ, 375−[383] index, [1] blank, [2−3] contents, [4] OPRAVY, [5] blank, [6] title page reproduced, [7−9] blank,. Fold. map inside rear cover.

Plates   Four b/w plates on coated paper following pp.16, 96, 192, 288.

Typography and paper $ 2 signed 2 2*.

Text   20 lines, 9 × 10 cm.

Paper   White, wove, unwatermarked, untrimmed, sheets bulk 2.5 cm.

Binding   White paper covers. On front cover: T.E. LAWRENCE | BOUŘE NAD ASIÍ | Vzpoura na poušti | [b/w photo of Arabs on horseback] | KNIHY OSUDÔ A PRÁGE, SVAZEK X. | ORBIS, PRAHA XII | Kč 45−. On spine: [running up, orange] T.E. LAWRENCE: BOUŘE NAD ASIÍ. On back cover: [pub. ads].

Published at   45.− Kć.

Notes   Hardbound edition same as above with following differences: [Collation]: 20.5 × 13.8 cm; [Binding]: Red cloth 12 s. Red. On front cover: [block and line pattern] [within black block at top, in red] SV.10 | KNIHY OSUDÚ A PRACE | [within black block at bottom, in red] T.E. LAWRENCE | BOUŘE | NAD ASIÍ. On spine: [running up] T.E. LAWRENCE: BOUŘE NAD ASIÍ. T.e. gray. Red and white head and tail bands, white silk place marker.

Copies   H, BPL.

A111   T.E. LAWRENCE, Oprøret I Ørkenen, Gyldendalske, 1928

First Danish Edition

T.E. LAWRENCE | OPRØRET I ØRKENEN | PAA DANSK | VED | PETER

DE HEMMER GUDME | [Oxford rule] | GYLDENDALSKE BOGHANDEL = NORDIEK | FORLAG – KØBENHAVN = MCMXXVIII

Collation 26.9 × 19.9 cm: [1]⁸ 2–16⁸, 128 leaves, pp.[1–5], 6–255, [1].

Contents Pp.[1] half-title, [2] blank, [3] title page, [4] issue statement, printer's credit, [5] –11 introduction, 12–255 text, [1] [translator's note].

Plates Sixteen b/w photos on coated paper printed on both sides following pp.[2], 16, 32, 48, 64, 80, 96, 112, 121, 144, 160, 176, 192, 208, 224, 240; fold map inside rear cover.

Typography and paper $ 1,2 signed Oprøret i Ørkenen 4,4*.

Text 20 lines, 10.4 × 12.7 cm.

Paper White, wove, unwatermarked, untrimmed, sheets bulk 2.5 cm.

Binding Tan paper covers. On front cover: [all in red] LAWRENCE§ | EGEN BERETNING OM | [b/w photo of camel grazing within single rule frame] | OPRØRET | I ØRKENEN | [thick, long rule] | GYLDENDALSKE BOGHANDEL. On spine: ¹[all in red] LAW | REN | CES | EGEN | BERETNING | OM | OPRØ- | RET | I | ØRKE- | NEN | [silhouette of rider on camel] | G.B. | N.F. | 1928. On back cover: [printer's device].

Notes Another issue, 1929, same as above, except that 1929 appears on title page and at foot of spine; 1928, 4000 copies; 1929, 5500 copies. Hardbound issue in red half-leather spine, mottled paper covered boards.

Copies AC, H, CAL.

A112 T.E. LAWRENCE, Arabië in Opstand, Leopold, 1927

First Dutch Edition

ARABIË IN OPSTAND | T.E. LAWRENCE | [cut] | *Geautoriseerde Bewerking van* | *Jhr. R.H.G. Nahuys* | [pub. device] | 'S-GRAVENHAGE MCMXXVII | H.P. LEOPOLD'S UITGAVERSMAATSCHAPPIJ

Collation 23.4 × 15.5 cm: [1]⁶ [2–16]⁸ [17]⁴, 130 leaves, pp.[i–iv], v–viii, [x–xii], 1–247, [1].

Contents [i] bastard title, [ii] blank, [iii] title page, [iv] original title, v–viii translator's note, [ix] contents, [x] blank, [xi] illustrations, [xii] blank, pp.1–247 text, [1] blank.

RT On verso ARABIË IN OPSTAND. On recto [according to chapter].

Plates Eight plates on coated paper, tipped in following pp.[ii], 16, 48, 80, 112, 144, 176, 224; fold map inside rear cover.

Text 20 lines, 7.6 (7.8) × 10.9 cm.

Paper White, wove, unwatermarked, all edges trimmed, sheets bulk 3.2 cm.

Binding   Tan cloth 57 l. Br. On front cover: [within frame of single black rules] [gilt] ARABIË | IN OPSTAND | [cut of TEL bust partially blind stamped, partially in black] | [gilt] T.E. LAWRENCE. On spine: [black rule] | [title and author's name gilt] ARABIË | IN | OPSTAND | T.E. LAWRENCE | [pub. device] | H.P. Leopold | [rule]. T.e. brown. End papers tan.

Copies   AC, Cal, H.

A113   T.E. LAWRENCE, Erämaan Kapina, Porissa, Satakunnan, Kirjatateollisuus Oy, 1928

First Finnish Edition

T.E. LAWRENCE | ERÄMAAN KAPINA | *TEKIJÄN VALTUUTTAMANA ENCLAANINK* | ELESTÄ | *SUOMENTANUT* | HIKKI TEITINEN | [pub. device] | PORISSA | SATAKUNNAN KIRJATEOLLISUUS OY

Collation   22 × 15 cm: [1]−28^8 29^4, 228 leaves, pp.[1−5], 6−451, [5].

Contents   Pp.[1] bastard title, [2] blank, [3] title page, [4] pub. device, [5]−8 preface, [9]−11 pub. note, [12] blank, [13]−451 text, [1] blank, [2−3] contents, [4−5] blank.

Plates   Frontispiece on coated paper preceding p.[1].

Typography and paper   \$ 1 signed 3-Erämaan Kapina.

Text   20 lines, 9 × 10 cm.

Paper   White, wove, unwatermarked, untrimmed, sheets bulk 3 cm.

Binding   Pictorial paper covers. [Black and red lettering] ERÄMAAN | KAPINA | T.E. LAWRENCE | [drawing taken from American dust wrapper in red and black]. On spine: [Oxford rule] | T.E. Lawrence | [Oxford rule] | Erämaan Kapina | [Oxford rule] | [pub. device]. On back cover: [blurb, within Oxford rule frame].

Published at   45.−.

Copies   H.

A114   T.E. LAWRENCE, La Révolte dans le Désert, Payot, 1928

First French Edition

COLLECTION DE MÉMOIRES, ÉTUDES ET DOCUMENTS | POUR SERVIR À | L'HISTOIRE DE LA GUERRE MONDIALE | [rule] | COLONEL T.-E. LAWRENCE | [short rule] | LA RÉVOLTE | DANS LE DÉSERT | (1916−1918) | TRADUIT DE L'ANGLAIS PAR B. MAYRA ET LE

L-COLONEL DE FONLONGUE | [short rule] | *Avec 8 illustrations et 1 carte hors texte* | [pub. device] | PAYOT, PARIS | 106, BOULEVARD ST-GERMAIN | [short rule] | 1928 | Tous droits réservés

Collation 22.8 × 14.3 cm: [1]⁸ 2–29⁸, 232 leaves, pp.[1–10], 11–463, [1].

Contents Pp.[1] blank, [2] blank, 3 title page, [4] issue, copyright statements, [5] contents, [6] illustrations, [7] preface, [8] blank, [9] –463 text, [1] blank.

RT On verso LA RÉVOLTE DANS LE DÉSERT. On recto [according to chapter].

Plates Eight illustrations on coated paper tipped in following pp.16, 80, 128, 192, 256, 320, 384, 432; 2 fold maps inside rear cover.

Typography and paper $ 1 signed 7 La Révolte dans le Désert.

Text 20 lines, 8.9 (9.1) × 9.9 cm.

Paper White, wove, unwatermarked, untrimmed, sheets bulk 2.5 cm.

Binding Tan paper covers 33 br. Pink. On front cover: [all in blue within single rule frame] COLLECTION DE MÉMOIRES, ÉTUDES ET DOCUMENTS | POUR SERVIR À | L'HISTOIRE DE LA GUERRE MONDIALE | [rule] | COLONEL T.-E. LAWRENCE | [short rule] LA RÉVOLTE | DANS LE DÉSERT | (1916–1918) | [short rule] | TRADUIT DE L'ANGLAIS PAR B. MAYRA | ET LE L-COLONEL DE FONLONGUE | [short rule] | *Avec 8 illustrations et 1 carte hors texte* | [pub. device] | PAYOT, PARIS. On spine: [in blue] [rule] | COLONEL | T.-E. LAWRENCE | [rule] | La Révolte | dans | le désert | [rule] | PRIX: | 32 fr. | [rule] | PAYOT, | PARIS | [short rule] | 1928 | [rule]. On back cover [list of titles in series].

Published at 32 fr., June 1928.

Notes List of impressions:
   2nd, 1929, same as above, with 1929 on title page and impression statement Avril 1929 on verso of title page.
   3rd, October 1930, same as above.
   4th, May 1935, same as above.
   5th, November 1935, sheets bulk 3.5 cm, otherwise as above.

Copies:AC, Cal, H.

A115 T.E. LAWRENCE, La Révolte dans le Désert, Payot, 1928

Publisher's Prospectus for First French Edition

PAYOT, 106. BOULEVARD SAINT-GERMAIN, 106, PARIS | [long rule] | COLONEL T.-E. LAWRENCE | [short rule] | LA RÉVOLTE | DANS

LE DÉSERT | (1916–1918) | Un volume in-8 illustré. . . . 32 fr.

Collation   18.5 × 11.8 cm: single leaf, printed on both sides.

Contents   Recto title, verso quotes from reviews.

Paper   Newsprint, wove, unwatermarked, all edges trimmed.

Published at   Free advertising flyer.

Copies   AC.

A116   T.E. LAWRENCE, Aufstand in der Wüste, List, [1927]

First German Edition

T.E. LAWRENCE | [double rule] | AUFSTAND | IN DER WÜSTE | DEUTSCH VON | DAGOBERT VON MIKUSCH | [star] | MIT 4 TIEFDRUCKBILDERN | UND EINER GELÄNDEKARTE | [pub. device] | EINZIG AUTORISIERTE AUSGABE |[double rule] | PAUL LIST VERLAG LEIPZIG

Collation   23.4 × 16.5 cm: π^6 1–22^8 23^2, 184 leaves, pp.[i–v], vi–[xii], 1–355, [1].

Contents   [i] bastard title, [ii] blank, [iii] title page, [iv] copyright statement, [v]–vi preface by G.B. Shaw, vii–xi translator's foreword, [xii] contents, 1–355 text, [1] ad.

RT   On both verso and recto [according to chapter].

Plates   Four b/w plates on coated paper printed on one side only following pp.[1], 64, 160, 256; fold map before rear free end paper.

Typography and paper $ 1,2 signed Aufstand in der Wüste, 3,3*.

Text   20 lines, 8.9 (9.2) × 10.9 cm.

Paper   White, wove, unwatermarked, all edges trimmed, sheets bulk 2.5 cm.

Binding   Tan rough cloth 33 br. Pink. On front cover: [in red] LAWRENCE | AUFSTAND IN DER WÜSTE. On spine: [two red rules] |[black decorated rule] | [crossed sword cut, in red] | [black decorated rule] | [moon and star in red] | [decorated black rule] | [white lettering on red rectangle] LAWRENCE | AUFSTAND | IN DER WÜSTE | [black decorated rule] | [crossed sword in red] | [black decorative rule] | [lance with banner, in red] | [double rule] | [pub. device over black decorative rule and six red rules]. T.e. tan. Red head and tail bands.

Published at   RM 4:80.

Copies   AC, Cal, H, UT.

A117 T.E. LAWRENCE, Aufstand in der Wüste, List, 1932?

Second German Edition

AUFSTAND | IN DER WÜSTE | VON | T.E. LAWRENCE | EINZIG AUTORISIERTE AUSGABE | [pub. device] | [rule] | PAUL LIST VERLAG · LEIPZIG

Collation   21 × 13.3 cm: [1] –23⁸ 24¹⁰, 194 leaves, pp.[1–4], 5–387, [1].

Contents   Pp.[1] bastard title, [2] blank, [3] title page, [4] translator's credit, issue, copyright statements, printer's credit, 5–6 G.B. Shaw preface, [7] contents, [8]–12 translator's introduction, [13]–384 text, [385]–387 translator's postscript, [388] ads.

RT   On both verso and recto [according to chapter].

Plates   Fold-out map preceding free end paper in back.

Typography and paper $ signed 1,2 Lawrence, Aufstand in der Wüste 19,19*.

Text   20 lines, 8.2 (8.5) × 9.7 cm.

Paper   White, wove, unwatermarked, all edges trimmed, sheets 2.7 cm.

Binding   Tan rough cloth 33 br. Pink. On front cover: T.E. LAWRENCE | [in red] Aufstand in der | [in red] Wüste. On spine: T.E. | Lawrence | [title in red] Aufstand | in der | Wüste | [pub. device]. T.e. grey. Brown head and tail bands.

Notes   19–26 auflage, introduction dated 1932.
   Another issue, 33–36 auflage 1935?, same as above, with following differences: [rule after pub. device on title page omitted]; [Collation]: 21.1 × 13 cm: [1]–24⁸ 25⁴ [26]⁴, 200 leaves, pp.[1–6] 7–400; [Contents]: pp.[1] bastard title, [2] blank, [3] title page, [4] translator's, binder's credits, issue, copyright statements, printer's credits, [5] contents, [6]–7 G.B. Shaw preface, [8] blank, [9]–20 translator's introduction dated July 1935, [21]–397 text, 398 Robert Graves's obituary of Lawrence, [399] ad, [400] blank; [Binding]: period following middle initial E is lacking on spine. Fold-out map is between pp.398–399.
   Another issue, 81–84 auflage, as immediately above with following differences: [Collation]: [1]–25⁸; [Contents]: p.[400] ad; [Binding]: darker brown.

Copies   AC, Cal.

A118 T.E. LAWRENCE, Aufstand in der Wüste, Deutsche Buch-Gemeinschaft, 1935

Third German Edition

T.E. LAWRENCE | AUFSTAND IN DER WÜSTE | Einzig autorisierte Ausgabe | [tapered rule] | Deutsche Buch-Gemeinschaft | G.M.B.H. | Berlin

Collation 18.6 × 12.5 cm: Ia^{12} 2−27^8 28^{12}, 232 leaves, pp.[I−IV], V−XXIII, [XXIV], 1−439, [1].

Contents [I] publisher's device, [II] blank, [III] title page, [IV] translator's, binder's, designer's credits, copyright statement, V contents, [VI] blank, VII−IX preface by G. B. Shaw, [X] blank, XI−[XXIV] introduction, 1−439 text, [1] ad.

RT On both verso and recto [according to subject of opening, both pages same].

Typography and paper \$ 1 signed 1,2 2 [fraktur] Lawrence, Aufstand in der Wüste, 2*.

Text 20 lines, 8.3 (8.6) × 9.1 cm.

Paper White, wove, unwatermarked, all edges trimmed, sheets bulk 2.5 cm.

Binding Buff 89 p. Y paper covered boards, green 151 d.g. G leather spine. On front cover: [lettering all in green] E·T·LAWRENCE *(sic)* | [drawing in brown of figures on camels] [next three lines script] Aufstand | in | der Wüste. On spine: [all in gilt] [rule] | [row of dots] | [rule] | E.T. *(sic)* | LAWRENCE | [rule] | [within brown rectangle, in script] Aufstand | in | der Wüste | [Oxford rule] | [row of dots] | [rule]. T.e. light tan. Pale yellow head and tail bands. White silk place marker. Folded map inside rear cover.

Notes Another issue same as above with the initials on binding corrected and a resetting of last page of text.

Copies AC, Cal.

A119 T.E. LAWRENCE, Aufstand in der Wüste, Deutsche Hausbucherei, 1957

Fourth German Edition (Book Club)

T.E. LAWRENCE | *Aufstand in der Wüste* | *DEUTSCHE HAUSBÜCHEREI* · *HAMBURG* · *BERLIN*

Collation 20.2 × 12.5 cm: [1–22]⁸ [23]⁹ (8 + 1) [24]⁸, 193 leaves, pp. [1–6], 7–384, [2].

Contents Pp.[1] pub. device, [2] blank, [3] title page, [4] translator's, designer's, binder's credits, [5] contents, [6] blank, 7–8 preface by G.B. Shaw, 9–19 biographical sketch of Lawrence, 20–383 text, [384] Graves' obituary of Lawrence, [1–2] translator's sources.

Text 20 lines, 8.3 × 9.3 cm.

Paper White, wove, unwatermarked, all edges trimmed, sheets bulk 3 cm.

Binding Yellow linen 97 v. g Y. On front cover: [within white smear, in red] aufstand | in der | wüste. On spine: [running down, in white] lawrence | [across, yellow within red rectanlge] t.e. | lawrence | aufstand | in der | wüste | [running down, in white] aufstand in der wüste. White silk place marker. Red head and tail bands. T.e. stained gray.

Copies AC.

A120 T.E. LAWRENCE, Aufstand in der Wüste, Fischer, 1957

Fifth German Edition

T.E. LAWRENCE | AUFSTAND IN DER WÜSTE | FISCHER BÜCHEREI

Collation 17.8 × 10.7 cm: [1–2]⁸ 3–23⁸ 24⁴, 188 leaves, pp.[1–6], 7–374, [2].

Contents Pp.[1] pub. device, [2] pub. blurb, [3] title page, [4] translator's credit, original title, issue statement, designer's, printer's credits, [5] contents, [6] blank, 7–[16] biog. sketch of TEL, [17–18] maps, [19] half-title, 20–374 text, [1–2] ads.

Typography and paper $ 1,2 signed 3/177, 3*.

Text 20 lines, 7.5 × 9 cm.

Paper White, wove, unwatermarked, all edges trimmed, sheets bulk 2 cm.

Binding Yellow paper 83 brill Y. Plastic coated. On front cover: Das berühmte Buch des | ⟩⟩ ungekrönten Königs von Arabiens ⟨⟨ | T.E. LAWRENCE | Aufstand | in der | Wüste | [pub. device] | FISCHER * BUCHEREI. On spine: 177 | [running down within white rectangle] T.E. LAWRENCE AUFSTAND IN DER WÜSTE | [below yellow rectangle] * * . On back cover: Das gute für jedermann | [within white rectangle, photo of Lawrence and blurb] | [below white rectangle] FISCHER * BÜCHEREI.

Copies AC.

A121   T.E. LAWRENCE, ha-Mered ba-midbar, Mizpah, 1931

First Hebrew Edition

[Running right to left] T.E. LAWRENCE | HA-MERED BA-MIDBAR | TURGAM MAYANGLIT | YAAKOV KOPLEVITZ | EEM HAKDAMA MAYAYT BERNARD SHAW | CHELEK RISHON | [pub. device] | SIFRIAT UNIVERSITAH LAAM | [broad bar] | HOTSAAT STARIM "MITSPEH" BAAM | TAF RESTI TSADL ALEPH TEL-AVIV

Collation   18.8 × 13 cm: Vol. 1, [1]–5¹⁶ 6⁸ 17¹⁶, 113 leaves, pp.[1–3], 4–210; Vol. 2, [1]–6¹⁶ 7¹⁰, 106 leaves, pp.[1–3], 4–212.

Contents   Vol. 1: pp.[1] title page, [2] copyright, publisher, printer's credits, [3]–5 G.B. Shaw introduction, [6] author's note, 7–210 text. Vol.2: pp.[1] title page, [2] copyright statement, printer's credit, [3]–212 text.

RT   On verso T.E. LAURENS. On recto HA-MERED BA-MIDBAR.

Typography and paper $ 1 signed 2.

Text   20 lines, 10.3 (10.5) × 9.8 cm.

Paper   White, wove, unwatermarked, all edges trimmed, sheets bulk 1.3 cm.

Binding   Blue buckram 183 d. Blue. On front cover: [gilt, running right to left] T.E. LAURENS | [short rule] | HA-MERED BA-MIDBAR. On spine: [gilt right to left] T.E. LAURENS | [rule] | HA-MERED | BA-MIDBAR | SIFRIAT | UNIVERSITAH | [rule].

Copies   LC, UCLA, H.

A122   THOMAS EDWARD LAWRENCE, Uppresinin Í Eydimörkinni, Islenzka, 1940

First Icelandic Edition

THOMAS EDWARD LAWRENCE | UPPREISNIN | Í EYÐIMÖRKINNI | BOGI OLAFSSON | ÞÝDDI | FYRRI HLUTINN | [pub. device] | HIÐ ISLENZKAÞ JODVINAFÉLAG | REYKJAVÍK · 1940 [Vol. II, 1941]

Collation   21.5 × 14 cm: Vol. I, π⁴ 1–11⁸, 92 leaves, pp.[I–V], VI–VII, [VIII], [1]–176; Vol. II, [12]–26⁸, 120 leaves, pp.[1–2], [177–179], 180–402, 403–404, [1–2].

Contents   Vol. I: prp.[I] bastard title, [II] blank, [III] title page, [IV] printer's credit, [V]–VII brief biography of Lawrence, [VIII] translator's note, pp.[1]–176 text. Vol. II: prp.[I] blank, [II] map, pp.[1] title page, [2] printer's credit, [3]–402 text, [1–8] four sheets with b/w illus. on one side only, 403–404 text, [1–2] blank.

RT On verso UPPREISNIN Í EYÐIMÖRKINNI. On recto [according to chapter].

Typography and paper $ 1 signed 8.

Text 20 lines, 8.1 (8.5) × 10.4 cm.

Paper White, wove, unwatermarked, all edges trimmed, sheets bulk 9 mm (Vol. I), 10 mm (Vol II).

Binding Vol.I, yellow paper covers 71 m. OY. On front cover: THOMAS EDWARD LAWRENCE | UPPRESININ | Í EYÐIMÖRKINNI | FYRRI HLUTINN | [pub. device]. Vol. II: blue paper covers 185 p. Blue.

Copies AC, INL.

A123   T.E.LAWRENCE, La Rivolta nel Deserto, Mondadori, 1930

First Italian Edition

T.E. LAWRENCE, [in red] LA RIVOLTA | NEL DESERTO | *Versione e piefazione di ARRIGO CAJUMI* | CON 6 illustrazioni e una carta | geografica | A MONDADORI | [pub. device] | EDITORE · 1930

Collation 22.5 × 14.5 cm: [1]^8 2–25^8 26^4 27^8, 212 leaves, pp.[I–VII], VII– [XVI], [1] –406, [2].

Contents Prp.[I–II] blank, [III] bastard title, [IV] blank, [V] title page, [VI] copyright statement, [VII] –XII translator's preface, [XIII] author's foreword, [XIV] blank, [XV] half title, [XVI] blank, [1] –398 text, 399–400 note by English editor, [fold map], [401] section title, [402] blank, [403] list of illustrations, [404] blank, [405] –406 contents, [1] colophon, [2] blank.

RT On verso *T.E. Lawrence – La rivolta nel deserto.* On recto [according to chapter].

Plates Six plates, tipped in following pp.32, 48, 144, 160, 272, 288; fold map after p.400.

Typography and paper $ 1 signed 9- LAWRENCE.

Text 20 lines, 7.4 (8) × 9 cm.

Paper White, wove, unwatermarked, top edge trimmed, sheets bulk 3.3 cm.

Binding Blue cloth 196s.p B. On front cover: [gilt] T.E. LAWRENCE | LA RIVOLTA | NEL DESERTO | MONDADORI. Blue & white striped head and tail bands. Pale green end papers bearing pub. device.

Published at   January 1930.

Notes   Reprinted February 1933.

Copies   Cal, H.

A124   T.E. LAWRENCE, La Rivolta nel Deserto, Mondadori, 1930

Publisher's Prospectus for First Italian Edition

[No title page]

Collation   Single leaf, pale green.

Contents   On one side blurb for *La Rivolta* within panelled rules frame. On verso: ad for D.H. Lawrence's books admonishing reader not to confuse D.H. and T.E. also within single rule frame.

Paper   5.8 × 9.7 cm, green, wove, unwatermarked, all edges trimmed.

Published at   Free advertising flyer.

Copies   Cal, H.

A125   T.E. LAWRENCE, La Rivolta nel Deserto, Mondadori, 1934

Second Italian Edition

T.E. LAWRENCE | [in red] LA RIVOLTA | [in red] NEL DESERTO | *Versione e prefazione* | *di* | *ARRIGO CAJUMI* | [pub. device] | A. MONDADORI MILANO

Collation   19.5 × 13 cm: [1]–25^8 26^{10}, 210 leaves, pp.[I–VII], VIII–XVI, [1]–400, [1–4].

Contents   [I–II] blank, [III] bastard title, [IV] blank, [V] title page, [VI] copyright, issue statements, [VII]–XII translator's preface, [XIII] author's note, [XIV] blank, [XV]–XVI contents, [1]–398 text, [399]–400 notes by English editor, [1] printer's colophon, [2–3]ads, [4] blank.

RT   On verso *T.E. Lawrence – La rivolta nel deserto.* On recto [according to chapter].

Typography and paper $1 signed 9- LAWRENCE.

Text   20 lines, 7.3 (7.9) × 9 cm.

Paper   White, wove, unwatermarked, top edge trimmed, sheets bulk 2.7 cm.

Binding   Brown cloth 43 m. r Br [top and bottom stripes (each 6cm)], in between 79 l. gy. y Brs stripe] [all run around both covers and spine]. On spine: [gilt on brown leather patch] [rule] | T.E. LAWRENCE | [short rule] | LA RIVOLTA | NEL DESERTO | [rule]. Brown head and tail bands. Sand simulated end papers.

Published at   July 1934.

Notes   Reprinted July 1935.

Copies   AC.

A126   T.E. LAWRENCE, La Rivolta nel Deserto, Mondadori, 1937

Third Italian Edition

T.E. LAWRENCE | LA | RIVOLTA | NEL DESERTO | *CON SEI TAVOLE | E UNA CARTA FUORI TESTO* | [double rule] | [pub. device] | A. MONDADORI · MILANO

Collation   18.3 × 12 cm: [1]⁸ 2–25⁸ 26¹⁰, 210 leaves, pp.[2], [I–VII], VIII, [IX], X–XIV, [XV–XVI], [1]–400, [2].

Contents   [1–2] blank, prp.[I–II] blank, [III] bastard title, [IV] blank, [V] title page, [VI] issue statement, printer's credit, [VII]–VIII contents, [IX–XIV] translator's note, [XV] author's note, [XVI] blank, [1]–398 text, 399–400 notes by English author, [1] printer's colophon, [2] blank.

RT   On verso *T.E. Lawrence – La Rivolta nel deserto.* On recto [in italics, according to chapter].

Plates   Six plates on coated paper following pp.48, 64, 160, 176, 288, 304.

Typography and paper $ 1 signed 3- Lawrence, 26, 26a- Lawrence.

Text   20 lines, 7.5 (8.1) × 9 cm.

Paper   White, wove, unwatermarked, all edges trimmed, sheets bulk 2.5 cm.

Binding   Blue cloth 183 d. Blue. On spine: [within gilt square, blue lettering] LA RIVOLTA | NEL DESERTO | under square, gilt] DI | T.E. | LAWRENCE | [gilt bar] Blue and white head and tail bands.

Published at   April 1937.

Copies   AC.

A127   T.E. LAWRENCE, Sabaku no Hanran, Kadogawa, 1966

First Japanese Edition

[Within double rule frame] Sabaku no Hanran | – – Arabia no Lawrensu Jiden – – | T.E. Lawrensu | Kashiwagura Toshizoo yaku | [pub. device] | Kadogawa Bunsho | 2364

Collation   15 × 10.5 cm: [1–22]⁸, 176 leaves, pp.[1–2], 3–346, [1–6].

Contents   Pp.[1] title page, [2] blank, 3–5 contents, [6] map, [7] half-title, [8] quote, 9–339 text, 340–345 translator's afterword, 346 brief biography of translator, [347] colophon, [1–5] pub. ads.

RT   On verso only, Sabaku no Hanran.

Plates   On coated paper frontis. before p.[1].

Text   20 lines, 5.5 (5.7) × 7.6 cm.

Paper   White, wove, unwatermarked, all edges trimmed, sheets bulk 1.3 cm.

Binding   Tan paper covers 73. p. OY. On front cover: [within pattern of floral cuts and double-rule] Kadogawa Bunsho | – – 2364 – – | Sabaku no Hanran | – – Arabia no Lawrensu Jiden – – | T.E. Lawrensu | Kashiwagura Toshizoo yaku | Kadogawa Shoten. On spine: [running down] Sabaku no Hanran | T.E. Lawrensu | Kashiwagura Toshizoo yaku | 2364. On back cover: [floral cut]. Brown silk place marker.

Published at   200 Yen.

Copies   AC.

A128   T.E. LAWRENCE, Săcelsanās Tuksnesī, Culbis, Riga 1935

First Lettish Edition

Pulkvedis Tomass E. Laurenss | Sacelsanās tuksnesī | *No anglu valodas tulkojis* | P. REINHOLDS | 1935 | [double rule] | *Izdevis A. Gulbis Rīgā*

Collation   18.7 × 11.5 cm: [1]–3⁸ 4⁴ 1–16⁸ 17⁴, 160 leaves, pp.[I–II], III–LIII, [1–3], 1–264.

Contents   Prp.[I] title page, [II] printer's credit, III–IV contents, V–LIII brief biography by P.R., pp.[1] blank, [2] half title, [3] blank, 1–264 text.

Plates   Eleven b/w plates printed on both sides, one before prp.I, others following pp.LII, 16, 48, 80, 128, 176, 208, 240, 256, 264.

Typography and paper $ 1,2 signed 2,2*.

Text 20 lines, 7.6 × 9 cm.

Paper White, wove, unwatermarked, all edges trimmed, sheets bulk 2 cm.

Binding Buff paper covers. On front cover: [photo of Lawrence] | [in white] Pulkvedis Tomasse E. Laurens | [in red] Sacelšanās tuksnesi. On back cover: [quotes from critics].

Notes Lettish translation of *Revolt in the Desert*.

Copies NYPL.

A129 T.E. LAWRENCE, Rebelión en el Desierto, Diana, 1952

First Mexican Edition

T.E. LAWRENCE | REBELIÓN | EN EL DESIERTO | Traducción directa del inglés por ELISABETH MULDER | EDICIÓN ILUSTRADA | EDITADO POR: | EDITORIAL DIANA, S.A. | TLACOQUEMECATL 73 MEXICO D.F.

Collation 18.6 × 14 cm: [1–13][^{16}, 208 leaves, pp.[1–4], [2], 5–32, [2], 33–48, [2], 49–80, [2], 81–96, [2], 97–128, [2], 129–144, [2], 145–176, [2], 177–192, [2], 193–224, [2], 225–256, [2], 257–288, [2], 289–320, [2], 321–336, [2], 337–368, [2], 369–382, [2], [4]; illustrations are printed on gatherings but not included in pagination.

Contents Pp.[1–2] blank, [3] bastard title, [4] blank, [5] photo of Kennington bust of Lawrence, [6] title page, [7] copyright, issue statements, [8] –377 text, [378] blank, [379] list of illustrations, [380] blank, [381] –382 contents, [1] colophon, [2] blank.

RT On verso REBELIÓN EN EL DESIERTO. On recto [according to chapter].

Text 20 lines, 7.3 (7.5) × 10.1 cm.

Paper White, wove, unwatermarked, all edges trimmed, sheets bulk 2.8 cm.

Binding Green cloth 141 s.G. On front cover: [in silver, within double wavy rule frame within fancy decorative corners] T.E. LAWRENCE | *REBELION EN* | *EL DESIERTO* | [cut] | EDITORIAL DIANA, S.A. | TLACOQUEMECATL, 73 | México, D.F. On spine: [double wavy rule] T.E. | LAWRENCE | [double wavy rule] | [double wavy rule] | REBELION | EN EL | DESIERTO |[double wavy rule]| [double wavy rule] | DIANA, S.A. | [double wavy rule]. End papers pale blue with publisher's device.

Published at June 1952.

Notes Reprinted August 1957, August 1962 and November 1963.

Copies Cal.

A130   T.E. LAWRENCE, Rebelión en el Desierto, Diana 1964

Second Mexican Edition

T.E. LAWRENCE | REBELIÓN | EN EL DESIERTO | 5a. EDICIÓN | EDICIÓN ILUSTRADA | EDITORIAL DIANA, S.A. | TLACOQUEMECATL 73 MEXICO, D.F.

Collation   13.9 × 19.4 cm: [1–13]^{16}, 208 leaves, pp.[1–4], [2], [5–7], 8–32, [2], 33–48, [2], 49–80, [2], 81–96, [2], 97–128, [2], 129–144, [2], 145–176, [2], 177–192, [2], 193–224, [2], 225–256, [2], 257–288, [2], 289–320, [2], 321–336, [2], 337–368, [2], 369–382, [4].

Contents   Pp.[1–2] blank, [3] bastard title, [4] blank, [5] title page, [6] translator's credit, issue statement, printer's credit, [7]–377 text, [378] blank, [379] list of illustrations, [380] blank, [381]–382 list of contents, [1] printer's statement, [2–4] blank.

RT   On verso REBELIÓN EN EL DESIERTO. On recto [according to chapter].

Text   20 lines, 7.3 (7.5) × 10 cm.

Paper   White, wove, unwatermarked,all edges trimmed, sheets bulk 3 cm.

Binding   Red paper covered boards 40 s. r Br. On spine: [in white running up] Rebelión en el Desierto | T.E. | Lawrence | [across at bottom] DIANA.

Published at   July 1964.

Notes   Variant binding: On front cover: [all in white] T.E. LAWRENCE | REBELION | EN EL DESIERTO. On spine: [all in white] T.E. | LAWRENCE | [running up] REBELION EN EL DESIERTO | [across] DIANA.

Copies   AC.

A131   T.E. LAWRENCE, Oprøret I Ørkenen, Gyldendal Norsk, 1939

First Norwegian Edition

T.E. LAWRENCE | OPRØRET I ØRKENEN | GYLDENDAL NORSK FORLAG | [rule] OSLO 1939

Collation   19.8 × 13.7 cm: [1]^8 2–12^8 13^6, 102 leaves, pp.[1–5], 6–204.

Contents   Pp.[1] bastard title, [2] blank, [3] title, [4] translator's, printer's credits, [5]–202 text, [203–204] blank.

RT   On verso: T.E. Lawrence. On recto: Oprøret i ørkenen.

Plates Eight b/w plates on coated paper, printed on both sides following pp.16, 32, 48, 64, 112, 128, 160, 176.

Typography and paper $ 1 signed 2.

Text 20 lines, 8.3 (8.7) × 10 cm.

Paper White, wove, unwatermarked, all edges trimmed, sheets bulk 2.8 cm.

Binding Patterned paper covered boards, brown leather spine and corners. On spine: [gilt] T.E. LAWRENCE | OPRØRET | I ØRKENEN. T.e. brown, red and green striped head and tail bands.

Copies Cal.

A132   T.E. LAWRENCE, Burźa nad Azja, Groszowa, 1928

First Polish Edition

[All in green] T.E. LAWRENCE | B. PULKOWNIK ARMJ | ANCIELSKI | BURZA NAD AZJA | (REWOLT [sic] IN THE DESERT) | ZAKOŃCZENIE | POWIEŚCI | « BUNT ARABOW » | [pub. device] | WARSZAWA | BIBLJOTEKA GROSZOWA | [rule]]

Collation 19 × 13 cm: π^2 [1] – 18^8 [19]^4, 148 leaves, pp.[1–4], [1]–295, [1].

Contents Prp.[1] bastard title, [2] blank, [3] title page, [4] pub. credit, pp.[1]–295 text, [1] illus.

Plates Eight b/w photos printed on one side only following pp.16, 32, 80, 96, 144, 160, 208, 224.

Typography and paper $ 1 signed Burza nad Azja 2.

Text 20 lines, 9 × 9 cm.

Paper White, wove, unwatermarked, untrimmed, sheets bulk 2 cm.

Binding Pictorial paper covers. On front cover: [next to circle frame within which is Kennington Cheshire portrait of Lawrence] T. LAWRENCE [stencil lettering] | [within double frame, drawing of riders on camels] | BURZA | NAD AZJA. On spine: [running up] T. LAWRENCE Burza nad Azja. On back cover: [pub. device].

Notes Companion volume with *Bunt Arabow* (A133), both volumes together comprise full text of *Revolt in the Desert*.

Copies Cal, H.

A133   T.E. LAWRENCE, Bunt Arabów, Groszowa, 1928

First Polish Edition (Vol. 2)

[All in blue] T.E. LAWRENCE | B. PUŁKOWNIK ARMJI ANGIELSHIEJ | BUNT ARABÓW | (REWOLT [sic] IN THE DESERT) | pub.device | WARSZAWA | BIBLJOTEKA GROSZOWA | [long rule]

Collation   19 × 13 cm: π^2 [1]^8 2–17^8, 138 leaves, pp.[1–4], 1–272.

Contents   Prp.[1] bastard title, [2] blank, [3] title page, [4] contents, pp.1–272 text.

Plates   Five b/w plates on coated paper following pp.32, 48, 96, 240, 256.

Typography and paper $ 1 signed Bunt Arabów 16.

Text   20 lines, 4.5 × 8.9 cm.

Paper   White, wove, unwatermarked, untrimmed, sheets bulk 1.7 cm.

Binding   White paper covers. On front cover: [green] T.E. LAWRENCE | [drawing of Arab on horse] | BVNT | ARA= | BÓW [next to photo of Kennington pastel of Lawrence in circle]. On spine: [running up] T.E. Lawrence: Bunt Arabów. On back: [pub. device].

Notes   Vol. 2 to accompany *Burźa nad Azja* (A132).

Copies   H.

A134   T.E. LAWRENCE, Revolta ïn Deşert, Fundaţia Pentru Literaturǎ şi Artǎ, 1934

First Romanian Edition •

COLONEL T.E. LAWRENCE | REVOLTA ÏN DEŞERT | Traducere din limba englezǎ de Mircea ELIADE | [star] | [pub. device] | BUCUREŞTI | FUNDAŢIA PENTRU LITERATURǍ ŞI ARTǍ „REGELE CAROL II" | 39, bulevardul lascar catarşi, 39 | 1934

Collation   18 × 13.5 cm: Vol. I, [1]–16^8, 128 leaves, pp.[1–5], 6–[250], [1–3]; Vol. II, [i]–12^8 13^{10}, 106 leaves, pp.[1–5], 6–210, [1–2].

Contents   Vol. I: pp.[1] bastard title, [2] issue, copyright statements, [3] title page, [4] blank, [5]–13 translator's preface, [14] blank, [15]–249 text, [250] blank, [1] contents, [2] colophon, [3–6] blank. Vol. II: pp. [1] bastard title, [2] issue and copyright statements, [3] title page, [4] blank, [5]–210 text, [1] contents, [2] colophon.

RT   On both recto and verso REVOLTA ÏN DEŞERT.

Typography and paper $ 2 signed 5,5*, 5/II,5.

Text   20 lines, 9 (9.4) × 10 cm.

Paper White, wove, unwatermarked, all edges trimmed, sheets bulk 3 cm.

Binding Pictorial paper covers. On front cover: [in white] BIBLIOTECA ENERGIA | COLONEL T.E. LAWRENCE | [in semi-circle, swash] Revolta în | deșert | [in white] FUNDAȚIA PENTRU LITERATURĂ ȘI ARTĂ „REGELE CAROL II". On spine: I [II] | [running up] REVOLTA ÎN DEȘERT | [across] I [II]. On back: [photos] | 2 Vol. Lei 60.

Published at Lei 60.

Copies H.

A135   T.E. LAWRENCE, Vosstanie v pustyne, Mospoligrafa, [1929?]

First Russian Edition

[On left of double title pages] T.E. LAURENCE | REVOLT IN THE | DESERT. [on right of double title pages] T. LOURENS | VOSSTANIE | V PUSTYNE | Sokrashchenyi perebod s angliiskovo | YA. CHERNYAKA | pod redaktsiei i s predsloviem | IRANDUSTA | 5- 10 Tns. | MOSKOVSKII RABOCHII | MOSKVA-LENINGRAD

Collation 19 × 13.5 cm: [1]–22^8, 23^2, 176 leaves, pp.[1–6], 7–354, [2].

Contents [1] pub. device, [2–3] title pages, [4] issue statement, pub. address, [5–6] contents, 7–[22] translator's preface, 23–354 text, [1] map, [2] pub. ads.

Typography and paper $ 1,2 signed 2,2*.

Text 20 lines, 9 × 10 cm.

Paper White wove, unwatermarked, all edges trimmed sheets bulk 1.2 cm.

Binding Only copy seen rebound.

Copies CPL.

A136   T.E. LAWRENCE, Rebelión en el Desierto, Juventud, 1940

First Spanish Edition

T.E. LAWRENCE | REBELIÓN | EN EL DESIERTO | TRADUCCION DIRECTA DEL INGLES | POR | ELISABETH MULDER | EDICIÓN ILUSTRADA | [pub. device] | EDITORIAL JUVENTUD, S.A. | Madrid – Barcelona – Buenos Aires

Collation 24.5 × 17 cm: [1]–20^8, 160 leaves, pp.[1–5], 6–319, [1].

Contents Pp.[1] bastard title, [2] blank, [3] title page, [4] copyright, issue statements, printer's credit, [5]–319 text, [1] blank.

RT On verso REBELIÓN EN EL DESIERTO. On recto [according to chapter].

Plates Twenty-nine plates on uncoated paper, printed on one side only, following pp.2, 8, 24, 32, 40, 48, 64, 80, 88, 96, 104, 112, 128, 144, 152, 160, 168, 176, 184, 192, 200, 208, 216, 224, 240, 256, 272, 296, 304.

Typography and paper $ 1 signed 1 2- REBELIÓN EN EL DESIERTO.

Text 20 lines, 8.3 (8.5) × 12.8 cm.

Paper White, wove, unwatermarked, all edges trimmed, sheets bulk 2 cm.

Binding Black cloth. On front cover: [gilt stamped John drawing of Lawrence]. On spine: REBELION | EN EL | DESIERTO | · | T·E· | LAWRENCE |[cut] | · | EDITORIAL | JUVENTUD. Decorated end papers in rose and blue. Blue and white head and tail bands.

Published at December 1940.

Copies AC.

A137 T.E. LAWRENCE, Rebelión en el Desierto, Juventud, 1957

Second Spanish Edition

T.E. LAWRENCE | REBELIÓN | EN EL DESIERTO | [pub. device] | EDITORIAL JUVENTUD, S.A. | Provenza, 101 – Barcelona

Collation 17.5 × 11.3 cm: [1]–22^8, 176 leaves, pp.[1–4], 5–347, [5].

Contents Pp.[1] bastard title, [2] series title, editor's note, [3] title page, [4] copyright, issue statements, printer's credit, 5–[347] text, [1] blank, [2–5] pub. ads.

Plates Four b/w plates on coated paper, printed on both sides, following pp.176.

Typography and paper $ 1 signed 2 REBELIÓN EN EL DESIERTO.

Text 20 lines, 6.9 × 9 cm.

Paper White, wove, unwatermarked, all edges trimmed, sheets bulk 1.8 cm.

Binding Pictorial paper covers. On front cover: [all in white] T.E. LAWRENCE | [series device in green and white] | el desierto | la | incredíble | historia | de | LAWRENCE | DE ARABIA | Narrada | por | él | mismo | [running up on left side] rebelión en. On spine: 24 | [running up] REBELION EN EL DESIERTO T.E. Lawrence | [long rule] | [at foot, design in green and black] | Z. On back cover: [blurb] | [series device] | Colección de bolsillo | Editorial Juventud.

Published at Ptas 55, February 1957.

Notes List of impressions:
2nd, March 1962.
3rd, July 1965, as above.

Copies AC, Cal.

A138 T.E. LAWRENCE, Uppror i Öknen, Bonniers, 1927

First Swedish Edition

UPPROR I ÖKNEN | AV | T.E. LAWRENCE | ÖVERSATT OCH FÖRSEDD MED EN INLEDNING AV | STEN SELANDER | [pub. device] | STOCKHOLM | ALBERT BONNIERS FÖRLAG

Collation 23.8 × 15.7 cm: [1]–28⁸, 224 leaves, pp.[1–5], 6–445, [446–448].

Contents Pp.[1] bastard title, [2] blank, [3] title page, [4] printer's credit, 5–10 translator's note, 11–445 text, [446] blank, [447–448] contents.

Typography and paper $ 1 signed 2- Lawrence, Uppror i öknen.

Text 20 lines, 8.7 × 10 cm.

Paper White, wove, unwatermarked,coated, all edges trimmed, sheets bulk 2.3 cm.

Binding Pictorial paper covers. On front cover: *T.E. Lawrence* | Uppror | i öknen | STOCKHOLM · ALBERT BONNIERS FORLAG.

Copies H, Cal.

1928

The Imperial Camel Corps With Colonel Lawrence

In the first decade following the War, D.G. Pearman, Lowell Thomas, Laurence Gotch and perhaps others, gave lantern-slide presentations on the Arab campaign. Pearman also marketed his glass slides through Newton & Co. Few sets are to be found today. There is a set in a private California collection and another is reported to be in the Imperial War Museum. The warehouse in which Newton's stock was stored was bombed during the Second World War and most sets destroyed. Though not common, the booklet itemising the slides seems to exist in larger numbers.

Perhaps it was used more in the nature of a sales catalogue/prospectus than as a user's guide. On pages 3–4 there appears a printed letter from Lawrence to Pearman. On the strength of that letter it is included in the canon.

A139   D.G. PEARMAN, The Imperial Camel Corps With Colonel Lawrence, Newton, 1928

First English Edition

THE IMPERIAL CAMEL CORPS | WITH COLONEL LAWRENCE | Illustrated by a series of 89 lantern slides; | AND | LAWRENCE AND THE ARAB REVOLT | Illustrated by a series of 70 lantern slides.| Lecture Notes by Captain D.G. Pearman. | Price 2s. 6d. | [rule] | *STRICTLY COPYRIGHT.* | [rule] | Messrs. Newton have much pleasure publishing these | new and exclusive lecture sets which are of exceptional | interest dealing with Colonel Lawrence and his work among | the Arabs during the Great War, and with the Imperial Camel | Corps which assisted the Arabs in their revolt against the | Turks. | The photographs and notes have been provided by Capt. | D.G. Pearman, a member of the Expedition, and the sets | are published by arrangement with him and with the kind | permission of Colonel Lawrence and his Trustees.

Collation   21.8 × 14.2 cm: [1]^{22}, 22 leaves, pp.[1], 2–44.

Contents   Pp.[1] title page, 2 author's note, 3–4 copy of letter from Lawrence to Pearman, 5–42 text, 43–44 list of slides.

Text   20 lines, 7.3 × 10.3 cm.

Paper   White, wove, unwatermarked, all edges trimmed, sheets bulk 2 mm.

Binding   Grey paper wrappers 22 r. Gray. On front cover: [within frame of decorative cuts] THE IMPERIAL CAMEL CORPS | WITH COLONEL LAWRENCE | Illustrated by a series of 89 lantern slides; | AND | LAWRENCE AND THE ARAB | REVOLT Illustrated by a series of 70 lantern slides | Lecture Notes by Captain D.G.Pearman. | Price 2s. 6d. | [rule] | *STRICTLY COPYRIGHT.* | [pub. device] | *Published only by:-* | Messrs. NEWTON & CO., LTD., | 43 Museum Street, | London, W.C. 1.

Published at   2s. 6d.

Notes   Prefatory letter from Lawrence dated 16-2-28, no. 342, pp.3–4, in Garnett, *The Letters.*

Copies   AC, Cal, H, UT.

1930

Prospectus for 'Her Privates We'

Frederick Manning's book, *Her Privates We,* was issued anonymously in 1930. Lawrence guessed the identity of the author and both telephoned and wrote to the publisher praising the book. The gist of the telephone call and of the letter's contents was incorporated into this advertising leaflet.

A140   FREDERICK MANNING, Her Privates We, Peter Davies, 1930

Publisher's Advertising Pamphlet

[Within Oxford rule frame] COLONEL | LAWRENCE | *and others* | *on* | "HER PRIVATES WE" | by | Private 19022 | *This pamphlet is free of charge*

Collation   16.5 × 10.1 cm: [1]⁸, 8 leaves, unpaged.

Contents   Pp.[1] title page, [2] contents, [3–6] publisher's note, including conversation and letter from T.E. Lawrence, [7–14] extracts from reviews, [15] order form, [16] blank.

RT   On both verso and recto [according to contents of page].

Text   20 lines, 7 (7.4) × 6.8 cm.

Paper   Bright yellow, wove, unwatermarked, all edges trimmed, sheets bulk 1 mm.

Published at   Free advertising flyer.

Copies   AC, Cal, UT.

1932

The Odyssey

Inspired by reading *Seven Pillars of Wisdom,* Bruce Rogers persuaded Lawrence to undertake a new translation of *The Odyssey.* Begun in 1928 and published in 1932, the translation was undertaken during Lawrence's free time while he was serving in the ranks. It was published in a beautiful edition of 530 copies by Emery Walker, Wilfred Merton and Bruce Rogers.

After this edition no other English editions were published until 1935. An American edition was published in 1932 by the Oxford University Press. Issued in both limited and trade issues, the American edition badly hurt sales of the English 1932 edition. Copies of the latter were still available even after Lawrence's death in 1935. When a trade edition appeared in England in 1935 it was initially the American sheets with an English title page. Oxford also acquired the remaining stock of the 1932 limited edition which they advertised for sale as well. The many variant states of this 1935 English edition are difficult to unravel.

A141   HOMER, The Odyssey, privately printed, 1932

First English Edition

THE ODYSSEY OF | HOMER | [gold roundel] | PRINTED IN ENGLAND | 1932

Collation   29.3 × 20.2 cm: 1⁶ 2–23⁸, 182 leaves, unpaged.

Contents   Leaves [1] blank, [2] title page, [3] invocation of Muse, [4–180] text, [181–182] translator's note, colophon on verso of [182] *'Printed and published by* | *Sir Emery Walker, Wilfred Merton and Bruce Rogers* | *16 Clifford's Inn, London* | *530 copies'*.

RT   On verso ODYSSEY. On recto [according to book] BOOK III.

Text   20 lines, 12.5 (12.7) × 12.3 cm. Set in 16 pt. Monotype Centaur.

Paper   Grey handmade paper by J.B. Green, watermarked, top edge trimmed, sheets bulk 2.5 cm.

Binding   Full black Niger morocco. On spine: [gilt] THE | ODYSSEY | OF | HOMER | 1932. T.e. gilt. In slip case as issued.

Published at   £12.12s, Autumn 1932.

Notes   Limited to 530 copies, 500 for sale by subscription. Contains 26 roundels printed in black on gold leaf at the head of each book and title page, tissue guards before each roundel. Commissioned and designed by Bruce Rogers.

Copies   AC, Cal, UT, H.

A142   HOMER, The Odyssey, 1932

Publisher's Prospectus

The Odyssey | A NEW TRANSLATION

Collation   29.5 × 20.5 cm: single fold, pp.[1–4].

Contents   Pp.[1–2] text of prospectus and title, [3] specimen page from book, [4] blank.

Paper Mould-made, watermarked, same paper as in final published volume.

Copies AC, Cal.

A143   HOMER, The Odyssey, Oxford University Press, 1932

Publisher's Prospectus

This Advertisement appeared in Publishers Weekly of October 29th, 1932 | T.E. SHAW | *As "Lawrence of Arabia"*| *he gave us* | [etc.]

Collation   25.5 × 17.8 cm: single leaf printed on one side only.

Paper   White, wove, unwatermarked, all edges trimmed.

Copies   AC, Cal.

A144   HOMER, The Odyssey, Oxford University Press, 1935

Second English Edition (First Trade Edition)

THE ODYSSEY OF | HOMER | TRANSLATED BY T.E. SHAW | (COLONEL T.E. LAWRENCE) | [85 d. Y roundel positioned 1 cm from line of type above it] | OXFORD UNIVERSITY PRESS | LONDON: HUMPHREY MILFORD

Collation   23.1 × 16 cm: [1]^{10} [2–21]^8, 170 leaves, pp.[1–12], [1]–327, [1].

Contents   Prp.[1–2] blank, [3] bastard title, [4] blank, [5] title page, [6] issue statement, printer's credit, [7]–9 translator's note, [10] blank, [11] invocation of the Muse, [12] blank, [1]–327 text, [1] blank.

RT   On verso ODYSSEY. On recto [according to book].

Text   20 lines, 10 (10) × 10.5 cm.

Paper   White, wove, unwatermarked, top edge trimmed, sheets bulk 2 cm.

Binding   Blue buckram, 173 m. g B. On front cover: [gold roundel]. On spine: [gilt] THE | ODYSSEY | OF HOMER | [star] | T.E. SHAW | (T.E. LAWRENCE) | OXFORD. T.e. gilt. Blue and white head and tail bands. White end papers.

Published at   10s 6d, August 1935.

Notes   Another state, as above, with following differences: roundel on title page is 2.7 cm below line of type above it. Shorter format 23 × 15.5 cm, for sheets. Colour of roundel is 72 d. OY. [Typography]: top and bottom edges trimmed.
   Another state, same as that immediately above, with the following

differences: [Collation]: 22.3 × 14.5 cm. Cancelled t.p, intro by Finley, map end papers.

Another issue: same as two listed immediately above, with following differences: [Collation]: 21.9 × 14 cm: 1–19⁸ 20⁴ 21–22⁸, 172 leaves, pp.[1–12], 1–327, [3], [Contents]: prp.[1] bastard title, [2] blank, [3] title page, [4] issue statement, Printed in U.S.A., [5]–6 introduction, [7–9] translator's note, [10] blank, [11] invocation of Muse, [12] blank, pp.[1]–327 text, [1–3] blank; [Typography and paper]: sheets bulk 2.5 cm; [Binding]: Brown buckram 55 s. Or. On spine: [gilt] HOMER'S | ODYSSEY | T.E. SHAW | OXFORD. Map end papers.

Another state, as 2nd variant issue above, with following diferences: [Collation]: 1–20⁸ 21⁴ 22⁸, 172 leaves. Map end papers are present but tipped in before and after free end papers. Trial binding?

Another state, published in full blue or brown morocco.

Copies   AC, Cal, UT, Ho.

A145   HOMER, The Odyssey, Oxford University Press, 1935

Publisher's Prospectus for Second English Edition

Mr. Humphrey Milford | ANNOUNCES THE PUBLICATION | EARLY IN AUGUST | OF THE FIRST UNLIMITED | ENGLISH EDITION OF | [in blue] T.E. LAWRENCE'S | [in blue] TRANSLATION OF | [in blue] THE ODYSSEY | AT | [in blue] 10s 6D NET | NOTE.– A few copies of the first English edition | printed by Emery Walker on hand-made paper, | bound in black Niger, and limited to 500 copies | are still available at £10 16s net. | *BOTH EDITIONS ARE DESIGNED BY | MR.BRUCE ROGERS.* | [in blue] OXFORD UNIVERSITY PRESS | LONDON: HUMPHREY MILFORD | 1935

Collation   22 × 14 cm: single fold leaflet, pp.[1–4].

Contents   Pp.[1] title page, [2–3] text, [4] order form.

Paper   White, wove, unwatermarked, all edges trimmed.

Copies   H.

A146   HOMER, The Odyssey, Oxford University Press, 1955

Third English Edition, World's Classics

THE ODYSSEY OF | HOMER | *Translated from the Greek* | by | T.E. SHAW | (LAWRENCE OF ARABIA) | *With an Introduction by* | SIR MAURICE BOWRA | [series device] | *Geoffrey Cumberlege* | OXFORD UNIVERSITY PRESS | *London Toronto*

Collation   14.9 × 9.3 cm: [A]¹⁰ B–O¹⁶ P['14], 232 leaves, pp.[2], [i–v], vi–xviii, 1–442, [1–2].

Contents Prp.[1–2] blank, *series, bastard title,* [ii] printer's credit, [iii] title page, [iv] biographical note on T.E. Lawrence, [v]–vi contents, [vii]–xvi introduction, xvii extracts from T.E. Lawrence letters, [xviii] blank, pp.[1] invocation of Muse, [2] blank, [3]–437 text, [438] blank, [439]–442 translator's note, [1–2] blank.

RT On verso THE ODYSSEY. On recto [according to number of book].

Typography and paper $ 1 signed 550 E.

Text 20 lines, 7.8 (7.9) × 7.7 cm.

Paper Thin white, wove, unwatermarked, all edges trimmed, sheets bulk 1.5 cm.

Binding Blue linen 183 d. Blue. On front cover: [pub. device, blind stamped]. On spine: [gilt] THE | ODYSSEY | OF | HOMER | [star] | *Translated by* | T.E. SHAW | OXFORD.

Published at 6s.

Notes No. 550 of The World's Classics series (reprint of Hesperides series, A151).

Copies AC, Cal.

A147 HOMER, The Odyssey, Oxford University Press, 1932

Uncorrected Proof of First American Edition

THE ODYSSEY OF | HOMER | NEWLY TRANSLATED INTO ENGLISH PROSE | NEW YORK | OXFORD UNIVERSITY PRESS | 1932

Collation 24.7 × 16.5 cm: π^2 π^2 [1–19]^8 20^3, pp.[1–4], [329]–[332], [1]–[328].

Contents Prp.[1] title page, [2] blank, [3] invocation of the Muse, [4] blank, [329]–331 translator's note, pp.[332] blank, pp.[1]–327 text, [328] blank.

RT On verso ODYSSEY. On recto [according to number of book].

Text 9.8 (10) × 10.5 cm.

Paper White, laid, watermarked, all edges trimmed, sheets bulk 1.9 cm.

Binding Blue paper covers 182 m. Blue. On front cover: [in only copy seen it appears that a paper label had once been glued to front cover].

Copies H.

A148   HOMER, The Odyssey, Oxford University Press, 1932

First American Edition (Limited)

THE ODYSSEY OF | HOMER | NEWLY TRANSLATED INTO ENGLISH
PROSE | [gilt roundel] | NEW YORK | OXFORD UNIVERSITY PRESS |
1932

Collation   25.3 × 16.5 cm: [1–22]^8 [22]^4, 172 leaves, pp.[1–12], 1–327,
[1–6].

Contents   Prp.[1–2] blank, [3] bastard title, [4] blank, [5] title page, [6]
copyright statement, [7–9] translator's note, [10] blank, [11] invocation of
the Muse, [12] blank, pp.[1]–327 text, [1] blank, [2] 'THIS EDITION | IS
LIMITED TO THIRTY-FOUR COPIES | OF WHICH TWENTY-FIVE ARE
FOR SALE | THIS COPY NO.   , [3–6] blank.

RT   On verso THE ODYSSEY. On recto [according to number of book]
BOOK IV.

Text   20 lines, 10 (10.2) × 10.5 cm.

Paper   White, laid, watermarked, top edge trimmed, sheets bulk 2 cm.

Binding   Brown 43 m. r Br full crushed Morocco. On spine: THE |
ODYSSEY | OF | HOMER | OXFORD. T.e. gilt. Gold and red head and tail
bands.

Notes   Limited to 34 copies of which 25 are for sale, this copy no. 8. One of
11 in full morocco.
   Another copy, no. 1, [Binding]: full blue crushed morocco 187 d. gy. Blue.
Blue and white head and tail bands.

Copies   Cal, H, Ca, UT.

A149   HOMER, The Odyssey, Oxford University Press, 1932

First American Edition (Trade)

THE ODYSSEY OF | HOMER | NEWLY TRANSLATED INTO ENGLISH
PROSE | [blue roundel] | NEW YORK | OXFORD UNIVERSITY PRESS |
1932 [roundel is 1.3 cm from line above]

Collation   23.1 × 15.2 cm: [1–19]^8 [20]^{10} [21]^8, 170 leaves, pp.[1–12], 1–327,
[1].

Contents   Prp.[1–2] blank, [3] bastard title, [4] blank, [5] title page, [6]
copyright statement, [7–9] translator's note, [10] blank, [11] invocation of
the Muse, [12] blank, pp.[1]–327 text, [1] blank.

RT   On verso ODYSSEY. On recto BOOK [IV].

Text   20 lines, 10 (10) × 10.5 cm. Set in Janson.

Paper White, wove, unwatermarked, top edges trimmed, sheets bulk 2.2 cm.

Binding Blue buckram 187 d. gy B. On front cover: [gilt roundel, ship and ocean gilt, background blue]. On spine: [gilt] [Oxford rule] | THE | ODYSSEY | OF | HOMER | OXFORD. T.e. light yellow. Yellow and blue head and tail bands.

Published at $3.50, 25 November 1932.

Notes Another issue, 25 review copies. Same as above with following differences: [Collation]: 24.2 × 15.8 cm: [1]⁶ [2–20]⁸ [21]⁴ [22]⁸, 170 leaves, pp.[1–12], 1–327, [1]; [Paper]: all edges trimmed, sheets bulk 2cm [Binding]: [no roundel on front cover]. On spine: [on white paper label] [decorative line] | THE | ODYSSEY | OF | HOMER | [decorative rule].
   List of impressions:
   2nd, November 1932, same as above, with following differences: [roundel on title page is 1.5 cm. from line above]. [Contents]: verso of title page designer's credit, issue statement, printer's credit. [Binding]: [no Oxford rule at top of spine]. Roundel 1.5 cm. from line of type above it.
   3rd, December 1932, as above, with following differences. Roundel on front cover has blue ship and sea, background is gold. Sheets bulk 2 cm. All impressions through the 3rd contain the points listed below: p.31, 3rd line from bottom, read 'not' for 'lost'; p.72, 4th line from top, read 'of' for 'for'; p.73, 4th line from top, read 'from' for 'for'.
   4th, December 1932, as above, with following differences: roundel on title page is yellow d. OY and black; [Collation]: [1]¹⁰ [2–21]⁸; [Binding]; blue buckram 108 gy. Blue smooth cloth.
   5th, January 1933, as fourth impression above.

Copies AC, Cal, UT, LC.

A150 HOMER, The Odyssey, Oxford University Press, 1934

First American Edition (Popular Edition)

THE ODYSSEY OF | HOMER | NEWLY TRANSLATED INTO ENGLISH PROSE | [roundel in black] | NEW YORK | OXFORD UNIVERSITY PRESS

Collation 22.2 × 14.2 cm: [1–21]⁸ [22]⁴, 172 leaves, pp.[1–12], [1]–327, [5].

Contents Prp.[1] bastard title, [2] blank, [3] title page, [4] copyright, issue statements, printer's credit, [5–6] introduction, [7–9] translator's note, [10] blank, [11] invocation of the Muse, [12] blank, pp.[1]–327 text, [1–5] blank.

RT On verso ODYSSEY. On recto [according to book] BOOK [IV].

Text 20 lines, 9.9 (10) × 10.5 cm.

Paper   White, wove, unwatermarked, all edges trimmed, sheets bulk 2.3 cm.

Binding   Brown cloth 55 s. Br. On front cover: [black roundel]. On spine: THE | ODYSSEY | OF | HOMER | OXFORD. T.e. brown. End papers: maps in brown.

Notes   List of impressions:
   2nd, (7th impression), 1937, same as above except, t.e. is unstained.
   3rd, (8th impression), 1937, same as above, with following differences: [Collation]: [1–20]⁸ [21]⁴ [22]⁸; T.e. orange.

   4th, (9th impression), 1939.
   5th, (10th impression), 1940, same as above, with following differences: THE ODYSSEY OF | HOMER | NEWLY TRANSLATED INTO ENGLISH PROSE | BY T.E. SHAW | LAWRENCE OF ARABIA | [black roundel] | NEW YORK | OXFORD UNIVERSITY PRESS; [Binding]: T.e. unstained.
   6th, (11th impression), 1944, same as above, with following differences: [Paper]: sheets bulk 2 cm.
   7th, (12th), as above.
   8th, (13th), as above.
   9th, (14th), 1947, as above, with following differences, [Binding]: brown cloth 38 d.r O.

Copies   AC, Cal.

A151   HOMER, The Odyssey, Oxford University Press, 1940

Second American Edition (Hesperides Edition)

THE ODYSSEY OF HOMER | TRANSLATED FROM THE | GREEK BY T.E. SHAW | [in red, within brackets] [LAWRENCE OF ARABIA] | NEW YORK | OXFORD UNIVERSITY PRESS | 1940

Collation   18.4 × 12.3 cm: [1]⁴ [2–29]⁸, 228 leaves, pp.[8], [1–3], 4–442, [6].

Contents   Prp.[1] series title, [2] list of titles in series, *2500 COPIES OF THIS VOLUME PRINTED AT* | THE WALPOLE PRINTING OFFICE | MOUNT VERNON, N.Y', [3] bastard title, [4] blank, [5] title page, [6] copyright statement, [7] extracts from T.E. Shaw letters, [8] blank, pp.[1] invocation of Muse, [2] blank, [3]–437 text, [438] blank, [439]–442 translator's note, [1–6] blank.

RT   On verso THE ODYSSEY. On recto BOOK [THREE].

Text   20 lines, 7.8 (8) × 7.6 cm.

Paper   White, laid, unwatermarked, top edges trimmed, sheets bulk 2.8 cm.

Binding   Brown cloth 55 dull s. Br. On spine: [gilt] HOMER'S | ODYSSEY | T.E. SHAW |[pattern of spaced cuts] | [gilt rule at top and bottom running around both covers and spine]. T.e. gilt.

Published at $3.00.

Notes Limited to 2500 copies, designed by Bruce Rogers. Hesperides Series – only title printed. Reprinted in England in World's Classics.

Copies AC, Cal, UT.

A152 HOMER, The Odyssey, Editions for the Armed Services, Inc., 1945?

Third American Edition (Armed Services Edition)

[Within double rule frame divided into two panels by vertical rule] [in left panel] PUBLISHED BY ARRANGEMENT WITH | OXFORD UNIVERSITY PRESS | NEW YORK | [pub. device] *All rights reserved* | COPYRIGHT, 1932, BY BRUCE ROGERS | [in right panel] THE ODYSSEY OF | HOMER | *Newly Translated into English Prose* | By T.E. SHAW | LAWRENCE OF ARABIA | *Editions for the Armed Services, Inc.* | A NON-PROFIT ORGANIZATION ESTABLISHED BY | THE COUNCIL ON BOOKS IN WARTIME, NEW YORK | [below frame, lower left] 925

Collation 11.2 × 16.3 cm: [1–12]^{16}, 192 leaves, pp.[1–2], 3–384.

Contents Pp.[1] title page, copyright statement, [2] *Manufactured in the United States of America*, 3–4 introduction, 5–8 translator's note, 9 invocation of the Muse, 10 map, 11–384 text.

Text 20 lines, 7.7 × 6.3 cm double column format, both columns 13.1 cm.

Paper White, wove, newsprint, unwatermarked, all edges trimmed, sheets bulk 1 cm.

Binding Pictorial paper covers: [on left half] 925 | [picture of book with black cover tilted to left on its cover in white] THE | ODYSSEY | OF | HOMER | TRANSLATED BY | T.E. SHAW | (LAWRENCE OF ARABIA) | [in blue circle near lower left corner of drawing in white] ARMED | SERVICES | EDITION | [on right half, in white] THE | ODYSSEY | OF | HOMER | TRANSLATED BY | T.E. SHAW | (LAWRENCE OF ARABIA) | [seven lines, in yellow, detailing overseas Armed Services editions] | [across in yellow at bottom] THIS IS THE COMPLETE BOOK – NOT A DIGEST. On spine: [running down] SHAW – THE ODYSSEY OF HOMER | [across at bottom in yellow] 925. On back cover: [within frame of red lines with white stars, lengthy blurb]. Inside front cover: [official statement]. Inside rear cover: [list of titles in series].

Published at Donated to armed services during Second World War.

Copies AC, Cal.

A153 HOMER, The Odyssey, Oxford University Press, 1956

Fourth American Edition (Paperback Edition)

THE ODYSSEY OF | HOMER | TRANSLATED INTO ENGLISH PROSE | BY | T.E. SHAW | (Colonel T.E. Lawrence) | [pub. device] | A GALAXY BOOK | NEW YORK · OXFORD UNIVERSITY PRESS | 1956

Collation 20.5 × 13.5 cm: [1–22]⁸, 164 leaves, pp.[1–8], [1], 2–327, [1].

Contents Prp.[1] bastard title, [2] blank, [3] title page, [4] design credit, copyright, issue statements, [5–7] translator's note, [8] invocation of the Muse, pp.[1]–327 text, [1] blank.

RT On verso ODYSSEY. On recto [according to number of book] [BOOK IV].

Text 20 lines, 9.6 (9.7) × 10.2 cm.

Paper White, wove, unwatermarked, all edges trimmed, sheets bulk 1.6 cm.

Binding Brown paper covers 43 m. r Br. On front cover: THE ODYSSEY | OF | HOMER | [first five words in white] Translated into English prose by T.E. SHAW | [in white] (Colonel T.E. Lawrence) | GB2 $1.50. On spine: [running down] THE ODYSSEY OF HOMER T.E. SHAW | [across in white, series device] | GB2. On back cover: [blurb].

Published at $1.50.

Copies AC, Cal.

A154 HOMER, The Odyssey, Limited Editions Club, 1981

Fifth American Edition

[In red] THE ODYSSEY | [in red] OF HOMER | [rule] | TRANSLATED BY | T.E. SHAW | *Lawrence of Arabia* | WOOD ENGRAVINGS BY | *Barry Moser* | PREFACE BY | *Jeremy M. Wilson* | THE LIMITED EDITIONS CLUB

Collation 27.5 × 17.3 cm: [1–23]⁸ [24]⁴, 188 leaves, pp.[i–x], xi–xxi, [xxii–xxiv], 1–301, [5], plates included in gatherings.

Contents Prp.[i–ii] blank, [iii] bastard title, [iv] frontispiece, [v] title page, [vi] copyright statement, [vii] contents, [viii] blank, [ix] list of illustrations, [x] blank, xi–xviii preface by J.M. Wilson, xix–xxi translator's note by T.E. Lawrence, [xxii] blank, [xxiii] invocation of the Muse, in red, [xxiv] illustrations, pp.1–300 text, [301] 'Two thousand copies of this edition of | THE ODYSSEY OF HOMER | in the translation by Lawrence of Arabia have been printed for | the members of The Limited Editions Club by the Hampshire | Typothetae in West Hatfield, Massachusetts, the type having | been composed in San Francisco by Mackenzie-Harris and cast | in metal by Michael & Winifred Bixler, in Boston. Barry Moser, | who planned the typographic format and executed the wood | engravings, and Jeremy M. Wilson, who wrote the preface, | here sign | [signatures] this copy, which is number [mss. number].'

Plates Of the 25 plates, 23 are included in the gatherings but not counted in pagination. Frontis. and first plate are included in pagination. Woodcuts follow pp.14, 26, 50, 64, 80, 90, 106, 120, 126, 138, 158, 166, 186, 190, 204, 218, 242, 252, 262, 268, 282, 290, 297.

Text 20 lines, 10.2 × 10.6 cm. Set in 13pt Van Dijck, headings Albertus.

Paper Soft-white, wove, unwatermarked, all edges trimmed, sheets bulk 3.3 cm.

Binding 77 m. y Br cloth. On front cover: [red rectangle 19.2 × 10.8 cm]. On spine: [in red, running down] THE ODYSSEY OF HOMER. On back cover: [red rectangle]. End papers buff, red head and tail bands. Boxed as issued.

Notes Limited to 2000 copies. Illustrations by Barry Moser. Signed by Moser and Wilson.

Copies AC, Cal, UT.

Arabia Felix

Lawrence's third and last introductory essay is a foreword to Bertram Thomas's book of the first crossing by a European of the Empty Quarter of Arabia Felix only a few months before a similar crossing by H.St John Philby. Lawrence admired the feat (*The Letters*, no. 435). The foreword was written with the aid of G.B. Shaw (Howard, *Jonathan Cape, Publisher*, p.150).

A155   BERTRAM THOMAS, Arabia Felix, Cape, 1932

First English Edition

ARABIA FELIX: | ACROSS THE EMPTY QUARTER OF ARABIA | *by* BERTRAM THOMAS | O.B.E. [Mil.]; formerly Wazir to H.H. the Sultan of Muscat | and Oman, sometime Political Officer in Iraq, and Assistant | British Representative in Trans-Jordan. Founder's Medallist | of the Royal Geographical Society; Burton Memorial Medallist | of the Royal Asiatic Society; Gold Medallist of the Royal | Geographical Society of Antwerp; and Cullum Gold Medal of | the American Geographical Society | WITH A FOREWORD BY | T.E. LAWRENCE (T.E.S.) | AND APPENDIX BY | Sir ARTHUR KEITH, F.R.S., M.D., Etc. | CONTAINING ALSO | MAPS, CHARTS, DIAGRAMS | AND ILLUSTRATIONS COMPLEMENTARY | TO THE TEXT | [pub. device] | LONDON: | JONATHAN CAPE, THIRTY

BEDFORD SQUARE | & AT 91 WELLINGTON STREET W. TORONTO |
1932

Collation   23.5 × 16 cm: [a] –b⁸ A –U⁸ X –2B⁸, 216 leaves, pp.[i–iv], v–xxix,
[xxx–xxxii], 1–397, [3].

Contents   Prp.[i] bastard title, [ii] list of author's works, [iii] title page, [iv]
issue statement, printer's, papermaker's, binder's credits, v–x contents,
xi–xiii illustrations, [xiv] blank, xv–xviii foreword, [xix] dedication, [xx]
blank, xxi–xxii preface, xxiii–xxvii introduction, [xxviii] blank, xxix poem,
[xxx] blank, xxxi half-title, [xxxii] blank, pp.1–299 text, [300] blank, 301–
383 appendixes, [384] blank, 385–397 index, [1–3] blank.

RT   On both verso and recto [according to subject of page].

Plates   Forty-eight b/w photos, coated on one side and printed on one side,
following pp.ii, 2, 10, 24 double, 34, 38, 42, 48, 50, 54, 62, 70, 74, 80, 82, 98,
104, 108, 122, 128, 136, 138, 140, 142, 150, 156, 170, 174, 178, 192, 194, 216, 222,
224, 226, 236, 238, 244, 294, 296, 298, 310, 326 double, 330, 332 double, fold
map inside rear cover.

Typography and paper $ 1 signed B.

Text   20 lines, 9.9 (10) × 11.2 cm.

Paper   White, wove, unwatermarked, top edge trimmed, sheets bulk 3.5
cm.

Binding   Brown buckram 54 br. O. On spine: [gilt] ARABIA | FELIX |
[cut] | BERTRAM | THOMAS | JONATHAN CAPE. On back cover: [blind
stamped pub. device]. Fold. map inside rear cover. T.e. tan. Following p.378
of smaller size than sheets, ad for *Arabia Deserta*.

Published at   25s, February 1932.

Notes   List of impressions:
2nd, February 1932, as above, with following differences: [Binding]:
gold-brown cloth 35 s. r. O. On spine: [gilt] ARABIA | FELIX | [cut] |
BERTRAM | THOMAS | [pub. device]. T.e. brown.
3rd, 1936, new and cheaper edition, same as above with following
differences: [Collation]: first and last sheets paste down end papers;
[Binding]: Linen 30 gy r O. On spine: [at foot, only pub. device]. Back
cover: [blind stamped pub. device]. Fold-out map between pp.384–385.
   Lawrence's preface reprinted in *Now and Then*, Spring 1932, and in *Then
and Now*, 1935, pp.93–96.

Copies   AC, Cal, H, UT.

A156   BERTRAM THOMAS, Arabia Felix, Readers' Union, 1938

Second English Edition

ARABIA FELIX: | ACROSS THE EMPTY QUARTER OF ARABIA | by BERTRAM THOMAS | O.B.E. [Mil.]; formerly Wazir to H.H. the Sultan of Muscat | and Oman sometime Political Officer in Iraq, and the Assistant | British Representative in Trans-Jordan. Founder's Medallist | of the Royal Geographical Society; Burton Memorial Medallist | of the Royal Asiatic Society; Gold Medallist of the Royal | Geographical Society of Antwerp; and Cullum Gold Medal of | the American Geographical Society | WITH A FOREWORD BY | T.E. LAWRENCE (T.E.S.) | [pub. device] | READERS' UNION LTD. | BY ARRANGEMENT WITH | JONATHAN CAPE

Collation   21.7 × 14.5 cm: A–K^{16}, 160 leaves, pp.[i–iv], v–xvi, 1–304.

Contents   Prp.[i] bastard title, [ii] list of works by author, [iii] title page, [iv] note on Readers' Union edition, printer's credit, v contents, vi illustrations, vii–ix foreword by T.E. Lawrence, x dedication, xi preface, xii–xv introduction, xvi poem by Walter de la Mare, pp.1–299 text, [300] topographical terms, 301–304 index.

RT   On both recto and verso [according to subject of page].

Plates   9 photographs, on coated paper printed on one side only, following pp.ii, 14, 81, 112, 127, 145, 176, 241, 272; fold map following p.296.

Typography and paper $ 1 signed 1,5 B,B*.

Text   20 lines, 9.8 (9.9) × 11 cm.

Paper   White, wove, unwatermarked, all edges trimmed, sheets bulk 2.5 cm.

Binding   Yellow brown 76 l. y Br. cloth. On front cover: [all in red] ARABIA | FELIX | [red cuts along left side]. On spine: [all in red] ARABIA | FELIX | BERTRAM | THOMAS | READERS' | UNION. T.e. red brown.

Notes   Abridged, lacks appendixes (pp.301–383 of original edition).

Copies   AC, Cal.

A157   BERTRAM THOMAS, Arabia Felix, Scribner's, 1932

First American Edition

ARABIA FELIX | ACROSS THE "EMPTY QUARTER"| OF ARABIA | by | BERTRAM THOMAS | *O.B.E. [Mil.]; formerly Wazir to H.H. the Sultan of Muscat and Oman, sometime | Political Officer in Iraq, and Assistant British*

Representative in Trans-Jordan. | *Founder's Medallist of the Royal Geographical Society; Burton Memorial Medallist* | *of the Royal Asiatic Society; Gold Medallist of the Royal Geographical Society of* | *Antwerp; and Cullum Medallist of the American Geographical Society, New York* | WITH A FOREWORD BY | Colonel T.E. LAWRENCE | [T.E.S.] | AND AN APPENDIX BY | Sir ARNOLD KEITH, F.R.S., M.D. | CONTAINING ALSO | MAPS, CHARTS, DIAGRAMS, AND | ILLUSTRATIONS COMPLEMENTARY | TO THE TEXT | NEW YORK | CHARLES SCRIBNER'S SONS | 1932

Collation 23.5 × 16 cm: [1–27]^8, 216 leaves, pp.[i–vi], vii–xxix, [xxx–xxxii], 1–397, [3].

Contents Prp.[i] bastard title, [ii] list of author's works, [iii] title page, [iv] copyright, issue statements, [v] dedication, [vi] blank, vii–xii contents, xiii–xv list of illustrations, [xvi] blank, xvii–xx foreword by T.E. Lawrence, xxi–xxii preface, xxiii–xxvii introduction, [xxviii] blank, xxix poem, [xxx] blank, [xxxi] half title, [xxxii] blank, pp.1–299 text, [300] blank, 301–384 appendixes, 385–397 index, [1–3] blank.

RT On both verso and recto [according to subject of page].

Plates Fifty-six photographs on coated paper, printed on one side only, following pp.[ii], 2, 10, 16, 24 double, 34, 38, 42, 48, 50, 54, 72 double, 78, 80, 82, 96, 104, 108, 122, 126, 136, 138, 140, 142, 150, 152, 156, 170, 174, 176, 178, 192, 194, 206, 222, 224, 226, 236, 238, 244, 256, 294, 296, 298 double, 310, 326 triple, 330, 332 triple.

Text 20 lines, 9.8 (9.9) × 10.8 cm.

Paper White, wove, unwatermarked, all edges trimmed, sheets bulk 3.8 cm.

Binding Maroon cloth 262 gy. p R. On front cover: [gilt] ARABIA | FELIX | [cut] | BERTRAM | THOMAS. On spine: [gilt] ARABIA | FELIX | [cut] | BERTRAM | THOMAS | SCRIBNERS. T.e. light tan.

Published at $5.00, 1 February 1932.

Notes List of impressions:
    2nd, March 1932, same as above, with following difference: [Binding]: Blue cloth 182 m Blue.
    3rd, March 1932.
    4th, March 1932, maroon cloth 262 gy. p Br [on dust wrapper of this issue inside rear flap the statement: The Gold Medal of the National Geographical Society in Washington, is printed over].
    A specially made-up state, same as above with added item: tipped inside fly leaf single fold menu: [within double rule frame] AN AMERICAN | ARABIAN NIGHT | ATOP THE | EMPIRE STATE BUILDING | IN | BAGHDAD*ON*THE*HUDSON | IN HONOR OF | BERTRAM THOMAS | *February 22, 1932 Shawal 15, 1350 H.;* [Contents]: pp.[1] title, [2] menu, 3 [list of major guests for the evening], [4] blank. Most copies have signatures of guests of honour near their printed names [it is presumed

that each person attending the dinner was given a copy of the book with the menu tipped in].

Copies   AC, Cal.

Two Hundred Class Royal Air Force Seaplane Tender

Lawrence requested posting out of the country during the time *Revolt in the Desert* was to be available in Great Britain. He was sent to India in July 1927, initially to Karachi, and later further north to Miranshah. In early January 1929 he was returned home due to sensational press accounts that he was involved in an attempt to overthrow the government in Afghanistan. In Britain once more he was posted to Mount Batten, RAF station, Plymouth. Here for five years under Wing Command Sydney Smith he found a measure of happiness. The record of these years is to be found in Smith, *The Golden Reign* (1940). In the autumn of 1930 he was assigned to development of high-speed tenders for flying boats which were to double as rescue craft. He continued in this work with the Marine Craft Section until his discharge from the service in February 1935. The *Two Hundred Class Royal Air Force Seaplane Tender* technical manual was written in lieu of the official manual to be developed later (never issued). The text bears all the marks of Lawrence's characteristic clarity of style, providing the essential information needed for operation of the craft. Very few copies of the original exist. Only a portion of it is contained in *The Essential T.E. Lawrence* (1951).

A158   T.E. LAWRENCE, The Two Hundred Class Royal Air Force Seaplane Tender, 1932

First English Edition

THE | 200 CLASS ROYAL AIR FORCE | SEAPLANE TENDER | [short rule] | PROVISIONAL ISSUE OF NOTES. MARCH, 1932.

Collation   38 × 25.5 cm: prp.[1–4], pp.1–81, [1–37].

Contents   Prp.[1] title page, [2] copy of leaf of original manuscript, [3] letter by H. Wilkins, [4] contents, pp.[1] particulars of craft, 2–65 text, 66–83 index, pp.[1–37] appendixes.

Text   Copy of typed original.

Paper   White, wove, unwatermarked, all edges trimmed, sheets bulk 1 cm.

Binding   73 p OY paper covers. On front cover: [title, as above] in purple.

Published at   March 1932.

Notes Some of text reprinted in _The Essential T.E. Lawrence_, pp.300–304. Full text reprinted in _The History of Royal Air Force Marine Craft 1918–1986_, Appendix 16, The 200 Class Seaplane Tender, Canimpex Publishing, London, 1986, pp.135–171.

Copies AC, Cal, H, UT.

No Decency Left

Under the pseudonym "Barbara Rich", Robert Graves and Laura Riding wrote this 'future world' novel. Needing a technical description of an autogyro, they obtained a word picture of it and a description of its capabilities from T.E. Lawrence (pp.153–5).

A159 BARBARA RICH, No Decency Left, Cape, 1932

First English Edition

NO DECENCY LEFT | BY | BARBARA RICH | [pub. device] | JONATHAN CAPE | THIRTY BEDFORD SQUARE | LONDON

Collation 19 × 12 cm: [A]^8 B–S^8, 144 leaves, pp.[1–8], 9–287, [288].

Contents Pp.[1] bastard title, [2] blank, [3] title page, [4] issue statement, printer's, papermaker's, binder's credits, [5] dedication, [6] blank, [7] half-title, [8] blank, 9–[288] text.

Typography and paper $ 1 signed B.

Text 20 lines, 9.1 × 9 cm.

Paper White, wove, unwatermarked, top and fore edge trimmed, sheets bulk 2.5 cm.

Binding Salmon 53 m Orange cloth. On front cover: [cut in blue]. On spine: [all in blue] NO | DECENCY | LEFT | [star] | BARBARA | RICH | JONATHAN CAPE. On back cover: [blind stamped pub. device].

Published at 7s 6d.

Notes Barbara Rich is pseudonym of Robert Graves and Laura Riding. T.E. Lawrence wrote a technical description of the autogyro on pp.153–155. He is mentioned on pp.178, 258.
    Reprinted March 1932.
    Reprinted April 1932.
    Reprinted March 1935.
    Lawrence's contribution reprinted in _T.E. Lawrence to His Biographer, Robert Graves_, pp.168–169.

Copies Cal.

1933

Letters From T.E. Shaw to Bruce Rogers

Bruce Rogers and William Rudge printed this short collection of 39 letters and issued it privately in an edition of 200 copies. Many of the copies are signed by Rogers who apparently gave them as gifts. The letters are for the most part those written by Lawrence during the period he was translating *The Odyssey* and are of major importance in relation to that work.

A160 T.E. LAWRENCE, Letters From T.E. Shaw to Bruce Rogers, 1933
First American Edition

[In brown] LETTERS | [in brown] *from T.E. Shaw to Bruce Rogers*

Collation 20.8 × 14.1 cm: [1]⁴ [2–6]⁸, 44 leaves, unpaged.

Contents Pp.[1–4] blank, [5] title page, [6] *'Copyright 1933 by Bruce Rogers | All rights reserved | 200 copies privately printed at the | Press of William Edwin Rudge | from type set by Bertha M. Goudy',* [7–8] introduction by Bruce Rogers, [9–44] text.

Text 20 lines, 15.1 × 10.5 cm.

Paper Buff, wove, unwatermarked, all edges trimmed, sheets bulk 5 mm.

Binding Brown linen 78 d. y Br. On spine: [gilt, running up] *LETTERS.*

Notes Limited to 200 copies. Companion volume to *More Letters From T.E. Shaw to Bruce Rogers,* 1936 (A165). Text printed in brown using italics. Letters written to Rogers during period of Lawrence's translation of *The Odyssey.*

Copies AC, Cal, H, UT.

1935

Announcement Card to Correspondents

When he retired from the RAF in February 1935, Lawrence had a card printed stating his intention not to write much in the future, in an attempt to control his correspondence. Perhaps this is a reflection of his general despondency at the time.

A161   T.E. LAWRENCE, Announcement card to correspondents, 1935

First English Printing

To tell you that in future I shall | write very few letters. | T.E.S.

Collation   9 × 11.4 cm: single card printed on one side only, letterpress.

Paper   Buff, woven, unwatermarked, all edges trimmed.

Notes   Sent to friends and correspondents after Lawrence retired from RAF in 1935.

Copies   Cal, H, UT.

Then and Now

Jonathan Cape, Lawrence's publisher from its earliest years, published an occasional periodical *Now and Then*. A number of the articles published were gathered together into a collection as *Then and Now* in 1935, the year of Lawrence's death. The collection contains one article by Lawrence, the preface for *Arabia Felix*, and two articles about him.

A162   JONATHAN CAPE LTD., Then and Now, Cape, 1935

First English Edition

THEN AND NOW | A Selection of articles, stories & | poems, taken from the first fifty | numbers of 'Now & Then' 1921–1935 | together with | Some illustrations, and cer- | tain other work now printed | for the first time | [cut] | JONATHAN CAPE | Thirty Bedford Square London | 1935

Collation   19 × 12 cm: [A]^8 B–O^8, 112 leaves, pp.[1–5], 6–224.

Contents   [1] bastard title, [2] blank, [3] title page, [4] printer's, binder's credits, 5–8 contents, 9–10 illustrations, 11–12 introduction, 13–218 text, 219–224 bibliographies.

RT   On verso [according to chapter]. On recto [according to author of chapter].

Typography and paper $ 1 signed B.

Text   20 lines, 8.4 (8.5) × 9 cm.

Paper   White, wove, unwatermarked, all edges trimmed, sheets bulk 1.5 cm.

Binding   Stiff red paper 36 deep r O. On front cover: [running around

square formed by white rectangle in centre, in white] THEN |
1921–1935 | NOW | 1921–1935 | [within square printed over red
ampersand] a selection of | articles, stories | and poems | reprinted
from | NOW AND THEN | together with | certain illustra- | tions
and | other work | now printed | for the first | time by | Jonathan
Cape | [red rule along inner margin]. On spine: THEN | & | NOW |
1921 | 1935 | [running up, in white] THEN AND NOW | [across at bottom,
printer's device]. On back cover: [in white] THEN AND NOW | [another
white rectangle] contributors include | [red rule] | H.G. Wells Arnold
Bennett Hugh | [red rule] | Walpole D.H. Lawrence George | [red rule]
Bernard Shaw The Rt. Hon. Stanley | [red rule] | Baldwin John Middleton
Murry | [red rule] | T.E. Shaw [T.E. Lawrence] The Very | [red rule] | Rev.
W.R. Inge H.M. Tomlinson | [red rule] | E.M. Forster A.C. Benson. Andre |
[red rule] | Maurois St. John Ervine W.H. | [red
rule] | Davies Hilaire Belloc Edmund | [red rule] | Blunden Henry
Williamson | [red rule] | H.E. Bates Herbert Read | [red rule] | William
Plomer W.H. | [red rule] | Auden Stephen Spender | [red rule] | [below
rectangle in white] JONATHAN CAPE. All edges slate grey.

Published at   Free of charge.

Notes   Contains: W.H. Auden, "T.E. Lawrence", pp.21–22; T.E. Shaw,
"Arabian Traveller", pp.93–96 (reprint of preface to Thomas' *Arabia Felix*);
G.B. Shaw, ' "Revolt in the Desert"and its Author', pp.121–131.

Copies   AC, Cal.

River Niger

Contains a prefatory letter by Lawrence. This deservedly forgotten novel
has to its credit between its covers only the letter by Lawrence.

A163   SIMON JESTY, pseud., River Niger, Boriswood, 1935

First English Edition

SIMON JESTY | RIVER NIGER | A NOVEL | With a prefatory letter
by | T.E. LAWRENCE | BORISWOOD : LONDON

Collation   19 × 12.5 cm: [A]^8 B–S^8, 144 leaves, pp.[1–10], 11–288.

Contents   Pp.[1–2] blank, [3] bastard title, publisher's device], [4] list of
author's works, [5] title page, [6] printer's credits, issue, copyright
statements, [7–9] contents, [10] acknowledgments, 11–13 prefatory letter,
[14] publisher's disclaimer,[15], quote, [16] blank, [17] half-title, [18] blank,
[19] section title, [20] blank, 21–287 text, [1] blank.

RT   On verso *River Niger.* On recto [according to chapter].

Typography and paper $ 1 signed G.

Text   20 lines, 7.8 (8) × 9 cm.

Paper   White, wove, unwatermarked, all edges trimmed, sheets bulk 2.5 cm.

Binding   Yellow cloth 82 v. Y. On spine: [in red, double wavy rule] | SIMON JESTY | [in blue] river | [in blue] niger | [in red, next three lines] prefaced by | T.E. | LAWRENCE | [in red, double wavy rule] | [triple blue wavy rule running down] | [double red wavy rule, across] | [in blue] BORISWOOD. On back cover: [pub. device, blind stamped]. T.e. blue grey

Published at   7s 6d, October 1935.

Notes   Another issue, limited, large paper same as above, with following differences: [Collation]: 19.5 × 13.2 cm; [Paper]: Pannekoek all-rag, laid, watermarked, top edge trimmed; [Binding]: red Niger 13 deep red. T.e. gilt; [Price]: 25s.

Copies   AC, Cal, H, UT.

A164   Simon Jesty, River Niger, Boriswood, 1935

Publisher's Prospectus for First English Edition

RIVER | [red rule] | prefaced by T.E. Lawrence of Arabia | [red rule] | NIGER

Collation   12.5 × 9.5 cm: single-fold leaflet, unpaged [1–4].

Contents   Pp.[1] title page, [2–3] blurb including extracts from Lawrence's letter, [4] order form.

Paper   White, laid, unwatermarked, all edges trimmed.

Published at   Free advertising flyer.

Notes   Lawrence wrote prefatory letter.

Copies   H.

1936

More Letters From T.E. Shaw to Bruce Rogers

This is a companion volume to *Letters From T.E. Shaw to Bruce Rogers* (1933). This volume adds 13 letters to the 39 in the first volume. The two volumes are most often sold as a set. Most of the letters are not contained in *The Letters of T.E. Lawrence*. Handset and printed by Rogers.

A165   T.E. LAWRENCE, More Letters From T.E. Shaw to Bruce Rogers, 1936

First American Edition

MORE LETTERS | from T.E. Shaw to Bruce Rogers

Collation   20.6 × 13.7 cm: [1–5]⁴ [6]², 22 leaves including pastedown end papers, unpaged.

Contents   Pp.[1–8] blank, [9] title page, [10] *'Copyright 1936 by Bruce Rogers | All rights reserved | 300 copies privately printed | by permission of the | Trustees of the late T.E. Shaw | Printed in U.S.A.'*, [11–18] text, [19–22] blank.

Text   20 lines, 15.2 × 10.1 cm, all italic, all in brown ink.

Paper   Buff, wove, unwatermarked, all edges trimmed, sheets buff, wove, unwatermarked, all edges trimmed, sheets bulk 2 mm.

Binding   Brown linen deep y. Br. On spine: [gilt, running up] *MORE LETTERS*. All edges light brown.

Notes   Limited to 300 copies. Companion volume to *Letters From T.E. Shaw to Bruce Rogers*, 1933 (A160).

Copies   AC, Cal, H, UT, Ho.

The Mint

One of Lawrence's avowed purposes in joining the RAF, though not the only one, was to write of the ranks from the inside. He began immediately making notes when he enlisted in 1922. With his dismissal from the RAF in January 1923, because of unfavourable publicity, the project was set aside, not to be taken up again until he was posted to India in 1927, during which interval he had overseen the publication of *Seven Pillars of Wisdom* and the abridging of it as *Revolt in the Desert* for Cape. While in India he edited the text of his earlier notes and began revisions. In March 1928 he sent a clean copy of the revised text to Edward Garnett. Garnett had copies typed which were circulated to a small circle, among them Air Marshal Trenchard. Cape wished to publish it and claimed the right under an agreement to have first right of refusal to Lawrence's next book after *Revolt*. To forestall them Lawrence asked for an advance of £1,000,000, thus successfully preventing Cape from exercising their option. Trenchard's concerned response led Lawrence to guarantee that it would not be published at least until 1950. Later revisions were made by Lawrence in the last months of his life with a possible view to publication in a private edition on a handpress.

The manuscript found its way to America and, in 1936, in order to control publication, it was found necessary to have a copyright edition published in the USA. As with the earlier copyright edition of *Seven Pillars of Wisdom*, a prohibitive price was set to prevent sales, in this case $500,000 per copy. The edition was 50 copies, ten of which were for sale. A sensational scoop occurred when the editor of the *Saturday Review*, H.S. Canby, knowing that two copies had been sent to the Library of Congress, visited that institution demanding to read the book, which right was ultimately granted him. One copy was 'sold' to Lawrence's literary agent in England for $1.00 in an attempt to secure copyright there. This was later deemed not to have met the reasonable requirements of the public for that purpose.

The manuscript used for the American edition was not the last state of the text. A revised manuscript was found later and formed the basis for the text which was set in type by Cape in 1948. It was only published in 1955 in the USA and England after the death of an officer described unfavourably in the text. The American edition was first issued in a limited edition of 1000 copies. Cape published 2000 limited de luxe copies and a trade issue of the same edition which had all objectionable words lifted out of the text leaving blank spaces. In 1973 a definitive edition, edited with a preface by J.M. Wilson, and including the objectionable words and names as they appeared in the manuscript, was published by Cape. These names had been changed in some cases due to fear of libel suits.

A166 T.E. LAWRENCE, The Mint, Doubleday, Doran, 1936

First American Edition (Copyright)

[In red] THE MINT | NOTES MADE IN THE R.A.F. DEPOT BETWEEN | AUGUST AND DECEMBER 1922, AND AT | CADET COLLEGE IN 1925 | By | 352087 A/c ROSS | REGROUPED AND COPIED IN 1927 AND | 1928 AT AIRCRAFT DEPOT, KARACHI | GARDEN CITY, NEW YORK | [in red] DOUBLEDAY, DORAN & COMPANY | MCMXXXVI

Collation 28.5 × 20 cm: π^2 [1–12]^8 [1]^1, 204 leaves, pp.[2], [i–iv], v–vii, [viii], [1–2], 3–199, [200], [2].

Contents Prp.[1] bastard title, [2] blank, title page, [ii] copyright statement, printer's credits, [iii] dedication, [iv] blank, v–vii contents, [viii] blank, pp.[1] half-title, [2] blank, 3–199 text, [200] blank, [1] colophon, 'This edition of | THE MINT | is limited to 50 copies, | of which 10 copies are for sale. | THIS IS NUMBER [mss. #]', [2] blank.

Text 20 lines, 10 × 12.4 cm.

Paper Mould-made, watermarked, top edge trimmed, sheets bulk 1.5 cm.

Binding Blue 191 b. Grey paper covered boards, vellum spine (4 cm) and small corners. On spine: [within single rule on black leather patch, running down, gilt] THE MINT. T.e. gilt. End papers blue. Red and gold head band.

Published at $500,000, 25 September 1936.

Notes Published to protect copyright, limited to 50 copies, text of this edition follows that of the typescript made by Edward Garnett.

Copies Cal, H, UT.

A167   T.E. LAWRENCE, The Mint, Doubleday, 1955

Second American Edition (Uncorrected Proofs)

The Mint | NOTES MADE IN THE R.A.F. DEPOT | BETWEEN AUGUST AND DECEMBER, 1922 | AND AT CADET COLLEGE IN 1925 BY | T.E. Lawrence (352087 A/c ROSS) | REGROUPED AND COPIED IN 1927 AND 1928 AT AIRCRAFT DEPOT, KARACHI | Doubleday & Company, Inc., Garden City, N.Y. 1955

Collation   23.5 × 15.5 cm: [1–16]^8, 128 leaves, pp.[2], [1–6], 7–254.

Contents   Prp.[1–2] blank, pp.[1] bastard title, [2] blank, [3] title page, [4] copyright statement, printer's credit, [5] dedication, [6] blank, 7–9 contents, [10] blank, 11–15 note by A.W. Lawrence, [16] blank, [17] section title, [18] blank, 19–250 text, 251 postscript, [252–254] blank.

RT   On verso THE MINT. On recto [according to section].

Text   20 lines, 10 (10.2) × 10.2 cm.

Paper   Cream, wove, unwatermarked, all edges trimmed, sheets bulk 2 cm.

Binding   White paper covers glued to sheets. On front cover: [within frame of yellow rectangle] THE | MINT | T.E. LAWRENCE | [below frame] REVIEWERS' EDITION | *T.E. Lawrence's* THE MINT | *will be published February 21, 1955,* | *in an edition of 1000 numbered copies* | *priced at $20.00.* | DOUBLEDAY AND COMPANY, INC., GARDEN CITY, NEW YORK. T.e. pale yellow.

Notes   Text revised by A.W. Lawrence after publication of 1936 edition.

Copies   Cal.

A168   T.E. LAWRENCE, The Mint, Doubleday, 1955

Second American Edition (Limited Issue)

The Mint | NOTES MADE IN THE R.A.F. DEPOT | BETWEEN AUGUST AND DECEMBER, 1922 | AND AT CADET COLLEGE IN 1925 BY | T.E. Lawrence (352087 A/c ROSS) | REGROUPED AND COPIED IN 1927

AND | 1928 AT AIRCRAFT DEPOT, KARACHI | Doubleday & Company, Inc., Garden City, N.Y. 1955

Collation   23.5 × 15.6 cm: π¹ [1−16]⁸, 129 leaves, pp.[1−4], [1−6], 7−250, [4].

Contents   Prp.[1−2] blank, [3] *'This edition is limited to one thousand copies | of which this is copy number* [stamped #]', [4] blank, pp.[1] half title, [2] blank, [3] title page, [4] copyright statement, [5] dedication, [6] blank, 7−9 contents, 10 blank, 11−15 note by A.W. Lawrence, [16] blank, [17] section title, [18] blank, 19−250 text, [1] postscript, [2−4] blank.

RT   On verso THE MINT. On recto [according to chapter].

Text   20 lines, 9.8 (10.1) × 10.1 cm.

Paper   Buff, wove, unwatermarked, all edges trimmed, sheets bulk 1.8 cm.

Binding   Blue cloth 175 v.d. g B. On front cover: [gilt] THE MINT | [long rule]. On spine: [running down] T.E. LAWRENCE | [across] The | Mint | [running down] DOUBLEDAY. T.e. and end papers bright yellow 82 v. Y. Head and tail bands blue and yellow. Boxed as issued.

Published at $20.00.

Notes   Limited to 1000 copies.

Copies   AC, Cal, UT, Ho.

A169   T.E. LAWRENCE, The Mint, Doubleday, 1957

Second American Edition

THE MINT | NOTES MADE IN THE R.A.F. DEPOT | BETWEEN AUGUST AND DECEMBER, 1922, | AND AT CADET COLLEGE IN 1925 BY | T.E. Lawrence (352087 A/c ROSS) | REGROUPED AND COPIED IN 1927 AND | 1928 AT AIRCRAFT DEPOT, KARACHI | Doubleday & Company, Inc., Garden City, N.Y., 1957

Collation   23.4 × 15 cm: [1−16]⁸, 128 leaves, pp.[2], [1−6], 7−250, [4].

Contents   Prp.[1−2] blank, pp.[1] bastard title, [2] blank, [3] title page, [4] copyright statement, [5] dedication, [6] blank, 7−9 contents, [10] blank, 11−15 note by A.W. Lawrence, [16] blank, [17] section title, [18] blank, 19−250 text, [1] postscript, [3−4] blank.

RT   On verso THE MINT. On recto [according to section].

Text   20 lines, 9.9 (10.2) × 10.2 cm.

Paper   White, wove, unwatermarked, all edges trimmed, sheets bulk 1.8 cm.

Binding   Black cloth. On spine: [running down, in red] T.E. Lawrence

Doubleday | [across between name and pub. name, in white] THE | MINT. Red and gold head and tail bands.

Published at $7.50.

Copies AC, Cal.

A170 T.E. LAWRENCE, The Mint, Norton, 1963

Third American Edition

The Mint | NOTES MADE IN THE R.A.F. DEPOT | BETWEEN AUGUST AND DECEMBER, 1922, | AND AT CADET COLLEGE IN 1925 BY | T.E. Lawrence (352087 A/c ROSS) | REGROUPED AND COPIED IN 1927 AND | 1928 AT AIRCRAFT DEPOT, KARACHI | [pub. device] | The Norton Library | W.W. NORTON & COMPANY INC | NEW YORK

Collation 19.7 × 12.8 cm: guillotined sheets, 128 leaves, pp.[1–8], 7–250, [4].

Contents Prp.[1] bastard title, [2] blank, [3] biographical sketch, [4] blank, [5] title page, [6] copyright, issue statements, pub. pledge, [7] dedication, [8] blank, pp.7–9 contents, [10] blank, 11–15 note by A.W. Lawrence, [16] blank, [17] section title, [18] blank, 19–250 text, [1] postscript, [2–4] pub. ads.

RT On verso THE MINT. On recto [according to section].

Text 20 lines, 9.5 (9.8) × 9.8 cm.

Paper White, wove, unwatermarked, all edges trimmed, sheets bulk 1.4 cm.

Binding Pictorial paper covers. On front cover: [all in white except for pub. device] $ 1.25 | N196 | T.E.LAWRENCE | THE MINT | "I DEEM HIM ONE OF THE | GREATEST BEINGS ALIVE IN | OUR TIME...WE SHALL NEVER | SEE HIS LIKE AGAIN. HIS | NAME WILL LIVE IN HISTORY"| – WINSTON CHURCHILL | [pub. device] | [running down] Finegold. On spine: [running down, author's name in brown] T.E. LAWRENCE THE MINT NORTON | [across at bottom] N196 | [pub. device within black rectangle]. On back cover: [within brown rectangle] THE MINT | [nine-line blurb] | [italics, designer's credit] | [within brown banner, pub. device and address].

Published at $1.25.

Notes Second issue has price on front cover changed to $1.95. Verso of title page bears issue code 34567890.

Copies AC, Cal.

A171   T.E. LAWRENCE, The Mint, Cape, 1948

Uncorrected Proofs for proposed First English Edition

THE MINT | *A day-book of the R.A.F. Depot between* | *August and December 1922* | *with later notes by* | 352087 A/c ROSS | [pub. device] | JONATHAN CAPE | THIRTY BEDFORD SQUARE | LONDON

Collation   24.5 × 18.5 cm: [A] –N⁸, 106 leaves, pp.[1–4], 5–207, [1].

Contents   Pp.[1] bastard title, [2] blank, [3] title page, [4] issue statement, printer's credit, 5–7 contents, [8] blank, [9] dedication, [10] blank, [11] section title, [12] blank, 13–206 text, 207 postscript, [1] blank.

RT   On verso THE MINT. On recto [according to section].

Typography and paper $ 1 signed B.

Text   20 lines, 8.7 (9) × 12.2 cm.

Paper   White, wove, unwatermarked, all edges trimmed, sheets bulk 8 mm.

Binding   Grey paper wrappers. On front cover: THE MINT | 352087 A/c ROSS | [pub. device] | Uncorrected Proof. On spine: [running up] THE MINT. On back cover: The Alden Press (Oxford) Ltd. | Oxford.

Notes   The type was set in anticipation of publishing in 1950 but this was delayed until 1955 when an individual mentioned in the book died, thus avoiding danger of a libel suit.

Copies   Cal, H.

A172   T.E. LAWRENCE, The Mint, Cape, 1955

First English Edition (Limited Issue)

T.E. LAWRENCE | [in red] THE MINT | *A day-book of the R.A.F. Depot between* | *August and December 1922* | *with later notes* | by | 352087 A/c ROSS | LONDON | JONATHAN CAPE 30 BEDFORD SQUARE

Collation   25.5 × 19.5 cm: π² [A]⁸ B–N⁸ χ², 112 leaves, pp.[1–6], [1–2], 3–206, [4].

Contents   Prp.[1] patterned end paper pasted to this leaf, [2] blank, [3–4] blank, [5] 'THE MINT | THIS EDITION IS | LIMITED TO TWO | THOUSAND COPIES | FOR SALE | COPY NUMBER:' | [pub. device], [6] list of author's works, pp.[1] title page, [2] issue statement, printer's, papermaker's, binder's credits, 3–5 contents, 6 blank, 7–10 note by A.W. Lawrence, 11 section title, 12 dedication, 13–206 text, [1–3] blank, [4] patterned end paper pasted to this leaf.

RT   On verso THE MINT. On recto [according to section].

Typography and paper $ 1 signed B.

Text   20 lines, 9.8 (9.9) × 12.2 cm.

Paper   White, laid, unwatermarked, top edges trimmed, unopened, sheets bulk 2 cm. First and last gatherings are different paper than other gatherings.

Binding   Blue buckram 187 d. gy. B. dark blue pigskin spine. On spine: [gilt] T.E. | LAWRENCE | [cut] THE | MINT | 352087 | A/C | ROSS | [pub. device]. T.e. gilt. Blue and white marbled end papers. Boxed as issued. Blind rule along edge of leather both covers.

Published at   £3 14s, February 1955.

Notes   Limited to 2000 numbered copies.

Copies   AC, Cal, UT.

A173   T.E. LAWRENCE, The Mint, Cape, 1955

First English Edition

T.E. LAWRENCE | [in red] THE MINT | *A day-book of the R.A.F. Depot between* | August and December 1922 | *with later notes* | by | 352087 A/c ROSS | LONDON | JONATHAN CAPE 30 BEDFORD SQUARE

Collation   24.8 × 18.5 cm: [A]⁸ B−N⁸, 108 leaves, pp.[1−2], [1−2], 3−206.

Contents   Prp.[1] bastard title, [2] other works by author, pp.[1] title page, [2] issue statement, printer's, binder's, papermaker's credits, 3−5 contents, [6] blank, 7−10 note by A.W. Lawrence, 11 section title, 12 dedication, 13−206 text.

RT   On verso THE MINT. On recto [according to section].

Typography and paper $ 1 signed B.

Text   20 lines, 9.8 (9.9) × 12.2 cm.

Paper   White, wove, unwatermarked, all edges trimmed, sheets bulk 1.5 cm.

Binding   Blue buckram 187 d. gy. B. On front cover: [blind stamped bird]. On spine: T.E. | LAWRENCE | [cut] | THE | MINT | 352087 | A/C | ROSS | [pub. device]. T.e. blue.

Published at   17s 6d, February 1955.

Notes   All objectionable words omitted from text by lifting type, leaving blank spaces.
      2nd impression, 1955, identical to above.

Copies   AC, Cal, UT.

A174   T.E. LAWRENCE, The Mint, Cape, 1955

Publisher's Prospectus for First English Edition

[Title page of published book reproduced]

Collation   25.5 × 19 cm: single-fold leaflet.

Contents   Pp.[1] title page, 2–3 text and ads for other Lawrence titles published by Cape, [4] more ads, order form.

Paper   White, wove, unwatermarked, all edges trimmed.

Published at   Free advertising flyer.

Copies   Cal, C.

A175   T.E. LAWRENCE, The Mint, Panther Books, 1962

Second English Edition

T.E. LAWRENCE | THE MINT | *A day-book of the R.A.F. Depot between* | August and December 1922 | *with later notes* | by | 352087 A/c ROSS | *A PANTHER BOOK*

Collation   17.3 × 10.8 cm: [A]^{16} B–F^{16}, 96 leaves, pp.[1–6], 7–192.

Contents   Pp.[1] quote from review of *The Mint*, [2] quotes from additional reviews, [3] title page, [4] issue statement, printer's credit, [5] contents, [6] blank, 7–10 note by A.W. Lawrence, [11] section title, [12] dedication, 13–191 text, [192] ads.

RT   On verso THE MINT. On recto [according to section].

Typography and paper $ 1 signed T-B.

Text   20 lines, 7 (7.1) × 9 cm.

Paper   White, wove, unwatermarked, all edges trimmed, sheets bulk 1.6 cm.

Binding   Multicolour paper covers glued to sheets. On front cover: [within white panel, at top] [pub. device] | [in grey] *Author of 'Seven Pillars of Wisdom'* | [wide red bar] [in red] T.E. [wide red bar] | [short blue bar, in blue] LAWRENCE [short blue bar] | [within grey panel at bottom, in green] The Mint | [in green] BY 352087 A/c ROSS | [in white] "Savage... brittle... | [in white] vivid...it is | [in white] bound to shock."| [in green] – H.E. BATES | [within green rectangle in lower right corner] 3/6. On spine: [running down, in white] T.E. LAWRENCE [in green] THE MINT [in white] BY 352087 A/C ROSS | [across at bottom, in white] PANTHER | [pub. device] | 1447. On back cover: [photo of Peter O'Toole and blurb for film, quotes from reviews, publisher's name and publisher's device. White and grey panels continued from front.

Published at   3s 6d, December 1962.

Notes   List of impressions:
2nd, 1963, as above.
3rd, 1969, as above, with following differences]: [justified right] T.E. Lawrence | THE MINT | a day- book of the R.A.F. depot between | August and December 1922 with later notes | by 352087 A/c ROSS | A Panther Book; [Collation]: 17.8 × 11 cm; [Contents]: | [within circle] Panther | [below circle] 028102. On spine: [running down] [title in white letters outlined in heavy black] THE MINT T.E. Lawrence Panther Books 029102. On back cover: [10 line blurb] | [2 line cover illustration credit] | U.K. 6/- (30p) AUSTRALIA 90c NEW ZEALAND 85c SOUTH AFRICA 75c; *Published at*   6/-.

Copies   AC, Cal.

A176   T.E. LAWRENCE, The Mint, Cape, 1972

Third English Edition, Uncorrected Proof

T.E. LAWRENCE | THE MINT | *A daybook of the R.A.F. Depot between* | *August and December 1922* | *with later notes* | by | 352087 A/C ROSS | [pub. device] | JONATHAN CAPE | THIRTY BEDFORD SQUARE LONDON

Collation   23.5 × 15.5 cm: [A–B]⁸ C–M⁸ [N]⁸, 104 leaves, pp.[1–4], 5–206, [2].

Contents   Pp.[1] bastard title, quotes from reviews pasted in, [2] list of author's works, [3] title page, [4] issue statement, printer's credit, 5–7 contents, [8] blank, [9] section title, [10] blank, 11–14 note by A.W. Lawrence, [15] dedication, [16] blank, [17] section title, [18] blank, 19–206 text, [1–2] blank.

RT   On verso THE MINT. On recto [according to section].

Typography and paper $ 1 signed B.

Text   20 lines, 9 (9.3) × 11 cm.

Paper   White, wove, unwatermarked, all edges trimmed, sheets bulk 3 cm.

Binding   Patterned yellow paper wrappers 102 mg Y, glued to sheets.

Published at   To be published at £2.95.

Copies   Cal.

A177   T.E. LAWRENCE, The Mint, Cape, 1973

Third English Edition

T.E. LAWRENCE | [Oxford rule] | THE MINT | [pub. device] | JONATHAN
CAPE | THIRTY BEDFORD SQUARE LONDON

Collation   23.3 × 15.2 cm: [A–B]⁸ C–N⁸, 104 leaves, pp.[1–8], 9–[206],
[1–2].

Contents   Pp.[1] bastard title, [2] list of author's works, [3] title page, [4]
issue statement, printer's credit, [5–7] contents, [8] blank, 9–12 note by
A.W. Lawrence, [13] title page of original manuscript, [18] blank, 19–[206]
text, [1–2] blank.

RT   On verso THE MINT. On recto [according to chapter].

Plates   Frontis., on coated paper, following p.[2].

Typography and paper $ 1 signed C.

Text   20 lines, 9.1 (9.3) × 11 cm.

Paper   White, wove, unwatermarked, all edges trimmed, sheets bulk 1.5
cm.

Binding   Heavy brown buckram 57 l. Br. On spine: [gilt] [double rule] |
T.E. | LAWRENCE | [cut] | THE | MINT | [double rule] | [pub. device]. T.e.
stained purple. Tan end papers.

Published at   £3.50.

Notes   Unexpurgated with minor text corrections including names used in
original manuscript.

Copies   AC, Cal.

A178   T.E. LAWRENCE, The Mint, Penguin, 1978

Fourth English Edition

T.E. LAWRENCE | [Oxford rule] | THE MINT | [Oxford rule] | [pub.
device] | PENGUIN BOOKS

Collation   18 × 11 cm: guillotined sheets glued to covers, 120 leaves,
pp.[1–4], 5–[232], [8].

Contents   Pp.[1] blurb, [2] blank, [3] title page, [4] issue, copyright
statements, printer's credit, sales restrictions, 5–7 contents, [8] blank, 9–13
preface by A.W. Lawrence, [14] blank, 15–25 preface by J.M. Wilson, [26]
blank, 27 notes, [28] blank, [29] title page of corrected edition, [30] blank,
[31] dedication, [32] blank, [33] section title, [34] blank, 35–232 text, [1–8]
ads.

RT On verso *The Mint*. On recto [according to section].

Text 20 lines, 8.1 (8.4) × 8.9 cm.

Paper White, wove, unwatermarked, all edges trimmed, sheets bulk 1.2 cm.

Binding Pictorial paper covers. On front cover: [all in white] [pub. device] Penguin Modern Classics | (352087) A/c Ross) T.E. LAWRENCE | [long rule] | The Mint | The Complete Unexpurgated Text | [John drawing of T.E. Lawrence]. On spine: [pub. device] | [in white] T.E. Lawrence (352087 A/c Ross) [in black] The Mint | ISBN 0 14 | 00.4505 8. On back cover: [first two lines white] Penguin Modern Classics [pub. device] | T.E. Lawrence (352087 A/c Ross) | [long rule] The Mint | The Complete Unexpurgated Text | Introduced by J.M. Wilson | [24-line blurb] | [prices and ISBN].

Notes Another issue, as above, with following differences: [Collation]: 19.7 × 12.8 cm; [Binding]: white paper covers [semi circle] PENGUIN MODERN CLASSICS | [pub. device, orange and black] | (352087 A/c Ross) | T.E. Lawrence | [rule] | The Mint | The Complete Unexpurgated Text | [orange rectangle containing John drawing of Lawrence]. On spine: [within orange rectangle at head] PMC | [pub. device] | [beneath rectangle Oxford rule] | [running down] T.E. Lawrence (352087 A/c Ross) The Mint | [Oxford rule] | [orange rectangle at foot, within rectangle running down] ISBN 0 14 | 00.4505 8. On back cover: [repeat of text on front cover] | Introduced by J.M. Wilson | [blurbs and credits] | [prices, ISBN].

Copies AC.

A179 T.E. LAWRENCE, El Troquel, Sur, 1955

First Argentine Edition (Limited Issue)

[In red] EL TROQUEL | APUNTES DIARIOS | tomados en el Cuarte de Tránsito de la R.A.F. | entre agosto y diciembre de 1922 | por | 352.087 A/C ROSS | T.E. LAWRENCE | *Con notas posteriores* | *Traduccion de* | VICTORIA OCAMPO | [pub. device] | BUENOS AIRES

Collation 24 × 16.5 cm: [1–19]⁸, 152 leaves, pp.[1–8], 9–297, [7].

Contents Pp.[1–2] blank, [3] bastard title, [4] blank, [5] title page, [6] original title, printer's credit, copyright statement, [7] dedication, [8] blank, 9–11 translator's note, [12] blank, 13–18 note by A.W. Lawrence, [19] section title, [20] blank, 21–292 text, [293] section title, [294] blank, 295–297 contents, [1–7] illustrations.

Text 20 lines, 9 (9.2) × 10 cm.

Paper White, wove, unwatermarked, no edges trimmed, sheets bulk 2 cm.

Binding Plain white paper wrappers, around these white dust wrapper. On front: [in red] T.E. LAWRENCE | EL TROQUEL | [pub. device] |

BUENOS AIRES. On spine: [in red] T.E. LAWRENCE | EL | TROQUEL | [pub. device] | BUENOS AIRES.

Published at $100. – m/aro.

Notes   Limited to 300 copies.

Copies   Cal.

A180   T.E. LAWRENCE, El Troquel, Sur, 1955

First Argentine Edition

[In green] EL TROQUEL | APUNTES DIARIOS | tomados en el Cuartel de Tránsito de la R.A.F. | entre agosto y diciembre de 1922 | por | 352.087 A/C ROSS | T.E. LAWRENCE | Con notas posteriores | Traducción de | VICTORIA OCAMPO | [pub. device] | BUENOS AIRES

Collation   20.7 × 13.8 cm: $[1-4]^8 [5-19]^8$, 152 leaves, pp.[1–9], 10–297, [7].

Contents   Prp.[1–2] blank, [3] bastard title, [4] blank, [5] issue, copyright statements, printer's credits, [6] dedication, [7] blank, [8–9] 10–11 translator's note, [12] blank, [13]–18 note by A.W. Lawrence, [19] section title, [20] blank, 21–292 text, [293] section title, [294] blank, 295–297 index, [1] blank, [2] printer's colophon, [3–7] blank.

RT   On verso T.E. LAWRENCE. On recto EL TROQUEL.

Text   20 lines, 9 (9.3) × 9.9 cm.

Paper   White, wove, unwatermarked, untrimmed, sheets bulk 2 cm.

Binding   Green paper 122 gy Y G. On front cover: [in black] T.E. LAWRENCE | [in white] EL TROQUEL | [pub. device] | BUENOS AIRES. On spine: T.E. LAWRENCE | [in white] EL | TROQUEL | [pub. device] | BUENOS AIRES. On back cover: $ 35. – m/aro.

Published at $35. – m/aro.

Copies   AC.

A181   T.E. LAWRENCE, Mønten, Schønberg, 1956

First Danish Edition

T.E. Lawrence | MØNTEN | [rule] | En dagbog fra | Royal Air Force's rekrutejr | mellem august og december 1922 | samt senere optegnelser af | Rekrut 352087 Ross | [pub. device] | DET SCHØNBERGSKE FORLAG | 1956

Collation   19.3 × 12 cm: $[1]^8 2–14^8 15^4$. 116 leaves, pp.[1–4], 5–229, [3].

Contents Pp.[1] pub. device, [2] blank, [3] title page, [4] original title, designer's credit, issue statement, printer's credit, 5–[11] introduction, [12] blank, 13–[18] remarks by A.W. Lawrence, [19] dedication, [20] blank, [21] section title, [22] blank, 23–[229] text, [1] blank, [2] list of books in series, [3] blank.

Typography and paper $ 1 signed 1,2 3 Mønten, 3*.

Text 20 lines, 8.2 × 8.6 cm.

Paper White, wove, unwatermarked, untrimmed, sheets bulk 1.4 cm.

Binding Red, white and brown patterned paper covers. On front cover: T·E | LAWRENCE | MØNTEN | SCHØNBERG | [pub. device]. On spine: [running down] T.E. LAWRENCE : MØNTEN | [across at bottom] [pub. device]. On back cover: [blurbs on T.E. Lawrence and *The Mint*].

Published at Kr. 15.75, March 1956.

Copies AC, Cal.

A182 T.E.LAWRENCE, La Matrice, Gallimard, 1955

First French Edition

[In half circle] DU MONDE ENTIER | T.E. LAWRENCE | LA | MATRICE | Journal du Dépot de la Royal Air Force | (août–décembre 1922) | suivi de notes ultérieures | *par le simple soldat Ross, matricule 352087* | (THE MINT) | *traduit de l'anglais par* | ETIEMBLE | [cut] | [pub. device] | GALLIMARD | 5, rue Sébastien-Bottin, Paris VIIᵉ

Collation 18.7 × 12.2 cm: [1]⁸ 2–18⁸, 144 leaves, pp.[1–9], 10–285, [3].

Contents Pp.[1–2] blank, [3] bastard title, [4] list of author's works, [5] title page, [6] issue, copyright statements, [7] dedication, [8] blank, [9]–15 preface, [16] blank, [17] section title, [18] blank, [19]–278 text, [279]–281 translator's note, [282] blank, 283–285 contents, [1] blank, [2] printer's colophon, [3] blank.

RT On verso LA MATRICE. On recto [according to section].

Typography and paper $ 1 signed 2.

Text 20 lines, 7.5 (7.8) × 8.1 cm.

Paper White, wove, unwatermarked, untrimmed, sheets bulk 1.7 cm.

Binding white paper covers. On front cover: [half-circle] DU MONDE ENTIER | T.E. LAWRENCE | [in red] LA | [in red] MATRICE | *traduit de l'anglais par* | ETIEMBLE | [cut] | [in red] [pub. device] | GALLIMARD. On spine: DU MONDE | ENTIER | T.E. | LAWRENCE | [in red] LA | [in red] MATRICE | [pub. device] | GALLIMARD. On back cover: [within diamond] H | T.E. LAWRENCE | [in red] LA MATRICE | [advertising blurb on book] | 600 fr. Baisse comprise + T.L.

Published at 600 fr.

Notes Another issue, 5^e, as above on ordinary paper, except has 5^e edition in italics at foot of title page.

Another issue, 7^e edition, identical to immediately above.

Another state, one of 150 on special paper as above, with following differences: [Paper]: white, wove, watermarked Lafume-Navarre nrf, untrimmed, sheets bulk 1.5cm; [Binding]: white paper. On front cover: [half-circle] DU MONDE ENTIER | [in red] CLI | [in red] T.E. LAWRENCE | [cut] | [in red] LA | [in red] MATRICE | *traduit de l'anglais par* | ÉTIEMBLE | [in red] [pub. device] | GALLIMARD. On spine: DU MONDE | ENTIER | CLI | [in red] LA | [in red] MATRICE | par | T.E. | LAWRENCE | [pub. device] | Gallimard. On back cover: [list of titles in series].

Copies AC, Cal, UT.

A183   T.E. LAWRENCE, La Matrice, Gallimard, 1966

Second French Edition

T.E. LAWRENCE | *La matrice* | *Journal du Dépôt de la "Royal Air Force"* | (août–décembre 1922) | *suivi de notes ultérieures* | par le simple soldat Ross, matricule 352087 | (THE MINT) | TRADUIT DE L'ANGLAIS PAR ÉTIEMBLE | ÉDITION INTÉGRALE ET CORRIGÉE | GALLIMARD

Collation   16.7 × 10.9 cm: [1]^{16} 2–8^{16}, 128 leaves, pp.[1–5], 6–255, [1].

Contents   Pp.[1] pub. blurb, [2] list of author's works available in French, [3] title page, [4] copyright notice, [5]–9 preface, [10] dedication, 11–251 text, [252] blank, 253–255 contents, [1] printer's colophon.

RT   On both recto and verso LA MATRICE.

Typography and paper $ 1 signed LA MATRICE 5.

Text   20 lines, 7.4 (7.7) × 8.5 cm.

Paper   White, wove, unwatermarked, all edges trimmed, sheets bulk 1.5 cm.

Binding   Orange paper covers 35 s. r O. On front cover: [stencil letters] POUR LES TYPES DE L'ARMÉE, IL N'Y A PAS D'HOMMES | SUR LA TERRE, RIEN QUE D'AUTRES TYPES DE L'ARMÉE… | MAIS IL NOUS ARRIVE DE VOIR DES ARBRES, LA LUMIÈRE | DES ÉTOILES, DES ANIMAUX, PARFOIS. J'AI VOULU METTRE | EN ÉVIDENCE A QUEL POINT NOUS VIVONS EN MARGE… | [in blue] T.E. LAWRENCE | [b/w photo of Lawrence] | [in blue] LA MATRICE | [in red] PAR L'AUTEUR DES SEPT PILIERS DE LA SAGESSE | [pub. series device]. On spine: [series device] | [running up within long oval, author's name in blue, title in red] T.E. LAWRENCE LA MATRICE | [at foot across 1558 | [star]. On back cover: [photo of Lawrence in service uniform before World War I]. All edges pale green.

Notes Another impression, 3e trimestre 1971, identical to above. Le Livre de Poche Series.

Copies AC, Cal.

A184 T.E. LAWRENCE, La Matrice, Gallimard, 1979

Third French Edition

T.E. Lawrence | La matrice | Journal du Dépôt | de la Royal Air Force | *(août–décembre 1922)* | suivi de notes ultérieures | *par le simple soldat Ross,* | *matricule 352 087* | *Traduit de l'anglais* | par Étiemble | Gallimard

Collation 19.1 × 12.5 cm: guillotined sheets glued to covers, [1–9], 10–251, [15].

Contents Pp.[1–2] blank, [3] series title, [4] blank, [5] title page, [6] copyright statement, [7] dedication, [8] blank, [9]–14 preface by A.W. Lawrence, [15] section title, [16] blank, [17]–248 text, [249]–251 note by translator, [1] blank, [2–4] contents, [5] blank, [6] list of author's works, [7] blank, [8–9] list of works in series, [10] printer's colophon, [11–15] blank.

RT On verso *La matrice*. On recto [according to section].

Text 20 lines, 8.3 (8.5) × 9.4 cm.

Paper White, wove, unwatermarked, all edges trimmed, sheets bulk 2.3 cm.

Binding White paper covers. On front cover: [in pink] T.E. | [in pink] Lawrence | [in blue] La | [in blue] matrice | L'IMAGINAIRE | [pink rectangle] | GALLIMARD. On spine: [running up, in pink] T.E. Lawrence [title in blue] La matrice | [running across at bottom] L'IMAGINAIRE | [pink rectangle] | GALLIMARD | 50. On back cover: [extract from text of book].

Notes Collection L'Imaginaire Series.

Copies AC, Cal.

A185 T.E. LAWRENCE, Unter Dem Prägestock, List, 1955

First German Edition

T.E. LAWRENCE | UNTER DEM PRÄGESTOCK | THE MINT | [pub. device] | PAUL LIST VERLAG MÜNCHEN

Collation   21.2 × 13 cm: [1–13]⁸ [14]¹⁰ [15]⁸, 122 leaves, pp.[1–8], 9–242, [2].

Contents   Pp.[1] bastard title, [2] blank, [3] title page, [4] original title, note by translator, designer's credit, copyright statement, printer's, binder's credits, [5] dedication, [6] blank, [7–8] contents, 9–18 foreword for German edition, 19–242 text, [1–2] publisher's ads.

Text   20 lines, 9 × 9.1 cm. Set in Garamond Antiqua Old Style.

Paper   White, wove, unwatermarked, all edges trimmed, sheets bulk 2.5 cm.

Binding   Black cloth. On front cover: [within gilt bars of various lengths, one bar for each line] T·E· | LAWRENCE | UNTER DEM | PRÄGESTOCK | [one blank bar]. On spine: [same five bars] ·T·E· | LAWRENCE | UNTER DEM | PRÄGE/ | STOCK | [at foot, gilt] [pub. device]. On back cover: [same five bars solid]. T.e. yellow. White head and tail bands.

Published at   15.80 DM.

Copies   AC, Cal.

A186   T.E. LAWRENCE, L'Aviere Ross, Garzanti, 1969

First Italian Edition

T.E. Lawrence | L'aviere Ross | Diario del periodo trascorso al deposito della RAF tra | l'agosoto e il | discembre del 1922, con annotazioni successive | Garzanti

Collation   18.9 × 12.5 cm: guillotined sheets glued to covers, pp.[1–6], 7–242, [6].

Contents   Pp.[1] series titles, [2] blank, [3] title page, [4] issue statement, translator's credit, original title, copyright statement, [5] dedication, [6] blank, 7–[11] introduction by A.W. Lawrence, [12] blank, [13] section title, [14] blank, 15–242 text, [1–3] contents, [4–5] list of titles in series, [6] printer's colophon.

Text   20 lines, 9 × 9.5 cm.

Paper   White, wove, unwatermarked, all edges trimmed, sheets bulk 2 cm.

Binding   Pictorial paper, fabric backed. On front cover: [in blue] L'AVIERE | ROSS | [long red rule] | THOMAS EDWARD LAWRENCE | [long red rule] | [within divided rectangle] R | B. On spine: [in white running up] GARZANTI L'AVIERE ROSS LAWRENCE. On back cover: [blurb, list of titles in series] | [within blue rectangle, in white] L. 850 | Copertina di | Fulvio Bianconi.

Published at Lire 850, July 1969.

Copies AC.

A187 T.E. LAWRENCE, Slagen till slant, Bonnier, 1955

First Swedish Edition

T.E. LAWRENCE | Slagen | till slant | *En dagbok från RAF-depån mellan augusti och | december 1922 jämte senare anteckningar av* | 352087 A/c ROSS | [long rule] | STOCKHOLM | ALBERT BONNIERS FÖRLAG

Collation 28.5 × 16 cm: [1] – 12⁸ 13¹⁰ 14⁸, 114 leaves, pp.[1–6], 7–226, [2].

Contents Pp.[1] bastard title, [2] blank, [3] title page, [4] translator's, printer's credits, issue statement, [5] dedication, [6] blank, 7–221 text, [222] blank, 223 postscript, [224] blank, [225]–226 contents [2] blank.

RT On verso *Slagen till slant*. On recto [according to chapter].

Typography and paper \$ 1,4 signed Lawrence, 5 Lawrence (13* Lawrence, 13† Lawrence).

Text 20 lines, 10.5 (10.7) × 11.3 cm.

Paper White, wove, unwatermarked, untrimmed, sheets bulk 1.5 cm.

Binding White paper covers. On front cover: [in red] T.E. LAWRENCE | (352087 A/C ROSS) | SLAGEN | TILL SLANT | [rule] | BONNIERS. On spine: [in red] T.E. | LAW- | RENCE | · | Slagen | till | slant. On back cover: 19:50, inb. 24:50.

Published at Kr. 19:50, bound Kr. 24:50.

Copies AC, Cal.

Crusader Castles

This was the first of the Golden Cockerel volumes of Lawrence's 'literary remains' to be published after his death. Lawrence gathered much of the material for this work on a solitary walking trek in the Near East in the summer of 1909. Lawrence's thesis in this work is counter to the accepted view that improvements in military architecture had been brought back from the Near East by the Crusaders: he believed rather that the improvements had been developed in Europe and taken by Crusaders to the Near East. This is a discussion not yet entirely settled.

Volume I contains Lawrence's Oxford thesis of 1910, the first written of his longer works. Volume II contains letters written to his family about military architecture accompanied by drawings made by Lawrence, together with photographs.

A188   T.E. LAWRENCE, Crusader Castles, Golden Cockerel, 1936 (Vol. I)

First English Edition

[All in red] CRUSADER | CASTLES | BY | T.E. LAWRENCE | THE | GOLDEN COCKEREL PRESS | 1936 | I. | THE THESIS

Collation   25 × 19 cm: π^1 a–b^4 c–d^8 e–g^{10} h^6 x^1, 62 leaves, pp.[2], [1–2], 3–18, [2], 19–20, [4], 21–22, [2], 23–24, [2], 25–26, [2], 27–30, [2],,31–32, [4], 33–34, [2], 35–36, [4], 37–38, [2], 39–40, [4], 41–42, [2], 43–44, [4], 45–46, [2], 47–48, [4], 49–50, [2], 51–52, [4], 53–54, [2], 55–56, [14], [2]. With the exception of first and last leaves, all unpaged leaves are illustrations.

Contents   Prp.[1–2] blank, pp.[1] title page, [2] 'Printed and published in Great Britain by Christopher Sandford, | Francis J. Newbery, and Owen Rutter at the Golden Cockerel Press, | 10 Staple Inn, London, and completed on the 20th May 1936. The | edition is limited to 1000 numbered copies printed in Perpetua type | on British mould-made paper. Number ', 3–5 preface, [6–7] facsimile of mss. pages of original, [8] blank, 9–10 contents, 11 note, 12 map, 13–56 text and illustrations, [1–14] illustrations, [1–2] blank. Two maps in linen pocket loosely inserted at back. Maps measure 48.5 × 36 cm.

Plates   Two fold maps in linen backed envelope loosely inserted inside rear cover.

Typography and paper $ 1 signed e.

Text   20 lines, 9.8 × 12.7 cm, set in 14pt Perpetua.

Paper   Mould-made paper, watermarked, top edge trimmed, sheets bulk 2.2 cm.

Binding   Half red morocco 16 d. Red, cream buckram boards 73 p.OY. On spine: CRUSADER | CASTLES | T.E. | LAWRENCE | [pub. device], bound by S. & S. [stamped inside front cover]. T.e. gilt. Red and yellow head and tail bands.

Published at   £3 3s, 20 May 1936.

Notes   Limited to 1000 copies for sale and 35 additional unnumbered copies.
   Another state; orange buckram 38 dr. O. [Library issue?]; 75 copies of this volume issued thus, presented to libraries and family. The word 'Number' is omitted from colophon.

Copies   AC, Cal, H, UT, NYPL.

A189   T.E. LAWRENCE, Crusader Castles, Golden Cockerel, 1936 (Vol. II)

First English Edition

[All in red] CRUSADER | CASTLES | BY | T.E. LAWRENCE | THE GOLDEN COCKEREL PRESS | 1936 | II. | THE | LETTERS

Collation   25 × 19 cm: π^1 [a]^4 b^4 c^6 d^4 e^8+1 f^8 g^{10}+1 h^6, 52 leaves, pp.[2], [1–4], 5–18, [2], 19–22, [2], 23–34, [2], 35–40, [8], 41–48, [2], 49–50, [4], 51–52, [4], 53–54, [4], 55–56, [2], 57–60, [4], 61–62, [2].

Contents   Prp.[1–2] blank, pp.[1] blank, [2] frontispiece, [3] title page, [4] 'Printed and published in Great Britain by Christopher Sandford, | Francis J. Newbery, and Owen Rutter at the Golden Cockerel Press | 10 Staple Inn, London, and completed on the 1st August 1936. The | edition is limited to 1000 copies printed in Perpetua type on British | mould-made paper.', 5–62 text and illustrations, [1–2] blank.

Typography and paper $ 1 signed e.

Text   20 lines, 9.8 × 12.7 cm. Set in 14pt Perpetua.

Paper   Mould-made paper, watermarked, top edge trimmed, sheets bulk 8 mm.

Binding   Half red morocco 16 d. Red, cream buckram boards 73 p.OY. On spine: CRUSADER | CASTLES | T.E. | LAWRENCE | [pub. device]. Bound by S & S.[stamped inside front cover]. T.e. gilt. Red and yellow head and tail bands.

Published at   £2 2s, August 1936.

Notes   Limited to 1000 copies for sale and 35 additional unnumbered copies. Vol. II printed two months after Vol. I.

Copies   AC, Cal, H, UT, Ho.

A190   T.E. LAWRENCE, Crusader Castles, Michael Haag, 1986

Second English Edition

CRUSADER CASTLES | BY | T.E. LAWRENCE | [outline letters] MICHAEL HAAG

Collation   24.5 × 19 cm: [1–26]^8, 112 leaves, pp.[1–4], 5–224.

Contents   Pp.[1] title page, [2] issue statement, preface, photos, cover design credits, pub. address, ISBN, [3] section title, [4] photo, 5–[13] preface, [14–17] maps, [18–19] photos of original mss. of table of contents, [20] blank, 21–22 contents, 23 explanation of references in the text, [24] maps, 25–[132] text of thesis, [133] section title, [134] illus., 135–224 text of letters.

Plates All illustrations in same gatherings as text, paginated.

Text 20 lines, 9.8 × 12.7 cm.

Paper White, wove, unwatermarked, all edges trimmed, sheets bulk 2.7 cm.

Binding Blue cloth 169 s.g B. On spine: [gilt, running down] CRUSADER CASTLES T.E. Lawrence | [across at foot, outline letters] MICHAEL | HAAG.

Published at £9.95 [$19.95].

Notes New edition with added illustrations and text. New preface by Michael Haag. Another issue paperback. On front cover: [all in white] CRUSADER | CASTLES | [long rule] | T.E. Lawrence | [photo of Lawrence superimposed on photo of Krac des Chevaliers]. On spine: [in white, running down] CRUSADER CASTLES T.E. Lawrence | [across at foot] [pub device] | [outline letters] MICHAEL | [outline letters] HAAG. On back cover: [5-paragraph blurb, publisher's name, ISBN numbers, and prices].

Copies AC, Cal.

A191 T.E. LAWRENCE, Crusader Castles, Doubleday, Doran, 1937

First American Edition

CRUSADER CASTLES | *THE LETTERS* | by | T.E. LAWRENCE | With a Preface by | MRS [sic] LAWRENCE | DOUBLEDAY, DORAN & COMPANY, INC. | *Garden City, New York* | MCMXXXVII

Collation 23 × 15.4 cm: [1]¹⁶, 16 leaves, pp.[2], 1–29, [1].

Contents Prp.[1] title page, [2] printer's credit, copyright, issue statements, pp.1–29 text, [1] blank.

RT On both verso and recto CRUSADER CASTLES.

Text 20 lines, 6.2 (6.5) × 11 cm.

Paper White, laid, watermarked, all edges trimmed, sheets bulk 3 mm.

Binding Two metal staples through centre gutter.

Notes Issued in an edition of 56 copies, 50 of which were for sale. Text of Vol. I only of English edition reprinted here. Issued to protect US copyright.

Copies AC, Cal, H, UT.

A Letter From T.E. Lawrence to His Mother

Three letters from Lawrence to his mother were published by the Corvinus Press in an edition limited to just 30 copies. As with all the Corvinus Press items, experimentation with format, paper, and type is the keynote.

A192 T.E. LAWRENCE, A Letter from T.E. Lawrence to His Mother, Corvinus, 1936

First English Edition

A LETTER | FROM | T.E. LAWRENCE | TO HIS | MOTHER

Collation 29 × 23 cm: [1–7]², [1]¹ [8–10]², 21 leaves, unpaged, includes paste down end papers.

Contents Leaves [1–3] blank, [4] title page, [5–12] text, [13] blank, [14–16] photos with tissue guards [17] blank, [18] '24 copies of this letter have been printed | for Mrs. Lawrence who received the | original from her son, at that time tour- | ing the castles and churches of France. | 12 copies numbered 1 to 12 have been | printed on Parchment Substitute paper, | and 12 copies numbered 13 to 24 have | been printed on Barcham Green | "Medway"paper. | This copy is number [mss. number] | Completed at the Corvinus Press during | August, 1936 Laus Deo', [19–21] blank.

Text 20 lines, 10.2 × 11.9 cm.

Paper Parchment substitute, white, laid, unwatermarked, top edge trimmed, sheets bulk 3 mm.

Binding Mottled paper covered boards, tan cloth spine 79 l. gy y Br. On spine: [gilt, running down] LETTER FROM T.E.L. TO HIS MOTHER. T.e. gilt. Boxed in black cloth slip case, as issued?

Published at August 1936.

Notes Limited to 24 copies. Nos. 1–12 parchment substitute, 13–24 Medway paper. Photos taken at Chartres by the author.

Copies Cal, H, Ca.

Letters From T.E. Shaw to Viscount Carlow

Another of the many fine press editions of Lawrence's writing which poured forth in the late 1930s. This Corvinus Press item is extremely limited. Only 17 copies were produced. Of the three letters contained in it, two appear in Garnett, *The Letters* (nos. 536 and 558).

A193   T.E. LAWRENCE, Letters From T.E. Shaw to Viscount Carlow, Corvinus Press, September 1936

First English Edition

LETTERS | FROM | T.E. SHAW | TO | VISCOUNT | CARLOW

Collation   24.5 × 16 cm: [1–5]⁴, 20 leaves, unpaged.

Contents   Pp.[1] blank, [2] title page, [3] blank, [4] – [14] text, [15] blank, [16] *Of this edition 17 copies have been issued, | hand set in 14-pt. Ratio Latein Kursiv type, | and printed on a hand press. All copies | are numbered and distributed as follows: | 2 copies on Parchment Substitute numbered | 1 and 2; 2 copies on Winchmore Blue | paper numbered 3 and 4; 2 copies on | Thistledown paper numbered 5 and 6; and | 11 copies on Milbourn hand made paper | numbered 7 to 17. None of these copies | are for sale. | Completed during September, 1936, at the | Corvinus Press. Laus Deo.,* [17–20] blank.

Text   10 lines, 7.3 × 9.4 cm, 14pt Ratio Latein Kursiv.

Paper   Buff, Milbourn handmade paper, watermarked, top edge trimmed, sheets bulk 5 mm.

Binding   Vellum. On front cover: [gilt] LETTERS | FROM | T.E. SHAW | TO | VISCOUNT | CARLOW. T.e. gilt. Two white silk ties. Boxed as issued.

Published at   September 1938.

Notes   Seventeen copies: copies 1–2 on parchment substitute paper, 3–4 Winchmore Blue paper, 5–6 Thistledown paper, 7–17 Milbourn handmade paper. Bindings of various coloured vellums.

Copies   Cal, UT.

1937

Diary of T.E. Lawrence, 1911

After graduating from Oxford with a First in History, Lawrence was employed, through the influence of D.G. Hogarth, at an archaeological dig in Northern Syria at Carchemish. During the 1911 'off-season' Lawrence went on a solitary journey on foot through Syria. The diary he kept on that journey was published by the Corvinus Press in 1937. This was the most ambitious and handsome volume published by the Corvinus Press, in an edition limited to 203 copies. The text was reprinted in *Oriental Assembly* (A220–A225). Some portions of the original mss. have never been published.

A194 T.E. LAWRENCE, Diary of T.E. Lawrence, Corvinus, 1937

First English Edition

THE DIARY | OF //T //E | LAWRENCE | MCMXI

Collation 29.5 × 23.5 cm: 1⁴ 2² 3⁴ 4² 5–9⁴ 10–11⁴ 12–14² 15–18⁴ 60 leaves, unpaged, includes paste down end sheets.

Contents Leaves [1–5] blank, [6] title page, [7] title note, [8] note concerning illustrations, [9] note on title, [10] note on text, [11] dedication, [12] half title, [13–31] text of diary, [32] blank, [33] section title, [34] blank, [35–41] text of letters, [42–53] illustrations, [54] 'Of this diary 203 copies have been printed, all of | which have been numbered. 150 copies only are for | sale. The type for the text is 18-point Bible Centaur. | The papers used are hand made by J.B. Green & | Son. 30 copies, numbered 1 to 30, have been printed on 'Medway' paper, and 130 copies, | numbered 71 to 200, have been printed on Parchment | substitute paper. There are also 3 copies, lettered A, | B, and C, printed on Papier d'Auvergne, green hand- | made parchment paper, and grey Japanese paper, | which are not for sale. | This is number | [mss. #] | Completed at the Corvinus Press during June 1937 | Laus Deo.

Text 20 lines, 14.3 × 11.7 cm, set in 18pt Bible Centaur.

Paper Parchment substitute paper, mould-made, watermarked, top edge trimmed, sheets bulk 1 cm.

Binding Mottled boards, brown leather spine. On spine: [gilt, running up] [cut] | THE DIARY OF T.E. LAWRENCE | [cut]. T.e. gilt, parchment corners, boxed as issued. Tissue guards before each plate.

Published at June 1937.

Notes The copies numbered 1–30 are the same as described above except as follows: [Binding]: Full white vellum. On front cover: [gilt] THE DIARY KEPT | BY T.E. LAWRENCE | WHILE TRAVELLING | IN ARABIA DURING | 1911. On spine: [running up, gilt] THE DIARY OF T.E. LAWRENCE. On back cover: [gilt cut of bird with worm in beak]. T.e. gilt, white silk ties.
  Reprinted in *Oriental Assembly* (1939).
  Three letters to his mother reprinted in *Home Letters* (1954).
  It is probable that three copies on special papers were printed.
  Another copy no. 13 (one of thirty on 'Canute' paper: [Binding]: full brown crushed morocco 41 deep r Br. On covers: [gilt rule along all outer edges. On spine: [raised bands with single gilt rules]. Green head and tail bands.

Copies AC, Cal, H, UT, Ho.

A195   T.E. LAWRENCE, The Diary of T.E. Lawrence, Doubleday, Doran, 1937

First American Edition

THE DIARY | OF T.E. LAWRENCE | [pub. device] | DOUBLEDAY, DORAN & COMPANY, INC. | *Garden City, New York* | MCMXXXVII

Collation   22.8 × 14.8 cm: [1]¹⁶, 16 leaves, pp.[1–6], 1–25, [1].

Contents   Prp.[1] title page, [2] 'PRINTED AT THE *Country Life Press*, GARDEN CITY, N.Y., U.S.A. | COPYRIGHT, 1937 | BY ARNOLD WALTER LAWRENCE | ALL RIGHTS RESERVED | FIRST EDITION', [3] note on text, [4] blank, [5] poem, [6] blank, pp.1–25 text, [1] blank.

RT   On both verso and recto THE DIARY OF T.E. LAWRENCE.

Text   20 lines, 7.7 (8) × 10.1 cm.

Paper   White, laid, watermarked, all edges trimmed, sheets bulk 3 mm.

Binding   None. Sheets fastened with two metal staples.

Notes   Issued in an edition of 56 copies, 50 of which are for sale, to secure American copyright.

Copies   AC, Cal, H, UT.

Two Arabic Folk Tales

A translation by Lawrence of two Arabic children's stories. It appears that this might have been part of 1911 language exercises by Lawrence who was working on improvement of his Arabic during this period. This is the only published text of these translations.

A196   T.E. LAWRENCE, trans. Two Arabic Folk Tales, Corvinus Press, 1937

First English Edition

[Cut] TWO ARABIC | FOLK TALES | Translated by | T.E. LAWRENCE | [decorative cut by Kennington, also used in *Diary 1911* (A194)]

Collation   33 × 23 cm: [1–6]⁴, (6 [–4] =5), 23 leaves, unpaged.

Contents   Leaf [1] paste down end paper, blank, [2–3] blank, [4] title page, [5–13] text of first tale, [14] title page, [15–20] text of second tale, [21] '30 copies of this book have | been printed on Millburn | hand-made paper and set | by hand in 36-pt. Tiemann | Type. One copy lettered | "A" on a Japanese yellow | paper is reserved for the | printer. All copies are |

numbered. | This is number | Completed during Decem- | ber, 1937, at the Corvinus | Press. Laus Deo.', [21] note, [1–3] blank, paste down end paper.

Text 10 lines, 13.5 × 15.1 cm, set in 36pt Tiemann.

Paper White, laid, watermarked, top edge trimmed, sheets bulk 5 mm.

Binding Brown buckram 56 deep Br. On front cover: [within gilt frame of single rule] TWO ARABIC FOLK | TALES | T.E. LAWRENCE. Spine blank. On back cover: [within single rule frame, gilt, pub. device]. T.e. gilt. Boxed as issued.

Published at December 1937.

Notes Thirty copies.
   Might have been translated by Lawrence as an Arabic exercise while in the Near East prior to the First World War.

Copies Cal, H, UT.

An Essay on Flecker

Written in 1925 with the intention of publication in a periodical, this article did not appear in print until 1937 when it was issued in this very limited edition of 30 copies. The poet James Elroy Flecker had been a friend of Lawrence's in Beirut before the war. None of the three appearances of this essay have been in trade editions. In addition to the two issues already mentioned, the essay is also contained in *Men In Print* (A229).

A198   T.E. LAWRENCE, An Essay on Flecker, Corvinus Press, 1937

First English Edition

AN ESSAY ON FLECKER | By T.E. Lawrence

Collation 29.3 × 20 cm: [1–5]⁴, 20 leaves, including pastedown end papers, leaves printed on rectos only.

Contents Leaves 1 blank, pastedown end paper, 2–5 blank, 6 title page, 7–14 text, 15 colophon, '30 copies of this book have been | printed on J.B. Green unsized | parchment paper. The setting of | the text is in 14 pt. Pastonschi | type. All copies are numbered. | Completed at the Corvinus Press | during the Coronation week of | King George the Sixth. | May, 1937. Laus Deo.', 16–19 blank, 20 pastedown end paper.

Text 20 lines, 9.8 × 7.6 cm, set in 14pt Pastonschi.

Paper J.B. Green unsized parchment, watermarked, 'J.B. Green', t.e. trimmed, sheets bulk 3 mm.

Binding White buckram 92 y. White. On front cover: [gilt, swash] AN ESSAY ON FLECKER | By T.E. Lawrence. T.e. gilt.

Published at May 1937.

Notes Limited to 30 copies, copies numbered 1–4 bound in full vellum with white silk ties.

One copy 'A' on white Japanese paper. Bound in white pigskin. On front cover: [within single rule frame] *AN ESSAY ON FLECKER* | By T.E. LAWRENCE. On spine: [two single rules] | [running up] AN ESSAY ON FLECKER | By T.E. LAWRENCE | [two single rules] | [cut] | [single rule].

One copy 'B' on papier de Marais. Smaller format 25.5 × 17.8 cm. Cream leather. On front cover: *AN ESSAY ON FLECKER* | *By T.E. LAWRENCE.* On spine: [two single rules] | AN | ESSAY | ON | FLECKER | BY | T.E. | LAWRENCE | [two single rules] | [cut]. Watered silk end papers. Title set in smaller face to correspond to reduced format.

Reprinted in *Men in Print* (1943).

Copies Cal, UT.

A199   T.E. LAWRENCE, An Essay on Flecker, Doubleday, Doran, 1937

First American Edition

AN ESSAY ON FLECKER | By | T.E. LAWRENCE | [pub. device] | DOUBLEDAY, DORAN & COMPANY, INC. | *Garden City, New York* | MCMXXXVII

Collation 22.9 × 15.2 cm: [1]⁴, 4 leaves, pp.[2], 1–4, [2].

Contents Prp.[1] title page, [2] printer's credit, copyright, issue statements, pp.1–4 text, [1–2] blank.

RT On both verso and recto AN ESSAY ON FLECKER.

Text 20 lines, 7.7 (7.9) × 10.2 cm.

Paper White, wove, watermarked, 'Utopian', all edges trimmed, sheets bulk 1 mm.

Binding Stapled with two metal staples in centre gutter.

Notes Fifty-six copies were printed to secure American copyright. In a letter dated 29 January 1938 A.W. Lawrence states that he requested 60 copies and thinks that 70 copies were printed.

Copies AC, Cal, H, UT.

Faisals Aufgebot

Paul List, the German publisher of many of Lawrence's works, published a small-format volume of extracts from *Seven Pillars of Wisdom*. It was reprinted in 1963 in an even smaller format.

A200   T.E. LAWRENCE, Faisals Aufgebot, List, [1937?]

First German Edition

T.E. Lawrence | Faisals Aufgebot | [pub. device] | Paul List Verlag Leipzig

Collation   18.8 × 12.8 cm: 1–4⁸, 32 leaves, pp.[1–2], 3–63, [1].

Contents   Pp.[1] title page, [2] translator's credit, copyright statement, printer's credit, 3–63 text, [1] list of titles in series.

Typography and paper $ 1 signed 2,2* (first gathering is only 1*).

Text   20 lines, 9 × 8.2 cm.

Paper   White, wove, heavy, unwatermarked, all edges trimmed, sheets bulk 6 mm.

Binding   Brown patterned paper covered boards. On front cover: [on white paper patch, within single rule frame] T.E. | LAWRENCE | [pub. device] | Faisals Aufgebot. On spine: [on white paper patch, within single rule frame, running up] Lawrence, Aufgebot | [across, at bottom] 11.

Published at   75 pfennig.

Notes   Extracted from *Seven Pillars of Wisdom*.

Copies   AC.

A201   T.E. LAWRENCE, Faisals Aufgebot, Reclam, 1963

Second German Edition

T.E. LAWRENCE | FAISALS AUFGEBOT | MIT EINEM NACHWORT | VON SCHROERS | PHILLIP RECLAM JUN. STUTTGART

Collation   15.4 × 9.7 cm: guillotined sheets, 32 leaves, pp.[1–2], 3–61, [62], [2].

Contents   Pp.[1] title page, [2] issue statement, 3–54 text, 55–[62] postscript, [1] chronology of T.E. Lawrence, [2] pub. ads.

Text   20 lines, 6.7 × 7.2 cm, set in Petit Garamond-Antiqua.

Paper   White, wove, unwatermarked, all edges trimmed, sheets bulk 2 mm.

Binding   Buff paper covers. On front cover: T.E. LAWRENCE | FAISALS |
AUFGEBOT | [thick rule] | RECLAM. On spine: [running down] [star]
LAWRENCE Faisals Aufgebot 8048 [star]. On back cover: [pub. device].

Notes   Extract from *Seven Pillars of Wisdom*.
   Universal Bibliothek No. 8048.

Copies   AC, Cal.

1938

The Letters of T.E. Lawrence

E.M. Forster first attempted editing the letters for publication, but gave up
the effort. It was then undertaken by Garnett (Howard, p.168). This edition
by David Garnett in 1938 is the major collection, rivalled and supplemented
only by the *Home letters of T.E. Lawrence and His Brothers* (1954). Minor
corrections were made during the run of the first impression and thus it
appears in two states. The extent of his interests and acquaintances is to be
found in this volume. A reprint of this collection by Spring Books (1964)
contains textual corrections and an introduction by Liddell Hart which
deals with the Aldington controversy.

A202   T.E. LAWRENCE, The Letters of T.E. Lawrence, Cape, 1938

First English Edition

THE LETTERS | of | [in red] T.E. LAWRENCE | Edited by | DAVID
GARNETT | [pub. device] | LONDON | JONATHAN CAPE 30 BEDFORD
SQUARE | & AT TORONTO

Collation   22.9 × 15.5 cm: [A]^8 B–ZZ^8 2A–2K^8, 488 leaves, pp.[1–6],
7–896.

Contents   Pp.[1–2] blank, [3] bastard title, [4] blank, [5] title page, [6] issue
statement, printer's, binder's, papermaker's credits, 7–24 contents, 25–27
list of recipients of letters, [28] blank, 29 illustrations, [30] blank, 31–32
preface, 33–34 note on the text, [35] section title, [36] blank, 37–41
introduction to part one, [42] blank, 43–873 text, [874] blank, 875 section
title, [876] blank, 877–896 index.

RT   On verso LETTERS OF T.E. LAWRENCE. On recto [according to
section].

Plates   Sixteen photos and drawings, tipped in, printed on one side only, following pp.4, 38, 102, 168, 233, 244, 409, 439, 495, 516, 532, 614, 619, 730, 840, 858; fold maps following pp.63, 185.

Typography and paper $ 1 signed B.

Text 20 lines, 8.1 (8.3) × 11 cm.

Paper Cream, wove, unwatermarked, top and fore edge trimmed, sheets bulk 4 cm.

Binding Brown buckram 57 l. Br. On spine: [gilt] THE | LETTERS | OF | T.E. | LAWRENCE | [cut] | [pub. device]. T.e. brown.

Published at 25s, November 1939.

Notes First state of first edition: letter on p.495 is signed T.E.L.; p.182, 9 lines from bottom, reads 'Baltic'.
   Second state: p.495 corrected signature T.E.S.; p.182 'Balkan'.
   Second impression, November 1938, same as above with dull unpolished buckram. Second line of footnote on p.495 reads: 'It differs from the version printed in *Lawrence and the Arabs*, which incorporated material provided by Lawrence'. Former sentence in first two states reads: 'It differs materially from the version printed by Graves in *Lawrence and the Arabs*'.
   Third impression, December 1938, as above except that the binding is 51 deep O.
   Dust wrapper of one copy bears statement First Cheaper Edition 15s.

Copies AC, Cal, UT, Ho.

A203 T.E. LAWRENCE, The Letters of T.E. Lawrence, Spring Books, 1964

Second English Edition

THE LETTERS | of | T.E. LAWRENCE | Edited by | DAVID GARNETT | With a foreword by | CAPTAIN B.H. LIDDELL HART | SPRING BOOKS · LONDON

Collation 21.6 × 13.5 cm: guillotined sheets, 448 leaves, pp.[1–4], 5–896.

Contents Pp.[1] bastard title, [2] frontispiece, [3] title page, [4] issue statement, printer's credit, 5–22 contents, 23–25 names of recipients of letters, 26–30 foreword, 31–32 preface, 33–34 note on the text, [35] section title, [36] map, 37–41 introduction to part one, [42] blank, 43–873 text, [874] blank, [875] section title, [876] blank, 877–896 index.

RT On verso LETTERS OF T.E. LAWRENCE. On recto [according to section].

Text 20 lines, 9 (9.1) × 11 cm.

Paper White, newsprint, wove, unwatermarked, all edges trimmed, sheets bulk 4.3 cm.

Binding   Brown orange 54 br. O simulated cloth covered boards. On spine: [gilt, running down] *The letters of* | T.E. LAWRENCE | *of Arabia* [across at bottom] SPRING BOOK.

Notes   Contains some corrections and additonal footnotes. New foreword for this edition by Liddell Hart.

Copies   AC, Cal.

A204   T.E. LAWRENCE, The Letters of T.E. Lawrence, Doubleday, Doran, 1939

First American Edition

THE LETTERS OF | T.E. LAWRENCE | Edited by | DAVID GARNETT | [pub. device] | New York | DOUBLEDAY, DORAN & COMPANY, INC. | MCMXXXIX

Collation   23 × 15.3 cm: [1–28]^{16}, 448 leaves, pp.[1–6], 7–896.

Contents   Pp.[1–2] blank, [3] bastard title, [4] blank, [5] title page, [6] printer's credit, issue code (CL) copyright, issue statements, 7–24 contents, 25–27 names of recipients of letters, [28] blank, 29 illustrations, [30] blank, 31–32 preface, 33–34 note on the text, [35] section title, [36] blank, 37–873 text, [874] blank, [875] section title, [876] blank, 877–896 index.

RT   On verso LETTERS OF T.E. LAWRENCE. On recto [according to section].

Plates   Sixteen photos and drawings on coated paper, printed on one side only, tipped in following pp.4, 44, 104, 168, 232, 244, 408, 440, 496, 516, 532, 616, 620, 728, 840, 856; fold maps following pp.64, 184.

Text   20 lines, 9.2 (9.3) × 11 cm.

Paper   White, wove, unwatermarked, all edges trimmed, sheets bulk 3.8 cm.

Binding   Blue cloth 187 d. gy. B. On front cover: [blind stamped, portrait head of T.E. Lawrence]. On spine: [gilt] THE | LETTERS OF | T.E. LAWRENCE | EDITED BY | DAVID GARNETT | [cut] | DOUBLEDAY DORAN. Buff end papers. T.e. blue. Red and yellow head and tail bands.

Published at $4.00.

Copies   AC, Cal, UT.

A205   T.E. LAWRENCE, Cartas de T.E. Lawrence, Sur, 1944

First Argentine Edition

CARTAS | de | T.E. LAWRENCE | *Reunidas por David Garnett* | [pub. device] | [in red] SUR | BUENOS AIRES

Collation   12.3 × 15 cm: [1–57]⁸ [58]⁶, 462 leaves, pp.[I–VII], VIII–XXV, [XXVI–XXVII], XXVIII–XXX, [XXXI–XXXII], [1–2], [1], 2–889, [1].

Contents   Prp.[I–II] blank, [III] bastard title, [IV] blank, [V] title page, [VI] original title, translator's credit, issue statement, [VII]–XXV contents, itemised list of letters, [XXVI] blank, [XXVII]–XXX list of recipients of letters, [XXXI] illustrations, [XXXII] blank, [1]–2 preface, [3]–4 note on text by David Garnett, [5] section title, [6] blank, [7]–862 text, [863]–889 index, [1] colophon.

RT   On verso CARTAS DE T.E. LAWRENCE. On recto [according to section].

Plates   Sixteen b/w photos on coated paper following pp.IV, 8, 72, 136, 200, 212, 380, 412, 470, 496, 512, 592, 598, 712, 828, 846; fold maps following pp.32, 152.

Text   20 lines, 8 (8.2) × 10.9 cm.

Paper   Buff, wove, unwatermarked, all edges trimmed, sheets bulk 6 cm.

Binding   Blue grey cloth 189 b. White. On front cover: [gilt, crossed swords as on first English trade edition of 1935 but without text]. On spine: [gilt] CARTAS | DE | T.E. LAWRENCE | SUR | BUENOS AIRES. Lavender and white head and tail bands.

Copies   Cal.

A206   T.E. LAWRENCE, Lettres de T.E. Lawrence, Gallimard, 1948

First French Edition (Limited)

Lettres | de | *T.E. LAWRENCE* | *traduites d'après l'édition anglaise par* | *ÉTIEMBLE et YASSU GAUCLÈRE* | *et enrichies de quatre lettres inédites* | [swash] nrf | GALLIMARD

Collation   22.5 × 14.2 cm: [1]⁸ 2–6⁸ [7]⁸ 8–53⁸, 424 leaves, pp.[i–vii], viii–x, [1]–184, [2], 185–186, [2], 187–834.

Contents   [i–ii] blank, [iii] bastard title, [iv] blank, [v] title page, [vi] *'Il a été tiré de cet ouvrage, sous la couverture de la collection* DU MONDE | ENTIER, cent cinquante-six exemplaires sur velin pur fil Lafuma Navarre, | dont cent cinquante numérotés de 1 à 150 et six, hors commerce, marques | A à F', copyright statement, [vii]–x translator's note, [1]–2 introduction, [3]–4 note on text, [5] section title, [6] blank, [7]–810 text, [811] section title, [812] blank, [813] list of plates, [814] blank, [815]–832 contents, [1] printer's colophon, [2] blank. Leaves between pp.184–185, 186–187 are maps, blank on verso.

RT   On both verso and recto LETTRES DE T.E. LAWRENCE.

Typography and paper $ 1 signed B.

Text   20 lines, 6.8 (6.9) × 9.9 cm.

Paper   Velin-purfil Lafuma Navarre, untrimmed, sheets bulk 4.5 cm.

Binding   Light weight grey paper 264 l. gray. On front cover: [letters form semi-circle] DU MONDE ENTIER | [red] LXXVI | [red] T.E. LAWRENCE | [cut] | [red] LETTRES | *Traduites d'après l'édition anglaise par* | ÉTIEMBLE ET YASSU GAUCLÈRE | *et enrichies de quatre lettres inédites* | [red, swash] nrf | GALLIMARD. On spine: DU MONDE | ENTIER | LXXVI | [red] LETTRES | par | T.E. LAWRENCE | [swash] nrf | GALLIMARD. On back cover: [list of titles in series].

Published at   December 1948.

Notes   One of 150 copies.

Copies   Cal.

A207   T.E. LAWRENCE, Lettres de T.E. Lawrence, Gallimard, 1948

First French Edition (Trade)

Lettres | de | T.E. LAWRENCE | traduites d'après l'édition par | ÉTIEMBLE et YASSU GAUCLERE | et enrichies de quatre lettres inédites | [swash] nrf | GALLIMARD | S.P.

Collation   22.5 × 14 cm: [1]⁸ 2–53⁸, 424 leaves, pp.[i–vii], viii–x, [1]–184, [2], 185–186, [2], 187–832, [2].

Contents   [i–ii] blank, [iii] bastard title, [iv] blank, [v] title page, [vi] issue, copyright statements, [vii]–x translator's note, [1]–2 introduction, [3]–4 note on text, [5] section title, [6] blank, [7]–810 text, [811] section title, [812] blank, [813] illustrations, [814] blank, [815]–832 contents, [1] printer's colophon, [2] blank.

RT   On both verso and recto LETTRES DE T.E. LAWRENCE.

Plates   Three plates, tipped in on coated paper, following pp.4, 38, 146.

Typography and paper $ 1 signed 2.

Text   20 lines, 6.7 (7) × 9.9 cm.

Paper   White, wove, unwatermarked, untrimmed, sheets bulk 5.5 cm.

Binding Tan paper covers. On front cover, [within triple rule frame, outer black, two inner red] *Lettres | de* | [in red] T.E. LAWRENCE | *traduites d'après l'édition anglaise par* | *ÉTIEMBLE et YASSU GAUCLÈRE* | *et enrichies de quatre lettres inédites* | [swash] nrf | GALLIMARD. On spine: [triple rule, one black, two red] | T.E. LAWRENCE | LETTRES | [swash] nrf | GALLIMARD | [triple rule, two red, one black]. On back cover: *S.P.* [within diamond] H | [within triple rules, one black, two red] [pub. list, ads in red and black].

Published at December 1948.

Notes 3ᵉ, i.e. 3rd impression, same as above, with following differences: on title page [below pub. name] *3ᵉ edition;* [Paper]: sheets bulk 5 cm; [Published at]: 1,150 fr.

Other issues, 9ᵉ and 10ᵉ, same as above, with similar differences noted for 3ᵉ; 10ᵉ published at 1,200 fr.

Copies AC, Cal.

A208   T.E. LAWRENCE, Selbstbildnis in Briefen, List, 1948

First German Edition

T.E. LAWRENCE | SELBSTBILDNIS | IN BRIEFEN | Herausgegeben von David Garnett | Deutsch von Hans Rothe | [pub. device] | PAUL LIST VERLAG MUNCHEN-LEIPZIG

Collation 21 × 13 cm: [1]⁸ 2–41⁸ 42⁴ x¹, 333 leaves, pp.[1–4], 5–662, [663–664], [2].

Contents Pp.[1] bastard title, [2] blank, [3] title page, [4] original title, issue statement, designer's credit, copyright statement, printer's, binder's credit, 5–6 foreword, 7–8 note on text, 9–657 text, [658] blank, 659–661 translator's note, [662] biographical note on T.E. Lawrence, [663] contents, [664] blank, [1–2] ads.

Typography and paper \$ 1,2 signed 2 Lawrence, Selbstbildnis, 2*.

Text 20 lines, 7.5 × 9.5 cm. Set in Garamond-Antiqua.

Paper White, wove, unwatermarked, all edges trimmed, sheets bulk 4 cm.

Binding Brown paper covered boards 63 l. br. Gy, black cloth spine. On front cover: [within frame of gilt single rules, swash] T.E. | [first letter swash] LAWRENCE | [next three lines swash] Selbstbildnis | in | Briefen. On spine: [gilt, within rectangle of single rules, swash] T.E. | [first letter swash] LAWRENCE | [next three lines swash] Selbstbildnis | in | Briefen | [pub. device]. T.e. yellow green.

Copies AC, Cal.

A209   T.E. LAWRENCE, Lettere di Thomas Edward Lawrence, Longanesi, 1942

First Italian Edition

LETTERE | DI | THOMAS EDWARD | LAWRENCE | [pub. device] | LONGANESI | EDITORE | ROMA

Collation   19.5 × 12.7 cm: [1]⁸ 2–23⁸, 184 leaves, pp.[1–8], 9–368.

Contents Pp.[1–2] blank, [3] series title, [4] blank, [5] title page, [6] copyright, issue statements, printer's credit, [7] section title, [8] blank, 9–14 preface, [15] section title, [16] blank, 17–362 text, [363–366] contents, [367] printer's colophon, [368] blank.

Typography and paper $ 1 signed 2 Lawrence.

Text   20 lines, 8.3 × 8.6 cm.

Paper   White, wove, unwatermarked, all edges trimmed, sheets bulk 2.5 cm.

Binding   Grey paper wrappers. On front cover: [in white] T.E. LAWRENCE | LETTERE DALL' ARABIA | [pub. device, in white]. On spine: [running up] LAWRENCE * LETTERE DALL' ARABIA. On back cover: [list of other titles in series].

Published at   30 Lire, 15 October 1942.

Notes   La Buona Societa, Biblioteca storica, v.2 .

Copies   Cal, LC.

T.E. Lawrence to His Biographer, Robert Graves
T.E. Lawrence to His Biographer, Liddell Hart

These volumes, published in editions of 500 each in both England and America, are remarkable documents showing Lawrence's intimate work with two of his biographers. The letters, manuscript commentary and corrections, reveal the nature of information Lawrence supplied and the interpretation he allowed the authors to derive from it. These volumes expose a process of biographical writing that is rarely documented.

A210   T.E. LAWRENCE, T.E. Lawrence to His Biographer, Robert Graves, Faber and Faber, 1938

First English Edition

[In brown] T.E. Lawrence | TO HIS BIOGRAPHER, | Robert Graves |

INFORMATION ABOUT HIMSELF IN THE FORM OF LETTERS, NOTES, AND ANSWERS TO QUESTIONS, | EDITED WITH A CRITICAL COMMENTARY. | [in brown] [cut] | FABER AND FABER LIMITED | 24 Russell Square | London

Collation 23 × 15.5 cm: π² [1–10]⁸ [11]¹⁰ [12]⁸, 100 leaves, pp.[1–2], [i–vi], vii–ix, [x], [1–2], 3–187, [1]; leaves with section titles not included.

Contents Prp.[1] blank, [2] *'This edition | is limited to 1,000 numbered and | signed copies for sale, of which 500 copies | are printed for Great Britain | This is number ',* [i] bastard title, [ii] blank, [iii] title page, [iv] copyright statement, printer's credit, [v] publisher's note, [vi] blank, vii–viii foreword, ix contents, [x] blank, pp.[1] section title, [2] blank, 3–187 text, [1] blank.

RT On verso T.E. LAWRENCE TO HIS BIOGRAPHER. On recto ROBERT GRAVES.

Plates Frontis. following prp.[ii].

Text 20 lines, 10.4 (10.6) × 11 cm.

Paper Cream, wove, unwatermarked, top edges trimmed, sheets bulk 1.6 cm.

Binding Red buckram 11 v. Red. On front cover: [within grey patch with triple gilt rule border] T.E. LAWRENCE | to his biographer | ROBERT GRAVES. On spine: [within grey patch in gilt] [triple rules] | T.E. | LAWRENCE | to his | biographer | ROBERT | GRAVES | [rule] | *Faber and | Faber.* T.e. gilt. Grey headband.

Notes Boxed as issued together with companion volume, *T.E. Lawrence to His Biographer, Liddell Hart;* "Limited to 1000 copies of which 500 are printed for Great Britain".

Copies AC, Cal, H, UT.

A211 T.E. LAWRENCE, T.E. Lawrence to His Biographer, Liddell Hart, Faber and Faber, 1938

First English Edition

[In brown] T.E. Lawrence | TO HIS BIOGRAPHER, | Liddell Hart | INFORMATION ABOUT HIMSELF, IN THE FORM | OF LETTERS, NOTES, ANSWERS TO QUESTIONS AND CONVERSATIONS. | [in brown] [cut] | FABER AND FABER LIMITED | 24 Russell Square | London

Collation 23 × 15.5 cm: π² [1–13]⁸ 14¹⁰ [15]⁸, 112 leaves, pp.[1–2], [i–vi], vii–viii, [ix–x], [1], 2–233, [1–3].

Contents Prp.[1] blank, [2] *'This edition | is limited to 1,000 numbered copies for sale, of which 500 copies | are printed for Great Britain | This is number ',* [i] bastard title, [ii] blank, [iii] title page, [iv] copyright statement, printer's credit, [v] pub. note, [vi] blank, vii–viii foreword, [ix] half title, [x] blank, pp.[1]–233 text, [1–3] blank.

RT On verso T.E. LAWRENCE TO HIS BIOGRAPHER. On recto LIDDELL HART.

Plates Two plates on coated paper, printed on one side only, following pp.[ii], 220.

Text 20 lines, 10.4 (10.6) × 11 cm.

Paper Cream, wove, unwatermarked, top edges trimmed, sheets bulk 2 cm.

Binding Grey cloth 23 d. r Gray. On front cover: [gilt, within red patch bordered by triple rule frame] T.E. LAWRENCE | to his biographer | LIDDELL HART. On spine: [gilt, within red patch] [triple rule] | T.E. | LAWRENCE | to his | biographer | LIDDELL | HART | [rule] | *Faber and* | *Faber.* T.e. gilt, red head band.

Notes Boxed as issued with companion volume, *T.E. Lawrence to His Biographer Robert Graves;* "Limited to 1000 copies 500 of which were printed for Great Britain".

Copies AC, Cal, H, UT.

A212 T.E. LAWRENCE, T.E. Lawrence to His Biographers, Faber, 1938

Publisher's Prospectus for First English Edition

[Within triple red rule frame] T.E. LAWRENCE | to his | biographers | LIDDELL HART | ROBERT GRAVES | *Information about himself, letters, notes and answers to questions* | *edited with his critical commentary* | FABER AND FABER

Collation 22 × 14.6 cm: single-fold leaflet, unpaged.

Contents Pp.[1] title, [2–3] text, [4] order form.

Paper Grey, laid, watermarked, all edges trimmed.

Published at Free advertising flyer.

Copies H.

A213   T.E. LAWRENCE, T.E. Lawrence to His Biographers, Cassell, 1963

Second English Edition

T.E. Lawrence | TO HIS BIOGRAPHERS | Robert Graves | AND | Liddell Hart | [pub. device] | CASSELL · LONDON

Collation   21.6 × 14 cm: [A]⁸ B–P¹⁶, 232 leaves, pp.[i–vi], vii–ix, [x], [1–2], 3–187, [1], [i], ii–iv, [1], 2–260, [2] (= 464 pp.).

Contents   Prp.[i] bastard title, [ii] blank, [iii] title page, [iv] issue, copyright statements, printer's credit, [v] half title, [vi] pub. device, vii–viii foreword, ix contents, [x] blank, pp.[1] section title, [2] blank, 3–187 text, [1] blank, prp.[i] half title, ii pub. note, iii–iv foreword, pp.[1]–233 text, [234] blank, 235–260 index, [1–2] blank.

RT   On verso T.E. LAWRENCE TO HIS BIOGRAPHER. On recto ROBERT GRAVES [LIDDELL HART].

Typography and paper $ 1 signed B.

Text   20 lines, 10 (10.1) × 10.5 cm.

Paper   White, wove, unwatermarked, all edges trimmed, sheets bulk 3 cm.

Binding   Brown cloth 57 l. Br. On spine: [gilt, running up] T.E. LAWRENCE | [across] TO HIS | BIOGRAPHERS | ROBERT | GRAVES | & | LIDDELL | HART | CASSELL.

Copies   AC, Cal, UT.

A214   T.E. LAWRENCE, T.E. Lawrence to His Biographer, Robert Graves, Doubleday, Doran, 1938

First American Edition

[In brown] T.E. Lawrence | TO HIS BIOGRAPHER, | Robert Graves, | INFORMATION ABOUT HIMSELF IN THE FORM | OF LETTERS, NOTES AND ANSWERS TO QUESTIONS, | EDITED WITH A CRITICAL COMMENTARY. | [in brown] [cut] | NEW YORK | Doubleday, Doran & Company, Inc. | MCMXXXVIII

Collation   23 × 15.5 cm: π² [1–10]⁸ [11]¹⁰ [12]⁸, 100 leaves, pp.[1–2], [i–vi], vii–ix, [x], [1–2], 3–187, [1]; leaves with section titles not included in pagination.

Contents   Prp.[1] blank, [2] 'This edition | is limited to 1,000 numbered and | signed copies for sale, of which 500 copies | are printed for the United States | This is number ', pp.[i] bastard title, [ii] blank, [iii] title page, [iv] copyright statement, printer's credit, [v] pub. note, [vi] blank, vii–viii foreword, ix contents, [x] blank, pp.[1] section title, [2] blank, 3–187 text, [1] blank.

RT   On verso T.E. LAWRENCE TO HIS BIOGRAPHER. On recto ROBERT GRAVES.

Text   20 lines, 10.4 (10.6) × 11 cm.

Paper   Cream, wove, unwatermarked, top edges trimmed, sheets bulk 1.6 cm.

Binding   Grey buckram 264 l.Gray. On front cover: [blind stamped] T.E. LAWRENCE | TO HIS BIOGRAPHER | ROBERT GRAVES. On spine: [alternating maroon and gilt rules] | [within maroon patch in gilt] [rule] | T.E. | LAWRENCE | TO HIS | BIOGRAPHER | ROBERT | GRAVES | DOUBLEDAY | DORAN | [alternating gilt and maroon rules]. T.e. gilt. Red and gold head band.

Published at $20.00 set.

Notes   Boxed as issued with companion volume, *T.E. Lawrence to His Biographer Liddell Hart;* Limited to 1000 copies of which 500 were printed for sale in US.

Copies   AC, Cal, H, UT, Ho.

A215   T.E. LAWRENCE, T.E. Lawrence to His Biographer, Liddell Hart, Doubleday, Doran, 1938

First American Edition

[In brown] T.E. Lawrence | TO HIS BIOGRAPHER | Liddell Hart | INFORMATION ABOUT HIMSELF IN THE FORM | OF LETTERS, NOTES, ANSWERS TO | QUESTIONS AND CONVERSATIONS. | [in brown, cut] | NEW YORK | Doubleday, Doran & Company, Inc.| MCMXXXVIII

Collation   23 × 15.5 cm: π^2 [1–13]^8 [14]^{10} [15]^8, 112 leaves, pp.[1–2], [i–iv], v–viii, [1], 2–233, [1–3].

Contents   Prp.[1] blank, [2] *'This edition | is limited to 1,000 numbered and signed copies for sale, of which 500 copies | are printed for the United States | This is number* ; [i] bastard title, [iii] blank, [iii] title page, [iv] copyright statement, printer's credit, [v] pub. note, [vi] blank, vii–viii foreword, ix contents, [x] blank, pp.[1] section title, [2] blank, 3–187 text, [1] blank.

RT   On verso T.E. LAWRENCE TO HIS BIOGRAPHER. On recto LIDDELL HART.

Text   20 lines, 10.4 (10.6) × 11 cm.

Paper   Cream, wove, unwatermarked, top edges trimmed, sheets bulk 1.6 cm.

Binding Grey buckram 264 l. Gray. On front cover: [blind stamped] T.E. LAWRENCE | TO HIS BIOGRAPHER | LIDDELL HART. On spine: [alternating maroon and gilt rules] | [within maroon patch, gilt] [gilt rule] | T.E. | LAWRENCE | TO HIS | BIOGRAPHER | LIDDELL HART | DOUBLEDAY | DORAN | [gilt rule] | [alternating maroon and gilt rules]. T.e. gilt. Red and gold head band.

Published at $20.00 set.

Notes Boxed as issued with companion volume, *T.E. Lawrence to His Biographer Robert Graves*; "Limited to 1000 copies of which 500 are printed for US".

Copies AC, Cal, H, UT, Ho.

A216 T.E. LAWRENCE, T.E. Lawrence to His Biographer, Liddell Hart [Robert Graves], Argus Bookshop, 1938

Book Dealer's Prospectus

[No title page.]

Collation 34.5 × 21.7 cm: single sheet, printed on one side only, mimeo.

Contents Order form at bottom.

Paper White, wove, unwatermarked, all edges trimmed.

Published at Free advertising flyer.

Copies Cal.

A217 T.E. LAWRENCE, T.E. Lawrence to His Biographers Robert Graves and Liddell Hart, Doubleday, 1963

Second American Edition

T.E. Lawrence | TO HIS BIOGRAPHERS | Robert Graves | AND | Liddell Hart | [cut] | DOUBLEDAY & COMPANY, INC. | GARDEN CITY, NEW YORK, 1963

Collation 20.8 × 14.3 cm: [1–16]⁸, 128 leaves, pp.[i–vi], vii–viii, [ix–x], [1] –187, [1], [i], ii–iv, [1], 2–223, [234], 235–260, [2].

Contents Prp.[i] bastard title, [ii] blank, [iii] title page, [iv] copyright statement, [v] half title, [vi] pub. note, vii–viii foreword, [ix] contents, [x] blank, pp.[1] section title, [2] blank, 3–187 text of Robert Graves section, [188] blank, prp.[i] section title, [ii] pub. note, iii–iv foreword, [1] –233 text of Liddell Hart section, [234] blank, 235–260 index, [1–2] blank.

RT   On verso T.E. LAWRENCE TO HIS BIOGRAPHER. On recto ROBERT
GRAVES [LIDDELL HART].

Text   20 lines, 10 × 10.5 cm.

Paper   White, wove, unwatermarked, all edges trimmed, sheets bulk 3 cm.

Binding   Brown cloth 38. d. r O, sand cloth spine 90 gy. Y. On spine:
[running down] T.E. LAWRENCE [next three words in brown] TO HIS
BIOGRAPHERS | *Robert Graves & B.H. Liddell Hart* [in brown]
[DOUBLEDAY]. Pale yellow head and tail bands.

Published at $6.50.

Copies   AC, Cal.

A218   T.E. LAWRENCE, T.E. Lawrence to His Biographers, Robert Graves and Liddell Hart, Greenwood Press, 1976

Third American Edition

T.E. Lawrence | TO HIS BIOGRAPHERS | Robert Graves | AND | Liddell
Hart | [pub. device] | GREENWOOD PRESS, PUBLISHERS | WESTPORT,
CONNECTICUT

Collation   21.5 × 13.8 cm: [1–12]^{16} [13]^8 [14–15]^{16} 232 leaves, pp.[1–2],
[i–vi], vii–[x], [1–2], 3–[188], [i]–iv, [1]–260.

Contents   Prp.[1] bastard title, [2]–[i] blank, [ii] frontispiece, [iii] title page,
[iv] CIP, copyright, issue statements, LC number, ISBN, [v] half title, [vi]
publisher's note, vii–viii foreword, ix contents, [x] blank, pp.[1] section
title, [2] blank, 3–187 text of Graves section, [188] blank, prp.[i] bastard title,
[ii] publisher's note, iii–iv foreword, pp.[1]–233 text of Liddell Hart section,
[234] blank, 235–260 index.

RT   On verso T.E. LAWRENCE TO HIS BIOGRAPHER. On recto ROBERT
GRAVES [LIDDELL HART].

Typography and paper   Original signatures present not related to gatherings
here.

Text   20 lines, 9.5 (9.6) × 10 cm.

Paper   White, wove, unwatermarked, all edges trimmed, sheets bulk 2.3
cm.

Binding   Blue cloth 183 d. Blue. On spine: [silver] LAWRENCE | [running
down] T.E. LAWRENCE TO HIS BIOGRAPHERS, ROBERT GRAVES AND
LIDDELL HART | [across] [pub. device]. Blue and white head and tail
bands.

Copies   University of Portland.

1939

Eight Letters From T.E. Lawrence

Letters written to Harley Granville-Barker. Only 50 copies were privately printed, intended as a Christmas gift. Only one of the letters in this slim volume is in *The Letters of T.E. Lawrence*. Although not so designated anywhere in the publication, this is a product of the Corvinus Press.

A219   T.E. LAWRENCE, Eight Letters From T.E. Lawrence, privately printed, 1939

First English Edition

EIGHT LETTERS | FROM | T.E.L. | PRIVATELY PRINTED | 1939

Collation   17 × 11.5 cm: [1–3]⁴, 12 leaves, pp.[1–2], 3–24.

Contents   Pp.[1] title page, [2] '*50 copies have been printed and the | type has been distributed.*', 3 preface, [4] blank, 5–24 text.

Text   20 lines, 10.5 × 7.7 cm.

Paper   White, wove, unwatermarked, top and bottom edges trimmed, sheets bulk 4 mm.

Binding   Grey paper wrappers 265 med Gray. On front cover: EIGHT LETTERS | FROM | T.E.L. | PRIVATELY PRINTED | 1939. Covers tied to sheets with cord.

Published at   Given as Christmas present.

Notes   Fifty copies printed by Corvinus Press.

Copies   Cal, H, UT.

Oriental Assembly

One of the last of the 'literary remains' volumes. *Oriental Assembly* was published in a trade edition by A.W. Lawrence and contains: the *Diary of MCMXI*; the first publication for the general public of the suppressed introductory chapter of *Seven Pillars of Wisdom*; two of Lawrence's newspaper/periodical articles; the preface to the Leicester Gallery catalogue; and 129 photos taken by Lawrence.

A220 T.E. LAWRENCE, Oriental Assembly, Williams & Norgate, 1939

First English Edition (Uncorrected proofs)

ORIENTAL | ASSEMBLY | by | T.E. Lawrence | [decorative cut] | Edited by | A.W. LAWRENCE | *With Photographs by* | *the Author* | LONDON | WILLIAMS AND NORGATE LTD. | GREAT RUSSELL STREET

Collation 21.7 × 14 cm: π^8 A–D^8, 12 plates E–I^8 K^{10}, plates L–S^8, 166 leaves, pp.[i–vi], vii–xiv, [xv–xvi], 1–292.

Contents Prp.[i–ii] blank, [iii] bastard title, [iv] blank, [v] title page, [vi] issue statement, printer's credit, vii foreword by A.W. Lawrence, [viii] blank, ix contents, [x] blank, xi–xiv illustrations, [xv] section title, [xvi] blank, pp.1–4 section foreword by A.W. Lawrence, 5–63 text, [64] blank, 12 plates (plate xv has caption Rum Kalat but no picture), 65 blank, except for page and signature numbers, 66 page number only, [67] section title, [68] blank, 69 section foreword by A.W. Lawrence, [70] blank, 71–97 text, [98] blank, [99] section title, [100] blank, 101 section foreword by A.W. Lawrence, [102] blank, 103–134 text, [135] section title, [136] blank, 137–146 text, [147] section title, [148] blank, 149–150 section foreword by A.W. Lawrence, 151–157 text, [158] blank, [159] section title, [160] blank, 161–162 section foreword by A.W. Lawrence, 163–164 index of persons and places in photographs, 165–292 plates.

RT On verso ORIENTAL ASSEMBLY. On recto [according to section].

Plates Thirteen plates on coated paper, b/w printed on one side only, captions on verso following pp.[iv], 62, 64 plates comprising pp.166–292.

Typography and paper $ 1 signed B, K K* 1,2.

Text 20 lines, 9.8 (10.3) × 9 cm.

Paper White, wove, unwatermarked, all edges trimmed, sheets bulk 2.3 cm.

Binding Only copy seen rebound.

Copies Cal, H.

A221 T.E. LAWRENCE, Oriental Assembly, Williams & Norgate, 1939

First English Edition

ORIENTAL | ASSEMBLY | BY | T.E. LAWRENCE | [decorative cut] | Edited by | A.W. LAWRENCE | *With Photographs by* | *the Author* | LONDON | WILLIAMS AND NORGATE LTD. | GREAT RUSSELL STREET

Collation   21.7 × 14 cm: π^8 A–D^8, 12 plates E–I^8 K^{10}, plates L–S^8, 166 leaves, pp.[i–vi], vii–xiv, [xv–xvi], 1–292, [p.16 minus 1, corrected in second impression].

Contents   Prp.[1–2] blank, [i] bastard title, [ii] blank, [iii] title page, [iv] issue statement, printer's credit, v foreword, [vi] blank, vii contents, [viii] blank, ix–xii illustrations, [xiii] section title, [xvi] blank, pp.1–4 editor's note by A.W. Lawrence, 5–62 text, [63] section title, [64] blank, 12 plates, [65] map, [66] blank, [67] section title, [68] blank, 69 editor's note by A.W. Lawrence, [70] blank, 71–97 text, [98] blank, [99] section title, [100] blank, 101 editor's note by A.W. Lawrence, [102] blank, 103–134 text, [135] section title, [136] blank, 137–138 editor's note by A.W. Lawrence, 139–146 text, [147] section title, [148] blank, 149–150 section foreword by A.W. Lawrence, 151–157 text, [158] blank, [159] section title, [160] blank, 161–162 section foreword by A.W. Lawrence, 163–164 index of persons and places in photographs, 165 blank, 166–291 plates, [292] blank.

RT   On verso ORIENTAL ASSEMBLY. On recto [according to section].

Plates   Frontis. following p.[iv], 12 plates following p.62, 64 plates comprising pp.165–292 all on coated paper, b/w printed on one side only.

Typography and paper $ 1 signed B, K K* 1,2.

Text   20 lines, 9.8 (10.3) × 9 cm.

Paper   White, wove, unwatermarked, all edges trimmed, sheets bulk 2.8 cm.

Binding   Brown buckram 77 m. y Br. On spine: [gilt] ORIENTAL | ASSEMBLY | T.E. | LAWRENCE | WILLIAMS | AND | NORGATE. T.e. black.

Published at   10s 6d, May 1939.

Notes   List of impressions:
   2nd, May 1939, identical to above, published at 12s 6d.
   3rd, August 1940, identical to above.
   4th, June 1944, as above, with following differences: this is a photolitho reproduction, [Collation]: 21.5 × 14 cm: A^8 B–L^8 L–O^8, 120 leaves, pp.[i–iv], v–[vi], vii, [viii], ix–xii, [xiii–xiv], pp.1–225 [1]; [Contents]: prp.[i] bastard title, [ii] blank, [iii] title page, [iv] issue statement, v foreword, [vi] blank, vii contents, [viii] blank, ix–xii illustrations, [xiii] section title, [xiv] blank, pp.1–4 editor's note, 5–62 text, [63] section title, [64] blank, 6 plates, [65] map, [66] blank, [67] section title, [68] blank, 69 editor's note, [70] blank, 71–97 text, [98] blank, [99] section title, [100] blank, 101 editor's note, [102] blank, 103–134 text, [135] section title, [136] blank, 137–138 editor's note, 139–146 text, [147] section title, [148] blank, 149–150 editor's note, 151–157 text, [158] section title, 159–160 editor's note, 161–162 index of persons and places in photographs 163–225 plates, [226] blank; [Typography and paper]: $ 1 signed B, E & F 1,8 E,E,E,F; [Paper]: sheets bulk 1.8 cm; [Plates]: frontis following prp.[ii], 6 plates

following p.64, 32 plates comprising pp.163–225, on coated paper, printed on both sides, captions below each photograph. [Binding]: maroon cloth 16 d. Red rough. On spine: [gilt] ORIENTAL | ASSEMBLY | T.E. | LAWRENCE | WILLIAMS | & | NORGATE. T.e. unstained.

5th, October 1945, identical to immediately above. Dust wrapper of this 5th impression is printed on verso of that for second.

Copies   AC, Cal, H, UT, Ho.

A222   T.E. LAWRENCE, Oriental Assembly, Williams & Norgate, 1939

Prospectus for First English Edition

ORIENTAL | ASSEMBLY | *By* | T.E. LAWRENCE | With about 120 photographs taken by the Author | *Notes by* A.W. LAWRENCE | Demy 8vo. 10/6 net.

Collation   22.2 × 14.2 cm: single fold, 2 leaves, pp.[1–4].

Contents   Pp.[1–2] title and blurb, contents, [3] specimen page, [4] order form.

Text   10 lines, 4.7 × 9.5 cm.

Paper   Buff, wove, unwatermarked, all edges trimmed.

Published at   Free advertising flyer.

Notes   Some copies have price overstamped with $4.00 on first and last pages, with Philip C. Duschnes' name and address stamped at head of order form.

Copies   AC, Cal.

A223   T.E. LAWRENCE, Oriental Assembly, Williams and Norgate, 1939

Prospectus for First English Edition (Argus Bookstore)

[No title page]

Collation   24.3 × 18.3 cm: single sheet, printed on one side only, mimeo.

Paper   White. wove, unwatermarked, all edges trimmed.

Published at   Free advertising flyer.

Copies   AC, Cal.

A224 T.E. LAWRENCE, Oriental Assembly, Williams & Norgate, 1947

Second English Edition

ORIENTAL | ASSEMBLY | by | T.E.Lawrence | [decorative cut] | Edited by | A.W. LAWRENCE | *With Photographs by* | *the Author* | LONDON | WILLIAMS AND NORGATE LTD. | GREAT RUSSELL STREET

Collation 21.6 × 13.7 cm: π^8 A–I^8 K^{10} L–O^8, 122 leaves, pp.[1–2], i–xvi, 1–228, [2].

Contents Prp.[1–2] blank, [i] bastard title, [ii] blank, [iii] title page, [iv] issue statement, printer's credit, v foreword by A.W. Lawrence, [vi] blank, vii contents, [viii] blank, ix–xii illustrations, xiii section title, pp.1–4 editor's notes, 5–62 text, [63] section title, [64] blank, 6 plates, [65] map, [66] blank, [67] section title, [68] blank, 69 editor's note, 70 blank, 71–97 text, [98] blank, [99] section title, [100] blank, 101 editor's note, [102] blank, 103–134 text, [135] section title, [136] blank, 137–138 editor's note, 139–146 text, [147] section title, [148] blank, 149–150 editor's note, 151–157 text, [158] blank, [159] section title, [160] blank, 161–162 editor's note, 163–164 index of persons and places in photographs, 165–227 photographs, [228] blank.

RT On verso ORIENTAL ASSEMBLY. On recto [according to section].

Plates Following p.[ii] 6 plates, following p.64, 32 plates comprising pp.163–225, on coated paper, printed on one side only, caption below.

Typography and paper $ 1 signed B K,K* 1,2.

Text 20 lines, 10.2 (10.2) × 9 cm.

Paper White, wove, unwatermarked, all edges trimmed, sheets bulk 1.7 cm.

Binding Red brown buckram, rough 43. m.r Br. On spine: ORIENTAL | ASSEMBLY | T.E. | LAWRENCE | WILLIAMS | & | NORGATE.

Notes This impression has new pictorial dust wrapper of white paper with statement | 'First Cheap Edition' | on spine.
   Another issue of this printing, same as above, with following differences: [Binding]: Red buckram 16 d. Red. Dust wrapper for this issue is same as earlier impressions, brown paper bearing statement 'Sixth Impression' on spine.

Copies AC, Cal.

A225 T.E. LAWRENCE, Oriental Assembly, Dutton, 1940

First American Edition

ORIENTAL | ASSEMBLY | by | T.E. Lawrence | [cut] | Edited by | A.W.

LAWRENCE | *With Photographs by* | *the Author* | NEW YORK | E.P. DUTTON & CO. INC. | 1940

Collation   21.7 × 14 cm: π^8 A–D^8, 12 plates E* I^8 K^{10}, plates L–S^8, 166 leaves, pp.[i–vi], vii–xiv, [xv–xvi], 1–292.

Contents   Prp.[1–2] blank, [i] bastard title] [ii] blank, [iii] title page, [iv] 'Printed in Great Britain', v foreword, [vi] blank, [vii] contents, [viii] blank, ix–xii illustrations, [xiii] section title, [xvi] blank, pp.1–4] editor's note, 5–62 text, [63] section title, [64] blank, 12 plates, [65] map, [66] blank, [67] section title, [68] blank, 69 editor's note, [70] blank, 71–97 text, [98] blank, [99] section title, [100] blank, 101 editor's note, [102] blank, 103–134 text, [135] section title, [136] blank, 137–138 editor's note, 139–146 text, [147] section title, [148] blank, 149–150 editor's note, 151–157 text, [158] blank, [159] section title, [160] blank, 161–162 editor's note, 163–164 index of persons and places in photos, [165] blank, 166–291 photos on rectos, captions on opposing versos [292] blank.

RT   On verso ORIENTAL ASSEMBLY. On recto [according to section].

Plates   Frontis. following p.[ii] 12 plates, following p.62, 64 plates comprising pp.165–292 on coated paper, b/w printed on one side only.

Typography and paper $ 1 signed B, K,K* 1,2.

Text   20 lines, 9.8 (10.3) × 9 cm.

Paper   White, wove, unwatermarked, all edges trimmed, sheets bulk 2.3 cm.

Binding   Brown buckram 38 d. r O. On spine: [gilt] ORIENTAL ASSEMBLY |[double rule] | *T.E. LAWRENCE* | DUTTON, white head and tail bands.

Published at $3.00.

Notes   There are two states of the dust wrapper.

Copies   AC, Cal, Ho.

Secret Despatches From Arabia

The majority of Lawrence's contributions to the *Arab Bulletin* are published in this volume. In addition to these items, 'Syrian Cross Currents', previously unpublished, is included; this was taken from a manuscript on Arab Bureau paper. Limited to 1000 copies this is the most extensive of the Golden Cockerel volumes by Lawrence.

A226 T.E. LAWRENCE, Secret Despatches From Arabia, Golden Cockerel Press, 1939

First English Edition

SECRET DESPATCHES | FROM ARABIA | BY T.E. LAWRENCE | Published by Permission of the Foreign Office | Foreword by A.W. Lawrence | THE GOLDEN COCKEREL PRESS

Collation   25 × 19 cm: [A]^8 B–L^8, 88 leaves, pp.[1–4], 5–173, [3].

Contents   Pp.[1] blank, [2] photo of Lawrence in Arab robes, [3] title page, [4] Printed in England, 5–7 Foreword by A.W. Lawrence, [8] blank, 9–10 contents, 11–171 text, 172–173 glossary, [1] blank, [2] colophon: Printed by Christopher Sandford and Owen Rutter at the Golden | Cockerel Press in Perpetua type on Arnold's mould-made paper. The | Edition is limited to 1,000 numbered copies, of which numbers 1–30 | are bound in white pigskin and accompanied by a collotype reproduc- | tion of part of T.E. Lawrence's manuscript of 'The Seven Pillars of | Wisdom'. Numbers 31–1000 are bound in 1/4 Niger. Number: , [3] blank.

Typography and paper $ 1 signed D.

Text   20 lines, 10 × 12.7 cm, set in 14pt Perpetua.

Paper   Laid, white, unwatermarked, top edge trimmed, sheets bulk 1.5 cm.

Binding   White linen boards, black quarter-Niger spine. On spine: [gilt] SECRET | DESPATCHES | T.E.|LAWRENCE | [pub. device]. White end papers. T.e. gilt. Boxed with glassine wrapper as issued.

Published at   £3 3s, September 1939.

Notes   One of 30, same as above with following differences: [Collation]: (25.2 × 19.5 cm): [1]^1 [A]^8 B–l^8 π^4 [1]^1, 92 leaves, pp.[1–4], 5–176, [1–8]; [Contents]: [1–2] blank, [rest as above until last page] [1] section title, [2–7] facsimile of manuscript of *Seven Pillars of Wisdom*, [8] blank, [1–2] blank; [Paper]: Sheets bulk 1.6 cm; [Binding]: white pigskin, [gilt fancy rule along all outer edges of boards. Boxed in white linen box; [Published at]: 15 gns; [Note]: has loosely inserted note from press that prospectus promised reproduction of one of despatches but the *Seven Pillars* collotype is substituted (chapter three of manuscript).
       A collection of articles from the *Arab Bulletin*.

Copies   AC, Cal, H, UT, Ho.

A227   T.E. LAWRENCE, Secret Despatches From Arabia, Golden Cockerel Press, 1939

Publisher's Prospectus

SECRET DESPATCHES | FROM ARABIA | BY T.E. LAWRENCE | WITH AN INTRODUCTION BY | A.W. LAWRENCE | Published by Permission | of the Foreign Office | PROSPECTUS | PRINTED IN GREAT BRITAIN AT | THE GOLDEN COCKEREL PRESS | ROLLS PASSAGE, LONDON, E.C. 4 | Note: To avoid disappointment, intending subscribers are requested | to place their orders, with remittance, early. It will be remembered | that *Crusader Castles* was heavily oversubscribed before publication.

Collation   25.4 × 17.9 cm: single leaf, pp.[1–2].

Contents   Pp.[1] title page, [2] blurb.

Text   20 lines, 9.9 (10.1) × 12.7 cm.

Paper   White, laid, watermarked, three edges trimmed.

Published at   Free advertising flyer.

Copies   AC, Cal.

A228   T.E. LAWRENCE, Secret Despatches From Arabia, Golden Cockerel Press, 1939.

Dealer's Prospectus

SECRET DESPATCHES | FROM ARABIA | BY T.E. LAWRENCE | WITH AN INTRODUCTION BY | A.W. LAWRENCE | [Published by Permission of the Foreign Office] | Philip C. Duschnes | 507 FIFTH AVENUE NEW YORK | *Note:* To avoid disappointment, intending subscribers are re- | quested to place their orders early. It will be remembered that | *Crusader Castles* was heavily oversubscribed before publication.

Collation   28 × 21.7 cm: single leaf printed on both sides.

Contents   Pp.[1] title page, [2] blurb.

Text   20 lines, 10 (11) × 12.7 cm.

Paper   White, laid, watermarked, all edges trimmed.

Published at   Free advertising flyer.

Copies   Cal.

1940

Men in Print

In 1927, by request of the editor, F. Yeats-Brown, Lawrence published five book reviews under the pseudonym of C.D. (Colin Dale) in the *Spectator*. Two of these are reprinted here, 'A Review of the Novels by D.H. Lawrence' and 'A Review of the Short Stories of H.G. Wells'. Also included are 'A Note on James Elroy Flecker', 'A Criticism of Henry Williamson's *Tarka The Otter*', and 'A Review of the Works of Walter Savage Landor'. The text of the Flecker essay printed here varies in some points from that published by the Corvinus Press.

A229   T.E. LAWRENCE, Men in Print, Golden Cockerel Press, 1940

First English Edition

MEN IN PRINT | ESSAYS IN LITERARY CRITICISM BY | T.E. LAWRENCE | INTRODUCTION BY | A.W. LAWRENCE | THE GOLDEN COCKEREL PRESS

Collation   25.3 × 19 cm: π^1 A–C^8 D^6 χ^1, 32 leaves, pp.[2], [1–8], 9–58, [59–60], [2].

Contents   Prp.[1–2] blank, pp.[1–2] blank, [3] title page, [4] printed in Great Britain, [5] contents, [6] blank, [7] section title, [8] blank, 9–15 introduction by A.W. Lawrence, [16] blank, [17] section title, [18] blank, 19–22 text of A Note on James Elroy Flecker [23] section title, [24] blank, 25–29 text of A Review of Novels by D.H. Lawrence, [30] blank, [31] section title, [32] blank, 33–38 text of A Review of Short Stories of H.G. Wells, [39] section title, [40] blank, 41–54 text of A Criticism of Henry Williamson's Tarka the Otter, [55] section title, [56] blank, 57–59 text of A Review of the Works of Walter Savage Landor, [60] 'Printed in the midst of war, by Christopher Sandford and Owen | Rutter at the Golden Cockerel Press, in Perpetua type on Arnold's | mould-made paper, and finished on the 16th day of July, 1940. The | Edition is limited to 500 numbered copies, of which Numbers 1–30 | are bound in full Niger and accompanied by a facsimile reproduction of T.E. Lawrence's manuscript of one of the essays. Numbers 31–500 | are bound in 1/4 Niger. Number: ' | [1–2] blank.

Typography and paper $ 1 signed C, D,D2.

Text   20 lines, 12 × 12.7 cm, set in 14pt Perpetua. Head titles 24pt titling.

Paper   White, laid, unwatermarked, top edge trimmed, sheets bulk 5 mm.

Binding White linen covered boards, 1/4 blue Niger 179 deep B. On spine: [gilt] MEN | IN | PRINT | T.E. | LAWRENCE | [pub. device]. T.e. gilt. Boxed in gray paper as issued.

Published at £2 2s.

Notes Limited to 500 numbered copies; numbers 31–500 are as described above; copies numbered 1–30 same as above, with following differences: [Collation]: A–C^8 D^6 x^6, pp.[2], [1–8], 9–58, [59–60], [1–10]; [Contents]: same as above, with added quire thus: pp.[1] section title, [2] blank, [3–8] on rectos only collotype facsimile of J.E. Flecker manuscript, [1–2] blank; [Binding]: Blue crushed morocco 179 deep B. Deep blue head and tail bands. All outer edges of boards gilt decorative rules. Inner sides of boards single rule along edges. [Published at]: 10 gns.

Copies AC, Cal, H, UT.

Selections From Seven Pillars of Wisdom

A text of extracts from *Seven Pillars of Wisdom*. It has been reprinted often, attesting to the continuing popularity of Lawrence's major work.

A230 T.E. LAWRENCE, Selections from Seven Pillars of Wisdom, Methuen, 1940

First English Edition

T.E. LAWRENCE | [Oxford rule] | *Selections from* | SEVEN PILLARS | OF WISDOM | *Edited by* | JOHN CULLEN | [pub. device] | *Abridged school edition* | METHUEN & CO. LTD., LONDON | *36 Essex Street, Strand, W.C. 2*

Collation 18.5 × 12.5 cm: π^8 [1]–8^8 9^{10} (9^8+ 9*^{2}), 82 leaves, pp.[i–vi], vii–xv, [xvi], 1–148.

Contents Pp.[i] bastard title, [ii] series listing, [iii] title page, [iv] issue statement, printer's credit, [v] editor's note, [vi] blank, vii contents, viii–xv introduction, [xvi] map, pp.1–141 text, 142–144 postscript, [145] section, 146–148 biographical notes.

RT On verso SEVEN PILLARS OF WISDOM. On recto [according to chapter].

Typography and paper $ 1 signed 8.

Text 8.7 (8.8) × 9.3 cm.

Paper White, wove, unwatermarked, all edges trimmed, sheets bulk 1 cm.

Binding Pale yellow cloth 87 Y. On front cover: [in brown between crossed swords, in script] the | sword | also means | clean-ness | & | death. On spine: [running down, in brown] SELECTIONS | FROM | SEVEN PILLARS OF WISDOM.

Notes Another impression, 'fourth edition' 1949, same as above, with following differences: [Binding]: 163 l. b. G. Blue green cloth.

Another impression, 1959, same as above, with following differences: [Binding]: Blue green cloth 159 brill b.G. On front cover: [in brown] *Selections from* | Seven Pillars | of Wisdom | [sword cut]. On spine: [running down] *Selections from* SEVEN PILLARS OF WISDOM. [Paper]: sheets bulk i cm.

Another impression, 1961, as above, with following differences: *Selections from* | *Seven Pillars of Wisdom* | [long rule] | T.E. LAWRENCE | *Edited by* | JOHN CULLEN | [pub. device] | METHUEN & CO LTD | *36 Essex Street, London WC2;* [Contents]: prp.[i] series and bastard titles; [Binding]: green paper simulated cloth covered boards 164 m. b G.

Another impression, as above, with following differences: [title page imprint] Methuen Educational Ltd. | LONDON · TORONTO · SYDNEY · WELLINGTON; [Collation]: 18.5 × 12.2 cm: [1]–3^{16} 4^{18} 5^{16}, 82 leaves, pp.xvi, 148, [signature remain for gatherings 1–9^8]; [Contents]: prp.[iv] issue statement, SBN, printer's credit; [Binding]: white and orange pictorial paper backed cloth. On front cover: Selections from | [in orange] SEVEN PILLARS | [in orange] OF WISDOM | T.E. Lawrence. On spine: LAWRENCE [in orange] Selections from Seven Pillars of Wisdom [in black] Methuen. On back cover: [pub. device] | Methuen Educational.

10th impression, 1961.

Copies AC, Cal.

A231 T.E. LAWRENCE, Selections from Seven Pillars of Wisdom, Brodie, 1963

Second English Edition

NOTES ON CHOSEN ENGLISH TEXTS | *General Editor:* NORMAN T. CARRINGTON, M.A. | T.E. LAWRENCE | SELECTIONS FROM | SEVEN PILLARS | OF WISDOM | (edited by John Cullen, Methuen's Modern Classics) | *By* | A.W. ENGLAND, B.A. | [pub. device] | © JAMES BRODIE LTD., LONDON AND BATH

Collation 18.3 × 12.5 cm: [1]^{16}, pp.[1–5], 6–62, [2].

Contents Pp.[1] title page, [2] map, [3] contents, [4] map, [5]–7 biographical note on Lawrence, 8–62 text, [1] blank, [2] printer's colophon.

RT On verso SEVEN PILLARS OF WISDOM. On recto [according to chapter].

Text 20 lines, 7.4 (7.5) × 9.3 cm.

Paper   White, wove, unwatermarked, all edges trimmed, sheets bulk 3 mm.

Binding   Grey paper wrappers 112 l. Ol Gy. On front cover: [within frame of ornaments] NOTES ON CHOSEN ENGLISH TEXTS | *General Editor:* NORMAN T. CARRINGTON, M.A. | T.E. LAWRENCE | SELECTIONS FROM | SEVEN PILLARS | OF WISDOM | (Edited by John Cullen, Methuen's Modern Classics) | *By* | A.W. ENGLAND, B.A. | JAMES BRODIE LTD., 15 QUEEN SQUARE, | BATH, SOMERSET, ENGLAND. On back cover: [list of titles in series]. Sheets fastened to wrappers with two steel staples.

Copies   AC, Cal.

1941

Selected Letters of T.E. Lawrence

An abridgement of the 1938 collected letters. Issued in the interest of providing books at a fraction of the price of the original editions. A well produced edition at an affordable price for the average reader.

A232   T.E. LAWRENCE, Selected Letters of T.E. Lawrence, World Books, 1941

First English Edition

SELECTED LETTERS | of | T.E. LAWRENCE | Edited by | DAVID GARNETT | WORLD BOOKS | 20 HEADFORT PLACE | LONDON, S.W. 1.

Collation   19.8 × 13.3 cm: [A]^{16} B–M^{16}, 192 leaves, pp.[1–6], 7–384.

Contents   Pp.[1–2] blank, [3] bastard title, [4] blank, [5] title page, [6] issue statement, printer's credit, 7–8 list of recipients of letters, 9 preface, [10] blank, 11–374 text, 375–384 index.

RT   On verso THE LETTERS OF T.E. LAWRENCE. On recto [according to section].

Typography and paper $ 1 signed E.

Text   20 lines, 8.5 (8.5) × 9.8 cm.

Paper   Thick, white, wove, unwatermarked, all edges trimmed, sheets bulk 2.5 cm.

Binding   Salt and pepper cloth. On spine: [in brown] LETTERS | OF | T.E. | LAWRENCE | Edited by | DAVID GARNETT | [pub. device].

Published at 2s 6d.

Notes Another issue, identical to above, except for following differences: Title page bears imprint THE REPRINT SOCIETY | LONDON; [Collation]: (19.7 × 13.5 cm): [A]^{16} B−L^{16} Z^{16}, 192 leaves, pp.[1−6], 7−384; [Binding]: brown buckram 55 s. Br. On spine: [gilt on black leather patch, within rules] LETTERS | OF | T.E. | LAWRENCE | Edited by | DAVID GARNETT. T.e. brown 3s 6d.

Copies AC, Cal, UT.

A233 T.E. LAWRENCE, Selected Letters of T.E. Lawrence, Cape, 1952

Second English Edition

SELECTED LETTERS | of | T.E. LAWRENCE | Edited by | DAVID GARNETT | [pub. device] | JONATHAN CAPE | THIRTY BEDFORD SQUARE | LONDON

Collation 20 × 13.2 cm: [A]^8 B−AA^8, 192 leaves, pp.[1−4], 5−384.

Contents Pp.[1] bastard title, [2] blank, [3] title page, [4] issue statement, printer's, binder's credits, 5−6 list of recipients of letters, 7 preface, [8] blank, 9−374 text, 375−384 index.

RT On verso THE LETTERS OF T.E. LAWRENCE. On recto [according to section].

Typography and paper $ 1 signed B L.T.E.L.

Text 20 lines, 8.5 (8.5) × 9.8 cm.

Paper White, wove, unwatermarked, all edges trimmed, sheets bulk 2 cm.

Binding Turquoise linen 173 M. g B. On spine: [gilt] SELECTED | LETTERS | of | T.E. | LAWRENCE | [at foot] [pub. device]. T.e. grey.

Published at 15s.

Notes Another state with cancelled title page to correct issue statement on verso. Issue statement for above reads: First Published 1938 | Reprinted 1952. Corrected state reads: The Letters of T.E. Lawrence | First Published 1938 | Second Impression November 1938 | Third Impression November 1938 | New Edition 1942 [sic] | Reprinted 1942 | Selected Letters of T.E. Lawrence | First Published 1952.

Copies AC, Cal, UT.

A233a   T.E. LAWRENCE, Selected Letters of T.E. Lawrence, Hyperion Press, 1978

First American Edition

SELECTED LETTERS | OF | T.E. LAWRENCE | Edited by | DAVID GARNETT | [pub. device] | HYPERION PRESS, INC. | *Westport, Connecticut*

Collation   21 × 13.5 cm: [1–24]¹⁶ , 192 leaves, pp.[1–4], 5–384.

Contents   Pp.[1] bastard title, [2] blank, [3] title page, [4] copyright statement, CIP, ISBN, 5–6 names of recipients of letters, 7 preface by David Garnett, [8] blank, 9–374 text, 375–384 index.

RT   On verso THE LETTERS OF T.E. LAWRENCE. On recto [according to section].

Typography and paper $ 1 signed S I.T.E.L. (these are from first printing and are for gatherings of 8).

Text   20 lines, 8.4 (8.5) × 9.7 cm.

Paper   White, wove, unwatermarked, all edges trimmed, sheets bulk 2.5 cm.

Binding   Green cloth 131 s.y. G. On spine: [gilt] [cut] | [running down] SELECTED LETTERS OF | T.E. LAWRENCE | Lawrence | [across at foot, pub. device]. Brown and white head and tail bands.

Copies   UCI.

1942

Shaw-Ede, T.E. Lawrence's Letters to H.S. Ede 1927–1935

The last of the four Golden Cockerel Lawrence titles. 'Produced in the midst of war' this book was published in an edition of 500 copies in 1942; 43 letters are contained in the volume, only six of which appear in the *The Letters of T.E. Lawrence.*

A234   T.E. LAWRENCE, Shaw-Ede, Golden Cockerel, 1942

First English Edition

SHAW-EDE | T.E. LAWRENCE'S LETTERS | TO H.S. EDE | 1927–1935 | FOREWORD AND | RUNNING COMMENTARY BY | H.S. EDE | THE GOLDEN COCKEREL PRESS

Collation   25.4 × 19 cm: [A]–D⁸, 32 leaves, pp.[1–4], 5–62, [2].

Contents Pp.[1–2] blank, [3] title page, [4] Printed in Great Britain, 5 foreword, [6] blank, 7–61 text, 62 'Printed by Christopher Sandford and Owen Rutter, at the Golden Cockerel Press, Rolls Passage, London, E.C. 4, in 14 pt. Perpetua type on | Arnold's mould-made paper, and finished on the 4th day of September, | 1942. The edition is limited to 500 numbered copies, of which num- | bers 1–30 are bound in full morocco and accompanied by facsimile re- | productions of five of the letters. Numbers 31–500 are bound in | quarter-morocco. Number: ', [1–2] blank.

Typography and paper $ 1 signed B.

Text 20 lines, 12 × 12.9 cm, set in 14pt Perpetua.

Paper Laid, unwatermarked, top edge trimmed, sheets bulk 6 mm.

Binding Buff cloth covered boards, quarter black Niger spine. On spine: [gilt] SHAW-EDE | T.E. | LAWRENCE'S | LETTERS | TO | H.S. EDE | [pub. device]. T.e. gilt.

Published at £3 12s.; With facsimiles £10 10s.; 4 September 1942.

Notes Of the 500 numbered copies produced, numbers 1–30 are bound in full morocco and accompanied by facsimile reproductions of five of the letters; nos. 1–30 as follows: [Collation]: facsimile of letters is added quire [E]^4 unpaged; [Contents]: following contents, as above: pp.[1] A FACSIMILE REPRODUCTION | of T.E. SHAW'S HANDWRITING | The MANUSCRIPT OF FIVE OF HIS | LETTERS TO H.S. EDE | Printed by the collotype process, | this supplement has been limited | to 30 copies to accompany the | first 30 copies of *Shaw-Ede*, [2–7] facsimiles of letters; [Binding]: full blue morocco 183 d. Blue. Boxed as issued in buff linen slip case. Outer edges of binding have gilt decorated rule.

Copies AC, Cal, H, UT.

A235 T.E. LAWRENCE, Shaw-Ede, Golden Cockerel Press, 1942

Publisher's Prospectus of First English Edition

PROVISIONAL SPECIFICATION OF | THE GOLDEN COCKEREL PRESS | BOOKS IN HAND : AUTUMN 1942 | (Subject to alteration in detail) | [pub. device]

Collation 21 × 13 cm: single sheet printed on both sides.

Paper Buff paper.

Published at Free advertising flyer.

Notes Another copy with Duschnes stamp at bottom on verso.

Copies Cal.

Lawrence av Arabien

This Swedish anthology edited by Gunnar Olinder parallels the *The Essential T.E. Lawrence* (1951), and precedes it by some nine years. This book and the Lönnroth biographical sketch (F159–F160) are both indications of a then current interest in Lawrence in Sweden.

A236   T.E. LAWRENCE, T.E. Lawrence av Arabien, Natur Och Kultur, 1942

First Swedish Edition

T.E. LAWRENCE | AV ARABIEN | EN ANTOLOGI | *Urvel och inledning av* | GUNNAR OLINDER | *Översättningen är utförd av Vera Olinder* | [rule] BOKFÖRLAGET NATUR OCH KULTUR

Collation   22.2 × 15.3 cm: [1]–16⁸ 17⁶, 134 leaves, pp.[1–4], 5–266, [1–2].

Contents   Pp.[1] bastard title, [2] blank, [3] title page, [4] printer's credit, 5–7 contents, [8] blank, 9–23 preface by Gunnar Olinder, [24] blank, 25–266 text, [1] glossary, [2] blank.

RT   On verso *Lawrence av Arabien*. On recto [in italics, according to section].

Plates   Frontispiece following p.[2] Kennington's 'Cheshire Cat'.

Typography and paper $ 1 signed T.E. Lawrence av Arabien 2;1,2 17,17*.

Text   20 lines, 9.1 (9.4) × 11 cm.

Paper   White, wove, unwatermarked, all edges trimmed, sheets bulk 2.5 cm.

Binding   Patterned paper covered boards, white cloth spine. On spine: [within blue rectangle, gilt] [rule] | GUNNAR OLINDER | [short rule] | LAWRENCE | AV ARABIEN | [at foot, blue rule]. White cloth corners.
   Paper issue: white paper covers. On front cover: GUNNAR OLINDER | [grey-green reproduction of Kennington pastel of Lawrence] | LAWRENCE | AV ARABIEN | *En antologi* | NATUR OCH KULTUR. On spine: [double rule] | NATUR | OCH | KULTUR | [double rule]. On back cover [blurb, list of other titles].

Published at   Paper Kr. 10, bound Kr. 13.

Copies   AC, Cal.

1951

The Essential T.E. Lawrence

An excellent introduction to Lawrence through selections from his correspondence and writings. The materials represented here include the only published extract up to that time from *The 200 Class Royal Air Force Seaplane Tender.* The editor, David Garnett, has contributed a fine preface, 'Patchwork Portrait'.

A237   T.E. LAWRENCE, The Essential T.E. Lawrence, Cape, 1951

Uncorrected Proofs of First English Edition

THE ESSENTIAL | T.E. LAWRENCE | Selected by | DAVID GARNETT | [pub. device] | JONATHAN CAPE | THIRTY BEDFORD SQUARE | LONDON

Collation   19.5 × 13.7 cm: [A] –T^8 U^4, 156 leaves. pp.[1–12], 13–311, [1].

Contents   Pp.[1–2] blank, [3] bastard title, [4] blank, [5] title page, [6] issue statement, printer's, binder's credits, [7] contents, [8] blank, [9] preface, [10] blank, [11] section title, [12] blank, 13–26 Patchwork Portrait of Lawrence by Garnett, [27] half-title, [28] blank, [29] section title, [30] blank, 31–311 text, [1] blank.

RT   On verso THE ESSENTIAL T.E. LAWRENCE. On recto [according to section].

Typography and paper $ 1 signed C E.T.E.L.

Text   20 lines, 7.5 (7.8) × 10 cm.

Paper   White, wove, unwatermarked, all edges trimmed, sheets bulk 1.2 cm.

Binding   Green paper 145 m. G. On front cover: THE ESSENTIAL | T.E. LAWRENCE | DAVID GARNETT | [pub. device] | Uncorrected Proof. On spine: THE ESSENTIAL T.E. LAWRENCE. On back cover: The Alden Press (Oxford) Ltd. | Oxford. T.e. red.

Published at   12s 6d.

Notes   Essential Series.

Copies   H.

A238 T.E. LAWRENCE, The Essential T.E. Lawrence, Cape, 1951

First English Edition

THE ESSENTIAL | T.E. LAWRENCE | selected with a Preface by | DAVID GARNETT | [pub. device] | JONATHAN CAPE | THIRTY BEDFORD SQUARE | LONDON

Collation   20 × 13.1 cm: [A]^8 B–U^8 X^4, 164 leaves, pp.[1–8], 9–328.

Contents   Pp.[1–2] blank, [3] bastard title, [4] blank, [5] title page, [6] issue statement, binder's credits, [7] contents, [8] blank, 9 preface, [10] blank, [11]–317 text, [318] blank, [319] section title, [320] blank, 321–328 index.

RT   On verso THE ESSENTIAL T.E. LAWRENCE. On recto [according to section].

Plates   Frontispiece following pp.[4].

Typography and paper   \$ 1 signed B. E.T.E.L.

Text   20 lines, 8.7 (8.8) × 10.2 cm.

Paper   White, wove, unwatermarked, all edges trimmed, sheets bulk 2.2 cm.

Binding   Red cloth 13 deep Red. On spine: [gilt] THE | ESSENTIAL | T.E. | LAWRENCE | [pub. device]. T.e. red.

Published at   12s 6d.

Notes   Later issues have red Daily Mail BOOK OF THE MONTH emblem on dust wrapper spine.
   2nd impression, identical to above.
   Essential Series.

Copies   AC, Cal, UT.

A239 T.E. LAWRENCE, The Essential T.E. Lawrence, Penguin, 1956

Second English Edition

THE ESSENTIAL | T.E. LAWRENCE | [star] | SELECTED | WITH A PREFACE BY | DAVID GARNETT | PENGUIN BOOKS | IN ASSOCIATION WITH | JONATHAN CAPE

Collation   18 × 11 cm: [A]^{16} B–E^{16} F^8 G–L^{16}, 168 leaves, pp.[1–11], 12–335, [1].

Contents   Pp.[1] bastard title, [2] list of author's works, [3] title page, [4] issue statement, printer's credit, [5] contents, [6] blank, [7] preface, [8]

blank, [9] section title, [10] blank, [11]–324 text, [325] section title, [326] blank, 327–335 index, [1] blank.

RT On both verso and recto pp.12–25 *Patchwork Portrait,* pp.27–335. On verso *The Essential T.E. Lawrence.* On recto [in italics, according to chapter].

Typography and paper $ 1 signed F.

Text 20 lines, 7.7 (7.9) × 9 cm.

Paper White, wove, unwatermarked, all edges trimmed, sheets bulk 1.5 cm.

Binding Red and white paper covers 255 s. p R. On front cover: [in red] PENGUIN BOOKS | [long rule] | The Essential | T.E. LAWRENCE | [wood cut of Lawrence beside pub. device] | Selected by | DAVID GARNETT | [long rule] | COMPLETE [price in red] 3/6 UNABRIDGED. On spine: [running up] David Garnett [in red pub. device] The Essential T.E. Lawrence | [across at bottom] 1015, [rules at top and bottom]. On back cover: [in red] PENGUIN BOOKS | [long rule] | [biographical sketch of Lawrence beside pub. dev.] | [long rule] | NOT FOR SALE IN THE U.S.A. Blurbs inside front and rear covers. Ad for *Passages From Arabia Deserta* inside rear cover.

Published at 3s 6d.

Copies AC, Cal, UT.

A240   T.E. LAWRENCE, The Essential T.E. Lawrence, Dutton, 1951

First American Edition

THE ESSENTIAL | T.E. LAWRENCE | Selected with a Preface by | DAVID GARNETT | [pub. device] | E.P. DUTTON & CO., INC. | *New York, 1951*

Collation 19.7 × 13.5 cm: [1–20]^8 X^4, 164 leaves, pp.[1–8], 9–328.

Contents Pp.[1–2] blank, [3] bastard title, [4] blank, [5] title page, [6] copyright, issue statements, [7] contents, [8] blank, 9 preface, [10] blank, [11]–317 text, [318] blank, [319] section title, [320] blank, 321–328 index.

RT On verso THE ESSENTIAL T.E. LAWRENCE. On recto [according to section].

Plates Frontispiece following p.[4].

Typography and paper Unsigned except for last quire, 1 X E.T.E.L.

Text 20 lines, 7.7 (7.8) × 10.2 cm.

Paper White, wove, unwatermarked, all edges trimmed, sheets bulk 2.3 cm.

Binding   Red cloth 16 d. Red. On front cover: [pub. device, blind stamped].
On spine: [gilt] THE | ESSENTIAL | T.E. | LAWRENCE | DUTTON.

Published at $3.75.

Copies   AC, Cal, Ho.

A241   T.E. LAWRENCE, The Essential T.E. Lawrence, Viking, 1963

Second American Edition

THE ESSENTIAL | T.E. LAWRENCE | selected with a Preface by | DAVID
GARNETT | [pub. device] | THE VIKING PRESS · NEW YORK CITY

Collation   19.7 × 13 cm:guillotined sheets, 158 leaves, pp.[1–8], 13–26, [2],
31–317, [1], 321–328.

Contents   Prp.[1] bastard title, [2] blank, [3] title page, [4] copyright, issue
statements, printer's credit, [5] contents, [6] preface, [7] section title, [8]
blank, pp.13–317 text, 318 blank, 321–328 index.

RT   On verso THE ESSENTIAL T.E. LAWRENCE. On recto [according to
section].

Text   20 lines, 7.8 (8.9) × 10.2 cm.

Paper   White, wove, unwatermarked, all edges trimmed, sheets bulk 1.5
cm.

Binding   Patterned paper covers. On front cover: [pub. device] The |
Essential | [name in red brown] T | E | Lawrence | A biography out of his
own writings: | *Seven Pillars of Wisdom; The Mint;* | and letters. Selected with
a preface by | David Garnett| $1.65. On spine: C141 | [running down] The
Essential [in brown] T.E. LAWRENCE David Garnett. On back cover:
[quotes from book and from critics within double rules rectangles], [below
second rectangle, identification of David Garnett] [in red, publisher's
address] [price].

Published at $1.65.

Notes   Second printing, September 1964, same as above with following
differences: impression note on verso of title page and word
BIOGRAPHIES added on back cover upper left corner, running up.
Compass Books C141.

Copies   AC, Cal.

A242   T.E. LAWRENCE, Les Textes Essentiels de T.E. Lawrence, Gallimard, 1965

First French Edition

Les textes | essentiels | de T.E. Lawrence | CHOISIS ET PRÉFACÉS PAR DAVID GARNETT | TRADUITS DE L'ANGLAIS PAR | ÉTIEMBLE ET YASSU GAUCLÈRE | nrf | GALLIMARD

Collation   20.6 × 14 cm: [1]^{16} 2–13^{16} 14^4 15^8, 220 leaves, pp.[1–9], 10–431, [9].

Contents   Pp.[1–2] blank, [3] bastard title, [4] blank, [5] title page, [6] issue statement, original title, copyright statement, [7] section title, [8] blank, [9]–29 preface, [30] blank, [31] half-title, [32] blank, [33] section title, [34] blank, [35]–431 text, [1] blank, [2] translator's note, [3] blank, [4] contents, [5] blank, [6] list of author's works, [7] blank, [8] printer's colophon, [9] blank.

RT   On verso LES TEXTES ESSENTIELS DE T.E. LAWRENCE. On recto [according to section].

Typography and paper $ 1 signed 2.

Text   20 lines, 8.2 (8.4) × 10 cm.

Paper   White, wove, unwatermarked, all edges trimmed, sheets bulk 2.5 cm.

Binding   White paper covers. On front cover: [forming half circle] DU MONDE ENTIER | [title in red] Les Textes | essentiels de | T.E. Lawrence | CHOISIS ET PRÉFACÉS PAR DAVID GARNETT | TRADUITS DE L'ANGLAIS PAR | ÉTIEMBLE ET YASSU GAULÈRE | [cut] | [in red] nrf | GALLIMARD. On spine: [in red] *du monde* | [in red] *entier* | [title in red] LES TEXTES | ESSENTIELS [first S is broken] | DE | T.E. | LAWRENCE | nrf | GALLIMARD. On back cover: [within diamond] H | T.E. LAWRENCE | [in red] Les Textes essentiels | [18-line blurb] | [in red] nrf | 19,50 F (+t.l.) | 20 F T.L.I. Covers have turned-in flaps with photos and biographical note on Lawrence.

Published at   20 F T.L.I., 5 March 1965.

Notes   Forty-three copies were printed on Lafuma-Navvare vélin pur and numbered 1–43 before the printing of the public edition.

Copies   AC, Cal, UT.

A243   T.E. LAWRENCE, Mosaik Meines Lebens, List, 1952

First German Edition

T.E. LAWRENCE | MOSAIK | MEINES LEBENS | Aus Briefen, Werken und anderen Dokumenten | ausgewahlt mit einer Einführung | von | DAVID GARNETT | [pub. device] | PAUL LIST VERLAG MÜNCHEN

Collation   20.6 × 13.3 cm: [1]⁸ 2–24⁸, 192 leaves, pp.[1–4], 5–377, [378], [6].

Contents   Pp.[1] bastard title, [2] blank, [3] title page, [4] translator's credit, original title, designer's credit, copyright statement, printer's, binder's credits, 5– [6] foreword, [7] section title, [8] blank, 9– [378] text, [1] contents, [2] bibliography, [3–6] publisher's ads.

Typography and paper $ 2 signed 1,2 ,5, Lawrence, Mein Leben,5*. 23*.

Text   20 lines, 7.5 × 9.5 cm.

Paper   White, wove, unwatermarked, all edges trimmed, sheets bulk 2.2 cm.

Binding   Golden brown cloth 74 s. y Br. On front cover: [gilt] T·E·LAWRENCE | MOSAIK MEINES LEBENS. On spine: [in black 23 parallel rules | [gilt] ·T·E· | LAWRENCE | MOSAIK | MEINES | LEBENS | [publisher's device] | [black rule]. T.e. brown. Yellow and white head and tail bands.

Notes   Another issue, as above, but title page imprint states Innsbruck as place of publication instead of Munich.

Copies   AC, Cal.

Der Glaube der Wüste

An attempt in German to provide a portrait of Lawrence, much in the same way as Garnett portrayed Lawrence in 'Patchwork Portrait' (*The Essential T.E. Lawrence*, A238), through extracts from his writings and letters. The main portion of the work is followed by an evaluation by Eugen Gottlob Winkler.

A244   T.E. LAWRENCE, Der Glaube der Wüste, Arche, 1951

First Swiss Edition

T.E. LAWRENCE | DER GLAUBE DER | WÜSTE | SEIN LEBEN IN SELBSZEUGNISSEN | Mit 4 abbildungen und einer | biographischen Würdigung von | EUGEN GOTTLOB WINKLER | [pub. device] | IM VERLAG DER ARCHE · ZÜRICH

Collation   19.2 × 11.4 cm: [1–10]⁸, 80 leaves, pp.[1–8], 9–159, [1].

Contents   Pp.[1] series title, [2] blank, [3] title page, [4] translator's credit, copyright statement, printer's credit, [5] contents, [6] blank, [7] editor's note, [8] blank, 9–154 text, 155–157 chronology of Lawrence's life, 158–159 bibliography, [1] ads.

Text   20 lines, 9 × 8.1 cm.

Paper   White, wove, unwatermarked, all edges trimmed, sheets bulk 1.4 cm.

Binding   Light green cloth 155 g Gray. On front cover: [gilt] DER | GLAUBE | DER | WÜSTE. On spine: [running up] T.E. LAWRENCE – DER GLAUBE DER WÜSTE.

Copies   AC, H.

1954

The Home Letters of T.E. Lawrence and His Brothers

This collection of letters, edited by his brother M.R. Lawrence, supplements the David Garnett collection of 1938. The letters included here for the most part cover his early years; fully two thirds of those included are from before the war. The two collections provide a remarkable picture of the range and scope of Lawrence's letter-writing from his youth to the end of his life. The letters of his brothers Frank and Will, both of whom died in the First World War, are also included. The whole reflects what was a truly remarkable family. This collection is a primary source for the pre-war correspondence of Lawrence.

A245   T.E. LAWRENCE, The Home Letters of T.E. Lawrence and His Brothers, Blackwell, 1954

Advance Proofs of First English Edition

[No title page]

Collation   22.8 × 15.5 cm: 1–45⁸ 46¹, 361 leaves, pp.[1–2], 3–722.

Contents   Pp.[1] half title, [2] blank, 3–722 text.

RT   On verso HOME LETTERS. On recto [according to section].

Typography and paper $ 1 signed H.L.-2 [23 misnumbered 22].

Text   20 lines, 9.1 (9.2) × 11 cm.

Paper White, wove, unwatermarked, all edges trimmed, sheets bulk 3 cm.

Binding Brown paper covers glued to sheets 79 l. gy. y Br. On front cover: [on white paper label pasted to cover, within frame made of ornamental cuts] THE HOME LETTERS OF | T.E. LAWRENCE AND | HIS BROTHERS | · | BASIL BLACKWELL.

Copies AC, Cal.

A246 T.E. LAWRENCE, The Home Letters of T.E. Lawrence and His Brothers, Blackwell, 1954

First English Edition

THE HOME | LETTERS OF | T.E. LAWRENCE | AND HIS | BROTHERS | [large outline letter, in red] | BASIL BLACKWELL | OXFORD | 1954

Collation 23 × 15.5 cm: π^8 [1] -45^8 46^6, 374 leaves, pp.[i–iv], v–xvi, [1–2], 3–731, [1].

Contents Prp.[i] bastard title, [ii] blank, [iii] title page, [iv] printer's, binder's credits, v contents, vi editor's note, vii–viii illustrations, ix publisher's note, x note by M.R. Lawrence, xi note on T.E. Lawrence's life, xii facsimile of Churchill letter, xiii–xvi allocution, pp.[1] section title, [2] blank, 3–392 text, [393] section title, [394] note on W.G. Lawrence, 395–397 foreword, [398] blank, 399–592 text, [593] section title, [594] note on F.H. Lawrence, 595 foreword, [596] blank, 597–722 text, 723–731 index, [732] blank.

RT On verso HOME LETTERS. On recto [according to section].

Plates Twenty photographs, tipped in, printed on both sides, following pp.ii, 32, 48, 64, 80, 96, 112, 128, 144, 160, 176, 192, 208, 224, 240, 256, 272, 394, 594.

Typography and paper $ 1 signed H.L.-2.

Text 20 lines, 9.1 (9.2) × 11 cm.

Paper White, wove, unwatermarked, all edges trimmed, sheets bulk 4.2 cm.

Binding Blue cloth 183 d. Blue. On spine: [gilt] THE | HOME | LETTERS | OF | T.E. | LAWRENCE | AND HIS | BROTHERS | BLACKWELL.

Published at £3 3s, 17 May 1954.

Notes Allocution, pp.xiii–xvi, by Winston Churchill is his speech at Oxford High School (1936) reprinted.

Copies AC, Cal, UT.

A247 T.E. LAWRENCE, The Home Letters of T.E. Lawrence and His Brothers, Macmillan, 1954

First American Edition

THE HOME | LETTERS OF | T.E. LAWRENCE | AND HIS | BROTHERS | [outline letters] L | THE MACMILLAN COMPANY | NEW YORK | 1954

Collation   23 × 15.5 cm: π^8 [1] –45^8 46^6, 374 leaves, pp.[i–iv], v–xvi, [1–2], 3–731, [1].

Contents   Prp.[i] bastard title, [ii] blank, [iii] title page, [iv] printer's, binder's credits, v contents, vi editor's note, vii–viii illustrations, ix publisher's note, x note by M.R. Lawrence, xi note on T.E. Lawrence, xii facsimile of Churchill letter, xiii–xvi allocution, pp.[1] section title, [2] blank, 3–392 text, [393] section title, [394] note on W.G. Lawrence, 395–397 foreword, [398] blank, 399–592 text, [593] section title, [594] note on F.H. Lawrence, 595 foreword, [596] blank, 597–722 text, 723–731 index, [732] blank.

RT   On verso HOME LETTERS. On recto [according to section].

Plates   Twenty photographs, printed on both sides, following pp.ii, 32, 48, 64, 80, 96, 112, 128, 144, 160, 176, 192, 208, 224, 240, 256, 272, 394, 594.

Typography and paper $ 1 signed H.L.-2.

Text   20 lines, 9.1 (9.2) × 11 cm.

Paper   White, wove, unwatermarked, all edges trimmed, sheets bulk 4.2 cm.

Binding   Blue cloth 183 d. Blue. On spine: [gilt] THE | HOME | LETTERS | OF | T.E. | LAWRENCE | AND HIS BROTHERS | BLACKWELL.

Published at $10.00, May 1954.

Notes   State one: bears American title page with large L in black on title page, on verso of title page, issue statement. Binding and dust wrapper bear Blackwell imprint as in English edition. Title page is tipped in on stub of original English edition title page. The other state has title page as integral part of first gathering.

Copies   AC, Cal.

1955

Leben Ohne Legende

This is a German collection of extracts from Lawrence's work, compiled by Rolf Schroers. It is roughly arranged by topic.

A248   T.E. LAWRENCE, Leben Ohne Legende, List, 1955

First German Edition

T.E. LAWRENCE | LEBEN OHNE LEGENDE | [pub. device] | PAUL LIST VERLAG MÜNCHEN

Collation   18 × 11.5 cm: [1–6]^{16}, 96 leaves, pp.[1–6], 7–184, [185], [7].

Contents   Pp.[1] bastard title, [2] biographical sketch of Lawrence, [3] title page, [4] translator's credit, issue, series, copyright statements, printer's credit, [5] contents, [6] blank, 7–[8]foreword, 9–[12] brief biography of T.E. Lawrence, 13–[14] chronology of T.E. Lawrence's life, 15–[185] text, [1–7] publisher's ads.

Text   20 lines, 7.4 × 8.7 cm, set in Garamond Antiqua Linotype.

Paper   White, wove, unwatermarked, all edges trimmed, sheets bulk 1 cm.

Binding   Yellow pictorial paper covers 66 v. OY. On front cover: T·E·LAWRENCE | [next three lines, white on purple patches] Leben | ohne | Legende | [on orange band across at foot] LIST *Bücher* | Lawrence: Gleichnis | des 20. Jahrhunderts. On spine: 55 | [running up] LAWRENCE [white on purple patch] Leben ohne [white on purple patch] Legende | [across at foot, pub. device]. On back cover: [at foot on orange band] LIST *Bücher*.

Published at   DM 1.90.

Copies   AC, Cal.

1959

From a Letter of T.E. Lawrence

Printed as a keepsake for the Double Crown Club in 1959 by the distinguished press, Officina Bodoni. A small number (approximately 70 to 75 copies) were printed. The text is included in *The Letters of T.E. Lawrence*.

A249   T.E. LAWRENCE, From a Letter of T.E. Lawrence, Officina Bodoni, 1959

First Italian Edition

FROM A LETTER | *of* | T.E. LAWRENCE

Collation   20 × 12.5 cm: $\pi^2\ 1^4\ x^2$, 8 leaves, pp.[1–4], [1–2], 3–4, [5], [1–2].

Contents Prp.[1–4] blank, pp.[1] title page, [2] blank, 3–[5] text, [1] blank, [2] 'Reprinted by kind permission of Jonathan Cape Limited from "Letters of T.E. Lawrence", London 1938. | Composed in Dante type, cast from punches cut | by Charles Malin, and printed by the designer | Giovanni Mardersteig at the Officina Bodoni in | Verona for presentation to the members of the | Double Crown Club | at the 150th dinner | 11 June 1959.' | [printer's device in red].

Text 20 lines, 9.9 × 7.5 cm, set in 14pt Dante type.

Paper White, laid, watermarked, top and fore edge trimmed, sheets bulk 1 mm.

Binding Pink paper folded around white board covers 28 l. y Pink. On front cover: [in grey] [printer's device]. Sheets glued to covers.

Published at Free keepsake, 11 June 1959.

Notes Not more than 75 copies. No. 21 in *Letters of T.E. Lawrence* (1938).

Copies Cal.

1960

Stéphane: T.E. Lawrence

A selection of Lawrence's writings, extracts ranging from one paragraph to many pages with much illustrative material and iconography. Text is in French. Stéphane [Roger Worms] also published two volumes of articles (E171 and E189), each of which contains essays on Lawrence.

A250   ROGER STEPHANE, T.E. Lawrence, Gallimard, 1960

First French Edition

[Within hand-drawn frame] LA BIBLIOTHÈQUE IDÉALE | Collection dirigée par Robert Mallet | [within hand drawn panel] T.E. LAWRENCE | [within second panel] par | Roger Stéphane | [within third panel] [swash] nrf | GALLIMARD

Collation 18.7 × 12 cm: [1]^8 2–17^8 18^4, 140 leaves, pp.[1–9], 10–275, [5].

Contents Pp.[1–2] blank, [3] bastard title, [4] series list, [5] title page, [6] copyright statement, [7] section title, [8] blank, [9]–254 text, [255] section title, [256] blank, [257]–264 list of Lawrence's works, [265]–266 iconography of Lawrence, [267] section title, [268] blank, [269]–272 illustrations, [273]–275 contents, [1] blank, [2] printer's colophon, [3–5] blank.

RT On verso LAWRENCE. On recto [according to section].

Plates Eight plates on coated paper, following pp.9, 48, 64, 112, 128, 192, 208, 240.

Typography and paper $ 1 signed 2.

Text 20 lines, 8.4 (9.1) × 8.1 cm.

Paper White, wove, unwatermarked, unopened, sheets bulk 2 cm.

Binding Red paper covers 13 deep Red. On front cover: [within hand drawn frame] LA BIBLIOTHÈQUE IDÉALE | [first row of panels running down] [panel one] Les sept piliers | de la | sagesse | [second panel] Les châteaux | des | croisades | [third panel] par | [fourth panel] Le désert de | Sin [fifth panel] Mélanges | orientaux | [sixth panel] La révolte | dans le désert | [second row of panels, first panel] La matrice | [second panel extends into third row and is white rectangle] T.-E. LAWRENCE | [third panel] Roger Stéphane | [fourth panel, reproduction of John drawing of Lawrence] | [fifth panel, swash] nrf | [third row, panel one] Lettres de | T.-E. Lawrence | [second panel] Secret | despatches | from Arabia | [third panel] Préface a | "Arabia deserta" | [fourth panel] Préface à | "Arabia félix" | [fifth pane;] Essai sur | Flecker | [beneath rows of panels within frame] GALLIMARD. On spine: [two panels within frame] [running up, first panel] LA BIBLIOTHÈQUE IDÉALE | [second panel] Roger Stéphane T. -E. LAWRENCE | [across at bottom, within frame, swash] nrf. On back cover: [panelled similarly to front cover with highlights from Lawrence's career in each].

Published at 9 NF + TL | 900F, April 21, 1955.

Notes Roger Stéphane was the pseudonym of Roger Worms.

Copies AC, Cal, LC.

1965

To S.A.

This is the introductory poem to *Seven Pillars of Wisdom*. Approximately 20 copies were printed in 1965 as a handpress exercise at the Library School of the University of California, Los Angeles.

A251   T.E. LAWRENCE, To S.A., privately printed, 1965

First American Edition

[In brown] TO S.A. | T.E. LAWRENCE

Collation   30.2 × 24.2 cm: single fold, 2 leaves, unpaged.

Contents   Pp.[1] title page, [2] blank, [3] poem, [4] blank.

Text   Set in: title 96pt Reiner, author's name 36pt Bembo, text 18pt Bembo.

Paper   Cream, wove, unwatermarked, all edges trimmed.

Published at   Not for sale.

Notes   Approximately 20 copies printed by Benjamin Whitten, Jr., at the printer's chapel, Library School, University of Los Angeles. Two states are reported: as above, and a few copies with gold sprinkled on the title page when the ink was still damp. None of the latter state have been found in the 12 copies examined.

Copies   AC, Cal.

The Voyages of Ulysses

A lavish coffee-table book with splendid plates of Mediterranean scenes captioned by text from Lawrence's translation of *The Odyssey*. Published in three editions, the American version is reduced in format, losing some of the impact of the Swiss and English editions.

A252   ERICH LESSING, The Voyages of Ulysses, Herder, 1965

First German Edition

[Two-page spread] [across both pages] THE VOYAGES OF ULYSSES | [on verso] With commentaries | by | PROFESSOR C. KERÉNYI | MICHEL GALL | HELLMUT SICHTERMANN | with selections from | T.E. Shaw's Translation of the Odyssey | and | Ithaka, den Peloponnes und Troja | by | Heinrich Schliemann | Pictorial and Literary Index | by | Cornelia Kerényi | [on recto] A photographic interpretation of Homer's classic | by | ERICH LESSING | HERDER-FREIBURG-BASEL-VIENNA

Collation   29.5 × 26 cm: [1–21]⁴ [22]⁶ [23–34]⁴ 138 leaves, pp.[1–4], 5–53, [54–200], 201–261, [262–276].

Contents   Pp.[1] blank, [2–3] title page, [4] translator's credit, text credit, copyright statement, [5] contents, [6] blank, 7–[11] publisher's preface, [12] blank, [13] section title, [14] brief biographical note on Gall, 15–38 text by Gall, [39] section title, [40] biographical note on Schliemann, 41–53 text, [54] blank, [55] section title for plates by Lessing, [56] biographical note on Lessing, [57–196] plates by Lessing (on coated paper, colour plates printed on both sides) [197] note on Lessing plates, [198] blank, [199] section title, [200] biographical note on Sichtermann, 201–261 text, [262] note on abbreviations in index, 263–276 pictorial and literary index.

Text 20 lines, 10.5 × 9.9 cm (20.8 cm double column).

Paper White, wove, unwatermarked, all edges trimmed, sheets bulk 2.3 cm.

Binding Grey oatmeal cloth. On front cover: [grey galley design]. On spine: [grey, running down] THE VOYAGES OF ULYSSES. Gold head and tail bands. Map end papers. Boxed as issued.

Published at DM 100.

Notes Extensive extracts from T.E. Lawrence's translation of *The Odyssey* are printed along with plates.

Copies AC, Cal.

A253 ERICH LESSING, The Voyages of Ulysses, Macmillan, 1966

First English Edition

[Two-page spread] [across both] THE VOYAGES OF ULYSSES | [on verso] With commentaries | by | PROFESSOR C. KERÉNYI | MICHEL GALL | HELLMUT SICHTERMANN | With selections from | T.E. Shaw's translation of the Odyssey | and | Ithaka, der Peloponnes und Troja| by | Heinrich Schliemann | Bibliography and archeological data| by | Cornelia Kerényi | [on recto] A photographic interpretation of Homer's classic | by | ERICH LESSING | MACMILLAN London · Melbourne | 1966

Collation 29.3 × 25.7 cm: [1–21]⁴ [22]⁶ [23–36]⁴, 186 leaves, pp.[1–4], 5–53, [54–200], 201–275, [276–292].

Contents Pp.[1] blank, [2–3]title pages, [4] original title, note, translator's credit, copyright, issue statements, 5 contents, [6] blank, 7–[11] pub. preface, [12] blank, [13] section title, [14] Gall biographical note, 15–38 text, [39] section title, [40] Schliemann biographical note, 41–53 text, [54] blank, [55] section title, [56] Lessing biographical note, 57–197 text and photos of section by Lessing, [198] blank, [199] section title, [200] Sichtermann biographical note, 201–228 text, [229] section title, 230–231 text, [232] blank, [233] section title, [234] Kerényi biographical note, 235–274 text, 275 notes on last section, [276] abbreviations for index, 277–289 index and bibliography, [290–292] blank.

Text 20 lines, 10.5 × 10 (20.9 cm double column).

Paper White, wove, unwatermarked, all edges trimmed, sheets bulk 2.5 cm. Photographic section on coated paper.

Binding Oatmeal cloth. On front cover: [grey galley design]. On spine: [in grey] [running down] THE VOYAGES OF ULYSSES. Map end papers, gold head and tail bands. Boxed as issued.

Published at £8 8s.

Copies AC, Cal.

A254 ERICH LESSING, The Adventures of Ulysses, Dodd, Mead, 1970

First American Edition

THE ADVENTURES | OF ULYSSES | HOMER'S EPIC IN PICTURES | BY ERICH LESSING | WITH AN INTRODUCTION | "HOMER AND HIS ODYSSEY" | BY KARL KERENYI | DODD, MEAD & COMPANY NEW YORK.

Collation 24 × 21 cm: [1]⁴ [2]⁴ 4 plates [3]⁴ 6 plates [4]⁴ 4 plates [5]⁴ 4 plates [6]⁴ 6 plates [7]⁴ 6 plates [8]⁴ 6 plates [9] – [10]⁴, 40 leaves, pp.[1–4], 5–67, [1–13].

Contents Pp.[1] bastard title, [2] blank, [3] title page, [4] credits, issue, copyright statements, 5–6 preface, [7] section title, [8] blank, 9–[15] foreword, [16] publisher's statement, [17] section title, [18] blank, [19]–67 text, [68] blank, [69] section title, [70] blank, [71] photo credits, [1–2] blank.

Text 20 lines, 6.5 × 15.7 cm.

Paper White, wove, unwatermarked, all edges trimmed, sheets bulk 3 cm.

Binding White cloth. On front cover: [trireme design in brown]. On spine: [running down] THE ADVENTURES OF ULYSSES | [across at foot, within single rule frame] DODD | MEAD. Gold head and tail bands.

Copies Murray.

1968

Evolution of a Revolt

A collection of Lawrence's contributions to newspapers and periodicals written at the end of the war and immediately following. The subjects are the Arab revolt and the consequences of it on the international level as seen by Lawrence.

A255 T.E. LAWRENCE, Evolution of a Revolt, Pennsylvania State University, 1968

First American Edition

EVOLUTION | OF A REVOLT | [rule] | *EARLY POSTWAR WRITINGS* | *OF*

T.E. LAWRENCE | [rule] | edited with an introduction by | STANLEY and RODELLE WEINTRAUB | 1968 | THE PENNSYLVANIA STATE UNIVERSITY PRESS | University Park and London

Collation 21.5 × 13.8 cm: [1–2]^{16} [3]^{16} [4–6]^{16}, 88 leaves, pp.[1–6], 7–175, [1].

Contents Pp.[1] bastard title, [2] blank, [3] title page, [4] copyright, authorisation statements, designer's credit, [5] dedication, [6] blank, 7–8 contents, 9–29 introduction, [30] blank, 31 notes on text and maps, [32] blank, 33–171 text, [172] blank, 173–175 index, [1] blank.

Plates Two plates on coated paper, printed on both sides, following pp.64, 80.

Text 20 lines, 8.4 × 9.8 cm.

Paper White, wove, unwatermarked, all edges trimmed, sheets bulk 2.2 cm.

Binding Orange and tan cloth 50 s. O and 33 br. Pink [top orange and bottom tan]. On spine: [running down] T.E. LAWRENCE EVOLUTION OF A REVOLT Pennsylvania State. Endpaper maps on 76 l. y Br. White head and tail bands.

Published at $5.95, April 1968.

Notes One copy with binding colours reversed exists; this is probably a binder's error.

Copies AC, Cal.

1971

Minorities

An anthology of poetry that appealed to Lawrence was collected by him between 1919 and 1927. It was published in 1971 with a biographical introduction by J.M. Wilson and a preface by the Poet Laureate, C. Day Lewis. A limited issue containing some facsimiles of the original mss. was published in an edition of 125 copies.

A256 T.E. LAWRENCE, compiler, Minorities, Cape, 1971

Uncorrected Proof of First English Edition

T.E. LAWRENCE | MINORITIES | [cut] | EDITED BY | J.M. WILSON | WITH A PREFACE BY | C. DAY LEWIS | [publisher's device] | JONATHAN CAPE | THIRTY BEDFORD SQUARE LONDON

Collation 21.7 × 14 cm: [A]⁸ B–R⁸, 136 leaves, pp.[1–6], 7–272.

Contents Pp.[1] bastard title, [2] list of author's works, [3] title page, [4] issue, copyright statement, ISBN, publisher's note, printer's credit, [5] contents, [6] blank, 7–9 acknowledgments, [10] blank, 11–12 abbreviations, 13–16 preface, 17–50 introduction, [51] blank, 52 note on contents, 53–64 titles of poems [65] half-title, [66] blank, 67–240 text, 241 section title, [242] blank, 243–265 notes, [266] blank, 267–268 index of authors, 269–272 index of first lines.

Typography and paper $ 1 signed B.

Text 20 lines, 9 × 9.3 cm.

Paper White, wove, unwatermarked, all edges trimmed, sheets bulk 1 cm.

Binding Yellow patterned paper 87 m. Y. On front cover: MINORITIES | T.E. LAWRENCE | [pub. device] | Uncorrected Proof. On spine: [running up] MINORITIES. On back cover: [printer's credit].

Notes There are six advance proofs made up of unsewn stapled gatherings and 40 as above.

Copies AC, Cal.

A257 T.E.LAWRENCE, compiler, Minorities, B. Rota and Cape, 1971

First English Edition (Limited issue)

T.E. LAWRENCE | MINORITIES | [cut] | EDITED BY | J.M. WILSON | WITH A PREFACE BY | C. DAY LEWIS | BERTRAM ROTA & JONATHAN CAPE | LONDON 1971

Collation 21.6 × 13.5 cm: [A]⁸ B–R⁸, 136 leaves, pp.[1–6], 7–272.

Contents Pp.[1] 'MINORITIES | A LIMITED EDITION | CONTAINING 24 FACSIMILES | OF LAWRENCE'S HOLOGRAPH | TRANSCRIPTIONS | THIS EDITION | CONSISTS OF 125 NUMBERED COPIES | OF WHICH 110 ARE FOR SALE | EACH COPY IS SIGNED BY THE POET LAUREATE | [mss. # and C.Day Lewis' signature]', [2] blank, [3] title page, [4] copyright statement, ISBN, pub. note, printer's credit, [5] contents, [6] blank, 7–9 acknowledgments, [10] blank, 11–12 abbreviations, 13–16 preface by C.Day Lewis, 17–51 introduction by J.M. Wilson, 52 note on contents, 53–64 list of poems, [65] section title, [66] blank, 67–240 text, 241–272 notes and index.

Plates One plate following p.[2] on coated paper, printed on one side only.

Typography and paper $ 1 signed B.

Text 20 lines, 9 × 9.3 cm.

Paper Cream, laid, unwatermarked, all edges trimmed, sheets bulk 2.5 cm.

Binding Grey cloth covered boards 22 r Gray, brown pigskin spine [front and back covers have vertical gilt rule 5mm in from left edge of cloth]. On spine: [within gilt bordered dark brown rectangle patch, in gilt, running down, each letter centred below one above] MINORITIES. T.e. gilt. red and gold head and tail bands. Grey silk place marker. Grey end papers. In glassine wrappers as issued.

Published at £20.

Notes Limited to 125 copies. Contains 24 facsimiles of Lawrence's holograph transcriptions of the poems. A few copies have Day Lewis' signature in ball-point pen.

Copies AC, Cal.

A258   T.E. LAWRENCE, compiler, Minorities, Cape, 1971

First English Edition

T.E. LAWRENCE | MINORITIES | [cut] | EDITED BY | J.M. WILSON | WITH A PREFACE BY | C. DAY LEWIS | [publisher's device] | JONATHAN CAPE | THIRTY BEDFORD SQUARE LONDON

Collation 21.7 × 14 cm: [A]⁸ B–R⁸, 136 leaves, pp.[1–6], 7–272.

Contents Pp.[1] bastard title, [2] list of author's works. [3] title page, [4] issue, copyright statements, ISBN, publisher's note, printer's credit, [5] contents, [6] blank, 7–9 acknowledgments, [10] blank, 11–12 abbreviations, 13–16 preface, 17–50 introduction, [51] blank, 52 note on contents, 53–64 titles of poems, [65] half-title, [66] blank, 67–240 text, 241 section title, [242] blank, 243–265 notes, [266]blank, 267–268 index of authors, 269–272 index of first lines.

Plates One plate following pp.[2] on coated paper, printed on one side only.

Typography and paper $ 1 signed B.

Text 20 lines, 9 × 9.3 cm.

Paper White, wove, unwatermarked, all edges trimmed, sheets bulk 1 cm.

Binding Dark blue cloth simulated paper 183 d.Blue, white linen simulated paper spine. On spine: [running down, within 168 brill g B rectangle, gilt] MINORITIES [cut] T.E. LAWRENCE | [across at bottom, gilt, pub. device]. Light blue e.p. T.e. blue.

Published at £2.50, November 1971.

Copies AC, Cal, UT.

A259   T.E. LAWRENCE, compiler, Minorities, Cape, 1971

Publisher's Advertising Poster

[At top, in white] Minorities | A personal anthology of Lawrence's favourite poems | with an Introduction and detailed notes by J.M. Wilson | and a Preface by C. Day Lewis. Included are nine poems | written in Lawrence's own hand, reproduced in facsimile | from his notebook, and a hitherto unpublished | frontispiece photograph of him signed 'T.E. Shaw'. | Published by Jonathan Cape| [photo of Lawrence superimposed on sample of page from Minorities mss.] | [running up right side] T.E. LAWRENCE.| [in yellow] designed by M. Mahon Printed in Great Britain

Collation   49.5 × 25 cm: printed on one side only, yellow background with black border.

Paper   White, wove, unwatermarked, all edges trimmed.

Published at   Free advertising poster.

Notes   Poster designed by M. Mahon.

Copies   AC.

A260   T.E. LAWRENCE, compiler, Minorities, Doubleday, 1972

First American Edition

T.E. Lawrence | MINORITIES | *Good Poems by Small Poets* | *and Small Poems by Good Poets* | EDITED BY J.M. WILSON | PREFACE BY C. DAY LEWIS | *Doubleday & Company, Inc.* | *Garden City, New York* | 1972

Collation   20.8 × 14 cm: [1–34]^8, 136 leaves, pp.[1–6], 7–272.

Contents   Pp.[1] bastard title, [2] photo of Lawrence, [3] title page, [4] list of Lawrence's works, permissions, ISBN, copyright, issue statements, [5] contents, [6] blank, 7–9 acknowledgments, [10] blank, 11–12 abbreviations, 13–16 preface, 17–50 introduction, [51] blank, 52 note on contents, 53–64 list of poems, [65] half-title, [66] blank, 67–240 text, [241] section title, [242] blank, 243–265 notes, [266] blank, 267–268 index of authors, 269–272 index of first lines.

Text   20 lines, 9.1 × 9.3 cm.

Paper   White, wove, unwatermarked, all edges trimmed, sheets bulk 1.7 cm.

Binding   Green cloth 149 p. G. On spine: [running down, compiler's name] *T.E. Lawrence:* MINORITIES | [line of decorative cuts] EDITED BY J.M.

WILSON | [across at bottom] *Doubleday*. Yellow head and tail bands. End papers dark blue.

Published at $10.00.

Copies AC, Cal.

1975

Five Hitherto Unpublished Letters

An inexpensively produced pamphlet of five of Lawrence's letters. Issued with much attempt at secrecy, privately issued in a short run, number unknown.

A261 T.E. LAWRENCE, T.E.L. Five Hitherto U' published Letters, privately printed 1975

First English Edition

T.E.L. | FIVE HITHERTO UNPUBLISHED LETTERS | PRIVATELY PRINTED 1975

Collation 17.5 × 14.4 cm: [1]¹⁰, 10 leaves, pp.[1–2], 1–16, [1–2].

Contents Prp.[1–2] blank, pp.[1–3] introductory letters by H.M.R.N., [4] blank, 5–13 text, 14–15 bibliography, 16 notes on people mentioned in letters, [1–2] blank.

Text 20 lines, 9.4 × 8.8 cm.

Paper White, wove, unwatermarked, all edges trimmed, sheets bulk 2 mm.

Binding Light blue paper covers 190 l. b Gray stapled to sheets, black cloth spine. On front cover: T. E. L. | FIVE HITHERTO UNPUBLISHED LETTERS | PRIVATELY PRINTED 1975.

Published at May 1975.

Notes Inside rear cover: Printed by Axminister Printing Co. Limited to 30 copies.

Copies AC, Cal.

1977

The Suppressed Introductory Chapter

A privately printed version of the text of the "suppressed" chapter of the 1926 edition of *Seven Pillars of Wisdom*.

A262   T.E. LAWRENCE, The Suppressed Introductory Chapter, privately printed 1977

First English Edition

THE SUPPRESSED | INTRODUCTORY CHAPTER | PRIVATELY PRINTED

Collation   24.2 × 17.5 cm: [1]⁶, unpaged.

Contents   Pp.[1–2] blank, serve as backing for wrappers, [3] title page, [4] foreword, [5–9] text, [10] 'The edition is twenty-five copies of which this is | No. | © 1977 | *ROBERT HATCH 4 CASTLE STREET TOTNES*', [11–12] blank, backing for wrappers.

Text   20 lines, 10.9 × 10.8 cm.

Paper   Mould-made, watermarked, all edges trimmed, sheets bulk 1 mm.

Binding   Red paper wrappers 12 s. Red tied to sheets by flax string. On front cover: THE SUPPRESSED | INTRODUCTORY CHAPTER. Wrappers overlap first and last sheets (8.2 cm).

Notes   Limited to 25 signed copies.

Copies   AC, Cal.

SECTION B

PERIODICAL ARTICLES
BY T.E. LAWRENCE

Lawrence began his published writing career while still a schoolboy. The initial items listed here reflect interests that we can trace to important themes in his later life. Following these articles there is a gap until 1919, at which time Lawrence published materials relating to the Arab campaign. Some of these were written at the request of friends, others to benefit individuals such as Robert Graves who were in need of the funds their sale could bring. Lawrence's contribution to the theory of guerrilla tactics in modern warfare are contained for the first time in these writings. His efforts at book reviewing in the *Spectator,* published over the pseudonym 'C.D.' (Colin Dale), are also to be found here.

B0001 L.ii (T.E. Lawrence), An Antiquarian and a Geologist in Hants, *Oxford High School Magazine,* March 1904, 1:6, pp.115–6.

B0002 Lawrence ii, Playground Cricket, *Oxford High School Magazine,* July 1904, 2:2, pp.29–30.

B0003 Two Calcolviphcians (T.E. Lawrence and C.F.C. Beeson), The Bachen, *Oxford High School Magazine,* , 3:5, pp.75–6.

B0004 Scroggs (C.F.C. Beeson), How to Win a Scholarship: advice from School Celebrities, *Oxford High School Magazine,* March 1907, 4:3, pp.56–7. *Note:* Contribution signed 'E. Lawrence'.

B0005 C.J.G. (T.E. Lawrence), The Kaer of Ibu Wardani, *Jesus College Magazine,* January 1913, 1:2, pp.37–9. *Notes:* A shortened version of this story is included in *Seven Pillars,* p.40; see also *Home Letters,* p.239.

B0006 T.E. Lawrence, Demolitions Under Fire, *Royal Engineers Journal,* January 1919, 29:1, pp.6–10. *Notes:* Reprinted in *The Essential T.E. Lawrence,* pp.209–14; *Evolution of a Revolt,* pp.56–62.

B0007 By an Eye Witness (T.E. Lawrence), Campaign of the Caliphs for Damascus, *Current History,* February 1919, 9(Part2):2, pp.348–57. *Note:* Reprinted in *Evolution of a Revolt,* pp.33–5.

B0008 T.E. Lawrence, France, Britain and the Arabs, *Observer,* 8 August 1920, p.10. *Notes:* Reprinted in *The Letters,* pp.311–15; *Evolution of a Revolt,* pp.92–5.

B0009 (T.E. Lawrence), The Changing East, *The Round Table,* September 1920, 10:40, pp.756–72. *Note:* Reprinted in *Oriental Assembly,* pp.71–97.

B0010 T.E. Lawrence, The Egyptian Problem by Sir Valentine Chirol, *Observer,* 19 September 1920, p.6. *Note:* review of V. Chirol, *The Egyptian Problem.*

B0011 T.E. Lawrence, Evolution of a Revolt, *Army Quarterly,* October 1920, 1:1, pp.55–69. *Notes:* Edited by Guy Dawnay. TEL gave Dawnay the article to help launch journal. Reprinted in *Oriental Assembly,* p.103–34; *The Essential T.E.Lawrence,* pp.214–20; *Evolution of a Revolt,* p.100–19.

B0012 T.E. Lawrence, A Set Piece: January 1918, *Army Quarterly,* April 1921, 2:1, pp.22–31. *Note:* Subject matter later included in *Seven Pillars.*

B0013 T.E. Lawrence, With Feisal at Court and Afield, *World's Work,* July 1921, 42:3, pp.277–88. *Note:* Reprinted in *Evolution of a Revolt,* pp.120–32.

B0014 T.E. Lawrence, Arabian Nights and Days, *World's Work,* August 1921, 42:4, pp.381–6 (Part I) and 516–20 (Part II). *Note:* Reprinted in *Evolution of a Revolt,* pp.133–159.

B0015 T.E. Lawrence, Adventures in Arabia's Delivrance, *World's Work,* October 1921, 42:6, pp.617–21. *Note:* Reprinted in *Evolution of a Revolt.*

B0016 T.E. Lawrence, Sherif Feisal: King of Irak, *The Landmark,* October 1921, 3:10, pp.642–6.

B0017 T.E. Lawrence, Massacre, *The Winter Owl,* November 1923, pp.5–14.

B0018 T.E. Lawrence, Massacre, *Living Age,* 3 May 1924, 321:4165, pp.858–64.

B0019 T.E. Lawrence, Fomenting Revolt in Arabia, *World's Work,* February 1927, 53:4, pp.369–92. *Note:* Illus.

B0020 T.E. Lawrence, Dynamiting Turks, *World's Work,* March 1927, 53:5, pp.513–33.

B0021 T.E. Lawrence, With Lawrence's Guerrillas, *World's Work,* April 1927, 53:6, pp.643–63. *Note:* Illus.

B0022 T.E. Lawrence, The Conquest of Damascus, *World's Work,* May 1927, 54:1, pp.36–53. *Note:* Illus.

B0023 (T.E. Lawrence), Seven Pillars of Wisdom an Anonymous Note on the Texts of Seven Pillars and Revolt in the Desert, *Now and Then,* Autumn 1927, 25, p.30. *Note:* Reprinted in *Now and Then,* 1935, *Letters,* no. 308.

B0024 C.D. (Colin Dale = T.E. Lawrence), D.H. Lawrence, *Spectator,* 6 August 1927, 139, p.223. *Note:* Reprinted in *Men in Print,* pp.23–29 and in *The Essential T.E. Lawrence,* pp.277–80.

B0025 C.D. (Colin Dale = T.E. Lawrence), Mixed Biscuits, *Spectator,* 20 August 1927, 139, pp.290–91.

B0026 C.D. (Colin Dale = T.E.Lawrence), A Critic of Critics Criticised, *Spectator,* 27 August 1927, 139, pp.321–2.

B0027 C.D. (Colin Dale = T.E.Lawrence), Hakluyt – First Naval Propagandist, *Spectator,* 10 September 1927, 139, pp.390–1.

B0028 C.D. (Colin Dale = T.E. Lawrence), The Wells Short Stories, *Spectator,* 25 February 1928, 140, pp.268–9. *Note:* Reprinted in *Men In Print,* pp.31–38.

B0029 J.C. (T.E. Lawrence), Ramping, *Royal Air Force College Journal,* Spring 1931, 11:1, pp.50–51. *Notes:* From *The Mint,* Part III, Chapter

16. First publication of any portion of the text.

B0030 T.E. Lawrence, Arabian Travellers, *Now and Then*, Spring 1932, 41, pp.22–4. *Note:* Reprint of preface to Bertram Thomas, *Arabia Felix*.

B0031 'S' (T.E. Lawrence), Putting the Weight in Ancient Days, *Journal of the Royal Air Force College*, Spring 1933, 13:1, pp.92–5. *Note:* Excerpt from *The Odyssey*, Book VIII.

B0032 T.E. Lawrence, Service Life, *British Legion Journal*, November 1933, 13:5, pp.160–1, 169. *Note:* Chapter from *The Mint*.

B0033 (T.E. Lawrence), "Lawrence of Arabia", *British Legion Journal*, December 1933, 13:6, p.208. *Notes:* Published apology for November article (B0032) published without permission. This second article was written by Lawrence and Wren Howard of Jonathan Cape.

B0034 T.E. Lawrence, Seven Pillars of Wisdom an Anonymous Note on the Texts of Seven Pillars of Wisdom and Revolt in the Desert, *Now and Then*, Summer 1935, 51, p.19. Reprinted in *Letters*, no. 308.

B0035 T.E. Shaw [T.E. Lawrence], Ramping, *R.A.F. College Magazine*, Cranwell, Autumn 1935, 15:2, pp.152–3. *Note:* Reprint of Spring 1931 article (B0029) with proper recognition of author.

B0036 T.E. Lawrence, Arabia Deserta: Vorwart zu dem Arabien-Buch von Charles Doughty, *Die Neue Rundschau*, July 1937, 48, pp.88–102.

B0037 T.E. Lawrence, Letters of T.E. Lawrence, *Atlantic Monthly*, February-March 1939, 163:2–3, pp.147–57, 327–37.

B0038 T.E. Lawrence, Cartas de T.E. Lawrence a Lionel Curtis, *Sur*, January 1943, 12, pp.7–27.

B0039 T.E. Lawrence, Lettres à Lionel Curtis, *Fontaine*, 1944, 37–40, pp.254–66. *Note:* Lawrence references also on pp.10–11.

B0040 T.E. Lawrence, AMG in Damascus, *Encore*, May 1945, 7:39, p.621–3.

B0041 T.E. Lawrence, Lettres Sur les Sept Piliers, *Valeurs*, October 1945, 3, pp.11–31.

B0042 T.E. Lawrence, The Mint (Fragmento), *Sur*, July–October 1947, 16, pp.247–51.

B0043 T.E. Lawrence, To S.A., *Sur*, July–October 1947, 16, pp.358–61. *Note:* Facsimile of holograph original, opposite translation by Ocampo.

B0044 T.E. Lawrence, Lettres, *Les Temps Modernes*, May–June, August 1948, pp.1944–75, 2177–98; 265–89.

B0045 T.E. Lawrence, Letter to Robert Graves, *World Review*, October 1949, 8, p.66.

B0046 T.E. Lawrence, Two Unpublished Letters to Ezra Pound, *Nine*, Summer 1950, 11:4, pp.180–2.

B0047 T.E. Lawrence, Théorie de la Guérrilla, *La Revue Internationale*, October–December 1950, 6:24, pp.251–63.

B0048 T.E. Lawrence, Huit Chapitres de: Le Mint, *Les Temps Modernes*, February–March 1952, 7:76 and 77, pp.1355–63, 1635–46.

B0049 T.E. Lawrence, Extracts from Lawrence's Thirty-Seven Articles, *Military Review*, October 1954, 34:7, pp.28–30.

B0050 T.E. Lawrence, The Fear, *New Republic*, 21 March 1955, 132:2, pp.18–19.

B0051 T.E. Lawrence, An Unpublished Letter of Lawrence of Arabia, *National Review*, 10 September 1963, 15:10, pp.203–5.

B0052 T.E. Lawrence, Some Unpublished Letters From T.E. Lawrence to Frederic Manning, *Southerly*, 1963, 23:4, pp.242–52. *Note:* Edited by L.T. Hergenhan.

SECTION C

NEWSPAPER ARTICLES
BY T.E. LAWRENCE

The first newspaper articles by Lawrence appeared as the First World War ended. The earliest dealt with the Arab campaign, but early in 1919 began advocacy for a change in British policy in the Middle East. These articles continued into 1920 and indicate a concern of Lawrence's that may have made Churchill's task of recruiting Lawrence into the Colonial Office easier. Churchill's attempt at resolving the problem of the Middle East culminated in the Cairo Conference of 1921. Following Lawrence's resignation from the Colonial Office, after the Cairo Conference, a period of some five years passed with no new contributions. The publication of *Revolt in the Desert* led to serialisation of the book in the *Daily Telegraph*.

The final articles listed here were stimulated by his accidental death.

C0001   T.E. Lawrence, Release of Damascus, *Palestine News*, 10 October 1918, p.6.

C0002   (T.E. Lawrence), The Arab March on Damascus, *The Times*, 17 October 1918, p.5.

C0003   T.E. Lawrence, The Arab Campaign, *The Times*, 26 November 1918, p.5.

C0004   T.E. Lawrence, The Arab Epic, *The Times*, 27–28 November 1918, pp.4, 7.

C0005   (T.E. Lawrence), The Syrian Question, *The Times*, 11 September 1919, p.11.

C0006   T.E. Lawrence, Secrets of the War on Mecca, *Daily Express*, 28 May 1920, p.1. *Note:* Reprinted in *Evolution of a Revolt*, pp. 92–95.

C0007   T.E. Lawrence, The War of the Departments, *Daily Express*, 29 May 1920, p.4. *Note:* Reprinted in *Evolution of a Revolt*, pp. 69–71.

C0008   T.E. Lawrence, The Middle East. How we are losing prestige, *Sunday Times*, 30 May 1920, p.11. *Note:* Reprinted in *Evolution of Revolt*, pp.72–77.

C0009   (T.E. Lawrence), To the Editors, *The Times*, 22 July 1920.

C0010   T.E. Lawrence, Arab Rights: Our Policy in Mesopotamia, *The Times*, 23 July 1920.

C0011   (T.E. Lawrence), Emir Feisal, *The Times*, 7 August 1920, p.9; 11 August 1920, p.9.

C0012   T.E. Lawrence, Ferment for Freedom, *Daily Herald*, 9 August 1920, p.2.

C0013   T.E. Lawrence, Mesopotamia: The Truth About the Campaign, *Sunday Times*, 22 August 1920, p.7. *Notes:* Reprinted: *Letters*, no.131; *The Essential T.E. Lawrence*, pp.225–7; *Evolution of a Revolt*, pp.96–9.

C0014 T.E. Lawrence, Arabian Politics: Resignation of Colonel Lawrence as Advisor, *Morning Post*, 20 July 1922, p.8. *Notes:* Letter from T.E. Lawrence to Sir John Shuckburgh. Letter reprinted in *The Letters*, pp.344–45. Article includes Churchill's reply.

C0015 T.E. Lawrence, Col. T.E. Lawrence Tired of Beastly Arabian Affairs, *Daily News* , 29 October 1923. *Note:* Letter to editor.

C0016 T.E. Lawrence, Revolt in the Desert, *Daily Telegraph*, 15 December 1926 – 10 January 1927. *Notes:* 1926: 15 December, pp.11–12; 16 December, pp.11–12; 17 December, pp.9–10; 18 December, pp.9–10; 20 December, pp.9–10; 21 December, pp.9–10; 22 December, pp.9–10; 23 December, pp.9–10; 24 December, pp.9–10; 28 December, pp. 9–10; 29 December, pp.9–10; 30 December, pp.9–10; 31 December, pp. 9–10. 1927: 1 January, p.9; 3 January, pp.9–10; 4 January, pp. 11–12; 5 January, pp.9–10; 6 January, p.10; 8 January, pp.9–10; 10 January, p.11.

C0017 T.E. Lawrence, Lawrence of Arabia Reply to A.T. Wilson, *Sunday Chronicle*, 1927.

C0018 T.E. Lawrence, Myself: by Lawrence, *Evening Standard*, 20 May 1935, pp.1–4. *Notes:* Reprinted in *T.E. Lawrence to His Biographer Robert Graves*, pp.180–184. Preceded by article by Robert Graves, *How This Document Was Written*, p.1.

C0019 T.E. Lawrence, Another Lawrence Letter, 20 May 1935, p.21.

C0020 T.E. Lawrence, Revolt in the Desert, *Evening Standard*, 23 May – 15 June 1935. *Notes:* Serialisation of extracts from *Revolt*, 11 parts: 22 May, p.1; 23 May, pp.22–23; 24 May, pp.22–23; 25 May, pp.10–11; 27 May, pp.22–23; 28 May, pp.22–23; 29 May, pp.22–23; 30 May, pp.23,30; 31 May, pp.23, 27; 1 June, pp.10–11; 3 June, pp.23, 26; 4 June, pp.23, 27; 5 June, pp.23, 27; 6 June, pp.23,27; 7 June, pp.23, 26; 8 June, pp.10–11; 11 June, pp.19, 22; 12 June, pp.19, 23; 13 June, p.19; 14 June, p.21; 15 June, pp.22–23.

C0021 T.E. Lawrence, Among the Bedouins, *Empire News*, 9 June 1935, p.7.

C0022 (T.E. Lawrence), T.E. Lawrence to His Friends, *The Times*, 10, 11, 12 November 1938; pp.17–18, 15–16, 13–14.

C0023 (T.E. Lawrence), The Mint, *Sunday Times*, 1955: 30 January, p.4; 6 February, p.4; 13 February, p.4.

C0024 T.E. Lawrence, The Great Race, *Motor Cycle News*, 10 November 1976.

SECTION D

INCIDENTAL WORKS CONTAINING WRITINGS OF T.E. LAWRENCE

Portions of Lawrence's published works are reprinted as chapters or sections in the following books.

D0001 Blacker, Irwin R., ed., *Behind the Lines*, Cassell, London 1956; xiv, 438 pp., 20.5 cm, red cloth. "Lawrence and the Arabs", pp.109–128.

D0002 Brockway, Wallace, and Winer, Bart K., eds, *A Second Treasury of the World's Great Letters*, Simon & Schuster, New York 1941; xl, 636 pp., 24.1 cm, deep blue cloth. "A Letter to Lionel Curtis", pp.568–573.

D0003 Brockway, Wallace, and Winer, Bart K., eds, *A Second Treasury of the World's Greatest Letters*, Heinemann, London 1950; xl, 592 pp., 23.8 cm, blue cloth. "A Letter to Lionel Curtis", pp.535–36, 539–40.

D0004 Brown, Oliver, *Exhibition*, Evelyn Adams & Mackay, London 1968; xii, 200 pp., 22.2 cm, purple cloth. Extracts from *Seven Pillars*, pp.77, 99, 100, 107, 218. Preface to *Catalogue for an exhibition of Arab Portraits by Eric Kennington*, 1921. Only complete reprint, pp.176–179. G.B. Shaw's Preface for *Exhibition of Illustrations of "Seven Pillars of Wisdom"*, 1927.

D0005 Jonathan Cape Ltd, *Then and Now*, Cape, London 1935; 226 pp., 18.8 cm, red and white paper covers. W.H. Auden, "T.E. Lawrence", pp.21–22, T.E.Lawrence, "Arabian Travellers", pp.93–96, G.B. Shaw, "*Revolt in the Desert* and Its Author", drawing of Lawrence facing p.128.

D0006 Congdon, Don, ed., *Combat: World War I*, Delacorte, New York 1964; xx, 428 pp., 22 cm, black cloth. "Blowing Up Trains" excerpt from *Seven Pillars of Wisdom*, pp.268–288.

D0007 Congdon, Don, ed., *Combat: World War I*, Dell, New York 1965; 448 pp., 16.2 cm, pictorial paper covers. "Blowing Up Trains" excerpt from *Seven Pillars of Wisdom*, pp.292–312.

D0008 Custot, Pierre, *Sturly*, Cape, London 1924; 128 pp., translated by Richard Aldington, 19.6 cm, grey paper covered boards, dark blue spine, paper label on spine. Blurb on front flap of dust wrapper is reputed to be by Lawrence.

D0009 De Weerd, H.A., *Great Soldiers of the Two World Wars*, Hale, London 1943; 260 pp., 21.9 cm. Excerpt from *Revolt in the Desert*, pp.92–100.

D0010 Elbogen, Paul, ed., *Dearest Mother*, Fischer, New York 1942; 2, 358 pp., 23.2 cm, grey cloth. Text of letter, pp.344–350.

D0010a Elliott-Bateman, Michael, *et al.*, *Revolt to Revolution*, Manchester University Press, 1974. "The Evolution of a Revolt", Chapter 5, pp.145–160.

D0011 Encyclopedia Britannica, 14th ed., London, 1936; 24 vols, 28.5 cm. T.E.Lawrence, "Science of Guerrilla Warfare", Vol. 10, pp.950–53; D.G. Hogarth, "T.E. Lawrence", Vol. 13, pp.798–99.

D0012 Golding, Louis, *In the Steps of Moses the Conqueror,* Rich and Cowan, London n.d. (1938); 368 pp., blue paper covered boards. T.E.Lawrence: pp.29, 48, 49, 51–52, 63, 120, 128–32, 153–155, 160, 194, 210, 213–214, 225, 245–247, 265, 276–277, 284–285, 288, 291–292, 294–295, 333–336, 339. Contains "Confession of Faith" by T.E. Lawrence.

D0013 Hanley, James, *Boy,* Boriswood, London January 1931; 272 pp., 19.2 cm, orange cloth. Blurb on dustwrapper.

D0014 Hanley, James, *Boy,* Boriswood, London, 4th impression, May 1934; 1st cheap edition, 274 pp., 19 cm, orange cloth. Blurb on dustwrapper.

D0015 Hausmann, Walter, *Reclam Lesestoffe Lehrpraktische Analyses Folge 6,* Reclam, Stuttgart 1967. "T.E. Lawrence: Faisals Aufgebot", pp.5–12.

D0016 Hemingway, Ernest, ed., *Men at War,* Crown, New York 1942; xxviii, 1076 pp., 21 cm, red cloth. "Torture" pp.303–308; "Blowing Up a Train", pp.522–528.

D0017 Higham, Thomas F., *From the Greek,* Clarendon Press, Oxford 1943; viii, 246 pp., 16.5 cm, tan cloth. Extracts from *The Odyssey,* pp.15–16, 18.

D0018 Higham, Thomas F., *The Oxford Book of Greek in Translation,* Clarendon Press, Oxford 1938; cxii, 782 pp., 17.1 cm, blue linen. T.E.Lawrence, pp.lxxii, 44(i), 45, 50, 52.

D0019 Israel Defense Forces, Chief Education Officer, *Victor Hugo, Julius Caesar, Stendhal, T.E. Lawrence, Virgil, Winston Churchill,* Ministry of Defense 1984; 132 pp., 21 cm, red and green paper covers, white lettering. "Blowing Up a Train", pp.85–100.

D0020 Jenkins, Alan C., *Eye-witness,* Collins- Lions, London 1974; 160 pp., 18 cm, pictorial paper covers. "Desert Raid. T.E. Lawrence", pp.142–151.

D0021 Keller, Helen Rex, *The Reader's Digest of Books,* Macmillan, New York 1938; 6, 1450 pp., 22 cm, blue cloth. Extract from *Revolt in the Desert,* pp.1291–1293.

D0022 Miller, David W., and Moore, Clark D., eds, *The Middle East Yesterday and Today,* Bantam, New York 1970; xx, 364 pp., 18 cm, pictorial paper covers. "The Arab Revolt", pp.137–147.

D0023 Reynolds, Quentin, and Leckie, Robert, eds, *With Fire and Sword,* Dial, New York 1963; 384 pp., 23.7 cm, orange cloth. "Blowing up a Train", pp.199–208.

D0024 Singer, Kurt D., ed., *The World's Greatest Spy Stories,* W.H. Allen, London 1954; 254 pp., 20.2 cm, black cloth. "Blowing up a Train", pp.243–251.

D0025 Stanley, Arthur, compiler, *The Golden Road,* Dent, London 1938; xii, 624 pp., 19.8 cm, wine cloth. "Noon and Night (1916–1918)", pp.245–250.

D0026 Steiner, George, ed., *Homer: A Collection of Critical Essays*, Prentice-Hall, Englewood Cliffs, NJ, 1962; xii, 180 pp., 10.3 cm, black paper covers. *T.E. Shaw – Translator's Note*, pp.153–55.

D0027 Thomas, Lowell, *Great True Adventures*, Arco, London 1955; xiv, 402 pp., 20.2 cm, maroon paper covered boards. "Adventure in Arabia", pp.93–111.

D0028 Thomas, Lowell, *Great True Adventures*, Arco, London 1958; 224 pp., 22.2 cm, red paper covered boards, simulated cloth. "Adventure in Arabia", pp.79–96.

D0029 Thomas, Lowell, *Great True Adventures*, Dell, New York 1959; 416 pp., 16.4 cm, pictorial paper covers. "Adventure in Arabia", pp.104–124.

D0030 Van Doren, Charles, ed., *Letters to Mother*, Allen & Unwin, London 1960; xviii, 350 pp., 24.2 cm, black cloth. Text of two letters [*The Letters*, nos. 21, 23, 1910], pp.65–69.

D0031 *The Weekend Library*, Doubleday Doran, Garden City, New York, 1930; x, 336 pp., 19.3 cm, orange cloth. Extracts from *Revolt in the Desert*, pp.75–105.

PART 2

BIOGRAPHY AND CRITICISM

Section E records those materials about Lawrence that have appeared in the sixty-three years since the first biography by Lowell Thomas. As in Part 1, the books make up the first section of this part. A second section (F) includes a lengthy listing of what are termed incidental works, i.e. works in which Lawrence is mentioned, chapters are included on him, or whole portions of up to one third of the work deal with him in some fashion. Journal articles comprise a third section (G) and newspaper articles a fourth (H).

The entries in Section F are uneven; many of them are relatively unimportant works, but they have been included for the sake of completeness. Throughout all the sections there are many items dealing with critical analysis of one or more of the works described or with the David Lean film. Exhaustive inclusion may well be a criticism levelled at this portion of the work. It has been felt preferable to err in that regard rather than omit material of use to readers.

SECTION E

BOOKS ABOUT
T.E. LAWRENCE

Lowell Thomas, 1920–1929

The writing on Lawrence during the first decade following the First World War is dominated by the work of Lowell Thomas. Thomas' public association with Lawrence began with his lantern-slide lectures on the Middle Eastern campaigns. Beginning in 1919, the lectures, especially in London, were an immediate success. There are a great many pieces of ephemera associated with the lectures, many of which are represented here. After leaving England, Thomas went on a world tour with his lectures, which in turn were highly successful.

Following his world tour, and as a natural consequence of the success it enjoyed, Thomas published the first biography on Lawrence, much to the subject's regret. Thomas spent only a few weeks, at most, in Akaba during the war and met Lawrence on only a few occasions then and afterwards. This book is today well remembered by those then in their youth. Its popularity kept it in print for many years.

In 1927, three years after publication of his Lawrence biography, Thomas published *The Boys' Life of Colonel Lawrence*, one of the first two juvenile biographies on Lawrence. This work set the tone for the many juveniles on Lawrence to follow.

Thomas' world tour had included Australia and it is no surprise that in the same year as Thomas' "Boys' Life' another juvenile work was published in Australia, Roseler's *Prince of Mecca*. Roseler is a pseudonym of E.V.Timms, a well known and respected novelist in his day.

With publication of *Revolt in the Desert* in 1927, Cape sensed that they had stimulated a market for an 'authorised' biography, which could at the same time serve as an antidote to Thomas' work. Lawrence's friend, Robert Graves, was in need of funds at the time and Lawrence persuaded Cape to commission him to write the biography. Graves received extensive help from Lawrence as is attested in *T.E. Lawrence to His Biographer, Robert Graves* (1938).

The publication of *Seven Pillars of Wisdom* (1926) by subscription and *Revolt in the Desert* (1927), gave rise almost immediately to an attempt at bibliography. The information contained in the German Reed work *Annotations on Some Minor Writings* perpetuated some persistent myths, among them – that there are only 100 copies of the 1926 edition and that 'complete' copies are bound in full leather and 'incomplete' in half leather.

One book published that year included Lawrence along with two other figures from the war period. *Three Persons* is one of the first hostile essays on Lawrence. Lawrence took exception to it, "He patronised me, I thought, damn him. What does he know about prose that he dare praise mine?' (*The Letters*, p.651).

1921?

E001 LOWELL THOMAS, With Allenby in Palestine, 192–?

Programme for Slide Lecture

[All in purple] [Royal Coat of Arms] | ROYAL OPERA HOUSE | COVENT GARDEN. | PROPRIETORS . . . . THE GRAND OPERA SYNDICATE. LTD. | [double rule] | Commencing Thursday Evening, August 14th, and Nightly at 8:30. | .. Matinees Wednesday, Thursday and Saturday at 2:30.. | [double rule] | PERCY BURTON | (by arrangement with the Grand Opera Syndicate) | presents | LOWELL THOMAS | in | His Illustrated Travelogue of the British Campaign | *AMERICA'S TRIBUTE TO BRITISH VALOUR* | With Allenby in Palestine | including | THE CAPTURE OF JERUSALEM | and | THE LIBERATION OF HOLY ARABIA

Collation   25.5 × 19 cm: single-fold leaflet, back page blank.

Published at   3d.

Copies   Cal.

E002 LOWELL THOMAS, With Allenby in Palestine, [1920?]

Programme for Slide Lecture

[All in brown] QUEEN'S HALL, | LANGHAM PLACE, REGENT ST. W. | Sole Lessees ... ... CHAPPELL & CO., Ltd. | [double rule] | COMMENCING FRIDAY, DECEMBER 26th, | MATINEES AT 2.30, EVENINGS AT 8.30 For Dates see Next Page. | [double rule] | PERCY BURTON | presents | *AMERICA'S TRIBUTE TO BRITISH VALOUR* | IN THE PERSON OF | LOWELL THOMAS | [within single-rule frame, photo of Thomas in uniform wearing abba] | In his Illustrated Travelogue of the British Campaigns: | "With Allenby in Palestine | and Lawrence in Arabia."

Collation   25.5 × 19 cm: single-fold leaflet.

Contents   Pp.[1] title page, [2] list of show dates, outline of part one, WITH ALLENBY IN PALESTINE, [3] outline of part II, WITH LAWRENCE IN ARABIA, ad for *Strand* magazine article on Lawrence, by Thomas, [4] credits, outline of programme of music.

Paper   White, wove, unwatermarked, all edges trimmed.

Published at   6d.

Copies   AC.

E003 LOWELL THOMAS, With Allenby in Palestine and Lawrence in Arabia, 1919

Programme for Slide Lecture

[All in brown] [Royal Coat of Arms] | ROYAL ALBERT HALL, | KENSINGTON | [short double rules] | Matinee at 2:20. Evenings at 8. | For dates of Representations, see Daily Papers. | [short double rules] | PERCY BURTON | presents | *AMERICA'S TRIBUTE TO BRITISH VALOUR* | IN THE PERSON OF | LOWELL THOMAS | [photo of LT in mufti, within single rule frame] | In his Illustrated Travelogue of the British Campaigns: | "With Allenby in Palestine | and Lawrence in Arabia"

Collation   25.5 × 19 cm: single-fold leaflet, 4 pp.

Contents   [1] title page, [2–3] programme text, [4] credits.

Published at   6d.

Copies   Cal.

E004 LOWELL THOMAS, With Allenby in Palestine and Lawrence in Arabia, n.d.

Programme for Slide Lecture

[Within frame of fancy rules, printed over photo of Thomas, all in red] LOWELL THOMAS | Creator of "With Allenby in Palestine and | Lawrence in Arabia"| *The Modern Master of the Magic Carpet.*

Collation   28 × 23 cm: [1]⁹, 18 leaves, pp.[1–2], 1–16, [1–2].

Contents   Prp.[1] title cover, [2] blank, pp.1–16 text, testimonies, quotes from reviews, etc., pp.[1] blank, [2] half title.

Paper   White, wove, unwatermarked, all edges trimmed.

Copies   H.

E005 LOWELL THOMAS, With Allenby in Palestine and Lawrence in Arabia, 1919

Programme for Slide Lecture

[All in blue] [Old English lettering at top] Philharmonic Hall | [within very elaborate frame & pictorial design] PERCY BURTON | PRESENTS | LOWELL THOMAS | (IN PERSON) | in his world famous travelogue: | "With Allenby in Palestine | and Lawrence in Arabia"| TWICE DAILY, 2:30 & 8:30. SUNDAY 8.

Collation   28.8 × 22.8 cm: [1]⁶, 6 leaves, unpaged.

Contents   [First and last leaves, herringbone cellophane sheets. First sheet has small blue sticker in white] 6D. | Please see that | this seal is |

Unbroken | pp.1 [photo of Lowell Thomas in Arab garb], [2] blank, 3 title page, 4 synopsis of programme, 5 within elaborate frame ads for other travelogues, 6 extracts from reviews, 7 blank, 8 advertisement sheets on slick paper, 1st and last sheets white, inner sheets buff. Two holes punched through with blue cord tie.

Published at   6d.

Copies   Cal.

1924

E006   LOWELL THOMAS, With Lawrence in Arabia, Century, 1924

First American Edition

WITH LAWRENCE | IN ARABIA | BY | LOWELL THOMAS | ORIGINAL PHOTOGRAPHS TAKEN BY H.A. CHASE, | F.R.G.S., AND BY THE AUTHOR | [cut] | THE CENTURY CO. | *New York & London*

Collation   19.8 × 13 cm: [1]^{10} [2–26]^8 [27]^4, 214 leaves, pp.[2], [i–vi], vii–xvii, [xviii], [1–2], 3–408.

Contents   [1–2] blank, prp.[i] bastard title, [ii] blank, [iii] title page, [iv] copyright statement, [v] dedication, [vi] blank, vii–xii foreword, xiii–xiv contents, xv–xvii illustrations, [xviii] blank, [1] half-title, [2] blank, 3–408 text.

RT   On verso WITH LAWRENCE IN ARABIA. On recto [according to chapter].

Plates   Thirty-two photographs on coated paper, printed on both sides, following pp.2, 8, 32, 48, 64, 96, 112, 160, 176, 180, 188, 224, 240, 260, 268, 288, 304, 308, 312, 316, 320, 324, 328, 332, 352, 356, 364, 384, 388, 396, 400, 404.

Text   20 lines, 10 (10.1) × 9.8 cm.

Paper   White, thick, wove, unwatermarked, all edges trimmed, sheets bulk 3.5 cm.

Binding   Brown cloth 54 br. O. On front cover: [within black frame, forming arch, framing picture of desert scene with rider on camel with sky in blue] | WITH | LAWRENCE | IN ARABIA | LOWELL | THOMAS. On spine: WITH | LAWRENCE | IN | ARABIA | [cut] | LOWELL | THOMAS | [cut, with blue sky background] | THE | CENTURY | CO. Orange head and tail bands.

Notes   Later impressions differ as follows: [Collation]: 20.2 × 13.3 cm; [Plates]: same as above, except for arrangement, following pp.2, 8, 32, 44, 52, 62, 68, 82, 104, 132, 150, 156, 178, 204, 206, 210, 214, 220, 228, 238, 250, 258, 268, 274, 282, 290, 298, 306, 310, 324, 378, 404; [Binding]: Orange cloth 39 gy. r O. Earlier copies have spine imprint 1 cm above bottom edge of spine.

Copies   AC, Cal, UT, Ho, LC.

E007   LOWELL THOMAS, With Lawrence in Arabia, Garden City, [193–?]

Second American Edition

[Within single rule frame] A STAR BOOK | [long rule across entire frame] | WITH LAWRENCE | IN ARABIA | By | LOWELL THOMAS | Original Photographs | Taken by H.A. Chase F.R.G.S. | And by the Author | [series device] | [long rule across entire frame] | GARDEN CITY PUBLISHING COMPANY | GARDEN CITY, NEW YORK

Collation   20.5 × 14.2 cm: [1–6]^{16} [7–14]^8 [15–16]^{16} [17]^4 [18]^{16}, 212 leaves, pp.[i–vi], vii–xiv, [1–2], 3–408, [2].

Contents   Prp.[i] bastard title, [ii] blank, [iii] title page, [iv] copyright statement, [v] dedication, [vi] blank, vii–xii foreword, xiii–xiv contents, pp.[1] half-title, [2] blank, 3–408 text, [1–2] blank.

RT   On verso WITH LAWRENCE IN ARABIA. On recto [according to chapter].

Plates   Eight plates on coated paper, printed on both sides except for frontispiece, following pp.ii, 42, 74, 106, 154, 202, 250, 298.

Text   20 lines, 9.9 (10.2) × 9.8 cm.

Paper   Thick,white, wove,unwatermarked, all edges trimmed, sheets bulk 3 cm.

Binding   Smooth brown cloth 54 br. O. On spine: [in blue] WITH | LAWRENCE | IN | ARABIA | [cut] | LOWELL | THOMAS | [cut of Lawrence in abba] | GARDEN CITY | PUBLISHING CO. Top edge purple.

Published at $2.50.

Notes   Star series: there are a variety of differences in issues in this series, some of them are noted here:
[Collation]: 20.7 × 14 cm: [1–12]^{16} [13]^4 [14]^{16}, 212 leaves, pp.[i–vi], vii–xiv, [1–2], 3–408, [1–2]; [Binding]: On spine: WITH | LAWRENCE | IN | ARABIA | [cut] | LOWELL | THOMAS | GARDEN CITY | PUBLISHING CO. T.e. light brown.
Another issue: [Collation]: 20.5 × 14 cm: [1–24]^8 [25]^8 [26–27]^8, 212 leaves; [Paper]: sheets bulk 3.5 cm; [Binding]: On spine: [in blue, same as immediately above].
Another issue: [Collation]: 20.5 × 14.2 cm: [1–23]^8 [24]^{12} [25]^8 212 leaves, pp.[4], vii–xiv, [1–2], 3–408, [4]; [Contents]: prp.[1] title page, [2] copyright statement, [3] dedication, [4] blank, vii–xii foreword, xii–xiv contents, pp.[1] half-title, [2] blank, 3–408 text, [1–4] blank; [Plates]: 8 plates on coated paper, printed on both sides, except frontispiece. Frontispiece before first page, others following pp.4, 36, 52, 132, 148, 244, 260.
Another issue: as immediately above, with following differences: [Collation]: 19.9 × 14 cm:; [Binding]: brown cloth 45 l.gy r Br.
Another issue, 1942: [Collation]: 19.5 × 14 cm: [1–13]^{16} 208 leaves, pp.[2], vii–xiv, 3–408; [Contents]: prp.[1] title page, [2] copyright statement, vii–xii foreword, xiii–xiv contents, 3–408 text; [Paper]: sheets

bulk 3 cm; [Plates]: 4 plates on coated paper printed on both sides following pp.24, 56, 152, 184; [Binding]: Brown cloth 38 d. r O. smooth cloth, [spine lettering in blue]. T.e. light brown.

Another issue, same as immediately above, except spine lettering in black.

Copies   AC, Cal, UT.

E008   LOWELL THOMAS, With Lawrence in Arabia, Colliers, n.d.

Third American Edition

LOWELL THOMAS | WITH LAWRENCE | IN ARABIA | *Illustrated With Original Photographs* | *Taken by H.A. Chase, F.R.G.S.,* | *And by Lowell Thomas* | [pub. device] | PUBLISHED BY | P.F. Collier & Son Corporation, New York | BY SPECIAL ARRANGEMENT WITH | D. Appleton-Century Co., Inc. | NEW YORK

Collation   20.3 × 13.8 cm: [1–12]^{16} [13]^4 [14]^{16}, 212 leaves, pp.[i–vi], vii–xiv, [1–2], 3–408, [2].

Contents   Prp.[i] bastard title, [ii] blank, [iii] title page, [iv] copyright statement, [v] dedication, [vi] blank, vii–xii foreword, xiii–xiv contents, pp.[1] half-title, [2] blank, 3–408 text, [1–2] blank.

RT   On verso WITH LAWRENCE IN ARABIA. On recto [according to chapter].

Plates   Eight plates on coated paper, printed on both sides except frontispiece, following pp.ii, 42, 74, 106, 154, 202, 250, 298.

Text   20 lines, 9.8 (10.1) 9.7 cm.

Paper   White, wove, unwatermarked, all edges trimmed, sheets bulk 3 cm.

Binding   Green leather simulated cloth 151 d. gy. G. On front cover: [logo of Lowell Thomas Adventure Library]. On spine: [white] [rule] | [within gilt rectangle, in green] LOWELL | THOMAS | [below double white rule] | [gilt] WITH | LAWRENCE | IN ARABIA | [double white rule] | [within gilt rectangle, in green] COLLIER | [white rule]. Yellow and green head and tail bands.

Notes   Another issue, same as above, with following differences: [Collation]: 20.5 × 14 cm: [1]^8 [2]^4 [3–13]^{16} [14]^8 [15]^{16}. [Typography and paper]: sheets bulk 2.5 cm.

Copies   AC, Cal.

E009   LOWELL THOMAS, With Lawrence in Arabia, Grosset & Dunlap, 1955

Fourth American Edition

LOWELL THOMAS | [tapered rule] | WITH LAWRENCE | IN ARABIA | [tapered rule] | [series device] | NEW YORK | GROSSET & DUNLAP | *Publishers*

Collation   20.8 × 14 cm: [1–7]¹⁶ [8]²⁰ [9–10]¹⁶, 164 leaves, pp.[i–xii], [1], 2–316.

Contents   Prp.[i] bastard title, [ii] titles in series, [iii] title page, [iv] copyright statement, [v–viii] preface, [ix–x] contents, [xi] half-title, [xii] blank, pp.[1]–316 text.

RT   On verso WITH LAWRENCE IN ARABIA. On recto [according to chapter].

Text   20 lines, 9.2 (9.5) × 10.1 cm.

Paper   White, wove, unwatermarked, all edges trimmed, sheets bulk 3 cm.

Binding   Cloth simulated paper covered boards 60 l.gy. Br., 15 m. Red cloth spine. On front cover: [series design cut]. On spine: LOWELL | THOMAS | WITH | LAWRENCE | IN | ARABIA | GROSSET | & | DUNLAP. T.e red.

Notes   Great Adventures Library Series.

Copies   AC, Cal.

E010   LOWELL THOMAS, With Lawrence in Arabia, Popular Library, 1961

Fifth American Edition

WITH | LAWRENCE | IN ARABIA | LOWELL THOMAS | POPULAR LIBRARY NEW YORK | NED L. PINES President | FRANK P. LUALDI Publisher

Collation   17.6 × 10.7 cm: [1]⁸ 2–16⁸, 128 leaves, pp.[1–5], 6–256.

Contents   Pp.[1] extract from book, [2] brief biography of Lowell Thomas, [3] title page, [4] issue, copyright statements, 5–8 foreword, 9–253 text, [1] ad, [2] blank, [3] ad.

Text   20 lines, 7 × 8.9 cm.

Paper   Wove, unwatermarked, all edges trimmed, sheets bulk 1.3 cm.

Binding   Pictorial paper covers. On front cover: [in white] SP116 | [in white] 50¢ | by LOWELL THOMAS | [three-line quote from *NY Times Rev.*] | [in white, series device] | [in red brown] WITH | LAWRENCE | IN ARABIA | Watch for the great Columbia picture. On spine: [in white] SP116 | [in white] 50¢ | [running down] WITH LAWRENCE IN ARABIA [author's name in white] LOWELL THOMAS | [across at bottom] [rule in white] |

POPULAR | SPECIAL. On back cover: With Lawrence In Arabia | [nine line blurb] | ORIGINALLY PUBLISHED AT $4.00 BY APPLETON-CENTURY-CROFTS, INC. | [in white] POPULAR [pub. device] LIBRARY | Litho in U.S.A. [All edges green.]

Published at 50¢.

Notes Another impression, same as above, with following differences: [Title page desc.]: [names of president and publisher omitted]; [Collation]: 17.5 × 10.6 cm; [Contents]: pp.[2] blank, last three pages ads; [Binding]: [first line of front cover in white] 445-08165-075 75¢, title in red. On spine: [redesigned pub. device] | [running down in white] POPULAR | LIBRARY | WITH LAWRENCE IN ARABIA LOWELL THOMAS | [in white] 445-08165-075. On back cover: [line reading ORIGINALLY PUB. AT $4.00 etc. is omitted; [Published at]: 75¢.

Copies AC, Cal, UT.

E011 LOWELL THOMAS, With Lawrence In Arabia, Doubleday, 1967

Sixth American Edition

New Enlarged Edition | WITH | LAWRENCE | IN | ARABIA | BY LOWELL THOMAS | *Original photographs taken by H.A. Chase, F.R.G.S.* | *and by the Author* | DOUBLEDAY & COMPANY, INC. | GARDEN CITY, N.Y. | 1967

Collation 20.8 × 14 cm: [1–11]¹⁶, 176 leaves, pp.[i–vii], viii–xxx, [1], 2–320, [2].

Contents Prp.[i] bastard title, [ii] list of author's works, [iii] title page, [iv] copyright statement, [v] dedication, [vi] blank, [vii]–xix, foreword, [xx] blank, [xxi]–xxii contents, [xxiii]–xxv illustrations, [xxvi] blank, [xxvii]–xxx introduction, [1]–320 text, [1–2] blank.

RT On verso *With Lawrence in Arabia*. On recto [in italics, according to chapter].

Plates Thirty-two b/w photographs, printed on both sides except frontispiece. Frontispiece before prp.i, others in fours following pp.66, 130, 194, 258.

Text 20 lines, 9.1 (9.2) × 10.3 cm.

Paper White, wove, unwatermarked, top and bottom edges trimmed, sheets bulk 2.3 cm.

Binding Black cloth. On spine: LOWELL | THOMAS | [running down] With Lawrence in Arabia | [across] Doubleday. Yellow head and tail bands.

Notes Book Club edition same as above with following difference: [Binding]: Tan leather simulated cloth 53 m O. T.e. light yellow.

Copies AC, Cal, UT, LC.

E012 LOWELL THOMAS, With Lawrence in Arabia, Hutchinson, [1925]

First English Edition

WITH LAWRENCE | IN ARABIA | by | LOWELL THOMAS | With Frontispiece and 64 other Illustrations. | LONDON: HUTCHINSON & CO. | PATERNOSTER ROW

Collation 23 × 15 cm: [A]^8 B–U^8, 160 leaves, pp.[i–iv], v–xiii, [14], 15–317, [3].

Contents [i] bastard title, [ii] blank, [iii] title page, [iv] dedication, v–viii foreword, ix–x contents, xi–xiii illustrations, [14] publisher's statement, 15–317 text, [3] blank.

RT On verso WITH LAWRENCE IN ARABIA. On recto [according to chapter].

Plates Sixty-five photographs, on coated paper, following pp.11, 18, 32, 40, 48, 62, 86, 100, 120, 130, 132, 136, 140, 158, 170, 176, 186, 188, 192, 208, 222, 232, 244, 256, 264, 280, 288, 294, 308, 310, 314. All but frontispiece printed both sides.

Typography and paper $ 1 signed B.

Text 20 lines, 8.4 (9.1) × 10.5 cm.

Paper White, wove, unwatermarked, all edges trimmed, sheets bulk 3.5 cm.

Binding Red cloth 13 deep Red. On front cover: [double blind rules along all four outer edges]. On spine: [gilt] [double rule] WITH | LAWRENCE | IN | ARABIA | LOWELL | THOMAS | HUTCHINSON | [double rule].

Notes Another copy has 15 m Red binding. The 4th edition, i.e. impression, is same as above except it has issue statement on title page above imprint. The 6th to 11th editions are as 4th.

Copies AC, Cal, UT.

E013 LOWELL THOMAS, With Lawrence in Arabia, Hutchinson, n.d.

First English Edition (Twelfth Impression)

WITH LAWRENCE IN ARABIA | By | LOWELL THOMAS | *With Frontispiece and 64 other Illustrations.* | *TWELFTH EDITION* | LONDON: | HUTCHINSON & CO. (Publishers), LTD. | PATERNOSTER ROW

Collation 21.5 × 14 cm: [A]^8 B–U^8, 160 leaves, pp.[i–iv], v–xiii, [14–15], 16–316, [3].

Contents Pp.[i] half-title, [ii] blank, [iii] title page, [iv] dedication, v–viii foreword, ix–x contents, xi–xiii illustrations, xiv publisher's statement, [15] –317 text, 318–320 blank.

RT On verso WITH LAWRENCE IN ARABIA. On recto [according to chapter].

Plates Sixty-five photos on coated paper following pp.ii, 18, 32, 40, 48, 62, 86, 100, 120, 130, 132, 136, 140, 158, 170, 176, 186, 188, 192, 208, 220, 222, 232, 244, 256, 264, 280, 288, 294, 308, 310, 314. All but frontispiece printed on both sides.

Typography and paper $ 1 signed G.

Text 20 lines, 8.9 (9.1) × 10.5 cm.

Paper White, wove, unwatermarked, all edges trimmed, sheets bulk 2 cm.

Binding Red cloth 12 s. Red. On spine: WITH | LAWRENCE | IN | ARABIA | [cut] | LOWELL | THOMAS | HUTCHINSON. T.e. grey.

Notes 14th to 24th editions (impressions) as above; 25th impression as above with following differences: [Plates]: following pp.ii, 16, 32, 48, 56, 64, 72, 80, 96, 104, 112, 128, 136, 144, 160, 168, 176, 192, 196, 204, 208, 224, 228, 236, 240, 256, 264, 276, 284, 288, 304, 312; [Binding]: blue cloth 182 m. Blue. On front cover: [black rules along outer edges, all sides]. On spine: [same as above except double rules top and bottom]. One copy seen lacks cut between author's name and title. 26th impression same as 12th above with following differences: [Binding]: 180 v. l B polished cloth. 27th impression same as above with following differences: 168 brill g B. Publisher's name on spine of 12th edition is smaller than those following.

Copies AC, Cal.

E014   LOWELL THOMAS, With Lawrence in Arabia, Hutchinson, n.d.[1933?]

78th thousand

WITH | LAWRENCE IN ARABIA | by | LOWELL THOMAS | *78th THOUSAND* | *London:* | HUTCHINSON & CO. (Publishers), LTD.

Collation 17.7 × 11.5 cm: [A]–I^{16} x^2, 146 leaves, pp.[i–x], xi–xvi, [xvii–xviii], 19–288, [2], 1st leaf paste-down end papers.

Contents Pp.[i–iv] blank, [v] bastard title, [vi] list of author's works, [vii] title page, [viii] printer's credit, [ix] dedication, [x] blank, xi–xiv foreword, xv–xvi contents, [xvii] publisher's disclaimer that T.E.Lawrence is the source of facts contained in text, [xviii] blank, 19–288 text, [1–4] publisher's ads.

Typography and paper $ 1,5 signed L. in A.B, L. in A. B*.

Text 20 lines, 7 × 8.9 cm.

Paper White, wove, unwatermarked, all edges trimmed, sheets bulk 1.7 cm.

Binding White oatmeal cloth. On front cover: [in blue] WITH | LAWRENCE | IN | ARABIA | LOWELL THOMAS. On spine: WITH | LAWRENCE | IN | ARABIA | LOWELL | THOMAS | HUTCHINSON'S |

BOOKLOVER'S | LIBRARY.

Published at   2s.

Notes   Series: Hutchinson's Booklover's Library no. 16.
85th thousand, same as above, with following differences: [Binding]:
Light tan 31 p. y Pink buckram.
107th thousand [1935], same as 78th thousand, with following
differences: [Collation]: [A] – K^{16} x^4, 148 leaves, pp.i–xviii, 19–288, [8];
[Contents]; [i–ix] [same as above] [x] publisher's disclaimer, xi–xiv
foreword, xv within rules, note of death and appreciation by Lord Allenby,
[xvi] blank, xvii–xviii contents, 19–288 text, [1–8] ads; [Binding]: same as
85th thousand.
117th thousand [1936], same as 107th thousand above.

Copies   AC, Cal.

E015   LOWELL THOMAS, With Lawrence in Arabia, Hutchinson, n.d.[1935]

First English Edition (97th thousand)

WITH | LAWRENCE | IN ARABIA | [rule] | by | LOWELL THOMAS |
[rule] | WITH FRONTISPIECE AND 30 OTHER | ILLUSTRATIONS | 97th
THOUSAND | HUTCHINSON & CO. | *(Publishers) Ltd.* | LONDON | [rule]

Collation   21.5 × 13.5 cm: [A] – Q^8, 128 leaves, pp.[1–10], 11–254, [2].

Contents   [1] half-title, [2] blank, [3] title page, [4] printer's credit, [5]
dedication, [6] publisher's disclaimer, [7–8] contents, [9–10] illustrations,
11–14 foreword, 15–254 text, 255 obituary notice of TEL and appreciation
by Lord Allenby, [256] blank.

RT   On verso WITH LAWRENCE IN ARABIA. On recto [according to
chapter].

Plates   Sixteen plates on coated paper, following pp.[2], 16, 36, 52, 64, 82,
98, 114, 130, 146, 160, 178, 194, 208, 224, 238; printed on both sides except for
frontis.

Typography and paper $ 1 signed B.

Text   20 lines, 7.8 (7.9) × 10 cm.

Paper   White, wove, unwatermarked, all edges trimmed, sheets bulk 3.2
cm.

Binding   Blue cloth 182 m Blue. On front cover: [black rules along outer
edges]. On spine: [double rule] | WITH | LAWRENCE | IN | ARABIA |
[cut] | LOWELL | THOMAS | HUTCHINSON | [double rule].

Published at   3s 6d.

Notes   Some of illustrations here do not appear in earlier impressions.
105th thousand [1936?], same as above, with following differences:
[Plates]: 17 plates on coated paper, printed on both sides except for frontis.,
following pp.[2], 14, 32, 48, 64, 80, 96, 112, 128, 144, 160, 176, 192, 208, 224,

240; [Binding]: light blue cloth 185 p. Blue.

132nd thousand, same as 105th thousand above, with following differences: [Binding]: 199 l. p B.; another copy has no rules on front cover 15 m. Red polished cloth.

Copies Cal.

E016 LOWELL THOMAS, With Lawrence in Arabia, Hutchinson, n.d.

101st thousand

WITH | LAWRENCE IN ARABIA | by | LOWELL THOMAS | *101st Thousand* | *London.* | HUTCHINSON & CO. (Publishers), LTD.

Collation 17.5 × 11 cm: [A]⁸ [B]⁸ C–S⁸, 144 leaves, pp.[i–x], xi–xviii, 19–288.

Contents Pp.[i–iv] end papers, [v] bastard title, [vi] list of author's works, [vii] title page, [viii] printer's credit, [ix] dedication, [x] disclaimer by publisher, xi–xiv foreword, [xv] within single rule frame, Allenby's statement on Lawrence's death, [xvi] blank, xvii–xviii contents, 19–288 text.

Typography and paper $ 1 signed C.

Text 7 × 9 cm.

Paper White, wove, unwatermarked, all edges trimmed, sheets bulk 2 cm.

Binding White cloth. On front cover: [all in blue] WITH LAWRENCE | IN ARABIA | LOWELL THOMAS. On spine: WITH | LAWRENCE | IN | ARABIA | LOWELL | THOMAS | HUTCHINSON'S | BOOKLOVER'S | LIBRARY.

Copies Murray.

E017 LOWELL THOMAS , With Lawrence In Arabia, Hutchinson, 1939

Second English Edition (Pocket Library)

Lowell Thomas | [tapered rule] | WITH LAWRENCE | IN ARABIA | *172nd THOUSAND* | [tapered rule] | HUTCHINSON & CO. | *(Publishers), Ltd.* | LONDON

Collation 17.7 × 10.5 cm: [A] –H¹⁶, 128 leaves, pp.[1–7], 8–251, [1–2].

Contents Pp.[1] bastard title, [2] blank, [3] title page, [4] pub. note, printer's credit, [5] dedication, [6] pub. note, 7–10 foreword, xi–xii contents, 12–251 text, [1] obituary note on Lawrence, [2] ad.

RT On verso WITH LAWRENCE IN ARABIA. On recto [according to chapter].

Typography and paper $ 1 signed B.

Text 20 lines, 6.2 (6.3) × 8.7 cm.

Paper White, wove, unwatermarked, all edges trimmed, sheets bulk 2.3 cm.

Binding Only copy examined has been rebound.

Copies AC.

E018 LOWELL THOMAS, With Lawrence in Arabia, Arrow, 1962

Third English Edition

WITH | LAWRENCE | IN ARABIA | LOWELL THOMAS | *With a new Introduction by the author* | [pub. device] | ARROW BOOKS

Collation 17.8 × 11 cm: guillotined sheets, 128 leaves, pp.[1–8], 9–256.

Contents Pp.[1] bastard title, [2] blank, [3] title page, [4] issue, copyright statements, printer's credit, [5] dedication, [6] blank, [7–8] contents, 9–18 foreword, 19–[256] text.

Plates Eight plates on coated paper, printed on both sides following p.128.

Text 20 lines, 7.2 × 8.8 cm.

Paper White, wove, unwatermarked, all edges trimmed, sheets bulk 1.5 cm.

Binding Pictorial paper covers. On front cover: [in white] WITH | LAWRENCE | IN ARABIA | by | [in white] LOWELL THOMAS | *The book that launched* | *the Lawrence legend* | [within red circle on yellow oval, in red] Arrow 3/6 | NET. On spine: [within red circle, in red] 3/6 | [in red] 669 | [running down] WITH LAWRENCE IN ARABIA | [in red] Lowell Thomas | [across] [publisher's device]. On back cover: [information on motion picture]. All edges yellow.

Published at 3s 6d.

Copies AC, Cal.

E019 LOWELL THOMAS, Med Lawrence I Arabien, Gyldendal, 1928

First Danish Edition

LOWELL THOMAS | MED LAWRENCE I | ARABIEN | [cut] | [Oxford rule] | GYLDENDALSKE BOGHANDEL//NORDISK | FORLAG//KØBENHAVN//MCMXXVIII

Collation 25.2 × 19 cm: [1]^8 2–12^8, 13^4, 100 leaves, pp.[1–5], 6–197, [1–3].

Contents Pp.[1] bastard title, [2] blank, [3] title page, [4] translator's, printer's credits, issue statement, [5]–197 text, [1–3] blank.

Plates Sixteen b/w photographs on coated paper, printed on both sides following pp.[3], 12, 16, 32, 48, 64, 80, 96, 112, 128 double, 144, 166, 176 double, 192.

Typography and paper $ 1,2 signed Med Lawrence i Arabien 3,3*.

Text 20 lines, 10.4 × 12.8 cm.

Paper White, wove, unwatermarked, all edges trimmed, sheets bulk 2 cm.

Binding Marbled paper covered boards, brown leather spine 40 s r Br. On spine: [gilt] [4 line rule] | [cut] | [4 line rule] | LOWELL | THOMAS | [short rule] | MED | LAWRENCE | I | ARABIEN | [4 line rule] | [cut] | [4 line rule] | [cut] | [4 line rule] | [cut] | [4 line rule]. Dark olive end papers, marbled edges, red and gold head and tail bands.

Copies Cal.

E020   LOWELL THOMAS, La Campagne du Colonel Lawrence, Payot, 1933

First French Edition

COLLECTION DE MÉMOIRES, ÉTUDES ET DOCUMENTS | POUR SERVIR À | L'HISTOIRE DE LA GUERRE MONDIALE | [rule] | LOWELL THOMAS | [rule] | LA CAMPAGNE | DU | COLONEL LAWRENCE | *(ARABIE DÉSERTE 1916–1919)* | [pub. device] | PAYOT, PARIS | 106, BOULEVARD ST-GERMAIN | [short rule] | 1933 | *Tous droits réservés*

Collation 22.8 × 14.5 cm: [1]⁸ 2–19⁸, 152 leaves, pp.[1–7], 8–297, [7].

Contents Pp.[1–2] blank, [3] bastard title, [4] list of titles in series, [5] title page, [6] printer's statement, 7–297 text, [1] illustrations, [2] contents, [3] blank, [4–5] ads, [6–7] blank.

RT On both verso and recto [according to chapter].

Typography and paper $ 1 signed LOWELL THOMAS 2.

Text 22.7 × 14.3 cm.

Paper White, wove, unwatermarked, untrimmed, sheets bulk 2 cm.

Binding Bluish grey paper covers 264 1. Gray. On front cover: [in blue, within single rule frame], COLLECTION DE MÉMOIRES ÉTUDES ET DOCUMENTS | POUR SERVIR À | L'HISTOIRE DE LA GUERRE MONDIALE | [rule] | LOWELL THOMAS | [short rule] | LA CAMPAGNE | DU | COLONEL LAWRENCE | *(ARABIE DÉSERTA 1916–1919)* | [short rule] | *Avec huit photographies hors textes* | [short rule] | [pub. device] | PAYOT, PARIS. On spine: [rule] | LOWELL | THOMAS | [rule] | La | Campagne | du | Colonel | Lawrence | [rule] | PRIX: | 24 fr. | [rule] | PAYOT | PARIS | [rule]. On back cover: [list of other titles offered by publisher].

Published at 24 fr.

Copies AC, Cal.

E021   LOWELL THOMAS, Æfintýri Lawrence Í Arabíu, Leiftur, 1940

First Icelandic Edition

LOWELL THOMAS | ÆFINTÝRI LAWRENCE | Í ARABÍU | PÁLL SKÚLASON | ÞYDDI | [pub. device] | H.F. LEIFTUR, REYKJAVÍK

Collation   24.2 × 17 cm: [1–13]⁸, 104 leaves, pp.[1–5], 6–208.

Contents   Pp.[1–2] blank, [3] title page, [4] ISAFOLDARPRENTSMIDJA H.F., [5] –208 text.

Plates   Twelve b/w plates, on coated paper, printed on both sides following pp.16, 32, 48, 64, 80, 96, 112, 128, 144, 160, 176, 192.

Typography and paper $ 1,5 signed *Lawrence 3,4; 4,5; etc.*

Text   20 lines, 9 × 12.7 cm.

Paper   White, wove, unwatermarked, all edges trimmed, sheets bulk 1.5 cm.

Binding   Green cloth 164 m. g B. On spine: [Oxford rule] | LOWELL | THOMAS | [rule] | Æfintýri | Lawrence | Í Arabíu | [Oxford rule]. T.e green.

Copies   INL.

E022   LOWELL THOMAS , Med Lawrence I Arabien, Beckmans, 1926

First Swedish Edition

LOWELL THOMAS | [short rule] | MED LAWRENCE | I ARABIEN | [short rule] | BEMYNDIGAD ÖVERSÄTTNING AV | *KARIN JENSEN* | *F. LIDFORSS* | [short rule] | MED ILLUSTRATIONER | [pub. device] | *STOCKHOLM* | [long tapered rule] | J. BECKMANS BOKFÖRLAG

Collation   24 × 16 cm: [1] –16⁸, 128 leaves, pp.[1–7], 8–256.

Contents   Pp.[1–2] blank, [3] bastard title, [4] blank, [5] title page, [6] printer's credit, [7] –8 contents, 8–10 illustrations, [11] –256 text.

Plates   Forty-four plates following pp.4, 16 double, 24, 28, 32 double, 40 double, 48 double, 56, 64, 80, 96, 104 double, 112 double, 120, 136 double, 140 double, 144 double, 152 double, 160 double, 168 double, 176 double, 216, 224, 232 double, 240, 248 triple, 252 double.

Typography and paper $ 1 signed 128 26 3.

Text   20 lines, 8.6 × 10.2 cm.

Paper   White, wove, unwatermarked, uncut, sheets bulk 2 cm.

Binding   White paper covers. On front cover: LOWELL THOMAS | [in red] MED LAWRENCE | [in red] ARABIEN | [colour drawing] | [long, red rule] | J. BECKMANS BOKFÖRLAG | STOCKHOLM. On spine: LOWELL | THOMAS | [in red] MED | [in red] LAWRENCE | [in red] I | [in red] ARABIEN | [pub.device] | J. BECKMANS | BOKFÖRLAG. On back cover: [tapered rule] | Pris Kr. 7:50 | [tapered rule].

Published at Kr. 7:50.

Copies AC, Cal.

1927

E023   LOWELL THOMAS, The Boy's Life of Colonel Lawrence, Century [1927]

First American Edition

The Boys' Life | *of* | COLONEL LAWRENCE | By | LOWELL THOMAS | Author of "With Lawrence in Arabia," "Beyond | Khyber Pass," etc. | Illustrated | [pub. device] | THE CENTURY CO. | *New York London*

Collation   18.6 × 12.7 cm: [1–19]⁸, 152 leaves, pp.[i–iv], v–[viii], [1–2], 3–293, [3].

Contents   Prp.[i] bastard title, [ii] blank, [iii] title page, [iv] copyright statement, v contents, [vi] blank, vii illustrations, [viii] blank, pp.[1] half-title, [2] map, 3–293 text, [1–3] blank.

RT   On verso LIFE OF COLONEL LAWRENCE. On recto [according to chapter].

Plates   Eight photos on coated paper, printed on one side only following pp.ii, 16, 56, 112, 160, 176, 240, 256.

Text   20 lines, 11.3 (11.4) × 8.5 cm.

Paper   White, wove, unwatermarked, all edges trimmed, sheets bulk 2.5 cm.

Binding   Dark green cloth 126 d Ol G. On front cover: [all in pale green] *The* BOYS' LIFE | *of* | COLONEL | LAWRENCE | [cut of T.E. Lawrence's bust with red abba] | LOWELL THOMAS. On spine: [all in white] *The* | BOYS' | LIFE | *of* | COLONEL | LAWRENCE | [cut] | LOWELL | THOMAS | THE | CENTURY | CO.

Published at $2.00.

Notes   List of impressions: 1st, September 1927, as above; 2nd, November 1927, as above except sheets bulk 2.7 cm; 3rd, May 1928; 4th and 5th impressions as above; 6th, 1933, as above with following differences: [Title page]: [same down to imprint] [pub. device of Appleton-Century] | D. APPLETON-CENTURY COMPANY | INCORPORATED | NEW YORK LONDON; [Binding]: [at foot of spine] APPLETON | CENTURY. Dust wrapper has only Century imprint on spine.

Copies   AC, Cal, LC.

E024 LOWELL THOMAS, The Boys' Life of Colonel Lawrence, Appleton Century, 1938

Second American Edition

THE BOYS' LIFE OF | COLONEL LAWRENCE | BY | LOWELL THOMAS | [pub. device] | D. APPLETON-CENTURY COMPANY | INCORPORATED | NEW YORK 1938 LONDON

Collation 19.1 × 13 cm: [1–19]^8 [20]^6, 158 leaves, pp.[i–iv], v–vi, [vii–x], 1–303, [3].

Contents Prp.[i] bastard title, [ii] list of author's works, [iii] title page, [iv] copyright statement, v–vi contents, [vii] illiustrations, [viii] blank, [ix] half-title, [x] map, pp.1–303 text, [1–3] blank.

RT On verso LIFE OF COLONEL LAWRENCE. On recto [according to chapter].

Plates Eight plates on coated paper, printed on one side only, following pp.24, 50, 116, 156, 162, 184, 232.

Text 20 lines, 11.4 (11.4) × 8.5 cm.

Paper White, wove, unwatermarked, all edges trimmed, sheets bulk 2.8 cm.

Binding Orange cloth 35 s. r O. On front cover: *The* BOYS' LIFE | *of* | COLONEL | LAWRENCE | LOWELL THOMAS. On spine: *The* | BOYS' | LIFE | *of* | COLONEL | LAWRENCE | [cut] | LOWELL | THOMAS | APPLETON | CENTURY.

Copies AC, Cal, LC.

E025 LOWELL THOMAS, The Boys' Life of Colonel Lawrence, Roy, 1959

Third American Edition

THE BOYS' LIFE OF | COLONEL LAWRENCE | *By* | LOWELL THOMAS | | ROY PUBLISHERS – NEW YORK

Collation 18.5 × 12 cm: [A]^8 B–K^8, 80 leaves, pp.[1–8], 9–160.

Contents Pp.[1] summary of text, [2] list of author's works, [3] title page, [4] LC number, printed in Great Britain, [5–6] contents, [7] illustrations, [8] map, 9–160 text.

RT On verso THE BOYS' LIFE OF COLONEL LAWRENCE. On recto [according to chapter].

Plates Seven photographs on coated paper, printed on both sides, following pp.16, 32, 48, 64, 80, 96, 128.

Typography and paper $ 1 signed D.

Text 20 lines, 8.4 (8.5) × 9.3 cm.

Paper White, wove, unwatermarked, all edges trimmed, sheets bulk 2 cm.

Binding Medium orange paper covered boards 53 m ered boards 53 m O. On front cover: THE BOYS' LIFE OF | COLONEL LAWRENCE | LOWELL THOMAS. On spine: THE BOYS' | LIFE OF | COLONEL | LAWRENCE | LOWELL | THOMAS | ROY.

Published at $3.00.

Copies Cal.

E026 LOWELL THOMAS, The Boys' Life of Colonel Lawrence, Hutchinson, 1927

First English Edition

THE BOYS' LIFE OF | COLONEL LAWRENCE | By | LOWELL THOMAS | WITH 31 ILLUSTRATIONS | HUTCHINSON & CO. (Publishers) LTD. | PATERNOSTER ROW, LONDON, E.C.

Collation 18.6 × 12.2 cm: [A]^8 B–S^8, 144 leaves, pp.[i–ii], [1–4], 5–285, [286].

Contents Prp.[i–ii] blank, [1] bastard title, [2] blank, [3] title page, [4] printer's credit, 5–6 contents, 7–8 list of illustrations, 9–[286] text.

RT On verso THE BOYS' LIFE OF COL. LAWRENCE. On recto [according to chapter].

Plates Thirty-one photographs on coated paper, printed on both sides except frontis., following pp.2, 14, 26, 44, 54, 94, 102, 114, 136, 142, 152, 198, 210, 228, 244, 256.

Typography and paper $ 1 signed B.

Text 20 lines, 10.5 (10.8) × 8.3 cm.

Paper White, wove, unwatermarked, all edges trimmed, sheets bulk 3 cm.

Binding Red cloth 13 deep Red. On front cover: [blind rules along all edges]. On spine: [Oxford rule] | THE BOYS' | LIFE OF | COLONEL | LAWRENCE | LOWELL | THOMAS | Hutchinson | [Oxford rule]. Map end papers.

Notes Second edition, i.e. 2nd impression, as above, has edition statement on title page; 5th edition, i.e. impression, same as above, with following differences: [Paper]: sheets bulk 2.7 cm; [Binding]: Rose cloth 15 M. Red; 11th edition, i.e. impression, same as above. Each impression bears issue statement on title page just above imprint.

Copies AC, Cal.

E027   LOWELL THOMAS, En Vovehals, Gyldendalske, 1932

First Danish Edition

LOWELL THOMAS | EN VOVEHALS | THOMAS EDWARD LAWRENCE | ARABIENS UKRONEDE KONGE | [cut] | GYLDENDALSKE BOGHANDEL-NORDISK | FORLAG-KØBENHAVN-MCMXXXII

Collation   18.5 × 13 cm: [1]⁸ 2–9⁸, 72 leaves, pp.[1–5], 6–144.

Contents   Pp.[1] bastard title, [2] blank, [3] title page, [4] translator's note, issue statement, printer's credit, [5]–144 text.

Plates   Eight plates on coated paper, printed on one side only, following pp.2, 16, 32, 48, 64, 80, 112, 128.

Typography and paper $ 1,2 signed En Vovehals 2,2*.

Text   20 lines, 8.3 × 9.1 cm

Paper   White, thick, wove, unwatermarked, all edges trimmed, sheets bulk 2.2 cm.

Binding   Green cloth 150 gy G. On front cover: [frame of single rules, gilt]. On spine: [rule] LOWELL | THOMAS | EN | VOVEHALS| GYLDENDAL | [rule].

Published at   Kr 2.00 paper; Kr 2.50 hardbound.

Copies   AC, Cal.

E028   DAVID ROSELER, Lawrence, Prince of Mecca, Cornstalk, 1927

First Australian Edition

LAWRENCE | PRINCE OF MECCA | BY | DAVID ROSELER | AUSTRALIA: | CORNSTALK PUBLISHING COMPANY | 89 CASTLEREAGH STREET, SYDNEY | 1927

Collation   18.2 × 12 cm: A–P⁸, 120 leaves, pp.[1–8], 1–227, [1–5].

Contents   Prp.[1] bastard title, [2] blank, [3] title page, [4] printer's credit, [5] contents, [6] blank, [7] maps and illustrations, [8] blank, pp.[1]–227 text, [1] printer's colophon, [2–5] blank, includes free and pastedown end papers.

RT   On verso LAWRENCE, PRINCE OF MECCA. On recto [according to chapter].

Plates   Four plates on coated paper, frontispiece in colour, following pp.2, 110, 182, 198.

Typography and paper $ 1 signed B.

Text   20 lines, 9.9 (10) × 8.5 cm.

Paper   White, wove, unwatermarked, all edges trimmed, sheets bulk 3 cm.

Binding   Red cloth 13 deep Red. On front cover: [within single rule frame]
LAWRENCE | PRINCE OF MECCA | DAVID ROSELER. On spine:
LAWRENCE | PRINCE | OF MECCA | DAVID | ROSELER |
CORNSTALK | COMPANY.

Published at   6d.

Notes   Another state of which the title page reads: LAWRENCE | PRINCE
OF MECCA | BY | DAVID ROSELER | *(E.V. Timms)* | *Second Edition* |
AUSTRALIA: | CORNSTALK PUBLISHING COMPANY |
CASTLEREAGH STREET, SYDNEY | 1927. This is the first impression with
a cancelled title page. Present title page is attached to the stub of the one
removed.

Copies   AC, Cal, LC.

E029   ROBERT GRAVES, Lawrence and the Arabs, Cape, 1927

Uncorrected proofs of First English Edition

LAWRENCE AND THE | ARABS | *By* | ROBERT GRAVES | [pub. device] |
ILLUSTRATIONS EDITED BY | ERIC KENNINGTON | MAPS BY | HERRY
PERRY | LONDON | JONATHAN CAPE 30 BEDFORD SQUARE

Collation   20 × 13.5 cm: [A]^8 B–U^8 Z^8 AA–EE^8 FF^4, 228 leaves, pp.[2],
[1–2], 3–454.

Contents   Prp.[1] bastard title, [2] quote, pp.[1] title page, [2] issue
statement, printer's credit, 3–4 list of illustrations, 5–7 introduction, [8]
blank, [9] half-title, [10] blank, 11–448 text, 449–454 index.

RT   On both verso and recto]: LAWRENCE AND THE ARABS.

Plates   Twenty-seven plates tipped in following pp.[1], 48, 72, 92, 118, 142,
156, 178, 196, 212, 254, 260, 274, 278, 298, 308, 326, 342, 346, 358, 370, 386, 402,
428, maps 60, 164, 226, 336.

Typography and paper $ 1 signed B.

Text   20 lines, 9.1 (9.2) × 10 cm.

Paper   White, wove, unwatermarked, all edges trimmed, sheets bulk 3.1
cm.

Binding   Brown paper covers 57 l. Br. On front cover: [within frame of
ornamental cuts] LAWRENCE AND | THE ARABS | ROBERT GRAVES |
[cut] | ADVANCE COPY ONLY | NOT FOR SALE.

Copies   Cal.

E030 ROBERT GRAVES, Lawrence and the Arabs, Cape, 1927

First English Edition

LAWRENCE AND THE | ARABS | *By* | ROBERT GRAVES | [pub. device] | ILLUSTRATIONS EDITED BY | ERIC KENNINGTON | MAPS BY | HERRY PERRY | LONDON | JONATHAN CAPE 30 BEDFORD SQUARE

Collation 20 × 13.5 cm: [A]⁸ B–U⁸ Z⁸ AA–EE⁸ FF⁴, 228 leaves, pp.[2], [1–2], 3–454.

Contents Prp.[1] bastard title, [2] quote, pp.[1] title page, [2] issue statement, printer's credit, 3–4 list of illustrations, 5–7 introduction, [8] blank, [9] half-title, [10] blank, 11–448 text, 449–454 index.

RT On both verso and recto: LAWRENCE AND THE ARABS.

Plates Twenty-seven plates tipped in following pp.[1], 48, 72, 92, 118, 142, 156, 178, 196, 212, 254, 260, 274, 278, 298, 308, 326, 342, 346, 358, 370, 386, 402, 428, maps 60, 164, 226, 336.

Typography and paper $ 1 signed B.

Text 20 lines, 9.1 (9.2) × 10 cm.

Paper White, wove, unwatermarked, all edges trimmed, sheets bulk 3.1 cm.

Binding Tan buckram 57 l. Br. On spine: [gilt] LAWRENCE | AND THE | ARABS | [cut] | ROBERT | GRAVES | JONATHAN CAPE [rough cloth]. On back cover: [pub. device, blind stamped].

Published at 7s 6d, 17 November 1927.

Notes There are variant colours of cloth bindings: 55 s Br, 38 dr O, 54 b. O. The first and second impressions contain an advertising sheet bound in following p.448 (ad for *Arabia Deserta*), 19 × 12.5 cm. In later impressions variant binding colours continue 72 d YO.

List of impressions: 2nd and 3rd, 1927 (some copies of third impression are bound in polished cloth); 4th impression 1928. American title: *Lawrence and the Arabian Adventure*.

Copies AC, Cal, UT, LC.

E031 ROBERT GRAVES, Lawrence and the Arabs, Cape, 1927

Publisher's Prospectus for First English Edition

PUBLICATION DAY: NOVEMBER 17TH | [photo] |"T.E. LAWRENCE," 1926 | LAWRENCE | AND THE ARABS | *by* | ROBERT GRAVES | With twenty-four illustrations and four maps in two colours | 460 pages Large Crown 8vo. 7s.6d. net

Collation 22.2 × 14.8 cm: single fold, 2 leaves, pp.[1–4].

Contents   Pp.[1] title page, [2–3] blurbs, [4] list of illustrations and order form.

Text   10 lines, 4.7 × 9.7 cm.

Paper   Coated, white, wove, unwatermarked, all edges trimmed.

Published at   Free advertising flyer.

Copies   Cal.

E032   ROBERT GRAVES, Lawrence and the Arabs, Cape, 1934

Second English Edition (Concise)

LAWRENCE AND THE | ARABS | *By* | ROBERT GRAVES | Author of | *Good-bye to All That* | [pub. device] | [within brackets] CONCISE EDITION | LONDON | JONATHAN CAPE 30 BEDFORD SQUARE | AND AT TORONTO

Collation   17.8 × 11.4 cm: [A]^{16}, B–I^{16*8}, 154 leaves, pp.[1–10], 11–228, [16].

Contents   Pp.[1] bastard,series titles, [2] series statement, [3] title page, [4] issue statement, printer's credit, [5] note, [6] blank, [7] map. [8] blank, [9] half-title, [10] blank, 11–228 text,[1–16] pub. ads.

Typography and paper $ 1 signed L.A. B, L.A. I,L.A. I* [fifth leaf].

Text   20 lines, 7.3 × 8.9 cm.

Paper   White, wove, unwatermarked, all edges trimmed, sheets bulk 1.8 cm.

Binding   Grey brown buckram 79 1 gy yBr. On front cover: [in brown] LAWRENCE | AND THE ARABS | ROBERT GRAVES. On spine: [in brown] LAW- | RENCE |AND THE | ARABS | ROBERT | GRAVES | JONATHAN | CAPE.

Published at   2s.

Notes   List of impressions: 2nd, February 1935; 3rd, May 1935; 4th, June 1935; 5th, August 1935, added quire of 10 leaves at end; 6th, September 1935; 8th, March 1936; 9th, September 1937, added quire of 12 leaves at end; 10th, 10 October 1939. Florin books series.

Copies   AC, Cal.

E033   ROBERT GRAVES, Lawrence and the Arabs, Cape, 1935

Second English Edition (Children's Edition)

LAWRENCE | AND THE | ARABS | BY | ROBERT GRAVES | [pub. device] | ILLUSTRATIONS EDITED BY | ERIC KENNINGTON |

JONATHAN CAPE | THIRTY BEDFORD SQUARE | LONDON

Collation   20 × 13.5 cm: [A]⁸, B–S⁸, 114 leaves, pp.[1–6], 7–8, [9–10], 11–228.

Contents   Pp.[1] bastard title, [2] blank, [3] title page, [4] issue statement, printer's, papermaker's credits, [5] author's note, [6] blank, 7 illustrations, 8 maps, [9] half-title, [10] map, 11–228 text.

Plates   Fifteen photos on coated paper, printed on one side only, following pp.28, 36, 80, 92, 122, 134, 170, 186, 207, 228, 236, 242, 250, 278, 284.

Typography and paper $ 1 signed L.A. B.

Text   20 lines, 7.8 × 8.8 cm.

Paper   White, wove, unwatermarked, all edges trimmed, sheets bulk 3 cm.

Binding   Orange-red cloth 27 deep y Pink. On front cover: [outline lettering] ROBERT GRAVES | JONATHAN | CAPE. On back cover: [pub. device].

Published at   2s.

Copies   Cal.

E034   ROBERT GRAVES, Lawrence and the Arabs, Cape, 1938

Second English Edition (concise edition in larger format)

LAWRENCE | AND THE | ARABS | By | ROBERT GRAVES | [pub. device] | ILLUSTRATIONS EDITED BY | ERIC KENNINGTON | JONATHAN CAPE | THIRTY BEDFORD SQUARE | LONDON

Collation   19.9 × 13.6 cm: [A]⁸ B–S⁸, 144 leaves, pp.[1–6], 7–288.

Contents   Pp.[1] bastard title, [2] blank, [3] title page, [4] impression statement, printer's, binder's, papermaker's credits, [5] note, [6] blank, 7 illustrations, 8 maps, [9] half-title, [10] map, 11–288 text.

Plates   Sixteen plates on coated paper, printed on one side only, following pp.2, 28, 36, 80, 92, 122, 134, 170, 186, 206, 228, 235, 242, 250, 278, 284.

Typography and paper $ 1 signed L.A. C.

Text   20 lines, 7.8 × 8.9 cm.

Paper   White, wove, unwatermarked, all edge trimmed, sheets bulk 2.8 cm.

Binding   Red cloth 15 m. Red. On front cover: [outline type] LAWRENCE AND THE ARABS. On spine: [outline letters] LAWRENCE | AND THE | ARABS | ROBERT | GRAVES | JONATHAN | CAPE. On back cover: [publisher's device].

Published at   March 1938.

Copies   AC.

E035   ROBERT GRAVES, Lawrence and the Arabs, Cape, 1935

Third English Edition (Life and Letters Series)

THE LIFE AND LETTERS SERIES NO. 71 | [tapered rule] | ROBERT GRAVES | LAWRENCE | AND THE ARABS | With eight illustrations and four maps | London – JONATHAN CAPE – Toronto

Collation   20.1 × 13.3 cm: [A]^{16} B–I^{16}x^{10}, 154 leaves, pp.[1–10], 11–288, [20].

Contents   Pp.[1] series, bastard titles, [2] note on series, [3] title page, [4] issue statement, printer's credit, [5] author's note, [6] blank, [7] list of illustrations, [8] blank, [9] half-title, [10] map, 11–288 text, [1]–18 list of titles in series, [19] printer's credit, [20] blank.

Plates   Eight plates on paper coated on one side only, following pp.2, 28, 92, 170, 198, 236, 250, 282.

Typography and paper $ 1 signed L.A. B, 5 signed B*.

Text   20 lines, 7.8 × 8.9 cm.

Paper   White, wove, unwatermarked, all edges trimmed, sheets bulk 2 cm.

Binding   Green buckram 145 m. G. On front cover: [gilt] LAWRENCE AND THE ARABS | [series device]. On spine: LAWRENCE | AND THE | ARABS | [series device] | ROBERT | GRAVES | JONATHAN CAPE.

Published at   4s 6d.

Notes   Re-issued February 1937, same as above with following differences: [Binding]: Green cloth 159 gy. G. On back cover: [pub. device blind stamped]. [Published at]: 4s 6d.

Copies   AC, Cal.

E036   ROBERT GRAVES, Lawrence and the Arabs, Longmans, Green, 1940

Fourth English Edition

[Within frame of decorative rules] LAWRENCE AND THE | ARABS | By | ROBERT GRAVES | CONCISE EDITION PREPARED BY | W.T. HUTCHINS, M.A. | LONGMANS, GREEN AND CO. | LONDON · NEW YORK · TORONTO

Collation   16.5 × 11 cm: [A]^{16} B–F^{16}, 96 leaves, pp.[i–viii], ix–xi, [xii], 1–179, [1].

Contents   Prp.[i] bastard title, [ii] list of works in series, [iii] blank, [iv] frontispiece, [vi] title page, [vii] illustrator's credits, issue statement, printer's credit, [vii] acknowledgments, [viii] map, ix–xi prologue, [xii] blank, pp.1–179 text, [1] blank.

RT On both verso and recto LAWRENCE AND THE ARABS.

Typography and paper $ 1,5 signed B,B*.

Text 20 lines, 7.7 (7.9) × 8.9 cm.

Paper White, wove, unwatermarked, all edges trimmed, sheets bulk 1 cm.

Binding Green paper covered boards 127 gy Ol G. On spine: [gilt, swash] Lawrence | and the | Arabs | [series device] | [swash] Longmans.

Notes First published in this series (The Heritage of Literature Series) in 1940, reprinted in this photolithographic issue in 1941.

Copies AC.

E037 ROBERT GRAVES, Lawrence and the Arabian Adventure, Doubleday, Doran, 1928

First American Edition

[Outline lettering] LAWRENCE | AND THE ARABIAN | ADVENTURE | By | ROBERT GRAVES | ILLUSTRATIONS EDITED BY ERIC KENNINGTON | [rule] | DOUBLEDAY, DORAN & COMPANY, INC. | GARDEN CITY, NEW YORK, 1928

Collation 22 × 14.7 cm: [1–26]⁸, 208 leaves, pp.[1–12], 1–400, [4].

Contents Prp.[1–2] blank, [3] bastard title, [4] two-line quote, [5] title page, [6] copyright statement, printer's credit, issue statement, [7–8] illustrations, [9–11] introduction, [12] blank, pp.1–400 text, [1–4] blank.

RT On both verso and recto LAWRENCE AND THE ARABIAN ADVENTURE.

Plates Twenty-four plates, mostly photos, on coated paper, printed on one side only, following pp.[4], 32, 56, 76, 96, 116, 132, 148, 164, 176, 184, 186, 216, 224, 236, 268, 284.

Text 20 lines, 8.6 (8.8) × 10.2 cm.

Paper White, wove, unwatermarked, top edges trimmed, sheets bulk 3 cm.

Binding Brown linen 57 l.Br. On spine: [gilt] LAWRENCE | & THE | ARABIAN | ADVENTURE | [cut of figure riding camel] | ROBERT | GRAVES | DOUBLEDAY | DORAN. Map end papers in blue and red. T.e. brown.

Published at $ 3.00.

Notes The first printing of this edition bears the statement 'First Edition' beneath the copyright statement on the verso of the title page. Subsequent printings do not. English title: *Lawrence and the Arabs*.

Copies AC, Cal, UT, Ho.

E038   ROBERT GRAVES, Lawrence and the Arabs, Nelson, 1941

First Canadian Edition

LAWRENCE AND THE | ARABS | *By* | ROBERT GRAVES | Author of | *Good-bye to All That* | [CONCISE EDITION] [brackets present] | LONDON | JONATHAN CAPE 30 BEDFORD SQUARE | Published in Canada by | THOMAS NELSON AND SONS LIMITED | TORONTO

Collation   16.8 × 11.5 cm: [1–9]^{16}, 144 leaves, pp.[1–10], 11–288.

Contents   Pp.[1] series, bastard titles, [2] blank, [3] title page, [4] issue, copyright statements, printer's credit, [5] note, [6] blank, [7] map, [8] blank, [9] series title, [10] blank, 11–288 text.

Text   20 lines, 7.1 × 9 cm.

Paper   White, wove, unwatermarked, all edges trimmed, sheets bulk 2.5 cm.

Binding   Orange cloth 37 m. r O. On front cover: LAWRENCE | AND THE ARABS | ROBERT GRAVES. On spine: LAW- | RENCE | AND THE | ARABS | ROBERT | GRAVES | NELSON.

Notes   Nelson's Collegiate Classics. Printed in Canada.

Copies   AC.

E039   ROBERT GRAVES, Lawrence et les Arabes, Gallimard, 1933

First French Edition

LAWRENCE | ET LES ARABES | *par ROBERT GRAVES* | Traduit de l'anglais | par Jeanne Roussel | S.P. | nrf | PARIS | Librairie Gallimard | 43, rue de Beaune (VIIme)

Collation   18.8 × 12 cm: [1]^8 2–19^8, 152 leaves, pp.[1–2], p.[1–5], 6–297, [5].

Contents   Prp.[1–2] blank, pp.[1] bastard title, [2] blank, [3] title page, [4] blank, 5–8 introduction, 9–297 text, [1] blank, [2] printer's colophon, [3–5] blank.

RT   On both recto and verso LAWRENCE ET LES ARABES.

Typography and paper $ 1 signed 6.

Text   20 lines, 8.3 (8.3) × 8.2 cm.

Paper   White, wove, unwatermarked,all edges untrimmed, sheets bulk 1.5 cm.

Binding   Tan paper covers. On front cover: [semicircle] LAWRENCE | [small circle] ET LES ARABES [small circle] | [in red] *par ROBERT GRAVES*| Traduit de l'anglais | par Jeanne Roussel | [in red] nrf | [lettering on red runner forming large U running from between the dots at either end of second line of title] | LES CONTEMPORAINS VUS DE PRÈS | LIBRAIRIE GALLIMARD – 43, RUE DE BEAUNE (VIIE) | S.P. On spine: Lawrence | et | les | Arabes | [in red] par | ROBERT | GRAVES | nrf | [red dot]. On back cover: [list of works in series].

Copies AC.

E040 ROBERT GRAVES, Lawrence at les Arabes, Gallimard, 1962

Second French Edition

ROBERT GRAVES | Lawrence | et les Arabes | TRADUIT DE L'ANGLAIS | PAR JEANNE ROUSSEL | nrf | GALLIMARD

Collation 20.5 × 14 cm: [1]^8 2–16^8 17^6, 134 leaves, pp.[1–7], 8–264, [4].

Contents Pp.[1–2] blank, [3] series title, [4] blank, [5] title page, [6] copyright, issue statements, [7]–9 introduction, [10] blank, [11]–264 text, [1] printer's colophon, [2–4] blank.

RT On both verso and recto LAWRENCE ET LES ARABES.

Typography and paper $ 1 signed 5.

Text 20 lines, 8.2 (8.5) × 9.9 cm.

Paper White, wove, unwatermarked, all edges trimmed, sheets bulk 1.7 cm.

Binding White paper covers. On front cover: [in red] LEURS FIGURES | [long rule] | *Robert Graves* | [next two lines in red] LAWRENCE | ET LES ARABES | [b/w photo of Kennington bust of Lawrence within frame of double embossed rule] | [in red] nrf | [long rule] | GALLIMARD. On spine: [in red] LEURS | [in red] FIGURES | [rule] | *Robert* | *Graves* | [in red] LAWRENCE | [in red] ET LES | [in red] ARABES | [in red] nrf | [rule] | GALLIMARD. On back cover: [list of titles in series].

Published at 11 nf + t.i.

Notes Leurs Figures series.

Copies AC, Cal.

E041 ROBERT GRAVES, Arabia no Lawrensu, Heibon-Sha, 1963

First Japanese Edition

[Running down] Toyo Bunko 5 Heibonsha | [long rule] | Arabia no Lawrensu | R.Graves | Ono Shinobu yaku | [long rule]

Collation 16.8 × 11.3 cm: [1–21]^8 [22]^4, 172 leaves, pp.[1–6], [1–2], 3–335, [1–5].

Contents Prp.[1] title page, [2] typographer's and binder's credit, [3–6] contents, pp.[1–2] maps, 3–327 text, 328–329 Lawrence chronology,

330–335 annotated bibliography, [1] blank, [2] colophon, [3–5] publisher's ads.

RT On verso only [according to chapter].

Text 20 lines, 5.8 × 7.5 cm.

Paper White, wove, unwatermarked, all edges trimmed, sheets bulk 1.5 cm.

Binding Green cloth 125 m. Ol G. On front cover: [blind stamped publisher's device]. On spine: [gilt, running down] Arabia no Lawrensu [rule]R. Graves Ono Shinobu yaku Toyo Bunko 5 | [across] Heibonsha. Green silk place marker. Boxed as issued.

Published at 450 Yen, 10 October 1963.

Notes Toyo Bunko series: 5th impression, 25 August 1965, as above; 11th impression, 10 June 1970, as above.

Copies AC.

E042 ROBERT GRAVES, Arabia no Lawrensu, Kadogawa, 1970

Second Japanese Edition

[Within double rule frame] Arabia no Lawrensu | R. Graves | Ono Shinobu yaku | [pub. device] | Kadogawa Bunko | 2692

Collation 15 × 10.5 cm: [1–18]⁸, 144 leaves, pp.[1–2], 3–286, [1–2].

Contents Pp.[1] title page, [2] blank, 3–4 contents, 5 map, [6] blank, 7–277 text, 278–280 Lawrence chronology, 281–286 annotated bibliography, [1] colophon, [2] publisher's statement.

RT On verso Arabia no Lawrensu.

Plates Frontispiece on coated paper before p.[1].

Text 20 lines, 5.5 (5.7) × 7.5 cm.

Paper White, wove, unwatermarked, all edges trimmed, sheets bulk 1 cm.

Binding Tan paper covers 73 p. OY. On front cover: [all in brown, floral cut with two double rules to either side] | Kadogawa Bunko | -2692- | Arabia no Lawrensu | R. Graves | Ono Shinobu yaku |[three floral cuts with multiple double rules to either side] | = Kadogawa Shoten = | [floral cut with double rules to either side]. On spine: [running down] Arabia no Lawrensu | R.Graves | Ono Shinobu yaku |2692. On back cover: [in brown, floral cut]. Brown silk place marker.

Published at 180 Yen, 30 October 1970.

Copies AC.

1928

E043 T. GERMAN-REED, Bibliographical Notes on T. E. Lawrence's Seven Pillars of Wisdom and Revolt in the Desert, Foyle, 1928

First English Edition

BIBLIOGRAPHICAL NOTES | ON | T.E. LAWRENCE'S | SEVEN PILLARS OF WISDOM | AND | REVOLT IN THE DESERT | BY T. GERMAN-REED | [cut] | LONDON MCMXXVIII | W. & G. FOYLE LIMITED | CHARING CROSS ROAD, W.C. 2

Collation   19.5 × 13 cm: [1–4]⁴, 16 leaves, pp.[1–10], One–Sixteen, [1–4].

Contents   Prp.[1–4] blank, [5] bastard title, [6] *'This Edition is limited to Three hundred and | seventy five copies of which Three hundred | and fifty are for sale. This is No. | The Decoration is from | a Wood Engraving by | PAUL NASH',* [7] title page, [8] blank, [9] dedication, [10] blank, pp.1–16 text, [1] blank, [2] printer's colophon, [3–4] blank.

Text   10 lines, 3.8 × 7.8 cm.

Paper   White, laid, watermarked, top edge trimmed, sheets bulk 3 mm.

Binding   Brown cloth 58 m. Br. On front cover: [gilt] BIBLIOGRAPHICAL NOTES | ON | T.E. LAWRENCE'S | SEVEN PILLARS OF WISDOM | AND | REVOLT IN THE DESERT.

Published at   5s.

Notes   Limited to 375 copies of which 350 were for sale. Paul Nash wood engraving.   Page numbers of text are in words not numerals.

Copies   AC, B, BPL, H, Cal, Can, UT, LC.

E045 T. GERMAN-REED, Bibliographical Notes On T.E. Lawrence's Seven Pillars of Wisdom and Revolt in the Desert, Folcroft, 1976

American Reprint Edition

BIBLIOGRAPHICAL NOTES | ON | T.E. LAWRENCE'S | *SEVEN PILLARS OF WISDOM* | AND | *REVOLT IN THE DESERT* | BY T. GERMAN-REED | [cut] | *FOLCROFT LIBRARY EDITIONS/ 1976*

Collation   22.2 × 16.2 cm: [1–2]⁶, 12 leaves, pp.[1–8], One–Sixteen.

Contents   Prp.[1] bastard title, [2] limitation statement 1st ed, title page decoration credit, [3] title page, [4] blank, [5] original title page for Foyle edition, [6] blank, [7] dedication, [8] blank, pp.One–Sixteen text.

Text   20 lines, 8.4 × 7.7 cm.

Paper   White, wove, unwatermarked, all edges trimmed, sheets bulk 2 mm.

Binding   Green buckram 126 d. Ol G. On spine: [running down, gilt] T.E. LAWRENCE'S SEVEN PILLARS OF WISDOM [cut] GERMAN-REED.

Published at $8.50.

Copies   AC, LC.

E046   T. GERMAN-REED, Bibliographical Notes on T.E. Lawrence's Seven Pillars of Wisdom and Revolt in the Desert, Norwood, 1977

Second American Edition

BIBLIOGRAPHICAL NOTES | ON | T.E. LAWRENCE'S | *SEVEN PILLARS OF WISDOM* | AND | *REVOLT IN THE DESERT* | *BY T. GERMAN-REED* | [cut by Paul Nash] | *NORWOOD EDITIONS / 1977*

Collation   21.5 × 16 cm: [1]¹², 12 leaves, pp.[1–8], One–Sixteen.

Contents   Prp.[1] bastard title, [2] limitation statement, illustrator's credit, [3] title page, [4] blank, [5] title page of original edition, [6] blank, [7] dedication, [8] blank, pp.One–Sixteen text.

Text   20 lines, 7.8 × 7.7 cm.

Paper   Buff, wove, unwatermarked, all edges trimmed, sheets bulk 2 mm.

Binding   Green buckram 151 d. g Gray. On spine: [gilt, running down] NOTES ON T.E. LAWRENCE'S SEVEN PILLARS OF WISDOM [cut] GERMAN-REED.

Copies   SJSU.

1929

E047   ANDREW MACPHAIL, Three Persons, Murray, 1929

First English Edition

THREE PERSONS | By | ANDREW MACPHAIL | LONDON | JOHN MURRAY, ALBEMARLE STREET, W.

Collation   21.9 × 13.9 cm: [A]⁸ B–P⁸ Q⁶, 126 leaves, pp.[i–iv], v–xi, [xii], [1–2], 3–240.

Contents   Prp.[i] bastard title, [ii] copyright statement, [iii] title page, [iv] issue statement, v–viii preface, ix contents, x blank, xi illustrations, [xii] blank, pp.[1] section title, [2] reference to another published work on person under consideration, 3–235 text, 236–240 index.

RT   On verso [according to subject of section by name]. On recto [according to chapter within section].

Plates Three plates on coated paper, printed on one side only, following prp.xii, pp.100, 192.

Typography and paper $ 1 signed C.

Text 20 lines, 9.5 (9.6) × 9.3 cm.

Paper White, wove, unwatermarked, all edges trimmed, sheets bulk 2.5 cm.

Binding Dark blue cloth 204 gy p B. On front cover: [frame of blind rules along outer edges]. On spine: [gilt] [rule] | THREE | PERSONS | [dot within circle] | MACPHAIL | [rule] | JOHN MURRAY.

Published at February 1929.

Notes Errata slip tipped in after prp.viii; Section III Colonel Lawrence, The Myth – The Truth, pp.193–235; 2nd impression, March 1929, as above.

Copies AC, Cal, UT.

E048   ANDREW MACPHAIL, Three Persons, Carrier, 1929

First American Edition

THREE | PERSONS | [rule] | SIR ANDREW MACPHAIL | [pub. device] | NEW YORK & MONTREAL | LOUIS CARRIER & CO. | LONDON: JOHN MURRAY | 1929

Collation 22 × 14.5 cm: [1–22]⁸, 176 leaves, pp.[2], [1–4], 5–346, [4].

Contents Prp.[1–2] blank, pp.[1] bastard title, [2] list of author's works, [3] title page, [4] copyright statement, printer's credit, 5–8 preface, 9 preface to third edition, [10] blank, 11 contents, [12] blank, 13 illustrations, [14] blank, 15–340 text, 341–346 index, [1–4] blank.

RT On verso [according to subject of section by name]. On recto [according to chapter within section].

Plates Three plates on coated paper, printed on one side only, following pp.16, 160, 284.

Text 20 lines, 11.3 (11.6) × 9.3 cm.

Paper White, wove, thick, unwatermarked, all edges trimmed, sheets bulk 3 cm.

Binding Blue-black cloth. On front cover: [author's signature blind stamped]. On spine: [gilt] [double rule] | THREE | PERSONS | · | MACPHAIL | [double rule] | CARRIER.

Published at March 1929.

Notes Another issue same as above with following differences: [Binding]: Light blue 182 m Blue cloth. [front cover and spine are in black ink]; Section III Colonel Lawrence – The Myth – The Truth, pp.283–338.

Copies AC, Cal.

Juveniles: the first wave, 1930–1934

With the publication of Lowell Thomas' *Boys' Life*... and the work by Roseler, an ever-increasing stream of Lawrence boy adventure stories began which has not yet run completely dry. Gurney Slade's *In Lawrence's Bodyguard* is the first fictional work having Lawrence as the motif, one of three books written by Stephen Bartlett, under the psuedonym of Slade. All three are a natural outgrowth of the Thomas and Roseler biographies.

Steuben's *Emir Dynamit*, based on the Graves biography, is a German boys' adventure book focusing on the Arab campaign. Four years after his first book on Lawrence, Slade's second *Led by Lawrence*, appeared.

The mid-point of the decade saw the third Lawrence biography published and the second 'authorised' work by Liddell Hart, perhaps the most respected of the military writers of his time. Liddell Hart began the work with some reservations as to Lawrence's military reputation and finished a life-long admirer, vigorously defending him at the time the Aldington biography appeared (1955). Lawrence aided in the writing of this work; the record of this co-operation can be found in *T.E. Lawrence to His Biographer, Liddell Hart* (1938). He also wrote the dust wrapper blurb used for the first impression which was later dropped in favour of quotes from reviews.

1930

E050 GURNEY SLADE, In Lawrence's Bodyguard, Stokes, 1930

First American Edition

IN LAWRENCE'S | BODYGUARD | [decorative rule] | By GURNEY SLADE | *With four illustrations in line by* | WILLIAM SIEGEL | [publisher's device] | [decorative rule] | FREDERICK A. STOKES COMPANY | NEW YORK MCMXXX

Collation 18.7 × 12.7 cm: [1–18]⁸, 144 leaves, prp.[i–vi], vii–ix, [x–xiv], pp.1–267, [7], plates are included in pagination, text printed on verso of each.

Contents Prp.[i] bastard title, [ii–iii] blank, [iv] plate, [v] title page, [vi] copyright, vii–viii preface, ix contents, [x] blank, [xi] illustrations, [xii] blank, [xii] half-title, [xiv] blank, pp.1–267 text, [1–7] blank.

RT On verso [between rules] *In Lawrence's Bodyguard*. On recto [between rules, according to chapter].

Plates Four b/w plates counted into pagination, with text printed on verso following pp.[ii], 58, 126, 232, on coated paper.

Text 20 lines, 9.3 (9.6) × 8.9 cm.

Paper White, wove, unwatermarked, all edges trimmed, sheets bulk 2.5 cm.

Binding Blue cloth 197 deep p.B. On front cover: [in orange] IN LAWRENCE'S BODYGUARD | [rule] | GURNEY SLADE. On spine: IN | LAWRENCE'S | BODYGUARD | [thick rule] | SLADE | STOKES. Map end papers, in blue.

Published at $1.75, 15 September 1930.

Notes Gurney Slade was the pseudonym of Stephen Bartlett; 2nd impression, 26 November 1930, as above; 3rd, 15 December 1932; 4th, 28 September 1936, as above with following differences: [Collation]: [1–17]^8 [18]^6, 142 leaves prp.[i–vi], vii–ix, [x–xiv], pp.1–267, [3].

Copies AC.

E051   GURNEY SLADE, In Lawrence's Bodyguard, Stokes, 1930

First American Edition [Second Printing]

IN LAWRENCE'S | BODYGUARD | [decorative rule] | By GURNEY SLADE | *with four illustrations in line by* | WILLIAM SIEGEL | [pub. device] | decorative rule] | FREDERICK A. STOKES COMPANY | NEW YORK MCMXXX

Collation 18.7 × 12.7 cm: [1–16]^8 [17]^{10}, 138 leaves, prp.[i–vi], vii–ix, [x–xiv], pp.1–267, [3]; plates included in pagination, text printed on verso of each.

Contents Prp.[i] bastard title, [ii] blank, [iii–iv] plate, [v] title page, [vi] copyright, issue statements, vii–viii preface, ix contents, [x] blank, [xi] illustrations, [xii] blank, [xiii] half-title, [xiv] blank, 1–267 text, [1–3] blank.

RT On verso [between rules] *In Lawrence's Bodyguard*. On recto [between rules, according to chapter].

Plates Four b/w plates on coated paper, counted in pagination, between iii–iv, 58–61, 126–129, 232–235. Plates have text printed on one side. Frontispiece is coloured.

Text 20 lines, 9.3 (9.6) × 8.9 cm.

Paper White, wove, unwatermarked, all edges trimmed, sheets bulk 2.5 cm.

Binding Blue cloth 197 deep p. B. On front cover: [in orange] IN LAWRENCE'S | BODYGUARD | [rule] | GURNEY SLADE. On spine: IN | LAWRENCE'S | BODYGUARD | [thick rule] | GURNEY | SLADE | STOKES. Map end papers, in blue.

Notes Order of plates has been changed. In 1st edition "A Huge Turk was about to cleave him in two" has been placed following p.126, with text of p.128 on verso, and the "The party came to a halt and surveyed Irwin critically" has been made the frontispiece. Also in the 2nd impression, in the lower right corner below the caption, within brackets, the page from which the caption was taken is given. Gurney Slade was the pseudonym of Stephen Bartlett.

Copies AC, Cal.

E052   GURNEY SLADE, In Lawrence's Bodyguard, Warne, 1931

First English Edition

IN LAWRENCE'S | BODYGUARD | BY | GURNEY SLADE | *Author of* | "The Pearlers of Loren," | "Marling Ranges," & c. | [pub. device] | FREDERICK WARNE & CO.LTD. | 1–4, BEDFORD COURT, LONDON, W.C. 2

Collation   18.8 × 13 cm: [A]⁸ B–S⁸, 144 leaves, pp.[i–iv], v–vii, [viii], 9–288.

Contents   [i] bastard title, [ii] blank, [iii] title page, [iv] copyright statement, 1931, v–vi preface, vii contents, [viii] blank, 9–288 text, [at foot p.288] *Printed for the Publishers by Simson & Co. Ltd., Hertford.*

RT   On verso IN LAWRENCE'S BODYGUARD. On recto [according to chapter].

Plates   Four plates on paper coated on one side only. Frontispiece coloured, tipped in following p.[iii], others pp.48, 200, 252.

Typography and paper $ 1 signed F.

Text   20 lines, 9.1 (9.4) × 8.8 cm.

Paper   White, wove, unwatermarked, all edges trimmed, sheets bulk 3.5 cm.

Binding   Dark red orange cloth 38 d. r O. On front cover: [in brown, within border frame of single rule] IN LAWRENCE'S | BODYGUARD | BY | GURNEY SLADE | [cut of rider on camel]. On spine: [rule] | IN | LAWRENCE'S | BODYGUARD | · | GURNEY SLADE | [cut] · WARNE · [rule].

Notes   Another copy 13 deep Red, otherwise same as above, has advertisement gathering at rear. Another issue, same as above, with following differences: IN LAWRENCE'S | BODYGUARD | BY | GURNEY SLADE | *Author of* | "Led by Lawrence," | "Through the Never-Never," | "The Delta Patrol," Etc. | [pub. device] | FREDERICK WARNE & CO LTD. | 1–4, BEDFORD COURT, LONDON, W.C. 2.; Copyright statement on verso of title page contains no date, p.288 [at foot] *Printed for the Publishers by* | *Wyman & Sons, Ltd., London, Fakenham and Reading:* [Binding]: 37 m.r O. Gurney Slade was the pseudonym of Stephen Bartlett. Treasure Library Services.

Copies   AC, Cal.

E053   GURNEY SLADE, In Lawrence's Bodyguard, Warne, n.d.

English Reprint

IN LAWRENCE'S | BODYGUARD | BY | GURNEY SLADE | *Author of* | "Led by Lawrence," | "Through the Never-Never," | The Delta Patrol, Etc. | [pub. device] | FREDERICK WARNE & CO. LTD. | 1–4, BEDFORD COURT, LONDON, W.C. 2

Collation   18.6 × 12.4 cm: [A]⁸ B−S⁸, 144 leaves, p.288.

Contents   Pp.[i] bastard title, [ii] blank, [iii] title page, [iv] copyright statement, printer's credit, v−vi preface, vii contents, [viii] blank, 9−288 text.

RT   On verso IN LAWRENCE'S BODYGUARD. On recto [according to chapter].

Typography and paper $ 1 signed Q.

Text   20 lines, 9.2 (9.3) × 8.9 cm.

Paper   White, wove, unwatermarked, all edges trimmed, sheets bulk 2.9 cm.

Binding   Red cloth 30 d. y Pink. On front cover: [running down left side zig-zig rule] | IN LAWRENCE'S | BODYGUARD | GURNEY | SLADE. On spine: [zig-zag rule] | IN | LAWRENCE'S | BODYGUARD | [zig-zag rule] | GURNEY | SLADE | [zig-zag rule] | WARNE | [zig-zag rule].

Notes   Gurney Slade was the pseudonym of Stephen Bartlett.

Copies   Cal.

1931

E054   LAURENCE M. GOTCH, Lawrence, the Uncrowned King of the Arabs, 1931

Admission ticket to slide lecture

[Swash] Admit Bearer | to Lantern Lecture | LAWRENCE | The Uncrowned King | of Arabia | *Laurence* M. Gotch, F.R.I.B.A., | in | STATIONERS' HALL | (Entrance Stationers' Court, Ludgate Hill, E.C.) | on Tuesday, 20th October, 1931, at 5.30 p.m. | *In Aid of the Widows' Friend Society* | RESERVED SEAT TWO SHILLINGS AND SIXPENCE

Collation   9 × 11.5 cm.

Typography and paper   Card.

Paper   White, wove, unwatermarked, all edges trimmed.

Copies   BPL.

E056   FRITZ STEUBEN, Emir Dynamit, Kosmos, 1931

First German Edition

Fritz Steuben | Emir Dynamit | Bilder aus dem Leben des Obersten Lawrence | Berechtigte Bearbeitung der von | Lawrence autorisierten Biographie | Lawrence and the Arabs | von Robert Graves | Mit 8 Kunstdrucktafeln | und mehreren Kartenskizzen | [pub. device] | Fünfte Auflage | [tapered rule] | Kosmos, Gesellschaft der Naturfreunde | Franckh'ische Verlagshandlung, Stuttgart

Collation 19.4 × 13 cm: [1] −10⁸, 80 leaves, pp.[1−6], 7−157, [3].

Contents Pp.[1] bastard title, [2] blank, [3] title page, [4] copyright statement, picture, designer's, printer's credits, [5] foreword, [6] contents, list of illustrations, 7−157 text, [1−3] ads.

Plates Eight b/w plates on coated paper, printed on one side only, following pp.2, 16, 48, 64, 80, 96, 128, 144.

Typography and paper $ 1 signed Graves-Steuben Emir Dynamit 2.

Text 20 lines, 8.2 × 9.5 cm.

Paper White, wove, unwatermarked, all edges trimmed, sheets bulk 1.8 cm.

Binding Light yellow grey cloth 79 l. gy. y. Br. On front cover: [in blue, cut of Lawrence in Abba] | [swash] Emir | [swash] Dynamit. On spine: [running up] Graves-Steuben / Emir Dynamit. Black head and tail bands. Illustrated end papers.

Published at RM 4.80.

Copies AC.

1934

E057   GURNEY SLADE, Led by Lawrence, Warne, 1934

First English Edition

LED BY LAWRENCE | BY | GURNEY SLADE | [pub. device] | FREDERICK WARNE AND CO. LTD. | LONDON AND NEW YORK

Collation 19.3 × 13 cm: [A]⁸ B−S⁸, 144 leaves, pp.[1−4], 5−288.

Contents [1] bastard title, [2] list of author's works, [3] title page, [4] copyright statement, 5−6 preface, 7 contents, 8 glossary, 9−288 text.

RT On verso LED BY LAWRENCE. On recto [according to chapter].

Typography and paper $ 1 signed B.

Text 20 lines, 11.1 (11.2) × 8.5 cm.

Paper White, wove, unwatermarked, all edges trimmed, sheets bulk 3.5 cm.

Binding Red cloth 36 deep r O. On front cover: [rules along all outer edges of covers] | [within smaller frame of single rules] LED BY | LAWRENCE | · | GURNEY | SLADE. On spine: [outer edges of spine frame of single rule] LED BY | LAWRENCE | [short rule] | GURNEY | SLADE | · | WARNE. Another copy seen with green cloth 136 m. y G.

Notes Another copy has advertising gathering in back. Another issue, Magnet Library issue (1934?), same as above with following differences: [Contents]: preface is all on p.5; [Plates]: frontispiece in colour; [Binding]: turquoise cloth, 167 vl b G. On front cover: [in blue, zig-zag double rule running up left side] | LED BY | LAWRENCE | GURNEY | SLADE. On spine: [in blue] [zig-zag double rule] | LED BY | LAWRENCE | [zig-zag double rule] | GURNEY | SLADE | [zig-zag double rule] | WARNE | [zig-zag double rule]; [Published at]; 3s 6d. Gurney Slade was the pseudonym of Stephen Bartlett. Albion Library Series.

Copies AC, Cal.

E058 BASIL HENRY LIDDELL HART, 'T.E. Lawrence' in Arabia and After, Cape, 1934

First English Edition

'T.E. LAWRENCE' | *In Arabia and After* | *by* | LIDDELL HART | [pub. device] | JONATHAN CAPE | THIRTY · BEDFORD · SQUARE | LONDON

Collation 22 × 14.5 cm: [A]⁸ B–U⁸ X–EE⁸ FF⁴, 228 leaves, pp.[2], [1–2], 3–454.

Contents Prp.[1] bastard title, [2] list of author's works, pp.[1] title page, [2] printer's credits, 3–4 contents, 5 illustrations, [6] blank, 7–9 preface, [10] dedication, [11] section title, [12] blank, 13–448 text, 449–454 index.

RT On verso 'T.E. LAWRENCE'. On recto [according to chapter].

Plates Twelve b/w photographs tipped in, following prp.[2], pp.[1], 124, 128, 132, 140, 150, 180, 224, 234, 258, 326, 360. Fold map following pp. 50, 178, 198, 210, 282.

Typography and paper $ 1 signed H.

Text 20 lines, 9.1 (9.2) × 10.2 cm.

Paper Buff, wove, unwatermarked, top and fore edges trimmed, sheets bulk 3 cm.

Binding Red orange buckram 36 deep r O. On front cover: [gilt] 'T.E. LAWRENCE'. On spine: [gilt] 'T.E. LAWRENCE' | LIDDELL | HART | JONATHAN | CAPE. On back cover: [pub. device, blind stamped]. T.e. russet.

Published at 7s 6d, March 1934.

Notes List of impressions: 2nd, March 1934, and 3rd, March 1934, same as above; Reissued in Academy Books – 4th, May 1935; 5th, May 1935; 6th, June 1935; 7th, September 1935 – all as above with following differences: [title page same down to author's name]| [series device] | JONATHAN CAPE | THIRTY BEDFORD SQUARE | LONDON; [Collation]: [four-leaf quire of ads at end]; [Contents]: prp.[1] has series device added after bastard title,[2] lists titles in series replacing list of author's works; [Binding]: gilt lettering on front cover omitted, yellow series device in lower right corner. Lettering on spine is in yellow with publisher's device substituted for publisher's name at foot. Cloth 16 d. red; [Published at]: 7s 6d.

New and enlarged edition, list of impressions: 1st, December 1935; 2nd,

March 1936; 3rd, September 1936; 4th, November 1937; 5th, January 1939 – these are all as 1935 Academy printings with following differences: [Collation]: [A]⁸ B–U⁸ X–HH⁸, 248 leaves, pp.[2], [1–2], 3–491, [1]. [Contents]: added gatherings are to accommodate material added after Lawrence's death, replacing the section EPILOGUE with 'Postscript', 'The Man of Reflection', 'The Man of Action' and 'The Message'. [Published at]: 7s 6d. Blurb on dustwrapper of first impression was written by Lawrence, dropped from all subsequent issues.

Second 'authorised' biography, *see* Liddell Hart, *T.E. Lawrence to His Biographer'.*

Copies AC, Cal, UT.

E059   BASIL HENRY LIDDELL HART, 'T.E. Lawrence' in Arabia and After, Cape, 1940

Second English Edition (reissue in smaller format)

'T.E. LAWRENCE' | In Arabia and After | by | LIDDELL HART | [pub. device] | JONATHAN CAPE | THIRTY BEDFORD SQUARE | LONDON

Collation   22.2 × 14.5 cm: [A]⁸ B–HH⁸, 248 leaves, pp.[2], 1–491, [3].

Contents Prp.[1] bastard title, [2] blank, pp.[1] title page, [2] issue statement, publisher's, printer's, papermaker's, binder's credits, 3–4 contents, 5 illustrations, 6 dedication, 7–10 preface and special note for civilian readers, 11 section title, [12] blank, 13–482 text, 483 section title, [484] blank, 485–491 index, [1–3] blank. Has added chapter IV of Book Four p.434–460 inserted before Epilogue renamed 'The Man of Reflection'.

RT On verso 'T.E. LAWRENCE'. On recto [according to chapter].

Plates Eleven plates on coated paper, printed on one side only, following pp.124, 128, 132, 140, 150, 180, 224, 234, 326, 360, 438. Fold. maps following pp.50, 178, 198, 210, 242.

Typography and paper $ 1 signed AA.

Text 20 lines, 9 (9.1) × 10.1 cm.

Paper White, wove, unwatermarked, top and fore edge trimmed,sheets bulk 2.5 cm.

Binding Green cloth 150 gy G. On spine: [in silver] 'T.E. | LAWRENCE' | LIDDELL | HART | [at foot, publisher's device]. T.e. green.

Published at 10s 6d, September 1940.

Notes Reissued November 1943, September 1945 and March 1948, above with following differences: November 1943 and September 1945: [Collation]: 19.9 × 13.5 cm; [Plates]: seven plates printed on one side only, following pp.128, 180, 224, 234, 326, 360, 438. Fold. maps following pp.50, 178, 198, 210, 282; [Typography and paper]: all edges trimmed, sheets bulk 2.1 cm; [Binding]: Green cloth 145 m. G; [Published at]: 12s 6d. March 1948: [Collation]: 19.9 × 13.5 cm; [Plates]: no plates, maps follow pp.37, 51,

63, 83, 179, 199, 211, 271, 283; [Binding]: green cloth 165 d bG.

Another impression, February 1961, same as above except sheets bulk 2.5 cm.

Another impression, June 1964, same as above with following differences: [Collation]: [A]^{16} B–P^{16} Q^8; [Paper]: sheets bulk 3 cm; [Published at]: 42s; has added Chapter IV in Book Four, pp.434–460, inserted before the epilogue, which is expanded and retitled 'The Man of Reflection'.

Copies   AC, Cal.

E060   BASIL HENRY LIDDELL HART, 'T.E. Lawrence' in Arabia and After, Cape, 1965

Third English Edition (Paperback reissue)

LIDDELL HART | 'T.E.Lawrence' | in Arabia and After | JONATHAN CAPE | THIRTY BEDFORD SQUARE LONDON

Collation   19.7 × 12.3 cm: guillotined sheets glued to paper covers, 250 leaves, pp.[2], 494, [4].

Contents   Prp.[1] bastard title. [2] blank, pp.[1] title page, [2] issue, copyright statements, printer's credit, 3–4 contents, [5] dedication, [6] blank, 7–10 preface, [11] section title, [12] blank, 13–482 text, 483–489 index, [490–494] maps, [1–3] list of books in paperback series, [4] blank.

RT   On verso 'T.E. LAWRENCE'. On recto [according to chapter].

Text   20 lines, 8.7 (8.8) × 9.7 cm.

Paper   White, wove, unwatermarked, all edges trimmed, sheets bulk 2.5 cm.

Binding   Pictorial paper covers. On front cover: B.H. LIDDELL HART 18s | IN U.K. ONLY | [brown] JONATHAN | [brown] CAPE | [brown] PAPERBACK | T.E. Lawrence. | In Arabia and | After. On spine: JCP. 38 | [running down] B.H. LIDDELL HART | T.E. Lawrence: In Arabia and After. | [in white] JONATHAN | CAPE | PAPERBACK. On back cover: B.H. LIDDELL HART | [quote from three reviews] | [running up] Cover design by Jan Pienkowski.

Published at   18s, November 1965.

Notes   Also hardbound in green cloth binding.

Copies   Cal.

E061   BASIL HENRY LIDDELL HART, Colonel Lawrence, the Man Behind the Legend, Dodd, Mead, 1934

First American Edition

[Decorative rule] | COLONEL LAWRENCE | THE MAN BEHIND THE

LEGEND | *By* | LIDDELL | HART | [cut] | WITH ILLUSTRATIONS AND MAPS | [cut] | DODD, MEAD & COMPANY | NEW YORK 1934 | [decorative rule]

Collation 23.5 × 16 cm: [1–20]⁸ [21]⁴ [22–25]⁸, 196 leaves, pp.[i–iv], v–ix, [x], [1–2], 3–382.

Contents Prp.[i] bastard title, [ii] blank, [iii] title page, [iv] copyright statement, printer's credit, v–vi preface, vii–viii contents, ix illustrations, [x] blank, pp.[1] section title, [2] blank, 3–365 text, [366] blank, 367–382 index.

RT On verso COLONEL LAWRENCE. On recto [according to chapter].

Plates Twenty-two b/w photos on coated paper, printed on one side only, following pp.i, 34, 50, 62, 78, 102, 118, 122, 134, 142, 174, 182, 192, 198, 206, 222, 230, 254, 268, 280, 326.

Text 20 lines, 9.2 (9.4) × 11.5 cm.

Paper White, wove, unwatermarked, top and bottom edges trimmed, sheets bulk 4 cm.

Binding Green cloth 151 D. gy. G. On front cover: [gilt] [thick rule] | COLONEL | LAWRENCE | THE MAN BEHIND THE LEGEND | [thick rule] | LIDDELL HART | [thick rule]. On spine: [gilt] COLONEL | LAWRENCE | [cut] LIDDELL | HART | DODD, MEAD | & COMPANY. T.e. salmon. Pale green end papers.

Published at $3.75, April 1934.

Notes List of impressions: 2nd, as above, with following differences: On verso of title page issue statement is added: Published April 1934; 2nd, April 1934, [Binding]: front cover blind stamped; 3rd, April 1934, as above; 4th, April 1934, as above; 5th, November 1935, as above. Another copy of fifth printing in variant binding 265 med. Gy cloth with all lettering in black. T.e. unstained and end papers white. Plates following pp.ii, 24, 34, 42, 56, 58, 102, 118, 122, 134, 140, 142, 154, 164, 182, 216, 222, 224, 230, 254, 326, 358. English title: '*T.E. Lawrence' In Arabia and After*.

Copies AC, Cal, UT, Ho, LC.

E062 BASIL HENRY LIDDELL HART, Colonel Lawrence of Arabia, Halcyon, 1937

First American Edition (reprint)

THE MAN BEHIND THE LEGEND | COLONEL | LAWRENCE | [OF ARABIA] | NEW AND ENLARGED EDITION | BY | LIDDELL HART | ILLUSTRATED | WITH MAPS AND PHOTOGRAPHS | [publisher's device] | HALCYON HOUSE: NEW YORK

Collation 23.9 × 16 cm: [1–27]⁸ [28]⁴, 220 leaves, pp.[i–iv], v–[x], [1–2], 3–24, [1–2], 25–34, [1–2], 35–42, [1–2], 43–56, [1–2], 57–58, [1–2], 59–140, [1–2], 141–154, [1–2], 155–164, [1–2], 217–224, [1–2], 225–406, [1–4]. Maps on unpaged leaves, verso blank.

Contents Prp.[i] bastard title, [ii] blank, [iii] title page, [iv] copyright, issue statements, printer's credit, v–vi preface, vii–viii contents, ix illustrations, [x] blank, pp.[1] section title, [2] blank, 3–390 text, 391–406 index, [1–4] blank.

RT On verso COLONEL LAWRENCE. On recto [according to chapter].

Plates Twelve b/w photos on coated paper, printed on one side only, following pp.ii, 102, 118, 122, 134, 142, 182, 222, 230, 254, 326, 358. Ten maps on leaves of text, but not paginated, following pp.24, 34, 42, 56, 140, 154, 164, 216, 224.

Text 20 lines, 9.2 (9.3) × 11.5 cm.

Paper White, simulated wove, unwatermarked, top and bottom edges trimmed, sheets bulk 4 cm.

Binding Blue cloth 179 deep Blue. On front cover: [blind stamped] COLONEL | LAWRENCE | THE MAN BEHIND THE LEGEND | LIDDELL HART |. On spine: [gilt] COLONEL | LAWRENCE | [cut] | LIDDELL | HART | [pub. device] | HALCYON HOUSE.

Published at $1.69, January 1937.

Notes This issue cited as 6th printing. English title: 'T.E. Lawrence' in Arabia and After.

Copies AC, Cal, UT, LC.

E064 BASIL HENRY LIDDELL HART, T.E. Lawrence, Gyldendalske, 1938

First Danish Edition

LIDDELL HART | T.E. LAWRENCE | I ARABIEN OG EFTER | PAA DANSK VED | IVER GUDME | KØBENHAVN | [rule] | GYLDENDALSKE BOGHANDEL | NORDISK FORLAG | 1938

Collation 24.8 × 16.5 cm: [1]⁸ 2–24⁸, 192 leaves, pp.[1–5], 6–380, [4].

Contents [1] bastard title, [2] blank, [3] title page, [4] translator's credit, original title, copyright, issue statements, printer's credit, [5]–6 foreword, 7 note to reader, [8] blank, [9] section title, [10] blank, 11–380 text, [1–2] contents, [3–4] publisher's ads.

Plates Eleven b/w photos on coated paper, printed on one side, following pp.3, 96, 104, 112, 120, 136, 172, 176, 248, 288, 352. Five maps on coated paper following pp.40 (folded), 144, 152, 168, 224.

Typography and paper $ signed 1 T.E. Lawrence 2,2*.

Text 20 lines, 9 × 11.5 cm.

Paper White, wove, unwatermarked, all edges trimmed, sheets bulk 3 cm.

Binding Pictorial paper covers. On front cover: [white] T.E. LAWRENCE | AF LIDDELL HART | GYLDENDAL. On spine: LIDDELL | HART | T.E. LAW- | RENCE | GYLDEN | DAL. On back cover: [within frame of single rules, blurb]

Notes Copies printed: 4000.

Copies AC, Cal.

E065 BASIL HENRY LIDDELL HART, La Vie Du Colonel Lawrence, Nouvelle Revue Critique, 1935

First French Edition

Captaine B.-H. LIDDELL HART | LA VIE | DU COLONEL | LAWRENCE | *(Lawrence in* (sic) *Arabia)* | TRADUIT DE L'ANGLAIS PAR | *HENRI THIES* | [pub. device] | *BIBLIOTHÈQUE D'HISTOIRE* | *POLITIQUE, MILITAIRE ET NAVALE* | ÉDITIONS de la NOUVELLE REVUE CRITIQUE

Collation 23 × 14 cm: [1]⁸ 2–20⁸, 160 leaves, pp.[1–7], 8–317, [3].

Contents Pp.[1–2] blank, [3] bastard title, [4] list of titles in series, [5] title page, [6] blank, [7]–8 pub. note, [9]–10 preface, [11] section title, [12] map, 13–317 text, [1] list of maps. [2] table of contents, [3] printer's colophon.

RT On both verso and recto LA VIE DU COLONEL LAWRENCE.

Typography and paper $ 1 signed 6.

Text 20 lines, 8.4 (8.7) × 10 cm.

Paper White, wove, unwatermarked, untrimmed, sheets bulk 2.5 cm.

Binding Tan paper covers. On front cover: [green Oxford rule] | Capitaine B.-H. LIDDELL HART | [long rule] | LA VIE | DU COLONEL | LAWRENCE | [pub. device, in green] | *BIBLIOTHÈQUE D'HISTOIRE* | POLITIQUE, MILITAIRE ET NAVALE | [green] ÉDITIONS de la NOUVELLE REVUE CRITIQUE. On spine: [green Oxford rule] | Capitaine | B.-H. | LIDDELL HART | [rule] | La | Vie du | colonel (sic) | Lawrence | [rule] | Exemplaire | sur Vélin | supérieur | [rule] | PRIX | 25 franc. | [rule] Bibliothèque | d'Histoire | [rule] | [green Oxford rule] | 050.1909 | MH [in diamond frame]. On back cover: [within rules, blurb on book and list of titles in series].

Published at 25 francs.

Copies AC.

E066 BASIL HENRY LIDDELL HART, Oberst Lawrence, Schlegel, 1935

First German Edition

Liddell Hart | Oberst Lawrence | Der Kreuzfahrer des 20. Jahrhunderts | *Ins Deutsche übertragen von Theodor Lücke* | Mit 13 Bildern und einer Karte | auf Tafeln | [pub. device] | [rule] | Vorhut=Verlag Otto Schlegel GmbH | Berlin SW 68

Collation 21.7 × 14.5 cm: [1]⁸ 2-17⁸ 18⁴, 140 leaves, pp.[1–8], 9–279, [1].

Contents Pp.[1] bastard title, [2] blank, [3] title page, [4] original title, copyright statement, typographer's, printer's credits, [5] contents, [6] blank, [7] section title, [8] blank, 9–279 text, [1] ad.

Plates Four photos on coated paper, printed on both sides, following pp.80, 96, 176, 192.

Typography and paper $ 1,2 signed 2 [fraktur] Liddell Hart, Oberst Lawrence,2*.

Text 20 lines, 8.9 × 10.4 cm.

Paper White, wove, unwatermarked, all edges trimmed, sheets bulk 2.5 cm.

Binding Red cloth 12 s. red. On front cover: [within black rectangle which itself is within double rule frame, in red] OBERST | LAWRENCE. On spine: [triple rules] | [within black rectangle] LIDDELL | HART | OBERST | LAWRENCE | [triple rule] | [ten alternating multiple rules and asterisks]. T.e. light tan. Gold head and tail bands.

Published at Paper RM 5; Cloth RM 6.

Copies AC, Cal.

E067 BASIL HENRY LIDDELL HART, Lorens tes Arabias, Oikos, 1973

First Greek Edition

[Double page] [on left page] 'O titlos tox Prototxpoy | H. Liuddell Hart | T.E. Lawrence: | In Arabia and | After | Copyright: by JONATHAN CAPE, LONDON | Dia tey ellenthahe metarastes: D. Darema. [on right page] LIDDELL HART | Lorens | tes | Arabias | METAPHRASTES: | D.P. KOSTELENOS | EKDOTIKOS OIKOS | DEM. DAREMA | IPPOKRATOYS 42 | ATHENA 1973

Collation 22.8 × 15.5 c): [1]–32⁸, 256 leaves, pp.[1–15], 16–503, [1–9].

Contents Pp.[1] blank, [2] frontispiece, [3] bastard title, [4] English title page, [5] title page, [6] blank, [7–10] prefaces, [11–12] contents, [13] half-title, [14] blank, [15]–503 text, [1] blank, [2–6] maps, [7] blank, [8] printer's colophon, [9] blank.

RT On verso T.E. Lorens. On recto [according to chapter].

Typography and paper $ 1 signed 3.

Text 20 lines, 9 (9.4) × 10.8 cm.

Paper White, wove, unwatermarked, all edges trimmed, sheets bulk 3.5 cm.

Binding Red leather simulated fabric. On front cover: [gilt] LIDDELL HART | LORENS | TES ARABIAS. On spine: [gilt] [triple rules] L. HART | LORENS | TES | ARABIAS [gilt, triple rules].

Copies Rosen.

Death of Lawrence, 1935

On 15 May 1935, Lawrence was involved in a fatal motorcycle accident near his cottage, Clouds Hill in Dorset.

During the year of his death a number of items were published. A committee was formed almost immediately to raise funds for a memorial. Eric Kennington was commissioned to sculpt a bust which is now housed in the crypt of St Paul's, and A.W. Lawrence got two publishing projects underway; the collected letters and a group of essays written by Lawrence's friends and acquaintances. Printed letters soliciting contributions for each were sent out. Thus began the period of publication of Lawrence's literary remains.

Three biographies appeared in rapid succession as well: Charles Edmonds' (Carrington) book *T.E. Lawrence*; Kiernan's *Lawrence of Arabia*, a juvenile biography, many times reprinted, which unlike the other two, does not carry the biography beyond the end of the war; Robinson's *Lawrence, the Story of His Life*, the author of which took part in the Arab campaign and was with Lawrence during part of it.

In Italy, a biography by Roodes was also published in 1935. It has never been translated. In the USA, Julian Arnold, a latter-day Frank Harris, who hob-knobbed with the famous and near-famous and was eager to write of these acquaintances, published a small essay on his meeting Lawrence.

A second attempt to deal with the Lawrence biography appeared under the authorship of G. (John Gawsworth, pseudonym of Terence Ian Fytton Armstrong). It is one half of the very limited information on the Lawrence canon available at the time.

CARCHEMISH

REPORT ON THE EXCAVATIONS AT DJERABIS
ON BEHALF OF THE BRITISH MUSEUM

CONDUCTED BY

C. LEONARD WOOLLEY, M.A.

AND

T. E. LAWRENCE, B.A.

PART I

INTRODUCTORY

BY

D. G. HOGARTH, M.A., F.B.A.

PRINTED BY ORDER OF THE TRUSTEES

SOLD AT THE BRITISH MUSEUM

AND BY MESSRS. LONGMANS AND CO., 39 PATERNOSTER ROW
MR. BERNARD QUARITCH, 11 GRAFTON STREET, NEW BOND STREET, W.
MESSRS. ASHER AND CO., 14 BEDFORD STREET, COVENT GARDEN
AND MR. HUMPHREY MILFORD, OXFORD UNIVERSITY PRESS, AMEN CORNER, LONDON

1914

Plate 1 *Carchemish:* the report of the work completed in 1914 at the archeological site of Carchemish where Lawrence worked in conjunction with D.G. Hogarth and C.L. Woolley from 1911 to 1914.

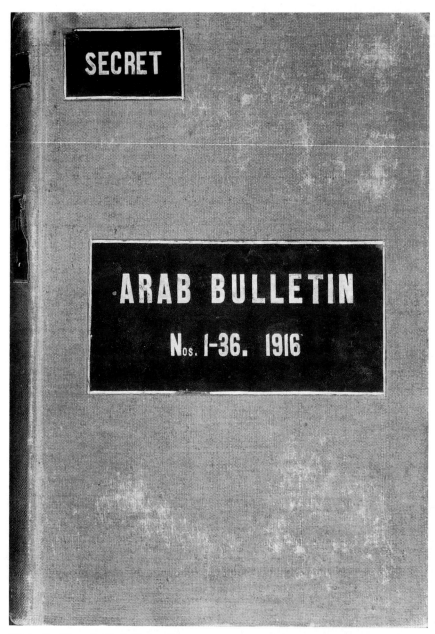

Plate 2 The *Arab Bulletin* 1916–18 issued by the Intelligence Bureau in Cairo. It contains many articles by Lawrence; some of them are the first appearance in print of material later used in *Seven Pillars of Wisdom*. It was reprinted in 1986.

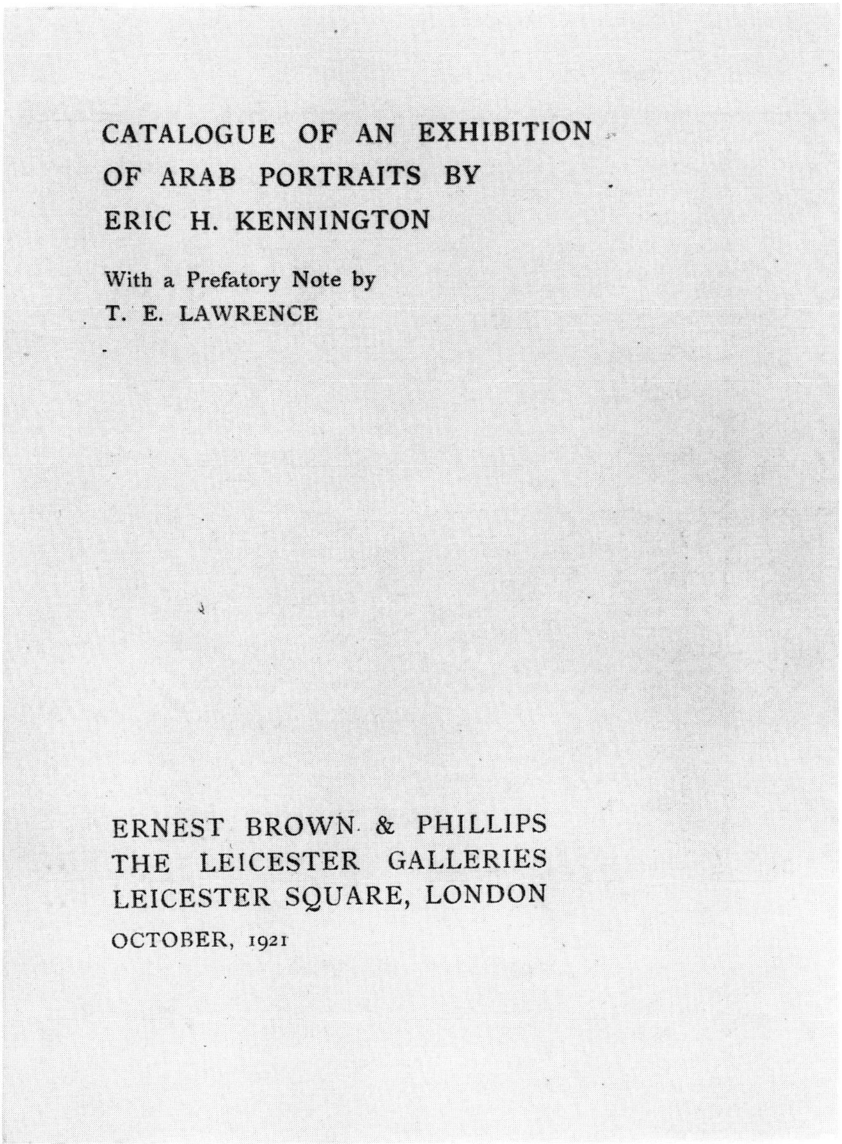

CATALOGUE OF AN EXHIBITION
OF ARAB PORTRAITS BY
ERIC H. KENNINGTON

With a Prefatory Note by
T. E. LAWRENCE

ERNEST BROWN & PHILLIPS
THE LEICESTER GALLERIES
LEICESTER SQUARE, LONDON
OCTOBER, 1921

Plate 3 *Catalogue of an Exhibition of Arab Portraits by Kennington,* Leicester Galleries, 1921. This rare catalogue contains introductory material by both Lawrence and G.B. Shaw.

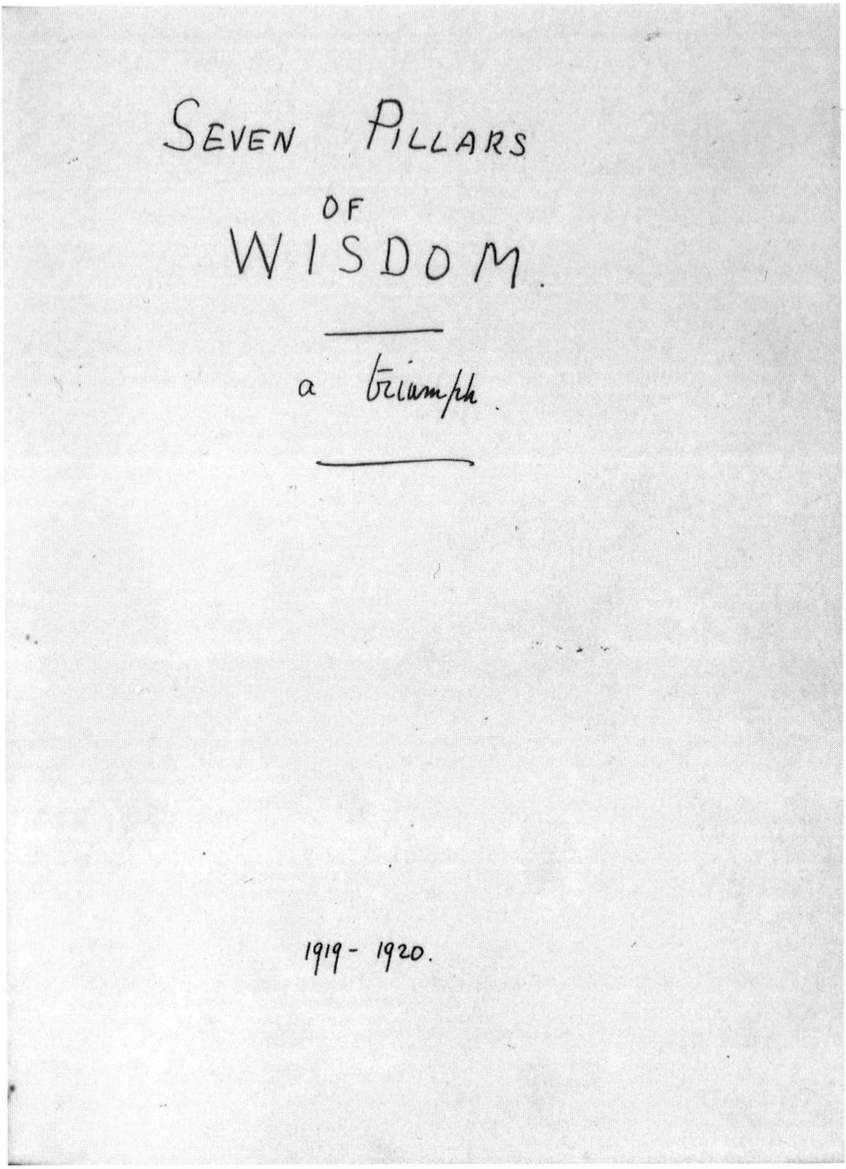

SEVEN PILLARS
OF
WISDOM.

a triumph.

1919 - 1920.

Plate 4 Title page of the 1922 'Oxford' edition of *Seven Pillars of Wisdom*, 1919–20. The first printing of this book was eight copies.

LETTERS
FROM
T E SHAW
TO
VISCOUNT
CARLOW

TWO ARABIC
FOLK TALES

Translated by
T. E. LAWRENCE

A LETTER

FROM

T· E·

LAWRENCE

TO HIS

MOTHER

AN ESSAY ON FLECKER
By T. E. LAWRENCE

Plate 5 Four examples of Lawrence works issued by the Corvinus Press in very limited editions.

THE ODYSSEY OF
HOMER

PRINTED IN ENGLAND

1932

Plate 6 The Emery Walker/Bruce Rogers 1932 edition of Lawrence's translation of *The Odyssey*. Considered by some as one of the beautiful books of this century.

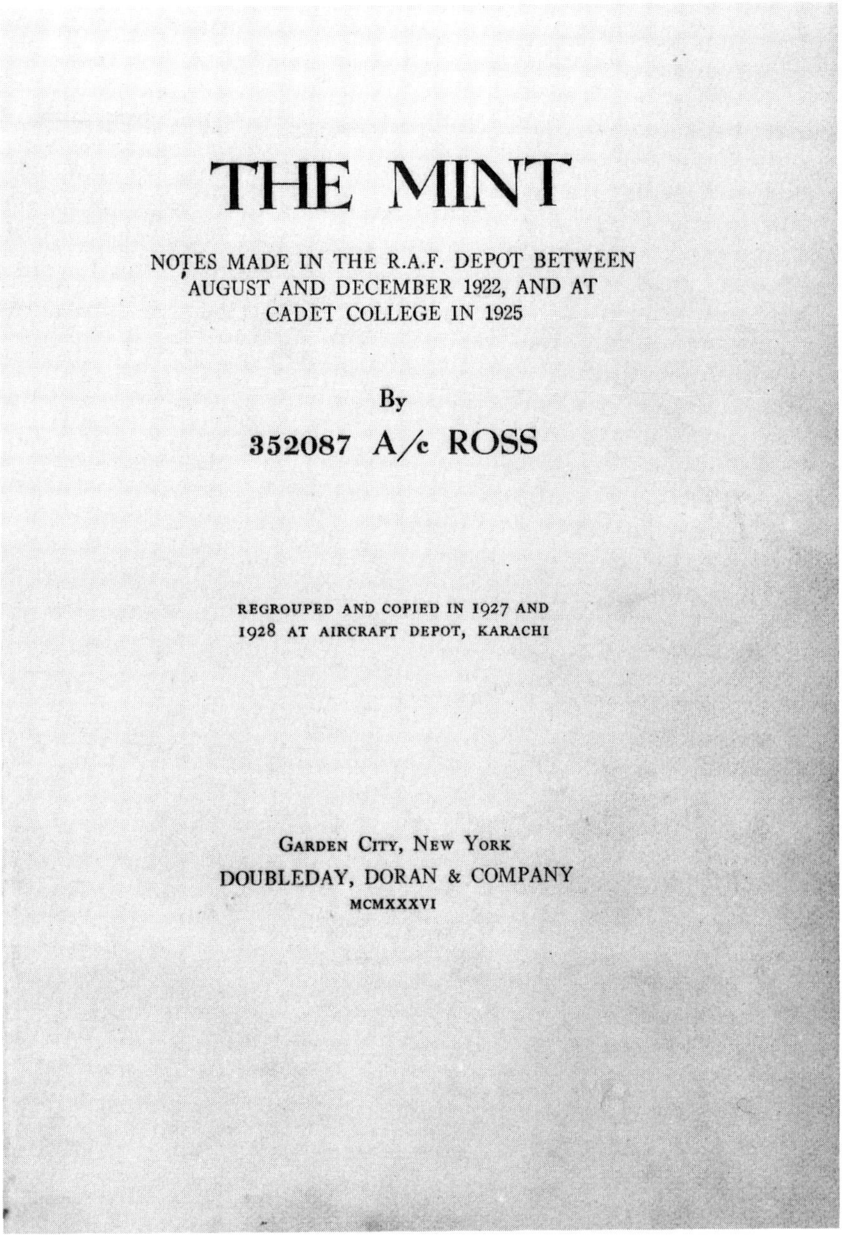

THE MINT

NOTES MADE IN THE R.A.F. DEPOT BETWEEN
AUGUST AND DECEMBER 1922, AND AT
CADET COLLEGE IN 1925

By

352087 A/c ROSS

REGROUPED AND COPIED IN 1927 AND
1928 AT AIRCRAFT DEPOT, KARACHI

GARDEN CITY, NEW YORK
DOUBLEDAY, DORAN & COMPANY
MCMXXXVI

Plate 7   The 1936 U.S. 'copyright' edition of *The Mint*. This was published in America 19 years before the first U.K. edition, to protect the American copyright.

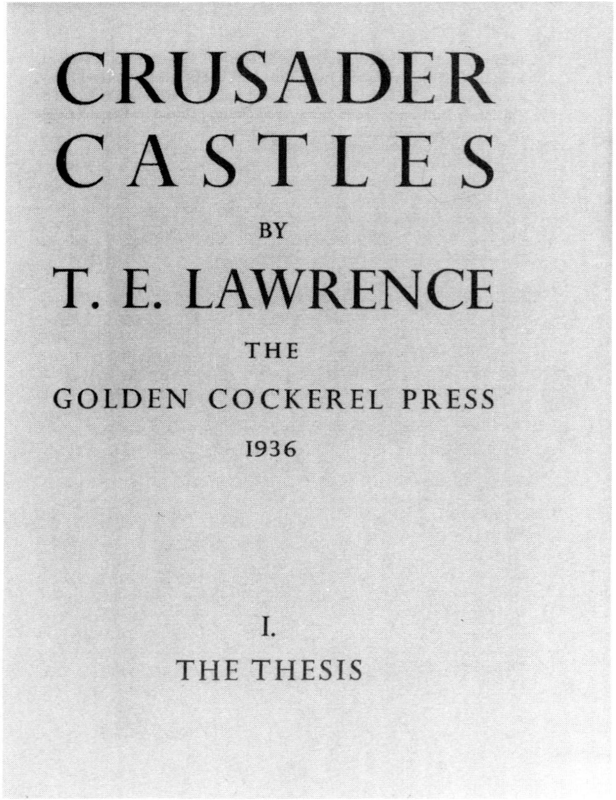

CRUSADER
CASTLES

BY

T. E. LAWRENCE

THE

GOLDEN COCKEREL PRESS

1936

I.

THE THESIS

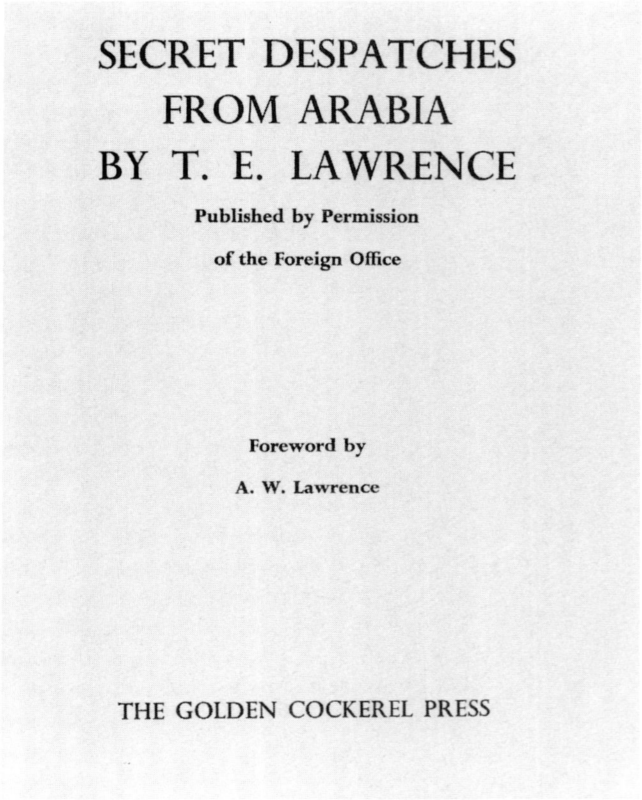

SECRET DESPATCHES
FROM ARABIA
BY T. E. LAWRENCE

Published by Permission
of the Foreign Office

Foreword by
A. W. Lawrence

THE GOLDEN COCKEREL PRESS

Plate 8 Two of the five books by Lawrence published by the Golden Cockerel Press after Lawrence's death.

Steel

Chariots

in the Desert

S. C. ROLLS

**The Story of an
Armoured-Car Driver
with the Duke of Westminster in
Libya and in Arabia with**

T. E. LAWRENCE

EIGHTEENTH FINCHLEY SCOUT GROUP

THE "T. E. LAWRENCE" ROVER CREW

THE SAINT PAUL'S CATHEDRAL
BUST OF LAWRENCE OF ARABIA
BY ERIC KENNINGTON

"THE FIRST
FIVE YEARS"

PRICE ONE SHILLING

Plate 9 *Left*: S.C. Rolls' book of war memoirs; his Rolls-Royce armoured car unit joined Lawrence in the Arabian campaign of August 1917. *Right*: A scarce leaflet published by the 18th Finchley Scout Group named after Lawrence.

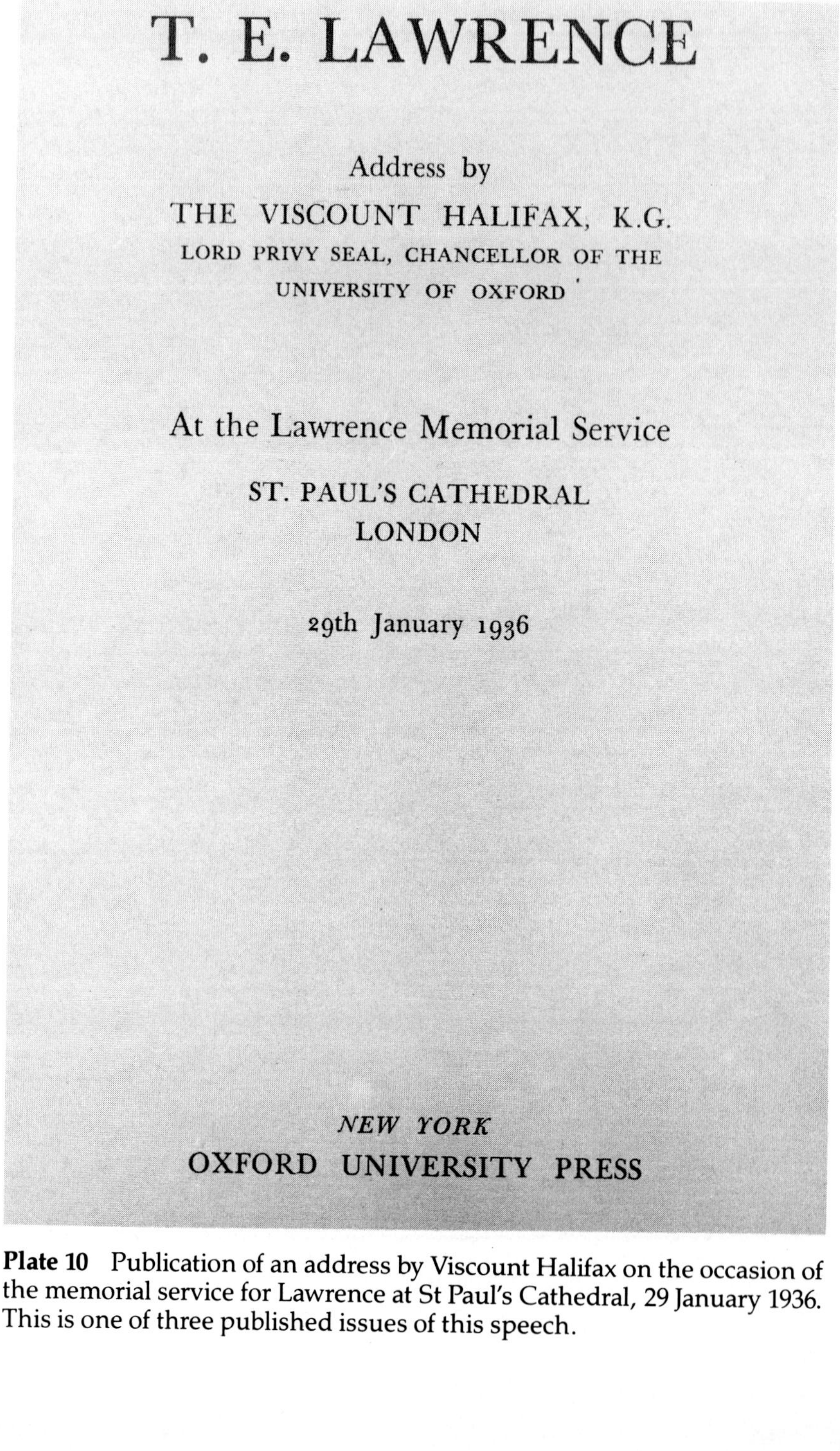

T. E. LAWRENCE

Address by

THE VISCOUNT HALIFAX, K.G.
LORD PRIVY SEAL, CHANCELLOR OF THE
UNIVERSITY OF OXFORD

At the Lawrence Memorial Service

ST. PAUL'S CATHEDRAL
LONDON

29th January 1936

NEW YORK
OXFORD UNIVERSITY PRESS

Plate 10 Publication of an address by Viscount Halifax on the occasion of the memorial service for Lawrence at St Paul's Cathedral, 29 January 1936. This is one of three published issues of this speech.

Stig Steuben

Emir Dynamit

Bilder aus dem Leben des Obersten Lawrence

Berechtigte Bearbeitung der von
Lawrence autorisierten Biographie

Lawrence and the Arabs

von Robert Graves

Mit 8 Kunstdrucktafeln
und mehreren Kartenskizzen

Fünfte Auflage

Kosmos, Gesellschaft der Naturfreunde
Franckh'sche Verlagshandlung, Stuttgart

Plate 11 A German boys' book based on the Graves biography, published in 1931.

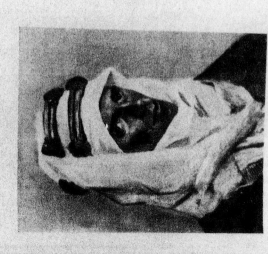

T. E. LAWRENCE

GLAUBE
DER WÜSTE

MIT BIBLIOGRAPHIE · BILDTEIL · LEBENSBERICHT

DIE ARCHE

GÖTEBORGS HÖGSKOLA
FORSKNINGAR OCH FÖRELÄSNINGAR

Erik Lönnroth

LAWRENCE
AV ARABIEN

ÖKENKRIGAREN OCH POLITIKERN

ALBERT BONNIERS FÖRLAG

Plate 12 Two western European works: Lönnroth's *Lawrence av Arabien* (later translated into English) and *Glaube der Wüste* (1951), a Swiss publication of collected portions of Lawrence's work.

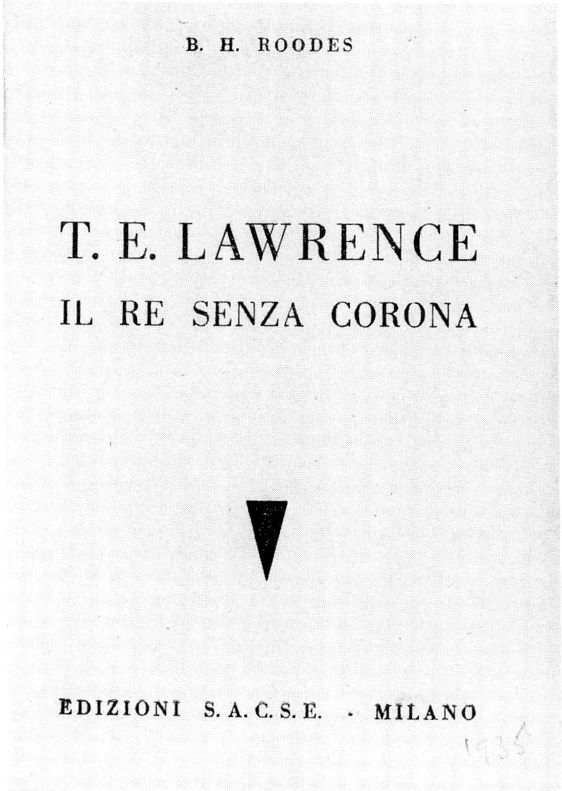

B. H. ROODES

T. E. LAWRENCE
IL RE SENZA CORONA

▶

EDIZIONI S. A. C. S. E. · MILANO

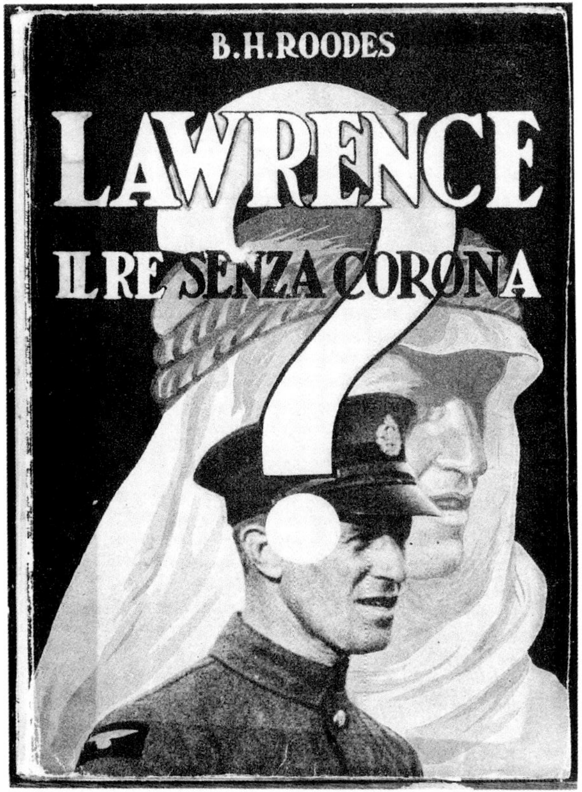

Plate 13 *Lawrence Il Re Senza Corona* by B.H. Roodes, an original Italian work published in 1935.

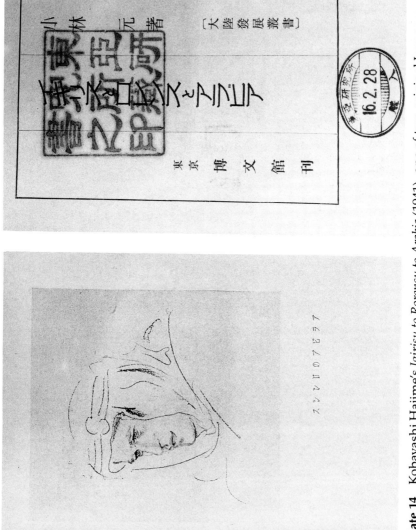

Plate 14 Kobayashi Hajime's *Igirisu to Rorensu to Arabia* (1941), one of two original Japanese works published in the 1940s.

TÜRK DÜŞMANI

Casus Lâvrens

VE

BENZERLERİ

EMEKLİ ALBAY

AZİZ HUDAİ AKDEMİR

Milli Mücadelede Atatürk'ün İstanbul İstihbarat Şefi

Bu eserimi, Milli Mücadelenin sayılı kahramanlarında Kara Salih Sakarya'ya ithaf ediyorum.

A. H.

Muallim Fuad Gücüyener Yayınevi
Büyük Postahane Karşısında Meydancık Hanında
P. K. 210 — İstanbul

Türk Düşmanı

CASUS
LAVRENS

ve

BENZERLERİ

Casus Lavrens Arab kıyafetinde

Plate 15 Akdemir's *Türk Düşmanı*, vehemently anti-Lawrence, published in Turkey in 1950.

Plate 16 Serez' *Lawrence ve Arap İsyanı* (1965), another Turkish work denouncing T.E. Lawrence.

1935

E068 LAWRENCE OF ARABIA COMMITTEE, Lawrence of Arabia Memorial, London, 1935

First English Edition

LAWRENCE OF ARABIA | MEMORIAL

Collation   19.5 × 11.5 cm: single-fold leaflet, unpaged.

Contents   Pp.[1] title page, [2–3] text, [4] blank.

Paper   Buff, wove, unwatermarked, all edges trimmed.

Published at   Free solicitation flyer, August 1935.

Notes   Sent as appeal to raise funds for St Paul's Cathedral memorial. Committee listed at end of text: Allenby, Herbert, Baker, Churchill, Curtis, John, G.B. Shaw, Wrench.

Copies   AC, Cal.

E069 not used   ARNOLD WALTER LAWRENCE, Letters of T.E. Lawrence (T.E. Shaw) 1935

E070 ARNOLD WALTER LAWRENCE, Letters of T.E. Lawrence, [1935?]

Printed letter

LETTERS OF T.E. LAWRENCE | *(T.E. Shaw).*

Collation   25.5 × 20.4 cm: single sheet printed on one side.

Text   20 lines, 6.2 (9) × 11.1 cm.

Paper   White, wove, unwatermarked, all edges trimmed.

Published at   Free solicitation letter.

Notes   Printed letter circulated to friends of T.E. Lawrence soliciting letters for the projected 'Letters of T.E. Lawrence' to be published by Cape. Announces the administrators of the Lawrence Trust. Letter is 20 lines in length.

Copies   Cal, UT.

E071 not used   ARNOLD WALTER LAWRENCE, T.E. Lawrence (T.E. Shaw)

E072 ARNOLD WALTER LAWRENCE, T.E. Lawrence (T.E. Shaw), [1935?]

Printed Letter

T.E. LAWRENCE *(T.E. Shaw)*.

Collation   25.5 × 20.5 cm: single sheet printed on one side.

Text   20 lines, 6.5 × 12.9 cm.

Paper   White, wove, unwatermarked, all edges trimmed.

Published at   Free solicitation letter.

Notes   Printed letter circulated by A.W. Lawrence soliciting contributions for a collection of reminiscences by T.E. Lawrence's friends to be published later in *T.E. Lawrence by His Friends* by Cape. Letter is 50 lines in length.

Copies   Cal, UT.

E073 REGINALD HUGH KIERNAN, Lawrence of Arabia, Harrap, 1935

First English Edition

LAWRENCE OF | ARABIA | By | R.H. Kiernan | AUTHOR OF | "THE FIRST WAR IN THE AIR," ETC. | *With Maps and Illustrations* | [publisher's device] | GEORGE G. HARRAP & CO. LTD. | LONDON BOMBAY SYDNEY

Collation   19.7 × 13 cm: [A]^8 B–M^8 N^4, 100 leaves, pp.[2], [i–iv], v–x, 11–198.

Contents   Prp.[1–2] blank, bastard title, [ii] blank, [iii] title page, [iv] dedication, copyright statement, v–vi introduction, vii contents, [viii] blank, ix maps and illustrations, [x] blank, 11–186 text, 187–195 appendixes, [196] blank, 197–198 bibliography.

RT   On verso LAWRENCE OF ARABIA. On recto [according to chapter].

Plates   Eight b/w photographs on coated paper, printed on one side only, following pp.ii, 44, 72, 104, 146, 160, 164, 172.

Typography and paper $ 1 signed B.

Text   20 lines, 9.8 (9.9) × 9 cm.

Paper   White, wove, unwatermarked, all edges trimmed, sheets bulk 2.2 cm.

Binding   Orange cloth 50 s. O. On spine: LAWRENCE | OF | ARABIA | [cut] | R.H. KIERNAN | [pub. device] | HARRAP.

Published at   July 1935.

Notes   2nd impression, September 1935, as above except publisher's device on spine reduced in size; January 1936, July 1936, July 1937 and November 1938 impressions same as 2nd impression above; 7th impression, March 1941, as above with following differences: [Collation]: 19.5 × 13 cm; [Text]: 20 lines, 9.6 (9.8) × 8.9 cm; [Paper]:sheets bulk 2 cm;

[Binding]: Orange cloth 51 deep O. No. pub. device on spine; 8th impression, August 1942.

Copies AC, Cal, UT, LC.

E074 REGINALD HUGH KIERNAN, Lawrence of Arabia, Harrap, 1945

Ninth English Impression

LAWRENCE OF | ARABIA | *By* | R.H. KIERNAN | AUTHOR OF | "LLOYD GEORGE" "BADEN-POWELL" | ETC. | *With Maps and Illustrations* | [pub. device] | GEORGE G. HARRAP & CO. LTD. | LONDON TORONTO BOMBAY SYDNEY

Collation 18.2 × 12.3 cm: [A]⁸ B–M⁸, 96 leaves, pp.[1–6], 11–196.

Contents Prp.[1] title page, [2] dedication, issue statement, printer's credit, [3–4] introduction, [5] contents, [6] blank, pp.11–186 text, 187–195 appendixes, 196 bibliography.

RT On verso LAWRENCE OF ARABIA. On recto [according to chapter].

Plates Four plates on coated paper, printed on both sides following p.28.

Typography and paper $1 signed B.

Text 20 lines, 9.7 (9.8) × 9 cm.

Paper White, wove, unwatermarked, all edges trimmed, sheets bulk 1 cm.

Binding Orange cloth 51 deep O. On spine: [in brown] LAWRENCE | OF | ARABIA | [cut] | R.H. | KIERNAN | HARRAP.

Notes Dust wrapper states 10th impression, March 1947, as above with following differences: MAPS AND ILLUSTRATIONS p.10; other impressions: May 1949 and November 1951; 13th impression, June 1955, as above with following difference: [Binding]: grey paper covered boards.

Copies AC, Cal.

E075 REGINALD HUGH KIERNAN, Lawrence of Arabia, McKay, 1935

First American Edition

LAWRENCE OF | ARABIA | *By* | R.H. KIERNAN | AUTHOR OF | "THE FIRST WAR IN THE AIR" ETC. | *With Maps and Illustrations* | PHILADELPHIA | DAVID McKAY COMPANY SOUTH WASHINGTON SQUARE

Collation 19.5 × 13 cm: [A]⁸ B–M⁸ N⁴, 100 leaves, pp.[1–2], [I–IV], V–IX, [10], 11–198.

Contents Prp.[1–2] blank, pp.[I] bastard title, [II] blank, [III] title page, [IV] dedication, printer's credit, V–VI introduction, VII contents, [VIII] blank, IX maps and illustrations, [10] blank, 11–186 text, 187–195 appendixes, [196]

blank, 197–198 bibliography (bibliographical note).

RT   On verso LAWRENCE OF ARABIA. On recto [according to chapter].

Plates   Eight b/w plates printed on coated paper, following pp.2, 44, 72, 104, 146, 160, 164, 172.

Typography and paper $ 1 signed B.

Text   20 lines, 9.7 (9.9) × 8.8 cm.

Paper   White, wove, thick, unwatermarked, all edges trimmed, sheets bulk 2.3 cm.

Binding   Orange linen 34 v. r O. On spine: [in black] LAWRENCE | OF | ARABIA | [cut] | R.H. | KIERNAN | McKAY.

Copies   AC.

E076   REGINALD HUGH KIERNAN, Lawrence of Arabia, Folcroft, 1977

Second American Edition

LAWRENCE OF | ARABIA | *By* | R.H. KIERNAN | AUTHOR OF | "THE FIRST WAR IN THE AIR", ETC. | *With Maps and Illustrations* | *FOLCROFT LIBRARY EDITIONS/ 1977*

Collation   22.2 × 16 cm: guillotined sheets, 103 leaves, pp.[1–8], [i–iv], v–ix, [10], 11–198.

Contents   Prp.[1–4] blank, [5] bastard title, [6–7] blank, [8] frontispiece, pp.[i] title page,[ii] dedication, original issue, copyright statements, publisher's credit, [iii–iv] blank, v–vi introduction, vii contents, [viii] blank, ix illustrations, [10] blank, 11–186 text, 187–195 appendixes, [196] blank, 197–198 bibliography.

Typography and paper $ 1 signed H (signatures of original edition).

Text   20 lines, 9.7 × 8.8 cm.

Paper   Buff, wove, unwatermarked, all edges trimmed, sheets bulk 1.8 cm.

Binding   Dark green buckram 146 d. G. On spine: [gilt, running down] [cut] LAWRENCE OF ARABIA [cut] KIERNAN [cut].

Notes   Reprint of first English edition.

Copies   LC.

E077   G.(Terence Ian Fytton Armstrong), Annotations on Some Minor Writings of "T.E. Lawrence", Eric Partridge, 1935

First English Edition

ANNOTATIONS | ON SOME MINOR WRITINGS OF | "T.E.

LAWRENCE" | BY | G | ERIC PARTRIDGE, LTD. | AT SCHOLARTIS PRESS | THIRTY MUSEUM STREET, LONDON | 1935

Collation   18.5 × 12 cm: [1–2]⁸, 16 leaves, pp.[2], [i–vi], vii–x, 11–28, [4].

Contents   Prp.[1–2] blank, [i] half-title, [ii] 'This Edition is limited to | Five hundred copies of which | Four hundred and fifty are | for sale. Copy No...' , [iii] blank, [iv] drawing of T.E. Lawrence, [v] title page, [vi] printer's credit, vii prefatory note, [viii] blank, ix–xi index, 11–28 text, [1–4] blank.

Text   20 lines, 7 (8.1) × 9.3 cm.

Paper   White, wove, all edges trimmed, unwatermarked, sheets bulk 3 mm.

Binding   Orange cloth 68 s.OY. On front cover: ANNOTATIONS ON SOME | MINOR WRITINGS OF | "T.E. LAWRENCE".

Published at   5s.

Notes   Limited to 500 copies of which 450 were for sale. G. is John Gawsworth, i.e. T.I.F. Armstrong. Frontispeice drawing by F. Carter.

Copies   AC, Cal, BPL, H, UT, LC.

E078   JULIAN BIDDULPH ARNOLD, Lawrence of Arabia, Stricker, 1935

First American Edition

[In green] *Lawrence of Arabia* | JULIAN | BIDDULPH | ARNOLD | THOMAS PERRY STRICKER | *Los Angeles : Mcmxxxv*

Collation   19.2 × 13.3 cm: [1]¹⁰, 10 leaves, pp.[1–6], i–ii, [1–2], 3–10, [1–2].

Contents   Prp.[1] bastard title, [2] blank, [3] title page, [4] copyright, 'This first edition consists of | 500 copies, printed from | hand composed foundry type | & bound at Los Angeles, | California.', [5] section title, [6] blank, i–ii forenote, pp.[1] half-title, [2] blank, 3–10 text, [1–2] blank.

Text   20 lines, 9.8 × 8.5 cm.

Paper   Laid, deckle fore-edge, watermarked, white, top and bottom edges trimmed, sheets bulk 2 mm.

Binding   Light brown paper wrappers l y.Br. Green cords securing cover to sheets. On front cover: [all in green] *Lawrence of Arabia* | *JULIAN* | *BIDDULPH* | *ARNOLD.*

Notes   Limited to 500 copies. Text is essentially the material on Lawrence contained in *Giants and Dressing Gowns*, Argus, Chicago, 1942.

Copies   AC, Cal, LC.

E079   CHARLES EDMONDS, T.E. Lawrence, Davies, 1935

First English Edition

T.E. LAWRENCE | BY | CHARLES EDMONDS | AUTHOR OF 'A SUBALTERN'S WAR' | [five line quote] | PETER DAVIES LIMITED | 1935
Collation   19.2 × 13 cm: [1–12]^8, 96 leaves, pp.[1–4], 5–192.

Contents   Pp.[1] bastard title, [2] blank, [3] title page, [4] issue statement, printer's credit, 5–6 preface, 7 contents, 8 chronology of Lawrence's life, 9–189 text, 190 bibliographical note, 191–192 index.

RT   On verso T.E. LAWRENCE. On recto [according to chapter].

Plates   B/w photo frontispiece following p.2.

Typography and paper $ 1 signed, each gathering is signed with a C.

Text   20 lines, 9.2 (9.3) × 8.6 cm.

Paper   White, wove, unwatermarked, all edges trimmed, sheets bulk 2 cm.

Binding   Black cloth. On spine: [double rule] | [double rule] | [within green rectangle, gilt] | T.E. | LAWRENCE | * | CHARLES | EDMONDS | [double rule] | [single rule] | [within green rectangle] DAVIES | [double rule]. T.e. green.

Published at   5s, November 1935.

Notes   Author's name was the pseudonym of Charles Edmond Carrington. Another issue: light blue cloth 181 l. Blue. On spine: [all in black with no coloured rectangles]. T.e. unstained, otherwise as above.

Copies   AC, Cal, LC.

E080   CHARLES EDMONDS, T.E. Lawrence, Nelson, 1936

Second English Edition

T.E. LAWRENCE | BY | CHARLES EDMONDS | *Author of 'A Subaltern's War'* | [quote from Marshal Saxe] | THOMAS NELSON & SONS LTD | LONDON EDINBURGH PARIS MELBOURNE | TORONTO AND NEW YORK

Collation   17 × 11 cm: [1]^8 2–12^8, 96 leaves, pp.[1–4], 5–192.

Contents   Pp.[1] series and bastard titles, [2] blank, [3] title page, [4] copyright, issue statements, 5–6 preface, 7 contents, 8 chronology of Lawrence's life, 9–189 text, 190 bibliographical note, 191–192 index of personal names.

RT   On verso T.E. LAWRENCE. On recto [according to section].

Typography and paper $ 1 signed 3.

Text   20 lines, 9.1 (9.4) × 8.7 cm.

Paper   White, wove, unwatermarked, all edges trimmed, sheets bulk 1.5 cm.

Binding   Grey cloth 264 l. Gray. On spine: [in red] T.E. | LAW- | RENCE | CHARLES | EDMONDS | NELSON. T.e. grey.

Published at   November 1935.

Notes   No. 9 in publisher's series Short Biographies; 2nd impression, March 1938, same as above except lettering on spine in black; another impression, April 1942, same as above except t.e. is green. Author's name was the pseudonym of Charles Edmond Carrington.

Copies   AC, Cal, UT.

E081   CHARLES EDMONDS, T.E. Lawrence, Appleton-Century, 1936

First American Edition

T.E. LAWRENCE | (OF ARABIA) | BY | CHARLES EDMONDS | [five-line quote from Marshal Saxe] | [pub. device] D. APPLETON-CENTURY COMPANY | INCORPORATED | NEW YORK LONDON | 1936

Collation   18.9 × 13 cm: [1–12]^8, [13]^{10}, 106 leaves, pp.[i–iv], v–x, 1–199, [3].

Contents   [i] bastard title, [ii] list of titles in series, [iii] title page, [iv] copyright statement, v–vi preface, vii contents, viii blank, ix maps, x chronology of Lawrence's life, pp.1–194 text, 195–196 bibliographical note, 197–199 index of personal names, [1–3] blank.

RT   On verso T.E. Lawrence. On recto [according to chapter].

Plates   B/w photo frontispiece following prp.[ii].

Text   20 lines, 9.8 (9.9) × 8.5 cm.

Paper   White, wove, unwatermarked, top and bottom edges trimmed, sheets bulk 1.9 cm.

Binding   Black cloth. On spine: [all gilt] [double rule] | [double rule] | [within red rectangle] T.E. | LAWRENCE | * | CHARLES | EDMONDS | [below rectangle, double rule] | [single rule] | [within red rectangle] APPLETON | CENTURY | [below rectangle, double rule]. T.e. red.

Published at $1.50.

Notes   Charles Edmonds was the pseudonym of Charles Edmond Carrington.

Copies   AC, Cal, LC.

E082   CHARLES EDMONDS, T.E. Lawrence, Haskell House, 1977

Second American Edition

T.E. LAWRENCE | BY | CHARLES EDMONDS | AUTHOR OF 'A

SUBALTERN'S WAR' | [quote] | [publisher's device] | HASKELL HOUSE PUBLISHERS LTD. | *Publishers of Scarce Scholarly Books* | Brooklyn, NY | 1977.

Collation   20.3 × 13.5 cm: [1–5]^{16}, 96 leaves, pp.[1–4], 5–[192].

Contents   Pp.[1] bastard title, [2] blank, [3] title page, [4] publisher's credit, CIP, 5–6 preface, 7 contents, 8 brief chronology of Lawrence's life, 9–189 text, 190 bibliographical notes, 191–192 index.

RT   On verso T.E. LAWRENCE. On recto [according to chapter].

Typography and paper $ 1 signed C, (signatures of original edition).

Text   20 lines, 9.2 (9.3) × 8.5 cm.

Paper   White, wove, unwatermarked, all edges trimmed, sheets bulk 2 cm.

Binding   Blue cloth 195 brill.p B. On spine: [in white running down] T.E. LAWRENCE CHARLES EDMONDS.

Notes   Reprint of first English edition. Charles Edmonds was the pseudonym of Charles Edmond Carrington.

Copies   AC, LC.

E083   EDWARD ROBINSON, Lawrence, Oxford, 1935

First English Edition

LAWRENCE | *THE STORY OF HIS LIFE* | *by* | EDWARD ROBINSON | *With an Introductory note by* | A.W. LAWRENCE | *Illustrated with a Coloured Frontispiece* | *and 32 pages of plates* | [publisher's device] | *LONDON · NEW YORK · TORONTO* | OXFORD UNIVERSITY PRESS

Collation   19 × 13 cm: [A]^8 B–P^8 Q^6, 126 leaves, pp.[1–7], 8–250, [2].

Contents   [1] bastard title, [2] blank, [3] title page, [4] printer's credit, [5] introductory note, [6] map, [7]–8 preface, 9–10 list of illustrations, 11–250 text, [1–2] blank.

RT   On both verso and recto LAWRENCE.

Plates   Twenty b/w photos tipped in, two leaves each following pp.2, 24, 56, 88, 120, 152, 184, 216, 248.

Typography and paper $ 1 signed C.

Text   20 lines, 9.7 (9.8) × 8.8 cm.

Paper   White, wove, unwatermarked, all edges trimmed, sheets bulk 2.8 cm.

Binding   Brown cloth 54 br O. On front cover: [brown stamped] LAWRENCE | [roundel of camel rider]. On spine: [in brown] LAWRENCE | [cut] | EDWARD | ROBINSON [cut] | OXFORD. T.e. brown.

Notes   List of impressions: 2nd and 3rd, 1935, as above; 4th, 1945, same as above with following differences: last plates follow p.246; sheets bulk 1.4 cm. On spine: [in brown] LAW- | RENCE | EDWARD |ROBINSON | OXFORD; 5th, 1948, same as above with following differences:

LAWRENCE | *THE STORY OF HIS LIFE* | EDWARD ROBINSON |
GEOFFREY CUMBERLEGE | OXFORD UNIVERSITY PRESS; [Paper]:
buff, simulated laid, sheets bulk 2 cm; [Plates]: last plates follow p.248;
[Binding]: red cloth 36 d.r O. On front cover: LAWRENCE | [roundel of
camel rider]. On spine: LAW- | RENCE | EDWARD | ROBINSON |
OXFORD; [Published at]: 6s, lacks A.W. Lawrence's introductory note.

Copies   AC, Cal, UT, LC.

E084   EDWARD ROBINSON, Lawrence, Folcroft, 1979

First American Edition

LAWRENCE | *THE STORY OF HIS LIFE* | By | EDWARD ROBINSON | *With
an Introductory Note by* | A.W. LAWRENCE | *Illustrated with a Coloured
Frontispiece* | *and 32 pages of plates* | [pub. device] | THIS IS A LIMITED
EDITION OF 150 COPIES | FOLCROFT LIBRARY EDITIONS/ 1979

Collation   22.3 × 16 cm: [1–18]^16, 128 leaves, pp.[1–6], [1–7], 8–250.

Contents   Prp.[1–2] blank, [3] bastard title, [4–5] blank, [6] frontis., [1] title
page, [2] blank, [3] title page of original edition, [4] pub. address, issue
statement of original edition, [5] introductory note by A.W. Lawrence, [6]
map, [7–8] preface, [9]–10 illustrations, [11]–250 text.

RT   On both verso and recto LAWRENCE.

Plates   Those of first issue are included in gatherings, but not paginated.

Typography and paper $ 1 signed B these are from first issue.

Text   9.8 (9.8) × 9 cm.

Paper   Buff, wove, unwatermarked, all edges trimmed, sheets bulk 2 cm.

Binding   Green buckram 137 d. y Gr. On spine: [gilt, running down]
LAWRENCE [cut] ROBINSON. End papers white.

Copies   Cal.

E085   B.H. ROODES, Lawrence Il Re Senza Corona, S.A.C.S.E., 1935

First Italian Edition

B.H. ROODES | T.E. LAWRENCE | IL RE SENZA CORONA | [cut] |
EDIZIONI S.A.C.S.E. – MILANO

Collation   18.5 × 12.8 cm: [1]–19^8, 152 leaves, pp.[1–4], 5–302, pp.[1–2].

Contents   Pp.[1] bastard title, [2] blank, [3] title page, [4] copyright
statement, printer's credit, 5–302 text, [1] blank, [2] printer's colophon.

RT   On verso B.H. ROODES. On recto T.E. LAWRENCE.

Typography and paper $ 1 signed 5-LAWRENCE.

Text   20 lines, 8 (8.5) × 9 cm.

Paper White, wove, unwatermarked, all edges trimmed, sheets bulk 2.2 cm.

Binding White paper covers [pictorial front cover with green background in white] B.H. ROODES | LAWRENCE | [1st 4 letters in white, rest in green] IL RE SENZA CORONA. On spine: B.H. | ROODES | [Oxford rule] | [running up] T.E. LAWRENCE | [Oxford rule] | S.A.C.S.E. | MILANO.

Copies H.

E086   John & Edward Bumpus Ltd., T.E. Lawrence A Bibliographical Note, Bumpus, 1935

First English Edition

T.E. LAWRENCE | A BIBLIOGRAPHICAL NOTE | SEVEN PILLARS | OF WISDOM | Complete and unabridged with | 48 illustrations 30/ | JOHN & EDWARD BUMPUS Ltd. | *Booksellers to His Majesty The King* | 477 OXFORD STREET, W.1

Collation   13.7 × 9 cm: single-fold leaflet, [1–4].

Contents   Pp.[1] title page, [2] three-paragraph description on Lawrence, [3–4] list of Lawrence's works and list of works about him.

Paper   Buff, wove, watermarked, all edges trimmed.

Published at   Free flyer.

Copies   AC.

Assessment begins: Biography I, 1936

The year following Lawrence's death saw the beginning of what has become referred to by critics as the Lawrence 'industry'. Two juvenile boy adventure books appeared: Slade's *Lawrence in the Blue* (the third and last book by Slade) and Shumway's *Lawrence the Arabian Knight*. The latter appeared in England under the title *War in the Desert*.

The committee formed in 1935 to raise funds for a Lawrence memorial was successful in its efforts and a service was held in St Paul's Cathedral in 1936 for the unveiling of the Kennington bust. The address was given by Viscount Halifax. The text of his speech was published by Oxford University Press, both in England and the USA, and was reprinted by Cape for readers of *Now and Then*.

Vyvyan Richards, a close friend of Lawrence from their Oxford days, published an account of that friendship. Richards and Lawrence had long-standing, but never realised, plans to print fine books in the manner of the Kelmscott Press.

A Swedish selection of Lawrence's work in translation also appeared during this year. It predates the Garnett collection, *The Essential T.E. Lawrence* (1951), a similar effort, by some 16 years. The first of the limited 'fine press' books issued through the Corvinus and Golden Cockerel

Presses was the Liddell Hart/Storrs essays under the title *Lawrence of Arabia* by the Corvinus Press. A truly private press, the first effort of the press was the Liddell Hart piece separately printed. It was deemed unsuccessful apparently, and when combined with the Storrs essay was issued on 22 May.

The world-wide interest in Lawrence is reflected in an abscure essay by Miquel Marsicovétere y durán published in Guatemala. In Palestine a Hebrew work on Lawrence also appeared: Assaf *Laurens b'chayyim ub'agada*. The Golden Cockerel Press brought out *Crusader Castles* this year and the publication was covered prominently in the press prospectuses. Maggs Brothers issued a catalogue offering the manuscript of the Robert Graves biography and related materials such as correspondence between Lawrence and Graves.

1936

E087   GURNEY SLADE, Lawrence in the Blue, Stokes, 1936

First American Edition

LAWRENCE | IN THE BLUE | GURNEY SLADE | AUTHOR OF | "IN LAWRENCE'S BODYGUARD" | [pub. device] | FREDRICK A. STOKES COMPANY | NEW YORK MCMXXXVI

Collation   18.7 × 12.7 cm: [1–2]^8 [3–16]^8 [17]^4 [18]^8, 140 leaves, pp.[i–iv], v–vii, [viii], 1–269, [3].

Contents   Prp.[i] bastard title, [ii] blank, [iii] title page, [iv] copyright statement, v–vi foreword, vii illustrations, [viii] map, pp.1–269 text, [1–3] blank.

RT   On both verso and recto [between rules] LAWRENCE IN THE BLUE.

Plates   Three drawings on coated paper, printed on one side only, following pp.ii, 164, 242.

Text   20 lines, 9.7 (10.1) × 8.7 cm.

Paper   White, wove, unwatermarked, all edges trimmed, sheets bulk 3 cm.

Binding   Blue cloth 182 m. Blue. On front cover: [in red] LAWRENCE | IN THE BLUE | [rule] | GURNEY SLADE. On spine: [in red] LAWRENCE | IN | THE BLUE | [rule] | SLADE | STOKES.

Notes   Gurney Slade was the pseudonym of Stephen Bartlett.

Copies   AC, Cal.

E088   GURNEY SLADE, Lawrence in the Blue, Warne, 1936

First English Edition

LAWRENCE | IN THE BLUE | BY | GURNEY SLADE | AUTHOR OF "IN LAWRENCE'S BODYGUARD" | "LED BY LAWRENCE," ETC.,ETC. | [publisher's device] | FREDRICK WARNE AND CO., LTD. | LONDON

AND NEW YORK

Collation   19.2 × 13 cm: [A]^8 B–S^8 x^8, 152 leaves, pp.[1–4], 5–288, [1]–16.

Contents   Pp.[1] bastard title, [2] copyright statement, [3] title page, [4] map, 5–6 foreword, 6–288 text, [1–16] publisher's ads.

RT   On both verso and recto LAWRENCE IN THE BLUE.

Plates   Four plates on coated paper, printed on one side only, following pp.2 (colour), 96, 176, 260.

Typography and paper $ 1 signed B.

Text   20 lines, 11.3 (11.5) × 9 cm.

Paper   White, wove, unwatermarked, all edges trimmed, sheets bulk 3.8 cm.

Binding   Orange cloth 37 m. rO. On front cover: [within black rule frame] LAWRENCE | IN THE BLUE | BY | GURNEY SLADE | [line drawing of Lawrence in Arab robes, lower right corner]. On spine: [thick rule] | LAWRENCE | IN THE | BLUE | · | GURNEY SLADE | [cut] | · WARNE · | [thick rule].

Notes   Gurney Slade was the pseudonym of Stephen Bartlett. Albion Library Series.

Copies   AC, Cal, LC.

E090   HARRY IRVING SHUMWAY, Lawrence the Arabian Knight, Page, 1936

First American Edition

LAWRENCE | THE ARABIAN KNIGHT | BEING THE LIFE STORY OF | THOMAS EDWARD LAWRENCE | By | HARRY IRVING SHUMWAY | *AUTHOR OF "ALBERT:. THE SOLDIER KING," ETC.* | Illustrated by Paul Quinn | [cut] L.C. PAGE & COMPANY | Publishers –:– Boston

Collation   19.5 × 13.5 cm: [1–22]^8, 176 leaves, pp.[2], [i–vi], vii–xii, 1–330, [8].

Contents   [1] bastard title, [2] list of author's works, prp.[1] blank, [ii] frontis., [iii] title page , [iv] copyright, issue statements, printer's credits, [v] dedication, [vi] blank, vii–viii contents, ix–x illustrations, [xi] map, [xii] drawing, 1–330 text, [1–7] publisher's ads, [8] blank.

RT   On verso [double rule] | LAWRENCE THE ARABIAN KNIGHT | [single rule]. On recto [according to chapter].

Text   20 lines, 9.8 (10.1) × 8.4 cm.

Paper   White, wove, unwatermarked, all edges trimmed, sheets bulk 3 cm.

Binding   Orange cloth 35 s. r O. On front cover: [in brown] [decorated rule] | LAWRENCE | THE ARABIAN KNIGHT | [cut] | HARRY IRVING SHUMWAY | [decorated rule]. On spine: [in brown] [decorated rule] | LAWRENCE | [rule] | THE ARABIAN | KNIGHT | SHUMWAY | PAGE | [short rule] | BOSTON | [decorated rule].

Published at $1.75.

Notes   Text same as that of Shumway, *War in the Desert*, Collins, n.d. 1938.

Copies   AC, Cal, LC.

E091   HARRY IRVING SHUMWAY, War in the Desert, Collins, 1938

First English Edition

WAR IN THE DESERT | *by* | HARRY IRVING SHUMWAY | *Illustrated by Paul Quinn* | [cut] | COLLINS | LONDON AND GLASGOW

Collation   19.6 × 13.3 cm: [A]⁸ B–Q⁸, 128 leaves, pp.[1–8], 9–256.

Contents   Pp.[1] bastard title, [2] list of titles in series, [3] title page, [4] printer's, binder's credits, [5–6] contents, [7–8] illustrations,. 9–256 text.

Text   20 lines, 9.8 × 8.8 cm.

Paper   White, laid, unwatermarked, all edges trimmed, sheets bulk 1.9 cm.

Binding   Rough red buckram 12 s Red. On front cover: [cut]. On spine: WAR | IN THE | DESERT | HARRY | IRVING | SHUMWAY | COLLINS. T.e. pink.

Notes   Published in USA under title: *Lawrence the Arabian Knight*. Another binding green cloth 141 s. G with black cut on front cover and spine lettering.

Copies   AC, Cal, LC.

E092   HARRY IRVING SHUMWAY, War In the Desert, Collins, 1940

Second English Edition

[Within elaborate ornamental frame] *The Laurel and Gold Series* | WAR IN | THE DESERT | *The Story of* | *Lawrence of Arabia* | *by* | HARRY IRVING SHUMWAY | *Illustrated* | *Collins Clear-Type Press*

Collation   15.3 × 10 cm: [A]¹⁶ B–G¹⁶, 112 leaves, pp.[1–4], 5–224.

Contents   Pp.[1] series title, [2] quote within elaborate ornamental frame, [3] title page, [4] issue statement, printer's credit, 5 contents, [6] illus., [7]–224 text.

RT   On verso WAR IN THE DESERT. On recto [according to chapter].

Typography and paper $ 1 signed W.D., D.

Text   20 lines, 7.8 (8.1) × 7.9 cm.

Paper   White, wove, unwatermarked, all edges trimmed, sheets bulk 2 cm.

Binding   Green cloth 136 m.y G. On front cover: [gilt, series device]. On spine: [all in gilt] [double rule] | [within decorative frame, running down] WAR IN THE DESERT | [below frame, running across] 92 | COLLINS | [double rule].

Published at January 1940.

Notes A 2nd impression, May 1941; 3rd impression, July 1945.

Copies AC.

E093 ST. PAUL'S CATHEDRAL, Form of Service, London, 1936

First English Edition

ST. PAUL'S CATHEDRAL. | [short rule] | FORM OF SERVICE | USED AT | THE UNVEILING OF THE MEMORIAL| TO | THOMAS EDWARD LAWRENCE | LAWRENCE OF ARABIA | [short rule] | WEDNESDAY, 29th JANUARY, 1936 | AT 5:30 P.M.

Collation 21.5 × 13.8 cm: [1]⁴, 4 leaves, pp.[1–3], 4–7, [8].

Contents Pp.[1] title page, [2] photo of bust of Lawrence, [3] –8 order of service.

Text 20 lines, 10.5 × 9 cm.

Paper White, wove, unwatermarked, all edges trimmed, sheets bulk 1 mm.

Binding Two metal staples.

Published at 29 January 1936.

Copies AC, Cal, UT.

E094 EDWARD FREDERICK LINDLEY WOOD, 3rd VISCOUNT HALIFAX, T.E. Lawrence, Oxford University Press, 1936

First English Edition

[Outline lettering] T.E. LAWRENCE | [rule] | AN ADDRESS | *by the* | VISCOUNT HALIFAX K.G. | LORD PRIVY SEAL | CHANCELLOR OF THE UNIVERSITY OF OXFORD | *delivered at* | ST. PAUL'S CATHEDRAL | *on Wednesday, 29 January* | 1936 | *Price 6d. net* | OXFORD UNIVERSITY PRESS | LONDON : HUMPHREY MILFORD

Collation 21.4 × 14.3 cm: [1]⁵, 10 pages, pp.[2], 1–7, [3]; includes covers.

Contents Prp.[1] front cover and title page, [2] blank, pp.1–7 text, [1] printer's colophon, [1–2] blank back cover.

Text 20 lines, 9.5 × 9.4 cm.

Paper White, wove, unwatermarked, all edges trimmed, sheets bulk 1 mm.

Binding 79 l. gy. y Br paper different from sheets. On front cover: [title page]. Linen-thread stitching.

Published at 6d, February 1936.

Notes Another state, same as above, with following differences: no covers, on last page in addition to printer's colophon: PRINTED BY PERMISSION OF THE AUTHOR | AND THE OXFORD UNIVERSITY PRESS | FOR PRESENTATION BY JONATHAN CAPE TO THE READERS OF | *NOW AND THEN* | MCMXXX | VI. Sheets fastened with two metal staples. Reprinted in *R.A.F. Cadet College Journal*, Autumn 1936.

Copies AC, Cal, UT, Ho.

E095 EDWARD FREDERICK LINDLEY WOOD, 3rd VISCOUNT HALIFAX, T.E. Lawrence, Oxford University Press, 1936

First American Edition

T.E. LAWRENCE | Address by | THE VISCOUNT HALIFAX, K.G. | LORD PRIVY SEAL, CHANCELLOR OF THE | UNIVERSITY OF OXFORD | at the Lawrence Memorial Service | ST. PAUL'S CATHEDRAL | LONDON | 29th January 1936 | *NEW YORK* | OXFORD UNIVERSITY PRESS

Collation 21.7 × 14.4 cm: [1]⁶, 12 pages, pp.[1–2], 3–10, [11–12].

Contents Pp.[1] title page, [2] copyright statement, 3–10 text, [11–12] blank.

RT On both verso and recto T.E. LAWRENCE.

Text 20 lines, 10 (10) × 9.8 cm.

Paper White, wove, unwatermarked, all edges trimmed, sheets bulk 2mm.

Binding 60 l. gy. Br paper covers fastened by cord to sheets. On front cover: [same as title page].

Published at 40 cents.

Copies AC, Cal, LC.

E096 VYVYAN RICHARDS, Portrait of T.E. Lawrence, Cape, 1936

Uncorrected Proof of First English Edition

PORTRAIT OF | T.E. LAWRENCE | BY | VYVYAN RICHARDS | [pub. device] | JONATHAN CAPE | THIRTY BEDFORD SQUARE | LONDON.

Collation 19.5 × 13.5 cm: [A]–Q⁸, 168 leaves, pp.[1–4], 5–252, [2].

Contents Pp.[1] bastard title, [2] blank, [3] title page, [4] issue statement, printer's, paper maker's, binder's credits, [5] contents, [6] blank, 7 illustrations, [8] blank, 9–13 introduction, [14] blank, 15 acknowledgments, [16] blank, [17] half-title, [18] blank, 19–252 text, [1–4] blank.

RT On verso [according to chapter].

Typography and paper $ 1 signed B.

Text 20 lines, 9.8 (.9.9) × 9.8 cm.

Paper White, wove, unwatermarked, all edges trimmed, sheets bulk 1 cm.

Binding Green paper 149 p. G. On front cover: PORTRAIT OF | T.E. LAWRENCE | BY | VYVYAN | RICHARDS | [pub. device] | Advance Proof | Does not contain Proof Reader's marks. On spine: [running up] PORTRAIT OF T.E. LAWRENCE

Copies Can.

E097 VYVYAN RICHARDS, Portrait of T.E. Lawrence, Cape, 1936

First English Edition

PORTRAIT OF | T.E. LAWRENCE | *THE LAWRENCE OF* | *THE SEVEN PILLARS OF WISDOM* | BY | VYVYAN RICHARDS | [pub. device] | JONATHAN CAPE | THIRTY BEDFORD SQUARE | LONDON

Collation 20.2 × 13.5 cm: [A]^8 B–Q^8, 128 leaves, pp.[1–4], 5–255, [1].

Contents Pp.[1] bastard title, [2] blank, [3] title page, [4] issue statement, printer's, papermaker's, binder's credits, 5 contents, [6] blank, 7 illustrations, [8] blank, 9–13 introduction, [14] blank, 15 acknowledgments, [16] blank, 17 half-title, [18] blank, 19–252 text, 253–255 index, [1] blank.

RT On verso PORTRAIT OF T.E. LAWRENCE. On recto [according to chapter].

Plates Six b/w photographs on coated paper, printed on both sides, following pp.2, 54, 94, 124, 192, 246.

Typography and paper $ 1 signed B.

Text 20 lines, 9.8 (10) × 9.8 cm.

Paper White, wove, unwatermarked, top and fore edges trimmed, sheets bulk 2.3 cm.

Binding Blue buckram 179 deep B. On spine: [gilt] PORTRAIT | OF T.E. | LAWRENCE | VYVYAN | RICHARDS | [publisher's device]. T.e. dark blue.

Published at 8s 6d, July 1936.

Notes A 2nd impression, November 1936, same as above with impression statement added to verso of title page.

Copies AC, Cal, H, UT, LC.

E098 MAGGS BROTHERS, Colonel Lawrence of Arabia Catalogue, 1936

First English Edition

COLONEL LAWRENCE | OF | ARABIA | HIS ORIGINAL MANUSCRIPT AUTOBIOGRAPHY | AND | CORRESPONDENCE WITH ROBERT GRAVES | IN CONNECTION WITH | THE PUBLICATION OF | "LAWRENCE AND THE ARABS" | INCLUDING | GRAVES' ORIGINAL

TYPESCRIPT | WITH COPIOUS CORRECTIONS BY COLONEL LAWRENCE HIMSELF | MAGGS BROS. LTD. | *Booksellers by Appointment to His Majesty* | 34 & 35 CONDUIT STREET, LONDON, W. | 1936

Collation 27.8 × 21.9 cm: [1]¹⁰, pp.[6], 1–11, [3].

Contents Prp.[1–2] blank, [3] title page, [4] printer's credit, [5] foreword, [6] blank, pp.[1–11] text, 1–3 blank.

RT Both verso and recto COLONEL LAWRENCE OF ARABIA.

Text 20 lines, 9.2 (10) × 11.7 cm.

Paper White, wove, unwatermarked, all edges trimmed, sheets bulk 3 mm.

Binding Tan 73 p. OY paper wrappers, stapled with two metal staples to sheets. On front cover: [same as title page].

Notes Detailed description of the 18-page mss. by Lawrence as submitted to Graves for his biography of Lawrence.

Copies AC, Cal.

E099 GEORG WASMUTH SEJERSTED, Lawrence og hans Arabere, Aschehoug, 1936

First Norwegian Edition

GEORG WASMUTH SEJERSTED | LAWRENCE | OG HANS ARABERE | ANNET OPLAG | [pub. device] | OSLO | FORLAGT AV H. ASCHEHOUG & CO. (W. NYGAARD) | 1936

Collation 20.2 × 12.7 cm: [1]⁸ 2–13⁸ 14⁶, 110 leaves, pp.1–220.

Contents Pp.[1] bastard title, [2] blank, [3] title page, [4] copyright statement, printer's credit, [5] contents, [6] blank, [7]–13 foreword, [14] blank, 15–218 text, [219] bibliography, [220] blank, fold map sewn in last sheets.

Plates Eight plates printed on both sides following pp.16, 32, 64, 80, 96, 120, 168, 200.

Typography and paper $ 1 signed 2-Lawrence.

Text 20 lines, 9 × 9.1 cm.

Paper White, wove, unwatermarked, all edges trimmed, sheets bulk 2 cm.

Binding Tan cloth 79 l, gy. y Br. On front cover: [in brown, figure on camel]. On spine: [4 rules] | [cut] | G. WASMUTH | SEJERSTED | LAWRENCE | OG HANS | ARABERE | [rule] | [cut] | [4 rules]. Brown and white striped head and tail bands.

Copies Cal, LC.

E100   B.H LIDDELL-HART, Lawrence of Arabia, Corvinus Press, 1936

First English Edition (trial setting)

LAWRENCE | *"The Artist in War and Letters"* | *By Captain B. H. Liddell Hart*

Collation   29 × 23.5 cm: [1]¹⁰, pp.[1–20], including covers.

Contents   Pp.[1] cover title, [2] blank, [3] title page, [4] blank, [5–14] text, [15] blank, [16] *'LAWRENCE* | *"Himself"* | *By Sir Ronald Storrs',* [17–20] blank.

RT   Both verso and recto LAWRENCE, "THE ARTIST IN WAR & LETTERS."

Text   20 lines, 11.8 (12.1) × 11.8 cm. Set in 12pt Centaur.

Paper   White, laid, watermarked, untrimmed, sheets bulk 2 mm.

Binding   Stapled with three metal staples along left edges.

Published at   March 1936.

Notes   This is believed to be the first publication of the Corvinus Press cited in a checklist in the Bodleian Library. The presence of the title page for the Ronald Storrs piece that appears with it in the May 1936 publication seems to indicate that this item is perhaps only a trial impression later abandoned in favour of larger type (18pt Centaur). Ten copies were printed. This appears, in fact, to be a trial setting with type re-set for the May publication.

Copies   Cal.

E101   BASIL HENRY LIDDELL HART and RONALD STORRS, Lawrence of Arabia, Corvinus Press, 1936

Edition: First English Edition

LAWRENCE | OF ARABIA | [swash] By | [swash] Capt. Liddell Hart and Sir Ronald Storrs

Collation   29 × 23 cm: [1]⁴ [2–3]² [4–7]⁴, 24 leaves, unpaged.

Contents   Leaf [1–2] blank, [3] recto title page, verso blank, [4] recto section title, verso blank, [5] recto printer's note, verso blank, [6] recto section title, verso blank, [7–12] text of Lawrence 'The Artist in War and Letters' by Liddell Hart, [13] blank, [14] recto section title, verso blank, [15–19, recto of 20] text of Lawrence 'Himself' by Storrs, [20 verso] blank, [21] recto, 'THIS VOLUME has been set in 18pt Centaur Type | with Arrighi Italic and printed in a hand press. The | edition comprises 128 numbered copies, all signed by | the Authors and distributed as follows: 24 specially | marked copies, printed for the authors on Barcham | Green 'Boswell' hand made paper, numbered 1 to | 24: 25 copies on Barcham Green 'Boswell' paper, | numbered 25 to 49: 6 copies on Winchmore Blue | paper, numbered 50 to

55: and 70 copies on Barcham | Green "Medway' hand made paper numbered 56 to 125. Also 3 copies on various papers lettered A to C, | printed for the exclusive use of the printer. The | edition was bound by Sangorski & Sutcliffe. | This copy is number .... | Completed at the CORVINUS PRESS the Twenty- | second day of May 1936. Laus Deo'.

Text 20 lines, 15.5 × 12 cm. Set in 18 pt Centaur type.

Paper Winchmore Blue Paper, laid, watermarked, top edge trimmed, sheets bulk 3 mm.

Binding Blue paper-covered boards 199 l.pB, blue cloth spine and corners 175 v.dB. On spine: [running up] LAWRENCE OF ARABIA. On both covers: [gilt rule along inner edges of covers. T.e. gilt.

Published at 22 May 1936.

Notes Another copy: one of 70 copies on Medway paper same as above with following differences: [Paper]: Barcham Green 'Medway' Paper, sheets bulk 5 mm; [Binding]: Mottled boards, tan cloth spine and corners. On front cover: [gilt design lower left corner]. On spine: [gilt, running up] LAWRENCE OF ARABIA. Boxed as issued.

Another copy: one of 24 specially marked copies, printed for the authors on Barcham Green 'Medway' hand-made paper. Same as above except that verso of last sheet of text reads: "This copy is one of 12 printed for Capt. B.H. Liddell Hart".

Copies AC, Cal, H, UT.

E102 MIGUEL MARSICOVÉTERE Y DURÁN, Lawrence de Arabia, Minima, 1936

First Guatemalan Edition

BIBLÍOTECA MINIMA | [long rule] m. marsicovétere y durán | LAWRENCE DE ARABIA | editorial mínima | guatemala, c.a. | 1936

Collation 11.1 × 10 cm: 22 leaves, pp.[1–4], 5–45, [1–3].

Contents Pp. [1] front cover, [2] blank, [3] title page, [4] blank, 5–45 text, [1] blank, [2–3] back cover.

Text 20 lines, 7.1 × 7.2 cm.

Paper White, wove, unwatermarked, untrimmed, sheets bulk 3 mm.

Binding White paper. On front cover: [in brown] BIBLIOTECA MINIMA | [long rule] | LAWRENCE DE ARABIA | [in brown] editorial mínima | guatemala, c.a. | 1936. On back cover: [publisher's list].

Notes Essay on Lawrence, pp.5–16, dated 1934.

Copies UT.

E104   MICHAEL ASSAF, Laurens b'chayyim ub'agada, Davar, 1935/1936

First Hebrew Edition

MICHAEL ASSAF | LAURENS B'CHAYYIM UB'AGADA | HOTSAAT "DAVAR", TEL-AVIV, RESH TSADI VAV

Collation   19.8 × 14 cm: [1–7]¹⁶, 112 leaves, pp.[1–2], 3–224.

Contents   Pp.[1] title page, [2] copyright statement, typesetter's, binder's credits, [3]–223 text, 224 contents.

Plates   Three b/w plates, frontispiece before pp.[1], two following p.224.

Text   20 lines, 10.3 × 10.8 cm.

Paper   White, wove, unwatermarked, all edges trimmed, sheets bulk 1.3 cm.

Binding   Grey cloth. On front cover: MICHAEL ASSAF | LAURENS B'CHAYYIM UB'AGADA. On spine: ASSAF | LAURENS | "DAVAR". T.e. blue. Grey head and tail bands.

Copies   LC.

E105   GOLDEN COCKEREL PRESS, Some News from the Golden Cockerel Press, 1936

Prospectus including Crusader Castles

SOME NEWS | FROM | [remainder underlined] *THE* | *GOLDEN* | *COCKEREL* | *PRESS*

Collation   16 × 9.5 cm: double-fold leaflet, printed on one side, 4 leaves, pp.[1–8].

Contents   Pp.[1] notice of *Crusader Castles*, [2–3] blank, [4–5] notice of other titles, [6–7] blank, [8] further text on additional titles.

Paper   White, wove, unwatermarked, all edges trimmed.

Published at   Free advertising flyer.

Copies   UT.

Recognition: Biography II, 1937–1939

The year 1937 saw a continuing number of publications stimulated by Lawrence's death. Reginald Sims compiled from memory *The Doings of T.E.*, which are short anecdotes related by Lawrence to Sims and his wife during his many visits to Sims' home.

T.E. Lawrence by His Friends contains contributions by many of the important, and some less well known, people in Lawrence's life. It provides a portrait of the man from many angles from youth to maturity.

Two books of poetry appeared in 1937 with relation to Lawrence. One is a book of verse by a close friend from pre-war days, E.H.R. Altounyan. The book is dedicated to the memory of Lawrence. The second verse volume is a retelling of the Lawrence campaign in verse by Seldon Rodman.

S.C. Rolls' *Steel Chariots in the Desert,* was written by a driver for a section of armoured cars which in the later stages of the desert campaign joined Lawrence.

A pamphlet issued at the time of the unveiling of the memorial to Lawrence by his former High School in Oxford is the printed text of the speech given by Sir Winston Churchill on the occasion. The memorial itself is a statue by Lady Kennet.

The sole publication about Lawrence to appear in 1938 is Duval's, the first full-scale attempt at a descriptive bibliography. It overlooked some items and was issued just a few months too soon to include others such as the collected letters (a risk inherent in all bibliographies).

In 1939 Vyvyan Richards produced a second work on Lawrence. A briefer account than his first book, it is often confused with the earlier Cape volume. This much abbreviated account has often been reprinted, most recently by Icon books and by Scholastic Books in America. In these editions it was published under the title of the 1936 Cape work, adding greatly to confusion in libraries and bibliographies.

Following Lawrence's campaign trail 30 years later, Glen, *In the Steps of Lawrence of Arabia,* retraced Lawrence's movements and met a number of individuals among the Arabs involved in the events of the campaigns. Some of these provided memories.

Two souvenir items appeared in 1939. Heffer and Sons issued a prospectus offering the Thomas Wright bas-relief plaques of T.E. Lawrence and Rupert Brooke. A pamphlet published by the National Trust as a souvenir information piece describes Lawrence's cottage, Clouds Hill. (The cottage had been given by A.W. Lawrence to the National Trust in 1938.) The pamphlet has been issued in new covers from time to time.

1937

E106 REGINALD G. SIMS, The Doings of T.E., privately printed, 1937

First English Edition

[No title page, hand-written on front cover] The Doings of T.E.

Collation 24.1 × 19 cm: 46 leaves, printed on one side only, carbon or mimeo.

Contents Leaves [1–2] Explanation Apology, [3–6] The Dirty Lorry, [7–8] Woods bust of TEL, [9–11] The Stranded Battleship, [12–13] The Visit, [14–16] The Fire Report, [17–18] The Salute, [19–22] The Fracture, [23] Telephone Wire, [24] Unique Items, [25–28] Two Minutes Silence, [29–30] La Position, [31–34] Speed, [35–36] BOOM, [37–38] Literary Recognition, [39] Purple and Fine Linen, [40] Finance, [41–42] Train Wrecking, [43–44] Fish & Chips, [45] HA HA, [46] Et Puis Bon-Soir, (loose) The Business Instinct.

Text Typed, double-spaced, many mss. corrections.

Paper White, wove, unwatermarked, all edges trimmed, sheets bulk 3 mm.

Binding Buff stiff board, tied to sheets by linen cord through three holes in tab at back.

Published at January 1937.

Notes This copy sent to Mrs. Lawrence by Sims, 3 March 1937. Another copy, same as above, with following differences: 5. The Visit, 18. Fish and Chips, 19.Ha-Ha, 20. The Business Instinct, 21. Train Wrecking, 22. Odd Phrases, 23. Et Puis Bon Soir, 24. Illusions, 25. [untitled], 26. Audition Aidiet. [The last three added in 1966].

Copies Cal.

E107   ARNOLD WALTER LAWRENCE, compiler, T.E. Lawrence by His Friends, Cape, 1937

First English Edition

T.E. LAWRENCE | BY HIS FRIENDS | EDITED BY | A.W. LAWRENCE | [publisher's device] | JONATHAN CAPE | THIRTY BEDFORD SQUARE | LONDON

Collation 22 × 14.5 cm: [A]^8 B–NN^8 OO^{10}, 298 leaves, pp.[1–4], 5–596.

Contents Pp.[1] bastard title, [2] blank, [3] title page, [4] issue statement, printer's, papermaker's, binder's credits, 5–6 preface, 7–10 contents, 11 illustrations, [12] blank, 13 chronology of T.E. Lawrence, [14] blank, [15] section title, [16] blank, 17–595 text, 596 blank.

RT On verso [according to section]. On recto [name of author of piece].

Plates Eight plates on paper heavier than sheets, printed on one side only, following pp.2, 48, 154, 190, 234, 266, 376, 572.

Typography and paper $ 1 signed NN, OO, OO*.

Text 20 lines, 9.2 (9.3) × 10.6 cm.

Paper White, wove, unwatermarked, top edges trimmed, sheets bulk 3 cm.

Binding Wine red 41 deep r Br Buckram. On spine: [gilt] T.E. LAWRENCE | BY | HIS | FRIENDS | [pub. device] |. T.e. red.

Published at 15s.

Notes List of impressions: 2nd, June 1937; 3rd, September 1937; 4th, January 1938 – all as above; 5th, 1939, as above with following differences: [Binding]: dark brown buckram 56 deep Br. T.e. brown. Another copy of 1st impression, 14 v. deep Red binding.

Copies AC, Cal, UT, Ho, LC.

E108 ARNOLD WALTER LAWRENCE, T.E. Lawrence by His Friends, Cape, 1954

Second English Edition

T.E. LAWRENCE | BY HIS FRIENDS | EDITED BY | A.W. LAWRENCE | [pub. device] | JONATHAN CAPE | THIRTY BEDFORD SQUARE | LONDON

Collation 22.2 × 14.5 cm: [A]^8 B–U^8, 160 leaves, pp.[1–6], 7–319, [1].

Contents Pp.[1–2] blank, [3] bastard title, [4] blank, [5] title page, [6] issue statement, printer's, binder's credits, 7 preface, [8] blank, 9–11 contents, [12] blank, 13 chronology of T.E.Lawrence, [14] blank, [15] half-title, [16] blank, [17] section title, 18–23 introduction, [24] section title, 25–319 text, [1] blank.

RT On verso [according to section]. On recto [according to author of piece].

Typography and paper $ 1 signed B.

Text 20 lines, 9.2 (9.2) × 10.5 cm.

Paper White, wove, unwatermarked, top and fore-edge trimmed, sheets bulk 1.8 cm.

Binding Maroon buckram 241 m. r P. On spine: [gilt] T.E. LAWRENCE | BY | HIS FRIENDS | [pub. device]. T.e. maroon.

Published at 16s.

Notes Another issue, identical to above, with following differences: title lettering is within blind stamped rectangle on spine of binding. This is an abridgment of the first English edition.

Copies AC, Cal, UT, LC.

E109 ARNOLD WALTER LAWRENCE, ed., T.E. Lawrence by His Friends, Doubleday, Doran, 1937

First American Edition

T.E. Lawrence | BY HIS FRIENDS | EDITED BY A.W. LAWRENCE | [pub. device] | Doubleday, Doran & Company, Inc. | GARDEN CITY 1937 NEW YORK

Collation 22.8 × 15.3 cm.: [1–15]^{16}, [16]^{20} [17]^{16}, 276 leaves, pp.[i–iv], v–xiv, [1–2], 3–538.

Contents Prp.[i] bastard title, [ii] blank, [iii] title page, [iv] printer's credit, copyright and issue statements, v–vi preface, vii–x contents, xi–xii chronology of T.E. Lawrence's life, xiii illustrations, [xiv] blank, [1] section title, [2] blank, 3–538 text.

RT On verso [according to section]. On recto [name of author of section].

Text 20 lines, 8.5 (8.7) × 10.5 cm.

Paper White, wove, unwatermarked, top and bottom edges trimmed, sheets bulk 3.4 cm.

Binding Brown buckram 55 s.Br. On front cover: [gilt, script lettering over blind stamped leaf cut] TEL. On spine: [within brown rectangle with single rules border, gilt] T.E. | LAWRENCE | *BY HIS* | *FRIENDS* | [below rectangle] [large gilt design] | DOUBLEDAY DORAN. T.e. brown. Buff end papers.

Published at $4.00.

Notes First impression is denoted by statement FIRST EDITION as last line on verso of title page. This statement is lacking in later impressions.

Copies AC, Cal.

E110 ARNOLD WALTER LAWRENCE, ed., T.E. Lawrence by His Friends, McGraw-Hill, 1963

Second American Edition

[Pub. device] | T.E. Lawrence by His Friends | A new selection of memoirs | edited by A.W. Lawrence | McGraw-Hill Book Company, Inc. | New York Toronto London

Collation 20.2 × 13.4 cm: guillotined sheets, 200 leaves, pp.[1–8], 9–397, [3].

Contents Pp.[1] bastard title, two quotes from reviews, [2] list of titles in series, [3] frontispiece John painting of TEL, [4] blank, [5] title page, [6] issue statement, [7] preface to new edition, [8] blank, 9–11 contents, 12 chronology of TEL, 13 section title, 14–19 introduction, 20 section title, 21–397 text, [1–3] blank.

RT On verso [according to section]. On recto [name of author of piece within section].

Text 20 lines, 8.8 (8.9) × 10.3 cm.

Paper White, wove, unwatermarked, all edges trimmed, sheets bulk 2.8 cm.

Binding Pictorial paper covers. On front cover: McGRAW-HILL PAPERBACKS | T.E. Lawrence | by His Friends | [pub. device] | edited by A.W. Lawrence | A new selection of memoirs by: | George Bernard Shaw Chaim Weizmann | Winston Churchill E.M. Forster | W.H. Auden Ernest M. Dawson | Lord Halifax David Garnett | Sheikh Hamoudi L.B. Namier | Robert Graves Lowell Thomas | and others | [within circle] $2.65. On spine: McGRAW-HILL | [within black square publisher's device] | PAPERBACKS | [running down] T.E. Lawrence A.W. Lawrence, editor | by His Friends Man, not myth...Biographical Impressions $2.65. On back cover: [blurb including quote by Churchill] | McGraw-Hill Paperbacks [in blue, publisher's device] 36721.

Published at $2.65.

Notes Thirty articles in first edition omitted from this edition. Auden piece was new for this edition.

Copies AC, Cal.

E111 ARNOLD WALTER LAWRENCE ed., T.E. Lawrence by His Friends, Gordian Press, 1980

Third American Edition

T.E. Lawrence | BY HIS FRIENDS | EDITED BY A.W. LAWRENCE | [publisher's device] | GORDIAN PRESS | NEW YORK | 1980

Collation 22.9 × 15 cm: [1–2]¹⁶ [3]⁴ [4]⁸ [5–20]¹⁶, 284 leaves, pp.[i–ii], [1–2], [iii–iv], [1–2], 3–34, [1–2], 35–130, [1–2], 131–162, [1–2], 163–202, [1–2], 203–234, [1–2], 235–332, [1–2], 333–514, [1–2], 515–538.

Contents Prp.[i] bastard title, [ii] blank, [1] blank, [2] frontispiece, [iii] title page, [iv] issue, copyright statements, CIP, v–[vi] preface by A.W. Lawrence, vii–x contents, xi–xii chronology, xiii illustrations, [xiv] blank, [1] section title, [2] blank, 3–538 text including unpaged leaves for illustrations as shown in collation.

RT On verso [according to section]. On recto [name of author of piece within section].

Text 20 lines, 8.5 (8.7) × 10.5 cm.

Paper White, wove, unwatermarked, all edges trimmed, sheets bulk 3 cm.

Binding Brown cloth 57 l. Br. On spine: [gilt] [double rule] | T.E. | LAWRENCE | BY HIS | FRIENDS | [pub. device] | GORDIAN | [double rule]. Red and gold head and tail bands.

Copies PPL, LC.

E112 ARNOLD WALTER LAWRENCE, ed., Oberst Lawrence, List, 1938

First German Edition

OBERST LAWRENCE | geschildert von seinen Freunden | Herausgegeben von | A.W. LAWRENCE | [pub. device] | PAUL LIST VERLAG LEIPZIG

Collation 21.2 × 13.2 cm: π⁸ 1–21⁸, 176 leaves, pp.[I–VI], VII–XVI, 1–331, [4].

Contents Prp.[I–II] blank, [III] bastard title, [IV] blank, [V] title page, [VI]translator's, designer's, printer's credits, original title, issue, copyright statements, VII–XVI introduction by Lord Halifax, pp.1–330 text, 331–332 biographical outline of Lawrence's life, [1–4] publisher's ad.

Plates Four photos on coated paper, printed on one side only, following pp.IV, 72, 168, 248.

Typography and paper $ 1 signed 1 Lawrence, Freunde, 1*.

Text 20 lines, 7.7 × 9.5 cm.

Paper White, wove, unwatermarked, all edges trimmed, sheets bulk 2.8 cm.

Binding Black cloth, [within recessed rectangle, gilt] T.E.L. On spine: [gilt] [all swash] OBERST | LAWRENCE | geschildert | von | seinen | Freunden | [pub. device]. T.e. light brown, white head and tail bands.

Copies AC, Cal, LC.

E113   E.H.R. ALTOUNYAN, Ornament of Honour, Cambridge, 1937

First English Edition

[Within single rules] ORNAMENT | OF | HONOUR | [decorative cut] | 1937 | CAMBRIDGE | AT THE UNIVERSITY PRESS

Collation   20 × 14.5 cm: π^4 $1-7^8$ 8^{10}, 70 leaves, pp.[1–8], [1–2], 3–131, [1].

Contents   Prp.[1–2] blank, [3] bastard title, [4] pub. statement, [5] title page, [6] acknowledgments, [7] dedication T.E. LAWRENCE, [8] blank, pp.[1] section title, [2] blank, 3–131 text, [1] printer's credit.

Typography and paper $ 1,2 signed AO 2, 2-2.

Text   20 lines, 10.1 × 8.2 cm.

Paper   Laid, watermarked, top and fore-edges trimmed, sheets bulk 1.4 cm.

Binding   Rust paper-covered boards 76 l.y Br. red cloth spine 40 s. r Br. On spine: [within paper patch, all in red] [rule] | Ornament | [rule] | of Honour | [rule] | ALTOUNYAN | * | Cambridge.

Published at   7s 6d.

Notes   A replacement spine label pasted inside back cover.

Copies   AC, Cal, UT.

E114   SAM COTTINGHAM ROLLS, Steel Chariots in the Desert, Cape, 1937

First English Edition

STEEL CHARIOTS | IN THE DESERT | *The Story of an Armoured-Car* | *Driver with the Duke of Westminster* | *in Lybia and in Arabia with* | T.E. LAWRENCE | BY | S.C. ROLLS | [pub. device] | JONATHAN CAPE | THIRTY BEDFORD SQUARE | LONDON

Collation   20 × 13.5 cm: [A]^8 B–S^8, 144 leaves, pp.[1–6], 7–[288].

Contents   Pp.[1–2] blank, [3] bastard title, [4] long quote from *Seven Pillars of Wisdom* [5] title page, [6] issue statement, publisher's, papermaker's, binder's credits, 7–8 contents, 9 list of illustrations, [10] blank, 11–12 excerpt from text, 13 preface, [14] blank, [15] half title, [16] blank, 17–286 text, [287–288] blank.

RT   On verso STEEL CHARIOTS IN THE DESERT. On recto [according to chapter].

Plates   Six b/w plates on coated paper, printed on one side only, following pp.31, 58, 98, 188, 212.

Typography and paper $ 1 signed B.

Text   20 lines, 9.1 (9.3) × 10.3 cm.

Paper   White, wove, unwatermarked, all edges trimmed, sheets bulk 2.2 cm.

Binding   Brown cloth 39 gy r O. On spine: [gilt] STEEL | CHARIOTS | IN THE | DESERT | [cut] | S.C. ROLLS | [publisher's device]. T.e. light brown.

Published at   10s 6d.

Notes   Later included in the Odyssey Library series by publisher, no. 28; given a pink dustwrapper for the series.

Copies   AC, Cal, H, Ho, LC.

E115   SELDEN RODMAN, Lawrence, the Last Crusade, Viking, 1937

Uncorrected Proof of First American Edition

BANK 48 SLIDE 2 | *Lawrence* | THE LAST CRUSADE | A DRAMATIC NARRATIVE POEM | BY SELDEN RODMAN | NEW YORK · THE VIKING PRESS: MCMXXXVII

Collation   22.7 × 15 cm: guillotined sheets glued to plain board covers, 133 leaves [1–7] 11–129 [4].

Contents   Leaf [1] bastard title, [2] title page, [3] rules, pub. device to be used in title page layout, [4] issue, copyright statements, [5] dedication, [6] quote from Macleish, [7] section title, 11–129 text, [1–4] notes.

RT   On even pages LAWRENCE: THE LAST CRUSADE. On odd pages [according to book].

Text   20 lines, 10.7 (10.7) × 9.1 cm.

Paper   Newsprint, unwatermarked, all edges trimmed, sheets bulk 1 cm.

Binding   Plain brown paste board sheets glued to text sheets.

Copies   Cal, UT.

E116   SELDEN RODMAN, Lawrence, the Last Crusade, Viking, 1937

First American Edition

[Within frame of yellow rules which cross at corners] *Lawrence* | [yellow rule] | THE LAST CRUSADE | A DRAMATIC NARRATIVE POEM | BY SELDEN RODMAN | [pub. device in yellow] NEW YORK · THE VIKING PRESS: MCMXXXVII

Collation   23.5 × 15.5 cm: [1–9]^8, 72 leaves, pp.[1–2], [1–10], 11–129, [13].

Contents   Prp.[1–2] blank, pp.[1] bastard title, [2] blank, [3] title page, [4] issue, copyright statements, printer's, distributor's credits, [5] dedication, [6] blank, [7] quote, [8] blank, [9] section heading, [10] quote, 11–129 text, [1] blank, [2] section title, [3] blank, [4–6] notes, [7] blank, [8] map, [9–13] blank.

RT   On verso LAWRENCE: THE LAST CRUSADE. On recto [according to section].

Text   20 lines, 10.6 (10.7) × 9 cm.

Paper White, wove, unwatermarked, all edges trimmed, sheets bulk 1.5 cm.

Binding Grey cloth 264 l. Gray. On front cover: [gilt cut]. On spine: [gilt, running down] RODMAN [cut] LAWRENCE, THE [cut] VIKING | LAST CRUSADE. T.e. yellow.

Published at $2.50.

Copies AC, Cal, H, Ho.

E117 OXFORD HIGH SCHOOL FOR BOYS, Proceedings at the Unveiling of the Memorial to Lawrence of Arabia, Thornton, 1937

First English Edition

CITY OF OXFORD | HIGH SCHOOL FOR BOYS | PROCEEDINGS AT THE | UNVEILING OF THE | MEMORIAL TO | LAWRENCE OF ARABIA | 3 OCTOBER 1936 | [school seal] | OXFORD | J. THORNTON & SON | 1937

Collation 22.7 × 17.8 cm: [1]^{12}, 12 leaves, pp.[1–2], 3–23, [1].

Contents Pp.[1] title page, [2] foreword (seven lines), 3–23 text, [1] printer's colophon.

Plates One, wrapped around gathering, frontispiece on coated paper, precedes first leaf.

Text 20 lines, 14.1 × 11.5 cm.

Paper White, laid, watermarked, top edge trimmed, sheets bulk 3 mm.

Binding Tan heavy paper covers sewn to sheets by cord stabbed through gutter, 76 l. y Br. On front cover: [same as title page, in blue].

Notes The first issue has a foreword of 7 lines and printer's colophon states the printing was by John Johnson. Another issue, same as above, with following differences: no imprint on title page; [Contents]: same as above but foreword has 12 lines; printer's colophon notes that printer was Charles Batey; [Paper]: white, wove, unwatermarked, top and fore-edges trimmed; [Binding]: greyish paper covers (much lighter than above) also with no imprint below school seal.

Copies AC, Cal, H, UT.

E118 OXFORD HIGH SCHOOL FOR BOYS, Proceedings at the Unveiling of the Memorial to Lawrence of Arabia, Thornton, 1936

Publisher's Prospectus

No title page.

Collation 10.6 × 15.4 cm: post card printed on both sides.

Contents [On verso] announcement and address of publisher; [on recto] Post Card [short rule].

Paper Thick, white, wove, unwatermarked, all edges trimmed.

Copies AC.

1938

E119 ELIZABETH W. DUVAL, T.E. Lawrence, a Bibliography, Arrow, 1938

First American Edition

T.E. LAWRENCE | A BIBLIOGRAPHY | BY ELIZABETH W. DUVAL | ARROW EDITIONS · NEW YORK

Collation 25.5 × 16.5 cm: [1–3]⁸ [4]¹⁰ [5–6]⁸, 50 leaves, pp.[1–2], [1–4], 5–95, [3].

Contents Prp.[1] half-title, [2] blank, pp.[1] title page, [2] copyright notice, [3] contents, [4] blank, 5–6 foreword, [7] section title, [8] blank, [9] section title, 10–93 text, 94–95 index, [96] colophon, [97–98] blank.

Text 10 lines, 4.9 × 11 cm.

Paper White, laid, watermarked (Freefolk), bottom edges trimmed, sheets bulk 8 mm.

Binding Green 156 d. g G paper-covered boards, tan rough weave cloth spine. Paper label on spine: [within single rule frame, running down] T.E. LAWRENCE · A BIBLIOGRAPHY · DUVAL. Boxed in grey slip case and glassine dust wrapper as issued.

Published at $7.50.

Notes Limited to 500 copies, unnumbered.

Copies AC, Cal, BL, H, UT, Ho, LC.

E120 ELIZABETH W. DUVAL, T.E. Lawrence, a Bibliography, Arrow 1938

Prospectus for First American Edition, issued by Argus Bookstore

No title page.

Collation 24.3 × 18.3 cm: single sheet; printed on one side only, mimeo.

Contents Order form at bottom.

Paper White, wove, unwatermarked, all edges trimmed.

Copies Cal.

E121   ELIZABETH W. DUVAL, T.E. Lawrence, a Bibliography, Haskell House, 1972

Reprint of First American Edition

T.E. LAWRENCE | A BIBLIOGRAPHY | BY ELIZABETH W. DUVAL | [publisher's device] | HASKELL HOUSE PUBLISHERS LTD | *Publishers of Scarce Scholarly Books* | NEW YORK N.Y. 10012 | 1972

Collation   21.5 × 14 cm: [1–3]^{16}, 48 leaves, pp.[1–4], 5–95, [1].

Contents   Pp.[1] title page, [2] issue statement, LC and SBN numbers, [3] contents, [4] blank, 5–6 foreword, [7] section title, [8] blank, [9] section title, 10–93 text, 94–95 index, [1] colophon.

Text   10 lines, 5.2 × 10.3 cm.

Paper   White, wove, unwatermarked, all edges trimmed, sheets bulk 9 mm.

Binding   Brown cloth 94 l.ol Br. On front cover: T.E. LAWRENCE | A BIBLIOGRAPHY | BY ELIZABETH W. DUVAL | [pub. device] | HASKELL | HOUSE. Red and yellow head and tail bands.

Published at   January 1972.

Copies   AC, LC.

E122   MEULENIJZER, VICTOR, Le Colonel Lawrence, Rex, 1938

First Belgian Edition

VICTOR MEULENIJZER | Le Colonel | Lawrence | agent de l'Intelligence Service | EDITIONS REX | 33, RUE DES CHARTREUX | BRUXELLES

Collation   17.5 × 11.3 cm: I–XIV^8 XV^7 [–1], 119 leaves, pp.[1–7], 8–235, [1–3].

Contents   Pp.[1] signature, [2] blank, [3] bastard title, [4] blank, [5] title page, [6] blank, [7] –235 text, [1] blank, [2–3] contents.

RT   On both verso and recto *Le Colonel Lawrence*.

Typography and paper $ 1 signed LE COLONEL LAWRENCE I.

Text   20 lines, 7.1 (7.6) × 8.3 cm.

Paper   White, wove, unwatermarked, all edges trimmed, sheets bulk 1 cm.

Binding   White paper covers. On front cover: VICTOR MEULENYSER [*sic*] | [yellow rectangle] | LE COLONEL | LAWRENCE | [script type] Agent de l'Intelligence Service | [yellow rectangle containing drawing] | COLLECTION NATIONALE. On back cover: [publisher's ads, blurb].

Copies   LC.

E123 FREDERICK SANDERS, Lawrence of Arabia an Analysis of a Man of Destiny, privately printed, 1938

First English Edition

LAWRENCE OF ARABIA | AN ANALYSIS OF A MAN OF DESTINY | BY | FREDERICK SANDERS. | (PRIVATE EDITION) | 1938

Collation   25 × 19 cm: 104 leaves, i–xi, 1–95 sheets typed on one side only.

Contents   Prp.i bastard title, ii title page, iii contents, iv 9-line poem quote, v–vii acknowledgements, viii–ix introduction, x half title, xi 7-line poem quote, pp.1–93 text, 94 7-line poem quote, 95 THE | END.| ...

Typography and paper   Typed sheets duplicated.

Paper   White, wove, unwatermarked, all edges trimmed, sheets bulk 1 cm.

Binding   Maroon 44 dr r Br. On front cover: [gilt] LAWRENCE | OF | ARABIA | (PRIVATE EDITION). On spine: LAWRENCE OF ARABIA By F. Sanders. All edges red speckled.

Notes   Six copies. A copy was sent to each of the following: Admiral Evans, Churchill, A.W. Lawrence, British Museum Library, F.W.T. Sanders, G.B. Shaw.

Copies   Cal, BPL.

1939

E124 VYVYAN RICHARDS, T.E. Lawrence, Duckworth, 1939

First English Edition

[Within frame of Oxford rules] T.E. LAWRENCE | *By* VYVYAN RICHARDS | Great Lives | DUCKWORTH | 3 HENRIETTA STREET | LONDON W.C. 2

Collation   18.5 × 11 cm: [A]⁸ B–I⁸, 72 leaves, pp.[1–4], 5–144.

Contents   Pp.[1] bastard title, [2] blank, [3] title page, [4] issue statement, printer's credit, 5–6 contents, 7–10 chronology of T.E. Lawrence, 11–143 text, 144 bibliography.

RT   On verso T.E. LAWRENCE. On recto [according to chapter].

Typography and paper $ 1 signed B.

Text   20 lines, 9.1 (9.3) × 8 cm.

Paper   Buff, laid, unwatermarked, all edges trimmed, sheets bulk 1 cm.

Binding   Red cloth 40 s. r Br. On spine: [gilt] T.E. | LAWRENCE | VYVYAN | RICHARDS | DUCKWORTH.

Published at   2s.

Notes 2nd impression, 1940, as above. Another impression, 1949, same as above with following differences: [Contents]: pp.[2] woodcut portrait of T.E. Lawrence; [Paper]: wove; [Binding]: Red cloth 12 s. Red. On spine: [gilt] T.E. | LAWRENCE | RICHARDS | DUCKWORTH. Another impression, 1954, same as 1949 above, with following differences: [Binding]: Red cloth simulated paper covered boards; [Published]: 5/- net. Great Lives Series no. 84.

Copies AC, Cal, UT, LC.

E125   VYVYAN RICHARDS, T.E. Lawrence, Icon, [1963]

Second English Edition

VYVYAN RICHARDS | T.E. LAWRENCE | ICON BOOKS LIMITED

Collation 18.2 × 10.7 cm: [A]^{16} B^{16} [C–D]^{16}, 64 leaves, pp.[1–8], 9–128.

Contents Pp.[1] bastard title, publisher's device, [2] issue statement, designer's credit, copyright statement, printer's credit, [3] title page, [4–5] chronology of Lawrence's life, [6] blank, [7] contents, [8] blank, 9–126 text, 127–128 bibliography.

Typography and paper $ 1 signed B.

Text 20 lines, 9 × 8.8 cm.

Paper White, wove, unwatermarked, all edges trimmed, sheets bulk 8 mm.

Binding Pictorial paper covers. On front cover: [within white rectangle across top] an Icon book | T.E. LAWRENCE [pub. device] | Vyvyan Richards. On spine: [across] [rule] | [running down] an Icon book B6 | [across, rule] | [running down] T.E. LAWRENCE Vyvyan Richards [pub. device] | [across at bottom, within circle 3/6]. On back cover: [rule] an Icon book | [pub. device] | T.E. LAWRENCE | [rule] | [blurb and quote from *TLS*].

Published at 3s 6d.

Copies AC, Cal.

E126   VYVYAN RICHARDS, Portrait of T.E. Lawrence, Scholastic Books, 1964

First American Edition

Portrait of | T.E. Lawrence | By VYVYAN RICHARDS | Cover Design by Dom Lupo | SCHOLASTIC [publisher's device] BOOK SERVICES | Published by Scholastic Book Services, a division | of Scholastic Magazines, Inc., New York, N.Y.

Collation 16.3 × 10.4 cm: guillotined sheets glued to covers, 80 leaves, pp.[I–II], III–VIII, [2], 1–148, [2].

Contents Prp.[I] title page, [II] price, issue statement, III–V chronology of

Lawrence's life, [VI] blank, VII–VIII contents, pp.[1] blank, [2] map, 1–145 text, [146] blank, 147–148 bibliography, [1–2] blank.

RT On verso *A Portrait of T.E. Lawrence.* On recto [in italics, according to chapter].

Text 20 lines, 7.9 (8.6) × 8 cm.

Paper White, wove, unwatermarked, all edges trimmed, sheets bulk 8 mm.

Binding Pictorial paper covers. On front cover: [in yellow] Portrait of | [in white] T.E. Lawrence | [in pale blue] By VYVYAN RICHARDS | [next two lines pale blue] 35c | T543. On spine: [running down] [publisher's device in blue] [in blue] T543 [next two words yellow] Portrait of T.E. LAWRENCE. Richards. On back cover: [five-line blurb in white] | [two-line quote in yellow] | [in white] SCHOLASTIC BOOK SERVICES, NEW YORK | [publisher's device, in yellow]. All edges yellow.

Published at 35 cents.

Notes Some first printing copies have correction label pasted over issue statement on p.II, otherwise identical; 2nd printing, April 1967, same as above except that issue statement has been corrected; 3rd printing, September 1971, new cover: *Portrait of* | T.E. LAWRENCE | *by Vyvyan Richards* | SBS SCHOLASTIC BOOK SERVICES | New York Toronto London Auckland Sydney; [Collation]: 16.2 × 10.7 cm: guillotined sheets glued to covers, 80 leaves, pp. [i–ii] iii–viii [ix–x] 1–148 [2]: [Contents]: prp.[1] title page, [ii] copyright, issue statements, iii–v chronology of Lawrence's life, [vi] blank, vii–viii contents, [ix] blank, [x] map, pp.1–45 text, [146] blank, 147–148 bibliography, [1–2] blank; [RT]: On verso *A Portrait of T.E. Lawrence.* On recto [according to chapter]; [Text]:20 lines, 7.6 (8.2) × 8 cm; [Paper]: white, wove, unwatermarked, all edges trimmed, sheets bulk 7 mm; [Binding]: white paper covers. On front cover: [rectangle still from film, within which, in orange] *Portrait of* | [lighter orange] T.E. LAWRENCE | [in white] UNCROWNED KING OF THE ARABS | [in orange] *by Vyvyan Richards* | [in white] T543 60c. On spine: [running down] T543 *Portrait of* T.E. LAWRENCE *Richards.* On back cover: [within single rule rectangle] six-line quote from Sheikh Hamoudi, five-line blurb, photo of O'Toole as Lawrence, cover photo credit; [Published at]: 60c.

Copies AC, Cal.

E127 VYVYAN RICHARDS, Portrait of T.E. Lawrence, Haskell House, 1976

First American Edition (reprint of 1964 Scholastic Books edition)

Portrait of | T.E. Lawrence | By VYVYAN RICHARDS | Cover Design by Dom Lupo | [pub. device] | HASKELL HOUSE PUBLISHERS Ltd. | *Publishers of Scarce Scholarly Books* | Brooklyn, NY | 1976

Collation 20.3 × 13.2 cm:guillotined sheets glued to covers, 80 leaves, pp.[i–ii], iii–viii, [ix–x], 1–148, [2].

Contents   Prp.[i] title page, [ii] CIP, iii–v chronology, [vi] blank, vii–viii contents, [ix] blank, [x] map, pp.1–145 text, [146] blank, 147–148 bibliography, [2] blank.

Text   20 lines, 7.7 (8.3) × 8 cm.

Paper   White, wove, unwatermarked, all edges trimmed, sheets bulk 1.2 cm.

Binding   Light brown cloth 60 l. gy. Br. On spine: [running down] Portrait of | T.E. Lawrence VYVYAN RICHARDS. Black and white head and tail bands. Bright orange end papers.

Published at $10.95.

Copies   AC.

E128   DOUGLAS GLEN, In the Steps of Lawrence of Arabia, Rich & Cowan, 1939

First English Edition

IN THE STEPS OF | LAWRENCE OF ARABIA | *By* | DOUGLAS GLEN | [publisher's device] | LONDON | RICH & COWAN, LTD. | 37 BEDFORD SQUARE W.C. 1

Collation   19.6 × 13.5 cm: [A]^8 B–U^8, 160 leaves, pp.[i–iv], v–x, 11–320.

Contents   Pp.[i] bastard title, [ii] blank, [iii] title page, [iv]printer's, binder's, papermaker's credits, v–viii contents, ix–x illustrations, 11–317 text, 318–320 index.

Plates   Thirty-two b/w photos tipped in on coated paper, printed on one side, following pp.[ii], 14, 17, 32, 37, 44, 49, 64, 69, 76, 81, 96, 113, 128, 133, 140, 145, 160, 177, 192, 209, 224, 229, 236, 241, 256, 261, 268, 273, 288, 309, 316.

Typography and paper $ 1 signed B.

Text   20 lines, 8.8 × 9.4 cm.

Paper   White, wove, unwatermarked, all edges trimmed, sheets bulk 3 cm.

Binding   Golden brown cloth 54 br. O. On spine: [gilt] IN THE STEPS | OF | LAWRENCE | OF ARABIA | [cut] | DOUGLAS GLEN | Rich & Cowan.

Copies   AC, Cal, UT, LC.

E129   W. HEFFER & SONS LIMITED, Prospectus for Lawrence Portrait Plaque

Publisher's prospectus

TWO ATTRACTIVE | PORTRAIT PLAQUES | [photo of plaque] | A Plaque of | T.E. LAWRENCE

Collation   21 × 13.5 cm: single leaf printed on both sides.

Contents Pp.[1] title page, description of plaque, [2] information on Rupert Brooke plaque and order form.

Paper Buff, wove, unwatermarked, all edges trimmed.

Published at Free advertising flyer.

Copies AC.

E130 NATIONAL TRUST, Clouds Hill, National Trust, 1939

First English Edition

CLOUDS HILL | Published by | THE NATIONAL TRUST | FOR PLACES OF HISTORIC INTEREST OR NATURAL BEAUTY | 7 Buckingham Palace Gardens, S.W.I

Collation 18.3 × 12.3 cm: [1]⁸, 8 leaves, pp.[1] – 14, [1–2].

Contents Pp.[1] title page, 2–10 Liddell Hart essay, 'T.E. Lawrence of Arabia and Clouds Hill', 11–14 list of contents of Clouds Hill, [1] contribution form, [2] blank.

Plates One b/w frontispiece before p.[1].

Text 10 lines, 3.5 × 9 cm.

Paper White, wove, unwatermarked, all edges trimmed, sheets bulk 2 mm.

Binding Green paper wrappers 163 l. b Green. On front cover: CLOUDS HILL | [pub. device] | *Price Threepence* | 1939. On back cover: Geo Barber & Son Ltd. London, E.C. 4.

Published at 3d.

Notes Lawrence's cottage 'Clouds Hill' was given to the National Trust by A.W. Lawrence in 1938.

Copies UT.

E131 NATIONAL TRUST, Clouds Hill, National Trust, 1946

Second English Edition

CLOUDS HILL | A PROPERTY OF THE NATIONAL TRUST | *Second Edition* | Published by | COUNTRY LIFE LTD. | 2–10 Tavistock Street, London, W.C. 2 | for | THE NATIONAL TRUST | 42 Queen Anne's Gate; London, S.W. 1.

Collation 18.5 × 12.3 cm: [1]⁸, 16 leaves, pp.[1] – [16].

Contents [1] title page, 2–11 text, 12–15 catalogue of contents of cottage, [16] blurb.

Plates Two b/w plates on coated paper, printed on both sides, following p.8.

Text   20 lines, 20.8 × 18.8 cm.

Paper   Newsprint, white, wove, unwatermarked, all edges trimmed, sheets bulk 2 mm.

Binding   Green paper covers 137 d. y Gr.

Notes   Lawrence's cottage 'Clouds Hill' was given to the National Trust by A.W. Lawrence in 1938.

Copies   Can.

E132   NATIONAL TRUST, Clouds Hill, National Trust, 1955

Third English Edition

CLOUDS HILL | DORSET | A Property of the National Trust | 1955 | London | COUNTRY LIFE LIMITED | For the National Trust

Collation   18.3 × 12.2 cm: [1]^{10}, 10 leaves, pp.[1] – 18, [2].

Contents   Pp.[1] title page, 2–18 text, [1–2] National Trust ads.

Plates   Two plates on coated paper, printed on both sides, following p.10.

Text   20 lines, 7.7 × 8.8 cm.

Paper   White, wove, unwatermarked, all edges trimmed, sheets bulk 2 mm.

Binding   Green paper covers 137 d.y.G. Covers stapled to sheets by two metal staples. On front cover: [in white] CLOUDS HILL | DORSET | [in white, oak leaf cut] | [in white] THE NATIONAL TRUST. Blurb on Clouds Hill and admission prices on inner front cover.

Notes   Another issue, 1964, as above with following differences: [date on title page changed to 1964]; [Collation]: 18.5 × 12 cm: [1]^{12}, 12 leaves, pp.[1]–19 [1–4]; [Contents]: [1] title page, 2–19 text, [20] blank, [1–2] National Trust ad., [3–4] blank; [Paper]: sheets bulk 3 mm; [Binding]: On front cover: [in white] CLOUDS HILL | DORSET | [white oak leaf cut] | [in white] THE NATIONAL TRUST. Blurb on inner front cover is revised, prices no longer appear. Another issue, 1965, same as 1964.

Copies   AC, Cal.

E133   NATIONAL TRUST, Clouds Hill, National Trust, 1970

Fourth English Edition

Clouds Hill | *Dorset* | THE NATIONAL TRUST | 1970

Collation   21.5 × 13.8 cm: [1]^{10}, 10 leaves, pp.1–20.

Contents   Pp.[1] title page, [2] blurb on Clouds Hill, cover, photo, printer's credits, 3–20 text.

Text   20 lines, 9.8 × 10.2 cm.

Paper White, wove, unwatermarked, all edges trimmed, sheets bulk 2 mm.

Binding Yellow paper covers 68 s OY. Covers stapled to sheets with two metal staples. On front cover: Clouds Hill | [reproduction of John oil of TEL in Arab dress, b/w] | THE NATIONAL TRUST. On back cover: [oak leaf cut].

Copies AC, Cal.

E134 NATIONAL TRUST, Clouds Hill, 1977

Fifth English Edition

Clouds Hill | *Dorset* | THE NATIONAL TRUST | 1977

Collation 21.5 × 14 cm: [1]^{12}, 24 leaves, pp.[1–2], 3–24.

Contents Pp.[1] title page, [2] location, cover illustrator's, photographer's, printer's credits, 3 contents, introduction, 4–6 preface by A.W. Lawrence, 7–11 description of cottage, 12–21 Liddell Hart essay, 22 chronology of Lawrence's life, 23–24 information on National Trust.

Plates Two b/w plates printed on both sides, following pp.8, 16.

Text 20 lines, 9.8 × 10.2 cm.

Paper White, wove, unwatermarked, all edges trimmed, sheets bulk 2 mm.

Binding Olive paper wrappers 95 m Ol Br. On front cover: Clouds Hill | [drawing of Lawrence by Augustus John] | THE NATIONAL TRUST. On back cover: [oak leaf symbol of trust].

Copies UCLA.

Interlude of War: Foreign Biography, 1940–1945

The 1940s began with juvenile biographical efforts by Burbidge, *The Mysterious A.C.2*, and Gorman, *With Lawrence to Damascus*, a semi-fictional account stressing the adventure of the desert campaign. Due to war conditions the format of these books is almost that of pamphlets.

One of a number of Lawrence studies first published in a language other than English is Nakano's Japanese-language *Lawrence of Arabia*. Another is Léon Boussard's biographical study in which the fact of Lawrence's illegitimacy was presented in print for the first time. No published translation has been made of either work.

Wing Commander Sydney Smith was Lawrence's C.O. at Mount Batten. A portrait of Lawrence during his stay there is given by the Wing Commander's wife, Clare Sydney Smith, *The Golden Reign*. The first edition contains many photographs unpublished in later editions, and a number of letters by Lawrence are reproduced in the text.

Storrs, one-time Political Governor of Palestine, and war-time friend of Lawrence's, extracted a chapter on Lawrence from his autobiography

Orientations (1937), combined it with some material on Palestine, and published it in the Penguin series under the title *Lawrence of Arabia, Zionism and Palestine*. Another friend of Lawrence's, Henry Williamson, wrote an appreciation containing a number of Lawrence letters with commentary by Williamson: *Genius of Friendship*. It was Williamson who was the recipient of the last correspondence sent by Lawrence; his accident occurred just after sending Williamson a telegram. Proofs of this book contain a dedication to Leonard Mosley, the British Fascist. The intended dedication was omitted from the published book.

An M.A. thesis presented to the University of Southern California by Nancy Holmes, using the more readily available sources, appeared in 1942. It was soon followed by another, more successful, work also by a woman. Victoria Ocampo wrote and published, in 1942, her *338171 T.E.* Ocampo was a highly regarded Argentine woman of letters. Of her work, A.W. Lawrence wrote, "The most profound and best balanced of all portraits of my brother". This was soon followed by Virignia de Castro e Almeida's *Lawrence e os Arabes*.

The foreign biographical studies for the first half of the 1940s were completed with the publication of Eric Lönnroth's *Lawrence av Arabien*. This is a study of Lawrence in Swedish, later translated, as was Ocampo.

1940

E136 WILLIAM F. BURBIDGE, The Mysterious A.C. 2, Crowther, 1940

First English Edition

THE MYSTERIOUS A.C. 2 | A Biographical Sketch of | LAWRENCE | OF ARABIA | *by* | WM. F. BURBIDGE | A | JOHN CROWTHER | PUBLICATION | Made and Printed in Great Britain by | BOBBY & CO. LTD., Printers, MARGATE, for | JOHN CROWTHER LTD., BOGNOR REGIS and | 14, HENRIETTA PLACE, LONDON, W. 1, ENGLAND | [rule] AGENTS: NEW YORK · TORONTO · MELBOURNE

Collation 20.3 × 12.5 cm: [A]^8 B^8 C^4, 20 leaves, pp.[1–4] Five-Forty.

Contents Pp.[1] title page, [2] list of titles in series, [3] map, [4] contents, 5–40 text.

RT On verso [long rule] | LAWRENCE OF ARABIA *Page Ten* | [long rule]. On recto [long rule] | [according to chapter] | [long rule].

Typography and paper $ 1 signed B.

Text 20 lines, 8.4 (9.4) × 8.8 cm.

Paper White, wove, unwatermarked, all edges trimmed, sheets bulk 2 mm.

Binding Grey paper wrappers 155 g. Gray, glued to sheets. On front cover: [all in white] [short double rule] THE MYSTERIOUS A.C. 2 [short double rule] | A | BIOGRAPHICAL SKETCH OF | LAWRENCE | OF ARABIA |

BY | WM. F. BURBIDGE | [double rule] TRAVEL [double rule] | 1/6. On spine: [grey lettering on white, running up] JOHN CROWTHER LTD. LAWRENCE OF ARABIA WM. F. BURBIDGE. On back cover: [book production war economy standard emblem].

Published at 1s 6d.

Copies AC, Cal, UT, LC.

E137 YOSHIO NAKANO, Arabia no Lawrensu, Iwanami-shinso, 1940

First Japanese Edition

[Within hand-drawn frame with four-winds corners] Nakano Yoshio sho | Arabia no Lawrensu | Iwanami Shinsho | 73

Collation 17.3 × 11.1 cm: [1–14]⁸, 112 leaves, pp.[1–4], 1–4, [1–4], 1–205, 1–5.

Contents Prp.[1] title page, [2] blank, [3] frontispiece [4] blank, 1–4 preface, 1 contents, [2] blank, [3] map, [4] blank, pp.1–202 text, 203–205 bibliography, [1] blank, [2] colophon, [3] publisher's statement, [inside back cover] publisher's ad.

Text 20 lines, 6.3 × 7.8 .cm

Paper White, wove, unwatermarked, all edges trimmed, sheets bulk 1 cm.

Binding Orange paper covers 39 gy. r O. On front cover: Nakano Yoshio sho | Arabia no Lawrensu | [in white pub. device] | Iwanami Shinsho | 73. On spine: [running down] Arabia no Lawrensu Nakano Yoshio Sho | [cut] | 73. On back cover: [different publisher's device]. Brown silk place marker.

Published at 50 yen.

Notes A 4th impression, 5 December 1963, with new introduction, pp.i–x, on verso RT, modern Chinese characters used, 8 pp. ads in rear, price 150 Yen (the three separately numbered prp. sequences are now i–xii). Another issue, 8th impression, 10 May 1965, as immediately above. Another issue 1971.

Copies AC, H.

E138 CLARE SYDNEY SMITH, The Golden Reign, Cassell, 1940

First English Edition

THE GOLDEN REIGN | THE STORY OF MY FRIENDSHIP WITH | "LAWRENCE OF ARABIA" by | CLARE SYDNEY SMITH | *With 25 half-tone Illustrations* | [pub. device] | *CASSELL* | and Company, Ltd. | London, Toronto, Melbourne | and Sydney

Collation   20.6 × 13.3 cm: [A]⁸ B–P⁸ Q¹⁰, 130 leaves, pp.[i–iv], v–vii, [viii], 1–252.

Contents   Prp.[i] bastard title, [ii] blank, [iii] title page, [iv] issue statement, printer's credit, v–vi foreword, by T.E. Lawrence's mother, vii illustrations, [viii] blank, 1–247 text, [248] blank, 249–252 index.

RT   On both verso and recto THE GOLDEN REIGN.

Plates   Eight photographs on coated paper, printed on both sides, following pp.[ii], 14, 32, 66, 110, 118, 136, 172; photo of Mount Batten from air deleted (p.15).

Typography and paper $ 1,2 signed Q,Q*.

Text   20 lines, 9.9 (10) × 9.3 cm.

Paper   Thick, white, wove, unwatermarked, all edges trimmed, sheets bulk 2.5 cm.

Binding   Sage green cloth 149 p. Gr. On spine: [gilt] THE | GOLDEN | REIGN | CLARE | SYDNEY | SMITH | CASSELL.

Published at   12s 6d.

Notes   Contains 50 letters by T.E.Lawrence, p.241.

Copies   AC, Cal, H, UT, LC.

E139   CLARE SYDNEY SMITH, The Golden Reign, Cassell, 1949

Second English Edition

[Double page] [on verso, within decorated purple frame] [cut | POCKET LIBRARY | *Published by* | CASSELL & CO. LTD. | LONDON | TORONTO · MELBOURNE · SYDNEY | WELLINGTON. | [On recto within decorated purple frame] THE | GOLDEN | REIGN | *The story of my friendship with* | "LAWRENCE OF ARABIA" | CLARE SYDNEY SMITH

Collation   17.2 × 11 cm: [A]¹⁶, B–F¹⁶, 96 leaves, pp.[1–7], 8–190, [2].

Contents   Pp.[1] bastard title, [2] series title, [3] title page, [4] issue statement, printer's credit, [5] foreword, by T.E. Lawrence's mother, [6] blank, [7]–185 text, [186] blank, [187]–190 index, [1–2] blank.

RT   On both verso and recto *The Golden Reign.*

Plates   One b/w photo following p.32.

Typography and paper $ 1 signed B.

Text   20 lines, 6.9 (7.2) × 8 cm.

Paper   White, wove, thin, unwatermarked, all edges trimmed, sheets bulk 1 cm.

Binding   Patterned maroon and buff cloth. On front cover: [gilt] THE GOLDEN | REIGN | CLARE SYDNEY | SMITH. On spine: [gilt] THE | GOLDEN | REIGHN | CLARE | SYDNEY | SMITH | [rule] | CASSELL. Green end papers. T.e. blue.

Published at 6s.

Notes No. 47 Pocket Library series.

Copies AC, Cal.

E140 CLARE SYDNEY SMITH, The Golden Reign, Cassell, 1978

Third English Edition

THE | GOLDEN | REIGN | [short Oxford rule] THE STORY OF MY FRIENDSHIP WITH | 'LAWRENCE OF ARABIA' | CLARE SYDNEY | SMITH | CASSELL | LONDON

Collation 19.7 × 12.8 cm: [1–6]^{16}, 96 leaves, pp.[1–6], 7–190, [2].

Contents Pp.[1] bastard title, [2] blank, [3] title page, [4] copyright, issue statements, ISBN, printer's credit, [5] foreword by T.E. Lawrence's mother, [6] facsimile of note to author, 7–185 text, [186] blank, 187–190 index, [1–2] blank.

RT On both verso and recto *The Golden Reign*.

Text 20 lines, 7.7 (8) × 9.2 cm.

Paper White, wove, unwatermarked, all edges trimmed, sheets bulk 1.6 cm.

Binding Black cloth. On spine: [within rectangle of Oxford rules, running down, gilt] THE GOLDEN REIGN CLARE SYDNEY SMITH. White end papers.

Published at £4.25.

Copies AC, Cal, LC.

E141 RONALD STORRS, Lawrence of Arabia, Zionism and Palestine, Penguin, 1940

First English Edition

LAWRENCE OF ARABIA | ZIONISM AND PALESTINE | BY | SIR RONALD STORRS | [pub. device] | PENGUIN BOOKS | HARMONDSWORTH MIDDLESEX ENGLAND | 41 EAST 28th STREET, NEW YORK, U.S.A.

Collation 18 × 11.2 cm: [A]^{16} B–D^{16}, 64 leaves, pp.[i–iv], v–viii, 9–128.

Contents Pp.[i] bastard title, biographical note on author, publisher's note, [ii] portrait of author, further biographical note, [iii] title page, [iv] issue statement, printer's credit, v–vi introduction, vii–viii biographical summary of T.E. Lawrence's life, 9–37 text of Lawrence of Arabia section, [38] blank, [39] section title, [40] blank, 41–128 text of Zionism and Palestine section.

Typography and paper $ 1 signed B.

Text 20 lines, 7.6 (7.8) × 8.5 cm.

Paper White, wove, unwatermarked, all edges trimmed, sheets bulk 8 mm.

Binding Blue and white panelled paper covers 182 m. Blue. On front cover: [within rhomboid] PENGUIN | BOOKS | [within central white panel] LAWRENCE OF ARABIA | SIR | RONALD | STORRS | ZIONISM AND PALESTINE. On spine: [running up, top panel] SIR RONALD STORRS | [middle panel] LAWRENCE OF ARABIA | ZIONISM AND PALESTINE | [bottom panel, across] [pub. device] | 288. On back cover: [same as front cover except that an Arabic seal printed beside author's name is replaced by Hebrew seal].

Published at March 1940.

Notes A 2nd impression, June 1941; 3rd impression, November 1943, same as above with following differences: [Collation]: [A]^{16} B–C^{16}, 48 leaves, 96 pp.; [Contents]: pp.[1] bastard title, blurb, [2] illustration of author, [3] title page, [4] issue statement, printer's credit, 5 preface, [6] blank, vii Lawrence biographical note, [8] blank, 9–30 text of Lawrence section, [31] section title, [32] blank, 33–96 text of Zionism and Palestine section; [Typography and paper]: sheets bulk 4 mm.

Copies AC, Cal, UT, LC.

E142 J.T. GORMAN, With Lawrence to Damascus, Oxford, 1940

First English Edition

GREAT EXPLOITS | WITH LAWRENCE | TO DAMASCUS | By | MAJOR J.T. GORMAN | [publisher's device] | OXFORD UNIVERSITY PRESS | LONDON · NEW YORK · TORONTO

Collation 18.4 × 12.4 cm: [A] –C^8, 24 leaves, pp.[1–4], [1]–44.

Contents Prp.[1] bastard title, [2] frontis., [3] title page, [4] printer's credit, pp.[1] –44 text.

RT On both verso and recto WITH LAWRENCE TO DAMASCUS.

Typography and paper $ 1 signed B.

Text 20 lines, 8.3 (8.5) × 8.8 cm.

Paper White, wove, unwatermarked, all edges trimmed, sheets bulk 5 mm.

Binding Pictorial paper covers wrapped around boards. On front cover: [in white] GREAT EXPLOITS | [within frame of weapons, on green background] WITH | LAWRENCE | TO | DAMASCUS | · | By | Major J.T. Gorman | [below frame in white] OXFORD UNIVERSITY PRESS. On back cover: [within frame of white, on green background, list of titles in series].

Notes Great Exploits series; 2nd impression, 1941, as above.

Copies AC.

1941

E143 LÉON BOUSSARD, Le Secret du Colonel Lawrence, Editions Mont-Louis, 1941

First French Edition

LE SECRET DU COLONEL | LAWRENCE

Collation 18.7 × 11.8 cm: [1–8]^8, 64 leaves, pp.[1–11], 12–124, [4].

Contents Pp.[1–2] blank, [3] title page, [4] copyright statement, [5] two quotes, Stendahl and Lawrence, [6] note on issue, [7] dedication, [8] blank, [9] section title, [10] blank, 11–18 preface, [19] section title, [20] blank, 21–124 text, [1] section title, [2] blank, [3] printer's colophon, [4] blank.

Text 20 lines, 7.5 × 8 cm.

Paper White, wove, unwatermarked, all edges trimmed, sheets bulk 7 mm.

Binding Tan paper wrappers 76 l.y Br. On front cover: LÉON BOUSSARD | LE SECRET DU COLONEL | [green and black lettering] LAWRENCE | [cut within green rule frame] | EDITIONS MONT-LOUIS | CLERMONT – FERRAND – PARIS | [short rule] | 1941. On spine: [running up] LE SECRET DU COLONEL LAWRENCE | [across at foot] 10fr.

Published at 10 Francs.

Notes The first book to record Lawrence's illegitimacy.

Copies AC.

E144 LÉON BOUSSARD, Le Secret du Colonel Lawrence, A.M., 1946

Second French Edition

LÉON BOUSSARD | LE SECRET | DU COLONEL | LAWRENCE | Editions A.M. | PARIS 1946

Collation 18.8 × 12 cm: [1]^8, 2–10^8, 80 leaves, pp.[1–8], 9–[152], [8].

Contents Pp.[1–2] blank, [3] bastard title, [4] author's note, [5] title page, [6] limitation statement, 50 copies on vélin paper, [7] two quotes, TEL and Stendhal, [8] blank, 9–13 foreword by author, 14–[152] text, [1–2] blank, [3] contents, [4] blank, [5] printer's colophon, [6–8] blank.

RT On both recto and verso *LE SECRET DU COLONEL LAWRENCE* .

Typography and paper $ 1 signed 2.

Text 20 lines, 7 (7.5) × 8.5 cm.

Paper White, wove, unwatermarked, untrimmed, sheets bulk 8 mm.

Binding Brown paper covers 57 l. Br. On front cover: LE COLONEL | [white rule] | LAWRENCE | SON ACTIVITÉ SECRÈTE | ET PUBLIQUE EN | ASIE MINEURE | AVEC UN PORTRAIT PAR AUGUSTUS JOHN | [2 white rules]. On spine: [running up] LE COLONEL LAWRENCE.

Published at 55 Francs.

Notes Another issue, as above, with following differences: [Binding]: white paper. On front cover: *LEON BOUSSARD* | [in yellow brown] le se | cret | du co | lonel | [imprinted over last two lines, on slant] Lawrence. On back cover: Prix 55fr. *Notes* Fifty copies printed on papier velin, numbered 1–50.

Copies Cal, H, UT, LC.

E144a LÉON BOUSSARD, Le Secret du Colonel Lawrence, Simpson, 1947

First Canadian Edition

LÉON BOUSSARD | LE SECRET | DU COLONEL | LAWRENCE | LES ÉDITIONS B.D. SIMPSON | Montréal

Collation 19.3 × 12.4 cm: 1–11⁸ 12⁴ 13⁸, 100 leaves, pp.[1–8], 9–196, [1–4].

Contents Pp.[1] [gathering signature], [2] blank, [3] bastard title, [4] blank, [5] title page, [6] author's note, [7] quotes Stendhal and Lawrence, [8] blank, 9–14 preface, 15–196 text, [1] contents, [2–4] blank.

RT On both verso and recto *LE SECRET DU COLONEL LAWRENCE*.

Typography and paper $ 1 signed LE SECRET DU COLONEL...— 2.

Text 20 lines, 9.2 (9.6) × 8.5 cm.

Paper White, wove, unwatermarked, untrimmed, sheets bulk 1.5 cm.
Binding White paper covers. On front cover: *LÉON BOUSSARD* | [in red] LE SECRET | [in red] *du* | [in red] COLONEL LAWRENCE | [b/w reproduction of John painting of Lawrence] | ÉDITIONS B.D. SIMPSON. On spine: [red rule] | LÉON | BOUSSARD | [red rule] | LE | SECRET | *du* | [in red] COLONEL | [in red] LAWRENCE | *ÉDITIONS* | B.D. | SIMPSON | MONTRÉAL | [red rule]. On back cover: [printer's mark].

Notes Preface signed January 1947. Chapter 8 entitled 'Un simple soldat' in earlier editions is here titled 'La Frère lai de la RAF'.

Copies Cal.

E145 HENRY WILLIAMSON, Genius of Friendship, Faber & Faber, 1941

Uncorrected Proof of First English Edition

GENIUS OF FRIENDSHIP | 'T.E. LAWRENCE' | [cut] | HENRY | WILLIAMSON | FABER AND FABER | 24 Russell Square | London

Collation 24.8 × 15.5 cm: [A]–E⁸, 40 leaves, pp.[1–8], 9–78, [79–80].

Contents Pp.[1–4] blank, [5] bastard title, [6] blank, [7] title page, [8] issue statement, printer's credit, 9–78 text, [79–80] blank.

Typography and paper $ 1 signed B W.G.F.

Text   20 lines, 12 × 10.2 cm.

Paper   White, wove, unwatermarked, all edges trimmed, sheets bulk 4 mm.

Binding   Blue paper 172 l. g B. On front cover: GENIUS OF | FRIENDSHIP | 'T.E. LAWRENCE' | by | HENRY WILLIAMSON | [between rules] PROOF COPY | FABER AND | FABER.

Notes   Dedicated to Leonard Mosley [omitted in published edition].

Copies   Cal, LC.

E146   HENRY WILLIAMSON, Genius of Friendship, Faber and Faber, 1941

First English Edition

GENIUS OF FRIENDSHIP | 'T.E. LAWRENCE' | [cut] | HENRY | WILLIAMSON | FABER AND FABER LIMITED | 24 Russell Square | London

Collation   25.5 × 16.2 cm: [A]^8 B–E^8, 40 leaves, pp.[1–8], 9–78, [79–80].

Contents   Pp.[1–4] blank, [5] bastard title, [6] blank, [7] title page, [8] issue statement, printer's credit, 9–78 text, [79–80] blank.

Typography and paper $ 1 signed B W.F.G.

Text   20 lines, 11.9 × 10.2 cm.

Paper   White, wove, watermarked, top edge trimmed, remainder deckle edge, sheets bulk 5 mm.

Binding   Golden brown linen 54 br. O. On spine: [gilt, running down] GENIUS OF FRIENDSHIP: 'T.E. LAWRENCE ' | BY HENRY WILLIAMSON | [across at foot] F & F. End papers white, of heavier stock than sheets.

Published at   10s 6d, November 1941.

Notes   2nd impression, December 1941, as above, but paper has smoother finish. Another state of 1st impression exists with variant binding material, 43 m/ r Br polished cloth – precedent not known.

Copies   Ac, Cal, UT.

E147   NANCY HOLME, The Career of T.E. Lawrence, University of Southern California, 1941

Unpublished Master's Thesis

THE CAREER OF T.E. LAWRENCE | [rule] | A Thesis | Presented to | the Faculty of the Department of History | University of Southern California | [rule] | In Partial Fulfillment | of the Requirements for the Degree | Master of Arts | [rule] | by | Nancy Holme | June 1941

Collation Eight × 11 sheets, 112 leaves, pp.[i–ii], iii–ix, 1–103.

Contents Prp.[i] title page, [ii]–iii preface, iv–ix contents, pp.1–96 text, 97–103 bibliography.

Typography and paper Typewritten double-spaced on single sheets.

Paper Sheets bulk 1.3 cm.

Binding Black buckram. On spine: [gilt] HOLME.

Copies AC, USC.

E147A HAJIME KOBAYASHI, Igirisu to Rorensu to Arabia, Hakubunkan kan, 1941

First Japanese Edition

[Within 3-panelled rule frame, running down] Kobayashi, Hajime | [Co tai riku | hatten | Gyoshol | Igirisu to Rorensu to Arabia | Tokyo Hakubunkan | kan.

Collation 18.8 × 15.5 cm: 1–25⁸, 26⁸ (–4), 214 leaves, pp.1–8, [1]–415, [15].

Contents Prp.[1] introduction, 2–3 blank, 4–5 author's note, 6–8 contents, pp.[1] bastard title, [2] blank, [3] section title, 4–415 text, [1–9] bibliography, [10–13] maps, [14–15] ads.

Plates Two b/w printed on both sides before p.1.

Text 20 lines, 7.3 × 9.4 cm.

Paper White, wove, unwatermarked, all edges trimmed, sheets bulk 2.5 cm.

Binding White paper.

Copies LC.

1942

E148 VICTORIA OCAMPO, 338171 T.E., Sur, 1942

First Argentine Edition (Limited issue)

VICTORIA OCAMPO | [in red] 338171 | [stencil letters] T.E. | *EDITIONS DES LETTRES FRANÇAISES* | SAN MARTIN 689 [in red, underlined] SUR BUENOS AIRES | 1942

Collation 20.8 × 14.9 cm): [1–8]⁸ [9]¹⁰, 74 leaves, pp.[1–12], 13–144, [145–148].

Contents Pp.[1–2] blank, [3] bastard title, collect. des amis des Lettres Françaises, [4] blank, [5] title page, [6] 'Il a été tiré à part 20 exemplaires sur papier Whatman', copyright notice, [7] advertisement, [8] blank, [9] dedication to Roger Caillois, [10] blank, [11] quote from F. Doubleday, [12] blank, 13–[145] text, [146] blank, [147] contents, [148] printer's colophon.

Text   20 lines, 10.5 × 8.6 cm.

Paper   White, laid, unwatermarked, untrimmed, sheets bulk 1 cm.

Binding   White paper wrappers. On front cover: [in blue] VICTORIA OCAMPO | [in red] 338171 | [in blue outline letters] T.E. | *EDITIONS DES LETTRES FRANÇAISES* | SAN MARTIN 689 [in red] Sur [in blue] BUENOS AIRES | 1942. On spine: [in blue] VICTORIA | OCAMPO | [in red] 338171 | [in blue] T.E. | EDITIONS | DES LETTRES | FRANÇAISES. On back cover: [all in blue, ads for other titles in series].

Published at $ 4 m/arg.

Copies   Cal, LC.

E149   VICTORIA OCAMPO, 338171 T.E., Sur, 1942

First Argentine Edition

VICTORIA OCAMPO | [in red] 338171 | [stencil letters] T.E | [publisher's device] | BUENOS AIRES

Collation   19.5 × 14 cm: 65 leaves, pp.[1–10], 11–126, [1–4].

Contents   Pp.[1–2] blank, [3] bastard title, [4] blank, [5] title page, [6] copyright statement, [7] dedication, [8] blank, [9] quote by Florence Doubleday, [10] blank, 11–126 text, [1] blank, [2] printer's colophon, [3–4] blank.

Text   20 lines, 11.8 × 8.6 cm.

Paper   White, wove, unwatermarked, all edges trimmed, sheets bulk 1 cm.

Binding   White paper covers. On front cover: VICTORIA OCAMPO | [in red] 338171 | T.E. | SUR. On spine: VICTORIA | OCAMPO | [in red] 338171 | T.E | SUR. on back cover: [list of other titles in series].

Published at   5 November 1942.

Copies   UT.

E150   VICTORIA OCAMPO, 338171 T.E., Sur, 1963.

Second Argentine Edition

Victoria Ocampo | [in red] 338171 | [stencil lettering] T.E. | *(Lawrence de Arabia)* | SUR

Collation   19.5 × 12 cm: [1–7]⁸ [8]⁴ [9]⁸, 68 leaves, pp.[1–10], 11–128, [1–8].

Contents   Pp.[1–2] blank, [3] bastard title, [4] blank, [5] title page, [6] deposit number, printing statement, [7] dedication, [8] blank, [9] quotation from Florence Doubleday, [10] blank, 11–14 prologue by A.W. Lawrence, 15–128 text, [1] section title, [2] blank, [3] contents, [4] blank, [5–6] list of author's works, [7] colophon, [8] blank.

Text   20 lines, 9.8 × 8.5 cm.

Paper   White, wove, unwatermarked, all edges trimmed, sheets bulk 9 mm.

Binding White paper covers. On front cover: Victoria Ocampo | [in red] 338171 | [stencil lettering] T.E. | *(Lawrence de Arabia)* | SUR. On spine: VICTORIA | OCAMPO | [in red] 338171 | T.E.

Published at 17 December 1963.

Notes Variant title page as follows: VICTORIA OCAMPO | [in red] 338171 | [in stencil lettering] T.E [*sic*] | *(Lawrence de Arabia)* | Prologo de | A.W. Lawrence | [publisher's device] | BUENOS AIRES.

Copies UCB.

E151 VICTORIA OCAMPO, 338171 T.E. Lawrence of Arabia, Gollancz, 1963

Uncorrected Proof of First English Edition

338171 T.E. | (LAWRENCE OF ARABIA) | by | VICTORIA OCAMPO | Translated by | DAVID GARNETT | LONDON | VICTOR GOLLANCZ | 1963

Collation 19.8 × 13 cm: [1–4]^{16}, 64 leaves, pp.[1–13], 14–128.

Contents Pp.[1] bastard title, [2] blank, [3] title page, [4] issue, copyright statements, translator's, printer's credits, [5] dedication, [6] blank, [7] translator's note, [8] blank, [9] quote, [10] blank, [11] contents, [12] blank, [13]–15 introduction, [16] blank, [17]–128 text.

RT On verso 338171 T.E. On recto [according to section].

Text 20 lines, 10.3 (10.8) × 9.7 cm.

Paper White, wove, unwatermarked, all edges trimmed, sheets bulk 9 mm.

Binding Blue paper wrappers 190 l. b Gray. On front cover: [within frame of Oxford rules] VICTOR GOLLANCZ LTD. | LONDON | 338171 T.E. | VICTORIA OCAMPO | The Garden City Press Ltd., Letchworth, Herts.

Copies Cal.

E152 VICTORIA OCAMPO, 338171, T.E. Lawrence of Arabia, Gollancz, 1963

First English Edition

338171 T.E. | (LAWRENCE OF ARABIA) | by | VICTORIA OCAMPO | Translated by | DAVID GARNETT | LONDON | VICTOR GOLLANCZ LTD. | 1963

Collation 9.5 × 12.5 cm: [1]^{16} 2–4^{16}, 64 leaves, pp.[1–13], 14–128.

Contents Pp.[1] bastard title, [2] blank, [3] title page, [4] issue, copyright statements, translator's, printer's credits, [5] dedication, [6] blank, [7] translator's note, [8] blank, [9] quote, [10] blank, [11] contents, [12] blank, [13]–15 introduction, [16] blank, [17]–128 text.

RT On verso 338171 T.E. On recto [according to section].

Typography and paper $ 1 signed 2- T.E.

Text 20 lines, 10.3 × (10.8) × 9.7 cm.

Paper White, wove, unwatermarked, all edges trimmed, sheets bulk 9 mm.

Binding Brown cloth 37 mr O. On spine: [gilt, running down] 338171 T.E. * VICTORIA OCAMPO.

Published at 15s, July 1963.

Notes A 2nd impression, August 1963, as above. Written in French in 1942. The present translation is that text with the additional notes of the Spanish translation published in 1951, together with an introduction by A.W. Lawrence.

Copies AC, Cal, LC.

E153   VICTORIA OCAMPO, 338171, T.E. (Lawrence of Arabia), Dutton, 1963

First American Edition (Review issue)

338171 T.E. | *(Lawrence of Arabia)* | by | VICTORIA OCAMPO | Translated by | DAVID GARNETT | [publisher's device] | NEW YORK | E.P. DUTTON & CO., INC. | 1963

Collation 18.8 × 12.5 cm: [1–4]^{16}, 64 leaves, pp.[1–13], 14–128.

Contents Pp.[1] bastard title, [2] blank, [3] title page, [4] copyright, issue statements, [5] dedication, [6] blank, [7] translator's note, [8] blank, [9] quote from Florence Doubleday, [10] blank, [11] contents, [12] blank, [13]–15 introduction, [16] blank, [17]–128 text.

RT On verso 338171 T.E. On recto [according to chapter].

Text 20 lines, 9.2 (9.7) × 9.1 cm.

Paper White, wove, unwatermarked, all edges trimmed, sheets bulk 1 cm.

Binding White paper covers glued to sheets. Original DW pasted around cover.

Copies AC.

E154   VICTORIA OCAMPO, 338171 T.E. (Lawrence of Arabia), Dutton, 1963

First American Edition

338171 T.E. | *(Lawrence of Arabia)* | by | VICTORIA OCAMPO | Translated by | DAVID GARNETT | [publisher's device] | NEW YORK | E.P. DUTTON & CO., INC. | 1963

Collation 18.3 × 12.5 cm: [1–4]^{16}, 64 leaves, pp.[1–13], 14–128.

Contents Pp.[1] bastard title, [2] blank, [3] title page, [4] copyright, issue statements, original publication credit, [5] dedication, [6] blank, [7] translator's note, [8] blank, [9] quote, [10] blank, [11] contents, [12] blank, [13]–15 introduction, [16] blank, [17]–128 text.

RT On verso 338171, T.E. On verso [according to chapter].

Text 20 lines, 10 (10.5) × 9.3 cm.

Paper White, wove, unwatermarked, all edges trimmed, sheets bulk 1 cm.

Binding Orange cloth 34 v. r O. On spine: [running down] OCAMPO 338171 T.E. DUTTON | (*Lawrence of Arabia*).

Published at $3.00, October 1963.

Notes Another issue, 2nd impression, November 1963, as above.

Copies AC, Cal, UT, LC.

E155   VICTORIA OCAMPO, 338171 T.E. (Lawrence of Arabia), Dutton, 1963

Publisher's Prospectus for First American Edition

No title page.

Collation 14 × 20.5 cm: single leaf printed on both sides.

Contents [Recto] name of publisher and address, [verso] quotes from reviews superimposed on drawing of Lawrence in Arab headdress.

Paper Pasteboard, unwatermarked, all edges trimmed.

Published at Free advertising flyer.

Copies AC.

E156   VICTORIA OCAMPO, 338171 T.E., Gallimard, 1947

First French Edition

VICTORIA OCAMPO | 338171 | T.E. | (LAWRENCE D'ARABIE) | *nrf* | GALLIMARD

Collation 18.8 × 11.8 cm: [1]⁸ 2–8⁸ 9⁴, 68 leaves, pp.[1–10], 11–130, [6].

Contents Pp.[1–2] blank, [3] bastard title, [4] blank, [5] title page, [6] copyright statement, [7] dedication, [8] blank, [9] quote, [10] blank, 11–130 text, [1] section title, [2] blank, [3] contents, [4] blank, [5] printer's colophon, [6] blank.

RT On verso 338.171 – T.E. On recto [according to chapter].

Typography and paper $ 1 signed 3.

Text 20 lines, 9.8 (10) × 8.2 cm.

Paper White, wove, unwatermarked, untrimmed, sheets bulk 8 mm.

Binding White paper covers. On front cover: [within triple rules (one black, two red)] | VICTORIA OCAMPO | [in red] 338171 | [in red] T.E. | (*LAWRENCE D'ARABIE*) | *nrf* | GALLIMARD. On spine: [triple rule (one black, two red)] | [running up] VICTORIA OCAMPO. – [in red] – T.E. (LAWRENCE D'ARABIE) | [triple rule (one black, two red)]. On back cover: [within triple rules (one black, two red)] [list of works by Valery Larbaud].

Notes Septième edition as above.

Copies AC, LC.

1943

E157 VIRGINIA de CASTRO e ALMEIDA, Lawrence e os Arabes, Livraria Classica Editone, 1943

First Portuguese Edition

LAWRENCE | E OS ARABES [Lisbon]

Collation 19 × 12 cm: [1] –5^8, 40 leaves, pp.[1–11], 12–77, [3].

Contents Pp.[1] series title, [2] printer's credit, [3] title page, [4] blank, [5] list of author's works, [6] advertisements, [7–8] leaf missing, [9] section title, [10] blank, [11] –25 introduction, [26] blank, [27] section title, [28] blank, [29] –58 text, [59] –77 appendixes, [1] blank, [2] contents, [3] blank.

RT On both verso and recto *LAWRENCE E OS ARABES.*

Typography and paper $ 1 signed 2.

Text 20 lines, 7.5 (8.2) × 8.1 cm.

Paper White, wove, unwatermarked, all edges trimmed, sheets bulk 5 mm.

Binding Orange and yellow paper covers 67 brill. OY and 89 p.Y. On front cover: VIRGINIA DE CASTRO E ALMEIDA | [over white dagger] COLECCAO | GIADIO | LAWRENCE | E OS | ARABES | [within signle rule frame] OS ARABES EO SEU PROBLEMA | EM 1914 * MENTALIDADE BRI- | TANICA * LAWRENCE: A SUA | FORSA E A SUA FRAQUEZA; | A SUA VITORIA E A SUA | DERROTA * A SORTE DOS ARA- | BES DEPOIS DO SEU SACRIFI- | CIO * MARTIRIO DE LAWRENCE | * DOCUMENTACAO. | [over white rectangle] FIGURAS | NOTAVELS | LIVARARIA CLASSICA EDITORA. On spine: [running up] V. DE CASTRO E ALMEIDA-LAWRENCE E OS ARABES | [across at top] | 3. On back cover: [list of titles in series].

Copies Cal, LC.

E158 VIRGINIA de CASTRO E ALMEIDA, Lawrence e os Arabes, Livraria Classica, 1943

First Portugese Edition

D. VIRGINA DE CASTRO E ALMEIDA | LAWRENCE | E OS ARABES | 1943 | LIVRARIA CLASSICA EDITORA | A.M. Teixeira & C.a(s) (Filhos) | 17, Praca d os Restauradores, 17-LISBOA

Collation   19 × 12.3 cm: [1]–5⁸, 40 leaves, pp.[1–11], 12–77, [1–3].

Contents   Pp.[1] series title, [2] printer's credit, [3] bastard title, [4] blank, [5] list of author's works, [6] pub. ad, [7] title page, [8] blank, [9] section title, [10] blank, [11]–77 text, [1] blank, [2] contents, [3] blank.

RT   On both verso and recto *LAWRENCE E OS ARABES.*

Typography and paper $ 1 signed 2.

Text   20 lines, 7.5 (8.2) × 8 cm.

Paper   White, wove, unwatermarked, untrimmed, sheets bulk 5 mm.

Binding   Yellow and tan paper covers. On front cover: VIRGINIA DE CASTRO E ALMEIDA | COLECCAO | GIADIO | LAWRENCE | E OS | ARABES | [within rectangle of single rules] OS ARABES E O SEU PROBLEMA | EM 1914 % MENTALIDADE BRI- | TANIC * LAWRENCE A SUA FORCA E A SUA FRAQUEZA: | A SUA VITORIA E A SUA | DERROTA * A SORTE DOS ARA- | BES DEPOIS DO SEU SACRIFI- | CIO * MARTIRIO DE LAWRENCE | * DOCUMENTACAO | FIGURAS | NOTAVELS | LIVRARIA CLASSICA EDITORA. On spine: [sword cut] | 3 | [running up within white rectangle] V.DE CASTRO A ALMEIDA– LAWRENCE DE ARABES | [across] SERIE | VIII. On back cover: [list of titles in series].

Notes   GIADO collection no.3.

Copies   LC.

E159   ERIK LÖNNROTH, Lawrence av Arabien, Bonniers, 1943

First Swedish Edition

GÖTESBORGS   HÖGSKOLA | FORSKNINGAR   OCH FÖRELÄSNINGAR | [long rule] | LAWRENCE | AV ARABIEN | ÖKENKRIGAREN OCH POLITIKERN | AV | ERIK LÖNNROTH | [pub. device] | STOCKHOLM | ALBERT BONNIERS FÖRLAG

Collation   19.5 × 12.5 cm: [1]⁸ 2–6⁸ 7⁴, 52 leaves, pp.[1–6], 7–100, [4].

Contents   Pp.[1] bastard title, [2] note on text, [3] title page, [4] issue statement, [5] foreword, [6] blank, 7–13 introduction, 14–[101] text, [1] blank, [2] contents, [3] blank.

RT   On both verso and recto [according to chapter].

Typography and paper $ 1 signed 2 *Lönnroth Lawrence.*

Text   20 lines, 9.1 (9.2) × 9.6 cm.

Paper   White, wove, unwatermarked, untrimmed, sheets bulk 5 mm.

Binding   Tan paper covers. On front cover: GÖTEBORGS HÖGSKOLA | [in red] FORSKNINGAR OCH FÖRELÄSNINGAR | [Oxford rule] | *Erik Lönnroth* | [in red] LAWRENCE | [in red] AV ARABIEN | ÖKENKRIGAREN OCH POLITIKERN | ALBERT BONNIERS FÖRLAG. On spine: [running down] LÖNNROTH | LAWRENCE AV ARABIEN. On back cover: T.E.

Lawrence | [lengthy blurb] | [long rule] | ALBERT BONNIERS FÖRLAG | *Pris 3:75.*

Published at SK 3:75.

Copies AC, Cal.

E160 ERIK LÖNNROTH, Lawrence of Arabia, Vallentine, Mitchell, 1956

First English Edition

ERIK LÖNNROTH | LAWRENCE | *of* | ARABIA | AN HISTORICAL APPRECIATION | [publisher's device] | VALLENTINE, MITCHELL · LONDON

Collation 21.6 × 13.8 cm: [A]^8 B–F^8 G^4 H^8, 60 leaves, pp.[i–iv], v–xviii, 1–102.

Contents Prp.[i] bastard title, [ii] blank, [iii] title page, [iv] issue, copyright statements, translator's, printer's credits, v contents, vi map. vii–viii foreword, ix–xviii introduction, pp.1–98 text, 99 cartoon, 100–102 index.

RT On verso *Lawrence of Arabia.* On recto [according to chapter].

Typography and paper $ 1 signed B.

Text 20 lines, 9.9 (10.2) × 10.2 cm. Set in 12 and 14pt Bookprint.

Paper White, wove, unwatermarked, all edges trimmed, sheets bulk 1 cm.

Binding Blue cloth 181 l. Blue. On spine: [in maroon] ERIK LÖNNROTH ... LAWRENCE OF ARABIA.

Published at 13s 6d.

Copies AC, Cal, H.

First Ebbing: Forgotten Biography, 1945–1949

After the war little was published on Lawrence. Interest in him seemed to have been exhausted. A work which did appear during this period and which has experienced some neglect is the second book on Lawrence by Edward Robinson, *Lawrence the Rebel* (1946).

An Iranian work by Shiftah is an interpretation of Lawrence's role in an imaginative espionage effort in Iran. Another foreign-language publication appeared in Germany; Rolf Schroers was commissioned to write *T.E. Lawrence Schicksal und Gestalt,* and later was employed as editor and translator of other Lawrence items for Paul List, the German publishers of Lawrence. Neither work has been translated.

1946

E164   EDWARD ROBINSON, Lawrence the Rebel, Lincolns-Praeger, 1946

First English Edition

LAWRENCE | THE | REBEL | BY | EDWARD ROBINSON | [publisher's device] | LINCOLNS-PRAEGER (PUBLISHERS) LTD.| LONDON

Collation   21.2 × 13.7 cm: [A]^8 B–N^8 O^{10}, 114 leaves, pp.[1–4], 5–228.

Contents   Pp.[1] title page, [2] issue, copyright statements, printer's credits, [3] introduction, [4] dedication, 5–225 text, 226 list of works from which quotes are taken, 227–228 index.

Plates   Frontispiece preceding p.[1].

Typography and paper $ 1 signed B.

Text   20 lines, 8.5 × 9.8 cm.

Paper   White, wove, unwatermarked, all edges trimmed, sheets bulk 1.3 cm.

Binding   Green cloth 149 p. G. On spine: [gilt] LAWRENCE | THE | REBEL | BY | EDWARD | ROBINSON | LINCOLNS – | PRAEGER | LONDON.

Copies   AC, Cal, UT, LC.

E165   EDWARD ROBINSON, Lawrence the Rebel, Folcroft, 1979

First American Edition

LAWRENCE | THE | REBEL | BY | EDWARD ROBINSON | THIS IS A LIMITED EDITION OF 150 COPIES | FOLCROFT LIBRARY EDITIONS/ 1979

Collation   Prp.[1] blank, [2] photo, [3] title page, [4] blank, pp. [1] title page of original edition, [2] issue, copyright statements, printer's credit, [3] introduction, [4] dedication, 5–225 text, 226 acknowledgments, 227–228 index.

Text   20 lines, 8.5 × 10.2 cm.

Paper   Buff, wove, unwatermarked, all edges trimmed, sheets bulk 1.5 cm.

Binding   Olive cloth 108 d. Ol. On spine: [gilt] [cut] | [running down] LAWRENCE THE REBEL [cut] ROBINSON [cut].

Notes   Reprint of Lincoln-Prager edition of 1946.

Copies   Wesleyan University.

1947

E166   NASR A SHIFTAH, Sih mard-i ajib, 1947?

First Iranian Edition

[Pictorial title page, in blue, running right to left] [running diagonally] Sih mard-i ajib | [within single rule frame panel] (yek dastan-e-haghighi va khandani) | 1. chegooneh Lawrence vared-e-Iran shod? | 2. Ghegooneh Sytmesghoo shooresh nemood? | 3. Chegooneh Seyyed Farhad as Zendan farar kard? | va ertebat-e-in seh mozoo beham | [within second panel framed by single rules] Nevisandeh va gerdavarandeh: Nasra Shiftah

Collation   19 × 13.5 cm: [1–7]^8, 56 leaves, pp.[1–4], [1–3], 4–105, [1–3].

Contents   Prp.[1] title page, [2] photo, [3] half-title, topics covered, credits, [4] dedication, pp.[1] half-title, note by critic, [2] preface, [3]–105 text, [1] photo of Lawrence, [2–3] blank.

Text   20 lines, 9 × 10.5 cm.

Paper   White, wove, newsprint, unwatermarked, all edges trimmed, sheets bulk 5 mm.

Binding   Only copy seen rebound.

Copies   UCLA.

1949

E167   Rolf Schroers, T.E. Lawrence Schicksal und Gestalt, Dorn, 1949

First German Edition

Rolf Schroers | T.E. LAWRENCE | SCHICKSAL UND GESTALT | Biographische Studie | [pub. device] | WALTER DORN VERLAG BREMEN – HORN

Collation   18.8 × 12 cm: [1]–12^8 13^4, 100 leaves, pp.[1–5], 5–198, [199–200].

Contents   Pp.[1] T.E. Lawrence, [2] dedication, [3] title page, [4] copyright statement, printer's credit, [5] 16-line quote from Hugo von Hofmannsthal, [6] blank, 7–8 foreword, 9–196 text, 197–[199] notes, [200] blank.

Plates   Following p.[2] on coated paper, b/w reproduction of John drawing of Lawrence; following p.[200] on coated paper, b/w map of Near East.

Typography and paper $ 1,2 signed 2,2*.

Text   20 lines, 8.2 × 8 cm.

Paper   White wove, unwatermarked, all edges trimmed, sheets bulk 1 cm.

Binding   Tan 76 1. y Br paper covered boards, green 127 gy. OL G cloth spine. On front cover: [all in green] *Rolf Schroers* | T.E. LAWRENCE |

SCHICKSAL UND GESTALT | WALTER DORN VERLAG BREMEN-
HORN . On spine: [on small paper patch, all in green] SCHROERS | T.E. |
LAWRENCE. T.e.gray & red head band, yellow tail band.
Copies H, SUA, UNW.

E168   E. ALFRED JONES, The T.E. Lawrence Silver Cup, n.p. , n.d.

First English Edition

The T.E. Lawrence Silver Cup by E. Alfred Jones
Collation   30 × 24.8 cm: [1]², unpaged.
Contents   Leaves printed on one side only; leaf 1 has b/w photo of cup,
mounted; leaf 2 has six-paragraph description.
Paper   White, wove, unwatermarked, all edges trimmed.
Copies   AC, Cal.

Reawakening of Interest, 1950–54

The apparent decline of interest in Lawrence ended suddenly in the early
1950s. In the first half of the decade two important Lawrence books were
published. The first is Garnett's *The Essential T.E. Lawrence* (1950), which
opened the decade, and the second is Aldington's biography which
appeared in France in 1954 and in England in 1955 bridging the mid-decade
years.

In between these works came a variety of minor items. A scout group
named for Lawrence issued a pamphlet giving a brief history of the
adoption of the name and the history of the group. In France Roger
Stéphane (pseudonym of Roger Worms), published a study of three literary
adventurers: Lawrence, Malraux and von Salomon. A virulently anti-
Lawrence treatise was published in Istanbul in 1950 written by Aziz H.
Akdemir.

The fortunes of Jonathan Cape were strongly tied to Lawrence works.
They published many titles, and kept them in print for many years. With
the return to more normal conditions after the war, the publishing industry
in England began to reawaken. A Lawrence prospectus described here
reflects the renewal of marketing vigour by the company.

The Imperial War Museum has, since 1952, issued a variety of hand lists
of materials related to Lawrence from their collections.

After a lapse of some years authors rediscovered Lawrence as a subject
for juvenile books. John Thomas' *True Book About Lawrence of Arabia* (1953) is
the first post-war attempt. It has been followed by a throng of others.
Stéphane included a second essay on Lawrence in a collection *Théâtre de
Destin* (1953).

Richard Aldington's *Lawrence of Arabia* has caused a greater controversy than any other work published on Lawrence. First published in French, some passages were altered when it was published in England. Aldington's literary career was much damaged by the controversy surrounding the book. The effort to prevent its being published in England at all was considerable on the Continent as well as in the English-speaking world. Ripples of the controversy remain with us today.

1950

E170   The "T.E. Lawrence' River Crew, 1950

First English Edition

[On front cover] EIGHTEENTH FINCHLEY SCOUT GROUP | [rule] | [scout badge cut] | THE "T.E. LAWRENCE" RIVER CREW | [photo of Kennington bust of Lawrence] | THE SAINT PAUL'S CATHEDRAL | BUST OF LAWRENCE OF ARABIA | BY ERIC KENNINGTON | "THE FIRST | FIVE YEARS"| PRICE ONE SHILLING

Collation   22.2 × 14.3 cm: [1]⁶, 6 leaves, pp.[1–12].

Contents   Pp.[1] foreword, [2] photo, [3] 'Founding of the crew', [4] photos, [5] service, [6] photo, [7] 'Recollection of TEL by Leonard H. Green', [8] photo, [9] 'Travel and the Crew', [10] photo, [11] 'What of the Future?', [12] addresses.

Text   5 lines, 2.8 × 10 cm.

Paper   Slick, white, wove, unwatermarked, all edges trimmed, sheets bulk 1 mm.

Binding   Tan paper wrappers 73 p OY. Covers attached to sheets by two metal staples.

Published at   1s.

Copies   Cal.

E171   ROGER STÉPHANE, Portrait de L'Aventurier, Sagittaire, 1950

First French Edition

ROGER STÉPHANE | PORTRAIT DE | L'AVENTURIER | T.E. LAWRENCE | MALRAUX VON SALOMON | précédé d'une étude de | JEAN-PAUL SARTRE | [pub.device] | SAGITTAIRE

Collation   18.8 × 12 cm: [1]⁸ 2–18⁸ [19]⁴, 148 leaves, pp.[1–9], 10–290, [6].

Contents   Pp.[1–2] blank, [3] bastard title, [4] list of author's works, [5] title page, [6] issue, copyright statements, [7] dedication, [8] two quotes, [9]–285 text, 287–290 bibliography, [1–2] contents, [3–4] blank, [5] printer's colophon, [6] blank.

RT   On both verso and recto *PORTRAIT DE L'AVENTURIER.*

Typography and paper $ 1 signed 3.

Text 20 lines, 7.5 (8.1) × 8 cm.

Paper White, wove, unwatermarked, all edges trimmed, sheets bulk 1.5 cm.

Binding Tan paper. On front cover: [within red rule frame] ROGER STÉPHANE | [in red] PORTRAIT DE | [in red] L'AVENTURIER | T.E. LAWRENCE | MALRAUX, VON SALOMON | précédé d'une étude de | JEAN-PAUL SARTRE | [publisher's device in red] SAGITTAIRE. On spine: ROGER | STÉPHANE | [title all in red] PORTRAIT | DE | L'AVEN- | TURIER | SAGITTAIRE. On back cover: [within red rule frame] [pub. ads] | [below rule at bottom] H[in diamond] 450Frs.

Published at 450 Francs.

Notes Roger Stéphane was the pseudonym of Roger Worms.

Copies AC, Cal, H, LC.

E172 ROGER STÉPHANE, Portrait de L'aventurier, Grasset, 1965

Second French Edition

ROGER STÉPHANE | PORTRAIT DE | L'AVENTURIER | *T.E. LAWRENCE* | *MALRAUX-VON SALOMON* | précédé d'une étude de | JEAN-PAUL SARTRE | BERNARD GRASSET ÉDITEUR | 61 RUE DES SAINTS-PÈRES, VI | PARIS

Collation 18.5 × 12.7 cm: [1] –8^{16}, 9^6, 134 leaves, pp.[1–11], 12–264, [4].

Contents Pp.[1–2] blank, [3] bastard title, [4] quote from *Seven Pillars*, [5] title page, [6] issue, copyright statements, [7] dedication, [8] blank, [9] quote from *Seven Pillars*, [10] blank, [11] –30 preface, [31] –255 text, [256] blank, [257] –261 bibliography, [262] blank, [263] –264 contents, [265] printer's colophon, [266–268] blank.

RT On verso *PORTRAIT DE L'AVENTURIER*. On recto [according to chapter].

Typography and paper $ 1 signed 8, (9,9*).

Text 20 lines, 8.3 (8.7) × 8 cm.

Paper White, wove, unwatermarked, all edges trimmed, sheets bulk 1.9 cm.

Binding Pictorial paper covers. On front cover: [in white] T.E. LAWRENCE VON SALOMON ANDRÉ MALRAUX | *Roger Stéphane* | PORTRAIT DE L'AVENTURIER | *Grasset*. On spine: *Roger* | *Stéphane* | [running up] PORTRAIT DE L'AVENTURIER | [across at foot] *Grasset*. On back cover: H[in diamond] | 15,00F | IICO[in oval] Grou-Radenez Paris (14,59 F h.t.).

Published at 15 Francs.

Notes 26 special copies were printed: 1–12 Alfa Numérotes, 13–26 Hors Commerce HC 1–HC XIV. Roger Stéphane was the pseudonym of Roger Worms.

Copies Cal, LC.

E173 ROGER STÉPHANE, Portrait de L'Aventurier Bourgois, 1965

Third French Edition

PORTRAIT DE | L'AVENTURIER | T.E. LAWRENCE | MALRAUX-VON SALOMON | PAR | ROGER STÉPHANE | Précédé d'une étude de | JEAN-PAUL SARTRE | [within rectangular box] 10 18 | CHRISTIAN BOURGOIS | DOMINIQUE DE ROUX

Collation 17.7 × 10.8 cm: [1–10]¹⁶, 160 leaves, pp.[1–9], 10–311, [312–320].

Contents Pp.[1] UNION GÉNÉRALE D'ÉDITIONS, [2] blank, [3] title page, [4] copyright statement, [5] dedication, [6] blank, [7] quotes, [8] blank, [9]–33 preface by Sartre (1950), [34] blank, [35]–311 text, [312] blank, [313]–316 bibliography, [317] contents, [318] blank, [319] printer's colophon, [320] blank.

RT On both recto and verso *PORTRAIT DE L'AVENTURIER*.

Text 20 lines, 9.2 (9.5) × 7.7 cm.

Paper White, wove, unwatermarked, all edges trimmed, sheets bulk 2 cm.

Binding Pictorial paper covers. On front cover: [in white] Roger Stéphane | Portrait de | l'aventurier | [in yellow] 10 18. On spine: [running up,in yellow] 10 18. [in black] Roger Stéphane: Portrait de l'adventurier | [across at top] 669. On back cover: [blurb taken from Sartre preface].

Notes Roger Stéphane was the pseudonym of Roger Worms.

Copies Cal.

E174 ROGER STÉPHANE, Portrait de l'aventurier, Bourgois, 1972

Third French Edition

PORTRAIT DE | L'AVENTURIER | T.E. LAWRENCE | MALRAUX-VON SALOMON | PAR | ROGER STÉPHANE | précédé d'une étude de | JEAN-PAUL SARTRE | [series device] | CHRISTIAN BOURGOIS | DOMINIQUE DE ROUX

Collation 17.7 × 10.7 cm: guillotined sheets glued to covers, 160 leaves, pp.[1–9], 10–316, [1–4].

Contents Pp.[1] publisher's address, [2] blank, [3] title page, [4] copyright statement, [5] dedication, [6] blank, [7] quotes from Montaigne and Lawrence, [8] blank, [9]–33 preface by Sartre, [34] blank, [35]–311 text, [312] blank, [313]–316 index, [1] contents, [2] blank, [3] printer's colophon, [4] blank.

RT On both verso and recto *PORTRAIT DE L'AVENTURIER*.

Text 20 lines, 9 (9.5) × 7.5 cm.

Paper White, wove, unwatermarked, all edges trimmed, sheets bulk 2.5 cm.

Binding Pictorial paper covers. On front cover: [all in white] Roger Stéphane | [double yellow bars] | Portrait de | l'aventurier | [photos of Malraux and Lawrence divided by yellow vertical bar] | [series device]. On spine: 669 | [running up] [three squares] [series device] Roger Stéphane : Portrait de l'aventurier. On back cover: [extract from Sartre preface, cover design credit, photo credits, series device].

Note Roger Stéphane was the pseudonym of Roger Worms.

Copies UCSB.

E175   ROGER STÉPHANE, Retrato del Aventurero, Ediciones de la Flor, 1968

First Argentine Edition

RETRATO DEL | AVENTURERO | *Roger Stéphane* | *Con un estudio preliminar de* | *Jean-Paul Sartre.* | EDICIONES DE LA FLOR [pub. device]

Collation   19.3 × 12 cm: guillotined sheets glued to covers, 95 leaves, pp.[1–10], 11–185, [1–5].

Contents   Pp.[1–2] blank, [3] bastard title, [4] blank, [5] title page, [6] original title, translator's, designer's credits, copyright statement, [7] dedication, [8] blank, [9] quote, [10] blank, 11–24 Sartre foreword, 25–182 text, 183–185 bibliography, [1] blank, [2] section title, [3] blank, [4] contents, [5] printer's colophon.

Text   20 lines, 8.5 × 9 cm.

Paper   White, wove, unwatermarked, all edges trimmed, sheets bulk 1.2 cm.

Binding Pictorial paper covers. On front cover: Roger Stéphane | [in blue] RETRATO DEL | AVENTURERO | [pub. device] Ediciones de la Flor. On back: [all in blue, blurb].

Note Roger Stéphane was the pseudonym of Roger Worms.

Copies BPL.

E176   AZIZ HUDAI AKDEMIR, Türk Düşmani, Casus Lâvrens ve Benzerleri, Yayinevi, 1950

First Turkish Edition

TÜRK DÜŞMANI | Casus Lâvrens | VE | BENZERLERI | EMEKLI ALBAY | AZIZ HUDAI AKADEMIR | Millî Mücadelede Atatürk'ün İstanbul İstihbarat Şefi | Bu eserini, Millî Mücadelenin sayili kahramanlarinda Kara Salih | Sakarya'ya ithaf ediyorum. | A.H. | [pub. device] | Muallin Fuad Gücüyener Yayinevi | Büyük Postahane Karşisinda Meydanck Haninda | P.K. 210 – İstanbul

Collation   19.5 × 13.5 cm: [1]–4⁸, 32 leaves, pp.[1–2], 3–57, [1–7].

Contents Pp.[1] title page, [2] quote, publisher's statement, 3–57 text, [1] publisher's ad, [2] list of titles in series, [3–7] ads.

Plates One b/w preceding p.[1].

Typography and paper $ 1 signed Casus Lâvrens ve Benzerleri F.2.

Text 20 lines, 9.1 × 10.8 cm.

Pap?r White, wove, unwatermarked, all edges trimmed, sheets bulk 4 mm.

Binding White paper covers. On front cover: [in red] Türk Düşmani | [in red] Casus | [in blue] Lavrens | [in red] VE | [in red] *BENZERLERI* | [in blue, photo of Lawrence] | [in red] Casus Lavrens Arab Kiyafetinde.

Published at March 1950.

Copies LC.

1951

E177 VICTORIA OCAMPO, Lawrence de Arabia Y Otros Ensayos, Aquilar, 1951

First Spanish Edition

VICTORIA OCAMPO | LAWRENCE | DE ARABIA | Y | OTROS ENSAYOS | [pub. device] | AGUILAR, S.A. DE EDICIONES | MADRID * 1951

Collation 11.8 × 8 cm: [1]¹⁶ 2–17¹⁶ 18⁶, 278 leaves, pp.[1–12], 13–550, [1–6].

Contents Pp.[1–4] blank, [5] title page, [6] blank, [7] half-title, [8] copyright statement, printer's credit, [9] section title, [10] blank, [11]–23 prologue ending with a list of author's works, [24] blank, [25] section title, [26] blank, [27]–30 'testimonios', [31]–546 text of all essays, [547] section title, [548] blank, [549] contents, [1–6] blank.

RT On verso VICTORIA OCAMPO. On recto [according to essay].

Plates Sepia photo of author as frontispiece, following p.[6].

Typography and paper $ 1 signed OCAMPO. *2.

Text 20 lines, 5.1 (5.4) × 6.3 cm.

Paper White, thin, wove, unwatermarked, all edges trimmed, sheets bulk 1 cm.

Binding Dark brown 243 v.d. Br leather. On front cover: [blind stamped rule devices] | [blind stamped pub. device]. On spine: [in silver, 8 rules] | [decorative rule device] | Victoria | Ocampo | LAWRENCE | DE ARABIA Y | OTROS ENSAYOS | [decorative rule device] | [publisher's device flanked by parallel rules]. On back cover: [blind stamped as front cover]. Red and white head and tail bands. Red silk place marker. T.e. pale pink. Brown end papers with multiple decorative cuts.

Notes   338171 T.E. (Lawrence de Arabia), pp.[35]–128; 18 other essays
follow, none related to Lawrence.
Copies   CM, LC.

1952

E178   JONATHAN CAPE LIMITED, Prospectus for all of their T.E. Lawrence titles, [1952?]

Publisher's prospectus

[In maroon] T.E. | [maroon] LAWRENCE | [quotes from Wavell and
Churchill] | [crossed sword design in maroon]
Collation   17.9 × 11.5 cm: two-fold leaflet, pp.[1–6].
Contents   Pp.[1] title page, [2] blurb for *Seven Pillars of Wisdom*, [3] blurb for
T.E. Lawrence by His Friends, [4] blurb for *Selected Letters of T.E. Lawrence*, [5]
blurbs for Liddell Hart *'T.E. Lawrence' in Arabia and After*, and Garnett *The
Essential T.E. Lawrence*, [6] order form.
Paper   White, wove, unwatermarked, all edges trimmed.
Published at   Free advertising flyer.
Copies   AC, Cal.

E179   IMPERIAL WAR MUSEUM, Thomas Edward Lawrence, 1952

First Compilation

Thomas Edward Lawrence: A List of References by and on Colonel T.E.
Lawrence in the Imperial War Museum Library, London, IWM, 1952
Collation   33 × 21 cm: 2 leaves, pp.[1–4].
Paper   White, wove, unwatermarked, all edges trimmed, stapled in upper
left corner.
Published at   Free handout.
Copies   BL.

E180   IMPERIAL WAR MUSEUM, Colonel Lawrence Collection, 1964

Second Compilation

[All underlined] COLONEL LAWRENCE COLLECTION
Collation   33 × 21 cm: 10 leaves, unpaged.
Published at   Free flyer.
Notes   Lists photographs for sale by the IWM taken by Lawrence during

the Arabian campaign. Another state: four-page list on same size paper designated R.343/69.

Copies AC.

E181 IMPERIAL WAR MUSEUM,
Thomas Edward Lawrence, 1964

Second Compilation

IMPERIAL WAR MUSEUM LIBRARY | THOMAS EDWARD LAWRENCE. | A list of references by and on | Colonel T.E. Lawrence. | In the Imperial War Museum Library.

Collation 32.5 × 20.5 cm: 2 leaves, pp.1–3, [4].

Contents Pp.1 title, text begins, 2–3 text continued, 4 blank.

Typography and paper Typed sheets.

Paper White, wove, unwatermarked, all edges trimmed.

Binding Stapled upper left corner.

Published at Free flyer.

Copies AC, Cal.

E182 IMPERIAL WAR MUSEUM,
Colonel T.E. Lawrence, 1966

Third Compilation

Bibliography BIO. 51 | IMPERIAL WAR MUSEUM | COLONEL T.E. LAWRENCE | A SHORT LIST OF REFERENCES | ARRANGEMENT |

Collation 33 × 20.5 cm: 5 leaves, prp.1–2, pp.[1], 2–7, [1].

Contents Prp.[1] title contents and notes, [2] blank, pp.[1]–7 text, [1] blank.

Text Typed sheets.

Paper White, wove, unwatermarked, all edges trimmed, sheets bulk 1 mm.

Binding Stapled upper left corner.

Published at Free flyer.

Notes Cyclostyled list of IWM holdings. Lower right corner prp.[1] VR/RS/9/1966.

Copies AC, Cal, BL.

E183   IMPERIAL WAR MUSEUM,
Colonel T.E. Lawrence, 1975

[Rule] | Booklist No. 1076A: Colonel T.E. Lawrence – Addenda | London, Imperial War Museum, 1975

Collation   30 × 21 cm: 1 leaf, pp.1–2.

Text   Typed sheets.

Paper   White, wove, unwatermarked, all edges trimmed.

Published at   Free flyer.

Notes   Supplement to 1966 list.

Copies   AC.

E184   IMPERIAL WAR MUSEUM,
Thomas Edward Lawrence, 1964

IMPERIAL WAR MUSEUM. | BOOK LIST No. 1076 | T.E. LAWRENCE – NEWSCUTTINGS

Collation   32.5 × 20.5 cm: 1 leaf.

Text   Typed sheets.

Published at   Free flyer.

Notes   20 May 1965.

Copies   AC.

E185   IMPERIAL WAR MUSEUM,
Thomas Edward Lawrence, 1964

IMPERIAL WAR MUSEUM THOMAS EDWARD LAWRENCE. | A list of references by and on | Colonel T.E. Lawrence. | In the Imperial War Museum Library. | (booklist no. 1076)

Collation   32.5 × 20.5 cm: 2 leaves, pp.1–3, [4].

Contents   Pp.1 title, text begins, 2–3 text continued, 4 blank.

Text   Typed sheets.

Paper   White, wove, unwatermarked, all edges trimmed.

Binding   Stapled in upper left corner.

Published at   Free flyer.

Copies   AC.

E186   IMPERIAL WAR MUSEUM, T.E. Lawrence, 1966

IMPERIAL WAR MUSEUM | BOOKLIST NO.

1106. | T.E. LAWRENCE – ADDITIONS TO OUR CYCLOSTYLED BIBLIOGRAPHY | [22 titles] | All these items are in the Imperial War Museum except the | three marked with an asterisk.

Collation 30 × 21 cm: 3 leaves, [1] pp.1–2.

Text Typed sheets.

Published at Free flyer.

Copies AC.

E186a JAMES L. BUNNELL, T.E. Lawrence and Anglo-Arab Diplomacy, 1914–1922, Vanderbilt University

First American Edition

T.E. LAWRENCE AND ANGLO-ARAB | DIPLOMACY, 1919–1922 | By | James L. Bunnell | A Thesis | Submitted to the Faculty of the Graduate | School of Vanderbilt University in | partial Fulfillment of the require- | ments for the degree of Master | of Arts. | June, 1952 | Approved by Date |

Collation 22.5 × 28 cm: 125 leaves, pp.[2], 1–123.

Contents Prp.[1] title page, [2] contents, pp.[1]–5 preface, 6–115 text, 116 map, [117]–120 appendix, [118]–123 bibliography.

Typography and text Photocopy of typed original.

Paper White, wove, unwatermarked, all edges trimmed, sheets bulk 2 cm.

Binding Black cloth. On spine: [gilt] Bunnell.

Copies AC.

1953

E187 JOHN THOMAS, The True Book About Lawrence of Arabia, Muller, 1953

First English Edition

THE TRUE BOOK ABOUT | LAWRENCE OF ARABIA | by | JOHN THOMAS | *Illustrated by* | G.H. CHANNING | FREDERICK MULLER LTD. | LONDON

Collation 18.5 × 12.1 cm: [1]^{16} 2–4^{16} 5^8, 72 leaves, pp.[1–6], 1–136, [2].

Contents Prp.[1] bastard title, [2] frontis., [3] title page, [4] issue statement, printer's credit, [5] contents, [6] blank, pp.1–136 text, [1–2] blank.

RT On verso TRUE BOOK ABOUT LAWRENCE OF ARABIA. On recto [according to chapter].

Typography and paper $ 1 signed 2.

Text 20 lines, 9.2 (9.3) × 9.5 cm.

Paper   White, wove, unwatermarked, all edges trimmed, sheets bulk 1.5 cm.

Binding   Brown cloth 54 br O. On spine: [gold] *The* | *True* | *Book about* | LAWRENCE | of | ARABIA | JOHN | THOMAS | FREDERICK | MULLER. T.e. brown. Spine height 19 cm.

Notes   Another issue, as above, with spine lettering in what appears to be aluminium (silver?), reprinted 1954, 1955, 1956, 1957, 1959, 1962. The 1962 reprint has fo!.¸wing differences: TRUE BOOKS | *Editor:* Vernon Knowles | [long rule] | THE TRUE BOOK ABOUT | LAWRENCE OF ARABIA | *by* | JOHN THOMAS | *Illustrated by* | G.H. CHANNING | FREDERICK MULLER LIMITED | LONDON; [Collation]: 18.5 × 12 cm: [1]⁸ 2–9⁸, 72 leaves, pp.[1–6], 1–136, [2]; [Binding]: cloth simulated paper covered boards, light brown 76 l. y Br. T.e. not stained. Has only MULLER at foot instead of FREDERICK | MULLER [spine height is 1 mm higher than 1953 issue].

Copies   AC, Cal.

E188   JOHN THOMAS, The True Story of Lawrence of Arabia, Children's Press, 1964

First American Edition

The true story of | LAWRENCE | [in brown] OF ARABIA | BY JOHN THOMAS | CHILDREN'S PRESS, CHICAGO

Collation   21.6 × 15 cm: [1–9]⁸, 72 leaves, pp.[1–14], 15–141, [3].

Contents   Pp.[1] blank, [2–3] double page spread illus, [4] blank, [5] bastard title, [6] illustrations, [7] title page, [8] issue, copyright statements, [9] contents, [10] blank, [11] foreword, [12] blank, [13] half-title, [14] section title, 15–137 text, 138 credits, 139 brief biographies of author, artist, 140–141 index, [1–2] map, [3] blank.

Text   20 lines, 12 × 11 cm.

Paper   White, wove, unwatermarked, all edges trimmed, sheets bulk 1.2 cm.

Binding   Pictorial cloth. On front cover: [in brown] THE TRUE STORY OF | [in white] LAWRENCE OF ARABIA. On spine: [running down] [in white] LAWRENCE OF ARABIA | [across] CHILDREN'S | PRESS.

Published at $3.50.

Notes   No fly leaves; 2nd printing, 1965, as above.

Copies   AC, Cal, LC.

E189   ROGER STÉPHANE, Théâtre de Destin, La Table Ronde, 1953

First French Edition

ROGER STÉPHANE | THÉÂTRE | DE | DESTIN | Pièces | [publisher's device] | LA TABLE RONDE | *8, RUE GARANCIÈRE, 6e* | PARIS

Collation   19 × 12 cm: π⁴ 1–18⁸ 1¹, 149 leaves, pp.[8], i–vi, 1–282, [2].

Contents   Prp.[1–2] blank, [3] bastard title, [4] list of author's works, [5] title page, [6] copyright notice, [7] dedication, [8] blank, prp.i–vi preface, pp.[1] section title, 'Le Destin Le Jour', 2–78 text, [79] section title, 'Le Destin de Rossel', 80–175 text, [176] blank, 177 section title, 'Lawrence, Moine laic, 178–282 text, [1] printer's colophon, [2] blank.

RT   On both verso and recto [according to title of play].

Typography and paper $ 1 signed 3.

Text   20 lines, 8.2 (8.9) × 8.2 cm.

Paper   White, wove, unwatermarked, untrimmed, sheets bulk 2 cm.

Binding   White paper wrappers. On front cover: [thick rule] | [in red] ROGER STÉPHANE | [red rule] | THÉÂTRE | DE | DESTIN | [thick red rule] | [red publisher's device] | LA TABLE RONDE | [in red] PARIS. On spine: ROGER STÉPHANE | [thick red rule] | THÉÂTRE | DE | DESTIN | [red publisher's device] | [thick red rule] | LA TABLE | RONDE. On back cover: [list of publications].

Published at   525 Francs.

Notes   Stéphane was the pseudonym of Roger Worms.

Copies   AC, Cal.

1954

E190   RICHARD ALDINGTON, Lawrence L'Imposteur, Amiot-Dumont, 1954

First French Edition

"TOUT LA VILLE EN PARLE" | [double rule] | RICHARD ALDINGTON | LAWRENCE | L'IMPOSTEUR | *T.E. Lawrence,* | *"THE LEGEND AND THE MAN"* | traduit de l'Anglais par | *Gilberte MARCHEGAY, Jacques RAMBAUD, Jean ROSENTHAL* | *AMIOT-DUMONT* | *Paris*

Collation   21.4 × 15.8 cm: [1]¹⁶ 2–10¹⁶ 11⁶, 166 leaves, pp.[1–7], 8–330, [2].

Contents   Pp.[1–2] blank, [3] bastard title, [4] cover photo credit, [5] title page, [6] copyright statement, [7]–10 letter by author, [11] section title, [12] blank, [13]–325 text, [326] blank, [327]–330 bibliography, [1] printer's colophon, [2] blank.

RT   On both verso and recto: *LAWRENCE L'IMPOSTEUR.*

Typography and paper $ 1 signed 2.

Text   20 lines, 7.5 × 7.9 cm.

Paper   White, wove, unwatermarked, untrimmed, sheets bulk 1.9 cm.

Binding   Yellow paper covers 89 p.Y. on front cover: *toute la ville* [cut] *en* [cut] | *parle* | [within white oval] RICHARD ALDINGTON | LAWRENCE | L'IMPOSTEUR | [within white oval] AMIOT [star] DUMONT [photo of Lawrence along right side]. On spine: RICHARD ALDINGTON |

LAWRENCE | L'IMPOSTEUR | *Toute la ville* | *en parle* | AMIOT | DUMONT | [yellow bar]. On back cover: [list of pub. titles in series].

Copies AC, Cal.

E191 RICHARD ALDINGTON, Lawrence of Arabia, Collins, 1955

Uncorrected proof copy of First English Edition

LAWRENCE | OF | ARABIA | A Biographical Enquiry | by | RICHARD ALDINGTON | Untruthful! My nephew Algernon? | Impossible! He is an Oxonian. | OSCAR WILDE | COLLINS | ST. JAMES'S PLACE, LONDON | 1955

Collation 21 × 14 cm: [A]⁸ B–2E ⁸, 224 leaves, pp.[1–10], 11–448.

Contents Pp.[1] bastard title, [2] blank, [3] title page, [4] printer's credit, [5] dedication, [6] blank, [7–8] contents, [9] illustrations, [10] list of maps, 11–14 introductory letter by author, [15] section title, [16] blank, 17–388 text, 389–391 maps, 392–420 list of sources, 421–425 bibliography, 426 acknowledgments, 427–448 index.

RT On verso *Lawrence of Arabia* [Part 2 [etc.]. On recto CHAP. 2 [etc.] *A Biographical Enquiry*.

Plates Ten photographs, on coated paper, following pp.2, 48, 80, 96, 128, 144, 256, 268, 272, 384.

Typography and paper $ 1 signed L.O.A. C.

Text 20 lines, 9.7 (9.9) × 11 cm.

Paper White, wove, unwatermarked, all edges trimmed, sheets bulk 2.7 cm.

Binding Brown paper covers 76 l.y Br.

Copies Cal.

E192 RICHARD ALDINGTON, Lawrence of Arabia, Collins, 1955

First English Edition

LAWRENCE | OF | ARABIA | A Biographical Enquiry | by | RICHARD ALDINGTON | Untruthful! My Nephew Algernon? | Impossible! He is an Oxonian. | OSCAR WILDE | COLLINS |ST. JAMES'S PLACE, LONDON | 1955

Collation 21 × 14 cm: [A]⁸ B–2E⁸, 224 leaves, pp.[1–10], 11–448.

Contents Pp.[1] bastard title, [2] blank, [3] title page, [4] printer's credit, [5] dedication, [6] blank, [7–8] contents, [9] illustrations, [10] list of maps, 11–14 introductory letter by author, [15] section title, [16] blank, 17–388 text, 389–391 maps, 392–420 list of sources, 421–425 bibliography, 426 acknowledgments, 427–448 index.

RT On verso *Lawrence of Arabia* [Part 2 [etc.]. On recto CHAP. 2 [etc.] *A Biographical Enquiry.*

Plates Ten photographs, on coated paper, following pp.2, 48, 80, 96, 128, 144, 256, 268, 272, 384.

Typography and paper $ 1 signed L.O.A. C.

Text 20 lines, 9.7 (9.9) × 11 cm.

Paper White, wove, unwatermarked, all edges trimmed, sheets bulk 2.7 cm.

Binding Black cloth. On spine: [gilt] *LAWRENCE | OF | ARABIA | * |* RICHARD | ALDINGTON | COLLINS.

Published at 25s, January 1955.

Notes On page 332 an errata slip is tipped in. In early issues this is a 12 × 2.4 cm slip whiter than sheets. Later copies of the first edition have a slip 7.7 × 4 cm on paper same as the sheets. In later issues sheets bulk 3 cm. A 2nd impression, January 1955, has issue statement added to verso of title page.

Copies AC, Cal, UT, Ho, LC.

E193   RICHARD ALDINGTON, Lawrence of Arabia, Collins, 1969

First English Edition (1969 reprint)

LAWRENCE | OF | ARABIA | A BIOGRAPHICAL ENQUIRY BY | *RICHARD ALDINGTON* | INTRODUCTION BY | *CHRISTOPHER SYKES* | *Untruthful! My nephew Algernon? | Impossible! He is an Oxonian.* | OSCAR WILDE | COLLINS | ST. JAMES'S PLACE, LONDON | 1969

Collation 21 × 13.7 cm: [A]⁸ B¹² C–2E⁸, 228 leaves, pp.[1–8], [1]–448.

Contents Prp.[1] bastard title, [2] blank, [3] title page, [4] dedication, issue and copyright statements, printer's credit, [5] illustrations, [6–8] maps, pp.[1] half-title, 2–10 introduction, 11–14 introductory letter, [15] section title, [16] blank, 17–390 text, [391] section title, 392–420 list of sources, 421–425 bibliography, 426 acknowledgments, 427–448 index.

RT On verso *Lawrence of Arabia.* On recto *A Biographical Enquiry.*

Typography and paper $ 1 signed L.O.A. C, L.O.A. B, L.O.A. B2.

Text 20 lines, 8.7 (8.8) × 10.9 cm.

Paper White, wove, unwatermarked, all edges trimmed, sheets bulk 2.8 cm.

Binding Black cloth. On spine: [gilt] *LAWRENCE | OF | ARABIA* | [star cut] | RICHARD | ALDINGTON | COLLINS [publisher's name at foot is in larger type than 1955 ed.).

Published at 42s.

Notes Reissued to coincide with publication of *The Secret Lives of Lawrence of Arabia* (E301). Contains new introduction by Christopher Sykes.

Copies AC, Cal, LC.

E194   RICHARD ALDINGTON, Lawrence of Arabia, Collins, 1955

Publisher's Prospectus

A Biographical Enquiry | [photo of T.E. Lawrence] | LAWRENCE OF ARABIA

Collation   21 × 13.4 cm: single-fold leaflet, pp.[1–4].

Contents   [1] title page, [2–3] blurb running to both pages. At bottom of second page, order form, [4] 'COLLINS 25s'.

Paper   White, wove, unwatermarked, all edges trimmed.

Published at   Free advertising flyer.

Copies   AC.

E195   RICHARD ALDINGTON, Lawrence of Arabia, Four Square, 1957

Second English Edition

LAWRENCE OF ARABIA | RICHARD ALDINGTON | Untruthful! My nephew Algernon? |Impossible! He is an Oxonian. | OSCAR WILDE | A FOUR [pub. device] SQUARE BOOK

Collation   17.8 × 11.3 cm: A–N^{16}, 208 leaves, pp.[1–7], 8–416.

Contents   Pp.[1] blurb, [2] issue statement, printer's credit, [3] title page, [4] dedication, [5–7] maps, 8–11 introduction, [12] blank, 13–384 text, 385–413 sources, 414–416 bibliography.

Typography and paper $ 1 signed A.

Text   20 lines, 7 × 9.3 cm.

Paper   White, wove, unwatermarked, all edges trimmed, sheets bulk 2.5 cm.

Binding   Pictorial paper covers. On front cover: [upper right corner, running up] FOUR [publisher's device] SQUARE BOOKS | [running across] LAWRENCE OF | ARABIA | RICHARD ALDINGTON | Was Lawrence quite the genius the world believes? | [publisher's device] A FOUR SQUARE BIOGRAPHY 3/6. On spine: [running down] A FOUR SQUARE [publisher's device] BOOK [within black rectangle, in white] LAWRENCE OF ARABIA | RICHARD | ALDINGTON [publisher's device]. On back cover: [front cover repeated, in white].

Published at   3s 6d.

Notes   This edition has added notes in the form of footnotes and a postscript; 2nd impression, May 1958; 3rd impression, 1960, as above with following differences: [Binding]: pictorial paper covers. On front cover: [upper right corner] [publisher's device] | [upper left corner] 3'6 | [in white] ? LAWRENCE | ROSS | HERO | HUMBUG | [ochre] LAWRENCE | OF | ARABIA | [brown] RICHARD ALDINGTON | MORTELMANS. On spine:

[running down] FOUR SQUARE [white] LAWRENCE OF ARABIA |
RICHARD ALDINGTON | [across at bottom, in white] 3. On back cover:
[upper right corner, pub. device, 14-line blurb]. The 2nd impression sheets
bulk 2 cm.

Copies   AC, Cal.

E196   RICHARD ALDINGTON, Lawrence of Arabia, Four Square Books, 1957

Publisher's Prospectus

[Reproduction of 1957 paperback title page]

Collation   7.5 × 5 cm: pasteboard card printed on both sides.

Contents   [Recto] full colour reproduction of cover for paperback, [verso]
blurb.

Paper   Pasteboard, all edges trimmed.

Published at   Free advertising card.

Copies   AC.

E197   RICHARD ALDINGTON, Lawrence of Arabia, Penguin, 1971

Third English Edition

RICHARD ALDINGTON | [double rule] | Lawrence | of Arabia | [double
rule] | A BIOGRAPHICAL INQUIRY | INTRODUCTION BY
CHRISTOPHER SYKES | [two-line quote from Oscar Wilde] | [pub. device]|
PENGUIN BOOKS

Collation   17.7 × 10.8 cm: [A]^{16} B–Q^{16}, 256 leaves, pp.[1–12], 13–503, [504],
[1–8].

Contents   Pp.[1] biographical note on author, [2] blank, [3] title page, [4]
issue, copyright statement, printer's credits, [5] dedication [6] blank, [7]
contents, [8] blank, [9] illustrations, [10–12] maps, 13–23 introduction, [24]
blank, 25–29 introductory letter by author, [30] blank, [31] section title, [32]
blank, 33–443 text, [444] blank, 445–477 notes, [478] blank, 479–482
bibliography, 483 acknowledgements, [484] blank, 485–[504] index, [1]
blurb on publisher, [2] blank, [3–8] publisher's ads.

Plates   Four photographs, printed on both sides, following p.256.

Typography and paper $ 1 signed T-LOA-B.

Text   20 lines, 7.7 × 9 cm.

Paper   White,wove,unwatermarked,all edges trimmed,sheets bulk 2 cm.

Binding   Pictorial paper covers. On front cover: [in white] [publisher's
device] Pelican Biographies | Richard Aldington | [long rule] | Lawrence of
Arabia. On spine: [in blue green, running down] Richard Aldington

Lawrence of Arabia 140212639 | [across at foot, blue green] [publisher's device]. On back cover: [blurb and publisher's series note].

Published at   12s.

Copies   AC.

E198   RICHARD ALDINGTON, Lawrence of Arabia, Regnery, 1955

First American Edition

LAWRENCE | OF | ARABIA | *A Biographical Enquiry* | *by* | RICHARD ALDINGTON | *Untruthful! My nephew Algernon?* | *Impossible! He is an Oxonian.* | OSCAR WILDE | HENRY REGNERY COMPANY | CHICAGO 1955

Collation   21 × 14 cm: [1–14]¹⁶ [15]⁸, 232 leaves, pp.[1–8], 11–48, [2], 49–80, [2], 81–96, [2], 97–128, [2], 129–144, [2], 145–256, [2], 257–272, [2], 273–368, [2], 369–384, [2], 385–448.

Contents   Prp.[1] bastard title, [2] photo of Lawrence, [3] title page, [4] copyright, [5–6] contents, [7] illustrations, [8] maps, pp.11–14 introductory letter by author, [15] section title, [16] blank, 17–388 text, [389–391] maps, 392–420 sources, 421–425 bibliography, 426 acknowledgements, 427–448 index.

RT   On verso: *Lawrence of Arabia.* On recto *A Biographical Enquiry.*

Text   20 lines, 8.6 (8.8) × 11 cm.

Paper   White, wove, unwatermarked, all edges trimmed, sheets bulk 2.9 cm.

Binding   Blue cloth 182 m. Blue. On spine: [gilt] RICHARD ALDINGTON | [star cut] | LAWRENCE | OF | ARABIA | REGNERY.

Published at $5.00.

Notes   No errata slip as in English edition, corrections have been made in text. Illustrations present on unpaged leaves as shown in collation.

Copies   AC, Cal, UT.

E199   RICHARD ALDINGTON, Lawrence of Arabia, Greenwood, 1976

Second American Edition

LAWRENCE | OF | ARABIA | *A Biographical Enquiry* | *by* | *RICHARD ALDINGTON* | *Untruthful! My nephew Algernon?* | *Impossible! He is an Oxonian.* | OSCAR WILDE | [pub. device] | GREENWOOD PRESS, PUBLISHERS | WESTPORT, CONNECTICUT

Collation   21.2 × 13.5 cm: [1–29]¹⁶, 232 leaves, pp.[1–2], [1–10], 11–448, [2].

Contents Prp.[1] bastard title, [2] pp.[1] blank, [2] frontispiece, [3] title page, [4] CIP, issue statement, LC, ISBN numbers, [5] dedication, [6] errata note, [7–8] contents, [9] illustrations, [10] maps, 11–14 introduction, [15] section title, [16] blank, 17–388 text, [389–391] maps, 392–420 list of sources, 421–425 bibliography, 426 acknowledgements, 427–488 index, [1–2] blank.

RT On verso *Lawrence of Arabia.* On recto *A Biographical Enquiry.*

Plates Plates from original edition are on same sheets as text but not counted in pagination.

Typography and paper $ signed L.O.A. O [signatures of original issue].

Text 20 lines, 8.1 (8.4) × 10.4 cm.

Paper White, wove, unwatermarked, all edges trimmed, sheets bulk 2.4 cm.

Binding Blue cloth 177 brill. B.

Copies CSUS.

E200 RICHARD ALDINGTON, Lawrence de Arabia, Sudamericana, 1956

First Argentine Edition

RICHARD ALDINGTON | LAWRENCE | DE ARABIA | UNA INVESTIGACIÓN BIOGRÁFICA | *Traduction de* | GUILLERMO WHITELOW | EDITORIAL SUDAMERICANA | BUENOS AIRES

Collation 21 × 15.4 cm: [1–32]⁸, 256 leaves, pp.512.

Contents Pp.[1–2] blank, [3] bastard title, [4] BIOGRAFÍAS, [5] title page, [6] copyright statement, original title, [7] quote, [8] blank, [9] dedication, [10] blank, [11]–15 prefatory letter, [16] blank, [17]–468 text, [469]–473 bibliography, [474] blank, [475]–[508] notes, [509] contents, [510] printer's colophon, [511–512] blank.

RT On verso RICHARD ALDINGTON. On recto LAWRENCE DE ARABIA.

Text 20 lines, 8.3 (8.5) × 9.5 cm.

Paper White, wove, (simulated laid), unwatermarked, all edges trimmed, sheets bulk 2.5 cm.

Binding Pink cloth 27 deep y Pink. On front cover: [gilt, cut]. On spine: [gilt, double rule] | R. ALDINGTON | LAWRENCE DE ARABIA | EDITORIAL | SUD AMERICANA | [double rule]. Orange and white head and tail bands. Dark brown patterned end papers.

Copies Cal.

E201   RICHARD ALDINGTON, Der Fall T.E. Lawrence, Rinn, 1955

First German Edition

RICHARD ALDINGTON | Der Fall T.E. Lawrence | *Eine kritische Biographie* | [thick rule] | *Deutsch von Ursula zu Hohenlohe* | VERLAG HERMANN RINN

Collation   22 × 14 cm: [1–22]^8, 176 leaves, pp.[1–4], 5–349, [3].

Contents   Pp.[1] bastard title, [2] blank, [3] title page, [4] original title, copyright statement, printer's credit, 5–9 pub. preface, [10] blank, 11–341 text [342] blank, 343–345 maps, [346] blank, 347–349 related bibliography, [1] blank, [2] contents, [3] blank.

Text   20 lines, 8.2 × 10 cm.

Paper   White, wove, unwatermarked, all edges trimmed, sheets bulk 2.7 cm.

Binding   Red grey cloth 22 r Gray. On spine: [grey lettering within red triangle, running up] DER FALL T.E. LAWRENCE. T.e. grey. White head and tail bands.

Published at   DM 15.80.

Notes   Another state, as above, with following differences: [Collation]: 22 × 14.5 cm; [Binding]: Brown oatmeal cloth. On front cover: [in red] RICHARD ALDINGTON | DER FALL T.E. LAWRENCE. On spine: [in red] running up] ALDINGTON/DER FALL T.E. LAWRENCE. T.e. unstained. Red head and tail bands.

Copies   AC, Cal.

E202   RICHARD ALDINGTON, Lawrence de Arabia, Planeta, 1977

First Spanish Edition

Richard Aldington | LAWRENCE | DE ARABIA | UNA INVESTIGACIÓN BIOGRÁFICA | [pub. device]| Editorial Planeta | Barcelona | Editorial Sudamericana | Buenos-Aires

Collation   18.2 × 10 cm: guillotined sheets glued to sheets, pp.[1–8], 9–349, [350–352].

Contents   Pp.[1] series title, [2] blank, [3] title page, [4] original title, translator's credit, copyright statement, designer's, cover artist's, printer's credits, ISBN, [5] quote, [6] blank, [7] dedication, [8] blank, 9–12 letter to Alister Kershaw, 13–[346] text, 347–[350] bibliography, contents, [351–352] blank.

Text   20 lines, 9 × 8 cm.

Paper   White, wove, unwatermarked, all edges trimmed, sheets bulk 2.1 cm.

Binding   pictorial paper covers. On front cover: [in red] Richard |

Aldington | LAWRENCE | DE | ARABIA | [in white] Planeta | [colour photo]. On spine: [running up, all in white] Richard Aldington LAWRENCE DE ARABIA | [across] 13 | MAYOR | [publieher's device]. On back cover: [in white blurb].

Copies UCB, Cal.

Aldington: The Controversy, 1955–59

A far more balanced and reflective study than Aldington's, by Béraud-Villars, appeared in 1955. The pamphlet by Liddell Hart, *T.E. Lawrence, Aldington and the Truth* is an offprint of an article in *London Magazine* where a major skirmish of the public debate over the Aldington book took place. It refutes some of the main points of the book. Liddell Hart worked hard and long to distribute the text of it as widely as possible. There are at least three issues of the offprint.

A third biography, following quickly upon the heels of Aldington and Béraud-Villars was published in America, *The Desert and the Stars* by Flora Armitage. A postscript commenting on Aldington's work was added when the book was being prepared for press.

The French critic Cohen entered the Aldington fray somewhat tardily in 1956. His article in *Homme et Mondes* was issued as an offprint. His position is generally one of support for Aldington. This might be considered as one of the last salvoes of the Aldington affair, though echoes are found even now in the literature. A dramatic treatment of the Lawrence theme, *T.E. Lawrence, was written in German by zur Nedden.*

Another of the many boys' adventure books on the Arab campaigns is Kennett, Prince Dynamite.

1955

E204   JEAN BÉRAUD-VILLARS, Le Colonel Lawrence, ou, La recherche de l'absolu, Michel, 1955

First French Edition

JEAN BERAUD VILLARS | LE COLONEL | LAWRENCE | OU | LA RECHERCHE DE L'ABSOLU | ÉDITIONS | ALBIN MICHEL | 22, RUE HUYGHENS | PARIS

Collation 20 × 13 cm: [1]⁸, 2–26⁸, 208 leaves, pp.[1–9], 10–411, [5].

Contents Pp.[1–2] blank, [3] bastard title, [4] list of author's works, [5] title page, [6] issue,copyright statements, [7] dedication, [8] blank, [9]–10 preface, [11] section title, [12] blank, [13]–395 text, [396] blank, [397] bibliographic summary, [398] blank, [399]–402 works of Lawrence, [403] tables, [404] blank, [405] editor's note, [406] blank, [407] table of maps, [408] blank, [409]–411 contents, [1] blank, [2] printer's colophon, [3–5] blank.

RT On verso *LE COLONEL LAWRENCE*. On recto [in italics, according to chapter].

Typography and paper $ 1 signed 3.

Text 20 lines, 8.2 (8.5) × 9.5 cm.

Paper White, wove, unwatermarked, untrimmed, sheets bulk 2.3 cm.

Binding Pictorial paper covers. On front cover: [in brown] JEAN BERAUD VILLARS | [in white] LE COLONEL | [in white] LAWRENCE | [in white] *OU LA RECHERCHE DE L'ABSOLU* | ÉDITIONS | ALBIN | MICHEL. On spine: [triple brown rule] | [in brown] JEAN | [in brown] BERAUD VILLARS | LE | COLONEL | LAWRENCE | [triple brown rule] | ÉDITIONS | [in brown] ALBIN | [in brown] MICHEL | PARIS | [triple brown rule] | [underlined] 900 F. On back cover: [publiehr's ad.]

Published at 900 Francs.

Notes Another special issue, 35 copies on vélin de Lana, 10 copies numbered 1–10, as above, with the following differences: sheets bulk 3 cm; [Binding]: On spine: exemplaire | sur vélin de Lana. On back cover: [blank].

Copies AC, Cal, LC.

E205   JEAN BÉRAUD-VILLARS, T.E. Lawrence, Sidgwick and Jackson, 1958

First English Edtion

T.E. LAWRENCE | OR | THE SEARCH FOR THE ABSOLUTE | *By* | JEAN BERAUD VILLARS | TRANSLATED FROM THE FRENCH BY | PETER DAWNAY | SIDGWICK AND JACKSON LIMITED | LONDON

Collation 21.7 × 13.5 cm: [1]⁸ 2–22⁸ 23¹⁰, 186 leaves, pp.[i–ix], x–xii, [1–3], 4–358, [2].

Contents Prp.[i] bastard title, [ii] blank, [iii]title page, [iv] issue, copyright statements, printer's credit, [v] dedication, [vi] acknowledgments, [vii] pub. note, [viii] blank, [ix]–x contents, [xi]–xii preface, pp.[1] section title, [2] blank, [3]–353 text, [354] blank, [355]–358 bibliography, [1–2] blank.

RT On verso T.E. LAWRENCE. On recto [according to chapter].

Plates Frontispiece following p.ii.

Typography and paper $ 1 signed 2.

Text 20 leaves, 8.4 (8.4) × 10.1 cm.

Paper White, wove, unwatermarked, all edges trimmed, sheets bulk 2.2 cm.

Binding Peach cloth 71 m.OY. On spine: [running up] T.E. LAWRENCE VILLARS | [across at foot] *Sidgwick* | & | *Jackson.*

Published at 30s.

Notes Another issue, 1965, as above, with following differences: [Contents]: no acknowledgement on prp.[vi]; [Binding]: blue cloth 181 l.Blue. On spine: [in silver] T.E. LAWRENCE | Jean Beraud | Villars | Sidgwick | & Jackson. T.e. yellow. Dust wrapper different from first issue.

Copies AC, Cal, UT, LC.

E206 JEAN BÉRAUD-VILLARS, T.E. Lawrence, Duell, Sloan & Pearce, 1959

First American Edition

T.E. LAWRENCE | OR | THE SEARCH FOR THE ABSOLUTE | *By* | JEAN BERAUD VILLARS | TRANSLATED FROM THE FRENCH BY | PETER DAWNAY | DUELL, SLOAN & PEARCE, INC | NEW YORK

Collation 21.4 × 13.8 cm: [1]⁸ 2–22⁸ 23¹⁰, 186 leaves, pp.[i–ix], x–xii, [1–3], 4–358, [2].

Contents Prp.[i] bastard title, [ii] blank, [iii] title page, [iv] issue, copyright statements, printer's credit, [v] dedication, [vi] acknowledgments, [vii] pub. note, [viii] blank, [ix]–x contents, [xi]–xii preface, pp.[1] section title, [2] blank, [3]–353 text, [354] blank, [355]–358 bibliography, [1–2] blank.

RT On verso T.E.LAWRENCE. On recto [according to chapter].

Plates Frontispiece following p.[iv].

Typography and paper $ 1 signed 1,5 23+ 23*.

Text 20 lines, 8.4 (8.5) × 10.1 cm.

Paper White, wove, unwatermarked, all edges trimmed, sheets bulk 2.3 cm.

Binding Orange cloth 25 s.r.O. On spine: [running down] T.E. LAWRENCE by JEAN BERAUD VILLARS | [across at bottom] Duell, Sloan | and Pearce.

Copies AC, Cal, Ho, LC.

E207 JEAN BÉRAUD-VILLARS, Pulkownik Lawrence, Ministerstwa Obrony Narodowej, 1960

First Polish Edition

[Within frame of single rules with orange dot corners] *Jean* | [underlined] *Béraud-Villars* | [short bar] | PULKOWNIK | [printed over orange bar] LAWRENCE | [printed over orange bar] CZYLI | POSZUKIWANIE | [printed over orange bar] ABSOLUTU | PRZELOZYL | JERZY LISOWSKI | WYDAWNICTWO | MINISTERSTWA OBRONY NARODOWEJ | 1960

Collation 19 × 12 cm: [1]–27⁸, 216 leaves, pp.[1–2], 3–428, [2].

Contents Pp.[1] title page, [2] original title, translator's credit, copyright statement, various credits, 3–[6] preface, [7] quote, [8] blank, 9–[426] text, [427]–428 contents, [1–2] blank.

Typography and paper $ 1 signed 2 – Pulkownik Lawrence.

Text 20 lines, 9.2 × 9.5 cm.

Paper White, wove, unwatermarked, all edges trimmed, sheets bulk 2.8 cm.

Binding Only copy seen was rebound in library binding.

Copies DPL.

E208 JEAN BÉRAUD-VILLARS, El Coronel Lawrence, Sancla, 1964

First Spanish Edition

Jean Beraud Villars | EL CORONEL LAWRENCE | O | LA BUSQUEDA DE LO ABSOLUTO | SANCLA EDICIONES

Collation   21 × 15 cm: [1] –21⁸ 22⁴, 172 leaves, pp.[1–6], 7–342, [2].

Contents   Pp.[1–2] blank, [3] bastard title, [4] blank, [5] title page, [6] translator's credit, copyright statement, printer's credit, 7–8 prologue, 9–342 text, [1–2] contents.

Typography and paper $1 signed 22.

Text   20 lines, 8.4 × 10.5 cm.

Paper   White, thick, wove, unwatermarked, all edges trimmed, sheets bulk 2.5 cm.

Binding   Blue cloth 200 m. p Blue. On spine: [gilt] JEAN | BERAUD | VILLARS | [running up] EL CORONEL LAWRENCE | [across] LAWRENCE | DE | ARABIA. Blue and white head and tail bands.

Copies   BPL.

E209   BASIL HENRY LIDDELL HART, T.E. Lawrence, Aldington and the Truth, 1955

Reprint from *London Magazine*

B.H. LIDDELL HART | T.E. Lawrence, Aldington | and the Truth | [decorative rule] | REPRINTED FROM | THE LONDON MAGAZINE | APRIL 1955 | (With three additional passages inset, correcting | further points misrepresented in Aldington's book)

Collation   21.5 × 13.6 cm: [1]⁶, 6 leaves, pp.[1–2], 1–[10].

Contents   Prp.[1] title page, [2] blank, pp.1–[10] text, p.[10] printer's colophon at foot.

RT   On verso B.H. LIDDELL HART. On recto T.E. LAWRENCE ALDINGTON AND THE TRUTH.

Text   20 lines, 7 (7.2) × 10.1 cm.

Paper   Buff, wove, unwatermarked, all edges trimmed, sheets bulk 1 mm.

Binding   Two metal staples.

Published at   Distributed free.

Notes   Printed by Parrott & Son, Henley-on-Thames.

Copies   AC, Cal.

E210 BASIL HENRY LIDDELL HART, T.E. Lawrence, Aldington and the Truth, 1955

Reprint from *London Magazine*

LIDDELL HART | T.E. Lawrence, Aldington | and the Truth | [double rule] | REPRINTED FROM | THE LONDON MAGAZINE | APRIL 1955

Collation   21.5 × 14 cm: [1]⁶, 6 leaves, pp.[1–2], 1–9, [1].

Contents   Prp.[1] title page, [2] blank, pp.1–9 text, [1] printer's colophon.

RT   On verso B.H. LIDDELL HART. On recto T.E. LAWRENCE, ALDINGTON AND THE TRUTH.

Text   20 lines, 7.7 (7.9) × 10.1 cm.

Paper   Light buff, wove, unwatermarked, all edges trimmed, sheets bulk 1 mm.

Binding   Two metal staples.

Published at   Distributed free.

Notes   Printed by Shenval Press, London Hertford and Harlow.

Copies   AC, Cal, UT.

E211 BASIL HENRY LIDDELL HART, Aldington's "Lawrence", 1955

ALDINGTON'S 'LAWRENCE' | His Charges – and Treatment of Evidence

Collation   25.2 × 19.8 cm: Sheets printed on one side, pp.[1], 2–7[1].

Contents   Pp.[1] title and beginning of text, 2–7 text. [1] blank.

Text   Typed single-spaced, stapled in upper left corner.

Paper   White, wove, unwatermarked, all edges trimmed, sheets bulk 1 mm.

Published at   Distributed free.

Notes   Apparently duplicated by Liddell Hart and sent by him to interested parties.

Copies   AC.

E212 FLORA ARMITAGE, The Desert and The Stars, Holt, 1955

First American Edition

[Cut] | THE Desert | AND | The Stars | [cut] | A Biography of | Lawrence of Arabia | by Flora Armitage | [cut] | *Illustrated with Photographs* | Henry Holt and Company New York

Collation   21 × 14 cm: [1–10]^{16}, 160 leaves, pp.[i–vii], viii–ix, [10–15], 16–318, [2].

Contents   Prp.[i] bastard title, [ii] blank, [iii] title page, [iv] copyright, issue statements, LC number, printer's credit, [v] acknowledgement, [vi] blank, [vii]–ix preface, [10] blank, [11] contents, [12] blank, [13] half-title, [14] quote, [15]–308 text, [309]–312 bibliography, [313]–318 index, [1–2] blank.

RT   On verso only [according to chapter].

Plates   Two photographs on coated paper, printed on both sides, following p.160.

Text   20 lines, 9 (9.5) × 10.5 cm.

Paper   White, wove, unwatermarked,all edges trimmed, sheets bulk 2.8 cm.

Binding   Light brown cloth 57 l.Br, dark brown cloth spine 42 m. r Br. On spine: [gilt] Armitage | [running down] [cut] THE [swash] Desert | AND [swash] The Stars [cut] | [across at bottom] HOLT. Yellow and brown head and tail bands.

Published at $4.00.

Notes   A 2nd printing, September 1955, as above.

Copies   AC, Cal, Ho, LC.

E213   FLORA ARMITAGE, The Desert and the Stars, Faber and Faber, 1956

First English Edition

The Desert and the Stars | *A Portrait of T.E. Lawrence* | by | FLORA | ARMITAGE | [ornamental rule] | FABER AND FABER | 24 Russell Square | London

Collation   21.8 × 14 cm: [A]^8 B–X^8, 168 leaves, pp.[1–6], 7–334, [2].

Contents   Pp.[1–2] blank, [3] bastard title, [4] blank, [5] title page, [6] issue statement, printer's credit, 7 contents, [8] blank, 9 quote, [10] blank, 11 acknowledgments, [12] frontis. credit, 13–323 text, 324–327 bibliography, [328] blank, 329–334 index, [1–2] blank.

RT   Both verso and recto [according to chapter].

Plates   Frontispiece following p.4.

Typography and paper $ 1 signed B.

Text   20 lines, 9 (9.4) × 10.2 cm.

Paper   White, wove,unwatermarked,all edges trimmed, sheets bulk 2.2 cm.

Binding   Orange cloth 69 deep OY. On spine: [gilt, within gilt-edged blue oval] The | Desert | and | the | Stars | [below oval] Flora | Armitage | Faber and | Faber.

Notes   Another issue, as above, with following differences: [Binding]: Red paper cloth simulated covered boards 13 deep Red. On spine: [same, in black].

Copies   AC, Cal, UT.

E214 FLORA ARMITAGE, Lawrence D'Arabie, Payot, 1957

First French Edition

BIBLIOTHÈQUE HISTORIQUE | [rule] | F. ARMITAGE | [short rule] | LAWRENCE D'ARABIE | LE DÉSERT ET LES ÉTOILES | [short rule] | TRADUCTION DE S.M. GUILLEMIN | [rule] | [pub. device] | PAYOT, PARIS | 106, BOULEVARD SAINT-GERMAIN | [short rule] | 1957 | Tous droits de traduction, de reproduction et d'adaption réserves pour tous pays. | Flora Armitage: The Desert and the Stars, Faber and Faber, Publishers, London

Collation   22.7 × 14.2 cm: [1]⁸ 2–22⁸, 176 leaves, pp.[1–7], 8–339, [1–13].

Contents   Pp.[1–2] blank, [3] bastard, [4] list of works in series, [5] title page, [6] quote, [7]–329 text, 330–333 bibliography, 334–339 index, [1] blank, [2] contents, [3] blank, [4–11] pub. ads. [12–13] blank.

RT   Both verso and recto [according to chapter].

Typography and paper $ 1, signed F. ARMITAGE-LAWRENCE D'ARABIE 2.

Text   20 lines, 8.2 (8.4) × 10.5 cm.

Paper   White, wove, unwatermarked, untrimmed, sheets bulk 2.3 cm.

Binding   Tan paper covers 71 m.OY. On front cover [in brown within frame of single rules] BIBLIOTHÈQUE HISTORIQUE | [long rule] | F. ARMITAGE | [short rule] | LAWRENCE D'ARABIE | LE DÉSERT ET LES ÉTOILES | [line drawing by John within yellow triangle] | *TRADUCTION DE S.M. GUILLEMIN* | PAYOT, PARIS. On spine: [rule] F. ARMITAGE | [rule] | Lawrence d'Arabie | [rule] | 1,300 fr. | [rule] | [publisher's device] | [rule] | Payot | Paris | 1957 | [rule]. On back cover: [within frame of single rules, list of publisher's titles in series] | [below frame] IMP. GROU-RADEMEZ, 11, RUE DE SÈVRES, PARIS 6 – 93705 2-57.

Published at   1,300 francs.

Copies   AC, Cal.

E215 FLORA ARMITAGE, Lawrence d'Arabie, Payot, 1980

Second French Edition

Flora Armitage | Lawrence | D'Arabie | Le Désert et les Étoiles | Traduit de l'Anglais par S.M. Guillemin | Payot | 106, boulevard Saint Germain 75006 Paris

Collation   18 × 11 cm: [1]–11¹⁶, 176 leaves, pp.[1–7], 8–339, [340–342], [10].

Contents   Pp.[1] pub. device, [2] blank, [3] bastard title, [4] blank, [5] title page, [6] 9-line quote from Coleridge, issue, copyright statements, [7]–329 text, [330]–333 bibliography, [334]–339 index, [340] blank, [341] table of contents, [342] list of titles in series, [1–10] pub. ads.

RT   On both verso and recto [according to chapter].

Typography and paper $ 1 signed *Lawrence d'Arabie 2*.

Text   20 lines, 6.8 (7) × 8.7 cm.

Paper   White, wove, unwatermarked, all edges trimmed, sheets bulk 2.3 cm.

Binding   Pictorial paper covers. On front cover: [in blue] F. Armitage | [in blue] Lawrence | d'Arabie | [in white, short rule] | [in white] Payot | [in white, short rule]. On spine: [rule] | 11 | [rule] | [running up] | F. *Armitage* [title in blue] Lawrence d'Arabie | [at foot, across, publisher's device]. On back cover: [blurb, series title].

Copies   AC.

E216   FLORA ARMITAGE, Lawrence von Arabien, List, 1963

First German Edition

FLORA ARMITAGE | LAWRENCE | VON ARABIEN | *Die Wüste und die Sterne* | [pub. device] | LIST VERLAG MÜNCHEN

Collation   20.8 × 13 cm: [1–23]⁸ [24]¹⁰, 194 leaves, pp.[1–6], 7–387, [1].

Contents   Pp.[1] bastard title, [2] blank, [3] title page, [4] translator's credit, original title, frontis. caption, typographer's credit, copyright statement, printer's and binder's credits, [5] contents, [6] quote, 7–375 text, [376] blank, 377–382 notes, 383–387 name index, [1] publisher's ad.

Plates   Seven b/w plates, on coated paper, printed on one side only, following pp.2, 48, 64, 176, 192, 304, 320.

Text   20 lines, 8.2 × 9 cm.

Paper   White, wove, unwatermarked, all edges trimmed, sheets bulk 2.8 cm.

Binding   White cloth 92 y.White. On front cover: [within black rectangle superimposed on gold rectangle, in gilt] F. ARMITAGE | LAWRENCE | VON | ARABIEN | *Die Wüste* | *und die Sterne*. On spine: [continuation of gilt and black design repeating the author's name and title as on front cover] | [publisher's device below at foot]. White silk head and tail bands, white silk place marker.

Copies   AC, Cal.

1956

E217   GUSTAVE COHEN, Affaire Aldington contre Lawrence d'Arabie, 1956

Offprint of *Hommes et Mondes* **article**

[On front cover] GUSTAVE COHEN | AFFAIRE ALDINGTON | *contre* | LAWRENCE d'ARABIE | [three rules] | EXTRAIT DE | HOMMES ET MONDES | TOME XXIX – No 116 – MARS 1956

Collation   24.2 × 15.7 cm: [1]⁸ including covers, pp.[1–2], 1–14.

Contents   Prp.[1] title page, [2] blank, pp.1–11 text, [12–14] blank.

Text   20 lines, 8.3 (8.7) × 11.3 cm.

Paper   Wood pulp, white, wove, unwatermarked, all edges trimmed, sheets bulk 1 mm.

Binding   Brown 71 m OY paper heavier than sheets, stapled with two staples to sheets. On front cover: title page as above.

Copies   Cal.

1958

E218   OTTO C.A. zur NEDDEN, T.E. Lawrence, Staats, 1958

First German Edition

T.E. LAWRENCE | (LAWRENCE VON ARABIEN) | *Die Legende seines Lebens* | *für die Bühne gestaltet von Otto C.A. zur Nedden* | VERLAG FR. STAATS GMBH WUPPERTAL-BARMEN

Collation   19.5 × 13 cm: [1]⁸ 2–11⁸, 88 leaves, pp.[1–10], 11–173, [3].

Contents   Pp.[1] bastard title, [2] blank, [3] title page, [4] blank, [5] quote, [6] copyright statement, [7] list of characters, [8] scenes, [9] time symbols, [10] section title, 11–173 text, [1] biographical note, [2] copyright statement, [3] blank.

Typography and paper $ 1 signed 2 2 Lawrence, 2*.

Text   20 lines, 7.4 × 8.6 cm.

Paper   White, wove, unwatermarked, all edges trimmed, sheets bulk 1.4 cm.

Binding   Oatmeal cloth. On front cover: [in red] T.E. LAWRENCE *Bühnenlegende*. On spine: [in red, running up] *Otto C.A. zur Nedden* T.E. LAWRENCE. Red and white striped head and tail bands. Cream coloured end papers.

Copies   AC, Cal.

E219   JOHN KENNETT, Prince Dynamite, Blackie & Son, 1958

First English Edition

[Cut] | [decorative rule] | *Prince Dynamite* | THE STORY OF LAWRENCE OF ARABIA | [fancy rule] JOHN KENNETT | [outline rule] | *Illustrations by* | GILBERT DUNLOP | *Decoration by* | BIRO | [pub. device] | BLACKIE & SON LIMITED | [italics] London & Glasgow

Collation   18.4 × 14 cm: [1]⁸ 2–5⁸, 40 leaves, pp.[8], 1–69, [3].

Contents   Prp.[1] bastard title, [2] frontispiece drawing of TEL, [3] title page, [4] printer's credit, series list, [5] contents, [6] blank, [7] biographical data on TEL, [8] blank, pp.1–69 text, [1–3] blank.

RT   On verso PRINCE DYNAMITE. On recto [according to chapter].

Typography and paper $ 1 signed 2 (G674).

Text   20 lines, 8.9 (9.2) × 10.5 cm.

Paper   White, wove, unwatermarked, all edges trimmed, sheets bulk 1 mm.

Binding   Pictorial cloth. On front cover: [in white] Great Endeavour | *Prince Dynamite* | THE STORY OF LAWRENCE OF ARABIA | JOHN KENNETT. On spine: [running up] [series device in white] [in white] BLACKIE | *Prince Dynamite* | THE STORY OF LAWRENCE OF ARABIA | KENNETT. On back cover: Blackie | [in white] [publisher's device] [running up] Prince Dynamite.

Notes   Great Endeavour, a series of biographical readers for secondary schools.

Copies   AC, Cal.

The Film: Stimulation of the Legend, 1960–1962

The film *Lawrence of Arabia* by Columbia Films stimulated publication of a number of works on Lawrence. These range from two more juveniles – Bond, *The Lawrence of Arabia Story* (a biography), and Cadell, *The Young Lawrence of Arabia* (an attempt to go beyond the standard juvenile biography) – to the dramatic work by Terence Rattigan. Rattigan was selected in the mid-1950s to write the script for the film. When this fell through, he later turned it into the play *Ross*. When the Rattigan script was rejected, Robert Bolt was commissioned to produce another which was used in the film.

Souvenir publications continued with leaflets: *To the Dear Memory of T.E. Lawrence* and *Lawrence and All Souls*. The University of Texas Humanities Research Center published a catalogue of an exhibition they held in 1962 of their Lawrence materials. It contains much useful information and is now considered a collector's item. Souvenir programmes for the film itself were also issued in a variety of forms, most of them elaborate slick promotional pieces. There are a variety of states as well as a variety of ephemeral items associated with the film.

One of two biographies published almost on the eve of the release of the film is Nutting's *Lawrence of Arabia*. It has been widely translated.

A French work by Benoist-Méchin, *Lawrence d'Arabie*, accepts the belief that Lawrence harboured a strong hatred for the French. It contains a detailed 'chronology' and an extensive bibliography. Another, privately printed, French work was by Adam: *Les Echecs de T.E. Lawrence*.

A.W. Lawrence published a portion of the other side of the correspondence contained in *Letters of T.E. Lawrence* (1938). An offending sentence on the dust wrapper of the first impression was eliminated by substitution of a less offensive letter for the 2nd impression.

In addition to the two French items, a third non-English language work was Mousa: *Lawrence wa al Arab*. He made a strong argument for the Arab viewpoint on Lawrence. Published in Jordan in 1962 it was eventually translated In 1966.

Robert Payne's *Lawrence of Arabia* is the second of the biographies directly intended to ride the wave of the film's popularity. It was first published as a paperback in America and later in hardbound form in England.

1960

E221   GEOFFREY BOND, The Lawrence of Arabia Story, Arco, 1960

First English Edition

The | Lawrence of Arabia | Story | *by* | GEOFFREY BOND | LONDON | ARCO PUBLICATIONS | 1960

Collation   18.5 × 12.2 cm: [A]^{16} B–E^{16}, 80 leaves, pp.[1–8], 9–160.

Contents   Pp.[1] bastard title, [2] list of author's works, [3] title page, [4] issue, copyright statements, printer's credit, [5] contents, [6] blank, [7] half-title, [8] blank, 9–160 text.

RT   On verso 12 THE LAWRENCE OF ARABIA STORY. On recto [according to chapter].

Text   20 lines, 8.5 (8.6) × 8.8 cm.

Paper   White, wove, unwatermarked, all edges trimmed, sheets bulk 1.3 cm.

Binding   Black cloth simulated paper covered boards 114 Ol Black. On spine: [running down] The Lawrence of Arabia Story. *Geoffrey Bond* | [across at bottom] ARCO.

Published at   10s 6d.

Copies   AC, Cal.

E222   TERENCE RATTIGAN, Ross, Hamish Hamilton, 1960

First English Edition

ROSS | *A Dramatic Portrait* | BY | TERENCE RATTIGAN | [publisher's device] | HAMISH HAMILTON | LONDON

Collation   18.4 × 12.2 cm: [1]^{16} 2–3^{16} 4^{16} (–4^{16}), 63 leaves, pp.[1–8], 9–122, [2].

Contents   Pp.[1] bastard title, [2] list of author's works, [3] title page, [4] issue, copyright statements, acknowledgments, printer's credit, [5] dedication, [6] blank, [7] list of characters and setting, [8] list of cast of first production, 9–122 text, [1–2] blank.

RT   On verso ROSS. On recto ACT I [II].

Typography and paper $ 1 signed 3.

Text 20 lines, 7.7 (7.9) × 9.3 cm.

Paper White, wove, unwatermarked, all edges trimmed, sheets bulk 8 mm.

Binding Red cloth simulated paper covered boards 12 s. Red. On spine: [silver, running down] ROSS [star] *TERENCE RATTIGAN HAMISH HAMILTON.*

Published at 12s 6d.

Notes As above,2nd (November 1961) and 3rd impressions.

Copies AC, Cal, LC.

E223   TERENCE RATTIGAN, Ross, French, 1960

Second English Edition

ROSS | A play in Two Acts | by | TERENCE RATTIGAN | SAMUEL [publisher's device] FRENCH | LONDON

Collation 21.2 × 13.8 cm: [A] –B^{16} C^8 D^{16}, 56 leaves pp.[1–6], 1–103, [3].

Contents Prp.[1] title page, [2] copyright statement, printer's credit, [3] cast list, [4] synopsis of scenes, [5] blank, [6] copyright statement, pp.1–84 text, 85–93 furniture and property list, 94–97 lighting plot, 98–100 effects plot, 101–103 costumes plot, [1–3] blank.

RT On both verso and recto ROSS.

Plates Three b/w plates on coated paper, printed on both sides, following p.6.

Typography and paper $ 1 signed D.

Text 20 lines, 7.3 (7.5) × 10.1 cm.

Paper White, wove, unwatermarked, all edges trimmed, sheets bulk 5 mm.

Binding Blue paper wrappers 172 l.g B. glued to sheets. On front cover: [in maroon] ROSS | A play | TERENCE RATTIGAN | [within maroon rectangle running along spine in blue] [publisher's device] | French's | Acting | Edition. On spine: [maroon, running down] ROSS 6s net.

Published at 6s.

Copies AC, UT.

E224   TERENCE RATTIGAN, Ross, Random House, 1962

First American Edition

ROSS | A | Dramatic | Portrait | by | Terence | Rattigan | [publisher's device] | RANDOM HOUSE: | NEW YORK

Collation 20.6 × 13.9 cm: π^2, 1–6^{16}, 98 leaves, pp.[1–14], [1–2], 3–180, [2].

Contents   Prp.[1] bastard title, [2] blank, [3] list of author's works, [4–5] double-page title page, on verso photo, on recto photo portion and wording of title page, [6] issue, copyright statements, photo credits, [7] dedication, [8] blank, [9] acknowledgements, [10] blank, [11] cast of first American performance, [12] blank, [13] setting of play, [14] blank, pp.[1] section title, [2] blank, 3–180 text, [1–2] blank.

RT   On both verso and recto ROSS.

Plates   Two b/w photos on coated paper, tipped in following pp.68, 104.

Text   20 lines, 8.2 (8.3) × 8.6 cm.

Paper   White, wove, unwatermarked, top edges trimmed, sheets bulk 2 cm.

Binding   64 br Grey paper covered boards, black cloth spine. On front cover: [publisher's device blind stamped]. On spine: [gilt] TERENCE | RATTIGAN | [within oblong running top to bottom] ROSS | RANDOM | HOUSE. T.e. yellow.

Published at $3.50, April 1962.

Notes   Title page on coated paper, tipped in. Another issue: differs in following details: [Collation]: 21 × 14 cm: pp.[1–12], 180, [8]; [Contents]: prp.[1] bastard title, [2–3] title page, [4] copyright statement, photographer's credit, [5] dedication, [6] blank, [7] acknowledgments, [8] blank, [9] cast of characters, [10] blank, [11] setting, [12] blank, pp.[1] section title, [2] blank, 3–180 text, [1–8] blank; [Plates]: following pp.64, 112; [Paper]: sheets bulk 1.9 cm; [Binding]: Pink 27 deep y Pink paper covered boards, 33 br Pink cloth spine. On spine: [running down, gilt] TERENCE | RATTIGAN | [within black rectangle] ROSS | *RANDOM* | HOUSE. Pale yellow head and tail bands.

Copies   AC, Cal, UT, LC.

E225   TERENCE RATTIGAN, Ross, 1960

Programme for Première Performance

THEATRE ROYAL | HAYMARKET | [short rule] | *ROSS* | *A Dramatic Portrait* | *by* | TERENCE RATTIGAN | [short rule] | *Programme* | [short rule] | First Performance | Thursday, May 12th 1960

Collation   21.5 × 14 cm: [1]⁶, 6 leaves, pp.[1–12].

Contents   Pp.[1] title page, [2] ad, [3] picture of Alec Guinness as TEL, [4] biography of Guinness, [5] ad, [6] list of characters, [7] credits, [8] history of Haymarket, [9] ad, [10] biographies of actors, [11] ad, [12] credits.

Paper   White, wove, coated, stapled with two metal staples, all edges trimmed sheets bulk 1 mm.

Published at   1s.

Copies   Cal.

E225a   TERENCE RATTIGAN, Ross, Wezarat Alalaalam, 1971

First Kuwaiti Edition

[In drawing of scroll, within black circle in white] 22 | Men al-Masarah | [within black rectangle in white] awal voyliah 1971 | [beneath rect.] Sharaaiah | Ross | aw | Lawrence al Arab | Taaleef Terence Rattigan | Taraagamah wa Takdeem: Muhammed Kamal Kamali | Murragah: D. Muhammed Samir abd al-Hamid | Tassdur an: Wezarat Alalaalam – al Kuwait.

Collation   20.5 × 13.5 cm: guillotined sheets glued to paper covers, 140 leaves, pp.[1–6], 7–278, [2].

Contents   Pp.[1–2] blank, [3] title page, [4] blank, [5] English title page, [6] blank, 7–32 introduction, 33 cast of characters, [34] blank, 35–273 text, [274] blank, [275] contents, [276] blank, 277–278 publishers ads, [279] government printing office statement, [280] blank.

Text   10 lines, 6.9 × 7.1 cm.

Paper   White, wove, unwatermarked, edges trimmed, sheets bulk 1.3 cm.

Binding   Pictorial paper covers. On front cover: [within white rectangle in purple] Men al-Masarah alalammy | [beneath rectangle] Ross | aw | Lawrence al Arab | Teeleef Terence Rattigan | Taragamah wa Takdeem: Muhammed Kamal Kamali | Murragah: D. Muhammed Samir abd al-Hamid. On spine: [running down] ROSS Lawrence al-Arab Jalif Terence Rattigan. On back cover: [publisher's blurb] | [price].

Published at   100 fils.

Notes   Introduction by translator: Muhammed Kamal Kamali.

Copies   AC

E226   TERENCE RATTIGAN and ANATOLE de GRUNWALD, Lawrence of Arabia, 1960

First Film Script

LAWRENCE OF ARABIA | [long line] | [row of asterisks] | [long line] | by | Terence Rattigan and Anatole de Grunwald

Collation   28.3 × 21.8 cm: 205 leaves, typed on one side only, punched with covers held together by metal brads.

Contents   Prp.[1] title page, [2] quotes from *T.E. Lawrence by His Friends*, pp.1–263 text.

Text   From typed original.

Paper   White, wove, unwatermarked, all edges trimmed, sheets bulk 2 cm.

Binding   Orange paper covers.

Notes   Original script for Lean film (rejected). Another version written by Robert Bolt was used for the film.

Copies   Cal.

E227 JAMES CADELL, The Young Lawrence of Arabia, Parrish, 1960

First English Edition

The Young | Lawrence | of Arabia | JAMES CADELL | *Illustrated by* | *William Randell* | MAX PARRISH · LONDON

Collation 19.8 × 13 cm: [A]^{16} B–C^{16} D^8 E^{16} includes pastedown end papers, 72 leaves, pp.[1–6], 7–139, [5].

Contents Pp.[1] bastard title, [2] blank, [3] title page, [4] issue, copyright statements, [5] contents, [6] dedication, 7–139 text, [1–5] blank.

RT On verso THE YOUNG LAWRENCE OF ARABIA. On recto [according to chapter].

Typography and paper $ 1 signed B.

Text 20 lines, 9.2 (9.3) × 9.3 cm.

Paper White, wove, unwatermarked, all edges trimmed, sheets bulk 1.3 cm.

Binding Red orange cloth 39 gy r O. On spine: [gilt] The | Young | Lawrence | of Arabia | JAMES | CADELL | MAX | PARRISH.

Published at 10s 6d.

Notes A 2nd impression, 1962, as above; 3rd impression, 1965, as above with following differences: [Binding]: brown paper covered boards, simulated cloth, 55s Br. White end papers. James Cadell is a pseudonym of Ronald Wills Thomas.

Copies AC, Cal.

E228 JAMES CADELL, The Young Lawrence of Arabia, Roy, 1961

First American Edition

The Young | Lawrence | of Arabia | JAMES CADELL | *Illustrated by* | *William Randell* | ROY PUBLISHERS, NEW YORK

Collation 19.8 × 13 cm: [A]^{16} B–C^{16} D^8 E^{16}, 72 leaves, pp.[1–6], 7–139, [5], includes paste-down end papers.

Contents Pp.[1] bastard title, [2] blank, [3] title page, [4] issue, copyright statements, [5] contents, [6] dedication, 7–139 text, [1–5] blank.

RT On verso THE YOUNG LAWRENCE OF ARABIA. On recto [according to chapter].

Typography and paper $ 1,signed B.

Text 20 lines, 9.2 (9.3) × 9.3 cm.

Paper White, wove, unwatermarked, all edges trimmed, sheets bulk 1.4 cm.

Binding Brown cloth simulated paper covered boards 54 br.O. On spine:

[gilt] The | Young | Lawrence | of Arabia | JAMES | CADELL | ROY.
Published at $3.00.
Copies AC, Cal, LC.

E229 JAMES CADELL, Lawrence de Arabia, Santillana, 1963

First Spanish Edition

JAMES CADELL | Lawrence de Arabia | [rule] | [publisher's device] | NOVELA | [rule] | santillana
Collation 17.8 × 10.3 cm: [1] – 10⁸, 80 leaves, pp.[1–4], 5–160.
Contents Pp.[1–2] blank, [3] title page, [4] original title, translator's credit, copyright statement.
Typography and paper $ 1 signed El joven…3.
Text 20 lines, 8.9 × 9 cm.
Paper White, wove, unwatermarked, all edges trimmed, sheets bulk 1 cm.
Binding Only copy examined rebound.
Notes James Cadell is a pseudonym of Ronald Wills Thomas.
Copies LAPL.

E230 To The Dear Memory of T.E. Lawrence, n.p., [1960?]

[First three lines old English type] To the dear Memory | of | T.E. Lawrence | *(Lawrence of Arabia)* | *Born May* [sic] *1888 Died May 1935.* | *Cloud's* (sic) *Hill Cottage,* | *Dorset.*
Collation 28.7 × 18 cm: single-fold leaflet.
Contents Pp.[1] title page, [2] text within frame of ornamental cuts, [3] two b/w photos glued in with disjointed captions in italics, [4] blank.
Text 10 lines, 6.3 × 8.9 cm.
Paper White, wove, unwatermarked, all edges trimmed.
Notes Contains two textual errors p.[1], line 5, TEL was born in August not May; and p.[2], line 10 replace 'collision… with' with 'near'.
Copies AC, Cal.

E231 JOHN S.G. SIMMONS, Lawrence and All Souls, All Souls, Oxford, [1960?]

Information Leaflet

LAWRENCE AND ALL SOULS
Collation 27.9 × 21.5 cm: single sheet printed on one side only.

Contents Brief summary of T.E. Lawrence and All Souls connection.

Text 20 lines, 4.9 × 13.2 cm.

Paper White, wove, unwatermarked, all edges trimmed.

Published at Free information sheet.

Copies AC, Cal.

1961

E232 ANTHONY NUTTING, Lawrence of Arabia, Hollis & Carter, 1961

First English Edition

LAWRENCE | OF | ARABIA | *The Man and the Motive* | by | ANTHONY NUTTING | LONDON | HOLLIS & CARTER | 1961

Collation 21.6 × 13.7 cm: [1]⁸ 2–16⁸, 128 leaves, pp.[1–5], 6–256.

Contents Pp.[1] bastard title, [2] blank, [3] title page, [4] copyright statement, printer's, binder's credits, [5]–6 contents, [7] illustrations, [8] acknowledgments, [9]–16 prologue, [17]–247 text, [248]–249 bibliography, [250] blank, [251] section title, [252]–256 index.

RT On recto LAWRENCE OF ARABIA. On verso [according to chapter].

Plates Seven photos on coated paper, printed on both sides, except frontispiece following pp.2, 32, 48, 80, 96.

Typography and paper $ 1 signed L.A.-3.

Text 20 lines, 9.5 (9.6) × 9.8 cm.

Paper White, wove, unwatermarked, all edges trimmed, sheets bulk 1.8 cm.

Binding Orange cloth 50 s. O. On spine: [gilt] [all swash] Lawrence | of | Arabia | the Man | and the | Motive | Anthony | Nutting | Hollis & | Carter. T.e. salmon.

Published at 21s.

Notes A 2nd impression, November 1961, as above except for issue statement and dedication added to verso of title page.

Copies AC, Cal, H, LC.

E233 ANTHONY NUTTING, Lawrence of Arabia, Trust, 1961

Second English Edition

ANTHONY NUTTING | [rule] | LAWRENCE | OF ARABIA | The Man & The Motive | TRUST BOOKS

Collation   17.6 × 10.8 cm: [A]¹⁶ B–G¹⁶ H¹⁶, 128 leaves, pp.[1–9], 10–256.

Contents   Pp.[1] advertisement, [2] copyright statement, [3] title page, [4] dedication, [5]–6 contents, [7–8] maps, [9]–16 prologue, 17–247 text, 248–249 bibliography, acknowledgements, [250–254] index, [255–256] ads.

RT   On verso LAWRENCE OF ARABIA. On recto [according to chapter].

Plates   Four b/w photographs printed on both sides following p.128.

Typography and paper $ 1 signed B.

Text   20 lines, 8.2 (8.4) × 9.2 cm.

Paper   White, wove, unwatermarked, wood pulp, all edges trimmed, sheets bulk 1.5 cm.

Binding   Pictorial paper covers. On front cover: [all in white] TRUST Publishing 3'6 | profits | donated to Illustrated | OXFAM | ANTHONY NUTTING | LAWRENCE | OF ARABIA | Legend or phony? | The battle of words | goes on long after | Lawrence's death. On spine: [all in white] TRUST | BOOKS | [within black rectangle, within white rectangle, running down] LAWRENCE OF ARABIA Anthony Nutting | T8. On back cover: [photos from film and blurbs].

Published at   3s 6d.

Copies   AC, Cal.

E234   ANTHONY NUTTING, Lawrence of Arabia, Mayfair, 1962

Third English Edition

Anthony Nutting | [rule] | LAWRENCE OF ARABIA | The Man & the Motive | MAYFAIR BOOKS

Collation   17.5 × 10.9 cm: guillotined sheets, glued to covers, pp.[1–9], 10–256.

Contents   Pp.[1] blank, [2] copyright statement, [3] title page. [4] dedication, [5–6] contents, [7–8] map, [9]–16 prologue, 17–247 text, [248]–249 bibliography, acknowledgments, [250–251] blank, [252]–256 index.

RT   On verso LAWRENCE OF ARABIA. On recto [according to chapter].

Plates   Four plates on coated paper, printed on both sides, following p.128.

Text   20 lines, 8.3 (8.4) × 9.2 cm.

Paper   White, wove, unwatermarked, all edges trimmed, sheets bulk 1.5 cm.

Binding   Pictorial paper covers. On front cover: [within purple rectangle upper left corner, in white] MAYFAIR | 3'6 | Illustrated | [red] ANTHONY NUTTING | LAWRENCE | OF [blue] ARABIA | [in blue] Legend or Phony? | The battle of words | goes on long after | Lawrence's death. On spine: [running down] MAYFAIR LAWRENCE OF [in blue] ARABIA | [running across] 58 | [running down, in red] Anthony Nutting | [across] 3'6.

On back cover: [photos and blurb].

Published at 3s 6d.

Copies Cal.

E235 ANTHONY NUTTING, Lawrence of Arabia, Potter, 1961

First American Edition

LAWRENCE | OF | ARABIA | *The Man and the Motive* | by | ANTHONY NUTTING | [pub. device] | CLARKSON N. POTTER, INC./PUBLISHER | NEW YORK

Collation 21.7 × 14 cm: [1]⁸ 2–16⁸, 128 leaves, pp.[1–5], 6, [7–9], 10–256.

Contents Pp.[1] bastard title, [2] blank, [3] title page, [4] copyright statement, printer's, binder's credits, [5] –6 contents, [7] illustrations, [8] acknowledgments, [9] –16 prologue, [17] –247 text, [248] –249 bibliography, [250] blank, [251] section title, [252] –256 index.

RT On verso LAWRENCE OF ARABIA. On recto [according to chapter].

Plates Seven b/w plates on coated paper, printed on both sides except for frontispiece, following pp.2, 32, 48, 80, 96, 192, 208.

Typography and paper $ 1 signed L.A. -2.

Text 20 lines, 21.5 (21.7) × 9.7 cm.

Paper White, wove, thick, unwatermarked, all edges trimmed, sheets bulk 1.8 cm.

Binding 68 s. OY Orange yellow cloth. On spine: [gilt] LAWRENCE | OF | ARABIA | The Man and the | Motive | ANTHONY | NUTTING | [pub. device] | Clarkson N. | Potter. Plain end papers.

Published at $5.00.

Notes Another state, as above, but also has map end papers. Another issue, same as above, with following differences: [Collation]: 21.7 × 13.8 cm; [Binding]: T.e. pink. First edition printed and bound in England.

Copies AC, Cal, LC.

E236 ANTHONY NUTTING, Lawrence of Arabia, Potter, 1961

First American Edition (second state)

LAWRENCE | OF | ARABIA | *The Man and the Motive* | by | ANTHONY NUTTING | [pub. device] | CLARKSON N. POTTER, INC. /PUBLISHER | NEW YORK

Collation 20.9 × 14 cm: [1–7]¹⁶ [8]⁸ [9]¹⁶, 136 leaves, pp.[1–5], 6, [7–8], [2], 9–256 plus 14 unnumbered pages with illustrations (see below), totalling 272 pp.

Contents Pp.[1] bastard title, [2] blank, [3] title page, [4] copyright statement, printer's credit, [5]–6 contents, [7] illustrations, [1] acknowledgments, [2] blank, [8]–16 prologue, [17]–247 text, [248]–249 bibliography, [250] blank, [251] section title, [252]–256 index.

RT On verso LAWRENCE OF ARABIA. On recto [according to chapter].

Plates Plates are part of gatherings but not counted in pagination. There are seven following pp.2, 32, 48, 80, 96, 192, 208, these are not indicated in list of illustrations.

Text 20 lines, 9.4 (9.5) × 9.5 cm.

Paper White, wove, unwatermarked, all edges trimmed, sheets bulk 1.8 cm.

Binding 90 gy. Y Gray yellow cloth. On spine: [in brown, running down] LAWRENCE OF ARABIA | [across] *The Man* – *and the* | *Motive* | ANTHONY | NUTTING | [pub. device] | *Clarkson N.* | *Potter.* Maps on end papers.

Published at $5.00.

Notes One copy examined has publisher's device in yellow on spine. This issue is a photoreproduction of first state, described above, which was printed and bound in England. Sheets printed in USA.

Copies AC, Cal, UT.

E237   ANTHONY NUTTING, Lawrence of Arabia, Bramhall, 1961

First American Edition (Reprint)

LAWRENCE OF | ARABIA | *The Man and the Motive* | by | ANTHONY NUTTING | BRAMHALL HOUSE | NEW YORK

Collation 20.3 × 13.8 cm: unsewn gatherings, 136 leaves, pp.[1–12], [9], 10–256 *(sic)* plus 14 unnumbered pages, totalling 272 pp.

Contents Prp.[1–2] blank, [3] bastard title, [4] photo of Lawrence, [5] title page, [6] copyright statement, [7–8] contents, [9] illustrations, [10] blank, [11] acknowledgments, [12] blank, [9]–16 prologue, [17]–247 text, [248]–249 bibliography, [250] blank, [251] section title, [252]–256 index.

RT On verso LAWRENCE OF ARABIA. On recto [according to chapter].

Plates Plates are part of gatherings, but not paginated, following pp.4, 32, 48, 80, 192, 208.

Text 20 lines, 9.6 (9.7) × 9.8 cm.

Paper White, wove, unwatermarked, edges trimmed, sheets bulk 1.7 cm.

Binding Yellow paper covered boards 84 s Y. On spine: [running down] NUTTING LAWRENCE OF ARABIA | THE MAN AND THE MOTIVE | [across at bottom] BRAMHALL | HOUSE.

Copies AC.

E238   ANTHONY NUTTING, Lawrence of Arabia, Signet, 1962

Second American Edition

LAWRENCE | OF | ARABIA | *THE MAN AND THE MOTIVE* | By Anthony Nutting | [publisher's device] | *A SIGNET BOOK* | PUBLISHED BY | THE NEW AMERICAN LIBRARY

Collation   18 × 10.5 cm: guillotined sheets, 129 leaves, pp.[1–6], 7–252, [4].

Contents   Pp.[1] biographical blurb on Lawrence, [2] list of other Signet biographies, [3] title page, [4] copyright, issue statements, acknowledgments, [5–6] contents, [7–13] prologue, 14–240 text, 241–242 bibliography, 243–252 index, [1–4] publisher's ads.

RT   On verso *LAWRENCE OF ARABIA*. On recto [in italics, according to chapter].

Plates   Four b/w photographs, printed on both sides, following p.128.

Text   20 lines, 7.7 × 8.2 cm.

Paper   White, wove, unwatermarked, all edges trimmed, sheets bulk 1.5 cm.

Binding   White paper covers. On front cover: SIGNET BOOKS [along top part of oval containing price, in white] 75c | T2106 | *ANTHONY NUTTING* | [wide red bar] | *LAWRENCE* | *of ARABIA* | [wide red bar] | [five and a half-line quote from review in London *Sunday Times*] | [square containing colour portrait of TEL, along right side of portrait square, running up] A SIGNET BOOK Complete and Unabridged. On spine: [within black square, in white, within white oval] SIGNET | [below square] T | 2106 | [in red running down] LAWRENCE OF ARABIA [author's name in grey] Anthony Nutting. On back cover: [blurb on Lawrence] | [wide red bar] | [biographical sketch and photo of author] | [in red] PUBLISHED BY THE NEW AMERICAN LIBRARY. All edges red.

Published at   75c, December 1962.

Notes   List of impressions: 4th, February 1963; 5th, April 1963; 6th, June 1963.

Copies   AC, Cal.

E239   ANTHONY NUTTING, Lawrence van Arabie, Scheltens & Giltay, 1961

First Dutch Edition

ANTHONY NUTTING | [in blue] LAWRENCE | [in blue] VAN ARABIË | VERTALING DOLF KONING | [in blue] [pub. device] | SCHELTENS & GILTAY – AMSTERDAM

Collation   21 × 14.5 cm: [1–15]⁸, 120 leaves, pp.[1–4], 5–238, [2].

Contents   Pp.[1] bastard title, [2] blank, [3] title page, [4] copyright, photo credits, 5–6 contents, 7–13 foreword, [14] map, 15–238 text, [1–2] blank.

Plates Four b/w plates on coated paper, printed on both sides, following pp.16, 32, 160, 176.

Text 20 lines, 8.2 × 10 cm.

Paper White, wove, unwatermarked, all edges trimmed, sheets bulk 2 cm.

Binding Yellow cloth 87 m. Y. On front cover: [in brown] LAWRENCE | van ARABIË. On spine: [in brown] ANTHONY | NUTTING | [running down] LAWRENCE van ARABIË | [across at foot] SCHELTENS | & GILTAY | AMSTERDAM. Grey head and tail bands.

Published at G. 6.90.

Copies AC.

E240   ANTHONY NUTTING, Lawrence D'Arabie, Fayard, 1962

First French Edition

Lawrence | d'Arabie | LAWRENCE OF ARABIA | PAR | Anthony Nutting | TRADUIT DE L'ANGLAIS PAR | HÉLÈNE PASQUIER | FAYARD

Collation 22 × 13.2 cm: [1] –8^{16} 9^8, 136 leaves, pp.[1–7], 8–[263], [1–7].

Contents Pp.[1–2] blank, [3] bastard title, [4] blank, [5] title page, [6] original title, copyright statement, [7–13] prologue, [14] blank, [15]–[263] text, [1–2] contents, [3] colophon, [4] blank, [5] printer's mark, [6–7] blank, [fold map inside rear cover].

Typography and paper $ 1 signed 9.

Text 20 lines, 9 × 20 cm.

Paper Thick, white, wove, unwatermarked, all edges trimmed, sheets bulk 1.8 cm.

Binding Pictorial paper covers. On front cover: [in brown] *Anthony Nutting* | LAWRENCE | [brown] D'ARABIE | FAYARD. On spine: [running up] *fayard* [in brown] *Lawrence d'arabie* [black] *anthony nutting*. On back: [photo of Lawrence].

Published at 14,50 francs.

Copies Can.

E241   ANTHONY NUTTING, O Lorens tis Aravias, Skarabeos, [1962]?

First Greek Edition

ANTONY NATTING | O LORENS TIS ARAVIAS | *Metafrasi: EIR. GIAKA* | [pub. device] | EKDOSEIS SKARAVEOS

Collation 20 × 12.7 cm: [1] –15^8, 120 leaves, pp.[1–5], 6–237, [3].

Contents Pp.[1] bastard title, [2] blank, [3] title page, [4] printer's credit, [5]–12 preface, 13–237 text, [1–3] blank.

RT On verso ANTONY NATTING. On recto O LORENS TIS ARAVIAS.

Typography and paper $ 1 signed 2.

Text 7.8 (8.2) × 9 cm.

Paper White, wove, unwatermarked, all edges trimmed, sheets bulk 2 cm.

Binding Green paper covers 141 s. G. On front cover: PAGOSMIA VIVLIOTHIKI | [within white rectangle with double rule frame] ANTONY NATTING | O LORENS | TIS ARAVIAS | METAFRASI EIR. GIAKA | [beneath rectangle] [pub. device] | Drach. 30 | EKDOSEIS SKARAVEOS. On spine: 1–2 | [running up, within white rectangle] ANTONY NATTING O LORENS TIS ARAVIAS | [running across] EKDOSEIS | E.S. On back cover: [blurb].

Published at 30 Drachma.

Copies AC.

E242 ANTHONY NUTTING, Lorence ish arav, Hotzat Saphim, 1963

First Israeli Edition

[Text runs right to left] ANTONY NATING | LORENCE ISH ARAV | IVRIT : N. BA'AL-GALIL | [rule] | HOTZAT SEFARIM "SAPHIH,, BA'AM [two identical title pages: one on verso, one on recto of opening]

Collation 16.5 × 11.5 cm: guillotined sheets glued to covers, 96 leaves, pp.[1–4], 5–[185], [1–7].

Contents Pp.[1] bastard title, [2–3] double title pages, [4] original title, copyright statement, publisher's, distributor's, printer's, cover designer's credits, 5–11 preface, 12–[185] text, [1–7] ads.

Text 20 lines, 10.5 × 8 cm.

Paper White, wove, unwatermarked, all edges trimmed, sheets bulk 1 cm.

Binding Multicoloured pictorial paper covered boards. On front cover: [upper left corner, slanted, in red] MA'ADVRA SHENIA | SEFER RAV MEHER | ATA SERET RAV ROSHEM | ANTONY NATING | LORENCE | ISH | ARAV. On spine: [running down] ANTONY NATING LORENCE ISH ARAV | [across at foot] [pub device] | HOTZAT SAPHIM. On back cover: LORENCE ISH ARAV | ANTONY NATING | SEFER MERRATEC | OBZERVER | [three line quote from review] | DAILY TELEGRAM | GA'ON | NOHEL | ISH HAZON | HARPATCAN | SEFER ZEHOOSRAT | V'YOOTZAG BARETZ |1.50| DFOOS | LITO-OFSET LEON | TEL AVIV, DEREH PETAH-TIKVA 308.

Published at 1.50 shekels.

Notes 2nd printing, paperback, otherwise same as above.

Copies AC.

E243   ANTHONY NUTTING, Lawrence di Arabia, Calderini, 1963

First Italian Edition

lawrence | di arabia | di Anthony Nutting | *Traduzione de G. Malagoli* | Edizione Calderini

Collation   21 × 13 cm: π⁶ 1⁸ [2–3]⁸ 4–12⁸ 13⁶, 108 leaves, pp.[I–VI], VII–XIV, 1–201, [1].

Contents   Prp.[I–II] blank, [III] title page, [IV] original title, copyright, printer's credit, [V] acknowledgments, [VI] blank, VII–VIII contents, IX–XIV introduction, pp.1–201 text, [1] blank.

Plates   Ten photographs on coated paper, printed on both sides, following pp.14, 30, 46, 62, 78, 94, 126, 142, 174, 190.

Typography and paper $ 1,2 signed 13,13*.

Text   20 lines, 7.3 × 10 cm.

Paper   White, wove, unwatermarked, simulated laid paper, all edges trimmed, sheets bulk 1.2 cm.

Binding   Pictorial cloth. On front cover: [in white] lawrence | [in orange] di arabia | [in white] di Anthony Nutting. On spine: [running up] Anthony Nutting LAWRENCE DI ARABIA. On back cover: [in white] lawrence | [orange] di arabia | [in white] di Anthony Nutting | [illegible line] | [lengthy blurb] | EDIZIONI | CALDERINI | BOLOGNA. Map end papers. Blue head and tail bands.

Copies   AC.

E244   ANTHONY NUTTING, Lawrence de Arabia, Plaza & Janés, 1963

First Spanish Edition

LAWRENCE | DE ARABIA | El hombre y la circunstancia | *por ANTHONY NUTTING* | [pub. device] | PLAZA & JANÉS, S.A. | EDITORES | BUENOS AIRES – BARCELONA – MEXICO, D.F. | BOGOTA – RIO DE JANEIRO

Collation   18.5 × 11.7 cm: [1]–17⁸, 136 leaves, pp.[1–5], 6–262, [1–10].

Contents   Pp.[1–2] blank, [3] title page, [4] original title, credits, issue, copyright statements, [1]–12 prologue, [13]–262 text, [1–2] contents, [3–6] ads, [7] printer's colophon, [8–10 blank].

RT   On verso ANTHONY NUTTING. On recto LAWRENCE DE ARABIA.

Plates   Eight b/w plates on coated paper, printed on both sides, following pp.32, [48], 80, 96, 128, 144, 176, 192; folded map following p.[4].

Typography and paper $ 1 signed 10-2162.

Text   20 lines, 7.5 (7.8) × 9.5 cm.

Paper   White, wove, unwatermarked, all edges trimmed, sheets bulk 2 cm.

Binding   Only copy seen rebound.

Copies   LAPL.

E245   JACQUES BENOIST-MÉCHIN, Lawrence D'Arabie, Clairefontaine, 1961

First Swiss Edition

BENOIST-MÉCHIN, [outline type] LAWRENCE D'ARABIE | OU | LE RÊVE | FRACASSÉ | ÉDITIONS CLAIREFONTAINE | LAUSANNE

Collation   20 × 14.3 cm: [1–17]⁸ [18]⁴, 142 leaves, prp.[1–6], 9–277, [9].

Contents   Prp.[1] bastard title, [2] list of author's works, [3] title page, [4] copyright statement, [5] AVANT-PROPOS, [6] blank, 9–[14] preface, [15] quotes, from Goethe and Lawrence, [16] blank, 17–[197] text, [198] blank, [199] ANNEXES, [200] blank, [201] CHRONOLOGIE, [202] blank, 203–[251] chronology of Lawrence's life, [252] blank, [253] Hashimite genealogy, [254] blank, [255] NOTES ET COMMENTAIRES, [256] blank, 257–266 notes, [267] BIBLIOGRAPHIE. [268] blank, 269–270 Lawrence's works, 271–[273] works about Lawrence, 274–275 studies of Lawrence, periodicals, 276–277 historical works related to the study of Lawrence, [1] blank, [2] ICONOGRAPHIE, [3] blank, [4] illustrations, [5] blank, [6] contents, [8] blank, [9] printer's colophon.

RT   On verso LAWRENCE D'ARABIE. On recto [according to chapter].

Plates   Eight photographs on coated paper, following pp.2, 64, 80, 88, 112, 128, 144, 184. Folded map following p.3.

Text   20 lines, 9.0 (9.1) × 9.5 cm.

Paper   White, wove, unwatermarked, all edges trimmed, sheets bulk 2 cm.

Binding   Pictorial paper covers. On front cover: [in white] Benoist-Méchin | Lawrence | [in yellow] d'Arabie | [white] ou | le | rêve | fracassé. On spine: Benoist-Méchin | Lawrence | d'Arabie | ou | le rêve | fracassé | Clairefontaine.

Notes   Another issue: differs from above as follows: [Collation]: 21.3 × 13.8 cm guillotined sheets, pp.[1–10], 11–278, [2]. [Contents]: pp.[1–2] blank, [3] bastard title, [4] list of author's works, [5] title page, [6] copyright statement, [7] quotes by Lawrence and Goethe, [8] blank, [9] section title, [10] blank, 11–199 text, [200] blank, [201] ANNEXES, [202] blank, [203] section title, [204] blank, 205–253 chronology, [254] Hashimite genealogy, [256] blank, [257] section title, [258] blank, 259–268 notes, [269] section title, [270] blank, 271–279 bibliography, [280] blank, [281] section title, [282] blank, [283] illustrations, [284] blank, [285–286] contents, [287] blank, [288] printer's statement, [289–290] blank. [Plates]: p.3 otherwise as above; [Binding]: On spine: Benoist- | Méchin | Lawrence.

Copies   AC, Cal.

E246   JACQUES BENOIST-MÉCHIN,
Lawrence von Arabien, Kohlhammer, 1967

First German Edition

BENOIST-MÉCHIN | Lawrence | von | Arabien | DER ENTSCHWINDENE TRAUM | W. KOHLHAMMER VERLAG | STUTTGART BERLIN KÖLN MAINZ

Collation   21.1 × 13.3 cm: [1–15]^8, [16]^6, 126 leaves, pp.[1–6], 7–252.

Contents   Pp.[1] publisher's name and device, [2] blank, [3] title page, [4] translator's, typographer's, printer's credits, copyright statement, [5] contents, [6] blank, 7–173 text, 174–184 notes, [185] section title, [186] blank, 187–247 chronology of Lawrence's life, 248 Hashimite genealogy, 249 bibliography and iconography, [250] blank, 251–252 index.

Text   20 lines, 9 × 9.5 cm.

Paper   White, wove, unwatermarked, all edges trimmed, sheets bulk 2 cm.

Binding   Orange cloth 102 mg Y. On spine: [broad white rule] | [within black rectangle in white] Benoist- | Méchin | [broad white rule] | [in white] Law- | rence | [broad white rule]. Black head and tail bands.

Copies   AC, Cal, LC.

E247   JACQUES BENOIST-MÉCHIN, Lawrence d'Arabia, Abruzzini, 1963

First Italian Edition

BENOIST-MÉCHIN | LAWRENCE D'ARABIA | O IL SOGNO | INFRANTO | EDIZIONI ITALIANE ABRUZZINI | ROMA

Collation   21.1 × 14.7 cm: guillotined sheets glued to covers, 145 leaves, pp.[1–8], 5–282, [4].

Contents   Prp.[1–2] blank, [3] series titles, [4] blank, [5] bastard title, [6] blank, [7] title page, [8] original title, copyright statement, translator's credit, pp.1–10 preface, [11] quotes, [12] blank, 13–193 text, [194] blank, [195] section title, [196] blank, [197] section title, [198] blank, 199–246 chronology of Lawrence's life, 247 Hashimite genealogy, [248] blank, [249] section title, [250] blank, 251–261 notes, [262] blank, [263] section title, [264] blank, 265–273 bibliography, [274] blank, [275] section title, [276] blank, [277] fold. map, [278] blank, 279 illus., [280] blank, 281 contents, [1] blank, [2] printer's colophon, [3–4] blank.

Plates   Eight plates on coated paper, printed on one side only, following pp.6, 56, 80, 88, 112, 128, 144, 184.

Text   20 lines, 9 × 10 cm.

Paper   White, wove, unwatermarked, all edges trimmed, sheets bulk 1.8 cm.

Binding Pictorial paper covers. On front cover: [in white] Benoist-Méchin | [in white] Lawrence | [in orange] d'Arabia | [in white] o il sogno | infranto | EDIZIONI ITALIANE | ABRUZZINI. On spine BENOIST-MÉCHIN | Lawrence | d'Arabia | il sogno | infranto | Storie | de guerra. Covers have turned in flaps with blurbs and advertising.

Published at Lire 1.800.

Copies AC.

1962

E248 PAUL ADAM, Les Echecs de T.E. Lawrence, privately printed, [Barbizon], 1962

First French Edition

Les Echecs | de | T.E. Lawrence [title hand-lettered] | Paul ADAM

Collation 20.5 × 15.1 cm: guillotined sheets, 103 leaves, pp.[1–6], 1–198, [2].

Contents Prp.[1] title page, [2] blank, [3] map, [4] blank, [5] table of contents, [6] blank, pp.[1]–5 chronology of Lawrence's life, [6] blank, [7]–184 text, 185–198 notes, [1] corrections, [2] blank.

Text 20 lines, 8.3 × 12.2 cm.

Paper White, wove, unwatermarked, all edges trimmed, sheets bulk 1.8 cm.

Binding Grey cloth 93 y. gray.

Notes Limited to about 250 copies.

Copies AC, Cal.

E249 ROBERT BOLT, Lawrence of Arabia, unpublished, 1962

Filmscript

LAWRENCE OF ARABIA

Collation 28 × 21 cm: mimeo sheets printed on one side only, [1] 142 [125] 1,269 leaves.

Contents Pp.[1] title page, pp.1–142 part one, 1–125 part 2, 1 printer's statement. Printed by Scripts Limited | [pub. device] | 187 Wardour Street | London W 1. | [phone number].

Text 20 lines, 9.7 × 15.2 cm.

Paper White, wove, unwatermarked, all edges trimmed, sheets bulk 2.5 cm.

Binding Heavy blue 204 gy. p B paper with window for title.

Copies AC, Cal.

E250   ARNOLD WALTER LAWRENCE, ed., Letters to T.E. Lawrence, Cape, 1962

Uncorrected Proof of First English Edition

LETTERS | to | T.E. LAWRENCE | edited by | A.W. LAWRENCE | [pub. device] | LONDON | JONATHAN CAPE 30 BEDFORD SQUARE

Collation   22.9 × 15.3 cm: [A]^8 B–N^8 O^4, 108 leaves, pp.[1–10], 11–214, [2].

Contents   Pp.[1] portion of preface by A.W. Lawrence, [2] blank, [3] title page, [4] issue, copyright statements, printer's, binder's, papermaker's credits, [5–6] contents, [7–8] preface, [9] half-title, [10] note, 11–214 text, [1–2] blank.

Typography and paper $ 1,signed B.

Text   20 lines, 9.2 × 11.1 cm.

Paper   White, wove, unwatermarked, all edges trimmed, sheets bulk 7 mm.

Binding   Yellow paper wrappers 87 m. Y with white publisher's device pattern. On front cover: LETTERS TO | T.E. LAWRENCE | A.W. LAWRENCE | Uncorrected Proof. On spine: [running down] LETTERS TO T.E. LAWRENCE. On back cover: The Alden Press (Oxford) Ltd.

Copies   AC, UT.

E251   ARNOLD WALTER LAWRENCE, ed., Letters to T.E. Lawrence, Cape, 1962

First English Edition

LETTERS | to | T.E. LAWRENCE | Edited by | A.W. LAWRENCE | [pub. device] | LONDON JONATHAN CAPE 30 BEDFORD SQUARE

Collation   23 × 15.3 cm: [A]^8 B–O^8, 112 leaves, pp.[1–10], 11–216, [2], includes 6 leaves of facsimiles unnumbered (see below) 224 pp.

Contents   Pp.[1] bastard title, [2] blank, [3] title page, [4] issue statement, printer's, binder's, papermaker's credits, [5–6] contents, [7–8] preface, [9] half-title, [10] note, 11–214 text, 215–216 index, [1–2] blank.

Plates   Facsimiles on both sides of three leaves, unnumbered, following pp.24, 120, 160; part of gatherings but not paginated.

Typography and paper $ 1 signed B.

Text   20 lines, 9.1 × 11 cm.

Paper   White, wove, unwatermarked, all edges trimmed, sheets bulk 1.5 cm.

Binding   Golden Brown cloth 74 s. y Br. On spine: [gilt] LETTERS | TO | T.E. | LAWRENCE | [cut] | [publisher's device]. End papers facsimiles of signature of writers of letters. T.e. brown.

Published at 35s.

Notes Errata slip on p.105. Another impression with corrections, 1964, as above with following differences: T.E. LAWRENCE on title page is cordova and not red; on verso of title page impression note and note that corrections were mainly by Audrey Sutherland. No errata slip on p.105. The 1st impression bears dust wrapper different from the 2nd, reproduced under printed matter is a facsimile of a letter to TEL from Augustus John. The first state contains an inquiry from John 'What are your latest views on sex? and life?' The second state reproduces a less troublesome letter. Another state; the 1964 issue was also found in a variant binding as follows: slate grey paper covered boards. T.e. grey. Red T.E. LAWRENCE on title page.

Copies AC, Cal, UT.

E252 ALISTAIR MACLEAN, All About Lawrence of Arabia, Allen, 1962

First English Edition

[In yellow] *All About* | LAWRENCE | OF ARABIA | By | ALISTAIR MacLEAN | *Illustrated by* | GIL WALKER | [in yellow] [pub. device] W.H. ALLEN | LONDON, 1962

Collation 21.5 × 14 cm: [1]–5^{16}, includes pastedown end papers, 80 leaves, pp.[1–12], 1–148.

Contents Prp.[1–2] paste-down end paper, [3–4] free end paper, [5] bastard title, [6] illustrations, [7] title page, [8] acknowledgments, copyright statement, publisher's imprint, [9] contents, [10] blank, [11] maps. [12] blank, pp.[1] half-title, [2] blank, 3–[135] text, [136] text, 137 bibliography, [138] blank, 139–141 index, [142–144] blank, [145–146] free end paper, [147–148] paste down end paper.

RT On verso ALL ABOUT LAWRENCE OF ARABIA. On recto [according to chapter].

Plates Nine plates on coated paper, frontispiece is in colour, all others b/w, (all are stills from film) following pp.7, 68.

Typography and paper $ 1 signed, 2.

Text 20 lines, 9.8 (9.9) × 10.1 cm.

Paper Buff, wove, unwatermarked, all edges trimmed, sheets bulk 1.7 cm.

Binding Blue 197 deep p B cloth simulated paper covered boards. On spine: [silver] All | About | Lawrence of | Arabia | MacLean | [pub. device] | W.H. ALLEN. Yellow illustrated end papers.

Copies Cal.

E253   ALISTAIR MACLEAN, Lawrence of Arabia, Random, 1962

First American Edition

[Double page spread, running across both pages in brown] [swash] Lawrence of Arabia | [on recto leaf] ALISTAIR MACLEAN | ILLUSTRATED BY | GIL WALKER | [series device] | RANDOM HOUSE · NEW YORK [on verso drawing of Lawrence]

Collation   21 × 14.3 cm: [1–6]^{16} including paste down end papers, 96 leaves, pp.[1–10], [1–2], 3–177, [5].

Contents   Prp.[1–4] paste down and free end papers, [5] bastard title, [6–7] title pages, [8] acknowledgments, copyright statement, L C number, printer's, designer's credits, [9] contents, [10] list of maps, pp. [1] half title, [2] blank, 3–[172] text, 173 list of other books about Lawrence, [174] blank, 175–177 index, [178] blank, [1–4] free and paste down end papers.

RT   On verso LAWRENCE OF ARABIA. On recto [in italics, according to chapter].

Text   20 lines, 11.1 (11.5) × 9.9 cm.

Paper   White, wove, unwatermarked, all edges trimmed, sheets bulk 1.5 cm.

Binding   Beige buckram 90 gy. Y. On front cover: [swash, in blue] Lawrence of Arabia | [gold sword cut]. On spine: [within blue rectangle, gilt] MacLEAN | [running down] Lawrence of Arabia | [series device, gilt on blue circle] | [beneath, gilt] RANDOM | HOUSE. T.e. red.

Published at $1.95.

Notes   Issued in World Landmark Books Series. Another issue, same as above with following differences: [Contents]: prp.[5] short biographical sketch of T.E. Lawrence instead of bastard title; [Binding]: pictorial cloth. On front cover: Lawrence of Arabia | [first three words in red] BY ALISTAIR MACLEAN ILLUSTRATED BY GIL WALKER | W-52 | [series device]. On spine: MacLEAN | [running down] Lawrence of Arabia | [across at bottom] W-52 | [series device] | RANDOM | HOUSE. On back cover: 12 s. Red. Another issue, same as immediately above, with following differences: [Contents]: prp.[8] last line 5 764; [Binding]: Back cover 34 v. r O.

Copies   AC, Cal, LC.

E254   ALISTAIR MACLEAN, Lawrence d'Arabie, Nathan 1969

First French Edition

ALISTAIR MacLEAN | [within black rectangle, in white] LAWRENCE | D'ARABIE | ADAPTÉ PAR | NOELLE BRUN | FERNAND NATHAN

Collation   13.3 × 15.5 cm: [1–10]^8, 160 leaves, pp.[1–4], 5–160.

Contents   Pp.[1] bastard title, [2] frontispiece, [3] title page, [4] map, original title, copyright statement, 5–158 text, 159 photo, illustration credits, 160 contents, printer's colophon.

RT On both verso and recto [according to chapter].

Text 20 lines, 9 (9.4) × 10.8 cm.

Paper White, wove, unwatermarked, all edges trimmed, sheets bulk 1.5 cm.

Binding Brown cloth 77 m. y Br. On front cover: [in white] LAWRENCE D'ARABIE | [pictorial paper label pasted into stamped rectangle]. On spine: [in white] ALLISTAIR *(sic)* MACLEAN | LAWRENCE D'ARABIE. End papers brown. Brown and gold head and tail bands.

Published at April 1969.

Copies AC.

E255 SULEIMAN MOUSA, Lawrence wa al Arab, Monalef, 1962

First Jordanian Edition

[Running right to left] Suleiman Mousa | Lawrence wa al Arab | Wighat Nazir Arabia | [triple rule] | Al-Tabaa Al Oula | [dot] | Gamie Al Hekouk Mahfouza Lil Monalef | Amman Nissan, 1962

Collation 23.7 × 16.5 cm: [1–20]⁸ [21]², 162 leaves, pp.[1–8], 9–324.

Contents Pp.[1] title page, [2] blank, [3] poem, [4] blank, [5] acknowledgments, [6] list of works by author, [7–8] introduction, [9]–316 text, 317 Arabic bibliography, 318 English bibliography, 319 illus, charts, maps, [320] blank, 321–324 contents.

Text 20 lines, 16.2 × 12.7 cm.

Paper Wood pulp, wove, white, unwatermarked, all edges trimmed, sheets bulk 2.5 cm.

Binding Pictorial paper covers. On front cover: Lawrence | wa al Arab | Wighat Nazir Arabia | Suleiman Mousa. On spine: [running down] Lawrence wa al Arab Suleiman Mousa. On back cover: [short biography of Lawrence, quotes, price 400 Jordanian pennies].

Published at 400 Jordanian pennies.

Copies AC, Cal.

E256 SULEIMAN MOUSA, T.E. Lawrence, an Arab View, Oxford University Press, 1966

First English Edition

T.E. | LAWRENCE | AN ARAB VIEW | [Oxford rule] | Suleiman Mousa | Translated by Albert Butros | *London* | OXFORD UNIVERSITY PRESS | *New York Toronto* | 1966

Collation　21.7 × 13.8 cm: [1]^8 2–18^8 19^4 20^8, 156 leaves, pp.[i–v], vi–x, [1], 2–301, [1].

Contents　Prp.[i] bastard title, [ii] blank, [iii] title page, [iv] issue statement, printer's credit, [v]–vi contents, [vii]–x preface, [1]–278 text, [277]–287 comment by A.W. Lawrence, [288]–290 bibliography, [291]–301 index, [1] blank.

RT　On verso T.E. LAWRENCE. On recto [according to chapter].

Typography and paper　$ 1 signed T.E.L. -2.

Text　20 lines, 8.5 (8.6) × 10.6 cm.

Paper　White, wove, unwatermarked, all edges trimmed, sheets bulk 2.4 cm.

Binding　Black cloth. On spine: [gilt] T.E. | LAWRENCE | AN ARAB | VIEW | SULEIMAN | MOUSA | OXFORD.

Published at　35s, July 1966.

Notes　Another issue, 1967 impression, same as above except date is removed from title page. Published at £2.00.

Copies　AC, Cal.

E257　SULEIMAN MOUSA, T.E. Lawrence, An Arab View, Oxford University Press, 1966

First American Edition

T.E. | LAWRENCE | AN ARAB VIEW | [Oxford rule] | Suleiman Mousa | Translated by Albert Butros | 1966 | OXFORD UNIVERSITY PRESS | LONDON AND NEW YORK

Collation　21.5 × 13.8 cm: [1–10]^{16}, 160 leaves, pp.[i–v], vi–x, [xi–xii], [1], 2–301, [7].

Contents　Prp.[i] bastard title, [ii] blank, [iii] title page, [iv] copyright statement, [v]–vi contents, [vii]–x preface, [xi] half-title, [xii] blank, [1]–278 text, [279]–287 comment by A.W. Lawrence, [288]–290 bibliography, [291]–301 index, [1–7] blank.

RT　On verso T.E LAWRENCE. On recto [according to chapter].

Text　20 lines, 8.5 (8.6) × 10.6 cm.

Paper　White, wove, unwatermarked, all edges trimmed, sheets bulk 1.9 cm.

Binding　Yellow 84 s. Y cloth. On front cover: [blind stamped circular design]. On spine: [in brown] [decorative rule] | T.E. | LAWRENCE | An Arab | View | [rule] | MOUSA | [decorative rule] | OXFORD. Brown and yellow head and tail bands.

Published at　$6.50, July 1966.

Copies　AC, Cal.

E258   SULEIMAN MOUSA, T.E. Lawrence, an Arab View, Oxford University Press, 1966

Publisher's Prospectus

No title page.

Collation   21.7 × 14 cm: single sheet printed on one side only.

Paper   White, wove, unwatermarked, all edges trimmed.

Published at   Free advertising flyer.

Copies   AC.

E259   SULEIMAN MOUSA, Songe et mensonge de Lawrence, Sindbad, 1973

First French Edition

Suleiman Moussa [*sic*] | Songe et mensonge | de Lawrence | *Traduit de l'anglais* | *par Hélène Houssemaine* | *et précédè de* | Lawrence vu par les Arabes | *par Vincent Montiel* | [pub. device] | Sindbad | 1 et 3 rue Feutrier | Paris 18

Collation   22.5 × 14 cm: [1–9]^{16}, [10]^{24}, [11]^{16}, 184 leaves, pp.[1–11], 12–351, [9].

Contents   Pp.[1–2] blank, [3–4] series titles, [5] bastard title, [6] blank, [7] title page, [8] original title, copyright statements, [9] section title], [10] blank, [11]–33 preface, [34] blank, [35] half-title, [36] blank, [37]–40 foreword, [41]-327 text, [328] section title, [329] blank, [330]–340 comment on text by A.W. Lawrence, [341]–342 response by author, [343] section title, [344–345] blank, [346] blank, [347]–351 bibliography. [1] blank, [2–4] contents, [5] blank, [6] issue statement, [7–9] blank.

RT   On recto only [according to chapter].

Text   20 lines, 8.8 (10.1) × 10.2 cm.

Paper   Paper verge , laid, unwatermarked, all edges trimmed, sheets bulk 2.5 cm.

Binding   Pink paper 254 v.p. R. On front cover: Suleiman Moussa [*sic*] | Songe et mensonge | de Lawrence | Précédè de | Lawrence vu par les Arabes | par Vincent Monteil | [Kennington cartoon drawing of Lawrence in white] | LA BIBLIOTHÈQUE ARABE | Sindbad. on spine: [running up] Sindbad | Suleiman Moussa [*sic*] – Songe et mensonge de Lawrence. On back cover: [blurb, brief biography of author]. Front and back covers have turned in flap with other titles in series printed on them.

Published at   October 1973.

Copies   AC.

E260   ROBERT PAYNE, Lawrence of Arabia, Pyramid, 1962

First American Edition

[Swash] Lawrence | [swash] of Arabia | A TRIUMPH | by Robert Payne | author of "The Gold of Troy" | and "Gershwin" | [pub. device] | PYRAMID | BOOKS | 444 Madison Avenue, New York 22, New York

Collation   18 × 10.7 cm: [1–12]⁸, 96 leaves, pp.[1–6], 7–190, [2].

Contents   Pp.[1] advertising blurb, [2] blank, [3] title page, [4] dedication, acknowledgment, issue, copyright statements, printer's credit, [5] contents, [6] map, 7–190 text, [1] publisher's ads, [2] publisher's device.

RT   On both verso and recto LAWRENCE OF ARABIA.

Text   20 lines, 6.7 (6.8) × 8.8 cm.

Paper   White, wove, unwatermarked, all edges trimmed, sheets bulk 1.2 cm.

Binding   Pale pink 31 p. y Pink paper covers. On front cover: [in red] PYRAMID BOOKS- R-685 50c | ROBERT PAYNE'S | [in blue] fabulous story of the immortal | [in blue, swash] Lawrence | [in blue, swash] of Arabia |[drawing of Lawrence wrapped in Union Jack]. On spine: [in red] R-685 | [in purple, runnning down] LAWRENCE OF ARABIA [author's name in blue] ROBERT PAYNE | [across at foot in red] [triangle] | [in red] PYRAMID | [in red] BOOKS. On back cover: [advertising blurb, drawing of dagger, cover design credit]. All edges orange.

Published at   50c, January 1962.

Notes   Another issue, 2nd impression, February 1963, identical to above with following differences: [Binding]: [on front cover, under title] SEE THE BRILLIANT NEW FILM EPIC | "LAWRENCE OF ARABIA". Number has been changed to R-838 on both front cover and spine. Another issue, 3rd printing, July 1963, same as 2nd printing above.

Copies   AC, Cal, UT, LC.

E261   ROBERT PAYNE, Lawrence of Arabia, Hale, 1966

First English Edition

ROBERT PAYNE | [outline letters] LAWRENCE | [outline letters] OF ARABIA | A Triumph | *Illustrated and* | *with map* | [publisher's device] | ROBERT HALE · LONDON

Collation   21.5 × 13.9 cm: A⁸ B–Q⁸, 128 leaves, pp.[i–xi], xii–xiii, [xiv–15], 16–256.

Contents   Prp.[i] bastard title, [ii] list of author's works, [iii] title page, [iv] copyright, issue statements, printer's credits, [v] dedication, [vi] blank, [vii] contents, [viii] map, [ix] illustrations, [x] blank, [xi]–xiii introduction, [xiv] blank,[15]–250 text, [251]–256 index.

RT On verso LAWRENCE OF ARABIA: A TRIUMPH. On recto [according to chapter].

Plates Six b/w photographs, on coated paper, following pp.80, 96, 128, 144, 192, 208.

Typography and paper $ 1 signed B.

Text 20 lines, 9 (9.1) × 9.7 cm.

Paper Buff, imitation laid paper, wove, all edges trimmed, unwatermarked, sheets bulk 2.3 cm.

Binding Red 13 deep Red paper covered boards. On spine: [gilt] [Oxford rule] | LAWRENCE | OF | ARABIA | A Triumph | [cut] | ROBERT | PAYNE | [Oxford rule] | [cut] | ROBERT | HALE.

Published at 35s.

Copies AC, Cal, LC.

E262 ROBERT PAYNE, Lawrence d'Arabia, Volpe, 1966

First Italian Edition

Robert Payne | LAWRENCE | D'ARABIA | [pub. device] | I CONTEMPORANEI | DELLA VOLPE EDITORE – MILANO

Collation 22 × 14 cm: [1] – 13⁸ 14¹⁰, 114 leaves, pp.[1–4], 5–224, [1–4].

Contents [1] bastard title, [2] blank, [3] title page, [4] original title, translator's credit, copyright, issue statements, series notice, 5–8 chronology of Lawrence's life, 9–215 text, 216 bibliography, [217] section title, 218–224 index, [1] printer's colophon, [2] blank, [3] list of titles in series, [4] blank.

RT On verso [according to chapter]. On recto LAWRENCE D'ARABIA.

Plates Sixteen b/w plates, printed on both sides, following p.48.

Typography and paper $ 1 signed 4 *Lawrence d'Arabia* (14,14** 1,2).

Text 20 lines, 8.3 (8.6) × 10.5 cm.

Paper White, wove, unwatermarked, all edges trimmed, sheets bulk 1.7 cm.

Binding White leather simulated cloth. On front cover: [gilt] ROBERT PAYNE | LAWRENCE | D'ARABIA | DELLA VOLPE EDITORE. On spine: [spine black] [raised gilt rules] [between 1st and 2nd rules, in white] LAWRENCE | D'ARABIA | [between 7th and 8th gilt rules] [pub. device] | [between 14th and 15th gilt rules] DELLA VOLPE. Yellow head and tail bands.

Notes Series: I Contemporanei no. 14.

Copies UT.

E262a ROBERT PAYNE, Arabia no Rorensu, Chi Ruma, Shobo, 1963

First Japanese Edition

LAWRENCE OF ARABIA | by | Robert Payne

Collation 18.5 × 11.5 cm: [1–21]⁶, 126 leaves, pp.[1–4], 5–249, [1–2].

Contents Pp.[1] title page, [2–3] contents, [4] acknowledgements, 5–247 text, 248–249 bibliography, [1–2] copyright, translator's credit, publisher's information.

Paper White, wove, unwatermarked, all edges trimmed, sheets bulk 2 cm.

Binding Only copy seen rebound.

Published at 380 Yen, 24 December 1963.

Copies LC.

E263 ROBERT PAYNE, Lawrence de Arabia, Bruguera, 1962

First Spanish Edition

ROBERT PAYNE | LAWRENCE | DE ARABIA | [publisher's device] | EDITORIAL BRUGUERA, S.A. | BARCELONA – BUENOS AIRES – BOGOTÁ

Collation 20.7 × 13.5 cm: [1] –22⁸, 176 leaves, pp.[1–6], 7–345, [346–352].

Contents Pp.[1] bastard title, [2] blank, [3] title page, [4] issue, copyright statements, printer's credit, [5] dedication, [6] map, 7–345 text, [346] blank, [347] section title, [348] blank, [349] contents, [350–352] blank.

Text 20 lines, 9 × 10 cm.

Paper White, wove, unwatermarked, all edges trimmed, sheets bulk 2 cm.

Binding Light yellow brown cloth 76 l. y Br. On front cover: [in blue] ROBERT | PAYNE | LAWRENCE | de ARABIA. On spine: [across at top, in blue] ROBERT | PAYNE | [running up, in blue] LAWRENCE DE ARABIA | [across at bottom, in blue] BRUGUERA. Blue and white head and tail bands. White end papers.

Copies Cal, UT.

E264 ROBERT PAYNE, Lawrence de Arabia, Bruguera, 1968

Second Spanish Edition

Lawrence | de | Arabia | ROBERT PAYNE | [publisher's device] | EDITORIAL BARCELONA | BRUGUERA S.A. | BOGOTA | BUENOS AIRES | CARACAS | MEXICO | RIO DE JANEIRO

Collation 17.5 × 10.5 cm: [1]¹⁶ 2¹⁶ 3⁸ 4–6¹⁶ 7⁸ 8–10¹⁶ 11⁸ 12¹⁶, 168 leaves, pp.[1–6], 7–336.

Contents Pp.[1] bastard title, [2] blank, [3] title page, [4] original title, copyright, issue statements, printer's credit, 5 dedicatory letter, [6] blank, [7]–336 text.

Typography and paper $ 1 signed LAWRENCE.

Text 20 lines, 7.3 × 8.5 cm.

Paper Pulp, wove, unwatermarked, all edges trimmed, sheets bulk 2 cm.

Binding White paper covers glued to sheets. On front cover: [running around 2½ sides beginning at lower left corner in light green] BRUGUERA LIBRO AMIGO. [repeated four times, ending half way down right border] | [within blue circle, in white] A | [next two lines in red] ROBERT | PAYNE | Lawrence | de | [in red] Arabia | [in red] eb | [colour still from film of O'Toole as Lawrence in Arab dress]. On spine: LAWRENCE DE ARABIA | [in red] ROBERT PAYNE | [across at bottom] BRUGUERA. On back cover: [publisher's blurb, address, price].

Published at 40 ptas.

Notes A 2nd impression, 1971, same as above, with following differences: no RIO DE JANEIRO on title page; [Price]: 50 ptas.

Copies AC, Cal.

E265 UNIVERSITY OF TEXAS, Humanities Research Center, T.E. Lawrence/ Fifty Letters, 1962

First American Edition

[To right of John drawing of T.E. Lawrence] T.E. LAWRENCE/ *Fifty Letters: 1920–35.* AN EXHIBITION: | OCTOBER FIRST TO DECEMBER FIFTEENTH 1962 | *Held at* THE HUMANITIES RESEARCH CENTER, THE UNIVERSITY OF TEXAS

Collation 17.8 × 25.5 cm: [1]²⁰, 20 leaves, pp.1–36, [37–38], [2].

Contents Pp.1 title page, 2 blank except for page number, 3–[38] text, [1–2] blank.

Text 20 lines, 7.9 × 10.2 (21.3 cm) double column format.

Paper Buff, wove, unwatermarked, all edges trimmed, sheets bulk 3 mm.

Binding Light brown 76 l. y Br pictorial paper wrappers stapled to sheets. On front cover: T.E. LAWRENCE/ *Fifty Letters: 1920–35.* On back cover: [left side running up] [University logo] THE HUMANITIES RESEARCH CENTER, THE UNIVERSITY OF TEXAS.

Notes 2000 copies.

Copies AC, Cal, UT, LC.

E266 COLUMBIA PICTURES, Lawrence of Arabia, Columbia Pictures, 1962

American Souvenir Program

[Double-page spread, in white on verso] COLUMBIA PICTURES

PRESENTS [On Recto] THE SAM SPIEGEL AND DAVID LEAN PRODUCTION OF LAWRENCE | OF | ARABIA

Collation   31.5 × 24 cm: [1]²⁰, 20 leaves, unnumbered, includes covers.

Contents   Pp.[1] cover, [2–3] title pages, [4] publisher, art director, writer, photographer credits, copyright statement, [5] quote from Winston Churchill, [6–18] text and photos many leaves with view windows, [19–20] back cover.

Text   20 lines, 8.5 × 9.1 cm, double column.

Paper   White, wove, unwatermarked, all edges trimmed, sheets bulk 4 mm.

Binding   Pictorial paper wrappers stapled to sheets. On front cover: LAWRENCE | OF | ARABIA | [rectangle photo from film, Lawrence chasing servant in quicksand scene].

Notes   Another copy has lighter violet coloured end papers. Another issue reported with different photo [Arabs attacking train]. Another issue?: single-fold format with cover as above but containing only a resetting of a portion of the text on verso of first leaf and advertisement and credits on recto of second leaf, rear cover chronology and bibliography.

Copies   AC, Cal, UT.

E267   COLUMBIA PICTURES, Lawrence of Arabia, 1962

Souvenir Program

LAWRENCE | OF | ARABIA | [photo of Alec Guinness as Feisal on horseback challenging enemy plane bombing his camp]

Collation   31 × 24 cm: [1]¹⁴, 28 unnumbered pages.

Contents   Pp.[1] front cover and title page, [2] quote from Churchill, [3] half-title, [4–25] text and photographs, [26] film credits, [27] colophon, [28] blank, back cover.

Text   20 lines, 8.4 × 9.7 cm.

Paper   White, wove, unwatermarked, all edges trimmed, sheets bulk 2 mm.

Binding   Covers same stock as sheets, stapled with two metal staples.

Notes   Colour stills used are different from other souvenir programs, no view window page at beginning of text section.

Copies   AC, Cal.

E268   COLUMBIA PICTURES, Lawrence of Arabia, 1962

Royal World Première Performance Souvenir Programme

[First two lines in red] ROYAL WORLD | PREMIÈRE | *to aid S.S.A.F.A. and SAVE THE CHILDREN FUND* | *in the gracious presence of* | HER MAJESTY

THE QUEEN | HIS ROYAL HIGHNESS THE DUKE OF EDINBURGH | *Columbia Pictures presents The Sam Spiegel-David Lean production of* | [in red] LAWRENCE OF ARABIA | Odeon Theatre Leicester Square, Monday December 10th 1962

Collation 33 × 24.5 cm: [1]^{15}, 30 leaves, unpaged, includes covers.

Contents [Front cover], pp.[1] title, [2] caption of photo on next page,[3] b/w portrait of Queen Elizabeth II, [4] caption of photo on next page, [5] b/w portrait of Duke of Edinburgh, [6–20] advertisements, [21–30] text of programme on rectos, ads on versos, [31–58] advertising, [59–60] blank covers.

Text 9.1 × 12.6 cm.

Paper White, coated, wove, unwatermarked, all edges trimmed, sheets bulk 5 mm.

Binding White paper covers stapled to sheets. See title transcription above for wording on front cover.

Published at December 1962.

Copies AC, Cal.

E269   COLUMBIA PICTURES, Advance Information–Campaign Book, [1962]

Film Campaign Book (England)

[In red] ADVANCE INFORMATION– CAMPAIGN BOOK | The Unique Film Experience | [reproduction of film poster] | Certificate 'A' Running Time 3 hrs. 26 mins. 46 secs. | 1st Half 129 mins. 40 secs. (includes Overture) 2nd Half 77 mins. 6 secs. (Additional Playout Music 2 mins. 34 secs.) | [long rule in red] | COLUMBIA PICTURES CORPN. LTD. FILM HOUSE, 142 WARDOUR STREET, LONDON, WIV 4AH | [long rule in red]

Collation 32.2 × 24 cm: single fold with two separate sheets loosely inserted, 8 pp.

Contents Pp.[1] title page, [2] editorial stereos, accessories available, technical credits, [3] sample posters, [4] blank, [5–6] your selling campaign, [7] the story, the cast, samples of posters, [8] sample of poster.

Text Considerable variation in type and layout.

Paper Coated, white, wove, unwatermarked, all edges trimmed, sheets bulk less than 1 mm.

Copies AC, Cal.

E270   COLUMBIA PICTURES,
A Teacher's Guide to Lawrence of Arabia, 1963

First American Edition

[White lettering on brown rectangle across top] A TEACHER'S GUIDE TO | LAWRENCE OF ARABIA

Collation   23.6 × 16.3 cm: [1]⁴, 4 leaves, pp.[1]–8.

Contents   Pp.[1] title page and beginning of text, 2–8 text.

Text   20 lines, 6.6 × 11.3 cm double column.

Paper   White, wove, unwatermarked, all edges trimmed, sheets bulk less than 1 mm.

Binding   Sheets stapled with two metal staples.

Notes   Maps and illustrations in text.

Copies   AC, Cal.

E271   COLUMBIA PICTURES, Lawrence of Arabia
Poster, 1963

Marquee poster for theatres showing film

ACADEMY AWARD WINNER! | BEST PICTURE OF THE YEAR! | [single rule rectangle frame to right] WINNER OF | 7 | ACADEMY | AWARDS | [double rule] | BEST PICTURE | BEST DIRECTION | BEST CINEMATOGRAPHY | (Colour) | BEST ART DIRECTION | (Colour) | BEST MUSICAL SCORE | (Original) | BEST FILM EDITING | BEST SOUND | [below rectangle] COLUMBIA PICTURES presents | The SAM SPIEGEL-DAVID LEAN production of | LAWRENCE OF ARABIA | STARRING | ALEC GUINNESS · ANTHONY QUINN · JACK HAWKINS · JOSE FERRER | ANTHONY QUAYLE · CLAUDE RAINS · ARTHUR KENNEDY WITH | · OMAR SHARIF as 'Ali' | AND INTRODUCING | PETER O'TOOLE as 'LAWRENCE' · SCREEN PLAY ROBERT BOLT · | PRODUCED BY | SAM SPIEGEL · | DIRECTED BY | DAVID LEAN · | A HORIZON PICTURE BY | TECHNICOLOR | PHOTOGRAPHED IN | [in red] SUPERB PANAVISION 70 | w/c | Copyright 1963 by Columbia Pictures Corporation. All Rights Reserved.

Collation   35.7 × 56 cm.

Contents   Multicolour poster with drawing of battle scene as background for b/w drawing of white-robed Lawrence with upraised sword.

Paper   Heavy poster stock.

Copies   AC, Cal.

E272 COLUMBIA PICTURES, Lawrence of Arabia Film Posters, 1962

Series of four small posters for film, as follows: (1) Behind long dune attacking Turkish train; (2) Arab horsemen (attack on Akaba?); (3) Arabs looting horses from Turkish train; (4) Drawing of head of Lawrence in Arab head-dress. Figures of characters in film are emerging from behind.

Collation 28.1 × 35.5 cm.

Paper Heavy white wove, unwatermarked, all edges trimmed.

Copies AC.

E273 COLUMBIA PICTURES, Poster from film, 1971

Large Foyer Picture

Columbia Pictures | Presents | THE SAM SPIEGEL-DAVID LEAN | Production of | [in red, swash] LAWRENCE OF ARABIA | [in red] STANDS ALONE! | etc [all on yellow background]

Collation 102.6 × 68 cm: single sheet printed on one side only.

Paper White, wove, unwatermarked, all edges trimmed.

Copies AC.

Post Film, 1963–64

In the years following its release, the film, often shown on television, has been a watershed for a new generation who discovered Lawrence through it as a first exposure. Many new collections were stimulated by the film as were a number of dissertations and books. One of the first of the latter is Weintraub's *Private Shaw and Public Shaw,* a study of the relationships between G.B. Shaw and T.E. Shaw.

Comic books inevitably appeared following the popularity of the film. They are represented here by French, Dutch and English publicatons. One of the participants in the making of the film wrote of his experiences, *Single Bed for Three,* which gives the reader some idea of the conditions under which the film was made.

The year 1964 saw additional items published as a direct or indirect response to the film. Jehanne's (Theodora Duncan) *Seven Poems Dedicated to T.E. Lawrence,* privately printed in an edition of 100 copies, is the second book of poetry dedicated to his memory, the first being Altounyan (1937). The pseudonym is taken from *Richard Yea and Nay,* a book favoured by Lawrence in his youth. Urbina's *Lawrence de Arabia* is a popular rendering of the Lawrence story which also appeared in 1963. One of the strangest of the Lawrence-associated items is Sherwood's *Post Mortem Journal,* a piece of 20th-century occult literature. It is ostensibly the result of Lawrence's spirit speaking through an automatic writing medium.

The souvenir list was added to with the appearance of Broughton's first publication, *Lawrence of Arabia and Wareham,* a popular retelling of Lawrence's life in the local area.

1963

E275 STANLEY WEINTRAUB, Private Shaw and Public Shaw, Braziller, 1963

First American Edition

PRIVATE SHAW | *and* | PUBLIC SHAW | [long rule] | *a dual portrait of* | *Lawrence of Arabia and G.B.S.* | [long rule] | *by* STANLEY WEINTRAUB | GEORGE BRAZILLER *New York, 1963*

Collation 21.2 × 14.5 cm: [1–10]^{16}, 160 leaves, pp.[i–xii], xiii–xvi, [xvii–xviii], 1–302.

Contents Prp.[i] bastard title, [ii] facsimile of GBS inscription,[iii] title page, [iv] copyright, issue statements, printer's credit, [v] dedication, [vi] blank, [vii] quote from Rilke, [viii] blank, [ix] contents, [x] blank, [xi] illustrations, [xii] blank, xii–xvi foreword, [xvii] half-title, [xviii] blank, 1–276 text, 277–281 epilogue, [282] blank, 283–287 appendix, 288–294 references, 295–296 bibliography, 297–302 index.

RT On verso *Private Shaw and Public Shaw.* On recto [in italics, according to chapter].

Text 20 lines, 9.1 (9.5) × 9.7 cm.

Paper White, wove, unwatermarked, all edges trimmed, sheets bulk 2.5 cm.

Binding Light blue linen 168 brill. g B. On spine: [within black rectangle, gilt] *Private* | SHAW | *and Public* | SHAW | [below rectangle, gilt] *Stanley* | *Weintraub* | [in black] *George* | *Braziller.* T.e. light blue.

Published at $5.00.

Notes Another impression, second printing, as above.

Copies AC, Cal, UT, LC.

E276 STANLEY WEINTRAUB, Private Shaw and Public Shaw, Cape, 1963

Advance Proof of First English Edition

PRIVATE SHAW | *and* | PUBLIC SHAW | [rule] | *a dual portrait of* | *Lawrence of Arabia and G.B.S.* | [rule] | *by* STANLEY WEINTRAUB | [pub. device] | JONATHAN CAPE *Thirty Bedford Square London*

Collation 21.6 × 14.5 cm: [1–20]^{8}, 160 leaves, pp.[i–xii], xiii–xvi, [xvii–xviii], 1–302.

Contents Prp.[i] bastard title, [ii] facsimile of GBS inscription in Lawrence's copy of *Saint Joan*, [iii] title page, [iv] issue, copyright statements, printer's credit, [v] dedication, [vi] blank, [vii] quote, [viii] blank, [ix] contents, [x] blank, [xi] illustrations, [xii] blank, xiii–xvi foreword, [xvii] half-title, [xvii] blank, 1–281 text, [282] blank, 283–287 appendix, 288–294 references, 295–296 bibliography, 297–302 index.

RT On verso *Private Shaw and Public Shaw*. On recto [dates for each chapter].

Text 20 lines, 9.1 (9.5) × 9.7 cm.

Paper White, wove, unwatermarked, all edges trimmed, sheets bulk 2.2 cm.

Binding Red paper covers 15 m Red. On front cover: [pasted on label with blurb].

Copies Cal.

E277 STANLEY WEINTRAUB, Private Shaw and Public Shaw, Cape, 1963

First English Edition

PRIVATE SHAW | *and* | PUBLIC SHAW | [rule] | *a dual portrait of* | *Lawrence of Arabia and G.B.S.* | [rule] | *by* STANLEY WEINTRAUB | [publisher's device] | JONATHAN CAPE *Thirty Bedford Square London*

Collation 21.6 × 14.5 cm: [1–20]⁸, 160 leaves, pp.[i–xii], xiii–xvi, [xvii–xviii], 1–302.

Contents Prp.[i] bastard title, [ii] facsimile of GBS inscription in Lawrence's copy of *Saint Joan*, [iii] title page, [iv] issue, copyright statements, printer's credit, [v] dedication, [vi] blank, [vii] quote, [viii] blank, [ix] contents, [x] blank, [xi] illustrations, [xii] blank, xiii–xvi foreword, [xvii] half-title, [xviii] blank, 1–281 text, [282] blank, 293–287 appendix, 288–294 references, 295–296 bibliography, 297–302 index.

RT On verso *Private Shaw and Public Shaw*. On recto [dates for each chapter].

Text 20 lines, 9.1 (9.5) × 9.7 cm.

Paper White, wove, unwatermarked, all edges trimmed, sheets bulk 2.2 cm.

Binding Blue paper covered boards 182 m. Blue. On spine: [gilt] PRIVATE | SHAW | AND | PUBLIC | SHAW | [cut] | STANLEY | WEINTRAUB | [publisher's device]. T.e. black.

Published at 30s.

Notes Another state, same as above, with following differences: [Binding]: black paper covered boards. T.e. unstained.

Copies AC, Cal.

E278 LAWRENCE D'ARABIE, O.D.E.J, n.d.

First French Edition

[In red] Lawrence | [in red] d'Arabie | [cut] | [in blue] SÉRIE ÉLÉPHANT BLANC

Collation 25 × 17.8 cm: guillotined sheets glued to covers, 32 leaves, unpaged [1–64].

Contents Pp.[1] title page, [2] within decorative frame, series list, copyright statements, [3–32] text, [33] title of Prince Vaillant [*sic*], [34] within decorative border, series list, copyright statement, [35–64] text.

Typography and paper Sheets are comic strip panels with text in balloons.

Text Alternate double spreads are in colour. Hand lettered.

Binding Paper covered boards. On front cover: [series device] [in red] Lawrence | [in red] d'Arabie. On back cover: [series device] Prince Vaillant | "L'ILE DU TONNERRE".

Copies AC.

E279 Lawrence, Dell Comic Books, 1963

First American Edition

[Within blue rectangle upper left corner, in orange] DELL | 12 | [in light blue rectangle just below first one] 12-426-308 | [first word, red brown lettering, with white outline on first letter] Lawrence | DESERT WAR! | ARAB REVOLT! | THE UNBELIEVABLE | STORY OF | LAWRENCE | OF | ARABIA!

Collation 26 × 17.7 cm: [1]^{16}, 32 pages, unpaged.

Contents [Front cover] title page, [verso of front cover] b/w introduction to Lawrence, pp.1–32 text in form of panel cartoons, [inside rear cover] b/w filler of panels depicting water as resource in desert, [back cover] ad. for film.

Paper Newsprint, white, wove, unwatermarked, all edges trimmed, sheets bulk 2 mm.

Binding Covers are pictorial paper covers stapled to sheets with two metal staples.

Published at 12 cents.

Notes This comic book depended upon the film for sales, but does not follow that version.

Copies AC, Cal.

E280 HOWARD KENT, Single Bed for Three, Hutchinson, 1963

First English Edition

HOWARD KENT | Single Bed for Three | A 'LAWRENCE OF ARABIA'

NOTEBOOK | [publisher's device] HUTCHINSON OF LONDON

Collation 21.2 × 13.8 cm: [A]⁸ B–N⁸, 104 leaves, pp.[1–8], 9–208.

Contents Pp.[1] bastard title, [2] blank, [3] title page, [4] issue, copyright statements, printer's credit, [5–6] contents, [7] illustrations, [8] blank, 9–208 text.

RT On verso SINGLE BED FOR THREE. On recto [according to chapter].

Plates Five b/w photographs on coated paper, printed on both sides except for frontispiece, following pp.2, 52, 60, 128, 144.

Typography and paper $ 1 signed B.

Text 20 lines, 9.2 (9.2) × 9.8 cm. Set in Bembo.

Paper White, Antique wove, unwatermarked, all edges trimmed, sheets bulk 1.8 cm.

Binding Brown 40 s.r Br cloth. On spine: [gilt] HOWARD | KENT | [within red rhomboid] Single | bed | for | three | [below rhomboid, at foot] [pub. device] | HUTCHINSON.

Copies AC, Cal.

E281 ENRIQUE MARTINEZ FARINAS,
Lawrence de Arabia, G.P., 1963

First Spanish Edition

LAWRENCE | DE | ARABIA | [rule] | TEXTO: ENRIQUE M. FARIÑAS | [rule] | PORTADA: COBOS | [rule] | ILLUSTRACIONES: VILARROYA | [rule] | Difundido por | PLAZA EJANÉS, S.A. | Barcelona: Enrique Granados, 86–88 | Buenos Aires: Montevideo, 333 | Mexico D.F.: Ayuntamiento, 162–B | Bogotá: Carrera 8.a(s) Núms. 17–41 | EDICIONES G.P. – BARCELONA

Collation 15.7 × 8 cm: [1]–5⁸, 40 leaves, pp.[1–2], 3–[76], [1–4].

Contents Pp.[1] title page, [2] pub. ad., copyright statement, printer's credit, 3–[76] text, [1–4] list of titles in series.

Typography and paper $ 1 signed 4-LAWRENCE.

Text 20 lines, 6.6 × 6.8 cm.

Paper White, wove, unwatermarked, all edges trimmed, sheets bulk 6 mm.

Binding Pictorial paper covers. On front cover: ENCICLOPEDIA | POPULAR | ILUSTRADA | [in yellow] | Enrique M. Farinas | [in white] El | rey | sin | corona | [in red] LAWRENCE | [in white] | DE ARABIA. On back cover: ¿UN AVEN- | TURERO? | ¿UN POLITICO? | ¿UN HEROE? | La fabulosa | aventura del | hombre quel «invento» el | Oriente Medio | y conquistó para | la Gran Bretaña | el Imperio | del Petróleo. | [rest in blue] LA TIERRA | EL PENSAMIENTO | ENCICLOPEDIA POPULAR ILUSTRADA | EL HOMBRE | 7 PTD. | Las Musas.

Published at 7 PTAS.

Copies LC.

E282   JAMES DUNN, The Adventures of Lawrence of Arabia, Horowitz, 1963

First Australian Edition

[Double-page spread] The adventures of | Lawrence of Arabia | JAMES DUNN | [silhouette drawing] | HOROWITZ PUBLICATIONS INC. | LONDON | MELBOURNE · SYDNEY

Collation   17.8 × 11.5 cm: guillotined sheets, 64 leaves, pp.[1–4], 7–130.

Contents   Pp.[1] blank, [2–3] title page, [4] issue, publisher's statements, printer's credits, pp.7–8 prologue, 9–129 text, 130 bibliography.

Text   20 lines, 6.3 × 8.8 cm.

Paper   White, pulp, wove, unwatermarked, all edges trimmed, sheets bulk 9 mm.

Binding   Yellow paper covers 86 l.Y. On front cover: LAWRENCE 4'6 | 45-/ | PB164 | [in red] WINSTON CHURCHILL SAID: | "I deem him one of the | greatest being alive | in our time. I do not | see his like anywhere." | [drawing of O'Toole with sword, on orange square]. On spine: [in red, running down] LAWRENCE OF ARABIA, [in blue-green] JAMES DUNN. On back cover: [excerpts from text].

Published at   45 cents.

Notes   Another impression 1965 as above.

Copies   Cal.

1964

E283   JEHANNE (Theodora Duncan), Seven Poems Dedicated to T.E. Lawrence, privately printed, 1964

First American Edition

SEVEN POEMS | dedicated to | T.E. LAWRENCE | By Jehanne

Collation   21.8 × 13.9 cm: [1]⁶, 6 leaves, unpaged.

Contents   Pp.[1] title page, [2] copyright notice, [3] untitled poem, [4] blank, [5–11] text, [12] 'This edition is limited to | 100 copies of which this is | copy number ____'.

Text   10 lines, 4 × 10.5 cm.

Paper   White, wove, unwatermarked, all edges trimmed, sheets bulk 1 mm.

Binding   57 l. Br. paper wrappers. On front cover: SEVEN POEMS | Dedicated to | T.E. Lawrence | · | By Jehanne. Brown cord run through two holes in spine.

Notes   Limited to 100 copies. Jehanne is the pseudonym of Theodora Duncan.

Copies   AC, Cal, UT.

E284 PEDRO A. URBINA, Lawrence de Arabia, Instituto de Artes Gráficas, 1964

First Spanish Edition

[Wide rule] | [cut] PEDRO A. URBINA [cut] | [wide rule] | *Lawrence | de Arabia* | [wide rule] | COLECCION [next word within black oval, in white] auriga SERIE AMARILLA | [wide rule] | instituto de artes gráficas [vertical rule] I.D.A.G. | [wide rule]

Collation 19.5 × 16.5 cm: [1] – 10^8, 80 leaves, pp.[1–4], 5–152, [1–8].

Contents: [1–2] blank, [3] title page, [4] adaptor's, illustrator's credits, issue, copyright, distributor's statements, 5–152 text, [1] contents, 2–8 blank.

Plates Nine colour plates, printed on one side only, following pp.[4], 45, 58, 70, 84, 110, 122, 144, 148; fold map following p.146.

Typography and paper $ 1 signed 7.

Text 20 lines, 9.9 × 6.8 double column 14.3 cm.

Paper White, wove, unwatermarked, all edges trimmed, sheets bulk 1 cm.

Binding Only copy seen rebound.

Notes Urbina is listed as the 'adapter' in credits on verso of title page.

Copies LAPL.

E285 JANE SHERWOOD, Post-Mortem Journal, Spearman, 1964

First English Edition

Post-Mortem Journal | *Communications from T.E. Lawrence* | JANE SHERWOOD | NEVILLE SPEARMAN |.LONDON 1964.

Collation 18.5 × 12.3 cm: [A]^{16} B–D^{16}, 62 leaves, pp.[1–8], 9–128.

Contents Pp.[1] bastard title, [2] blank, [3] title page, [4] copyright statement, printer's credits, [5] half-title, [6] blank, [7] contents, [8] blank, 9–13 introduction, [14] blank, 15–128 text.

RT On verso *Post-Mortem Journal*. On recto [in italics, according to chapter].

Typography and paper $ 1 signed B.

Text 20 lines, 9.1 (9.4) × 8.9 cm.

Paper White, wove, unwatermarked, all edges trimmed, sheets bulk 1.3 cm.

Binding Orange cloth 72 d. OY. On spine: [running down] Jane Sherwood POST-MORTEM JOURNAL Spearman.

Published at 15s.

Copies AC, Cal.

E286   JANE SHERWOOD, Post-Mortem Journal, Spearman, 1964

Publisher's prospectus

POST- | MORTEM | JOURNAL | Communications from T.E. Lawrence | through the mediumship of Jane Sherwood

Collation   19.2 × 12.3 cm: single leaf printed on both sides.

Contents   [Recto] title page, same as dust wrapper of book, [verso] blurb and order form.

Text   20 lines, 8.6 × 10.1 cm.

Paper   White, coated, unwatermarked, all edges trimmed.

Published at   Free advertising flyer.

Copies   AC.

E287   HARRY BROUGHTON, Lawrence of Arabia and Wareham, Pictorial Museum, 1964

First English Edition

LAWRENCE OF ARABIA | AND WAREHAM | COMPILED BY HARRY BROUGHTON | (Sometime Mayor of Wareham) | [seal of city] | PICTORIAL MUSEUM, WAREHAM, DORSET

Collation   20 × 13 cm: [1]⁶, 6 leaves, unpaged.

Contents   Pp.[1] front cover, [2] blank, [3] title page, [4] photos, [5] text, 6–7 map, [8] photos, [9] Lawrence data, [10] Wareham data, [11] photos, [12] back cover.

Text   20 lines, 9.2 × 9.2 cm.

Paper   White, wove, unwatermarked, all edges trimmed, sheets bulk 1 mm.

Binding   White paper covers stapled to sheets with two metal staples. On front cover: LAWRENCE OF ARABIA | AND WAREHAM | [b/w photo of Lawrence in Arab robes] | *Picture: Hutchinson & Co. (Publishers) Ltd., London.* On back cover: ANGLEBURY PRESS, WAREHAM.

Copies   AC, Cal.

E288   ANDRÉ THIBAULT, Colonel Lawrence et L'Arabie, Charpentier, 1964

First French Edition

ANDRÉ THIBAULT | COLONEL | LAWRENCE | ET L'ARABIE | Couverture de J. GILLY | [pub. dev.] | LIBRAIRIE CHARPENTIER | PARIS

Collation   16.5 × 11.5 cm: guillotined sheets, 96 leaves, pp.1–188, [1–4].

Contents Pp.[1] title page, [2] copyright statements, [3]–4 preface, [5] map, [6] blank, [7]–188 text, [1] blank, [2–3] list of titles in series, [4] printer's colophon.

RT On both verso and recto COLONEL LAWRENCE ET L'ARABIE.

Text 20 lines, 8.2 (8.5) × 8 cm.

Paper White, wove, unwatermarked, all edges trimmed, sheets bulk 1 cm.

Binding Pictorial paper covers. On front cover: [in white] COLONEL LAWRENCE | ET L'ARABIE | [at bottom] [publisher's device], [within rhomboid] *Texte Intégral*. On spine: [running up] A. THIBAULT · COLONEL LAWRENCE ET L'ARABIE | [at foot, running across] [pub. device] | 30. On back cover COLONEL LAWRENCE ET L'ARABIE | [21-line brief biography of Lawrence] | [publisher's device].

Published at 30 July 1964.

Copies Rosen.

Evaluation: Beginnings of Scholarship, 1965–1969

In 1965 yet two more juveniles appeared: Barbary, *Lawrence and His Desert Raiders*, a retelling of the Arab campaign, and Dunn, *The Adventures of Lawrence of Arabia*, the second Australian juvenile after Roseler (1927). Two anti-Lawrence Turkish books were also published: Kutay, *Lavrens'e Karsi Kuscubasi*, and Serez, *Lawrence ve Arap İsyani*.

In 1966, Bayard L. Kilgour '27 presented his outstanding Lawrence collection ot the Houghton Library at Harvard. The lists described here show it to be not only rich in manuscript materials but it contains, as well, many of the extremely rare items, among them a copy of the Oxford edition of *Seven Pillars of Wisdom* (1922). This year also saw the publication of another Broughton work, *Lawrence of Arabia and Dorset*, another local-interest pamphlet.

An awakening of interest on the part of scholarship was seen in 1967. An Honours thesis, a Master's thesis, and a doctoral dissertation on Lawrence were all produced during this period by Stephen King. Houston's *A Checklist of Lawrence* is an attempt at garnering from all available national bibliographies a checklist of Lawrence materials. The following year, Dr Frank Baxter had copies made of his *An Annotated Checklist of a Collection of Writings by and About T.E. Lawrence*. Baxter, an accomplished Professor of English assembled one of the finer Lawrence collections.

Theodora Duncan published a second collection of her poems, *Ten Poems More Dedicated to T.E. Lawrence*. This is a companion volume to her earlier collection of poems (1964).

The year 1969 saw the appearance in book form of an earlier version of the text that had appeared in serial form in the *Sunday Times* (1968), Knightley and Simpson's *The Secret Lives of Lawrence of Arabia*. The foreign rights were readily snapped up. This book appeared in more translations than all other Lawrence books except, perhaps, Lawrence's own *Seven Pillars* and *Revolt*. The book did not retain quite all of the material contained in the newspaper articles.

1965

E289   JAMES BARBARY, Lawrence and His Desert Raiders, Parrish, 1965

First English Edition

[Double-page spread] *Lawrence | and his | Desert Raiders* | JAMES BARBARY | Illustrated by | ELMA CAMERON | [line drawing] MAX PARRISH · LONDON

Collation   18.5 × 12.3 cm: [1]⁸ 2–6⁸, 48 leaves, pp.[1–4], 5–95, [96].

Contents   Pp.[1] bastard title, [2–3] title page,[4] contents, copyright statement and printer's credit, 5–[96] text.

Typography and paper $ 1 signed L.D.R. -2.

Text   20 lines, 8.3 × 8.8 cm.

Paper   White, unwatermarked, all edges trimmed, sheets bulk 1 mm.

Binding   Blue cloth simulated paper covered boards 169 s.g B. On spine: [within gilt elipse, running down] *Lawrence and his Desert Raiders* JAMES BARBARY *Parrish*.

Published at   10s 6d, May 1965.

Copies   AC, Cal.

E290   JAMES BARBARY, Lawrence and His Desert Raiders, Meredith, 1968

First American Edition

[Two-page spread] LAWRENCE AND HIS | [Arab dagger] DESERT | RAIDERS | JAMES BARBARY | *Illustrated by ELMA CAMERON* | [Also by James Barbary | THE ENGINE AND THE GUN | *MEREDITH PRESS New York*

Collation   20.5 × 13.7 cm: [1–6]⁸, 48 leaves, pp.[1–4], 5–96.

Contents   Pp.[1] bastard title, [2–3] title page, [4] copyright, issue statements, printer's credits, 5 contents, [6] blank, [7] half-title, [8] map, 9–96 text.

RT   On verso Lawrence and His Desert Raiders. On recto [according to chapter] .

Text   20 lines, 10.3 (10.5) × 10.2 cm.

Paper   White, wove, unwatermarked,all edges trimmed, sheets bulk 5 mm.

Binding   Tangerine paper covered boards, 71 m.OY, brick red cloth spine 38 d.r.O. On spine: [running down, gilt] JAMES BARBARY *Meredith Press* | LAWRENCE AND HIS DESERT RAIDERS. Tangerine end papers.

Published at $3.95.

Copies   AC, Cal, LC.

E291 CĒMĀL KUTAY, Lavrens'e Karşi Kuşçubaşi, Unan, 1965

First Turkish Edition

Cemal Kutay | Lavrens'e Karşi | KUŞÇUBAŞI | [pub. device] | Nesreden: Mustafa UNAN | Tarih Ysymlari Müessesesi – Istanboul, Nuruosmaniye C. | No: 78/A – Telefon: 22 78 10 – Posta Kutusu 167 – Istanboul

Collation 15.5 × 11.5 cm: [1]–20^8, 160 leaves, pp.[1–3], 4–320.

Contents Pp.[1] title page, [2] author's note, [3]–[12] preface, [13]–320 text.

RT On both verso and recto LAVRENS'E KARŞI KUŞÇUBAŞI.

Typography and paper $ 1 signed Fr.2.

Text 20 lines, 8.1 (8.6) × 8.9 cm.

Paper White, newsprint, wove, unwatermarked, all edges trimmed, sheets bulk 1.6 cm.

Binding Black embossed cloth. On front cover: [all in white] [within single rule frame] Cemal Kutay | [within second single rule frame] Lavrens'e Karşi | KUŞÇUBAŞI. On spine: [spine overprinted all in white, all lettering in white on black background rectangles] [across] Cemal Kutay | [running up] Lavrens'e Karşi | Kuşçubaşi. White and orange head and tail bands. Orange cloth place marker.

Copies UCLA, LC.

E292 NACI SEREZ, Lawrence ve Arap İsyani, Arkin Kítabeví, 1965

First Turkish Edition

T.E. LAWRENCE | ve | ARAP İSYANI | NACI SEREZ | [pub. device] | ARKIN KÍTABEVÍ | Ankara Cad. 60, İstanbul.

Collation 19 × 13.7 cm: [1]–9^8 10^6, 78 leaves, pp.[1–6], 7–154, [1–2].

Contents Pp.[1] bastard title, [2] frontis., [3] title page, [4] copyright statement, [5] contents, [6] blank, 7–154 text, [1] bibliography, [2] blank.

Typography and paper $ 1 signed F.4.

Text 20 lines, 7.4 × 9.9 cm.

Paper White, wove, unwatermarked, all edges trimmed, sheets bulk 8 mm.

Binding Pictorial paper covers. On front cover: [in white] Naci Serez | [in white] LAWRENCE | [in white] ve Arap İsyani | [in yellow] ARKIN KÍTABEVÍ – İSTANBUL.

Copies LC.

1966

E293   HARVARD UNIVERSITY, List of Items Presented to Harvard by Bayard L. Kilgour '27

Volumes presented by | Bayard L. Kilgour, Jr. '27 | 225 East Fourth Street | Cincinnati, Ohio 45202

Collation   30 × 21 cm: 34 leaves.

Typography and paper   Typed sheets.

Copies   AC.

E294   HARVARD UNIVERSITY, Manuscripts Presented to Harvard by Bayard L. Kilgour '27

Manuscripts presented by | Mr. Bayard L. Kilgour | 225 East Fourth Street| Cincinnati, Ohio 45202

Collation   30 × 21 cm: 53 leaves.

Typography and paper   Typed sheets.

Copies   AC.

E295   HARRY BROUGHTON, Lawrence of Arabia and Dorset, Pictorial Museum, 1966

First English Edition

LAWRENCE OF ARABIA | AND DORSET | COMPILED BY HARRY BROUGHTON | *(Sometime Mayor of Wareham)* | [seal of city] | PICTORIAL MUSEUM, WAREHAM, DORSET

Collation   20.5 × 13 cm: [1]^{10}, 10 leaves, unpaged.

Contents   Pp.[1] title page, [2] photo, [3–20] text and photos.

Text   20 lines, 7.7 × 9.3 cm.

Paper   White, wove, coated, unwatermarked, all edges trimmed, sheets bulk 2 mm.

Binding   White paper covers stapled to sheets by two metal staples. On front cover: LAWRENCE OF ARABIA | AND DORSET | [b/w photo of Lawrence in Arab robes] | *Picture: Hutchinson & Co. (Publishers) Ltd., London.* On back cover: Anglebury Press, Wareham.

Published at   3d, 13 May 1966.

Copies   AC, Cal, LC.

E296 HARRY BROUGHTON, Lawrence of Arabia and Dorset, Pictorial Museum, 1966

Publisher's Prospectus

LAWRENCE OF ARABIA | AND DORSET | [photo of Lawrence in Arab robes]

Collation 20.6 × 12.9 cm: single leaf printed on both sides.

Contents Pp.[1] title, [2] blurb and order form.

Paper White, wove, unwatermarked, all edges trimmed.

Published at Free advertising flyer.

Copies AC.

1967

E297 STEPHEN H. KING, Thomas Edward Lawrence and Classical Statesmanship, 1967

Unpublished Honors Thesis

CLAREMONT MEN'S COLLEGE | THOMAS EDWARD LAWRENCE | AND CLASSICAL STATESMANSHIP | A REPORT TO | HAROLD W. ROOD | AND | O.W. PHELPS | BY | STEPHEN H. KING | FOR | HONORS THESIS X190 | APRIL 19, 1967

Collation 27.8 × 21.5 cm: 95 leaves, ii, 93 pp. typed on one side only.

Contents Prp.[i] title page, ii contents, pp.1–12 introduction, 13–85 text, 86–90 appendixes, 91–93 bibliography.

Text 20 lines, 16.4 × 14.9 cm.

Paper White, wove, unwatermarked, all edges trimmed, sheets bulk 5 mm.

Copies AC, Cal.

E298 GUYLA BOND HOUSTON, A Checklist of Lawrenciana, Privately Issued, 1967

First American Edition

THOMAS EDWARD LAWRENCE (1888–1935) | A checklist of Lawrenciana, 1915–1965 | By | Guyla Bond Houston | November 1967

Collation 28.2 × 21.5 cm: 158 leaves, pp.[6], 1–148, [4]; xeroxed sheets printed on one side only.

Contents Pr.leaf [1–2] blank, [3] title page, on verso copyright statement, compiler's address, [4] introduction, [5] contents, [6] blank, leaves 1–148 text, [1] blank, [2–3] sources consulted, [4] blank.

Paper   White, wove, unwatermarked, all edges trimmed, sheets bulk 1.5 cm.

Binding   Smead pressboard covers attached with thin metal connectors through holes in sheets. Colour varies. On front cover: [paper patch with gold edges, typed] THOMAS EDWARD LAWRENCE | (1888–1935) | A Checklist of Lawrenciana, | 1915–1965 | By | Guyla Bond Houston.

Notes   Three supplements, as follows: 1st supplement, 1970, 1–10 leaves; 2nd supplement, 1975, 1–12 leaves; 3rd supplement, 1978, 1–59 leaves.

Copies   AC, Cal, B, BL, H, LC.

E298a   JAMES G. COATES, The Influence of T.E. Lawrence on British Foreign Policy in the Middle East 1918–1922, McGill University, 1967

Canadian Master's Thesis

THE INFLUENCE OF T.E. LAWRENCE | ON BRITISH FOREIGN POLICY IN THE MIDDLE EAST 1918–1922 | by | James G. Coates | A Thesis | Submitted to the Faculty of Graduate Studies | of McGill University | in partial fulfillment of the degree of Master of Arts | December, 1966 |©James G. Coates, 1967

Collation   28 × 21.5 cm: typed sheets one side only, 160 leaves, pp.[1–3], i–vii, 1–151.

Contents   Prp.[1–2] permission sheet, [3] half-title, i title page, ii quote from Lawrence, iii–iv preface, v–vii contents, pp.1–134 text, 135–138 appendixes, 139–151 bibliography.

Typography and paper   Typed original photocopied one side of sheet.

Paper   White, wove, unwatermarked, all edges trimmed.

Note   AC.

1968

E9299   FRANK C. BAXTER, An Annotated Check-list of a Collection of Writings By and About T.E. Lawrence, privately printed, 1968

First American Edition

An Annotated Check-List | of | A Collection of Writings By and About | T.E. LAWRENCE | (Lawrence of Arabia) | With many Other Things Collateral to the Story | of his Military, Literary and Personal Life | and to the History of the Arab Revolt | and the Palestine Campaign | of World War I | "Wisdom hath builded a house; she | hath hewn out her seven pillars." | Gathered over Four Decades | by | Frank C. Baxter | Los Angeles | 1968 | Sixty Copies | (Copyright, 1968, by Frank C. Baxter)

Collation 31 × 21.1 cm: 104 leaves, pp.[1–4], 1–99, [1].

Contents Leaf [1] title page, [2] foreword, [3] contents, [4] section title, leaves 1–99 text, [1] blank.

Text Mimeo of typed original.

Paper White, wove, unwatermarked, all edges trimmed, sheets bulk 1 cm.

Binding Green paper covers 145 m.G, black cloth hinge at top. On front cover: An Annotated Check-List | of | A Collection of Writings By and About | T.E. LAWRENCE | (LAWRENCE OF ARABIA) | With Many Other Things Collateral to the Story | of his Military, Literary, and Personal Life | and to the History of the Arab Revolt | and the Palestine Campaign | of World War I | Frank C. Baxter | Los Angeles | 1968.

Notes Privately printed, 60 copies not for sale.

Copies AC, Cal, B, BL, H, UT, LC.

E300 JEHANNE (Theodora Duncan), Ten Poems More Dedicated to T.E. Lawrence, 1968

First American Edition

TEN POEMS MORE | dedicated | to | T.E. LAWRENCE | by Jehanne | [cut]
Collation 22.2 × 14.3 cm: [1]⁸, pp.[1–16].

Contents Pp.[1] blank, [2] copyright statement, [3] title page, [4–14] text, [15] 'This edition is limited to | 50 copies, of which this | is No.____'.

Text 10 lines, 3.6 × 7.3 cm.

Paper Light buff, unwatermarked, all edges trimmed, sheets bulk 2 mm.

Binding Tan paper covers 76 l. y Br. On front cover: TEN POEMS MORE | Dedicated to T.E. Lawrence | · | by Jehanne [deep brown silk cord attaches sheets to cover through two holes punched in spine].

Notes Limited to 50 copies.

Copies AC, Cal.

1969

E301 PHILLIP KNIGHTLEY and COLIN SIMPSON, The Secret Lives of Lawrence of Arabia, Nelson, 1969

Uncorrected Proof of First English Edition

The Secret Lives of | [outline type] LAWRENCE | [outline type] OF ARABIA | *Phillip Knightley and Colin Simpson* | Nelson
Collation 23 × 15 cm: [1–18]⁸ [19]², 146 leaves, pp.[i–xii], 1–278, [2].

Contents Prp.[i] bastard title, [ii] blank, [iii] title page, [iv] copyright, issue statements, [v] contents, [vi] plates, [vii] publisher's note, [viii]–ix acknowledgments, [x] blank, [xi] quote by Lawrence, [xii] blank, pp.[1]–6 introduction, [7]–276 text, [277]–278 bibliography, [1–2] blank.

RT   On verso THE SECRET LIVES OF LAWRENCE OF ARABIA. On recto [according to chapter].

Plates   Sixteen photographs on coated paper, following pp.4, 20, 84, 100, 164, 180, 244, 260.

Text   20 lines, 8.3 (8.8) × 11 cm.

Paper   White, wove, unwatermarked, all edges trimmed, sheets bulk 2.2 cm.

Binding   Green paper wrappers 150 gy G. On front cover: [same as title page with addition of:] UNCORRECTED | PROOF COPY [in centre under authors' names].

Notes   Second page proofs have blue paper wrappers 185 p Blue.

Copies   AC, Cal.

E302   PHILLIP KNIGHTLEY and COLIN SIMPSON, The Secret Lives of Lawrence of Arabia, Nelson, 1969

First English Edition

The Secret Lives of | [outline type] LAWRENCE | [outline type] OF ARABIA | *Phillip Knightley and Colin Simpson* | Nelson

Collation   22.4 × 15 cm: [1]⁸ 2–19⁸, 152 leaves, pp.[i–viii], ix–[x], [1], 2–293, [1].

Contents   Prp.[i] bastard title, [ii] blank, [iii] title page, [iv] copyright, issue statements, [v] contents, [vi] plates, [vii] section title, [viii]–ix acknowledgments, [x] quote from Lawrence, [1]–6 introduction, [7]–276 text, [277]–278 bibliography, [279]–293 index, [1] blank.

RT   On verso THE SECRET LIVES OF LAWRENCE OF ARABIA. On recto [according to chapter].

Plates   Sixteen photographs on coated paper, following pp.54, 62, 70, 94, 254.

Typography and paper $ 1 signed 2.

Text   20 lines, 8.2 (8.9) × 10.8 cm.

Paper   White, wove, unwatermarked, all edges trimmed, sheets bulk 2.3 cm.

Binding   Black cloth. On spine: [in blue, running down] PHILLIP KNIGHTLEY COLIN SIMPSON | THE SECRET LIVES OF LAWRENCE OF ARABIA | [across at bottom] NELSON. End papers photograph.

Published at   42s, September 1969.

Notes   A 2nd impression, September 1969, incorporates corrections on p.275 and contains impression statement on verso of title page. Another impression, Literary Guild, same as above with following differences: [on title page, imprint reads] THE LITERARY GUILD | LONDON; [Binding]:

51 deep O. On spine: [across at bottom, pub. device]. White end papers. Text is same as first impression above, uncorrected. Another state has white end papers, issued for launching party. Based on articles published in *Sunday Times*, 1968. Major revisions in published book.

Copies AC, Cal, LC.

E303 PHILLIP KNIGHTLEY and COLIN SIMPSON, The Secret Lives of Lawrence of Arabia, Nelson, 1969

Publisher's Prospectus

[In blue] THE [next word in red within red triangle] SECRET [the rest in blue] SECRET LIVES OF LAWRENCE OF ARABIA

Collation 35 × 25.5 cm: single-fold folder with second leaf having flap turned in and stapled to form pocket.

Contents Pp.[1] title, blurb in blue and red, outline figure of Lawrence with British flag superimposed, [2] in white on dark blue continuation of blurb, [3] in white on dark blue list of countries expected to purchase rights, flap has photo of Lawrence used for outline on front cover, [4] brief biographies of authors and photo of Lawrence on motorcycle with Union Jack superimposed on headlight lens.

Text 20 lines, 11.3 × 9.7 cm. (double column).

Paper Heavy, wove, unwatermarked, all edges trimmed.

Notes Inserted in pocket formed by flap on second leaf: (1) copy of note from A.W. Lawrence to Keeper of Mss, Bodleian, giving permission for Simpson to read materials on TEL held there, 14.8 × 15.5 cm; (2) dustwrapper intended for first issue of book (not used); (3) copies of the four issues of the *Sunday Times* articles on T.E. Lawrence used as the basis for the later book, reduced in size, each article single sheet printed on both sides, 32 × 24 cm; (4) a 16-page synopsis (chapter by chapter) of the book stapled at upper left corner appear to be enlargements of original typed copy, sheets printed on one side only, 33 × 20.5 cm.

Copies AC, Cal.

E304 PHILLIP KNIGHTLEY and COLIN SIMPSON, The Secret Lives of Lawrence of Arabia, Collins, 1969

Publisher's broadside

Press release. The Secret Lives of Lawrence of Arabia, by Phillip Knightley and Colin Simpson. London, 1969.

Collation 32.5 × 20.5 cm.

Paper White, wove, unwatermarked, all edges trimmed.

Copies AC, Cal.

E305   PHILLIP KNIGHTLEY and COLIN SIMPSON, The Secret Lives of Lawrence of Arabia, Nelson, 1969

Publisher's broadside

The Secret Lives of Lawrence of Arabia. [by] Phillip Knightley & Colin Simpson. London 1969

Collation   23.5 × 18.5 cm.

Notes   Accompanied by photographic print of Lawrence in Arab dress, given to press at the launching party for book.

Copies   AC, Cal.

E306   PHILLIP KNIGHTLEY and COLIN SIMPSON, The Secret Lives of Lawrence of Arabia, Nelson, 1969

Publisher's prospectus

Collation   29.8 × 20.4 cm: single sheet printed on one side only.

Paper   Yellow, wove, unwatermarked, all edges trimmed.

Copies   AC.

E308   PHILLIP KNIGHTLEY and COLIN SIMPSON, The Secret Lives of Lawrence of Arabia, Panther, 1971

Second English Edition

Phillip Knightley and | Colin Simpson | The Secret Lives of | Lawrence of Arabia | A Panther Book

Collation   17.8 × 11.5 cm: guillotined sheets glued to covers, 168 leaves, pp.[1–8], 9–331, [5].

Contents   Pp.[1] blurb, [2] brief biographies on authors, [3] title page, [4] issue, copyright statements, printer's credit, [5] contents, [6] illustrations, [7] acknowledgments, [8] – 10 formal acknowledgments, [11] – 17 introduction, [18] blank, [19] – 314 text, [315] – 316 bibliography, [317] – 331 index, [1–4] publisher's ads, [5] list of authors on publisher's list.

RT   On verso THE SECRET LIVES OF LAWRENCE OF ARABIA. On recto [according to chapter].

Text   20 lines, 6.9 (7.1) × 8.8 cm.

Paper   White, wove, unwatermarked, all edges trimmed, sheets bulk 2 cm.

Binding   White paper. On front cover: Phillip Knightley and Colin Simpson | [in red] The Secret Lives | [in red] of Lawrence | [in red] of Arabia | An explosive examination of a 20th Century legend | [painting of Lawrence in Arab robes, colour] | Illustrated [within oval] Panther | 586 03433 1. On spine: [running down, in red] The Secret Lives of Lawrence of Arabia | Phillip Knightley and Colin Simpson | Panther 586 03433 1. On back cover: [lengthy blurb, title in gold, cover illustrator's credit].

Published at   40p, February 1971.

Copies   AC, Cal.

E309   PHILLIP KNIGHTLEY and COLIN SIMPSON, The Secret Lives of Lawrence of Arabia, McGraw-Hill, 1970

First American Edition

[Within double rules] THE SECRET LIVES OF | LAWRENCE | OF ARABIA | PHILLIP KNIGHTLEY AND COLIN SIMPSON | [reproduction of John drawing of T.E. Lawrence] | [four-line quote from *Seven Pillars of Wisdom*] | McGRAW-HILL BOOK COMPANY | NEW YORK ST. LOUIS SAN FRANCISCO | MEXICO PANAMA

Collation   22.8 × 15 cm: [1–11]¹⁶, 176 leaves, pp.[i–vii], viii, [ix], x–xiv, [1–2], 3–333, [5].

Contents   Prp.[i] bastard title, [ii] blank, [iii]title page, [iv] copyright, issue statements, [v] contents, [vi] blank, [vii] –viii acknowledgments, [ix] –xiv introduction, pp.[1] section title, [2] blank, 3–316 text, 317–318 bibliography, 319–333 index, [1] blank, [2] note on the authors, [3–5] blank.

RT   On verso THE SECRET LIVES OF LAWRENCE OF ARABIA. On recto [according to chapter].

Plates   Sixteen b/w photos on coated paper, printed on both sides, following p.178.

Text   20 lines, 8.4 (8.8) × 10.8 cm.

Paper   White, wove, unwatermarked, all edges trimmed, sheets bulk 3 cm.

Binding   Black cloth. On front cover: [within blind stamped square, gilt line cut of John's drawing of T.E. Lawrence in Arab head dress]. On spine: [all gilt] [rule] | [Arabic lettering] | [rule] | [running down] THE SECRET LIVES OF LAWRENCE | OF ARABIA | PHILLIP KNIGHTLEY AND COLIN SIMPSON | [rule] | [Arabic lettering] | [rule] | [across] McGRAW-HILL. End papers [black with gold Arabic lettering]. Black and white tail and head bands.

Published at $8.95.

Notes   A 2nd printing identical to above. Another issue, Book club edition, smaller format resetting of type, same as above, with following differences: [Collation]: 21 × 13.7 cm: 1–11¹⁶, 176 leaves, pp.[i–v], vi, [vii], viii, [ix], x–xv, [xvi], [1–3], 4–334, [2]; [Contents]: [i] bastard title, [ii] blank, [iii] title page, [iv] issue, copyright statements, [v]–vi contents, [vii]–viii acknowledgments, [ix]–xv introduction, [xvi] blank, pp.[1] section title, [2] blank, [3]–316 text, [317]–319 bibliography, [320] blank, [321]–334 index, [1–2] blank; [RT]: on verso THE SECRET LIVES OF LAWRENCE OF ARABIA, on recto [according to chapter]; [Text]: 20 lines 8.6 (8.8) × 10.3 cm; [Paper]: white, wove, unwatermarked, top and bottom edges trimmed, sheets bulk 2.5 cm.

Copies   AC, Cal, LC.

E310   PHILLIP KNIGHTLEY and COLIN SIMPSON, The Secret Lives of Lawrence of Arabia, Bantam, 1971

Second American Edition

The Secret Lives of | LAWRENCE OF ARABIA | [rule] | Phillip Knightley and Colin Simpson | [four-line quote from *Seven Pillars of Wisdom*] | [publisher's device] | A NATIONAL GENERAL COMPANY

Collation   17.8 × 10.7 cm: [guillotined sheets], 176 leaves, pp.[i–vi], vii–xv, [xvi–xviii], 1–332, [2].

Contents   Prp.[i] quotes from reviews, [ii] blank, [iii] title page, [iv] copyright, issue statements, [v] contents, [vi] blank, vii–viii acknowledgments, ix–xv introduction, [xvi] blank, [xvii] half-title, [xviii] blank, pp.1–311 text, [312] blank, 313–314 bibliography, 315–332 index, [1] biographical note on authors, [2] publisher's ads.

RT   On both verso and recto THE SECRET LIVES OF LAWRENCE OF ARABIA.

Plates   Eight photographs on uncoated paper, printed on both sides, following p.158.

Text   20 lines, 7 (7.1) × 8.8 cm.

Paper   White, wove, unwatermarked, all edges trimmed, sheets bulk 2 cm.

Binding   Black paper covers. On front cover: [first 6 lines in white] THE ONLY BOOK WITH THE DISTURBING, | *NEWLY-REVEALED* | TRUTH ABOUT THE BRITISH "PRINCE OF MECCA" | SOLDIER, AUTHOR, STATESMAN, | 20TH-CENTURY LEGEND | [rule] | BY PHILLIP KNIGHTLEY AND COLIN SIMPSON | [6 lines in gold] the | Secret Lives | of | Lawrence | of | Arabia | [photo of Lawrence within frame of gold and white] | [in white] FULLY ILLUSTRATED. On spine: [publisher's device within white rectangle with rounded corners] | [remaining in gold except author s'names] NON- | FICTION | [rule] | $1.50 | [running down] | the Secret Lives of Lawrence of Arabia | [across in white] KNIGHTLEY | AND | SIMPSON | [running down in gold] 553.05796.150. On back cover: [within rules in gold] Lawrence | of | Arabia | [nine lines in white] ARCHAEOLOGIST, AUTHOR, SAVANT, | SOLDIER, INTIMATE OF POETS AND KINGS, | AN INTELLECTUAL WHO | WAS ALSO A MAN OF ACTION... | OR | PATHOLOGICAL LIAR, HOMOSEXUAL, IRISH NOBODY, TRAITOR, | A FOREIGN OFFICE LACKEY IN | FANCY DRESS? | [below line, in white, ten-line blurb]. All edges stained yellow.

Published at $1.50.

Copies   AC, Cal.

E311   PHILLIP KNIGHTLEY and COLIN SIMPSON, Het Geheim Leven van Lawrence of Arabia, Elsevier, 1970

First Dutch Edition

PHILLIP KNIGHTLEY | COLIN SIMPSON | Het geheim leven | van |

Lawrence of Arabia | [pub. device] | ELSEVIER-AMSTERDAM-BRUSSEL MCMLXX. [all lines justified to left]

Collation   20.4 × 13.2 cm: [1–15]⁸, 120 leaves, pp.[1–6], 7–239, [240].

Contents   Pp.[1] bastard title, [2] blank, [3] title page, [4] original title, copyright statement, [5] contents, [6] blank, 7–[12] introduction, 13–[240] text.

Text   20 lines, 7.2 × 10.5 cm.

Paper   White, wove, unwatermarked, all edges trimmed, sheets bulk 2 cm.

Binding   Orange cloth 50 s. O. On spine: P. KNIGHTLEY | C. SIMPSON | [gilt rule] | [within black rectangle, gilt] HET GEHEIM | LEVEN VAN | *Lawrence* | *of* | *Arabia* | [gilt rule] | ELSEVIER. Grey head and tail bands. T.e. grey.

Published at   255.-.

Copies   AC.

E312   PHILLIP KNIGHTLEY and COLIN SIMPSON, Les Vies Secrètes de Lawrence d'Arabie, Laffont, 1970

First French Edition

PHILLIP KNIGHTLEY | COLIN SIMPSON | LES VIES SECRÈTES | DE | LAWRENCE D'ARABIE | traduit de l'anglais par Paule et Raymond Olcina | [publisher's device] | ROBERT LAFFONT | 6, place Saint-Sulpice, 6 | PARIS-VIe

Collation   24 × 15.4 cm: [1]¹⁶ 2–13¹⁶, 208 leaves, pp.[1–9], 10–415, [1].

Contents   Pp.[1–2] blank, [3] bastard title, [4] blank, [5] title page, [6] original title, copyright statement, [7] quote from *Seven Pillars*, [8] blank, [9]–17 introduction, [18] blank, [19]–408 text, [409] acknowledgments, [410] blank, [411]–412 acknowledgments, [413]–415 bibliography, [1] printer's colophon.

RT   On verso LES VIES SECRÈTES DE LAWRENCE D'ARABIE. On recto [according to chapter].

Plates   Eight plates on coated paper, printed on both sides, following pp.128, 256.

Typography and paper $ 1 signed 3.

Text   20 lines, 9.6 (9.8) × 11.4 cm.

Paper   White, wove, unwatermarked, all edges trimmed, sheets bulk 2.5 cm.

Binding   Pictorial paper covers. On front cover: [in blue] LES VIES SECRÈTES DE | [in red] LAWRENCE D'ARABIE | PHILLIP KNIGHTLEY COLIN SIMPSON | [collage, illustration] | [in red] ROBERT LAFFONT. On spine: PHILLIP KNIGHTLEY | [rule] | COLIN | SIMPSON | [running up] [first four words in blue, the rest in red] LES VIES SECRÈTES DE LAWRENCE D'ARABIE | [across at bottom] [pub. device] | ROBERT |

LAFFONT. On back cover: [14-line blurb] | [photo] | [red rule] Imp. Chanyenay 70-111-876. 500-2600. Covers have printed flaps turned in.

Published at   February 1969.

Copies   AC, Cal.

E313   PHILLIP KNIGHTLEY and COLIN SIMPSON, Das Geheim Leben des Lawrence von Arabien, Hoffmann und Campe, 1969

First German Edition

Colin Simpson – Phillip Knightley | DAS [next word within slanted rules] GEHEIM LEBEN | DES LAWRENCE | VON ARABIEN | Aus dem Englischen von Paul Baudisch | Hoffmann und Campe

Collation   22 × 14.5 cm: [1–18]⁸ [19]¹⁰ [20]⁸, 162 leaves, pp.[1–6], 7–322, [323], [1].

Contents   Pp.[1] pub. device, [2] blank, [3] title page, [4] original title, acknowledgments, copyright statement, typographer's, binder's, printer's credits, [5–6] contents, 7–13 introduction, [14] blank, 15–319 text, 320–321 acknowledgments, 322–[323] bibliography, [1] blank.

Plates   Nine photos on coated paper, printed on both sides except for frontispiece, following pp.2, 160.

Text   20 lines, 8.2 × 10.6 cm.

Paper   White, wove, unwatermarked, all edges trimmed, sheets bulk 3.2 cm.

Binding   76 l. y. Br brown cloth. On front cover: [stamped figure of Lawrence]. On spine: [running up] DAS [next word within frame of single rule, the whole on a slant] GEHEIM LEBEN DES LAWRENCE VON ARABIEN. Red head and tail bands.

Published at   DM 24.

Copies   AC, Cal.

E314   PHILLIP KNIGHTLEY and COLIN SIMPSON, Das Geheim Leben des Lawrence von Arabien, Hoffmann und Campe, 1969

Publisher's Prospectus

No title page.

Collation   29.8 × 20.8 cm: single sheet printed on one side only.

Paper   Coated paper, white, wove, unwatermarked, all edges trimmed.

Published at   Free advertising flyer.

Copies   Cal.

E315 PHILLIP KNIGHTLEY and COLIN SIMPSON, Le Vite Segrete di Lawrence D'Arabia, Mondadori, 1970

First Italian Edition

Phillip Knightley – Colin Simpson | [in blue] LE VITE SEGRETE | [in blue] DI LAWRENCE D'ARABIA | Traduzione di Attilio Veraldi | con 22 illustrationi fuori testo | e due cartine nel testo | ARNOLDO MONDADORI EDITORE

Collation 21 × 15.5 cm: [1]^{16} 2–6^{16} 7^8 8–12^{16} 13^4 14^{16}, 196 leaves, pp.[1–6], 7–382, [383], [9].

Contents Pp.[1] 'LE SCIE', [2] blank, [3] title page, [4] copyright, issue statements, original title, [5] half-title, [6] blank, 7–[8] acknowledgments, [9] quote from *Seven Pillars of Wisdom*, [10] blank, 11–[19] introduction, [20] blank, 21–[366] text, 367–[368] bibliography. [369] section title, [370] blank, 371–[383] index, [1] illustrations, [2–3] contents, [4] blank, [5] printer's colophon, [6–9] publisher's list.

RT On verso LE VITE SEGRETE DI LAWRENCE D'ARABIA. On recto [according to chapter].

Typography and paper $ 1 signed 3./.

Text 20 lines, 9.3 (9.3) × 11.3 cm.

Paper White, wove, simulated laid paper, wove, unwatermarked, all edges trimmed, sheets bulk 2.3 cm.

Binding Red cloth 15 m. Red. On spine: [gilt, running down] Phillip Knightley – Colin Simpson . Le Vite segrete di Lawrence d'Arabia | [across at bottom] [pub. device]. Boxed as issued. Red and white head and tail bands.

Published at Lire 3000, August 1970.

Copies AC.

E316 PHILLIP KNIGHTLEY and COLIN SIMPSON, Arabia no Lawrensu no Himitsu, Hayakawa, 1971

First Japanese Edition

[Pub. device] | [wide brown rule] | Arabia no Lawrensu no Himitsu | Fuilpu · Naitoli, Kolin · Shimpson/Muramatsu Sentaro yaku | HAYAKAWA NON FICTION | [long brown rule]

Collation 18.8 × 13 cm: [1–23]^8, 184 leaves, prp.[1], pp.[1–16] plates, [17–18], 19–371, III–I, [1–10].

Contents Prp.[1] title page, 2 [blank], pp.[1–16] b/w plates, [17] half-title [18] quote from *Seven Pillars of Wisdom*, 19–20 acknowledgments, [21–22] contents, 23–30 introduction, 31–371 text, III–I Bibliography [1] colophon, [2–8] pub. ad., [9–10] blank.

Plates Eight plates on coated paper, printed on both sides, included in pagination after title page and before text.

Text   20 lines, 5.3 × 9.5 cm.

Paper   White, wove, unwatermarked, all edges trimmed, sheets bulk 2 cm.

Binding   Putty coloured paper covered boards 93 y. Gray. On front cover: The Secret Lives of | [outline letterings next two lines] LAWRENCE | OF ARABIA. On spine: [running down] Arabia no Lawrensu no Himitsu | Fuilip · Naitoli | Kolin · Shimpson | Muramatsu Setaro yaku | [across] Hayakawa Shobo. Maroon and white head and tail bands. Maroon and black place marker.

Published at   900 yen.

Notes   Another impression, 31 March 1971.

Copies   AC.

E317   PHILLIP KNIGHTLEY and COLIN SIMPSON, Lawrence of Arabia, Gyldendal Norsk, 1970

First Norwegian Edition

[Title in outline lettering] LAWRENCE | OF ARABIA | MANNEN OG MYTEN | *Av Phillip Knightley og Colin Simpson* | Oversatt av Carl Hambro | Gyldendal Norsk Forlag · Oslo

Collation   22.5 × 15 cm: [1]⁸ 2–21⁸, 168 leaves, pp.[1–7], 8–336.

Contents   Pp.[1] bastard title, [2] blank, [3] title page, [4] original title, printer's credit, issue statement, [5] contents, [6] blank, [7]–14 introduction, [15]–333 text, [334] translator's note, [335]–336 bibliography.

RT   On both verso and recto [according to chapter].

Plates   Four plates on coated paper, printed on both sides, following p.128.

Typography and paper $ 1 signed 2 Lawrence of Arabia.

Text   20 lines, 9 (9.2) × 10.8 cm.

Paper   White, wove, unwatermarked, all edges trimmed, sheets bulk 2.5 cm.

Binding   Black cloth. On front cover: [blind stamped, within blind stamped frame of single rule] LAWRENCE | OF ARABIA. On spine: [within red rectangle, gilt] Phillip | Knightley | og | Colin | Simpson | [short rule] | LAWRENCE | OF ARABIA. T.e. salmon. Blue and white head and tail bands.

Published at   75,00 kr.

Copies   AC.

E318   PHILLIP KNIGHTLEY and COLIN SIMPSON, La Vida Secreta de Lawrence de Arabia, Bruguera, 1970

First Spanish Edition

La vida secreta de | Lawrence de Arabia | [rule] | PHILLIP KNIGHTLEY |

COLIN SIMPSON | [within black rectangle in white] [pub. device] | EDITORIAL BRUGUERA, S.A. | BARCELONA · BOGOTA · BUENOS AIRES · CARACAS · MEXICO · RIO DE JANEIRO

Collation   20.8 × 13.5 cm: [1–20]⁸, 160 leaves, pp.[1–6], 7–320.

Contents   Pp.[1] bastard title, [2] blank, [3] title page, [4] original title, copyright statement, translator's credit, issue statement, printer's credit, [5] contents, [6] quote from *Seven Pillars of Wisdom*, 7–8 acknowledgments, 9–15 introduction, 16–316 text, 317–320 index.

Text   20 lines, 7.5 × 10 cm.

Paper   White, wove, unwatermarked, all edges trimmed, sheets bulk 2 cm.

Binding   Blue cloth 179 deep B. On front cover: [gilt] CIRCULO AZUL. On spine: [decorative rule] | C. SIMPSON | P. KNIGHTLEY | [decorative rule] | [running up] La vida secreta de Lawrence de Arabia | [across at foot] BRUGUERA. Blue and white head and tail bands.

Published at   275.00 pesetas, June 1970.

Copies   AC, Cal.

E319   PHILLIP KNIGHTLEY and COLIN SIMPSON, Lawrence av Arabien, Nordstedt & Söners, 1969

First Swedish Edition

Phillip Knightley och Colin Simpson | *Lawrence av Arabien* | *Hans hemliga liv* | Översattning av Vera Olinder | P.A. Nordstedt & Söners Forlag Stockholm

Collation   22.2 × 14 cm: 1–10¹⁶, 160 leaves, pp.[1–4], 5–318, [2].

Contents   Pp.[1] bastard title, [2] blank, [3] title page, [4] original title, copyright statement, 5–11 introduction, 12–314 text, [315] map, 316–[318] index, [1–2] blank.

RT   On both sides [according to chapter].

Plates   Six plates on coated paper, printed on both sides, following p.160.

Typography and paper $ 1,5 signed 2-Lawrence av Arabien, 2* Lawrence av Arabien.

Text   20 lines, 9 × 10.5 cm.

Paper   White, wove, unwatermarked, untrimmed, sheets bulk 1.8 cm.

Binding   Pictorial paper covers. On front cover: *Phillip Knightley och Colin Simpson* | [in white] Lawrence | av Arabien | Hans hemliga liv. On spine: [running down] *Phillip Knightley* och *Colin Simpson* Lawrence av Arabien. On back cover: [photo of Lawrence].

Published at   45 SKr.

Copies   AC.

E320   STEPHEN KING, Thomas Edward Lawrence in the City of Artisans, Claremont Graduate School, 1969

Unpublished M.A. Thesis

THOMAS EDWARD LAWRENCE | IN THE CITY OF ARTISANS | By | Stephen H. King | Presented to the General Faculty of | the Claremont Graduate School in | Partial fulfillment of the requirements | for the degree of Master of Arts: | We certify that we have read this document | and approve it as adequate in scope and | quality for the degree of Master of Arts: | [long rule] | Examiner | [signature] | [long rule] | Faculty Reader | [signature] | [long rule] | Faculty Advisor | Date [long rule, date] May 21, 1969

Collation   27.3 × 21 cm: 85 leaves, pp.[1–4], 1–81.

Contents   Prp.[1] title page, [2–3] abstract, [4] contents, pp.1–63 text, pp.64–76 appendixes, 77–81 bibliography.

Paper   8 × 11 sheets, double-spaced typing.

Binding   Black buckram. On spine: [gilt, running down] KING.

Copies   AC, Cal.

E321   THEDORA DUNCAN, Theodora Duncan Collection of T.E. Lawrence, n.p., [1969]

No title page.

Collation   8 × 10 inches: 341 leaves.

Text   Typed originals photocopied.

Paper   White, wove, unwatermarked, three holes in left margin.

Binding   Three-ring binder.

Published at   Not for sale.

Notes   This is a list of the Duncan collection made just prior to its sale in 1969. Most items are annotated in detail.

Copies   AC, Cal.

E322   HARRY BROUGHTON, Lawrence of Arabia, The Facts Without the Fiction, Wareham Pictorial Museum, 1969

First English Edition

LAWRENCE OF ARABIA | The Facts without the Fiction | by | Harry Broughton

Collation   20.5 × 13 cm: [1]⁴, 4 leaves, unpaged.

Contents   Pp.[1] title page, [2–8] text.

Text   20 lines, 7.2 × 9.2 cm.

Paper   White, wove, unwatermarked, all edges trimmed, sheets bulk 1 mm.

Binding   White paper wrappers stapled to sheets by two metal staples. On front cover: LAWRENCE OF ARABIA | The Facts without the Fiction | by | Harry Broughton.

Notes   A 2nd edition, as above, with following differences: [after last line of title page is added] SECOND EDITION | AUGUST 1972; [Collation: 19.5 × 21.7 cm; [Binding]: covers of rough paper.

Copies   AC, Cal.

E323   Al-'Umari, Lurans Kama 'Ariftuh, dar Al-Nahar, 1969

First Syrian Edition

[Within single rule frame, running right to left] Sobhi Al-'Umari | Lurans | Kama Ariftuh | dar Al-Nahar Lil Nashr

Collation   19.2 × 13.5 cm: guillotined sheets, 128 leaves, pp.[1–6], 7–247, [9].

Contents   Pp.[1–2] blank, [3] bastard title, [4] blank, [5] title page, [6] copyright statement, 7–8 contents, 9–15 preface, 16–247 text, [1] blank, [2–6] maps, [7–9] blank.

Plates   Two b/w plates on coated paper, printed on both sides, following p.128.

Text   20 lines, 12.2 × 10.3 cm.

Paper   White, wove, unwatermarked, all edges trimmed, sheets bulk 1.3 cm.

Binding   Pictorial paper covers. On front cover: Sobhi Al-'Umari | [in red] Lurens | Kama Ariftuh | [drawing of Lawrence within yellow frame]. On back cover: [lengthy blurb and brief biography of Lawrence].

Copies   UCLA, UoC, LC.

Scholarship Continues, 1970–74

With the advent of the 1970s additional scholars began to pay attention to Lawrence. In the first half of the decade at least four dissertations appeared. Steve Tabachnick, one of the most prolific scholars in the Lawrence field, began his still growing list of works with a term paper, 'A House Divided', for a graduate course taught by Stephen Spender. A dissertation was written by O'Donnell, 'The Dichotomy of Self in T.E. Lawrence's *Seven Pillars of Wisdom*'. O'Donnell points out interesting parallels in the work of Lawrence and Conrad, among other matters. In 1979 it was revised and published as *Confessions of T.E. Lawrence*.

Anti-western material continued to appear in the Near East. Zahdi al-

Fatah's *Lurens al-Arab ala Khuta Hirtzil* is a very angry denunciation of
Lawrence, using extensive quotes linking Lawrence to ardent Zionism.

A second dissertation was Tabachnick's, 'T.E. Lawrence's *Seven Pillars of
Wisdom* as a Work of Art'. It is a detailed study of *Seven Pillars of Wisdom* as a
literary masterpiece. In Israel a popular rendering in Hebrew of the
Lawrence story by Scheyer, *The Revolt in the Desert and Afterwards* appeared.

The marked upsurge of interest in Lawrence scholarship is also reflected
in the continued issuing of checklists and bibliographies: Disbury's *T.E.
Lawrence of Arabia A Collector's Checklist* is an ambitious attempt to cover the
work by and about Lawrence. It was published at about the same time as
Clements' *T.E. Lawrence A Reader's Guide,* which is the first published
attempt since Duval to provide a descriptive bibliography.

Along with Tabachnick, Jeffrey Meyers was one of the two most prolific
writers in the 1970s. He published a detailed study of the composition of
Seven Pillars of Wisdom, originally included as a chapter in *The Wounded
Spirit,* and published in revised form in *PMLA* (October 1973). Meyers also
published *T.E. Lawrence: A Bibliography.* This is a checklist of very broad
scope and was first published in *Bulletin of Bibliography* (January-March
1972).

Other Lawrence scholarship appeared on the scene in 1974. Charles
Grosvenor completed a senior honors thesis; Friedman's 'The Challenge of
Destiny' is a third doctoral dissertation relating Malraux's work to
Lawrence. Short studies were written by two of Tabachnick's students at
the Ben Gurion University of the Negev (Feinglass, 'T.E. Lawrence and the
Heroic Narrative Mode', and Bograd, *T.E. Lawrence: An Appreciation of His
Military Leadership*).

Another comic book appeared in Holland, Dooley's *Lawrence van Arabie.*
A privately printed study by a US Army Reserve Officer – Butler's *The
Guerrilla Strategy of Lawrence and Mao* – was published in a limited edition
at the mid-point of the decade. This is one of three studies of Lawrence
written at the Army War College.

1970

E325   STEPHEN ELY TABACHNICK, A House Divided, 1970

Unpublished Term Paper

A House Divided: | The "Crisis of Belief" in T.E. Lawrence's <u>Seven Pillars of
Wisdom</u> | Term Paper | Modern British Literature | Mr. Spender

Collation   24 leaves, prp.[1], pp.[1], 2–21, [2].

Contents   Prp.[1] title page, pp.[1]–21 text, [1] postscript, [2] bibliography.

Typography and paper   Typed 8 × 11 sheets on one side only.

Notes   Submitted for a course given at University of Connecticut, taught by
Stephen Spender.

Copies   AC, Cal.

E326 THOMAS JAMES O'DONNELL, The Dichotomy of Self in T.E. Lawrence's Seven Pillars of Wisdom, University of Illinois, 1970

Unpublished Ph. D. Dissertation

THE DICHOTOMY OF SELF IN T.E. LAWRENCE'S | SEVEN PILLARS OF WISDOM | THESIS | Submitted in partial fulfillment of the requirements | for the degree of Doctor of Philosophy in English | in the Graduate College of the | University of Illinois at Urbana-Champaign, 1970 | Urbana, Illinois

Collation 21 × 16 cm: guillotined sheets glued to covers, 247 leaves, pp.[2], [i–ii], iii–iv, 1–242.

Contents Prp.[1] copyright statement, [2] cataloging information, [i] title page, [ii] signature sheets, iii acknowledgments, iv contents, pp.1–232 text, 233–242 bibliography, 242 vita sheet.

Text 20 lines, double-spaced typed, reduced through photocopying.

Paper White, wove, unwatermarked, all edges trimmed, sheets bulk 1.7 cm.

Binding Dark blue paper covers 197 deep p b. [white paper label pasted on front cover, within frames of orange decorative rules and single rules] THE DICHOTOMY OF SELF IN | T.E. LAWRENCE'S SEVEN | PILLARS OF WISDOM | T.J. O'Donnell, 1970 | [long rule] | *Published on demand by* | UNIVERSITY MICROFILMS | *University Microfilms Limited, High Wycombe, England | A Xerox Company, Ann Arbor, Michigan, USA.*

Copies AC.

1971

E327 FATIH, ZUHDI AL-, Lurins al-Arab ala Khuta Hirtzil, Dar Al Na-fa-is, 1971

First Lebanese Edition

Zuhdi Al Fateh | Lurins Al-Arab | Ala Khuta Hirtzil| Takarir Lurins Al-Sirria | Tawzih | Dar Al Na-fa-is | Bayrout S.B. 6347

Collation 19 × 13.5 cm: guillotined sheets glued to pages, [1–6], 7–160.

Contents Pp.[1] quote from Koran, [2] blank, [3] bastard title, [4] blank, [5] title page, [6] copyright, issue statements, 7 quotes from Lawrence and Menachin Begin, [8] blank, 9 quotes from Toynbee and Eugene Rostow, [10] blank, 11 quotes from 'Communist Manifesto' and 'National Arabism', [12] blank, 13 quote from Lawrence in both English and Arabic translation from *Secret Despatches*, [14] blank, 15 –158 text, 159–160 contents.

Text 20 lines, 10.3 × 9 cm.

Paper White, wove, unwatermarked, all edges trimmed, sheets bulk 8 mm.

Binding   Pictorial paper covers. On front cover: Zuhdi Al Fateh | [in red] Lurins Al-Arab | Ala Khota Hirtzil | Takarir Lurins Al-Sirria. On back cover: [publisher's blurb, price].

Published at   400 Lebanon Piastres.

Copies   NYPL.

1972

E328   STEPHEN ELY TABACHNICK, T.E. Lawrence's Seven Pillars of Wisdom As a Work of Art, 1972

Unpublished Ph.D. Dissertation

T.E. LAWRENCE'S SEVEN PILLARS OF WISDOM AS A WORK OF ART | Stephen Ely Tabachnick, A.B.,M.A. | University of California at Berkeley, 1966 | University of Chicago, 1967 | A Dissertation | Submitted in Partial Fulfillment of the | Requirements for the Degree of | Doctor of Philosophy | at | The University of Connecticut | 1971

Collation   20.9 × 15.8 cm: 204 leaves, guillotined sheets glued to covers, pp.[2], [i], ii, [1], iii–iv, 1–196, [2].

Contents   Prp.[1] copyright statement, cataloging information, [i] title page, [ii] approval page, [2] pub. note, iii acknowledgments, iv contents, pp.1–179 text, 180 section title, 181–188 appendixes, 189 section title, 190–196 bibliography, [1–2] errata.

Text   Typed double-spaced, reduced in photoduplication.

Paper   White, wove, unwatermarked, all edges trimmed, sheets bulk 1.3 cm.

Binding   Black paper covers glued to sheets. On front cover: [white paper label pasted on, within orange decorative rule frame and black single rule frame] T.E. LAWRENCE'S SEVEN | PILLARS OF WISDOM AS | WORK OF ART. | S.E. Tabachnick, 1972 | [long rule] | *Published on demand by* | UNIVERSITY MICROFILMS | *University Microfilms Limited, High Wycombe, England* | *A Xerox Company, Ann Arbor, Michigan, USA.*

Copies   AC.

E329   AMRAM SCHEYER, Laurens ul'Acharav Hemered Bamidbar, v'Hotsa'at Sheba, 1972

First Israeli Edition

AMRAM SCHEYER | LAURENS | U'L'ACHARAV HEMERED BAMIDBAR | SIFRIAT POALIM BA'AM | V'HOTSA'AT SHEBA

Collation   21.2 × 13.6 cm: [1–8]^8 [9]^4, 68 leaves, pp.[1–4], 5–136.

Contents   Pp.[1] bastard title, [2] frontispiece, [3] title page, [4] English translation of author and title, copyright statement, printer's credit, 5 acknowledgements, 6 three-line quotes from *The Mint*, 7 foreword, [8]

blank, 9–131 text, [132] blank, 133 selected bibliography, [134] blank, [135–136] index.

Text 9.5 × 9 cm.

Paper White, wove, unwatermarked, all edges trimmed, sheets bulk 1 cm.

Binding Yellow paper covered boards 83 Brill Y. On front cover: Amram Scheyer | [running down] LAURENS U'L'ACHARAV HAMERED BAMIDBAR | SIFRIAT POALIM BA'AM. On spine: [running down] AMRAM SCHEYER * LAURENS SIFRIAT POALIM BA'AM. On back cover: [blurb and publisher's name].

Notes English title: The Revolt in the Desert and Afterwards.

Copies AC, LC.

E330 DAVID G. DISBURY, T.E. Lawrence of Arabia, A Collector's Booklist, privately printed, 1972

First English Edition

T.E. LAWRENCE (of Arabia) | A Collector's Booklist | Compiled by David G. Disbury | Part I The Writings of T.E. Lawrence | Part II The Writings of T.E. Lawrence reviewed | Part III Books on and about T.E. Lawrence | David G. Disbury, | 44 Hythe Park Road, | Thorpe Lea, | Egham, | Surrey, | TW20 8DA

Collation 25 × 20.3 cm: single sheets stapled together, 38 leaves, unpaged.

Contents Pp.[1] title page, [2] blank, [3] section title, [4] blank, [5–78] text.

Text Photocopy of typed original.

Paper White, bond, unwatermarked, all edges trimmed, sheets bulk 5 mm.

Binding 70 l.OY tan paper covers, black cloth spine. On front cover: T.E. Lawrence | of Arabia | A Collector's Booklist | compiled by | DAVID G. DISBURY.

Published at £1.50, October 1972.

Copies AC, Cal, B, BL, LC.

E331 FRANK CLEMENTS, T.E. Lawrence, A Reader's Guide, David & Charles, 1972

First English Edition

T.E. Lawrence: | *a reader's guide* | *Frank Clements* | [pub. device] | *David & Charles: Newton Abbot*

Collation 21.5 × 13.8 cm: [A]⁸ B–N⁸, 104 leaves, pp.[1–4], 5–208.

Contents Pp.[1] bastard title, [2] blank, [3] title page, [4] ISBN number, copyright statement, printer's credit, 5 contents, [6] blank, 7 author's notes, [8] blank, 9–10 arrangement and terms used in text, [11] section title, [12] blank, 13–23 introduction, [24] blank, [25] section title, [26] blank, 27–200 text, 201 appendix, 202–208 index.

RT On verso *T.E. Lawrence: A Reader's Guide.* On recto [according to chapter].

Typography and paper $ 1 signed B [on page 203 the 3 is inverted].

Text 20 lines, 9.2 (9.4) × 10.2 cm. Set in 12pt Aldine Bembo.

Paper Thick, white, wove, unwatermarked, all edges trimmed, sheets bulk 1.8 cm.

Binding Red cloth 12 s.Red. On spine: [running down, gilt] T.E. Lawrence: a reader's guide | Frank Clements | [across at bottom] DAVID & | CHARLES.

Published at £3.50.

Copies AC, Cal, LC.

1973

E332   FRANK CLEMENTS, T.E. Lawrence: A Reader's Guide, Archon, 1973

First American Edition

T.E. Lawrence: | *a reader's guide* | *Frank Clements* | *Archon Books* | *1973*

Collation 21.6 × 13.8 cm: [A]^8 B–N^8, 104 leaves, pp.[1–4], 5–208.

Contents Pp.[1] bastard title, [2] blank, [3] title page, [4] CIP, copyright, issue statements, 5 contents, [6] blank, 7 author's note, [8] blank, 9–10 arrangement and terms used in text, [11] section title, [12] blank, 13–23 introduction, [24] blank, [25] section title, 27–200 text, 201 appendix, 202–208 index.

RT On verso *T.E. Lawrence: a reader's guide.* On recto [in italics, according to section].

Typography and paper $ 1 signed B.

Text 20 lines, 9.1 × 9.2 cm.

Paper Thick, white, wove, unwatermarked, all edges trimmed, sheets bulk 1.9 cm.

Binding Red cloth 12 s.Red. On spine: [running down, gilt] T.E. Lawrence: a reader's guide | Frank Clements | [across at bottom] ARCHON.

Published at $8.50, February 1973.

Copies AC, Cal, UT, LC.

E333   FRANK CLEMENTS, T.E. Lawrence, a Reader's Guide, Shoe String Press, 1973

Distributor's Prospectus

No title page.

Collation 21.5 × 14 cm: single sheet printed on one side only.

Paper Yellow, wove, unwatermarked, all edges trimmed.

Published at Free advertising flyer.

Copies AC.

E334 DOUGLAS ORGILL, Lawrence, Ballantine, 1973

First American Edition

[In white] Lawrence | [in white] Douglas Orgill | [publisher's device] [lettering superimposed on b/w photo of Lawrence in Arab robes]

Collation 20.8 × 13.5 cm: guillotined sheets glued to covers, 80 leaves, pp.[1–5], 6–159, [1].

Contents Pp.[1] bastard title, [2] montage of photos of Lawrence b/w, [3] title page, [4] credits, copyright, issue statements, address of publisher, [5] contents, 6–7 introduction, 8–159 text, [1] bibliography.

Text 20 lines, 7 × 6 cm, double column format 12.3 cm.

Paper White, wove, unwatermarked, all edges trimmed, sheets bulk 1 cm.

Binding Pictorial paper covers. On front cover: [all in white except publisher's device, serial number and price] Lawrence | Douglas Orgill | Ballantine's Illustrated History [publisher's device extending down into next line] war leader 03222.5 | of the Violent Century [lower half of publisher's device] book No 18 $1. On spine: [running down, all in white except serial number, publisher's device and price] LAWRENCE OF ARABIA Douglas Orgill war leader | book No 18 345.03222.5 | [across at bottom] [publisher's device] | $1. On back cover: [all in white except publisher's device and price] [seven-line blurb] [last two lines same as front cover omitting serial number].

Published at $1.00.

Copies AC, Cal, LC.

E335 JEFFREY MEYERS, The Wounded Spirit, Brian & O'Keefe, 1973

Uncorrected Proof of First English Edition

The Wounded | Spirit | A STUDY OF | *Seven Pillars of Wisdom* | JEFFREY MEYERS | [ornamental leaf cut] | *With a Preface by* | SIR ALEC KIRKBRIDE | K.C.M.G., C.V.O., O.B.E., M.C. | 'A wounded spirit who can bear?' | PROVERBS 18:14 | MARTIN BRIAN | & O'KEEFE | LONDON

Collation 21.5 × 14 cm: [A]⁸ B–M⁸ N⁴, 100 leaves, pp.[1–6], 7–197, [3].

Contents Pp.[1] bastard title, [2] list of author's works, [3] title page, [4] issue statement, ISBN, copyright statement, printer's credit, [5] dedication, [6] blank, 7 contents, [8] blank, 9–10 preface, 11–15 introduction, [16] blank, 17–140 text, 141–147 appendixes, 148 Biblical allusions, [149] section title, [150] blank, [151] preface to bibliography, [152] blank, 153–197 bibliography, [198–200] blank.

RT On verso THE WOUNDED SPIRIT. On recto [according to chapter].

Typography and paper $ 1, signed B.

Text   20 lines, 8.4 (8.5) × 10.2 cm.

Paper   White, wove, unwatermarked, all edges trimmed, sheets bulk 1.4 cm.

Binding   Grey paper covers glued to sheets. On front cover: [same as title page]. On spine: [running down] THE WOUNDED SPIRIT.

Copies   AC, Cal.

E336   JEFFREY MEYERS, The Wounded Spirit, Brian & O'Keefe, 1973

First English Edition

The Wounded | Spirit | A STUDY OF | *Seven Pillars of Wisdom* | JEFFREY MEYERS | [ornamental leaf cut] | *With a Preface by* | SIR ALEC KIRKBRIDE | K.C.M.G., C.V.O., O.B.E., M.C. | 'A wounded spirit who can bear?' | PROVERBS 18:14 | MARTIN BRIAN | & O'KEEFE | LONDON

Collation   21.8 × 13.5 cm: [A]⁸ B−L⁸ [M]⁴ N⁸, 100 leaves, pp.[1−6], 7−200.

Contents   Pp.[1] bastard title, [2] list of author's works, [3] title page, [4] issue statement, ISBN, copyright statement, printer's credit, [5] dedication, [6] blank, 7 contents, [8] blank, 9−10 preface, 11−15 introduction, [16] blank, 17−140 text, 141−147 appendixes, 148 Biblical allusions, [149] section title, [150] blank, [151] preface to bibliography, [152] blank, 153−197 bibliography, [198−200] index.

RT   On verso THE WOUNDED SPIRIT. On recto [according to chapter].

Plates   Fold map following p.[16].

Typography and paper $ 1, signed B.

Text   20 lines, 8.4 (8.5) × 10.2 cm.

Paper   White, wove, unwatermarked, all edges trimmed, sheets bulk 1.4 cm.

Binding   Rose cloth 255 s. p R. On spine: [gilt, running down] The Wounded Spirit [leaf cut] JEFFREY MEYERS | [across at bottom] MB | & | O'K.

Published at   £3.00, May 1973.

Notes   The bibliography here is a slightly different version of the bibliography published by the Garland Press and in the *Bulletin of Bibliography* by the same author.

Copies   AC, Cal, LC.

E337   PETER MANSFIELD, Lawrence and His Legacy, BBC TV and Time-Life, 1973

First English Edition

[First three letters within rhomboids and next two within another] B B C tv

TIME-LIFE BOOKS 25p | No. 75 | [display type, yellow with brown borders] THE | BRITISH | EMPIRE | [John's drawing of Lawrence] | LAWRENCE | AND HIS LEGACY | Australia & New Zealand 70c South Africa 70c Canada 95c

Collation 29.8 × 23.1 cm: [1]^{16}, 16 leaves, pp.[2], 2073–2100, [2].

Contents Prp.[1] title page on front cover, [2] credits, ads, contents, pp.2073–2100 text, [1] picture of uniform, [2] back cover, blank.

Text 20 lines, 7.6 (7.7) × 6.3 cm. (triple column 20.7 cm).

Paper White, slick, wove, unwatermarked, all edges trimmed, sheets bulk 2 mm.

Binding Grey paper covers, fastened to sheets by two staples. On front cover: [title page].

Published at 26d.

Notes Part of series, THE BRITISH EMPIRE, no. 75.

Copies AC, Cal.

E337a   HOWARD M. GABBERT, Lawrence and Mao Together, Army War College, 1973

First American Edition

AD-778 891 | LAWRENCE AND MAO TOGETHER | Howard M. Gabbert | Army War College | Carlisle Barracks, Pennsylvania | 3 August 1973

Collation 27.8 × 21.5 cm: 35 single sheets stapled together, prl.[1], I–III, i–ii, leaves 1–28, [1].

Contents Prl.[1] title page, I–II security classification leaves, III second title page, i abstract, ii contents, leaves 1–19 text, 20–21 appendix, 22–24 notes, 25–28 bibliography, [1] film date.

Text Photocopy of typed original.

Paper White, wove, unwatermarked, all edges trimmed sheets bulk 5 mm.

Binding Sheets stapled together with two steel staples.

Copies AC, Cal.

E337b   JOHN B. COTTINGHAM JR., A Comparison of the Guerilla Strategies of Mao and Lawrence, Army War College, 1973

First American Edition

AD-778 885 | A COMPARISON OF THE GUERILLA STRATEGIES OF MAO AND LAWRENCE | John B. Cottingham, Jr. | Army War College | Carlisle Barracks, Pennsylvania | 19 November 1973

Collation 27.8 × 21.5 cm: 33 leaves, prp.[1], ia–ib, i, pp.1–28, [1].

Contents   Prp.[1] title page, ia second title page, ib abstract, i security classification page, pp.1–22 text, 23–25 footnotes, 26–28 bibliography, [1] filming statement.

Text   Photocopy of typed original.

Paper   White, wove, unwatermarked, all edges trimmed, sheets bulk 3 mm.

Binding   Sheets fastened together by two steel staples.

Copies   AC, Cal.

E337c   OLIVER J. BUTLER, An Examination of the Guerrilla Strategies of Lawrence and Mao, Army War College, 1973

First American Edition

AD-778 887 | AN EXAMINATION OF THE GUERRILLA | STRATEGIES OF LAWRENCE AND MAO | Oliver J. Butler, Jr. | Army War College | Carlisle Barracks, Pennsylvania | 15 October 1973

Collation   27.8 × 21.6 cm: 59 leaves, prp.[1], ib, ii–iii, ppo.1–52, i–ia, [1].

Contents   Prp.[1] title page, [ib] second title page, ii contents, iii abstract, 1–43 text, 44–49 footnotes, 50–52 bibliography, i–ia security classification pages, [1] filming statement.

Text   Photocopy of typed original.

Paper   White, wove, unwatermarked, all edges trimmed, sheets bulk 5 mm.

Binding   Sheets fastened together by two steel staples.

Copies   AC, Cal.

E337d   OLIVER J. BUTLER, The Guerrilla Strategies of Lawrence and Mao, 1974

Second American Edition

THE GUERRILLA STRATEGIES | OF | LAWRENCE AND MAO | An Examination | by | Colonel Oliver J. Butler, Jr. | Infantry | United States Army Reserve | Houston, Texas | May, 1974

Collation   22.3 × 15 cm: guillotined sheets sewn to covers, 57 leaves, pp.[1], 1–5, 1–50, [1].

Contents   Leaf [1] blank, i title page, ii quote, iii dedication, iv contents, v preface, 1–3 introduction, 4–38 text, 39–44 footnotes, 45–47 bibliography, 48–50 brief biography of author.

Text   20 lines, 13.8 × 11 cm.

Paper   White, wove, unwatermarked, all edges trimmed, sheets bulk 1 cm.

Binding Pale blue buckram 180 v.l. Blue. On front cover: [gilt] THE GUERRILLA STRATEGIES | OF | LAWRENCE AND MAO | [cut] | Colonel Oliver J. Butler Jr. On spine: [gilt, running down] THE GUERRILLA STRATEGIES OF LAWRENCE AND MAO | [rule, across] | [running down] Butler.

Published at Privately printed, not for sale.

Copies LC.

1974

E338 JEFFREY MEYERS, T.E. Lawrence: A Bibliography, Garland, 1974

First American Edition

T.E. Lawrence: | A | *Bibliography* | Jeffrey Meyers | *Garland Publishing, Inc., New York & London* | [publisher's device] | 1974

Collation 21.5 × 14 cm: [1]⁸ [2]⁴ [3–4]⁸, 28 leaves, pp.[1–6], [1–2], 3–48, [1–2].

Contents Prp.[1] bastard title, [2] blank, [3] title page, [4] copyright statement, CIP, [5] dedication, [6] blank, pp.[1] preface, [2] – [48] text, [1–2] blank.

Text Photocopy of typed original, double spaced.

Paper White, wove, unwatermarked, all edges trimmed, sheets bulk 3 mm.

Binding Red cloth 12 s. Red. On spine: [double rules] | [running down] Meyers *T.E. Lawrence: A Bibliography* | [across] [publisher's logo] | [running down] Garland | [across, double rules].

Published at $10.00, August 1974.

Copies AC, Cal, B, BL, H, Ca, UT, LC.

E339 CHARLES M. GROSVENOR, The Aesthetic T.E. Lawrence, unpublished, 1974

Unpublished Senior Honors Thesis

THE AESTHETIC T.E. LAWRENCE | [rule] | A Thesis Presented to | The Faculty of the Department of Art | of | Bates College | [rule] | In Partial Completion | of the Requirements | of the Bachelor of Arts Degree | in Art | [rule] | Charles M. Grosvenor, Jr. | 11 March 1974

Collation 27.2 × 21 cm: 156 leaves, pp.[5], i–ii, 1–111, [1–38].

Contents Pp.[1] title page, [2] TEL quote, [3] frontispiece, [4] acknowledgments, [5] contents, i–ii list of illustrations, 1–83 text, 84–91 appendixes, 92–99 notes to text, 100–111 references, [1–38] illustrations.

Typography and paper Typed, double spaced.

Paper Sheets 8 × 11, white, wove, unwatermarked, all edges trimmed, sheets bulk 1.5 cm.

Binding Black cloth.

Published at 11 March 1974.

Copies AC, Cal.

E340 JOHN S. FRIEDMAN, The Challenge of Destiny, New York University, 1974

Unpublished Ph.D. Dissertation

The Challenge of Destiny: A Comparison | of T.E. Lawrence's and André Malraux's Adventure Tales | John Saul Friedman | February, 1974 | A dissertation in the Department of Comparative | Literature submitted to the faculty of the Graduate | School of Arts and Science in partial fulfillment | of the requirements for the degree of Doctor of | Philosophy at New York University | Approved: | [signature] | [rule] | Advisor

Collation 21 × 15.5 cm: guillotined sheets glued to covers, 216 leaves, pp.[4], 1–212.

Contents Prp.[1] copyright statement, [2] cataloging information, [3] title page, [4] dedication, pp.1–191 text, 192–212 bibliography.

Text Photocopy of original typed double-spaced dissertation.

Paper White, wove, unwatermarked, all edges trimmed, sheets bulk 1.4 cm.

Binding Blue buckram 187 d. gy B. On spine: [runing down] THE CHALLENGE OF DESTINY [star] FRIEDMAN.

Copies AC.

E341 AVRAHAM FEINGLASS, T.E. Lawrence and the Heroic Narrative Mode, unpublished, 1974

B.A. Honours Paper, Ben Gurion University of the Negev

"I am become a name..." | T.E. LAWRENCE and the Heroic Narrative Mode | Clash of Cultures in Twentieth Century British Literature | Dr. E. Tabachnick | September 25, 1974 | Avraham Feinglass

Collation 8 × 11 inches: 62 leaves, pp.[1–2], [1]–49, [50], i–x.

Contents Prp.[1] title page, [2] half-title, quotes, pp. [1]–49 text, [50] blank, i–vii footnotes, viii–x bibliography.

Typography and paper Photocopy of typed original.

Copies AC, Cal.

E342 MICHAEL BOGRAD, T.E. Lawrence: an appreciation of his military leadership, unpublished, 1974

B.A. Honours Paper, Ben Gurion University of the Negev

Michael Bograd | June 1974 | T.E. Lawrence: | An Appreciation of his | Military Leadership

Collation 57 leaves, pp.[1], 2–57.

Contents Pp.[1] title page and start of text, 2–57 text.

Typography and paper Sheets 8 × 11, typed on one side only.

Copies AC, Cal.

E343 ELLIOTT DOOLEY, Lawrence van Arabië, Amsterdam Boek, 1974

Dutch Comic Book

[All in white] WERELDBEROEMDE VERHALEN | Lawrence | van Arabië | [four-colour drawing] | ELLIOTT DOOLEY | [in upper right corner within white rule square with star symbol in centre, in circular format] TOPPERS IN STRUP

Collation 26.5 × 18.5 cm: [1]^{16}, unpaged.

Contents Pp.[1] title page, [2–31] text, [32] series, publication information.

Text Comic book in panels, four-colour strip.

Paper White, newsprint, wove, unwatermarked, all edges trimmed, sheets bulk 2 mm.

Binding Front cover is title page.

Published at 1.25 Francs.

Copies AC, Cal.

E344 ELLIOT DOOLEY, Lawrence of Arabia, King Features, 1978

First American Edition

Elliot Dooley | LAWRENCE | OF | ARABIA | [drawing] | Adapted by Dr. Anne Mueser

Collation 26.3 × 18.8 cm: 18^1, 18 leaves, pp.[2], 1–30.

Contents Prp.[1] title page, [2] issue, copyright statements, pp.1–30 text.

Typography and text Strip comic book format.

Paper White, wove, unwatermarked, all edges trimmed, sheets bulk 5 mm.

Binding Pictorial paper covers. On front cover: *Elliot Dooley* |

LAWRENCE | OF ARABIA. On back cover: ILLUSTRATED | CLASSICS |
[list of 32 titles in series]. [drawings above and below list]. [Inner sides of
front cover map, inner sides of back cover brief biography of Lawrence].

Notes   No. 24 in series, ILLUSTRATED CLASSICS.

Copies   Rosen.

Scholarship Continues: Continued, 1975–79

More academic work appeared in the second half of the decade, as well as
a variety of other materials. A second work by the Weintraubs, *Lawrence of
Arabia, the Literary Impulse,* examines the literary wellsprings of Lawrence's
career as a writer. Phillip Knightley also published a second volume on
Lawrence, *Lawrence of Arabia,* a juvenile biography that stands in marked
contrast to his earlier *Secret Lives* (1969). This is much briefer and directed at
a different audience.

Charles Grosvenor, drawing upon his earlier honours thesis at Bates
College, produced *The Portraits of T.E. Lawrence,* the first of its type. Given
the many portraits of Lawrence, it is surprising that no one had earlier
attempted an iconography.

With the publication of Mack's *A Prince of Our Disorder,* yet another
biography appeared. It won the author a Pulitzer Prize for biography. More
new ground is covered in its pages than any biography to date.

Two books for young people appeared. As with Knightley (1975), Brent's
T.E. Lawrence, a juvenile photobiography, is a more strictly factual account
of the Lawrence story than is found in many earlier juveniles, which
tended to stress the 'heroic adventurer'. It presents many photos couched
in a text in which fuller presentation of his life story wins out over the 'boy's
adventure' theme. Graves' *Lawrence of Arabia and His World,* another well
illustrated biography, also has a less emotional view of some aspects of
Lawrence's life.

In 1976 a periodical was begun by Jeremy Wilson, *T.E. Lawrence Studies,*
and one issue was published. This promised to serve as a clearing house
for those interested in Lawrence studies. It is to be regretted that no other
issues have appeared.

An analysis of the Arab campaign by Konrad Morsey, *T.E. Lawrence und
der arabische Aufstand 1916/1918,* was published in Germany. Morsey uses
material in governmental archives not examined before. Another German
work, Stöger's *Wüste in Flammen,* is a juvenile that continues the factual
presentation found in works by Knightley, Graves and Brent.

The continued interest in Lawrence, by now well established, began to
diversify. Desmond Stewart, a writer on Near-Eastern affairs published *T.E.
Lawrence* about a year before his death. Phillips' *T.E. Lawrence* is a vanity-
press publication, and only a few copies appear to have been printed. A
study of Lawrence's life in the ranks is Montgomery Hyde's *Solitary in the
Ranks.* A slim volume of Lawrence's childhood in the the City of Oxford is
Marriott's *The Young Lawrence of Arabia.*

Steve Tabachnick's *T.E. Lawrence* is a study of the Lawrence canon for the
Twayne author's series. It examines the important works and places them

in the context of 20th-century British prose writing. A counterpart to Tabachnick's work is Maurice Larès' dissertation and subsequent book, *T.E. Lawrence, La France et Les Français*. It includes much long-buried French material. The bibliography it contains is the authoritative one to date, of French-language publications.

Three more juveniles appeared in rapid succession, continuing a tendency to appear in clumps. All three revert to the adventure genre: Davis' *Ned*, Bory's *Lawrence d'Arabie* in France, and Allen's *Lawrence of Arabia*. It is interesting that the last work appeared in England and the USA under two different authors' names; Allen in England and Ebert in the USA. Eden's *The Murder of Lawrence of Arabia*, is a fictional treatment of Lawrence's death. It accepts, as a premise, the black car theory.

1975

E346   STANLEY WEINTRAUB and RODELLE WEINTRAUB, Lawrence of Arabia, The Literary Impulse, Louisiana State University, 1975

First American Edition

[Double-page spread] [left page] LOUISIANA STATE UNIVERSITY PRESS| BATON ROUGE. [right page, swash] Lawrence | OF | [swash] Arabia | THE LITERARY IMPULSE | *Stanley Weintraub & Rodelle Weintraub*

Collation   21.5 × 14 cm: [1–6]^{16}, 96 leaves, pp.xvi, 1–175, [1].

Contents   Prp.[i] bastard title, [ii–iii] title page, [iv] ISBN and LC number, copyright statement, designer's and printer's credits, [v] quote, [vi] blank, [vii] dedication, [viii] blank, [ix] contents, [x] blank, xi–xiii preface, [xiv] blank, xv acknowledgments, xvi blank, pp.1–153 text, [154] blank, 155–161 notes, [162] blank, 163–169 selected bibliography, [170] blank, 171–175 index, [1] blank.

RT   On verso LAWRENCE OF ARABIA. On recto [in italics, according to chapter].

Text   20 lines, 9.8 (9.9) × 9.8 cm.

Paper   White, wove, unwatermarked, all edges trimmed, sheets bulk 1.2 cm.

Binding   Orange cloth 35 s. r O. On spine: [across at top, in brown] Weintraub | *and* | Weintraub | [running down, gilt] LAWRENCE OF ARABIA | [across at bottom, publisher's device]. Brown and white head and tail bands.

Published at $8.50 November 1984

Copies   AC, Cal, UT, LC.

E347 STANLEY AND RODELLE WEINTRAUB, Lawrence of Arabia the Literary Impulse, Louisiana State University, 1975

Publisher's Prospectus

[Dark brown, swash] Lawrence | of | Arabia | *Stanley Weintraub* | & | *Rodelle Weintraub* | Louisiana State | University Press

Collation   21.7 × 9.9 cm: single-fold leaflet printed on both sides.

Contents   Pp.[1] title page, [2–3] blurb, on page 3 also short blurb on *Saint Joan* by same author, [4] order form.

Paper   Yellow, wove, unwatermarked, all edges trimmed.

Published at   Free advertising flyer.

Copies   AC.

E348 PHILLIP KNIGHTLEY, Lawrence of Arabia, Sidgwick & Jackson, 1975

Uncorrected galley proofs

Lawrence | of | Arabia | Phillip Knightley | [publisher's device] | SIDGWICK & JACKSON | LONDON

Collation   20 × 13 cm: [1–7] [11] 12–78 leaves.

Contents   Leaf [1] list of author's works, [2] bastard title, [3] title page, [4] copyright statement, binder's, printer's credits, [5] dedication, [6] contents, [7] illustrations, [11]–78 text.

RT   On verso LAWRENCE OF ARABIA. On recto [according to chapter].

Text   20 lines, 10 (10) × 9 cm.

Paper   White, wove, unwatermarked, all edges trimmed, sheets bulk 7 mm.

Binding   White paper covers, sheets and covers glued at top edge. On front cover: Lawrence | of | Arabia | Phillip Knightley | [publisher's device] | SIDGWICK & JACKSON | LONDON.

Notes   No illustrations except map inside rear cover.

Copies   AC, Cal, LC.

E349 PHILLIP KNIGHTLEY, Lawrence of Arabia, Sidgwick & Jackson, 1976

First English Edition

Lawrence of Arabia | *by* | Phillip Knightley | [publisher's device] | SIDGWICK & JACKSON | LONDON

Collation   19.6 × 12.6 cm: [A]^8 B^8 C^{10} D–E^8, 42 leaves, pp.[1–11], 12–84.

Contents   Pp.[1] bastard title, [2] list of author's works, [3] title page, [4] copyright statement, ISBN number, printer's credit, [5] dedication, [6]

blank, [7] contents, [8] blank, [9–10] illustrations, 11–78 text, [79] map, [80] blank, [81] –84 index.

RT On recto LAWRENCE OF ARABIA. On verso [according to chapter].

Plates Eight plates on coated paper, printed on both sides, in twos following pp.16, 32, 52, 68.

Typography and paper $ 1 signed A C,C*.

Text 20 lines, 9.8 (9.8) × 8.8 cm.

Paper White, wove, unwatermarked, all edges trimmed, sheets bulk 8 mm.

Binding Tangerine cloth 67 bril OY cloth covered boards. On spine: [running down] Lawrence of Arabia Phillip Knightley | [running across at foot] [publisher's device] | Sedgwick | & Jackson.

Published at £2.25.

Copies AC, Cal.

E350   PHILLIP KNIGHTLEY, Lawrence of Arabia, Nelson, 1977

First American Edition

LAWRENCE | of ARABIA | by Phillip Knightley | [publisher's device] | THOMAS NELSON INC., PUBLISHERS | Nashville/New York

Collation 20.4 × 13.5 cm: [1–6]⁸, 48 leaves, pp.[1–8], 9–96.

Contents Pp.[1] bastard title, [2] blank, [3] title page, [4] copyright, issue statements, CIP, [5] dedication, [6] blank, [7] contents, [8] map, 9–91 text, 92–96 index.

RT On verso LAWRENCE OF ARABIA. On recto [according to chapter].

Text 20 lines, 9.8 (10.2) × 9.7 cm.

Paper White, wove, unwatermarked, all edges trimmed, sheets bulk 6 mm.

Binding Red cloth 12 s. Red. On front cover: [in white] LAWRENCE |of ARABIA. On spine: [running down, white] KNIGHTLEY LAWRENCE OF ARABIA | [across at bottom] [publisher's device] | [semi-circle] NELSON. Red and white head and tail bands.

Published at $5.95.

Copies AC, Cal, LC.

E351   CHARLES GROSVENOR, The Portraits of T.E. Lawrence, Otterden Press, 1975

First American Edition

THE PORTRAITS | OF | [in red] T.E. LAWRENCE | By | CHARLES GROSVENOR | [pub. device] | THE OTTERDEN PRESS

Collation   28 × 21.6 cm: 46 leaves, pp.[1–8], [1]–82, [1–2].

Contents   Prp.[1–2] blank, [3] bastard title, [4] frontispiece, [5] title page, [6] photo credits, copyright statement, pub. address, [7] dedication, [8] blank, pp.[1]–3 introduction, 4–82 text, [1] edition limitation statement, [2] blank.

RT   On both verso and recto [according to section].

Text   20 lines, 18.8 (18.9) × 16.1 cm.

Paper   White, wove, unwatermarked, all edges trimmed, sheets bulk 6 mm.

Binding   Tan paper covers 76 l y. Br. On front cover: THE PORTRAITS | OF | [in red] T.E. LAWRENCE | [colour portrait of T.E. Lawrence with white border, pasted on] | By CHARLES GROSVENOR. On spine: [running down] THE PORTRAITS OF T.E. LAWRENCE GROSVENOR. On back cover: [publisher's device] | THE OTTERDEN PRESS

Published at $15.00.

Notes   Limited to 200 copies.

Copies   AC, Cal, UT, LC.

E352   JOHN E. MACK, A Prince of Our Disorder, Little, Brown, 1975

Uncorrected Proof of First American Edition

John E. Mack | [Oxford rule] | A PRINCE OF | OUR DISORDER | [Oxford rule] | The Life of T.E. Lawrence | WITH MAPS AND ILLUSTRATIONS | LITTLE, BROWN AND COMPANY | BOSTON-TORONTO

Collation   23.5 × 14.5 cm: guillotined sheets glued to covers, 266 leaves pp.[12], [ix]–xxvi, 1–502.

Contents   Prp.[1–2] blank, [3] statement of uncorrected proof, [4] blank, [5] bastard title, [6] list of acknowledgments, [7] title page, [8] copyright, issue statements, [9] dedication, [10] blank, [11] quotes from G.B. Shaw and T.E. Lawrence, [12] blank, [ix]–xii contents, xiii–xiv illustrations, xv–xxvi introduction, pp.[1] section title, [2] blank, 3–453 text, [454] blank, [455] section title, [456] blank, 457–464 appendixes, 465–520 chapter notes, 521–529 bibliography, [530] blank.

Text   20 lines, 9.6 × 11.4 cm.

Paper   White, wove, unwatermarked, all edges trimmed, sheets bulk 3.1 cm.

Binding   Orange yellow paper 71 m. OY. On front cover: [same as title page].

Copies   AC, Cal.

E353   JOHN E. MACK, A Prince of Our Disorder, Little Brown, 1976

First American Edition

John E. Mack | [Oxford rule] | A PRINCE OF | OUR DISORDER | The Life of T.E. Lawrence | [Oxford rule] | WITH MAPS AND ILLUSTRATIONS | [publisher's device] | LITTLE, BROWN AND COMPANY | BOSTON-TORONTO

Collation 23.4 × 15.5 cm: [1–19]^{16}, 312 leaves, pp.i–xxviii, 1–561, [3].

Contents Prp.[i] blank, [ii] list of author's works, [iii] bastard title, [iv] John drawing of TEL, [v] title page, [vi] copyright, issue statements, CIP, printer's credit, [vii] dedication, [viii] blank, [ix] quotes by G.B.Shaw and T.E. Lawrence, [x] blank, [xi]–xii acknowledgments, [xiii]–xiv contents, [xv]–xvi illustrations, [xvii]–xxviii introduction, pp.[1] section title, [2] blank, [3]–460 text, [461] section title, [462] blank, [463]–467 appendix, [468] blank, [469] section title, [470] blank, [471]–526 chapter notes, [527] section title, [528] blank, [529]–537 bibliography, [538] blank, [539] copyright acknowledgments, [540] blank, [541]–561 index, [1–3] blank.

RT On recto [according to section]. On verso [according to chapter title].

Plates Two gatherings of plates, in eights bound in, following pp.132, 420.

Text 20 lines, 8.5 (8.8) × 11,5 cm.

Paper White, wove, unwatermarked, all edges trimmed, sheets bulk 3.7 cm.

Binding Red cloth 15 m. Red. On front cover: [blind-stamped publisher's device]. On spine: [gilt] John E. Mack | [within black patch with double gilt rule top and bottom] A PRINCE | OF OUR | DISORDER. | [below rectangle] The Life of | T.E. Lawrence | [at foot] Little, Brown.

Published at $15.00, February 1975.

Copies AC, Cal, UT, LC.

E354 JOHN E. MACK, A Prince of Our Disorder, Little, Brown, 1978

First American Edition (Paperback)

JOHN E. MACK | [double rule] | A PRINCE OF | OUR DISORDER | The Life of T.E. Lawrence | [double rule] | WITH MAPS AND ILLUSTRATIONS | [publisher's device] | LITTLE, BROWN AND COMPANY | BOSTON-TORONTO

Collation 19.3 × 12.5 cm: guillotined sheets glued to covers, 296 leaves, pp.[i–xi], xii–xxviii, [xxix–xxx], [1–2], 3–[562].

Contents Prp.[i] blank, [ii] list of author's works, [iii] bastard title, [iv] drawing of T.E. Lawrence by John, [v] title page, [vi] copyright, issue statements, CIP, designer's credit, [vii] dedication, [viii] blank, [ix] quotes, [x] blank, [xi]–xii acknowledgments, [xiii]–xiv contents, [xv]–xvi illustrations, [xvii]–xxviii introduction, [xxix–xxx] maps, pp.[1] section title, [2] blank, 3–467 text, [468] blank, [469] section title, [470] blank, [471]–526 chapter notes, [527] section title, [528] blank, [529]–537 bibliography, [538] blank, [539] copyright acknowledgments, [540] blank, [541]–561 index, [562] blank.

RT On verso [according to section]. On recto [according to chapter].

Plates   Sixteen b/w plates on same stock as text, printed on both sides, following pp.132, 420; probably counted in gatherings.

Text   20 lines, 7.3 (8.2) × 10 cm.

Paper   White, wove, unwatermarked, all edges trimmed, sheets bulk 3 cm.

Binding   Pink paper covers 31 p. y Pink. On front cover: JOHN E.MACK | [in deep red] A PRINCE OF | [in deep red] OUR DISORDER | The Life of T.E. Lawrence | [within single rule frame, colour reproduction of John drawing of Lawrence] | [in red] Winner of the Pulitzer Prize for Biography. On spine: [running down, title in deep red] A PRINCE OF OUR DISORDER | JOHN E. MACK [publisher's device] Little Brown. On back cover: $6.95 | [quotes from reviews] | [ISBN number].

Published at $6.95.

Copies   AC, Cal.

E355   JOHN E. MACK, A Prince of Our Disorder, Weidenfeld & Nicolson, 1976

First English Edition

John E. Mack | [Oxford rule] | A PRINCE OF | OUR DISORDER | The Life of T.E. Lawrence | [Oxford rule] | WEIDENFELD AND NICOLSON | LONDON

Collation   23.3 × 15.5 cm: [1–17]¹⁶ [18]⁸ [19]¹⁶, 296 leaves, pp.[i–xi], xii–xxviii, [1–3], 4–564.

Contents   Prp.[i] blank, [ii] works by author, [iii] half title, [iv] frontispiece, drawing of TEL by John, [v] title page, [vi] copyright, ISBN, printer's and binder's credits, [vii] dedication, [viii] blank, [ix] quotes, [x] blank, [xi]–xii acknowledgments, [xiii]–xiv contents, [xv]–xvi illustrations, [xvii]–xxviii introduction, pp.[1] section title, [2] blank, [3]–460 text, [461] section title, [462] blank, [463]–467 appendix, [468] blank, [469] section title, [470] blank, [471]–526 chapter notes, [527] section title, [528] blank, [529]–537 bibliography, 538 blank, [539] copyright acknowledgments, [540] blank, [541]–561 index, [562–564] blank.

RT   On verso [in italics, according to section]. On recto [in italics, according to chapter].

Plates   Sixteen plates on coated paper, printed on both sides, following p.132.

Text   20 lines, 8.4 (8.8) × 11.4 cm.

Paper   White, wove, unwatermarked, all edges trimmed, sheets bulk 3.4 cm.

Binding   Wine red buckram 14 v. deep Red. On spine: [gilt] A PRINCE | OF OUR | DISORDER | The Life of | T.E. Lawrence | John E. Mack | Weidenfeld | & Nicolson. Red & white head and tail bands. Map end papers in blue.

Published at   £6.95, December 1976.

Copies   AC, Cal.

E356 PETER BRENT, T.E. Lawrence, Weidenfeld & Nicolson, 1975

First English Edition

GREAT LIVES | T.E. LAWRENCE | *Peter Brent* | Introduction by Elizabeth Longford | [photo of dagger and sheath] | Weidenfeld and Nicolson London

Collation 24.8 × 17 cm: [1–3]^8 [4]^4 [5–15]^8, 116 leaves, pp.[1–6], 7–232.

Contents Pp.[1] series title, [2] portrait of T.E.Lawrence, [3] title page, [4] copyright statement, credits, [5] contents, [6] blank, 7–8 introduction, [9] blank, 10–11 two-page photo spread, on right page section title 12–223 text, [224] blank, 225 further reading, 226–228 list of illustrations, 229–232 index.

Text 20 lines, 9 × 10.4 cm.

Paper White, wove, unwatermarked, all edges trimmed, sheets bulk 2.2 cm.

Binding Maroon cloth 16 d. Red. On front cover: [within gilt fancy scroll work, gilt] GREAT | LIVES. On spine: [running down within rectangle formed by double gilt rules on three sides and fancy scroll work at bottom] T.E. Lawrence Peter Brent | [within fancy scroll work] GREAT | LIVES | [across at foot] Weidenfeld & Nicolson. Pictorial end papers.

Published at £3.25.

Notes Another binding state 20 d. gy Red. Peter Brent is the pseudonym of Peter Kilner.

Copies AC, Cal, LC.

E357 PETER BRENT, T.E. Lawrence, Putnam, 1975

First American Edition

T.E. Lawrence | [swash] Peter Brent | Introduction by Elizabeth Longford | [photo] | G.P. Putnam's and Sons. New York

Collation 25 × 17 cm: [1–5]^8 [6]^4 [7–15]^8, 116 leaves, pp.[1–6], 7–232.

Contents Pp.[1] bastard title, [2] photo of Lawrence, [3] title page, [4] issue, copyright statements, credits, SBN, LC numbers, [5] contents, [6] blank, 7–8 introduction, 9 blank, [10–11] double-spread photo and section title, 12–223 text, [224] blank, 225 list of further reading, 226–228 list of illustrations, 229–232 index.

Text 20 lines, 9 × 10.3 cm.

Paper White, wove, unwatermarked, all edges trimmed, sheets bulk 1.8 cm.

Binding Maroon cloth 16 d. red. On front cover: [within art nouveau frame] T.E. Lawrence. On spine: [within double rule frame, gilt] T.E. Lawrence Peter Brent | [at foot, across, within fancy frame] Putnam. Pictorial end papers.

Published at $12.95.

Notes   Peter Brent is the pseudonym of Peter Kilner.

Copies   AC, LC.

1976

E358   RICHARD GRAVES, Lawrence of Arabia and His World, Scribners, 1976

First American Edition

RICHARD PERCEVAL GRAVES | LAWRENCE OF ARABIA | and his world | CHARLES SCRIBNER'S SONS | NEW YORK

Collation   23.2 × 18.2 cm: 1–8⁸, 64 leaves, pp.[1–6], 7–128.

Contents   Pp.[1] bastard title, [2] frontispiece, [3] title page, [4] author's note, copyright statement, printer's credit, [5] dedication, [6] quotes, 7–113 text, [114] blank, 115–116 chronology, 117–118 bibliography, 119–123 illustrations, 124–127 index, [128] blank.

Text   20 lines, 8.7 × 10.4 cm.

Paper   White, wove, unwatermarked, all edges trimmed, sheets bulk 1 cm.

Binding   Olive green cloth 107 m. OL On spine: [gilt, running down] LAWRENCE OF ARABIA and his world | RICHARD PERCEVAL GRAVES | [at foot, running down] SCRIBNERS.

Published at $8.95.

Notes   Thames and Hudson appears on front of dust wrapper, Scribners is at foot on spine of dust wrapper.

Copies   AC, Cal, LC.

E359   RICHARD GRAVES, Lawrence of Arabia and His World, Thames and Hudson, 1976

First English Edition

RICHARD PERCEVAL GRAVES | LAWRENCE OF ARABIA | and his world | [publisher's device] | THAMES AND HUDSON | LONDON

Collation   23.2 × 18.2 cm: 1–8⁸, 64 leaves, pp.[1–6], 7–128.

Contents   Pp.[1] bastard title, [2] frontispiece, [3] title page, [4] author's note, copyright statement, printer's credit, [5] dedication, [6] quotes, 7–113 text, [114] blank, 115–116 chronology, 117–118 bibliography, 119–123 illustrations, 124–127 index, [128] blank.

Text   20 lines, 8.7 × 10.4 cm.

Paper   White, wove, unwatermarked, all edges trimmed, sheets bulk 1 cm.

Binding   Olive green cloth 107 m. OL. On front cover: [gilt, publisher's device]. On spine: [running down, gilt] LAWRENCE OF ARABIA and his world | RICHARD PERCEVAL GRAVES | [across at foot] THAMES | AND | HUDSON. White silk head and tail bands.

Published at £3.50, October 1976.

Notes Title page cancel pasted on to stub of American title page.

Copies AC, Cal, LC.

E359a RICHARD GRAVES, Lawrence de Arabia, Saluat, 1976?

First Spanish Edition

LAWRENCE DE | ARABIA | RICHARD PERCEVAL GRAVES | Prólogo | MANUEL DIEL ALEGRIA | SALUAT

Collation Guillotined sheets glued to covers, 92 leaves, pp.[1–4], 5–183, [1].

Contents Pp.[1] bastard title, [2] blank, [3] title page, [4] original title, translator's credit, copyright statement, ISBN, printer's credit, 5 contents, 6 illustrations, 7–175 text and illustrations, [176] blank, 177–179 chronology, [180] blank, 181–182 literature, 183 bibliography, [184] list of works in series.

Text 20 lines, 7 × 10 cm.

Paper White, wove, unwatermarked, all edges trimmed, sheets bulk 1.7 cm.

Binding Pictorial paper covers LAWRENCE | DE ARABIA | RICHARD P. GRAVES | [rule] | BIBLIOTECA SALVAT DE | [rule] | GRANDES BIOGRAFIAS. On spine: [running down, in white] LAWRENCE DE ARABIA Richard P. Graves | [across at foor] 6 | SALVAT.

Copies Rosen.

E360 JEREMY M. WILSON, T.E. Lawrence, Ashmolean Museum. 1976

First English Edition

T.E. LAWRENCE | "LAWRENCE OF ARABIA" | *set of slides with a commentary and* | *biographical notes by* | J.M. WILSON | ASHMOLEAN MUSEUM, OXFORD | 1976

Collation 17.8 × 12 cm: [1]¹⁶, 16 leaves, pp.[1–6], 1–24, [2]; folded plastic slide holder for six slides and identifying information attached to back cover.

Contents Prp.[1] bastard title, [2] frontispiece, [3] title page, [4] copyright, ISBN, publisher's device, designer's, printer's credits, [5] acknowledgments, [6] plate 1, pp.1–20 text and plates, 21 plate 5, 22 notes, 23 plate 6, 24 illustrations, 1–2 blank.

Text 20 lines, 8.2 × 8.8 cm Set in 10/11 pt. Theme.

Paper White, wove, unwatermarked, all edges trimmed, sheets bulk 2 mm.

Binding   Pictorial paper covers, stapled to sheets with two metal staples.
On front cover: T.E. LAWRENCE | "LAWRENCE OF ARABIA" | SET OF 6
SLIDES WITH A COMMENTARY | [photo of T.E.L.'s dagger and belt] |
ASHMOLEAN MUSEUM OXFORD. On back cover: ISBN.

Published at   £1.50, January 1971.

Copies   AC, Cal.

E361   BERNARD T. WARD, Lawrence of Arabia &
Pole Hill, Chingford Historical Publication No. 3, 1976

Lawrence of Arabia & | *Pole Hill, Chingford* | by | *Bernard T. Ward* | (Reprinted
from Essex Journal, Vol. 9, No. 3) | [photo of Pole Hill Cottage] | The
'Cloister' built by Vyvyan W. Richards and the boys from Bancroft's School
after | the first hut had been destroyed by fire.

Collation   21.2 × 14.9 cm: [1]⁴, 4 leaves, unpaged.

Contents   Pp.[1] title page, [2–6] text, [7] photo, acknowledgments,
bibliography, [8] map, colophon.

Text   8 lines, 3.2 × 11.2 cm.

Paper   White, wove, unwatermarked, all edges trimmed, sheets bulk 1
mm.

Binding   Stapled together with two metal staples.

Published at   15p.

Copies   AC.

E362   T.E. LAWRENCE STUDIES, n.p., 1976

Prospectus for Periodical

T.E. Lawrence | Studies

Collation   21 × 10.2 cm: tri-fold leaflet.

Paper   Buff, wove, unwatermarked, all edges trimmed.

Notes   Prospectus for English periodical (issued by Jeremy Wilson) to be
published irregularly (see next item).

Copies   AC, Cal, UT.

E363   T.E. LAWRENCE STUDIES, Vol. 1, No. 1, Spring 1976

No title page.

Collation   No. 1, 21 × 13.8 cm: 84 pp.

Contents   Pp.1 references, ISSN, printer's credit, limitation statement, 3–10
J.M. Wilson, Sense and Nonsense in The Biography of T.E. Lawrence,
11–20 Denis Boak, Malraux and T.E. Lawrence, 21–32 André Malraux,

'N'Etait-ce Donc Que Cela?', 33–43 R.G. Sims, The Sayings and Doings of T.E., 44–53 J.M. Wilson, Catalogue Raisonné of Works by, About and Relating to T.E. Lawrence, 54–58 Works Received and Forthcoming 1975–1976, 58–59 English Editions of Works by T.E. Lawrence In Print, 60 Where to Obtain Current English Editions By Post, 60–63 Register of Current Research, 63 Related Biographical Studies, 63–84 Reviews, inside rear cover, acknowledgments, announcements.

Binding Tan paper covers 73 p. OY.

Published at $14.50 for one-year subscription.

Notes Issue no. 1 only issue published to date.

Copies AC, Cal, Ca.

E364 T.E. LAWRENCE STUDIES, "For Sale and Wanted", vol. 1- 1976

T.E. LAWRENCE STUDIES Vol. I No 1 Spring 1976 | "FOR SALE AND WANTED". Supplement SENT AIRMAIL TO SUBSCRIBERS

Collation 21 × 10 cm: tri-fold leaflet, three sheets, pp.1–18.

Contents Pp.[1] title page, ordering information, contents, 2–18 list of items.

Text Photocopy of typed original.

Paper Green, wove, unwatermarked, all edges trimmed.

Notes No. 2 issued 1977, unpaged.

Copies AC, Cal.

E365 KONRAD MORSEY, T.E. Lawrence und der arabische Aufstand 1916/18, Biblio, 1976

First German Edition

Konrad Morsey | T.E. Lawrence | und der arabische | Aufstand 1916/18 | Biblio Verlag · Osnabrück 1976

Collation 2.9 × 15.7 cm: guillotined sheets glued to covers, pp.[2], i–xii, 1–474.

Contents Prp.[1–2] blank, [I] series title, [II] series information, [III] title page, [IV] copyright, printer's statements, V–VIII contents, [IX] foreword, [X] note by author, XI abbreviations, pp.[1] section title, [2] blank, [3]–287 text, [288] blank, [289] section title, [290] blank, 291–388 notes, [389] section title, [390] blank, 391–457 bibliography, [458] section title, [459] blank, [460–474] illustrations and maps.

Text 20 lines, 8.9 × 10 cm.

Paper White, wove, unwatermarked, all edges trimmed, sheets bulk 2.5 cm.

Binding Silver paper, glued to sheets. On front cover: Konrad Morsey |
T.E. Lawrence | und der arabische | Aufstand 1916/18 | 7 Studien zur
Militärgeschichte, Militär- | wissenschaft und Konfliktsforschung. On
spine: [running down] Morsey · T.E. Lawrence und der arabische
Aufstand 1916/18. StMK7.

Copies AC, Cal, LC.

1977

E366   AUGUST K. STÖGER, Wüste in Flammen, Hoch, 1977

First German Edition

AUGUST K. STÖGER | Wüste in Flammen | Lawrence von Arabien- |
weisser Bruder der Beduinen | HOCH-VERLAG · DUSSELDORF

Collation 21.7 × 14 cm: [1–10]⁸, 80 leaves, pp.[1–4], 5–159, [160].

Contents Pp.[1] title page, [2] ISBN, typographer's credit, copyright
statement, printer's credit, [3] frontispiece, [4] blank, 5 contents, [6] map,
7–158 text, 159 bibliography, [160] ad.

Text 20 lines, 8.4 × 10.2 cm.

Paper White, wove, unwatermarked, all edges trimmed, sheets bulk 1.8
cm.

Binding Yellow green cloth l. Y G. On front cover: Wüste | in | Flammen.
On spine: [running up] Stöger Wüste in flammen. Black and white head
and tail bands.

Published at 14 DM.

Notes Boys' adventure book.

Copies AC, Cal.

E366a   DESMOND STEWART, T.E. Lawrence,
Harper & Row, 1977

Uncorrected Proofs of First American Edition

T.E. LAWRENCE | BY | DESMOND STEWART | HARPER & ROW,
PUBLISHERS | New York, Hagerstown, San Francisco, London

Collation 21.1 × 16.8 cm: guillotined sheets glued to covers, 177 leaves,
pp.[1–6], [i–xi], xii, [1–3], 4–334, [1–2].

Contents Prp.[1–2] blank, [3] bastard title, [4] list of author's works, [i–ii]
blank, [iii] title page, [iv] copyright statement, [v] dedication, [vi] blank, vii
contents, [viii] blank, [ix] ILLUSTRATIONS, [x] blank, [xi]–xii
acknowledgements, pp.[1] section title, [2] blank, [3]–305 text, [306–307]
blank, [308] section title, [309]–334 notes, [335] section title, [306] blank.

RT On verso *T.E. Lawrence.* On recto [in italics, according to chapter].

Text 10.2 (10.5) × 17.4 cm.

Paper White, wove, unwatermarked, all edges trimmed, sheets bulk 1.8 cm.

Binding Pale green paper wrappers 122 gy. Y G. On front cover: T.E. LAWRENCE | BY | DESMOND STEWART | UNCORRECTED PROOF | Title: T.E. LAWRENCE | Author: Desmond Stewart | Characterization: nonfiction | Probable publication date: August 1977 | Probable price: $15.00 | Illustrations: 16 black and white | Approximate length: 448 pages | ISBN: 0-06-014123-9 | [rule] | Reviewers are reminded | that changes may be made | in this proof copy before books are printed. If any | material from this book is to be quoted in a review, | the quotation should be checked against the final bound book. | HARPER & ROW, PUBLISHERS | New York, Hagerstown, San Francisco, London.

Published at Not for sale.

Copies Cal, Rosen.

E367 DESMOND STEWART, T.E. Lawrence, Hamish Hamilton, 1977

First English Edition

T.E. LAWRENCE | BY | DESMOND STEWART | [publisher's device] | HAMISH HAMILTON | LONDON

Collation 23.4 × 15.5 cm: [1]^{16} 2–11^{16} 12^8, 168 leaves, pp.[i–xii], 1–352, [4].

Contents Prp.[i–ii] blank, [iii] bastard title, [iv] list of author's works, [v] title page, [vi] issue, copyright statements, SBN, printer's credit, [vii] dedication, [viii] blank, [ix] contents, [x] blank, [xi–xii] illustrations, pp.[1] section title, [2] blank, [3]–306 text, [307] section title, [308] blank, [309]–334 note incorporating bibliography, [335]–337 acknowledgments, [338] blank, [339]–352 index, [1–4] blank.

RT On verso T.E. LAWRENCE. On recto [according to section].

Plates Six b/w plates on coated paper, printed on both sides, following pp.84, 180, 212.

Typography and paper $ 1 signed 1 5*.

Text 20 lines, 8.3 (8.5) × 11.1 cm.

Paper White, wove, unwatermarked, all edges trimmed, sheets bulk 2.5 cm.

Binding Brown paper 64 br. Gray. On spine: [gilt] [thick rule] | T.E. | Lawrence | [diamond] | DESMOND | STEWART | [publisher's device at foot]. T.e. orange.

Published at £7.50, June 1977.

Copies AC, Cal, LC.

E368 DESMOND STEWART, T.E. Lawrence, History Book Club, 1977

Book Club Prospectus

[In brown] T.E. LAWRENCE | A New Biography | BY DESMOND

STEWART | [in brown] *The brilliant yet bizarre personality behind* | [in brown]
Lawrence of Arabia's romantic mystique | [photo of Lawrence in Arab dress
within black rule frame] | [beneath frame] another new selection from The
History Book Club November 1977

Collation   20.7 × 13.5 cm: single-fold leaflet.

Contents   Pp.[i] title page, [2] repeat of title, order information, picture of
book, [3–4] blurb notes on author, reviewer and quote from review, photo
of Lawrence.

Text   20 lines, 7 × 10.1 cm.

Paper   White, wove, unwatermarked, all edges trimmed.

Published at   Free advertising flyer.

Copies   AC.

E369   DESMOND STEWART, T.E. Lawrence, Paladin/Granada, 1979

Second English Edition

Desmond Stewart | T.E. Lawrence | PALADIN | GRANADA PUBLISHING |
London Toronto Sydney New York

Collation   19.5 × 12.8 cm: guillotined sheets glued to paper covers, 184
leaves, pp.[i–xi], xii, [1–3], 4–352, [4].

Contents   Prp.[i–ii] blank, [iii] brief biography of author, [iv] blank, [v] title
page, [vi] ISBN, copyright, issue statements, printer's credit, [vii]
dedication, [viii] blank, [ix] contents, [x] blank, [xi]–xii illustrations, pp.[1]
section title, [2] blank, [3]–306 text, [307]–334 notes, incorporating
bibliography, [335]–337 acknowledgments, [338] blank, [339]–352 index,
[353] blank, [1–3] ads.

RT   On verso *T.E. Lawrence.* On recto [in italics, according to chapter].

Plates   Eight b/w plates printed on both sides, following p.148.

Text   20 lines, 7.6 (7.8) × 10 cm.

Paper   White, wove, unwatermarked, all edges trimmed, sheets bulk 1.8
cm.

Binding   White paper covers glued to sheets. On front cover: DESMOND
STEWART | [long brown rule] | [in brown] T.E. LAWRENCE | [long brown
rule] | [colour drawing of Lawrence] | [publisher's device] | 0 586 08306 5.
On spine [running down] *DESMOND STEWART* | [in brown] T.E.
LAWRENCE PALADIN GRANADA. On back cover: [7 quotes and blurb].

Published at   £1.95, February 1979.

Copies   AC, Cal.

E370   DESMOND STEWART, T.E. Lawrence, Harper & Row, 1977

First American Edition

[Stencil lettering] T.E. LAWRENCE | [rule] | [stencil lettering] by Desmond

Stewart | [rule] | HARPER & ROW, PUBLISHERS | NEW YORK, HAGERSTOWN, SAN FRANCISCO, LONDON

Collation 23.3 × 16 cm: [1–9]¹⁶ [10]⁸ [11–12]¹⁶, 168 leaves, pp.[i–xi], xii, 1–352, [4].

Contents Prp.[i–ii] blank, [iii] bastard title, [iv] list of author's works, [v] title page, [vi] acknowledgments, copyright, edition statements, [vii] dedication, [viii] blank, [ix] contents, [x] blank, [xi]–xii illustrations, pp.[1] section title, [2] blank, 3–306 text, 307–334 notes incorporating bibliography, 335–337 acknowledgments, [338] blank, 339–352 index, [1–4] blank.

RT On verso T.E. LAWRENCE. On recto [according to section].

Plates Six plates on coated paper, printed on both sides, in groups of two following pp.84, 180, 212.

Text 20 lines, 8.7 (9) × 11.6 cm.

Paper White, wove, unwatermarked, all edges trimmed, sheets bulk 2.9 cm.

Binding Yellow cloth 90 gy Y. On spine: [running down, stencil lettering, gilt] T.E. LAWRENCE Desmond Stewart | [across at foot] Harper | & Row. Brown and white head and tail bands. Grey end papers.

Published at $15.00, November 1977.

Copies AC, Cal, LC.

E371   DESMOND STEWART, Lawrence von Arabien, Claassen, 1979

First German Edition

Desmond Stewart | LAWRENCE VON ARABIEN | Eine Biographie | claassen

Collation 21.4 × 14 cm: guillotined sheets glued to case, 224 leaves, pp.[1–10], 11–441, [7].

Contents Pp.[1] bastard title, [2] blank, [3] title page, [4] original title, copyright statement, translator's credit, issue statement, German copyright statement, printer's credit, ISBN, [5] dedication, [6] blank, [7] contents, [8] blank, [9] section title, [10] blank, 11–441 text, [1–7] ads.

Plates Eight plates on coated paper, printed on both sides, following p.224.

Text 20 lines, 8.9 × 10.5 cm. Set in Garamond.

Paper White, wove, unwatermarked, all edges trimmed, sheets bulk 4 cm.

Binding Medium orange paper covered boards 53 m O. On spine: [within dark brown rectangle] Stewart | Lawrence | von | Arabien | claassen. White silk head and tail bands.

Published at DM 38.

Copies AC.

E371a   DESMOND STEWART, Lawrence von Arabien, Heyne, 1977

Second German Edition

Desmond Stewart | [rule] | LAWRENCE | VON ARABIEN | Magien und Abenteurer | Wilhelm Heyne Verlag | München

Collation   17.9 × 11.5 cm: guillotined sheets glued to covers, 224 leaves, pp.[1–7], 8–447, [1].

Contents   Pp.[1] bastard title, [2] list of author's works, [3] title page, [4] original title, copyright and other credits, ISBN, [5] contents, [6] dedication, [7] section title, 8–393 text, 394 acknowledgements, [395] section title, 396 abbreviations, 397–420 notes, 421–437 chronology, 438–[448] index.

Plates   Eight b/w photos printed on both sides, following pp.96, 160, 298, 352.

Text   20 lines, 7.9 × 9 cm.

Paper   White, wove, unwatermarked, all edges trimmed, sheets bulk 2.4 cm.

binding   Pictorial paper covers. On front cover: [in pale yellow] HEYNE BIOGRAPHIEN | [vert. pennant design] | Desmond Stewart | [in white, rule] | [in pale yellow] LAWRENCE | VON ARABIEN | [in white, rule] | [in white] Magier und Abenteurer. On spine: [in white] 91 | [remainder pale yellow] HEYNE | BIOGRA- | PHIEN | [running up, in white] Desmond Stewart [in pale yellow] LAWRENCE VON ARABIEN. | [across at foot, in yellow] 1280 | [in yellow] [vert. pennant design]. On back cover: [in yellow] HEYNE BIOGRAPHIEN | [vert. pennant design] | [blurb, all in white] | DM 12.80.

Published at   DM 12.80.

Copies   Rosen.

E372   JILL M. PHILLIPS, T.E. Lawrence, New York, Gordon Press, 1977

First American Edition

T.E. LAWRENCE: | [rule] | PORTRAIT OF | THE ARTIST AS HERO | Controversy and Caricature in the | biographies of "Lawrence of Arabia" | by Jill M. Phillips | [publisher's device] | GORDON PRESS | NEW YORK | 1977

Collation   22.8 × 15 cm: [1–14]^{16}, 224 leaves, pp.[2], [1–10], 11–446.

Contents   Prp.[1] bastard title, [2] blank, pp.[1] blank, [2] frontispiece, [3] title page, [4] copyright, CIP, [5] dedication, [6] blank, [7] quote from GBS play, [8] blank, [9] contents, [10] blank, 11 note on transliteration, [12] blank, 13 note on publication, [14] blank, 15–16 acknowledgments, 17 introduction, [18] blank, 19–22 preface, 23–30 author's introduction, [31] section title, [32] blank, [33] quote, [34] blank, 35–315 text, [316] blank, [317] section title, [318] blank, 319–416 annotated bibliography, [417] section title, [418] blank, 419–427 additional bibliography, [428] blank, [429] section title, [430] blank, 431–439 appendixes, [440] blank, 441 quote, [442–446] blank.

Text Photocopy of typed original.

Paper White, wove unwatermarked, all edges trimmed, sheets bulk 2.1 cm.

Binding Red cloth 11 v. red. On front cover: [gilt] T.E. | LAWRENCE: | PORTRAIT OF THE | ARTIST AS HERO | JILL M. PHILLIPS. On spine: [running down, gilt] T.E. LAWRENCE: | PORTRAIT OF THE ARTIST AS HERO | PHILLIPS | [across at foot] [publisher's device] | GORDON | PRESS. Orange and red head and tail bands. White end papers.

Published at $55.00.

Notes This book is the product of a vanity press operation and only a few copies appear to have been printed.

Copies AC, Cal.

E372a HARFORD MONTGOMERY HYDE, Solitary in the Ranks, Constable, 1977

Unedited Proofs of First English Edition

SOLITARY | IN THE RANKS | Lawrence of Arabia | As Airman and Private Soldier | H. Montgomery Hyde | Constable London

Collation 21.5 × 14 cm: [1–9]^{16}, 144 leaves, pp.[1–9], 10–288.

Contents Pp.[1] bastard title, [2] title page, [3] title page, [4] copyright statement, ISBN, printer's, binder's credits, [5] dedication, [6] quote from Lawrence, [7] contents, [8] blank, [9]–10 illustrations, [11]–13 acknowledgements, [14] blank, 15–16 foreword, 17–258 text, [259]–272 sources and notes, [273]–277 bibliography, [278] blank, [279]–288 index.

RT On verso *Solitary in the Ranks*. On recto [according to title of chapter].

Text 20 lines, 9.1 (9.7) × 10 cm.

Paper White, wove, unwatermarked, all edges trimmed, sheets bulk 2 cm.

Binding White paper. On front cover: [same as title page]. On spine: [running down] SOLITARY IN THE RANKS.

Copies Cal.

E373 HARFORD MONTGOMERY HYDE, Solitary in the Ranks, Constable, 1977

First English Edition

SOLITARY | IN THE RANKS | Lawrence of Arabia | as Airman and Private Soldier | H. Montgomery Hyde | Constable London

Collation 21.6 × 13.8 cm: [A]–I^{16}, 144 leaves, pp.[1–9], 10–288.

Contents   Pp.[1] bastard title, [2] list of books by author, [3] title page, [4] copyright statement, ISBN, printer's, binder's credits, [5] dedication, [6] quote from T.E. Lawrence, [7] contents, [8] blank, [9]–10 illustrations, [11]–13 acknowledgments, [14] blank, 15–16 foreword, 17–258 text, [259]–272 sources and notes, [273]–277 bibliography, [278] blank, [279]–288 index.

RT   On recto *Solitary in the Ranks*. On verso [in italics, according to chapter].

Plates   Twenty-five plates on coated paper, frontispiece one side only, others both sides, following pp.2, 32, 96 and 160 in groups of eight.

Typography and paper $ 1 signed B.

Text   20 lines, 9.1 (9.7) × 10 cm. Set in 12pt Monotype Fournier.

Paper   White, wove, unwatermarked, all edges trimmed, sheets bulk 2 cm.

Binding   Blue cloth 182 m. Blue. On spine: [gilt] H. | Mont- | gomery | Hyde | [cut] | SOLITARY | IN THE | RANKS | [cut] | Lawrence | of | Arabia | as airman | and | private | Soldier | Constable. Grey end papers.

Published at   £6.95, November 1977.

Copies   AC, Cal, LC.

E374   HARFORD MONTGOMERY HYDE,
Solitary in the Ranks, Atheneum, 1978

First American Edition

H. MONTGOMERY HYDE | SOLITARY | IN THE RANKS | Lawrence of Arabia | as Airman and | Private Soldier | Atheneum | NEW YORK | 1978

Collation   22.4 × 14.7 cm: [1–10]^{16}, 160 leaves, pp.[1–2], [2], [3–9], 10–16, [2], 17–32, [8], 33–96, [8], 97–160, [8], 161–291, [292].

Contents   Prp.[1] blank, [2] list of author's works, pp.[1] bastard title, [2] frontispiece, [3] title page, [4] CIP, copyright, printer's credits, issue statement, [5] dedication, [6] quote from Lawrence letter, [7] contents, [8] blank, [9]–10 illustrations, [11]–13 acknowledgments, [14] blank, [15]–16 foreword, [1] half title, [2] blank, [17] –258 index, 259–272 sources and notes, 273–277 selected bibliography, [278] blank, 279–288 index, [289–290] blank, 291 biography of author, [292] blank.

RT   On verso *Solitary in the Ranks*. On recto [in italics, according to chapter].

Plates   Twenty-six plates on same paper as text, integral to sheets but unpaged. Frontispiece printed on one side only, others on both sides of each sheet, following pp.2, 32, 96, 160. All but frontispiece contain four leaves each.

Text   20 lines, 9.1 (9.6) × 10.1 cm.

Paper   White, wove, unwatermarked, all edges trimmed, sheets bulk 2 cm.

Binding   Blue linen 175 v.d. gB. On spine: [gilt, running up] SOLITARY IN THE RANKS: T.E. Lawrence | as Airman and Private Soldier [italics] by H.

MONTGOMERY HYDE | [across at foot] Atheneum. Blue end papers, yellow and orange head and tail bands. T.e. yellow.

Published at $ 11.95.

Copies   AC, Cal, LC.

E375   PAUL J. MARRIOTT, The Young Lawrence of Arabia, privately printed by author, 1977

First English Edition

OXFORD'S LEGENDARY SON– | THE YOUNG | LAWRENCE OF ARABIA | 1888–1910 | by | PAUL J. MARRIOTT

Collation   21 × 14.5 cm: [1–7]^8, 56 leaves, pp.I–VIII, 1–33, [2], 32–100, [2].

Contents   Prp.I title page, II ISBN, printer's credit, III dedication, quote from Lawrence, IV contents, V illustrations, VI maps and charts, VII acknowledgments, VIII map, pp.1–89 text, 90–94 bibliography, 95–100 index, [2] blank.

Plates   Integral part of gatherings, numbered in pagination with exception noted in collation pagination.

Text   20 lines, 7.7 × 11 cm.

Paper   White, wove, unwatermarked, all edges trimmed, sheets bulk 5 mm.

Binding   White paper covers glued to sheets. On front cover: THE YOUNG | LAWRENCE OF ARABIA | 1888–1910 | [b/w photo of Lawrence] | T.E LAWRENCE | PAUL J. MARRIOTT.

Published at   £3.50, April 1977.

Notes   Copies printed, 600.

Copies   AC, Cal, LC.

1978

E376   STEPHEN ELY TABACHNICK, T.E. Lawrence, Twayne, 1978

First American Edition

T.E. LAWRENCE | By STEPHEN ELY TABACHNICK | *Ben-Gurion University of the Negev* | [publisher's device] | TWAYNE PUBLISHERS | A DIVISION OF G.K. HALL & CO. BOSTON

Collation   20.3 × 13.5 cm: [1–2]^{16} [3]^8 [4–6]^{16}, 88 leaves, pp.[1–14], 15–174, [2].

Contents   Pp.[1] series statement, [2] photo of Lawrence, [3] title page, [4] copyright, issue statements, CIP, [5] dedication, [6] blank, [7] contents, [8] biography of author, [9–10] preface, [11] acknowledgments, [12] blank, [13–14] chronology, 15–151 text, 152–156 notes and references, 157–165 selected bibliography, [166] blank, 167–174 index, [175–176] blank.

RT On verso T.E. LAWRENCE. On recto [in italics, according to chapter].

Text 20 lines, 7.7 (8.1) × 10.1 cm.

Paper White, wove, unwatermarked, all edges trimmed, sheets bulk 1.4 cm.

Binding Red buckram 40 s. r Brown. On front cover: [gilt] T.E. LAWRENCE | Stephen Ely Tabachnick | [publisher's device]. On spine: [gilt] TEAS | [publisher's device] | [thick rule] | 233 | [thick rule] | [running down] T.E. LAWRENCE | [rule] | [running down] Stephen Ely | Tabachnick | [thick rule] | TWAYNE. Red and yellow head and tail bands.

Published at September 1978.

Copies AC, Cal, UT, LC.

E377 MAURICE LARÈS, T.E. Lawrence, La France et Les Français, Université de Lille, 1978

First French Edition of Dissertation

MAURICE LARÈS | T.E. LAWRENCE | LA FRANCE ET LES FRANÇAIS | TOME I | THÈSE PRESENTÉE DEVANT L'UNIVERSITÉ DE PARIS III | –LE 6 NOVEMBRE 1976– | SERVICE DE RÉPRODUCTION DES THÈSES | UNIVERSITÉ DE LILLE III | –1978–

Collation 23.8 × 15.8 cm: guillotined sheets glued to covers; Vol. 1, [1–8] 1–643 [3]; Vol. 2, [6] 645–1316 [3].

Contents Vol. 1: prp.[1–2] blank, [3] frontis., [4] blank, [5] title page, [6] blank,[7]contents, [8] blank, pp.[1] quote from T.E. Lawrence, note on abbreviations, 2–4 acknowledgments, 5–10 introduction, 11 contents of section 1, 12 bibliography, 13–643 text, 1–3 blank. Vol. 2: prp.[1–2] blank, [3] title page, [4] blank, [5] contents, [6] blank, pp.645 contents of section, 646–1197 text, 1198–1306 general bibliography, 1307–1308 table of contents, 1309–1315 addenda, 1316 general table of contents, [1–3] blank.

Typography and paper Typed pages photocopied and reduced, printed on both sides.

Paper White, wove, unwatermarked, all edges trimmed, sheets bulk 4 cm (both volumes).

Binding White paper covers glued to sheets. On front cover: [same as title page above, except that author's name and title are in blue]. On spine: [running up, title in blue] T.E. LAWRENCE, LA FRANCE ET LES FRANÇAIS MAURICE LARÈS | [across at foot] * [**].

Copies AC, Cal.

E378 MAURICE LARÈS, T.E. Lawrence, la France et les Français, Sorbonne, 1980

First French Edition

Maurice Larès | Docteur ès Lettres et Sciences humaines | T.E. Lawrence, |

la France | et les Français | Publications de la Sorbonne | Imprimerie nationale | Paris 1980

Collation   24 × 16 cm: 1–36^8, 288 leaves, pp.[i–vi], vii–xvi, 560.

Contents   Prp.[i–ii] blank, [iii] bastard title, [iv] blank, [v] title page, [vi] frontispiece, vii dedication, [viii] blank, ix quote from TEL and note on footnotes, [x] blank, xi–xii contents, xiii–xvi introduction, pp.[1] section title, [2] blank, [3]–516 text, 517–532 general bibliography, 533–555 index, [556] blank, 557–558 contents, [559] *'Il a été tiré de cet ouvrage:* | *4 exemplaires sur papier Japon numérotés de 1 à 4* | *40 exemplaires sur papier vergé,* | *numérotés de 5 à 44,* | *et 40 exemplaires sur papier buffant,* | *numérotés de 45 à 84, signés par l'auteur* | *EXEMPLAIRE* ', [560] printer's colophon.

RT   On verso T.E. Lawrence, la France et les Français. On recto [according to chapter].

Typography and paper $ 1,2 signed 3,3.

Text   20 lines, 7.4 (8) × 11.5 cm.

Paper   White, wove, unwatermarked, all edges trimmed, sheets bulk 2.5 cm.

Binding   White paper covers. On front cover: Maurice Larès | T.E. Lawrence, | la France | et les Français | [orange band 5cm high across full width of cover, within which, Sorbonne crest] | [below band] Université de Paris iii Sorbonne nouvelle Série Sorbonne 7 | Publications de la Sorbonne | Imprimerie nationale. On spine: Maurice | Larès | [running up] T.E. Lawrence, | la France et les Français | [across at bottom] [pub. device]. On back cover: [within orange band, publisher's device].

Published at   200 fr.

Notes   Another copy, one of 40 copies on papier vergé, numbered 5–44, signed by author. Paper is laid, sheets bulk 3 cm. Another copy, one of 40 copies on papier bouffant, numbered 45–84, signed by the author. Sheets bulk 3 cm.

Copies   AC, Cal.

E379   PAXTON DAVIS, Ned, Atheneum, 1978

First American Edition

[Double-spread pictorial] *NED by Paxton Davis* | DRAWINGS BY HAROLD LITTLE | ATHENEUM · NEW YORK · 1978

Collation   21 × 13.7 cm: [1–3]^{16} [4]^{12} [5]^{16}, 76 leaves, pp.[1–10], 1–140, [2].

Contents   Prp.[1] blank, [2] list of author's works, [3] bastard title, [4–5] title pages, [6] copyright statement, LC, ISBN numbers, printer's, designer's credits, issue statement, [7] dedication, [8] blank,[9] contents,[10] blank, pp.[1] section title, [2] blank, 3–140 text, [1] afterword, [2] blank.

RT   On both verso and recto [according to section].

Text   20 lines, 11.2 (11.6) × 9.2 cm.

Paper   White, wove, unwatermarked, all edges trimmed, sheets bulk 9 mm.

Binding Blue cloth 168 brill g.B. On spine: [running down, gilt] *Paxton Davis* NED *Atheneum.* Tan end papers.

Published at $7.95.

Copies AC, Cal, LC.

E380 JEAN-FRANÇOIS BORY, Lawrence d'Arabie, Paris, L'Ecole des Loisirs, 1978

First French Edition

Jean-François Bory | Lawrence | d'Arabie | Illustré par Régis Loisel | [pub. device] | l'ecole des loisirs | 11, rue de Sèvres, Paris 6e

Collation 19 × 12.3 cm: [1–16]⁸, 64 leaves, pp.[1–4], 5–121, [7].

Contents Pp.[1] bastard title, [2] brief biographies of author and illustrator, copyright statement, [3] title page, [4] illus, 5–121 text, [1–2] double-spread map, [3–6] Ads, [7] blank.

Text 20 lines, 9.8 × 10 cm.

Paper White, wove, unwatermarked, all edges trimmed, sheets bulk 1.3 cm.

Binding Pictorial paper covers. On front cover: [upper left corner, in red and white, publisher's device] | Jean-François Bory | Lawrence | d'Arabie. On spine: [running up] Bory Lawrence d'Arabie 9 à 12 ans [the rest in red] renard poche 50. On back cover: [blurb and ISBN number].

Copies AC.

E381 KENNETH ALLEN, Lawrence of Arabia, Macdonald, 1978

First English Edition

Lawrence of | Arabia | written by | Kenneth Allen | illustrated by | Roy Schofield | Macdonald Educational

Collation 20 × 14.5 cm: [1]¹⁶, 16 leaves, 32 pages.

Contents Pp.[1] title page, 2–32 text.

Text 20 lines, 13.7 × 8.8 cm.

Paper White, wove, unwatermarked, all edges trimmed, sheets bulk 3 mm.

Binding Pictorial paper wrappers, stapled to sheets with two metal staples. On front cover: [upper left corner on red band running diagonally] Macdonald | Adventures | [across] Lawrence of | Arabia. On back cover: [blurb, ISBN number and price].

Published at 45p.

Copies AC, Cal.

1979

E382   RICHARD EBERT, Lawrence of Arabia, Raintree Publishers, 1979

First American Edition

[Silhouette lettering] Lawrence | of Arabia | By | Richard Ebert | Illustrations by | Roy Schofield | [publisher's device] Raintree Publishers | Milwaukee · Toronto · Melbourne · London

Collation   22.8 × 15.2 cm: [1]¹⁶, 16 leaves, pp.[1–3], 4–31, [32].

Contents   Pp.[1] bastard title, [2] copyright, issue, CIP statements, [3] title page, 4–31 text, [32] blank.

Text   20 lines, 13.2 × 10.1 cm.

Paper   White, wove, unwatermarked, all edges trimmed, sheets bulk 2 mm.

Binding   Red cloth 13 deep Red. On front cover: Lawrence | of Arabia | [four-colour drawing]. On spine: [running down] Ebert Lawrence of Arabia [publisher's device] Raintree. On back cover: ISBN 0-8393-0150-2.

Published at $6.95.

Notes   This is essentially the same book as the one by Allen published by Macdonald in England. There are extra illustrations included in this edition. Text is the same. Why a different author's name is used is not known.

Copies   AC, Cal, LC.

E383   THOMAS J. O'DONNELL, The Confessions of T.E. Lawrence, Ohio University Press, 1979

First American Edition

THE CONFESSIONS OF | T.E. LAWRENCE | THE ROMANTIC HERO'S | PRESENTATION OF SELF | BY | THOMAS J. O'DONNELL | [publisher's device] | Ohio University Press | Athens, Ohio

Collation   23 × 15.2 cm: [1–4]¹⁶ [5]⁸ [6–7]¹⁶, 104 leaves, pp.[i–ix], x, [xi–xii], [1–2], 3–196.

Contents   Prp.[i] bastard title, [ii] frontispiece, [iii] title page, [iv] copyright, CIP, [v] dedication, [vi] blank, [vii] acknowledgments, [viii] quote from *Seven Pillars of Wisdom*, [ix]–x preface, [xi] contents, [xii] reference abbreviations, pp.[1] half title, [2] blank, 3–182 text, 182–189 bibliography, 190 blank, 191–196 index.

RT   On verso The Confessions of T.E. Lawrence. On recto [according to chapter].

Text   20 lines, 9 (9.5) × 10.1 cm.

Paper   White, wove, unwatermarked, all edges trimmed, sheets bulk 1.2 cm.

Binding Deep pink cloth 27 deep y Pink. On spine: [gilt, running down] O'DONNELL THE CONFESSIONS OF T.E. LAWRENCE | [across at bottom] [publisher's device] OHIO | UNIVERSITY | PRESS.

Published at $13.95, December 1978.

Copies AC, Cal, LC.

E384 MATTHEW EDEN, The Murder of Lawrence of Arabia, Crowell, 1979

First American Edition

THE MURDER | OF LAWRENCE | OF ARABIA | [long rule with decorative cut at end] | A NOVEL BY *Matthew Eden* | THOMAS Y. CROWELL, PUBLISHERS | ESTABLISHED 1834 | NEW YORK

Collation 22.9 × 15.2 cm: [1–9]^{16}, 144 leaves, pp.[10], 1–271, [7].

Contents Prp.[1–2] blank, [3] bastard title, [4] list of author's works, [5] title page, [6] copyright, issue statements, typographer's credit, CIP, [7] author's note, [8] blank, [9] half-title, [10] blank, pp.1–271 text, [1–7] blank.

Text 20 lines, 9 × 10.6 cm.

Paper White, wove, unwatermarked, all edges trimmed, sheets bulk 1.9 cm.

Binding Black cloth spine, very dark grey paper-covered boards, 266 d. Gy. On spine: [gilt, running down] THE MURDER OF *Matthew Eden* | LAWRENCE OF ARABIA CROWELL. On front cover: [lower right corner blind-stamped publisher's device]. End papers s R O.

Published at $9.95.

Copies AC, Cal, LC.

E385 MATTHEW EDEN, The Murder of Lawrence of Arabia, New English Library, 1979

First English Edition

THE MURDER OF | LAWRENCE | OF ARABIA | A NOVEL BY MATTHEW EDEN | [publisher's device] | NEW ENGLISH LIBRARY | [rule] | TIMES MIRROR

Collation 21 × 13.8 cm: [1–16]^{16}, 128 leaves, pp.1–256.

Contents Pp.[1] bastard title, [2] blank, [3]title page, [4] copyright,issue statements, CIP, printer's, typesetter's credits, 5 author's note, 6 blank except for page number, 7–256 text.

Text 20 lines, 7.8 × 10.2 cm.

Paper White, wove, unwatermarked, all edges trimmed, sheets bulk 3 cm.

Binding Black simulated cloth paper-covered boards. On spine: [gilt, running down] THE MURDER OF LAWRENCE OF ARABIA | [across]

MATTHEW | EDEN | [publisher's device] | NEW | ENGLISH | LIBRARY.
Published at £5.95, February 1980.
Copies AC, Cal.

Continuing Diversity, 1980–87

The years of this decade have seen a wide variety of publications, ranging from a poster by the National Portrait Gallery depicting Lawrence and Oscar Wilde before the façade of the NPG building, to a miniature consisting of a brief essay on Lawrence's interest in printing and fine books (O'Brien *T.E. Lawrence and Fine Printing*).

Larès' *Lawrence d'Arabie et les Châteaux des Croisés* is one of the shorter pieces by this prolific French scholar. The Hamlin and Brun work, *Lawrence von Arabien*, is the script of a radio broadcast for popular consumption.

Another Italian volume is Boccozzi's *Lawrence d'Arabia*, an illustrated book picking up on the adventure of the Arab campaign. Yet another volume of poems based on aspects of Lawrence's life is MacEwen's *T.E. Lawrence Poems*. Weeks' *T.E. Lawrence* is a short essay describing Lawrence's editing of a forgotten literary work.

Another short piece by Larès, *Texte et Traductions*, compares versions of translations of a Malraux text on Lawrence, an interesting study of the acts of omission and word choice by translators.

A recent dissertation by a student working under Weintraub is Allen's *The Medievalism of T.E. Lawrence (of Arabia)*. It traces the influence of Lawrence's early interest in the Middle Ages and his later life and work. This was followed by a collected work of original contributions treating a wide variety of topics conceived and edited by Tabachnick, *The T.E. Lawrence Puzzle*.

Triad Films of Australia with *Lawrence of Arabia the Master Illusionist* produced a television film special. Michael Yardley's *Backing Into the Limelight* is a popular biography of Lawrence. Two shorter works are Knight's *Colonel T.E. Lawrence (Lawrence of Arabia) Visits Mr. and Mrs. Thomas Hardy* and a reprint in fine dress of an article by Hugh Walpole, *Seven Pillars of Wisdom T.E. Lawrence in Life and Death*. Rumours of manuscripts seeking publishers as well as dissertations now being written, all point to more titles being added to the bibliography in the near future. Even as this book was being typeset, Rodney Legg resurrects the black-car mystery in *Lawrence of Arabia in Dorset (1987)*.

1980

E387 NATIONAL PORTRAIT GALLERY, Poster, 198-?

Poster for National Portrait Gallery

In colour, photo of front façade of gallery with figures of Oscar Wilde and T.E. Lawrence superimposed in street before entrance.

Collation 75 × 50 cm.

Paper   White, wove, unwatermarked, all edges trimmed.

Copies   AC, Cal.

E388   PHILIP M. O'BRIEN, T.E. Lawrence and Fine Printing, Hillside Press, 1980

First American Edition

T.E. LAWRENCE | AND FINE PRINTING | by | Philip M. O'Brien | [cut, in red] | THE HILLSIDE PRESS | BUFFALO, NEW YORK | 1980

Collation   5.5 × 5 cm: [1–8]⁴, 32 leaves, pp.[1–11], [1–2], 3–39, [1–14]; includes free and paste-down end papers.

Contents   Prp.[1–4] free and paste-down end papers [5] bastard title, [6] frontispiece, [7] title page, [8] copyright statement, [9] dedication, [10] blank, [11] 'This edition limited to | 375 numbered copies of | which this is number', pp.[1] blank, [2]–39 text, [1–6] bibliography, [7] note on author, [8] blank, [9] *'The text for this book was | set by hand in 6 pt. Roman | Century type and printed on | Rives imported paper at the | Hillside Press in cooperation | with Lorson's Books & Prints | Fullerton, CA. in the month | of March, 1980.',* [10–14] blank.

Text   20 lines, 3.7 × 3.3 cm.

Paper   White, wove, unwatermarked, all edges trimmed, sheets bulk 5 mm.

Binding   Pale yellow leatherette cloth 87 m Y. On front cover: [gilt] TEL. On spine: [running down] *T.E. Lawrence and Fine Printing.*

Published at $12.50, March 1980.

Notes   Limited to 375 copies plus specials: 26 lettered copies A–Z, 3 binder's, 11 presentation copies. Special issue has added frontispiece drawn and printed by author and extra colophon printed by author. Extra frontispiece precedes bastard title, extra colophon follows original colophon. Extra colophon reads: This is copy   of 26 lettered | copies with special binding by | Kater-Crafts Bookbinders, Pico | Rivera, CA. This colophon and | extra frontispiece printed by the | author at the Bonibel Press, | Whittier College, | June 1980. Sheets bulk 7 mm. [Binding]: white vellum spine and corners. Blue paper covered boards 187 d. gy B. On front cover: [gilt roundel from Bruce Rogers edition of Odyssey]. On spine: [across, gilt rule] [running down] T.E. LAWRENCE AND FINE PRINTING | [across, rule]. Marbled end papers. Boxed as issued.

Copies   AC, Cal, LC.

E389   MAURICE LARÈS, Lawrence d'Arabie et les Châteaux des Croisés, 1980

First French Edition

PUBLICATIONS DE L'ASSOCIATION DES MÉDIÉVISTES DE L'ENSEIGNMENT SUPÉRIEUR | [long rule] 6 [long rule] | [white label

pasted over original Michel LARÈS] Maurice LARÈS | LAWRENCE
D'ARABIE | et les | CHÂTEAUX DES CROISÉS | [drawing of T.E.
Lawrence] | PARIS | 1980

Collation 29.6 × 21 cm: guillotined sheets glued to covers, 61 leaves, pp.[1],
2–122. Does not count covers. Title page is front cover.

Contents [Front cover] title page, [verso of front cover] *'De ce volume tiré* | *à
trois cents exemplaires,* | *cet exemplaire est le* | *numéro',* pp.[1] half-title, 2–3
contents, 4 facsimile of original title page of *Crusader Castles,* 5–6
introduction, 7–86 text, 87 contents of bibliographic section, 88–105
bibliographies, 106 contents of indexes, 107–117 indexes, 118–119 contents,
[120] blank, 121–122 list of titles in series.

Typography and paper Photocopy of typed double-spaced original.

Paper White, wove, unwatermarked, all edges trimmed, sheets bulk 7
mm.

Binding White paper covers glued to sheets, heavier stock than sheets. On
front cover: [title page as above]. On back cover: Dépôt legal: 2 trimestre
1980 | ISBN 2-901 198-02-3 IMPRIMERIE DU C.R.P. D'AMIENS.

Notes Limited to 300 copies.

Copies AC.

E390 ARMAND HAMELIN & JEAN-MICHEL BRUN, Lawrence von Arabien – Auf den Spuren Abenteurers. Sender frei Berlin, 1980

Script of radio broadcast

SENDER FREIES BERLIN | FS-Politik/ Dokumentation I und II |
LAWRENCE VON ARABIEN | Auf den Spuren eines Abenteurers

Collation 29.7 × 21 cm: photocopy of original typed sheets, text on one
side only, pp.[1], 1–24, [1].

Contents Prp.[1] title page, pp.1–23 text, [1] Radio Station cover sheet for
document.

Paper White, wove, unwatermarked, all edges trimmed.

Copies AC, Cal.

1981

E391 CINO BOCCAZZI, Lawrence d'Arabia, Rusconi, 1981

First Italian Edition

Cino Boccazzi | LAWRENCE | D'ARABIA | L'AVVENTURIERO |
DELL'ASSOLUTO | Rusconi

Collation 21 × 13 cm: [1–15]⁸ 16⁴, 124 leaves, pp.[1–4], [1–6], 7–235, [1–9]; includes paste-down end papers.

Contents Prp.[1–4] blank end papers, pp.[1] series title, [2] other works by author, [3] title page, [4] issue, copyright statements, credits, [5] section title, [6] blank, 7–226 text, 227–229 chronology of Lawrence's life, [230] blank, 231–234 bibliography, 235 biography note on author, [1] blank, [2] contents, [3] blank, [4] list of titles in series, [5] colophon, [6–9] blank.

Plates Eight plates, first four in colour, on coated paper, printed on one side only, caption on verso, following pp.28, 44, 76, 92, 140, 156, 188, 204.

Text 20 lines, 9 × 9.4 cm.

Paper White, wove (simulated laid), unwatermarked, all edges trimmed, sheets bulk 2 cm.

Binding Red cloth 36 d r Orange. On spine: [gilt, running up] Cino Boccazzi Lawrence d'Arabia Rusconi. Red head and tail bands.

Published at 14,000 Lire.

Copies AC, Cal.

1982

E392   GWENDOLYN MacEWEN,
The T.E. Lawrence Poems, Mosaic Press, 1982

First Canadian Edition

[Within single rule frame] THE | T.E. LAWRENCE | POEMS | Gwendolyn MacEwen | [John sketch of TEL] | [publisher's device] | Mosaic Press/Valley Editions | "Publishers for Canadian Committee"

Collation 22.8 × 15.2 cm: guillotined sheets glued to covers, [1–10] [1–2] 3–70.

Contents Prp.[1] bastard title, [2] blank, [3] title page, [4] ISBN, CIP, copyright statement, printer's, typographer's, cover artist's, binder's credits, [5] foreword, [6] author's note, [7–8] contents, [9–10] blank, pp.[1] section title, [2] blank, 3–70 text.

Paper Buff, wove, unwatermarked, all edges trimmed, sheets bulk 5 mm.

Binding Brown paper covers 44 d. r Br. On front cover: [within orange single rule frame, in white] THE | T.E. LAWRENCE | POEMS | [within orange rectangle, drawing of TEL by John] | [in white] Gwendolyn MacEwen. On spine: [running down, in white] THE T.E. LAWRENCE POEMS Gwendolyn MacEwen [across, in orange] [publisher's device]. On back cover: [within orange single rule frame, extract from foreword and brief biography of author].

Published at Hardbound $12.95, paperbound $6.95.

Notes Hardbound issue same as above with following differences: brown buckram 62 d gy Br. On spine: [gilt, running down] THE T.E. LAWRENCE POEMS Gwendolyn MacEwen | [across] [publisher's device].

Copies AC, Cal, Can.

1983

E393 DONALD WEEKS, T.E. Lawrence, privately printed, 1983

First English Edition

T.E. LAWRENCE | *an* | *hitherto* | *unknown* | *biographical* / | *bibliographical* | *note by* | Donald Weeks | *Privately printed* | EDINBURGH | 1983

Collation 24.8 × 16 cm: [1]⁷, 14 leaves, pp.[1−6], [1−4], 5−16, [6].

Contents Prp.[1−5] blank, [6] frontispiece pp.[1] title page, [2] copyright statement, [3] dedication, [4] blank, 5−16 text, [1] 'EDITION LIMITED TO TWO HUNDRED AND THIRTY COPIES, | PRINTED IN BEMBO TYPE ON SOMMERVILLE LAID PAPER | BY THE TRAGARA PRESS, EDINBURGH, FOR DONALD WEEKS. | THIRTY COPIES FOR PRESENTATION BY THE AUTHOR', [2−6] blank.

Text 20 lines, 9.5 × 10.2 cm.

Paper White, laid, unwatermarked, all edges trimmed, sheets bulk 3 mm.

Binding Green paper wrappers, turned in end flaps 105 g.gy Y. On front cover: [white paste-on patch, within frame of single rules] T.E. LAWRENCE.

Published at $12.50.

Copies AC, Cal.

E394 MAURICE LARÈS, Texte et Traductions, privately published, 1983

First French Edition

TEXTE ET TRADUCTIONS PRÉSENTÉS PAR | MAURICE LARÈS | DÉCEMBRE 1983

Collation 29.3 × 21.8 cm: guillotined sheets glued to covers, 61 leaves.

Contents Leaf [1] blank, [2] title page, [3] blank, [4−59] text, [1−2] blank.

Text Photocopy of typed original.

Paper White, wove, unwatermarked, all edges trimmed, sheets bulk 5 mm.

Binding Maroon buckram 16 d. Red.

Published at December 1983.

Copies AC, Cal.

E395 MALCOLM DENNIS ALLEN, The Medievalism of T.E. Lawrence ("of Arabia"), 1983

Unpublished Ph.D. Dissertation

The Pennsylvania State University | The Graduate School | Department of English | The Medievalism of T.E. Lawrence ("of Arabia") | A Thesis in |

English | by | Malcolm Dennis Allen | Submitted in Partial Fulfillment | of the Requirements | for the Degree of | Doctor of Philosophy | August 1983 | © 1983 by Malcolm Dennis Allen | [statement granting University reproduction rights] | signature [underlined] | Malcolm Dennis Allen

Collation   21.5 × 16 cm: guillotined sheets glued to covers, pp.[1–6], [i–iv], v–[x], [1]–[210].

Contents   Prp.[1] publisher's statement, [2] blank, [3] CIP, [4] blank, [5] publisher's statement, [6] blank, [i] title page, [ii] committee signatures, [iii–iv] abstract, v–[vi] contents, [vii]–ix preface, [x] notes, pp.[1]–202 text, [203]–209 bibliography, [210] vita.

Text   Photo reproduction of typed original.

Paper   White, wove, unwatermarked, edges trimmed, sheets bulk 1.2 cm.

Binding   Blue paper covers 201 d. pB. On front cover: [typed label] THE MEDIEVALISM OF T.E. | LAWRENCE ("OF ARABIA") | ALLEN, MALCOLM DENNIS | DEGREE DATE 1983.

Copies   AC.

E395a   Laurens al-Arab, al-Mararef Mousse, 1983

First Lebanese Edition

Laurens al-Arab | Dar wa Matameh al-Moustakabel | b-Fagalah wa al-Askandria | Mousse al-Mararef Tabaaka | wa alnasher b-Beirut

Collation   20 × 13.5 cm: guillotined sheets glued to covers, 54 leaves, pp.[1–4], 5–107, [1–3].

Contents   Pp.[1] photo of Lawrence, [2] series note, [3] title page, [4] blank, 5–107 text, [1] blank, [2] English and Arabic bibliographies, [3] printer's statement.

Text   20 lines, 13.8 × 10.4 cm.

Paper   White, wove, unwatermarked, edges trimmed, sheets bulk 5 mm.

Binding   Pictorial paper covers. On front cover: [in white] Laurens | al-Arab. On back cover: [b/w photo of Lawrence] | Moustakabel b-Fagalah wa Askandria | Mousse al-Mararef b-Beirut | [two rows of photos of other persons treated in series].

Published at   75 piastres.

Copies   AC, Rosen.

1984

E396   STEPHEN E. TABACHNICK, ed.,
T. E. Lawrence Puzzle, University of Georgia, 1984

First American Edition

[Within arabesque frame] THE | T◆E◆LAWRENCE | P◆U◆Z◆Z◆L◆E |

EDITED BY | STEPHEN E.| TABACHNICK | THE UNIVERSITY OF | GEORGIA PRESS | ATHENS | 1984 | [cut]

Collation 23 × 15.5 cm: [1–16]¹⁶, 176 leaves, pp.[i–v], vi–vii, [viii–x], [1]–342.

Contents Prp.[i] bastard title, [ii] blank, [iii] title page, [iv] copyright statement, designer's credit, paper permanency statement, CIP, ISBN, [v]–vii contents, [viii] blank, [ix] acknowledgments, x abbreviations, pp.[1]–311 text, [312] blank, [313]–321 bibliography, [314] blank, [315]–324 brief biography of contributors, [325]–342 index.

RT On verso [according to author of chapter]. On recto [according to chapter].

Text 20 lines, 9 (9.5) × 11 cm. Set in 11 on 13 pt. Goudy Old Style.

Paper White, wove, unwatermarked, all edges trimmed, sheets bulk 2 cm.

Binding Green cloth 146 d. G. On spine: [silver] [arabesque panel] | The T.E. | Lawrence | Puzzle | [cut] EDITED BY | *Stephen E.* | *Tabachnick* | [arabesque panel] | [cut] | [arabesque panel] | GEORGIA | [arabesque panel]. Green and white head and tail bands. Pale green end papers.

Published at $22.50.

Notes Contributors: Stephen E. Tabachnick, A Fragmentation Artist, pp.1–49; M.D. Allen, Lawrence's Medievalism, pp.53–70; Thomas J. O'Donnell, The Assertion and Denial of the romantic will in *Seven Pillars of Wisdom*, pp.71–95; Keith M. Hull, Seven Pillars of Wisdom, pp.96–114; Stephen E. Tabachnick, The Waste Land in *Seven Pillars of Wisdom*, pp.115–123; Jeffrey Meyers, T.E. Lawrence: The Mechanical Monk, pp.125–136; Rodelle Weintraub, T.E. Lawrence: Technical Writer, pp.137–156; Charles Grosvenor, The Subscriber's *Seven Pillars of Wisdom*, pp.159–184; Konrad Morsey, T.E. Lawrence: Strategist, pp.185–203; Gideon Gera, T.E. Lawrence: Intelligence Officer, pp.204–219; Maurice Larès, T.E. Lawrence and France: Friends or Foes?, pp.220–242; Aaron Klieman, Lawrence as Bureaucrat, pp.243–268; Stanley Weintraub, Lawrence of Arabia: The Portraits from Imagination 1922–1979, pp.269–292; Philip M. O'Brien, Collecting T.E. Lawrence Materials, pp.293–311.

Copies AC, Cal.

1985

E397   TRIAD FILMS, Lawrence of Arabia: The Master Illusionist, PTV Publications, 1985

First American Edition

[Underlined] *Transcript* | LAWRENCE | OF ARABIA: | The Master Illusionist | [long rule] | Produced by Triad Films Pty., 141 Benshurst Street, Willoughby, NSW 2068, Australia | Distributed by Trans Action, 5 Sherwood Street, London, WIV 7RA, England | [long rule]

Collation 21.5 × 17.5 cm: 1⁸, 8 leaves, pp.[1–2], 1–10, [1–4].

Contents Prp.[1] front cover, [2] credits, pp.1–10 text, [1–3] list of other transcripts in series, [4] back cover used as address page in mailing.

Text Reduction of typed original.

Paper 90 gy Y paper, wove, unwatermarked, all edges trimmed, sheets bulk 1 mm.

Binding Covers same paper as sheets stapled in centre gutter with two staples.

Published at $4.00.

Notes Transcription of television movie of same title.

Copies AC, Cal.

E398 MICHAEL YARDLEY, Backing into the Limelight, Harrap, 1985

First English Edition

Backing into | the Limelight | A Biography of | T.E. Lawrence | Michael Yardley | Harrap London

Collation 23.3 × 15.6 cm: [1–7]^{16} [8]^8 [9]^{16}, 136 leaves, pp.[1–9], 10–267, [1–5].

Contents Pp.[1] bastard title, [2] blank, [3] title page, [4] dedication, issue, copyright statements, ISBN, typographer's, printer's, binder's credits, [5] contents, [6] blank, [7–8] illustrations, [9]–10 acknowledgments, [11]–15 preface, [16] blank, [17] section title, [18] blank, [19]–235 text, [236] blank, [237]–249 notes, [250] blank, [251]–257 bibliography, [258] blank, [259]–267 index, [1–5] blank.

RT On verso *Backing into the Limelight.* On recto [according to chapter].

Plates Sixteen plates on coated paper, printed on both sides, in groups of four following pp.32, 96, 128, 192.

Text 20 lines, 8.2 (8.6) × 11.4 cm.

Paper White, wove, unwatermarked, all edges trimmed, sheets bulk 2.2 cm.

Binding Black cloth. On spine: [gilt, running down] Backing into the Limelight | A Biography of T.E. LAWRENCE Michael Yardley | [across at foot] Harrap.

Published at £12.95.

Copies AC, Cal.

E398a MICHAEL YARDLEY, T.E. Lawrence, Stein and Day, 1987

First American Edition

A BIOGRAPHY | T.E. LAWRENCE | MICHAEL YARDLEY | [publisher's device] | STEIN AND DAY | *Publishers:/NEW YORK*

Collation 23.6 × 15.5 cm: 1⁸, [2–17]¹⁶, 138 leaves, pp.[1–2], [1–19], 20–267, [1–7].

Contents Prp.[1] bastard title, [2] blank, pp.[1] title page, [2] dedication, issue, copyright statements, CIP, [3] contents, [4] blank, [5–6] illustrations, [7–8] acknowledgements, [9–13] preface, [14] blank, [15] half-title, [16] blank, [17] section title, [18] blank, [19]–235 text, [236] blank, [237]–249 notes, [250] blank, [251]–257 bibliography. [258] blank, [259]–267 index, [1–7] blank.

RT On recto [in italics, according to chapter].

Plates Sixteen b/w photos, printed on both sides, following p.150.

Text 20 lines, 8.3 (8.7) × 11.3 cm.

Paper White, wove, unwatermarked, all edges trimmed, sheets bulk 2.2 cm.

Binding Yellow paper-covered boards 89 p. Y., black cloth spine. On front cover: [publisher's device, blind stamped]. On spine: [gilt, running down] YARDLEY T.E. LAWRENCE | [across at bottom] [publisher's device] | STEIN | AND | DAY. Black and white head and tail bands.

Published at $22.95.

Copies AC, Cal.

E399 RONALD D. KNIGHT, Colonel T.E. Lawrence (Lawrence of Arabia), Bat and Bull Press, 1985

First English Edition

COLONEL | T.E. LAWRENCE | (LAWRENCE OF ARABIA) | VISITS | MR & MRS | THOMAS HARDY | RONALD D KNIGHT

Collation 21 × 16 cm: [1]⁶², 62 leaves, pp.[i–ii], iii–[x], 1–112, [1–2].

Contents Prp.[i] title page, [ii] list of author's works, copyright statement, ISBN, iii–iv list of illustrations and acknowledgments, v–viii introduction, ix list of abbreviations, [x] map, 1–5 prologue, 6–108 text, 109–112 bibliography, [1–2] ads for other works by author.

Plates B/w illustrations printed on same sheets as text.

Text Photo reproduction of original typed sheets.

Paper White, wove, unwatermarked, all edges trimmed, sheets bulk 7 mm.

Binding White paper wrappers stapled to sheets by two steel staples. On front cover: [in green] COLONEL | T.E. LAWRENCE | (LAWRENCE OF ARABIA) | [photo of TEL] | [in green] VISITS | [photos of Mr. & Mrs. Hardy] | [in green] MR & MRS | THOMAS HARDY | RONALD D KNIGHT. On back cover: [photo of author] | [brief biography of author] | £2.95 net in U.K. ISBN: 0 903769 98 0.

Published at £2.95.

Copies AC, Cal.

E400   MAGGS BROTHERS, T.E. Lawrence, 1985

First English Edition (Dealer's Catalogue)

Catalogue 1055 | Books by and about | T.E. LAWRENCE | including | Manuscript Material and | Original Art | [Royal Coat of Arms] | BY APPOINTMENT TO | HER MAJESTY THE QUEEN | MAGGS BROS. LTD., LONDON. | PURVEYORS OF RARE BOOKS | & MANUSCRIPTS | MAGGS BROS. LTD. | 50 Berkeley Square, London W1X 6EL | Telephone: 01-493-7160 Cables: Bibliolite | London | © Maggs Bros Ltd.

Collation   21 × 16.5 cm: [1]⁸ [2]⁶ [3]⁸, 22 leaves, pp.[1–4], 5–43, [1].

Contents   Pp.[1] title page, [2] contents, [3] introduction by J.M. Wilson, [4] illus., 5–38 text of catalogue, 39 list of references cited, 40–43 index, [1] blank.

Text   20 lines, 7.9 × 12.6 cm.

Paper   White, wove, unwatermarked, all edges trimmed, sheets bulk 3 mm.

Binding   B/w pictorial wrappers. On front cover: [all in white] Catalogue 1055 | T.E. LAWRENCE | [photo of Kennington bust of Lawrence] | MAGGS BROS. LTD. On back cover: [photo of a number of books offered in catalogue].

Published at   March 1985.

Copies   AC, Cal.

E401   HUGH WALPOLE, Seven Pillars of Wisdom
T.E. Lawrence in Life and Death, Rota, 1985

First English Edition

HUGH WALPOLE | SEVEN PILLARS | OF WISDOM | T.E. LAWRENCE IN LIFE AND DEATH | WITH AN INTRODUCTION BY | RUPERT HART-DAVIS | BERTRAM ROTA | 1985

Collation   26 × 17.5 cm: [1] ¹², 12 leaves, pp.[1–24].

Contents   Pp.[1–2] blank, [3] bastard title, [4] blank, [5] title page, [6] cover illustration credit, copyright statement, ISBN, publisher's address, [7] section title, [8] blank, [9–11] introduction by Rupert Hart-Davis, [12] blank, [13] section title, [14] blank, [15–18] text, [19–20] blank, [21] 'This edition of 100 numbered copies is | published to commemorate the 50th anniversary of | T.E. Lawrence's death. | Set in Monotype Garamond 156 | and printed at I.M. Imprimit, London, | in May 1985. | This is number', [22–24] blank.

Text   20 lines, 10.4 × 11.8 cm.

Paper   White, laid, unwatermarked, all edges trimmed, sheets bulk 2 mm.

Binding   Tan paper wrappers 91 d. gy. Y. stitched to sheets. On front cover of wrap-around paper cover of same stock as binding, paste on white paper reproduction of John drawing of Lawrence 1919.

Published at   £25, May 1985.

Copies   AC, Cal.

1986

E402   E. THURLOW LEEDS, Recollections of T.E.L., Bonibel Press, 1986

First American Edition

[In brown] Recollections of | [in brown] T.E.L. | by E. Thurlow Leeds | [cut in brown] | *with a frontispiece* | *linocut of T.E. Lawrence* | *by Wm Erik Voss* | The Bonibel Press | CALIFORNIA | 1986

Collation   26.7 × 18 cm: [1]⁸, 8 leaves, prp.[1–6] pp.1–8, [1–2].

Contents   Prp.[1] bastard title, [2] frontispiece, [3] title page, [4] copyright statement, [5] preface, [6] blank, pp.[1–8] text, [1] blank, [2] colophon.

RT   On verso RECOLLECTIONS. On recto OF T.E.L.

Typography and paper   Set in 14 pt. Caslon.

Text   20 lines, 12.6 (12.7) × 11 cm.

Paper   White, laid, watermarked, top edge trimmed, sheets bulk 2 mm.

Binding   Violet 213 v.p.V. paper wrappers. On front cover: [in brown, linocut of T.E. Lawrence by Wm. Voss (same as frontispiece)].

Published at   Not for sale.

Notes   [Colophon]: [press device, in brown] *70 copies hand-set in 14-point* | *Caslon by students of Whittier College,* | *California, and printed on a Vandercook proof* | *press. 30 copies are printed on Henry* | *Moore hand-made paper, and 40* | *copies on Ragston paper.* | COPY NO. | *The printers are:* | *Ji-Hyun, Stefanie Perrie Diamond,* | *James O. Ettinger, Kent H. Gilbert, Denise A.* | *Haag, Frank H.G. Haun, Vaughn J. King, Pedro* | *Morales, Philip M. O'Brien, Patti L. O'Dea,* | *Robert F. Olsabeck, Michael S. Pelly, John* | *Randle, & Wm Erik Voss.* There were only 64 copies finally completed, 37 copies of the Henry Moore paper issue, and 27 of the Ragston paper. There are six copies made from spoiled sheets. Philip M. O'Brien had no part in the printing, but tried to stay out from underfoot.

Copies   AC, Cal, HL.

E403   VYVYAN RICHARDS, T.E. Lawrence Book Designer, Fleece Press, 1986

First English Edition

[In blue] T.E. Lawrence | *Book Designer* | *his friendship with* | [in blue] Vyvyan Richards | *Fleece Press*

Collation   18.5 × 14.5 cm: [1–4]⁴, 16 leaves, prp.[1–10] pp.[1]–20, [1–2].

Contents   Prp.[1–2] blank, [3] bastard title, [4] wood cut frontispiece, [5] title page, [6] printer's credit, ISBN, frontispiece credit, [7] publisher's note, [8] blank, [9] half-title, [10] blank, [1]–20 text, [1] [in blue] "*T.E. Lawrence: Book Designer* | was printed in an edition of 250 copies, on | Velin Arches Blanc by Simon Lawrence, who | also set the 14pt Caslon, at his Fleece

Press | in Wakefield. 200 copies are bound in quarter | cloth and Sage
Reynolds paste paper over | boards, & 50 are bound in quarter sheepskin |
parchment and paste paper, signed by Peter | Reddick, who engraved the
frontispiece | portrait of T.E. Lawrence. The book was | bound in Otley by
Smith Settle. | Two copies were printed on vellum, or | rather sheepskin
parchment, and full-bound | by Angela James. One of these is contained |
in a solander box with trial efforts on sheep- | skin parchment & relevant
correspondence', [2] blank.

RT   On verso *T.E. Lawrence.* On recto *Book Designer.*

Text   20 lines, 11.8 (11.8) × 8.8 cm.

Paper   White, wove, unwatermarked, untrimmed, sheets bulk 5 mm.

Binding   16 d. Red cloth spine, patterned paper-covered boards. On spine:
[paper label pasted on spine, running down] *T.E. Lawrence: Book Designer.*

Notes   Another state 50 copies bound as above except spine in white
parchment with spine lettering gilt.

Copies   AC, Cal.

E404   VALERIE M. THOMPSON, 'Not a Suitable Hobby for an Airman'–, Orchard, 1986

First English Edition

'NOT A SUITABLE HOBBY | FOR AN AIRMAN'– | T.E. LAWRENCE AS
PUBLISHER | V.M. THOMPSON | [publisher's device] | ORCHARD
BOOKS

Collation   21 × 15 cm: [guillotined sheets glued to covers], 96 leaves,
pp.[1–2], [i–iv], v–xii, [xiii–xiv], 1–173, [1–3].

Contents   Prp.[1–2] blank, [i] bastard title, [ii] frontispiece, [iii] title page,
[iv] issue, copyright statements, ISBN, printer's credit, v contents, [vi]
blank, vii–ix notes and abbreviations, [x] blank, xi–xii introduction,
[xiii–xiv] blank, pp.1–143 text, [144] blank, 145–168 appendixes, 169–173
references, [1–3] blank.

Text   20 lines, 8.5 × 10.7 cm.

Paper   White, wove, unwatermarked, all edges trimmed, sheets bulk 1 cm.

Binding   76 l. y Br brown paper covers. On front cover: 'NOT A SUITABLE
HOBBY | FOR AN AIRMAN'– | T.E. LAWRENCE AS PUBLISHER |
[crossed swords device from Seven Pillars] | V.M. THOMPSON. On spine:
[running down] NOT A SUITABLE HOBBY FOR AN AIRMAN – T.E.
LAWRENCE AS PUBLISHER V.M. THOMPSON | [across at bottom, pub.
device]. On back cover: ISBN.

Copies   AC, Cal.

E405 TERENCE RATTIGAN, Ross, Proscenium Publications, 1986

Theatre Programme

[All in orange] [Royal Coat of Arms] | THE OLD VIC | [rule] | [swash] Ross | by Terence Rattigan

Collation 21.5 × 13.5 cm: [1]^{12} pp.[1–24].

Contents [1–2] ads, [3] credits, [4] ads, [5] synopsis of Arab revolt with map, [6–11] 'What's in a Name' by Dick Benson-Gyles, [12] list of acts and scenes, [13] cast list, [14–19] brief biographies of cast, [20] production team, [21] photos of play, [22] ad, [23] credits and acknowledgements, [24] services and facilities, [inside rear cover] short history of The Old Vic.

Text Varies.

Paper White, wove, unwatermarked, coated, all edges trimmed, sheets bulk 2 mm.

Binding Pictorial paper wrappers, title page front cover, stapled to sheets with two metal staples. Back cover colour ad.

Copies AC.

E406 CHARLES BLACKMORE, In the Footsteps of Lawrence of Arabia, Harrap, 1986

First English Edition

IN THE FOOTSTEPS OF | LAWRENCE | OF ARABIA | CHARLES BLACKMORE | Harrap · London

Collation 24.6 × 17.5 cm) [1–10]^8, 80 leaves, pp.[1–6], 7–160.

Contents Pp.[1] [bastard title, [2] issue, copyright statements, printer's credit, acknowledgements, [3] contents, [4]–18 introduction, 19–160 text.

RT On verso *In the Footsteps of Lawrence of Arabia*. On recto [in italics, according to day of trip].

Plates Eight coloured plates, two each following pp.24, 56, 104, 120; printed on both sides.

Text 20 lines, 8.2 (9.3) × 9.5 cm.

Paper White, wove, unwatermarked, all edges trimmed, sheets bulk 1 cm.

Binding Blue cloth 183 d, Blue. On spine: [gilt, running down] IN THE FOOTSTEPS OF LAWRENCE OF ARABIA Blackmore | [across at foot] HARRAP.

Published at £9.95.

Copies AC, Cal.

1987

E407 RODNEY LEGG, Lawrence of Arabia in Dorset, Dorset Publishing Co./Wincanton Press, 1987

First English Edition

LAWRENCE | OF ARABIA | IN DORSET | RODNEY LEGG | [on left at foot] [colophon] DORSET PUBLISHING COMPANY | KNOCK-NA-CRE, MILBORNE PORT | SHERBORNE, DORSET DT9 5HJ | [on right at foot] [colophon] | WINCANTON PRESS | NATIONAL SCHOOL, NORTH STREET | WINCANTON, SOMERSET BA9 9AT

Collation 25 × 17.5 cm: [1–7]⁸, 56 leaves, pp.[1–2], 3–109, [110–112].

Contents Pp.[1] title page, 2 author's other titles, dedication, issue, copyright, restriction statements, publisher's address, ISBN, 3 contents and photo of Lawrence, [4–5] map, [6] photo of Lawrence, 7–109 text and photos, [110] reproduction of John drawing, beginning of index, [111–112] index continued.

RT On verso LAWRENCE OF ARABIA. On recto [according to section]

Plates Forty-seven photos on text paper distributed throughout text; two maps, pp.[4–5], 71; Kennington cartoon, p.[44]; letter reproductions, pp.38, 42.

Text 20 lines, 9.1 (9.4) × 14 cm.

Paper White, wove, unwatermarked, all edges trimmed, sheets bulk 8 mm.

Binding Pictorial drawn-on cover. On front cover: [in yellow] LAWRENCE | [in white] OF ARABIA | [in yellow] IN DORSET | [in white] RODNEY LEGG [plus two b/w photos of Lawrence and full-colour photo of Clouds Hill]. On spine: [running down] [in yellow] LAWRENCE [in white] OF ARABIA [in yellow] IN DORSET [in white] RODNEY LEGG [dpc colophon]. On back cover: [blurb, ISBN]

Published at £7.95, November 1987. Note that the issue date and copyright on page 3 is given as 1988. Copies were, however, on sale in Dorset shops in November 1987.

Copies AC.

SECTION F

INCIDENTAL BOOKS CONTAINING CHAPTERS AND REFERENCES TO T.E. LAWRENCE

Lawrence is constantly mentioned in works on the Middle East; often the references are quite cursory and many such are represented here. However, there are quite a few that are substantial. No attempt has been made in the details that follow to distinguish the two kinds of reference. This section is admittedly incomplete, though it is hoped that few items of importance have been omitted. Where the Lawrence references make up whole chapters they are identified by the chapter title.

F0001 H.H.A., *Letters of the Earl of Oxford and Asquith to a Friend*, Bles, London 1933.

F0002 'Abdallah, King of the Hashemite Kingdom of the Jordan, *Memoirs of King Abdullah*, Cape, London 1950; 280 pp., 20.5 cm, red cloth. TEL: pp.18, 23, 91, 157, 165, 170, 200, 225.

F0003 'Abdallah, King of Jordan, *Memoirs of King Abdullah*, Philosophical Library, New York 1950; 280 pp., 20.5 cm, red cloth. TEL: pp.18, 23, 91, 157f, 165f, 170ff, 200ff, 225.

F0004 Adam, Colin Forbes, *Life of Lord Lloyd*, Macmillan, London 1948; x, 318 pp., 22 cm, blue cloth. TEL: pp.64, 87–89, 96, 199–200, 211–12, 216, 262–6, 279.

F0005 Adams, Michael, *The Middle East*, Blond, London 1971; xiv, 634 pp., 23.3 cm, blue paper covered boards. TEL: pp.273, 561.

F0006 Addison, William, *Epping Forest*, Dent, London 1945; 2 , i–xii, 240 pp., 15 leaves of photos, 22 cm, green cloth. TEL: pp.224–5.

F0007 Aglion, Raoul, *War in the Desert*, Holt, New York 1941. TEL: pp.77, 85, 86, 88, 140.

F0008 Alaglouni, Mohamed Ali, *Zekriah an Althawara Al Arabia Al-Koubra Marshourat Makteh*, Al- Houria Press, Amman 1956; 24.4 cm, white paper covers. TEL: pp.36, 45–51.

F0009 Aldanov, Mark A., *Yunost' Pavla Stroganova i Drugia Charakteristiki*, n.p., Belgrade n.d. TEL: Korol 'Feisal i polkovnik Laurens', pp.122–53.

F0010 *Alden's Oxford Guide*, Alden, Oxford; 164 pp., 17.2 cm, pictorial paper covers. TEL: pp.58, 112.

F0011 Aldington, Richard, *Life for Life's Sake*, Viking Press, New York 1941; 2, 414 pp., 22 cm, brown cloth. TEL: pp.267–8.

F0012 Aldington, Richard, and Durrell, Lawrence, *Literary Lifelines*, Viking, New York 1981; 240 pp., 23.3 × 15 cm, red cloth spine, black paper covered boards.
TEL: pp.7, 10, 11, 20, 23, 24, 25, 32, 33, 39, 53, 79, 87, 89, 92, 98, 99, 103, 112, 115, 124, 140, 142, 143, 150, 151, 163, 170, 173, 177, 190, 204.

F0013 Aldington, Richard, *A Passionate Prodigality*, New York Public Library, 1975; xvi, 364 pp., limited to 1500 copies, 25.2 cm, maroon cloth.
TEL: pp.3–5, 6–8, 9, 10–23, 26–8, 30–46, 48–53, 56, 58, 60, 63–4, 66–7, 69–85, 88, 90, 92, 98–103, 106–7, 109, 113–4, 116–7, 119, 120–21, 123, 124, 129, 131, 133, 135, 137, 141–2, 145–7.

F0014 Aldridge, James, *Heroes of the Empty View*, Knopf, New York 1954; x, 432 pp., 21.7 cm, maroon cloth .
TEL: Main character modelled on Lawrence.

F0015 Al Ghossian, *Mozakrati an al Thawara Al Arabia*, Al Taraki Press, Damascus 1956; 23.9 cm, brown paper covers.
TEL: p.229

F0016 Ali Shah, Ikbal, *The Controlling Minds of Asia*, Herbert Jenkins, 1937; 312 [8] pp., blue cloth.
TEL: pp.169, 181.

F0017 Allan, Mea, *Palgrave of Arabia*, Macmillan, London 1972; 320 pp., 22.3 cm, brown cloth.
TEL: p.206

F0018 Allen, Sir Richard, *Imperialism and Nationalism in the Fertile Crescent*, Oxford University Press, New York 1974.
TEL: pp.234, 249, 250.

F0019 Al Madi, Monib, and Mousa, Suliman, *Tarikh Alourdon Fi Alkarn Al Eishrin*, Amman 1959; 23.3 cm, brown paper covers.
TEL: pp.34, 35

F0020 Al-Marayat, A., *The Middle East: Its governments and politics*, Duxbury, Belmont, California, 1972; xvi, 491, 25 pp., 23.5 cm, beige cloth.
TEL: pp.232, 257.

F0021 Al Shaar, Ammen Abou, *Mozakerat Al Malek Abdullah*, Al Hasimaiate Press, Amman 1965; 23.5 cm, multicoloured paper covers.
TEL: pp.121, 133–5.

F0022 Altounyan, Taqui, *In Aleppo Once*, Murray, London 1969; viii, 196 pp., 22.5 cm, red buckram.
TEL: pp.8, 42.

F0023 The American Boy, *American Boy Adventure Stories*, Sun Dial Press, New York 1928; x, 408 pp., 20.3 cm, blue cloth.
TEL: Benge Atlee, pp.17–45, 'The Bridge at Tel-el-Shehab'.

F0024 *American Heritage History of World War I*, American Heritage, New York 1964; 384 pp., 5 cm, blue-grey paper-covered boards, blue buckram spine.
TEL: pp.184, 218, 262.

F0025 American Heritage and UPI, *Churchill*, American Heritage, New

York 1964; 144 pp., 28.5 cm, white paper covered pictorial boards. TEL: p.52.

F0026 Amory, Cleveland, and Bradlee, Frederick, eds, *Vanity Fair*, Viking, New York 1960; 328 pp., 30.4 cm, patterned paper covered boards, red cloth spine. TEL: p.138, photograph.

F0027 Anderson, M.S., *The Eastern Question, 1774–1923*, Macmillan, London 1968; xxii, 438 pp., 22.4 cm, brown linen. TEL: p.339.

F0028 *Annual Report of the Curators of the Bodleian Library for 1972–1973*, Supplement no.5 of University Gazette, Vol. CIV, June 1974; 50 pp., 21.7 cm, grey paper wrappers. TEL: pp.17, 27. *Ibid.*, 1973–1974, Supplement no.4, Vol.CV, June 1975; 64 pp. TEL: pp.19, 21.

F0029 Antonius, George, *The Arab Awakening*, Hamish Hamilton, London 1938 (2nd impression); 4, 472 pp., 22.3 cm, green cloth. TEL: pp.132, 211, 215–7, 221–2, 224, 231–2, 316–7, 319–24, 369, 437.

F0030 Antonius, George, *The Arab Awakening*, Lippincott, Philadelphia 1939; 4, 472 pp., 22.5 cm, brown cloth. TEL: pp.132, 211, 215–7, 221–2, 224, 231–2, 283–4, 316–7, 319–20, 331–2, 369.

F0031 Antonius, George, *The Arab Awakening*, Capricorn, New York 1965; 10, 13–471, 1 pp., 18.4 cm, pictorial paper covers. TEL: pp.122, 211, 215–7, 221–2, 224, 231–2, 283–4, 316–7, 319–24, 369.

F003 Arab Horse Society, *The Arab-Breed Register, 1929*, n.p. 1929; 72 pp., 18.3 cm, brown cloth. TEL: p.68.

F0033 Arabian American Oil Company, *Aramco Handbook*, Haarlem, 1960; 343 pp., illustrated, 28.5 cm. TEL: pp.70, 283.

F0034 Arabian American Oil Company, *Aramco Handbook Oil and the Middle East*, Dhahran, Saudi Arabia 1968; 279 pp., illustrated, 28.5 cm. TEL: pp.62, 267–8.

F0035 Arberry, A.J. *British Orientalists*, Collins, London 1943; orange paper covered boards, 22.2 cm. TEL: pp.20, 22.

F0036 Archer, Sir Geoffrey, *Personal and Historical Memoirs of an East African Administration*, Oliver & Boyd, London 1963; xiii, 260 pp., blue cloth, 24.3 cm. TEL: pp.118–22, 125–7

F0037 Archer, Jules, *Legacy of the Desert*, Little, Brown, Boston 1976. TEL: pp.23, 68–9, 72–3.

F0038 Arendt, Hannah, *The Origins of Totalitarianism*, Harcourt & World, New York 1966. TEL: pp.134, 218–21, 327.

F0039 Armstrong, Harold Courtney, *Grey Steel: J.C. Smuts,* Arthur Barker, London (Special edition for the Book Club) 1937; 408 pp., 22 cm, cream paper covered boards, red cloth spine.
TEL: p.10.

F0040 Armstrong, Harold Courtney, *Grey Wolf: Mustafa Kemal,* Barker, London January 1932; 352 pp., 22.3 cm, dark blue cloth.
TEL: pp.104, 106, 107, 267.

F0041 Armstrong, Harold Courtney, *Lord of Arabia,* Barker, London 1934; 308 pp., 22.2 cm, light blue cloth.
TEL: pp.140, 172, 187, 189, 209, 210, 224.

F0042 Armstrong, Harold Courtney, *Lord of Arabia,* Penguin Books, Harmondsworth, England, 1938; 18 cm, pictorial paper covers.
TEL: pp.111, 135, 146, 147, 163, 175.

F0043 Armstrong, Margaret, *Trelawny,* Macmillan, 1940.
TEL: p.366.

F0044 Arnold, Julian B., *Giants in Dressing Gowns,* Argus, Chicago 1942; 4, viii, 242 pp., 22.9 cm, blue cloth.
TEL: pp.140–44, "Arabian Adventure".

F0045 Arnold, Julian B., *Giants in Dressing Gowns,* Macdonald, London 1945; 176 pp., 22.1 cm, black cloth.
TEL: pp.103–6, "Arabian Adventure".

F0046 Asad, Muhammad, *The Road to Mecca,* Simon & Schuster, New York 1954; xi, 400 pp., 24 cm, tan buckram spine, green boards.
TEL: pp.166, 261.

F0047 Asad, Muhammad, *The Road to Mecca,* Reinhardt, London 1954; 2, xiv, 384 pp., 22.2 cm, slate cloth.
TEL: pp.155, 243.

F0048 Ashley, Maurice, *Churchill as Historian,* Scribner's, New York 1968; viii, 248pp., 21.7 cm, black cloth.
TEL: pp.9, 72, 104, 161, 225, 227.

F0049 *Aspects de la littérature européenne depuis 1945,* du Seuil, Paris 1952.
TEL: pp.120–33, d'Astrog, "Lawrence, Notre Frère".

F0050 Asprey, Robert B., *War in the Shadows,* Doubleday, Garden City, New York, 1975; 2 volumes, 24 cm, tan paper covered boards, black cloth spine, boxed as issued.
TEL: pp.xxxiii, 279–95, 332, 421, 423, 447, 654, 657, 680, 992, 1009, 1102, 1130.

F0051 *Auction Catalog of the Estate of Colin L. Campbell,* Goleta, California, 13 June 1941; 6, 42 pp., 27 cm, grey paper wrappers.
TEL: pp.28–31. Sale of a copy of 1927 *Seven Pillars of Wisdom.*

F0052 Auden, Wystan Hugh, and Isherwood, Christopher, *The Ascent of F6 and On the Frontier,* Faber, London 1958; 192 pp., 18.4 cm, red paper covers.
TEL: Character in "The Ascent of F.6".

F0053 Aunert, Uri, *Israel without Zionists,* Macmillan, New York 1968; 6, 218 pp., 21.8 cm, bright blue cloth.
TEL: pp.60, 61, 137.

F0054 Bain, James S., *A Bookseller Looks Back,* Macmillan, London 1940;

xvi, 304 pp., 22.8 cm, green cloth.
TEL: pp.262, 263, 264, 265, 266, 286, 287.

F0055   Baker, Sir Herbert, *Architecture and Personalities*, Country Life, London 1944; xii, 224 pp., 25.2 cm, blue cloth.
TEL: pp.195–7.

F0056   Baker, Hettie Gray, *Bookplates*, Hyacinth Press, Cleveland 1947; 16 leaves, mounted samples, 24 cm, tan paper wrappers.
TEL: p.10, zinc plate BP, "Hettie Gray Baker's Lawrenciana' for collection presented to Dartmouth College.

F0057   Baldwin, Hanson W., *World War I, An Outline History*, Harper Row, New York 1962; x, 182pp., 21.7 cm, grey cloth boards, black spine.
TEL: pp.121, 136–7.

F0058   Bardens, Dennis, *Churchill in Parliament*, A.S.Barnes, South Brunswick 1967; 384 pp., 21.5 cm, black cloth.
TEL: p.145.

F0059   Barker, A.J., *The Neglected War: Mesopotamia, 1914–1918*, Faber, London 1967; 536 pp., 22.4 cm, black cloth.
TEL: p.366.

F0060   Barker, Sir Ernest, *Age & Youth*, Oxford University Press, London 1953; xii,348 pp., 22.2 cm, green cloth.
TEL: pp.60–61.

F0061   Barnes, Eric Wollencott, *The Man Who Lived Twice*, Scribner's, 1956.
TEL: p.285.

F0062   Barrow, General Sir George, *The Fire of Life*, Hutchinson, London 1942; viii, 256 pp., 23.5 cm, rose cloth.
TEL: pp.209, 212, 213, 214.

F0063   Barsley, Michael, *The Orient Express*, Stein & Day, New York 1966; xiv, (2), 16–210 pp., illustrated, 24.3 cm, deep pink paper covered boards, black cloth spine.
TEL: pp.68, 157.

F0064   Barzun, Jacques, *The Modern Researcher*, Harcourt Brace, World, New York 1970; xviii, 430 pp., 21.4 cm, white paper covers.
TEL: pp. 37, 50–51.

F0065   Bates, Herbert Ernest, *Edward Garnett*, Parrish, London 1950; 88 pp., 19 cm, brown cloth
TEL: p.79.

F0066   Bath Assembly Rooms and the Museum of Costume, *An Illustrated Souvenir with a History of the Assembly Rooms, the Story of the Collection, and a Guide to the Exhibition*, Spa Committee of the Bath City Council, Bath, England 1965; 44 pp., 24.6 cm, gold paper covers.
TEL: p.37.

F0067   Baulin, Jacques, *The Arab Role in Africa*, Penguin, Baltimore; 144 pp., 18 cm, pictorial paper covers glued to sheets.
TEL: pp.115, 139.

F0068   Beach, Joseph Warren, *The Making of the Auden Canon*, University of Minnesota Press, Minneapolis 1957; viii, 316 pp., 22.2 cm, bright yellow cloth.
TEL: pp.73, 120.

F0069 Beaverbrook, William Maxwell Aitken, 1st Baron, *The Decline and Fall of Lloyd George*, Duell, Sloan and Pearce, New York 1963; 320 pp., 24 cm, black cloth.
TEL: p.33.

F0070 Bedford, Sybille, *Aldous Huxley*, Knopf/Harper, New York 1975.
TEL: pp.455, 456.

F0071 Begg, Robert Campbell, *The Secret of the Knife*, Jarrold, Norwich 1966; 2, x, 164 pp., 24 cm, blue cloth.
TEL: pp.42, 161.

F0072 Behrman, Samuel Nathaniel, *Portrait of Max*, Random, New York 1960; xvi, 320pp., 23.9 cm, blue cloth.
TEL: p.279.

F0073 Bell, Gertrude M.L., *The Letters of Gertrude Bell*, Benn, London 1927; 2 volumes, 24.3 cm, blue cloth.
TEL: pp.i, 305, 353, 360, 372, 468, 519, 645.

F0074 Bell, Gertrude M.L., *The Letters of Gertrude Bell*, Boni & Liveright, New York 1927; 2 volumes, 24.9 cm, blue buckram.
TEL: Volume I, pp.305, 353, 360, 372; Volume II, pp.468, 519, 645.

F0075 Bell, Gertrude M.L., *Letters of Gertrude Bell*, Penguin, Harmondsworth 1939; 2 volumes, 18.2 cm, blue and white paper covers.

F0076 Bell, Gertrude, *Persian Pictures*, Liveright, New York 1928; 198 pp., 22 cm.
TEL: Reference to Lawrence on dust wrapper.

F0077 Bell, Gertrude, *Persian Pictures*, Benn, London 1947; 157 pp., 22 cm.
TEL: p.7.

F0078 Belmont, Eleanor, *(Robson) Fabric of Memory*, Farrar, Straus 1957.
TEL: pp.205, 256–7.

F0079 Beloff, Max, *Imperial Sunset*, Knopf, New York 1970; 4, xiv, 396pp., 24 cm, blue buckram.
TEL: pp.256, 257, 297, 298, 326.

F0080 Ben-Horin, Eliahu, *The Middle East*, Norton, New York 1943; 252 pp., 21 cm, yellow cloth.
TEL: pp.12, 50, 55, 85, 120, 136, 145.

F0081 Bennett, Arnold, *The Journals of Arnold Bennett*, Cassell, London 1933.
TEL: p.174. Index confuses D.H. Lawrence and T.E. Lawrence.

F0082 Benoist-Méchin, Jacques, *Arabian Destiny*, Elek, London 1957; x, 298 pp., 22.2 cm, blue cloth (also red cloth).
TEL: pp.133, 137, 150, 152, 153, 157, 158, 170, 172, 173.

F0083 Benoist-Méchin, Jacques, *Arabian Destiny*, Essential Books, Fair Lawn, New Jersey, 1958; x, 298 pp., blue cloth.
TEL: pp.133, 137, 150, 152, 153, 157, 158, 170, 172, 173.

F0084 Benoist-Méchin, Jacques, *Le Loup et le léopard*, Editions Albin Michel, Paris 1954; 464 pp., 20.5 cm, pictorial paper covers.
TEL: Volume 1, p.50.

F0085 Bentley, Nicolas, *A Choice of Ornaments*, Deutsch, London 1959; 351 pp., 22 cm, golden brown cloth.
TEL: pp.25, 245, 334.

F0086   Bentley, Wilder, *The Printer to the Poet*, Archetype Press, Berkeley 1937; 8 pp., limited to 350 copies, 25.6 cm, printed paper, wrappers tied by cord to sheets.
TEL: p.6.

F0087   Bentwich, Norman, *My 77 Years*, Jewish Publication Society, Philadelphia 1961; 344 pp., 21 cm.
TEL: pp.33, 42, 69, 196.

F0089   Berg, Dave, *Mad's Dave Berg Looks at the U.S.A.*, Warner, New York 1977; 112 pp., 18 cm, pictorial paper covers.
TEL: p.66.

F0090   Berger, Monroe, *The Arab World Today*, Doubleday, Garden City, New York, 1962; 480 pp., 21.5 cm, sand-coloured cloth.
TEL: pp.36, 61, 72, 329.

F0091   Bernstein, Burton, *Sinai*, Viking, New York 1982.
TEL: pp.15, 17, 42, 53.

F0092   Bertram, Anthony, *Paul Nash*, Faber & Faber, London 1955; 336 pp., 24 cm, maroon buckram.
TEL: pp.74, 111, 112, 137, 310.

F0093   *The Bibliophile's Almanack for 1928*, Fleuron, London 1927; 2, 92 pp., 1 of 120 copies, 20 cm, white paper covered boards, brown cloth spine.
TEL: pp.35–41, Herbert Read, 'Seven Pillars of Wisdom'.

F0094   *The Bibliophile's Almanack for 1928*, Fleuron, London 1927; 14–85 pp., [1–15 pp.], 19.6 cm, grey-olive green cloth. No issue statement p.2, paper not handmade, price at foot of front cover.
TEL: pp.35–41, Herbert Read, "The Seven Pillars of Wisdom".

F0095   Birdwood, William R., *Nuri As-Said*, Cassell, London 1959; xiv, 306 pp., 22.3 cm, black cloth.
TEL: pp.33, 41, 47–51, 54, 56–7, 58, 64–5, 69–76, 78–84, 86–88, 102–104, 112–3, 116, 119–20, 123–5, 132, 182.

F0096   Birkenhead, 2nd Earl of (Frederick W.F. Smith), *Halifax*, Houghton Mifflin, Boston 1966; xiv, 626 pp., 23.6 cm, black cloth.
TEL: p.123.

F0097   Bishop, Edward, *The Debt We Owe*, Longmans, London 1969; xii, 164 pp., 22.2 cm, blue paper covered boards.
TEL: pp.14, 16–18, 121.

F0098   Black, Donald, *Red Dust*, Cape, London 1931; 304 pp., 20.5 cm, red linen.
TEL: pp.275, 289.

F0099   Blackledge, William James, *Legion of the Marching Madmen*, Sampson, Low, Marston, London 1936; xii, 244 pp., 22.8 cm, red cloth.
TEL: pp.243–4.

F0100   Blackmur, Richard Palmer, *The Expense of Greatness*, Arrow, New York 1940; 6, 306 pp., 21.5 cm, maroon cloth.
TEL: pp.1–36, 'The Everlasting Effort. A Citation of T.E. Lawrence'.

F0101   Blackmur, Richard Palmer, *The Expense of Greatness*, Peter Smith Gloucester, Mass., 1958; 6, 366 pp., 21 cm, red cloth.

TEL: pp.1–36, 'The Everlasting Effort. A Citation of T.E. Lawrence'.

F0102 Blackmur, Richard Palmer, *The Lion and the Honeycomb*, Harcourt Brace, New York 1955; viii, 310 pp., 20.3 cm, pictorial cloth.
TEL: pp.97–123.

F0103 Blaiklock, E.M., ed., *The Zondervan Pictorial Bible Atlas*, Zondervan Press, Grand Rapids, Michigan, 1969; xx, 492, 16 pp., 24.8 cm, brown cloth.
TEL: p. 14.

F0104 Blankfort, Michael, *Behold the Fire*, New American Library, New York 1965; xviii, 398 pp., 21.5 cm, orange cloth.
TEL: pp.149, 153, 185–6, 270.

F0105 Blankfort, Michael, *Behold the Fire*, Heinemann, London 1966; xiv, 346 pp., 22 cm, black cloth.
TEL: pp.133–43, 146, 337, 345.

F0106 Blankfort, Michael, *Behold the Fire*, New American Library, New York 1966; 384 pp., 17.8 cm, pictorial paper covers.
TEL: pp.151, 162–7, 170–71, 268, 369.

F0107 Blumenfeld, Ralph David, *All in a Lifetime*, Benn, London 1931; x, 278 pp., 22.2 cm, blue cloth.
TEL: p.136.

F0108 Blumenfeld, Ralph David, *R.D.B.'s Procession*, Nicholson & Watson, London 1935; 4, 332 pp., 20.3 cm, yellow-green cloth.
TEL: p.115.

F0109 Blunt, Wilfrid, *Cockerell*, Hamilton, London 1964; 10, ix–xviii, 388 pp., 23 cm, brown cloth.
TEL: pp.102–3, 207–8, 212, 220, 335, 351, 358, 359.

F0110 Blunt, Wilfrid, *Cockerell*, Knopf, New York 1965; xviii, 388 pp., 21.9 cm, deep maroon.
TEL: pp.101–3, 207–8, 212, 220, 335, 351, 358, 359.

F0111 Blythe, Ronald, *The Age of Illusion*, Houghton, Mifflin, Boston 1964; 10, 298 pp., 22 cm, orange cloth.
TEL: Dust wrapper, Chapter 4, pp.63–82, 'Sublimated Aladdin'.

F0112 Boak, Denis, *André Malraux*, Oxford University Press, Oxford 1968; 2, xiv, 268 pp., 22.3 cm, blue linen.
TEL: pp.1, 9n, 30, 34, 48, 147–8, 3–5, 7, 209–11.

F0113 Bodley, Ronald, and Hearst, Lorna, *Gertrude Bell*, Macmillan, New York 1940; xii, 260 pp., 22 cm, orange-yellow cloth.
TEL: pp.18, 36, 81, 119, 120, 129, 131, 147, 152, 175, 193, 204.

F0114 Bodley, Ronald V.C., *Wind in the Sahara*, Coward-McCann, New York 1944; xviii, 3–224 pp., 21.5 cm, black cloth.
TEL: Dustwrapper blurb.

F0115 Bodley, Ronald V.C., *Wind in the Sahara*, Creative Age Press, New York 1944; xviii, 3–224 pp., 21 cm.
TEL: pp.3–22+.

F0116 Bodley, Ronald V.C., *Wind in the Sahara*, Robert Hale, London 1947; 280 pp., 22 cm, blue cloth .
TEL: Dustwrapper blurb.

F0117 Bodleian Library, Oxford, *Annual Report 1973–1974*, Bodleian

Library, Oxford 1975.

F0118 Boisdeffre, Pierre de, *Les Ecrivains de la Nuit*, Plon, Paris 1973; 308 pp., 20.8 cm, black cloth.
TEL: pp.189–208, 'La Recherche du Châtiment, T.E. Lawrence'.

F0119 Bolitho, Hector, *The Angry Neighbours*, Barker, London 1957; 160 pp., 22.5 cm, brown paper-covered boards.
TEL: pp.77, 105, 135, 137–9.

F0120 Bolitho, Hector, *A Biographer's Notebook*, Macmillan, New York 1950.
TEL: pp.89.

F0121 Bolitho, Hector, *Older People*, Cobden-Sanderson, London 1935; 296 pp., 22.4 cm, green cloth.
TEL: pp.221, 252, 254, 257–60,

F0122 Bolitho, Hector, *Older People*, Appleton-Century, New York 1935; 296 pp., 22.5 cm, green cloth.
TEL: pp.252, 257–60.

F0123 Bond, Michael, *Samuel Shepheard of Cairo*, Michael Joseph, London 1957; 240 pp., 27 cm.
TEL: p.150.

F0124 Bonnell, F.W., and Bonnell, F.C., *Conrad Aiken: A Bibliography*, Huntington Library, San Marino 1982.
TEL: p.186.

F0125 Bonsal, Stephen, *Suitors and Suppliants*, Prentice-Hall, New York 1946; xviii, 302 pp., 23.5 cm, blue cloth.
TEL: pp.32ff, 54, 56–7, 287, 34–5, 33, 51.

F0126 Boothby, Robert, *Recollections of a Rebel*, Hutchinson, London 1978; 272 pp., blue cloth.
TEL: pp.73–5.

F0127 *The Borough and District of Wareham*, Burrow, Cheltenham n.d.; 48 pp., 18 cm, printed paper covers.
TEL: p.28, illustration of TEL's effigy.

F0128 Bott, Alan, *Eastern Flights*, Penguin, Harmondsworth 1940; 160 pp., pictorial paper covers.
TEL: pp.156–7, 160.

F0129 Bottomley, Gordon, *Poet & Painter*, Oxford University Press, 1955; xx, 280 pp., 22 cm, green cloth.
TEL: pp.155–6.

F0130 Bowden, Tom, *The Breakdown of Public Security*, Sage, London 1977.
TEL: pp.110, 148.

F0131 Bowen, Norman R., ed., *Lowell Thomas, the Stranger Everyone Knows*, Doubleday, Garden City, New York, 1968; xx, 188 pp., 23.7 cm, tan cloth.
TEL: pp.37–43, Gove Hambidge, 'He Was with Lawrence in Arabia'.

F0132 Bowman, Humphrey, *Middle-East Window*, Longmans Green, London 1942; 2, xxii, 348 pp., 20.3 cm, blue cloth.
TEL: pp.xxi, 180, 181, 184, 330.

F0133 Boyars, Arthur, and Bary, Harmon, eds, *Oxford Poetry 1948*, Blackwell, Oxford 1948; 64 pp., 19 cm, paper wrappers.
TEL: p.12, L.J. Arundel, 'T.E. Lawrence'.

F0134 Boyle, Andrew, *Trenchard,* Collins, London 1962; 768 pp., 23.5 cm, orange cloth (also blue simulated leather).
TEL: pp.377–8, 383–4, 391, 427–30, 459–60, 515–6, 538–41, 580, 595, 613, 684.

F0135 Boyle, Andrew, *Trenchard,* Norton, New York 1962; 768 pp., 23.5 cm.
TEL: pp.377–8, 383, 391, 427–30, 459, 460, 515–6, 538–41, 574–5, 580, 595.

F0136 Boyle, William, *My Naval Life, 1886–1941,* Hutchinson, London 1943; 208 pp., 23.4 cm, blue cloth.
TEL: pp.90, 100, 102, 103.

F0137 Bradley, Russell, *The Siege,* Viking, New York 1970; 352 pp., 22 cm, mustard paper covered boards, yellow cloth spine.
TEL: pp.250, 253, 297.

F0138 Bray, Norman Napier Evelyn, *A Paladin of Arabia,* Unicorn Press, London 1936; xviii, 430 pp., 22 cm, black cloth.
TEL: pp.297, 298, 372.

F0139 Bray, Norman Napier Evelyn, *Shifting Sands,* Unicorn Press, London 1934; xii, 312 pp., 22 cm, black cloth .
TEL: pp.44, 101, 112, 118, 132, 137, 138, 140, 141, 142, 143, 144, 153, 155, 166, 236, 240, 301, 302.

F0140 Bremond, Edouard, *Le Hedjaz dans la Guerre Mondiale,* Payot, Paris 1931; 352 pp., 22.7 cm, printed paper wrappers.
TEL: pp.7, 9, 12, 71, 73, 75–6, 85–7, 91, 93, 102, 109, 119, 121, 122, 138, 160–62, 185n, 212–3, 216–7, 220, 222, 226, 235, 236, 238–9, 261, 270–71, 273–4, 278–9, 285–90, 294–5, 298, 300–2,309+.

F0141 Brent, Peter, *Far Arabia,* Readers Union, Newton Abbot 1978; 14, 242 pp., 21.5 × 13.2 cm, grey cloth.
TEL: pp.14, 19–20, 74, 125, 132, 144, 171, 178, 181, 188, 192, 195, 197–9, 202.

F0142 Brent, Peter, *Far Arabia,* Weidenfeld & Nicolson, London 1977; xiv, 240 pp., 22.3 cm, brown cloth.
TEL: pp.14, 19–20, 74, 125, 132, 144, 171, 178, 181, 188, 192, 195, 197–9, 202.

F0143 Brian, Denis, *Tallulah, Darling,* Macmillan, New York 1980.
TEL: pp.4, 51, 52, 130.

F0144 Briant, Keith, *Oxford Limited,* Farrar & Rinehart, New York 1938; xiv, 306 pp., 21.2 cm, bright blue cloth.
TEL: p.162.

F0145 Bridges, Thomas Charles, and Tiltman, H. Hessell, *Heroes of Modern Adventure,* Harrap, London 1927; x, 278 pp., 21.5 cm, blue cloth.
TEL: Chapter 13, pp.174–93, 'Lawrence of Arabia'.

F0146 Bridges, Thomas Charles, and Tiltman, H. Hessall, *Heroes of Modern Adventures,* Little Brown, Boston 1927; x, 278 pp., 22.5 cm, brown cloth.
TEL: Chapter 13, pp.174–93, 'Lawrence of Arabia'.

F0147 Brock, Ray, *Ghost on Horseback,* Duell Sloan, New York 1954; viii,

408 pp., 21 cm, black cloth.
TEL: pp.184, 185.

F0148 Brodie, Fawn, *The Devil Drives*, W.W. Norton, New York 1967; 390 pp., 24 cm.
TEL: pp.59, 104–5, 349.

F0149 Brodrick, Alan Houghton, *Near to Greatness*, Hutchinson, London 1965; 272 pp., 21.6 cm, blue cloth.
TEL: pp.17, 18, 177–83, 185.

F0150 Brook-Shepherd, Gordon, *Nov. 1918*, Collins, London 1981; 464 pp., black cloth.
TEL: pp.159, 161–2, 163n, 166, 171, 174–5, 177–9.

F0151 Brophy, John, *Flesh and Blood*, Dent, London 1931; 256 pp., 18.8 cm, brown cloth.
TEL: Main character based on Lawrence.

F0152 Brophy, John, *Flesh and Blood*, Fridberg, Dublin 1948; 128 pp., 18.5 cm, patterned white paper wrappers.
TEL: 'Mr. Brophy now feels free to admit that the chief character of this story, while not a portrait, is to some extent derived from his friend T.E. Shaw – "Lawrence of Arabia".' c.f. dust jacket.

F0153 Brophy, John, *The Human Face*, Prentice-Hall, New York 1946; vi, 250 pp.
TEL: pp.v–vi, 50, 67, 225.

F0154 Brophy, John, ed., and Partridge, Eric, *Songs and Slang of the British Soldier 1914–1918*, E. Partridge, London 1930 (2nd edn); viii, 224 pp., 22.2 cm, orange cloth.
TEL: p.vi.

F0155 Brown, Carl, and Itzkowitz, Norman, eds, *Psychological Dimensions of Near Eastern Studies*, Darwin Press, Princeton, New Jersey 1977; 384 pp., 25 cm, blue cloth.
TEL: pp.27–59, John E. Mack, 'T.E. Lawrence and the Uses of Psychology in Biography of Figures'.

F0156 Brown, Cecil, *Suez to Singapore*, Random House, New York 1942; xii, 548 pp., 23.2 cm, tan buckram.
TEL: pp.17, 43, 55, 61, 71, 120.

F0157 Brown, Christopher, and Thesing, William, *English Prose and Criticism, 1900–1950*, Gale, Detroit 1983.
TEL: pp.271–8 bibliography.

F0158 Brownlow, Kevin, *The Way West and the Wilderness*, Knopf, New York 1979; 2, xviii, 602 pp., 26.7 cm, black cloth.
TEL: pp.444–6, 449, 450–1.

F0159 Brownigg, Sir Douglas, *Unexpected (a book of memories)*, Hutchinson, London 1942; 172 pp., 23 cm, brown cloth.
TEL: pp.58, 59.

F0160 Brunton, Paul, *A Hermit in the Himalayas*, Weiss, New York 1971.
TEL: pp.34–5, 138.

F0161 Buchan, John (Baron Tweedsmuir), *The Clearing House*, Hodder & Stoughton, London 1946; xiv, 234 pp., 22.7 cm, blue paper covered boards.
TEL: pp.84–9.

F0162 Buchan, John (Baron Tweedsmuir), *The Courts of the Morning,* Hodder & Stoughton, London 1929; 406, 10 pp., 19.2 cm, blue cloth.
TEL: Main character based on Lawrence.

F0163 Buchan, John (Baron Tweedsmuir), *Greenmantle,* Doran, New York 1916; 348 pp., 18 cm, deep maroon.

F0164 Buchan, John (Baron Tweedsmuir), *A History of the Great War,* Houghton Mifflin, Boston 1923; 4 volumes.
TEL: Vol. 3, p.489; Vol. 4, p.356.

F0165 Buchan, John (Baron Tweedsmuir), *Julius Caesar,* Davies, London 1932; 172 pp., 19.9 cm, black cloth also green cloth.
TEL: Dedication, p.5, 'To My Friend, Aircraftsman T.E. Shaw'.

F0166 Buchan, John (Baron Tweedsmuir), *Julius Caesar,* Daily Express Publications, London 1938; 4, 152, 4 pp., 19 cm, brown leather simulated cloth.
TEL: Dedication, p.5, 'To My Friend, Aircraftsman T.E. Shaw'.

F0167 Buchan, John (Baron Tweedsmuir), *The King's Grace 1910–1935,* Hodder & Stoughton, London 1935; 285 pp., 19 cm, tan cloth.
TEL: pp.231, 245.

F0168 Buchan, John (Baron Tweedsmuir), *Memory-Hold-the-Door,* Hodder & Stoughton, London 1940; 328 pp., 23 cm, green cloth.
TEL: pp.106, 151, 183, 211, 212, 213, 214, 215, 216, 217, 218.

F0169 Buchan, John (Baron Tweedsmuir), *Pilgrim's Way,* Houghton Mifflin, Cambridge, Mass., 1940; viii, 344 pp., 20 cm, light red cloth and yellow cloth.
TEL: pp.103, 148, 184, 210–17.

F0170 Buchan, Susan, *John Buchan By His Wife and Friends,* Hodder & Stoughton, 1947; 304 pp., 22.9 cm, black cloth.
TEL: pp.162, 192–5, 230.

F0171 Buchan, William, *John Buchan,* Harrap, 1985.

F0172 Buell, Frederick, *W.H. Auden as a Social Poet,* Cornell University Press, Ithaca 1973; xii, 204 pp., 21.5 cm, tan cloth.
TEL: pp.15, 17, 18–19, 22, 88, 134.

F0173 Bullard, Sir Reader, *Britain and the Middle East,* Hutchinson University Library, London 1951.
TEL: pp.74, 87, 144.

F0174 Bullard, Sir Reader, *The Camels Must Go,* Faber, London 1961; 304 pp., 22 cm, red cloth.
TEL: pp.88–9, 103, 190, 117, 121, 122, 158–9.

F0175 Bullock, Alan and Woodings, R.B. eds, *Twentieth Century Culture,* Harper & Row, New York.
TEL: pp.430.

F0176 Burgoyne, Elizabeth, *Gertrude Bell,* Benn, London 1958; 2 volumes, 22 cm, brown cloth.
TEL: Vol. 1, pp.1, 27, 278; Vol. 2, pp.28, 30, 33, 37–8, 108–10, 114, 162–5, 216, 227, 254.

F0178 Busch, Briton Cooper, *Britain, India and the Arabs, 1914–1921,* University of California Press, Berkeley 1971; 2, xii, 528 pp., 22.3 cm, black cloth.

TEL: pp.67, 85, 102, 105, 106, 171, 178, 185, 195n, 199f, 201, 263, 272, 274f, 282, 289, 293, 299, 302, 322, 323, 325, 328, 330, 332, 336f, 339, 340f, 348, 344, 361, 365, 384, 407f, 416, 458, 465f, 467, 469, 471, 482.

F0179 Butler, Grant C., *Beyond Arabian Sands*, Devin-Adair, New York 1964; 223 pp., 21 cm, oatmeal cloth.
TEL: pp.15, 19–20, 99, 191–2.

F0180 Butler, Grant C., *Kings and Camels*, Devin-Adair, New York 1960; xii, 212 pp., 21 cm, brown paper covered boards, green cloth spine.
TEL: p. 206.

F0181 Butler, James Ramsay Montagu, *Lord Lothian (Philip Kerr) 1882–1940*, Macmillan, London 1960; xiv, 386 pp., 22.5 cm, black cloth.
TEL: pp.245–246

F0182 Calde, Mildred, and French, Francesca, *The Gobi Desert*, Hodder & Stoughton, London 1942; 22.2 cm, blue cloth.
TEL: Contains Lawrence quote.

F0183 Callan, Edward, *Auden: A Carnival of Intellect*, Oxford University Press, New York 1983.
TEL: pp.106–7, 250.

F0184 Campbell Johnson, Alan, *Viscount Halifax*, Washburn, New York 1941; 576 pp., 22.5 cm, red cloth (also issued in blue cloth).
TEL: pp.90, 97, 389–90.

F0185 Campbell, Olwen Ward, *The Lighted Window*, Heffer & Sons, Cambridge 1940; 82 pp., 19.2 cm, plain tan paper covered boards.
TEL: t.p., pp.9–36, 'Some Reflections on the Life of T.E. Lawrence'.

F0187 Canning, John, ed., *100 Great Modern Lives*, Odhams Books, London 1965; 640 pp., 22.7 cm, grey buckram.
TEL: pp.516–20, 'Thomas Edward Lawrence, 1888–1935'.

F0188 Cartland, Barbara, *Ronald Cartland*, Hutchinson, London 1945; 160 pp., 21.8 cm, red cloth.
TEL: p. 62.

F0189 Carlow, Michael, and Hodson, Gillian, *Terence Rattigan*, Quartet Books, London 1979; 360 pp., deep blue cloth.
TEL: pp.24, 236–7, 250–56, 263–4, 265, 267, 269, 303, 320, 324, 360–61.

F0190 Carmichael, Amy, *The Widow of the Jewels*, Society for the Promotion of Christian Knowledge, London 1928; 96 pp., 19 cm, green linen.
TEL: p.V, "T.E. Lawrence of 'The Revolt in the Desert' makes the foreword of this book."

F0191 Carpenter, Humphrey, *W.H. Auden*, Houghton Mifflin, Boston 1981.
TEL: pp.193–4.

F0192 Carr, Winifred, *Hussein's Kingdom*, Frewin, London 1966; 176 pp., 21.8 cm, brown paper-covered boards.
TEL: pp.12, 82, 86, 87, 93, 105, 108, 110–11.

F0193 Carruthers, Douglas, *Arabian Adventure*, Witherby, London 1953.
TEL: pp.10, 14, 79, 80, 124, 158.

F0194 Carver, Michael (Field Marshal Lord), ed., *The War Lords*, Little

Brown, Boston 1976.
TEL: pp.xiv, xvi, 156–7.

F0195 Casey, Robert, *Baghdad and Points East*, J.H. Sears, New York 1928; xiv, 304 pp., 23.8 cm, olive cloth.
TEL: p. 34.

F0196 *Catalogue of the Edward Clark Library*, Privately printed for Napier College of Commerce and Technology, Lothian Regional Council, 1976; 2 volumes, 25.5 cm.
TEL: Vol. 2, pp.285, 322.

F0197 Catlin, George, *For God's Sake! Go*, Colin Smythe, Gerrards Cross 1972.
TEL: pp.21, 294–5.

F0198 Cottrell, Leonard, *Lost Cities*, Holt, Rinehart & Winston, New York 1961; 254 pp., 21.7 cm, light blue linen.
TEL: p. 87.

F0199 Caudwell, Christopher, *Studies in a Dying Culture*, Dodd Mead, New York 1938; xxviii, 228 pp., 18.7 cm, red cloth.
TEL: pp.20–43, 'T.E. Lawrence, a Study in Heroism'.

F0200 Caudwell, Christopher, *Studies and Further Studies in a Dying Culture*, Dodd Mead, New York 1958 reprint (1938, 1949); 2, xxvi, 256 pp., 21 cm, light brown cloth.
TEL: pp.xv, 20–43, 'T.E. Lawrence, A Study in Heroism'.

F0201 Caudwell, Christopher, *Studies in a Dying Culture*, Current Book Distributors, Sydney 1949; 128 pp., 21.5 cm, brown paper wrappers.
TEL: pp.7, 10; 24–35, 'T.E. Lawrence, a Study in Heroism'.

F0202 Ceram, C.W., *Gods, Graves and Scholars*, Knopf, New York 1951; 2, xii, 426, xxiv pp., 21.8 cm, blue cloth.
TEL: pp.212, 308.

F0203 Ceram, C.W., *The March of Archaeology*, Knopf, New York 1958.
TEL: p.232.

F0204 Ceram, C.W., *Narrow Pass, Black Mountain*, Readers Union, London 1957; 22.2 cm, orange cloth.
TEL: pp.41, 63–4.

F0205 Ceram, C.W., *The Secret of the Hittites*, Knopf, New York 1956; 2, xxii, 282, xiv pp., 21.7 cm, green cloth and red cloth.
TEL: pp.43, 66.

F0206 Chalfont, Alun, Baron, *Montgomery of Alamein*, Atheneum, New York 1976; xvi, 368 pp., 24 cm, light blue cloth.
TEL: pp.31–2.

F0207 Channon, Sir Henry, *Chips*, Weidenfeld & Nicolson, London 1967; 10, 498 pp., 24.8 cm, black cloth.
TEL: pp.34, 289.

F0208 Charrier, Paul, *Gordon of Khartoum*, Lancer Books, New York 1965; 224 pp., 17.9 cm, pictorial paper covers.
TEL: Front cover, pp.12, 13, 128, 134.

F0209 Childs, J. Rive, *Foreign Service Farewell*, University of Virginia Press, Charlottesville 1969.
TEL: pp.52, 143, 144, 183, 184.

F0210 Churchill, Winston S., *Great Contemporaries*, Putnam's, New York 1937; 2, x, 300 pp., 23.6 cm, blue cloth.
TEL: pp.129–40, 'Lawrence of Arabia'.

F0211 Churchill, Winston S., *Great Contemporaries*, Reprint Society, London 1941; viii, 344 pp., 19.1 cm, yellow cloth.
TEL: pp.127–42, 'Lawrence of Arabia'.

F0212 Churchill, Winston S., *Great Contemporaries*, Thornton Butterworth, London 1937; 336 pp., 22 cm, blue buckram.
TEL: pp.155–67, 'Lawrence of Arabia'.

F0213 Churchill, Winston S., *Great Contemporaries*, Butterworth, London October 1937 (4th impression); 336 pp., 22 cm, blue cloth.
TEL: pp.155–67, 'Lawrence of Arabia'.

F0214 Churchill, Winston S. *Great Contemporaries*, University of Chicago Press, Chicago 1937; 388 pp., pictorial paper covers.
TEL: 'Lawrence of Arabia'.

F0215 Churchill, Winston S., *Great Contemporaries*, Macmillan, London 1942; vi, 288 pp., 20 cm, dark blue cloth.
TEL: pp.113–25, 'Lawrence of Arabia'.

F0216 Churchill, Winston S., *Great Contemporaries*, Fontana Books, London 1959; 320 pp., 18 cm, multicoloured paper covers.
TEL: pp.127–38, 'Lawrence of Arabia'.

F0217 *Churchill, Winston S., His Complete Speeches, 1897–1963*, edited by Robert Rhodes James, 8 volumes, Chelsea 1974.
TEL: Vol. IV, pp.3355, 3533, 5610, 5715, 5791, 5792, 5793, 6134, 7374, 7779.

F0218 Churchill, Winston, in Gilbert, Martin, *Winston S. Churchill*, Heinemann, London 1977.
TEL: Vol. 4, pt 1, pp.xviii, xix; pt 2, pp.1124, 1295, 1298, 1306, 1314, 1316, 1336, 1348, 1355, 1357–8, 1359, 1368, 1370, 1381, 1396, 1398, 1403, 1405, 1412, 1414; pt 3, pp.510, 514, 515–6, 527–8, 532, 534, 538, 544, 545–6, 549, 552, 553, 556, 587, 813–4, 815, 889–90, 895.

F0219 Clayton, Sir Gilbert Falkingham, *An Arabian Diary*, University of California Press, Berkeley 1969; 2, xiv, 384 pp., 23.7 cm, sand cloth.
TEL: pp.23, 29, 33, 65, 69, 25, 40, 60–61, 64, 65, 67, 68.

F0220 Collins, R.J. (Major-General), *Lord Wavell*, Hodder & Stoughton, London 1947.
TEL: p.87.

F0221 Collis, Maurice, *Nancy Astor*, Faber & Faber, London 1960; 240 pp., 2.3 cm, purple cloth.
TEL: pp.150f, 217.

F0222 Collis, Maurice, *Nancy Astor*, Dutton, New York 1960; 2, 238 pp., 21.5 cm, blue cloth; second printing orange cloth..
TEL: pp.150f, 217.

F0223 Colmer, John, *E.M. Forster*, Routledge, 1975.
TEL: pp.112, 129, 19.

F0224 Connell, John, *The "Office"*, St. Martin's, New York, 1958.
TEL: pp.24, 32.

F0225 Connell, John, *Wavell*, Collins, London 1964; 576 pp., 23.5 cm, grey cloth.
TEL: pp.132, 159, 175–6, 185.

F0226 Connell, John, *Wavell*, Harcourt Brace & World, New York 1965
(First American edition); 576 pp., 24 cm, black cloth.
TEL: pp. 132, 159, 175–6, 185.

F0227 Contemporary British Literature, 1943.
TEL: pp. 321–2.

F0229 Cook, Albert, *The Meaning of Fiction*, Wayne State University Press,
Detroit 1960; 2, xii, 322 pp., 22.2 cm, black cloth.
TEL: pp. 273–9.

F0230 Cook, Bruce, *Dalton Trumbo*, Scribners, New York 1977.
TEL: p. 280.

F0231 Coolidge, Olivia, *Winston Churchill*, Houghton Mifflin, Boston 1960.
TEL: pp. 80–81.

F0233 Cottrell, Leonard, *Concise Dictionary of Archaeology*, Hawthorne,
New York 1971; xxvi, 430 pp., 25.3 cm, brown cloth.
TEL: p. 392.

F0234 Courcel, Martin de, *Malraux, Life and Work*, Harcourt Brace
Jovanovich, New York 1976; x, 286 pp., 24 cm, black cloth.
TEL: pp. 6, 32, 33, 34, 140, 145–8, 166, 188, 214, 216–7.

F0235 Coward, Noel. *Future Indefinite*, Heinemann, London 1954; viii, 338
pp., 22 cm.
TEL: pp. 257–9.

F0236 Coward, Noel, *Future Indefinite*, Doubleday, Garden City, New
York, 1954; 344 pp., 21.5 cm, black cloth.
TEL: pp. 263–5.

F0237 Cowles, Virginia, *Winston Churchill*, Harper, New York 1953; xiv, 378
pp., 21.8 cm, black cloth.
TEL: p. 235.

F0239 Crafford, F.S., *Jan Smuts*, Doubleday, Doran, Garden City, New
York, 1943; xiv, 322 pp., 23.5 cm, brown cloth.
TEL: pp. 181, 229.

F0240 Craster, Sir Edmund, *History of the Bodleian Library*, Clarendon
Press, Oxford 1952.
TEL: pp. 301–3.

F0241 Crawford, Osbert Guy Stenhope, *Said and Done*, Phoenix House,
London 1955; 316 pp., 22.1 cm, green cloth.
TEL: pp. 72, 198.

F0242 Cresswell, Walter D'Arcy, *The Letters of D'Arcy Cresswell*, University
of Canterbury Press, Christchurch, NZ, 1971; 256 pp., 22.3 cm, tan
paper covered boards.
TEL: pp. 47–9.

F0243 Crossman, Richard, *Palestine Mission*, Harper, New York 1947.
TEL: pp. 103, 104.

F0244 Crutchlow, William, *Tale of an Old Soldier*, Hale, London 1937; 288
pp., 19 cm, salmon cloth.
TEL: Chapter 8, pp. 175–89.

F0245 Cummings, Edward Estlin, *The Enormous Room*, Cape, London
1928; 336 pp., 21 cm, purple paper covered boards.
TEL: Dustwrapper, pp. 7–8.

F0246 Cunard, Nancy, *These Were the Hours*, Southern Illinois University Press, Carbondale 1969.
TEL: p.143.

F0247 Cunliffe, J.W., *English Literature in the Twentieth Century*, Macmillan, New York 1934; 8, 341, 3 pp., 22 cm, red cloth boards, brown cloth spine.
TEL: pp.275–80, 'T.E. Lawrence, 1888–'.

F0248 Curtis, Michael, *People and Politics in the Middle East*, Transaction Books, New Brunswick, New Jersey 1971; 6, 330 pp., 20.4 cm, pictorial paper covers.
TEL: pp.170–71.

F0249 Dane, Edmund, *British Campaigns in the Nearer East, 1914–1928*, Hodder & Stoughton, London 1919; xvi, 240 pp., 22.3 cm, blue cloth.
TEL: Vol. 2, p.22.

F0250 Daugherty, Charles Michael, *The Great Archaeologists*, Crowell, New York 1962; 2, xiv, 144 pp., 21.5 cm, light blue cloth.
TEL: p.96.

F0251 Day-Lewis, Cecil, compiler, *Anatomy of Oxford*, Cape, London 1938; 320 pp., 20.5 cm, blue cloth.
TEL: pp.242–3.

F0252 Deacon, Richard, *A History of the British Secret Service*, Taplinger, New York 1969.
TEL: pp.234–5.

F0253 Deardon, Seton, *Burton of Arabia*, New York National Travel Club 1937; 2, 334 pp., 22.5 cm, black cloth.
TEL: pp.86, 320.

F0254 de Chair, Somerset, *The Golden Carpet*, Golden Cockerel, London 1943; 130 pp., 25.7 cm, cream linen, green leather spine (limited to 500 copies).
TEL: pp.7–9.

F0255 de Chair, Somerset, *The Golden Carpet*, Faber and Faber, London 1943; 224 pp., 22.7 cm, yellow linen.
TEL: pp.5, 6, 15, 32, 33, 106, 173, 206.

F0256 de Chair, Somerset, *The Golden Carpet*, Harcourt Brace, New York 1945; xvi, 254 pp., pl., 21 cm, black cloth.
TEL: pp.5, 26, 113, 193, 232.

F0257 De Gaury, Gerald, *Arabia Phoenix*, Harrap, London 1946; 172 pp., 20.2 cm, orange/brown cloth. Preface by Freya Stark.
TEL: p.106.

F0258 De Gaury, Gerald, *Arabian Journey*, Harrap, London 1950; 192 pp., 20.2 cm, tangerine cloth.
TEL: pp.88, 135.

F0259 De Gaury, Gerald, *Rulers of Mecca*, Harrap, London 1951; 321 pp., 22.3 cm, brown cloth.
TEL: p.273.

F0260 De Gaury, Gerald, *Three Kings in Baghdad, 1921–1958*, Hutchinson, London 1961; 232 pp., 21.7 cm, pink cloth.
TEL: pp.16, 18–19, 22, 23, 40, 74, 184, 205.

F0261   De la Bere, Rupert, *A History of the Royal Air Force College,* Cranwell 1934; 64 pp., 19 cm, blue cloth.
TEL: p.55.

F0262   Delderfield, E.P., *Visitors' Guide to the County of Dorset,* Raleigh Press, Exmouth n.d.; 48 pp., 18.5 cm, pictorial paper covers.
TEL: pp.33, 37, 40–41.

F0263   Desmond, Shaw, *Personality and Power,* Rockliff, London 1950; viii, 344 pp., 22.3 cm, green cloth.
TEL: p.103.

F0264   Deuel, Leo, ed., *Treasures of Time,* Souvenir Press, London 1962; 320 pp., 22.2 cm, brown cloth.
TEL: pp.147, 258, 269.

F0265   Devas, Nicolette, *Two Flamboyant Fathers,* W. Morrow, New York 1967; 288 pp., 21.5 cm, patterned paper covered boards, black cloth spine.
TEL: pp.90–91, 159, 276.

F0266   *Dictionary of National Biography 1931–1940,* Oxford University Press, London 1949.
TEL: pp.528–31 Ronald Storrs.

F0267   Dinning, Hector, *Nile to Aleppo,* Macmillan, New York 1920; 288 pp., 25.7 cm, brown linen illus.
TEL: pp.224–32, "Working with Lawrence". Colour portrait facing p.25.

F0268   Dinning, Hector, *Nile to Aleppo,* Allen & Unwin, London 1920; 288 pp., 24.8 cm, brown and green cloth.
TEL: Chapter 12, pp.224–32, "Working with Lawrence". Colour portrait facing p.25.

F0269   Dixon, Alec, *Tinned Soldier,* Cape, London 1941; 4, 7–314 pp., 20.5 cm, light maroon cloth.
TEL: pp.294–309.

F0270   Dixon, C. Aubrey, and Heilbrunn, Otto, *Communist, Guerilla Warfare,* Allen & Unwin, London 1954.
TEL: pp.26, 90, 192.

F0271   Donaldson, Jay Robert, *Zanies,* New Century, Ne Jersey 1982; xxiv, 464 [8] pp.
TEL: pp.216–9.

F0272   Donaldson, Norman and Betty, *How Did They Die?,* Greenwich House, New York 1980; [18], 398 pp., tan cloth.
TEL: pp.218–20.

F0273   Doran, George H., *Chronicles of Barabbas, 1884–1934,* Harcourt Brace, New York 1935; xvi, 416 pp., 22.2 cm, blue cloth.
TEL: pp.294, 395–7..

F0274   Doran, George H., *Chronicles of Barabbas, 1884–1934,* Methuen, London 1935; xvi, 376, 8 pp., 22.3 cm, black cloth.
TEL: pp.184–6, 279.

F0275   *Dorset Year Book 1952–1953.*
TEL: pp.112–7, Llewellyn Pridham, "Lawrence of Arabia, a man of mystery".

F0276 *Dorset Year Book for 1968–1969*, Society of Dorset Men, 1968; 200 pp., 25 cm, pictorial paper cover.
TEL: p.128.

F0277 Doubleday, Frank, *A Few Indiscreet Recollections*, Privately published, December 1927; 57 copies, 19.5 cm.
TEL: pp.77–88, "The Strange Character, Colonel Lawrence".

F0278 Doubleday, Frank Nelson, *The Memoirs of a Publisher*, Garden City, New York 1972; xvi, 304 pp., 21.5 cm, maroon cloth.
TEL: pp.253–63.

F0279 Douglas of Kirtleside, Sholto, 1st Baron, *Combat and Command*, Simon & Schuster, New York 1966; 21.8 cm, 808 pp.
TEL: pp.484–6, 247–8.

F0280 Douie, Charles, *Beyond the Sunset*, Murray, London 1935; 320 pp., 19 cm, black cloth.
TEL: pp.25–6.

F0281 Downey, Farifax D., *Burton*, Scribner's, New York 1931.
TEL: pp.vii, 88.

F0282 Drabble, Margaret, *The Genius of Thomas Hardy*, Knopf, New York 1976.
TEL: pp.38, 52.

F0283 Du Cann, Charles Garfield Lott, *The Loves of George Bernard Shaw*, Barker, London 1963; 288 pp., 22.3 cm, brown cloth.
TEL: pp.172–7, 185, 190, 197.

F0284 Du Cann, Charles Garfield Lott, *The Loves of George Bernard Shaw*, Funk & Wagnalls, New York 1963; 2, xii, 306 pp., 21.5 cm, pink cloth.
TEL: pp.173–9, 192, 200.

F0285 Dudley-Gordon, Tom (pseudonym), *I Seek My Prey in the Waters*, Doubleday Doran, Garden City, New York 1943; xiv, 298 pp., 22 cm, blue cloth.
TEL: p.1+?

F0286 Duff, Douglas V., *Bailing With a Teaspoon*, J. Long, London 1953; 224 pp., 21.8 cm, red cloth.
TEL: pp.87, 99.

F0287 Duffy, James Dennis, *Arabia Literaria*, Univeristy of Toronto Press, Toronto 1964; 4, 1, 398 pp., black cloth.
TEL: pp.257–344, "Thomas Edward Lawrence".

F0288 Dukore, Bernard F., *Bernard Shaw, Playwright*, University of Mississippi Press, Columbia 1973; xiv, 314 pp., 24 cm, tan cloth.
TEL: p.20.

F0289 Dunbar, Janet, *J.M. Barrie, the Man behind the Image*, Houghton Mifflin, Boston 1970; xvii, 414 pp., 23.5 cm, brown cloth.
TEL: p.258.

F0290 Dunbar, Janet, *Mrs. G.B.S.*, Harrap, London 1963; 328 pp., 22.8 cm, grey tweed cloth.
TEL: pp.7, 9, 261–2, 265–99, Chapter 17, "T.E. Lawrence (1922–1925)".

F0291 Dunbar, Janet, *Mrs. G.B.S., a Portrait*, Harper & Row, New York

1963 (1st edition); xiv, 306 pp., 21.8 cm, brown cloth.
TEL: pp.xi, xiii, 231–3, 236–70, Chapter 17, 'T.E. Lawrence (1922–1935)'.

F0292 Dunn, George, *Ten Days Off*, Cape, London 1937.
TEL: pp.287, 55.

F0293 Durrell, Lawrence, *Spirit of Place*, Dutton, 1969.
TEL: pp.16, 133, 138–9, 141.

F0294 Duschnes, Philip C., *Bruce Rogers* (Address of the 25th Annual Meeting of the Brown University Libraries, 25 March 1963), Stinehour Press, Luneburg, Vermont, 1965; 2, 26 pp., 23.3 cm, brown wrappers.
TEL: pp.1, 2, 18.

F0295 Dutton, Ralph, *Wessex, Dorset*, Batsford, London 1950; viii, 128 pp., 21.8 cm, green cloth.
TEL: pp.66, 69.

F0296 E.E.T., Miss (Hardy's parlour maid – Ellen E. Titterington), *The Domestic Life of Thomas Hardy*, Toucan Press, Beaminster, Dorset 1963; 20 pp., 18.7 cm, grey wrappers.
TEL: pp.7, 9, 13, 15, 18.

F0297 Eade, Charles, ed., *Churchill by his Contemporaries*, Hutchinson, London 1954; 528 pp., 23.5 cm, blue cloth.
TEL: pp.274–5, 292, 497.

F0298 Eade, Charles, ed., *Churchill by his Contemporaries*, Reprint Society, London 1955; xvi, 368 pp., 20.3 cm, yellow cloth.
TEL: pp.185, 198, 341.

F0299 Easton, Malcolm, *The Art of Augustus John*, David R. Godine, Boston 1975; viii, 216 pp., 28.6 cm, black linen.
TEL: pp.168–9, 'T.E. Lawrence, 1919. Pencil on Paper'.

F0300 Edmonds, Sir James Edward, *A Short History of World War I*, Oxford University Press, London 1951; 2, xxxiv, 456 pp., 22.3 cm, purple cloth.
TEL: p.376.

F0301 Eickelman, Dale F., *The Middle East, an anthropological approach*, Prentice-Hall, Englewood Cliffs, New Jersey, 1981.
TEL: pp.24, 68.

F0302 Elliott-Bateman, Michael, *The Fourth Dimension of Warfare*, Praeger, New York 1970; xii, 184 pp., 21 cm, red cloth.
TEL: pp.27, 29, 31, 37, 41, 131, 138, 140–41, 148, 160, 166–8, 172, 174.

F0303 Ellis, Harry B., *The Arabs*, World Publishers, Cleveland, Ohio, 1958; 128 pp., 24 cm, yellow cloth.
TEL: p.107.

F0304 Ellis, Harry B., *Heritage of the Desert*, Ronald, New York 1956; 311 pp., maps, 21 cm.
TEL: pp.6, 59.

F0305 Ellis, Peter Berresford, and Williams, Piers, *By Jove, Biggles*, Allen, London 1981; xii, 306 pp., 21.5 red cloth.
TEL: pp.107–11.

F0306 *Encyclopedia Britannica*.
TEL: 1965, 'T.E. Lawrence, Thomas Edward', by Glubb Pasha; 1974

Macropaedia, Vol.10, 'Lawrence, T.E.', by Stanley Weintraub, pp.725–7.

F0307 *Encyclopedia Judaica.*
TEL: 1971, Vol. 9, 'Lawrence, Thomas Edward', by D.Ef., pp.1488–9.

F0308 *Encyclopedia Universalis.*
TEL: Vol. 10, 'T.E. Lawrence. L'auteur d'une épopée moderne', by R. Étiemble, pp.854–5.

F0309 Engel, Claire-Eliane, *Profils anglais, romances de guerre,* Suisse, Baconniers-Neuchatel 1946; 19.6 cm.
TEL: pp.127–145, Le Colonel Lawrence et la culture Française; portrait of Lawrence following p.160.

F0310 Engle, Anita, *The Nili Spies,* Hogarth Press, London 1959; 248 pp., 22.2 cm, brown cloth.
TEL: pp.15, 54, 101, 102, 134, 157, 175, 229–38.

F0311 Entwistle, William J., and Gillett, Eric, *The Literature of England,* Longmans, Green, London 1948 (2nd edition); xli, 310 pp., 19 cm, tan cloth.
TEL: pp.225, 228–9, 273, 292, 271, 272, 291.

F0312 Erskine, Mrs Steuart, *King Faisal of Iraq,* Hutchinson, London 1933; 4, 300 pp., 23.7 cm, maroon cloth.
TEL: pp.40, 50, 51, 52, 53, 56, 57, 59, 61, 71, 77, 80, 83, 84, 87, 92, 99, 146.

F0313 Étiemble, René, *Hygiène des Lettres I – Premières Notions,* Gallimard, Paris 1952.
TEL: pp.239–55 , 'Lawrence d'Arabie'; pp.256–68, 'Un saint en salopette'.

F0314 Étiemble, René, *Hygiène des Lettres III – Savoir et Gout,* N.R.F., Paris 1958.
TEL: pp.174–210, 'Aldington l'Imposteur'; 'Le Matrice', pp.211–28.

F0315 Esin, Emel, *Mecca the blessed; Madinah the radiant,* Crown, New York 1963; 224 pp., oatmeal cloth.
TEL: pp.189–90.

F0316 Evans, Bergen, *Spoor of Spooks,* Knopf, New York 1954.
TEL: p.85.

F0317 Evans, Laurence, *United States Policy and the Partition of Turkey 1914–1924,* Johns Hopkins University Press, Baltimore 1965.
TEL: pp.24–5, 121, 122, 141–2, 148.

F0318 Evans, Tony, and Green, Candida, *English Cottages,* Weidenfeld & Nicolson, London 1982; 160 pp., 19.2 cm, ochre cloth.
TEL: pp.76 (Clouds Hill).

F0319 Evenari, Michael, *The Negev,* Harvard University Press, Cambridge, Mass, 1971; xii, 346 pp., 26 cm, yellow cloth.
TEL: pp.9, 95, 180, 334.

F0320 *Explorers All,* Oxford University Press, London 1942; 48 pp., 19 cm, red paper covers.
TEL: Front cover photo, pp.35–9.

F0321 Eydoux, Henri Paul, *In Search of Lost Worlds,* World Pub., New York

1971; 344 pp., 27 cm, violet cloth.
TEL: pp.75, 100.

F0322 Fabre-Luce, Alfred, *Deuil au Levant,* Librairie Arthème Fayard, Paris 1950; 329 pp., 18.7 cm, pictorial paper covers.
TEL: pp.39ff.

F0323 Fadiman, Clifton, *Any Number Can Play,* World Pub. Co., Cleveland, Ohio 1957; 2, 414 pp., 22 cm, grey cloth.
TEL: p.193.

F0324 Fagon, Brian M. *Ride to Babylon,* Little, Brown, Boston 1979; xx, 300 pp., cream paper-covered boards, brown cloth spine.
TEL: pp.227, 237, 248, 228–31, 233, 236, 247, 250.

F0325 Falls, Cyril, *Armageddon: 1918,* J.B. Lippincott, Philadelphia 1964; xx, 204 pp., 21 cm, black cloth.
TEL: pp.11, 16, 35, 41, 104, 106, 121, 168, 100–102, 107, 108, 109, 120, 123–31, 135, 136–7, 87, 175, 143, 57, 24.

F0326 Falls, Cyril, *Armageddon: 1918,* Weidenfeld & Nicolson, London 1964; 216 pp., 22.2 cm, red cloth.
TEL: pp.23, 120, 121, 125, 127, 128, 129, 130, 141, 149, 151, 156, 157, 158, 189.

F0327 Falls, Cyril, *A Hundred Years of War,* Duckworth, London 1953.
TEL: pp.279–89.

F0328 Farago, Ladislas, *Arabian Antic,* Sheridan House, New York 1938; 21.8 cm.

F0329 Farago, Ladislas, *Palestine at the Cross-Roads,* Putnam, New York 1937; x, 286 pp., 22.2 cm, light green cloth.
TEL: pp.155–7, 160, 209, 244, 252.

F0330 Farago, Ladislas, *Palestine on the Eve,* Putnam, London 1936; x, 286 pp., 22 cm, red cloth.
TEL: pp.155–7, 160, 209, 224, 252, 210, 234, 254, 259, 263.

F0331 Farmer, Bernard J., *Bibliography of the Works of Sir Winston S. Churchill,* [published by the author] London 1958; [1], 1–65 pp., 26.5 cm, brown cloth.
TEL: pp.1, 56.

F0332 Farson, Daniel, *Henry,* Michael Joseph, London 1982; x, 246 pp.
TEL: pp.57–9, 97–101, 102, 195.

F0333 Fedden, Robin, and Thomson, John, *Crusader Castles,* John Murray, London 1950; 129 pp., 21.7 cm, dark green cloth.
TEL: pp.41, 84.

F0334 Fedden, Robin, *English Travellers in the Near East,* British Council and National Book League, London 1958; 44 pp.
TEL: pp.34–8, 'T.E. Lawrence'.

F0335 Fedden, Robin, *The Phoenix Land,* Braziller, New York 1965; xii, 276 pp., 22.2 cm, orange cloth.
TEL: pp.174, 185n.

F0336 Fedden, Robin, *Syria,* Robert Hale, London 1956; xii, 244 pp., 22.2 cm, blue cloth.
TEL: p.153.

F0337 Ffoulkes, Charles John, *Arms and the Tower,* Murray, London 1939;

xii, 248 pp., 22 cm, green cloth.
TEL: pp.29–30, 126, 207.

F0338 Field, Henry, *Arabian Desert Tales*, Synergetic Press, Santa Fe, New Mexico, 1976; viii, 176 pp., 21.5 cm, pictorial paper covers.
TEL: pp.45–9, 'Lawrence of Arabia Draws a Map'.

F0340 *Fifty Mutinies, Rebellions and Revolutions*, Odhams Press, London 1938; 704 pp., 21.7 cm, blue cloth.
TEL: pp.561–71, M.E. Langman, 'The Arab Revolt'.

F0341 Finley, John, *A Pilgrim in Palestine*, Scribner, New York 1919; 251 pp., 21 cm.
TEL: pp.197–9.

F0342 Fisher, William Bayne, *The Middle East*, Methuen, London 1950; 2, xiv, 516 pp., 22.2 cm, green cloth.
TEL: pp.152, 168.

F0343 Fishman, Jack, *My Darling Clementine*, Pan, London 1963; 384 pp., 17.7 cm, pictorial paper covers.
TEL: pp.78–81.

F0344 Fishman, Jack, *My Darling Clementine*, McKay, New York 1963; xvi, 384 pp., 22 cm, black cloth.
TEL: pp.67–9.

F0345 Fishman, Jack, *My Darling Clementine*, Avon Books, New York 1963; 480 pp., 18.2 cm, pictorial papers.
TEL: pp.97–100.

F0346 Fitch, Noel Riley, *Sylvia Beach and the Lost Generation*, Norton, New York 1983.
TEL: p.107.

F0347 Fitzsimons, M.A., *Empire by Treaty*, Notre Dame Press, Notre Dame, Indiana, 1964; xvi, 240 pp.
TEL: pp.17, 22, 25, 27.

F0348 Flecker, James Elroy, *The Letters of J.E. Flecker to Frank Savery*, Beaumont Press, London 1926; 310 copies, 126 pp., 23 cm, pictorial paper covered boards, vellum spine.
TEL: p.33.

F0349 Flecker, James Elroy, *Some Letters from Abroad*, Heinemann, London 1930; xiv, 192 pp., 22.2 cm, black cloth.
TEL: pp.ix, 59, 64–5. Frontispiece is photograph of Flecker taken by Lawrence. Photo of Lawrence opposite p.64.

F0350 Flesch, Rudolf, *How to Write, Speak and Think More Effectively*, Harper, New York 1960.
TEL: pp.204–5.

F0351 Fletcher, Arnold, *Afghanistan, Highway of Conquest*, Cornell University Press, Ithaca, New York, 1965.
TEL: pp.223–4.

F0352 *Folios of New Writing*, Hogarth Press, London 1941; 192 pp., 21.7 cm, violet cloth.
TEL: pp.44–51, Henry Green, 'Apologia'.

F0353 Folk, Edges-Estes, *A Catalogue of the Library of Charles Lee Smith*, Wake Forest College Press, Wake Forest, New Cambden, 1950; xxx,

656 pp., 26.2 cm, maroon cloth.
TEL: pp.91, 352, 353, 390.

F0354 Foot, Sir Hugh, *A Start in Freedom,* Hodder & Stoughton, London 1964; 256 pp., 22.9 cm, grey cloth.
TEL: pp.65, 66, 67, 70, 74, 170.

F0355 Foot, M.R.D., *Resistance,* McGraw-Hill, New York 1977.
TEL: pp.20, 47, 118, 129, 138, 158.

F0356 Forbes, Rosita, *Appointment in the Sun,* Cassell, London 1949; 484 pp., 22.2 cm, red cloth.
TEL: p.14, 53, 54, 18, 55, 237.

F0357 Forbes, Rosita, *Gypsy in the Sun,* Cassell, London 1944; 381, 3 pp., 22.3 cm, red cloth.
TEL: pp.23, 57–8, 63.

F0358 Forster, Edward Morgan, *Abinger Harvest,* Harcourt, Brace, New York 1936; x, 374 pp., 22.3 cm, brown cloth.
TEL: pp.141–7, 'T.E. Lawrence'.

F0359 Forster, Edward Morgan, *Abinger Harvest,* Arnold, London 1936; viii, 352 pp., 22.5 cm, black linen.
TEL: pp.139–44, 'T.E. Lawrence'.

F0360 Forster, Edward Morgan, *Abinger Harvest,* Arnold, London 1961 (reprint of pocket edition); 400 pp., 17 cm, blue-green cloth.
TEL: pp.165–71, 'T.E. Lawrence'.

F0361 Forster, Edward Morgan, *The Eternal Moment,* Sidgwick & Jackson, London 1928; 8, 188 pp., 18.5 cm, maroon cloth, 1500 copies.
TEL: p.5, Dedication 'To T.E. in the absence of anything else'.

F0362 Forster, Edward Morgan, *The Eternal Moment,* Harcourt Brace, New York 1928; 248 pp., 19.5 cm, blue cloth.
TEL: Dedication, p.5.

F0363 Forster, Edward Morgan, *The Life to Come and Other Stories,* Arnold, London 1972; xxi, 240 pp., 22 cm, black cloth.
TEL: p.xii.

F0364 Forster, Edward Morgan, *Two Cheers for Democracy,* Arnold, London 1951; 372 pp., 22.2 cm, blue cloth.
TEL: pp.281, 282, 286, 287, 289, 291; pp.352–5, 'Clouds Hill'.

F0365 Forster, Edward Morgan, *Two Cheers for Democracy,* Harcourt Brace, New York 1951; xvi, 368 pp., 21 cm, blue-grey cloth.
TEL: pp.ix, 239, 263, 265, 267, 274, 279, 280, 282, 284; pp.344–7, 'Clouds Hill'.

F0366 Forster, Edward Morgan, *Two Cheers for Democracy,* Arnold, London 1972; xiv, 410 pp., 22.2 cm, black cloth.
TEL: pp.230, 257, 272, 274, 276, 260, 261, 267–8, 339, 341 'Clouds Hill'.

F0367 Fowles, John, *The Magus,* Dell, New York 1967; 698 pp., 17 × 11 cm, pictorial paper covers.
TEL: p.41.

F0368 Fox, Ralph, *Ralph Fox, a Writer in Arms,* Lawrence & Wishart, London 1937; vii, 254 pp., 19 cm, black cloth.
TEL: pp.88–95, "Lawrence, the twentieth century hero".

F0369 *Foylibra*, Foyles Bookshop, London 1963.
TEL: p.10.
F0370 Frankfurter, Felix, *Felix Frankfurter Reminisces*, Reynal, New York 1960.
TEL: pp.155–6.
F0371 Freedland, Michael, *Peter O'Toole*, St. Martin's, New York 1982; xx, 216 pp., brown cloth.
TEL: Film, pp.47, 70–90, 105, 116, 118, 152, 156, 160, 186, 187, 193, 223, 227, 229; Lawrence, pp.47, 69, 71, 72–9, 93, 85, 90, 94–5, 107, 119, 187.
F0372 Freemantle, Anne, *Loyal Enemy*, Hutchinson, London 1938; 448, 4 pp., 22 cm, maroon cloth.
TEL: pp.35, 36, 37, 39, 47, 53, 55, 61, 134 234, 262, 263, 264, 265, 266, 327.
F0373 Freeth, Zahra, *Explorers of Arabia.*, Allen & Unwin, London 1978; 308 pp., 24 cm, brown cloth.
TEL: pp.223, 267.
F0374 Friends of Dartmouth Library, *Final Report 1959–1960*, Hanover, New Hampshire 1960; 19 pp., 22.5 cm.
TEL: p.1, Portrait of Lawrence by unknown artist given to library by Friends of the Library.
F0375 Froembgen, Hanns, *Kemal Ataturk*, Jarrolds, Norwich 1937; 286 pp., 22.1 cm, grey cloth.
TEL: pp.64, 65, 67, 70, 71, 72.
F0376 Froembgen, Hanns, *Kemal Ataturk*, Hillman-Curl, New York 1937; 288 pp., 24 cm, brown cloth.
TEL: pp.73, 74, 76, 79, 81, 82.
F0377 Fuller, John, *A Reader's Guide to W.H. Auden*, Farrar, Straus & Giroux, New York 1970; 288 pp., 21 cm, brown cloth.
TEL: pp.44, 90, 93, 105, 146, 266.
F0378 Furlong, William B., *GBS/GKC*, Pennsylvania State University Press, University Park 1970.
TEL: pp.7, 176.
F0379 Furst, Herbert, ed. *The Woodcut. An Annual*, Fleuron, London 1927.
TEL: pp.53, Blair Hughes Stanton engraving for *Seven Pillars*.
F0380 Fysh, Hudson, *Qantas Rising*, Angus & Robertson, London 1965 xii, 296 pp., 24.2 cm, blue paper covered boards.
TEL: pp.53–4.
F0381 Gabrieli, Francesco, *The Arab Revival*, Random, New York 1961; 178 pp., 21 cm.
TEL: pp.68–70, 90–91, 129.
F0382 Gabrieli, Francesco, *The Arabs*, Hawthorn, New York 1963; viii, 216 pp., 21 cm, tan cloth.
TEL: p.191.
F0383 Galante, Pierre, *Malraux*, Cowles, New York 1971; xvi, 272 pp., 23.5 cm, violet cloth.
TEL: p.202.
F0384 Garcia Calderon, Ventura, *The White Llama*, Golden Cockerel Press, London 1938; 124 pp., 20.9 cm, orange pictorial wrapper.

TEL: Mention on dustwrapper.

F0385 Gardner, Brian, *Allenby,* Cassell, London 1965; xx, 316 pp., 22 cm, red cloth.
TEL: pp.xiv, xv,1 29, 227, 229, 260, 264, 269–70, 271, ix, 117, 141–2, 143–4, 162, 165, 178, 203, 13, 131, 139–41, 143, 158, 189, 200–11, 260, xvii, xviii, 131–2, 140, 134, 135–7, 138, 151–2, 159, 169, 171, 182, 187–91, 192, 215, 224, 238, 239, 273, 274.

F0386 Gardner, Brian, *Allenby of Arabia,* Coward-McCann, New York 1966; xxxiv, 318 pp., 22 cm, black cloth.
TEL: pp.xiv, xv, 129, 227, 229, 260, 265, 269–70, 271, 16, 117, 141–44, 162, 165, 176, 13, 139–41, 200–211, xvii–xviii, 131–2, 134, 135, 137, 151–2, 158, 159, 169, 171, 182, 187–92, 24, 238, 239, 273–4. Introduction of Lawrence by Lowell Thomas on dustwrapper. Chapter 10, pp.200–211, 'Allenby and Lawrence'.

F0387 Gardner, Brian, *Churchill in Power,* Houghton Mifflin, Boston 1970; xviiii, 350 pp., 21.9 cm, red cloth.
TEL: pp.76, 102, 122.

F0388 Garnett, David, *The Familiar Faces,* Chatto & Windus, London 1962; xvi, 224 pp., 22.3 cm, russet cloth.
TEL: pp.xii, 90, 91, 102, 113, 151, 155, 168, 172, 180, 192.

F0389 Garnett, David, *The Familiar Faces,* Harcourt Brace & World, New York; xvi, 224 pp., 22.5 cm, brown cloth.
TEL: pp.90–91, 102–15, 168–9.

F0390 Garnett, David, *Flowers of the Forest,* Chatto & Windus, London 1955; 12, 252 pp., 22.2 cm, red cloth.
TEL: pp.15, 83, 154.

F0391 Garnett, David, *The Flowers of the Forest,* Harcourt Brace, New York 1956; 14, 256 pp., 21 cm, grey cloth.
TEL: pp.15, 83, 154.

F0392 Garnett, David, *Great Friends,* Macmillan, London 1979; 240 pp., 24.6 cm, brown cloth.
TEL: pp.191–202, 'T.E. Shaw'.

F0393 Gates, Norman Timmuns, *A Checklist of the Letters of Richard Aldington,* Southern Illinois University Press, Carbondale, and Feiffer & Simons, London 1977; xvi, 176 pp., 53.7 cm, blue cloth.
TEL: pp.45+?

F0394 Gellhorn, Eleanor Cowles, *McKay's Guide to the Middle East,* D. McKay, New York 1965; xviii, 238 pp., 21.2 cm, blue cloth.
TEL: p.191.

F0395 Gilbert, Mark, *Isle of Purbeck,* Saint Catherine Press, London 1948; xii, 68 pp., 13.6 cm, pictorial paper covers.
TEL: pp.53, 55.

F0396 Gilbert, Vivian, *The Romance of the Last Crusade,* Appleton, New York 1925; 10, 238 pp., 19.5 cm, blue cloth.
TEL: p.217.

F0397 Gilmer, Walker, *Horace Liveright,* Lewis, New York 1970 xiv, 290 pp., 22 cm, blue cloth.
TEL: pp.36, 99.

F0398 *Girl Television and Film Annual,* Longacre Press, London 1962; 128

pp., 25.5 cm, blue paper covered boards.
TEL: Film, pp.80–85, Jean Westbourne, "Lawrence of Arabia' film.

F0399 Girvan, I. Waveney, *A Bibliography and a Critical Survey of the Works of Henry Williamson*, Alcuin Press, Chipping Campden, Glos. 1931; 56 pp., 22.7 cm, patterned cloth covered boards, brown and white coarse cloth spine. Limited to 428 copies.
TEL: p.33.

F0400 Gittings, Clare, *Brasses and Brass Rubbing*, Blandford Press, London 1970; 104 pp., 22 cm, pictorial paper covered boards.
TEL: p.7.

F0401 Gittings, Robert, *Thomas Hardy's Later Years*, Little, Brown, Boston 1978.
TEL: pp.194, 204, 297.

F0402 Glubb, Sir John Bagot, *Britain and the Arabs*, Hodder & Stoughton, London 1959; 496 pp., 22.7 cm, blue cloth.
TEL: pp.80, 82–3, 86, 88–9, 165, 191, 480.

F0403 Glubb, Sir John Bagot, *The Empire of the Arabs*, Prentice-Hall, Englewood Cliffs, New Jersey, 1965; 384 pp., 23 cm, blue cloth.
TEL: p.241.

F0404 Glubb, Sir John Bagot, *The Great Arab Conquests*, Prentice-Hall, Englewood Cliffs, New Jersey, 1964; 384 pp., 23.5 cm, brown cloth.
TEL: p.61.

F0405 Glubb,Sir John Bagot, *The Great Arab Conquest*, Hodder & Stoughton, London 1963; 384 pp., pictorial paper covered boards.
TEL: p.61.

F0406 Glubb, Sir John Bagot, *A Short History of the Arab Peoples*, Stein & Day, New York 1969; 320 pp., 22.8 cm, blue cloth spine, blue paper covered boards.
TEL: p.273.

F0407 Glubb, Sir John, *A Soldier with the Arabs*, Hodder & Stoughton, London 1957; 448 pp., 22 cm, paper wrappers.
TEL: pp.24, 179, 279.

F0408 Glubb, Sir John Bagot, *A Soldier with the Arabs*, Harper, New York 1957; 458 pp., 21.8 cm, slate cloth, orange cloth spine.
TEL: pp.24, 179, 279.

F0409 Glubb, Sir John Bagot, *The Story of the Arab Legion*, Hodder & Stoughton, London 1948; 372 pp., 23 cm, tangerine cloth.
TEL: pp.7, 59, 187, 198, 324, 347.

F0410 Glubb, Sir John Bagot, *War in the Desert*, Norton, New York 1961; 352 pp., 21.5 cm, brown cloth boards, tan cloth spine.
TEL: p.59.

F0411 Glubb, Pasha, *War in the Desert*, Hodder & Stoughton, London 1960 352 pp., blue cloth.
TEL: p.59.

F0412 Glueck, Nelson, *Rivers in the Desert*, Farrar, Straus & Cudahy, New York 1959; xvi, 304 pp., 23.5 cm, maroon cloth.
TEL: pp.33, 34, 74, 261, 263.

F0413 Glueck, Nelson, *Rivers in the Desert*, Grove Press, New York 1960; 2, xvi, 310 pp., 25.3 cm, pictorial paper covers.

TEL: pp.33, 34, 74, 261, 263.

F0414 Goertzel, Victor, *Cradles of Eminence*, Little, Brown, Boston 1962.
TEL: pp.217, 218, 328.

F0415 Golden Cockerel Press, *Autumn Books from the Workshop of the Golden Cockerel Press*, GCP, London 1939; 36 pp., 18.3 cm.
TEL: p.3, announcement of *Secret Despatches from Arabia* (A226).

F0416 Golden Cockerel Press, *Chanticleer, a bibliography of the Golden Cockerel Press, 1921–1936*, Golden Cockerel Press, London 1936; 2, 48, 2 pp., 26.2 cm, orange patterned cloth boards, green morocco spine (one of 300 copies).
TEL: p.48.

F0417 *Golden Cockerel Press News*, GCP, London 1940; 12 unnumbered pages, 25 cm, orange paper covers.
TEL: Back cover, ad for *Men In Print*, (A229).

F0418 Golden Cockerel Press, *Some News from the Golden Cockerel Press*, GCP, London 1936; 8 pp., 9.5 cm, unbound.
TEL: pp.4–5, announcing a delay in the publication of, *Crusader Castles*, Vol. 1, and the publication of Vol. 2; A188–9).

F0419 Golding, Harry, ed., *The Wonder Book of Daring Deeds*, Ward Lock, London 1937; 256 pp., 25 cm, pictorial paper covered boards, red and green cloth spine, illus.
TEL: pp.27–36, "Lawrence of Arabia".

F0421 Goldschmidt, Arthur, *A Concise History of the Middle East*, Westview Press, Boulder, Colorado, 1979.
TEL: pp.191, 192, 193, 194.

F0422 Goodman, Susan. *Gertrude Bell*, Berg, Leamington Spa 1985; vi, 122, 20.5 cm, blue cloth.
TEL: pp.72, 73, 74, 77, 81, 93, 95, 96, 97, 105.

F0423 Gordon, John William Jr., *Special Forces For Desert Warfare*, University Microfilms, Ann Arbor 1985; [8], xiii, 302 pp., 20.7 cm,, black paper covers.
TEL: Chapter II, "Special Forces in the Desert: The Lawrence Legend and the Light Car Patrols", pp.34–73.

F0424 Grant, Christina Phelps, *The Syrian Desert*, Macmillan, New York 1938; xvi, 412 pp., 24.2 cm, brown cloth.
TEL: pp.3, 30, 118, 119, 301, 146n.

F0425 Graves, Philip Perceval, *The Life of Sir Percy Cox*, Hutchinson, London 1941; 352 pp., 23.8 cm, black cloth.
TEL: pp.19, 200–203, 219, 245, 259, 278, 280, 281, 283, 284, 340.

F0426 Graves, Philip. P., *Palestine: The Land of Three Faiths*, Doran, 1924; Introduction by D.G.Hogarth.
TEL: p.112, plate facing p.220.

F0427 Graves, Philip, P.,*Palestine: The Land of Three Faiths*, Cape, London 1923; 286 pp., 22.5 cm, blue cloth.

F0428 Graves, Robert, *Claudius the God*, Smith & Haas, New York 1935; 584 pp., 21.8 cm, black cloth.
TEL: p.6.

F0429 Graves, Robert, *The Crowning Privilege*, Cassell, London 1955.
TEL: pp.121–5.

F0430   Graves, Robert, *Difficult Questions, Easy Answers*, Cassell, London 1972; viii, 216 pp., 22 cm, brown cloth.
TEL: pp.17, 167–8.

F0431   Graves, Robert, *Good-bye to All That*, Cape, London 1929; 448 pp., 20.6 cm, deep pink cloth, 1st unexpurgated issue.
TEL: pp.371–3, 439, Sassoon poem on pp.342–3.

F0432   Graves, Robert, *Good-bye to All That*, Cape, London 1929 (2nd impression); 448 pp., pp.341–3 blank, 20 cm, orange linen.
TEL: pp.371–3, 439.

F0433   Graves, Robert, *Good-bye to All That*, Cape & Smith, New York 1929; x, 430 pp., 22.2 cm, maroon cloth.
TEL: pp.357–64, 371.

F0434   Graves, Robert, *Good-bye to All That*, Doubleday & Co., Garden City, New York, 1957; 10, 350 pp., 18.2 cm, pictorial paper covers.
TEL: pp.297–309, 310, 322, 323–4, 325, 338.

F0435   Graves, Robert, *Good-bye to All That*, Cassell, London 1961 (3rd rev. ed.); viii, 308 pp., 22.3 cm, black cloth.
TEL: pp.263–75.

F0436   Graves, Robert *I, Claudius*, Smith & Haas, New York 1934; 496 pp., 22 cm, blue cloth.
TEL: p.9, dedication "Aircraftsman T.E. Shaw".

F0437   Graves, Robert, *I, Claudius*, Modern Library, New York 1937; x, 428, 10 pp., 18.4 cm, brown cloth.
TEL: pp.v, ix.

F0438   Graves, Robert, and Hodge, Alan, *The Long Week-end*, W.W. Norton, New York 1963; 2, 478 pp., 19.7 cm, pictorial paper covers.
TEL: pp.x, 70, 71, 84, 135, 209, 217–9.

F0439   Graves, Robert, *My Head! My Head!*, Martin Secker, London 1928; 141 pp., green linen.
TEL: Dedication: 'To T.E. Lawrence'.

F0440   Graves, Robert, *On English Poetry*, Heinemann, London 1922; 152 pp., 20.8 cm, patterned paper covered boards.
TEL: Dedication: "To T.E. Lawrence of Arabia and All Souls College, Oxford,...".

F0441   Graves, Robert, *The Pier-Glass*, M. Secker, London 1921; 64 pp., 19.5 cm, patterned paper covered boards.
TEL: p.13, "The Pier-Glass (to T.E. Lawrence, who helped me with it)".

F0442   Graves, Robert, *The Pier-Glass*, Knopf, New York 1921; 64 pp., 16.1 cm, orange paper covered boards (another issue: green cloth).
TEL: Dedication: "The Pier-Glass. (To T.E. Lawrence, who helped me with it)", pp.14–6.

F0443   Graves, Sir Robert Windham, *Storm Centres of the Near East*, Hutchinson, London 1933; 4, 7–388 pp., 23.7 cm, maroon cloth.
TEL: pp.299, 310 *et seq.*

F0444   Great Britain, Imperial War Museum, *Handbook*, HMSO, London 1967; 56 pp., 21.4 cm, red paper covers.
TEL: p.35.

F0445 Great Britain, Imperial War Museum, *James McBey, 1883–1959, Exhibition Catalogue,* Graphis Press, London 1977; 16 pp., 20 cm, pictorial wrappers.
TEL: pp.5, 8.

F0446 Great Britain, Imperial War Museum, *19th Report of the Director General,* HMSO, London 1937; 58 pp., 32.5 cm.
TEL: pp.12, 14, 16, 25, 27, 31, 46–8.

F0447 Great Britain, Imperial War Museum, *A Short Guide to the Imperial War Museum,* HMSO, London 1956 (2nd ed.); 54 unnumbered pages, 18.2 cm, grey paper wrappers.
TEL: "Lawrence of Arabia", section 58.

F0448 *Great Contemporaries,* Cassell, London 1935; 464 pp., 22.3 cm, green cloth.
TEL: pp.213–29, "Lawrence of Arabia, the (almost) free man", by B.H. Liddell Hart.

F0449 *Great Soviet Encyclopedia,* Macmillan.
TEL: Vol. 15, p.97.

F0450 Gregory, Lady Augusta (Persse), *Lady Gregory's Journals, 1916–1930,* Putnam, London 1946; 344 pp., 21 cm, blue cloth.
TEL: pp.212–21.

F0451 Gregory, Maundy, *Honours for Sale,* Richards Press, London 1954; 244 pp., 21.5 cm, red cloth.
TEL: pp.123–4.

F0452 Grierson, Edward, *Death of the Imperial Dream,* Doubleday, Garden City, New York, 1972; xii, 348 pp., 21.5 cm, deep red cloth.
TEL: pp.180, 186.

F0453 Griggs, John, *Nancy Astor,* Sidgwick & Jackson, London 1980; 192 pp.
TEL: pp.113, 117.

F0454 Guarmani, Carlo, *Northern Najd,* Argonaut Press, London 1938; xliv, 136 pp., 26.3 cm, brown buckram, white cloth spine, limited to 475 copies.
TEL: pp.xxv, xxvii, 78n.

F0455 Guedalla, Philip M., *Mr. Churchill,* Hodder & Stoughton, London 1941; 348 pp., 19.2 cm, green cloth.
TEL: pp.218–9.

F0456 Guedalla, Phillip M. *Mr. Churchill,* Reynal & Hitchcock, 1942.
TEL: pp.216–7.

F0457 Guinn, Paul, *British Strategy and Politics, 1914–1918,* Clarendon Press, Oxford 1965; xvi, 360 pp., 22.2 cm, blue cloth.
TEL: pp.276, 317.

F0458 Gullett, Henry Somer, *Australian Imperial Force in Sinai and Palestine, 1914–1918,* Angus & Robertson, Sydney 1923; xvi, 846 pp., 22.1 cm, dark maroon cloth.
TEL: pp.382, 205, 381, 383, 686–7, 723, 738, 739, 743, 763, 769, 772.

F0459 Gunther, John, *Inside Asia,* Harper & Bros, New York 1939; xii, 604 pp., 22 cm, black cloth (another, oatmeal cloth).
TEL: pp.523, 536, 543, 544, 574.

F0460 Gunther, John, *Inside Asia*, Hamish Hamilton, London 1939; 660 pp., 22.5 cm, brown cloth.
TEL: pp.572, 585, 593, 594, 625.

F0461 Gurney, O.R., *The Hittites*, Penguin, Baltimore 1962; xvi, 240 pp., 18 cm, pictorial paper covers.
TEL: p.8.

F0462 Haddad, George, *Fifty Years of Modern Syria and Lebanon*, Dar-al-Hayat, Beirut 1950; vi, 264 pp., 23.3 cm, tan paper covers.
TEL: pp.54, 59, 60.

F0463 Haffenden, John, ed., *W.H. Auden*, Routledge & Kegan Paul, London 1983.
TEL: pp.8, 19, 189, 212, 226, 234.

F0464 Hagedorn, Hermann, *The Book of Courage*, Winston, Chicago 1929; ii–xv, 412 pp., 23.7 cm, blue cloth with pictorial labels.
TEL: pp.343–57, "Lawrence of Arabia".

F0465 Halifax, Edward Frederick Lindley Wood (3rd Viscount), *Speeches on Foreign Policy*, Oxford University Press, London 1940; 2, x, 268 pp., 22 cm, blue linen.
TEL: pp.27–32, "Lawrence of Arabia", address delivered 29 January 1936 at the unveiling of a memorial tablet to Lawrence.

F0466 Hall, Melvin, *Journey to the End of an Era*, Scribner, New York 1947; x, 438 pp., 23.4 cm, blue cloth variant binding.
TEL: pp.317, 319–21.

F0467 Hall, Melvin, *Journey to the End of an Era*, Werner Laurie, London 1948; 8, 46- pp., 22.1 cm, blue green cloth.
TEL: pp.336, 339, 340.

F0468 Hall, William H., *The Near East*, Interchurch Press, New York 1920; x, 230 pp., 18.7 cm, brown paper covers.
TEL: p.16.

F0469 Halliburton, Richard, *Seven League Boots*, Bobbs-Merrill, Indianapolis 1935; 420 pp., 24 cm, blue cloth.
TEL: p.366.

F0470 Hamilton, Alastair, *The Appeal of Facism*, Avon, New York 1973; 352 pp., 17.8 cm, pictorial paper covers.
TEL: p.302n.

F0471 Hammerton, Sir John Alexander, *Other Things Than War*, Macdonald, London 1943; 204 pp., 22.2 cm, yellow cloth.
TEL: pp.156–7.

F0472 Hamnett, Nina, *Laughing Torso*, Constable, London 1932; 22.5 cm, x, 328 pp., limited to 92 copies.
TEL: p.119.

F0473 Hancock, Percy Stuart Peache, *The Archaeology of the Holy Land*, Fisher Unwin, London 1916; 384 pp., 22.5 cm, blue cloth.
TEL: pp.19, 113, 114, 145.

F0475 Hansen, Thorkild, *Arabia Felix*, Harper & Row, New York 1964; 384 pp., 24.3 cm, blue cloth.
TEL: p.328.

F0476 Harding, G. Lankester, *The Antiquities of Jordan*, Praeger, New York

1967; 216 pp., 22.3 cm, black cloth.
TEL: pp.52, 113, 145, 156, 164.

F0477 Hardinge, Helen, *The Path of Kings*, Blandford Press, London 1953; 224 pp., 20.8 cm, brown cloth.
TEL: p.35.

F0478 Hardwick, Michael, *The Bernard Shaw Companion*, Murray, London 1973; xvi, 196 pp.,20.5 cm, grey paper covered boards.
TEL: p.191.

F0479 Hardwick, Michael and Mollie, *Writers' Houses*, Phoenix House, London 1968; x, 102 pp., 26 cm, brown cloth.
TEL: pp.52–6, "Clouds Hill, Wool, Dorset. T.E. Lawrence 1923–1935".

F0480 Hardy, Florence Emily, *The Later Years of Thomas Hardy, 1892 -1928*, Macmillan, New York 1930; xii, 292 pp., 24.5 cm, green cloth.
TEL: pp.236, 239, 249–50.

F0481 Hardy, Florence Emily, *The Life of Thomas Hardy, 1840–1928*, Macmillan, London 1962; xiv, 470 pp., 23.2 cm, green cloth.
TEL: pp.424, 426, 434.

F0482 Hardy, Thomas, *Life and Work of Thomas Hardy*, University of Georgia Press, Athens, Georgia, 1985.
TEL: pp.457, 459, 468.

F0483 Harriman, Florence Gaffray (Hurst), *From Pinafores to Politics*, Holt, New York 1923; 8, 360 pp., 24 cm, green cloth.
TEL: pp.305–7.

F0484 Harrop, Dorothy A., *A History of Gregynog Press*, Private Libraries Association, London 1980; 282 pp., 24 cm.
TEL: pp.36, 52, 74, 76.

F0485 Hart-Davis, Rupert, *Hugh Walpole*, Macmillan, London 1952; xiv, 501 pp., 22.4 cm, green cloth.
TEL: pp.195, 278, 279.

F0486 Harvard University, Houghton Library, *The Houghton Library 1942–1967*, Harvard College Library. Cambridge 1967; xvi, 256 pp., 37 cm, black cloth.
TEL: pp.80–81, "T.E. Lawrence".

F0487 Hasluck, Eugene Lewis, *Foreign Affairs*, Basis Books, London 1940; 2, xvii, 356 pp., 19.5 cm, pictorial paper covered boards.
TEL: p.225.

F0488 Hassall, Christopher, *Edward Marsh*, Longmans, London 1959; xvi, 732 pp., 23 cm, blue cloth.
TEL: pp.456, 459, 476, 484, 485, 499, 530, 539, 544–5, 549–50, 563, 565.

F0489 Hassall, Christopher, *A Biography of Edward Marsh*, Harcourt Brace, New York 1959; xvi, 736 pp., 22.2 cm, blue cloth.
TEL: pp. 456, 459, 476, 484, 485, 499, 530, 539, 544–5, 563, 565.

F0490 Hatton, Sydney Frank, *The Yarn of the Yeoman*, Hutchinson, London 1930; 284 pp., 22.5 cm, brown cloth.

F0491 *Have You Read 100 Great Books?*, Jasper Lee Co., New York 1950; 144 pp., 27.4 cm, grey cloth.
TEL: pp.35, 54, 57, 82.

F0492 Hawkes, Jacquetta, *The World of the Past*, Knopf, New York 1963; 2 volumes boxed, 24.5 cm, cream cloth boards, blue buckram spine. TEL: Vol. 1, pp.117–8; Vol. 2, pp.175–6, 201.

F0493 Hazard, Harry W., *The Arabian Peninsula*, Doubleday, Garden City, New York, 1959; 64 pp., 21 cm, pictorial paper covers. TEL: p.19.

F0494 Heer, Friedrich, *The Intellectual History of Europe*, World, Cleveland 1966. TEL: p.323.

F0495 Heir-Davies, Harry, *Autobiography of Captain Harry Hier-Davies of London*, n.p., n.d.; [10], iv, 179, [3] pp., red cloth spine, grey paper boards. TEL: pp.106–14.

F0496 Heliburn, Carolyn G., *The Garnett Family*, Allen & Unwin, London 1961; 216 pp., 22.3 cm, red cloth. TEL: pp.63, 140–42.

F0497 Heliburn, Carolyn G. *The Garnett Family*, Macmillan, New York 1961; 216 pp., 22.3 cm, maroon cloth. TEL: pp.63, 140–42.

F0498 Henderson, Archibald, *George Bernard Shaw*, Appleton Century, 1956. TEL: p.174.

F0499 Herwig, Holger H., and Heyman, Neil M., *Biographical Dictionary of World War I*, Greenwood, Westport 198?. TEL: pp.221–2.

F0500 Higgins, Trumbull, *Winston Churchill and the Dardanelles*, Macmillan, New York 1963; xii, 308 pp., 21.8 cm, black cloth spine, red cloth covered boards. TEL: pp.61, 203.

F0501 Highet, Gilbert, *The Classical Tradition*, Oxford University Press, 1949. TEL: pp.488–90.

F0502 Hirsch, Foster, *The Hollywood Epic*, Tantivy Press, South Brunswick 1978. TEL: pp.37, 40, 106–8, 113.

F0503 Hirschorn, Clive, *The Warner Bros. Story*, Crown, New York 1979. TEL: pp.344–5, 354.

F0504 Hitti, Philip K., *History of Syria*, Macmillan, New York 1951; xxvi, 780 pp., 22.5 cm, green cloth. TEL: pp.610, 699.

F0505 Hitti, Philip K., *History of the Arabs*, Macmillan, London 1951; xxiv, 824 pp., 22.4 cm, maroon cloth. TEL: pp.7, 20.

F0506 Hitti, Philip K., *Lebanon in History*, Macmillan, London 1957; xx, 548 pp., 22.7 cm, green cloth. TEL: pp.486.

F0507 Hitti, Philip K., *The Near East in History*, Van Nostrand, Princeton, New Jersey, 1961; xviii, 574 pp., 23.5 cm, tan cloth boards, green spine.

TEL: pp.400, 464, 505.

F0508 Hochhuth, Rolf, *Soldiers,,* Grove Press, New York 1968; 256 pp., 17.8 cm, pictorial paper covers.
TEL: pp.100–101, 179.

F0509 Hodgson, Geraldine, *The Life of James Elroy Flecker,* Blackwell, Oxford 1925; 288 pp., 22.5 cm, blue linen.
TEL: p.176.

F0510 Hoffman, Hester R., *Bookman's Manual,* R.R. Bowker, New York 1958 (8th rev. ed.); xvi, 992 pp., 23.5 cm, brown cloth.
TEL: pp.517, 579.

F0511 Hogarth, David George, *Hittite Problems and the Excavation of Carchemish,* British Academy and Oxford University Press, London 1912; 16 pp., 25 cm, grey wrappers.
TEL: p.10.

F0512 Hogarth, David George, *Life of Charles M. Doughty,* Oxford University Press, London 1928; x, 216 pp., 23.8 cm, green buckram.
TEL: pp.89, 92, 132, 137, 174, 185, 196–8, 200, 204.

F0513 Hogarth, David George, *The Life of Charles M. Doughty,* Oxford University Press, London 1928; xii, 216 pp., fold map. 27 cm, green buckram.
TEL: pp.89, 92, 132, 137, 174, 185, 196–8, 200, 204.

F0514 Hogarth, David George, *The Life of Charles M. Doughty,* Doubleday, Doran, Garden City, New York 1929; xii, 216 pp., 26.7 cm, brown cloth.
TEL: pp.89, 92, 132, 137, 174, 185, 196–8, 200, 204.

F0516 Holden, David, *Farewell to Arabia,* Walker, New York 1966.
TEL: pp.11, 47, 83, 128.

F0517 Holden, David, and Johns, Richard, *The House of Saud,* Holt Rinehart & Winston, New York 1981.
TEL: pp.53, 55, 60–61, 65, 72–3, 116–7.

F0518 Hole, Edwyn, *Syrian Harvest,* Hale, London 1956; 224 pp., 22.2 cm, blue cloth.
TEL: pp.49, 50.

F0519 Holmboe, Knud, *Desert Encounter,* Putnam, New York 1937; xviii, 268 pp., 22 cm, red orange cloth.
TEL: p.vii.

F0520 Holmes, Oliver Wendell, *The Holmes–Einstein Letters,* St. Martin, New York 1964.
TEL: pp.267, 269.

F0521 Holmes, Oliver Wendell, *The Holmes–Laski Letters,* Harvard University Press, 1953.
TEL: pp.943, 1056.

F0522 Holroyd, Michael, *Augustus John,* Heinemann, London 1975; Vol. 2, xviii, 270 pp., 24 cm, brown cloth.
TEL: pp.40, 76, 86, 96, 101, 125, 137, 179.

F0523 Holroyd, Michael, *Lytton Strachey,* Holt Rinehart & Winston, New York 1968.
TEL: p.484.

F0524 Homerus, *The Odyssey,* New American Library, New York 1963; 304 pp., 18 cm, pictorial paper.
TEL: p.iv.

F0525 Hope, Stanton, *Arabian Adventurer,* Hale, London 1951; 336 pp., 22.1 cm, blue cloth.
TEL: pp.12, 27, 281, 282.

F0526 Hopkinson, Arthur Wells, *Pastor's Progress,* Joseph, London 1943; 224 pp., 22.3 cm, dark red.
TEL: pp.16ff.

F0526a Hopkinson, Arthur W., *Pastor's Progress,* Faith Press, London 1958 (revised and enlarged edition); 240 pp., 22.5 cm, green cloth.
TEL: pp.16ff.

F0527 Horne, Alistair, *A Savage War of Peace,* Viking, New York 1977.
TEL: pp.18, 89.

F0528 Hoskins, Halford L., *The Middle East,* Macmillan, New York 1956; viii, 312 pp., 21.3 cm, black cloth.
TEL: pp.100, 120.

F0529 Hottinger, Arnold, *The Arabs,* University of California Press, Berkeley 1963; 344 pp., 25 cm, brown cloth.
TEL: pp.214, 215–6, 220.

F0530 House, Edward Mandell, ed., *What Really Happened at Paris,* Scribner, New York 1921; xvi, 528 pp., 23.3 cm, black cloth.
TEL: pp.184, 185, 432.

F0531 Howard, Harry N., *The King-Crane Commission,* Khayats, Beirut 1963; 2, xvi, 37 pp., 22.4 cm, green cloth.
TEL: pp.3, 10, 35, 36, 43, 71, 92, 266.

F0532 Howard, Leslie Ruth, *A Quite Remarkable Father,* Harcourt Brace, New York 1959; x, 308 pp., 21 cm, black cloth.
TEL: pp.161–2, 244.

F0533 Howard, Michael S., *Jonathan Cape, Publisher,* Cape, London 1971; 352 pp., 24 cm, brown buckram.
TEL: pp.50, 81–96, 109, 143–5, 148–9, 151–8, 168, 213–4, 269.

F0534 Howard, Philip, *Weasel Words,* Oxford University Press, New York 1979.
TEL: p.44.

F0535 Howarth, David, *The Desert King,* Collins, London 1964; 256 pp., 22.5 cm, brown cloth.
TEL: pp.73, 78, 80, 87, 94, 95, 97, 99, 100, 102, 104, 106, 108, 133, 147, 174.

F0536 Howarth, David, *The Desert King,* McGraw-Hill, New York 1964; 312 pp., 22 cm, rough tan cloth-covered boards, black cloth spine, simulated leather.
TEL: pp.1–3, 87, 92, 95, 106–18, 119, 124, 126–7, 136, 152, 193.

F0537 Howe, Irving, *Israel, the Arabs and the Middle East,* Bantam, New York 1972; viii, 440 pp., 17.7 cm, pictorial paper covers.
TEL: pp.143n, 146–7, 228n.

F0538 Howe, Irving, *A World More Attractive,* Horizon Press, New York 1963; xli, 308 pp., 22 cm, orange cloth boards, brown cloth.
TEL: pp.1–39, "T.E. Lawrence: the problem of heroism".

F0539 Howe, Lionel, *The Churches of Wareham, Dorset,* British Publishing Co., Gloucs. 1953; 32 pp., 19.1 cm, blue paper covers, illus.
TEL: pp.24–5.

F0540 Howe, Quincy, *A World History of Our Times,* Simon & Schuster, 1949.
TEL: Vol. 1, pp.569, 604.

F0541 Howells, Roy, *Churchill's Last Years,* McKay, New York 1966.
TEL: pp.66–7.

F0542 Humes, James C., *Churchill,* Stein & Day, New York 1980.
TEL: pp.142, 266.

F0543 Hussein, King of Jordan, *Uneasy Lies the Head,* Heinemann, London 1962; xii, 236 pp., 22 cm, red cloth.
TEL: pp.73, 163, 213.

F0544 Huxley, Julian, *From an Antique Land,* Crown, New York 1955 (2nd imp.); 312 pp., 22.5 cm, blue cloth.
TEL: pp.82, 119, 140, 182, 309.

F0545 Huxley, Julian, *From an Antique Land,* Harper & Row, New York 1966; 14, 8–336 pp., 22.5 cm, blue cloth.
TEL: pp.82, 119, 140, 182, 309.

F0546 Hynes, Samuel, *The Auden Generation,* Bodley Head, London 1976; 432 pp., 21.4 cm, tan cloth.
TEL: pp.190–92, 238, 240.

F0547 *In Memory of Dorothy Walker, 2 April 1878–1920,* n.p., September 1963; privately printed 1963, 33 pp.
TEL: pp.20, 21, 28, 29.

F0548 Inchbald, Geoffrey, *Imperial Camel Corps,* Johnson, London 1970; xviii, 166 pp., 22.2 cm, deep maroon cloth.
TEL: pp.ix, 85, 105, 112, 129, 142.

F0549 Ingrams, Doreen, compiler, *Palestine Papers, 1917–1922,* Braziller, New York 1972; xii, 198 pp., 21.5 cm, red cloth.
TEL: pp.48, 68, 127.

F0550 Ingrams, Doreen, compiler and annotater, *Palestine Papers, 1917–1922,* J. Murray, London 1972; xii, 198 pp., 22.2 cm, red paper covered boards.
TEL: pp.48, 68, 127.

F0551 Ingrams, Harold, *Arabia and the Isles,* Praeger, New York 1966; x, 400 pp., 22.1 cm, brown cloth.
TEL: pp.3, 4, 22n, 34, 38, 47–52, 57–8, 61, 64, 65, 74, 93.

F0552 Ingrams, Harold, *Arabia and the Isles,* John Murray, London 1943; tan cloth 23.5 cm.

F0553 Isherwood, Christopher, *Christopher and His Kind,* Farrar Straus, & Giroux, New York 1977.
TEL: pp.106, 242, 258.

F0554 Isherwood, Christopher, *Exhumations,* Methuen, London 1966; 12, 256 pp., 22.3 cm, blue cloth (another copy grey cloth).
TEL: pp.22–4, "T.E. Lawrence by his friends, edited by A.W. Lawrence".

F0555 Isherwood, Christopher, *Exhumations,* Simon & Schuster, New York

1966; xii, 254 pp., 22 cm, blue cloth.
TEL: pp.22–4.

F0556 Ishmael, Tareq Y., *Governments and Politics of the Contemporary Middle East*, Parsey?, 1970.
TEL: pp.285, 286, 386.

F0557 Izzeddin, Nejla, *The Arab World*, Henry Regnery, Chicago 1963; xvi, 416 pp., 26 cm, brown cloth.
TEL: pp.97, 104, 206, 353–4.

F0558 Jablonski, Edward, *The Great War*, Whitman Pub. Co., Racine, Wisconsin, 1965; 216 pp., 19.7 cm, pictorial paper covered boards.
TEL: pp.43–65, "El Aurens, Thomas Edward Lawrence".

F0559 Jackson, Esther, *Art of the Anglo-Saxon Age*, N.H. and R.R. Smith, Peterborough 1964; xvi, 176 pp., 24.2 cm, green cloth.
TEL: pp.154.

F0560 Jarche, James, *People I Have Shot*, Methuen, London 1934; xvi, 240 pp., 19 cm, orange cloth.
TEL: pp.226–9, photo facing p.228.

F0561 Jarvis, Claude Scudamore, *Arab Command*, Hutchinson, London 1942; 2, 158 pp., 23.3 cm, blue cloth.
TEL: pp.78–87, "Lawrence's Return to Trans Jordan", pp.9, 24, 26, 29–36, 39–40, 42–3, 45–54, 78, 80–86, 93, 95, 134, 151, 153.

F0562 Jarvis, Claude Scudamore, *Desert and Delta*, Murray, London 1938; viii, 320 pp., 2.2 cm, yellow cloth.
TEL: pp.33, 44, 186.

F0563 Jarvis, Claude Scudamore, *Half a Life*, Murray, London 1943 (1st ed.); viii, 216 pp., 22.2 cm, green cloth.
TEL: pp.93.

F0564 Jarvis, Claude Scudamore, *Three Deserts*, Murray, London 1936 (1st ed.); x, 314 pp., 22.3 cm, green cloth.
TEL: pp.129, 130, 132, 164, 295–303.

F0565 Jarvis, Claude Scudamore, *Three Deserts*, Dutton, New York 1937; x, 316 pp., 22.3 cm, brown cloth.
TEL: pp.129, 130, 132, 164, 295–303.

F0566 Jefferson, George, *Edward Garnett*, Cape, London 1982; x, 350 pp.
TEL: pp.197–9, 200–201, 325n.

F0568 *Jesus College Record, 1966*, Oxford, 1967; 48 pp., 23.5 cm, grey paper wrappers.
TEL: p.29.

F0569 John, Augustus Edwin, *Chiaroscuro*, Cape, London 1952; 288 pp., 23.5 cm, red cloth.
TEL: pp.77, 153, 238, 239, 244–7.

F0570 John, Augustus Edwin, *The Drawings of Augustus John*, Borden Publishing Co., Alhambra, California, 1967; 48 pp., 30 cm, pictorial paper covers stapled to sheets.
TEL: p.26.

F0571 John, Evan, *Time in the East*, Heinemann, London 1946; xvi, 230 pp., 22 cm, dark brown cloth.
TEL: pp.xiii, 12, 50, 125.

F0572 John, Robert and Hadawi, Sami, *The Palestine Diary,* New World Press, New York; 2 volumes, 4, xiii–xvi, 428 pp., 24.7 cm, maroon cloth, simulated leather.
TEL: pp.40, 41f, 44–5f, 46, 47, 50, 57, 93, 94, 96, 101, 102, 113, 126, 131, 151, 166, 168, 169.

F0573 Johnson, Foster Macy, Harry, Charles, and Hornby, St.John, *English Gentlemen,* Bayberry Hill Press, Meriden, Conn., 1973; 75 copies, 4, 40 pp., 26.8 cm, marbled boards, red cloth spine.
TEL: pp.15–18.

F0574 Jones, Thomas, *A Diary with Letters, 1931–1950,* Oxford University Press, London 1954; 2, xlvi, 584 pp., 22.5 cm, dark brown cloth.
TEL: pp.1, 67, 143, 148, 149n, 173–4, 196, 519–20.

F0575 Jones, Thomas, *Lloyd George,* Oxford University Press, London 1951; xii, 332 pp., 22.5 cm, green linen.
TEL: pp.115, 154.

F0576 Joseph, Bernard, *British Rule in Palestine,* Public Affairs Press, Washington DC 1949; viii, 280 pp., 23.5 cm, blue cloth.
TEL: pp.9, 19, 27, 63, 74, 107, 123, 258.

F0577 Juterczenka, Manfred von, *Nahost am Mikrofon,* Schwaan, Düsseldorf 1970.
TEL: pp.12–14, "Erinnerungen an Lawrence von Arabien".

F0578 Kahn, David, *The Codebreakers,* Macmillan, New York 1970 (6th printing); 2, xviii, 1164 pp., 24.5 cm, cardovan cloth boards, blue cloth spine.
TEL: p.312.

F0579 Kamm, Josephine, *Daughter of the Desert,* Bodley Head, London 1956; 192 pp., 20.5 cm, brown paper covered boards.
TEL: pp.77, 119, 151.

F0580 Katz, Samuel, *Battleground,* Bantam, New York 1973; xiv, 274 pp., 18 cm, pictorial paper covers.
TEL: pp.50, 51, 55, 68, 224.

F0581 Kavaler, Lucy, *The Astors,* Dodd Mead, New York 1966.
TEL: p.220.

F0582 Kearsey, A., *A Summary of the Strategy and Tactics of the Egypt and Palestine Campaign with Details of the 1917–1918 Operations Illustrating the Principles of War,* Gale & Polden, Aldershot n.d.; 8, 104 pp., 12 field maps, 21.5 cm, brown paper.
TEL: pp.9, 93.

F0583 Kedourie, Elie, *England and the Middle East,* Bowes & Bowes, London 1956; viii, 9–236 pp., 22.1 cm, red cloth.
TEL: pp.89, 94–9, 100–103, 118, 119, 120, 125–7, 135–6, 139, 178–9, 180, 193, 198.

F0584 Keegan, John and Darracott, Joseph, *The Nature of War,* Holt Rinehart, New York 1981.
TEL: p.72.

F0585 Keith, Agnes Newton, *Children of Allah,* Michael Joseph, London 1966.
TEL: p.121.

F0586 Kelly, J.B., *Arabia, the Gulf and the West*, Basic Books, New York 1980. TEL: pp.1, 259.

F0587 Kennet, Kathleen (Bruce) Young, Lady, *Self-portrait of an Artist*, J. Murray, London 1949; 368 pp., 22.2 cm, blue cloth. TEL: pp.125, 188–99, 246–7, 268, 295–6, 302–3, 359; Illustrations, pp.260, 300.

F0588 Kennington, Eric H., *Drawing the R.A.F,* Oxford University Press, London 1942; 144 pp., 24.5 cm, blue cloth. TEL: pp.11, 12–32, text opposite plate 20.

F0589 Kiernan, Reginald Hugh, *The Unveiling of Arabia*, Harrap, London 1937; 359 pp., 22.5 cm, dark green cloth. TEL: pp.119–20, 149, 151, 174, 242, 276, 292, 295, 288, 302–3.

F0590 Kimche, Jon, *Palestine or Israel*, Secker & Warburg, London 1973; xx, 364 pp., 24 cm, brown cloth. TEL: pp.x, 15, 20, 38, 43, 68, 71–2, 124, 154, 162–3, 165–6, 170, 175–9, 181–3, 191.

F0591 Kimche, Jon, *The Second Arab Awakening*, Holt Rinehart & Winston, New York 1970; 288 pp., 21.5 cm, black simulated leather. TEL: pp.70, 82, 144, 155–6, 180, 12–14.

F0592 Kimche, Jon, *Seven Fallen Pillars*, Secker & Warburg, London 1950; xxii, 326 pp., 22 cm, orange cloth. TEL: pp.22, 23–4, 26, 28, 42, 45, 57, 62, 83, 100, 105, 106, 299.

F0593 Kimche, Jon, *Seven Fallen Pillars*, Praeger, New York 1953; xxvi, 442 pp., 22 cm, black cloth. TEL: pp.xix, xxiii, 24–5, 29–30, 113, 403.

F0594 Kimche, Jon, *There Could Have Been Peace*, Dial Press, New York 1973; xx, 362 pp., 23.5 cm, black cloth. TEL: pp.15, 20, 38, 43, 68, 71–2, 124, 154, 162–3, 165–6, 170, 175–9, 181–183, 191.

F0595 King, Francis, *E.M. Forster and His World*, Scribner's, New York 1978. TEL: pp.62, 76, 86, 87, 88.

F0596 King, Stephen Hessor, 'British Succesor States in the Post War Middle East', Claremont Graduate School, Claremont, California, 1978; vii, 534 pp., unpublished dissertation. TEL: Chapter VI, TE Lawrence and Arab Nationalism; Chapter VII, Lawrence, Faisal and the Arab Cause at the Paris Peace Conference – a French immorality play.

F0597 Kirkbride, Sir Alec S., *An Awakening*, Eng. Univ. Press of Arabia, Tavistock 1971; 6, 134 pp., 22.3 cm, red cloth. TEL: pp.3, 6, 13–16, 22–4, 32, 34–5, 40, 45, 48, 51, 55, 58, 64, 68–72, 75–8, 82–3, 86, 90, 93, 95–7, 113, 116–9.

F0598 Kirkbride, Sir Alec S., *A Crackle of Thorns*, Murray, London 1956; [10], 202 pp., 22.2 cm, red cloth. TEL: pp.2, 5, 6, 7, 8, 9, 10, 11.

F0599 Klieman, Aaron S., *Foundations of British Policy in the Arab World: the Cairo Conference of 1921*, Johns Hopkins University Press, Baltimore 1970; xiv, 322 pp., 23.6 cm, cream cloth. TEL: pp.84, 93, 96, 107–8, 109, 117, 119, 126, 129,152–3, 163–4, 168, 210, 211, 219, 221–7, 230, 233, 248.

F0600   Knight, G.Wilson, *Neglected Powers*, Routledge & Kegan Paul, London 1971; 2, 518 pp., 22.2 cm, red cloth.
TEL: pp.25, 53, 55–7, 64–6, 71, 79, 80, 84, 88, 160n, 217, 466, 65; pp.309–51, "T.E. Lawrence".

F0601   Knightley, Phillip, *First Casualty*, Harcourt, New York 1975.
TEL: pp.123, 150, 289, 306.

F0602   Knowles, John, *Double Vision*, Secker & Warburg, London 1964; 10, 210 pp., 20.2 cm, blue cloth simulated paper covered boards.
TEL: pp.108–121, film.

F0603   Koestler, Arthur, *The Thirteenth Tribe*, Picador, London 1976; 224 pp., 19.2 cm, pictorial paper covers.
TEL: p.179.

F0604   Kolisko, Eugen, *Reincarnation and Other Essays*, King, Littlewood & King, London 1940; 200 pp., 19 cm, black cloth.
TEL: pp.24, 54–65, "Lawrence of Arabia".

F0605   Komroff, Manuel, *True Adventures of Spies*, Little, Brown, Boston 1954; [10], 220 pp.
TEL: pp.109–127 G. Chap, "Prince Dynamite".

F0606   Konody, Paul George, *Sir William Orpen, Artist and Man*, Seeley Service, London 1932; 288 pp., 23.7 cm, green cloth.
TEL: Plate IX, 1919 Colonel A.[*sic*] E. Lawrence.

F0607   Korda, Michael, *Charmed Lives*, Random House, New York 1979.
TEL: pp.340, 346–7.

F0608   Kraus, René, *The Men Around Churchill*, Lippincott, New York 1941.
TEL: pp.234–5.

F0609   Kraus, René, *Winston Churchill*, New York Literary Guild, 1941; 416 pp., 22 cm, red cloth.
TEL: pp.250–53.

F0610   Kubie, Nora, *Road to Nineveh*, Cassell, London 1965.
TEL: pp.43–4, 178.

F0611   Kulik, Karol, *Alexander Korda*, W.H. Allen, London 1975; 14, 410 pp., 22 cm, red paper covered boards.
TEL: pp.189–90, 191, 385.

F0612   Kulik, Karol, *Alexander Korda*, Arlington House, New Rochelle, New York 1975; 14, 407 pp., 22.2 cm, orange paper covered boards.
TEL: pp.189–91, 385.

F0613   Kunitz, Stanley, and Haycroft, Howard, *Twentieth Century Authors*, Wilson, New York 1942.
TEL: pp.798–9.

F0614   Kuysman, Dan, *Genesis 1948*, New American Library, New York 1972; 832 pp., 17.8 cm, blue paper covers.
TEL: p.712.

F0615   Laffin, John, *Swifter than Eagles*, Blackwood, Edinburgh 1964; xii, 280 pp., 22 cm.
TEL: pp.220–21.

F0616   Lahr, John, *Coward the Playwright*, Methuen, London 1982.TEL: pp.1, 7, 60, 96.

F0617   Landau, Rom, *Search for Tomorrow*, Nicholson & Watson, London 1938; xx, 404 pp., 22.5 cm, bright blue cloth.

TEL: pp.9, 57, 144, 200, 222.
F0618 Lane, Arthur E., *An Adequate Response. The War Poetry of Wilfred Owen and Siegfried Sassoon*, Wayne State University Press, Detroit 1972; 192 pp., 23.7 cm, brown cloth.
TEL: pp.170–72.
F0619 Laquer, Walter, *Guerrilla*, Little, Brown, Boston 1976.
TEL: pp.ix, xi, 154–6, 169, 170–71.
F0620 Laquer, Walter Ze'Ev, *The Guerilla Reader, a Historical Anthology*, Temple University Press, Philadelphia 1977; viii, 248 pp., 10.8 cm, black cloth.
TEL: pp.126–38, "Thomas Edward Lawrence: The Lessons of Arabia".
F0621 Laquer, Walter Ze'ev, *The Middle East in Transition*, Praeger, New York 1958; xx, 516 pp., 21.5 cm, black linen.
TEL: p.188.
F0622 Le Vien, Jack, and Lewis, Peter, *The Finest Hours*, Harrap, London 1964; 160 pp., 18.7 cm, blue cloth.
TEL: p.48.
F0623 Lawrence, David Herbert, *Lady Chatterley's Lover*, Grosset & Dunlap, New York 1934; 330 pp., 20.3 cm, black cloth.
TEL: p.301, "C.E. Florence".
F0624 Lawrence, David Herbert, *Lady Chatterley's Lover*, Grove Press, New York 1959; 2, xlii, 372 pp., 20.9 cm, beige cloth.
TEL: pp. 339, "Colonel C.E. Florence".
F0625 Leach, Sally, compiler, *The Scholar at Work*, Historical Research Center, University of Texas, Austin 1975; 56 pp., 23 cm, tan paper covers.
TEL: p.37.
F0626 Leavis, F.R., *The Common Pursuit*, New York University Press, New York 1964.
TEL: p.152.
F0627 Leed, Eric J., *No Man's Land*, Cambridge University Press, Cambridge 1979.
TEL: pp.26, 56, 135, 200, 239.
F0628 Legman, G., ed., *The New Limerick*, Crown, New York 1977.
TEL: pp.129, 493.
F0629 Lehmann, John, *The Whispering Gallery*, Longmans, Green, London 1955.
TEL: pp.175, 270–71, 306–7.
F0630 Lenczowski, George, *The Middle East in World Affairs*, Cornell University Press, Ithaca, New York 1962; 24 cm, tan brown buckram.
TEL: pp.58,96ff.
F0631 Lengyel, Emil, *The Changing Middle East*, Day, New York 1960; 378 pp. 21.6 cm, black cloth.
TEL: pp.22, 159.
F0632 Lengyel, Emil, *Turkey*, Random, New York 1941; x, 474 pp., 23.5 cm, blue cloth.
TEL: pp.331, 333–7, 353–5.

F0633 Lengyel, Emil, *World Without End*, John Day, New York 1953; 10, 374 pp., 21.8 cm, black cloth or grey cloth.
TEL: pp.11, 100, 104ff, 109, 112, 117ff, 130, 186, 195, 199, 328, 345.

F0634 Lesley, Cole, *The Life of Noel Coward*, Penguin, Harmondsworth 1978; xvi, 560 pp., 18.1 cm, pictorial paper covers.
TEL: pp.7, 149–52, 155, 156, 195.

F0635 Leslie, Shane, *Mark Sykes*, Cassell, London 1923; xii, 308 pp., 24.2 cm, blue cloth.
TEL: pp.248, 249, 282.

F0636 Levin, Meyer, *The Story of Israel*, Putnam's, New York 1972; 240 pp., 17.4 cm, pictorial paper covers.
TEL: pp.107, 114, 115–16, 122, 175.

F0637 Lewin, Ronald, *Rommel as Military Commander*, Ballantine, New York 1970; xiv, 338 pp., 17.8 cm, pictorial paper covers.
TEL: pp.66, 313, 314.

F0638 Lewis, Alun, *The Last Inspection*, Allen & Unwin, London 1943 (2nd imp.); 224 pp., pink cloth, 18.8 cm, another copy red cloth.
TEL: pp.189–96, "Dusty Hermitage".

F0639 Lewis, C. Day, *The Buried Day*, Chatto & Windus, London 1960.
TEL: pp.219, 232.

F0640 Lewis, Wyndham, *Blasting and Bombadiering*, Eyre & Spottiswoode, London 1937; 8, 312 pp., 22 cm, orange cloth.
TEL: pp.14, 150, 152–4; "Lawrence of Arabia", pp.241–8.

F0641 Lewis, Wyndham, *Blasting and Bombadiering*, Calder & Boyars, London 1967; 8, 343 pp., 21 cm, green paper covered boards.
TEL: p.13; "Lawrence of Arabia", pp.237–45.

F0642 Lias, Godfrey, *Glubb's Legion*, Evans, London 1956; 232 pp., 22 cm, blue cloth.
TEL: pp.4, 16, 18, 21, 23, 26, 28, 30, 31, 32, 34, 35, 38, 44, 61, 62, 64, 65, 68, 69, 71, 77, 80, 87, 88, 93, 109, 110, 113, 128, 137, 151, 159, 143–4, 163, 192.

F0643 Liddell Hart, B.H., *The British Way of Warfare*, Faber, London 1932; 205 pp., 21.8 cm, red cloth.

F0644 Liddell Hart, B.H., *Defense of the West*, Morrow, New York 1950; 2, x, 340 pp., 22 cm, sand cloth.
TEL: pp.62, 63, 66, 257.

F0645 Liddell Hart, B.H., *The Ghost of Napoleon*, Faber & Faber, London 1933; 200 pp., 21 cm, grey cloth.
TEL: Dedication: "To 'T.E.' who trod this road before 1914."

F0646 Liddell Hart, B.H., *History of the First World War*, Pan Books, London 1970; 18, 560 pp., 18.5 cm, pictorial paper covers.
TEL: pp.212, 307, 378, 436ff.

F0647 Liddell Hart, B.H., *The Liddell Hart Memoirs*, Putnam's, New York 1965; 2 volumes, 22.4 cm,, blue cloth.
TEL: Vol. 1, pp.84–5, 150, 154, 301, 339–56, 357; Vol. 2, pp.13, 181–2, 13; Vol. 1, Chapter 15, "Lawrence and Lloyd George", pp.339–56.

F0648 Liddell Hart, B.H., *The Memoirs of Captain Liddell Hart*, Cassell, London 1965; 2 volumes, 21.8 cm, green cloth.

TEL: Vol. 1, pp.84–5, 150, 154, 301, 339–56, 357; Vol. 2, pp.181–2, 13; Vol. 1, Chapter 15, "Lawrence and Lloyd George", pp.339–56.

F0649 Liddell Hart, B.H., *The Real War, 1914–1918*, Little, Brown, Boston 1930; xiv, 510 pp., 20.5 cm, green cloth, also grey paper.
TEL: pp.331, 443, 444, 447.

F0650 Liddell Hart, B.H., *Reputations, Ten Years After*, Little, Brown, Boston; xii, 316 pp., 21.7 cm, black cloth .
TEL: pp.253–4.

F0651 Liddell Hart, B.H., *Strategy*, Praeger, New York 1954; 2, 426 pp., 21.5 cm, black cloth.
TEL: pp.17, 18, 137, 197–200, 224, 363.

F0652 Liddell Hart, B.H., *The Tanks*, Praeger, New York 1959; 2 volumes, 22.2 cm, black cloth.
TEL: Vol. 1, pp.20, 209, 213.

F0653 Liddell Hart, B.H., *This Expanding War*, Faber and Faber, London 1942; 278 pp., 22.4 cm, black cloth.
TEL: pp.64, 216, 244.

F0654 Liddell Hart, B.H., *Through the Fog of War*, Random House, New York 1938; x, 382 pp., 20.8 cm, grey cloth.
TEL: pp.24, 75, 89, 96, 160.

F0655 Liddell Hart, B.H., *The Way to Win Wars*, Faber & Faber, London 1952; 256 pp., 18.2 cm, pictorial paper covers.
TEL: pp.130, 212, 213, 237.

F0656 Lidstone, G. H. ed., *On Guard! A History of the 10th (Torbay) Battalion, Devonshire Home Guard*, Torquay Times & Devonshire Press [1946]; 136 pp., 22.3 cm, brown cloth.
TEL: p.18.

F0657 Life Magazine. *The Unforgettable Winston Churchill*, Time, New York 1965; 128 pp., 28.5 cm, pictorial paper covers.
TEL: p.74.

F0658 Lilienthal, Alfred M., *The Zionist Connection*, Dodd Mead, New York 1978.
TEL: p.20.

F0659 Lindbergh, Anne Morrow, *The Flower and the Nettle*, Harcourt Brace Jovanovich, New York 1976.
TEL: pp.532–3.

F0660 Lindbergh, Charles A., *The Wartime Journals of Charles A. Lindbergh*, Harcourt Brace Jovanovich, New York 1970; xx, 1938 pp., 24.2 cm, blue cloth.
TEL: p.157.

F0662 Littlefield, David W., *The Islamic East and North Africa*, Colorado Libraries Unlimited, Littleton 1977.
TEL: pp.73–4.

F0663 Litvinoff, Barnet, *Weizmann*, Putnam, New York 1976.
TEL: pp.96, 98, 122–3, 127.

F0664 Lloyd, Seton, *Mounds of the Near East*, Edinburgh University Press, 1963; 120 pp., 25.8 cm, pink cloth.
TEL: pp.52, 87.

F0665 Lloyd, Seton. *Twin Rivers*, Oxford University Press, London 1943;

viii, 230 pp., 22 cm, blue cloth.
TEL: pp.151, 205–6, 211.

F0666 Lloyd George, David, *The Truth About the Peace Treaties,* Gollancz, London 1938; 2 volumes, 22.8 cm, blue cloth.
TEL: Vol. 2, pp.755, 1021, 1028, 1035, 1038, 1140.

F0667 Lloyd George, David, *War Memories,* Odhams, London 1938; 2 volumes, 21.5 cm, simulated red leather cloth.
TEL: Vol. 2, pp.1076–7.

F0668 Lockhart, Sir Robert Bruce, *The Dreamers 1915–1938,* Macmillan, London 1973; 436, [4] pp., maroon cloth spine, light maroon paper covers.
TEL: pp.315, 320–21.

F0669 Longgood, William F. *Suez Story,* Greenberg, New York 1957; xviii, 174 pp., 21.5 cm, yellow cloth.
TEL: p.8.

F0670 Lonnroth, Erik, *En Annan Uppfattning,* Bonniers, Stockholm 1949; 208 pp.
TEL: pp.190–207, "Thomas Edward Lawrence".

F0671 Love, Kennet, *Suez, the Twice Fought War,* McGraw-Hill, New York 1960; xviii, 768 pp., 23.5 cm, black leather simulated cloth.
TEL: pp.31, 32, 193, 266.

F0672 Lucas, Edward Verrall, *Post-Bag Diversions,* Methuen, London 1934; xii, 256 pp., 20.7 cm, black cloth.
TEL: p.183.

F0673 Lucas, Frank, *Cecile,* Chatto & Windus, London 1930; 8, 404 pp., 21.5 cm, blue cloth.
TEL: Dedication, p.5, "To the Author of 'The Seven Pillars of Wisdom'."

F0674 Luce, Robert B., *Faces of Five Decades,* Simon & Schuster, New York 1964; 24 cm, black paper-covered boards, tan cloth spine.
TEL: pp.346–53, "Robert Graves, Lawrence Vindicated".

F0675 Lunt, James, *The Barren Rocks of Aden,* Harcourt Brace & World, New York 1966; 196 pp., 22.4 cm, brown cloth..
TEL: pp.20, 32, 170, 178, 183, 184, 189.

F0676 Lyell, Thomas, *The Ins and Outs of Mesopotamia,* A.M. Philpot Ltd, London 1923.
TEL: pp.109, 202.

F0677 McConnell, Frank, *Storytelling and Mythmaking,* Oxford University Press, New York 1979.
TEL: pp.122–9, 262–3, 278–9.

F0678 McCormick, Donald, *The Mark of Merlin,* Holt Rinehart & Winston, New York 1964.
TEL: pp.216–7.

F0679 McCormick, Donald, *The Mystery of Lord Kitchener's Death,* Putnam, London 1959; 224 pp., 20.3 cm, black cloth.
TEL: p.82.

F0680 McDowell, Frederick P.W., *E.M. Forster,* Twayne, Boston 1982.
TEL: pp.11, 135, 140.

F0681 McEntee, Girard Lindsley, *Military History of the World War*, Scribner's, New York 1943.
TEL: p.447.

F0682 Mackenzie, Compton, *My Life and Times*, Chatto & Windus, London 1963–1971; 10 volumes, 8, 294, 2 pp., 22.3 cm, blue cloth.
TEL: Vol. V, pp.127, 155; Vol. VI, pp.55–6.

F0683 McKinnon, Ian, *Garroot*, Cape, London 1933; 252 pp., 20.5 cm, yellow cloth.
TEL: p.6.

F0684 McKnight, Gerald, *Verdict on Schweitzer*, Day, New York 1964.
TEL: pp.38, 179.

F0685 Maclean, Fitzroy, *Eastern Approaches*, Cape, London 1949; 544 pp., 20.5 cm, red cloth.
TEL: pp.193–4.

F0686 Maclean, Fitzroy, *Eastern Approaches*, Times, New York 1965; 568 pp., 20.4 cm, pictorial paper cover.
TEL: pp.x, 164.

F0687 Maclean, Norman, *His Terrible Swift Sword*, Gollancz, London 1942; 88 pp., 19.7 cm, blue cloth.
TEL: pp.73–7.

F0688 MacLeish, Archibald, *Collected Poems 1917–1953*, Houghton Mifflin, Boston 1936.

F0689 Macmillan, George, and Falls, Cyril, *Military Operations Egypt and Palestine*, HMSO, London 1928; 3 volumes, 23.5 cm, red cloth.
TEL: Vol. 1, pp.233, 235, 236, 239, 240; Vol. 2, pp.260, 398, 400.

F0690 Madame Tussaud's Ltd, London, *Madame Tussaud's Exhibition*, London, 1958; 12 pp., 20.5 cm, pictorial covers.
TEL: p.7.

F0691 Madsen, Axel, *Malraux*, Morrow, New York 1976; 384 pp., 24.2 cm, tan paper-covered boards, black cloth spine.
TEL: pp.21, 147–8, 223–4, 233, 237, 254–5.

F0692 Magill, Frank N., ed., *Masterplots*, Salem, New York 1964.
TEL: Vol. 13, pp.3435–7, "Seven Pillars of Wisdom".

F0693 Main, Ernest, *Iraq*, Allen & Unwin, London 1935; 4, 268 pp., 24.4 cm, green cloth.
TEL: Chapter III, pp.50–77, "Lawrence and the Arabs of Iraq".

F0694 Malraux, André, *Antimémoires*, Gallimard, Paris 1967; 612 pp., 20.6 cm, white paper covers.

F0695 Malraux, André, *Anti-memoirs*, Holt, Rinehart, Winston, New York 1968; 10, 438 pp., 21.7 cm, black cloth.
TEL: pp.8, 54, 65, 74, 268.

F0696 Malraux, André, *Anti-memoirs*, Bantam, New York 1970; 10, 524 pp., 17.8 cm, black paper covers.
TEL: pp.9, 65, 78, 91, 323.

F0697 Malraux, André, *Le Miroir des limbes*, Gallimard, Paris 1975; 240 pp., 18.6 cm, white paper covers, 475 copies printed.
TEL: p.218.

F0698 Malraux, André, *Les Noyers d'Altenburg,* Gallimard, Paris 1948; 10, 282 pp., 21.8 cm, brown paper covers.

F0699 Mannin, Ethel, *A Lance for the Arabs,* Hutchinson, London 1963; 172 pp., 21.5 cm, black cloth.
TEL: p.168.

F0700 Mannin, Ethel, *The Lovely Land,* Travel Book Co., London 1965; 204 pp., 21.5 cm.
TEL: pp.52, 73, 100, 102.

F0701 Manning, Frederick, *Scenes and Portraits,* Davies, London 1930; 8, 292 pp., 21.5 cm, brown buckram slip case, limited to 250 copies.
TEL: Dedication: 'Apologia di! To T.E. Shaw', pp.267–91.

F0702 Mansfield, Peter, *Ottoman Empire and Its Successors,* St. Martin's, New York 1973.
TEL: pp.44, 53, 56.

F0703 Marcosson, Isaac F., *Turbulent Years,* Dodd Mead, New York 1938.
TEL: p.147.

F0704 Marlowe, John, *Rebellion in Palestine,* Cresset, London 1946; 280 pp., 22 cm, red cloth.
TEL: pp.30–31, 43, 48, 55.

F0705 Marsh, Edward and Hassall, Christopher, *Ambrosia and Small Beer,* Harcourt, Brace and World, New York 1944.
TEL: p.233.

F0706 Marsh, Sir Edward, *A Number of People,* Harper, New York 1939; 24.5 cm, brown cloth (another copy red cloth, another yellow).
TEL: pp.234–9, 344–5.

F0707 Martin, Gilbert and Churchill, Randolph S., *W.S. Churchill,* Houghton Mifflin, New York 1977.
TEL: Vol.5, pp.14–15, 56, 318–9, 329, 364, 707, 789.

F0708 Marwick, Arthur, *Britain and the Century of Total War,* Little, Brown, Boston 1968.
TEL: p.57.

F0709 Mason, Harold Andrew, *To Homer Through Pope,* Barnes & Noble, New York 1972; viii, 216 pp., 22.3 cm, grey paper boards.
TEL: pp.192, 197, 198, 199, 202.

F0710 Massey, Raymond, *A Hundred Different Lives,* Little, Brown, Boston 1979; 448 pp., 24 cm, red cloth boards, black cloth spine.
TEL: p.62.

F0711 Massey, William Thomas, *Allenby's Final Triumph,* Constable, London 1920; xii, 348 pp., 22.7 cm, blue cloth.
TEL: pp.61, 201, 246, 249, 263, 272, 274, 275, 342–3.

F0712 Massignon, Louis, *Parole Donnée,* Union Generale d'Editions, Paris 1970; 512 pp., 18 cm, pictorial paper covers.
TEL: pp.312–18, "L'Entrée à Jerusalem avec Lawrence en 1917".

F0713 Massignon, Louis, *Opera Minora,* Dar Al–Maaref, Beirut 1963; 3 volumes.
TEL: Vol. 3, pp.423–7, "Mes Rapports avec Lawrence en 1917".

F0714 Maugham, Robin, *Approach to Palestine,* Falcon, London 1947; 99 pp., 19 cm, rust and cream boards.

F0715 Maugham, Robin, *Nomad,* Chapman & Hall, London 1947; 244 pp., 19 cm, pale yellow.
TEL: pp.30, 39, 49, 52–3, 83, 112, 133, 167, 200, 206, 236.

F0716 Maugham, Robin, *Nomad,* Viking, New York 1948; 6, 186 pp., 21 cm, tan.
TEL: pp.19, 26, 34, 36, 37, 60, 82, 98, 99, 125, 150, 155, 178.

F0717 Maxwell, Elsa, *I Married This World,* Heinemann, London 1955; viii, 130 pp., 22.1 cm.
TEL: pp.,105.

F0718 Mee, Arthur, *Dorset,* Hodder & Stoughton, London 1945 (3rd imp.); x, 336 pp., 20.3 cm, red cloth.
TEL: pp.165f, 273.

F0719 Mee, Charles L., Jr., *The End of an Order,* Dutton, New York 1980.
TEL: pp.84–7, 192, "Feisal, and Lawrence of Arabia".

F0720 Meinertzhagen, Richard, *Army Diary, 1899–1926,* Oliver and Boyd, Edinburgh 1960; viii, 304 pp., 22.8 cm, red cloth.
TEL: p.296.

F0721 Meinertzhagen, Richard, *Middle East Diary, 1917–1956,* Cresset, London 1959; xii, 376 pp., 22.3 cm, blue cloth.
TEL: pp.15, 27, 28, 29, 30, 31, 33, 34, 35, 36, 37, 38, 39, 40, 41, 42, 43, 95, 96, 98, 99, 117, 118, 198, 246, 349, 364.

F0722 Meinertzhagen, Richard, *Middle East Diary, 1917–1956,* Yoseloff, New York 1960; xii, 378 pp., 24 cm, deep red cloth.
TEL: pp.15, 27, 28, 29, 30, 31, 33, 34, 35, 36, 37, 38, 39, 40, 41, 42, 43, 95, 96, 98, 99, 117, 246, 349, 364.

F0723 *Men of Turmoil,* Minton, Balch & Co., New York 1935; 8, 376 pp., 24.1 cm, brown boards, tan cloth spine.
TEL: pp.99–122, Liddell Hart, "Lawrence of Arabia".

F0724 Mendelson, Edward, *Early Auden,* Viking, New York 1981; xxiv, 408 pp., brown cloth.
TEL: pp.135, 181–2, 185, 210, 214, 216, 218, 239, 244, 245, 251, 313.

F0725 Mendelson, Edward, *Early Auden,* Faber & Faber, London 1981; xxiv, 408 pp., grey paper covered boards.
TEL: pp.135, 181–2, 185, 210, 214, 216, 218, 239, 244, 245, 251, 313.

F0726 Meulen, Daniel van der, *The Wells of Ibn Sa'ud,* Praeger, New York 1957; x, 270 pp., 22.2 cm, green cloth.
TEL: pp.5, 9, 10, 69–70, 78–9, 80–83, 257.

F0727 Meyers, Jeffrey, *D. H. Lawrence and the Experience of Italy,* University of Pennsylvania Press, Philadelphia 1982.
TEL: pp.161–2, 184.

F0728 Meyers, Jeffrey, *Disease and the Novel, 1880–1960,* St. Martin's, New York 1984.
TEL: p.98.

F0729 Meyers, Jeffrey, *A Fever at the Core,* Barnes & Noble, New York 1976; 2, 174 pp., 22.2 cm, black cloth.
TEL: pp.113–42, 20, 25, 54, 81,143–7, 150, 153–6,160,169; "T.E. Lawrence, (1888–1935)", pp.153–6.

F0730 Meyers, Jeffrey, ed., *Hemingway,* Routledge & Kegan Paul, London

1982.
TEL: pp.368–9, Carlos Baker review of "Men at War".
F0731   Meyers, Jeffrey, *Married to Genius*, Barnes & Noble, New York 1977; 214 pp., 22 cm, black buckram.
TEL: pp.38–57.
F0732   Meynell, Francis, *My Lives*, Random, New York 1971; 336 pp., 22.2 cm, brown cloth.
TEL: pp.172–3.
F0733   Meynell, Viola, *The Best of Friends*, Rupert Hart-Davis, London 1956; x, 11–308 pp., 22.2 cm, green cloth.
TEL: pp.v, 29, 32, 34, 80, 123, 124, 223, 224.
F0734   Meynell, Viola, *Friends of a Lifetime*, Cape, London 1940; 384 pp., 23 cm, blue cloth.
TEL: pp.247, 252, 253, 257, 311, 313, 314, 312, 249; "Thomas Edward Lawrence", pp.357–73.
F0735   Michie, Allen A., *Retreat to Victory*, Alliance Books, Chicago 1942.
F0736   *The Middle East*, Royal Institute of International Affairs, London 1954; xviii, 590 pp., 22 cm, green cloth.
TEL: pp.22, 24, 353, 469–70.
F0737   Mikusch, Dagobert von, *Gasi Mustafa Kemal*, List, Leipzig 1929; viii, 336 pp., 24.3 cm, orange cloth.
TEL: p.221.
F0738   Millar, Ronald, *Kut*, Secker & Warburg, London 1969; viii, 324 pp., 22.2 cm, maroon cloth.
TEL: pp.133, 252, 253, 257, 259, 265, 266, 270, 271, 273, 274, 275.
F0739   Miller, Alice (Duer), *I Have Loved England*, Putnam's, New York 1941; unpaged, 26.1 cm, blue cloth.
TEL: Photo of ghost on stairway at Raynham.
F0740   Miller, David Hunter, *My Diary at the Conference at Paris, with Documents*, Appeal Printing Co., New York (printed for author) 1924; 21 volumes.
TEL: Vol. 1, pp.74–5, +?
F0742   Miller, Edward, *That Noble Cabinet*, Ohio University Press, 1974.
TEL: p.330.
F0743   Miller, Wright Watts, *Books, an Introduction to Reading*, Pitman, London 1932; xx, 224 pp., 19.5 cm, green cloth.
TEL: p.14.
F0744   Millgate, Michael, *Thomas Hardy, a Biography*, Random, New York 1982.
TEL: pp.442, 549, 550, 554, 561, 576.
F0745   Minchin, Neville, *The Silver Lady*, G.T. Foulis, London 1961; 180 pp., 22.2 cm, black paper covered boards.
TEL: pp.94, 96, 97, 99, 104.
F0746   *Modern Literary Manuscripts from King's College, Cambridge* (exhibition catalogue), Fitzwilliam Museum, Cambridge 1976; unpaged, 14.8 cm, pictorial paper covers.
TEL: Item 71, photo of effigy.
F0747   Molnar, Thomas, *Sartre, Ideologue of our Time*, Funk & Wagnalls,

New York 1968.
TEL: p.10.

F0748 Monegal, Emir Rodriguez, *Jorge Luis Borges*, Dutton, New York 1978.
TEL: pp.286, 292.

F0749 Monroe, Elizabeth, *Britain's Moment in the Middle East, 1914–1956*, Chatto & Windus, London 1963; 256 pp., 2.3 cm, black cloth.
TEL: pp.36, 46–7, 55, 61, 65, 67–8, 117, 140.

F0750 Monroe, Elizabeth, *Britain's Moment in the Middle East, 1914–1956*, Methuen, London 1965; 262 pp., 21.7 cm, pictorial paper covers.
TEL: pp.36, 46–7, 55, 61, 65, 67–8, 117, 140.

F0751 Monroe, Elizabeth, *Philby of Arabia*, Faber & Faber, London 1973; 332 pp., 22.3 cm, brown cloth.
TEL: pp.52, 58, 71, 95, 100, 103, 106, 114, 115–7, 120, 153, 284.

F0752 Montgomery, Bernard L. (Field Marshal Viscount Montgomery), *A History of Warfare*, World, Cleveland 1968; 584 pp., 25.3 cm, black cloth.
TEL: pp.21, 489, 494.

F0753 Moody, William Vaughn and Lovett, Robert M., *A History of English Literature*, Scribner, New York 1956.
TEL: pp.484–5.

F0754 Moorehead, Alan, *African Trilogy*, Hamish Hamilton, London 1955; 592 pp., light blue cloth.
TEL: pp.144, 168, 169.

F0755 Moorehead, Alan, *The March to Tunis*, Harper, New York 1965; 16, 492 pp., 22 cm, black cloth.
TEL: pp.144, 168, 169.

F0756 Moorehead, Alan, *Mediterranean Front*, Hamish Hamilton, London 1941; 304 pp., 22 cm, green cloth.
TEL: pp.243, 285, 288.

F0757 Moorehead, Alan, *The White Nile*, Harper & Row, New York 1971; 368 pp., 26 cm, brown cloth.
TEL: p.254.

F0758 Moran, (Charles McMoran Wilson) Lord, *Churchill*, Houghton Mifflin, Boston 1966; xviii, 787 pp., 21.8 cm, blue cloth.
TEL: pp.113, 561, 827.

F0759 Morris, James, *The Hashemite Kings*, Pantheon, New York 1959; 14,210 pp., 21.5 cm, red cloth.
TEL: pp.33–8, 40, 43f, 47–50, 52f, 59, 61, 63f, 72, 86, 87f, 93.

F0760 Morris, James, *The Hashimite Kings*, Faber, London 1959; 232 pp., 22.2 cm, red cloth.
TEL: pp.49–54, 56, 59, 60, 63–4, 66, 68–9, 75, 77, 79–81, 84, 88, 95,104, 106–7, 110.

F0761 Morris, James, *Islam Inflamed*, Pantheon, New York 1957; 3, 326 pp., 23.5 cm, orange cloth.
TEL: pp.136, 142, 162, 167, 314.

F0762 Morris, James, *Oxford*, Faber, London 1965; 2, 296 pp., 22.3 cm, yellow cloth.
TEL: pp.19, 46, 98, 106, 160, 259, 265.

F0763   Morris,James, *Oxford*, Harcourt Brace & World, New York 1965; 302
        pp., 22 cm, bright blue cloth.
        TEL: pp.19, 46, 98, 106, 160, 259, 265.
F0764   Morris, James, *Sultan in Oman*, Pantheon, New York 1957; xii, 148
        pp., 21.6 cm, tan cloth boards, black cloth spine.
        TEL: pp.58, 84, 115.
F0765   Morton, H.V., *In the Steps of St Paul*, Rich & Cowan, London 1936;
        xvi, 440 pp., 19.2 cm, black cloth.
        TEL: p.26.
F0766   Morton, H.V., *In the Steps of the Master*, Rich & Cowan, London
        1934; xii, 388 pp., 19.5 cm, black cloth.
        TEL: pp.245, 280, 296.
F0767   Morton, H.V., *Middle East*, Methuen, London 1941; x, 326 pp., 19
        cm, red cloth.
        TEL: p.9.
F0768   Morton, H.V., *Middle East*, Dodd Mead, New York 1944; x, 374 pp.,
        22 cm, blue cloth.
        TEL: p.10.
F0769   Mosley, Leonard, *Dulles*, Dial Press, New York 1978; xii, 532 pp.,
        23.5 cm, blue simulated leather.
        TEL: pp.71–2.
F0770   Mosley, Leonard, *Gideon Goes to War*, Barker, London 1955.
        TEL: pp.12, 16–17, 127.
F0771   Mosley, Leonard, *Power Play*, Penguin, 1974.
        TEL: pp.42, 281.
F0772   Moss, Howard, *Instant Lives*, Avon, New York 1976; 127 pp., 17.9
        cm, pictorial paper covers.
        TEL: pp.,77–8, "Lawrence of Arabia".
F0773   Mountfort, Guy, *Portrait of a Desert*, Houghton Mifflin, Boston 1965;
        192 pp., 24.5 cm, tan cloth.
        TEL: pp.38, 50, 58, 78–9, 107, 108, 133, 147, 166, 125 (film).
F0774   Mountfort, Guy, *Portrait of a Desert*, Collins, London 1969; 192 pp.,
        24.5 cm, buff and red cloth.
        TEL: pp.38, 50, 56, 78–9, 107–8, 133, 147, 166, 125.
F0775   Mousa, Suleiman *Al Hussein Ben Ali wa Al Thawara Al Arabia Al
        Koubra*, Dar El Nasher, Amman 1957.
        TEL: pp.112–13.
F0776   Muggeridge, Malcolm, *Chronicles of Wasted Time*, Morrow, New York
        1973; 288 pp., 24.1 cm, green paper covered boards, black cloth
        spine.
        TEL: p.79.
F0777   Muggeridge, Malcolm, *The Sun Never Sets*, Random House, New
        York 1940; 6, 394 pp., 23 cm, red and blue buckram.
        TEL: pp.40–42, 203.
F0778   Muir, Ramsay, *A Brief History of Our Own Times*, G. Philip & Son,
        London 1934; x, 306 pp., 22.5 cm, green cloth.
        TEL: pp.189, 193, 196, 213.
F0779   Mumby, Frank Arthur, *Publishing and Bookselling*, Cape, London,

and Bowker, New York, 1949 (2nd imp.); 440 pp., 22.7 cm, brown cloth.
TEL: pp.303, 313, 325.

F0780 Mundy, Talbot, *Jimgrim and Allah's Peace*, Appleton-Century, New York 1936; vii, 280 pp., 19.7 cm, yellow cloth.

F0781 *Le mythe d'Étiemble*, Didier-Erudition, Paris 1980; 366, (2) pp., white paper.
TEL: pp.143–56, Maurice Larés, "La science et l'art militaires de T.E. Lawrence"; pp.143–55, Vincent Monteil, "Étiemble et Lawrence d'Arabie".

F0782 Namier, L.B. *In the Margin of History*, Macmillan, London 1939; 20.7 cm.
TEL: pp.271–303, "Lawrence as I Knew him, 'Seven Pillars of Wisdom', His Letters"; photo following p.172.

F0783 Napier, Priscilla. *A Late Beginning*, Hamish Hamilton, London 1986.

F0784 Neave, Dorina L., *Remembering Kut*, Barker, London 1937; x, 322 pp., 22.4 cm, blue cloth.
TEL: pp.75–6, 107–113, 115.

F0785 Neave, Dorina L., *Romance of the Bosphorus*, Hutchinson, London 1949; 256 pp., 23.5 cm, red cloth.
TEL: pp.152, 233.

F0786 Nelson, Nina, *Shepheard's Hotel*, Barrie & Rockliff, London 1960; xvi, 220 pp., 22.2 cm, maroon cloth.
TEL: pp.2, 5, 73, 81, 84, 86–7, 89, 90, 213–4.

F0787 Nelson, Nina, *Shepheard's Hotel*, Macmillan, New York 1960; xvi, 220 pp., 22.2 cm, maroon cloth.
TEL: pp.2, 5, 73, 81, 84, 86–7, 89, 90, 213–4.

F0788 Nevakivi, Jukka, *Britain, France and the Arab Middle East 1914–1920*, University of London, Athlone Press, London 1969; xiv, 286 pp., 22.4 cm, dark blue linen.
TEL: pp.8, 45, 59, 62, 70–73, 85–8, 97, 105, 108–9, 111–12, 115, 134–5, 137–9, 141–4, 149, 175, 180, 200–201, 209, 258.

F0789 Newins, Edward, and Wright, T., *World Without Time*, John Day, New York 1969; 320 pp., 22 cm, sand cloth.
TEL: pp.13–14.

F0790 Newman, Edward W.P., *The Middle East*, Bles, London 1926; xvi, 304 pp., 25.8 cm, violet cloth.
TEL: p.124.

F0791 Newton & Co., Ltd, *The Film-slide System*, London, n.d.; 84 pp., 21.8 cm, yellow wrappers.
TEL: p.57, "Colonel Lawrence and his Magnificent Exploit in Arabia" (catalogue of film-reels).

F0792 Newton & Co., Ltd, *Supplementary List of Lantern Slides*, Newton & Co., London n.d. (late 1930s); 72 pp., 21.8 cm, illus.
TEL: pp.41–3, lists slides of series: "The Imperial Camel Corps with Colonel Lawrence", "Lawrence and the Arab Revolt".

F0793 Nicolson, Sir Harold, *Diaries and Letters*, Atheneum, New York 1966–1967; 512 pp. (Vol. 2, War Years 1939–1945), 24.5 cm, blue

cloth.
TEL: pp.66–7, 361.
F0794 Nicolson, Sir Harold, *Diaries and Letters, 1930–1939,* Collins, London 1966; 448 pp., 23.5 cm, yellow buckram.
TEL: p.154.
F0795 Nicolson, Sir Harold, *Peacemaking, 1919,* Constable, London 1933; 2, x, 380 pp., 22.5 cm, blue cloth.
TEL: pp.141, 142.
F0796 Nitschke, August, *Der Fiend,* Kohlhammer, Stuttgart, 1964; 268 pp., red cloth, 21.5 cm.
TEL: pp.163–93, "Politik im Dienst der Abstraktion, Thomas Edward Lawrence".
F0797 Nobile, Philip, ed., *Favorite Movies: Critics' Choice,* Macmillan, New York 1973; x, 301 pp., 24 cm, blue cloth.
TEL: pp.77–86, 247.
F0798 Nockolds, Harold, *The Magic of a Name,* Clymer, Los Angeles 1966; 10, 283 pp., 21 cm, pictorial paper covers.
TEL: pp.110, 111, 112, 113.
F0799 Nonesuch Press, *Bodkin Permitting,* Nonesuch Press, London 1929; 2, 30 pp., 20.1 cm, marbled paper wrappers.
TEL: pp.4–5.
F0800 Nonesuch Press, *The Nonesuch Century,* Nonesuch Press, London 1936; [2], xii, [2], 80 pp., 30.8 cm, green buckram.
TEL: pp.47–8.
F0801 Norman, Charles, *Ezra Pound,* Macmillan, New York 1960; xviii, 494 pp., 21.5 cm, brown cloth.
TEL: pp.225, 226.
F0802 Nutting, Anthony, *The Arabs,* Potter, New York 1964; vi, 424 pp., 23.6 cm, blue cloth.
TEL: pp.288, 301, 341.
F0803 Nutting, Anthony, *The Arabs,* Mentor, New York 1965; 416 pp., 18 cm, pictorial covers.
TEL: pp.283, 297, 335.
F0804 Nutting, Anthony, *Gordon,* Reprint Society, London 1967; 288 pp., 20.5 cm, orange paper covered boards.
TEL: pp.282–3.
F0805 Nutting, Anthony, *Gordon,* C.N. Potter, New York 1966; 10, 338 pp., 22.3 cm, red cloth.
TEL: pp.318–9.
F0806 Nutting, Anthony, *No End of a Lesson,* C.N. Potter, New York 1967; 208 pp., 21.5 cm, black cloth.
TEL: p.30.
F0807 Ocampo, Victoria, *Testimonios, Septima serie (1962–1967),* Sur, Buenos Aires 1967; 296 pp., 19.6 cm, white wrappers.
TEL: pp.63–6, "Servir sin ser Premiado"; pp.66–83, "El Aurens en el Deisier dela Pantalla"; pp.83–8, "O'Toole Interpreta un Guion de Robert Bolt"; pp.89–103, "El Unicornio enuna Cabelleriza"; pp.103–4, "Propositos de Lawrence de Arabia"; pp.113–8, "Horoes con y sin Eseatandra".

F0808 O'Casey, Sean, *The Letters of Sean O'Casey,* Macmillan, New York 1975.
TEL: Vol. 1, pp.xx, xxii, 371, 498–9, 594, 683–4, 883; Vol. II, pp.64, 585, 603, 608, 823.

F0809 Oliver, Jocelyn, ed., *Achievement,* Collins, London 1937; viii, 256 pp., 27 cm, red cloth.
TEL: pp.243–9, Edward Robinson, "Lawrence of Arabia".

F0810 Osanka, Franklin Mark, ed., *Modern Guerrilla Warfare,* Free Press of Glencoe, New York 1962; xxiv, 520 pp., 24 cm, red cloth.
TEL: pp.5–6, 18, 21, 32, 168.

F0811 O'Shea, Raymond, *The Sand Kings of Oman,* Methuen, London 1947; xx, 212 pp., 22.3 cm, red cloth.
TEL: pp.xv, 1, 70, 86, 180, 193, 196, 197.

F0812 Overseas Press Club of America, *Men Who Make Your World,* Dutton, New York 1949.
TEL: p.276.

F0813 Owen, David Lloyd, *The Desert My Dwelling Place,* London, Cassell 1957; 272 pp., 21.7 cm, red cloth.
TEL: pp.23, 46.

F0814 Owen, Frank, *Tempestuous Journey,* Hutchinson, London 1954; 784 pp., 23.5 cm, blue cloth.
TEL: p.547.

F0815 Oxford University, *Jesus College, Oxford. Short Guide for Visitors,* Holywell Press, Oxford n.d.; 4 pp., 25 × 13 cm.
TEL: p.4.

F0816 Page, B., Leitch, D., and Knightley, P., *Philby,* Book of the Month Club, London 1969; 296 pp., 22.3 cm, orange paper-covered boards.
TEL: pp.29, 37–8.

F0817 Palestine Exploration Fund, *World of the Bible,* Victoria and Albert Museum, London 1965; xii, 73 pp., 23 cm, white paper covers.
TEL: p.15.

F0818 Panichas, George Andrew, *Promise of Greatness,* Cassell, London 1968; xxxvi, 572 pp., 23.5 cm, black cloth.
TEL: p.xxiii.

F0819 Panichas, George Andrew, *Promise of Greatness,* Day, New York 1968; xxxvi, 572 pp., 23.5 cm, green cloth.
TEL: p.xxiii.

F0820 Papen, Franz von, *Memoirs,* Deutsch, London 1952; x, 630 pp., 22 cm, black cloth.
TEL: pp.68, 77, 80, 83.

F0821 Papen, Franz von, *Memoirs,* Dutton, New York 1953; 6, 634 pp., 22 cm, black cloth.
TEL: pp.68, 77, 80, 83.

F0822 Parker, E.W. and A.R. Moon, *Encounters,* Longmans Green, London 1951; 192 pp., 16.7 cm, maroon cloth.
TEL: pp.152–6, extract from Grave s *Lawrence of Arabia.*

F0823 Parkes, James, *A History of Palestine,* Gollancz, London 1949; 392 pp., 22.3 cm, green cloth.
TEL: pp.283, 286.

F0824 Patai, Raphael, *The Kingdom of Jordan,* Princeton University Press, Princeton, New Jersey 1958; x, 316 pp., 22.1 cm, yellow cloth.
TEL: pp.33–5.

F0825 Patch, Blanche, *Thirty Years with G.B.S,* Gollancz, London 1951; 256 pp., 22.3 cm, orange cloth (also green).
TEL: pp.35, 68, 69, 71, 76, 77, 78, 79, 80, 81, 82, 84, 85, 86, 87, 113, 127, 160, 239; Chapter V, pp.76–87, "Lawrence of Arabia".

F0826 Patch, Blanche, *Thirty Years with G.B.S,* Dodd, Mead, New York 1951; 320 pp., 21 cm, blue cloth.
TEL: pp.42, 83, 84, 87, 93, 94, 96, 97, 98, 99, 100, 101, 102, 103, 164, 106, 105, 154, 194, 290.

F0827 Payne, Robert, *Mao Tse–Tung,* Schuman, New York 1950.
TEL: pp.274–5.

F0828 Payne Robert, *A Portrait of André Malraux,* Prentice-Hall, Englewood Cliffs 1970; xii, 484 pp., 23.6 cm, red cloth.
TEL: pp.62, 296–300.

F0829 Pearson, Hesketh, *Bernard Shaw,* Collins, 1945.
TEL: pp.392–3.

F0830 Pearson, Hesketh, *G.B.S. a full-length Portrait,* Garden City, New York 1946; 6, ix–xii, 390 pp., 22 cm, maroon cloth.
TEL: pp.355–7.

F0831 Pearson, Hesketh, *G.B.S. A Postscript,* Harper, New York 1950; x, 138 pp., 21.8 cm, red cloth.
TEL: pp.67, 72, 91–2, 107.

F0832 Pearson, Hesketh, *G.B.S. a Postscript,* Collins, London 1951; 192 pp., 21.6 cm, russet cloth.
TEL: pp.94, 104, 131.

F0833 Pearson, Hesketh, *George Bernard Shaw,* Atheneum, New York 1963; 11, 16–484 pp., 18.5 cm, pictorial paper covers.
TEL: pp.384–5, 414, 445, 465.

F0834 Peniakoff, Vladimir, *Popski's Private Army,* Cape, London 1950; 572 pp., 20.5 cm, brown cloth.
TEL: pp.15–16 and dustwrapper.

F0835 Penzer, Norman Mosley, *An Annotated Bibliography of Sir Richard Francis Burton,* Philpot, London 1923; xvi, 352 pp., 26.5 cm, brown buckram, 500 copies.
TEL: pp.7, 9.

F0836 Perez, Don, *The Middle East Today,* Holt Rinehart & Winston, New York 1978.
TEL: pp.106, 140, 431, 432.

F0837 Peter, Laurence J. *Why Things Go Wrong,* Morrow, New York 1985; 208 pp., 21 cm, blue cloth spine, white paper covered boards.
TEL: p.126.

F0838 Peyre, Henri, *Literature and Sincerity,* Yale University Press, New Haven 1963.
TEL: pp.121, 139.

F0839 Phelps, Robert, *The Literary Life,* Farrar, Straus & Giroux, New York 1968; 20, 244 pp., 28 cm, blue cloth.
TEL: pp.90–91, 108, 113, 138, 153, 154, 155, 158, 169.

F0840 Philby, Harry St J.B., *Arabia of the Wahabis*, Constable, London 1928; xvi, 424 pp., 22.5 cm, olive green cloth.
TEL: pp.220, 332, 375.

F0841 Philby, Harry St J.B., *Arabia of the Wahabis*, Arno, New York 1973; 10, xiii–xvi, 431 pp., 22.3 cm, violet cloth.
TEL: pp.220, 332, 375.

F0842 Philby, Harry St J.B., *Arabian Days*, Hale, London 1948; xvi, 336 pp., 24.7 cm, blue cloth.
TEL: pp.xvi, 49, 99, 100, 101, 127, 140, 142, 153, 157, 158, 163, 175, 181, 182, 196, 207, 208, 209, 210, 211, 228, 231, 241, 250, 266, 289, 302, 314.

F0843 Philby, Harry St J.B., *Arabian Jubilee*, Hale, London 1952; xiv, 280 pp., 23.5 cm, black cloth.
TEL: pp.51, 58, 67, 174.

F0844 Philby, Harry St J.B., *Arabian Jubilee*, Day, New York 1953; xvi, 280 pp., 23.6 cm, black cloth.
TEL: pp.51, 58, 65, 174.

F0845 Philby, Harry St J.B., *Arabian Oil Ventures*, Middle East Institute, Washington DC 1964; xiv, 134 pp., 23.5 cm, blue cloth.
TEL: pp.12–14.

F0846 Philby, Harry St J.B., *Forty Years in the Wilderness*, Hale, London 1957; xvi, 272 pp., 23.4 cm, blue cloth.
TEL: pp.51, 73, 74, 79, 82–109, 251; Chapter V, pp.82–109, "T.E. Lawrence and His Critics".

F0847 Philby, Harry St J.B., *The Land of Midian*, Benn, London 1957; xiv, 288 pp., 21.5 cm, green paper green cloth.
TEL: pp.4, 123, 169, 234, 241.

F0848 Philby, Harry St J.B., *A Pilgrim in Arabia*, Hale, London 1946; 4, 200 pp., 22.2 cm, red cloth.
TEL: p.70.

F0849 Philby, Harry St J.B., *A Pilgrim in Arabia*, Golden Cockerel Press, 1934; 192 pp., 25.7 cm, linen boards, red leather spine.
TEL: p.66.

F0850 Philby, Harry St J.B., *Sa'udi Arabia*, Benn, London 1955; xx, 396 pp., 22 cm, blue cloth.
TEL: pp.275, 280, 285.

F0851 Philby, Harry St J.B., *Sheba's Daughters*, Methuen, London 1939; xx, 486 pp., 24 cm, green cloth.
TEL: pp.vii, 404.

F0852 Phillips, Cabell, *The New York Times Chronicle of American Life*, Macmillan, New York 1969.
TEL: p.402.

F0853 Phillips, Wendell, *Oman, a history*, McKay, New York 1966; xiv, 320 pp., 21 cm, orange cloth.
TEL: pp.34, 98–9, 209, 216–7.

F0854 Phillips, Wendell, *Oman, a History*, Reynal & Co., London 1967; xiv, 246 pp., 22.9 cm, deep red linen.
TEL: pp.178–9.

F0855 Pickard, Roy, *Hollywood Gold*, Talinger, New York 1979.
TEL: p.90.

F0856 Picon, Gäetan, *L'Usage de la lecture,* Mercure de France, Paris 1960; 2, 1–268 pp., 19.3m white paper covers.
TEL: pp.49–54, "Lawrence et L'Innocence de L'Action".

F0857 Pilgrim Trust, London, *Recording Britain,* Oxford University Press, London 1946–49; Volumes 3–4, 25.4 cm, red cloth.
TEL: Vol. 3, p.108; Vol. 4, p.114.

F0858 Plowden, Joan M.C., *Once in Siniai,* Methuen, London 1940; xvi, 302 pp., fold map at rear, 22.4 cm, black cloth.
TEL: pp.1, 19, 20, 36, 40, 125, 146, 185–6.

F0859 Poll, Bernhard, *Deutsches Schicksal 1914–1918,* Weidmannsche, Berlin 1937.
TEL: pp.235–6.

F0860 Portland, 6th Duke of ([William J.A.C.J. Cavendish-Bentinck), *Men Women and Things,* Faber, London 1938 (2nd imp.); xx, 424 pp., 28.3 cm, blue cloth.
TEL: p.52.

F0861 *Portmadoc Urban and District Guide,* Watkins, Portmadoc n.d.; 108 pp., 21 cm, pictorial paper covers.
TEL: p.45.

F0862 Pound, Ezra, *The Cantos of Ezra Pound,* New Directions, New York 1948; 4, 118 pp., 21.8 cm, black cloth.
TEL: p.22 of Pisan Cantos.

F0863 Pound, Ezra, *The Letters of Ezra Pound, 1907–1941,* Harcourt, Brace, New York 1950; xxvi, 358 pp., 20.3 cm, white paper covers.
TEL: pp.152–4.

F0864 Powell, Edward A., *By Camel and Car to the Peacock Throne,* Century, New York 1923; 2, xxii, 392 pp., 20.1 cm, orange cloth.
TEL: p.196.

F0865 Powell, Edward A., *By Camel and Car to the Peacock Throne,* Garden City, New York n.d.; 2, xiv, 392 pp., 20.9 cm, orange-brown cloth.
TEL: p.196.

F0866 Powell, Lawrence Clark, *Books in My Baggage,* World, Cleveland, Ohio 1960.
TEL: pp.61, 197.

F0867 Powell, Lawrence Clark, *Books in My Baggage,* Constable, London 1960; 136 pp., 22 cm, blue cloth.
TEL: p.61.

F0868 Presland, John, *Deedes Bey,* Macmillan, London 1942; xiii, 360 pp., 22.4 cm, blue cloth.
TEL: pp.179, 220, 237, 238–40, 250, 251, 252, 254, 256, 271, 278, 290.

F0869 Presley, John W., *The Robert Graves Manuscripts and Letters at Southern Illinois University, An Inventory,* Whitson Pub. Co., Troy, New York, 1976; 4, viii, 266 pp., 23.6 cm, blue cloth.
TEL: pp.792, 832, 834–5.

F0870 Preston, Richard Martin Peter, *The Desert Mounted Corps,* Houghton Mifflin, Boston 1923; xxiv, 356 pp., 22.5 cm, sand cloth.
TEL: pp.130, 195, 255, 257, 278.

F0871 Prigent, Simone, *Qui Est-Ce?,* Hachette, Paris 1971.
TEL: Item 121.

F0872 Pritchett, V.S., *Books in General*, Chatto & Windus, London 1953; viii, 260 pp., 19 cm, blue linen.
TEL: pp.37–42, "A Portrait of T.E. Lawrence".

F0873 Pritchett, V.S., *The Tale Bearers*, Vintage Books, New York 1980; 228 pp., 20.4 cm, brown paper covers.
TEL: pp.54–63, "T.E. Lawrence".

F0874 Pritchett, V.S., *The Tale Bearers*, Random House, New York 1980; 224 pp., 21.5 cm, red paper covered boards, black cloth spine.
TEL: pp.54–63, "T.E. Lawrence".

F0875 Prittie, Terence, *Israel*, Penguin Books, Baltimore 1967; 6, 266 pp., 18 cm, pictorial paper covers.
TEL: pp.172–3.

F0876 *Progress of Nations*, Department of Rehabilitation, Disabled American Veterans of the World War, Chicago 1933.
TEL: pp.260–63.

F0877 Pustay, John S., *Counter-Insurgency Warfare*, Free Press, 1965.
TEL: pp.23, 24, 25, 28, 58, 214.

F0878 *Quarto Club Papers, 1928/1929*, Printed for the Members, New York 1930; 16, 128 pp., 2 cm, red marbled boards, black cloth spine, 140 copies.
TEL: pp.63–4.

F0879 Quennell, Peter, *The Wanton Chase*, New York 1980; 192 pp., 21.5 blue cloth, illus.
TEL: p.144.

F0880 Raban, Jonathan, *Arabia Through the Looking-Glass*, Collins, London 1979.
TEL: pp.15–16.

F0881 Randall, Rona, *Jordan and the Holy Land*, Muller, London 1968; xii, 244 pp., 22.3 cm, brown paper covered boards.
TEL: pp.35, 36, 37, 38, 42, 45, 47, 163, 165, 210.

F0882 Raswan, Carl R., *The Black Tents of Arabia*, Creative Age, New York 1947; xvi, 208 pp., 22 cm, brown cloth.
TEL: p.viii.

F0883 Raswan, Carl R., *The Black Tents of Arabia*, Little, Brown, Boston 1935; xiv, 208 pp., 24.6 cm, brown cloth.
TEL: p.viii.

F0884 Raswan, Carl R., *The Black Tents of Arabia*, Paternoster Library, London n.d.; 256 pp., 22.3 cm, green cloth.
TEL: pp.12, 204.

F0885 Raswan, Carl R., *The Black Tents of Arabia*, Farrar, Straus & Giroux, New York 1971; xvi, 208 pp., 21.5 cm, black paper covered boards.
TEL: p.viii.

F0886 Raymond, Ernest, *In the Steps of St Francis*, Rich & Cowan, London 1938; x, 378 pp., 20.4 cm, brown linen.
TEL: p.150.

F0887 Raymond, René, and Langdon, David, *Slipstream*, Eyre & Spottiswoode, London 1946; xii, 260 pp., 22.2 cm, blue cloth.
TEL: pp.98–101, Lord Kinross, "A.C. Shaw (Lawrence of Arabia)".

F0888 Read, Herbert, *A Coat of Many Colours*, Routledge, London 1945;

viii, 352 pp., 17.2 cm, red cloth.
TEL: pp.19–23, "Lawrence of Arabia"; pp.24–6, "The Seven Pillars of Wisdom".

F0889 Read, Herbert, *A Coat of Many Colours*, Readers' Union Routledge, London 1947; viii, 352 pp., 17 cm, green cloth.
TEL: pp.19–23, "Lawrence of Arabia"; pp.24–6, "The Seven Pillars of Wisdom".

F0890 Read, Herbert , *Vive Che!*, Lorrimer, London 1968.
TEL: p.120.

F0891 Reader's Digest, *Great Events of the 20th Century*, Reader's Digest Association, Pleasantville, New York, 1977.
TEL: p.118.

F0892 Reynolds, J.S. *Canon Christopher of St Aldates*, Abingdon Abbey Press, Oxford 1967; xxvi, 499 pp., 24.5 cm, red buckram.
TEL: p.346.

F0893 Rhondda, Viscountess, *Notes on the Way*, Macmillan, London 1937; viii, 224 pp., 19 cm.
TEL: pp.17–18, r e. Odyssey.

F0894 Rhys, Ernest, *Letters from Limbo*, Dent, London 1936; 2, xviii, 292 pp., 21.5 cm, red cloth.
TEL: pp.145–7, "Colonel T.E. Lawrence (1888–1935)".

F0895 Ridley, Maurice R., *Gertrude Bell*, Blackie, London 1941; 208 pp., 19.8 cm, brown cloth.
TEL: p.109.

F0896 Rigby, Douglas and Elizabeth, *Lock, Stock and Barrel*, Lippincott, 1944.
TEL: p.107.

F0897 Rihani, Ameen, *Around the Coasts of Arabia*, Constable, London 1930; xii, 364 pp., 22.6 cm, patterned cloth.
TEL: pp.96–8, 100, 111.

F0898 Rihani, Ameen, *Around the Coasts of Arabia*, Houghton Mifflin, Boston 1930; xii, 364 pp., 22.3 cm, blue cloth.
TEL: pp.96–8, 100, 111.

F0899 Rivington, Arabell, *Poems*, Privately printed by John Roberts Press, London 1973; 88 pp., 21.6 cm, green paper covers, 80 copies.
TEL: pp.7–44, a series of 27 verses written by author during several years' research on Lawrence. Notes on the poems in Part One contain many references to him.

F0900 Roberts, Glyn, *Most Powerful Man in the World*, Covici-Friede, New York 1938.
TEL: pp.292, 339, 340.

F0901 Robertson, Wilmot, *The Dispossessed Majority*, Cape Canaverel, 1976.
TEL: pp.192, 250, 477, 492.

F0902 Rogers, Bruce, *Paragraphs on Printing*, W.E. Rudge's Sons, New York 1943 2 × 188 pp., 28.2 cm, patterned paper-covered boards, oatmeal cloth spine, slipcase; large paper edition, four decorations in colour and printer's mark book. Book plate designed by Bruce Rogers. One of 199 copies, also regular issue in brown.
TEL: pp.148–60.

F0903 Rogers, Bruce, *Pi*, World Pub., Cleveland, Ohio 1953; x, 190 pp., 22 cm, maroon linen.
TEL: pp.51, 68, 69, 73, 74, 133.

F0904 Rogers, Bruce and Walker, Emery, *Typographical Partnership*, Carl H. Pforzheimer Library, Cambridge, England 1971; xvi, 48 pp., 29.2 cm, marbled paper covered boards, brown cloth spine, limited to 350 copies.
TEL: pp.xiii, 32, 35–6.

F0905 Rommel, Erwin, *The Rommel Papers*, Harcourt Brace, New York 1953; [4], vii–xxx, 548 pp., 22 cm, olive green cloth.
TEL: p.xiv.

F0906 Rosenblum, Ralph, and Karen, Robert, *When the Shooting Stops...and the Cutting Begins*, Viking, New York.
TEL: p.77.

F0907 Roskill, Stephen, *Hankey: Man of Secrets*, Collins, London 1970 (Volume 1), 1972 (Volume 2), 1974 (Volume 3); 23.3 cm, red cloth.
TEL: Vol. 2, pp.116–7, 119, 128.

F0908 Rothenstein, Sir John, *Summer's Lease*, Hamish Hamilton, London 1965; xii, 260 pp., 22.3 cm, red paper covered boards.
TEL: pp.64–72, 114, 115.

F0909 Rothenstein, Sir John, *Summer's Lease*, Holt Rinehart & Winston, New York 1966; xii, 260 pp., 21.5 cm, blue cloth.
TEL: pp.64–72, 114, 115.

F0910 Rothenstein, Sir William, *Men and Memories*, Faber & Faber, London 1932; 2 volumes, 21 cm, russet cloth (also black cloth 1939).
TEL: Vol. 2, pp.26, 367, 368, 382.

F0911 Rothenstein, Sir William, *Men and Memories*, Coward McCann, New York 1935; 2 volumes, 24.5 cm, white cloth.
TEL: Vol. 2, pp.26, 367, 368, 382.

F0912 Rothenstein, Sir William, *Men and Memories*, Tudor, New York 1937?; xx, 374, 4, 412 pp., 2 volumes in one, 24.5 cm, black linen.
TEL: Vol. II, pp.26, 367, 368, 382.

F0913 Rothenstein, Sir William, *Since Fifty*, Faber & Faber, London 1939; xvi, 352 pp., 24.5 cm, black cloth.
TEL: pp.8–12, 36, 69–72, 83–4, 104–6, 144, 153, 156, 225, 229, 263–6, 282, 284, 293, 329.

F0914 Rothenstein, Sir William, *Since Fifty*, Macmillan, New York 1940; xvi, 352 pp., 24.3 cm, blue linen.
TEL: pp.8–11, 12, 36, 69–82, 83–4, 104–6, 144, 153, 156, 225, 229, 263–6, 282, 284, 293, 329.

F0915 Rothenstein, Sir William, *Twenty-Four Portraits*, Allen & Unwin, London 1920; unpaged, 26 cm, grey-green paper covered boards, oatmeal cloth spine, limited to 2000 copies.
TEL: Portrait drawing with single page biography of him by Hogarth.

F0916 Rothenstein, Sir William, *Twenty-Four Portraits*, Harcourt, Brace, New York 1920; unpaged, 27 cm, green paper covered boards, green cloth spine, 2000 copies.
TEL: Portrait with short biography by Hogarth.

F0917 Rougemont, Denis de, *Dramatic Personages,* Holt Rinehart & Winston, New York 1964; xiv, 170 pp., 21.7 cm, grey cloth boards, white cloth spine.
TEL: pp.135–52, "Prototype E.T.L. *(sic)*".

F0918 Rousseaux, André, *Littérature du Vingtième Siècle,* Albin Michel, Paris 1955.
TEL: 4th series, pp.53–62, "La Mystique de T.E. Lawrence"; 6th series, pp.234–43, "La Fin de T.E. Lawrence ou Prométhée embourbé".

F0919 Rowse, A.L., *The Churchills,* Harper, New York 1958; xvi, 432 pp., 24.5 cm, red cloth boards, black cloth spine.
TEL: pp.328–9.

F0920 Rowse, A.L., *The English Spirit,* Macmillan, London 1944; x, 278 pp., 22.3 cm, orange cloth.
TEL: pp.55–7, 59–60, 255.

F0921 Rowse, A.L., *Homosexuals in History,* Carroll & Graf, New York 1977; xxvi, 350 pp., 21.5 cm.
TEL: pp.8, 137, 254–9.

F0922 Royal Institute of International Affairs. *The Middle East,* London & New York 1955; xviii, 590 pp., 22 cm, green cloth.
TEL: pp.22, 24, 353, 469–70.

F0923 Rumbold, Richard, *The Winged LIfe,* Weidenfeld, London 1954; 224 pp., 22.2 cm, bright blue cloth.
TEL: pp.29, 50, 197, 219.

F0924 Runyan, William McKinley, *Life Histories and Psychobiology,* Oxford University Press, New York 1982.
TEL: pp.195, 245.

F0925 Rustow, Dankwart A., *Middle Eastern Political Systems,* Prentice-Hall, New York 1971.
TEL: p.49.

F0926 Rutherford, Andrew, *The Literature of War,* Macmillan, London 1978; 12, 180 pp., 22.3 cm, blue cloth.
TEL: pp.38–63, 68, 105, 154.

F0927 Rutter, Owen, *Triumphant Pilgrimage,* Lippincott, Philadelphia 1937; 2, 296 pp., 21.8 cm, orange cloth.
TEL: pp.152, 166, 203, 204, 294.

F0928 Rutter, Owen, *Triumphant Pilgrimage,* Harrap, London 1937; 278 pp., 22.3 cm, maroon cloth.
TEL: pp.141, 155, 190, 191, 273.

F0929 Ryan, Peter, *The National Trust,* Dent, London 1969; xvi, 3, 84–160 pp., 35.6 cm, green cloth.
TEL: p.97, "Clouds Hill, Dorset".

F0930 Sachar, Howard M., *The Emergence of the Middle East 1914–1924,* Lane, 1969; 4, xiv, 518, xlviii pp., 24 cm, tan cloth.
TEL: pp.135, 137, 138, 139–40, 141–2, 145–9, 150–51, 173, 187, 233, 237, 240, 242, 254, 255, 261, 368, 376, 377, 378, 385, 401, 403–4.

F0931 Sachar, Howard M., *History of Israel,* Knopf, New York 1970.
TEL: pp.92, 121, 126.

F0932 St John Ervine, *Bernard Shaw,* William Morrow, New York 1956; xii,

628 pp., 24 cm, green cloth boards, black cloth spine.
TEL: pp.114, 522, 526, 580.

F0932a Saint-Laurent, Cecil, *Hortense 14–18,* Presses de la Cité, Paris 1965.
TEL: Chapter 4, pp.87–106; Chapter 6, pp.131–56; Chapter 8, pp.179–90; Chapter 13, pp.335–58.

F0933 Salmon, Edmond, and Worsfold, James, *The British Dominions Yearbook 1921,* Eagle, Star and British Dominion Insurance Co., London; 350 pp., 21.5 cm, blue paper covered boards, blue cloth spine.
TEL: p.23.

F0934 Salter, Arthur, 1st Baron, *Memoirs of a Public Servant,* Faber & Faber, London 1961; 356 pp., 22.3 cm, blue cloth.
TEL: pp.24, 142–5.

F0935 Sampson, George, *The Concise Cambridge History of English Literature,* Cambridge University Press 1949; xvi, 1096 pp., 20.5 cm, blue linen.
TEL: pp.1047–8.

F0936 Samuel, Herbert Louis Samuel, 1st Viscount, *Memoirs,* Cresset, London 1945; viii, 304 pp., 22.2 cm, orange cloth.
TEL: pp.155, 174, 179.

F0937 Sanger, Richard H., *The Arabian Peninsula,* Cornell University Press, Ithaca, New York, 1954; xvi, 296 pp., 24 cm, green cloth.
TEL: pp.6, 30, 78.

F0938 Sassoon, Sir Philip, *The Third Route,* Heinemann, London 1929; xiii, 292 pp., 22.7 cm, blue cloth.
TEL: pp.195, 206.

F0939 Sassoon, Sir Philip, *The Third Route,* Garden City, New York 1929; xvi, 282 pp., 23.5 cm, red cloth.
TEL: pp.195, 206.

F0940 Sassoon, Siegfried, *Siegfried's Journey, 1916–1920,* Faber, London 1945; 2, 224 pp., 20.5 cm, coral cloth.
TEL: pp.86–8.

F0941 Sassoon, Siegfried, *Siegfried's Journey, 1916–1920,* Viking, New York 1946 (second printing before publication); 2, 342 pp., 22 cm, tan cloth.
TEL: Dust wrapper and p.128.

F0942 *The Saturday Book, 3,* Hutchinson, London 1943; 280 pp.
TEL: pp.46–7, photo and ref.

F0943 *The Saturday Book, 11th year,* Hutchinson, London 1951; 280 pp., 23.5 cm, coarse rose cloth.
TEL: pp.174, Arabic poem by Emir Feisal, translated by Lawrence.

F0944 Savage, Raymond, *Allenby of Armageddon,* Hodder & Stoughton, London 1925; 308 pp., 23 cm, maroon cloth.
TEL: p.296.

F0945 Savage, Raymond, *Allenby of Armageddon,* Bobbs-Merrill, Indianapolis 1925; 308 pp., maroon cloth.
TEL: pp.276+.

F0946 (Scott), Kennet, Lady (Kathleen (Bruce) Young), *Homage,* Bles, London 1938; unpaged, 29 cm, blue cloth.

TEL: Plate XXV followed by three pages of commentary; A.W. Lawrence, p.[39].

F0947 Scott-James, R.A., *Fifty Years of English Literature 1900–1956*, Longmans, London 1951; x, 256 pp., 22 cm.
TEL: pp.167, 190–92.

F0948 Seaman, Lewis C.B., *Post-Victorian Britain: 1902–1951*, Methuen, London 1970; xii, 532 pp., 21.8 cm, orange cloth.
TEL: pp.140, 143–4.

F0949 Searight, Sarah, *The British in the Middle East*, Weidenfeld & Nicolson, London 1969; xvi, 216 pp., 24.7 cm, red cloth.
TEL: pp.139, 188, 190.

F0950 Searight, Sarah, *The British in the Middle East*, Atheneum, New York 1970; xvi, 216 pp., 24.8 cm, red cloth.
TEL: pp.139, 188, 190.

F0951 Seligo, Irene, *Zwischen Traum und Tat*, Societäts, Frankfurt 1938; 462, 2 pp., 21.3 cm, grey cloth.
TEL: pp.422–62, "Der Erbe, T.E. Lawrence".

F0951a Serjeant, R.B., and Bidwell, R.L., eds, *Arabian Studies VII*, Scorpion, London 1985.
TEL: pp.7–22, Sulaiman Mousa, "T.E. Lawrence and his Arab Contemporaries".

F0952 Seymour-Smith, Martin, *Robert Graves*, Holt Rinehart & Winston, New York 1982; xviii, 614 pp.
TEL: pp.6, 30, 75, 84–6, 89, 91, 93, 108–11, 115, 120–21, 132–5, 140, 141–3, 186, 212–3, 242, 253–5, 257–9, 374, 496–8.

F0953 Shaffer, Robert, *Tents and Towers of Arabia*, Dodd Mead, New York 1952; xii, 276 pp., 21 cm, black cloth.
TEL: pp.51, 213, 214, 216.

F0954 Shah, Ikbal Ali, Sidar, *The Controlling Minds of Asia*, Jenkins, London 1937; 320 pp., 21.7 cm, tan cloth.
TEL: pp.180–82.

F0955 Shah, Sayed Idries, *Destination, Mecca*, Rider, London 1957; 192 pp., 21.8 cm, maroon cloth.
TEL: pp.65, 73.

F0956 Sharif, Omar, *L'Éternel Masculin*, Stock, Paris 1976; 240 pp., 22 cm, pictorial paper covers.
TEL: pp.13, 37

F0957 Shaw, George Bernard, *Everybody's Political What's What*, Constable, London 1944; viii, 380 pp., 20.5 cm, brown cloth.
TEL: pp.320, 334.

F0958 Shaw, George Bernard, *Flyleaves*, Thomas Taylor, Austin, Texas, 1977; 2, 62, 4 pp., 28.8 cm, brown cloth, 350 copies printed by Henry Morris at the Bird & Bull Press.
TEL: pp.33–40.

F0959 Shaw, George Bernard, *Saint Joan, Major Barbara and Androcles and the Lion*, Modern Library, New York 1956; 6, 490 pp., 18.5 cm, red cloth.
TEL: Joan modelled on Lawrence.

F0960 Shaw, George Bernard, *Too True to Be Good, Village Wooing and On the Rocks*, Constable, London 1934; 2, vi, 276 pp., 20.8 cm, maroon cloth.
TEL: Main character Meek modelled on Lawrence.

F0961 Shaw, George Bernard, *Too True to Be Good, Village Wooing and On the Rocks*, Dodd, Mead, New York 1934; vi, 346 pp., 19.2 cm, black cloth.
TEL: Main character Meek modelled on Lawrence.

F0962 Sheean, Vincent, *Between the Thunder and the Sun*, Macmillan, London 1943; viii, 340 pp., 22 cm, red cloth.
TEL: pp.135, 136, 137, 138.

F0963 Sheean, Vincent, *Between the Thunder and the Sun*, Random House, New York 1943; 430 pp., 22 cm, red cloth.
TEL: pp.172, 173, 175.

F0964 Sheean, Vincent, *Personal History*, Houghton, New York 1969.
TEL: pp.381–5.

F0965 Sheean, Vincent, *In Search of History*, Hamish Hamilton, London 1935; viii, 448 pp., dark blue cloth.
TEL: pp.423, 424, 427.

F0966 Sheean, Vincent, *Personal History*, Literary Guild, New York 1935?; x, 404 pp., 22 cm, black cloth.
TEL: pp.381, 382, 385.

F0967 Sherer Herz, Judith, and Martin, Robert K., *E.M. Forster: Centenary Revaluations*, University of Toronto, Toronto 1982.
TEL: pp.19, 34, 223.

F0968 Sherwood, John, *No Golden Journey*, Heinemann, London 1973; xviii, 238 pp., 24 cm, brown cloth.
TEL: pp.xiii, 34, 146–8.

F0969 Shirer, William, *20th Century Journal*, Little, Brown, Boston 1984.
TEL: p.38.

F0970 Shotwell, James T., *At the Paris Peace Conference*, Macmillan, New York 1937; xii, 444 pp., 24 cm, blue cloth.
TEL: pp.108, 115, 121, 129, 131–2, 184, 191, 192, 197, 220, 225, 234, 313.

F0971 Sidebotham, Herbert, *Great Britain and Palestine*, Macmillan, London 1937; x, 310, [2] pp., blue cloth 22.4 cm.
TEL: p.20.

F0972 Silver, Alain, and Ursini, James, *David Lean and His Films*, Leslie Frewin, London 1974; 256 pp., 25.5 cm, brown cloth.
TEL: pp.161, 167–8, 176; Film, pp.83, 88, 132, 149–50, 161, 168, 169–75, 176–82, 198.

F0973 Silverberg, Robert, *If I Forget Thee O Jerusalem*, Pyramid, New York 1972; 640 pp., 17.8 cm, pictorial paper covers.
TEL: pp.85, 104, 110.

F0974 Sitwell, Osbert (Sir), *Laughter in the Next Room*, Little, Brown, Boston 1948.
TEL: pp.210–11.

F0975 Sloan, A., *Wanderings in the Middle East*, Hutchinson, London 1924;

318 pp., 24.8 cm, blue cloth.
TEL: pp.112, 118–47.

F0976 Smith, Janet Adam, *John Buchan*, Hart-Davis, London 1965; 526 pp., 22.3 cm, blue cloth.
TEL: pp.9, 27, 212, 224, 236, 241, 242–4, 262–3, 267, 280, 307, 326–7, 333, 341, 379.

F0977 Smith, Janet Adam, *John Buchan*, Little, Brown, Boston 1965; 2, 524 pp., 21.5 cm, black cloth.
TEL: pp.9, 207, 212, 224, 236, 241–4, 262–3, 280, 307, 326–7, 333, 341, 379.

F0978 Smith, R. Skilbeçk, *A Subaltern in Macedonia and Judea, 1916–1917*, Mitre Press, London 1930.

F0979 Smyth, Ethel, *Maurice Baring*, Heinemann, London 1938; xvi, 352 pp., 22.2 cm, brown cloth.
TEL: pp.57, 64, 185, 337–9.

F0980 Snipes, Katherine, *Robert Graves*, Ungar, New York 1973.
TEL: pp.viii, 6, 144–7.

F0981 Speaight, Robert, *William Rothenstein*, Eyre & Spottiswoode, London 1962; xvi, 444 pp., 21.3 cm, blue linen.
TEL: pp.305, 320, 352, 354, 365.

F0982 Spencer, William, *Political Evolution in the Middle East*, Lippincott, 1962.
TEL: pp.41–2, 300.

F0983 Spender, Stephen, *D.H. Lawrence, Novelist, Poet, Prophet*, Harper & Row, New York 1973; 6, 250 pp., 25.3 cm, red cloth.
TEL: p.136.

F0984 Sperber, Manès, *The Achilles Heel*, Deutsch, London 1959; 224 pp., 22 cm, brown paper covered boards.
TEL: pp.173–204, "False Situation: T.E. Lawrence and His Two Legends".

F0985 Sperber, Manès, *The Achilles Heel*, Doubleday, Garden City, New York, 1960; 224 pp., 22 cm, brown cloth.
TEL: pp.173–204, "False Situations: T.E. Lawrence and His Two Legends".

F0986 Sperber, Manès, *Le Talon d'Achille-Essais*, Calmann-Levy, Paris 1957.
TEL: pp.177–214, "Les Fausses Situations".

F0987 Stark, Freya, *Beyond Euphrates*, Murray, London 1951; xvi, 342 pp., 22.5 cm, green buckram.
TEL: pp.97, 209, 313–4.

F0988 Stark, Freya, *The Coast of Incense*, Murray, London 1953; xiv, 286 pp., 22.8 cm, green buckram.
TEL: pp.111, 113–4, 194, 255.

F0989 Stark, Freya, *The Freya Stark Story*, Coward McCann, New York 1953; x, 374 pp., 22 cm, dark blue cloth.
TEL: p.235.

F0990 Stark, Freya, *The Journey's Echo*, Murray, London 1963; xiv, 226 pp., 21 cm, green cloth.
TEL: p.xii.

F0991 Stark, Freya, *Letters from Syria,* Murray, London 1942; xii, 194 pp., 19 cm, green cloth.
TEL: pp.,39, 47, 53.

F0992 Stark, Lewis M., *Books Designed by Bruce Rogers,* New York Public Library, 1955; 16 pp., 22.5 cm, pink paper wrappers.
TEL: pp.11, 13, 15.

F0993 Steed, Wickham Henry, *Through Thirty Years,* Heinemann, London 1924; 2 volumes, 22.3 cm, blue linen.
TEL: Vol. 2, pp.300, 323.

F0994 Steiner, Morris J., *Inside Pan-Arabia,* Packard Co., Chicago; xvi, 240 pp., 21.5 cm, tan cloth.
TEL: pp.60, 79, 93, 161, 165, 200.

F0995 Stevenson, Frances, *Lloyd George,* Harper & Row, New York 1971; xiv, 338 pp., 24.4 cm, blue cloth.
TEL: pp.322.

F0996 Stewart, Desmond, *The Arab World,* Time, Inc., New York 1962; 160 pp., 28 cm, pictorial cloth covers.
TEL: pp.49 (photo), 112–14.

F0997 Stewart, Desmond, *The Middle East,* Doubleday, Garden City, New York, 1971; x, 422 pp., 24 cm, tan cloth covered boards, black cloth spine.
TEL: pp.203–4, 206–10, 234, 273–5.

F0998 Stirling, Walter Francis, *Safety Last,* Hollis & Carter, London 1953; viii, 252 pp., 22 cm, red cloth.
TEL: pp.67, 80–89, 92–4, 96, 162, 163; 245–8, "Lawrence of Arabia: A Personal Impression of a Comrade in the Great War". Portrait opposite p.88.

F0999 Stitt, George, *A Prince of Arabia,* Allen & Unwin, London 1948; 320 pp., 22.3 cm, orange cloth.
TEL: Dust wrapper.

F1000 Stock, Noel, *Life of Ezra Pound,* Pantheon Books, 1970.
TEL: pp.131–2, 229.

F1001 Stoddard, Lothrop, *The New World of Islam,* Scribner's, New York 1921; viii, 362 pp., 21 cm, green cloth.
TEL: pp.221, 230f, 234.

F1002 Stone, Wilfred, *The Cave and the Mountain,* Stanford University Press, 1966.
TEL: pp.288, 290, 346, 353, 360, 415.

F1003 Storrs, Sir Ronald, *Memoirs,* Putnam's, New York 1937; xviii, 566 pp., 23.5 cm, blue cloth.
TEL: pp.12, 38, 54, 74, 166–9, 186, 189, 202–4, 210–11, 238, 270, 281, 286, 293, 299, 371, 399, 417, 466–79, 513, 543, 550–51.

F1004 Storrs, Sir Ronald, *Orientations,* Nicholson & Watson, London 1937; xviii, 624 pp., 24.5 cm, dark blue cloth.
TEL: pp.11, 40, 56, 77, 176, 177, 179, 180, 199–200, 203, 218–21, 228–9, 261, 299, 312, 318, 325, 333, 412, 444, 463, 517–32, 568, 602, 609–10.

F1005 Storrs, Sir Ronald, *Orientations,* Reader's Union, London 1939;

xviii, 558 pp., 22.1 cm, green paper-covered boards.
TEL: pp.10, 36, 52, 71, 159–63, 180, 183, 196–9, 205–6, 233, 266, 277, 282–3, 288, 295, 364, 393, 410, 459–72, 505, 534, 541–2.

F1006 Strong, Leonard Alfred George, ed., *Sixteen Portraits of People Whose Houses Have Been Preserved by the National Trust*, Naldrett Press, London 1951; 248 pp., 22.2 cm, tan rough cloth.
TEL: pp.110–22, Sir Ronald Storrs, "T.E. Lawrence".

F1007 Sulzberger, C.L., *A Long Row of Candles*, Macmillan, Toronto 1969; 2, xviii,1070 pp., 24 cm, green cloth boards, blue buckram spine.
TEL: pp.193, 325–6, 397, 516, 723.

F1008 Summers, Claude, J., *Christopher Isherwood*, Unger, New York 1980.
TEL: pp.65, 100, 126, 145, 166.

F1009 Sutherland, L.W., *Aces and Kings*, Hamish Hamilton, London 1936; xii, 276 pp., 18.6 cm, blue cloth.
TEL: Chapter 5, pp.68–111, "Our Lawrence".

F1010 Sykes, Christopher, *Crossroads to Israel*, World, Cleveland 1965.
TEL: pp.17, 18, 19, 32, 47, 56, 57, 66, 160.

F1011 Sykes, Christopher, *Nancy*, Collins, London 1972; 544 pp., 23.5 cm, dark green cloth.
TEL: pp.308–11, 315, 349, 353, 360–61, 513, 520.

F1012 Sykes, Christopher, *Nancy*, Harper & Row, New York 1972; 544 pp., 21.8 cm, red cloth.
TEL: pp.308–11, 315, 349, 353, 360–61, 513, 520.

F1013 Sykes, Christopher, *Orde Wingate*, World, Cleveland 1959; 576 pp., 2.3 cm, beige cloth.
TEL: pp.122, 132–33, 167, 199, 209, 223, 224, 230, 250, 271, 291, 324, 541.

F1014 Sykes, Christopher, *Orde Wingate*, Collins, London 1959; 576 pp., 23.4 cm, red cloth.
TEL: pp.122, 132–33, 167, 199, 209, 223–4, 230, 250, 271, 291, 324, 541.

F1015 Sykes, Christopher, *Wassmuss, "The German Lawrence"*, Longmans, Green, London 1936; 2, xii,272 pp., 20.5 cm, oatmeal cloth.
TEL: Title page, 72, 114–5, 239, .

F1016 Sykes, Christopher, *Wassmuss, "The German Lawrence"*, B. Tauchnitz, Leipzig 1937; 248 pp., 18.1 cm, white printed paper covers, Vol. 5262 of Tauchnitz British and American Authors.

F1017 Sykes, Frederick, *From Many Angles*, Harrap, London 1943.
TEL: p.249.

F1018 Sykes, Sir Percy, *A History of Exploration from the Earliest Times to the Present Day*, Routledge, London 1934; 2, xiv, 376 pp., 25.5 cm, red cloth.
TEL: pp.xiii, 277, 293.

F1019 Sylvestre, Guy, *Sondanges*, Montreal, 1945.
TEL: pp.141–57, "Mésure de Lawrence".

F1020 Symes, Sir Stewart, *Tour of Duty*, Collins, London 1946; 27.1 cm, maroon cloth.
TEL: pp.29–33, 35.

F1021 Tabachnick, Stephen Ely, *Charles Doughty*, Twayne, Boston 1981; 183 pp., 21 cm, maroon buckram.
TEL: pp.26, 29, 32, 33, 42, 57, 65, 66, 69, 81, 82, 83, 122, 123, 127, 132, 156, 163, 165, 166, 168.

F1022 Talese, Gay, *Fame and Obscurity*, World Pub., New York 1970; x, 358 pp., 23.5 cm, green cloth.
TEL: pp.99–104 (film).

F1023 Targ, William, *Adventures in Good Reading*, Black Archer Press, Chicago 1940; xiv, 98 pp., 19,7 cm, buff cloth.
TEL: pp.67–8.

F1024 Taylor, A.J.P., *English History 1914–1945*, Oxford University Press, Oxford 1965.
TEL: pp.49, 179, 180, 605, 622.

F1025 Taylor, John Russell, *The Rise and Fall of the Well-Made Play*, Hill & Wang, New York 1967.
TEL: pp.156–7.

F1026 Taylor, John Russell, *Alec Guinness*, Little Brown, Boston 1984.
TEL: pp.30–31, 116, 122, 124, 125, 156.

F1027 Temple, Ruth Z., and Tucker, Martin, *A Library of Literary Criticism*, Vol. II, H–P, Unger, New York 1966.
TEL: pp.164–70, "T.E. Lawrence (1888–1935)".

F1028 Templewood, 1st Viscount (Samuel J.G.Hoare), *Empire of the Air*, Collins, London 1957; 320 pp., 21.5 cm, blue cloth.
TEL: pp.45, 47, 112, 152, 246, 255–8.

F1031 Tharaud, Jérome, *Le Chemin de Damas*, Plon, Paris 1928; 6, 292 pp., 18.8 cm, yellow paper covers.
TEL: pp.229–31, 248, 252, 280–81.

F1032 Thatcher, David, *Nietzsche in England, 1890–1914*, University of Toronto Press, 1970.
TEL: p.7.

F1033 *Theatre World Annual, No.11, 1 June 1 1959–61*, Macmillan, New York 1960; 176 pp., 25.5 cm, pink cloth.
TEL: pp.10, 15, 28, 144–8, "Ross".

F1034 Thesiger, Wilfred, *Arabian Sands*, Dutton, New York 1959; xvi, 336 pp., 22.8 cm, blue cloth spine, blue paper covered boards.
TEL: pp.1, 25, 68, 110.

F1035 Thesiger, Wilfred, *Arabian Sands*, Penguin Books, Harmondsworth 1964; 352 pp., 18.1 cm, pictorial paper covers.
TEL: pp.15, 39, 83, 97, 125.

F1036 Thesiger, Wilfred, *Arabian Sands*, Longmans Green & Co., London 1959; xiv, 270 pp., 20.6 cm, red cloth.

F1037 Thesiger, Wilfred, *The Last Nomad*, Dutton, New York 1980; 304, 2 pp., 27.5 cm, grey paper covered boards, white coarse linen spine.
TEL: pp.13, 32, 37, 297, 299.

F1038 Thomas, Bertram, *The Arabs*, Doubleday, Doran, Garden City, New York, 1937; x, 364 pp., 21.5 cm, orange cloth.
TEL: pp.222, 223, 284, 285, 289.

F1039 Thomas, Hugh, *Suez*, Harper & Row, New York 1967; 264 pp., 21.5

cm, black cloth.
TEL: pp.17, 24.

F1040 Thomas, Lowell, *Adventures Among Immortals*, Dodd Mead, New York 1937; x, 334 pp., 22.2 cm, orange cloth (also in blue cloth).
TEL: pp.v–vi; pp.264–79, "From Sherlock Holmes to T.E. Lawrence".

F1040a Thomas, Lowell, *Adventures Among Immortals*, Hutchinson, London 1938; 264 pp., 22.3 cm, maroon cloth.
TEL: pp.9, 206, 207, 208; Chapter XI, pp.199–210, "From Sherlock Holmes to T.E. Lawrence"; Portrait opposite p.192.

F1041 Thomas, Lowell, *Count Luckner*, Doubleday, New York 1928.
TEL: p.7.

F1042 Thomas, Lowell, *Good Evening Everybody*, Morrow, New York 1976; 352 pp., 24 cm, yellow cloth-covered boards, black cloth spine.
TEL: Chapter 6, pp.141–63, "With Lawrence in Arabia"; pp.83, 125, 130, 134, 136, 196, 198–9, 200, 202–4, 205–6, 208–11, 213, 216, 228, 235, 260–63, 265, 268, 286, 307, 310, 343.

F1043 Thomas, Lowell, *Pageant of Life*, Wilfred Funk, New York 1941; x, 278 pp., 23.6 cm, tan cloth.
TEL: pp.126–32.

F1044 Thomas, Lowell, *Sir Hubert Wilkins*, McGraw-Hill, New York 1961; 6, 298 pp., 21.9 cm, grey paper-covered boards, blue cloth spine.
TEL: pp.1–2, 296.

F1045 Thomas, Lowell, *With Allenby in the Holy Land*, Cassell, London 1938; 6, 202, 1 pp., 21 cm, black cloth.
TEL: pp.125–52, "Lawrence of Arabia Sweeps to the Right Flank".

F1045a *Thomas Hardy Yearbook, No.5 (1975)*, Toucan Press, Mount Durand, St Peter Port, Guernsey 1976, 108 pp., 22 cm, pictorial paper covers.
TEL: pp.35–8, M.H.C. Warner, "Lawrence of Arabia, Thomas Hardy and the Four Black Tea Sets".

F1046 *Thomas Hardy Yearbook, No.9*, (Marguerite Roberts, "Florence Hardy and The Max Gate Circle") Toucan Press, St Peter Port, Guernsey 1980; 96 pp., 22.6 × 15.5 cm, white paper covers.
TEL: Chapter 5, pp.43–90, "Barrie, Cockerell, and Lawrence".

F1047 Thompson, Edward, *Robert Bridges 1844–1930*, Oxford University Press 1944; viii, 132 pp., 22.1 cm, blue buckram.
TEL: p.102.

F1048 Thompson, Edward, *These Men, thy Friends*, Knopf, London 1927; 288 pp., 19.6 cm, patterned cloth boards, black cloth spine.
TEL: p.15.

F1050 Thompson, Reginald C., *Digger's Fancy, a Melodrama*, Sidgwick & Jackson, London 1938; 6, 70 pp., 19 cm, blue cloth.
TEL: Main character, Alan, is modelled in part on Lawrence, with whom the author worked on Carchemish excavations (noted by J.M. Wilson).

F1051 Thompson, Reginald Campbell, *A Pilgrim's Scrip*, John Lane, New York 1915; xii, 346 pp., 22.2 cm, red and brown cloth.
TEL: pp.vii, 294, 298, 321.

F1052 Thompson, Reginald W., *Winston Churchill*, Doubleday, Garden City, New York 1963; 344 pp., 21.5 cm, grey cloth boards, black cloth spine.
TEL: pp.17, 20, 212–3, 231.

F1053 Thompson, Sir Robert, *Revolutionary War in World Strategy*, Taplinger, New York 1970 x, 174 pp., 20.5 cm, black cloth.
TEL: p.16.

F1054 Thompson, Walter Henry, *Assignment: Churchill*, Farrar Straus & Young, New York 1955; 4, 310 pp., 21.5 cm, grey paper cloth, simulated covered boards.
TEL: pp.8–41.

F1055 Thompson, Walter H., *Sixty Minutes with Winston Churchill*, C. Johnson, London 1953; 92 pp., 19.1 cm, blue printed paper covered boards.
TEL: pp.11–12.

F1056 Thorpe, James, *Principles of Textual Criticism*, Huntington Library, San Marino, California, 1972; x, 214 pp., 23.5 cm, green cloth.
TEL: p.149.

F1057 Thoumin, Richard, *The First World War*, Secker & Warburg, London 1963; 544 pp., 22 cm, blue linen.
TEL: pp.407–11, 501, 530, 532, 535.

F1058 Thoumin, Richard, *The First World War*, Putnam's, New York 1964; 544 pp., 22.2 cm, black cloth.
TEL: pp.407–11, 501, 530, 532, 535.

F1059 Thurbon, Colin, *Mirror to Damascus*, Little, Brown, Boston 1968.
TEL: p.198.

F1060 Thurtle, Ernest, *Time's Winged Chariot*, Chaterson, Chaterson 1945; xii, 192 pp., 22 cm, black cloth.
TEL: pp.104–8.

F1061 Tibble, Anne, *Gertrude Bell*, A. & C. Black, London 1958; 96 pp., 20 cm, red paper-covered boards.
TEL: pp.88, 90.

F1062 Tidrick, Kathryn, *Heart-Beguiling Araby*, Cambridge University Press, London 1981; xii, 244 pp., 23.5 cm, orange cloth.
TEL: pp.39, 42, 126, 134, 142, 163, 164, 169, 170–72, 179–81, 185, 186, 187, 190, 191, 192, 207, 215–9.

F1063 Toy, Barbara, *The Highway of the Three Kings*, Murray, London 1968; xii, 188 pp., 22.2 cm, blue paper-covered boards.
TEL: pp.135–6, 146, 174.

F1064 Toynbee, Arnold J., *Acquaintances*, Oxford University Press, London 1967; viii, 312 pp., 22.5 cm, green cloth.
TEL: p.301; Chapter 14, pp.178–97, "Colonel T.E. Lawrence".

F1065 Trager, James, ed., *The People's Chronology*, Holt Rinehart & Winston, New York.
TEL: pp.772, 779, 828, 843, 882, 1094.

F1066 Tredell, Nicolas, *The Novels of Colin Wilson*, Barnes & Noble, New York 1982.
TEL: pp.28, 38, 39.

F1067   Trevor-Roper, Hugh, *The Hermit of Peking*, Macmillan, London 1979.
        TEL: pp.335–7.
F1068   Tschiffely, Aimé Felix, *Don Roberto*, Heinemann, London 1937; xx,
        460 pp., 22.2 cm, black cloth.
        TEL: p.353.
F1069   Tuohy, Frank, *Yeats*, Macmillan, New York 1976.
        TEL: pp.198–9.
F1071   Tweedsmuir, Lady Susan, *A Winter Bouquet*, Duckworth, London
        1955; 128 pp., 22 cm, dark green cloth.
        TEL: p.25.
F1073   Twitchell, Karl Saben, *Saudi Arabia*, Princeton University Press,
        Princeton, New Jersey, 1947; xiv, 194 pp., 20.5 cm, green cloth
        boards, tan cloth spine.
        TEL: pp.60, 97, 98, 103, 133.
F1073a University of Texas, Humanities Research Center, *A Creative Century
        (Exhibition catalogue)*, Austin, Texas 1964; 72 pp., 23.2 cm, pictorial
        grey paper covers.
        TEL: p.37.
F1073b University of Texas, Humanities Research Center, *An Exhibition on
        the Occasion of the Opening of the T.E. Hanley Library*, Research
        Center, University of Texas, Austin 1958; 16 pp., 25 cm, paper
        covers.
        TEL: p.13, copy of "Adventures of a Black Girl in Her Search for
        God" inscribed by Charlotte Shaw to T.E.S. (Colonel Lawrence).
F1074   University of Texas, Humanities Research Center, *Shaw Exhibition*,
        1977; 148 unnumbered pages, 25.5 cm, pictorial paper covers.
        TEL: pp.63, 64, 439, L36.
F1075   Uris, Leon, *The Haj*, Bantam, Toronto 1984; [14], 525, [5] pp., 17.5
        cm, pictorial paper covers.
        TEL: p.28.
F1077   Vaczek, Louis and Gail Buckland, *Travelers in Ancient Lands*, New
        York Graphic Society, Boston 1980; xx, 202 pp.
        TEL: pp.56, 58, 86, 88, 99, 184, 185, 186, 183, 195.
F1078   Van Doran, Carl, *American and British Literature since 1890*, Appleton
        Century Crofts, New York 1939.
        TEL: pp.304–5.
F1079   Van Loon, Hendrik Willem, *Air-Storming. A collection of 40 radio talks
        delivered by Hendrik Van Loon over the stations of the National
        Broadcasting Company*, Harcourt Brace, New York 1935; 8, 312 pp.,
        20.8 cm, blue cloth.
        TEL: pp.18–25, "May 23".
F1080   Van Paassen, Pierre, *Days of Our Years*, Hillman-Curl, New York
        1939; vi, 522 pp., 24.5 cm, blue cloth.
        TEL: pp.194, 196, 199, 200, 368, 403, 409.
F1081   Van Paassen, Pierre, *The Forgotten Ally*, Dial, New York 1943; 344
        pp., 21 cm, maroon cloth.
        TEL: pp.66, 70–71, 74–82, 97, 101, 116–8, 123, 143, 306–7.
F1082   Van Sinderen, Adrian, *The Lure of the Middle East*, Privately printed

(Yale University Press, New York), 1954; 144 pp., 26.1 cm, pictorial paper covered boards, blue cloth spine, limited to 700 copies. TEL: p.65.

F1083 Vansittart, Robert Gilbert, 1st Baron, *The Mist Procession*, Hutchinson, London 1958; 568 pp., 23.5 cm, blue cloth.
TEL: pp.166, 186, 205, 213, 214, 234, 246, 260, 317, 327, 365, 412, 431.

F1084 Vaughan, Agnes Carr, *Zenobia of Palmyra*, Doubleday, Garden City, New York 1967.
TEL: pp.92–3.

F1086 *Des Vivants et des Morts, Témoignages, 1948–1953*, Editions Universitaires, Paris 1954.
TEL: pp.297–303, "T.E. Lawrence héritier de Nietzsche".

F1087 Vredenburg, E., *East and West With the E.F.C.*, Tuck, London n.d.

F1088 Vulliamy, C.E., *English Letter Writers*, Collins, London 1946; 48 pp., 23.2 cm, brown paper covered boards.
TEL: pp.44–5.

F1089 Wallace, Irving, *et al.*, *The Intimate Sex Lives of Famous People*, Delacorte, New York 1981; 24 cm, purple cloth.
TEL: pp.362–4.

F1090 Wallace, Irving, *The Sunday Gentlemen*, Pocket Books, New York 1967; x, 518 pp., 17.7 cm, pictorial paper covers.
TEL: pp.286–7.

F1091 Walling, R.A.J., *The Story of Plymouth*, Morrow, New York 1950.
TEL: pp.265–6.

F1092 Ward, A.C., *Twentieth-Century English Literature 1901–1950*, Methuen, London 1956.
TEL: pp.71, 135, 224, 231.

F1093 Wareham Borough Council, *The Borough and District of Wareham. The Official Guide*, Cheltenham, n.d.; 40 pp., 18.5 cm, pictorial paper covers.
TEL: pp.17–18, illustration.

F1094 Wareham, Purbeck Rural District Council, *Wareham, Purbeck*, Wargrave Press 1964; 36 pp., 22 cm, pictorial paper covers.
TEL: pp.14–15, illustration.

F1095 Waterhouse, Francis A., *Gun Running in the Red Sea*, Sampson, Low Marston, London 1936; xii, 244 pp., 22.2 cm, red cloth.
TEL: pp.237–44, "Lawrence of Arabia Speaks".

F1096 Wathis, K.H., compiler/editor, *The Catalogue of the H.G. Wells Collection in the Bromley Public Library*, Borough of Bromley Public Library, London 1974; xii, 196 pp., 21.5 cm, brown cloth.
TEL: Item 923.

F1097 Watson, George, *Politics and Literature in Modern Britain*, Rowan, Littlefield, Totowa, New Jersey 1977.
TEL: pp.87–8, 91.

F1098 Watt, Ian, *Conrad*, University of California Press, Berkeley 1979.
TEL: p.31.

F1099 Waugh, Alec, *My Brother, Evelyn, and Other Profiles*, Cassell, London 1967; 8, 344 pp., 21.8 cm, red cloth.
TEL: pp.61, 69–70, 72.

F1100 Wavell, Archibald P. (Earl), *Allenby, a study in greatness*, Harrap, London 1940; 312 pp., 22.4 cm, red cloth.
TEL: pp.193, 230, 246, 253, 254, 269, 272, 283, 284n, 285, 286, 300n.

F1101 Wavell, Archibald P. (Earl), *Allenby, a Study in Greatness*, Oxford University Press, New York 1941; 314 pp., 22.2 cm, maroon cloth.
TEL: pp.193, 230, 246, 253, 254, 269, 272, 284, 286, 300.

F1102 Wavell, Archibald P. (Earl), *Allenby in Egypt*, Harrap, London 1943; 156 pp., 22.3 cm, dull red cloth.
TEL: pp.25n, 35, 130.

F1103 Wavell, Archibald P. (Earl), *Allenby in Egypt*, Oxford University Press, New York 1944; xiv, 162 pp., 22.2 cm, blue-grey cloth.
TEL: pp.17, 29, 135.

F1104 Wavell, Archibald P. (Earl), *Allenby: Soldier and Statesman*, White Lion, London 1974; 384 pp., 20.2 cm, black paper-covered boards.
TEL: pp.160–61, 193–4, 200, 213, 214, 228, 230, 240–41, 242, 243, 254.

F1105 Wavell, Archibald P. (Earl), *Allenby, Soldier and Statesman*, Harrap, London 1954; 384 pp., 20.5 cm, red cloth.
TEL: pp.160, 161, 193–4, 208, 213n, 214, 228, 230, 240–41, 242, 243, 254n.

F1106 Wavell, Archibald P. (Earl), *The Good Soldier*, Macmillan, London 1948; viii, 216 pp., 19 cm, tangerine cloth.
TEL: p.35; pp.57–56, "T.E. Lawrence".

F1107 Wavell, Archibald P. (Earl), *The Palestine Campaigns* [1914–1918], Constable, London 1928; xvi, 260 pp., 22.5 cm, red cloth.
TEL: pp.38, 54–6, 179, 199, 201, 203, 225, 229, 235, 235, 250, 251.

F1108 Wavell, Archibald P. (Earl), compiler, *Soldiers and Soldiering*, Cape, London 1953; 174 pp., 19.7 cm, red cloth.
TEL: pp.49, 106, 110, 145, 155.

F1109 Wayne, Philip, *The Personal Art*, Longman, London 1949; xii, 242 pp., 22 cm.
TEL: pp.235–7.

F1110 Weintraub, Stanley, *The Last Great Cause*, Weybright & Talley, New York 1968.
TEL: pp.41, 54, 71.

F1111 Weizmann, Chaim, *Trial and Error*, Hamish Hamilton, London 1949; 608 pp., 22.2 cm, tan buckram.
TEL: pp.98, 290, 292–4, 306, 489–90.

F1112 Weizmann, Chaim, *Trial and Error*, Harper, New York 1949; viii, 496 pp., 21.5 cm, black cloth.
TEL: pp.72, 234–6, 245, 398, 392.

F1113 Wells, H.G., *Experiment in Autobiography*, Macmillan, New York 1934; 24.2 cm, tan cloth.
TEL: p.602.

F1114 Werstein, Irving, *1914–1928: World War I*, Cooper Sq, New York 1964; 128 pp., 28 cm, pictorial paper covers, illus.
TEL: pp.102–3.

F1115 West, Anthony, *Principles and Persuasions*, Eyre & Spottiswoode,

London 1958; viii, 216 pp., 22.2 cm, pink cloth.
TEL: pp.51–5, "T.E. Lawrence".

F1116 West, Herbert Faulkner, *The Impecunious Amateur Looks Back*, Westholm, Hanover, New Hampshire, 1966; 10,234 pp., 500 copies. 22.5 cm, maroon cloth.
TEL: pp.65, 73–4, 135, 156, 181, 183.

F1117 West, Herbert Faulkner, *The Mind on the Wing*, Coward-McCann, New York 1947; xii, 308 pp., 21.4 cm, black cloth.
TEL: pp.19, 88, 90, 91, 92–3, 159, 205–6, 213, 222, 230, 275, 278.

F1118 West, Herbert Faulkner, *Sunny Intervals*, Westholm, Hanover, New Hampshire, 1972; 84 pp., 23.5 cm, blue paper boards, blue cloth spine, 400 copies.
TEL: pp.13, 24, 37, 39, 40, 49–50, 52–3, 69, 77.

F1119 Wester Wemyss, Lady Victoria, *The Life and Letters of Lord Wester Wemyss*, Eyre & Spottiswoode, London 1935; xii, 516 pp., 23.4 cm, blue cloth.
TEL: pp.275, 297, 336, 358–9, 410, 415.

F1121 Wetsgel, Meyer, and Carmichael, Joel, eds, *Chaim Weizmann*, Weidenfeld & Nicolson, London 1963; xii, 364 pp., 22.3 cm, black cloth.
TEL: p.174.

F1122 Wheeler, Sir Charles, *High Relief*, Country Life Books, Feltham, England, 1968; 144 pp., 22.1 cm, brown paper covered boards.
TEL: pp.58, 104.

F1123 White, Terence Hanbury, *The White/Garnett Letters*, Cape, London 1968; 320 pp., 22.3 cm, black cloth.
TEL: pp.15, 106, 242, 303, 304, 305, 308.

F1124 Whybrow, Stanley J.B., and Edwards, H.E., *Europe Overseas*, Basic Books, London 1940; xvi, 180 pp., 19 cm, pictorial paper covered boards.
TEL: pp.19–23.

F1125 Wilcox, Herbert, *Twenty-Five Thousand Sunsets*, Bodley Head, London 1967; [2], xiv, 234 pp., blue linen.
TEL: pp.172, 204, 58.

F1126 Willert, Arthur, *What Next in Europe*, Putnam, New York 1936; 10, 310 pp., 22.1 cm, brown cloth.
TEL: p.112.

F1127 Williams, Ann, *Britain France and the Middle East and North Africa*, Macmillan, New York 1968.
TEL: p.15.

F1128 Williamson, Audrey, *Bernard Shaw: Man and Writer*, Crowell-Collier, New York 1963; 224 pp.
TEL: pp.195–8, 216.

F1129 Williamson, Henry, *Devon Holiday*, Cape, London 1935; 320 pp., 20.5 cm, green cloth.
TEL: pp.7, 98–105, Lawrence is model for the character G.B. Everest.

F1130 Williamson, Henry, *The Gold Falcon*, Faber & Faber, London 1933;

416 pp., 19.5 cm, blue cloth.
TEL: pp.18, 22, 54, 56, 78, 123, 145, 235, 304–5, 329, 359. Lawrence is
the model for character G.B. Everest.

F1131   Williamson, Henry, *The Gold Falcon*, Smith & Haas, New York 1933;
416 pp., 19.8 cm, tan cloth.
TEL: Lawrence is the model for the character G.B. Everest.

F1132   Williamson, Henry, *Goodbye West Country*, Putnam, London 1937; 8,
400 pp., 22.2 cm, brown cloth.
TEL: pp.6, 19, 24, 29, 42, 118, 148, 162, 212, 228, 241, 252, 270, 271,
376, 382, 385–9, 399.

F1133   Williamson, Henry, *Goodbye West Country*, Little, Brown & Co.,
Boston 1938; 10, 370 pp., 22.7 cm, green cloth.
TEL: pp.148, 149, 164, 252, 346, 355, 356, 369.

F1134   Williamson, Henry, *The Patriot's Progress*, Macdonald, London 1968,
xxii, 198 pp., 20.3 cm, black paper-covered boards.
TEL: pp.1, 7–9.

F1135   Williamson, Henry, *Salar the Salmon*, Faber & Faber, London 1935;
320 pp., 19.5 cm, brown cloth.
TEL: Dedication to T.E. Lawrence and V.M. Yeates, p.9.

F1136   Williamson, Henry, *Salar the Salmon*, New American Library,New
York 1965; 192 pp., 18 cm, pictorial paper covers.
TEL: Dedication to T.E. Lawrence and V.M. Yeates, p.5.

F1137   Williamson, Henry, *Tarka the Otter*, Putnam's, London 1928 ("4th
edition, slightly revised following suggestions of T.E.L..."); viii, 256
pp., 19.5 cm, brown cloth.
TEL: p.iv.

F1138   Wilson, Sir Arnold Talbot, 1884–1940, *Loyalities: Mesopotamia,
1914–1917*, Oxford University Press, London 1930; 2 volumes, 25.5
cm, black cloth.
TEL: pp.98, 110, 161, 194, 312, 320.

F1139   Wilson, Sir Arnold Talbot, *Loyalties: Mesopotamia*, Oxford University
Press, London 1936; 2 volumes, 24.2 cm, brown buckram.
TEL: Vol. 1, pp.ix, 35, 70, 78, 92, 116, 210, 214, 244, 258, 267; Vol. 2,
pp.110, 194, 313, 330.

F1140   Wilson, Sir Arnold Talbot, *Thoughts and Talks, 1935–1937*, Right
Book Club, London 1938; xii, 392 pp., 19.1 cm, buff paper covered.
TEL: pp.33–5.

F1141   Wilson, Colin, *Beyond the Outsider*, Barker, London 1965.
TEL: pp.130, 134, 194, 208, 212, 217.

F1142   Wilson, Colin, *The Outsider*, Houghton Mifflin, Boston 1956; 288
pp., 21.3 cm, blue-patterned covered boards, blue cloth spine
(another copy brown cloth).
TEL: pp.71–84, 88, 90, 92–3, 101–2, 105–6, 110, 114–6, 120, 125, 137,
142, 144–5, 148, 151, 158, 165, 167, 172, 174, 181, 182, 183, 198, 202,
212, 220, 230, 232, 238–9, 268.

F1143   Wilson, Colin, *Religion and the Rebel*, Gollancz, London 1957; 336
pp., 20.2 cm, blue cloth.
TEL: pp.10, 11, 38, 39, 45, 61–2, 68, 80, 138, 142, 164, 175, 178, 194,
221, 254, 281, 290, 299, 316, 318.

F1144 Wilson, Colin, *Religion and the Rebel,* Houghton Mifflin, Boston 1957 (first printing); xii, 340 pp., 21 cm, grey cloth.
TEL: pp.3, 31, 61, 79, 102, 135, 138, 173, 176, 193, 213, 221, 222, 255, 261, 284, 293, 302, 319, 321.

F1145 Wilson, Colin, *Voyage to a Beginning,* Crown, New York 1969.
TEL: pp.7, 26, 316, 332–3.

F1146 Winckler, Paul A., ed., *Reader in the History of Books and Printing,* Information Handling Services, Englewood, Colorado, n.d.
TEL: p.396.

F1147 Winder, Richard Bayley, *Saudi Arabia in the Nineteenth Century,* Macmillan, London 1965; St Martin's, New York 1965; xiv, 314 pp., 22.7 cm, orange cloth.
TEL: pp.23, 91, 210.

F1148 Wingate, Sir Ronald, *Not in the Limelight,* Hutchinson, London 1959; 232 pp., 21.8 cm, brown cloth.
TEL: pp.62–3, 95.

F1149 Winsten, Stephen, *Days with Bernard Shaw,* Vanguard, New York 1949; 330 pp., 22.2 cm, blue cloth.
TEL: pp.144, 176, 267–8.

F1150 Winsten, Stephen, ed., *G.B.S. 90,* Hutchinson, London 1946; 200 pp., 23.5 cm, red cloth.
TEL: Photo opposite p.137.

F1151 Winsten, Stephen, *Jesting Apostle,* Dutton, New York 1957; 6, 234 pp., 23.5 cm, light blue cloth.
TEL: pp.8, 170, 171, 178, 179, 181, 183, 195.

F1153 Winsten, Stephen, *Shaw's Corner,* Hutchinson, London 1952; 240 pp., 21.5 cm, red cloth.
TEL: pp.21, 54, 82, 89, 181.

F1154 Winstone, Harry V. F., *Gertrude Bell,* Cape, London 1978; xiv, 322 pp., 22.3 cm, blue cloth.
TEL: pp.111, 115, 129, 161–6, 170ff, 182–3, 185, 191, 194–196, 199, 208–10, 218, 223–5, 228, 234ff, 243, 246, 248.

F1155 Winstone, Harry V. F., *Gertrude Bell,* Quartet, London 1978; xiv, 322 pp., 22.3 cm, blue cloth.
TEL: pp.111, 115, 129, 161–6, 170ff, 182–3, 185, 191, 194–6, 199, 208–210, 218, 223–5, 228, 234ff, 243, 246, 248.

F1156 Winstone, Harry V. F., *The Illicit Adventure,* Cape, London 1982; xvi, 528 pp., 21.5 cm.
TEL: pp.43, 69, 78, 106, 129, 166, 179, 206, 210, 240, 247, 280, 315, 323, 331, 335, 341, 351, 361.

F1157 Winstone, Harry, V. F., *Leachman O.C. Desert,* Quartet, London 1982; x, 246 pp., 23.3 × 15.3 cm, black cloth, illus.
TEL: pp.vii, viii, 148, 164ff, 175, 180ff, 206ff, 214, 215, 223.

F1158 Winterton, 6th Earl, *Fifty Tumultuous Years,* Hutchinson, London 1955; 232 pp., 23.7 cm, maroon cloth.
TEL: pp.10, 60, 64, 65–73, 140.

F1159 Winterton, 6th Earl, *Orders of the Day,* Cassell, London 1953; xiv, 370 pp., 21.8 cm, blue cloth.
TEL: pp.100–101, 201–2, 239.

F1160 Winterton, 6th Earl, *Pre–War*, Macmillan, London 1932; 2, x, 316 pp., 22.5 cm, blue linen.
TEL: pp.36, 131, 189.

F1160a Wintle, Justin, *Diaries of Parker Pash*, Quartet, London 1983.

F1161 Wintle, Justin, *Makers of Modern Culture*, Facts on File, New York 1981.
TEL: p.293.

F1162 Wisberg, Aubrey and Harold Waters, *Bushman at Large*, Green Circle Books, New York 1937; 20.7 cm, brown cloth.
TEL: p.200.

F1163 Wiseman, Thomas, *Cinema*, Cassell, London 1964; 28.5 cm, black cloth.
TEL: (Film), pp.117, 130, 149.

F1164 Wohl, Robert, *The Generation of 1914*, Harvard University Press, Cambridge 1979; xvi, 308 pp., 24.3 cm, brown cloth.
TEL: pp.116–21, 208, 226, 227, 229, 230.

F1165 Woolf, Virginia, *A Writer's Diary*, Harcourt Brace, New York 1954.
TEL: p.92.

F1166 Woolf, Virginia, *The Diary of Virginia Woolf, Vol. 4, 1931–1935*, Harcourt Brace Jovanovich, New York 1982.
TEL: pp.312.

F1167 Woolley, Sir C. Leonard, *As I Seem to Remember*, Allen & Unwin, London 1962; 116 pp., 19 cm, maroon cloth.
TEL: pp.17–20, 54, 88–93.

F1168 Woolley, Sir C.Leonard, *Dead Towns and Living Men*, Oxford University Press, London 1929; [2], viii, 260 pp., 22.3 cm, red cloth.

F1169 Woolley, Sir C.Leonard, *Dead Towns and Living Men*, Cape, London 1932; 8, 308 pp., 20.5 cm, green cloth. 2 added chapters to the 1929 edition.
TEL: pp.150–72.

F1170 Woolley, Sir C. Leonard, *Dead Towns and Living Men*, Cape, London 1932 (Life & Letters Series, No.29); x, 310, 48 pp., 20.7 cm, green cloth (two chapters added to the 1929 edition).
TEL: pp.150–72.

F1171 Woolley, Sir C. Leonard, *Dead Towns and Living Men*, Lutterworth, London 1954 (revised and enlarged ed.); 220 pp., 22.1 cm, maroon cloth.
TEL: pp.113–27, Frontispiece of Woolley and TEL at Carchemish.

F1172 Woolley, Sir C. Leonard, *Dead Towns and LIving Men*, Philosophical Library, New York 1956; 220 pp., 22.3 cm, brown cloth.
TEL: pp.viii (Frontispiece), 113–27.

F1173 Worth, Fred L., *Super Trivia Encyclopedia*, Brooke House, Los Angeles 1979.
TEL: p.293.

F1174 Wortham, Hugh Evelyn, *Mustapha Kemal of Turkey*, Holme, London 1930.
TEL: p.78.

F1175 Wortham, Hugh Evelyn, *Mustapha Kemal of Turkey*, Little Brown, Boston 1931; x, 254 pp., 21.2 cm, red cloth.

TEL: p.78.
F1176 Wouk, Herman, *Don't Stop the Carnival*, Doubleday, Garden City, New York 1965.
TEL: p.316.
F1177 Wren, Jack, *The Great Battles of World War I*, Grosset & Dunlap, New York 1971; xii, 436 pp., 30.3 cm, brown simulated leather.
TEL: p.332.
F1178 Wrench, John Evelyn, *Francis Yeats-Brown*, Eyre & Spottiswoode, London 1948; 8,2 96 pp., 22 cm, bright blue.
TEL: pp.72, 73, 112, 130–44, 199, 205, 228; Chapter VIII, "Y.B. and T.E. Lawrence", contains some letters by Lawrence.
F1179 Wrench, John Evelyn, *Struggle, 1914–1920*, Nicholson & Watson, London 1935; 504 pp., 22.5 cm, red cloth.
TEL: pp.361, 419, 446, 449, 467.
F1180 Yale, William, *The Near East*, University of Michigan Press, Ann Arbor 1958; [2], x, 486, xx pp., 24 cm, deep blue.
TEL: pp.47, 73, 244, 253, 255–60, 316, 319–20.
F1181 Yeates, Victor M., *Winged Victory*, Cape, London 1961; 6, 456 pp., 20.5 cm, blue simulated cloth paper-covered boards.
TEL: p.5, dust wrapper.
F1182 Young, Sir Hubert, *The Independent Arab*, Murray, London 1933; 2, xii, 346 pp., 22.7 cm, blue cloth.
TEL: pp.15–22, 72–3, 199, 243, 252, 291, 322, 136, 139, 142–3, 149, 151, 168, 169, 171, 175, 194–5, 198–9, 215, 240–41, 249, 140–41, 149, 154, 156–7, 158, 161–4, 167, 155–6, 203–5, 217–19, 221, 227–9, 229–31, 232–3, 242, 233, 238–9, 243–6, 248, 250, 251, 252, 279, 290, 291, 296, 313, 319, 325, 331.
F1183 Zehren, Erich, *The Crescent and the Bull*, Sidgwick & Jackson, London 1962.
TEL: p.159.
F1184 Zeine, Zeine N., *The Emergence of Arab Nationalism*, Khayats, Beirut 1966; xii, 205, 3 pp., 22.2 cm, purple cloth.
TEL: pp.132, 134, 139.
F1185 Zeine, Zeine N., *The Struggle for Arab Independence*, Khayats, Beirut 1960; 2, xiv, 298 pp., 23.7 cm, blue cloth.
TEL: pp.16, 21, 23, 26–7, 29, 30, 31, 53, 65, 68, 193–5, 198, 200–202, 205, 215.
F1186 Ziff, William B., *The Rape of Palestine*, Longmans Green, New York 1938; xvi, 622 pp., 22.2 cm, blue cloth.
TEL: pp.71–4, 78, 128, 216, 219, 224, 322, 371, 535–6.
F1187 Zinsser, William, *On Writing Well*, Harper & Row, New York 1980.
TEL: pp.98–9.
F1188 Zweig, Paul, *The Adventurer*, Basic Books, New York 1974; x, 278 pp., 21.8 cm, brown cloth.
TEL: pp.4, 15, 16, 26, 49, 82, 114, 171, 228–9, 230–37, 238, 240, 241, 244.
F1189 Zytaruk, George J., and Boulton, James T., *The Letters of D.H. Lawrence*, Cambridge University Press 1981.
TEL: p.403.

SECTION G

PERIODICAL ARTICLES
ABOUT T.E. LAWRENCE

This listing embraces all periodical items treating Lawrence as a subject. Thus articles on the man, his works, the 1962 Lean film, Middle Eastern politics, and reviews of books about him, are all to be found here. The intention has been to include all identifiable items whatever their source or value. Little has been excluded. Even so, there is unquestionably an embarassingly large number of items that belong here which have escaped notice.

The *Times Literary Supplement* has been abbreviated throughout to *TLS*.

G0001   *Palestine Exploration Quarterly*, July 1914, pp.121, 128.
G0002   D.G.H. (Hogarth), *Geographical Review*, 1915, 46, pp.55–6. *Note:* Review of *The Wilderness of Zin* (A004).
G0003   *Palestine Exploration Quarterly*, April 1915, p.61.
G0004   *Palestine Exploration Quarterly*, July 1915, pp.105, 121.
G0005   L. Dumont-Wilden, 'Le Front Arabe', *L'Illustration*, 20 October 1917, 75:3894, pp.400–403. *Note:* Lawrence not mentioned by name, his photo appears in article.
G0006   'Deux années de guerre en Arabie', *Bibliothéque universelle et revue suisse*, 1918, 92, pp.108–15.
G0007   Simon, 'Une Campagne au Hedjaz', *La Revue de Paris*, 1919, 5, pp.64–8.
G0008   'Long Awaited Liberation of Arabic Syria', *Review of Reviews*, 1919, 59.
G0009   *Palestine Exploration Quarterly*, January 1919, pp.4, 5.
G0010   William G. Shepard, 'An Arabian Knight's Story', *Red Cross Magazine*, July 1919, 14:7, pp.8–15.
G0011   'With General Allenby at Covent Garden Theatre', *The Sphere*, 23 August 1919, p.172. *Note:* Thomas slide lecture.
G0012   Lowell Thomas, 'War in the Land of Arabian Nights', *Asia*, September–October, December 1919, 19:9–10, 12, pp.829, 998–1012, 1205–12.
G0013   'Colonel Lawrence and the Hedjaz', *Current History*, November 1919, 11:2, pp.328–30. *Note:* Illus.
G0014   Maynard Owen Williams, Syria', *National Geographic*, November 1919, 36, pp.437–62, 551.
G0015   'How Young English Archaeologist Captured Damascus', *Literary Digest*, 27 December 1919, 63, pp.58, 60.
G0016   'The Arabian Army in Palestine', *Youth's Companion*, 28 December 1919, 93:51, p.724.

G0017 Lowell Thomas, 'The Uncrowned King of Arabia, Colonel T.E. Lawrence', *Strand Magazine*, January–April 1920, 1, pp.40–53, 141–53, 251–61, 330–38.

G0018 William T. Ellis, 'War's Most Romantic Figure', *Review of Reviews*, March 1920, 61, pp.308–9.

G0019 'Arabia's Uncrowned King', *Youth's Companion*, 4 March 1920, 94:10, p.132.

G0020 Luther R. Fowle, 'Prologue', *Asia*, April 1920, 20:3, pp.256–8.

G0021 Lowell Thomas, 'The Soul of the Arabian Revolution', *Asia*, April 1920, 20:3, pp.259–66. *Note:* Frontispiece.

G0022 W., 'Arabian Days and Nights', *Blackwood's Magazine*, May–June 1920, 207:mcciv–mcclvi, pp.585–608, 750–68.

G0023 Lowell Thomas, 'King Hussein and His Arabian Nights', *Asia*, May 1920, 20:4, pp.400–410.

G0024 Lowell Thomas, 'The Trojan Horse Enters Damascus', *Asia*, June 1920, 20:5, pp.517–25. *Note:* Illus.

G0025 D.G. Hogarth, 'Mecca's Revolt Against the Turk', *Century*, July 1920, 78, pp.401–11. *Note:* Illus.

G0026 Lowell Thomas, 'A Bedouin Battle in the City of Ghosts', *Asia*, July 1920, 20: 6, pp.597–665. *Note:* Illus.

G0027 Lowell Thomas, 'Thomas Lawrence, the Man', *Asia*, August 1920, 20: 7, pp.670–76. *Note:* Illus.

G0028 (Robert Graves), 'Isis Idol: Mr. T.E. Lawrence (Arabia and All Souls)', *Isis*, 27 October 1920, 514, p.5. *Note:* Illus.

G0029 'A New Battle of Petra', *Youth's Companion*, 24 March 1921, 95:12, p.188.

G0030 'Pole Hill', *Bancroftian*, 4 July 1921, 29:4, p.105.

G0031 'The Sensitive Arab', *Youth's Companion*, 14 July 1921, 95:24, p.378.

G0032 Col. Baron Friederich Kress von Kressenstein, 'The Campaign in Palestine – From the Enemy's Side', *Royal United Services Institute Journal*, August 1922, 67, pp.503–13.

G0033 William L. Westermann, 'Europe and the Arab World', *Asia*, September 1922, p.688.

G0034 Lt. Col. C.E. Vickery, 'Arabia and The Hedjaz', *Royal Central Asian Society Journal*, 1923, 10, pp.46–67.

G0035 *Asia*, January 1923, 23:1, pp.4–5.

G0036 Isaac Anderson, 'A New 1001 Nights in Arabia', *Literary Digest International Book Review*, January 1924, 2:2, pp.112–13. *Note:* Illus.

G0037 Lowell Thomas, 'Thomas Lawrence Incognito', *Asia*, November 1924, 24:11, pp.854–8. *Note:* Illus.

G0038 *Literary Review*, 22 November 1924, 5, p.2. *Note:* Portrait of Lawrence.

G0039 *Foreign Affairs*, 15 December 1924, 3, p.282.

G0040 *Booklist*, January 1925, 21, p.145. *Note:* Review, Thomas, *With Lawrence in Arabia* (E012).

G0041 C.K.S. (General Sir George MacMunn), 'The Uncrowned King of Arabia', *Sphere*, 8 August 1925, p.185.

G0042 'Trade Winds', *Saturday Review*, 7 November 1925, p.284. *Note:* Mention of *Seven Pillars of Wisdom*.

G0043 Edmund Chandler, 'Lawrence and the Hedjaz', *Blackwood's Magazine*, December 1925, 218, pp.733–61.

G0044 Edmund Chandler, 'Lawrence of the Hedjaz', *Atlantic*, March 1926, 137:3, pp.289–304.

G0045 'Colonel Lawrence's Manuscript', *Royal Central Asian Society Journal*, April 1926, 13:2, pp.165–8.

G0046 'Roderick Random', 'A London letter', *Saturday Review*, 10 April 1926, 2, pp.705–6.

G0047 'How the Turks Tortured Lawrence of Arabia', *Literary Digest*, 8 May 1926, 69, pp.50–56. *Note:* Illus.

G0048 *Apollo*, June 1926, pp.240, 319.

G0049 Raymond Savage, *Saturday Review*, 16 July 1926, p.942. *Note:* Letter to editor.

G0050 Hubert Young, 'Makik', *Cornhill Magazine*, October, November 1926, pp.409–28, 537–56.

G0051 'An Arabian Sand Storm', *Youth's Companion*, 4 November 1926, 100:44, pp.828–9.

G0052 'All Alone', *Collier's*, 6 November 1926, 78, p.12. *Note:* Portrait of Lawrence.

G0053 'Best Seller List', *Bookman*, 1927, p.211. *Note: Revolt in the Desert*, No. 11.

G0054 *Book of the Month Club News*, 1927. *Note:* Notice of *Revolt in the Desert* as Book of Month Selection.

G0055 L., 'Downing Street and Arab Potentates', *Foreign Affairs*, January 1927, 5:2, pp.233, 235.

G0056 Lowell Thomas, 'Lawrence of Arabia, Who He Was and What He Did', *World's Work*, February 1927, pp.362–8. *Note:* Illus.

G0057 'The Phoenix Nest', *Saturday Review*, 5 February 1927, 3, p.572. *Note:* Mention of *Revolt in the Desert*.

G0058 'The Phoenix Nest', *Saturday Review*, 19 February 1927, 3, p.602. *Note:* Mention of *Revolt in the Desert*.

G0059 'Thomas Lawrence The Soul of the Arabian Revolt, *Asia*, March 1927, 37:3, pp.179–82.

G0060 'Lawrence of Arabia', *Review of Reviews*, March 1927, 75, p.317. *Note:* Illus.

G0061 Lowell Thomas, 'Lawrence of Arabia', *Reader's Digest*, March 1927, 5:59, pp.649–50. *Note:* From *World's Work*, February 1927.

G0062 R. De la Bere, 'A Great Book', *Royal Air Force Cadet Magazine*, Spring 1927, 7:1, pp.24–30. *Note:* Review of *Seven Pillars of Wisdom* (A034); extract 'Feasting' from Chapter LXVI also included, pp.27–9.

G0063 G.B. Shaw, 'Revolt in the Desert and Its Author', *Now and Then*, Spring 1927, 33, pp.20–22.

G0064 *New Coterie*, Spring 1927, 5, pp.32, 44–5. *Note:* Photo of Kennington bust.

G0065 Lowell Thomas, 'Lawrence of Arabia as a Train Wrecker', *World's Work*, March 1927, 53:5, pp.511–12. *Note:* Illus.

G0066 'The Phoenix Nest', *Saturday Review*, 5 March 1927, 3, p.636. *Note:* Note on *Revolt in the Desert*.

G0067 'The Bowling Green', *Saturday Review*, 5 March 1927, pp.627–8. *Note:* Mention of *Revolt in the Desert*.

G0068 D. G. Hogarth, 'Lawrence and the Arabs', *TLS*, 10 March 1927, p.151.

G0069 *Illustrated London News*, 12 March 1927, p.432. *Note:* Review of *Revolt in the Desert* (A100).

G0070 'Lawrence the Nation Maker', *New Statesman*, 12 March 1927, pp.668–9. *Note:* Review of *Revolt in the Desert* (A100).

G0071 G. B. Shaw, 'The Latest From Colonel Lawrence', *Spectator*, 12 March 1927, p.429. *Note:* Review of *Revolt in the Desert* (A100).

G0072 Edward Shanks, 'The Greatest of Adventures', *Saturday Review*, 12 March 1927, pp.426–7. *Note:* Review of *Revolt in the Desert* (A100).

G0073 H. St. John Philby, 'Col. Lawrence's Books', *Observer*, 13 March 1927, p.9. *Note:* Review.

G0074 Leonard Woolf, 'The Epic of the Modern Man', *Nation and Atheneum*, 19 March 1927, 40:24, p.857. *Note:* Review of *Revolt in the Desert* A100.

G0075 'Personal Glimpses – Wrecking Turkish Trains With Lawrence of Arabia', *Literary Digest*, 19 March 1927, 92.

G0076 'Lawrence in Full', *Saturday Review*, 19 March 1927, 3, pp.426–7. *Note:* Review of *Revolt in the Desert* (A100).

G0077 John Buchan, 'Of Such is History', *Saturday Review*, 19 March 1927, 3, pp.659–60.

G0078 George Blake, 'Lawrence's Arabian Nights', *John O'London's*, 26 March 1927, 16:414, p.892. *Note:* Photo.

G0079 *Bookman*, April 1927, p.32a. *Note:* Portrait of Lawrence.

G0080 Lowell Thomas, 'How Lawrence Helped to Frame the Greatest Hoax Since the Trojan Horse', *World's Work*, April 1927, 53:6, pp.639–42. *Note:* Illus.

G0081 G.B. Shaw, 'This Man Lawrence', *World's Work*, April 1927, 53:6, pp.636–8. *Note:* Illus., reprint of GBS preface to Leicester Gallery Exhibition of 1921.

G0082 Chalmers Roberts, 'Lawrence of Arabia A Mystification – An Impression – A Tribute', *The World Today*, April 1927, 49, pp.441–5.

G0083 A.R.V. Barker, 'An Epic of the Desert War', *The World Today*, April 1927, 49, pp.445–50. *Note:* Review of *Revolt in the Desert* (A100).

G0084 'Glory of the Desert', *Saturday Review*, 2 April 1927, pp.689–92.

G0085 *Saturday Review*, 20 April 1927. *Note:* Note on *Seven Pillars of Wisdom*.

G0086 'Books of The Spring', *Saturday Review*, 23 April 1927, 3, p.773. *Note:* Mention of *Revolt in the Desert*.

G0087 Nouri Al-Said, 'Revolt in the Desert, Introduction to Arabic Version', *Near East and India*, 28 April 1927, 31, pp.496–7.

G0088 Sir Arnold Wilson, 'Revolt in the Desert', *Royal Central Asian Society Journal*, May 1927, 14, pp.282–5. *Note:* Review of *Revolt in the Desert* (A100).

G0089 Irving Brown, 'Arabia Desperata', *Bookman*, May 1927, 65:3, pp.340–43. *Note:* Review of *Revolt in the Desert* (A100).

G0090 Clennell Wilkinson, 'A Great Adventure, May 1927, 16:91, pp.62–9.

G0091 Charles Merz, *New Republic*, 25 May 1927, 51, pp.24–5. *Note:* Review of *Revolt in the Desert* (A100).

G0092 *The Bookman Advertiser*, June 1927, p.XIV. *Note:* Full page ad for *Revolt in the Desert*.

G0093 Lowell Thomas, 'The Chicago of Ancient Arabia, *World's Work*, June 1927, 54:2, pp.184–96. *Note:* Illus.

G0094 'Revolt', *The Dial*, July–December 1927, p.127. *Note:* Review of *Revolt in the Desert* (A100).

G0095 Poultney Bigelow, *American Historical Review*, July 1927, 32:4, pp.873–6. *Note:* Review of *Revolt in the Desert* (A100).

G0096 H.G. Dwight, 'Archaeologist Into Wrecker of Trains', *Yale Review*, July 1927, 16:4, pp.786–9.

G0097 C.M. Devers, 'With Lawrence of Arabia in the Ranks: Personal Recollections of a Private in the Tanks Corps', *The World Today*, July 1927, 50, pp.141–4.

G0098 Lowell Thomas, 'The White King of the Arabs', *St. Nicholas Magazine*, July–September 1927, 44:9–11, pp.667–70, 746, 768–72, 840–41, 853–7, 937–8.

G0099 Louis Gillet, 'Comment fut Inventé Emir Faycal', *Revue de Deux Mondes*, 15 July 1927, 40, pp.441–53.

G0100 *National Magazine*, August 1927, 55, pp.509, 546.

G0101 C.M. Devers, 'With Lawrence in the Tank Corps', *World's Work*, August 1927, pp.384–8. *Note:* Illus.

G0102 'Monthly Score', *Bookman*, September 1927, p.109. *Note:* Mention of *Revolt in the Desert*.

G0103 Flight-Cadet A. Will, 'Revolt in the Desert', *R.A.F. Cadet College Magazine*, Autumn 1927, 7:2, pp.157–9. *Note:* Review of *Revolt in the Desert* (A100).

G0104 *Women's City Club Magazine*, September 1927, 1:8, p.51. *Note:* Ad for Thomas, *The Boys' Life of Lawrence of Arabia* (E023).

G0105 'T.E. Lawrence Impaled', *Living Age*, 1 September 1927, 333:4313, pp.461–2.

G0106 Lowell Thomas, 'Lawrence Still a Man of Mystery', *St. Nicholas Magazine*, October 1927, 44:12, pp.970–71, 1023–24.

G0107 'In Defense of Lawrence', *Living Age*, 15 October 1927, 333, pp.745.

G0108 Bartlett Biebner, *Saturday Review*, 29 October 1927, 4, p.260. *Note:* Review of Thomas, *Boys' Life of Lawrence* (E023).

G0109 'Monthly Score', *Bookman*, November 1927, p.xxxvii. *Note:* Mention of *Revolt in the Desert*.

G0110 Lt.Gen. George MacMunn, 'The Truth About T.E. Lawrence', *The World Today*, November 1927, 50, pp.559–64.

G0111 *Wisconsin Library Bulletin*, November 1927, 23, p.262. *Note:* Review of Thomas, *Boys' Life of Lawrence* (E023).

G0112 *New Statesman*, 19 November 1927, 30, p.178. *Note:* Review of Graves, *Lawrence and Arabs* (E030), and Thomas, *Boys' Life of Lawrence of Arabia* (E026).

G0113 *Spectator*, 19 November 1927, 139, p.890. *Note:* Review of Graves, *Lawrence and the Arabs* (E030).

G0114 *Saturday Review*, 19 November 1927, 144, p.707. *Note:* Review of Graves, *Lawrence and the Arabs* (E030).
G0115 'Our Booking Agent', *Punch*, 23 November 1927, 173, p.586. *Note:* Review of Graves, *Lawrence and the Arabs* (E030).
G0116 *TLS*, 24 November 1927, p.882. *Note:* Review of Thomas, *Boys' Life of Colonel Lawrence* (E026).
G0117 Philby, H. St. John, 'The Lawrence Legend', *Observer*, 27 November 1927.
G0118 'Curzon Weeps', *Nation*, 30 November 1927, 125, p.591. *Note:* Illus.
G0119 'Monthly Score', *Bookman*, December 1927, p.480. *Note:* Mention of *Revolt in the Desert*.
G0120 George MacMunn, 'Gertrude Bell and T.E. Lawrence', *The World Today*, December 1927, 51, pp.36–40.
G0121 *TLS*, 1 December 1927, p.903. *Note:* Review of Graves, *Lawrence and the Arabs* (E030).
G0122 *Survey*, 1 December 1927, 59, p.330. *Note:* Review of Thomas, *Boys' Life of Colonel Lawrence* (E026).
G0123 *Nation and Atheneum*, 3 December 1927, 42, p.360. *Note:* Review of Graves, *Lawrence and the Arabs* (E030).
G0124 *Spectator*, 3 December 1927, 139, p.1009. *Note:* Review of Thomas, *Boys' Life of Colonel Lawrence* (E026).
G0125 'When Lawrence Said "No" to King George', *Literary Digest*, 10 December 1927, 95, pp.40–44. *Note:* Illus.
G0126 *The Periodical*, 15 December 1927, 72:142, p.210.
G0127 Louis Jalabert, 'Un aventurier et une aventure de grand style: le colonel Lawrence et la révolte arabe', *Etudes (Pères de la Compagnie de Jésus, Paris)*, 1928, 8, pp.433–58.
G0128 Will Vesper, 'Der Ungekrönte König von Arabien, *Die Schöne Literatur*, 1928, 29, pp.128–9.
G0129 *Booklist*, January 1928, 24, p.167. *Note:* Review of Lowell Thomas, *Boys' Life of Colonel Lawrence.*
G0130 *Palestine Exploration Quarterly*, January 1928, p.37.
G0131 'Monthly Score', *Bookman*, February 1928, p.707. *Note:* Mention of *Revolt in the Desert*.
G0132 Robert Graves, 'New Tales About Lawrence of Arabia', *World's Work*, February 1928, 55:4, pp.389–98. *Note:* Illus.
G0133 'Monthly Score', *Bookman*, March 1928, p.117. *Note:* Mention of *Revolt in the Desert*.
G0134 Robert Graves, 'Lawrence of Arabia as a Buck Private', *World's Work*, March 1928, 55:5, pp.508–16. *Note:* Illus.
G0135 Max Claus, 'Zeugen Unserer Zeit: T.E. Lawrence und J. Ortega Y Gasset', *Europäische Revue*, April–September 1928, 4:1, pp.324–5.
G0136 'Monthly Score', *Bookman*, April 1928, p.211. *Note:* Mention of *Revolt in the Desert*.
G0137 Robert Graves, 'The Real Colonel Lawrence', *World's Work*, April 1928, 55:6, pp.663–70. *Note:* Illus.
G0138 John Carton, 'Lawrence of Arabia; As Yet Unexplained', *New York Times Book Review*, 8 April 1928, p.5. *Note:* Review of Graves, *Lawrence and the Arabs* (E030).

G0139 *Pittsburgh Monthly Bulletin*, May 1928, 33, p.298. *Note:* Review of Graves, *Lawrence and the Arabs* (E030).

G0140 Robert Graves, 'The Making of a Conqueror', *World's Work*, May 1928, 56:1, pp.101–11. *Note:* Illus.

G0141 Leopold Weiss, 'Trouble in Arabia', *Living Age*, 1 May 1928, 334:4329, pp.806–13. *Note:* Originally published in *Neue Züericher Zeitung*, 18–22 March 1928.

G0142 'Literary Adventurer', *Literary Digest*, 12 May 1928, 97, p.24. *Note:* Illus.

G0143 *New Republic*, 16 May 1928, 54, p.399. *Note:* Review of Graves, *Lawrence and the Arabs* (E030).

G0144 George Fort Milton, 'Colonel Lawrence Again', *Nation*, 16 May 1928, 126, pp.567–8.

G0145 R.D. Williams, 'Lawrence of Arabia', *The Hound and the Horn*, Summer 1928, 1:4, pp.362–6. *Note:* Review of Graves, *Lawrence and the Arabs* (E030).

G0146 *St. Louis Library Bulletin*, June 1928, 26, p.194. *Note:* Review of Graves, *Lawrence and the Arabs* (E030).

G0147 *New York Herald Tribune Book Review*, 24 June 1928, p.7. *Note:* Review of Graves, *Lawrence and the Arabs* (E030).

G0148 *Booklist*, July 1928, 24, p.399. *Note:* Review of Graves, *Lawrence and the Arabian Adventure* (E037).

G0149 *National Geographic*, August 1928, pp.211, 213–15.

G0150 *Pratt Institute Quarterly*, Autumn 1928, p.41. *Note:* Review of Graves, *Lawrence and the Arabian Adventure* (E037).

G0151 D.B. MacDonald, 'Legendary Lawrence', *Yale Review*, Autumn 1928, 18:1, pp.176–7.

G0152 'Lawrence as an Arab Saint', *Outlook*, 10 October 1928, 150, p.936.

G0153 Louis Jalabert, 'Les 7 piliers de la sagesse. La confession du Colonel Lawrence', *Etudes (Pères de la Compagnie de Jésus, Paris)*, 1929, 228, pp.475–91.

G0154 , 'Spots in Spring Books', *Bookman*, 1929–1930, 46, pp.559–60. *Note:* Mention of *Revolt in the Desert*.

G0155 'Best Seller List', *Bookman*, 1929–1930, p.117. *Note:* *Revolt in the Desert*, No. 8.

G0156 M. Muret, *Journal des Débats*, 25 January 1929, 36, pp.158–60.

G0157 *Sphere*, 9 February 1929. *Note:* Photograph of Lawrence arriving at Plymouth.

G0158 'Turkophil', 'The Colonel Lawrence Bogy', *Near East and India*, 14 February 1929, 35, p.205.

G0159 *New Statesman*, 23 February 1929, 32, p.637. *Note:* Review of MacPhail, *Three Persons* (E047).

G0160 *Saturday Review*, 23 February 1929, 147, p.256. *Note:* Review of MacPhail, *Three Persons* (E047).

G0161 *TLS*, 28 February 1929, p.155. *Note:* Review of MacPhail, *Three Persons* (E047).

G0162 *Spectator*, 2 March 1929, 142, p.345. *Note:* Review of MacPhail, *Three Persons* (E047).

G0163 Charles-Eudes Bonin, 'T.E. Lawrence', *Larousse Mensuel Illustré*, April 1929, 266.

G0164 Xaver Schaukroff, *Der Gral*, April 1929, 23:7, pp.621–2. *Note:* Review of *Revolt in the Desert* A100.

G0165 'The Mysterious "Lawrence of Arabia"', *Current History*, April 1929, 30, pp.79–81.

G0166 R., 'Seven Pillars of Mystery', *Saturday Review*, 20 April 1929, pp.940–41.

G0167 *Saturday Review*, 4 May 1929, p.969. *Note:* Review of MacPhail, *Three Persons* (E047).

G0168 A. Small, 'Col. Lawrence and the Afghan Revolt', *Saturday Review*, 4 May 1929, 5, p.527.

G0169 *New York Herald Tribune Book Review*, 26 May 1929, p.18. *Note:* Review of MacPhail, *Three Persons* (E047).

G0170 *New York Times Book Review*, 7 July 1929, p.3. *Note:* Review of MacPhail, *Three Persons* (E047).

G0171 *Now and Then*, Autumn 1929, 29. *Note:* Contains Graves' Introduction to *The Enormous Room* (F0245).

G0172 G. Levi, 'Della Vida L'Arabia di Lawrence', *La Cultura*, 1930, n.s.9, p.352–66.

G0173 R. Rees, 'Lawrence a Britannia',*New Adelphi*, 1930, 3, pp.317–20.

G0174 G.B. Edwards, 'Lawrence, The Young Man', *New Adelphi*, 1930, 3, pp.310–16.

G0175 Benge Atlee, 'Lawrence of Arabia', *Battle Stories*, January 1930, pp.164–74. *Note:* Pulp magazine.

G0176 *Palestine Exploration Quarterly*, April 1930, pp.72, 73.

G0177 Clair Price, 'The Most Famous Privates in Any Army', *Reader's Digest*, March 1931, 98:107, pp.984–6.

G0178 *Atelier 1 (Studio 101)*, April 1931, p.233. *Note:* Portrait by W. Rothenstein.

G0179 Xavier de Hautecloque, 'L'Intelligence Service" anglais pendant la guerre', *Le Crapouillot*, June 1931, pp.35–8.

G0180 Kadmi-Cohen, 'Deux Grands Coloniaux Anglais. Lawrence et Philby', *Mercure de France*, August 1931, 229:795, pp.576–94.

G0181 Mrs. Becker, 'Reader's Guide', *Saturday Review*, 15 August 1931, 8, p.61. *Note:* Mention of *Revolt in the Desert*.

G0182 Lincoln Stephens, 'Armenians Are Impossible', *Outlook*, 14 October 1931, 159, pp.203–4, 222–4.

G0183 Evan David, 'War In the Desert', *War Stories*, December 1931, pp.98–105.

G0184 'T.E. Lawrence in a New Role', *Observer*, 1932.

G0185 Mrs. Belloc Lowndes, 'A Letter From England', *Saturday Review*, 13 February 1932, 8, p.526.

G0186 *New York Times Book Review*, 6 March 1932, pp.1, 22. *Note:* Review of Thomas, *Arabia Felix* (A157).

G0187 *TLS*, 28 April 1932. *Note:* Review of W. Rothenstein, *Men & Memories* (F0910).

G0188 'News from the States', *Saturday Review*, 27 August 1932, 9, p.71. *Note:* Note on *Seven Pillars of Wisdom*.

G0189 *Saturday Review,* 12 November 1932, 9, pp.233–5. *Note:* Review of *The Odyssey* (A149).

G0190 'Scholar Warrior', *Time,* 28 November 1932, pp.51–2. *Note:* Review of *The Odyssey* (A143).

G0191 *Bookmark,* December 1932, 75, p.832. *Note:* Portrait of Lawrence.

G0192 George Dangerfield, *Bookman,* December 1932, 75:8, pp.804, 806, 832, 857–9. *Note:* Review of *The Odyssey* (A149).

G0193 *Bookman,* December 1932, 75:8, p.IX. *Note:* Ad for *The Odyssey.*

G0194 Gilbert Murray, 'In Modern Dress', *Saturday Review,* 3 December 1932, 9, pp.281, 284. *Note:* Review of *The Odyssey* (A149).

G0195 *Saturday Review,* 3 December 1932, p.287. *Note:* Photo of *The Odyssey* with 'Sat Rev' scoop on book in background.

G0196 John H. Finley, 'The Odyssey of Col. Lawrence', *New York Times Book Review,* 18 December 1932, pp.1, 19. *Note:* Review of *The Odyssey* (A149).

G0197 'Lawrence of Arabia Translator to Homer', *Literary Digest,* 24 December 1932, 114, pp.13–14. *Note:* Review of *The Odyssey* (A149).

G0198 Henry Hazlitt, 'On Translating Homer', *Nation,* 31 December 1932, 135, pp.620–21.

G0199 Louis Lord, 'T.E. Shaw, The Odyssey of Homer', *Classical Journal,* 1933, 28, pp.533–6. *Note:* Review of *The Odyssey* (A149).

G0200 H. Fluckere, 'Lawrence: Lawrenciana', *Cahiers du Sud,* 1933, 20, pp.136–43.

G0201 'Literary Pictures of the Month', *Bookman,* January 1933, 76:1, p.55. *Note:* Drawing by Rothenstein.

G0202 Carl Purington Rollins', *Saturday Review,* 14 January 1933, 9, p.382. *Note:* Review of *The Odyssey* (A149).

G0203 H. Murray, *Canadian Forum,* February 1933, 13, pp.185–7. *Note:* Review of *The Odyssey* (A149).

G0204 Ernest Brennecke, Jr, 'English Arabs', *Commonweal,* 8 February 1933, 18, pp.406–8.

G0205 W.F. Stirling, 'Tales of Lawrence of Arabia', *Cornhill Magazine,* April 1933, n.s. 74, pp.494–510.

G0206 *Book Collector's Packet,* April 1933, 2:13, p.8.

G0207 C.M. Bowra, 'Two Translations', *New Stateman,* 8 April 1933, p.449.

G0208 Hannen Swaffer, 'Debunking Lawrence of Arabia', *Literary Digest,* 22 April 1933, 115, p.15.

G0209 *China Weekly Review,* 27 May 1933, 64, p.498. *Note:* Portrait of Lawrence.

G0210 A.T. Murray, 'The Odyssey of Homer Newly Translated Into English Prose by T.E. Shaw', *Classical Philology,* July 1933, 28, pp.225–7. *Note:* Review of *The Odyssey* (A149).

G0211 G.E. Harter, *Saturday Review,* 12 August 1933, 1, p.40. *Note:* Letter to editor re *The Odyssey.*

G0212 'T.E. Lawrence', *Saturday Review,* 7 October 1933, 10, p.172.

G0213 *Saturday Review,* 28 October 1933, 10, p.223. *Note:* Mention of *Wilderness of Zin* (A005) and *Carchemish* (A002).

G0214 Amy Loveman, 'The Clearing House', *Saturday Review,* 4 November 1933, p.243. *Note:* Mention of *The Odyssey.*

G0215 *Newsweek*, 13 January 1934, 3:2, p.15. *Note:* Photo of Lawrence in speedboat.

G0216 John H. Norton as told to J.B.L. Lam, 'I Flew Lawrence in War Crazed Arabia, Parts I–IV', *Liberty*, 15 and 22 January, 3 and 10 February, 1934, 9, pp.5–10, 22–7, 47–51, 42–7.

G0217 Sir John Surie, 'An Authoritative Biography', *John O'London's*, 4 March 1934. *Note:* Review of Liddell Hart, *'T.E. Lawrence' in Arabia and After* (E058).

G0218 'Lawrence and the Arabs', *TLS*, 8 March 1934, 33:1675, p.153. *Note:* Review of Liddell Hart, *'T.E. Lawrence' in Arabia and After* (E058).

G0219 *Spectator*, 9 March 1934, 152, p.382. *Note:* Review of Liddell Hart, *'T.E. Lawrence' in Arabia and After* (E058).

G0220 *New Statesman*, 10 March 1934, 7, p.344. *Note:* Review of Liddell Hart, *'T.E. Lawrence' in Arabia and After* (E058).

G0221 A.G. Macdonnell, 'T.E.L. A Lost Leader', *John O'London's*, 10 March 1934. *Note:* Review of Liddell Hart, *'T.E. Lawrence' in Arabia and After* (E058).

G0222 Col. Clive Rattigan, 'Lawrence the Soldier', *Saturday Review*, 31 March 1934, 157, p.350.

G0223 E. Wingfield-Stratford, 'Lawrence of Arabia an Authentic Hero', *Saturday Review*, 7 April 1934, 10, pp.603+.

G0224 *New York Times Book Review*, 8 April 1934, p.1. *Note:* Review of Liddell Hart, *Col. Lawrence, the Man behind Legend* (E061).

G0225 *New York Herald Tribune Book Review*, 8 April 1934, p.8. *Note:* Review of Liddell Hart, *Col. Lawrence, the Man behind the Legend* (E061).

G0226 Lincoln Kirstein, 'T.E. Lawrence', *New Republic*, 18 April 1934, 78, pp.279–80.

G0227 *Canadian Forum*, May 1934, 14, p.312. *Note:* Review of Liddell Hart, *Col. Lawrence, the Man behind the Legend* (E061).

G0228 *Booklist*, May 1934, 30, p.275. *Note:* Review of Liddell Hart, *Col. Lawrence, the Man behind the Legend* (E061).

G0229 'New Biography', *PW*, 12 May 1934, 126, pp.1772–3.

G0230 Amy Loveman, *Saturday Review*, 19 May 1934, 10, p.707. *Note:* Review of *Revolt in the Desert* (A107).

G0231 *Nation*, 23 May 1934, 138, pp.600, 602. *Note:* Review of Liddell Hart, *'T.E. Lawrence' in Arabia and After* (E058).

G0232 *Forum*, June 1934, 91, p.iv. *Note:* Review of Liddell Hart, *'T.E. Lawrence' in Arabia and After* (E058).

G0233 *Current History*, June 1934, 40, p.xii. *Note:* Review of Liddell Hart, *'T.E. Lawrence' in Arabia and After* (E058).

G0234 John F. Fiske, 'Lawrence as a Soldier', *American Review*, Summer 1934, 3:3, pp.398–402. *Note:* Review of Liddell Hart, *Col. Lawrence, the Man behind the Legend* (E061).

G0235 *Review of Reviews*, June 1934, 89, p.15. *Note:* Review of Liddell Hart, *Col. Lawrence, the Man behind the Legend* (E061).

G0236 *North American Review*, June 1934, 237, p.575. *Note:* Review of Liddell Hart, *Col. Lawrence, the Man behind the Legend* (E061).

G0237 William L. Langer, 'Lawrence As a Strategist', *Yale Review*, Summer 1934, 23:4, pp.827–9.

G0238 *Horn Book,* July 1934, 10, p.233. *Note:* Review of Liddell Hart, *Col. Lawrence, the Man behind the Legend* (E061).

G0239 *Foreign Affairs,* July 1934, 12:4, p.693. *Note:* Review of Liddell Hart, *Col. Lawrence, the Man behind the Legend* (E061).

G0240 *Cleveland Open Shelf,* July 1934, p.15. *Note:* Review of Liddell Hart, *Col. Lawrence, the Man behind the Legend* (E061).

G0241 P.E.G. Quercus, *Saturday Review,* 27 October 1934, 11, p.252. *Note:* Review of *The Odyssey* (A150).

G0242 *Outlook,* 26 November 1934, 138, p.512. *Note:* Review of Thomas,. *With Lawrence in Arabia* (E006).

G0243 'Soviet Imperialism in Afghanistan', *Foreign Affairs,* 1935, 13:3, p.701.

G0244 Laura Riding, 'The Cult of Failure: Rimbaud', *Epilogue,* 1935, 1, pp.65–6.

G0245 'Lawrence von Arabia', *Deutsche Zukunft,* 1935, 3, p.22.

G0246 K. Aebi, 'Lawrence of Arabia', *Schweitzer Monatshefte für Politik und Kultur (Zurich),* 1935, 15, pp.121–3.

G0247 A.M.R., 'T.E. Lawrence in Arabia and After', *Royal Central Asian Society Journal,* January 1935, 22:part 1, p.175.

G0248 *New York Herald Tribune Book Review,* 19 January 1935, p.8. *Note:* Review of Robinson, *Lawrence* (E083).

G0249 *National Geographic,* February 1935, 67:2, p.137.

G0250 Charles J. MacDonald, 'Vom Unbekanten Colonel Lawrence', *Hochland,* March 1935/1936, 33:1, pp.548–54.

G0251 'Lawrence: Alias Ross and Shaw.', *Newsweek,* 2 March 1935, 5:9, p.17. *Note:* Includes drawing by S.J. Woolf.

G0252 André Gybal, 'Révolte dans le désert ou l'étrange épopée du colonel Lawrence', *Paris-Midi,* 20 May 1935, pp.1, 2.

G0253 C.G.G., 'Lawrence of Arabia', *Aeroplane,* 22 May 1935, p.588.

G0254 Lord Allenby, 'Tribute to Lawrence Part I: In War', *Listener,* 22 May 1935, 13, p.857. *Note:* Front cover illus.

G0255 Sir Herbert Baker, 'Tribute to Lawrence Part II: In Peace', *Listener,* 22 May 1935, 13, p.858. *Note:* Front cover illus.

G0256 *Near East and India,* 23 May 1935, 44, p.632. *Note:* Obituary.

G0257 Francis Yeats-Brown, 'Lawrence as I Knew Him', *Spectator,* 24 May 1935, 154, pp.872–3.

G0258 'The Most Romantic Figure of the War', *Illustrated London News,* 25 May 1935, p.987. *Note:* Illus.

G0259 E. Bigelow Thompson, 'Lawrence Dies and a New Crop of Legends is Born', *Boston Evening Transcript Magazine Section,* 25 May 1935, pp.3, 5.

G0260 'Died: Col. Thomas Edward Lawrence', *Newsweek,* 25 May 1935, 5:21, p.28.

G0261 A. Moore, 'El Orens of Arabia', *New Statesman,* 25 May 1935, 9.

G0262 'Dramatic Life of "Lawrence of Arabia" Ends', *Literary Digest,* 25 May 1935, p.11.

G0263 '"Parlons un peu de mon épitaphe" par le colonel Lawrence', *Le Journal,* 25 May 1935, p.5.

G0264 'Passing of a Glamorous Figure', *Saturday Review,* 25 May 1935, 12:4, p.8. *Note:* Obituary.

G0265 An Oxford Friend, 'Lawrence of Arabia: Memories and a Tribute', *Observer*, 25 May 1935.

G0266 'Le Colonel Lawrence est mort', *Police-Magazine*, 26 May 1935, 235.

G0267 'Lawrence of Arabia – War's Spiritual Toll', *Christian Century*, 29 May 1935, 52, pp.717–8.

G0268 'Ulysses', *Jesus College Magazine*, June 1935, 4, p.27. *Note:* Also cartoon p.27.

G0269 J.G., 'T.E. Lawrence', *Jesus College Magazine*, June 1935, 4, pp.343–5.

G0270 Pierre Frédérix, 'Lawrence l'Arabe', *L'Europe Nouvelle (Paris)*, June 1935, 18, pp.522–3.

G0271 *English Review*, June 1935, 60, pp.654–6. *Note:* Obituary.

G0272 M.A. Aldanov, 'Le Roi Feycal et le Colonel Lawrence', *Revue de France*, June 1935, 15, pp.622–46.

G0273 Harry St. John Philby, 'Lawrence of Arabia: The Work Behind the Legend', *Review of Reviews (London)*, June 1935, 86, pp.15–17.

G0274 G.W.M. Dunn, 'T.E.', *Now and Then*, Summer 1935, 51, pp.7–8.

G0275 Jonathan Cape, 'T.E. Lawrence', *Now and Then*, Summer 1935, 51, p.7.

G0276 H.J. Hodgson, 'How *Seven Pillars of Wisdom* Was Printed', *The Monotype Recorder*, Summer 1935, 34:2, pp;17. 28–29.

G0277 *London Mercury and Bookman*, June 1935, 32, pp.103–4. *Note:* Obituary.

G0278 F.V. Morley, *Now and Then*, Summer 1935, 51. *Note:* Review of *Seven Pillars of Wisdom* (A042).

G0279 *L'Illustration*, 1 June 1935, 191, p.174. *Note:* Obituary.

G0280 *Saturday Review*, 1 June 1935, 160, p.143. *Note:* Obituary.

G0281 Christopher Morley, 'Bowling Green: Lawrence's *Revolt in the Desert*', *Saturday Review*, 1 June 1935, 12, pp.13+.

G0282 David Garnett, *New Statesman and Nation*, 1 June 1935.

G0283 'The Unknown Work by Colonel Lawrence', *Observer*, 2 June 1935. *Note:* Review.

G0284 A.T.P.W. & E.L.W., 'Lawrence in Oxford', *Oxford Magazine*, 6 June 1935, 53:22, pp.696–7.

G0285 *Observer*, 9 June 1935. *Note:* Statement that Cape will publish *Seven Pillars*.

G0286 E. Shillito, 'Lawrence of Arabia', *Christian Century*, 12 June 1935, 52, p.804.

G0287 *Public Opinion*, 12 June 1935. *Note:* Review of Thomas, *With Lawrence in Arabia* (E006).

G0288 Oswald G. Villard, 'Colonel Lawrence', *Nation*, 19 June 1935, 140, p.703.

G0289 *Saturday Review*, 22 June 1935, 12, pp.3–4, 15. *Note:* Review of Liddell Hart, *'T.E. Lawrence' in Arabia and After* (E061).

G0290 *New York Times Book Review*, 23 June 1935, 46, pp.55–6. *Note:* Review of *Seven Pillars of Wisdom* (A041).

G0291 René Arnaud, 'Lawrence l'Arabe ou la Guerre au Désert', *Les Annales Politiques et Littéraires*, 25 June 1935, 105, pp.632–5.

G0292 Ralph Fox, 'Lawrence, Twentieth-Century Hero', *Left Review*, July

1935, 1:10, pp.391–5.

G0293 *Apollo*, July 1935, p.2. *Note:* Portrait by Orpen.

G0294 Lord Allenby, 'Colonel T.E. Lawrence', *Royal Central Asian Society Journal*, July 1935, 22, p.333.

G0295 J. Lucas-Dubreton, 'La Vie Aventureuse du Colonel Lawrence', *Revue de Deux Mondes*, July 1935, 28, pp.168–89.

G0296 Varo Varanini, 'Pilsudski e Lawrence', *La Rassegna Italiana*, July 1935, pp.591–9.

G0297 S.F. Newcombe, 'T.E. Lawrence: Personal Reminiscences', *Palestine Exploration Quarterly*, July–October 1935, 67, pp.110–13, 159, 162–4.

G0298 L.B. Cross, 'Lawrence of Arabia', *Modern Churchman*, July 1935, 25, pp.236–42. *Note:* Review of *Seven Pillars of Wisdom* (A034).

G0299 L.B. Namier, 'Lawrence as a Friend', *Living Age*, July 1935, 348, pp.421–6.

G0300 '"Lawrence of Arabia" Alive?', *Literary Digest*, 6 July 1935, 120, p.8.

G0301 P.E.G. Quercus, *Saturday Review*, 20 July 1935.

G0302 'From Kinglake to Lawrence', *TLS*, 25 July 1935, p.1. *Note:* Review of *Seven Pillars of Wisdom* (A034).

G0303 David Garnett, *New Statesman*, 27 July 1935, 10, p.127. *Note:* Review of *Seven Pillars of Wisdom* (A034).

G0304 Eldon Rutter, 'Lawrence and His Epic', *Observer*, July 28, 1935.

G0305 E.M. Forster, 'T.E.', *Listener*, 31 July 1935, 14, pp.211–12. *Note:* Review of *Seven Pillars of Wisdom* (A034).

G0306 Anna McClure Sholl, 'Lawrence of Arabia', *Catholic World*, August 1935, 141, p.532.

G0307 Basil Jones, 'Shaw, Formerly Lawrence of Arabia', *Popular Flying*, August 1935, 4, pp.259–61, 286.

G0308 Robert Graves, 'Selbstbildnis von T.E. Lawrence', *Die Neue Rundschau*, August 1935, 46:2, pp.113–18.

G0309 A.S. Bryant, *TLS*, 1 August 1935. *Note:* Letter to editor.

G0310 'Lawrence of Arabia', *TLS*, 1 August 1935, 34:1748, pp.487, 491. *Note:* Review of *Seven Pillars of Wisdom* (A034).

G0311 'Numen Inest', *Spectator*, 2 August 1935, 155, p.193. *Note:* Review of *Seven Pillars of Wisdom* (A034).

G0312 M.E.T., 'Lawrence as Crusader', *John O'London's*, 10 August 1935.

G0313 'The Odyssey as a Novel', *TLS*, 15 August 1935, 34:1750, p.512. *Note:* Review of *The Odyssey* (A150).

G0314 E.E. Kellett, 'The Man of Many Devices', *Spectator*, 16 August 1935, 155, p.264. *Note:* Review of *The Odyssey* (A150).

G0315 *Illustrated London News*, 17 August 1935, p.276. *Note:* Review of *Seven Pillars of Wisdom* (A034).

G0316 'In Memory of T.E. Lawrence', *Near East and India*, 22 August 1935, 45, p.237.

G0317 Arthur Machen, 'Homer and His Translators', *John O'London's Weekly*, 24 August 1935, 33:854, pp.704, 720.

G0318 Ernest Barker, 'Homer's Odyssey in Lawrence's Version', *Observer*, 25 August 1935.

G0319 'News and Notes', *Bodleian Quarterly Review*, 3rd Quarter 1935, 8:87, pp.106–7.

G0320 Kenneth Williams, 'T.E. Lawrence – Fact and Legend', *Fortnightly,* September 1935, 144, pp.373–4. *Note:* Review.

G0321 Winston Churchill, 'Lawrence of Arabia', *Ex-Services of Malaya Magazine,* Autumn 1935, pp.19–20, 22–4.

G0322 B.H. Liddell Hart, 'Lawrence of Arabia', *Book of the Month Club News,* September 1935, pp.4–6.

G0323 Henry Seidel Canby, 'The Seven Pillars of Wisdom', *Book of the Month Club News,* September 1935, pp.2–3. *Note:* Lawrence picture on front cover.

G0324 Professor R.D.L.B. (De la Bere), 'Aircraftsman T.E. Shaw', *R.A.F. College Magazine,* Autumn 1935, 15:2, pp.178–83.

G0325 A.E. Prince, 'Lawrence of Arabia', *Queen's Quarterly (Kingston),* Autumn 1935, 42, pp.366–77.

G0326 *Pratt Institute Quarterly,* Autumn 1935, p.31. *Note:* Review of *Seven Pillars of Wisdom* (A041).

G0327 Lord Lloyd George, *National Review (England),* September 1935, 105, pp.342–6. *Note:* Review of *Seven Pillars of Wisdom* (A041).

G0328 *Christian Science Monitor (Weekly Magazine Section),* 4 September 1935, p.11. *Note:* Portrait.

G0329 H. Warner Allen, 'The Tragedy of Lawrence', *Saturday Review,* 7 September 1935, 160, p.143.

G0330 *Time,* 10 September 1935. *Note:* Review of *Seven Pillars of Wisdom* (A054).

G0331 *Listener,* 11 September 1935, p.456. *Note:* Review of *The Odyssey* (A150).

G0332 Clifton Fadiman, 'T.E. Lawrence', *New Yorker,* 28 September 1935, 11, pp.65–8. *Note:* Review.

G0333 'Lawrence', *Newsweek,* 28 September 1935. *Note:* Review of *Seven Pillars of Wisdom* (A054).

G0334 John H. Finley, 'Lawrence's Epic of Arabia', *New York Times Book Review,* 29 September 1935, p.1. *Note:* Review of *Seven Pillars of Wisdom* (A054), and ad.

G0335 Vincent Sheean, 'T.E. Lawrence: a Revelation and a Miracle', *New York Herald Tribune Books,* 29 September 1935, pp.1–2.

G0336 Henry Seidel Canby, 'The Last Great Puritan', *Saturday Review,* 29 September 1935, 12:22, pp.3–4, 14.

G0337 *Cleveland Open Shelf,* October 1935, p.17. *Note:* Review of *Seven Pillars of Wisdom* (A054).

G0338 'Lawrence Memorial Medal', *Royal Central Asian Society Journal,* October 1935, 22, p.523.

G0339 E.M. Forster, *Living Age,* October 1935, 349, pp.170–74. *Note:* Review of *Seven Pillars of Wisdom* (A054).

G0340 *Literary Digest,* 5 October 1935, 120, p.24. *Note:* Portrait.

G0341 'Among the Outstanding Books', *Literary Digest,* 5 October 1935. *Note:* Review of *Seven Pillars of Wisdom* (A054).

G0342 *Christian Science Monitor (Weekly Magazine section),* 9 October 1935, p.10. *Note:* Portrait.

G0343 Malcolm Cowley, 'Road to Damascus', *New Republic,* 9 October 1935, 74, pp.248–9.

G0344 Julian Arnold, 'Lawrence MS Bought by Wells', *Art News*, 26 October 1935, 34, p.4.

G0345 *Horn Book*, November 1935, 11, p.361. *Note:* Review of Robinson, *Lawrence* (E084).

G0346 Mary Colum, 'Lonely Leader', *Forum*, November 1935, 94, pp.279–80.

G0347 'The World's Books', *Current History*, November 1935, 43, p.iv. *Note:* Review of *Seven Pillars of Wisdom* (A054).

G0348 *Booklist*, November 1935, 32, p.60. *Note:* Review of *Seven Pillars of Wisdom* (A054).

G0349 *Atlantic Bookshelf*, November 1935, 156, p.26. *Note:* Review of Robinson, *Lawrence* (E084).

G0350 C.S. Coon, *Atlantic*, November 1935, 156, pp.14+. *Note:* Review of *Seven Pillars of Wisdom* (A054).

G0351 *Review of Reviews*, November 1935, 92, p.7. *Note:* Review of *Seven Pillars of Wisdom* (A054).

G0352 Ralph H. Isham, 'Panorama More Lawrence, Less Legend', *Town and Country*, November 1935, pp.43–4. *Note:* Mention of Korda and Disney for filming story of Arab campaign.

G0353 *Library Journal*, 1 November 1935, 60, p.829. *Note:* Review of Robinson, *Lawrence* (E083).

G0354 Mark Van Doren, 'Lawrence of England', *Nation*, 6 November 1935, 141, p.545.*Note:* Review of *Seven Pillars of Wisdom* (A041).

G0355 *New York Times Book Review*, 17 November 1935, p.31. *Note:* Review of Robinson, *Lawrence* (E083).

G0356 *Booklist*, December 1935, 32, p.115. *Note:* Review of Robinson, *Lawrence* (E083).

G0357 Hoffman Nickerson, 'Lawrence and Generalship', *American Review*, December 1935, 6:2, pp.129–54.

G0358 'T.E. Lawrence and the Streets in the Tropics', *Royal Institute of British Architects Journal*, 7 December 1935, 43, p.116.

G0359 *TLS*, 7 December 1935, p.834. *Note:* Reviews of Edmonds (E079), Kiernan (E073) and Robinson (E083).

G0360 Emile Mayer, 'Du Colonel Lawrence à la Guerre Italo-Ethiopienne', *Grande Revue*, 1936, 40, pp.188–98.

G0361 H.E. Friedrich, 'T.E. Lawrence Imperialist und Charackter', *Christliche Welt*, 1936, 50, pp.634–40.

G0362 'T.E. Lawrence Memorial Medal', *Royal Central Asian Society Journal*, 1936, 23, pp.412–13.

G0363 *Royal Academy Illustrated*, 1936, p.122. *Note:* Portrait by C. Wheeler.

G0364 Alfred Ehrentreich, 'Lawrence von Arabia', *Neuphilologische Monatschrift*, 1936, 7, pp.105–25.

G0365 *Now and Then*, 1936, 61. Note: Anouncement of *The Letters* (A202).

G0366 B.H. Liddell Hart, 'T.E. Lawrence: Through His Own Eyes and Another's', *Southern Review*, 1936, 2:1, pp.22–40.

G0367 Leon Abensour, 'T.E. Lawrence', *Larousse Mensuel Illustré*, January 1936, 347, pp.309–10.

G0368 *Catholic World*, January 1936, 142, p.496. *Note:* Review of *Seven Pillars of Wisdom* (A054).

G0369 Matilda C. Ghyka, 'Hamlet en Arabie', *La Revue de Paris*, January–February 1936, 43, pp.48–71.

G0370 'Four Best-Selling Personalities', *Literary Digest*, 11 January 1936, 121, p.28.

G0371 Stephan Bonsal, 'Lawrence – Speaks From the Grave', *Los Angeles Times Sunday Magazine*, 12 January 1936, pp.7–8. *Note:* Illus.

G0372 *National Review (England)*, February 1936, 106, pp.263–5. *Note:* Review of Liddell Hart and Storrs (E101)

G0373 'In Memory of T.E. Lawrence', *Great Britain and the East*, 6 February 1936, 46, p.175.

G0374 Frederick G. Kenyon, 'The Wilderness of Zin', *Now and Then*, Spring 1936, 53, pp.29–30.

G0375 'T.E.L.', *Now and Then*, Spring 1936, 53, pp.16, 20, 37.

G0376 Peter Munro Jack, 'The Mystery Colonel Lawrence', *Yale Review*, March 1936, 25:3, pp.637–8.

G0377 'The Wilderness of Zin', *TLS*, 14 March 1936, 1780, p.220. *Note:* Review.

G0378 E.G. Winkler, 'Oberst Lawrence', *Deutsche Zeitschrift (Munich)*, April 1936, 49, pp.241–56.

G0379 A.W. Smith, 'Lawrence and Clive', *Atlantic*, April 1936, 157:4, pp.447–56.

G0380 Francis Yeats-Brown, 'T.E., as Critic and Friend', *Atlantic*, April 1936, 157:4, pp.443–6.

G0381 P.R. Butler, 'T.E. Lawrence', *Quarterly Review*, April 1936, 266, pp.219–34. *Note:* Review of *Seven Pillars of Wisdom* (A042).

G0382 William Empson, 'Lawrence and Woolley', *Spectator*, 17 April 1936. *Note:* Review of *Wilderness of Zin* (A005).

G0383 *Booklist*, May 1936, 32, p.259. *Note:* Review of Edmonds, *T.E. Lawrence* (E079).

G0384 *Newsweek*, 9 May 1936, 19, p.15.

G0385 John Brophy, 'A Close Up of T.E. Lawrence', *Now and Then*, Summer 1936, 54, pp.25–6.

G0386 Christopher Morley, *Saturday Review*, 6 June 1936, pp.12, 14. *Note:* Memorial Fund.

G0387 *Saturday Review*, 13 June 1936, 14, p.21. *Note:* Mention of *Wilderness of Zin* (A007).

G0388 *New York Times Book Review*, 28 June 1936, p.12. *Note:* Review of Shumway, *Lawrence the Arabian Knight* (E090).

G0389 *TLS*, 4 July 1936, p.555. *Note:* Review of Richards, *Portrait of T.E. Lawrence* (E097).

G0390 'Latin Castles in Syria', *TLS*, 11 July 1936, p.578. *Note:* Review of *Crusader Castles* (A188).

G0391 Louis Gillet, 'El Aurens ou Lawrence l'Arabe', *Revue de Deux Mondes*, August 1936, 34, pp.688–700.

G0392 *London Studio*, August 1936, 12:(Studio 112). *Note:* Portrait by Kennington.

G0393 Lowell Thomas, 'Hell in the Holy Land', *Liberty*, 1 August 1936, pp.38–44.

G0394 Ernest Barker, *Observer*, 2 August 1936. *Note:* Review of Vol. 1 of

Crusader Castles (A188).

G0395 Francis Yeats-Brown, 'Lawrence of Arabia as Critic and Friend', *John O'London's*, 15 August 1936, 25, pp.689–90. *Note:* Photo, p.1.

G0396 *Saturday Review*, 22 August 1936, 14, p.12. *Note:* Portrait.

G0397 *New York Times Book Review*, 23 August 1936, p.2. *Note:* Review of Edmonds (E081).

G0398 Lord Halifax, 'Lawrence of Arabia', *R.A.F. Cadet College Journal*, Autumn 1936, 16:2, pp.178–81. *Note:* Text of speech at St Paul's.

G0399 *Palestine Exploration Quarterly*, October 1936, pp.231–4. *Note:* Review of *Crusader Castles* (A188–9).

G0400 'T.E. Lawrence's Expeditions', *TLS*, 3 October 1936, 35:1809, p.780. *Note:* Review of *Crusader Castles* (A188–9).

G0401 Edmund Chandler, *Saturday Review*, 3 October 1936, p.9. *Note:* Letter to editor.

G0402 A.C. Fifield, *Observer*, 1 November 1936. *Note:* Review of *Travels in Arabia Deserta* (A017).

G0403 *L'Europe Nouvelle (Paris)*, 7 November 1936, 19, pp.1117–8. *Note:* Review of *Seven Pillars of Wisdom* (A070).

G0404 N. Abrieu, *L'Europe Nouvelle (Paris)*, 14 November 1936, 19, pp.1141–3. *Note:* Review of *Seven Pillars of Wisdom* (A070).

G0405 'From Marco Polo to Lawrence', *TLS*, 21 November 1936, 1816, p.967. *Note:* Review of Slade, *Lawrence in the Blue* (E087).

G0406 Henry Seidel Canby, 'Lawrence After Arabia', *Saturday Review*, 21 November 1936, 15:4, pp.5–7.

G0407 'Lawrence: Review of His Book Scores News Beat by 14 Years', *Newsweek*, 28 November 1936, 8, p.41.

G0408 Winston Churchill, 'Mr. Churchill on T. E. Lawrence', *Now and Then*, Winter 1936, 55, p.26.

G0409 'Literary Coup', *Literary Digest*, 5 December 1936, 122, pp.25–6.

G0410 *Saturday Review*, 5 December 1936, p.59.

G0411 'Reviewer's Scoop', *Time*, 14 December 1936, 28, pp.91. *Note:* Review of *The Mint* (A166).

G0412 'Lawrence's Lat.', *News Review*, 24 December 1936, 2:50, p.30. *Note:* Mention of *The Mint* (A166).

G0413 'Presentation of the Lawrence Memorial Medal by the President', *Royal Central Asian Society Journal*, 1937, 24, pp.571–3.

G0414 Harvey Arthur DeWeerd, 'Was Lawrence a Great Soldier?', *Coast Artillery Journal (Washington)*, 1937, 80, pp.198–206.

G0415 Carl W. Ackerman, 'Prelude to War', *American Academy of Political & Social Science*, 1937, 192, p.38.

G0416 Sophie Freifrau von Wangenheim, 'Oberst Lawrence und der Aufstand der Araber im Weltkreig', *Zeitschrift für Politik*, 1937, 27, pp.417–37.

G0417 B., *Palestine Exploration Quarterly*, January 1937, pp.79–81. *Note:* Review of *Crusader Castles* (A188–9).

G0418 *National Geographic*, 1 January 1937, 71, pp.4, 60, 69, 79. *Note:* Ad for *Seven Pillars*, p.4.

G0419 Fred Allhoff, 'A Peek at Lawrence's $500,000 Book', *Liberty*, 23

January 1937, pp.51–3. *Note:* Illus.

G0420 Paul La Cour, 'En Uhaandterlig Krystal', *Tilskueren (Copenhagen)*, February 1937, 54, pp.102–12.

G0421 Horace Gregory, 'A Byronic Poem About a Modern History', *New York Herald Tribune Books*, 21 February 1937, p.2. *Note:* Review of Rodman, *Lawrence, the Last Crusade* (E115).

G0422 Muriel Rukeyser, 'Last Crusader', *New Republic*, 24 February 1937, 90, pp.88–9. *Note:* Review of Rodman, *Lawrence, the Last Crusade* (E115).

G0423 *Saturday Review*, 27 February 1937, 15, p.16. *Note:* Review of Rodman, *Lawrence, the Last Crusade* (E115).

G0424 *New York Times Book Review*, 28 February 1937, p.5. *Note:* Review of Rodman, *Lawrence, the Last Crusade* (E115).

G0426 *Booklist*, April 1937, 33, pp.238. *Note:* Review of Rodman, *Lawrence, the Last Crusade* (E115).

G0427 Eric H. Kennington, 'Lawrence An Unofficial Portrait', *Atlantic*, April 1937, 159:4, pp.406–15.

G0428 Irene Seligo, 'Gegenspieler von Lawrence', *Die Tat*, April 1937, 29:1, pp.45–52.

G0429 *Nation*, 10 April 1937, 144, p.417. *Note:* Review of Rodman, *Lawrence, the Last Crusade* (E115).

G0430 H.A. De Weerd, 'Was Lawrence a Great Soldier?', *Infantry Journal*, May–June 1937, 44:3, pp.196–204.

G0431 H.A. De Weerd, 'Was Lawrence a Great Soldier?', *Cavalry Journal*, May–June 1937, 46:3, pp.268–375.

G0432 *TLS*, 22 May 1937, p.393. *Note:* Review of *T.E. Lawrence By His Friends* (E107).

G0433 P.E.G. Quercus, 'Trade Winds', *Saturday Review*, 22 May 1937, p.24. *Note:* Short notice of limited edition of *Cancelled First Chapter of Seven Pillars of Wisdom*.

G0434 Ernest Barker, 'T.E. Lawrence by His Friends', *Observer*, 23 May 1937.

G0435 *Spectator*, 28 May 1937, 158, p.999. *Note:* Review of *T.E. Lawrence By His Friends* (E107).

G0436 David Garnett, *New Statesman*, 29 May 1937, 13, p.886. *Note:* Review of Altounyan, *Ornament of Honour* (E113) and *T.E. Lawrence by His Friends* (E107).

G0437 *Bachelor*, June 1937, 1:3, p.3. *Note:* Ad for *Seven Pillars of Wisdom*.

G0438 'To T.E. Lawrence', *TLS*, 19 June 1937, p.460. *Note:* Review of Altounyan, *Ornament of Honour* (E113).

G0439 Selden Rodman, 'They Knew Lawrence', *Saturday Review*, 26 June 1937, 16, p.6. *Note:* Review of *T.E. Lawrence by His Friends* (E109).

G0440 *New York Times Book Review*, 27 June 1937, p.5. *Note:* Review of *T.E. Lawrence By His Friends* (E109).

G0441 *Allez-Enseignez*, July 1937. *Note:* Review of French edition of *Seven Pillars of Wisdom* (A070).

G0442 *Wisconsin Library Bulletin*, July 1937, 33, p.128. *Note:* Review of Rodman, *Lawrence, the Last Crusade* (E116).

G0443 *Saturday Review*, 3 July 1937, 16, p.16. *Note:* Review of Altounyan, *Ornament of Honour* (E113).

G0444 *New York Herald Tribune Book Review,* 4 July 1937, p.6. *Note:* Review of
T.E. Lawrence by His Friends (E109).

G0445 Harold Rosenberg, 'T.E. Lawrence in Poetry', *Poetry,* August 1937,
50:5, pp.285–9. *Note:* Review of Rodman (E116) and Altounyan
(E113).

G0446 Jacques-Elian Finbert, 'Lawrence l'Arabe', *Le Risque,* 10 August 1937,
1:5, pp.13–15.

G0447 *New Republic,* 18 August 1937, 92, p.54. *Note:* Review of *T.E. Lawrence
by His Friends* (E109).

G0448 Hamish Miles, 'T.E. Lawrence: Contrast and Conflict', *Now and
Then,* Autumn 1937, 57, p.6.

G0449 *United Empire (Journal of the Royal Empire Society),* September 1937,
28:9, p.513.

G0450 *Booklist,* 1 September 1937, p.7. *Note:* Review of *T.E. Lawrence by His
Friends* (E109).

G0451 William Gilmore, 'A Wreath for Lawrence', *Nation,* 4 September
1937, p.246. *Note:* Review of *T.E. Lawrence by His Friends* (E109).

G0452 Christopher Lazare, *Nation,* 25 September 1937, 165, pp.328–9. *Note:*
Review of Altounyan (E113).

G0453 *Foreign Affairs,* October 1937, 16:1, p.188. *Note:* Review of *T.E.
Lawrence By His Friends* (E107).

G0454 Bernard Bromage, 'Difficulty of the Way: An Essay on T.E.
Lawrence', *Occult Review,* October 1937, 64, pp.255–61.

G0455 Ronald Storrs, 'Doughty, Lawrence and the Near East', *Listener,* 20
October 1937, 18:458, pp.865–6.

G0456 *Catholic World,* November 1937, 145, p.245. *Note:* Review of *T.E.
Lawrence by His Friends* (E107).

G0457 Jacques-Elian Finbert, 'Ma Première Rencontre avec Lawrence', *Le
Risque,* 25 November 1937, 1:12, pp.7–10.

G0458 Flodden W. Heron, 'Lost? Stolen? Cancelled? Literary Properties',
Colophon, Winter 1937, 2:2, pp.215–56. *Note:* Lawrence, pp.252–3.

G0459 Edward Garnett, 'Oberst Lawrence als Autor und Kritiker',
Europäische Revue, 1938, 14, pp.778–83.

G0460 *Bücherkünde,* 1938, pp.651–2. *Note:* Review of *T.E. Lawrence by His
Friends* E107).

G0461 A. Ehrentreich, 'Lawrence of Arabia in lichte Freunde', *Archiv für
den Studium den Neuren Sprachen,* 1938, 174, pp.81–4.

G0462 George Böse, *Die Literatur,* 1938/1939, 41, pp.121–2. *Note:* Review of
T.E. Lawrence By His Friends (E107).

G0463 Herbert Hagen, 'Lawrence, Bildnis Eines Forschers Politikers,
Soldaten und Menschen', *Volk im Werden (Hamburg),* 1938, 1,
pp.331–9.

G0464 Erich Müller, 'Utöpische und Apokalyptische Elemente der
Englische Gegenwart', *Stimmen Die Zeit,* 1938, 133, pp.307–14.

G0465 *Asia,* January 1938, 38:1, pp.41, 68.

G0466 Wyndham Lewis, 'Lawrence von Arabien', *Europäische Revue,*
March 1938, pp.200–205.

G0467 Kurt Hohoff, 'Lawrence von Arabien erregt Seit', *Hochland,* April
1938/1939, 36:7, pp.260–62.

G0468 Marcel Brion, 'Les Sept Piliers de la Sagesse par T.E. Lawrence', *Cahiers du Sud*, May 1938, 17, pp.400–404. *Note:* Review.

G0469 *Book Collector's Packet*, July 1938, 2:20, p.9. *Note:* Review.

G0470 H.T. Kirby, 'Lawrence of Arabia – Brass Rubber!', *Apollo*, July 1938, 28, pp.18–19.

G0471 C.G.G., 'F.W. Stent', *Aeroplane*, 6 July 1938, p.8.

G0472 Lowell Thomas, 'Perdition in the Mediterranean', *Liberty*, 23 July 1938, pp.12–13.

G0473 Eugen Kolisko, 'Reincarnation: Lawrence of Arabia', *Modern Mystic*, August 1938, 2, pp.298–301.

G0474 John Bruce, 'I Knew Lawrence Well', *Scottish Field*, August 1938, pp.20–21. *Note:* Illus.

G0475 E.M. Forster, 'Clouds Hill', *Listener*, 1 September 1938, 20:503, pp.426–7. *Note:* Illus.

G0476 'Exhibition at Clouds Hill', *TLS*, 24 September 24, 1938.

G0477 *Lancet*, 1 October 1938. *Note:* Obituary of MacPhail.

G0478 *British Medical Journal*, 1 October 1938, pp.723. *Note:* Obituary of MacPhail.

G0479 Z. Gaster, 'Lawrence and King Hussein: The 1921 Negotiations', *National and English Review*, 15 October 1938, 111, pp.512–5.

G0480 Goronwy Rees, 'Standards of Greatness', *Spectator*, 18 November 1938, 161, pp.847–8.

G0481 Phillip Duschnes, 'T.E. Lawrence and Dollars and Sense', *PW*, 19 November 1938, 134:21, pp.1817–9.

G0482 'T.E. Lawrence on Himself', *Observer*, 20 November 1938.

G0483 Ernest Barker, 'The Very Image', *Observer*, 20 November 1938.

G0484 C. Day Lewis, 'T.E. Lawrence', *Spectator*, 25 November 1938, 161, p.908. *Note:* Review of *Letters of T.E. Lawrence* (A202).

G0485 John Brophy, 'A Selfconcious Genius Made and Broken by War', *John o'London's*, 25 November 1938.

G0486 'T.E. Lawrence and His Letters', *TLS*, 26 November 1938, p.757.

G0487 *Book Collector's Packet*, December 1938, 3:4, p.7.

G0488 'The Letters of T.E. Lawrence', *Now and Then*, Winter 1938, 61, p.11.*Note:* Illus.

G0489 B.H. Liddell Hart, 'Lawrence of Arabia', *London Mercury*, December 1938, 39:230, pp.207–9. *Note:* Review of *Letters of T.E. Lawrence* (A202); also editorial notes, p.1.

G0490 Peter de Hemmer Gudme, 'Lawrence af Arabien, Myten, Manden og Strategen', *Tilskueren (Copenhagen)*, December 1938, 55, pp.372–88. *Note:* Review of Liddell Hart (E101).

G0491 Kenneth Williams, 'The Strange Self-Told Tales of T.E. Lawrence', *Great Britain and the East*, 1 December 1938, 51, p.597.

G0492 'Lawrence Speaking', *Punch*, 7 December 1938, p.642. *Note:* Review of *Letters of T.E. Lawrence* (A202).

G0493 Richard Hughes, 'The Lawrence Letters', *New Statesman*, 10 December 1938, 16, pp.1007–8. *Note:* Review of *Letters of T.E. Lawrence* (A202).

G0494 Sir John Squire, 'Colonel Lawrence Letter Writer', *Illustrated London*

News, 17 December 1938, p.1140. *Note:* Review of *Letters of T.E. Lawrence* (A202).

G0495 'First Editions of T.E. Lawrence', *TLS*, 24 December 1938, 37:1925, p.820. *Note:* Review of Duval, *A Bibliography* (E119).

G0496 'New Light on Lawrence', *Newsweek*, 26 December 1938, 12, pp.30–31. *Note:* Review of *T.E. Lawrence to His Biographers* (A210–11).

G0497 Wolf Schirrmacher, 'John Bull ungeschminkt', *Bücherkünde*, 1939, 6:8, pp.385–7.

G0498 *Quarterly Review*, 1939, 273, pp.180–81. *Note:* Review of *Oriental Assembly* (A220).

G0499 Ronald Storrs, 'Arabiens Ungekrönter König', *Nationalsozialistische Landpost*, 1939, 39.

G0500 Bruno Wachsmuth, 'Lawrence und der Freiheit der Araber', *Monatschrift für das Deutsche Geistesleben*, 1939, 41, pp.606–10.

G0501 Bruno Wachsmuth, 'Wer war Oberst Lawrence?', *Monatscrift für das Deutsche Geistesleben*, 1939, 41:2, pp.514–21.

G0502 Alfred Delp SJ, 'Der Kranke Held', *Stimmen Die Zeit*, 1939, 137, pp.76–82.

G0503 Harry Grindle, 'The Seven Pillars of Wisdom', *Central Literary Journal*, January 1939, 34, pp.23–30. *Note:* Review.

G0504 E.M.E.B., *Palestine Exploration Quarterly*, January 1939, pp.49–51. *Note:* Review of *The Letters of T.E. Lawrence* (A202); ad on back cover.

G0505 O. Williams, *National Review (England)*, January 1939, 112, pp.118–26. *Note:* Review of *Letters of T.E. Lawrence* (A202).

G0506 H.S. Canby, *Saturday Review*, 7 January 1939, 19, p.7. *Note:* Review of *T.E. Lawrence to His Biographers* (A214–5).

G0507 *New York Times Book Review*, 8 January 1939, p.1. *Note:* Review of *T.E. Lawrence To His Biographers* (A214–5).

G0508 *New York Herald Tribune Books*, 8 January 1939, p.2. *Note:* Review of *T.E. Lawrence to His Biographers* (A214–5).

G0509 'Lawrence the Chameleon', *TLS*, 14 January 1939, 38:1928, pp.17, 22. *Note:* Review of *T.E. Lawrence to His Biographers* (A210–11).

G0510 *Spectator*, 17 February 1939, 162, p.278. *Note:* Review of *T.E. Lawrence to His Biographers* (A210–11).

G0511 Clifton Fadiman, 'T.E. Lawrence', *New Yorker*, 11 March 1939, 15, p.78. *Note:* Review.

G0512 H.S. Canby, 'Sparks From Lawrence's Pen', *Saturday Review*, 11 March 1939, 19, p.6. *Note:* Review of *The Letters of T.E. Lawrence* (A204).

G0513 Herbert Gorman, 'Lawrence of Arabia As Revealed in His Own Words', *New York Review of Books*, 12 March 1939, p.3. *Note:* Review of *The Letters of T.E. Lawrence* (A204).

G0514 'T.E.', *Time*, 20 March 1939, 33, p.72. *Note:* Review of *T.E. Lawrence to His Biographers* (A214–5) and *Letters of T.E. Lawrence* (A204).

G0515 *New York Herald Tribune Books*, 26 March 1939, p.3. *Note:* Review of *The Letters of T.E. Lawrence* (A204).

G0516 Karl Rosenfedler, 'Männer und Machte des Britischen Weltreiches', *Nationalsozialistische Monatshefte*, April 1939, 10:109, pp.373–5.

G0517 *Booklist*, 1 April 1939, 35, p.251. *Note:* Review of *The Letters of T.E. Lawrence* (A204).

G0518 Mary Colum, 'The Artist as Leader', *Forum*, May 1939, 101, pp.268–9. *Note:* Review of *The Letters of T.E. Lawrence* (A204).

G0519 'Lawrence and the Arab Case', *TLS*, 27 May 1939. *Note:* Review of *Oriental Assembly* (A220).

G0520 *Pratt Institute Quarterly*, Summer 1939, p.28. *Note:* Review of *The Letters of T.E. Lawrence* (A204).

G0521 William Yale, 'Greatness of T.E. Lawrence', *Yale Review*, Summer 1939, 28:4, pp.819–22.

G0522 Fredson Bowers, 'Letters of a Man of Legend', *Virginia Quarterly Review*, Summer 1939, 15, pp.479–80. *Note:* Review of *The Letters of T.E. Lawrence* (A204).

G0523 *Time*, 5 June 1939, p.23.

G0524 Jerome et Jean Tharaud, 'La prodigieuse histoire du colonel Lawrence', *Conferencia*, 15 June 1939, 33:13, pp.3–16.

G0525 E.D., *Royal Central Asian Society Journal*, July 1939, 26:part 3, pp.526–8. *Note:* Review of *Oriental Assembly* (A220).

G0526 Sir Edward Marsh, 'A Number of People', *Harper's*, July 1939, 179, pp.173–4.

G0527 *Foreign Affairs*, July 1939, 17:4, p.820. *Note:* Review of *The Letters of T.E. Lawrence* (A202).

G0528 E.M. Reynaud, 'T.E. Lawrence d'après sa correspondance', *Étude Anglaise*, July 1939, 3, pp.234–44.

G0529 John Buchan, 'T.E. Lawrence', *Canadian Defense Quarterly*, July 1939, 16:4, pp.371–8.

G0530 A.W. Smith, *Atlantic*, July 1939, 164. *Note:* Review of *The Letters of T.E. Lawrence* (A204).

G0531 Lincoln Kirstein, 'Letters of T.E. Lawrence', *Nation*, 8 July 1939, 169, pp.47–8. *Note:* Illus. review.

G0532 Louis Gillet, 'L'Énigme du Colonel Lawrence', *Revue de Deux Mondes*, 15 September 1939, 53, pp.456–70.

G0533 *Book Collector's Packet*, October 1939, 3:10, p.5. *Note:* Announcement of *Secret Despatches* (A226).

G0534 Sir Hugh Walpole, 'T.E. Lawrence in Life and Death', *Broadsheet*, November 1939, pp.1, 2.

G0535 Josef Rick, 'Hitler und Lawrence', *Deutscher Kulturwart*, December 1939, p.30.

G0536 'December 1939 Selection: "Seven Pillars of Wisdom" by T.E. Lawrence (Vol. 2) also "What Was Lawrence's Secret?"', *Broadsheet*, December 1939, p.1.

G0537 Claire-Eliane Engel, 'Le Colonel Lawrence et la Culture Française', *Revue de Littérature Comparée*, January 1940, 20, pp.51–6.

G0538 William McCance, 'Lawrence: R.I.P.', *Picture Post*, 6 January 1940, 6, pp.12–14.

G0539 Ronald Storrs, 'Lawrence of Arabia', *Great Britain and the East*, 25 January 1940, 54, p.61.

G0540 'Lawrence on Arabia', *TLS*, 3 February 1940, 39:1983, p.62. *Note:* Review of *Secret Despatches* (A226).

G0541 Y.A. Dowse, 'Lawrence at Clouds Hill, *Chambers Journal*, March 1940, 9, pp.207–8.

G0542 Maynard Owen Williams, *National Geographic*, March 1940, 77:3, p.399.

G0543 Hans H. Bielstein, 'Wassmuss und Lawrence', *Westermanns Monatshefte*, March 1940, 84, pp.383.

G0544 'T.E. Lawrence: An Effigy in Wareham Church, Dorset', *Builder*, 22 March 1940, 158, pp.354, 359.

G0545 Ladislas Farago, 'No Nazi Revolt in the Desert', *Asia*, April 1940, p.176.

G0546 James Hanley, 'I Remember Lawrence of Arabia', *For Men Only*, April 1940, 14:53.

G0547 *Bodleian Library Record*, 1 April 1940, p.147. *Note:* Review of *The Letters of T.E. Lawrence* (A202).

G0548 Peter Jack, *New York Times Book Review*, 21 April 1940, p.5.

G0549 Ronald Storrs, 'T.E. Lawrence – The Man', *London Calling*, 22 June 1940, 35, pp.1–2.

G0550 'Ironside', *Foreign Affairs*, July 1940, 18:4, p.677.

G0551 Frank Flaherty, 'Brass Hat', *Popular Aviation*, July 1940, 27:1, p.78.

G0552 Stuart Lillico, 'A Mixed Bag of Lawrenceiana', *Saturday Review*, 24 August 1940, p.11.

G0553 'The Passion for Words', *TLS*, 28 September 1940, 39:2017, p.496. *Note:* Review of *Men in Print* (A229).

G0554 *Burlington Magazine*, October 1940, 77, pp.132–4. *Note:* Portrait by John.

G0555 Charles Wellington Furlong, 'Lawrence of Arabia and His Super Speedboat', *Blue Book*, December 1940, pp.2–3, 188–92. *Note:* Pulp magazine.

G0556 Winston Churchill, 'T.E. Lawrence – Hinn Ókrýndi Konungur Arabíu', *Vísir Sunnu-Dagsblad*, 1 and 8 December 1940, Blad 48, 49, pp.1–2 of each issue. *Note:* Apparently same article printed on two successive Sundays in Iceland.

G0557 Alfred Fabre-Luce, 'Deux Solitaires', *La Nouvelle Revue Française*, 1941, 29:326, pp.556–7.

G0559 L.H.L., 'Letters of T.E. Lawrence: Edited by David Garnett', *Broadsheet*, 14 January 1941, pp.1–2.

G0560 K.W. Marshall, '"T.E." By a Bookseller', *Bulletin of World Books*, February 1941.

G0561 K.W. Marshall, '"T.E." by a Bookseller', *Broadsheet*, February 1941.

G0562 Harold Albut, 'A New Lawrence of Arabia ', *World Digest*, February 1941, 22:8, pp.81–2.

G0563 J.L. Duncan, 'T.E. Lawrence: Portrait of an Englishman', *Dalhousie Review*, April 1941, 21, pp.71–6.

G0564 *MacLean's Magazine*, 15 June 1941, 54, p.11. *Note:* Portrait.

G0565 *World Digest*, July 1941, 27:5, p.25.

G0566 Oliver Warner, 'Scott, Lawrence and the Myth of British Decadence', *National Review (England)*, September 1941, 117, pp.314–7.

G0567 Martha Tucker, 'Devotee of the Desert', *New York Times Magazine*, 21 September 1941, p.26.

G0568 C.H. Warren, 'T.E. Lawrence of Arabia', *Bookman*, 1942, 72, p.32.

G0569 *Foreign Affairs*, July 1942, 20:4, pp.726, 727, 731.

G0570 Alfred Fabre-Luce, 'T.E. Lawrence. Lettres', *La Nouvelle Revue Française*, July 1942, 30:341.

G0571 W.J. Turner, 'Lawrence in the R.A.F.', *Spectator*, 30 October 1942, pp.413–4. *Note:* Review of *Shaw-Ede* (A234).

G0572 *Art News*, 15–31 December 1942, 41, p.25. *Note:* Short item on John's portrait.

G0573 Ezequiel Martinez Estrada, *SUR*, January 1943, 12, pp.100–107. *Note:* Review of Ocampo *338171 T.E.* (E148).

G0574 , 'T.E. Lawrence in Retreat', *TLS*, 2 January 1943, 42:2135, p.1. *Note:* Review of *Shaw-Ede* (A234).

G0575 *Art and Industry*, April 1943, 34, pp.98–101. *Note:* Photo of Kennington sculpture.

G0576 *National Geographic*, February 1944, 85:2, pp.247–8.

G0577 Lord Kinross (J.P.D. Balfour), 'Aircraftsman Shaw', *Royal Air Force College Journal*, March 1944, 2, pp.82–3.

G0578 *Studio*, February 1945, 129, p.51. *Note:* Portrait by W. Rothenstein.

G0579 *New York Times Magazine*, 1 July 1945, p.11.

G0580 Margot Hill, 'T.E. Lawrence, Some Trivial Memories', *Virginia Quarterly Review*, Autumn 1945, 21:4, pp.587–96.

G0581 Etiemble, 'T.E. Lawrence, *Oriental Assembly*, London 1939, Victoria Ocampo, *338191*, Buenos Aires, 1942', *Valeurs*, 1946, 5, pp.96–7.

G0582 Maynard Owen Williams, *National Geographic*, April 1946, 89:4, pp.478–9. *Note:* Mention of Lawrence.

G0583 *Art News*, December 1946, 45, p.45. *Note:* Herbert Gurschner portrait.

G0584 André Malraux, 'N'était-ce donc que cela?', *Editions du Pavois*, December 1946, pp.5–18.

G0585 André Malraux, 'N'est-ce donc que cela?', *Saisons*, Winter 1946–1947, 3, pp.9–24.

G0586 Henry Van Vyve, 'T.E. Lawrence, Héros modeste et orgueilleux', *Synthèses (Bruxelles)*, 1947, 3, pp.189–96.

G0587 H. Howarth, 'Silence in Zikhron', *Jewish Frontier*, June 1947, 14, pp.25–9.

G0588 Sir Ronald Storrs, 'The Spell of Arabia: Charles Doughty and T.E. Lawrence', *Listener*, 25 December 1947, 38, pp.1093–4.

G0589 Pierre Moinet, 'T.E. Lawrence en guerre', *Cheval de Troie*, 1948, 7–8, pp.1198–1214.

G0590 Emil Legnyel, 'Strains and Stresses in the Middle East', *American Academy of Political & Social Sciences*, 1948, 258, p.12.

G0591 Herbert Feis, 'Price of Greatness', *American Academy of Political & Social Science*, 1948, 246, p.36.

G0592 A.F. Johnson, 'Aircraftsman Shaw', *Royal Air Force Review*, 1948, 3:11, pp.7–8.

G0593 James H. Meisal, 'The Mystery of Airman Shaw', *Michigan Alumnus Quarterly Review*, July 1948, 54:24, pp.327–39.

G0594 André Malraux, '"Was That All, Then?"', _Transition (Paris)_, 1948, 2, pp.44–59.

G0595 Rolland P. Caillous, 'L'Echec de T.E. Lawrence', _Critique_, February 1948, 4, pp.97–107.

G0596 A. Blanc-Dufour, 'L'Agent Double', _Cahiers de Sud_, September 1948, 28, pp.546–9.

G0597 René Étiemble, 'Chronique Littéráire: Un Saint en Salopette', _Les Temps Modernes_, November 1948, 38, pp.878–86.

G0598 'Lawrence at Clouds Hill', _Everybody's Weekly_, 25 December 1948, p.15.

G0599 Hermann Hoffman, 'Oberst Lawrence', _Heimat und Glaube_, 1949, 1:5, p.4.

G0600 'Selbstbildnis T.E. Lawrence', _Deutsche Zeitung und Wirtschaftszeitung_, 1949, 4, p.15.

G0601 Denis de Rougemont, 'Modell T.E. Lawrence und Saint-Exupéry', _Merkur (Baden-Baden)_, 1949, 3:3, pp.229–41.

G0602 Gaëton Picon, 'Lawrence et l'innocence de l'action', _La Gazette des Lettres_, 1949, pp.49–54.

G0603 Hellmut Diwald, 'Die Einheit von Denken und Sein bei T.E. Lawrence und E. Jürgen', _Zeitschrift für Religions und Geistsgeschichte_, 1949/1950, 2:2.

G0604 A. Rousseaux, 'Lawrence d'Arabie', _France Illustration_, 19 March 1949, 5, p.28.

G0605 André Malraux, 'Le Démon de Absolu', _Liberté de L'Esprit_, April, May, June 1949.

G0606 Henri Perruchot, 'Lawrence et les Sept Piliers de la Sagesse', _Larousse Mensuel Illustré_, May 1949, 417, p.266.

G0607 Maurice Nadeau, 'T.E. Lawrence: Valet de Chambre de l'Idéal', _Mercure de France_, May 1949, 306, pp.124–8.

G0608 André Maurois, 'Destins Exemplaires. T.E. Lawrence', _Nouvelles Littéraires_, 5 May 1949.

G0609 Bertrand d'Astrog, 'Lawrence, notre frère', _Esprit_, June 1949, 17:6, pp.886–96.

G0610 Roger Stéphane, 'T.E. Lawrence: Lettres', _La Nef_, June 1949, 54.

G0611 Roger Stéphane, 'Les Dernières Années de T.E. Lawrence', _La Nef_, July 1949, 55, pp.26–36.

G0612 F.C. Gill, 'Lawrence, His Life', _Magazine of Wesleyan Methodist Church (London)_, July 1949, pp.322–6.

G0613 Pierre Frédérix, 'T.E. Lawrence', _La Revue de Paris_, August 1949, 56:8, pp.110–25.

G0614 André Malraux, 'The Demon of the Absolute', _World Review, London_, October–November 1949, 8, pp.33–7.

G0615 A.W.H.M., 'Aircraftsman Shaw – A Memory', _Journal of the Royal Air Force College_, November 1949, pp.132–3.

G0616 Carleton Coon, 'Point Four and the Middle East', _American Academy of Political & Social Science_, 1950, 270, p.87. _Note:_ Mention of Lawrence.

G0617 Louis Massignon, _Revue des Etudes Islamiques, Abstracts Islamica_,

1950, 9, pp.111–12. *Note:* Review of *The Letters of T.E. Lawrence* (A202).

G0618   Roger Stéphane, 'Lawrence et Son Corps', *Les Temps Modernes*, February 1950, 5:52, pp.1429–45.

G0619   A. Fabre-Luce, 'Le Colonel Lawrence et la France', *Les Oeuvres Libres*, May 1950, 48, pp.129–58.

G0620   Robert Graves, 'Revolt in the Desert', *Leader Magazine*, 10 June 1950, pp.31–4.

G0621   Hannah Arendt, 'The Imperialist Character', *Review of Politics*, July 1950, 12, pp.316–20.

G0622   Ronald Storrs, 'Das Retrospective Gepäck: Maurice Baring and T.E. Lawrence', *English*, Autumn 1950, 8:45, pp.112–16.

G0623   , 'A Modern Monumental Effigy: Kennington's Lawrence of Arabia', *Illustrated London News*, 16 September 1950, 217, p.452. *Note:* Illus.

G0624   Stephen Gardner, 'Clouds Hill', *Time & Tide*, 9 October 1950. *Note:* Poem.

G0625   P.H., 'Lawrence von Arabien und T.E. Shaw', *Englische Rundschau*, 1951, 9:233, pp.2–3.

G0626   T.E. Lawrence [pseudonym], 'Nile Mother and Mistress', *American Aphrodite*, 1951, 1:1, pp.64–9. *Note:* Not Lawrence's work.

G0627   W. Scawen Blunt, 'The Romantic as a Man of Action', *Adelphi*, 1951, 27:4, pp.330–33. *Note:* Review of *The Essential T.E. Lawrence* (A237).

G0628   André Malraux, 'Der Dämon des Absoluten', *Wort und Wahrheit*, 1951, 6, pp.593–604.

G0629   Maurice Nadeau, *Mercure de France*, January 1951, pp.111–15. *Note:* Review of *Portrait de l'aventurier* (E171).

G0630   Georges Seuffert, 'Lawrence, Homme Fasciste ou Athée Parfait', *Le Mal Pensants*, March–April 1951, 9, pp.272–85.

G0631   Sir Ronald Storrs, *Observer*, 8 April 1951.*Note:* Review of *The Essential T.E. Lawrence* (A237).

G0632   *Spectator*, 20 April 1951, 185, p.528. *Note:* Review of *The Essential T.E. Lawrence* (A237).

G0633   Arthur Calder-Marshall, 'Lawrence's Burden', *John O'London's*, 27 April 1951, p.254.

G0634   V.S. Pritchett, 'Self-Portrait of the Author from Selected Writings', *New Statesman*, 28 April 1951, 41, p.480. *Note:* Review of *The Essential T.E. Lawrence* (A237).

G0635   , 'Solitary Warrior', *TLS*, 1 June 1951, p.340. *Note:* Review of *The Essential T.E. Lawrence* (A237).

G0636   *TLS*, 8–29 June, 13–20 July, 1951, pp.357, 373, 389, 405, 437, 454. *Note:* Correspondence on Lawrence's knowledge of Arabic.

G0637   Peter de Mendelsohn, 'Lawrence von Arabien', *Die Literarische Deutschland*, 20 August 1951, 2:16, p.3.

G0638   'Snippets of a Hero', *Time*, 10 December 1951, 58, p.112. *Note:* Review of *The of Essential T.E. Lawrence* (A237).

G0639   Margret Boveri, 'T.E. Lawrence und die Angst', *Merkur (Stuttgart)*, 1952, 6:1, pp.99–100.

G0640   Gisela Uellenberg, 'Die Versuchung der Reinheit über T.E. Lawrence', *Merkur (Stuttgart)*, 1952, 6, pp.317–34.

G0641 Denis de Rougemont, 'Prototype T.E.L.', *La Table Ronde*, January 1952, 49, pp.32–44.

G0642 *Booklist*, 1 January 1952, 48, p.158. *Note:* Review of *The Essential T.E. Lawrence* (A240).

G0643 *New Yorker*, 5 January 1952, 24, p.74. *Note:* Review of *The Essential T.E. Lawrence* (A240).

G0644 *Picture Post*, 19 April 1952. *Note:* John's painting.

G0645 *Saturday Review*, 6 October 1952, pp.13–14.

G0646 Antiochus, 'Europe and the Middle East', *Cambridge Journal*, December 1952, 6:3, pp.131–59. *Note:* Reference to Lawrence.

G0647 Bruce Conde, 'What do the Arabs Think of Lawrence of Arabia?', *Al-Kulliyah (Beirut)*, December 1952, 27, pp.6–11.

G0648 Webster Evans, 'Lawrence of Arabia's Letters', *John O'London's*, 12 December 1952, p.1145.

G0649 Flora Armitage, 'The Home of Lawrence of Arabia', *Contemporary Review*, January 1953, 183:1045, pp.35–9.

G0650 *Partisan Review*, May–June 1953, 20:3, pp.327–8.

G0651 Henry Harrel-Courtès, 'Jean Béraud-Villars, poète de l'histoire épique', 27 May 1953.

G0653 Hans Gustave Guterbock, 'Carchemish', *Journal of Near Eastern Studies*, 1954, 13, pp.102–4.

G0654 James Milne, 'T.E. Lawrence in Buchan: a Little Known Episode', *Buchan Club: Transactions*, 1954, 17:3, pp.15–21.

G0655 Serge Caplain, 'Le Legendaire Colonel Lawrence ne fut-il qu'un Mythomane', 1954.

G0656 , 'Lawrence of Arabia: Venture in Debunking', *Newsweek*, 8 February 1954, 43, p.88.

G0657 'Lawrence: Lies or Legends?', *Newsweek*, 15 February 1954, pp.100, 102. *Note:* Illus.

G0658 Harvey Breit, 'The Dispute', *New York Times Book Review*, 28 February 1954, pp.8. *Note:* Review of Aldington *Lawrence l'imposteur* (E190).

G0659 Karlheinz Wallraf, 'T.E. Lawrence der Zweigeschtige', *Bücherei und Bildung*, March 1954, 6, pp.211–13.

G0660 Jean Béraud-Villars, 'Dédicace des "Sept Piliers de la Sagesse"', *Chercheurs et Curieux*, March 1954, 4:36, p.107.

G0661 'Lawrence's Defenders', *Newsweek*, 5 April 1954, 43, pp.97–8.

G0662 Henry Williamson, 'Threnos for T.E. Lawrence', *The European*, May–June 1954, xv–xvi:1,2, pp.44–61, 43–60.

G0663 Howard M. Sacher, 'The Declining World of T.E. Lawrence', *New Republic*, 10 May 1954, 130, pp.18–19.

G0664 Elie Kedourie, 'Colonel Lawrence', *Cambridge Journal*, June 1954, 7, pp.515–30.

G0665 Henry Williamson, 'T.E. Lawrence and His Brothers', *John O'London's*, 2 July 1954, 63:1564. *Note:* Review of *The Home Letters* (A246).

G0666 *Spectator*, 2 July 1954, p.30. *Note:* Review of *The Home Letters* (A246).

G0667 David Garnett, *Observer*, 4 July 1954. *Note:* Review of *The Home Letters* (A246).

G0668 Sir John Squire, 'A Nest of Eagles', *Illustrated London News*, 17 July 1954, 225, p.10. *Note:* Review of *The Home Letters* (A246).

G0669 *New Statesman*, 24 July 1954, 48, p.105. *Note:* Review of *The Home Letters* (A246).

G0670 Robert Graves, 'No. 2 Polstead Road', *New Statesman*, 24 July 1954, 48, pp.105–6.

G0671 'Richard Aldington: il m'a convaincu de la pureté de ses intentions', *Arts*, 4–10 August 1954.

G0672 *Listener*, 5 August 1954, 52:1327, pp.219, 221. *Note:* Review of *The Home Letters* (A246).

G0673 'Lawrence: Herunter von den Säulen', *Der Spiegel*, 11 August 1954, 8:33, pp.27–31. *Note:* Review of Aldington (E190).

G0674 'The Lawrence Family', *TLS*, 13 August 1954, p.516. *Note:* Review of *The Home Letters* (A246).

G0675 Peter Quennell, 'The T.E. Lawrence His Family Knew', *New York Times Book Review*, 29 August 1954, p.1. *Note:* Review of *The Home Letters* (A247).

G0676 *New York Herald Tribune Books*, 29 August 1954, p.3. *Note:* Review of *The Home Letters* (A247).

G0677 'The Vanished Galahads', *Time*, 30 August 1954, 64, pp.80,82. *Note:* Illus., review of *The Home Letters* (A247).

G0678 Charles J. Rollo, 'Elusive Genius', *Atlantic*, October 1954, 194, pp.86–97. *Note:* Review of *The Home Letters* (A247).

G0679 Oliver B. Patton, 'Col. T.E. Lawrence of Arabia', *Military Review*, October 1954, 34:7, pp.18–27.

G0680 *New Yorker*, 16 October 1954, 30, p.162. *Note:* Review of *The Home Letters* (A247).

G0681 Lewis Volger, 'Poet of the Arab Sands', *Saturday Review*, 16 October 1954, 37, p.21. *Note:* Illus., review of *The Home Letters* (A247).

G0682 *L'Express*, 20 November 1954. *Note:* Article on Aldington, *Lawrence of Arabia* (E192).

G0683 Jean Béraud-Villars, 'L'Affaire T.E. Lawrence', *La Table Ronde*, 26 November 1954, 83, pp.105–9. *Note:* Review of Aldington (E190).

G0684 René Lalou, 'T.E. Lawrence, the Legend and the Man', *Les Nouvelles Littéraires*, 9 December 1954.

G0685 Virginia Kirkus, *Virginia Kirkus*, 15 December 1954, 22, p.830. *Note:* Review of *The Mint* (A169).

G0686 *Historia*, 1955? *Note:* Review of Béraud-Villars, *Le Colonel Lawrence* (E204).

G0687 Peter Stadelmeyer, 'Die Aufzeichnungen von 352087 A/c die Enthüllungen des Richard Aldington', *Frankfurter Hefte*, 1955, 10:5, pp.371–3.

G0688 Nils Enkvist, 'T.E. Lawrence: En Kritiserad Hjälte', *Finsk Tidskrift*, 1955, 107–8, pp.140–44.

G0689 *British Book News*, 1955, p.923. *Note:* Review of *The Mint* (A173).

G0690 *Books Abroad*, 1955, 29, pp.473–4. *Note:* Review of *T.E. Lawrence by His Friends* (E108).

G0691 *La Revue Pour Tous*, 1955. *Note:* Review of Béraud-Villars (E204).

G0692 Herbert Hornstein, "'Weh dem, der Wüsten birgt'", *Neues Abendland*, 1955, 10:1, pp.689–93.

G0693 *Livres Choisis*, 1955. *Note:* Review of *The Mint* (A173).

G0694 A.R., *Biblio*, 1955. *Note:* Review of Aldington (E192).

G0695 Roland Hill, 'Arabiens "Ungekrönter König"', *Wort und Wahrheit*, 1955, 10, pp.334–9.

G0696 Josef Mühlberger, 'Der Späte Lawrence', *Welt und Wort (Tübingen)*, 1955, 10, p.145–6.

G0697 Wolfgang Koepper, 'Der Kleine und der Grosse Aufstand', *Texte und Zeichen*, 1955, 3, pp.246–50.

G0698 Burucoa, *Les Fiches Bibliographiques*, January 1955. *Note:* Review of Béraud-Villars (E204).

G0699 *Nouvelle Revue d'Outre Mer*, January 1955. *Note:* Review of Béraud-Villars (E204).

G0700 *Mercure de France*, January 1955. *Note:* Review of Aldington (E190).

G0701 Finbert, 'Le Secret des Mille Visages de Lawrence l'Inconnu', *Marco Polo (Monte-Carlo)*, January 1955.

G0702 'Lawrence: Hero or Imposter', *Tagespiegel*, 9 January 1955, p.6.

G0703 Faure, 'Le Secret de T.E. Lawrence, 20 January 1955.

G0704 Harold Nicolson, 'The Lawrence Legend', *Observer*, 30 January 1955. *Note:* Review of Aldington (E192).

G0705 J. Guthrie, 'Call Me Ishmael', *Literary Guide*, 30 January 1955. *Note:* Review of Aldington (E192).

G0706 A. Powell, 'Lawrence of Arabia', *Punch*, 2 February 1955. *Note:* Review of Aldington (E192).

G0707 Ronald Storrs, 'Lawrence of Arabia', *Listener*, 3 February 1955, 53:1353, pp.187–9. *Note:* Illus., review of Aldington (E192).

G0708 Eric Kennington, 'On Books and People', *Truth*, 4 February 1955, p.141. *Note:* Review of Aldington (E192).

G0709 'Mud on the White Robe', *TLS*, 4 February 1955. *Note:* Review of Aldington (E192).

G0710 H.M. Champress, 'Prince of Mecca', *Spectator*, 4 February 1955, 194, pp.131–2. *Note:* Review of Aldington (E192).

G0711 Richard Aldington, 'Why I Debunked The Lawrence Legend', *Illustrated*, 5 February 1955, pp.32–3.

G0712 David Garnett, 'Lawrence in the Dock', *New Statesman*, 5 February 1955, 49, pp.182–4.

G0713 C.E. Carrington, *Time & Tide*, 5 February 1955. *Note:* Review of Aldington (E192).

G0714 Blanche Patch, *Illustrated*, 10 February 1955, p.4. *Note:* Letter to editor.

G0715 Raymond Lacoste, 'Lapidation d'une idole', *Bulletin de Paris*, 11 February 1955.

G0716 Sir John Squire, 'The Case for the Prosecution', *Illustrated London News*, 12 February 1955, 136:3538, pp.224–6, 264. *Note:* Review of Aldington.

G0717 Philip Toynbee, 'Lawrence Into Ross', *Observer*, 13 February 1955. *Note:* Review of *The Mint* (A173).

G0718 'Autopsy of a Hero', *Time*, 14 February 1955, 65, p.29. *Note:* Review of Aldington (E198).

G0719 E.M. Forster, '"The Mint" by T.E. Lawrence', *Listener*, 17 February 1955, 53:1355, pp.279–80.

G0720 'Counterfeit or True?', *TLS*, 18 February 1955, p.99. *Note:* Review of Aldington (E192) and *The Mint* (A173).

G0721 Andrew Boyle, 'Lawrence a Man or Myth?', *New Statesman*, 19 February 1955, 49, pp.19–20. *Note:* Illus.

G0722 V.S. Pritchett, 'Ross At the Depot', *New Statesman*, 19 February 1955, 49, p.251. *Note:* Review of *The Mint* (A173).

G0723 J. Brooke, 'Men and Books – The Downward Urge', *Time & Tide*, 19 February 1955. *Note:* Review of *The Mint* (A173).

G0724 Christopher Derrick, 'Cliffs of Fall', *The Tablet*, 19 February 1955, p.180.

G0725 'Seven Pillars of Wisdom T.E. Lawrence's Icon Book', *Everybody's Weekly*, 19 February 1955.

G0726 Harvey Breit, 'Cross Section', *New York Times Book Review*, 20 February 1955, p.8. *Note:* Review of Aldington (E198).

G0727 Rob Lyle, *Truth*, 25 February, 11 and 18 March 1955. *Note:* Letters to editor.

G0728 *Spectator*, 25 February 1955, p.229. *Note:* Review of *The Mint* (A173).

G0729 'The Storm Over Lawrence', *Illustrated*, 26 February 1955, pp.6, 9. *Note:* Letters from G.F. Breese, B.H. Liddell Hart, etc., illus.

G0730 Mrs. Kennington, 'Lawrence, Was He a Woman Hater?', *Housewife*, Spring 1955.

G0731 Bernard de Fallois, 'Lawrence le Véridique', *La Revue de Paris*, March 1955, 62, pp.128–33.

G0732 Georges Perros, 'Choses Lues: Lawrence l'Imposteur', *Monde Nouveau*, March 1955, pp.103–5.

G0733 Lowell Thomas, *The Middle East Journal*, Spring 1955, 9:2, pp.197–8. *Note:* Review of Aldington (E192).

G0734 C.M. Woodhouse, 'T.E. Lawrence: New Legends For Old', *Twentieth Century*, March 1955, 157:937, pp.228–36.

G0735 'Lawrence of Arabia', *Truth*, 4 March 1955. *Note:* Review of Aldington (E192).

G0736 *Bulletin de Paris*, 11 March 1955. *Note:* Review of *The Mint* (A182).

G0737 Hans Bütow, 'Lawrence von Arabien', *Die Gegenwart*, 12 March 1955, 10:6, pp.173–5.

G0738 MPL, *Bulletin des Lettres (Lyon)*, 15 March 1955. *Note:* Review of Aldington (E190).

G0739 Robert Miquel, 'Une énigme qui bouleverse l'Angleterre: L'heros de légende ou imposteur?', *Point de Vue*, 17 March 1955.

G0740 R.C.O. Lovelock, 'The Mint – and the Metal: T.E. Lawrence's Life in the RAF', *Flight*, 18 March 1955, 67, p.356. *Note:* Review of *The Mint* (A173).

G0741 R.C. Preston, 'The Mint', *Aeroplane*, 18 March 1955, p.365. *Note:* Review.

G0742 Robert Cantwell, 'In Grave Adversity', *New York Times Book Review*, 20 March 1955, p.3. *Note:* Review of *The Mint* (A169).

G0743 *New York Herald Tribune Books,* 20 March 1955, p.3. *Note:* Review of *The Mint* (A169).

G0744 'Coin of the Realm', *Newsweek,* 21 March 1955, 45, pp.110–11. *Note:* Review of *The Mint* (A169).

G0745 Robert Graves, 'Lawrence Vindicated', *New Republic,* 21 March 1955, 132:2, pp.16–17, 20.

G0746 'Hero As Rookie', *Time,* 21 March 1955, 65, p.108. *Note:* Review of *The Mint* (A169).

G0747 Jürgen Rausch, 'Sterbensmüde vom Freien Willen T.E. Lawrence – ein Leben ohne Auftrag', *Deutsche Zeitung und Wirtschaftszeitung,* 26 March 1955, 10:24, p.22.

G0748 Albert-Marie Schmidt, 'Lawrence le Raté', *Reforme,* 26 March 1955.

G0749 *Saturday Night,* 26 March 1955, 70, p.14. *Note:* Illus.

G0750 René Lalou, 'Le Livre de la Semaine: La Matrice, de T.E. Lawrence', *Nouvelles Littéraires,* 31 March 1955.

G0751 'T.E. Lawrence: La Matrice', *Journal de la Société des Lecteurs,* April 1955.

G0752 *J'ai Lu,* April 1955. *Note:* Review of *The Mint* (A182).

G0753 Raymond Las Vergnas, 'Lettres Anglo-Américaines', *Hommes et Mondes,* April 1955.

G0754 'Comment', *Blackwood's Magazine,* April 1955, 277, pp.382–4. *Note:* Review of *The Mint* (A173).

G0755 J.D. Lunt, 'An Unsolicited Tribute', *Blackwood's Magazine,* April 1955, 277:1674, pp.289–96.

G0756 A.R., *Biblio,* April 1955. *Note:* Review of *The Mint* (A173).

G0757 Gabriel Puaux, 'La Ligue Arabe', *La Revue de Paris,* April 1955, 62, pp.69–81.

G0758 Silvio D'Arzo, 'T.E. Lawrence', *Paragone,* April 1955, 2, pp.72–6.

G0759 Herbert Tauber, 'Geheimnisse an T.E. Lawrence', *Der Monat,* April 1955, 7, pp.72–9.

G0760 B.H. Liddell Hart, 'T.E. Lawrence, Aldington and the Truth', *London Magazine,* April 1955, 2:4, pp.67–75.

G0761 'L'Égalité Véritable', *L'Express,* 2 April 1955.

G0762 Vincent Sheean, 'Ear to the RAF', *Saturday Review,* 2 April 1955, 38, pp.20–21. *Note:* Review of *The Mint* (A168).

G0763 John Haverstick, 'Behind the Book', *Saturday Review,* 2 April 1955, 38, p.21. *Note:* Review of *The Mint* (A168).

G0764 L.P. Hartley, 'A Failed Masterpiece', *Listener,* 14 April 1955, 53, pp.658–9. *Note:* Review of *The Mint* (A173).

G0765 Michel Mohrt, 'La métamorphose du colonel Lawrence "roi sans courronne" d'Arabie en simple soldat', *Bulletin de Paris,* 15 April 1955.

G0766 *New Republic,* 18 April 1955, 132, p.23. *Note:* Review of Aldington (E198).

G0767 John Rosselli, 'Was T.E. Lawrence a Fake?', *The Reporter,* 21 April 1955, 12, pp.49–51. *Note:* Review of Aldington (E198).

G0768 Linton Anselm, *Listener,* 21 April 1955, 53, p.713. *Note:* Letter to editor.

G0769 Vyvyan Richards, *Listener,* 21 April 1955, 53, p.713. *Note:* Letter to editor.

G0770 'La Fin d'une Légende', *Rivarol,* 28 April 1955.

G0771 R. Weltsch, 'Who Was the Founder of "Greater Arabia"?', *Yiddisher Kemfer,* 29 April 1955, 36, pp.6–8. *Note:* In Yiddish.

G0772 Charles J. Rollo, *Atlantic,* May 1955, 195:5, pp.82–3. *Note:* Review of *The Mint* (A168).

G0773 *Livres Choisis,* May 1955. *Note:* Review of *The Mint* (A182).

G0774 Meriel, 'Trois Aventures', May 1955.

G0775 *Sur,* May 1955, pp.42–72.

G0776 *Bibliographie de la France,* 3 May 1955. *Note:* announcement of Béraud-Villars, *Le Colonel Lawrence* (E204).

G0777 Jean Fannius, 'Héros ou Imposteur?', *Le Maroc,* 5 May 1955.

G0778 Lionel Curtis, *Listener,* 5 May 1955, 53, p.809. *Note:* Letter to editor.

G0779 Robert Graves, *New Republic,* 16 May 1955, 132, p.46. *Note:* Letter to editor.

G0780 *New Republic,* 23 May 1955, 132, p.23. *Note:* Letter to editor.

G0781 T. Birdde, *Listener,* 26 May 1955, 53, p.940. *Note:* Letter to editor.

G0782 Étiemble, 'Aldington L'Imposteur', *Les Lettres Nouvelles,* June 1955, 3:28, pp.873–91.

G0783 Bernard DeVoto, *Harper's,* June 1955, 210:1261, pp.13–14. *Note:* Review of *The Mint* (A168).

G0784 *Canadian Forum,* June 1955, 35, p.67. *Note:* Review of Aldington (E198).

G0785 Finbert, 'Européens dans La Mecque interdite', *Les Cahiers "Connaissance du Monde",* June 1955, 2e trimestre.

G0786 Pierre Frédérix, 'Lawrence l'Imposteur précéde d'une réponse de R. Aldington à de Fallois', *La Revue de Paris,* June 1955.

G0787 Rob Lyle, *London Magazine,* June 1955, 2:6, pp.75–81. *Note:* Letter to editor.

G0788 *Livres et Lectures (Issy-les-Moulineaux),* June 1955. *Note:* Review of Béraud-Villars (E204).

G0789 *Nouvelles Littéraires,* 9 June 1955. *Note:* Review of Béraud-Villars (E204).

G0790 P.P-L., *Bulletin des Lettres (Lyon),* 15 June 1955. *Note:* Review of Béraud-Villars (E204).

G0791 *Virginia Kirkus,* 15 June 1955, 23, p.411. *Note:* Review of Armitage, *The Desert and the Stars* (E212).

G0792 Robert Kemp, 'Atmosphères', *Nouvelles Littéraires,* 23 June 1955.

G0793 A. Lauras, *Etudes,* July 1955. *Note:* Review of *The Mint* (A182).

G0794 Jean Cathelin, 'La Littérature d'un Lawrence', *Correspondance,* July 1955, pp.257–61.

G0795 Pancho Picabia, "La dédicace de "Sept Piliers de la Sagesse"', *Chercheurs et Curieux,* July 1955.

G0796 Marcel Leibovici, 'T.E. Lawrence La Matrice', *La Nouvelle Revue Françaises,* July 1955, 31, pp.144–6.

G0797 J. Maclaren-Ross, 'The Mint', *London Magazine,* July 1955, 2:7, pp.71–4. *Note:* Review of *The Mint* (A173).

G0798 *Library Journal*, July 1955, 80, p.1578. *Note:* Review of Armitage (E212).

G0799 Guido Eeckels, 'Lawrence d'Arabie: L'Envers d'une Légende', *Synthèses (Bruxelles)*, July 1955, 10:10, pp.268–72.

G0800 Victoria Ocampo, 'Felix Culpa', *Sur*, July–August 1955, 235, pp.42–72.

G0801 Raymond Mortimer, 'Las Acusciones de Aldington', *Sur*, July–August 1955, 235, pp.39–42.

G0802 E.M. Forster, "El Troquel" de T.E. Lawrence', *Sur*, July–August 1955, 235, pp.31–8.

G0803 Sir Ronald Storrs, 'Lawrence y el Libro de Aldington', *Sur*, July–August 1955, 235, pp.22–30.

G0804 B.H. Liddell Hart, 'Lawrence, Aldington y le Verdad', *Sur*, July–August 1955, 235, pp.11–21.

G0805 Sir Winston Churchill, 'T.E. Lawrence', *Sur*, July–August 1955, 235, pp.2–11.

G0806 Jacques Delebacque, 'Le véritable Lawrence', *Aspects de la France*, 8 July 1955.

G0807 J.D.L., 'T.E. Lawrence – Another Point of View', *Spectator*, 9 July 1955, 195, p.42.

G0808 *Revue de Deux Mondes*, 15 July 1955, 40. *Note:* Review of Béraud-Villars (E204).

G0809 R. Bailly, *Larousse Mensuel Illustré*, August 1955. *Note:* Review of *The Mint* (A184).

G0810 René Lalou, 'Aldington, Jean Béraud-Villars', *Annales*, August 1955.

G0811 *Mercure de France*, August 1955. *Note:* Review of Béraud-Villars.

G0812 Ph.D., 'L'Aventure Imprimée', *Marco Polo (Monte-Carlo)*, August 1955.

G0813 Richard Aldington, 'A Reply to Captain Liddell Hart', *London Magazine*, August 1955, 2:8, pp.66–71. *Note:* Letter to editor.

G0814 *Bulletin de Paris*, 5 August 1955. *Note:* Review of Béraud-Villars (E204).

G0815 Robert Kemp, *Bulletin de la Société Littéraire des PTT*, 15 August 1955.*Note:* Review of Béraud-Villars (E204).

G0816 *New York Herald Tribune Book Review*, 28 August 1955. *Note:* Review of Armitage (E212).

G0817 *Roundel*, September 1955, 7, pp.41–5. *Note:* Review of *The Mint* (A169).

G0818 Manès Sperber, 'T.E. Lawrence et Ses Deux Légendes', *Preuves*, September 1955, 55, pp.5–19, illus.

G0819 'Analyses: Le Colonel Lawrence de Jean Béraud-Villars', *Le Papetier de France*, September 1955.

G0820 Hubert Juin, 'Chroniques', *La Table Ronde*, 3 September 1955.

G0821 Roger Grenier, 'La Livrée de la Mort', *La Table Ronde*, 3 September 1955, 93, pp.131–4.

G0822 Emil Lengyel, 'Enigma of the Sands', *Saturday Review*, 3 September 1955, 38, p.13. *Note:* Illus.

G0823 Selden Rodman, 'To Glory and Back', *New York Times Book Review*, 4 September 1955, p.7. *Note:* Review of Armitage (E212).

G0824 *Bibliographie de la France,* 22 September 1955. *Note:* Review of Béraud–Villars (E204).

G0825 *Revue Militaire d'Information,* 25 September 1955. *Note:* Review of Béraud-Villars (E204).

G0826 'Vincent Sheean', *New York Herald Tribune Book Review,* 25 September 1955, p.5. *Note:* Review of Aldington (E198).

G0827 Calvet Carron, *Éducation Nationale,* October 1955.*Note:* Review of Béraud-Villars.

G0828 *Bookmark,* October 1955, 15:1, p.3. *Note:* Notice of Armitage, *The Desert and The Stars* (E212).

G0829 Robert Kemp, *Biblio,* October 1955. *Note:* Review of Béraud-Villars.

G0830 Phoebe Lou Adams, *Atlantic,* October 1955, 196:4, pp.88. *Note:* Review of Armitage, *The Desert and the Stars* (E212).

G0831 'Le Procès T.E. Lawrence', *Annales,* October 1955.

G0832 Robert Kemp, *Livres de France,* October 1955. *Note:* Review of Béraud-Villars.

G0833 *Booklist,* 1 October 1955, 52, p.53. *Note:* Review of Armitage, *The Desert and the Stars.*

G0834 Carlos Baker, 'A Hero Challenged', *New York Times Book Review,* 2 October 1955, pp.24–5. *Note:* Review of Aldington (E198).

G0835 George Dangerfield, 'Parody of a Hero', *Nation,* 22 October 1955, 181, p.345.

G0836 Malcolm Muggeridge, 'Royal Soap Opera', *New Statesman,* 22 October 1955.

G0837 J.J. O'Conner, *America,* 29 October 1955, 94, p.134. *Note:* Review of Aldington, *Lawrence of Arabia* (E198).

G0838 Pierre de Boisdeffre, 'Le Colonel Lawrence ou la Tentation du Néant', *Etudes,* November 1955, 287, pp.168–82.

G0839 B.H. Liddell Hart, 'T.E. Lawrence Man or Myth?', *Atlantic,* November 1955, 196:5, pp.70–71.

G0840 *Practical Christianity,* November–December 1955, 237, p.16. *Note:* Mention of Lawrence.

G0841 A.G., *Nouvelle Revue d'Outre Mer,* November 1955. *Note:* Review of Béraud-Villars (E204).

G0842 A.R., *Etudes,* November 1955. *Note:* Review of Béraud-Villars (E204).

G0843 John Graham, 'With The Imperial Camel Corps', *Yeoman,* November 1955.

G0844 *Booklist,* 1 November 1955, 52, p.100. *Note:* Review of Aldington,*Lawrence of Arabia* (E198).

G0845 M.D., 'Le Colonel Lawrence ou la Recherche de L'Absolu', *Journal de la Marine Marchande (Paris),* 3 November 1955.

G0846 Emil Lengyel, 'Behind the Hero', *Saturday Review,* 12 November 1955, 38, pp.16, 144. *Note:* Review of Aldington (E198).

G0847 P.B., *Bulletin des Lettres (Lyon),* 15 November 1955. *Note:* Review of Béraud-Villars (E204).

G0848 M.A. Fitzsimons, 'Agonizing Reappraisal of T.E. Lawrence', *Commonweal,* 25 November 1955, 63:8, pp.202–4.

G0849 Étiemble, 'La Matrice (Ou la Réponse d'un Imposteur)', *Évidences,* December 1955, 7:53, pp.29–35.

G0850 Laurette S. Gabra, 'Le Colonel Lawrence ou la recherche de l'Absolu', *Le Rayon d'Égypte*, 4 December 1955.

G0851 Anthony West, 'The Fascination', *New Yorker*, 10 December 1955, 31, pp.215–20. *Note:* Review of Aldington (E198).

G0852 M.Y. Ben-Gavriel, 'Die Drei Deutschen Versüche den Suezkanal zu Erben', *Deutsche Rundschau*, 1956, 82:9, pp.947–50.

G0853 *British Book News*, 1956, p.678. *Note:* Review of *The Essential T.E. Lawrence* (A239).

G0854 *British Book News*, 1956, p.377. *Note:* Review of Armitage, *The Desert and The Stars* (E213).

G0855 Alfred Ehrentreich, 'T.E.Lawrence, The Mint ein Psycholgisches Problem', *Die Neuen Sprachen*, 1956, 5, pp.348–52.

G0856 Denis Marion, 'Un illustre Inconnu: T.E. Lawrence', *Critique*, January 1956, 14:104, pp.52–62. *Note:* Review.

G0857 Gustave Cohen, 'Affaire Aldington Contre Lawrence d'Arabie', *Hommes et Mondes*, March 1956, 116, pp.487–96.

G0858 Fritz Kraus, 'T.E. Lawrence – Legende und Wirklichkeit', *Deutsche Rundschau*, March 1956, 82, pp.279–85.

G0859 W.P. Snodgrass, *Western Review*, Spring 1956, 20:3, pp.237–9. *Note:* Review of *The Mint* (A168).

G0860 Étiemble, 'L'Année T.E. Lawrence', *Étude Anglaise*, April–June 1956, 9:2, pp.122–30. *Note:* Review.

G0861 *Canadian Army Journal*, April 1956, 10, pp.107–9. *Note:* Review of Aldington (E198).

G0862 Rob Lyle, 'Lawrence, Aldington and Some Critics', *Nine*, April 1956, 11, pp.39–42.

G0863 *TLS*, 13 April 1956. *Note:* Review of Armitage (E213).

G0864 André Garteiser, 'A Propos du Colonel Lawrence', *Hommes et Mondes*, May 1956, 116.

G0865 Paul Johnson, *New Statesman*, 5 May 1956. *Note:* Review of Armitage (E213).

G0866 *Time & Tide*, 19 May 1956. *Note:* Review of Armitage (E213).

G0867 *Military Review*, June 1956, 36, p.108. *Note:* Review of Aldington (E198).

G0868 R.A. Pavey, 'The Arab Revolt', *Marine Corps Gazette*, July 1956, 40, pp.48–52.

G0869 William Yale, *American Academy of Political & Social Science*, September 1956, 307, pp.167–8. *Note:* Review of Aldington, *Lawrence of Arabia* (E198).

G0870 Robert Graves, 'A Soldier's Homer', *New Republic*, 24 September 1956, 135, pp.17–19.

G0871 'Perspectives of the Arab World', *Atlantic*, October 1956, 198: 4. *Note:* Mention of Lawrence.

G0872 Wyndham Lewis, 'Perspectives on Lawrence', *Hudson Review*, Winter 1956, 8:4, pp.596–608. *Note:* Review of Aldington (E198) and Armitage (E212).

G0873 André Malraux, 'Lawrence and the Demon of the Absolute', *Hudson Review*, Winter 1956, 8:4, pp.519–32.

G0874 Anita Engle, 'The Mysterious S.A.', *New Statesman*, 22 December 1956, 52, pp.812–3.

G0875 S.H. Longrigg, *International Affairs*, 1957, 33, pp.337–8. *Note:* Review of Lönnroth (E160).

G0876 Paul Herre, *Historische Zeitschrift*, 1957, 183, pp.636–8. *Note:* Review of Aldington (E201).

G0877 Bertier de Sauvigny, '923-Arm-L', *Les Fiches Bibliographiques*, 1957. *Note:* Review of Armitage (E214).

G0878 *Echo de la Mode*, 1957, 30. *Note:* Review of Armitage (E214).

G0879 Jürgen Rausch, 'T.E. Lawrence oder die Schrecken der Freiheit', *Neue Deutsche Hefte*, 1957, 4:39, pp.591–602.

G0880 *Union Action*, 1957. *Note:* Review of Armitage (E213).

G0881 J. Leclant, *Les Livres*, January 1957. *Note:* Review of *Les Textes essentiels* (A242).

G0882 *Le Journal des Lettres*, 30 March 1957, p.10. *Note:* Review of Armitage (E214).

G0883 *Lectures Françaises*, April 1957. *Note:* Review of Armitage (E214).

G0884 *Guide de Lecteur*, May 1957. *Note:* Review of Armitage (E214).

G0885 Marvel Clavie, *Le Papetier-Libraire*, May 1957. *Note:* Review of Armitage (E214).

G0886 *La Nouvelle Revue Française*, May 1957. *Note:* Review of Armitage (E214).

G0887 *L'Education Familiale (Bruxelles)*, May 1957. *Note:* Review of Armitage (E214).

G0888 *Société Belge d'Etudes et d'Expansion (Liège)*, May–June 1957. *Note:* Review of Armitage (E214).

G0889 *La Sélection des Libraires de France*, May 1957. *Note:* Review of Armitage (E214).

G0890 *Bulletin critique du livre Français*, June 1957. *Note:* Review of Armitage (E214).

G0891 *La Revue de Paris*, June 1957. *Note:* Review of Armitage (E214).

G0892 *Réalités*, June 1957, 137, pp.51, 53.

G0893 *Palestine Exploration Quarterly*, July–December 1957, p.156.

G0894 *Mercure de France*, July 1957. *Note:* Review of Armitage (E214).

G0895 *Le Livre Français*, July–September 1957. *Note:* Review of Armitage (E214).

G0896 'Lawrence d'Arabie', *Amitiés France-Israel*, September 1957.

G0897 Pierre Lyautey, *Bulletin de l'Académie des Sciences d'outre-mer*, October 1957. *Note:* Review of Armitage (E214).

G0898 P.V., *Economie et Humanisme (Caliure)*, November–December 1957. *Note:* Review of Armitage (E214).

G0899 *Bulletin de l'Institut Pédagogique National*, November 1957. *Note:* Review of Armitage (E214).

G0900 L.R., *Revue de la Dé Nationale*, November 1957, p.1757.

G0901 Pierre Lyautey, 'Lawrence d'Arabie', *Bulletin de l'Académie des Sciences d'Outre-Mer*, November 1957.

G0902 *Marchés Tropicaux du Monde*, 2 November 1957. *Note:* Review of Armitage (E214).

G0903 F.B.?, *L'Insulaire*, December 1957. *Note:* Review of Armitage (E214).
G0904 *Feuillets Bibliographiques (Paris)*, 1958. *Note:* Review of Bourgois.
G0905 E.D., *Mer et Outre-Mer*, 1958:1ᵉ trimestre. *Note:* Review of Armitage (E214).
G0906 Charles Findley, 'The Amazing A.C.2', *Royal Air Force Flying Review*, January 1958, 13:5, pp.30–32. *Note:* Illus.
G0907 René Étiemble, 'Chronique Littéráire: 338.171 T.E.', *Les Temps Modernes*, March 1958, 30, pp.1708–20.
G0908 Charles Findley, 'The Amazing A.C.2', *Listener*, 5 June 1958, 59, pp.937–8. *Note:* Illus.
G0909 A.L., *Hobby (France)*, July–August 1958. *Note:* Review of Bourgois.
G0910 Helmüt Heissenbüttel, 'Ein Heiliger Unseres Jahrhunderts? Zun. 70. Geburtstag von T.E. Lawrence', *Deutsche Zeitung und Wirtschaftszeitung*, 16 August 1958, p.18.
G0911 *Revue Française de Science Politique*, September 1958, 8:3. *Note:* Review of Armitage (E214).
G0912 *Notes Bibliographiques (Paris)*, September 1958. *Note:* Review of Bourgois.
G0913 X. Pattyn, *Livres et Lectures (Issy-les-Moulineaux)*, September 1958. *Note:* Review of Bourgois.
G0914 *L'Athénée (Belgique)*, November–December 1958. *Note:* Review of Bourgeois.
G0915 *TLS*, 21 November 1958, p.670. *Note:* Review of Béraud-Villars (E205).
G0916 *New Statesman*, 20 December 1958, 56, p.891. *Note:* Review of Béraud-Villars (E205).
G0917 Herbert Punkik, 'Jordan – fra emirat til kongedømme', *Økonomig Politik*, 1959, 33:1, pp.27–8.
G0918 A.G. Prys-Jones, 'T.E. Lawrence as I Knew Him', *Wales*, March 1959, nn.s. no.7,, pp.47–53. *Note:* Listed in Contents as 'T.E. Lawrence at Oxford'.
G0919 *Library Journal*, 1 March 1959, 84, p.750. *Note:* Review of Béraud-Villars (E205).
G0920 D.W. Brogan, 'The Mystery and The Man', *New York Times Book Review*, 15 March 1959, p.32. *Note:* Review of Béraud-Villars (E205).
G0921 *New York Herald Tribune Book Review*, 15 March 1959, p.10. *Note:* Review of Béraud-Villars (E205).
G0922 William Sands, 'A Foreigner Under Faysal', *Saturday Review*, 11 April 1959, 42, pp.44–5. *Note:* Illus.
G0923 *New Yorker*, 2 May 1959, 35, p.163. *Note:* Review of Bérand-Villars (E205).
G0924 *Booklist*, 15 May 1959, 55, p.504. *Note:* Review of Bérand-Villars (E205).
G0925 Serge Talbot, 'Notre T.E. Lawrence', *Arcadie*, November 1959.
G0926 James N.M. MacLean, 'Lawrence of Arabia', *London Scottish Regimental Gazette*, December 1959, 64:768, pp.218–21.
G0927 Jukka Nevakivi, 'Arabien Krunnamaton Kuningas', *Historiallinen Aikakuskirja*, 1960, 58:1, pp.149–53.
G0928 Ernest Dawn, 'The Amir of Mecca al–Husayn Ibn'Ali and the

Origin of the Arab Revolt', *Proceedings of the American Philosophical Society,* 1960, 104, pp.11–34.

G0929 Col. Demange, 'La Guérilla', *Revue Militaire Générale,* February 1960, 2, pp.216–7.

G0930 J.T. Laird, 'T.E. Lawrence: The Problem of Interpretation', *Australian Quarterly,* March 1960, 32:1, pp.93–9.

G0931 'Romantic Riddle', *MD,* April 1960, 4:4, pp.221–7.

G0932 A. Brien, 'Ross', *Spectator,* 20 May 1960, 204, p.732. *Note:* Review of *Ross* (E222).

G0933 A. Alvarez, 'Arabia Deserta', *New Statesman,* 21 May 1960, 59, pp.748, 750. *Note:* Review of Rattigan (E222).

G0934 D.W., 'Elusive Lawrence', *The Tablet,* 21 May 1960, p.490.

G0935 *Time,* 23 May 1960. *Note:* Review of Rattigan (E222).

G0936 J.W. Trewin, 'Ross', *Illustrated London News,* 28 May 1960, 236, p.944. *Note:* Review of Rattigan (E222).

G0937 *Bancroftian,* June 1960, 59:5, p.70.

G0938 *La Vie des Métiers "Médecine",* June 1960. *Note:* Review of Stéphane, ed., *T.E. Lawrence* (A250).

G0939 Lucien Poirtier, 'Guerre et Littérature', *Revue Militaire d'Information,* July 1960, 318, pp.26–44.

G0940 Ray Lunt, 'Lawrence of Arabia Soldier-of-Fortune Who Became a Desert King', *Men,* July 1960, 9:7, pp.26–9, 82–3, 86–7. *Note:* Cover illus.

G0941 R.J. Merfield, *TV Times* (London ed.), 4–10 September 1960, 20:253, p.3. *Note:* Letter to editor.

G0942 Hector Bolitho, 'T.E. Lawrence and Lord Alfred Douglas', *Theatre World,* September 1960, 56:428, pp.30, 31. *Note:* Illus.

G0943 Lucien Poirier, 'Guerre et Litterature – Pt. II', *Revue Militaire d'Information,* October 1960, 320, pp.52–70.

G0944 Constantine Fitzgibbon, 'The Lawrence Legend', *Encounter,* November 1960, 15:5, pp.55–6.

G0945 *New Statesman,* 19 November 1960, 60, p.794. *Note:* Review of Cadell, *The Young Lawrence of Arabia* (E227).

G0946 *TLS,* 25 November 1960, p.xxvi. *Note:* Review of Cadell (E227).

G0947 Dilyara Zhantieva, 'Unmasking a False Hero', *Literaturnia Gazeta,* December 1960, 3.

G0948 'Le Balayeur du Désert', *Paris Match,* 1961. *Note:* Film.

G0949 'Glück durch Schmerz', *Der Spiegel,* 1961, 15:40, pp.95–7.

G0950 'Liebe zum Führer', *Der Spiegel,* 1961, 15:5, pp.43–7. *Note:* Film.

G0951 Bercovici, 'The Fabulous Fraud', *See Magazine,* January 1961, 19:3, pp.39–41, 72, 76, 78, 80, 81.

G0952 Alan Brien, 'London Lights Are All Aglow', *Theatre Arts,* February 1961, pp.59–60.

G0953 *Virginia Kirkus,* 1 February 1961, 29, p.108. *Note:* Review of Cadell (E227).

G0954 Denis Donoghue, 'London Letter: Moral West End', *Hudson Review,* Spring 1961, 14, pp.97–9. *Note:* Review of Rattigan (E222).

G0955 Thespis, *English,* Spring 1961, p.148. *Note:* Review of Rattigan (E222).

G0956 'Lawrence of Arabia: Why Have They Never Thought of This Before?', *Photoplay,* March 1961, p.17, 57. *Note:* Film.

G0957 R. Crouse, 'Yes, There is a Lowell Thomas', *Reader's Digest,* April 1961, pp.232–52.

G0958 *Abstracts of English Studies,* May 1961, 4:5, p.281, item 1357.

G0959 William K. Zinsser, 'In Search of Lawrence of Arabia', *Esquire,* June 1961, 55:6, pp.101–4. *Note:* Illus.

G0960 O'Toole, *Show Magazine,* June 1961, p.152. *Note:* Film.

G0961 *Time,* 14 June 1961. *Note:* Film.

G0962 'General Roundup', *Films and Filming,* 19 July 1961. *Note:* Notice of film.

G0963 *Tatler,* 19 July 1961. *Note:* Film.

G0964 'Lawrence d'Arabie', *Ciné Revue,* 21 July 1961, p.241. *Note:* Film.

G0965 'Discussing Plans for Spiegel's "Lawrence of Arabia"', *Box Office,* 24 July 1961, p.15.

G0966 'Lawrence of Arabia', *Independent Film News,* 29 July 1961. *Note:* Film.

G0967 *Sight and Sound,* Autumn 1961. *Note:* Film, illus.

G0968 Thierry Maulnier, 'Lawrence d'Arabie', *La Revue de Paris,* October 1961, 68:3, pp.152–5.

G0969 *TLS,* 20 October 1961, p.751. *Note:* Review of Nutting, *Lawrence of Arabia* (E232).

G0970 E. O'Brien, 'A Literary Lounger', *Illustrated London News,* 21 October 1961, p.690. *Note:* Review of Nutting (E232).

G0971 Malcolm Muggeridge, 'Poor Lawrence', *New Statesman,* 27 October 1961, 62, pp.604–6. *Note:* Review of Nutting (E232).

G0972 'Offstage', *Theater Arts,* November 1961, 45, pp.9, 78. *Note:* Film.

G0973 B.H. Liddell Hart, *TLS,* 3 November 1961, p.789. *Note:* Letter to editor.

G0974 *Library Journal,* 15 November 1961, 86, p.3946. *Note:* Review of Nutting (E232).

G0975 Ronald Bryden, 'Quest for Lawrence', *Spectator,* 17 November 1961, pp.716–7. *Note:* Review of Nutting (E232).

G0976 *Middle East Forum,* December 1961, p.62.

G0977 C. Mad, *Bulletin du Livre,* 1 December1961. *Note:* Review of Bénoist-Mechin, *Lawrence d'Arabia* (E245).

G0978 'Tortured Hero', *Time,* 1 December 1961, 78, pp.94–5. *Note:* Review of Nutting (E235).

G0979 'Enigma Who Toppled the Turks', *Saturday Review,* 23 December 1961, 44, p.22. *Note:* Review of Nutting (E235).

G0980 J. Hi , *La Nouvelle Revue de Lausanne,* 30 December 1961. *Note:* Review of Bénoist-Mechin (E245).

G0981 Stanley Weintraub, 'Political Motivation Wrapped in a Personal Enigma', *New York Times Book Review,* 31 December 1961, p.4. *Note:* Review of Nutting (E235).

G0982 *New York Herald Tribune Book Review,* 31 December 1961, p.6. *Note:* Review of Nutting (E235).

G0983 *Abstracts of English Studies,* 1962, 5:1, pp.38–9, item 207. *Note:* Review.

G0984 P.H., 'Lawrence of Arabia', Great Britain, 1962, pp.17–18. *Note:* Film.

G0985 *Time,* 5 January 1962, pp.62–3. *Note:* Review of Nutting (E235).

G0986 'Humanizing a Legend', *Newsweek,* 8 January 1962, 59, p.44. *Note:* Review of Rattigan (E224).

G0987 Richard Gilman, 'Myth, Fact and T.E. Lawrence', *Commonweal,* 10 January 1962, pp.435–6.

G0988 Keith Wheeler, 'The Romantic Riddle of Lawrence of Arabia', *Life,* 12 January 1962, 52, pp.94, 102, 104, 106, 108.

G0989 Henry Hewes, 'A Colonel of Truth', *Saturday Review,* 13 January 1962, 45:2, p.51. *Note:* Review of Rattigan (E224).

G0990 Robert Borstein, 'Little Night Music', *New Republic,* 22 January 1962, pp.20–22. *Note:* Review of Rattigan (E224).

G0991 Phillippe Diolé, 'En Colonel Shakespearien ', *Nouvelles Littéraires,* 25 January 1962, p.8.

G0992 'What's New', *Glamour,* February 1962.

G0993 Flora Armitage, *Life,* 2 February 1962, p.21. *Note:* Letter to editor.

G0994 Robert Bolt, 'Clues to the Legend of Lawrence', *New York Times Magazine,* 25 February 1962, pp.16–17, 45, 48, 50. *Note:* Illus.

G0995 John Simon, 'Theatre Chronicle', *Hudson Review,* Spring 1962, 15:1, pp.117–8. *Note:* Review of Rattigan (E224).

G0996 *Educational Theatre Journal,* March 1962, 14, pp.66–7. *Note:* Review of Rattigan (E229).

G0997 John Simon, 'Play Reviews', *Theatre Arts,* March 1962, pp.57–8, 59.

G0998 *Virginia Kirkus,* 15 March 1962, 30, p.287. *Note:* Review of Maclean, *Lawrence of Arabia* (E253).

G0999 John Simon, 'Terence Rattigan Talks to John Simon', *Theater Arts,* April 1962, 44:4, pp.22–4, 73–8.

G1000 *New York Herald Tribune Book Review,* 13 May 1962, p.27. *Note:* Review of Alistair Maclean (E253).

G1001 Irving Howe, 'Lawrence the Anti-Hero Hero', *Stanford Today,* Summer 1962, 1, pp.1–5. *Note:* Illus.

G1002 'Train Blown off the Rails for the Film "Lawrence of Arabia"', *Illustrated London News,* 30 June 1962, 240:6413, p.1042.

G1003 'For Auction at Christie's', *Illustrated London News,* 30 June 1962, 240:6413, p.1051. *Note:* Mention of Lawrence drawing in Augustus John sale.

G1004 John Knowles, 'All Out in the Desert', *Horizon,* July 1962, 4:6, pp.108–11. *Note:* Film.

G1005 'What do You Know About This Film?', *Photoplay,* July 1962, pp.28–9.

G1006 Henri Noguères, 'La biographie de Lawrence d'Arabie par J. Béraud-Villars', *Aux Carrefours de l'Histoire,* July 1962.

G1007 Chalmers A. Johnson, 'Civilian Loyalties and Guerrilla Conflict', *World Politics,* July 1962, 14:4, pp.646–61.

G1008 Herbert Read, 'Letters to T.E. Lawrence', *Listener,* 16 July 1962, 68, p.145. *Note:* Review of *Letters to TEL* (E251).

G1009 *TLS,* 20 July 1962, p.523. *Note:* Review of *Letters to TEL* (E251).

G1010 Christopher Sykes, 'Mystery Motorist', *Spectator,* 20 July 1962, p.89.

Note: Review of *Letters to TEL* (E251).

G1011 *Horn Book,* August 1962, 38, p.383. *Note:* Review of Maclean, *Lawrence of Arabia* (E253).

G1012 Eve Perch, 'Cumena', *Harper's Bazaar,* August 1962. *Note:* Review of film.

G1013 *Library Journal,* August 1962, 87, p.383. *Note:* Review of Maclean (E253).

G1014 *Punch,* 1 August 1962, p.177. *Note:* Review of *Letters to TEL* (E251).

G1015 *Hudson Review,* Autumn 1962, 15:3, pp.333–64.

G1016 'One-Way Correspondence', *Economist.* 11 August 1962, pp.531–532. *Note:* Review of 'Letters to Tel' (E251).

G1017 *New York Times Book Review.* 26 August 1962, p.26. *Note:* Review of Maclean (E253).

G1018 Irving Howe, 'T.E. Lawrence: The Problem of Heroism', *Hudson Review.* Autumn 1962, volume 15, issue 3, pp.333–364.

G1019 J.C., *Economie et Humanisme (Caliure).* September 1962. *Note:* Review of Bénoist-Mechin (E245).

G1020 William Burford, 'Lawrence/Ross/Shaw', *Texas Quarterly.* Autumn 1962, volume 5, issue 3, p.33.

G1021 Ann Bowen, 'T.E. Lawrence Collection at the University of Texas', *Texas Quarterly,* Autumn 1962, 5:3, pp.54–64.

G1022 Bertram Rota, 'Lawrence of Arabia and *Seven Pillars of Wisdom*', *Texas Quarterly,* Autumn 1962, 5:3, pp.46–53.

G1023 Gordon Mills, 'T.E. Lawrence as a Writer', *Texas Quarterly,* Autumn 1962, 5:3, pp.35–45.

G1024 'Lawrence of Arabia' Company on Location in Morocco as They Recreate the Final Charge of the Arabs', *Illustrated London News,* 1 September 1962, p.339.

G1025 *Booklist,* 1 September 1962, 59, p.42. *Note:* Review of Maclean (E253).

G1026 *Travel,* October 1962, pp.30, 32.

G1027 *Saturday Review,* 6 October 1962, pp.9, 14.

G1028 'Lawrence of Leeds', *Time,* 19 October 1962, 80, p.63.

G1029 William Boot, 'O'Toole of Arabia', *Scene,* 19 October 1962, 6, pp.10–13. *Note:* Illus.

G1030 E. Miller, 'Go At the World', *Seventeen,* November 1962, 21, pp.124–5+. *Note:* Film.

G1031 'War In The Desert', *Illustrated London News,* 17 November 1962, 241:6433, p.805. *Note:* Film.

G1032 *Journal of Society of Film and Television Arts ,* Winter 1962–63, 10:16, pp.1–24. *Note:* Illus., whole issue on film.

G1033 'People Are Talking About...', *Vogue,* December 1962, 140, p.122. *Note:* Mention of Lawrence in O'Toole article.

G1034 Elizabeth Bowen, 'Lawrence of Arabia', *Show,* December 1962, 2, pp.66–69, 132. *Note:* Film, ad for film p.101.

G1035 Peter Green, 'In Search of T.E. Lawrence', *Listener,* 6 December 1962, 68:1758, pp.980–81. *Note:* Illus.

G1036 John Coleman, 'El Aurens', *New Statesman,* 14 December 1962, 64, p.877. *Note:* Review of film.

G1037 'Baffling Hero of the Desert', *Life,* 14 December 1962, pp.118–9. *Note:* film.

G1038 Isabel Quigly, 'A Kind of Hero: Lawrence of Arabia', *Spectator,* 14 December 1962, 209, p.933. *Note:* Review of film.

G1039 Lowell Thomas, 'I Knew the Real Lawrence', *Family Weekly,* 16 December 1962, pp.10–11. *Note:* Illus.

G1040 A.W. Lawrence, 'The Fiction and the Fact', *Observer,* 16 December 1962, p.25.

G1041 Penelope Gilliatt, 'Blood, Sand and a Dozen Lawrences', *Observer,* 16 December 1962.

G1042 Eric Rhode, 'Two and a Half Pillars of Wisdom', *Listener,* 20 December 1962, 68:1760, p.1055. *Note:* Film.

G1043 'The Flawed Hero', *New Yorker,* 22 December 1962, 38, p.77. *Note:* Review of Mousa *TEL, An Arab View* (E257).

G1044 'All-Star All-Good', *Newsweek,* 24 December 1962, 60, p.64. *Note:* Film.

G1045 N. Wheeler, 'A Freudian Oasis', *Scene,* 27 December 1962.

G1046 Hollis Alpst, 'A Great One', *Saturday Review,* 29 December 1962, 45, pp.29–30. *Note:* Film, illus.

G1047 Robert Bolt, 'The Playwright In Films', *Saturday Review,* 29 December 1962, 45, pp.15–16.

G1048 James F. Fixx, 'The Spiegel Touch', *Saturday Review,* 29 December 1962, 45, pp.13–15. *Note:* Film.

G1049 J.F.J. von Rensburg, 'Lawrence of Arabia', *Kommando,* 1963, 14:6, pp.40–43.

G1050 Peter Baker, 'Lawrence of Arabia', *Film Guide,* 1963, pp.32–3.

G1051 *La Caravelle,* 1963. *Note:* Review of Bénoist-Mechin (E245).

G1052 *Abstracts of English Studies,* 1963, 6:2, pp.63, 388, 413, 521. *Note:* Items 315, 1903, 1904, 2302, 2573.

G1053 Jean Westbane, 'Lawrence of Arabia', *Television and Film Annual,* 1963, pp.81–4.

G1054 David Lean, 'Out of the Wilderness', *Films and Filming,* January 1963, 9:4, pp.8, 12–15. *Note:* Illus.

G1055 'Enigma Romantico/ Aventuras de Lawrence de Arabia', *MD en Espanol,* January 1963, 1:4.

G1056 *Ouest Médical,* January 1963. *Note:* Review of Bénoist-Mechin (E245).

G1057 *Time,* 4 January 1963, 81, p.58. *Note:* Review of film.

G1058 Dent, Alan, 'A Year to Remember', *Illustrated London News,* 5 January 1963, 242:6440, p.30.

G1059 Moira Walsh, 'Lawrence of Arabia', *America,* 5 January 1963, 108, pp.26–8. *Note:* Review of film.

G1060 Henry Hewes, 'All the King's Camels', *Saturday Review,* 5 January 1963, 46:1, p.31. *Note:* Review of film.

G1061 *Kinematograph Weekly,* 10 January 1963, p.14. *Note:* Ad for film.

G1062 Stanley Kauffmann, 'A Passion in the Desert', *New Republic,* 12 January 1963, 148, pp.26–8. *Note:* Review of film.

G1063 E. Jarry, *L'Aede,* 13 January 1963. *Note:* Review of Bénoist-Mechin (E245).

G1064 Philip T. Hartung, 'The Screen', *Commonweal,* 18 January 1963, 77:17, pp.439–40.

G1065 A. Dent, 'Dominant Influences', *Illustrated London News,* 19 January 1963, 242, p.100. *Note:* Review of film.

G1066 Robert Hatch, *Nation,* 19 January 1963, 196, pp.58–9. *Note:* Review of film.

G1067 'Women's Federation Playing Lawrence', 23 January 1963.

G1068 'The Mystery of Lawrence', *Senior Scholastic*, 30 January 1963, 82, p.11. *Note:* Illus.

G1069 Jay Jacobs, 'Fraud & Freud', *The Reporter*, 31 January 1963, 28, pp.48+. *Note:* Review of film.

G1070 Margaret Heideman, 'Hero and Anti-Hero', *Canadian Forum*, February 1963, 42, pp.259–60. *Note:* Review of *The Letters of TEL* (E250).

G1071 *Library Journal*, 1 February 1963, 88, p.563. *Note:* Review of Weintraub, *Private Shaw and Public Shaw* (E275).

G1072 *Bulletin du Livre*, 1 February 1963. *Note:* Review of *Seven Pillars of Wisdom*.

G1073 *TLS*, 1 February 1963, p.84. *Note:* Review of University of Texas, *Fifty Letters* (E265).

G1074 'Special Trailers on Lawrence', 4 February 1963.

G1075 William White, 'Lawrence/Ross/Shaw', *American Book Collector*, 6 February 1963, 13:6, p.6. *Note:* Letter to editor.

G1076 'Namesakes', *Newsweek*, 25 February 1963, 61, p.96. *Note:* Review of Weintraub (E275).

G1077 *National Review*, 26 February 1963, 14, pp.167–9. *Note:* Review of film.

G1078 *Christian Century*, 27 February 1963, 80, p.273. *Note:* Review of Weintraub (E275).

G1079 *Glamour*, March 1963, p.140–41.

G1080 Roger Sandall, 'Lawrence of Arabia', *Film Quarterly*, Spring 1963, pp.56–7.

G1081 Howard Rice, Jr., 'Additions to the Doubleday Collection: "Kipling, T.E. Lawrence, Conrad"', *Princeton University Library Chronicle*, Spring 1963, 24:3, pp.191–6. *Note:* Lawrence, pp.193–5.

G1082 Donald W. LaBadie, 'The Reel Lawrence', *Show*, March 1963, 3, p.31.

G1083 *Best Sellers*, 1 March 1963, 22, p.451. *Note:* Review of Weintraub (E275).

G1084 Harry T. Moore, 'Wit and the Wages of Wisdom', *Saturday Review*, 2 March 1963, 46, pp.23–4. *Note:* Review of Weintraub (E275).

G1085 'A Book a Week', *American Weekly*, 3 March 1963.

G1086 Trevor Armbristor, 'O'Toole of Arabia', *Saturday Evening Post*, 9 March 1963, 236, pp.22–5, 26, 28.

G1087 Marcel Matte, 'Un Témoin dépose la vérité Sur Lawrence d'Arabie', *Nouvelles Littéraires*, 14 March 1963, pp.1, 10.

G1088 '$30,800 First Week for "Arabia" in Tokyo', 21 March 1963.

G1089 Martin Seymour-Smith, 'Demi Coriolanus', *Spectator*, 22 March 1963, p.363.

G1090 D. MacDonald, 'Mr. Levin and Mr. Lawrence', *Esquire*, April 1963, 59, pp.36+. *Note:* Film.

G1091 *Critic*, April 1963, 21, p.70. *Note:* Review of Weintraub *Private Shaw and Public Shaw* (E275).

G1092 Beatrice Epstein, 'The Legend of T.E. Lawrence an Astrological Profile', *Prediction*, April 1963, 29:4, pp.10–12, 26. *Note:* Illus.

G1093 Terence Rattigan, 'Ross', *Theatre Arts*, April 1963, 46:4, pp.25–8.

Note: Illus.

G1094 Gerald Weales, 'Shaw and Lawrence', *Commonweal*, 5 April 1963, 78, pp.52–4.

G1095 *Economist*, 6 April 1963, 207, p.60. *Note:* Review of reprint of *TEL to His Biographers* (A213).

G1096 *Paris Match*, 6 April 1963, 730. *Note:* Film.

G1097 William Irvine, 'The Pen and the Sword Were Friends', *New York Times Book Review*, 7 April 1963, p.25. *Note:* Review of Weintraub (E275).

G1098 Kim Blauhome, 'Peter O'Toole', *Time*, 19 April 1963, pp.25, 54. *Note:* Review of film, p.67.

G1099 *Paris Match*, 27 April 1963, 733. *Note:* Film.

G1100 F.C., *Les Livres*, May 1963. *Note:* Review of French edition of *Seven Pillars* (A070).

G1101 F.C., *Bibl. de prof., élèves*, May 1963. *Note:* Review of Vol. I of pocket edition of *Seven Pillars* (A071).

G1102 Victoria Ocampo, 'Propositos de Lawrence de Arabia', *Sur*, May–June 1963, 282, pp.1–2.

G1103 Francois Vinneuil, 'Lawrence d'Arabie', *Les Spectacles du Monde*, May 1963.

G1104 'Lawrence', 1 May 1963.

G1105 *New York Herald Tribune Book Review*, 5 May 1963, p.7. *Note:* Review of Weintraub (E275).

G1106 *Library Journal*, 15 May 1963, p.1572.

G1107 Gerald McKnight, '99 Lives of Peter O'Toole', *American Weekly*, 26 May 1963. *Note:* Film mention.

G1108 *Holiday*, June 1963. *Note:* Photo of Lowell Thomas with Lawrence.

G1109 *Harper's*, June 1963, 226 , p.105. *Note:* Review of Weintraub (E275).

G1110 Pauline Kael, *Film Quarterly*, Summer 1963. *Note:* Review of film.

G1111 I.E. Brodie, 'Lawrence Was My Orderly', *NAAFI Review*, Summer 1963, 39, pp.6–7. *Note:* Illus.

G1112 Philip Stewart, 'Another Lawrence Myth', *Middle East Forum*, June 1963, 39, pp.17–18. *Note:* Illus.

G1113 *Mademoiselle*, June 1963, p.88. *Note:* Photo of O'Toole in Lawrence costume.

G1114 Stanley Rypins, 'Three Shaw-Centered Books', *Virginia Quarterly Review*, Summer 1963, 39:3, pp.514–8.

G1115 'Lawrence Looms as an Attendance Big Box Office Grosser', 3 June 1963.

G1116 Robert Graves, 'T.E. Lawrence and the Riddle of S.A.', *Saturday Review*, 15 June 1963, pp.16–17. *Note:* Illus.

G1117 *English Language Teacher*, July 1963, 17, pp.172–4. *Note:* Review of film.

G1118 Anis Sayigh, *Hiwar*, July–August 1963, 5, pp.15–23.

G1119 Richard M. Morris, *Saturday Review*, 6 July 1963, 46:27, pp.15. *Note:* Letter to editor.

G1120 Flora Armitage, *Saturday Review*, 6 July 1963, 46:27, p.15. *Note:* Letter to editor.

G1121 Barbara Foster, *Saturday Review*, 6 July 1963. *Note:* Letter to editor.

G1122 Andrew Churchill, 'The Soldier of Mystery', *Time & Tide*, 11 July

1963, p.25. *Note:* Review of Ocampo *338171* (E152).

G1123 *TLS,* 12 July 1963, p.504. *Note:* Review of Ocampo (E152).

G1124 Gay Talese, 'O'Toole of the Oulde Sod', *Esquire,* August 1963, 60, pp.76–8, 124.

G1125 Dean Lipton, 'The Lawrence of Arabia Myth', *Nexus,* August 1963, 1:2, pp.1–11. *Note:* Cover.

G1126 *Library Journal,* August 1963, 88, p.2891. *Note:* Review of reprint of *TEL to His Biographers* (A213).

G1127 *Southern Scene (Japan),* August 1963, pp.64–7. *Note:* Film.

G1128 Jocelyn Brooke, 'More About 338171', *Punch,* 7 August 1963, p.213. *Note:* Review of Ocampo (E152).

G1129 *New York Herald Tribune Books,* 18 August 1963, p.7. *Note:* Review of reprint of *TEL to His Biographers* (A213).

G1130 George Steiner, 'Once There Was a Hero', *New York Times Book Review,* 25 August 1963, p.3. *Note:* Review of *TEL to His Biographers* (A213).

G1131 Maryvonne Butcher, 'Riddle of the Sands', *The Tablet,* 31 August 1963, p.940.

G1132 Abraham N. Poliak, 'Lawrence and Arab Nationalism', *New Outlook,* September 1963, pp.42–8.

G1133 Harry Tatlock Moore, 'Richard Aldington in His Last Years', *Texas Quarterly,* Autumn 1963, 6:3, pp.60–74.

G1134 Victoria Ocampo, 'El Aurens en el Desierto de la Pantalla', *Sur,* September–October 1963, 284, pp.22–36.

G1135 *Newsweek,* October 1963. *Note:* Berlitz ad: What if Lawrence Hadn't Learned Arabic?

G1136 David Dixon, 'Very Superior', *Motorcycle,* 3 October 1963, pp.403–5.

G1137 Ivor Brown, 'G.B.S. and T.E.L.', *Observer,* 20 October 1963.

G1138 *TLS,* 25 October 1963, p.853. *Note:* Review of Weintraub (E277).

G1139 A.L. Rowse, 'Victoria Ocampo The Hero's Inner Life Was a Nightmare', *New York Times Book Review,* 27 October 1963, p.34. *Note:* Review of Ocampo (E152).

G1140 André Miguel, 'Quand un Arabe juge Lawrence', *Critique,* November 1963, 19:198, pp.946–57.

G1141 H.A. Corbett, 'A Critic In Action', *Royal United Service Institute Journal,* November 1963, 108:632, pp.366–70.

G1142 William Paul Haiber, 'To Gain the Rear', *Military Review,* November 1963, 43, pp.40–49.

G1143 *New Screen News,* 8 November 1963, pp.8–9. *Note:* Film.

G1144 'Cleaning Up After Lawrence', *Time,* 15 November 1963.

G1145 'Lawrence', *New Screen News,* 22 November 1963, p.19. *Note:* Film.

G1146 Stanley Weintraub, 'Legend Among the Bedouin', *Saturday Review,* 30 November 1963, 46, p.41. *Note:* Review of Ocampo (E153) and *TEL to His Biographers* (A217).

G1147 *The Jewish Digest,* December 1963, 9:3, p.11. *Note:* Mention of Lawrence.

G1148 Stanley Weintraub, 'How History Gets Rewritten: Lawrence of Arabia in the Theater', *Drama Survey,* Winter 1963, 2:3, pp.269–75.

G1149 'Lawrence of Arabia Prize Picture', *Movies Illustrated*, December 1963, pp.56–61.
G1150 *Library Journal*, 1 December 1963, 88, p.4626. *Note:* Review of Ocampo (E153).
G1151 'Royal Prince of "Lawrence of Arabia"', *Kinematograph*, 13 December 1963.
G1152 *Time*, 13 December 1963, 82: , pp.59–A, 59–B.
G1153 Richard Millatt, *Punch*, 26 December 1963. *Note:* Review of film.
G1154 *Library Journal*, 1964, 89, p.1855. *Note:* Review of Thomas, *The True Story...* (E188).
G1155 *Illustrated London News*, 4 January 1964. *Note:* Photo of Lawrence bust.
G1156 Jack Pearl, 'Lawrence of Arabia', *Impact*, February 1964, 13:5, pp.60–74. *Note:* Illus.
G1157 Jean Béraud-Villars, 'Lawrence d'Arabie, bourreau de soi-même', *Historia*, February 1964, pp.250–61.
G1158 Ann Sharpley, 'Lawrence of Arabia', *People* (Sunday newspaper supplement, *S.F. Examiner*), 9 February 1964.
G1159 Stanley Weintraub, 'Lawrence of Arabia', *Film Quarterly*, Spring 1964, 17, pp.51–4. *Note:* Review of film.
G1160 *Encounter*, March 1964, 22:3, p.34.
G1161 Frank Baxter, 'Some Notes on Lawrence of Arabia', *Coranto*, Spring 1964, 1:2, pp.24–30.
G1162 Rebecca West and Peter O'Toole, 'Rebecca West and Peter O'Toole' A Dialogue, *Redbook*, March 1964, 122:5, pp.56–7, 141, 146, 148–9. *Note:* Film.
G1163 F.C., *Bibl. de prof.*, *élèves*, March 1964. *Note:* Review of Vol. II of pocket edition of *Seven Pillars* (A171).
G1164 Larry Siegel, 'A Florence of Arabia Issue', *MAD*, April 1964, 86, pp.43–8.
G1165 *Harper's*, May 1964, 228:1368, p.121.
G1166 C.W. Robertson, 'Il Vero Volto di Lawrence d'Arabia', *Storia Illustrata*, May 1964, 12:78, pp.617–30.
G1167 Stanley Weintraub, 'The Two Sides of "Lawrence of Arabia": Aubrey and Meek', *Shaw Review*, May 1964, 7:2, pp.54–7.
G1168 'See-Saw In the Middle East', *Life*, 8 May 1964, pp.69, 72.
G1169 *Saturday Review*, 9 May 1964, 47:19, p.25. *Note:* Cartoon with Lawrence theme.
G1170 Lowell Thomas, 'The Real Lawrence of Arabia', *Reader's Digest*, June 1964, pp.252–74. *Note:* Another copy seen has variant cover.
G1171 Neil Ascherson, 'T.E. Lawrence', *New York Review of Books*, 2 June 1964. *Note:* Review of *TEL to His Biographers* (A217), illus.
G1172 David Footman, 'On to Damascus', *Spectator*, 12 June 1964, p.803. *Note:* Review of Falls, *Armaggedon 1918* (F0326).
G1173 Lowell Thomas, 'The Real Lawrence of Arabia', *Reader's Digest* (UK edition), July 1964, pp.154–74.
G1174 *MAD*, July 1964, 88. *Note:* Letter to editor on 'Florence of Arabia', (G1164).

G1175 'Romantic Riddle', *M.D. of Canada*, July 1964.
G1176 *TV Guide*, 11 August 1964. *Note:* Notice of Lowell Thomas and Lawrence in Jack Paar Show.
G1177 'Jack Paar Variety', *TV Guide*, 21 August 1964, p.A-83.
G1178 *Reader's Digest*, September 1964, p.232. *Note:* Cartoon.
G1179 Elie Kedourie, 'The Capture of Damascus 1 Oct 1918', *Middle Eastern Studies*, October 1964, 1:1, pp.66–83.
G1180 Stanley Weintraub, 'Bernard Shaw's Other Saint Joan', *Shavian*, October 1964, 2:10, pp.7–13.
G1181 *Library Journal*, 1 October 1964, 89, p.3686.
G1182 Alan and Lydia Taylor, 'A Reminiscence of Lawrence', *Viewpoints*, November 1964, 4:9, pp.22–4.
G1183 Leah Hewick, '"Painting" with Smoke', *New Zealand Woman's Weekly*, 9 November 1964.
G1184 Aleric Stacpole, 'Lawrence of Arabia', *Oxford Magazine*, 12 November 1964, p.94.
G1185 *National Geographic*, December 1964, 126:6, pp.838–40.
G1186 Philip W. Ireland, *Middle East Journal*, Winter 1964, 18: 1, pp.111–13. *Note:* Reviews of Nutting (E232) and Payne (E261).
G1187 *Observer*, 13 December 1964, p.15. *Note:* Mention of Lawrence.
G1188 Patrick Anderson, 'The Desert Prince: Letters of T.E. Lawrence', *Spectator*, 25 December 1964, 7122, p.875.
G1189 Daniel da Cruz, 'The Hedjaz Railroad: Its History', *Islamic Review*, 1965, 53:(9/10), 28–31.
G1190 *Abstracts of English Studies*, 1965, 8, p.97. *Note:* Item 523, review.
G1191 A. Stacpole, 'Lawrence', *Oxford Magazine*, 1965, Hilary 3, p.191.
G1192 Sheik Hassan Al-Tariff, 'One Thousand Vampires', *Man Magazine (Australia)*, 1965.
G1193 Capt. P.G. Boxhall, 'Two Studies in Destiny', *Army Quarterly*, January 1965, 89:2, pp.206–11.
G1194 '"Lawrence" has Tremendous Show Case', *Daily Cinema*, 1 January 1965. *Note:* Review of film.
G1195 *Look*, 12 January 1965, p.27. *Note:* Mention of Lawrence.
G1196 Theodora Duncan, 'Lawrence', *Oxford Magazine*, 21 January 1965, p.160.
G1197 *Time and Tide*, 21–27 January 1965, p.7. *Note:* Photo of Lawrence.
G1198 *John O'London's*, March 1965. *Note:* Illus. front cover from film.
G1199 Irene Gendzier, 'Notes on T.E. Lawrence', *The Middle East Journal*, Spring 1965, 19:2, pp.259–61.
G1200 James A. Notopoulus, 'The Tragic and Epic in T.E. Lawrence', *Yale Review*, Spring 1965, 54:3, pp.330–45.
G1201 Stanley Weintraub, 'Bernard Shaw's Other Saint Joan', *South Atlantic Quarterly*, Spring 1965, 64:2, pp.194–205.
G1202 Theodora Duncan, 'Lawrence and the War', *Oxford Magazine*, 4 March 1965, p.262.
G1203 D. Pastor Petit, 'La Vida y el Mito de T.E. Lawrence', *Destino*, 6 March 1965, pp.28–31.
G1204 *Motorcycle*, 25 March 1965, p.384. *Note:* Illus.

G1205 Anne Dooley, 'My Link With Lawrence of Arabia in Beyond', *Two Worlds*, April 1965, 78:3855, pp.112–14.
G1206 Roger à Grenier, 'Le Livre de la Mort', *Le Nouvel Observateur*, 8 April 1965.
G1207 Jacques Cabau, 'La Marie Stuart du Désert', *L'Express*, 12–18 April 1965.
G1208 Evan Butler, 'Lawrence of Arabia Without Allenby', *John O'London's*, May 1965, 80:9, pp.11–12.
G1209 H.C. Joynson, 'Critics of Lawrence of Arabia', *British Legion Journal*, May 1965.
G1210 Armand Rio, *Livres de France*, May 1965. *Note:* Extracts from *Les Textes essentiels* (A242).
G1211 Theodora Duncan, 'Lawrence: 30 Years After', *Viewpoints*, May 1965, 5:5, pp.15–16. *Note:* Illus.
G1212 'The Bull', *Economist*, 8–14 May 1965, pp.647–8.
G1213 *Bulletin critique du livre Français*, June 1965. *Note:* Review of *Les Textes essentiels* (A242).
G1214 *Railway Magazine*, June 1965, pp.346, 348.
G1215 'Middle East Treasure', *Viewpoints*, June–July 1965.
G1216 Yves Benot, *Europe*, July–August 1965. *Note:* Review of *Les Textes essentiels* (A242).
G1217 A. Hamilton, *Books and Bookmen*, July 1965, 10, p.48. *Note:* Review of *The Odyssey* (A144).
G1218 Emmanuelle Hubert, 'Lawrence d'Arabie archéologue', *Archeologia*, July–August 1965, 5, pp.81–4.
G1219 *Railway Magazine*, July 1965, p.408. *Note:* Mention of Lawrence.
G1220 Jean Duvignaud, 'Le Colonel Bousillé', *La Nouvelle Revue Française*, July 1965, 13:151, pp.113–21.
G1221 *Spécial*, 15 July 1965. *Note:* Review of *Les Textes essentiels* (A242).
G1222 D.H. Bradbury, *British Legion Journal*, August 1965. *Note:* Letter to editor.
G1223 M. Surfin, 'The Extraordinary Rolls-Royce', *Man's World*, August 1965.
G1224 A.W. Lawrence, *British Legion Journal*, September 1965. *Note:* Letter to editor.
G1225 *The Arab World*, September 1965, p.12.
G1226 James G. Coates, 'Further Notes on T.E. Lawrence', *The Middle East Journal*, Autumn 1965, 19:4, pp.556–7.
G1227 R. Las Vergnas, *Nouvelles Littéraires*, 16 September 1965. *Note:* Review of *Les Textes essentiels* (A242), illus. with photo of D.H. Lawrence.
G1228 *Viewpoints*, October 1965, 5:8, pp.5, 7.
G1229 *Life*, 15 October 1965, pp.135–6.
G1230 *John O'London's*, November 1965, 80:14, p.6.
G1231 André Miguel, *Cahiers du Sud*, November–December 1965, pp.351–2. *Note:* Review of *Les Textes essentiels* (A242).
G1232 Muriel Scarfe, 'Defending Lawrence', *British Legion Journal*, November 1965, 45:11.

G1233 Reid Gardner, *Life*, 5 November 1965. *Note:* Letter to editor.

G1234 *The Courier*, Winter 1965, 5:1, p.26.

G1235 Agnes Newton Keith, *Atlantic*, December 1965.

G1236 Jeanine Delpech, *Nouvelles Littéraires*, 23 December 1965. *Note:* Review of *Les Textes essentiels* (A242).

G1237 *Elle*, 30 December 1965. *Note:* Review of Stéphane, *Portrait de l'aventurier* (E173).

G1238 *Les Fiches Bibliographiques*, 1966, 11604. *Note:* Review of Stéphane (E173).

G1239 *Bulletin Bibliographique des Armées*, 1966, 1ᵉ trimestre. *Note:* Review of Stéphane (E173).

G1240 Denis Boak, 'Malraux and T.E. Lawrence', *Modern Language Review*, 1966, 61:2, pp.218–24.

G1241 Stanley Weintraub, 'A Man Who Knew Lawrence of Arabia', *Trenton Review*, 1966, 1, pp.45–60.

G1242 Leon Hugo, 'Shaw in Durban', *Shavian*, 1966, 3, pp.5–8.

G1243 David Walker, 'Lawrence of Arabia', *Isis*, January 1966, 26:1504, p.21. *Note:* Poem.

G1244 Jon Stallworthy, 'T.E. Lawrence', *Review of English Literature*, January 1966, 7:1, p.106. *Note:* Poem.

G1245 René Chabbert, 'Les Abstractions Aventurières de Roger Stéphane', *Le Spectacles du Monde*, January 1966, pp.60–62.

G1246 C.A. Doxiadic, *Saturday Review*, 1 January 1966.

G1247 'Portrait Without Death', *New Yorker*, 6 January 1966. *Note:* Review of Rattigan (E224).

G1248 R.M. Albérès, 'La grande clarté du XX siècle', *Nouvelles Littéraires*, 8 January 1966. *Note:* Review of Stéphane (E173).

G1249 Marcel Schneider, *Nouvelles Littéraires*, 13 January 1966. *Note:* Mention of Stéphane's book.

G1250 R.F. King, 'Another Lawrence: Air-Craftsman Shaw and Air-Cushion Aircraft', *Air-Cushion Vehicles*, February 1966, 7, pp.19–23.

G1251 R.F. King, 'Another Lawrence', *Flight International*, February 1966, supplement 24, pp.19–23.

G1252 *Bulletin critique du livre Français*, February 1966. *Note:* Review of Stéphane (E173).

G1253 *L'Armée*, February 1966. *Note:* Review of *Les Textes essentiels* (A242).

G1254 Judith Listowel, 'Clearing up After T.E. Lawrence', *Statist*, 18 February 1966, 190, pp.417–8.

G1255 Robert Kanters, 'Parmi les Livres. Du Côté de Montaigne et du Côté d'Augustin', *La Revue de Paris*, March 1966, pp.114–23.

G1256 Ilda (Espina) Cadiz–Avila, 'Lawrenciana: Recuerdos de Lawrence de Arabia', *El Mercurio* (Santiago, Chile), 20 March 1966.

G1257 Jean-Claude Lattes, 'Un portrait de l'aventurier selon Roger Stéphane', *Combat (France)*, 31 March 1966. *Note:* Review of Stéphane (E173).

G1258 'Eventyret I Orkenen', *Hete og Hjemme*, 22 April 1966, 16, pp.12–14. *Note:* Film.

G1259 'Writer's Collection Keeps Lawrence Legend Alive', *Around the*

Square, May 1966. *Note:* T. Duncan collection, house organ of Rexall Drug Stores.

G1260 *Abstracts of English Studies,* May 1966, 9:5, p.336. *Note:* Item 1784, review.

G1261 *France-Eurafrique,* 16 May 1966. *Note:* Review of Stéphane (E173).

G1262 *Abstracts of English Studies,* June 1966, 9:6, p.395. *Note:* Item 2081, review.

G1263 R.K. Shahani, 'Lawrence of Arabia', *United Services Institution Journal,* July–September 1966, 96:404, pp.240–44.

G1264 'Desert Dust Storm', *TLS,* 14 July 1966. *Note:* Review of Payne (E261) and Mousa (E256).

G1265 'Revolt From the Desert', *Economist,* 16 July 1966, p.259.

G1266 John Raymond, 'Arabia Novembera', *Punch,* 20 July 1966, p.123. *Note:* Review of Payne (E261) and Mousa (E256).

G1267 Ian Hamilton, 'Lawrence in an Arab Context', *Illustrated London News,* 30 July 1966. *Note:* Review of Mousa (E256).

G1268 *Books and Bookmen,* August 1966, p.31. *Note:* Review of Payne (E261).

G1269 *The Arab World,* August 1966, p.8.

G1270 'The Legend of Lawrence of Arabia Proves to be Just a Legend', *Eva,* 5 August 1966. *Note:* Review of Mousa (E256).

G1271 *TV Guide,* 17 August 1966, p.A-64. *Note:* Film.

G1272 William Buchan, 'Revolt in the Desert', *Spectator,* 26 August 1966, 7209, p.264.

G1273 Frank Procopio, 'The Gentle Assassins', *Infantry,* September–October 1966, 56: 5, pp.51–5.

G1274 Betty Tucker, *Popular Gardening,* 24 September 1966. *Note:* Letter to editor.

G1275 William Carter, 'The Pilgrim Railway', *Geographical Magazine,* October 1966, pp.422–33. *Note:* Illus.

G1276 Sir Ronald Wingate, 'T.E. Lawrence – A Pragmatic Study', *Royal United Services Institute Journal,* November 1966, 111, pp.344–5.

G1277 Roger à Grenier, 'Qui était Lawrence d'Arabie?', *Magazine Littéraire,* 28 November – 12 December 1966, 2, pp.21–2. *Note:* Review of Stéphane (E173).

G1278 Lucius Beebe, 'The Rolls Mystique', *Horizon,* Winter 1966, 8:1, pp.40–48.

G1279 N.F.W. (Betty Whitmore), 'Taking Time Off to Visit The Country Cottage of Lawrence of Arabia', *Redlands News,* December 1966, p.8. *Note:* Illus.

G1280 Stanley Weintraub, 'Wesker's Mint', *London Review,* Winter 1966, 1, pp.27–34.

G1281 'T.E.L. Find', *Observer,* 4 December 1966.

G1282 *Books Abroad,* 1967, 41, pp.486–7. *Note:* Review of Mousa (E282).

G1283 *Abstracts of English Studies,* 1967, 10, p.293. *Note:* Item 1645, review.

G1284 Yves Jouin, 'Hedjaz 1916–1918', *Revue Historique de L'Armée,* 1967, 23:4, pp.107–21.

G1285 Suleiman Mousa, 'The Role of Syrians and Iraqis in the Arab Revolt', *The Middle East Forum,* 1967, 43:1, pp.5–19.

G1286 *Sur,* 1967, pp.63–118.

G1287 Robin Fedden, 'Les châteaux des Croisés', *Archeologia,* January–February 1967, 14, pp.28–33.

G1288 J.D. Lunt, 'Lawrence of Arabia', *United States of India Journal,* January–March 1967. *Note:* Letter to editor.

G1289 Julian Symons, 'The Lost Heroes: T.E. Lawrence', *Sunday Times Magazine ,* 29 January 1967, p.23.

G1290 *Choice,* March 1967, pp.78, 80. *Note:* Review of Mousa (E256).

G1291 'March to Wadi-Aish', *Aramco World,* March–April 1967, pp.12–13. *Note:* Illus.

G1292 'Theft of *Mint* (From British Museum', *Library Journal,* 15 March 1967, p.1150.

G1293 G.B.H. Wightman, 'Symons and Lawrence', *New Statesman,* 31 March 1967, p.438.

G1294 *Gems and Minerals,* April 1967, 355, p.33.

G1295 Sam Wells, 'Lawrence of Arabia and the Brough Superior', *Cycle,* April 1967, 17:4, pp.50–53, 74–5.

G1296 *Barrack,* April 1967–1968, 1–18. *Note:* Journal of the Imperial Camel Corps, many references to Lawrence.

G1297 *America,* 6 May 1967, pp.688–90. *Note:* Review of Mousa (E256).

G1298 *Virginia Quarterly Review,* Summer 1967, 43:3, p.cxx. *Note:* Review of Mousa (E256).

G1299 *Observer,* 11 June 1967, pp.9, 10. *Note:* Illus.

G1300 'Lawrence of Princeton', *Vogue,* 12 June 1967.

G1301 Jock McGregor, *Motion Picture Exhibitor,* 21 June 1967. *Note:* Film.

G1302 'Arabia Deceptia', *Time,* 14 July 1967, p.24.

G1303 Maurice Samuel, 'If the Arabs Had Won', *Look,* 25 July 1967, p.80.

G1304 *Ladies Home Journal,* August 1967, pp.156.

G1305 *Doubleday Book Club,* August 1967. *Note:* Ad for Lowell Thomas (E011), illus.

G1306 Willam Dickinson, 'Master Guerrilla of Araby's Desert', *Army,* August 1967, 17:8, pp.66–7, 70, 72, 76–7. *Note:* Illus.

G1307 *Aramco World,* September–October 1967, p.17.

G1308 'Playboy Advisor', *Playboy,* September 1967, p.67.

G1309 *American Historical Review,* October 1967, 73:1, pp.188–9. *Note:* Review of Mousa (E257).

G1310 *Life,* 6 October 1967, p.3.

G1311 *TV Guide,* 6 October 1967, p.A-91. *Note:* Notice of film.

G1312 Edward Kern, 'The Desert Revolt Urged by a Legendary Englishman', *Life,* 20 October 1967, pp.54–5.

G1313 *National Geographic,* December 1967, p.79.

G1314 *L.A. Sky Writer,* 29 October 1967. *Note:* Photo of man who bought Rolls owned by Lawrence (?).

G1315 G.E. von Grunebaum, 'Suleiman Mousa T.E. Lawrence: An Arab View', *Der Islam,* 1968, 44, pp.278–80. *Note:* Review of Mousa (E256).

G1316 Maurice Larès, 'Secret Despatches From Arabia', *Échec à l'Obstacle,* 1968, 1ᵉ trimestre, no.13, pp.28–32.

G1317 *Library Journal,* 1968, 93, pp.1794. *Note:* Review of Barbary, *Lawrence and His Desert Raiders* (E289).

G1318 'Pre-Pillars', *TLS*, 1968. *Note:* Review of Weintraub, *Evolution of a Revolt* (A255).

G1319 J. Bakker, 'On T.E. Lawrence', *Levende Talen* (Holland), January 1968, 243, pp.12–23.

G1320 *The Arab World*, January–February 1968, p.3.

G1321 *Time*, 12 January 1968, pp.20. *Note:* Film.

G1322 *Encounter*, February 1968, 30:2, p.29.

G1323 'Rebuilding the Hejaz Railroad', *Jordan*, Spring 1968, 1, pp.9, 18.

G1324 *Abstracts of English Studies*, March 1968, 11:3, pp.148. *Note:* Item 958.

G1325 James L. Mrazek, 'The Philosophy of the Guerrilla Fighter', *Army Quarterly*, April 1968, 96:1, pp.64–74.

G1326 *Aramco World*, May–June 1968, p.34.

G1327 Colin Graham, 'An Investigation Into the Disturbing Facts of the Crash Which Killed Lawrence of Arabia', *Dorset*, Summer 1968, 2, pp.3–5.

G1328 *The Aryan Path*, June 1968, 39:6, p.265.

G1329 'Limited Edition of *The Mint* Disappears', *A/B Bookman's Weekly*, 24 June 1968, 41, p.2487.

G1330 'Lawrence of Arabia Papers', *A/B Bookman's Weekly*, 24 June 1968, 41, p.2486.

G1331 'Rare T.E. Lawrence Work Gone From British Museum', *Library Journal*, August 1968, 93, p.2783.

G1332 Eugenio Galvano, 'Lawrence of Arabia's Life was a Tragedy' (in Italian), *La Gazzetta del Populo* (Turin), 11 August 1968, p.3.

G1333 John Dayton, 'Le Chemin de Fer de Lawrence', *Historama (Saint-Quen)*, September 1968, 203-3, pp.87–8. *Note:* Illus.

G1334 Roger Delorme, 'La Véritable Histoire de Lawrence d'Arabie', *Historama (Saint-Quen)*, September 1968, 203-3, pp.79–86. *Note:* Illus.

G1335 Theodora Duncan, 'The Miracle', *Dorset*, Autumn 1968, 3, p.13. *Note:* Poem.

G1336 Maureen Cleave, 'Last of the Great Loners', *Holiday*, October 1968, 44:4, pp.70, 100–102.

G1337 Peter Kilduff, 'Carl Dixon's Scrapbook', *Cross & Cockade Journal*, Winter 1968, 9:4, p.382. *Note:* Many Lawrence references, including photo.

G1338 A.L. Tibawi, 'T.E. Lawrence, Feisal and Weizman', *Royal Central Asian Society Journal*, 1969, 61: pp.156–63.

G1339 *Abstracts of English Studies*, 1969–70, 13, pp.108, 576. *Note:* Items 595, 3007.

G1340 Michael Foss, 'Dangerous Guides: English Writers and the Desert', *New Middle East*, 1969, 9, pp.38–42.

G1341 A.L. Tibawi, 'T.E. Lawrence, Feisal and Weizman', *Middle East Forum*, 1969, 45:1, pp.81–90.

G1342 Richard W. Bailey, *Michigan Quarterly Review*, 1969, 8, pp.208–11. *Note:* Review of Weintraub (E255).

G1343 John E. Mack, 'The Inner Conflict of T.E. Lawrence', *TLS*, 8 February 1969, p.17.

G1344 William L. Langer, 'Discussion (of J.E. Mack's T.E. Lawrence)',

American Journal of Psychiatry, February 1969, 125, p.1092.
G1345 John E. Mack, *American Journal of Psychiatry,* February 1969, 125:8, pp.1083–92.
G1346 *Der Spiegel,* 10 February 1969, 23:7, p.90.
G1347 *Dorset,* Early Spring 1969, 5, p.13.
G1348 *Canvas,* April 1969, 3:12. *Note:* Portrait on front cover.
G1349 *Réalités,* April 1969, 221, p.93.
G1350 Irene l. Gendzier, 'The Lawrence Enigma', *American Journal of Psychiatry,* May 1969, 125:11, pp.1604–8.
G1351 *Mid–East,* May–June 1969, pp.7–8.
G1352 Major F.Q.X., 'Get That King!', *World Wide Adventure,* Summer 1969, 2:1, pp.45–8. *Note:* Fictitious exploit by Lawrence.
G1353 Anthony T. Sullivan, 'Obstinate Mr. Doughty', *Aramco World,* July–August 1969, pp.2–5.
G1354 Margaret Newby, 'Technique of Automatic Writing', *Prediction,* July 1969, pp.10–12.
G1355 'Death of a Hero', *Private Eye (London),* September 1969.
G1356 Sidney Sugarman, 'Finally After Half a Century of Legend: The Truth About T.E. Lawrence and the Arab Revolt', *Jewish Observer and Middle East Review* (London), 12 September 1969, pp.17–20.
G1357 Malcolm Muggeridge, 'A Legend That Dies Hard', *Observer,* 28 September 1969, p.29.
G1358 (Lebanon) Denise Ammoun, 'Le Piège Sioniste sera Brisé, October–November 1969.
G1359 Elizabeth Monroe, 'Imposter or Imperialist?', *TLS,* 2 October 1969, pp.1120–21. *Note:* Review of Knightley and Simpson, *The Secret Lives* (E302).
G1360 'New Legends Out of Old', *Economist,* 4 October 1969, 233, p.55. *Note:* Review of Knightley and Simpson (E302).
G1361 *Observer,* 5 October 1969, p.8.
G1362 Rolf Itelliaander, 'Die Geheimen Ängste des "Lawrence of Arabien"', *Welt am Sonntag,* 12 October 1969.
G1363 Peter Mansfield, 'Brown Dominions', *Listener,* 16 October 1969, 82:2116, p.528. *Note:* Review of Knightley and Simpson (E302).
G1364 R.D. Barnett, 'T.E. Lawrence and the British Museum', *TLS,* 16 October 1969, pp.1210–11.
G1365 Maurice Larès, 'Recherche de descendants Corbel, Fécelier, Martinet ayant connu famille Lawrence 1891–4; 1906–8', *Ouest-France,* 29 October 1969.
G1366 (Lebanon) Maha Arida, 'Lawrence d'Arabie ou Lawrence de Sion?', 30 October 1969.
G1367 Claud-Michel Cluny, 'Laurence *(sic)* d'Arabie', *Gazette Medicale de France,* 15 November 1969, 76:28, pp.5758–60.
G1368 *Réalités,* December 1969, 229, p.56.
G1369 Henk Ohne Sorgel, 'Lawrence von Arabien auf Defektem', *Die Welt der Literatur (Hamburg),* 4 December 1969.
G1370 David W. Littlefield, *Library Journal,* 15 December 1969, 94, pp.4520–21. *Note:* Review of Knightley and Simpson (E302).

G1371 Rolf Scheller, 'Den "Unbekante" Lawrence von Arabiens', *General-Anzeigen*, 18 December 1969.

G1372 'Lawrence', *Spandau Volksblat (Berlin)*, 21 December 1969.

G1373 *Bücherschiff (Kronberg, Taunes)*, Christmas 1969, 4. *Note:* Review of Knightley and Simpson (E302).

G1374 Claude Mauriac, *L'Express*, 28 December 1970 – 3 January 1971, 1016.

G1375 G.J.H. Van Gelder, 'Lawrence of Arabia or Lawrence of England', *International Spectator*, 1970, 24, pp.1119–32.

G1376 Raymond Lacoste, 'L'Angleterre et Israel de l'ère du Colonel Lawrence à 1969', *Ecrits de Paris*, 1970, 2, pp.66–81.

G1377 Michael Elliott-Bateman, 'The Form of Peoples' War', *Army Quarterly*, 1970, 100:1, pp.35–48. *Note:* Mention of Lawrence.

G1378 Forrest E. Hazard, 'The Ascent of F6: A New Interpretation', *Tennessee Studies in Literature*, 1970, 15, pp.165–75.

G1379 'Lawrence of Arabia, Illegitimate Son', *Eva*, January 1970.

G1380 *Virginia Kirkus Review*, 1 January 1970. *Note:* Review of Knightley and Simpson (E309).

G1381 *PW*, 19 January 1970. *Note:* Review of Knightley and Simpson (E309).

G1382 'Gewisse Dinge', *Der Spiegel*, 19 January 1970, 24:4, p.123. *Note:* Review of Knightley and Simpson (E313).

G1383 Andrew Wilson, 'Capt. Who Taught All the Generals', *Observer*, 1 February 1970.

G1384 'Died: Sir Basil Liddell Hart', *Newsweek*, 9 February 1970.

G1385 *Time*, 9 February 1970. *Note:* Obituary of Liddell Hart.

G1386 J. Béraud-Villars, 'Dédicace des "Sept Piliers de la Sagesse", *Chercheurs et Curieux*, March 1970, 20, pp.206–8. *Note:* Review of Knightley and Simpson (E312).

G1387 *Booknews*, March 1970. *Note:* Review of Knightley and Simpson (E302).

G1388 Theodore Duncan, 'An Arabic Folktale', *Barrack*, March 1970, 10, pp.5–6. *Note:* Features fictional Lawrence.

G1389 Jeffrey Meyers, 'E.M. Forster and T.E. Lawrence, a Friendship', *South Atlantic Quarterly*, Spring 1970, 69:2, pp.205–16.

G1390 Edward Said, 'Narrative', *Salmagundi*, Spring 1970, 12, pp.72–3.

G1391 Ralph Hollenbeck, *Parade of Books* (Kings Forest, New York), 8 March 1970. *Note:* Review of Knightley and Simpson (E309).

G1392 'Inspired by Lawrence of Arabia', *Time & Tide*, 12 March 1970.

G1393 George MacDonald Fraser, 'Backing Into the Limelight', *Chicago Tribune Book World*, 22 March 1970, 4:12, pp.4–5.

G1394 Stanley Weintraub, 'The Secret Lives of Lawrence of Arabia', *New York Times Book Review*, 22 March 1970, pp.8, 27.

G1395 George MacDonald Fraser, 'Backing Into the Limelight', *Washington Post Book World*, 22 March 1970, p.5. *Note:* Review of Knightley and Simpson (E309).

G1396 Edward Weeks, *Atlantic*, April 1970, 225, pp.123–4. *Note:* Review of Knightley and Simpson (E309).

G1397 Shelford Bidwell, 'A Military View of T.E. Lawrence', *Army Quarterly*, April 1970, 100, pp.71–3. *Note:* Review of Aldington (E193), Knightley and Simpson (E309) and Weintraub (E277).

G1398 *Time*, 13 April 1970, 65, p.79.

G1399 Eileen Kennedy, *Best Sellers*, 15 April 1970, 30:2, pp.25–6. *Note:* Review of Knightley and Simpson (E309).

G1400 W.T., 'How Lawrence Cut the Pie', *View Magazine*, 19 April 1970.

G1401 Francis Russell, 'The Unknown Lawrence', *National Review*, 21 April 1970, 22, pp.422–3.

G1402 Cécile Salanova, 'Lawrence d'Arabia: Du Mythe à la Réalité', *Plexus*, May 1970, 35, pp.24–36. *Note:* Illus.

G1403 Renée Winegarten, 'T.E. Lawrence: The End of the Legend', *Mainstream*, May 1970, 16, pp.57–65. *Note:* Review.

G1404 *Seaby's Coin and Medal Bulletin*, May 1970, p.163.

G1405 *America*, 2 May 1970, p.479. *Note:* Review of Knightley and Simpson (E309).

G1406 André Nouschi, 'Les bureaux, les hommes et la politique en Proche-Orient pendant et depuis la Première Guerre Mondiale', *Annales*, May–June 1970, 25:31, pp.768–74.

G1407 *Choice*, June 1970, 7, p.598. *Note:* Review of Knightley and Simpson E309.

G1408 Jeffrey Meyers, 'Nietzsche and Lawrence', *Midway*, Summer 1970, 11:1, pp.77–85.

G1409 William G. Cover, *Middle East Journal*, Summer 1970, 32:3, pp.361–2. *Note:* Review of Mack, *A Prince of Our Disorder* (E355).

G1410 J.R. Ackerley, 'E.M. Forster', *Observer*, 14 June 1970.

G1411 *Booklist*, 15 June 1970. *Note:* Review of Knightley and Simpson (E309).

G1412 Aram Bakshian, 'Garbo in Arabia', *National Review*, 25 June 1970, 28, p.693.

G1413 'New Faces of Lawrence', *Library of Book News*, July 1970.

G1414 *Treasure (Australia)*, 4 July 1970, 390, p.2. *Note:* Front cover.

G1415 Guy Dumur, 'Le Plus Musulman des Chrétiens', *Le Nouvel Observateur*, 13 July 1970, p.32.

G1416 *MD of Canada*, August 1970, p.106. *Note:* Review of Knightley and Simpson (E309).

G1417 G. Valensin, 'Le Comportement de l'Homosexuel', *Le Crapouillot*, August & September 1970, n.s. 12, pp.27–40.

G1418 John Mack, *The Middle East Journal*, Autumn 1970, 24, pp.520–21. *Note:* Review of Knightley and Simpson (E302).

G1419 'Clouds Hill', *Dorset*, Midsummer 1970, 13, p.17.

G1420 'The Sand of the Silence of T.E. Lawrence', *Newsfront*, Midsummer, September 1970, 14, pp.46–7, 16–17. *Note:* Parts 1 and 2.

G1421 Anthony West, 'The Summer of the Hero', *McCall's*, September 1970, 97:12, pp.84–5, 103–4, 114–6, 118–20, 122.

G1422 *Time*, 28 September 1970, p.25.

G1423 *Library and Book News*, October 1970, p.2. *Note:* Review of Knightley and Simpson (E302).

G1424 Jeffrey Meyers, 'T.E. Lawrence', *Commonweal*, 23 October 1970, 93:4, pp.100–104. *Note:* Review of Knightley and Simpson (E302).

G1425 Elizabeth Monroe, 'Round Table and Middle Eastern Peace Settlement', *The Round Table*, November 1970, 60:240, pp.479–90.

G1426 *Strategy and Tactics*, November–December 1970, 21. *Note:* Review of Knightley and Simpson (E302).

G1427 John Griggs, 'Orphans at No. 10', *Observer*, 6 December 1970, p.26.

G1428 Aileen W. Propes, *Library Journal*, 15 December 1970, 95, p.4246. *Note:* Review of *The Adventures of Ulysses*.

G1429 Edward W. Said, 'A Standing Civil War', *Hudson Review*, Winter 1970/1971, 23:4, pp.759–61.

G1430 James Lunt, 'Lawrence and the Arabs', *History of the First World War*, 1971, 6:6, pp.2392–401. *Note:* Special issue, front cover.

G1431 James Lunt, 'End in Palestine The Battle of Megeddo Arab Revolt', *History of the First World War*, 1971, 108, pp.3010–17.

G1432 James Lunt, 'The Arab Revolt', *History of the First World War*, 1971, 7:12.

G1433 J.D. Lunt, 'Los Arabes y Lawrence', *Historia Mundial del Siglo*, 1971, 2:22, pp.43–8.

G1434 Neville Braybrooke, 'Charles de Foucauld y Lawrence de Arabia: dos heroes des desierto', *Arbor*, 1971, 306, pp.21–5.

G1435 *Pictorial Knowledge*, 1971, 8:6, p.2639. *Note:* Portrait.

G1436 John Mack, 'Psychoanalysis and Historical Biography', *Journal of the American Psychiatric Association*, January 1971, 19:1, p.151.

G1437 'Assimil-Junior. Lawrence en bande dessinée et en cassette', *L'Express*, 4 January 1971, 1017.

G1438 *TLS*, 22 January 1971, p.105. *Note:* Mention of Lawrence.

G1439 *Aramco World*, February 1971, 22:1, pp.20–21. *Note:* Photo from film.

G1440 William I. Shaw, *Military Affairs*, February 1971, 35:1, p.41. *Note:* Review of Knightley and Simpson (E302).

G1441 Sidney Sugarman, 'Damn the Press', *Dorset* , Early Spring 1971, 17, pp.13–14.

G1442 Colin Graham, 'The Strange Relationship Between Thomas Hardy and Thomas Lawrence', *Dorset*, Early Spring 1971, 17, pp.11–12.

G1443 T.J. Henighan, 'T.E. Lawrence's *Seven Pillars of Wisdom*', *Dalhousie Review*, Spring 1971, 51, pp.49–59.

G1444 *L'Express*, 22–28 March 1971, 1028. *Note:* Article.

G1445 Malcolm Muggeridge, *Observer*, 28 March 1971.

G1446 Neville Braybrooke, 'Vocation in the Desert: Lawrence of Arabia and Charles de Foucauld', *Commonweal*, 2 April 1971, 94:4, pp.88–9.

G1447 *Abstracts of English Studies*, June 1971, 14:10, pp.642–3. *Note:* Item 3034.

G1448 *Reader's Digest*, July 1971, p.102.

G1449 Jack Wood, 'Lawrence of Arabia', *Cycle World*, October 1971, 10, pp.68–70+.

G1450 *Abstracts of English Studies*, October 1971, 15:2, p.103. *Note:* Item 479.

G1451 *New York Times Magazine*, 7 November 1971, p.38. *Note:* Photo.

G1452 D.A.M. Jones, 'Lawrence at Rest', *Listener*, 2 December 1971, 86, pp.771–2. *Note:* Review of *Minorities* (A258).

G1453 Uriel Dann, 'T.E. Lawrence in Amman 1921', *Abr-Nahrain*, 1972, XIII, pp.31–41. *Note:* Illus.

G1454 Jeffrey Meyers, 'T.E. Lawrence: A Bibliography', *Bulletin of Bibliography*, January–March 1972, 29:1, pp.25–36.

G1455 Robert Payne, 'On the Prose of T.E. Lawrence', *Prose*, Spring 1972, IV, pp.98–108. *Note:* Illus.

G1456 Keith N. Hull, 'T.E. Lawrence's Perilous Parodies', *Texas Quarterly*, Summer 1972, 15:2, pp.56–61.

G1457 William Kean Seymour, 'T.E. Lawrence's Private Anthology', *Contemporary Review*, September 1972, 221, pp.162–3.

G1458 Hugh Ford, *The Private Library*, Autumn 1972, p.121. *Note:* Article on Seizin Press.

G1459 *Booklist*, 15 November 1972, 69, p.271. *Note:* Review of *Minorities* (A260).

G1460 Bruce C. Merry, 'Thomas Hardy and T.E. Lawrence: Two English Sources for Beppe Fenoglio?', *Romance Notes*, Winter 1972, 14:2, pp.230–35.

G1461 Stephen E. Tabachnick, 'Two "Arabian" Romantics Charles Doughty and T.E. Lawrence', *English Literature in Translation*, 1973, 16:1, pp.11–25.

G1462 *Quarterly Journal of the Library of Congress*, January 1973, 30:1, p.92. *Note:* Photo.

G1463 Lowell Thomas, 'I Remember Lawrence of Arabia', *TV Guide*, 27 January – 2 February 1973, 21, pp.19–21.

G1464 *Los Angeles TV Times*, 28 January – 3 February, 1973, p.3. *Note:* Ad for rebroadcast of film.

G1465 *Economist*, 24 February 1973, 246, p.106. *Note:* Review of *The Mint* (A177).

G1466 *Colby Library Quarterly*, March 1973, Semester X:1, p.48.

G1467 *Abstracts of English Studies*, March 1973, 16:7, p.450. *Note:* Item 2003.

G1468 Graham Rigby, 'T.E. Lawrence and the Seizin Press', *The Private Library*, Spring 1973, 6:1, pp.16–21. *Note:* Illus.

G1469 Christopher Hollis, 'Unguarded Secret', *Spectator*, 17 March 1973, 230, pp.333–4.

G1470 *TLS*, 30 March 1973, p.357. *Note:* Review of *The Mint* (A177).

G1471 William Kean Seymour, 'T.E. Lawrence and "The Mint"', *Contemporary Review*, April 1973, 222, pp.220–21.

G1472 *Books and Bookmen*, April 1973, 18, p.80. *Note:* Review of *The Mint* (A177).

G1473 Jacob Alaric, 'The British Arabists', *History Today*, May 1973, 23:5, pp.373, 374.

G1474 *Books*, Summer 1973, 12, p.13.

G1475 Sig Sugarman, 'Hashemite Debt to Lawrence of Arabia', *International History*, July 1973, 7.

G1476 *Modern Maturity*, August–September 1973, 16:4, pp.12–13. *Note:* Article on Lowell Thomas.

G1477 'Man of Action, Man of Letters', *TLS*, 10 August 1973, p.925. *Note:* Review of *Seven Pillars of Wisdom* (A050).

G1478 Stanley and Rodelle Weintraub, 'Chapman's Homer', *Classical World,* September–October 1973, 67:1, pp.16–24.

G1479 Laura Jackson, 'The Cult of Connections', *The Private Library,* Autumn 1973, 6, pp.133–41.

G1480 Oscar Winters, *Paideuma* (University of Maine), Spring 1973, 2:1, p.146. *Note:* Reply to by Eva Hesse and John Haskins comments, Fall 1973, pp.3376–7.

G1481 Jeffrey Meyers, 'The Revisions of *Seven Pillars of Wisdom',* PMLA, October 1973, 88:5, pp.1066–82.

G1482 *Saturday Review,* 6 November 1973. *Note:* Lawrence cartoon.

G1483 Phillip Knightley, 'Aldington's Enquiry Concerning T.E. Lawrence', *Texas Quarterly,* Winter 1973, 16:4, pp.98–105.

G1484 George Woodcock, 'Arabia Infelix', *Queen's Quarterly,* 1974, 81, pp.605–10.

G1485 Hélène Houssemaine, *France-Pays Arabes,* January–February 1974, 40. *Note:* Review of Mousa *Songe et mensonge* ((E259).

G1486 Pierre Graziani, 'L'Orient des mythomanes', *France Pays Arabes,* January–February 1974, 40. *Note:* About Mousa (E259).

G1487 W.K.S., *Contemporary Review,* March 1974, 224, p.168. *Note:* Review of *Seven Pillars* (A050).

G1488 Jean Duvignaud, 'Un Arabe Juge Lawrence', *Le Nouvel Observateur,* 11 March 1974, p.58.

G1489 J.M. Wilson, 'T.E. Lawrence: Notes for Collectors', *Antiquarian Book Monthly Review,* April, May 1974, 3 and 4, pp.1–4 (Part 1), pp.3–6 (Part 2).

G1490 *Guardian,* 25 June 1974. *Note:* Note on *The Mint* (A177).

G1491 Rodelle and Stanley Weintraub, 'Moby Dick and the Seven Pillars of Wisdom', *Studies in American Fiction,* Autumn 1974, 2:2, pp.238–40.

G1492 *Quarterly Journal of the Library of Congress,* October 1974, 2, p.247. *Note:* Facsimile of Lawrence letter.

G1493 Edwin Samuel, 'A Recently Discovered Letter From T.E. Lawrence to My Father', *Contemporary Review,* December 1974, 225, pp.311–15.

G1494 *Abstracts of English Studies,* December 1974, 18:4, p.244. *Note:* Item 1196.

G1495 L.H., 'Aufstand in Der Wüste', *Westdeutscher Rundfunk Begleitheft,* 1975, pp.34–8.

G1496 Stephen Tabachnick, 'The Two Veils of T.E. Lawrence', *Studies in Twentieth Century,* 1975, 16, pp.89–110.

G1497 John S. Friedman, '"Lawrence of Arabia" and Zionism', *Jewish Spectator,* Spring 1975, 40, pp.43–146.

G1498 James W. Greenlee, 'Malraux, History and Autobiography: Seven Pillars of Wisdom Revisited', *Mélanges Malraux Miscellany,* Spring & Autumn 1975, 7:1 and 2, pp.18–35.

G1499 Randall Baker, 'Hejaz Stamps and Lawrence of Arabia', *Stamp Collecting,* 6 March 1975, pp.75–7.

G1500 Dhiela Pepper, *Library Journal*, 15 April 1975, 200, p.746. *Note:* Review of Meyers, *T.E. Lawrence: A Bibliography* (E338).

G1501 *America*, 1 May 1975, 134, p.386. *Note:* Review of Brent (E357).

G1502 Keith N. Hull, 'Lawrence of The Mint, Ross of the R.A.F.', *South Atlantic Quarterly*, Summer 1975, 74:3, pp.340–48.

G1503 Alain Damiani, 'T.E. Lawrence ou l'Honneur de Soi', *Nouvelles Littéraires*, 2 June 1975.

G1504 Pierre de Boisdeffre, 'Le secret de Thomas Edward Lawrence', *Nouvelles Littéraires*, 2 June 1975, 53:2488.

G1505 'Battle Album', *Battle*, July 1975, p.110. *Note:* Photo.

G1506 *Une Semaine de Paris*, July 1975, 372. *Note:* Notice of film broadcast.

G1507 'Announcement of Gift of T.E. Lawrence Collection to Honnold Library', *California Library Association Newsletter*, August 1975, 17:8.

G1508 John Glubb, 'Solitary Hero', *Books and Bookmen*, September 1975, pp.22–4. *Note:* Review of Brent (E356).

G1509 Keith N. Hull, 'Creeds, History, Prophets and Geography in *Seven Pillars of Wisdom*', *Texas Quarterly*, Autumn 1975, 18:3, pp.15–28.

G1510 J.M. Wilson, *TLS*, 19 September 1975, p.1063. *Note:* Letter to editor, request for Lawrence letters.

G1511 *New Yorker*, 22 September 1975, p.49.

G1512 *Paris Match*, 27 September 1975, p.40. *Note:* Drawing.

G1513 *New Yorker*, 20 October 1975, p.14.

G1514 'Who Really Killed Lawrence of Arabia?', *Headlines*, November 1975, 51, pp.42–4. *Note:* Illus., front cover.

G1515 *Best Sellers*, December 1975, 35, p.286. *Note:* Review of Brent (E357).

G1516 *New York Times Magazine*, 2 December 1975, p.15.

G1517 Bernard T. Ward, 'Lawrence of Arabia and Pole Hill', *Essex Journal*, 1976, 9:3.

G1518 R.L. Bidwell, 'Queries for Biographers of T.E. Lawrence', *Arabian Studies*, 1976, 3, pp.13–27.

G1519 Jeffrey Meyers, 'Xenophon and the *Seven Pillars of Wisdom*', *Classical Journal*, December–January 1976–1977, 72:2, pp.141–3.

G1520 Anthony Burton, 'Arranging the Minds of Men. T.E. Lawrence Theorist of War', *Army Quarterly*, January 1976, 10:1, pp.51–8.

G1521 *PW*, 26 January 1976, p.282. *Note:* Review of Mack (E353).

G1522 *Virgina Kirkus*, February 1976. *Note:* Review of Mack (E353).

G1523 Jane Larkin Crain, 'Nothing but a Great Man', *Saturday Review*, 21 February 1976, 23, pp.40–41. *Note:* Review of Mack (E353).

G1524 'Perpetual Attraction', *Book Seller*, 28 February 1976.

G1525 *Best Sellers*, March 1976, 35, p.386. *Note:* Review of Weintraub *Lawrence of Arabia: The Literary Impulse* (E346).

G1526 Stephen Tabachnick, 'T.E. Lawrence and Moby Dick', *Research Studies*, March 1976, 44:1, pp.1–12.

G1527 Kenneth Marshall, 'Customers & Friends: Memoirs of a Bookseller', *London Magazine*, March 1976, 15:6, pp.79–90.

G1528 *T.E. Lawrence Studies*, Spring 1976, 1:1.

G1529 Pamela G. Bonnell, *Library Journal*, 1 March 1976, 101, pp.719–20. *Note:* Review of Weintraub (E346).

G1530 Paul Zweig, 'A Prince of Our Disorder', *New York Times Book Review*, 21 March 1976, pp.1–2. *Note:* Review of Mack (E353).

G1531 Karen Trego, 'Portrait of Lawrence', *Chicago Sunday Times Bookweek*, 28 March 1976. *Note:* Illus.

G1532 V.S. Pritchett, 'The Athiest', *New York Review of Books*, 1 April 1976, 23, p.3.

G1533 Elizabeth P. Hayford, *Library Journal*, 1 April 1976, 101, p.886. *Note:* Review of Mack (E353).

G1534 Walter Clemons, 'Portrait of a Hero', *Newsweek*, 12 April 1976, 87, p.98. *Note:* Review of Mack (E353).

G1535 Robert Hughes, 'Self-Made Legend', *Time*, 12 April 1976, 107, pp.93–5. *Note:* Review of Mack (E353).

G1536 *Atlantic*, May 1976, 237, p.111. *Note:* Review of Mack (E353).

G1537 Frank X. J. Homer, *America*, 1 May 1976, p.386. *Note:* Review of Mack (E353).

G1538 *Street Lives*, 1 May 1976. *Note:* Review of Mack (E353).

G1539 Peter Rowley, 'More Light on Lawrence of Arabia', *Los Angeles Times Book Review*, 9 May 1976, p.4.

G1540 *New York Times Book Review*, 12 May 1976. *Note:* Ad for Mack (E353).

G1541 'Guilt Ridden', *Economist*, 15 May 1976, 259, p.121. *Note:* Review of Mack (E353.

G1542 Robert K. Morris, "In the Service of An Alien Race", *Nation*, 15 May 1976, 222, pp.600–601.

G1543 Phillip Knightley, 'Stripped', *New Statesman*, 21 May 1976, 91, p.684.

G1544 Quentin Oates, 'Critics Corner', *The Bookseller*, 22 May 1976, p.241.

G1545 Christopher Sykes, 'Lawrence of What?', *Observer*, 23 May 1976.

G1546 D.W. Harding, 'Lawrence, Twice a Hero', *Listener*, 27 May 1976, pp.683–4.

G1547 Lowell Thomas, 'I Did the First TV News Program in History', *TV Guide*, 29 May – 4 June 1976, pp.8–10.

G1548 Thomas J. O'Donnell, 'T.E. Lawrence and the Confessional Tradition', *Genre*, Summer 1976, IX:2, pp.135–52.

G1549 *Best Sellers*, June 1976, 36:3, p.82.

G1550 Jeffrey Meyers, *Sewannee Review*, Summer 1976, 84, pp.87–90. *Note:* Review of Mack (E353).

G1551 Paul Scott, 'Not so Much a Hero...', *Country Life*, 3 June 1976, p.1505.

G1552 Jan Morris, 'The Hard, Bright Flame', *Spectator*, 5 June 1976, pp.20–21.

G1553 John Glubb, 'Guilt-Haunted Hero', *Books and Bookmen*, July 1976, pp.40–44.

G1554 Anthony Ellis, 'Lawrence of Arabia Walked Back Into History', *Observer*, 8 August 1976, p.19.

G1555 Norman Dixon, 'Paradox of Arabia', *TLS*, 13 August 1976, p.1004.

G1556 Bernard Crick, 'Anglo-Spanish Attitude', *TLS*, 20 August 1976, p.1032. *Note:* Review of Meyers, *Fever at the Core* (F0729).

G1557 Anthony Storr, *Critic*, Fall 1976, 35, pp.91–3. *Note:* Review of Mack (E355).

G1558 *Choice*, September 1976, 13, pp.826, 830. *Note:* Review of Mack (E353) and Weintraub (E346).

G1559 Stephen E. Tabachnick, 'The T.E. Lawrence Revival in English Studies', *Research Studies*, September 1976, 44:3, pp.190–198.

G1560 Jeffrey Meyers, 'A Wanderer After Sensations', *Virginia Quarterly Review*, Autumn 1976, 52:4, pp.717–23.

G1561 Millicant Bell, *New Republic*, 4 September 1976, 175, pp.37–40. *Note:* Review of Mack (E353) and Weintraub (E346).

G1562 *Publisher's Weekly*, 8 November 1976, 210, p.11. *Note:* Notice for Richard Graves, *Lawrence of Arabia and His World* (E358).

G1563 Louis Allen, 'French Intellectuals and T.E. Lawrence', *Durham University Journal*, December 1976, 69:1, pp.52–66.

G1564 *Library Journal*, December 1976, 23, p.55. *Note:* Review of Knightley, *Lawrence of Arabia* (E349).

G1565 B.K. Martin, 'Ezra Pound and T.E. Lawrence', *Paideuma*, 1977, 6, pp.167–73.

G1566 John Thompson, *Book Collector's Market*, January–February 1977, 3:1, p.25. *Note:* Review of *T.E. Lawrence Studies* (E363).

G1567 A.S. Higgs, 'T.E. Lawrence: A Remoulding of the Legend', *Army Quarterly*, January 1977, 197, pp.71–4.

G1568 Elie Kedourie, 'The Surrender of Medina', *Middle Eastern Studies*, January 1977, 13:1, pp.124–43.

G1569 Bert Smith, 'An Exceptional Man', *The Wooden Boat*, January/February 1977, 14, pp.31–4.

G1570 Lisa Anderson, 'Explaining Lowell Thomas', *W Movies*, 7–14 January 1977, p.8.

G1571 *Library Journal*, 1 February 1977, pp.374–5. *Note:* Review of Graves (E358).

G1572 Stewart Humphries, 'At Sea With T.E. Lawrence', *Observer*, 20 February 1977, pp.8–9.

G1573 Maurice Larès, 'Le Colonel T.E. Lawrence, Le Moyen Orient et La France', *Guru*, March 1977, 3:3, pp.17–20.

G1574 *Best Sellers*, March 1977, 36:13, p.378. *Note:* Review of Graves (E358).

G1575 *The Periodical*, Spring 1977, 40:324, p.199.

G1576 Jeffrey Meyers, *Virginia Quarterly Reveiw*, Spring 1977, 53:2, p.50. *Note:* Review of Graves (E358).

G1577 *Publisher's Weekly*, 25 April 1977. *Note:* Pulitzer Prize winners, including Mack (E353).

G1578 Thomas J. O'Donnell, 'The Confessions of T.E. Lawrence: The Sadomasochistic Hero', *American Imago*, Summer 1977, 34:2, pp.115–32.

G1579 Elie Kedourie, 'The Real T.E. Lawrence', *Commentary*, July 1977, 64:1, pp.49–56.

G1580 *Best Sellers*, July 1977, 37, p.126. *Note:* Review of Knightley (E350).

G1581 'A Legend Shaken', *Economist*, 2 July 1977, 264, p.112. *Note:* Review of Stewart, *T.E. Lawrence* (E367).

G1582 Phillip Knightley, 'The Sandcastle', *New Statesman*, 8 July 1977, 94, p.56.

G1583 Francis King, 'Fact and Fantasy', *Spectator*, 9 July 1977, 239, p.19.

G1584 William Carroll Schwartz, 'T.E. On Film', *Mandate*, August 1977, 3:28, pp.48, 66, 68–9, 74, 76. *Note:* Homosexual magazine.

G1585 Paul-Francis Hartman, 'Arabian Knight: T.E. Lawrence', *Mandate*, August 1977, 3:28, pp.44–7. *Note:* Homosexual magazine.

G1586 Elizabeth P. Hayford, *Library Journal*, August 1977, 102, p.1634. *Note:* Review of Stewart (E370).

G1587 *Encounter*, September 1977, 49:3, p.53. *Note:* Review of Stewart (E367).

G1588 'Stranger Than Fiction', *Los Angeles Times Book Review*, September 1977.

G1589 *New Yorker*, 5 September 1977, 53, pp.89–90. *Note:* Review of Stewart (E367).

G1590 Nigel Dennis, 'Rigging The Lawrence Case', *New York Review of Books*, 29 September 1977, 24, pp.21–2.

G1591 *Commentary*, October 1977, 64, pp.10–18. *Note:* Response to Kedourie's article in July (G1579).

G1592 Robert Kirsch, 'T.E. Lawrence: Torn Between Ideals and Sordid Reality', *Los Angeles Times Book Review*, 9 October 1977.

G1593 *Best Sellers*, November 1977, 37, p.246. *Note:* Review of Stewart (E370).

G1594 Hugh Trevor-Roper, 'A Humbug Exalted', *New York Times Book Review*, 6 November 1977, pp.1, 34, 36, 38. *Note:* Review of Stewart (E370).

G1595 Robert Olson, *American Historical Review*, December 1977, 82:5, p.1302. *Note:* Review of Morsey, *T.E. Lawrence und der Arabische Aufstand* (E365).

G1596 Maurice Larès, 'L'Image de la France et des Francais pour T.E. Lawrence', *Relations Internationales*, 1978, 14, pp.159–70.

G1597 *Choice*, January 1978, p.1500. *Note:* Review of Stewart (E370).

G1598 Stanley Weintraub, 'Gift of Anonymity', *TLS*, 13 January 1978, p.29. *Note:* Review of Stewart (E367) and Montgomery Hyde, *Solitary in the Ranks* (E373.

G1599 'Snuggling With Lawrence', *New York Review of Books*, 9 February 1978, 24, p.46. *Note:* Review of Stewart (E367).

G1600 Desmond Stewart, *TLS*, 17 February 1978, p.202. *Note:* Letter to editor.

G1601 Maurice Larès, 'Deux Anti-Colonialistes: T.E. Lawrence et H. St. J.B. Philby', *Inter-Profs E.S.E.U.*, March 1978, 5, pp.8–15.

G1602 Maurice Larès, 'Deux Anti-Colonialistes', *Guru*, March 1978, 4:2, pp.32–8.

G1603 *Booklist*, 15 March 1978, p.116. *Note:* Review of Montgomery Hyde (E374).

G1604 Jeffrey Meyers, 'T.E. Lawrence: A Supplement', *Bulletin of Bibliography*, April–June 1978, 35:2, pp.84–7.

G1605 *Library Journal*, 15 May 1978, p.1055. *Note:* Review of Montgomery Hyde (E374).

G1606 Linda J. Travers, 'In Wisdom's House: T.E. Lawrence in the Near East', *Journal of Contemporary History*, July 1978, 13:3, pp.585–608.

G1607 Patricia Nell Warner, 'S.A.', *Blue Boy*, July, August 1978, pp.19–21, 33–5, 59; 30–31, 84, 89, 91, 98. *Note:* Fictionalised account of Lawrence in homosexual setting in Arabia.

G1608 Peter Quennell, 'Permissive Biography', *New York Times Book Review*, 1 September 1978, p.2.
G1609 *Smithsonian*, October 1978, 11:7.
G1610 *Publisher's Weekly*, 25 November 1978, p.60. *Note:* Review of Davis Ned, (E379).
G1611 Rex Benedici, 'Ned', *New York Times Book Review*, 31 December 1978, p.14. *Note:* Review of Davis (E379).
G1612 *Hamizrah Hedadash*, 1979, 28:1–2, pp.127–8. *Note:* Review in Hebrew of Morsey (E365).
G1613 *Publisher's Weekly*, 5 February 1979. *Note:* Review of Eden *The Murder of Lawrence of Arabia* (E384).
G1614 '5500 Pounds for *Seven Pillars of Wisdom*', *Book Auction News*, February 1979.
G1615 '*Seven Pillars* Sold for 5,500 Pounds', *Antiquarian Book Review*, February 1979.
G1616 Warren O. Ault, 'Oxford in 1907 (With a Glimpse of T.E. Lawrence)', *The American Oxonian*, Spring 1979, 66:2, pp.121–8.
G1617 Charles L. Parnell, 'Lawrence of Arabia's Debt to Seapower', *United States Naval Institute Proceedings*, April 1979, 105/8/918, pp.75–83. *Note:* Illus.
G1618 Uriel Dann, "Lawrence of Arabia' One More Appraisal', *Middle Eastern Studies*, May 1979, 15:2, pp.154–62.
G1619 D.A. Wilcox, 'Lawrence of Arabia Guerrilla Warrior!', *Combat Illustrated*, Summer 1979, 4:2, pp.67–75. *Note:* Portrait front cover.
G1620 Robert Obolski, 'Stamps and the History of the Hijaz', *Aramco World*, September–October 1979, pp.6–7. *Note:* Mention of Lawrence's role in first stamp issue.
G1621 William Russo, 'Lawrence of Arabia', *In Touch for Men*, November–December 1979, 44, pp.61–4.
G1622 'Erinnerungen an Lawrence of Arabia', *Britain Special* (Southern England Edition), March 1980, 31, p.1.
G1623 James W. Hamilton, 'Internal Consistency and the Scope of Interpretation in Psychohistory', *Psychohistory Review*, Spring 1980, 8:4, pp.37–42.
G1624 John E. Mack, *Psychohistory Review*, Spring 1980, 8:4, pp.43–5. *Note:* Response to James W. Hamilton (G1623).
G1625 Jean-Albert Fustel, 'L'aventure de Lawrence d'Arabie', *Miroir de l'Histoire*, March–April 1980, 316, pp.38–46.
G1626 John E. Mack, 'Lawrence and the Armenians', *Ararat*, Summer 1980, 221:3, pp.2–7.
G1627 Robert S. Gallagher, 'Good Evening Everybody', *American Heritage*, August/September 1980, pp.33–45. *Note:* Article on Lowell Thomas.
G1628 *Z Magazine*, October/November 1980, 7:5, pp.51–2. *Note:* Review of film.
G1629 *Smithsonian*, October 1980, pp.164–5. *Note:* Illus.
G1630 Michael Yardley, 'Clouds Hill and the Lawrence Legend', *Dorset*, 1981, 96, pp.4–16. *Note:* Front cover portrait.
G1631 *T.E. Lawrence Studies Newsletter*, 1981–, 1–.

G1632 T.W. Beaumont, 'Rank and File', *Journal of the Society for Army Historical Research*, Spring 1981, LVIV:237, pp.6–24.

G1633 *The Microbibliophile*, March 1981, 5:1, pp.10–11. *Note:* Review of O'Brien, *T.E. Lawrence and Fine Printing* (E388).

G1634 Roy Heman Chant, 'The Motor Cycle That Killed Lawrence of Arabia', *Dorset and West Magazine*, March 1981.

G1635 Albert Hourani, 'The Biffer of the French', *TLS*, 29 May 1981, p.609.

G1636 Eduardo Saccone, 'La Questione dell' "Ur Partigiano Johnny"', *Belfagor*, 30 September 1981, 36:5, pp.569–90.

G1637 *Changing times*, October 1981, p.88. *Note:* Joke.

G1638 Suleiman Mousa, 'Lawrence et le Rêve Arabe', *L'Histoire*, November 1981, 39, pp.25–35.

G1639 Louis Gardel, 'Lawrence et les Guichets du Rêve', *L'Histoire*, November 1981, 39, p.5.

G1640 Ralph Colp, Jr., *New York Times Book Review*, 1 November 1981, p.49. *Note:* Letter to editor.

G1641 *Antiquarian Book Monthly Review*, February 1982, 9:2(issue 94), p.47.

G1642 Lowell Thomas, *Michigan Quarterly Review*, Spring 1982, 21:2, pp.301–2. *Note:* Letter to editor.

G1643 Michael A. Anderegg, 'Lawrence of Arabia: The Man, The Myth, The Movie', *Michigan Quarterly Review*, Spring 1982, 21:2, pp.281–300.

G1644 Maurice Larès, 'Lawrence est de retour', *L'Histoire*, May 1982, 45, p.73.

G1645 George T. Foden, 'Strange Encounter', *Aeroplane Monthly*, June 1982, pp.320–23.

G1646 *Antiquarian Book Monthly Review*, October 1982, 9:102, p.392.

G1647 P. Tunbridge, '"SCOOP" Was Lawrence of Arabia a Contributor to Service Journal?', *Haltonian*, Winter 1982, 2, p.5.

G1648 Paul Collet, 'Blair Hughes-Stanton on Wood Engraving', *Matrix*, Winter 1982, 2, pp.45–50. *Note:* Hughes-Stanton did wood engravings for *Seven Pillars of Wisdom*.

G1649 Maurice Larès, 'Images Ethniques et Concept de Race chez Lawrence d'Arabie', *Etudes Inter-Ethniques*, 1983, 6, pp.111–59.

G1650 J. Thobie, 'Notes de Lecture', *Relations Internationales*, 1983, 34, pp.250–53. *Note:* Review of Larès, *T.E. Lawrence, La France, et Les Francais* (E377).

G1651 *ABMR's Booksellers Catalogue*, January 1983, 10:1, p.5. *Note:* Article on Aldington.

G1652 Albert Hourani, 'T.E. Lawrence and Louis Massignon', *TLS*, 8 July 1983, pp.733–4.

G1653 Ron Rosenbaum, 'The Great Mole Mystery', *Harper's*, October 1983, pp.46, 49–50.

G1654 Rudolf Bader, 'Lawrence of Arabia and H.H. Richardson', *Australian Literary Studies*, November 1983, pp.99–101.

G1655 Jeffrey Richards and Jeffrey Hulbert, 'Censorship in Action: The Case of "Lawrence of Arabia"', *Journal of Contemporary History*, January 1984, 19:1, pp.153–70.

G1656 Bert Smith, 'From Lawrence of Arabia: From Camels To Target Boats', *Waterfront*, February 1984, 5:7, pp.46, 82–3. *Note:* Illus.

G1657 M.H.N., 'The T.E. Lawrence Puzzle', *West Coast Review of Books*, May/June 1984, p.34. *Note:* Review.

G1658 Maurice Larès, 'De Lawrence à Learoyd', *Revue de Littérature Comparée*, May 1984, 1, pp.51–88.

G1659 Jeff Clew, 'The fatal fascination', *The Classic Motorcycle*, June 1984, pp.46–7.

G1660 Judith Miller, 'International Drawing', *New York Times Magazine*, 16 September 1984, p.109.

G1661 Sheila Ann Scoville, 'The T.E. Lawrence Puzzle', *Middle East Studies Association Bulletin*, December 1984, 18:2, pp.226–7. *Note:* Review.

G1662 Derrick Jensen, 'T.E. Lawrence Puzzle', *The Bloomsbury Review*, December 1984, 5:3. *Note:* Review of Tabachnick, *The T.E. Lawrence Puzzle* (E396).

G1663 Brian Holden Reid, 'Lawrence and the Arab Revolt', *History Today*, May 1985, 35, pp.41–5.

G1664 Brian Holden Reid, 'T.E. Lawrence and Liddell Hart', *History*, June, 1985, 70:229, pp.218–31.

G1665 *The T.E. Lawrence Society Newsletter*, December 1985 –, 1–:1–.

G1666 Jeremy M. Wilson, 'T.E. Lawrence and the Printing of *Seven Pillars of Wisdom*', *Matrix*, Winter 1985, 5, pp.55–69.

G1667 John Walsh, 'Napoleon in Burnous: the Lives of T.E. Lawrence', *Folio*, Spring 1986, pp.9–15.

G1668 Elizabeth Lambert, 'Historic Houses: Lawrence of Arabia', *Architectural Digest*, March 1986, pp.140–45, 203. *Note:* Photos.

G1669 Doug Dinford, 'Lawrence the Brough', *The Vintage M/C Club*, April 1986, p.232.

G1670 Suleiman Mousa, 'Arab Sources on Lawrence of Arabia: new evidence', *The Army Quarterly and Defense Journal*, April 1986, 116:2, pp.158–71.

G1671 C.D. Blackmore, 'Following Lawrence of Arabia', *British Army Review*, April 1986, 82.

G1672 S.R. Sonyel, 'Lawrence – the pro-Arab Zionist', *Impact International*, 27 June – 10 July 1986, 16:12, pp.11–13.

G1673 'Al Sir Al Ghamed Wara Moat Lawrence', *Asharq Al Awsat*, 27 August – 3 September 1986, 9, pp.16–17.

G1674 Guy Dumur, *L'Herne*. *Note:* Special issue on the death of Massignon.

G1675 W.T. Massey, 'I Saw Damascus Fall', *The Great War – I Was There*, Part 43, pp.1709–11.

G1676 J.R. Edmondton, 'On the Eve of Allenby's Final Victory', *The Great War – I Was There*, Part 43, pp.1698–1706.

G1677 S.C. Rolls, 'I Was With Lawrence of Arabia', *The Great War – I Was There*, Part 35?, pp.1408–16.

G1678 James Maueeri, 'De ? Meet With Lawrence of Arabia', *Film Daily*.

G1679 'The Seven Pillars of Wisdom', *Esquire*, November, pp.82, 124, 141–2.

G1680 'No Way to Treat a Lady', *Dorset, 69, p.13. Note:* Reproductions of newspapers at time of Lawrence's death, pp.23, 25, 27; dealer's sales list of Lawrence items, p.24.

G1681 Lowell Thomas, 'What Lawrence Wished for Thomas', *Dorset, 96, p.16.*

G1682 Byron Farwell, 'Inner Man', *Bookletter,* 2:16, *p.2. Note:* Illus.

G1683 A.M., *Biblio. de prof. pedag. Note:* Review of Bénoist-Mechin (E245).

G1684 Jeremy M. Wilson, 'T.E. Lawrence Books From the London Reference Collection of J.M. Wilson', *ABMR's Booksellers Catalogue,* Section I, p.VIII.

G1685 'Short article on *Seven Pillars of Wisdom* and *Secret Lives', A/B Bookman's Weekly.*

G1686 'Announcement of T.E. Lawrence collection at Honnold Library, Claremont College', *A/B Bookman's Weekly,* p.656.

G1687 Hugh Maclean, 'T.E. Lawrence: Hero', *Queen's Quarterly (Kingston),* Autumn 1 , 60, pp.367–83.

G1688 Giorgio Altarass, 'Il Leggendario Lawrence', *Oggi,* pp.49–50.

G1689 Robert Stephens, 'Lawrence and the Arabs', *Observer. Note:* Review of Mousa (E256).

G1690 Stanley Eichelbaum, 'The Legend of T.E. Lawrence', *Observer.*

G1691 A.W. Lawrence, 'Is the Cinema's Lawrence a Dramatic Disaster?', *Observer.*

G1692 Hal Burton, *Newsday,* p.26. *Note:* Review of Knightley and Simpson (E302).

G1693 J. Cournos, *New York Times Book Review. Note:* Review of *Oriental Assembly* (A225).

G1694 'Lawrence', *Life,* pp.30–31.

G1695 D.W. Littlefield, *Library Journal,* p.2283. *Note:* Review of Orgill *Lawrence* (E334).

G1696 'Blue Plaque to T.E. Lawrence', *Dorset,* pp.15–16.

G1697 Georges Reyer, 'Qui Etait le Vrai Lawrence?'.

G1698 Fredrick R. Karl, 'Death Seeker's Self-Portrait in Letters'.

G1699 John Morris, 'The Lawrence Enigma'. *Note:* Review of Aldington (E192).

G1700 'Sous un même Burnous deux Mondes s'Entrechoquent', pp.9–12. *Note:* Film.

G1701 Lt. Col. George Haig, 'Message to Damascus'.

G1702 'Hargon's Pictures Lawrence of Arabia'. *Note:* Illus.

G1703 Freda Bruce Lockhart, 'He's a Real Hero!'. *Note:* Illus.

G1704 '"Lawrence" Takes "Season" Record'.

G1705 'Est Le Mirage Lawrence d'Arabia'.

G1706 Peter Grosvenor, 'La Légende de Lawrence de Arabia Reculta una Legenda', p.36. *Note:* Review of film, illus.

G1707 W. Wei, 'Araber Gegen Turken in Weltkreig. T.E. Lawrence und der Araber's Aufstand in der Wüste', *Weltbühne,* 23:46, pp.747–50.

G1708 Douglas Brent, 'The British Prince of Mecca', p.13.

SECTION H

NEWSPAPER ARTICLES
ABOUT T.E. LAWRENCE

Interest in Lawrence has generated additional printed materials in the form of critiques, reviews and commentary. In recent years the film has added another major dimension. All of these are represented in the listing that follows.

As is the case with periodical articles, newspaper items about Lawrence present a serious problem to the bibliographer. It is impossible to come close to a complete listing. This problem, when added to the wish to gather articles covering all subjects related to Lawrence, greatly complicates the effort. Yet the merit of providing as much of the record as possible seems apparent and can be added to in the future.

H0001 Maynard Owen Williams, 'Unearthing Greatest Hittite Inscription World Has Seen for Three Thousand Years', *New York Sun*, 21 September 1913. *Note:* Report on Carchemish.

H0002 Maynard Owen Williams, 'Kalamazoo Boy in Startling Syrian Find! Buried Relic Dug up after 3,000 years. Greatest Hittite Inscription in World!', *Kalamazoo Gazette* (Michigan), 31 October 1913.

H0003 'Turkey Surrenders Absolutely', 1918.

H0004 Marcel Hutin, '"Les Bulgares fuient en désordre sur un front de 150 km. Les armeés turques de Palestine anéanties', *L'Écho de Paris*, 24 September 1918.

H0005 Pertinax, 'Les Revendications Arabes. La France et Syrie', *L'Echo de Paris*, 7 February 1919.

H0006 Pertinax, 'Il faut en finir avec l'affaire syrienne', *L'Écho de Paris*, 16 May 1919, p.1.

H0007 'Emir Feisal's Plea', *The Times*, 11 September 1919. *Note:* TEL letter to Ed.

H0008 'L'Accord Franco-Anglais', *Temps*, 17 September 1919.

H0009 Chekri Ganem, 'La Syrie et les droits du Hejaz', *Le Figaro*, 11 October 1919.

H0010 'By the Way', *Daily Express*, 4 March 1920.

H0011 '"Shaw" is Shaw's Guest', *New York Times*, 6 March 1920, p.10.

H0012 'Notre Action en Syrie', *Le Matin*, 29 July 1920.

H0013 'Resignation of Colonel Lawrence as Advisor', *Morning Post* (London), 20 July 1922, p.8.

H0014 'Colonel as Private Soldier', *Aldershot News*, 29 December 1922, p.7, col.4.

H0015 Leopold Weiss, 'Trouble in Arabia (in German)', *Züricher Zeitung*, 18–22 March 1924.

H0016 *New York Evening Post*, 22 November 1924, p.6. *Note:* Review of Thomas, *With Lawrence in Arabia* (E006).

H0017 'He Knew Lawrence of Arabia Well', *West Cumberland Times*, 1925.

H0018 'Book Costs $150 a Copy', *New York Times*, 16 February 1926, p.18.

H0019 'Col. Lawrence to Tell His Own Tale, 17 February 1926, p.18.

H0020 'Col. Lawrence's Holiday', *New York Times*, 24 July 1926, p.12.

H0021 'Prophesied Coup by Italy', *New York Times*, 20 September 1926, Part 12, p.11.

H0022 'Lawrence Explains Fall of Kut-El-Amara', *New York Times*, 20 October 1926, p.27.

H0023 'Lawrence Issues His Arabian Book', *New York Times*, 13 December 1926, p.6.

H0024 'The Arabian Epic', *The Times*, 13 December 1926.

H0025 D.G. Hogarth, 'Lawrence of Arabia – Story of his book – a lavish edition', *The Times*, 13 December 1926, pp.15–16.

H0026 John Buchan, 'Lawrence the Amazing', *Sunday Chronicle*, 19 December 1926. *Note:* Illus.

H0027 'Lawrence of Arabia', *Lincoln Echo*, 27 December 1926.

H0028 "Seven Pillars of Wisdom", 1927?

H0029 Ralph Strauss, 'Lawrence and the Arabs', *Sunday Times*, 1927. *Note:* Review of Graves, *Lawrence and the Arabs* (E030).

H0030 G.B. Shaw, 'Shaw Aircraftsman', 1927.

H0031 'Shereef Lawrence's Book', *New York Times*, 2 January 1927, Part II, p.8.

H0032 *Lawrence of Arabia*, 2 January 1927.

H0033 'Shaw Lauds Lawrence Conqueror of Arabia', *New York Times*, 4 February 1927, p.10.

H0034 Raymond Savage, 'Lawrence of Arabia in a New Disguise', *New York Times*, 7 March 1927, Part IV, pp.3, 22.

H0035 'Lawrence's War Book $20,000 a Copy Here, 8 March 1927, p.1.

H0036 'The Modest Author of a $20,000 Book', *New York Times*, 9 March 1927, p.24.

H0037 'To Print Parts of Lawrence Book', *New York Times*, 9 March 1927, p.8.

H0038 'New Book at £4,000 a Copy', *Daily Express*, 9 March 1927.

H0039 'New Book at £4,000 a Copy', *Sunday Times*, 6 March 1927.

H0040 'Colonel Lawrence's Book', *Sunday Times*, 6 March 1927.

H0041 'Lawrence Won't Lecture', *New York Times*, 10 March 1927, p.20.

H0042 Robert Lynd, 'Colonel Lawrence's Masterpiece', *Daily News* (London), 10 March 1927.

H0043 'Book of the Day', *The Times*, 10 March 1927. *Note:* Review of *Revolt in the Desert* (A102).

H0044 'Lawrence Copyright Seen in Danger', *New York Times*, 13 March 1927, Part II, p.9.

H0045 Ralph Strauss, 'Lawrence of Arabia', *Sunday Times*, 13 March 1927. *Note:* Review of *Revolt* (A102).

H0046 James Forman, 'Lawrence is Already a Legend', *New York Times*, 20 March 1927, Part III, pp.1, 34.

H0047 'Captured by Turks in the Holy Land', *New York Times*, 27 March 1927, Part II, p.11.

H0048 *Springfield Republican* (Mass), 26 May 1927, pp.7f. *Note:* Review of Graves (E030).

H0049 'Assails Lawrence on Arabian Record', *New York Times*, 24 July 1927, p.13.

H0050 'Lawrence of Arabia – Startling Attack on Uncrowned King', *Sunday Times*, 24 July 1927.

H0051 A.T. Wilson, 'Col. Lawrence's Critic', *Daily Express*, 29 July 1927.

H0052 Robert Graves, *Sunday Times*, 31 July 1927. *Note:* Reply to A.T. Wilson.

H0053 'How He Wanted For Turks to Kill Him', *Sunday Times*, 27 September 1927.

H0054 '£500 Paid For Book', *The Times*, 28 September 1927.

H0055 *Springfield Republican*, 1 November 1927, pd.10. *Note:* Review of Thomas, *Boys' Life of Col. Lawrence* (E023).

H0056 *New York World*, 6 November 1927, p.11. *Note:* Review of Thomas (E023).

H0057 *Boston Transcript*, 19 November 1927, p.4. *Note:* Review of Thomas (E023).

H0058 'Lawrence Bitter Over Fate of Arabs', *New York Times*, 24 November 1927, p.13.

H0059 'Lawrence the Enigma', *New York Times*, 25 November 1927, p.20.

H0060 'Lawrence of Arabia, Remarkable Tribute by King Feisal. Also Lawrence of Arabia. King Feisal Hopes for His Return to Iraq', *Daily Express*, November 1927.

H0061 '"Uncrowned King" as Private Soldier', *Daily Express*, 22 December 1927, p.1. *Note:* Illus.

H0062 *New York Sun*, 1928. *Note:* Lawrence's supposed activities in Afghanistan.

H0063 *New York Times*, 13 January 1928. *Note:* John painting.

H0064 Allen Raymond, 'British Air Fleet is Ready for Arabia', *New York Times*, 7 March 1928, pp.1, 6.

H0065 *New York World*, 1 April 1928, p.10. *Note:* Review of Graves (E037).

H0066 *Boston Transcript*, 4 April 1928, p.5. *Note:* Review of Robert Graves.

H0067 John Carter, 'Lawrence of Arabia As Yet is Unexplained', *New York Times*, 8 April 1928, Part IV, pp.5, 10.

H0068 '"Lawrence of Arabia"', *The Star* (London), 1 May 1928.

H0069 *New York Evening Post*, 14 July 1928, p.5. *Note:* Review of Graves (E037).

H0070 'Lawrence Still a Private', *New York Times*, 17 July 1928, p.10.

H0071 'Col. Lawrence Bobs Up Again', *Detroit Saturday Night*, 1 September 1928.

H0072 'Report Lawrence Now a Moslem Saint Spying on the Bolshevist Agents in India', *New York Times*, 27 September 1928, p.1.

H0073 'Colonel T.E. Lawrence', *Morning Post* (London), 27 September 1928.

H0074 Arthur F. Mam, 'Lawrence of Arabia Fights Soviet in India', *New York World*, 27 September 1928.

H0075 *New York Herald Tribune,* 1 October 1928. *Note:* Report of Lawrence's supposed activities in Afghanistan.

H0076 'Lawrence – A Legend Unveiled', *Evening Standard,* 19 October 1928, p.17.

H0077 'Lawrence Reported Writing a New Book on Middle East', *New York Times,* 2 November 1928, p.6.

H0078 T.P. Grieg, 'Seven Pillars of Wisdom: A Bibliographical Note', *Morning Post* (London), 14 November 1928.

H0079 'Lawrence of Arabia Seeking Peace in Waziristan', *Daily News,* 5 December 1928.

H0080 *Daily News and Westminister Gazette,* 5 December 1928. *Note:* Supposed activities in Afghanistan.

H0081 'Lawrence the Ubiquitous', *New York Times,* 11 December 1928, p.30.

H0082 'Lawrence Derides Reports of Spying', *New York Times,* 14 December 1928, p.7.

H0083 Francis Havelock, 'Colonel Lawrence and Trebitsch Lincoln', *Empire News,* 16 December 1928, p.3. *Note:* Supposed activities in Afghanistan.

H0084 'Lawrence of Arabia Arrest "Ordered" by Afghan Authorities', *Daily Herald,* 5 January 1929. *Note:* Supposed activities in Afghanistan.

H0085 'Lawrence of Arabia', *Daily Mail,* 5 January 1929.

H0086 'Lawrence of Arabia Afghan Arrest "Order" Unconfirmed', *Daily Herald,* 7 January 1929.

H0087 'Lawrence is Ordered to Britain From India', *New York Times,* 9 January 1929, p.2.

H0088 'Burn Lawrence in Effigy', *New York Times,* 22 January 1929, p.3.

H0089 'Amanullah Claims His Crown Again', *New York Times,* 29 January 1929, p.2.

H0090 'Lawrence of Arabia Hides in London', *New York Times,* 3 February 1929, p.3.

H0091 'Lawrence of Arabia. Home From India – Exclusive', *Sunday Pictorial,* 3 February 1929, p.1. *Note:* Photos.

H0092 *Daily News,* 4 February 1929. *Note:* Editorial on Lawrence–Afghanistan tempest.

H0093 'Tale of Lawrence Amuses Commons', *New York Times,* 7 February 1929, p.9.

H0094 'Lawrence Bobs Up to Confound Doubter, 9 February 1929, p.7.

H0095 'England's Mystery Man', *New York Times,* 23 February 1929, p.12.

H0096 'To Film "Lawrence of Arabia"', *New York Times,* 8 March 1929, p.9.

H0097 '$1,150 For Lawrence Book', *New York Times,* 16 March 1929, p.10.

H0098 'Private "Shaw" Working', *New York Times,* 11 April 1929, p.14.

H0099 E. Williamson, *New York Times,* 26 May 1929, Part III, p.5. *Note:* Letter to editor.

H0100 *Portland Evening Post,* 2 July 1929, p.5. *Note:* Review of MacPhail, *Three Persons* (E048).

H0101 R.L. Duffur, 'New Judgements on Three of the War's Big Reputations', *New York Times,* 7 July 1929, pt.IV, p.3. *Note:* Review of MacPhail (E048).

H0102 'Lawrence for Palestine', *New York Times,* 31 August 1929, p.14.

H0103 'Say Lawrence is In Area', *New York Times*, 2 September 1929, p.2.

H0104 'Wrongs of the Arabs', *New York Times*, 6 September 1929, p.24.

H0105 'Colonel Lawrence – A Denial', *Morning Post* (London), 28 December 1929.

H0106 T.B. Macauley, 'Colonel Lawrence Again in the News', *New York Times*, 2 March 1930, Part III, p.3.

H0107 'Turkey Astir at News Lawrence is in Region', *New York Times*, 1 May 1930, p.6.

H0108 'Links Col. Lawrence to Kurdish Revolt', *New York Times*, 9 July 1930, p.8.

H0109 J.B. Firth, 'T.E. Lawrence in a New Role: His View of the Odyssey', *Sunday Times*, May 1930.

H0110 'Man Who Might Have Conquered East', *'Unknown'*, October 1930.

H0111 'T.E. Lawrence Reappears', *New York Times*, 3 November 1930, p.7.

H0112 Walter Duranty, 'Plot to Start War Against the Soviet Charged in Moscow', *New York Times*, 12 November 1930, pp.1, 14.

H0113 'The Anti-Soviet Plot', *New York Times*, 13 November 1930, p.24.

H0114 'Lady Astor Rides Motorcycle Driven by Colonel Lawrence', *New York Times*, 17 November 1930, p.1.

H0115 Walter Duranty, '3 Plotters Confess At Moscow Trial; Europe Watches', *New York Times*, 27 November 1930, pp.1, 22.

H0116 'Lady Astor Defends Col. T.E. Lawrence', *New York Times*, 11 December 1930, p.9.

H0117 Clair Price, 'The Most Famous Private in Any Army', *New York Times*, 21 December 1930, Part V, p.6.

H0118 'Colonel Lawrence is Translating the "Odyssey" Into English Verse, But he May Not Publish it', *New York Times*, 27 December 1930, p.1.

H0119 'Lawrence's Version of Odyssey Ready', *New York Times*, 30 December 1930, p.23.

H0120 'A Modern Ascetic', *New York Times*, 31 December 1930, p.16.

H0121 'Col. T.E. Lawrence Eludes University Degree', *New York Times*, 7 January 1931, p.29.

H0122 'Lawrence Has New Hero Role', *Los Angeles Times*, February 1931.

H0123 'Turkish Press Links Lawrence in Revolt', *New York Times*, 2 February 1931, p.4.

H0124 'Col. Lawrence Hero of Fatal Air Disaster', *New York Times*, 11 February 1931, p.9.

H0125 'British Air Fatality Laid to "Novice" Pilot, *New York Times*, 19 February 1931, p.3.

H0126 'T E Lawrence Evidence on Blackburn Iris Flying Boat Disaster', *Western Weekly News*, 21 February 1931.

H0127 Abdul Shahbander, 'Lawrence in the Balance', *Al-Muqtataf* (Cairo), March–July 1931.

H0128 'Lawrence in Obituaries Again; Turks Hear He Died in Air Crash', *New York Times*, 12 March 1931, p.16.

H0129 Henry T. Russell, 'Desert Leader Tells Honor Refusals', *Pasadena Star News*, April 1931.

H0130 Henry T. Russell, 'Great Honors Refused by Soldier', *Pasadena Star News*, April 1931.

H0131 Henry T. Russell, 'Few Ambitions of Mystery Man Told', *Pasadena Star News*, April 1931.

H0132 Henry T. Russell, 'Veil is Lifted by Mystery Officer', *Pasadena Star News*, April 1931.

H0133 Henry T. Russell, 'Arab Revolt Head Tells Secrets', *Pasadena Star News*, April 1931.

H0134 'Lawrence Lauds Thomas', *New York Times*, 25 February 1932, p.19.

H0135 Fanny Butcher, 'T.E. Lawrence's Tale of Arabia', *Chicago Daily Tribune*, 28 September 1932, p.17. *Note:* Review of *Seven Pillars* (A052).

H0136 'Hails Lawrence "Odyssey"', *New York Times*, 6 November 1932, p.5.

H0137 'Lawrence May Visit Arabia Again, Says London News', *New York Times*, 29 November 1932, p.3.

H0138 'A Headlined Private', *New York Times*, 4 December 1932, Part 8, p.6.

H0139 'Led Air Raids For Lawrence, Killed', 1933?

H0140 Edwin C. Hill, 'Human Side of the New "Aircraftsman Shaw"', 1933.

H0141 'Col. Lawrence Seeks to Leave Air Force to Resume Writing', *New York Times*, 16 March 1933, p.15.

H0142 'Feisal, Twice King, Dreamt of Empire', *New York Times*, 9 September 1933, p.3.

H0143 G. Perkins, 'The Arab Revolt – Further Light on Feisal and Lawrence', *Morning Post* (London), 13 September 1933. *Note:* Letter to editor.

H0144 H. Heir Davies, 'Lawrence and Faisal: Their Encounter at Suez', *Morning Post* (London), 13 September 1933.

H0145 Henry T. Russell, 'Lawrence of Arabia Target of Air Bombs', 29 October 1933.

H0146 'British Planes Bomb Unsinkable Speedboat; Lawrence of Arabia Pilots New Test Craft', *New York Times*, 16 December 1933, p.17.

H0147 *Sunday Times*, 4 March 1934. *Note:* Review of Liddell Hart, *TEL in Arabia and After* (E058).

H0148 C.G. Poore, 'Colonel Lawrence Up to Now', *New York Times*, 8 April 1934, Part V, pp.1, 15.

H0149 *Boston Transcript*, 25 April 1934, p.2. *Note:* Review of Liddell Hart, *Col. Lawrence, the Man Behind the Legend* (E061).

H0150 J.M. Pughe, 'Lawrence of Arabia Talks (Exclusive)', *News Chronicle* (London), 11 May 1934, p.1.

H0151 '"Lawrence of Arabia" to be Filmed', *Yorkshire Daily News*, 22 May 1934.

H0152 'Lawrence's Story of Arabia Assailed', *New York Times*, 2 September 1934, p.12.

H0153 'Associates of Lawrence', *Galloway News*, 1935.

H0154 'Lawrence of Arabia', *Dumfries Standard*, 1935.

H0155 'T.E. Lawrence Leaves Book To Publish', 1935.

H0156 'Lawrence of Arabia One of His Last Letters', 1935.

H0157 'Lawrence of Arabia Appreciations', 1935.

H0158 'Secret Book of Lawrence of Arabia', 1935.

H0159 'Lawrence of Arabia Leaves £7,400', 1935.

H0160 Winston Churchill, 'Lawrence of Arabia Was a Man Not a Legend',

News of the World, 1935. *Note:* Illus.

H0161 '"Lawrence of Arabia" to Quit British Army', *New York Times*, 17 February 1935, p.8.

H0162 'Lawrence to Quit RAF', *Milwaukee Sentinel*, 17 February 1935.

H0163 'Lawrence Hero of Arab Revolt to Quit', *Milwaukee Journal*, 17 February 1935.

H0164 *Sunday Express*, 17 February 1935, p.5. *Note:* Letter re TEL.

H0165 'Lawrence Quits Army', *New York Times*, 2 March 1935, p.4.

H0166 'Lawrence of Arabia Discovered Again', *New York Times*, 2 March 1935.

H0167 'Lawrence Leaves Airforce', *Pasadena Star News*, 2 March 1935.

H0168 'Lawrence of Arabia Cycles Into Seclusion', *Wisconsin State Journal*, 3 March 1935.

H0169 'Lawrence of Arabia in Crash, Near Death', May 1935.

H0170 'Lawrence of Arabia', *Reporter* (Leeds, Yorkshire), May 1935.

H0171 'Lawrence of Arabia Dies', *New York Times*, May 1935, pp.1, 3.

H0172 'In the Desert', *Guardman* (Scotland), May 1935.

H0173 L.H. Ingham, 'Man Who Exercised a Remarkable Spell "Lawrence of Arabia"', *Western Morning News and Daily Gazette*, May 1935.

H0174 John MacKay, 'In the Desert Scots Driver's Tales of Lawrence's Exploits', *The Scotsman*, May 1935.

H0175 'Dishonest Thing', *New York Times*, 4 May 1935, p.15. *Note:* Mention of Lawrence.

H0176 'Mr. T.E. Shaw', *The Times*, 5–8 May 1935. *Note:* Series of articles.

H0177 '"Lawrence of Arabia"', *News Chronicle* (London), 8 May 1935, p.1.

H0178 Ferdinand Kuhn, 'Lawrence of Arabia Dying After Crash on Motorcycle', *New York Times*, 14 May 1935, pp.1, 4.

H0179 '"Lawrence of Arabia" Unconscious', *Leicester Mercury*, 14 May 1935, p.1.

H0180 'Lawrence of Arabia Very Ill', *Evening News* (London), 14 May 1935.

H0181 'Lawrence of Arabia Hurt in Highway Crash', *Chicago Tribune*, 14 May 1935.

H0182 *Daily Express*, 14 May 1935. *Note:* Report on Lawrence's accident.

H0183 'Lawrence of Arabia Unconscious', *Star* (London), 14 May 1935.

H0184 'Lawrence of Arabia Injured Seriously', *St. Paul Dispatch*, 14 May 1935.

H0185 Ferdinand Kuhn Jr., 'Lawrence Lingers But Hope is Faint', *New York Times*, 15 May 1935, pp.1, 18.

H0186 'Col. Lawrence Close to Death', *Milwaukee Sentinel*, 15 May 1935.

H0187 'Col. Lawrence is Badly Hurt', *Milwaukee Journal*, 15 May 1935.

H0188 'Surgeons Struggle to Save Lawrence', *Milwaukee Journal*, 15 May 1935.

H0189 'Col. Lawrence Fights for Life', *Duluth News Tribune*, 15 May 1935.

H0190 'An Author Brands Own Masterpiece', *Daily Cardinal* (Palo Alto, California), 15 May 1935.

H0191 'British King's Doctor Fighting...', *Chicago Tribune*, 15 May 1935.

H0192 'Lawrence of Arabia Guard Over State Papers', *Daily Mirror*, 15 May 1935, p.1.

H0193 *Daily Sketch*, 15 May 1935. *Note:* Report on Lawrence's accident.

H0194 'Condition of Lawrence of Arabia is Critical, 15 May 1935.
H0195 'Lawrence Facing the Crisis Today', *New York Times,* 16 May 1935, p.11.
H0196 'Col. Lawrence is Near Crisis', *Milwaukee State Journal,* 16 May 1935.
H0197 'Lawrence Clings to Life', *Milwaukee Sentinel,* 16 May 1935.
H0198 'Lawrence: Grave Anxiety', *Evening Standard,* 16 May 1935, p.1.
H0199 'Lawrence of Arabia Is Given Fighting Chance', *Chicago Tribune,* 16 May 1935.
H0200 'Lawrence: Grave Fears', *Star* (London), 16 May 1935, p.1. *Note:* Illus.
H0201 'Lawrence No Better but Hopes are Held', *New York Times,* 17 May 1935, p.23.
H0202 'Col. Lawrence is Still Unconscious', *Wisconsin News,* 17 May 1935.
H0203 'Lawrence of Arabia Still Unconsious', *New York Times,* 18 May 1935, p.8.
H0204 'Lawrence is Kept Closely Guarded', *Milwaukee Sentinel,* 18 May 1935.
H0205 'Scorn for Honors Marked Romantic Career of Lawrence, Hero of Arabia', *New York Times,* 19 May 1935, p.34.
H0206 'Lawrence Dies of Crash Injuries After a Six-Day Fight by Doctors', *New York Times,* 19 May 1935, pp.1, 34.
H0207 'Lawrence is Near Death', *Milwaukee Sentinel,* 19 May 1935.
H0208 'Col. Lawrence is Near Death', *Milwaukee Journal,* 19 May 1935.
H0209 'Lawrence of Arabia Dies of Motorcycle Injuries', *Los Angeles Times,* 19 May 1935.
H0210 *Sunday Express,* 19 May 1935. *Note:* Obituary.
H0211 'Lawrence Grave News Last Night', *Sunday Chronicle,* 19 May 1935, p.1.
H0212 'Intimate Friend: The Lawrence Nobody Knows', *Sunday Chronicle,* 19 May 1935, p.5. *Note:* Photo.
H0213 One Who Served Under Him, 'Lawrence of Arabia's Secret Power', *The People,* 19 May 1935. *Note:* Illus.
H0214 'Strangest Adventures of the War', *Morning Post,* 20 May 1935.
H0215 '"T.E."', *New York Times,* 20 May 1935, p.16.
H0216 Ferdinand Kuhn, 'Lawrence to Have a Simple Funeral', *New York Times,* 20 May 1935, pp.1, 10.
H0218 'Lawrence Dead: Britain Honors Hero of Arabia', *New York Herald Tribune,* 20 May 1935, p.1.
H0219 John Buchan', *New York Herald Tribune,* 20 May 1935. *Note:* Obituary.
H0220 'Lawrence, Scholar and Archaeologist in Early Life Freed Arabia from Turks', *New York Herald Tribune,* 20 May 1935.
H0221 'Death Brings New...', *Milwaukee Sentinel,* 20 May 1935.
H0222 'Nations Mourn', *Milwaukee Journal,* 20 May 1935.
H0223 L.B.Namier, 'Lawrence: As I Knew Him', *Manchester Guardian,* 20 May 1935, pp.9–10.
H0224 'All England Mourns Passing of Lawrence', *Los Angeles Times,* 20 May 1935.
H0225 '"Lawrence of Arabia" Led Colorful Life', *Los Angeles Examiner,* 20 May 1935, Section I, p.16. *Note:* Illus.

H0226 'The Real Lawrence', *Empire News*, 20 May 1935.
H0227 'Lawrence of Arabia Inquest Tomorrow', *Daily Telegraph*, 20 May 1935, p.14.
H0228 W.F. Stirling, 'Lawrence of Arabia', *Daily Telegraph*, 20 May 1935, p.12.
H0229 Sean Fielding, 'Last Fight For Life: Lawrence of Arabia Secrets Revealed', *Daily Mail*, 20 May 1935.
H0230 'Village Funeral for Lawrence of Arabia', *Morning Post*, 20 May 1935.
H0231 'How Lawrence Organized Revolt in the Desert', *Daily Telegraph*, 20 May 1935, p.9.
H0232 Lord Allenby, 'T.E. Lawrence', *Daily Express*, 20 May 1935. *Note:* Allenby broadcast.
H0233 *Daily Express*, 20 May 1935, p.12. *Note:* Letter to editor.
H0234 'Englishmen Urge', *Chicago Herald Examiner*, 20 May 1935.
H0235 John Gunther, 'Britannia's Greatest Names Join in Paying Tribute to "Lawrence of Arabia"', *Chicago Daily News*, 20 May 1935.
H0236 'Too Big For Wealth and Glory Lawrence the Soldier Dies to Live Forever', *Daily Sketch*, 20 May 1935, p.1. *Note:* P.3, Lawrence: The Last Hours.
H0237 'Continuous Use of Oxygen Fails to Revive Colonel Lawrence', *San Antonio Express*, 20 May 1935, p.1.
H0238 'Scholar Turned Fighter', *Toronto Telegram*, 20 May 1935. *Note:* Also, 'Lawrence Hides in Obscurity Even When Near Death, Famed Arabian Fighter Still Holding On'.
H0239 'Lord Allenby's Tribute', *The Times*, 20 May 1935, p.16.
H0240 Basil Henry Liddell Hart, 'A Genius of War and Letters; The Desert Revolt', *The Times*, 20 May 1935, pp.14–16.
H0241 'Lawrence Dead', *The Times*, 20 May 1935. *Note:* D16.
H0242 Ronald Storrs, 'The Lawrence I Knew', *Star* (London), 20 May 1935, p.4.
H0243 'Strategist of Desert Dies in Military Hospital', *Manchester Guardian*, 20 May 1935.
H0244 'T.E. Lawrence's Amazing Career', *San Francisco Examiner*, 20 May 1935.
H0245 'Lawrence of Arabia Dies of Injuries', Portland (Oregon) newspaper, 20 May 1935.
H0246 'Lawrence of Arabia', *Morning Post*, 20 May 1935. *Note:* Editorial.
H0247 'Lawrence Death', *News Chronicle* (London), 20 May 1935.
H0248 'Lawrence Man of Mysteries', *Daily Sketch*, 20 May 1935.
H0249 'T.E. Lawrence', *Manchester Guardian*, 20 May 1935. *Note:* Editorial.
H0250 'Death of T.E. Lawrence', *News Chronicle* (London), 20 May 1935.
H0251 'Lawrence of Arabia', *The Times*, 21 May 1935. *Note:* King's Tribute.
H0252 'Lawrence's Life Extolled by King', *New York Times*, 21 May 1935, p.9.
H0253 'News Broken to Mother', *The Times*, 21 May 1935.
H0254 'Mystery Shrouded Lawrence Secret Told by Friend', *New York Times*, 21 May 1935.
H0255 '"Uncrowned King's" Simple Burial', *Leicester Mercury*, 21 May 1935, pp.1, 16.
H0256 'Lawrence of Arabia Buried', *Evening News*, 21 May 1935, pp.1, 6.

H0257 'Lawrence of Arabia Funeral Today', *Daily Telegraph,* 21 May 1935, p.16.

H0258 E.F. Lawson, 'A Meeting with Lawrence', *Daily Telegraph,* 21 May 1935, p.14.

H0259 'Mystery of Car', *Evening Standard,* 21 May 1935.

H0260 'Arabian Hero's Mother Victim of China Reds', *Chicago Herald Examiner,* 21 May 1935.

H0261 'Mound Alone Marks Where Lawrence Lies, 21 May 1935.

H0262 'Britian Mourns T.E. Lawrence. British War Leader in Arabia', 21 May 1935.

H0263 'Conflicting Evidence at Lawrence Inquest', *Star* (London), 21 May 1935, p.9.

H0264 H.A.R. Philby, 'The New Arabia', *Star* (London), 21 May 1935, p.4.

H0265 'Inquest on "Lawrence of Arabia"', *Star* (London), 21 May 1935, p.1.

H0266 'Last Hours of Lawrence', *Daily Telegraph,* 21 May 1935.

H0267 'Lawrence Buried With Simple Rites', *New York Times,* 22 May 1935, p.19.

H0268 'Lawrence's Own Obituary', *Toronto Telegram,* 22 May 1935. *Note:* Also, 'Flag He Served So Well Shrouds Lawrence'.

H0269 'He Staked Himself', *New York Times,* 22 May 1935, p.18.

H0270 'Col. Buried Without a Word of Praise', *New York Herald Tribune,* 22 May 1935.

H0271 'Bury Lawrence in Simple Rites', *Milwaukee Journal,* 22 May 1935.

H0272 'Mystery of Black Car', *Daily Sketch,* 22 May 1935, p.5.

H0273 'Great and Humble Mourn "Col. Lawrence"', *Daily Sketch,* 22 May 1935, p.5. *Notes:* Illus.

H0274 'Lawrence Inquest: Car Mystery', *Daily Record and Mail,* 22 May 1935.

H0275 'Lawrence's Meadow Grave', *Daily Mirror,* 22 May 1935, p.1.

H0276 'Comrades Meet at Grave', *Daily Herald,* 22 May 1935. *Note:* Photo.

H0277 'Mystery Car', *Chicago Tribune,* 22 May 1935.

H0278 'Britain, Arabia Mourn Death of Col. Lawrence', *Chicago Tribune,* 22 May 1935.

H0279 'Lawrence of Arabia', *The Times,* 22 May 1935.

H0280 'T.E. Lawrence's Death', *News Chronicle and Manchester Guardian,* 22 May 1935.

H0281 'T.E. Lawrence Unreal Service', *News Chronicle* (London), 22 May 1935.

H0282 'Peer and Private Pay Tribute', *News Chronicle* (London), 22 May 1935, p.7.

H0283 *Morning Post,* 22 May 1935. *Note:* Letters to editor: Colin Templeton, Katherine Buck.

H0284 'Farewell to Lawrence', *Morning Post,* 22 May 1935.

H0285 H. de Winton Wigley, 'All Equal At Lawrence's Funeral', *News Chronicle* (London), 22 May 1935.

H0286 Walter Anderson, 'Memories of Lawrence', *Daily Telegraph,* 22 May 1935.

H0287 'No Military Ceremony at Funeral', 23 May 1935.

H0288 '"Lawrence of Arabia" His Own Story', *Yorkshire Evening Post,* 23 May 1935.

H0289 'I Did Not Die in 1935', *Yorkshire Evening News*, 23 May 1935? *Note:* Map of T.E. Lawrence's journeys; 1912–1913.

H0290 'New Lawrence of Arabia Letters', *The Star* (London), 23 May 1935, pp.1, 8.

H0291 S.C. Rolls, 'Lawrence of Arabia: A Northampton Comrade's Memories', *Northampton Independent*, 24 May 1935.

H0292 'Lawrence's Own Epitaph', *New York Times*, 26 May 1935, Section IV, p.5.

H0293 'The Simple Funeral of Lawrence of Arabia', *New York Times*, 27 May 1935, p.17.

H0294 'Britain Not Planning Lawrence Memorial', *New York Times*, 28 May 1935, p.25.

H0295 'Adopts Lawrence Medal', *New York Times*, 29 May 1935, p.23.

H0296 Walter Winchell, *Wisconsin State Journal*, 29 May 1935.

H0297 'Lawrence of Arabia', *The Times*, 30 May 1935. *Note:* Editorial.

H0298 'Lawrence's Book to Appear in Full', *New York Times*, 31 May 1935, p.13.

H0299 Arnold Walter Lawrence, 'Seven Pillars of Wisdom', *The Times*, 31 May 1935, p.16. *Note:* Publication plans discussed.

H0300 'Lawrence's Death Denied', June 1935.

H0301 'Memorial to Lawrence', *The Times*, 2 June 1935.

H0302 'Falsity is Denied', *New York Times*, 2 June 1935, Part IV, p.9.

H0303 'Lawrence Left a MSS.', *New York Times*, 3 June 1935, p.15.

H0304 A.J.L., 'The Last Portrait of Aircraftsman Shaw', *Daily Telegraph*, 3 June 1935. *Note:* Illus.

H0305 Raymond Savage, 'Lawrence's Writing', *The Times*, 13 June 1935.

H0306 'Insist Lawrence Lives', 14 June 1935.

H0307 'News and Views of London', *New York Times*, 16 June 1935. *Note:* Mention of Lawrence.

H0308 'These Names Make News', *Daily Express*, 19 June 1935.

H0309 'Lawrence's Essay', *Sunday Dispatch*, 23 June 1935.

H0310 Jacob de Haas, 'Lawrence of Arabia', *New York Times*, 23 June 1935, Part IV, p.9. *Note:* Letter to editor.

H0311 *Springfield Republican*, 30 June 1935, p.5e. *Note:* Review of *Seven Pillars* (A054).

H0312 E.M. Hopkins, 'Evolution of Iraq', *New York Times*, 30 June 1935, Part IV, p.9. *Note:* Letter to editor.

H0313 'Storrs and Lawrence', *New York Times*, 5 July 1935, p.12.

H0314 'Lawrence of Arabia', *New York Times*, 8 July 1935, p.14. *Note:* Letter to editor.

H0315 'Lawrence's Royalties Finance Education Fund', *New York Times*, 10 July 1935, p.19.

H0316 'Lawrence Fund Left to Orphans', *Milwaukee Sentinel*, 11 July 1935.

H0317 'Lawrence of Arabia Memorial', *Morning Post*, 24 July 1935.

H0318 'Britain Plans Memorial to Lawrence of Arabia', *New York Times*, 24 July 1935, p.1.

H0319 'Lawrence's Book is Due in the Fall', *New York Times*, 26 July 1935, p.13.

H0320 H.A.R. Philby, *Sunday Times*, 28 July 1935. *Note:* Review of *Seven Pillars of Wisdom* (A042).

H0321 Winston Churchill, 'Lawrence's Great Book', *Daily Mail*, 29 July 1935, p.8.

H0322 L.B. Namier, *Manchester Guardian*, 29 July 1935. *Note:* Review of *Seven Pillars of Wisdom* (A042).

H0323 'Seven Pillars of Wisdom', *The Times*, 29 July 1935. *Note:* Review.

H0324 J.B. Firth, 'How Lawrence of Arabia Saw Himself', *Daily Telegraph*, 29 July 1935. *Note:* Review of *Seven Pillars* (A042).

H0325 'Seven Pillars of Wisdom', *The Times*, 29 July 1935. *Note:* Review.

H0326 '$500,000 Price of Book, August 1935.

H0327 *Sunday Graphic and Sunday News*, 4 August 1935. *Note:* Notes on *Seven Pillars*.

H0328 'The Odyssey Lawrence's Unique Version', *The Scotsman*, 15 August 1935.

H0329 G. Grigson, 'Colonel Lawrence and His Unorthodox Views of Homer', *Morning Post* (London), 16 August 1935.

H0330 *The Times*, 16 August 1935. *Note:* Review of *The Odyssey* (A144).

H0331 *New York Times*, 24 August 1935, p.14. *Note:* Short note on memorial for Lawrence, no title.

H0332 'Lawrence Book Rips British', *Milwaukee State Journal*, 28 August 1935.

H0333 'Lawrence's Last Book', *Milwaukee Journal*, 28 August 1935.

H0334 'Lawence Book Price Set at $500,000', *Los Angeles Times*, 28 August 1935.

H0335 'Spirit of Lawrence of Arabia', *Milwaukee Journal*, 4 September 1935.

H0336 'Lawrence of Arabia', *Los Angeles Times*, 8 September 1935.

H0337 'Lawrence of Arabia Estate', *The Times*, 8 September 1935.

H0338 *Christian Science Monitor*, 14 September 1935, p.11. *Note:* Review of *Seven Pillars* (A054).

H0339 'Col. Lawrence Reports, Also A Col. Lawrence Manuscript', *Daily Telegraph*, 25 September 1935.

H0340 'Lawrence Report On Revolt is Sold', *New York Times*, 25 September 1935, p.26.

H0341 'Lawrence MSS', *Daily Telegraph*, 26 September 1935.

H0342 'Lawrence of Arabia', *Morning Post*, 26 September 1935.

H0343 'Arabs Offer Troops', *Milwaukee Sentinel*, 27 September 1935.

H0344 *New York Post*, 28 September 1935, p.7. *Note:* Review of *Seven Pillars* (A054).

H0345 *Boston Transcript*, 28 September 1935, p.1. *Note:* Review of *Seven Pillars* (A054).

H0346 John H. Finley, 'Lawrence's Epic of Arabia', *New York Times*, 29 September 1935, Part VI, pp.1, 15.

H0347 'Lawrence Clew Seen', *Los Angeles Times*, 6 October 1935.

H0348 'Lawrence's *Seven Pillars* Exceeds Fondest Hopes', 13 October 1935.

H0349 *Capitol Tribune*, 30 November 1935. *Note:* Q & A re TEL.

H0350 'T.E. Lawrence Notes Bring $500 in London', *Capitol Tribune*, 30 November 1935.

H0351 'Lawrence Cottage Kept as Memorial', *Chicago Tribune*, 29 December 1935.

H0352 'T.E. Lawrence Funeral', *Daily Telegraph*, 31 December 1935.

H0353 Edwin Muir, 'Aspects of an Enigmatic Personality', 1936. *Note:* Review of V. Richards, *Portrait* (E097).

H0354 Mary Johnson, *New York Times*, 5 January 1936, Part IV, p.9. *Note:* Letter to editor.

H0355 'Few Visit Lawrence Cottage', *New York Times*, 19 January 1936, Part IV, p.5.

H0356 'Lawrence Memorial', *The Times*, 29 January 1936.

H0357 'Lawrence of Arabia Threw His Sheikh's Robes into Thames', *Daily Mirror*, 30 January 1936.

H0358 'Lawrence of Arabia is Honored in London; Memorial Bust is Dedicated at St. Paul's', *New York Times*, 30 January 1936, p.13.

H0359 'Memorial Unveiled at St. Paul's', 30 January 1936.

H0360 Lord Halifax, 'Lawrence of Arabia', *The Times*, 31 January 1936. *Note:* Photo.

H0361 'Lawrence Letters Sold for $3,800 Here', *New York Times*, 31 January 1936, p.13.

H0362 *Christian Science Monitor*, 5 February 1936, p.14. *Note:* Review of Edmonds, *T.E. Lawrence* (E081).

H0363 'Did Lawrence Have Premonition of Death?', 8 March 1936.

H0364 *The Times*, 12 March 1936. *Note:* Review of *The Wilderness of Zin* (A006).

H0365 'Hero's Letters Shown', *Los Angeles Times*, 22 March 1936.

H0366 *Springfield Republican*, 29 March 1936, p.7. *Note:* Review of Edmonds (E081).

H0367 *Boston Transcript*, 29 April 1936, p.15. *Note:* Review of Shumway, *Lawrence, the Arabian Knight* (E090).

H0368 'Lawrence', *New York Herald Tribune*, 7 June 1936, p.7. *Note:* Review of Shumway.

H0369 Chaim Weizman , 'Arabs & Zionists', *The Times*, 10 June 1936, p.15. *Note:* Includes facsimile of TEL's note of Arab-Jewish Pact 1919.

H0370 *The Times*, 3 July 1936. *Note:* Review of *Crusader Castles* (E188).

H0371 Edward Shanks, 'Memories of T.E. Lawrence', *Sunday Times*, 5 July 1936. *Note:* Review of Richards (E097).

H0372 'Relics of Lawrence', *The Times*, 30 January 1936.

H0373 'Col. Lawrence Letters Sold', *Los Angeles Times*, 11 November 1936.

H0374 *Capitol Tribune*, 15 November 1936.

H0375 'New Lawrence Volume Causes Concern in Britain', *Los Angeles Times*, 5 December 1936, p.3.

H0376 'The £100,000 Book by Lawrence', *Evening Standard*, 17 December 1936. *Note:* Review of *The Mint* (A166).

H0377 'Lawrence Manuscript Sold to Pay a Blackmailer', *Evening Standard*, 16 January 1937.

H0378 *Boston Transcript*, 20 March 1937, p.4. *Note:* Review of Rodman, *Lawrence, the Last Crusade* (E116).

H0379 *Christian Science Monitor*, 24 March 1937, p.12. *Note:* Review of Rodman (E116).

H0380 *Manchester Guardian,* 20 April 1937. *Note:* Review of Altounyan, *Ornament of Honour* (E113).

H0381 *Manchester Guardian,* 21 May 1937. *Note:* Review of *TEL by His Friends* (E107).

H0382 Geoffrey Grigson, 'Lawrence of Arabia: The One-Man Monastery', *Morning Post,* 25 May 1937. *Note:* Review of *TEL By His Friends* (E107) and *Steel Chariots* (E114).

H0383 'T.E. Lawrence Notes Bring $500 in London', *New York Times,* 17 June 1937, p.33.

H0384 'Writer on Lawrence Sentenced in Fraud', *New York Times,* 17 June 1937, p.25.

H0385 *Springfield Republican,* 27 June 1937, p.7e. *Note:* Review of *TEL by His Friends* (E107).

H0386 *Christian Science Monitor,* 30 June 1937, p.10. *Note:* Review of *TEL by His Friends* (E107).

H0387 *Boston Transcript,* 10 July 1937. *Note:* Review of *TEL by His Friends* (E107).

H0388 *Boston Transcript,* 2 October 1937, p.2. *Note:* Review of Altounyan (E113).

H0389 *San Francisco Chronicle,* 31 October 1937, p.2.

H0390 'Gives Lawrence's Home', *New York Times,* 26 May 1938, p.23.

H0391 'T.E. Lawrence to His Friends', *The Times,* 17 November 1938, p.8.

H0392 'Lawrence of Arabia', *New York Times,* 19 November 1938, p.16.

H0393 'David Garnett's "Lawrence"', *New York Times,* 23 November 1938, p.20.

H0394 'T.E. Lawrence in His Letters', *The Times,* 26 November 1938.

H0395 *Christian Science Monitor,* 14 December 1938, p.10. *Note:* Review of *The Letters* (A204).

H0396 *Boston Evening Transcript,* 31 December 1938, p.2. *Note:* Review of Duval, *TEL, A Bibliography* (E119).

H0397 O. Karsten, 'T.E. Lawrence: Die Sieben Säulen der Weisheit', *Kölnische Zeitung,* 1939, 207–208.

H0398 L.B. Namier, *Manchester Guardian,* 7 January 1939. *Note:* Review of *The Letters* (A202).

H0399 H. Gorman, *The Times,* 7 January 1939. *Note:* Review of *TEL to His Biographers* (A210–11).

H0400 Edward Shanks, 'T.E. Lawrence on Self', *Sunday Times,* February 1939.

H0401 *Manchester Guardian,* 14 March 1939, p.7. *Note:* Review of *TEL to His Biographers* (A210–11).

H0402 Sam Chew, 'Greatness and Pettiness of T.E. Lawrence', *New York Herald Tribune,* 26 March 1939, Section IX, p.3. *Note:* Review of *The Letters* (A204).

H0403 'Lawrence Accused Himself of Deceit Held Pledges Worthless', *New York Times,* 23 May 1939, p.13.

H0404 *Boston Transcript,* 25 May 1939, p.1. *Note:* Review of *The Letters* (A204).

H0405 'Briton's Confession of Tricking Arabs Disclosed', *Los Angeles Times,* 28 May 1939.

H0406 'T.E. Lawrence on Elgar', *New York Times*, 4 June 1939, Part IX, p.6.

H0407 'Desert Woman Chieftain', *The People*, 2 July 1939.

H0408 'Buddy of Lawrence of Arabia Tells Wartime Experiences', *Los Angeles Times*, 16 July 1939, pp.1–2.

H0409 B.H. Liddell Hart, *London Mercury*, December 1939. *Note:* Review of *The Letters* (A202).

H0410 'Arab Revolt Celebrated', *News of The World*, 1940.

H0411 Winston Churchill, 'Lawrence of Arabia As I Knew Him', *Sunday Dispatch*, 19 May 1940, p.1. *Note:* Illus.

H0412 'Lawrence as Critic', *Manchester Guardian*, 4 October 1940.

H0413 *New York Times*, 29 June 1941, Section VI, p.2. *Note:* Review of *The Letters* (A204).

H0414 Martha Tucker, 'Devotees of the Desert', *New York Times*, 21 September 1941, Section VIII, p.26.

H0415 'Estate Bars Issuance of Lawrence Book', *New York Times*, 25 March 1944.

H0416 'Lettres sur les Sept Piliers', *Lettres Françaises* (Buenos Aires), 1 January 1945, 15, pp.21–35.

H0417 'Letters May Be Fakes', *Daily Mail*, 1 January 1945, p.3.

H0418 'Wilson, House and the Arabs in 1919', *New York Times*, 5 June 1945, p.18.

H0419 Lowell Thomas, 'Lawrence of Arabia and the False Lawrence', *Los Angeles Times*, 7 and 22 July 1945.

H0420 Edgar Morin, 'Les Héros désespérés ou le mal d'aujourd'hui', *Les Lettres Françaises*, 18 July 1947, pp.1, 3.

H0421 André Rousseaux, 'Les Lettres de T.E. Lawrence', *Le Figaro Littéraire*, 12 March 1949.

H0422 M. Brion, 'Lawrence d'Arabie et Son Secret', *Le Monde*, 14 April 1949, (13).

H0423 Joseph Garretson, 'More on Lawrence', *Cincinnati Enquirer*, 15 February 1950.

H0424 Émile Henroit, 'Le Portrait d'un Aventurier', *Le Monde*, 21 February 1951.

H0425 W.E. John, 'How Lawrence Joined the R.A.F.', *Sunday Times*, 8 April 1951, p.5.

H0426 Pierre de Boisdeffre, 'T.E. Lawrence Héritier de Nietzsche', *Le Journal de Genève*, 23–24 February 1952, 46, p.304.

H0427 B.H. Liddell Hart, 'Lawrence of Arabia A Genius', *The Times*, 20 May 1952, pp.15–16.

H0428 Alfred Taylor, 'Desert Lamb ', *?* (Leeds, Yorkshire), 1953.

H0429 'The House Over the Hedge', ____ *Post*, 1953. *Note:* London.

H0430 'Bridlington Memorial to Lawrence of Arabia', *Hull Daily Mail*, 24 September 1953.

H0431 'Bridlington Memorial to Lawrence of Arabia Unveiled', *Bridlington Free Press*, 25 September 1953, p.1.

H0432 *Evening Standard*, 19 January 1954, p.4. *Note:* Article on Aldington (E192).

H0433 'Le Colonel Lawrence, bouffon et bluffeur, faux héros et authentique mystificateur', *Aux Écoutes*, 29 January 1954.

H0434 'Pour Détruire la Légende de Lawrence', *Samedi-Soir*, 4 March 1954.
H0435 Richard Aldington, 'Lawrence d'Arabie fut-il un produit de la publicité?', *Le Figaro Littéraire*, 17 April 1954. *Note:* Part 3, Chapter II, Aldington (E190).
H0436 *The Times*, 30 June 1954. *Note:* Review of *The Home Letters* (A246).
H0437 *Sunday Times*, 4 July 1954. *Note:* Review of *The Home Letters* (A246).
H0438 *Springfield Republican*, 1 August 1954, p.4c. *Note:* Review of *The Home Letters* (A247).
H0439 *Christian Science Monitor*, 6 October 1954, p.9. *Note:* Review of *The Home Letters* (A247).
H0440 *Chicago Sunday Tribune*, 24 October 1954, p.6. *Note:* Review of *The Home Letters* (A247).
H0441 Jean Béraud-Villars, 'L'Affaire "Lawrence"', *Le Monde*, 26 November 1954.
H0442 Pia Pasca, 'T.E. Lawrence, imposteur ou mystificateur?', *Carrefour*, 1 December 1954.
H0443 R.C., *Le Maine Libre* (Le Mans), 7 December 1954. *Note:* Review of Aldington (E190).
H0444 Pierre Lamore, 'Controverse autour d'une légende. L'Affaire Lawrence', *Le Monde*, 8 December 1954.
H0445 *Franc-Tireur*, 16 December 1954. *Note:* Review of J. Béraud-Villars, *Le Colonel Lawrence* (E204).
H0446 Pierre Loewel, *L'Aurore*, 21 December 1954. *Note:* Review of Aldington (E190).
H0447 *Le Maine Libre* (Le Mans), 30 December 1954. *Note:* Announcement of Béraud-Villars.
H0448 H.P. Ziman Danzig, 'Self-Portrait of T.E. Lawrence', *Daily Telegraph*, 1955. *Note:* Review of *The Mint* (A173).
H0449 Don Davis, 'Misconception', *Christian Science Monitor*, 1955. *Note:* Letter to editor re Aldington.
H0450 *L'Écho-Liberté*, 4 January 1955. *Note:* Review of Béraud-Villars (E204).
H0451 Roger Giron, 'L'Homme le plus Mystérieux de l'Autre Guerre', *France Soir*, 7 January 1955.
H0452 'Lawrence – Held oder Hochstapler', *Der Tagespiegel*, 9 January 1955.
H0453 'Lawrence-Enthüllung in Paris Erscheinen', *Stuttgarter Zeitung*, 18 January 1955, p.2.
H0454 A.W. Lawrence, 'Lawrence of Arabia in the R.A.F.', *Sunday Times*, 23 January 1955, p.6.
H0455 A. Williams, 'The Making of *The Mint*', *Sunday Times*, 23 January 1955, p.6.
H0456 'Lawrence de Arabie, un imposteur?', *La Libre Belgique*, 26 January 1955.
H0457 *Aux Ecoutes*, 29 January 1955. *Note:* Review of Aldington (E190).
H0458 Raymond Mortimer, 'T.E. Lawrence Mr. Aldington's Charges', *Sunday Times*, 30 January 1955, p.5.
H0459 Lord Vansittart, 'The Lawrence Legend', *Daily Telegraph*, 31 January 1955. *Note:* Review of Aldington (E192); see also H0463.
H0460 B.H. Liddell Hart, 'Lawrence', *Sunday Chronicle*, 31 January 1955.

H0461 Robert Graves, 'The Lawrence I Knew', *News Chronicle* (London), 31 January 1955.

H0462 *Lire* (Algeria), February 1955. *Note:* Review of Aldington.

H0463 John Rosselli, 'The Devil's Advocate', *Manchester Guardian*, 1 February 1955. *Note:* Review of Aldington.

H0464 'Richard Aldington Defends His Book', *Daily Mail*, 1 February 1955.

H0465 'Lawrence and His Legend', *The Times*, 2 February 1955.

H0466 W.H. Brook, 'Lawrence Man and Legend', *Daily Telegraph*, 2 February 1955.

H0467 Jane Albert-Hesse, 'Autour du Mystère de Lawrence d'Arabie', 3 February 1955.

H0468 Gerard Andrieux, 'Lawrence l'Imposteur', *Paris-Casablanca*, 5 February 1955.

H0469 'Lawrence of Arabia', *The Times*, 6 February 1955, p.2.

H0470 Jock Chambers and Rev. Archibald McHandy, 'Lawrence of Arabia', *Sunday Times*, 6 February 1955. *Note:* Letter to editor.

H0471 *Noir et Blanc*, 7 February 1955. *Note:* Review of Aldington (E190).

H0472 *Observateur*, 10 February 1955. *Note:* Review of *The Mint* (A182).

H0473 'Enigma That Was Lawrence of Arabia', *Hull Daily Mail*, 12 February 1955.

H0474 H.E. Bates, 'The Mint is Bound to Shock', *News Chronicle (London)*, 14 February 1955. *Note:* Review of *The Mint* (A173).

H0475 F.B. Metcalfe, '540109 ex A/c2 Erk's Eyeview of Lawrence', *Manchester Guardian*, 17 February 1955, p.5. *Note:* Illus.

H0476 'Solitary in the Ranks', *The Times*, 17 February 1955. *Note:* Review of *The Mint* (A173).

H0477 H.D. Ziman, 'Damaging Self-Portrait of T.E. Lawrence', *Daily Telegraph*, 18 February 1955. *Note:* Review of *The Mint* (A173).

H0478 *Daily Telegraph*, 14 February 1955. *Note:* Letter to editor by Earl Winterton, Brian Stuart, W.F.Stirling, R. Gilman and Wallace Stokes.

H0479 Ronald Storrs, *Sunday Times*, 20 February 1955. *Note:* Review of *The Mint* (A173).

H0480 George Barrow, 'Desert Encounter With Lawrence', *Daily Telegraph*, February 1955.

H0481 'Lawrence Détestait la France parce Qu'il aimait Dahoum', *France-Dimanche*, 24 February 1955.

H0482 'Démolisseur de Lawrence d'Arabie', *La Presse*, 28 February 1955.

H0483 Sydney Smith, 'Why I Decided to Debunk a Hero', *Times of Brazil*, 1 March 1955.

H0484 Michel Chrestien, *La Semaine Internationale*, 9 March 1955. *Note:* Review of Aldington (E190).

H0485 'T.E. Lawrence dans son pays', *France-Observateur*, 10 March 1955. *Note:* Review of Aldington (E190).

H0486 *L'Écho d'Alger*, 15 March 1955. *Note:* Review of Aldington (E190).

H0487 Pierre Mazars, 'Du Fond de Son Tombeau, le Colonel Lawrence Répond a Son Détracteur Aldington', *Le Figaro*, 16 March 1955.

H0488 'Lawrence Confond ses Détracteurs', *Carrefour*, 16 March 1955. *Note:* Review of *The Mint* (A182).

H0489 *New York Times,* 20 March 1955, Section VII, p.3. *Note:* Review of *The Mint* (A168).

H0490 *New York Herald Tribune,* 20 March 1955. *Note:* Review of *The Mint* (A168).

H0491 *La Libre Belgique,* 23 March 1955. *Note:* Review of *The Mint* (A168).

H0492 Roger Stéphane, 'Les Mémoires d'Outre-Tombe de Lawrence', *France-Observateur,* 24 March 1955.

H0493 *Christian Science Monitor,* 24 March 1955, p.17. *Note:* Review of *The Mint* (A168).

H0494 Anne Manson, 'Le Matricule 338.171, c'était le Colonel Lawrence', *Paris-Presse,* 25 March 1955.

H0495 J. Brenner, 'La Matrice, de T.E. Lawrence', *Paris-Normandie* (Rouen), 25 March 1955.

H0496 *San Francisco Chronicle,* 27 March 1955, p.18. *Note:* Review of *The Mint* (A168).

H0497 *Springfield Republican,* 10 April 1955, p.6c. *Note:* Review of *The Mint* (A168).

H0498 G. Venaissin, *Combat (France),* 14 April 1955. *Note:* Review of *The Mint* (A168).

H0499 Michel Chrestien, 'Un fils de roi rampant', *La Semaine Internationale,* 26 April 1955.

H0500 Emile Bouvier, 'Les Gaieté s de l'Escadrille', *Midi Libre,* 27 April 1955.

H0501 'Lawrence's Friend Refuses to Sell His Letters', *?* (Yorkshire), May 1955.

H0502 Charly Guyot, 'Du Colonel Lawrence Au Soldat J.H. Ross', *Le Journal de Genève,* 8 May 1955.

H0503 J.P.A., 'T.E.L. Héros ou Imposteur?', *La Gazette de Lausanne,* 11 May 1955.

H0504 *L'Écho-Liberté,* 24 May 1955. *Note:* Review of Béraud-Villars, *Le Colonel Lawrence* (E204).

H0505 Y.B., *Lettres Françaises* (Buenos Aires), 26 May 1955. *Note:* Review of *The Mint* (A182).

H0506 *La Vigie* (Casablanca), 29 May 1955. *Note:* Review of Béraud-Villars (E204).

H0507 Gaston Laverne, '20ᵉ anniversaire: 1888–1935 T.E. Lawrence', *La Nation Belge,* 30 May 1955.

H0508 *La Croix du Nord et du Pas-de-Calais,* 3 June 1955. *Note:* Review of Béraud-Villars (E204).

H0509 Marcel Defosse, 'Lawrence, imposteur?', *Le Soir de Bruxelles,* 4 June 1955, no.154.

H0510 Émile Henroit, 'Un Portrait Français du Colonel Lawrence', *Le Monde,* 8 June 1955.

H0511 Pierre Mazars, 'Un "Lawrence" Sans Passion', *Le Figaro,* 8 June 1955.

H0512 *Le Berry Republicain,* 8 June 1955. *Note:* Review of Béraud-Villars (E204).

H0513 *Le Peuple (Bruxelles),* 8 June 1955. *Note:* Review of Béraud-Villars (E204).

H0514 Emile Henriot, 'Le Colonel Lawrence', *Dépêche Quotidienne d'Alger,*

10 June 1955.

H0515 René Tavernier, 'Lawrence. Soldat, Diplomate, Écrivain, demeure une figure attachante et étrange', *Prógrès,* 10 June 1955.

H0516 Pierre de Boisdeffre, 'De la Légende à l'Histoire', *L'Information,* 11 June 1955.

H0517 *Le Figaro Littéraire,* 11 June 1955. *Note:* Review of Béraud-Villars (E204).

H0518 Y.B., 'Du Colonel Lawrence aux pétroles de Kouweit', *Lettres Françaises* (Buenos Aires), 14 June 1955.

H0519 *Le Journal de Genève,* 15 June 1955. *Note:* Review of Béraud-Villars (E204).

H0520 André Brissaud, *Carrefour,* 15 June 1955. *Note:* Review of Béraud-Villars (E204).

H0521 *France-Tropiques,* 17 June 1955. *Note:* Review of Béraud-Villars (E204).

H0522 Paul Mansire, *Paris-Normandie (Rouen),* 17 June 1955. *Note:* Review of Béraud-Villars (E204).

H0523 *Ouest-France* (Rennes), 21 June 1955. *Note:* Review of Béraud-Villars (E204).

H0524 André D. Toledano, 'Le Colonel Lawrence Fut-Il un Imposteur?', *La Croix (Paris),* 27 June 1955.

H0525 *Mercure,* July 1955. *Note:* Review of *The Mint* (A182).

H0526 *Corse d'Aujourd'hui* (Hyères), July 1955. *Note:* Review of Béraud-Villars (E204).

H0527 André Rousseaux, 'Pour et Contre T.E. Lawrence', *Le Figaro Littéraire,* 2 July 1955.

H0528 *Nice-Matin,* 8 July 1955. *Note:* Review of Béraud-Villars (E204).

H0529 Richard Aldington, 'Le Légende du colonel Lawrence', *Le Monde,* 9 July 1955.

H0530 *Le Peuple* (Bruxelles), 11 July 1955. *Note:* Review of *The Mint* (A182).

H0531 *La Provençal* (Marseilles), 13 July 1955. *Note:* Review of Béraud-Villars (E204).

H0532 M. Prost, *Nouvelle Gazette* (Bruxelles, Namur), 31 July 1955. *Note:* Review of Béraud-Villars (E204).

H0533 'Encore Lawrence', *La Libre Belgique,* 3 August 1955. *Note:* Review of Béraud-Villars (E204).

H0534 *Nord-Éclair* (Lille), 5 August 1955. *Note:* Review of Béraud-Villars (E204).

H0535 Jules Romains, 'Une Figure de Grand Aventurier', *L'Aurore,* 11 August 1955.

H0536 Jules Romains, 'Un Aventurier d'un autre Style (Marco Polo)', *l'Aurore,* 18 August 1955.

H0537 G. Esquer, *Le Journal d'Alge,* 19 August 1955. *Note:* Review of Béraud-Villars (E204).

H0538 *Midi Libre,* 24 August 1955. *Note:* Review of Béraud-Villars (E204).

H0539 *Chicago Sunday Tribune,* 28 August 1955, p.2. *Note:* Review of Armitage, *The Desert and the Stars* (E212).

H0540 Jean Champomier, 'L'Homme Qui A Perdu Son Ombre', *L'Espoir* (Saint-Étienne), 2 September 1955.

H0541 *Christian Science Monitor,* 15 September 1955, p.13. *Note:* Review of

Armitage (E212).

H0542 'Le Colonel Lawrence à la Tribune de Paris', *Mon Programme*, 1 October 1955.

H0543 'M.-A.P.', *Invalide Liégeois*, 1 October 1955. *Note:* Review of Béraud-Villars (E204).

H0544 *Chicago Sunday Tribune*, 16 October 1955, p.4. *Note:* Review of Aldington.

H0545 *Marchés Coloniaux du Monde*, 17 October 1955. *Note:* Review of Béraud-Villars (E204).

H0546 *Christian Science Monitor*, 17 October 1955, p.9. *Note:* Review of Aldington (E198).

H0547 J.S., 'Le Prince de la Mecque', *Avenir de Tournaisis*, 2 November 1955.

H0548 *L'Écho de la Côte d'Azur et de la Principauté* (Nice), 5 November 1955. *Note:* Review of Béraud-Villars (E204).

H0549 Drion du Chapois, *Le Rappel* (Charleroi), 19 February 1956. *Note:* Article on Aldington and Béraud-Villars.

H0550 Peter D. Whitney, 'Row on Lawrence of Arabia Rages', *Los Angeles Times*, 7 March 1956.

H0551 Alec S. Kirkbride, 'T.E. Lawrence: A Memory of the Hedjaz 1918', *Manchester Guardian*, 20 August 1956, pp.4, 6.

H0552 Robert Kirsch, 'A U.S. Lawrence of Arabia', *Los Angeles Times*, 26 February 1957.

H0553 *Paris-Presse l'Intransigeant*, 30 May 1957. *Note:* Review of Armitage (E214).

H0554 David Catarivas, 'Un inépuisable sujet du nouveau sur le colonel Lawrence, *L'Observateur du Moyen-Orient*, 26 April 1957. *Note:* Review of Armtiage (E214).

H0555 Jean Mera, *République* (Toulon), 28 April 1957. *Note:* Review of Armitage (E214).

H0556 *Corse d'Aujourd'hui* (Hyères), May 1957. *Note:* Review of Armitage (E214).

H0557 *Le Soir de Bruxelles*, 11 May 1957. *Note:* Review of Armitage (E214).

H0558 P.F., *Carrefour*, 15 May 1957, 661. *Note:* Review of Armitage (E214).

H0559 *Les Débats de ce Temps*, 18 May 1957. *Note:* Review of Armitage (E214).

H0560 Joseph Capuano, 'Un nouveau livre sur le colonel Lawrence', *La Tribune de Genève*, 24 May 1957. *Note:* Review of Armitage (E214).

H0561 Felix Allouche, *L'Écho d'Israel*, 20 June 1957. *Note:* Review of Armitage (E214).

H0562 *La Gazette de Lausanne*, 20 July 1957. *Note:* Review of Armitage (E214).

H0563 *Nord-Éclair* (Lille), 8 August 1957. *Note:* Review of Armitage (E214).

H0564 *La Tribune Sioniste de France*, 25 October 1957. *Note:* Review of Armitage (E214).

H0565 A. Ben Hassen, 'Lawrence d'Arabie de F. Armitage', *L'Action* (Tunis), 2 December 1957.

H0566 J.B., *Le Journal de Genève*, 21 March 1958. *Note:* Review of Armitage.

H0567 *Forces Nouvelles*, July–August 1958. *Note:* Review of Bouregouis, *Lawrence, roi secret de l'Arabie*.

H0568 *Croix de Lorraine*, 4 July 1958. *Note:* Review of Bourgeois.

H0569 *Vers L'Avenir (Belgique)*, 17 August 1958. *Note:* Review of Bourgeois.

H0570 *La Tribune de Genève*, 23 August 1958. *Note:* Review of Bouregouis.

H0571 Earl Winterton, 'One Who Was There Remembers Derra', ? (Leeds, Yorkshire), 19 September 1958.

H0572 *Chicago Sunday Tribune*, 22 March 1959, p.4. *Note:* Review of Béraud-Villars.

H0573 *Springfield Republican*, 22 March 1959, p.40. *Note:* Review of Béraud-Villars.

H0574 *Christian Science Monitor*, 2 April 1959, p.5. *Note:* Review of Béraud-Villars.

H0575 'A Death Airs Origin of T.E. Lawrence', *New York Times*, 26 November 1959, p.2.

H0576 'Lawrence of Arabia', *Daily Mail*, 28 April 1960. *Note:* Photo.

H0577 Winston Churchill, 'T.E. Lawrence, le plus grand homme de notre temps, *Lettres et Spectacles*, 11 May 1960. *Note:* Essay from *TEL by His Friends*.

H0578 Yvon Hecht, 'Il y a vingt-cinq ans mourait un roi sans royaume', *Paris-Normandie* (Rouen), 13 May 1960.

H0579 Jacques Pateau, 'Rattigan Explains Lawrence of Arabia', *Los Angeles Times*, 18 May 1960, Part II, p.9.

H0580 Claude Mauriac, 'T.E. Lawrence et le Métier d'Artiste', *Le Figaro*, 18 May 1960.

H0581 'T.E. Lawrence, un tricheur qui a lu l'Ecclésiaste', *Paris-Presse l'Intransigeant*, 25 May 1960.

H0582 Harold Hobson, 'A Penetrating Rattigan Play', *Christian Science Monitor*, 28 May 1960.

H0583 Brice Abusson', *Le Matin d'Anvers*, 4 June 1960. *Note:* Review of Stéphane.

H0584 P.P., 'L'Énigme du XX Siècle', *La Libre Belgique*, 16 June 1960.

H0585 Jean Lacouture, 'Un Nouveau Portrait de T.E. Lawrence Par Roger Stéphane et Quelques Autres', *Le Monde*, 18 August 1960.

H0586 *Le Populaire du Centre*, 10 November 1960. *Note:* Review of Stéphane.

H0587 'David Lean en Jordanie', *Le Figaro*, 21 February 1961.

H0588 Arthur Cook, 'Why Mr. O'Toole Is Sleeping on His Face', *Daily Mail*, 7 March 1961, p.9.

H0589 Alian Delon, 'Joue un Fils du Desert', *Paris Journal*, 22 March 1961.

H0590 *New York Herald Tribune*, 14 May 1961, Section XII, p.30. *Note:* Review of Cadell, *Young Lawrence of Arabia* (E228).

H0591 '"Lawrence" Location Getting Film Supply', *Hollywood Reporter*, 23 May 1961.

H0592 'Filming Story of Lawrence of Arabia', *Ashburton Guardian* (New Zealand), 24 May 1961.

H0593 'Desert Journey', *Birmingham Mail*, 29 May 1961. *Note:* Film.

H0594 'C'est Arrivé Demain', *Arts*, 6 June 1961. *Note:* Film.

H0595 'Un Acteur Egyptien dans "Lawrence d'Arabie"', *Libération*, 11 June 1961.

H0596 'Cet Homme Balaye le Désert', *Le Journal du Dimanche*, 11 June 1961.

H0597 Louella Parsons, *Los Angeles Examiner*, 15 June 1961. *Note:* Note on film.

H0598 *Kine Weekly,* 22 June 1961. *Note:* Technical note of film.
H0599 'A Desert Journey with £10,000 in Gold', *Birmingham Mail,* 22 June 1961.
H0600 'Frozen Foods Support the "Seven Pillars of Wisdom"', *Merthyr Express,* 24 June 1961.
H0601 John R. Woolfenden, 'Desert Camera on the Trail of "Lawrence"', *New York Times,* 25 June 1961, section II, p.7.
H0602 '"Arabia" Press Moves Base', *Hollywood Reporter,* 28 June 1961.
H0603 *New York Post,* 29 June 1961. *Note:* Note on film.
H0604 'Camels in Old Compton Street', *Evening News* (London), 29 June 1961. *Note:* Film.
H0605 'Imported Sun into the Desert', *Daily Sketch,* 30 June 1961, p.9.
H0606 Harrison Carroll, 'Sam Spiegel Will Use 500 Camels for Background in "Lawrence of Arabia"', *Los Angeles Herald Examiner,* 7 July 1961.
H0607 'Sir Alec in "Lawrence of Arabia"', *The Citizen* (Gloucester), 8 July 1961.
H0608 'Photo of O'Toole as Lawrence', *Evening Mail,* 11 July 1961.
H0609 'Before & After – T.E. Lawrence & O'Toole', *Daily ? Weekly,* 16 July 1961.
H0610 Hamon Carroll, 'Plenty Hot on "Arabia" Location', *Boston Daily Record,* 17 July 1961.
H0611 William Werenth, 'Love, Rage Campaign for "Arabia" Outlined', *Motion Picture Daily,* 18 July 1961. *Note:* Film.
H0612 *Lancashire Evening Post,* 18 July 1961. *Note:* Film.
H0613 'Peter O'Toole Don Juan d'Arabie Affronte la Soif du Désert', *Cinémonde,* 18 July 1961.
H0614 'Spelling Above to T.E. Lawrence', 18 July 1961.
H0615 'Filming in the Desert', *Yorkshire Evening Post,* 19 July 1961.
H0616 F. Leslie Withers, 'It is tough being Lawrence', *Sunday Mercury* (Birmingham), 23 July 1961.
H0617 'A Desert Re-Union for Famous Trio', *Herald & Express,* 24 July 1961.
H0618 'Guinness Joins the "Lawrence" Team', *Oldham Evening Chronicle & Standard,* 26 July 1961.
H0619 *Edinburgh Evening News,* 28 July 1961. *Note:* Film.
H0620 *The Yorkshire Post,* 29 July 1961. *Note:* Technical notes on film.
H0621 Kate Cameron, 'London Alive with U.S. Film Workers', *Sunday News,* 30 July 1961. *Note:* Film.
H0622 Anthony Nutting, 'Lawrence of Arabia', *Sunday Times,* 10 September 1961.
H0623 K.J. Fielding, 'Lawrence's Confession', *The Times,* 17 September 1961.
H0624 Anthony Nutting, 'The Mirror of Degradation', *Sunday Chronicle,* 17 September 1961.
H0625 B.H. Liddell-Hart, 'Friday Supplement', October–November 1961? *Note:* Letter re a review of Nutting.
H0625 B.H. Liddell-Hart, 'Friday Supplement', October–November 1961? *Note:* Letter re a review of Nutting.
H0627 'Lawrence d'Arabie', *Le Figaro,* 1962. *Note:* Illus.

H0628 Cyril Connolly, 'Reflections of Greatness', 1962. *Note:* Review of *The Letters* (E251).

H0629 Pierre Cordey, 'Lawrence d'Arabie', *Feuille d'Avis de Lausanne*, 2 January 1962.

H0630 Peine Knickerbocker, 'Mysteries and Confusions: Surrealistic Portrait of Lawrence', *San Francisco Chronicle*, 11 February 1962, p.32. *Note:* Review of Nutting (E235).

H0631 Maxime Moirex, *La Voix du Nord*, 28 February 1962. *Note:* Review of Bénoist-Mechin (E245).

H0632 *La Provençal Dimanche*, 4 March 1962. *Note:* Review of Bénoist-Mechin (E245).

H0633 Robert Kirsch, 'T.E. Lawrence – Some New Light on the Face of a Hero', *Los Angeles Times*, 6 March 1962.

H0634 Philippe Secretan, 'La Chute de l'ange', *La Tribune de Genève*, 22 April 1962.

H0635 'Lawrence's House Shaken Up', *The Scotsman*, 11 June 1962.

H0636 Lowell Thomas, *San Francisco Chronicle (This Week)*, 24 June 1962, p.11. *Note:* Illus.

H0637 Howard Thompson, 'Producer of the Long Trek With "Lawrence of Arabia"', *New York Times*, 15 July 1962, p.5. *Note:* Film.

H0638 'In "Arabia" Some Blood, Some Tears', *Los Angeles Times*, 22 July 1962. *Note:* Review of film.

H0639 *The Times*, 26 July 1962, p.10. *Note:* Review of *Letters to TEL* (E251).

H0640 *Chicago Sunday Tribune*, 9 September 1962, p.9. *Note:* Review of MacLean (E253).

H0641 Herald Tudor, 'The Man Who Served With Lawrence in the Desert', *Birmingham Evening Mail*, 27 September 1962. *Note:* Photo, p.4.

H0642 Donald Zec, 'Lawrence', *Daily Mirror*, 17 November 1962.

H0643 André Renaudin, *Liberté Dimanche*, December 1962. *Note:* Review of film.

H0644 'Bolt Tries Film for Size', *Los Angeles Times Calendar*, 2 December 1962, p.1.

H0645 'Le Professeur Lawrence, frère du fameux "Lawrence d'Arabie" ', *Paris-Jour*, 5 December 1962.

H0646 'Pete O'Toole's Two Big Years', *Daily Express*, 7 December 1962.

H0647 Donald Zec, 'O'Toole of Arabia', *Daily Mirror*, 10 December 1962.

H0648 Jacqueline Tourreil, 'Première de Lawrence d'Arabie Devant la Reine d'Angleterre', *Le Figaro*, 11 December 1962.

H0649 Régine Gabbey, *Parisien Libéré*, 11 December 1962. *Note:* Film.

H0650 Patrick Gibbs, 'Two Styles Combined', *Daily Telegraph*, 12 December 1962.

H0651 Alan Dent, 'Lawrence of Arabia', *Sunday Telegraph*, 16 December 1962. *Note:* Film.

H0652 D. Powell, 'The Hero of the Desert', *The Times*, 16 December 1962.

H0653 'Lawrence of the Odeon', *Daily Mirror*, 17 December 1962.

H0654 *Evening Standard*, 18 December 1962. *Note:* Article on Kennington bust of TEL.

H0655 B.H. Liddell Hart, 'Lawrence of Arabia', *The Times*, 19 December 1962.
H0656 '"Lawrence" Film Opens With Fanfare', *Los Angeles Times*, 22 December 1962.
H0657 Melvin Maddocks, '"Lawrence of Arabia" as Screen Biography', *Christian Science Monitor*, 29 December 1962, p.4.
H0658 Ian Russell, 'Riddle of the "Arch Spy"', 1963.
H0659 'Full Length Portrait of Lawrence in the Desert', 1963.
H0660 'Lawrence of Arabia', *The Times*, 2 January 1963.
H0661 'Brother Rejects Lawrence Film', *New York Times*, 5 January 1963, p.1.
H0662 'Not Much Like Lawrence', *Oxford Mail*, 14 January 1963.
H0663 '1st Seven Pillars £310', *The Times*, 19 January 1963.
H0664 Clyde Gilmour, 'This Is a Triumph of Filmcraft', *Telegram* (Toronto), 31 January 1963, p.30.
H0665 Peter Worthington, '"That's the Way it Was" says a man who knows', *Telegram* (Toronto), 31 January 1963, p.30.
H0666 *Adam* (France), February 1963. *Note:* Film.
H0667 *Le Nouveau Candide*, 14 February 1963. *Note:* Review of *Seven Pillars* (A070).
H0668 Donald Stanley, 'The Old Friendship of Two Men Named Shaw', *San Francisco Examiner*, 24 February 1963. *Note:* Review of *Private Shaw and Public Shaw* (E275).
H0669 '"Lawrence d'Arabie" au Coeur de la Révolte', *Cinémonde*, 26 February 1963.
H0670 '"Lawrence d'Arabie" favori pour l'Oscar du Cinéma', *La Parisien*, 27 February 1963.
H0671 'Margaret est tenace:: elle veut voir "Lawrence d'Arabie" à Paris', *Paris-Jour*, 1 March 1963.
H0672 Jacques Parrot, 'La Véritable Histoire de Lawrence d'Arabie', *La Presse*, 7 March 1963.
H0673 John Jones, 'On the Lawrence Trail Again', *Sunday Telegraph*, 10 March 1963. *Note:* Review of *TEL to His Biographers*.
H0674 *Le Figaro*, 13–14 March 1963. *Note:* Film.
H0675 *New York Times*, 14 March 1963, p.8. *Note:* Review of Shaw, *Too True to Be Good*.
H0676 *Le Monde*, 14 March 1963. *Note:* Film.
H0677 Geoffrey Godsell, 'Shaw', *Christian Science Monitor*, 14 March 1963, p.11. *Note:* Review of Weintraub (E275).
H0678 *L'Aurore*, 14 March 1963. *Note:* Film.
H0679 Louis Chauvet, 'Lawrence d'Arabie', *Le Figaro*, 18 March 1963. *Note:* Film.
H0680 J. de Baroncelli, *Le Monde*, 19 March 1963. *Note:* Film.
H0681 Jean Fayard, *Le Figaro*, 19 March 1963. *Note:* Film.
H0682 Pierre Maracabru, 'Lawrence d'Arabie un Livre d'Images Pieuses', *Arts*, 20 March 1963.
H0683 Claude Mauriac, 'Lawrence d'Arabie de David Lean', *Le Figaro Littéraire*, 23 March 1963.
H0684 Henry Rabine, 'Mystérieux colonel Lawrence', *La Croix Dimanche*, 24 March 1963. *Note:* Film.

H0685 Jeander, 'Un héros? Un aventurier?...', *Libération*, 29 March 1963.
H0686 Franck Jotterand, 'Lawrence de David Lean', *La Gazette de Lausanne*, 30–31 March 1963. *Note:* Film.
H0687 *Adam (France)*, April 1963. *Note:* Film.
H0688 Georges Sadoul, 'Les Chameaux et l'Agent Secret', *Lettres Françaises* (Buenos Aires), 3 April 1963.
H0689 *Paris-Presse l'Intransigeant*, 4, 9–13, 17, 22–26 April 1963. *Note:* Serialisation of Bénoit-Mechin.
H0690 Brooks Atkinson, 'Critic At Large', *New York Times (Western Edition)*, 9 April 1963.
H0691 Jean Lacouture, 'T.E. Lawrence en Proie aux Images', *Le Monde*, 10 April 1963.
H0692 *La Cité (Bruxelles)*, 11 April 1963. *Note:* Review of *Seven Pillars* (A070).
H0693 *Parisien Libéré*, 16 April 1963. *Note:* Review of *Seven Pillars* (A070).
H0694 'Who Said Heroes Like Lawrence Had Vanished', *Sunday Express*, 17 April 1963.
H0695 R. Beaus, 'Lus et jugés. Des ouvrages de Valeur', *Le Havre Libre*, 23 April 1963.
H0696 *Les Échos*, 2 May 1963. *Note:* Review of French *Seven Pillars*.
H0697 *La Cité (Bruxelles)*, 8 May 1963. *Note:* Review of French *Seven Pillars*.
H0698 Eric Nicol, 'Eric of Arabia', *The Star* (London), 9 May 1963.
H0699 Philip Oakes, 'Stars on Location', *Sunday Times*, 19 May 1963. *Note:* Review of Kent, *Single Bed for Three* (E280).
H0700 'A Small "Trek"', *Evening Post*, 27 May 1963.
H0701 Edwin Howard, 'A.W. Lawrence on T.E. Film', *Memphis Press-Scimiter*, 29 May 1963.
H0702 Peterborough, 'London Day by Day', *Daily Telegraph*, 1 June 1963.
H0703 Claude Jannoud, 'T.E. Lawrence, l'Homme qui Réinventa le Guérilla', *La Nation*, 6 June 1963.
H0704 '3 T.E. Lawrence Letters come to light', *The Times*, 6 June 1963.
H0705 Brooks Atkinson, 'Critic at Large', *New York Times*, 14 June 1963. *Note:* Review of Weintraub (E275).
H0706 *Arts*, 26 June–2 July 1963. *Note:* Review of *Seven Pillars* (A049).
H0707 'Friendship of Shaw, Lawrence Discussed', *Evening Outlook* (Santa Monica), 15 July 1963. *Note:* Review of Weintraub (E275).
H0708 K.W. Gransden, 'Crippled Saint', 19 July 1963.
H0709 *Coronado Journal* (California), August 1963. *Note:* Review of Weintraub (E275).
H0710 'Lawrence's Library', *The Times*, August 1963.
H0711 'Another Shaw's Corner', *Daily Telegraph Reporter*, 5 August 1963.
H0712 *San Francisco Examiner*, 8 August 1963, p.28. *Note:* Film.
H0713 'Film Sends Visitors to Lawrence's Home', *Los Angeles Times*, 10 August 1963.
H0714 John Chamberlain, 'A Lawrence Needed to Lead Cubans', *San Francisco News Call Bulletin*, 24 August 1963. *Note:* Film, illus.
H0715 William H?, *San Francisco Chronicle*, 5 September 1963. *Note:* Review of *TEL to His Biographers* (A217).
H0716 Donald Stanley, 'The Real Lawrence', *San Francisco Examiner*, 8 September 1963.

H0717 Geoffrey Monkhouse, 'Retreat: Clouds Hill', *Manchester Guardian*, 10 September 1963, p.7.

H0718 *Nord-Eclair* (Lille), 11 September 1963. *Note:* Review of *Seven Pillars* (A070).

H0719 'Lawrence Exhibit Now on Display at USC Library', *The News*, 1 October 1963.

H0720 'Missing Pages of Lawrence's Manuscript Discovered', *Evening News and Star*, 21 October 1963. *Note: Revolt in the Desert.*

H0721 'Sidelights', *New York Times*, 29 October 1963. *Note:* Mention of Lawrence.

H0722 David Holloway, 'One Shaw to Another', *Daily Telegraph*, November 1963. *Note:* Review of Weintraub (E275).

H0723 O. Centlivres, 'Bénoist-Mechin Ou l'Histoire Passionnante', *Feuille d'Avis de Lausanne*, 1 November 1963.

H0724 'War Scenes for "Lawrence" Shot by 5 Cameras', *Los Angeles Times*, 11 December 1963.

H0725 Bosley Crowther, 'Pursuit of Bigness', *New York Times*, 28 December 1963. *Note:* Film.

H0726 *Oxford Mail*, 8 January 1964. *Note:* Film.

H0727 Cohey Black, 'Who's News', *Honolulu Star Bulletin*, 4 January 1964. *Note:* Film.

H0728 'Two Men Who Have a Century of Service', *Oxford Mail*, 10 January 1964.

H0729 'Lawrence Ban', *Daily Herald*, 14 January 1964.

H0730 Derich Gigs, 'The Enigma of Lawrence', *Oxford Mail*, 18 January 1964. *Note:* Film.

H0731 'Lawrence', *Oxford Mail*, 21 January 1964.

H0732 Terrence O'Flaherty, 'Dr. Frank Baxter', *San Francisco Chronicle*, 30 January 1964.

H0733 Anne Sharpley, 'Tell Me the Truth about Lawrence', *Las Vegas Sun*, 31 January 1964.

H0734 'A Lawrence Talks About that Legend', *?* (Leeds, Yorkshire), 10 April 1964.

H0735 'Light on Britain's...', *The Times*, 17 April 1964.

H0736 John Griffiths, 'The Age of the JAP', *Manchester Guardian*, 25 May 1964. *Note:* Photo of Lawrence on Brough.

H0737 'Letter of T.E. Lawrence in Bodleian', *Guardian*, 6 June 1964.

H0738 Bill Richardson, 'An 'American Lawrence' of Southwest Arabia', *San Francisco Chronicle*, 17 June 1964.

H0739 'Bodleian To Get T.E. Lawrence Letters', *Oxford Mail*, 6 July 1964.

H0740 '"Lost" Letters', *Daily Express*, 7 July 1964.

H0741 'Lawrence's Torse Saved for College', *Daily Telegraph*, 11 July 1964.

H0742 Robert Kirsch, 'Some Eminent Post-Victorians', *Los Angeles Times*, 14 July 1964.

H0743 Frédérick Kiesel, 'Duplicité Ou Incohérence', *La Cité (Bruxelles)*, 26 August 1964.

H0744 T.W. Beaumont, *News of the World*, 13 September 1964. *Note:* Letter to editor.

H0745 John E. Dayton, 'Tracking the Train Lawrence Wrecked', *The Times*,

4 December 1964, pp.13, 22.

H0746 Peter Hopkirk, 'The Train Lawrence Wrecked', *Sun*, 4 December 1964.

H0747 Peter Hopkirk, 'Lawrence of Arabia's Crash Bike sold for £1', *Sun*, 22 December 1964. *Note:* Photos.

H0748 Jonathan Stedell, 'Road to a Legend', 1965.

H0749 Anne Dooley, 'Lawrence of Arabia Writes From Beyond', *Psychic News*, 6 February 1965, 1705, p.1.

H0750 Henning Kehler, 'T.E. Lawrence's breve', *Berlingske Aftenavis Torsdag*, 11 February 1965. *Note:* Review of 2nd edition of *The Letters* (A203).

H0751 *Le Figaro Littéraire*, 4 March 1965. *Note:* Extracts from *Les Textes essentiels*.

H0752 *Aux Ecoutes*, 25 March 1965. *Note:* Review of *Les Textes essentiels* (A242).

H0753 *Le Monde*, 27 March 1965. *Note:* Review of *Les Textes essentiels* (A242).

H0754 *Le Tribune de Lausanne*, 28 March 1965. *Note:* Review of *Les Textes essentiels* (A242).

H0755 Marcel Brion, 'Les Textes Essentiels de T.E. Lawrence', *Le Monde*, 24 April 1965.

H0756 'Heroes of Tomorrow', *Women's Weekly* (UK), 27 April 1965. *Note:* Film.

H0757 H. de Lancker, *Les Beaux-Arts*, 29 April 1965. *Note:* Review of *Les Textes essentiels* (A242).

H0758 'Whittier College Exhibit of Duncan Collection', May 1965.

H0759 *La Libre Beligique*, 7 May 1965. *Note:* Review of *Les Textes essentiels* (A242).

H0760 'Lawrence Exhibit on Display', Temple City (California), 9 May 1965, p.17.

H0761 'T.E. Lawrence Exhibit at Whittier', *South Pasadena Reivew*, 10 May 1965, p.3.

H0762 'Lawrence Exhibit on at Whittier', *Gardena Valley News*, 13 May 1965, p.9.

H0763 'Memories of T.E.', *Yorkshire Post*, 18 May 1965.

H0764 Brian Murtough, 'The Steps of the Master are Hard to Find', *Sun*, 21 May 1965.

H0765 'Books – A Monument on Display at Whittier', *Los Angeles Times*, 23 May 1965.

H0766 'Lawrence Exhibit at Whittier College', *Hacienda Heights Highlander*, 26 May 1965.

H0767 'Library Features Exhibit of Lawrence of Arabia', *East Whittier Review*, 27 May 1965, p.40.

H0768 Ahmad Taroukh, 'What Would Lawrence Think?', *Tehran Journal*, 31 May 1965.

H0769 '"Lawrence of Arabia" gets Italian "Oscar"', *Los Angeles Times*, 5 June 1965.

H0770 Charly Guyot, 'Pour Connaître Lawrence d'Arabie', *Le Journal de Genève*, 12–13 June 1965.

H0771 Jack Tipp, *San Francisco Chronicle*, 18 June 1965. *Note:* Cartoon.

H0772 Franz Hellens, 'Textes Essentiels de T.E. Lawrence', *Le Soir*, 24 June 1965.
H0773 '"Lawrence" Team Reunited', *Los Angeles Times*, 25 June 1965.
H0774 *Evening Standard*, 30 July 1965. *Note:* Cartoon.
H0775 Peter Hopkirk, 'Secret Lives', *Calgary Herald*, 4 August 1965.
H0776 'Hedjaz Railroad', *New York Times*, 8 August 1965.
H0777 Thomas Jenkins, 'On A Desert Railway – a Blue Eyed Ghost', *Sunday Express*, 25 August 1965.
H0778 Anthony Wood, 'Diving Time on Trill Mill Stream', *Oxford Mail*, 18 October 1965.
H0779 Night Climber Mr. X, 'Oxford "Peaks"', *Oxford Mail*, 18 October 1965.
H0780 'Bought His Wives with Lawrence's Gold', *Keyhan Intern* (Tehran, Iran), 23 November 1965.
H0781 'He's Roamed the Desert for a Century', *Evening Standard*, 26 November 1965.
H0782 David Lancashire, 'Arabia Railway Hit by Lawrence Being Rebuilt', *Los Angeles Times*, 5 December 1965.
H0783 *Le Journal du Dimanche*, 12 December 1965. *Note:* Review of Stéphane *Portrait de l'aventurier* (E172).
H0784 D.P., 'Le Prix Sainte-Beuve à Robert Raviniaux et Roger Stéphane', *Le Figaro*, 15 December 1965.
H0785 *Parisien Libéré*, 15 December 1965. *Note:* Review of Stéphane (E172).
H0786 *Le Figaro Littéraire*, 16 December 1965. *Note:* Review of Stéphane (E172).
H0787 *La Croix*, 17 December 1965. *Note:* Review of Stéphane (E172).
H0788 'Roger Stéphane a complété son portrait de l'aventurier', *La Tribune de Lausanne*, 19 December 1965.
H0789 Matthieu Galey, 'La Gloire du Héros', *Arts*, 22 December 1965.
H0790 *Aux Écoutes*, 23 December 1965. *Note:* Review of Stéphane (E172).
H0791 Parria, 'Stéphane en est resté roi', *Minute*, 26 December 1965. *Note:* Review of Stéphane (E172).
H0792 Henry Bonnier, 'La Conquête Inutile', *Le Provençal*, 26 December 1965.
H0793 'Lawrence of Arabia Read Him', *Milwaukee Review*, 1966. *Note:* Review of Doughty, *Travels in Arabia Deserta* (A019).
H0794 *Montréal-Matin*, January 1966. *Note:* Review of Stéphane (E172).
H0795 *La Semaine à Paris*, January 1966. *Note:* Review of Stéphane (E172).
H0796 Jean-Etheir Blais, *Le Devoir de Montréal*, 22 January 1966. *Note:* Review of Stéphane (E172).
H0797 Jean Ladrière, 'Portrait de l'Aventurier, de Roger Stéphane', *Les Beaux-Arts*, 27 January 1966.
H0798 Pierre de Boisdeffre, 'Ou Sont les Aventuriers', *Notre Republique*, 27 January 1966.
H0799 J. O'N, 'Pour Enforcer un Culte Nécessaire', *Le Devoir de Montreal*, 12 February 1966.
H0800 Henri Petit, *Parisien Libéré*, 15 February 1966. *Note:* Review of Stéphane (E172).

H0801 André Major, 'Les Aventuriers', *Le Petit Journal,* 20 March 1966.

H0802 'Live Letters', *Daily Mirror,* 22 April 1966.

H0803 Les Perrin, 'His Brough is So Superior', *Daily Mirror,* 6 May 1966. *Note:* Letter to editor.

H0804 'The Sheep Had Three Necks!' *Daily Mirror,* 11 May 1966.

H0805 Noel Wain, 'Crash That Cost the World a Hero and Scarred a Man for Life', *Bournemouth Evening Echo,* 13 May 1966, p.26. *Note:* Photos.

H0806 Edmund Townshend, 'Talks Today on Lawrence's Railway', *Daily Telegraph,* 14 May 1966.

H0807 *Evening News,* 28 May 1966. *Note:* Article re attic used by TEL.

H0808 'Blue Plaque for Lawrence "Refuge"', *?* (Leeds, Yorkshire), 29 May 1966.

H0809 'Cottage of Trembling Memories', *Manchester Guardian,* 15 June 1966.

H0810 'Ton-up Pilgrims', *Sunday Chronicle,* 17 June 1966.

H0811 Robin Daniels, 'Celluloid Attempt to Pin Down a Legend', *Epsom & Ewell Herald,* 24 June 1966. *Note:* Review of film.

H0812 'Plaque to "Lawrence of Arabia"', *Daily Telegraph,* Summer 1966.

H0813 Michael Foot, 'Our Gritty Love Affair with the Desert', *Evening Standard,* 5 July 1966.

H0814 Lord Kinross, 'An Arab Slant to the Lawrence Legend', *Daily Telegraph,* 7 July 1966. *Note:* Review of Mousa, *TEL an Arab View* (E256) and Payne, *Lawrence of Arabia* (E266).

H0815 Peter Grosvenor, 'Lawrence a Nettle of Briars', *Daily Express,* 7 July 1966. *Note:* Review of Mousa (E256).

H0816 'Arab Angle', *The Times,* 7 July 1966. *Note:* Review of Mousa (E256).

H0817 Anthony Nutting, 'Sand in Our Eyes', *Sunday Telegraph,* 10 July 1966. *Note:* Review of Mousa (E256).

H0818 'For Lawrence', *Sun,* 25 September 1966. *Note:* About Clouds Hill.

H0819 Eric Newby, 'When Its Time to Say "No More Ruins"', *Observer Weekend Review,* 16 October 1966.

H0820 Alec Kirkbride, 'Arabs' Hero', *Sunday Chronicle,* 21 October 1966.

H0821 'Movie Film Suit', *New York Times,* 3 November 1966.

H0822 Roger Ebert, 'Man of Letters Sees Love Poetry Dying Out', *Los Angeles Times,* 5 December 1966, part VI, p.6.

H0823 Henry Bonnier, 'La Conquête de l'Inutile', *La Dépêche,* 28 December 1966.

H0824 '50 Years Later Lawrence', January 1967.

H0825 Katie Doyle, 'Lawrence of Arabia and Mount Batten', *The Independent* (Plymouth), 20 January 1967, pp.14–15.

H0826 Gabriel Gersh, 'Arab Unravels Lawrence Legend', *Los Angeles Times,* 29 January 1967. *Note:* Review of Mousa (E257).

H0827 Julian Symons, 'T.E. Lawrence', *The Times,* 29 January 1967. *Note:* Photo.

H0828 B.H. Liddell Hart, 'Propagandist', *The Times,* 5 February 1967. *Note:* Letter to editor, photo.

H0829 Gail Marzieh, 'An Arab Attacks Lawrence', *Cleveland Plain Dealer,* March 1967. *Note:* Review of Mousa (E257).

H0830 Malcolm Barker, 'Camel Men Plan a Reunion', *Yorkshire Evening Post*, 4 March 1967.

H0831 'Lawrence Makes the Dole', *Sun*, 23 March 1967.

H0832 'Bring Your Camel', *Yorkshire Evening Post*, 25 May 1967.

H0833 *Los Angeles Herald Examiner*, 5 June 1967. *Note:* Cartoon.

H0834 Malcolm Barker, 'They Rode Camels into Battle', *Yorkshire Evening Post*, 14 June 1967.

H0835 'Misgivings over Handcuffs', *The Times*, 30 June 1967.

H0836 Suleiman Mousa, 'T.E. Lawrence's Arabic', *The Times*, 30 June 1967, p.10.

H0837 'Pilot to T.E. Lawrence', *Yorkshire Evening Post*, 13 July 1967.

H0838 'Old Mid East Telegraph to Be Restored', *Los Angeles Times*, 1 August 1967.

H0839 'British Favorites', *Christian Science Monitor*, 18 August 1967, p.16.

H0840 'Lawrence Gift Refused', *Sun*, 15 September 1967.

H0841 'The Lincolnshire Yeomanry Goes Marching On', *Evening Telegraph*, 3 October 1967, p.5.

H0842 W.W. Skinner, 'Poor Worms', *Evening Express*, 29 October 1967. *Note:* Letter to editor.

H0843 Colin Graham, 'The Crash Which Killed Lawrence of Arabia', *Dorset*, Summer 1968, 2, pp.3–5.

H0844 '£950 a First Edition', 28 February 1968.

H0845 'Sir Harold Wernher's Copy of *Seven Pillars of Wisdom* to Quarich for £950, 29 February 1968.

H0846 'In Memoriam', *The Times*, 18 May 1968.

H0847 'T.E. Lawrence Book Is Missing', *Daily Telegram*, 26 May 1968.

H0848 Derek Humphrey, 'Rare Lawrence First Edition Vanishes', *Sunday Times*, 26 May 1968.

H0849 'Theft of MINT', *Los Angeles Times*, 27 May 1968.

H0850 'Still Searching', *Daily Express*, 28 May 1968.

H0851 'The Secret Lives of Lawrence of Arabia', *Sunday Times*, 2 June 1968.

H0852 'Pre-Pillars', *The Times*, 6 June 1968.

H0853 '*Secret Lives*' (Serialisation), *Sunday Times*, 9 June–14 September 1968. *Note:* 9 June, pp.49–50; 16 June, pp.49–50; 23 June, pp.45–46; 30 June, pp.45–46; 31 August, pp.21–22; 7 September, pp.45–46; 14 September, pp.49–50.

H0854 Robert Graves, 'The Riddle of "S.A." of the *Seven Pillars of Wisdom*', *Sunday Times*, 23 June 1968.

H0855 *Sunday Times*, 30 June 1968. *Note:* Letter to the editor.

H0856 'Lawrence of Arabia's Secret', *San Francisco Sunday Examiner and Chronicle* ('This World'), 30 June 1968. *Note:* Review of Knightley and Simpson, *Secret Lives* (H0853).

H0857 'T.E. Lawrence, a "classic case of masochism"', *Sunday Times*, 30 June 1968. *Note:* Letters to editor from Margaret Little, Marion F. Cameron, Martin Husbands.

H0858 'Lawrence Mystery of Black Car', *Sunday Times*, 7 July 1968, p.16. *Note:* Letter to editor.

H0859 C.L.A. Abbott, 'Who Slapped Lawrence of Arabia?', *Morning Herald*

(Sydney, Australia), 20 July 1968, p.20.

H0860 "'Fantasy" phase in the Life of Lawrence of Arabia', *Sunday Times*, 18 August 1968.

H0861 Bernard Cassen, 'Du Nouveau Sur Lawrence d' Arabie', *Le Monde*, 31 August 1968.

H0862 'Beduin, Thirst and Desert Travel', *The Times*, 2 September 1968.

H0863 'Lawrence Book on Sale Next Year', *Sunday Times*, 15 September 1968.

H0864 'American Buyers Take British Mss.', *New York Times*, 15 December 1968.

H0865 'Explorer and Desert Stayed Apart', *?* (Leeds, Yorkshire), 1969.

H0866 John E. Mack, 'Inner Conflict of T.E. Lawrence', *The Times*, 8 February 1969.

H0867 'No Deterrent', *Evening News*, 17 February 1969.

H0868 Jamal Kashani, 'S.A. The Spy in T.E.'s Life', *Iran Tribune*, 14 March 1969, p.47.

H0869 Colin Frame, 'The Finest Hours', *Evening News and Star*, 24 April 1969.

H0870 'Lawrence's Torse Saved for College', *Daily Telegraph*, 11 July 1969.

H0871 'Services Set for W.J. Miller Ex-Aide to Lawrence of Arabia', *Evening Tribune* (San Diego, California), 18 July 1969.

H0872 Peter Hopkirk, 'Were the Arabs Doublecrossed by Lawrence?', *The Times*, 29 July 1969, p.6.

H0873 Jon Kimche, *The Times*, 31 July 1969, p.9. *Note:* Letter to editor.

H0874 'Lawrence von Arabien', *Lubecker Nach...?*, 1 August 1969.

H0875 'War Lawrence ein Verater Arabiene?', *Hannoverishe Rundschau*, 1 August 1969.

H0876 'Das Geheim Leben des Lawrence von Arabien', *Pirmasener Zeitung*, 1 August 1969.

H0877 P. Knightley and C. Simpson, *The Times*, 4 August 1969, p.9.

H0878 Alan Harvey, 'Lawrence was He a Double Dealer?', *Toronto Telegram*, 16 August 1969.

H0879 'Lawrence Secrets to be Revealed', *Sunday Times*, 17 August 1969.

H0880 'Dorset Men in the ICC', *Dorset Evening Echo*, 28 August 1969.

H0881 '1st Edition of *Seven Pillars of Wisdom* for 1s 6d at Church Fete', *Daily Telegraph*, 29 August 1969.

H0882 'Woman Who Taught Lawrence Calls Him "Saint"', *Stars and Stripes*, 23 September 1969.

H0883 Elie Kedourie, 'New Light on Lawrence', *Sunday Times*, 28 September 1969.

H0884 'Schillern des Spiel in Britische Gold', *Esslinger Zeitung*, 30 September 1969.

H0885 'Lawrence Hero or Villain', *Cambridge Evening News*, October 1969.

H0886 Alex Natan, 'Entlaube Legende', *Die Zeit*, October 1969. *Note:* 41.

H0887 ' Hero with a Secret', *Evening News*, 1 October 1969.

H0888 R. Jones, *The Times*, 4 October 1969, p.4. *Note:* Review of Knightley and Simpson (E302).

H0889 'Lawrence Story', *Sunday Times*, 5 October 1969.

H0890 'How Lawrence Taught Me to Spy', *Evening News*, 8 October 1969.

H0891 Rob Bernhard, 'Die Geheimniss des T.E. Lawrence', *Frankfürter Neue Presse*, 11 October 1969.

H0892 *Cellesche Zeitung,* 11 October 1969. *Note:* Review of Knightley and Simpson, *Das Geheim Leben* (E313).

H0893 *Badisches Tagblatt,* 11 October 1969. *Note:* Review of Knightley and Simpson (E313).

H0894 'Neues Über T.E. Lawrence', *Schleswiger Nachrichten,* 15 October 1969.

H0895 Brian Lynch, 'Anti Hero', *Irish Press,* 18 October 1969.

H0896 'Wahrheit über Lawrence', *Neue Osnabrücke Zeitung,* 20 October 1969.

H0897 *Fuldaer Zeitung,* 21 October 1969. *Note:* Review of Knightley and Simpson (E313).

H0898 E.Z., 'Shatten der T.E. Lawrence', *Express* (Vienna), 25 October 1969.

H0899 *Reutlinger General-Anzeigen,* 25 October 1969. *Note:* Review of *Geheim Leben des Lawrence von Arabien.*

H0900 'A Friend of Lawrence', *Liverpool Post,* 27 October 1969.

H0901 B.H., 'An der Legende Geruttett', *Saarbrucker Zeitung,* 30 October 1969. *Note:* Review of Knightley and Simpson (E313).

H0902 *Pasauer Neue Presse,* 30 October 1969. *Note:* Review of Knightley and Simpson (E313).

H0903 *Nord See Zeitung* (Bremerhaven), 4 November 1969. *Note:* Review of Knightley and Simpson (E313).

H0904 'Lawrence's Letter for the War Museum', *Evening Standard,* 7 November 1969.

H0905 'Thought the Reputation of T.E. Lawrence...', *Evening Standard,* 7 November 1969.

H0906 'Empty Promises Point to War', *Sunday Times,* 9 November 1969.

H0907 *Cuxhavener Zeitung,* 13 November 1969. *Note:* Review of Knightley and Simpson (E313).

H0908 *Die Rheinpfalz* (Ludwigshafen), 17 November 1969. *Note:* Review of Knightley and Simpson (E313).

H0909 Werner Koch, 'Entzasuberung Einer Legende', *Die Zeit,* 21 November 1969, p.LIT 9. *Note:* Review of Knightley and Simpson (E313).

H0910 A.W. Lawrence, 'T.E. Lawrence', *The Times,* 22 November 1969, p.7.

H0911 'T.E. Lawrence Book Is Taken to Task', *Evening Standard,* 24 November 1969, p.14.

H0912 'Sluggish Lot', *The Times,* 24 November 1969.

H0913 'Lawrence Boom', *The Times,* 24 November 1969, p.10.

H0914 *Main-Post* (Wurtzburg), 26 November 1969. *Note:* Review of Knightley and Simpson (E313).

H0915 Gerhard Teschner, 'Held und unfernalischer Lügner', *Stuttgarter Zeitung,* 27 November 1969.

H0916 Martin Fagg, 'The Real Lawrence?', *Church Times,* 28 November 1969.

H0917 'Ein Abenteurerliches Leben', *Für Sie* (Hamburg), 2 December 1969.

H0918 *Mittel Bayerische Zeitung,* 3 December 1969. *Note:* Review of

Knightley and Simpson (E313).

H0919 *Nord Bayerischer Kurier*, 3 December 1969. *Note:* Review of Knightley and Simpsom (E313).

H0920 Henk Ohnesorge, 'Lawrence von Arabien auf defektem Sockel', *Die Welt*, 4 December 1969, p.3. *Note:* Review of Knightley and Simpson (E313).

H0921 Jack Smith, 'An Unwanted Cycle', *Los Angeles Times*, 10 December 1969.

H0922 *Buersche Zeitung*, 10 December 1969. *Note:* Review of Knightley and Simpson (E313).

H0923 'Yon's Lawrence of Arabia', 10 December 1969.

H0924 'Ein mysteriöses Leben', *Westfälische Nachrichten Munster*, 11 December 1969.

H0925 'Das Ende eine Legende', *Main-Echo* (Aschaffenburg), 12 December 1969.

H0926 *Das Kleine Blatt* (Wien), 13 December 1969. *Note:* Review of Knightley and Simpson (E313).

H0927 Harald Vocke, 'Bustrophedon', *Frankfürter Allgemeine Zeitung*, 20 December 1969, 295. *Note:* Review of Knightley and Simpson (E313).

H0928 'Geheimnisvolle Lawrence', *Bayern Kuner*, 20 December 1969.

H0929 Malcolm Bauer, "Lawrence of Arabia', 29 December 1970. *Note:* Review of Knightley and Simpson (E302).

H0930 'Das Fragewurdige Leben des Lawrence', *Aachener Volkszeitung*, 9 January 1970.

H0931 Jules Exner, 'Sieben Säulen der Unweisheit', *Rheinische Post* (Düsseldorf), 10 January 1970. *Note:* Review of Knightley and Simpson (E313).

H0932 'Motor Cycle Maker Dies', *Nottingham Evening Post*, 12 January 1970.

H0933 'Mr. George Brough', *Sunday Times*, 13 January 1970.

H0934 Walter Baumgartner, 'Lawrence von Arabien in Neuester Sicht', *Neue Züricher Zeitung*, 18 January 1970, p.51.

H0935 'Professor on a Camel', *Guardian*, 6 February 1970.

H0936 Bobby Mather, *Detroit Free Press*, 15 February 1970. *Note:* Review of Knightley and Simspon (E309).

H0937 'Lawrence', *Evening News*, 24 February 1970.

H0938 'New Evidence Effectively Shatters the Legend of a Gallant Liberator', *Grand Rapids Press*, Spring 1970.

H0939 'He Gave A/C Shaw a Rocket, 7 March 1970.

H0940 'T.E. Lawrence: Enigma Exposed', *The Light* (San Antonio, Texas), 8 March 1970.

H0941 Leonard Lyons, *New York Post*, 10 March 1970. *Note:* Review of Knightley and Simpson (E309).

H0942 Leonard Lyons, *Philadelphia Daily News*, 11 March 1970. *Note:* Review of Knightley and Simpson (E309).

H0943 Leonard Lyons, *Miami Beach Sun*, 13 March 1970. *Note:* Review of Knightley and Simpson (E309).

H0944 Leonard Lyons, *Lorain Journal* (Ohio), 13 March 1970. *Note:* Review of Knightley and Simpson (E309).

H0945 Leonard Lyons, *The Blade* (Toledo, Ohio), 14 March 1970. *Note:* Review of Knightley and Simpson (E309).

H0946 Leonard Lyons, *Times Herald Record* (Middleton, New York), 14 March 1970. *Note:* Review of Knightley and Simpson (E309).

H0947 Günter Blöcker, 'Reportage über Lawrence von Arabien', *Süddeutsche Zeitung,* 14 & 15 March 1970, 63. *Note:* Review of Knightley and Simpson (E313).

H0948 Frederick Kelly, 'T.E. Lawrence Agent of British Imperialism', *New Haven Register* (Conn.), 15 March 1970.

H0949 Leonard Lyons, *Morning Advocate* (Baton Rouge, Louisiana), 15 March 1970. *Note:* Review of Knightley and Simpson (E309).

H0950 J.B., 'Arab Liberator Lawrence's Legend Shattered', *Fort Lauderdale News Sun Sentinel* (Florida), 15 March 1970.

H0951 John Barkham, 'New Evidence Undercuts Hero', *The Blade* (Toledo, Ohio), 15 March 1970.

H0952 John Barkham, 'The End of Lawrence of Arabia', *Victoria Advocate* (Texas), 15 March 1970.

H0953 Gerald Meyer, 'Lawrence of Arabia Was a Spy', *St. Louis Post-Despatch,* 15 March 1970.

H0954 Leonard Lyons, *Cedar Rapids Gazette (Iowa),* 16 March 1970. *Note:* Review of Knightley and Simpson (E309).

H0955 Leonard Lyons, *Bayonne Times* (New Jersey), 16 March 1970. *Note:* Review of Knightley and Simpson (E309).

H0956 Leonard Lyons, *San Mateo Times* (California), 16 March 1970. *Note:* Review of Knightley and Simpson (E309).

H0957 Leonard Lyons, *Salt Lake Tribune,* 16 March 1970. *Note:* Review of Knightley and Simpson (E309).

H0958 John Barkham, 'The End of a Legend', *Hawkeye* (Burlingame, Iowa), 18 March 1970.

H0959 Leonard Lyons, *The Post-Standard* (Syracuse, New York), 19 March 1970. *Note:* Review of Knightley and Simpson (E309).

H0960 Thomas Lask, 'Man and Legend', *New York Times,* 21 March 1970, p.27.

H0961 Sam Laird, 'Lawrence Might-Have Been', *Courier-Post* (Camden, New Jersey), 21 March 1970.

H0962 Mary Wagner, 'Desert Enigma', *Burlingame Advance Star* (California), 21 March 1970.

H0963 Mary Wagner, 'Desert Enigma', *Palo Atlo Times,* 21 March 1970.

H0964 Leonard Lyons, 'Into the Lyons Den', *News* (Bangor,Maine), 21 March 1970.

H0965 Bobby Mather, 'Dark Side of Lawrence of Arabia', *Detroit Free Press,* 22 March 1970.

H0966 George MacDonald Fraser, 'Backing into the Limelight', *Chicago Tribune,* 22 March 1970.

H0967 George MacDonald Fraser, 'Backing Into the Limelight', *Washington Post,* 22 March 1970.

H0968 John Barkham, 'Lawrence Legend Shortened', *Times Union* (Albany, New York), 22 March 1970.

H0969 *Star Bulletin & Advertisor* (Honolulu), 22 March 1970. *Note:* Review of Knightley and Simpson (E309).

H0970 Maurice Duke, '"Different" Lawrence of Arabia Emerges from New Biography', *Richmond Times-Dispatch*, 22 March 1970. *Note:* Review of Knightley and Simpson (E309).

H0971 'New Light Shed on Lawrence of Arabia's Feelings', *Shelby Star* (North Carolina), 25 March 1970.

H0972 John Barkham, 'The Debunking of a Legend', *San Francisco Chronicle*, 25 March 1970.

H0973 Kelly Adrian, *Iowa Bookshelf*, 26 March 1970. *Note:* Review of Knightley and Simpson (E309).

H0974 'Lawrence of Arabia in a New Light', *Southfield Jewish News* (Michigan), 27 March 1970.

H0975 G.J. Advani, '"Debunking" T.E. Lawrence', *Chicago Daily News*, 28 March 1970.

H0976 Tom Donnelly, 'A Sound Spanking for a Hero', *Washington Daily News*, 29 March 1970.

H0977 John Barkham, 'Destroying the Lawrence Myth', *Sunday Record* (New Jersey), 29 March 1970.

H0978 *Sioux City Sunday Journal* (Iowa), 29 March 1970. *Note:* Review of Knightley and Simpson (E309).

H0979 John Barkham, 'Destroying the Lawrence Myth', *The Reader* (Hackensack, New Jersey), 29 March 1970.

H0980 Bobby Martin, 'New Data On Times, Trials of the "King of the Bedouins"', *Philadelphia Inquirer*, 29 March 1970.

H0981 Malcolm Bauer, '"Lawrence of Arabia" Seen in New Perspectives', *The Oregonian*, 29 March 1970.

H0982 Waka Tsunda, *Rosswell Record* (New Mexico), 30 March 1970. *Note:* Review of Knightley and Simpson (E309).

H0983 *Creston News Advertiser*, 31 March 1970, p.6. *Note:* Review of Knightley and Simpson (E309).

H0984 'Literary Guideposts', *Sulpher Springs News Telegram* (Texas), 31 March 1970. *Note:* Review of Knightley and Simpson (E309).

H0985 *State Times* (Baton Rouge, Louisiana), 31 March 1970. *Note:* Review of Knightley and Simpson (E309).

H0986 'Emotional Turmoil After War Deal', *Menominee Herald Leader* (Michigan), 1 April 1970.

H0987 *Manchester Herald* (Conn.), 1 April 1970. *Note:* Review of Knightley and Simpson (E309).

H0988 Adrian Kelly, *Cherokee Times* (Iowa), 1 April 1970. *Note:* Review of Knightley and Simpson (E309).

H0989 Waka Tsunda, *Biddleforne Saca Journal* (Maine), 1 April 1970. *Note:* Review of Knightley and Simpson (E309).

H0990 Waka Tsunda, *Baytown Texas Sun*, 1 April 1970. *Note:* Review of Knightley and Simpson (E309).

H0991 Waka Tsunda, 'Windfall Helped Pair with Lawrence Study', *Asbury Park, Evening Press* (New Jersey), 1 April 1970.

H0992 Waka Tsunda, 'T.E. Lawrence's Struggles Probed', ? (Alma, Michigan), 1 April 1970.

H0993 Waka Tsunda, *Sheboygan Press* (Wisconsin), 1 April 1970. *Note:* Review of Knightley and Simpson (E309).

H0994 Karl Oldberg, *Santa Monica Independent Journal*, 1 April 1970. *Note:* Review of Knightley and Simpson (E309).

H0995 *Oltumwa Courier* (Iowa), 1 April 1970. *Note:* Review of Knightley and Simpson (E309).

H0996 'Did Lawrence Want to Subjugate Arabs?', *Michigan City News Dispatch*, 2 April 1970.

H0997 'Lawrence Suffers Emotional Struggle After the Middle East', *Fort Walter Beach Playground News* (Florida), 2 April 1970.

H0998 Karl Oldberg, 'International History Is Novel', *Culver City Independent* (California), 2 April 1970.

H0999 *Statesville Record* (North Carolina), 2 April 1970. *Note:* Review of Knightley and Simpson (E309).

H1000 'T.E. Lawrence's Emotional Tussle', *North Pennsylvania Reporter*, 2 April 1970.

H1001 Mary Ann Riley, *News Telegraph* (Atlantic, Ohio), 2 April 1970. *Note:* Review of Knightley and Simpson (E309).

H1002 Waka Tsunda, *Kearney Hub* (Nebraska), 3 April 1970. *Note:* Review of Knightley and Simpson (E309).

H1003 *Hamilton Journal News* (Ohio), 3 April 1970. *Note:* Review of Knightley and Simpson (E309).

H1004 Waka Tsunda, 'Emotional Struggle after the Middle-East War Deal', *Carroll Town Democrat* (Missouri), 3 April 1970.

H1005 Waka Tsunda, 'Lawrence of Arabia Book Features New Facts', *Rochester Post-Bulletin* (Minnesota), 3 April 1970.

H1006 '"Secret Lives" Tells More of T.E. Lawrence', *Napa Register* (California), 4 April 1970. *Note:* Review of Knightley and Simpson (E309).

H1007 Waka Tsunda, *Muncie Press* (Indiana), 4 April 1970. *Note:* Review of Knightley and Simpson (E309).

H1008 Waka Tsunda, *Minot North Dakota News*, 4 April 1970. *Note:* Review of Knightley and Simpson (E309).

H1009 *Chronicle* (DeKalb, Illinois), 4 April 1970. *Note:* Review of Knightley and Simpson (E309).

H1010 Waka Tsunda, 'Lawrence Fought for British Empire', *Capital Journal* (Salem, Oregon), 4 April 1970.

H1011 Waka Tsunda, 'Eyes on Lawrence', *Berkeley Gazette* (California), 4 April 1970.

H1012 'Lawrence of Arabia Still Elusive Subject', *Beacon News* (New York), 4 April 1970.

H1013 'The Secret Lives of Lawrence of Arabia', *Anchorage Alaska Times*, 4 April 1970.

H1014 W.T., *Woodbridge News Tribune* (New Jersey), 4 April 1970. *Note:* Review of Knightley and Simpson (E309).

H1015 Waka Tsunda, 'Eyes on Lawrence', *Richmond Independent* (California), 4 April 1970.

H1016 'Thirty Books Later They're Still Dealing With Lawrence of Arabia', *Reno New Gazette* (Nevada), 4 April 1970.

H1017 Waka Tsunda, 'Lawrence of Arabia Still Elusive Subject', *Newburgh News*, 4 April 1970.

H1018 'New Data on Lawrence of Arabia', *Lexington Herald-Leader* (Kentucky), 5 April 1970.

H1019 Waka Tsunda, 'Psychodynamics of T.E. Lawrence', *Kalamazoo Gazette* (Michigan), 5 April 1970.

H1020 Waka Tsunda, 'A Fresh Look at Arabia's Lawrence', *Home News* (New Brunswick, New Jersey), 5 April 1970.

H1021 Waka Tsunda, 'Another Look at Lawrence', *High Point Enterprise* (North Carolina), 5 April 1970.

H1022 'Arabia's Lawrence New Light Shed', *Harrisburg Patriot News* (Pennsylvania), 5 April 1970.

H1023 'Lawrence's Emotional Struggle', *Florence News* (South Dakota), 5 April 1970.

H1024 'Lawrence of Arabia', *Council Bluffs Nonpareil* (Iowa), 5 April 1970. *Note:* Review of Knightley and Simpson (E309).

H1025 Waka Tsunda, 'Arabia's Lawrence in New Light', *Commercial Appeal* (Memphis, Tennessee), 5 April 1970.

H1026 'New Light on Lawrence, His Middle East Dealing', *Clarion-Ledger Jackson Daily News* (Missouri), 5 April 1970.

H1027 Waka Tsunda, 'Another Side of Lawrence of Arabia', *Bloomington Tribune and Star-Courier* (Indiana), 5 April 1970.

H1028 'Why Lawrence of Arabia Lied', *Billings Gazette* (Montana), 5 April 1970.

H1029 Waka Tsunda, 'More on Lawrence of Arabia', *Bay City Times* (Michigan), 5 April 1970.

H1030 Waka Tsunda, 'Englishman in Arab's Garb', *Springfield State Journal-Register* (Illinois), 5 April 1970.

H1031 W.T., 'Fabulous Lawrence of Arabia', *Springfield Republican*, 5 April 1970.

H1032 Waka Tsunda, 'Another Book is Written On Lawrence', *Salisbury Times* (Maryland), 5 April 1970.

H1033 Wak *(sic)* Tsunda, 'More to Say About Lawrence', *St. Petersburg Times* (Florida), 5 April 1970.

H1034 John Barkham, 'Lawrence Legend Furthered by Latest Co-op Efforts', *Rockford Register Star* (Illinois), 5 April 1970.

H1035 *Reading Eagle* (Pennsylvania), 5 April 1970. *Note:* Review of Knightley and Simpson (E309).

H1036 'Lawrence of Arabia "Secrets" Revealed', *Opelousas World* (Louisiana), 5 April 1970.

H1037 Waka Tsunda, 'Lawrence's Emotional Struggle After the Middle-East War Deal', *Opdika News* (Alabama), 5 April 1970.

H1038 Edwin Newman, 'Dissecting the Mystique of Lawrence of Arabia', *News and Observer* (Raleigh, North Carolina), 5 April 1970.

H1039 Joseph Landau, 'Hero or Mirage?', *Louisville Times* (Kentucky), 6 April 1970.

H1040 'Lawrence Emotional Struggle Examined', *Greensburg Tribune Review* (Pennsylvania), 6 April 1970.

H1041 Waka Tsunda, 'A Fascinating New Look at Lawrence of Arabia', *Chester Times* (Pennsylvania), 6 April 1970.

H1042 John Barkham, 'Lawrence of Arabia', *Middleton Press* (Conn.), 7 April 1970.

H1043 Waka Tsunda, 'Team Justifies Book on Lawrence', *Longmont Times-Call* (Colorado), 8 April 1970.

H1044 Kelly Adrian, *Fort Dodge Messenger and Chronicle* (Iowa), 8 April 1970. *Note:* Review of Knightley and Simpson (E309).

H1045 Waka Tsunda, 'Lawrence's Emotional Struggle', *Snyder News* (Texas), 8 April 1970.

H1046 Waka Tsunda, 'Two Newsmen Write Book About Lawrence of Arabia', *Easter Express* (Easter, Pennsylvania), 9 April 1970.

H1047 'Lawrence's Emotions After the Middle East War', *Vincennes Sun Commercial* (Indiana), 9 April 1970.

H1048 Waka Tsunda, 'Lawrence's Struggle After Middle East War', 9 April 1970.

H1049 Leonard Dubkin, 'Lawrence Has a New Dimension', *Skokie Life* (Illinois), 9 April 1970.

H1050 Waka Tsunda, 'Lawrence of Arabia New Material Shows His Other Side', *Mankato Free Press* (Minnesota), 10 April 1970.

H1051 Waka Tsunda, 'Lawrence of Arabia's Life Remains as Elusive as Ever', *Green Bay Press Gazzetter* (Wisconsin), 10 April 1970.

H1052 *Dubuque Iowa News*, 10 April 1970. *Note:* Review of Knightley and Simpson (E309).

H1053 Waka Tsunda, *Daily Observer* (Bricktown, New Jersey), 10 April 1970. *Note:* Review of Knightley and Simpson (E309).

H1054 W.T., *The Times Record* (Troy, New York), 11 April 1970. *Note:* Review of Knightley and Simpson (E309).

H1055 Waka Tsunda, 'Lawrence's Emotional Conflict', *Press-Register* (Clarkesdale, Mississippi), 11 April 1970. *Note:* Review of Knightley and Simpson (E309).

H1056 Waka Tsunda, 'Lawrence of Arabia Was Elusive', *Martinsville Bulletin* (Virginia), 12 April 1970. *Note:* Review of Knightley and Simpson (E309).

H1057 Carla L. Kausner, 'Lawrence: Friend of Arabs', *Kansas City Star*, 12 April 1970.

H1058 Waka Tsunda, 'Did He Doublecross the Arab?', *Detroit News*, 12 April 1970.

H1059 Alan Pryce-Jones, 'The Never Before Told Story of Lawrence of Arabia', *Detroit News*, 12 April 1970.

H1060 Richard E. Langford, *DeLand Sun News* (Florida), 12 April 1970. *Note:* Review of Knightley and Simpson (E309).

H1061 'Secret Lives of Lawrence Well Detailed', *Birmingham News* (Louisiana), 12 April 1970.

H1062 Waka Tsunda, 'Get Your Camels He's Off Again', *Ada Oklahoma News*, 12 April 1970.

H1063 'Book Analyses Lawrence Actions', *Winona News* (Minnesota), 12 April 1970.

H1064 W.T., 'Lawrence of Arabia – a whole new picture', *West Palm Beach Post-Times* (Florida), 12 April 1970.

H1065 'Did Lawrence Sell Out His Arab Buddies', *Stockton Record* (California), 12 April 1970.

H1066 *Sioux City Journal*, 12 April 1970. *Note:* Review of Knightley and Simpson (E309).

H1067 'Elusive Subject', *Niagara Falls Gazette*, 12 April 1970. *Note:* Review of Knightley and Simpson (E309).

H1068 Alan Branigan, 'Lawrence As Spy, Not Savior', *Newark Sunday News* (New Jersey), 12 April 1970.

H1069 Waka Tsunda, 'Lawrence's Emotional Struggle after the Middle-East War Deal', *Catskill Mail* (New York), 15 April 1970.

H1070 'Book on Lawrence of Arabia', *Spartenberg Journal* (South Carolina), 15 April 1970.

H1071 'Two Newsmen Probe Secrets of Lawrence of Arabia's Life', *Poughkeepsie Journal* (New York), 15 April 1970. *Note:* Review of Knightley and Simpson (E309).

H1072 Waka Tsunda, 'Lawrence After the Mid East', *Orangeburg Times and Democrat* (South Carolina), 16 April 1970.

H1073 'Lawrence's Emotional Struggle after the Middle East War Deal', *Enquirer Journal* (Monroe, North Carolina), 17 April 1970.

H1074 Waka Tsunda, 'New Book on Lawrence of Arabia', *Pawtucket Valley Times* (West Warwick, Rhode Island), 18 April 1970. *Note:* Review of Knightley and Simpson (E309).

H1075 Paul Leibson, *El Paso Times*, 19 April 1970. *Note:* Review of Knightley and Simpson (E309).

H1076 Loetta Libby Atkins, 'Will "Real" Lawrence Please Now Stand Up?', *Denver Post*, 19 April 1970.

H1077 J.G. McCall, 'The Man Behind the Legend', *Witchita Falls Times* (Kansas), 19 April 1970.

H1078 Hector Bolitho, 'Lawrence Minus the Legend', *Sunday Star* (Washington, DC), 19 April 1970.

H1079 'The Man Behind the Legend of Lawrence of Arabia', *San Raphael Independent* (California), 19 April 1970. *Note:* Review of Knightley and Simpson (E309).

H1080 'Paul Elder's Book Forum/Lawrence of Engima', *San Francisco Sunday Examiner & Chronicle* ('This World'), 19 April 1970.

H1081 'How Lawrence Cut the Pie', *Post-Crescent* (Appleton, Wisconsin), 19 April 1970.

H1082 Waka Tsunda, 'Lawrence of Arabia Had Benefit of New Material', *Newport News Press*, 19 April 1970.

H1083 Waka Tsunda, 'New Insights Offered', *Gallup Independent* (New Mexico), 20 April 1970.

H1084 *Owensboro Messenger-Inquirer* (Kentucky), 20 April 1970. *Note:* Review of Knightley and Simpson (E309).

H1085 Alan Pryce-Jones, 'Lawrence of Arabia Revisited', *Journal Herald* (Dayton, Ohio), 21 April 1970.

H1086 Ray Finocchiaro, 'The Many Aspects of Lawrence of Arabia', *Wilmington Morning News* (Delaware), 21 April 1970.

H1087 *Sacramento Mirror,* 22 April 1970. *Note:* Review of Knightley and Simpson (E309).

H1088 'Another Lawrence', *Columbia State* (South Carolina), 26 April 1970. *Note:* Review of Knightley and Simpson (E309).

H1089 Waka Tsunda, 'New Lawrence Study Fails to Solve Engima', *Call Chronicle* (Allentown, Pennsylvania), 26 April 1970.

H1090 *The State Columbus* (South Carolina), 26 April 1970. *Note:* Review of Knightley and Simpson (E309).

H1091 *Pueblo Colorado Star-Journal and Chieftain,* 26 April 1970. *Note:* Review of Knightley and Simpson (E309).

H1092 Waka Tsunda, 'Lawrence Still Elusive Figure', *Galveston News* (Texas), 27 April 1970.

H1093 Waka Tsunda, 'New Book on Lawrence of Arabia Looks at Origins of Middle East Problems', *Enquirer and New* (Battle Creek, Michigan), 28 April 1970.

H1094 'Zionist Position Delimited in the Knightley and Simpson New Volume Describing "The Secret Lives of Lawrence of Arabia"', *Detroit Jewish News,* 1 May 1970, p.19.

H1095 P.S., 'Zionist Position Delimited in the Knightley and Simpson New Volume Describing "The Secret Lives of Lawrence of Arabia"', *Southfield Jewish News* (Michigan), 1 May 1970.

H1096 Waka Tsunda, *San Mateo Times* (California), 2 May 1970. *Note:* Review of Knightley and Simpson (E309).

H1097 'New Material Aids Lawrence of Arabia Book', *Jackson Citizen Patriot* (Michigan), 3 May 1970.

H1098 John P. Brown, 'T.E. Lawrence', *Huntingdon Herald Advertiser* (West Virginia), 3 May 1970.

H1099 W.H., 'Lawrence of Arabia Still a Real Enigma', *Columbus Sunday Dispatch,* 3 May 1970.

H1100 Irene L. Gendzier, 'The Last Lawrence Veil', *Boston-Herald Traveler,* 3 May 1970.

H1101 Sidney Thomas, 'Lawrence's Mystery Remains Unsolved', *Atlanta Journal and Atlantic Constitution,* 3 May 1970.

H1102 *Merill Herald* (Wisconsin), 5 May 1970. *Note:* Review of Knightley and Simpson (E309).

H1103 W.T., *Wausau Record-Herald* (Wisconsin), 5 May 1970. *Note:* Review of Knightley and Simpson (E309).

H1104 Kelly Adrian, *Marshall Town Times-Republican* (Iowa), 6 May 1970. *Note:* Review of Knightley and Simpson (E309).

H1105 Owen Findsen, 'Lawrence Con Man of Desert Author Says', *Cincinnati Enquirer,* 7 May 1970.

H1106 Jeffrey Meyers, *Boston Globe,* 7 May 1970, p.39. *Note:* Review of Knightley and Simpson (E309).

H1107 *Lewiston Maine Journal,* 9 May 1970. *Note:* Review of Knightley and Simpson (E309).

H1108 Waka Tsunda, 'Lawrence of Arabia Seen in a New Light', *Elkhart Truth* (Indiana), 9 May 1970.

H1109 Waka Tsunda, 'New Material Available about Lawrence of Arabia', *Belleville Illinois News − Democrat,* 9 May 1970.

H1110 Douglas Sparks, 'Lawrence Led Fascinating Life-All of Them', *Musfreesboro News Journal* (Tennessee), 10 May 1970. *Note:* Illus., review of Knightley and Simpson (E309).

H1111 Waka Tsunda, 'Lawrence's Struggle After War', *Jackson Sun* (Tennessee), 10 May 1970.

H1112 Waka Tsunda, *Tucson Star-Citizen* (Arizona), 10 May 1970. *Note:* Review of Knightley and Simpson (E309).

H1113 John Leonard, *Scranton Times* (Pennsylvania), 10 May 1970. *Note:* Review of Knightley and Simpson (E309).

H1114 J. Michael Robson, 'T.E. Lawrence: A Hero More Complex Than Most', *Providence Journal* (Rhode Island), 10 May 1970.

H1115 Martin Pine, *Fresh Meadows Townsman* (Flushing, New York), 14 May 1970. *Note:* Review of Knightley and Simpson (E309).

H1116 Martin Pine, *Queen's Observer* (Jackson Heights, New York), 14 May 1970. *Note:* Review of Knightley and Simpson (E309).

H1117 Martin Pine, 'Generally Speaking', *Coney Island Times* (New York), 15 May 1970. *Note:* Review of Knightley and Simpson (E309).

H1118 'Public Library New Books', *Troy News* (Ohio), 15 May 1970. *Note:* Review of Knightley and Simpson (E309).

H1119 *Shreveport Times* (Louisiana), 17 May 1970. *Note:* Review of Knightley and Simpson (E309).

H1120 'Lawrence of Arabia Back on Book Shelves', *Somerset American* (Pennsylvania), 27 May 1970.

H1121 'Zionist Position Delimited in the Knightley and Simpson New Volume Describing "The Secret Lives of Lawrence of Arabia"', *American Jewish Ledger,* 29 May 1970.

H1122 Waka Tsunda, 'Fascinating Look at Some of Origins of Middle East', *Durham Herald* (North Carolina), 30 May 1970.

H1123 'The Secret's Out', *Sentinel* (Ansonia, Conn.), 4 June 1970.

H1124 Waka Tsunda, *Rockford Register-Republic* (Illinois), 6 June 1970. *Note:* Review of Knightley and Simpson (E309).

H1125 Gilbert Moore, *Redding Record-Searchlight* (California), 6 June 1970. *Note:* Review of Knightley and Simpson (E309).

H1126 'Arab Censors', *Los Angeles Times,* 9 June 1970.

H1127 Mrs. F.B. Manchester, 'Life of Lawrence of Arabia Filled With Mystery, Enigma', *Santa Barbara News-Press* (California), 14 June 1970. *Note:* Review of Knightley and Simpson (E309).

H1128 Peter Chronis, 'The Multiple Personae of Lawrence of Arabia', *Rocky Mountain News* (Denver, Colorado), 14 June 1970.

H1129 Waka Tsunda, 'A New Side of Lawrence of Arabia and the Arabs', *Rapid City Journal* (South Dakota), 14 June 1970. *Note:* Review of Knightley and Simpson (E309).

H1130 Waka Tsunda, *New Britain Herald* (Conn), 26 June 1970. *Note:* Review of Knightley and Simpson (E309).

H1131 Waka Tsunda, *Kokomo Tribune* (Indiana), 5 July 1970. *Note:* Review of Knightley and Simpson (E309).

H1132 Bill Hibbard, 'Lawrence of Arabia Again Some Secrets are Divulged', *Milwaukee Journal,* 6 July 1970. *Note:* Review of Knightley and Simpson (E309).

H1133 Waka Tsunda, 'Lawrence's Struggle Told After Mid-East War', *Van Wert Times Bulletin*, 8 July 1970.

H1134 Marianna F. Brose, 'Lawrence of Arabia: a return', *Arizona Republic*, 12 July 1970.

H1135 Betsy Lindau, *Pilot-Pines* (North Carolina), 15 July 1970, pp.2–3. *Note:* Review of Knightley and Simpson (E309).

H1136 Marianna F. Broese, 'Lawrence of Arabia: a Review', *Phoenix Republic*, 16 July 1970.

H1137 W.T., 'Lawrence's Emotional Struggle After the Middle East War Deal', *Waynesville Mountaineer* (North Carolina), 24 July 1970.

H1138 Flavio Poll, *Il Progresso Italo-Americano*, 24 July 1970. *Note:* Review of Knightley and Simpson (E309).

H1139 Louis Garros, 'Saladin, nous voici!', *Le Monde*, 26 & 27 July 1970.

H1140 Waka Tsunda, *Selma Times* (Alabama), 27 July 1970. *Note:* Review of Knightley and Simpson (E309).

H1141 'Lawrence Items at USC Library', *Los Angeles Times*, August 1970.

H1142 'T.E. Lawrence Exhibit Here', *Los Angeles Times*, August 1970.

H1143 Josof Digman, 'Best Biography of T.E. Lawrence?', *Courier Journal & Times* (Louisville, Kentucky), 2 August 1970.

H1144 Seymour B. Liebman, 'Secret Lives of Lawrence of Arabia', *Jewish Floridian*, 7 August 1970.

H1145 H.T. Hunt, 'Work Attempts to Assess Lawrence's Worth', *Columbus Enquirer* (Georgia), 17 August 1970.

H1146 Jean Lacouture, 'Le Cheikh Admirable', *Le Monde*, 22 August 1970.

H1147 'Pasadenan Shows Works on Lawrence', *Los Angeles Times*, 30 August 1970, p.4.

H1148 H. Hobson, *Christian Science Monitor*, 17 September 1970, p.9. *Note:* Review of Knightley and Simpson (E309).

H1149 'When Lawrence Made a Quiet Exit', *Yorkshire Post*, 28 October 1970.

H1150 *Milwaukee Journal*, 6 December 1970. *Note:* Review of Knightley and Simpson (E309).

H1151 'Lawrence of Arabia and Sex', *Los Angeles Times Calendar*, 1971.

H1152 Lois Lamplugh, 'Happy Years of T.E. Lawrence', *Western Morning News* (Plymouth), 22 January 1971, p.6.

H1153 Peter Hopkirk, 'Puzzle of Poems Lawrence Loved', *The Times*, 18 February 1971, p.15.

H1154 'Lawrence of Arabia', *Hollywood Independent*, 8 April 1971.

H1155 Stephen Farber, 'Look What They've Done to "Lawrence of Arabia" Now', *The Times*, 2 May 1971, p.11, Section 2.

H1156 Joyce B. Gregorian, 'A Stripped Lawrence', *Boston Globe*, 8 May 1971. *Note:* Letter to editor.

H1157 'Lawrence Papers Sold for $24,000', *New York Times*, 27 September 1971.

H1158 '£10,000 for Lawrence Letters', *Evening Standard*, 27 September 1971, p.6.

H1159 'Reopening Old Wounds', *Daily Telegraph*, 28 September 1971.

H1160 '£10,000 for letter', *Daily Mirror*, 28 September 1971.

H1161 Peter Hopkirk, '£10,000 for Service Papers of Lawrence', *The Times*, 28 September 1971, p.4.

H1162 R.R., 'Lawrence d'Arabie. Qui était le motocycliste?', *Télérama*, 30 September 1971.

H1163 R.R., 'Tribune de l'Histoire', *Télérama*, 30 September 1971.

H1164 'The Times Diary Lost Lawrence', *The Times*, 20 November 1971, p.12.

H1165 'Railway Cut by Lawrence of Arabia Still Crippled', *Los Angeles Times*, 4 June 1972, pp.4–5, Section A.

H1166 David Leitch, 'Lawrence was here or was it Mr. O'Toole?', *Sunday Times*, 24 December 1972, p.59.

H1167 *Sunday Times*, 1 March 1973, p.31, column 8. *Note:* Review of *The Mint* (A177).

H1168 Anthony Wood, 'Busts Link Two Unusual People', *Oxford Mail*, 26 June 1973, p.6. *Note:* Busts by Kennington and Willi Klopenstein.

H1169 'The Will to Power', *The Weekend Scotsman*, 14 July 1973. *Note:* Illus., review of Meyers, *Wounded Spirit* (E336).

H1170 'New Tablet for the "Shrine" at the Bottom of the Garden', *Daily Mail*, 17 August 1973, p.15. *Note:* Refers to house on Polstead Road with study for TEL in garden.

H1171 Keith Post, 'Sound Sense on T.E. Lawrence', _____ *Post*, September 1973.

H1172 Keith Bone, *Guardian*, 7 November 1973. *Note:* Review of Meyers (E336).

H1173 Jeffrey Meyers, *Guardian*, 7 November 1973. *Note:* Letter to editor.

H1174 Renaud Matignon, 'Lawrence d'Arabie. Grandeur et Misère des héros', *Le Figaro*, 9 July 1975.

H1175 *Pasadena Guardian*, 22 October 1975, 1:42, p.9. *Note:* Photo.

H1176 Geraldine Norman, 'Lawrence of Arabia First Edition for £11,100', *The Times*, 1976.

H1177 *Télé-Sept Jours*, 2 January 1976. *Note:* Review of television programme.

H1178 Stéphane Bijan, 'A Leffrinekweke, un jeune écrivain anglais, J.W. Wilson, prépare la "biographie officielle" de son légendaire compatriote Lawrence d'Arabie', *La Voix du Nord*, 17 February 1976, p.2. *Note:* Illus.

H1179 *Pasadena Star News*, 7 March 1976, p. A–7. *Note:* Review of Mack, *A Prince of Our Disorder* (E353).

H1180 M. Jennett, 'A Prince of Disorder', *Register* (New Hamden, Conn.), 21 March 1976. *Note:* Review of Mack (E353).

H1181 Alyn Brodsky, 'Lawrence of Arabia Enigmatic Hero', *Miami Herald*, 4 April 1976, p.7e. *Note:* Illus.

H1182 'Admiring View of Troubled Hero', *Des Moines Sunday Register*, 4 April 1976, p.3B.

H1183 Shaun O'Connell, 'The Complexities of T.E. Lawrence', *Boston Globe*, 4 April 1976. *Note:* Illus.

H1184 Roger Grooms, 'Lawrence: the Enigmatic "Ablest Soldier"', *Cincinnati Enquirer*, 11 April 1976, p.F9. *Note:* Illus.

H1185 John Richard, 'A Man With a Hump On His Mind', *Montréal Star*, 17 April 1976. *Note:* Illus.

H1186 Mack Paints, '"Human" Hero in Lawrence of Arabia', *Denver Post*, 18 April 1976. *Note:* Illus.

H1187 Margot Backas, 'The White Knight of the Desert', *Baltimore ?*, 18 April 1976. *Note:* Illus.

H1188 Hubert de Santana, 'Detailed Look At Lawrence', *Toronto Star*, 24 April 1976. *Note:* Review of Mack (E352).

H1189 Michael D. Hill, 'Skillfull Portrait of Enigmatic Hero', *Hartford Times*, 25 April 1976, p.35. *Note:* Illus.

H1190 Doris N. Taylor, 'Hero Legend Troublesome to Lawrence', *Sunday Oklahoma*, 25 April 1976.

H1191 Geoffrey Godsell, 'New Biography of Lawrence', *Christian Science Monitor*, 5 May 1976, p.23. *Note:* Review of Mack (E352).

H1192 Phillip Knightley, 'The Girl Who Snubbed Lawrence of Arabia', *Sunday Times*, 9 May 1976.

H1193 *Miami News*, 11 May 1976. *Note:* Illus., review of Mack (E352).

H1194 'The Face from the Desert that Haunted a Hero', *Daily Mail*, 13 May 1976.

H1195 E.C. Hodgkins, 'On the Couch', *The Times*, 13 May 1976.

H1196 Keith Robertson, 'Devastated Lawrence', *Oxford Mail*, 13 May 1976.

H1197 Robert Nye, 'Desert Songs', *The Scotsman*, 15 May 1976.

H1198 Donald B. Johnson, 'A Victim of the Dream', *Worcester Sunday Telegram*, 16 May 1976. *Note:* Illus.

H1199 Anthony Storr, 'Anatomy of Sacrifice', *Sunday Times*, 16 May 1976.

H1200 A.L. Rowse, 'Genius that Was, Lawrence', *Sunday Telegraph*, 16 May 1976.

H1201 Max Hastings, 'T.E. – A Mere Myth', *Evening Standard*, 18 May 1976, p.23.

H1202 Patrick Cosgrave, 'Lawrence the Man and the Legend', *Daily Telegraph*, 20 May 1976.

H1203 Bernard Dineen, 'Lawrence of Paradox', *Yorkshire Post*, 20 May 1976.

H1204 David Talbot, 'An American Last Word on Lawrence', *Birmingham Post*, 22 May 1976.

H1205 'Aircraftsman Shaw', *Sunday Telegraph*, 23 May 1976.

H1206 'Top Five Books', *Empire News*, 31 May 1976. *Note:* Review of Mack (E355).

H1207 W. Thesiger, 'In Defence of Lawrence', *Observer*, 6 June 1976.

H1208 C. Sykes, 'Lawrence of What?', *Observer*, 6 June 1976.

H1209 Richard Bensen-Gyles, 'Lawrence in Medical Hands', *Irish Times*, 12 June 1976.

H1210 Edmund Fuller, 'Reminiscences of an Old Pro', *Wall Street Journal*, 26 August 1976, p.10.

H1211 P. Albert DuHamel, 'Lawrence of Arabia', *Boston Herald American*, 12 December 1976, p.A40. *Note:* Photo.

H1212 *Los Angeles Times*, 11 June 1977. *Note:* Cartoon.

H1213 Colin Simpson, 'Lawrence Made Up Rape Story Says Author', *Sunday Times*, 12 June 1977, p.2. *Note:* Review of Stewart, *T.E. Lawrence* (E367).

H1214 'Lawrence of Arabia Slain, Author Claims', *?* (Long Beach, California), 13 June 1977.

H1215 'Lawrence of Arabia Slain', *Toronto Star*, 13 June 1977. *Note:* Review of Stewart (E367).

H1216 E.C. Hodgkins, 'The Monday Book', *The Times*, 4 July 1977.

H1217 Margaret Forster, 'Legend of Arabia?', *Evening Standard*, 5 July 1977, p.21.

H1218 Geoffrey Moorhouse, 'Peculiar Person', *Guardian*, 17 July 1977. *Note:* Review of Stewart (E367).

H1219 Tom Shales, 'Classics Cut up for Sitcom Set', *Los Angeles Times*, 13 August 1977, part II, p.17.

H1220 Nicholas Bormell, 'T.E. Lawrence: A Legend Built on Exaggeration', *Boston Sunday Globe Parade*, 9 October 1977, p.56.

H1221 'The Arabian Nights of T.E. Lawrence', *Gay Community News*, 22 October 1977, pp.8–9.

H1222 Julian Symons, 'The Man Who Backed Into the Limelight', *Sunday Times*, 4 December 1977. *Note:* Review of Montgomery Hyde, *Solitary in the Ranks* (E373).

H1223 David Legate, 'Last Word on Lawrence', *Montreal Star*, 21 January 1978. *Note:* Review of Stewart (E367).

H1224 Jack Smith, *Los Angeles Times*, 26 April 1978.

H1225 Jack Smith, *Los Angeles Times*, 3 May 1978.

H1226 'Quatre leaders de l'histoire (Jacques Bénoist-Mechin. Lawrence d'Arabie)', *Télé-Sept Jours*, 4 May 1978.

H1227 George MacDonald Fraser, 'Shifting Sands of Legend', *Manchester Guardian*, 21 May 1978. *Note:* Review of Stewart (E367) and Montgomery Hyde (E373).

H1228 William A. Henry, 'More on the Life of T.E. Lawrence', *Boston Globe*, 23 May 1978, p.24.

H1229 Robert Kirsch, 'T.E. Lawrence: The Inner Being', *Los Angeles Times*, 19 July 1978, part IV, p.4.

H1230 Jean-Marie Cavada et Michel Thoulouze, 'De Lawrence d'Arabie à Camp David', *Télé-Sept Jours*, 1979.

H1231 '20,863 Books Signed by Lawrence', 1979.

H1232 'Lawrence Faces the En-Dewrance Test', *Southern Evening Echo*, 5 January 1979.

H1233 'A New Memorial to Lawrence of Arabia', *Dorset Echo*, 15 March 1979.

H1234 Ken Adachi, *Toronto Star*, 18 June 1979. *Note:* Review of Eden, *The Murder of Lawrence of Arabia (E384)*.

H1235 Paul Giniewski, 'Lawrence d'Arabie contesté', *Le Figaro*, 27 August 1979.

H1236 Werner Birkenmaier, 'Der faschistischen Metaphysik sehr nahe', *Stuttgarter Zeitung*, 14 September 1979, p.16.

H1237 Peter Hennessy, 'Lawrence's Secret Arabian "slush fund"', *The Times*, 11 February 1980, p.12.

H1238 Harald Vocke, 'Kein Heldenkult Mit Lawrence', *Frankfürter Algemeine Zeitung*, 21 March 1980, 69, p.27.

H1239 Robert Fisk, 'T.E. Lawrence & Co. Slept Here', *The Times*, 5 April 1980, p.14.

H1240 J.M.G. Le Clézio, 'T.E. Lawrence mis à nu (sur Le Matrice)', *Le Monde*, 9 May 1980.

H1241 Pierre Lepape, 'Les mirages de Lawrence d'Arabie', *Télérama*, 31 December 1980, pp.6, 26–27, 37, 38, 42, 43.

H1242 Geneviève Coste, 'Mort sous un faux nom en 1935 Lawrence d'Arabie avait refusé d'être vice-roi des Indes', *Télé-Sept Jours*, 3–9 January 1981, pp.34–35, 40–41, 52–53.

H1243 Phillip Knightley, 'Another Twist in the Lawrence Tale', *Sunday Times*, 26 April 1981.

H1244 H.V.F. Winstone, 'Was Lawrence a Red Herring', *Sunday Times*, 10 May 1981.

H1245 Ken Adachi, *Toronto Star*, 1982. *Note:* Review of MacEwen, *T.E. Lawrence Poems* (E392).

H1246 Pierre Lepape, 'Introduction à "Un livre, des voix". Présentation de Pierre Sipriot. "Les Textes essentiels de T.E. Lawrence"', *Télérama*, 9 and 15 January 1982.

H1247 Howard Rosenberg, 'Lawrence: Death of 1,000 Cuts', *Los Angeles Times*, 12 July 1982, pp.1, 7.

H1248 *The Times*, November 1982. *Note:* Letter to editor re article by Janet de Gaynesford.

H1249 H.V.F. Winstone, 'Lawrence, and the Legend that Misfired', *The Times*, 6 November 1982, p.8.

H1250 Woodrow Wyatt, 'Tales From Arabian Nights', *Sunday Times*, 18 November 1982.

H1251 Howard Rosenberg, 'The Little Things that Meant a Lot', *Los Angeles Times Calendar*, 29 December 1982.

H1252 Hussein al-Jalili, 'Lawrence and the Presumed Connections With Arabs', *Daily al-Iraq*, 22 June 1983, p.4.

H1253 Massignon, Louis, 'My Contacts With Lawrence in 1917', *Daily al-Iraq*, 22 June 1983, p.4. *Note:* Translated by Dr. Akram Fadel.

H1254 Ian Ball, 'Lawrence Saw Philby's Father as "Rather a Red"', *Daily Telegraph*, 1 October 1983. *Note:* Illus.

H1255 Lucie Prinz, 'The Puzzle of T.E. Lawrence', *San Diego Union*, 1 April 1984. *Note:* Review.

H1256 Jon Kimche, 'Egypt's Taba claim based on forged British map of 1915', *Jerusalem Post (International Edition)*, 22 December 1984.

H1257 'Lawrence Death Probe 50 Years on', *?* (English), 29 January 1985.

H1258 Phillip Jordan, 'Lawrence of Arabia's bizarre double life', *Mail on Sunday*, 31 March 1985.

H1259 'Lawrence of Arabia: Legend in His Lifetime', *Dorset Evening Echo*, 13 May 1985, pp.10–11.

H1260 Glenys Roberts, 'Lawrence of the House Next Door', *London Standard*, 16 May 1985, p.25.

H1261 Michael Hegener, 'Lawrence na Arabia', *de Volkskraat* (Literary Supplement), 18 May 1985, p.1.

H1262 'Lawrence of Arabia: A Legend in His Lifetime', *Bournemouth Evening Echo*, 18 May 1985, pp.2–3.

H1263 Jacques Dars, 'Lawrence d'Arabie ou la recherche scrupuleuse de l'ascète', *Le Monde,* 22 May 1985.

H1264 'Great Interest in Lawrence Society', *Western Gazette* (Yeovil, England), 26 July 1985.

H1265 'Secret Lawrence admirer says it with flowers', *Dorset Evening Post,* 17 August 1985.

H1266 'Lawrence remembered: Mystery Roses Appear Again', *Western Gazette,* 23 August 1985.

H1267 Hugh A. Mulligan, 'Wiliam Ramsay Knew Lawrence and His Arabia', *Daily Press* (Newport News, Virginia), 7 July 1986.

H1268 John Rice, 'There's Little Evidence of Lawrence in Arabia', *Los Angeles Times,* 24 August 1986, part 1, p.4. *Note:* Early edition.

H1269 John Rice, 'Lawrence Isn't a Hero in Arabia', *San Francisco Chronicle,* 9 September 1986, p.16.

H1270 Adrian Lithgow, 'Last Mystery of Hero Lawrence', *Daily Mail,* 2 November 1986.

H1271 'Works of Burton, Lawrence Shown', *Los Angeles Times.*

H1273 'Jouera le personage le plus mystérieux de l'histoire moderne "Lawrence d'Arabie"', *Le Journal du Dimanche.*

H1274 Dolores Espina, 'Lawrenciana', *El Mercurio* (Santiago, Chile).

H1275 Tom Barensfeld, 'What Was T.E. Lawrence Really Like?', *Cleveland Press.*

H1276 Christopher G. Janus, 'The Grand Obsession of T.E. Lawrence', *Chicago Daily News. Note:* Illus.

H1277 Waka Tsunda, 'Look at Origins of Problems in Middle East', *Bridgeport Post* (Conn.).

H1278 Jeff Wylie, 'Thomas on Thomas', *Boston Sunday Herald Advertiser,* Section 5, p.A6.

H1279 Waka Tsunda, *Bodalusa News* (Louisiana). *Note:* Review of Knightley and Simpson (E379).

H1280 'Lawrence's Campaigns Relived by Old Comrades', *Yorkshire Post.*

H1281 'At Last a Memorial to Lawrence of Arabia', 16 May. *Note:* Illus.

H1282 Lord Astor, 'The Mother of "T.E.", Courageous Story of Mrs. Lawrence'.

H1283 Lewis Gannett, 'Books and Things Odysseus Lawrence Private Shaw'. *Note:* Review of *The Odyssey* (A114).

H1284 'How Lawrence of Arabia Died'. *Note:* Text in Russian.

H1285 'Une Femme par son ultime sacrifice a sauvé par amour Lawrence d'Arabie'.

H1286 Robert Payne, 'Other Places, Other Times', p.8.

H1287 Barrie Pitt, 'Prophet in Blue Blazer'.

H1288 Peter Grosvenor, 'Lawrence By a Woman Who Never Met Him'. *Note:* Review of Ocampo, *338171* (E152).

H1289 Kenneth Tynan, 'The Unravelling of Ross'.

H1290 Dr. Ernest Barker, 'The Last Gleanings'. *Note:* Review of *Oriental Assembly* (A221).

H1291 'Hero's Pillars Crumble. Destroy Legend of Lawrence', *Youngstown Vindicator* (Ohio).

H1292 Peter Worthington, 'Greater Man Than Lawrence of Arabia (Glubb Pasha)', *Toronto Telegram.*

INDEX

Explanatory note

Persons, places, societies and institutions have been indexed, except when appearing in the imprints of the publications. Titles of separate monograph works are included if at all distinctive. References are to item numbers.

A., H.H., F0001
A., J.P., H0504
Aachener Volkszeitung, H0930
A/B Bookman's Weekly, G1329–30, G1685–6
Abbott, C.L.A., H0859
Abdallah, King of Jordan, F0002–3
Abensour, Leon, G0367
Abingdon Abbey Press, F0892
'Abinger Harvest', F0359–60
ABMR's Booksellers Catalogue, G1651, G1684
Abr-Nahrain, G1453
Abrieu, N., G0404
Abruzzini, Italiane, (pub), E247
'Les Abstractions Aventurières de Roger Stéphane', G1245
Abstracts of English Studies, G0958, G0983, G1052, G1190, G1260, G1262, G1283, G1324, G1339, G1447, G1450, G1467, G1494
Abusson, Brice, H0583
'L'Accord Franco-Anglais', H0008
'Aces and Kings', F1009
'Achievement', F0809
'The Achilles Heel', F0984–5
Ackerley, J.R., G1410
Ackerman, Carl W., G0414
'Acquaintances', F1064
'A.C. Shaw (Lawrence of Arabia)', F0887
'Un Acteur Egyptien dans "Lawrence d'Arabie"', H0595
L'Action, H0565
'Las Acusciones de Aldington', G0801
Ada Oklahoma News, H1062
Adachi, Ken, H1234, H1245
Adam, Colin Forbes, E004
Adam, Paul, E248
Adam, H0666, H0687
Adams, Michael, F0005
Adams, Phoebe Lou, G0830
Addison, William, F0006
'Additions to the Doubleday Collection: Kipling, T.E. Lawrence' G1081
Adelphi, G0627
'An Adequate Response', F0618
'Admiring View of Troubled Hero', H1182
'Adopts Lawrence Medal', H0295

Adrian, Kelly, H0973, H0988, H1044, H1104
Advance Information – Campaign Book (Film), E269
Advani, G.J., H0795
'Adventure in Arabia', D0027–9
'The Adventurer', F1188
'Adventures Among Immortals', F1040–40a
'Adventures in Arabia's Deliverance', B0015
'Adventures in Good Reading', F1023
'The Adventures of Lawrence of Arabia', E283
'The Adventures of Ulysses', A254
Aebu, K., G0246
L'Aede, G1063
Aeroplane, G0253, G0471, G0741
Aeroplane Monthly, G1645
'The Aesthetic T.E. Lawrence', E339
'Affaire Aldington contre Lawrence d'Arabie', E217, G0857
'L'Affaire "Lawrence"', H0441
'L'Affaire T.E. Lawrence', G0683
'Afghanistan, "Highway of Conquest"', F0351
'African Trilogy', F0754
'Age and Youth', F0060
'The Age of Illusion', F0111
'The Age of the JAP', H0736
'L'Agent Double', G0596
Aglion, Raoul, F0006
'Agonizing Reappraisal of T.E. Lawrence', G0848
Aguilar (pub), E177
'AEfintýri Lawrence Í Arabííu', E021
Aiken, Conrad, F0124
'Air-Cushion Vehicles', G1250
'Aircraftsman Shaw', G0577, G0592, H1205
'Aircraftsman Shaw – A Memory', G0615
'Aircraftsman T.E. Shaw', G0324
'Air-Storming', F1079
Akdemir, Aziz Hudai, E176
Al-Fatih, Zuhdi, E327
Al Ghossim, F0015
Al Hasimaiate Press, F0021
al-Hayat, (pub), F0462
Al-Houria, (pub), F0008
'Al Hussein Ber Ali wa Al Thawara Al Arabia Al Koura', F0775
al-Jalili, Hussein, H1252

Al-Kulliyah, G0647
Al-Maaref (pub), F0713
Al Madi, Monib, F0019
Al-Marayat, Abid, F0020
Al-Mugtataf, H0127
Al Na-Faris, E327
al-Nahar (pub), E323
Al-Said, Nouri, G0087
Al Shaar, Ammon Abou, F0021
'Al Sir Al Ghamed Wara Moat Lawrence', G1673
Al Sirai Ghamed, G1672
Al-Tariff, Sheik Hassan, G1192
Al Tarraki (pub), F0015
Al-'Umari, E323
Alaglouni, Mohammed Ali, F0008
Alaric, Jacob, G1473
Albérès, R.M., G1248
Albert-Hesse, Jarre, H0467
'An Album of Illustrations to Colonel T.E.
   Lawrence's Seven Pillars of Wisdom', A098
Albut, Harold, G0562
Alcuin Press, F0399
Aldanov, Mark A., F0009, G0272
'Alden's Oxford Guide', F0010
Aldershot News, H0014
Aldington, Richard, D0008, E190–202, F0011–13,
   G0652, G0656, G0658, G0671, G0673, G0682–3,
   G0694, G0700, G0704–11, G0713, G0716, G0718,
   G0720, G0726, G0733, G0738, G0760, G0766–7,
   G0782, G0784, G0786, G0801, G0803–4, G0810,
   G0813, G0826, G0834, G0837, G0844, G0846,
   G0851, G0861–2, G0867, G0869, G0872, G0876,
   G1133, G1397, G1483, G1651, G1699, H0432,
   H0435, H0443, H0446, H0449, H0457–9,
   H0462–4, H0471, H0484–6, H0529, H0544,
   H0546, H0549
'Aldington l'Imposteur', F0314, G0782
'Aldington, Jean Béraud-Villars', G0810
'Aldington's Enquiry Concerning T.E. Lawrence',
   G1483
'Aldington's "Lawrence"', E211
'Aldous Huxley', F0070
Aldridge, James, F0014
'Alec Guinness', F1026
Alehoff, Fred, G0419
Alen (pub), F0305
'Alexander Korda', F0611–2
Ali Shah, Ikbel, F0016
'All About Lawrence of Arabia', E252–4
'All Alone', G0052
'All England Mourns Passing of Lawrence', H0224
'All Equal at Lawrence's Funeral', H0285
'All in a Lifetime', F0107
'All Out in the Desert', G1004
All Souls, Oxford, E231
'All the King's Camels', G1060
'All-Star All-Good', G1044
Allan, Mea, F0017
Allen, H. Warner, G0329
Allen, Kenneth, E381; see also Ebert, Richard, E382
Allen, Louis, G1563
Allen, Malcolm Dennis, E395–6
Allen, Richard, F0018
Allen & Unwin (pub), D0030, F0268, F0270, F0373,
   F0496, F0638, F0693, F0915, F0999, F1167
Allen, W.H., (pub), D0024, E252, F0611
Allenby, General Sir Edmond H.H., A011–2,
   F0385–6, F0944–5, F1100–105, G0255, G0294,
   H0231, H0239

'Allenby', F0385
'Allenby and Lawrence', F0386
'Allenby, a Study in Greatness', F1100–101
'Allenby in Egypt', F1102–3
'Allenby of Arabia', F0386
'Allenby of Armageddon', F0944–5
'Allenby: Soldier and Statesman', F1104–5
'Allenby's Final Triumph', F0711
Allez-Enseignez, G0441
Allgemeine Zeitung, H0927
Alliance Book (pub), F0735
Allouche, Felix, H0561
Alpst, Hollis, G1046
Altarass, Gloria, G1688
Altounyan, E.H.R., E113, G0436, G0438, G0443,
   G0445, G0452, H0380, H0388
Altounyan, Taqui, F0022
Alvarez, A., G0933
A.M. Éditions (pub), E144
'Amanullah Claims His Crown Again', H0089
'The Amazing A.C. 2', G0906, G0908
'Ambrosia and Small Beer', F0705
America, G0837, G1059, G1297, G1405, G1501,
   G1537
'American and British Literature Since 1890', F1078
American Aphrodite, G0626
American-Arabian Night, A187
American Book Collector, G1075
'The American Boy', F0023
'American Boy Adventure Stories', F0023
'American Buyers Take British Mss.', H0864
'American Heritage', G1627
American Heritage Editions, F0024–5
'American Heritage History of World War I', F0024
American Historical Review, G0095, G1309, G1595
American Imago, G1578
American Jewish Ledger, H1121
American Journal of Psychiatry, G1344–5, G1350
'An American Last Word on Lawrence', H1204
'An American "Lawrence" of Southeast Arabia',
   H0738
The American Oxonian, G1616
American Review, G0234, G0357
American Weekly, G1085, G1087
'AMG in Damascus', B040
Amiot-Dumont (pub), E190
'The Amir of Mecca al-Husayn Ibn 'Ali and the
   Origin of the Arab Revolt', G0923
Amitiés France-Israel, G0896
Ammoun, Denise, G1358
'Among the Bedouins', C0021
Amory, Cleveland, F0026
Amsterdam Boek (pub), E343
'An der Legende Gerüttelt', H0901
'Analyses: Le Colonel Lawrence de Jean Béraud-
   Villars', G0819
'Anatomy of Oxford', F0251
'Anatomy of Sacrifice', H1199
Anchorage Alaska Times, H1013
Anderegg, Michael A., G1643
Anderson, Isaac, G0036
Anderson, Lisa, G1570
Anderson, M.S., G0027
Anderson, Patrick, G1188
Anderson, Walter, H0286
André Malraux', F0112
Andrieux, Gérard, H0468
Angell, Olav, A084

'L'Angleterre et Israël de l'ère du Colonel Lawrence à 1969', G1376
'Anglo-Spanish Attitude', G1556
'The Angry Neighbours', F0119
Angus & Robertson (pub), F0380, F0458
Annales, G0831, G1406
Les Annales Politiquès et Littéraires, G0291
Annals, American Academy of Political & Social Science, G0415, G0590–1, G0616, G0869
'L'Année T.E. Lawrence', G0860
'An Annotated Bibliography of Sir Richard Francis Burton', F0835
'An Annotated Checklist of a Collection of Writings By and About T.E. Lawrence', E299
'Annotations on Some Minor Writings of T.E. Lawrence', E077
Announcement Card to Correspondents, A161
'Announcement of Gift of T.E. Lawrence Collection to Honnold Library', G1507
'Annual Report of the Curators of the Bodleian Library for 1972–1973', F0028
'Another Book is Written on Lawrence', H1032
'Another Lawrence', H1088
'Another Lawrence: Air-Craftsman Shaw and Air-Cushion Aircraft', G1250–51
'Another Lawrence Letter', C0019
'Another Lawrence Myth', G1112
'Another Look at Lawrence', H1021
'Another Shaw's Corner', H0711
'Another Side of Lawrence of Arabia', H1027
'Another Twist in the Lawrence Tale', H1243
Anselm, Linton, G0768
'Anti Hero', H0895
'Antimémoires', F0694
'Anti-memoirs', F0695–6
Antiochus, G0646
'An Antiquarian and a Geologist in Hants', B0001
Antiquarian Book Monthly Review, G1489, G1641, G1645
Antiquarian Book Review, G1614
'The Antiquities of Jordan', F0476
'The Anti-Soviet Plot', H0113
Antonius, George, F0029–31
'Any Number Can Play', F0323
Apollo, G0048, G0293, G0470
'The Appeal of Fascism', F0470
Appleton (pub), F0396
Appleton Century (pub), E024, E081, F0122, F0498, F0780
Appleton Century Crofts (pub), F1078
'Appointment in the Sun', F0356
'Approach to Palestine', F0714
'Arab Angle', H0816
'An Arab Attacks Lawrence', H0829
'The Arab Awakening', F0029–31
'The Arab Breed Register', F0032
'Arab Bulletin', A010–10a, A226
Arab Bureau, Cairo, A010–10a
'The Arab Campaign', C0003
'Arab Censors', H1126
'Arab Command', F0561
'The Arab Epic', C0004
Arab Horse Society, F0032
'Arab Liberator Lawrence's Legend Shattered', H0950
'The Arab March on Damascus', C002
'The Arab Revolt', D0022, F0340, G0868
'Arab Revolt Celebrated', H0410

'The Arab Revolt – Further Light on Feisal and Lawrence', H0143
'Arab Revolt Head Tells Secrets', H0133
'The Arab Revolt in Africa', F0067
'Arab Rights: Our Policy in Mesopotamia, C0010
'An Arab Slant to the Lawrence Legend', H0814
'Arab Source on Lawrence of Arabia: New Evidence', G1670
'Arab Unravels Lawrence Legend', H0826
'The Arab World', F0557, F0996, G1225, G1269, G1320
'The Arab World Today', F0090
'Un Arabe juge Lawrence', G1488
'Araber Gegen Turken in Weltkrieg. T.E. Lawrence und der Arabers Aufstand in der Wüste', G1707
'Arabia and the Hedjaz', G0034
'Arabia and the Isles', F0551–2
'Arabia Deceptia', G1302
'Arabia Deserta', A028, A250, G0933
'Arabia Deserta: Vorwart zu dem Arabien-Buch von Charles Doughty', B0036
'Arabia Desperata', G0089
Arabia Felix', A155–7, A250, B030, F0475, G0186
'Arabia Infelix', G1484
'Arabia Literaria', F0287
'Arabia no Lawrensu', E041–2, E262a
'Arabia no Lawrensu no Himitsu', E316
'Arabia Nova', G1266
'Arabia of the Wahabis', F0840–41
'Arabia Phoenix', F0257
' "Arabia" Press Moves Base', H0602
'Arabia Railway Hit By Lawrence Being Rebuilt', H0782
'Arabia Resa', A031
'Arabia, the Gulf and the West', F0586
'Arabia Through the Looking Glass', F0880
'Arabian Adventure', F0044–5, F0193
'Arabian Adventurer', F0525
Arabian-American Oil Company, F0033–4
'Arabian Antic', F0328
'The Arabian Army in Palestine', G0016
'Arabian Days', F0842
'Arabian Days and Nights', G0022
'Arabian Desert Tales', F0338
'Arabian Destiny', F0082–3
'An Arabian Diary', F0219
'The Arabian Epic', H0024
'Arabian Hero's Mother Victim of China Reds', H0260
'Arabian Journey', F0258
'Arabian Jubilee', F0843–4
'Arabian Knight: T.E. Lawrence', G1585
'An Arabian Knight's Story', G0010
'Arabian Nights and Days', B0014
'The Arabian Nights of T.E. Lawrence', H1221
'Arabian Oil Ventures', F0845
'The Arabian Peninsula', F0493, F0937
'Arabian Politics: Resignation of Colonel Lawrence as Advisor', C0014
'An Arabian Sand Storm', G0051
'Arabian Sands', F1034–5
Arabian Studies, G1518
'Arabian Studies VII', F0951a
'Arabian Travellers', B0030, D0005
'Arabia's Lawrence in New Light', H1025
'Arabia's Lawrence New Light Shed', H1022
'Arabia's Uncrowned King', G0019
'An Arabic Folktale', G1388

'Arabië in Opstand', A112
'Arabien Krunnamaton Kuningas', G0927
'Arabiens Ungekrönter König', G0499, G0695
'The Arabs', F0303, F0382, F0529, F0802-3, F1038
'Arabs and Zionists', H0369
'Arabs' Hero', H0820
'Arabs Offer Troops', H0343
'Aramco Handbook', F0033-4
Aramco World, G1291,G1307, G1326, G1353,
    G1439, G1620
Ararat, G1626
Arberry, A.J., F0035
Arcadie, G0925
'Archaeologist Into Wrecker of Trains', G0096
'The Archaeology of the Holy Land', F0473
Arche (pub), A244
Archeologia, G1218, G1287
Archer, Sir Geoffrey, F0036
Archer, Jules, F0037
Archetype Press, F0086
Architectural Digest, G1668
'Architecture and Personalities', F0055
Archiv für den Studium den Neuren Sprachen,
    G0461
Archive Editions (pub), A010a
Archon Books, E332
Arco (pub), D0027-8, E221
Arendt, Hannah, F0039, G0621
Argonaut Press, F0454
Argus Bookstore, A223, E120, F0044
Arida, Maha, G1366
Arizona Republic, H1134
Arlington House (pub), F0612
'Armageddon 1918', F0325-6
Armbistor, Trevor, G1086
Armed Service Edition, A152
L'Armée, G1253
'Armenians are Impossible', G0182
Armitage, Flora, E212-6, G0649, G0791, G0798,
    G0816, G0823, G0828, G0830, G0833, G0854,
    G0863, G0865-6, G0872, G0877-8, G0880-91,
    G0894-5, G0897-9, G0902-3, G0905, G0911,
    G0993, G1120, H0539, H0541, H0553-66
'Arms and the Tower', F0337
Armstrong, Harold Courtney, F0039-42
Armstrong, Margaret, F0043
Armstrong, Terence Ian Fytton, E077
Army, G1306
'Army Diary', F0720
Army Quarterly, B0011-12, G1193, G1325, G1377,
    G1397, G1520, G1567, G1670
Army War College (pub), E337a-c
Arnaud, René, G0291
Arno (pub), F0841
Arnold, Julian Biddulph, E078, F0044-5, G0344
Arnold (pub), F0359-60, F0363-4, F0366
'Around the Coasts of Arabia', F0897-8
Around the Square, G1259
'Arranging the Minds of Men: T.E. Lawrence
    Theorist of War', G1520
Arrow (pub), E018, F0100
Arrow Editions (pub), E119-20
Art and Industry, G0575
Art News, G0344, G0572, G0583
'The Art of Augustus John', F0299
'Art of the Anglo-Saxon Age', F0559
'The Artist as Leader', G0518
Arts, G0671,H0594, H0682, H0706, H0789

Arundel, L.J., F0133
The Aryan Path, G1328
'As I Seem to Remember', F1167
As-Said, Nuri, F0095
Asad, Muhammad, F0046-7
Asbury Park Evening Press, H0992
'The Ascent of F6 and the Frontier', F0052
'The Ascent of F6: A New Interpretation', G1378
Ascherson, Neil, G1171
Asharg Al Awsat Magazine, G1673
Ashburton Guardian, H0592
Asher & Co., A001-2
Ashley, Maurice, F0048
Ashmolean Museum, E360
Asia Magazine, G0012, G0020-1, G0023-4,
    G0026-7, G0033, G0035, G0037, G0059, G0465,
    G0545
Aspects de la France, G0806
'Aspects de la littérature européene depuis 1945',
    F0049
'Aspects of an Enigmatic Personality', H0353
Asprey, Robert B., F0050
Assaf, Michael, E104
'Assails Lawrence on Arabian Record', H0049
'The Assertion and Denial of the Romantic Will in
    Seven Pillars of Wisdom and The Mint', E396
'Assignment: Churchill', F1054
'Assimil-Junior. Lawrence en bonde dessinée et en
    cassette', G1437
'Associates of Lawrence', H0153
Astor, Lady Nancy, F0221-2, F0453
Astor, Lord, H1282
'The Astors', F0581
d'Astrog, Bertrand, F0049, G0609
'At Last a Memorial to Lawrence of Arabia', H1281
'At the Paris Peace Conference', F0970
Ataturk, Kemal, F0376
Atelier l, (Studio 101), G0178
L'Athénée, G0914
Atheneum (pub), E374, E379, F0206, F0793, F0833,
    F0879, F0950
'The Atheist', G1532
Atkins, Loetta Libby, H1076
Atkinson, Brooks, H0690, H0705
Atlanta Journal and Atlantic Constitution, H1101
Atlantic Bookshelf, G0349
'Atlantic Monthly, B037, G0044, G0350, G0379-80,
    G0427, G0530, G0678, G0772, G0830, G0839,
    G0871, G1235, G1396, G1536
Atlee, Benge, F0023, G0175
'Atmosphères', G0792
'Auction Catalog of the Estate of Colin L.
    Campbell', F0051
Auden, W.H., A162, D0005, E110, F0052, F0068,
    F0172, F0183, F0191, F0377, F0463, F0546
'Auden: A Carnival of Intellect', F0183
'The Auden Generation', F0546
'Aufstand in der Wüste', A116-20, F1495
Die Aufseichnungen von 352087 A/c die
    Enthüllungen des Richard Aldington', G0687
'Augustus John', F0522
Ault, Warren O., G1616
Aunert, Uri, F00522
L'Aurore, H0446, H0535, H0678
'Australian Imperial Force in Sinai and Palestine,
    1914-1918', F0458
Australian Library Studies, G1655
Australian Quarterly, G0930

'Autobiography of Captain Harry Heir-Davies of London', F0495
'Autopsy of a Hero', G0718
'An Author Brands Own Masterpiece', H0190
'An Authoritative Biography', G0217
'Autour du Mystère de Lawrence d'Arabie', H0467
'Autumn Books from the Workshop of the Golden Cockerel Press', F0415
Aux Carrefours de l'Histoire, G1006
Aux Écoutes, H0433, H0457, H0752, H0790
Avenir de Tournaisis, H0547
'L'Aventure de Lawrence d'Arabie', G1625
L'Aventure Imprimée', G0812
'Un Aventurier d'un Style (Marco Polo)', H0536
'Un aventurier et une aventure de grand style: le colonel Lawrence et la révolte arabe', G0127
'Les Aventuriers', H0801
'L'Aviere Ross', A186
Avon Books, F0345, F0470, F0772
'An Awakening', F0597
'A.W. Lawrence on T.E. Film', H0701

B., E.M.E., G0504
B., F., G0903
B.,P., G0847
B.,Y., H0505
BBC TV (pub), E337
Bakker, J., G1319
Bachelor, G0437
The Bachen, B003
Backas, Mergot, H1187
'Backing Into the Limelight', E398, G1393, G1395, H0966–7
Baconniers-Neuchâtel (pub), F0309
Baden, Rudolf, G1654
Badisches Tagblatt, H0893
'Baffling Hero of the Desert', G1037
'Baghdad and Points East', F0195
Bailey, Richard W., G1342
'Bailing With a Teaspoon', F0286
Bailly, R., G0809
Bain, James S., F0054
Baker, Carlos, G0834
Baker, Sir Herbert, F0055, G0254
Baker, Hettie Gray, F0056
Baker, Peter, G1050
Baker, Randall, G1499
Bakshian, Aram, G1412
'Le Balayeur du Désert', G0948
Baldwin, Hanson W., F0057
Baldwin, Stanley, A162
Balfour, J.P.P., *see* Lord Kinross
Ball, Ian, H1254
Ballantine (pub), E334, F0637
Bancroft School, E361
Bancroftian, G0030, G0937
Bankhead, Tallulah, F0143
Bantam Books, D0022, E310, F0537, F0580, F0696, F1075
Barbary, James, E289–90, G1317
Bardens, Dennis, F0058
Barensfeld, Tom, H1275
Baring, Maurice, F0979, G0622
Barker, A.J., F0059
Barker, A.R.V., G0083
Barker, Arthur (pub), F0039–41, F0119, F0283, F0784
Barker, Sir Ernest, F0060, G0318, G0394, G0434, G0483, H1290

Barker, Malcolm, H0830, H0834
Barkham, John, H0951–2, H0958, H0968, H0972, H0977, H0979, H1034, H1043
Barnes, Eric Wollencott, F0061
Barnes, A.S. (pub), F0058
Barnes & Noble (pub), F0709, F0729, F0731, F1066
Barnett, R.D., A003, G1364
Barrack, G1296, G1388
'The Barren Rocks of Aden', F0675
Barrie, J.M., F0289, F1046
Barrie and Rockliff (pub), F0786
'Barrie, Cockerell, and Lawrence', F1046
Barrow, Sir George, F0062, H0480
Barsley, Michael, F0063
Bartlett, Stephen, E050–53, E057, E087–8
Bary, Herman, F0133
Barzun, Jacques, F0064
Basis Books, F0487, F0585, F1124, F1188
Bat and Bull Press, E399
Bates, H.E., A162, A175, H0474
Bates College, E339
Batey, Charles, E117
Bath Assembly Room and Museum of Costume, F0066
Batsford (pub), F0295
Battle, G1505
'Battle Album', G1505
Battle Stories, G0175
'Battleground', F0580
Baudisch, Paul, E313
Bauer, Malcolm, H0929, H0981
Baulin, Jacques, F0067
Baumgartner, Walter, H0934
Bawden, Edward, A104
Baxter, Frank C., E299, G1161, H0732
Bay City Times, H1029
Bayberry Hill Press, F0574
Bayerische Zeitung, H0918
Bayern Kuner, H0928
Bayonne Times, H0955
Baytown Texas Sun, H0990
Beach, Joseph Warren, F0068
Beach, Sylvia, G0346
Beacon News, H1012
Beaverbrook, William M.A., F0069
Beaumont. T.W., G1632, H0744
Beaumont Press, F0348
Beaus, Luset, H0695
Les Beaux-Arts, H0757
Becker, Mrs., G0181
Beckmans (pub), E022
Bedford, Sybille, F0070
'A Bedouin Battle in the City of Ghosts', G0026
'Beduin, Thirst and Desert Travel', H0862
Beebe, Lucius, G1278
Beeson, C.F.C., B0003–4
'Before and After – T.E. Lawrence and O'Toole', H0609
Begg, Robert Campbell, F0071
Begin, Menachin, E327
'Behind the Book', G0763
'Behind the Hero', G0846
'Behind the Lines', D0001
'Behold the Fire', F0104–6
Behrman, Samuel Nathaniel, F0072
Belfagor, G1636
Bell, Gertrude Lowthian, F0073–7, F0113, F0176, F0422, F0895, F1061, F1154–5

Bell, Millicent, G1561
Belleville Illinois News-Democrat, H1109
Belloc, Hilaire, A162
Belmont, Eleanor, F0078
Beloff, Max, F0079
Ben-Gavriel, M.Y., G0852
Ben Gurion University of the Negev, E341–2
Ben Hassen, A., H0565
Ben-Horin, Eliahu, F0080
Benedici, Rex, G1611
Benn (pub), F0073, F0077, F0107, F0176, F0847,
    H0850
Bennett, Arnold, F0081
Bénoist-Mechin, Jacques, E245–7, F0082–4,
    G0977, G0980, G1019, G1051, G1056, G1063,
    G1683, H0631–2, H0699, H0723, H1226
'Bénoist-Mechin Ou l'Histoire Passionnante',
    H0724
Benot, Yves, G1216
Benson, A.C., A162
Bensen-Gyles, Richard, H1209
Bentley, Nicolas, F0085
Bentley, Wilder, F0086
Bentwich, Norman, F0087
Béraud-Villars, Jean, E204–8, G0651, G0660,
    G0683, G0686, G0691, G0698–9, G0776,
    G0788–90, G0808, G0810–11, G0814–15,
    G0819, G0824–5, G0827, G0829, G0832,
    G0841–2, G0847, G0915–16, G0919–21,
    G0923–4, G1006, G1157, G1386, H0441, H0444,
    H0447, H0450, H0504, H0506, H0508,
    H0512–13, H0517, H0519–23, H0526, H0528,
    H0531–4, H0537–8, H0543, H0545, H0548–9,
    H0572–4
Bercovici, G0951
Berg, Dave, F0089
Berg (pub), F0422
Berger, Monroe, F0090
Berghs, (pub), A031
Berkeley Gazette, H1011
Berlinske Aftenavis Torsdag, H0750
'Bernard Shaw', F0829, F0932
'The Bernard Shaw Companion', F0478
'Bernard Shaw: Man and Writer', F1128
'Bernard Shaw, Playwright', F0288
'Bernard Shaw's Other Saint Joan', G1180, G1201
Bernhard, Rob, H0891
Bernstein, Burton, F0091
Le Berry Républicain, H0512
Bertelsmann (pub), A074
Bertram, Anthony, F0092
Bertram Rota, A257
'Best Biography of T.E. Lawrence?', H1143
'The Best of Friends', F0733
Best Sellers, G1083, G1399, G1515, G1525, G1549,
    G1574, G1580, G1593
'Between the Thunder and the Sun', F0962–3
'Beyond Arabian Sands', F0180
'Beyond Euphrates', F0987
'Beyond the Outsider', F1141
'Beyond the Sunset', F0280
Biblio (pub). E365, G0694, G0756, G0829
Bibliographical Notes on T.E. Lawrence's Seven
    Pillars of Wisdom and Revolt in the Desert',
    E043–6
Bibliographie de la France, G0776, G0824
Bibliographie de prof. élèves, G1101, G1163
Bibliographie de prof. pedag., G1683

'A Bibliography and a Critical Survey of the Works
    of Henry Williamson', F0399
'Bibliography of the Works of Sir Winston S.
    Churchill', F0331
'The Bibliophile's Almanack for 1928', F0093–4
La Bibliothèque Idéale, A250
Bibliothèque universelle et revue suisse, G0006
Biddleforne Saca Journal, H0989
Bidwell, Robin L., A010a, F0951a, G1518
Bidwell, Shelford, G1397
Biebner, Bartlett, G0108
Bielstein, Hans H., G0543
'The Biffer of the French', G1635
Bigelow, Poultney, G0095
Bijan, Stéphane, H1178
Billings Gazette, H1028
'A Biographer's Notebook', G0120
'Biographical Dictionary of World War I', F0499
'La biographie de Lawrence d'arabie par J.
    Béraud-Villars', G1006
'A Biography of Edward Marsh', F0489
Bird and Bull Press, F0958
Birdde, T., G0781
Birdwood, William R., F0095
Birkenhead, Frederick, F0096
Birkenmaier, Werner, H1236
Birmingham Evening Mail, H0641
Birmingham Mail, H0593, H0599
Birmingham News, H1061
Birmingham Post, H1204
Biro, E219
Bishop, Edward, F0097
Black, A. & C. (pub), F1061
Black, Cohey, H0726
Black, Donald, F0098
Black Archer Press, F1023
'Black Tents of Arabia', F0882–5
Blacker, Irwin R., D0001
Blackie & Son (pub), E219, F0895
Blackledge, William James, F0099
Blackmore, C.D., G1671
Blackmur, Richard Palmer, F0100–102
Blackwell, Basil (pub), A245–7, F0133, F0509
Blackwood (pub), F0615
Blackwood's Magazine, G0022, G0043, G0754–5
The Blade, H0945, H0951
Blaiklock, E.M., F0103
'Blair Hughes-Stanton on Wood Engraving',
    G1648
Blais, Jean-Etheir, H0796
Blake, George, G0078
Blanc-Dufour, A., G0596
Blandford Press, F0400, F0477
Blankfort, Michael, F0104–7
'Blasting and Bombardiering', F0640–41
Blauhome, Kim, G1098
Bles (pub), F0001, F0790, F0946
Blöcker, Günter, H0947
Blond (pub), F0005
'Blood, Sand and a Dozen Lawrences', G1041
Bloomington Tribune and Star-Courier, H1027
Bloomsbury Review, G1662
'Blowing Up a Train', D0016, D0019, D0024
'Blowing Up Trains', D0006–7
Blue Book, G0555
Blue Boy, G1607
'Blue Plaque for Lawrence "Refuge"', H0808
'Blue Plaque to T.E. Lawrence', G1696

Blumenfeld, Ralph David, F0107–8
Blunden, Edmund, A162
Blunt, Wilfred S., F0109–10, G0627
Blythe, Ronald, F0111
Boak, Denis, E363, F0112, G1240
Bobbs-Merrill (pub), F0469, F0945
Boccazzi, Cino, E391
'Bodkin Permitting', F0799
Bodalusa News, H1279
Bodleian Library, F0028, F0117; Quarterly Review,
    G0319
'Bodleian to Get T.E. Lawrence Letters', H0739
Bodley, Ronald, F0113–16
Bodley Head (pub), A090–91, F0546, F0579, F1125
Bograd, Michael, E342
Boisdeffre, Pierre de, F0118, G0838, G1504, H0426,
    H0515, H0797
'A Bölcseseg Hét Pillere', A079
Bolitho, Hector, F0119–22
Bolt, Robert, E226, E249, E271, G0994, G1047,
    H0644
'Bolt Tries Film on For Size', H0644
Bompiani (pub), A080–1
Bond, Geoffrey, E221
Bond, Michael, H1172
Bone, Keith, H1172
Boni & Liveright (pub), A019–20, F0674
Bonibel Press, E388, E402
Bonin, Charles, G0163
Bonnell, F.W. & F.C., F0124
Bonnell, Pamela G., G1529
Bonnier, Albert, H0792
Bonnier, Henry, H0823
Bonniers, Albert (pub), A138, A187, E159, F0670
Bonsal, Stephen, F0125, F0371
'A Book a Week', G1085
'Book Analyses Lawrence Actions', H1063
Book Auction News, G1613
Book Collector's Market, G1566
Book Collector's Packet, G0206, G0469, G0487,
    G0533
'Book Costs $150 a Copy', H0018
Bookdealers' prospectuses, A216, A223, A228
'The Book of Courage', F0464
'Book of the Day', H0045
Book of the Month Club, F0816; Book of the
    Month Club News, G0054, G0322–3
'Book on Lawrence of Arabia', H1070
Bookseller, G1524, G1544
'A Bookseller Looks Back', F0054
Bookletter, G1682
Booklist, G0040, G0129, G1048, G0228, G0348,
    G0356, G0383, G0426, G0450, G0517, G0642,
    G0833, G0844, G0924, G1025, G1411, G1459,
    G1603
Bookman, G0053, G0079, G0089, G0107, G0109,
    G0119, G0131, G0133, G0136, G0154–5,
    G0192–3, G0201, G0568, G0828
The Bookman Advertiser, G0092
'Bookman's Manual', F0510
Bookmark, G0191
Booknews, G1387
'Bookplates', F0056
Books, G1474
'Books – A Monument on Display at Whittier',
    H0765
Books Abroad, G0690, G1282
'Books, an Introduction to Reading', F0743

Books and Bookmen, G1217, G1268, G1472,
    G1508, G1553
'Books Designed by Bruce Rogers', F0992
'Books in General', F0872
'Books in My Baggage', F0866–7
Boot, William, G1029
Boothby, Robert, F0126
Borden Pub. Co., F0570
Borges, Jorge Luis, F0748
Boriswood (pub), A163–4, D0013–14
Bormell, Nicholas, H1220
'The Borough and District of Wareham', F0127;
    'The Official Guide', F1093
Borstein, Robert, G0990
Bory, Jean-François, E380
Böse, George, G0462
Boston Daily Record, H0610
Boston Evening Transcript, Magazine Section,
    G0259, H0396
Boston Globe, H1106, H1156, H1183, H1228
Boston Herald American , H1211
Boston-Herald Traveller, H1100
Boston Sunday Globe Parade, H1220
Boston Sunday Herald Advertiser, H1278
Boston Transcript, H0057, H0066, H0149, H0345,
    H0367, H0379, H0387–8, H0404
Bott, Alan, F0128
Bottomley, Gordon, F0129
'Bought His Wives With Lawrence's Gold', H0780
Boulton, James T., F1189
Boure nad Asií, A110
Bourgeois, Willy, G0904, G0909, G0912–14,
    H0567–70
Bourgois, Christian (pub), E173–4
Boussard, Léon, E143–44a
Boveri, Margret, G0639
Bouvier, Emile, H0500
Bowden, Ann, G1021
Bowden, Tom, F0130
Bowen, Elizabeth, G1034
Bowen, Norman R., F0131
Bowers, Fredson, G0522
Bowes & Bowes (pub), F0583
Bowker, R.R., F0510, F0779
Bowman, Humphrey, F0132
Bowra, Sir Maurice, A146, G0207
Boxhall, Capt. P.G., G1193
'Boy', D0013–14
Boyars, Arthur, F0133
Boyle, Andrew, F0134, G0721
Boyle, William, F0136
Boys' adventure books, E023–7, E028, E050–53,
    E056–7, E073–6, E087–8, E090–92, E141,
    E187–8, E219, E221, E227–9, E252–4, E289–90,
    E348–50, E366, E379
'The Boys' Life of Colonel Lawrence', E023–7,
    G0108, G0111, G0116, G0122, G0124, G0129,
    H0055–7
Box Office, G0965
Bradbury, D.H., G1222
Bradlee, Frederick, F0026
Bradley, Russell, F0137
Bramhall House (pub), E237
Branigan, Alan, H1068
'Brass Hat', G0551
'Brasses and Brass Rubbing', F0400
Bray, Norman N.E., F0138–9
Braybrooke, Neville, G1446

Braziller, George (pub), E275, F0335, F0549
'The Breakdown of Public Security', F0130
Breese, G.F., G0729
Breit, Hervey, G0658–9, G0726
Bremond, Edouard, F0140
Brennecker, Ernest, G0204
Brenner, J., H0495
Brent, Douglas, G1708
Brent, Peter, E356–7, F0141–2, G1501, G1508,
    G1515
Brian, Denis, F0143
Brian & O'Keefe (pub), E335–6
Briant, Keith, F0144
'The Bridge at Tel-el-Shebab', F0023
Bridgeport Post, H1277
Bridges, Robert, F1047
Bridges, Thomas Charles, F0145–6
Bridlington Free Press, H0431
'Bridlington Memorial to Lawrence of Arabia',
    H0430
'Bridlington Memorial to Lawrence of Arabia
    Unveiled', H0431
'A Brief History of Our Own Time', F0778
'A Brief Record of the Advance of the Egyptian
    Expeditionary Force', A011–12
Brien, A., G0932, G0952
'Bring Your Camel', H0832
Brion, Marcel, G0468, H0422, H0755
Brissaud, André, H0520
'Britain and the Arabs', F0402
'Britain and the Century of Total War', F0708
'Britain and the Middle East', F0173
'Britain, Arabia Mourn Death of Col. Lawrence',
    H0278
'Britain, France and the Arab Middle East', F0788
'Britain, France and the Middle East and North
    Africa', F1127
'Britain, India and the Arabs', F0178
'Britain Mourns T.E. Lawrence. British War
    Leader in Arabia', H0262
'Britain Not Planning Lawrence Memorial', H0294
'Britain Plans Memorial to Lawrence of Arabia',
    H0318
Britain Special, G1622
'Britannia's Greatest Names Join in Paying Tribute
    to "Lawrence of Arabia"', H0235
'Britain's Moment in the Middle East', F0749–50
'British Air Fatality Laid to "Novice" Pilot', H0125
'British Air Fleet is Ready For Arabia', H0064
'The British Arabists', G1473
British Army Review, G1671
British Book News, G0689, G0853–4
'British Campaigns in the Nearer East', F0249
British Council (pub), F0334
'The British Dominions Yearbook 1921', F0933
The British Empire, E337
'British Favorites', H0839
'The British in the Middle East', F0949–50
'British King's Doctor Fighting', H0191
British Legion Journal, B0032–3, G1209, G1222,
    G1224, G1232
British Medical Journal, G0478
British Museum, A001–3
'British Orientalists', F0035
'British Planes Bomb Unsinkable Speed Boat;
    Lawrence of Arabia Pilots New Test Craft',
    H0146
'The British Prince of Mecca', G1708

'British Role in Palestine', F0576
'British Seek High Honor for Lawrence of Arabia',
    H1298
'British Strategy and Politics, 1914–1918', F0457
'British Successor States in the Post-War Middle
    East', F0596
'The British Way of Warfare', F0643
'Briton's Confession of Tricking Arabs Disclosed',
    H0405
Broadsheet, G0534, G0536, G0588–9, G0561
Brock, Roy, F0147
Brockway, Wallace, D0002–3
Brodie, Fawn, F0148
Brodie, I.E., G1111
Brodie (pub), A231
Brodrick, Alan Houghton, F0149
Brogan, D.W., G0920
Bromage, Bernard, G0454
Bromley Public Library, F1096
Brook, W.H., H0466
Brooke, J., G0723
Brooke, Jocelyn, G1128
Brooke, Rupert, E129
Brooke House (pub), F1173
Brook-Shepherd, Gordon, F0150
Brophy, John, F0151–4, G0385, G0483
Brose, Marianna F., H1134, H1136
'Brother Rejects Lawrence Film', H0661
Broughton, Harry, E287, E295–6, E322
Brown, Carl, F0155
Brown, Cecil, F0156
Brown, Christopher, F0157
Brown, Ernest and Phillips, A032, A099
Brown, Irving, G0089
Brown, Ivor, G1137
Brown, John P., H1098
'Brown Dominions', G1363
Brownlow, Kevin, F0158
Brownrigg, Sir Douglas, F0159
Bruce, John, G0474
'Bruce Rogers', F0294
Bruguera (pub), E263–4, E318
Brun, Jean-Michel, E390
Brun, Nöelle, E254
Brunten, Paul, F0160
Bryant, A.S., G0309
Bryden, Ronald, G0975
Buchan, John, F0161–71, F0976–7, G0077, G0529,
    G0654, H0026, H0219
Buchan, Susan, (Lady Tweedsmuir), F0170
Buchan, William, F0171, G1272
'Buchan Club: Transactions', G0654
Bücher Künde, G0460, G0497
Bücherei und Bildung, G0659
Büchershiff, G1373
Buck, Katherine, H0283
Buckland, Gail, F1077
'Buddy of Lawrence of Arabia Tells Wartime
    Experiences', H0408
Buell, Fredrick, F0172
Bueresche Zeitung, H0922
Builder, G0544
'Les Bulgares fuient en désordre sur un Front de
    150km. Les Armées turques de Palestine
    anéanties', H0004
'The Bull', G1212
Bullard, Sir Reader, F0173–4
Bulletin Bibliographique des Armées, G1239

Bulletin critique du livre Française, G0890, G1213, G1252
Bulletin de l'Académie des Sciences d'outre-mer', G0897, G0901
'Bulletin de la Société Littéraire des P.T.T.', G0815
Bulletin de l'Institut Pédagogique National', G0849
Bulletin de Paris, G0715, G0736, G0765, G0814
Bulletin des Lettres (Lyon), G0738, G0790, G0847
Bulletin du Livre, G0977, G1072
Bulletin of Bibliography, E336, G1454, G1604
Bulletin of World Books, G0560
Bullock, Alan, F0175
Bumpus Ltd., J. & E., E086
Bunnell, James L., E186a
'Bunt, Arabów', A133; *see also* Burzá nad Azja
Burbidge, William H., E136
'Les bureaux, les hommes et la politique en Proche-Orient pendant et depuis la Première Guerre Mondiale', G1406
Burford, William, G1020
Burgoyne, Elizabeth, F0176
'The Buried Day', F0639
Burlingame Advance Star, H0962
Burlington Magazine, G0554
'Burn Lawrence in Effigy', H0088
Burr, John, F1124
Burton, Anthony, G1520
Burton, Hal, G1692
Burton, Sir Richard Francis, F0253, F0281, F0835, H1271
'Burton', F0281
'Burton of Arabia', F0253
Burucoa, G0698
'Bury Lawrence in Simple Rites', H0271
'Burzá nad Azja', A132; *see also* Bunt Arabów
Busch, Briton Cooper, F0178
'Bushman at Large', F1162
'Busts Link Two Unusual People', H1168
'Bustropheden', H0927
Butcher, Fanny, H0135
Butcher, Maryvonne, G1131
Butler, Evan, G1208
Butler, Grant, F0179–80
Butler, J. R. M., F0181
Butler, Oliver J., E337c–d
Butler, P.R., G0381
Bütow, Hans, G0737
Butros, Albert, E256–7
Butterworth (pub), F0213
'By Camel and Car to the Peacock Throne', F0864–5
'By Jove, Biggles', F0305
'By the Way', H0010
'A Byronic Poem About a Modern Hero', G0421

C., F., G1100–101, G1163
C., J., G1019
C., J. (pseudonym for TEL), B0029
C., L., H0173
Cabau, Jacques, G1207
Cadell. James, E227–9, G0945–6, G0953, H0590
Cadiz-Avila, Ilda (Espina), G1256
Les Cahiers "Connaissance du Monde"', G0785
Cahiers du Sud, G0200, G0468, G0596, G1231
Caillous, Rolland P., G0595
Cajumi, Arrigo, A123, A125
Calde, Mildred, F0182
Calder & Boyars (pub), F0641

Calder-Marshall, Arthur, G0633
Calderini (pub), E243
Calgary Herald, H0775
California Library Association Newsletter, G1507
Call Chronicle, H1089
'Call Me Ishmael', G0705
Callan, Edward, F0183
Calmann-Levy (pub), F0986
Cambridge Evening News, H0885
Cambridge Journal, G0646, G0664
Cambridge University, E113, F0627, F0935, F1062, F1189
'Camel Men Plan a Reunion', H0830
'Camels in Old Compton Street', H0604
'The Camels Must Go', F0174
Cameron, Elma, E289–90
Cameron, Kate, H0621
Cameron, Marion F., H0857
'La Campagne du Colonel Lawrence', E020
'The Campaign in Palestine – From the Enemy's Side', G0032
'Campaign of the Caliphs for Damascus', B0007
Campbell, Colin L., F0051
Campbell, Olwen Ward, F0185
Campbell Johnson, Alan, F0184
Canadian Army Journal, G0861
Canadian Defense Quarterly, G0529
Canadian Forum, G0203, G0227, G0784, G1070
Canby, Henry Seidal, G0323, G0336, G0406, G0506, G0512
'Cancelled First Chapter of Seven Pillars of Wisdom' (ghost), G0433
Canning, John, F0187
'Canon Christopher of St. Aldates', F0892
'The Cantos of Ezra Pound', F0862
Cantwell, Robert, G0742
Canvas, G1348
Cape, Jonathan, G0275
Cape (pub), A005–6, A013–18, A041–5, A047–51, A094–5, A100–102, A155, A159, A162, A171–4, A176–7, A202, A233, A237–9, A249, A256–9, D0005–6, E029–35, E058–60, E094, E096–7, E107–8, E114, E178, E250–51, E276–7, F0002, F0098, F0245, F0251, F0269, F0292, F0427, F0431–3, F0533, F0559, F0569, F0683, F0685, F0734, F0779, F0834, F1108, F1123, F1129, F1154, F1156, F1169–70, F1181, G0285
Cape & Smith (pub), F0433
Capital Journal, H1010
Capitol Tribune, H0349–50
Caplain, Serge, G0655
Capricorn (pub), F0031
'Captain Who Taught All the Generals', G1383
'The Capture of Damascus 1 Oct. 1918', G1179
'Captured by Turks in Holy Land', H0019
Capuano, Joseph, H0560
La Caravelle, G1051
Carchemish, A001–3, G0213, G0653
'The Career of T.E. Lawrence', E147
'Carl Dixon's Scrapbook', G1337
Carlow, Michael, F0189
Carlow, Viscount, A193
Carmichael, Amy, F0190
Carmichael, Joel, F1121
Carroll & Graf (pub), F0921
Carpenter, Humphrey, F0191
Carr, Winifred, F0192
Carrefour, H0442, H0488, H0520, H0558

Carrier, Louis, (pub), E048
Carrington, Charles E., E079–82, G0713, H0362, H0360
Carroll, Hamon, H0610
Carroll, Harrison, H0606
Carroll Town Democrat, H1004
Carron, Calvet, G0827
Carruthers, Douglas, F0193
'Cartas de T.E. Lawrence', A205
'Cartas de T.E. Lawrence a Lionel Curtis', B0038
Carter, F., E077
Carter, John, H0067
Carter, William, G1275
Cartland, Barbara, F0188
Cartland, Ronald, F0188
Carton, John, G0138
Carver, Michael (Field Marshal Lord), F0194
'The Case for the Prosecution', G0716
Casey, Robert, F0195
Cassell (pub), A213, D0001, E138–40, F0081, F0095, F0356–7, F0385, F0430, F0435, F0448, F0610, F0635, F0648, F0813, F0818, F1045, F1099, F1159, F1163
Cassen, Bernard, H0861
Castro e Almeida, Virginia de, E157–8
'Catalogue of An Exhibition', A032, D0004
'Catalogue of the Edward Clark Library', F0196
'The Catalogue of the H.G. Wells Collection in the Bromley Public Library', F1096
'A Catalogue of the Library of Charles Lee Smith', F0353
'Catalogue Raisonné of Work by, about and relating to T.E. Lawrence', E363
Catarivas, David, H0554
Cathelin, Jean, G0794
Catholic World, G0306, G0368, G0456
Catlin, George, F0197
Catskill Mail, H1069
Caudell, Christopher, F0199–201
Cavada, Jean-Marie, H1230
Cavalry Journal, G0431
'The Cave and the Mountain', F1002
'Cecile', F0673
Cedar Rapids Gazette, H0954
'Cei Sapte Stâlpi', A087
Cellesche Zeitung, H0892
'Celluloid Attempt to Pin Down a Legend', H0811
'Censorship in Action: The Case of "Lawrence of Arabia"', G1655
Centlivres, O., H0723
Central Literary Journal, G0503
Century (pub), E006, E023, F0864
Century Magazine, G0025
Ceram, C.W., F0202–5
'C'est Arrivé Demain', H0594
'Cet Homme Balaye le Désert', H0596
Chabbert, René, G1245
'Chaim Weizmann', F1121
Chalfont, Alun (Lord), F0206
'The Challenge of Destiny', E340
Chamberlain, John, H0714
Chambers, Jock, H0470
Chambers Journal, G0541
'Les Chameaux et l'Agent Secret', H0688
Champonier, Jean, H0540
Champress, H.M., G0710
Chandler, Edmund, G0043–4, G0401
'The Changing East', B0009

'The Changing Middle East', F0631
Changing Times, G1637
Channon, Sir Henry, F0207
Chant, Roy Heman, G1634
'Chanticleer', F0416
Chapman & Hall (pub), F0715
'Chapman's Homer', G1478
Chapois, Drion du, H0549
'Charles Doughty', F1021
'Charmed Lives', F0607
Charpentier (pub), E288a
Charrier, Paul, F0208
Chase, H.A., E006–8, E011
'Les Châteaux des Croisades', A240, G1287
Chaterson (pub), F1060
Chatto & Windus (pub), F0388, F0390, F0682, F0749, F0872
Chauvet, Louis, H0679
'A Checklist of Lawrenciana', E298
'A Checklist of the Letters of Richard Aldington', F0393
'Le Cheikh Admirable', H1146
'Le Chemin de Damas', F1031
'Le Chemin de Fer de Lawrence', G1333
Chercheurs et Curieux, G0660, G0795
Chernyaka, Ya., A135
Cherokee Times, H0988
Chester Times, H1041
Chesterton, G.K., F0378
Cheval de Troie, G0589
Chew, Sam, H0402
Chi Ruma, Shabo (pub), E262a
'Chiaroscuro', F0569
Chicago Daily News, H0235, H0975, H1276
Chicago Daily Tribune, H0135
Chicago Herald Examiner, H0234, H0260
'The Chicago of Ancient Arabia', G0093
Chicago Sunday Times Bookweek, G1531
Chicago Sunday Tribune, H0440, H0539, H0544, G0572, H0640
Chicago Tribune, H0181, H0191, H0199, H0277–8, H0351, H0966
Chicago Tribune Book World, G1393
'Children of Allah', F0585
Children's Press, E188
Childs, J. Rive, F0209
China Weekly Review, G0209
Chingford Historical Publication, E361
'Chips', F0207
Choice, G1290, G1407, G1557, G1597
'A Choice of Ornaments', F0085
'Choses Lues: Lawrence l'Imposteur', G0732
Chrestien, Michel, H0484, H0499
Christian Century, G0267, G0286, G1078
Christian Science Monitor, H0338, H0362, H0379, H0386, H0395, H0449, H0493, H0541, H0546, H0554, H0582, H0657, H0677, H0839, H1148, H1191; Weekly Magazine Section, G0328, G0342
Christliche Welt, G0361
'Christopher and His Kind', F0553
'Christopher Isherwood', F1008
Chronicle, H1009
'Chronicles of Barabbas', F0273–4
'Chronicles of Wasted Time', F0776
'Chronique Littéráire 338.171 T.E.', G0902
'Chronique Littéráire: Un Saint en Salopette', G0597

'Chroniques', G0820
Chronis, Peter, H1128
Church Times, H0916
'The Churches of Wareham, Dorset', F0539
Churchill, Andrew, G1122
Churchill, Sir Winston S., A170, A246, C0014,
  E110, E266–7, E282, F0210–18, F0230, F0237,
  F0298, F0331, F0387, F0455–6, F0500, F0541–2,
  F0608–9, F0657, F0707, F0758, F1052, F0154–5,
  G0321, G0408, G0556, G0805, H0160, H0322,
  H0411, H0577
'Churchill', F0025, F0455, F0543, F0758
'Churchill as Historian', F0048
'Churchill by His Contemporaries', F0297–8
'Churchill in Parliment', F0058
'Churchill in Power', F0387
'The Churchills', F0919
'Churchill's Last Years', F0541
'La Chute de l'ange', H0634
Cincinnati Enquirer, H0423, H1105, H1184
Ciné Revue, G0964
Cinema, F1163
Cinémonde, H0613, H0669
La Cité, H0692, H0697, H0743
The Citizen, H0607
'Civilian Loyalties and Guerrilla Conflict', G1007
Claassen (pub), E371
Clairefontaine (pub), E245
Claremont Graduate School, E320, F0596
Claremont Men's College, E297
Clarion-Ledger Jackson Daily News, H1026
Classic Motorcycle, G1659
Classical Journal, G0199, G1519
Classical Philology, G0210
'The Classical Tradition', F0501
Classical World, G1478
'Classics Cut up for Sitcom Set', H1219
'Claudius the God', F0428
Claus, Max, G0135
Clavie, Marvel, G0885
Clayton, Sir Gilbert F., F0219
'Cleaning Up After Lawrence', G1144, G1254
'The Clearing House', F0161
Cleave, Maureen, G1336
Clements, Frank, E331–3
Clemons, Walter, G1534
Cleveland Open Shelf, G0240, G0337
Cleveland Plain Dealer, H0829
Cleveland Press, H1275
Clew, Jeff, G1659
'Cliffs of Fall', G0724
'A Close Up of T.E. Lawrence', G0385
'Clouds Hill', E130–34, F0364–6, G0475, G0624,
  G1419
'Clouds Hill and the Lawrence Legend', G1630
'Clouds Hill, Dorset', F0929
'Clouds Hill, Wool, Dorset. T.E. Lawrence
  1923–1935', F0479
'Clues to the Legend of Lawrence', G0994
Clung, Claud-Michel, G1367
Clymen (pub), F0798
Coast Artillery Journal, G0414
'The Coast of Incense', F0988
'A Coat of Many Colours', F0888–9
Coates, James G., E298a, G1226
Cobden-Sanderson (pub), F0121
Cockerell, Sir Sydney, F0109–10, F1046
'Cockerell', F0109–10

'The Code Breakers', F0578
Cohen, Gustave, E217, G0857
'Coin of the Realm', G0744
Colby Library Quarterly, G1466
Coleman, John, G1036
'Collected Poems 1917–1953', F0688
'Collecting T.E. Lawrence Materials', E396
Collet, Paul, G1648
Colliers (pub), E008
Collier's, G0052
Collins (pub), E091–2, E191–4, E304, F0035,
  F0134, F0150, F0225, F0535, F0774, F0794, F0809,
  F0829, F0832, F0907, F1011, G1014, F1020, F1028,
  F1088
Collins, Major-General R.J., F0220
Collins-Lions, D0020
Collis, Maurice, F0221–2
Colmer, John, F0223
'Colonel as a Private Soldier', H0014
'Le Colonel Bousillé', G1220
'Col. Buried Without a Word of Praise', H0270
'Colonel Lawrence', G0664
'Le Colonel Lawrence', E122, G0288, G0686,
  G0691, G0698–9, G0776, G0788–90, G0808,
  G0811, G0814–15, G0824–5, G0827, G0829,
  G0832, G0841–2, G0847, G0915–16, G0919–21,
  G0923–4, G1006, H0445, H0447, H0450, H0504,
  H0506, H0508, H0512–14, H0517, H0519–23,
  H0526, H0531–4, H0537–8, H0543, H0545,
  H0548–9, H0572–4
'Colonel Lawrence – a Denial', H0105
'Du Colonel Lawrence à la Guerre Italo-
  Ethiopienne', G0360
'Le Colonel Lawrence à ia Tribune de Paris', H0542
'Colonel Lawrence Again', G0144
'Colonel Lawrence Again in the News', H0106
'Colonel Lawrence and His Magnificent Exploit in
  Arabia', F0791
'Colonel Lawrence and His Unorthodox Views of
  Honor', H0329
'Colonel Lawrence and the Afghan Revolt', G0168
'Colonel Lawrence and the Hedjaz', G0013
'Colonel Lawrence and Trebitsch Lincoln', H0083
'Du Colonel Lawrence Au Soldat J. H. Ross',
  H0502
'Du Colonel Lawrence aux Pétroles de Koweit',
  H0518
'Col. Lawrence Bobs up Again', H0071
'The Colonel Lawrence Bogy', G0158
'Le Colonel Lawrence, bouffon et bluffeur, faux
  héros et authentique mystificateur', H0433
'Col. Lawrence Close to Death', H0186
'Colonel Lawrence Collection', E180
'Le Colonel Lawrence est mort', G0266
'Colonel Lawrence et l'Arabie', E288a
'Le Colonel Lawrence et la France', G0619
'Le Colonel Lawrence et la Culture Française',
  F0309, G0537
'Col. Lawrence Fights for Life', H0189
'Le Colonel Lawrence fut-il un Imposteur', H0524
'Col. Lawrence is Badly Hurt', H0187
'Col. Lawrence is Near Crisis', H0196
'Col. Lawrence is Near Death', H0208
'Col. Lawrence is Still Unconscious', H0202
'Colonel Lawrence is Translating the "Odyssey'
  Into English Verse, But He May Not Publish It',
  H0118
'Colonel Lawrence Letter Writer', G0494

'Col. Lawrence Letters Sold', H0373
'Colonel Lawrence of Arabia', E098
'Le Colonel Lawrence, ou, la recherche de l'absolu', E204, G0845, G0850
'Le Colonel Lawrence ou la Tentation de Néant', G0838
'Col. Lawrence Reports, Also a Col. Lawrence Manuscript', H0339
'Col. Lawrence Seeks to Leave Air Force to Resume Writing', H0141
'Colonel Lawrence, the Man Behind the Legend', E061–2, G0224–5, G0228, G0231–6, G0238–41, G0289
'Col. Lawrence to Tell His Own Story', H0019
'Colonel Lawrence Up to Now', H0148
'Colonel Lawrence's Book', H0040
'Col. Lawrence's Books', G0073
'Col. Lawrence's Critic', H0051
'Col. Lawrence's Holiday', H0020
'Colonel Lawrence's Manuscript', G0045
'Colonel Lawrence's Masterpiece', H0044
'A Colonel of Truth', G0989
'En Colonel Shakespearien', G0991
'Colonel T.E. Lawrence', E182–3, F1064, G0294, H0073
'Colonel T.E. Lawrence (1888–1935)', F0894
'Col. T.E. Lawrence Eludes University Degree', H0121
'Colonel T.E. Lawrence (Lawrence of Arabia)', E399
'Le Colonel T.E. Lawrence, Le Moyen Orient et la France', G1573
'Col. T.E. Lawrence of Arabia', G0679
'Col. T.E. Lawrence Tired of Beastly Arabian Affairs', C0015
Colophon, G0458
Colorado Libraries Unlimited (pub), F0662
Colp, Ralph, G1640
Colum, Mary, G0346, G0518
Columbia Pictures, E266–73
Columbia State, H1088
Columbus Enquirer, H1145
Columbus Sunday Dispatch, H1099
Comarnescu, Petru, A087
Combat (France), G1257, H0498
'Combat and Command', F0279
Combat Illustrated, G1619
Combat: World War I, D0006–7
'Comment Fut Inventé "Emir Faycal"', G0099
Commentary, G1579, G1591
Commercial Appeal, H1025
Communications and Studies Inc. (pub), A064
'The Common Pursuit', F0626
Commonweal, G0204, G0848, G0987, G1064, G1094, G1424, G1446
'Communist, Guerrilla Warfare', F0270
'A Comparison of the Guerrilla Strategies of Mao and Lawrence', E337b
'The Complexities of T.E. Lawrence', H1183
'Le Comportement de l'Homosexuel', G1417
'Comrades Meet at Grave', H0276
'The Concise Cambridge History of English Literature', F0936
'Concise Dictionary of Archaeology', F0233
'A Concise History of the Middle East', F0421
Conde, Bruce, G0647
'Condition of Lawrence of Arabia is Critical', H0194

Coney Island Times, H1117
Conferencia, G0524
'Confession of Faith', D0012
'Confessions of T.E. Lawrence', E383
'The Confessions of T.E. Lawrence: The Sadomasochistic Hero', G1578
'Conflicting Evidence at Lawrence's Inquest', H0263
Congdon, Don, D0006–7
Connell, John, F0224–6
Connolly, Cyril, H0628
'The Conquest of Damascus', B0022
'Le Conquête de l'Inutile', H0823
'Conrad', F1098
'Conrad Aiken: A Bibliography', F0124
Constable (pub), E372a, E373, F0473, F0711, F0795, F0840, F0867, F0897, F0957, F0960, F1107
'Contemporary British Literature', F0227
Contemporary Review, G0649, G1457, G1471, G1487, G1493
'Continuous Use of Oxygen Fails to Revive Colonel Lawrence', H0237
'The Controlling Minds of Asia', F0016, F0954
'Controverse autour d'une légende l'Affaire Lawrence', H0444
Cook, Albert, F0229
Cook, Arthur, H0588
Cook, Bruce, F0230
Coolidge, Olivia, F0231
Coon, Carleton S., G0350, G0616
Cooper Square (pub), F1114
Coranto, G1161
Corbett, H.A., G1141
Cordey, Pierre, H0629
Cornell University Press, F0172, F0351, F0630, F0937
Cornhill Magazine, G0050, G0205
Cornstalk (pub), E028
'El Coronel Lawrence', E208
Coronado Journal (CA), H0709
Correspondance, G0794
Corse d'Aujourd'hui, H0526, H0556
Corvinus Press, A192–4, A196, A198, A219, E100–101
Cosgrove, Patrick, H1202
Coste, Geneviève, H1242
'Cottage of Trembling Memories', H0809
Cottingham, John B., E337b
Cottrell, Leonard, F0233, F0198
Council Bluffs Nonparile, H1024
'Count Luckner', F1042
'Counterfeit or True?', G0720
'Counter-Insurgency Warfare', F0877
Country Life, F0055, F1122, G1551
Courcel, Martin de, F0234
Courier, G1234
Courier Journal and Times, H1143
Courier-Post, H0961
Cournos, J., G1693
'Courts of the Morning', F0162
Cover, William G., G1409
Covici-Friede (pub), F0900
Coward, Noel, F0235–6, F0634
Coward McCann (pub), F0114, F0386, F1117, F0911, F0989
'Coward the Playwright', F0616
Cowles, Virginia, F0237
Cowles (pub), F0383

Cowley, Malcolm, G0343
Cox, Sir Percy, F0425
'A Crackle of Thorns', F0598
'Cradles of Eminence', F0414
Crafford, F.S., F0239
Crain, Jane Larkin, G1523
Le Crapouillot, G0179, G1417
'Crash that Cost the World a Hero and Scarred a Man for Life', H0805
'The Crash Which Killed Lawrence of Arabia', H0843
Craster, Edmund, F0240
Crawford, O. G. S., F0241
Creative Age Press, F0115, F0882
'A Creative Century', F1073a
'Creeds, History, Prophets and Geography in Seven Pillars of Wisdom', G1509
'The Crescent and the Bull', F1183
Cresse (pub), F0721
Cresset (pub), F0704, F0936
Cresswell, Walter D'Arcy, F0242
Creston News Advertiser, H0983
Crick, Bernard, G1556
'Crippled Saint', H0708
Critchfield, Richard, H1295
Critic, G1091
'A Critic In Action', G1141
'A Critic of Critics Criticized', B0026
'A Criticism of Henry Williamson's Tarka the Otter', A229
'Critics of Lawrence of Arabia', G1209
Critique, G0595, G0856, G1140
La Croix, H0525, H0787
Croix de Lorraine, H0568
La Croix Dimanche, H0684
La Croix du Nord et du Pas-de-Calais, H0508
Cross, L.B., G0298
Cross and Cockade Journal, G1337
'Cross Section', G0726
Crossman, Richard, F0243
'Crossroads to Israel', F1010
Crouse, R., G0957
Crowell-Collier (pub), F1128
Crowell, Thomas Y. (pub), E384, F0250
Crown (pub), D0016, F0315, F0503, F0544, F0628, F1145
'The Crowning Privilege', F0429
Crowther, Bosley, H0725
Crowther, John (pub), E136
'Crusader Castles', A188–91, A227–8, E161–2, F0333, G0390, G0394, G0399–400, G0417, H0370
Crutchlow, William, F0244
Culbis (pub), A128
Cullen, John, A230
'The Cult of Connections', G1480
'The Cult of Failure: Rimbaud', G0244
La Culture, G0172
Culver City Independent, H0998
Cumberlege, Geoffrey, A146
'Cumena', G1012
Cummings, Edward E., F0245
Cunard, Nancy, F0246
Cunliffe, J.W., F0247
Current Book Distributors (pub), F0201, G0233
Current History, B0007, G0013, G0165, G0347
Curtis, Lionel, D0002–3, G0778
Curtis, Michael, F0248
'Curzon Weeps', G0118

Custot, Pierre, D0008
'Customers and Friends: Memories of a Bookseller', G1527
Cuxhavener Zeitung, H0907
Cycle, G1295
Cycle World, G1449

D., C., see Dale, Colin
D., E., G0525, G0905
D., M., G0845
da Cruz, Daniel, G1189
Daily al-Iraq, H1252–3
Daily Cardinal, H0190
Daily Cinema, G1194
Daily Express, C0006–7, H0010, H0038, H0051, H0060–61, H0182, H0232–3, H0308, H0646, H0740, H0815, H0850
Daily Express Pubs., F0166
Daily Herald, C0012, H0084, H0086, H0276, H0729
Daily Mail, H0085, H0229, H0322, H0417, H0464, H0576, H0588, H1170, H1194, H1270
Daily Mirror, H0192, H0275, H0357, H0642, H0647, H0653, H0802–4, H1160
Daily News, C0015, H0043, H0079, H0092
Daily News and Westminster Gazette, H0080
Daily Observer, H1053
Daily Press, H1267
'Daily Record and Mail', H0274
Daily Sketch, H0193, H0236, H0248, H0272–3, H0605
Daily Telegraph, C0016, H0227–8, H0231, H0257–8, H0266, H0286, H0304, H0324, H0339, H0341, H0352, H0459, H0466, H0477–8, H0480, H0650, H0702, H0722, H0741, H0806, H0812, H0814, H0881, H1157, H1159, H1202, H1254
Daily Telegraph and Morning Post, H0870
Daily Telegraph Reporter, H0711
Dale, Colin (pseudonym for T.E. Lawrence), B0024–8
Dalhousie Review, G0563, G1443
'Dalton Trumbo', F0230
'Damaging Self-Portrait of T.E. Lawrence', H0477
Damiani, Alain, G1503
'Damn the Press', G1441
'Der Dämon des Absoluten', G0628
Dane, Edmund, F0249
Dangerfield, George, G0192, G0835
Daniels, Robert, H0811
'Dangerous Guides: English Writers and the Desert', G1340
Dann, Uriel, G1453, G1618
Danzig, H.P. Ziman, H0448
'Dark Side of Lawrence of Arabia', H0965
Darracott, Joseph, F0584
Dars, Jacques, H1263
Darwin Press, F0155
D'Arzo, Silvio, G0758
Daugherty, Charles Michael, F0250
'Daughter of the Desert', F0579
Davar (pub), E104
David, Evan, G0183
David, Max, H1272
David, W., D0023
David & Charles (pub), E331
'David Garnett's "Lawrence"', H0393
'David Lean and His Films', F0972
'David Lean en Jordanie', H0587
Davies, Peter (pub), E079, F0165, F0701

Davies, W.H., A162
Davis, Don, H0449
Davis, Leslie, G0964
Davis, Parton, E379, G1610–11
Dawn, Ernest, G0928
Dawray, Guy, B0011
Dawnay, Peter, E205–6
Dawson, Ernest M., E110
Day, John (pub), F0631, F0633, F0684, F0789, F0818, F0844
'Days of Our Years', F1080
'Days With Bernard Shaw', F1149
Dayton, John, G1333, H0745
de Fonblanque, Lt.-Colonel, A114
De Gaury, Gerald, F0257–60
de Hautecloque, Xavier, G0179
De La Bere, Rupert, F0261, G0062, G0324
Deacon, Richard, F0252
'Dead Towns and Living Men', F1168–72
Deardon, Seton, F0253
'Dearest Mother', D0010
'A Death Airs Origin of T.E. Lawrence', H0575
'Death Brings News...', H0221
'Death of A Hero', G1355
'Death of the Imperial Dream', F0452
'Death of T.E. Lawrence', H0250
'Death Seeker's Self-Portrait in Letters', G1698
Les Débats de ce Temps, H0559
'The Debt We Owe', F0097
'Debunking Lawrence of Arabia', G0208
'The Debunking of a Legend', H0972
'Debunking T.E. Lawrence', H0975
de Chair, Somerset, F0254–6
'The Decline and Fall of Lloyd George', F0069
'The Declining World of T.E. Lawrence', G0663
'Dédicace des "Sept Piliers de la Sagesse"', G0660, G0795, G1386
Dedications to T.E. Lawrence, F0165–6, F0361–2, F0439–42, F0645, F0673, F0701, F1135–6
Deedes, Sir Wyndham, F0868
'Deedes Bey', F0868
'Defending Lawrence', G1232
'Defense of the West', F0644
Defosse, Marcel, H0509
Delacorte (pub), D0006, F1089
DeLand Sun News, H1060
Delebacque, Jacques, G0806
Dedenfield, E.P., F0262
Dell (pub), A061, D0007, D0029, F0367
Dell Comic Books, E279
'Della Vida L'Arabia di Lawrence', G0172
Delon, Alain, H0589
Delorme, Roger, G1334
Delp, Alfred, G0502
Delpech, Jeanine, G1236
Demange, Col., G0929
'Demi Coriolanus', G1079
'Démolisseur de Lawrence d'Arabie', H0482
'Demolitions Under Fire', B0006
'Le Démon de Absolu', G0605
'The Demon of the Absolute', G0614
Dennis, Nigel, G1590
Dent, Alan, G1058, G1065, H0651
Dent (pub), D0025, F0006, F0151, F0894, F0929
Denver Post, H1076, H1186
La Dépêche, H0823
Dépêche Quotidienne d'Alger, H0514
'Les Dernières Années de T.E. Lawrence', G0611

Derrick, Christopher, G0724
'Desert and Delta', F0562
'The Desert and the Stars', E212–16, G0791, G0798, G0816, G0823, G0828, G0830, G0833, G0854, G0865, G0866, G0872, G0877–8, G0880–91, G0894–5, G0897–9, G0902–3, G0905, G0911, H0539, H0541, H0553–66
'Desert Camera on the Trail of "Lawrence"', H0601
'Le Desert de Sin', A008, A250
'Desert Dust Storm', G1264
'Desert Encounter', F0519
'Desert Encounter With Lawrence', H0840
'Desert Enigma', H0962–3
'Desert Journey', H0593
'A Desert Journey With £10,000 in Gold', H0599
'The Desert King', F0535–6
Desert Lamb, H0428
'Desert Leader Tells Honor Refusals', H0129
'The Desert Mounted Corps', F0870
'The Desert My Dwelling Place', F0813
'The Desert Prince: Letters of T.E. Lawrence', G1188
'Desert Raid. T.E. Lawrence', D0020
'A Desert Re-Union for Famous Trio', H0617
'The Desert Revolt Urged by a Legendary Englishman', G1312
'Desert Songs', H1197
'Desert Woman Chieftain', H0407
Des Moines Sunday Register, H1182
Desmond, Shaw, F0263
'Destination, Mecca', F0955
Destino, G1203
'Destins Exemplaires. T.E. Lawrence', G0608
'Destroying the Lawrence Myth', H0977, H0979
'Detailed Look at Lawrence', H1188
Detroit Free Press, H0936, H0965
Detroit Jewish News, H1094
Detroit News, H1058–9
Detroit Saturday Night, H0071
Deuel, Leo, F0264
'Deuil au Levant', F0322
Deutsch (pub), F0085, F0821, F0984
Deutsche Buch-Gemeinschaft (pub), A118
Deutsche Hausbucherei (pub), A119
Deutsche Rundschau, G0852, G0858
Deutsche Zeitschrift, G0378
Deutsche Zeitung und Wirtschaftszeitung', G0600, G0747, G0910
Deutsche Zukunft, G0245
Deutscher Kulturwart, G0535
'Deutsches Schicksal 1914–1918', F0859
'Deux années de guerre en Arabie', G0006
'Deux Anti-Colonialistes', G1602
'Deux Anti-Colonialistes: T.E. Lawrence et H. St. J.B. Philby', G1601
'Deux Grandes Coloniaux Anglais – Lawrence et Philby', G0180
'Deux Solitaires', G0557
Devas, Nicolette, F0265
'Devastated Lawrence', H1196
Devers, C.M., G0097, G0100
'The Devil Drives', F0148
'The Devil's Advocate', H0463
Devin-Adair (pub), F0179–80
Le Devoir de Montréal, H0796, H0799
'Devon Holiday', F1129
'Devotee of the Desert', G0567, H0414
DeVoto, Bernard, G0783

De Weerd, Harvey A., D0009, G0414, G0430–31
'D. H. Lawrence', B0024
'D.H. Lawrence and the Experience of Italy', F0727
'D.H. Lawrence, Novelist, Poet, Prophet', F0983
Dial (pub), D0023, F0023, F0594, F0769, F1081
The Dial, G0094
Diana (pub), A129–30
'Diaries and Letters', F0793–4
'Diaries of Parker Pasha', F1160a
'Diary of T.E. Lawrence', A194–5
'The Diary of Virginia Woolf', F1166
'A Diary With Letters', F0574
'The Dichotomy of Self in T.E. Lawrence's Seven Pillars of Wisdom', E326
Dickinson, William, G1306
'Dictionary of National Biography', F0266
'Did He Doublecross the Arab?', H1058
'Did Lawrence Have Premonition of Death?', H0363
'Did Lawrence Sell Out His Arab Buddies?', H1065
'Did Lawrence Want to Subjugate Arabs?', H0996
Didier-Erudition (pub), F0781
'Died: Col. Thomas Edward Lawrence', G0260
'Died: Sir Basil Liddell Hart', G1384
'"Different" Lawrence of Arabia Emerges from New Biography', H0970
'Difficult Questions, Easy Answers', F0430
'Difficulty of the Way: An Essay on T.E. Lawrence', G0454
'Digger's Fancy', F1050
Digman, Josef, H1143
Dineen, Bernard, H1203
Dinford, Doug, G1669
Dinge, Gewisse, G1382
Dinning, Hector, F0267–8
Diolé, Philippe, G0991
Disabled American Veterans of the World War (pub), F0876
Disbury, David, E330
'Discussing Plans for Spiegel's "Lawrence of Arabia"', G0965
'Disease and the Novel', F0728
'Dishonest Thing', H0175
'The Dispossessed Majority', F0901
'The Dispute', G0658
'Dissecting the Mystique of Lawrence of Arabia', H1038
'Diving Time on Trill Mill Stream', H0778
Diwald, Hellmut, G0603
Dixon, Alec, F0269
Dixon, C. Aubrey, F0270
Dixon, Carl, G1337
Dixon, David, G1136
Dixon, Norman, G1555
Djerabis, *see* Jerablus
'Dr. Frank Baxter', H0732
Dodd, Mead & Co. (pub), A090, A092, A254, E061, F0199–200, F0581, F0658, F0703, F0768, F0826, F0953, F0961, F1040
'The Doings of T.E.', E106
'The Domestic Life of Thomas Hardy', F0296
'Dominent Influences', G1065
'Don Roberto', F1068
Donaldson, Betty, F0272
Donaldson, Jay Robert, F0271
Donaldson, Norman, F0272
Donnelly, Tom, H0976

Donoghue, Denis, G0954
'Don't Stop The Carnival', F1176
Dooley, Anne, G1205, H0749, H0297
Dooley, Elliott, E343–4
Doran, George H., F0273–4
Doran (pub), A052, A105–8, F0163, F0426
Dorn, Walter, E167
'Dorset', F0718, G1317, G1335, G1347, G1419, G1441–2, G1630, G1680–81, G1696, H0843
Dorset and West Magazine, G1634
Dorset Echo, H1233
Dorset Evening Echo, H0880, H1259
Dorset Evening Post, H1265
'Dorset Men in the ICC', H0880
Dorset Sun, H0843
'Dorset Year Book', F0275–6
Double Crown Club, A249
Doubleday, Florence, E149–50
Doubleday, Frank, F0277–8
Doubleday (pub), A062, A167–9, A217, A260, E011, F0050, F0090, F0131, F0236, F0434, F0451, F0493, F0985, F0997, F1041, F1052, F1084, F1176
Doubleday Book Club, G1305
Doubleday, Doran (pub), A053–9, A097, A107, A166, A191, A195, A199, A204, A214–15, A217, D0031, E037, E109, F0239, F0285, F0514, F1038
'Double Vision', F0602
Doughty, Charles M., A013–31, F0512–14, F1021, G0402, G0455, G0588, G1353, G1461, H0793
'Doughty, Lawrence and the Near East', G0455
Douglas of Kirtleside, Lord, F0279, G0942
Douie, Charles, F0280
Dover (pub), A026
Downey, Fairfax, F0281
'Downing Street and Arab Potentates', G0055
Dowse, Y.A., G0541
Doxiadic, C.A., G1246
Doyle, Katie, H0825
Drabble, Margaret, F0282
Drama Survey, G1148
'Dramatic Life of "Lawrence of Arabia" Ends', G0262
'Dramatic Personages', F0917
'Drawing the R.A.F.', F0588
'The Drawings of Augustus John', F0570
'The Dreamers 1915–1938', F0668
'Die Drei Deutschen Versuche den Suez-Kanal zu Erben', G0852
Drugy, Tom, A086
Du Cann, Charles G. L., F0283–4
'Du Fond de Son Tombeau, le Colonel Lawrence Répond a Son Detra', H0487
Du Monde Entier, A206–7
Du Mont (pub), A030
Dubkins, Leonard, H1049
Dubuque Iowa News, H1052
Duckworth (pub), E124, F0327, F1071
Dudley-Gorden, Tom (pseud.), F0285
Duell, Sloan & Pearce (pub), E206, F0069, F0147
Duff, Douglas V., F0286
Duffur, R.L., H0101
Duffy, James Dennis, F0287
Du Hamel, Albert, H1211
Duke, Maurice, H0970
'Dulles', F0769
Duluth News Tribune, H0189
Dumfries Standard, H0154
Dumont-Wilden, L., G0005

Dumur, Guy, G1415, G1674
Dunbar, Janet, F0289–91
Duncan, J.L., G0563
Duncan, Theodora, E283, E300, E321, G1196, G1202, G1211, G1259, G1335, G1388, H0758
Dunlop, Gilbert, E219
Dunn, G.W.M., G0274
Dunn, George, F0292
Dunn, James, E282
'Duplicité Ou Incohérence', H0743
Duranty, Walter, H0112, H0115
Durham Herald, H1122
Durham University Journal, G1563
Durrell, Lawrence, F0012, F0293
Duschnes, Philip, A228, A235, F0294, G0481
'Dusty Hermitage', F0638
Dutton, Ralph, F0295
Dutton, E.P. (pub), A225, A240, E153–5, F0222, F0293, F0565, F0719, F0748, F0812, F0821, F1034, F1037, F1151
Duval, Elizabeth W., E119–21, G0495, H0396
Duvingaud, Jean, G1220, G1488
Duxbury (pub), F0020
Dwight, H.G., G0096
'Dynamiting Turks', B0020

Eade, Charles, F0297–8
'Ear to the R.A.F.', F0762
'Early Auden', F0724–5
East Whittier Review, H0767
'East and West With the E.F.C.', F1087
Easter Express, H1046
'Eastern Approaches', F0685–6
'Eastern Flights', F0128
'The Eastern Question', F0027
Easton, Malcolm, F0299
Ebert, Richard, E382; *see also* Allen, Kenneth, E381
Ebert, Roger, H0822
Échec à l'Obstacle, G1316
Les Echecs de T.E. Lawrence, E248, G0595
L'Écho d'Alger, H0486
L'Écho de la Côte d'Azur et de la Principauté, H0548
Écho de la Mode, G0878
L'Écho de Paris, H0004–6
L'Écho d'Israel', H0561
L'Écho-Liberté, H0450, H0504
Les Échos, H0696
L'Ecole des Loisirs (pub), E380
Economie et Humanisme (Caliure), G0898, G1019
Economist, G1016, G1095, G1212, G1265, G1360, G1465, G1541, G1581
Ecrits de Paris, G1376
'Les Ecrivains de la Nuit', F0118
Ede, H.S., A234–5
Eden, Matthew, E384–5, G1615, H1234
Edinburgh Evening News, H0619
Edinburgh University Press, F0664
Editions du Pavois, G0584
Edmonds, Charles (pseudonym), E079–83, G0359, G0383, G0397
Edmonds, Sir James E., F0300
Edmonton, J.R., G1676
L'Education Familiale, G0887
Éducation Nationale, G0827
Educational Theatre Journal, G0996
'Edward Garnett', F0065, F0566
'Edward Marsh', F0488

Edwards, G.B., G0174
Eeckels, Guido, G0799
L'Égalité Véritable', G0761
'The Egyptian Problem by Sir Valentine Chirol', B0010
'Egypt's Taba Claim Based on Forged British Map of 1915', H1256
Ehrentreich, Alfred, G0364, G0461, G0855
Eichelbaum, Stanley, G1690
Eickleman, Dale F., F0301
'Eight Letters From T.E. Lawrence', A219
Eighteenth Finchley Scout Group, E170
'Ein Abenteurliches Leben', H0917
'Ein Mysteriöses Leben', H0924
'Die Einheit von Denken und Sein bei T.E. Lawrence und E. Jürgen', G0603
Einstein, Albert, F0521
'El Aurens', G1036
'El Aurens en el Desierto de la Pantalla', F0807, G1134
'El Aurens ou Lawrence l'Arabe', G0391
'El Aurens, Thomas Edward Lawrence', F0558
Elbogen, Paul, D0010
Elek (pub), F0082
Eliade, Mircea, A134
Elkhart Truth, H1108
Elle, G1237
Elliott-Bateman, Michael, D0010a, F0302, G1377
Ellis, Anthony, G1554
Ellis, Harry B., F0303–4
Ellis, Peter Berresford, F0305
Ellis, William T., G0018
El Nasher (pub), F0775
'El Orens of Arabia', G0261
El Paso Times, H1075
Elsevier (pub), E311
'Elusive Genius', G0678
'Elusive Lawrence', G0934
'Elusive Subject', H1067
'The Emergence of Arab Nationalism', F1184
'The Emergence of the Middle East 1914–1924', F0930
'E.M. Forster', F0223, F0680, G1410
'E.M. Forster and His World', F0595
'E.M. Forster and T.E. Lawrence, A Friendship', G1389
'E.M. Forster: Centenary Revaluations', F0967
'Emir Dynamit', E056
'Emir Fesial', C0011
'Emir Fesial's Plea', H0007
'Emotional Struggle After the Middle-East War Deal', H1004
'Emotional Turmoil After War Deal', H0986
'Empire By Treaty', F0347
Empire News, C0021, H0083 H0226, H1206
'Empire of the Air', F1028
'The Empire of the Arabs', F0403
Empson, William, G0382
'Empty Promises Point to War', H0906
'En Annan Uppfattning', F0670
Encore, B0040
'Encore Lawrence', H0533
Encounter, G0944, G1160, G1322, G1587
'Encounters', F0822
Encyclopedia Britannica, D0011, F0306
Encyclopedia Judaica, F0307
Encyclopedia Universalis, F0308
'The End of a Legend', H0958

'The End of an Order', F0719
'The End of Lawrence of Arabia', H0952
'Des Ende eine Legende', H0925
Engel, Claire-Éliane, F0309, F0537
'England and the Middle East', F0583
'England's Mystery Man', H0095
Engle, Anita, F0310, G0874
Englische Rundschau, G0625
English, G0622, G0955
'English Arabs', G0204
'English Cottages', F0318
'English Gentlemen', F0573
'English History 1914–1945', F1024
English Language Teacher, G1117
'English Letter Writers', F1088
'English Literature in the Twentieth Century', F0247
English Literature in Translation, G1461
'English Prose and Criticism', F0157
English Review, G0271
'The English Spirit', F0920
'English Travellers in the Near East', F0334
'Englishman in Arab's Garb', H1030
'Englishmen Urge', H0234
'The Enigma of Lawrence', H0730
'Enigma Romantico/Aventuras de Lawrence de Arabia', G1055
'Enigma That Was Lawrence of Arabia', H0473
'Enigma Who Toppled the Turks', G0979
'L'Énigme du XX Siècle', H0584
'L'Énigme du Colonel Lawrence', G0532
Enkvist, Nils, G0688
'The Enormous Room', F0245
Enquirer and News, H1093
Enquier Journal, H1073
'Entlaube Legende', H0886
'L'Entrée à Jerusalem avec Lawrence en 1917', F0712
Entwistle, William J., F0311
'Entzasuberung Einer Legende', H0909
'An Epic of the Desert War', G0083
'The Epic of the Modern Man', G0074
Epilogue, G0244
'Epping Forest', F0006
Epsom and Ewell Herald, H0811
Epstein, Beatrice, G1092
'Erämaan Kapina', A113
'Der Erbe, T.E. Lawrence', F0951
'Eric of Arabia', H0698
'Erinnerungen an Lawrence of Arabia', G1622
'Erinnerungen an Lawrence von Arabien', F0577
Erskine, Mrs. Stuart, F0312
Ervine, St. John, A162
Esin, Emel, F0315
Espina, Dolores, H1274
L'Espoir, H0540
Esprit, G0609
Esquer, G., H0537
Esquire, G0959, G1090, G1124, G1679
'An Essay on Flecker', A198–9, A250
Essential Books (pub), F0083
'The Essential T.E. Lawrence', A237–43, B0006, B0011, B0024, C0013, G0627, G0631–2, G0634–5, G0638, G0642–3, G0853, G0881, G1210, G1213
Essex Journal, E361, G1517
Esslinger Zeitung, H0884
'Est Le Mirage Lawrence d'Arabia', G1705

'Estate Bars Issuance of Lawrence Book', H0415
'L'Éternal Masculin', F0956
'The Eternal Moment', F0361–2
Etiemble, René, A182–4, A206–7, A242, F0308, F0313–14, F0781, G0581, G0597, G0782, G0849, G0860, G0907
'Etiemble et Lawrence d' Arabie', F0781
Étude Anglais, G0528, G0860
Etudes, G0793, G0838, G0842
Etudes Inter-Ethniques, G1649
Etudes (Pères de la Compagnie de Jésus, Paris), G0127, G0152
Europäische Revue, G0135, G0459, G0466
Europäischer Buchklub (pub), A076
Europe, G1216
'Europe and the Arab World', G0033
'Europe and the Middle East', G0646
L'Europe Nouvelle, G0270, G0403–4
'Europe Overseas', F1124
The European, G0662
'Européens dans La Mecque interdite', G0785
Eva, G1270, G1379
Evans, Bergen, F0316
Evans, Laurence, F0317
Evans, Tony, F0318
Evans, Webster, G0648
Evans Brothers (pub), F0642
Evelyn Adams & Mackay (pub), D0004
Evenari, Michael, F0319
Evening Echo, H0805, H1262
Evening Mail, H0608
Evening News, H0180, H0256, H0604, H0807, H0867, H0887, H0890, H0937
Evening News and Star, H0720, H0869
Evening Outlook, H0707
Evening Post, H0700
Evening Standard, C0018, C0020, H0076, H0198, H0259, H0376–7, H0432, H0654, H0774, H0781, H0813, H0904–5, H0911, H1158, H1201, H1217
Evening Telegraph, H0841
Evening Tribune, H0871
'Eventyret I Orkenen', G1258
'Everybody's Political What's What', F0957
Everybody's Weekly, G0598, G0725
'The Everlasting Effort', F0100–102
Évidences, G0849
'Evolution of A Revolt' A255, B0006–8, B0011, B0013–15, C0006–8, C0013, D0010a, C1318, G1342, G1397
'Evolution of Iraq', H0312
'An Examination of the Guerrilla Strategies of Lawrence and Mao', E337c
'An Exceptional Man', G1569
'Exhibition', D0004
'Exhibition at Clouds Hill', G0476
'An Exhibition on the Occasion of the Opening of the T.E. Henley Library', F1073b
Exner, Jules, H0930
'The Expense of Greatness', F0100–101
'Experiment in Autobiography', F1113
'Explaining Lowell Thomas', G1570
'Explorer and Desert Stayed Apart', H0865
'Explorers All', F0320
'Explorers of Arabia', F0373
Express, H0898
L'Express, G0682, G0761, G1207, G1374, G1437, G1444
Ex-Services of Malaya Magazine, G0321

'Extracts From Lawrence's Thirty-Seven Articles', B0049
'The Extraordinary Rolls-Royce', G1223
'Exhumations', F0554–5
Eydoux, Henri Paul, F0321
Eye Witness, B0007, D0020
'Eyes on Lawrence', H1011, H1015
Eyre & Spottiswoode (pub), F0640, F0887, F0981, F1115, F1119–20, F1178
Ezequiel Martinez Estrada, G0573
'Ezra Pound', F0801
'Ezra Pound and T.E. Lawrence', G1565

F., P., H0558
'F.W. Stent', G0471
Faber & Faber (pub), A210–12, E145–6, E213, F0052, F0059, F0092, F0174, F0227, F0255, F0643, F0645, F0653, F0655, F0725, F0751, F0760, F0762, F0764, F0860, F0910, F0913, F0934, F0940, F1130, F1135
Fabre-Luce, Alfred, F0322, G0557, G0570, G0619
'The Fabulous Fraud', G0951
'Fabulous Lawrence of Arabia', H1031
'The Face From the Desert that Haunted a Hero', H1194
'Faces of Five Decades', F0674
'Fact and Fantasy', G1583
Facts on File (pub), F1161
Fadiman, Clifton, F0323, G0332, G0511
Fagg, Martin, H0916
Fagon, Brian M., F0324
'A Failed Masterpiece', G0764
Faisal, King of Iraq, *see* Feisal
'Faisals Aufgebot', A200–201, D0015
Faith Press, F0526a
Falcon (pub), F0714
'Der Fall T.E. Lawrence', E201
Fallois, Bernard de, G0731
Falls, Cyril, F0325–7, F0689
'False Situation: T.E. Lawrence and His Two Legends', F0984–5
'Falsity is Denied', H0302
'Fame and Obscurity', F1022
'Famed Arabian Fighter Said Holding On', H0238
'The Familiar Faces', F0388–9
Family Weekly, G1039
Fannius, Jean, G0777
'"Fantasy" Phase in the Life of Lawrence of Arabia', H0860
Farago, Ladislas, F0328–30, G0845
'Far Arabia', F0141–2
Farber, Stephen, H1155
Fariñas, Enrique Martinez, E281
Farmer, Bernard J., F0331
Farrar & Rinehart, F0144
Farrar, Straus (pub), F0078
Farrar, Straus & Cudahy (pub), F0412
Farrar, Straus & Giroux (pub), F0377, F0553, F0839, F0885
Farrar, Straus & Young (pub), F1054
Farson, Daniel, F0332
'Farewell to Arabia', F0516
Farwell, Byron, G1682
'Der faschistischen Metaphysik sehr nahe', H1236
'Fascinating Look at Some of the Origins of Middle East', H1122
'A Fascinating New Look at Lawrence of Arabia', H1041

'The Fascination', G0851
'The Fatal Fascination', G1659
Faure, G0703
'Les Fausses Situations', F0986
'Favorite Movies: Critic's Choice', F0797
Fayard, Jean, G0681
Fayard, Arthème (pub), E240, F0322
'The Fear', B0050
Fedden, Robin, F0333–6, G1287
'Une Femme par son ultime sacrifice a sauvé par amour Lawrence', H1285
Feinglass, Avraham, E341
Feis, Herbert, G0591
Feisal, King of Iraq, E267, F0312, F0719, G1338, H0060, H0142
'Feisal and Lawrence of Arabia', F0719
'Feisal, Twice King, Dreamt of Empire', H0142
'Felix Culpa', G0800
'Felix Frankfurter Reminisces', F0370
'Ferment for Freedom', C0012
Ferrer, Jose, E271
Feuille d'Avis de Lausanne, H0629, H0723
Feuillets Bibliographiques, G0904
'A Fever at the Core', F0729, G1556
'Few Ambitions of Mystery Man Told', H0131
'A Few Indiscreet Recollections', F0277
'Few Visit Lawrence Cottage', H0355
Ffoulkes, Charles John, F0337
Les Fiches Bibliographiques, G0698, G0877, G1238f
'The Fiction and the Fact', G1040
Field, Henry, F0338
Fielding, K.J., H0623
Fielding, Sean, H0229
'Der Fiend', F0796
Fifield, A.C., G0402
'Fifty Mutinies, Rebellions and Revolutions', F0340
'Fifty Tumultuous Years', F1158
'50 Years Later Lawrence', H0824
'Fifty Years of English Literature 1900–1956', F0947
'Fifty Years of Modern Syria and Lebanon', F0462
'£5500 for Seven Pillars of Wisdom', G1613
Le Figaro, H0009, H0487, H0511, H0580, H0587, H0627, H0648, H0674, H0679, H0687, H0784, H1174, H1235
Le Figaro Littéraire, H0421, H0435, H0517, H0527, H0683, H0751, H0786
Film Daily, G1678
'Film is Renewing Legend of "Lawrence of Arabia"', H1271
Film Quarterly, G1080, G1110, G1159
Film Scripts, E226, E249
'Film Sends Visitors to Lawrence's Home', H0713
'The Film Slide System', F0791
'Filming in the Desert', H0615
'Filming Story of Lawrence of Arabia', H0592
Films and Filming, G0962, G1054
'Un Fils de Roi Rampant', H0499
'La Fin de T.E. Lawrence ou Promethée Embourbé', F0918
'La Fin d'une Légende', G0770
'Finally After Half a Century of Legend: the Truth About T.E. Lawrence and the Arab Revolt', G1356
Finbert, Jacques-Elian, G0446, G0457, G0701, G0785
Findley, Charles, G0906, G0908

Finchley Scouts, *see* Eighteenth Finchley
Findser, Owen, H1105
'The Finest Hours', F0622, H0869
Finley, John, F0341, F0196, G0334, H0346
Finsk Tidskrift, G0688
Fiocchiaro, Roy, H1086
'The Fire of Life', F0062
'First Casualty', F0601
'1st Edition of Seven Pillars of Wisdom for 1s and 6p at Church Fete', H0881
'First Editions of T.E. Lawrence', G0495
'1st Seven Pillars', H0663
'The First World War', F1057–8
Firth, J.B., H0109, H0324
Fischer (pub), A120, D0010
Fisher, William Payne, F0342
Fisher Unwin (pub), F0473
Fishman, Jack, F0343–5
Fisk, Robert, H1239
Fiske, John F., G0234
Fitch, Noel Riley, F0346
Fitzgibbon, Constantine, G0944
Fitzsimons, M.A., G0848
Fitzsimmons, M.H.A., F0347
'540109 ex A/c2 Eyeview of Lawrence', H0475
'Five Hitherto Unpublished Letters', A261
'£500 Paid for a Book', H0054
'$500,000 Price of Book', H0326
Fixx, James F., G1048
'Flag He Served So Well Shrouds Col. Lawrence', H0268
Flaherty, Frank, G0551
'The Flawed Hero', G1043
Flecker, James Elroy, A229, F0348–9, F0509
Fleece Press, E403
Flesch, Rudolf, F0350
'Flesh and Blood', F0151–2
Fletcher, Arnold, F0351
Fleuron (pub), F0093–4
Flight, G0740
Flight International, G1251
Flor, Editions de la (pub), E175
'A Florence of Arabia Issue', G1164
'Florence Hardy and the Max Gate Circle', F1046
Florence News, H1023
Florin Books, E032
'Flower and the Nettle', F0659
'Flowers of the Forest', F0390–91
Fluckere, H, G0206
'Fly Leaves', F0958
Foden, George T., G1645
Folcroft (pub), E045, E076, E084, E165
Folio, G1667
Folio Society (pub), A104
'Folios of New Writing', F0352
Folk, Edges-Estes, F0353
'Following Lawrence of Arabia', G1671
'Fomenting Revolt in Arabia', B0019
Fontaine, B0039
Fontana Books (pub), F0216
Foot, Sir Hugh, F0354
Foot, M.R.D., F0355
Foot, Michael, H0813
Footman, David, G1172
'For God's Sake! Go!', F0197
'For Lawrence', H0818
For Men Only, G0546
'For Sale and Wanted', E364

Forbes, Rosita, F0356–7
Forces Nouvelles, H0567
Ford, Hugh, G1458
'Foreign Affairs', F0487
Foreign Affairs Magazine, G0039, G0055, G0239, G243, G0453, G0527, G0550, G0569
'Foreign Service Farewell', F0209
'A Foreigner Under Faysal', G0922
'Forest Giant', A094–7
'The Forgotten Ally', F1081
'The Form of People's War', G1377
'Form of Service Used at the Unveiling of the Memorial to Thomas Edward Lawrence (Lawrence of Arabia)', E093
Forman, James, H0046
Forster, E.M., A162, E110, F0223, F0358–66, F0595, F0680, G0305, G0399, G0475, G0719, G0802, G1389, G1410
Forster, Margaret, H1217
Fort Dodge Messenger and Chronicle, H1044
Fort Lauderdale News Sun Sentinel, H0950
Fort Walter Beach Playground News, H0997
Fortnightly, G0320
'Forty Years in the Wilderness', F0846
The Forum, G0232, G0346, G0518
Foster, Barbara, G1121
Foss, Michael, G1340
Foulis, G.T. (pub), F0745
'Foundations of Arab Revolt', A035–6
'Foundations of British Policy in the Arab World', F0599
'Four Best-Selling Personalities', G0370
Four Square (pub), E195–6
'The Fourth Dimension of Warfare', F0302
Fowle, Luther R., G0020
Fowles, John, F0367
Fox, Ralph, F0368, G0292
Foyle (pub), E043
'Foyles Bookshop', F0369
'Foylibra', F0369
'Das Fragewürdige Leben des Lawrence', H0930
'A Fragmentation Artist', E396
Frame, Colin, H0869
Franc-Tireur, H0445
'France, Britain and the Arabs', B0008
France-Dimanche, H0481
France-Eurafrique, G1261
France Illustration, G0604
France-Observateur, H0485, H0492
France-Pays Arabe, G1485–6
France Soir, H0451
France-Tropiques, H0521
'Francis Yeats-Brown', F1178
Frankfurter, Felix, F0370
Frankfürter Allgemeine Zeitung, H1238
Frankfürter Hefte, G0687
Frankfürter Neue Presse, H0891
Fraser, George MacDonald, G1393, G1395, H0966–7, H1227
'Fraud and Freud', G1069
Frédérix, Pierre, G0270, G0613, G0786
Free Press, F0877
Free Press of Glencoe, F0810
Freedland, Michael, F0371
Freemantle, Anne, F0372
Freeth, Zahra, F0373
French, Francesca, F0182
French, Samuel (pub), E223

'French Intellectuals and T.E. Lawrence', G1563
'A Fresh Look at Arabia's Lawrence', H1020
Fresh Meadows Townsman, H1115
'A Freudian Oasis', G1045
Frewin, Leslie (pub), F0192, F0972
'The Freya Stark Story', F0989
Fridberg (pub), F0152
Friedman, John S., E340, G1497
Friedrich, H.E., G0361
'A Friend of Lawrence', H0900
'Friends of Dartmouth Library', F0374
'Friends of a Lifetime', F0734
'Friendship of Shaw, Lawrence Discussed', H0707
Froembgen, Hanns, F0375-6
'From a Letter of T.E. Lawrence', A249
'From an Antique Land', F0544-5
'From Kinglake to Lawrence', G0302
'From Many Angles', F1017
'From Marco Polo to Lawrence', G0405
'From Pinafores to Politics', F0483
'From Sherlock Holmes to T.E. Lawrence',
    F1040-40a
'From the Greek', D0017
'Le Front Arabe', G0005
'Frozen Foods Support the "Seven Pillars of
    Wisdom"', H0600
'Full Length Portrait of Lawrence in the Desert',
    H0659
Fuller, Edmond, H1210
Fuller, John, F0377
Fundaţia Pentru Literatur (pub), A087, A134
'Funeral of Lawrence', H0284
Funk, Wilfred (pub), F1043
Funk & Wagnalls (pub), F0284, F0747
Für Sie, H0917
Furlong, Charles Wellington, G0555
Furlong, Williams B., F0378
Furst, Herbert, F0379
'Further Notes on T.E. Lawrence', G1226
Fustel, Jean-Albert, G1625
'Future Indefinite', F0235-6
Fysh, Hudson, F0380

G., E077
G., A., G0841
G., C. G., G0253, G0471
G., C. J., B0005
G., J., G0269
Gabbert, Howard M., E337a
Gabbey, Régine, H0649
Gabra, Laurette S., G0850
Gabrieli, Francesco, F0382
'Les Gaietés de l'Escadrille', H0500
Galante, Pierre, F0383
Galaxy Book, A153
Gale (pub), F0157
Gale & Polden (pub), F0582
Galey, Matthieu, H0789
Gall, Michel, A252-3
Gallagher, Robert S., G1627
Gallimard (pub), A182-4, A206-7, A242, A250,
    E156, F0313, F0694, F0697-8
Galloway News, H0153
Gallup Independent, H1083
Galvano, Eugenio, G1332
Galveston News, H1092
Ganem, Cherki, H0009
Gannett, Lewis, H1283

'Garbo in Arabia', G1412
Garcia Calderon, Ventura, F0384
Garden City (pub), A060, A109, E007, F0830,
    F0865, F0939
Gardena Valley News, H0762
Gardner, Brian, F0385-7
Gardner, Reid, G1233
Gardner, Stephen, G0624
Garland Press, E336, E338
Garnett, David, A202-5, A208, A232-3a,
    A237-43, E110, E151, E152-4, E178, F0388-91,
    F1123, G0282, G0303, G0436, G0481-4,
    G0488-9, G0492-4, G0512-15, G0517-18,
    G0520, G0522, G0527, G0530-31, G0559, G0617,
    G0627, G0631-2, G0634-5, G0638, G0642-3,
    G0667, G0712, G0853, G0881, G1071, G1210,
    G1213, H0393, H0395, H0398, H0402, H0404,
    H0409, H0413, H0750-51, H0755, H0757, H0759,
    H1246
Garnett, Edward, A024, A028, F0065, F0566,
    G0459
Garnett, Richard, A090-94
'The Garnett Family', F0496-7
Garretson, Joseph, H0423
'Garroot', F0683
Garros, Louis, H1139
Garteiser, André, G0864
Garzanti (pub), A186
'Gasi Mustafa Kemal', F0737
Gaster, Z., G0479
Gates, Norman T., F0393
Gauclère, Yassu, A206-7, A242
Gawsworth, John (pseudonym), E077
Gay Community News, H1221
Gaynesford, Janet de, H1248
Le Gazette de Lausanne, H0503, H0562, H0626,
    H0686
Gazette des Lettres, G0602
Gazette Médicale de France, G1367
Le Gazzetta del Populo, G1332
'G.B.S. a Full Length Portrait', F0830
'G.B.S. A Postscript', F0831-2
'G.B.S. and T.E.L.', G1137
'GBS/GKC', F0378
'G.B.S. 90', F1150
'Gegenspieler von Lawrence', G0428
Die Gegenwart, G0737
'Das Geheim Leben des Lawrence von Arabien',
    H0876
'Des Geheim Leben des Lawrence von Arabien',
    E313-14, H0891-3, H0897, H0899, H0901-9,
    H0914, H0918-20, H0922, H0947
'Die Geheimen Ängste des "Lawrence von
    Arabien"', G1362
'Die Geheimniss des T.E. Lawrence', H0891
'Geheimnisse an T.E. Lawrence', G0759
'Geheimnisvolle Lawrence', H0928
Gellhorn, Eleanore Cowles, F0394
Gems and Minerals, G1294
Gendzier, Irene L., G1199, G1350, H1100
'The Generation of 1914', F1164
General-Anzeigen, G1371
'General Roundup', G0962
'Genesis 1948', F0614
'Genius of Friendship', E145-6
'The Genius of Thomas Hardy', F0282
'A Genius of War and Letters', H240
'Genius That Was, Lawrence', H1200

Genre, G1548
'The Gentle Assassins', G1273
'George Bernard Shaw', F0498, F0833
Geographical Magazine, G1275
Geographical Review, G0002
'Mr. George Brough', H0953
Gera, Gideon, E396
German-Reed, T., E043–6
Gersh, Gabriel, H0826
'Gertrude Bell', F0113, F0176, F0422, F0895, F1061, F1154–5
'Gertrude Bell and T.E. Lawrence', G0120
'Get That King', G1351
'Get Your Camels He's Off Again', H1062
'The Ghost of Napoleon', F0645
'Ghost on Horseback', F0147
Ghyka, Matilda C., G0369
'Giants in Dressing Gowns', E078, F0044–5
Gibbs, Patrick, H0650
'Gideon Goes to War', F0770
'Gift of Anonymity', G1598
Gigs, Derich, H0730
Gilbert, Mark, F0396
Gilbert, Martin, F0218
Gill, F.C., G0612
Gillet, Louis, G0099, G0391, G0532
Gillett, Eric, F0311
Giliatt, Penelope, G1041
Gilman, Richard, G0987, H0478
Gilmer, Walker, F0397
Gilmore, William, G0451
Gilmour, Clyde, H0664
Giniewski, Paul, H1235
'Girl Television amd Film Annual', F0398
'The Girl Who Snubbed Lawrence of Arabia', H1192
Giron, Roger, H0451
Girvan, I. Waveney, F0399
Gittings, Clare, F0400
Gittings, Robert, F0401
'Gives Lawrence's Home', H0390
Glamour, G0992, G1079
'Der Glaube der Wüste', A244
Glen, Douglas, E128
'La Gloire de Héros', H0789
'To Glory and Back', G0823
'Glory of the Desert', G0084
Glubb, Sir John Bagot, F0366, F0402–11, F0642, G1508, G1553
'Glubb's Legions', F0642
'Glück durch Schmerz', G0949
Glueck, Nelson, F0412–13
'Go At the World', G1030
The Gobi Desert, F0182
Godine, David R. (pub), F0299
'Gods, Graves and Scholars', F0202
Godsell, Geoffrey, H0677, H1191
Goertzel, Victor, F0414
'The Gold Falcon', F1130–31
'The Golden Carpet', F0254–6
Golden Cockerel Press, A188–9, A226–9, A234–5, E161–2, F0254, F0384, F0416–18, F0849
'Golden Cockerel Press News', F0417
'The Golden Reign', E138–40
'The Golden Road', D0025
Golden, Harry, F0419
Golding, Louis, D0012
Goldschmidt, Arthur, F0421

Gollancz, Victor (pub), E151–2, F0666, F0687, F0823, F0825, F1143
'Good Evening Everybody', F1042, G1627
'The Good Soldier', F1106
'Good-bye to All That', F0430–35
'Goodbye West Country', F1132–3
Goodman, Susan, F0422
Gordian Press (pub), E111
Gordon, John William Jr., F0423
'Gordon', F0804–5
'Gordon of Khartoum', F0208
Gordon Press, E372
Gorman, Herbert, G0513, H0399
Gorman, J.T., E142
Gotch, Laurence M., E054
Goudy, Bertha M., A160
Government Press and Survey of Egypt, A011
'Governments and Politics of the Contemporary Middle East', F0556
G.P. (pub), E281
Graham, Colin, G1327, G1442, H0843
Graham, John, G0843
Der Gral, G0164
'The Grand Obsessions of T.E. Lawrence', H1276
Grand Rapids Press, H0938
'La grande clarté du XX siècle', G1248
Grande Revue, G0360
Gransden, K.W., H0708
Grant, Christina Phelps, G0424
Graphics Press, F0440
Grasset, Bernard (pub), E172
'In Grave Adversity', G0942
Graves, Philip Perceval, F0425–7
Graves, Richard Perceval, E358–9, G1562, G1571, G1574, G1576
Graves, Robert, A119, A159, A210, A213–14, A217–18, B0017, B0044, C0018, E029–42, E056, E098, E110, F0428–42, F0674, F0869, F0980, G0028, G0112–15, G0121, G0123, G0132, G0134, G0137–40, G0143, G0145–8, G0150, G0171, G0308, G0425, G0494, G0506–10, G0514, G0620, G0670, G0745, G0779, G0870, G1095, G1115, G1126, G1129–30, G1146, G1171, H0029, H0048, H0052, H0065–6, H0069, H0399, H0401, H0461, H0673, H0715, H0854; see also Barbara Rich
Graves, Sir Robert Windham, F0443
'Gray Steel', F0039
Graziani, Pierre, G1486
'A Great Adventure', G0090
'Great and Humble Mourn "Col. Lawrence"', H0273
'The Great Arab Conquests', F0404–5
'The Great Archaeologists', F0250
'The Great Battles of World War I', F1177
'A Great Book', G0062
Great Britain. Colonial Office, A033
Great Britain. General Staff, Geographical Section, War Office, A009
Great Britain. Imperial War Museum, E179–86, F0444–7
'Great Britain and Palestine', F0971
'Great Britain and the East', G0373, G0491, G0539
'Great Contemporaries', F0210–16, F0448
'Great Events of the 20th Century', F0891
Great Exploits, E142
'Great Friends', F0392
'Great Honors Refused by Soldier', H0130

'Great Interest in Lawrence Society', H1264
'The Great Mole Mystery', G1653
'A Great One', G1016
'The Great Race', C0024
'Great Soldiers of the Two World Wars', D0009
Great Soviet Encyclopedia, F0449
'Great True Adventures', D0027–9
'The Great War', F0558
'The Great War – I Was There', G1674–7
'Greater Man Than Lawrence of Arabia', H1292
'The Greatest of Adventures', G0072
'Greatness and Pettiness of T.E. Lawrence', H0402
'Greatness of T.E. Lawrence', G0521
Green, Candida, F0318
Green, Leonard H., E170
Green, Peter, G1035
Green Bay Press Gazetter, H1051
Green Circle Books (pub), F1162
Greenberg (pub), F0669
Greenlee, James W., G1498
'Greenmantle', F0163
Greensburg Tribune Review, H1040
Greenwich House (pub), F0272
Greenwood Press, A218, E199
Gregg, T.P., H0078
Gregorian, Joyce B., H1156
Gregory, Horace, G0421
Gregory, Lady Isabella Augusta (Perse), F0450
Gregory, Maundy, F0451
Grenier, Roger à, G0821, G1208, G1277
'Grey Wolf', F0040
Grierson, Edward, F0452
Griffiths, John, H0736
Griggs, John, F0453, G1427
Grigson, Geoffrey, H0329, H0382
Grindle, Harry, G0508
Grooms, Roger, H1184
Grosset and Dunlop (pub), E009, F0623, F1177
Grosvenor, Charles M., E339, E351, E396
Grosvenor, Peter, G1706, H0815, H1287
Groszowo (pub), A132–3
Grove Press, F0413, F0508, F0624
Grunebaum, G.E. von, G1315
Grunwald, Anatole de, E226
Guardian, G1490, H0737, H0935, H172–3
Guardman, H0172
Guarmani, Carlo, F0454
Gudme, Iver, E064
Gudme, Peter de Hemmer, G0490
Guedalla, Philip M., F0455–6
Guerre et Littérature, G0939, G0943
'Guerrilla', F0619
'La Guérrilla', G0929
'The Guerrilla Reader', F0620
'The Guerrilla Strategies of Lawrence and Mao', E344
Guide de Lecteur, G0884
Guillemin, S.M., E214–15
'Guilt-Haunted Hero!', G1553
'Guilt Ridden', G1541
Guinn, Paul, F0457
Guinness, Alec, E225, E267, E271, F1026, H0607, H0618
'Guinness Joins the "Lawrence Team"', H0618
Gullett, Henry Somer, F0458
'Gun Running in the Red Sea', F1095
Gunther, John, F0459–60, H0235
Gurney, O.R., F0461

Gurschner, Herbert, G0583
Guru, G1573, G1602
Güterbock, Hans Gustave, G0653
Guthrie, J., G0705
Guy, P.L.O., A002
Guyot, Charly, H0502, H0770
Gybal, André, G0252
Gyldendalske (pub), A068–9, A084, A111, E019, E027, E064
Gyldendalske Norsk (pub), A131, E317
'Gypsy In the Sun', F0356

H., B., H0901
H., L., G1496
H., P., G0625, G0984
Haag, Michael (pub), A190
Haas, Jacob de, H0310
Hachette (pub), F0871
Hacienda Heights Highlander, H0766
Hadawi, Sami, F0572
Haddad, George, F0462
Haffenden, John, F0463
Hagedorn, Hermann, F0464
Hagen, Herbert, G0463
Haiber, William Paul, G1142
Haig, George, G1701
'Hails Lawrence Odyssey', H0136
'The Haj', F1075
Hajime, Kobayashi, E147a
'Hakluyt – First Naval Propagandist', B0027
Hakubunkan Kan (pub), E147a
Halcyon House (pub), E062
Hale, Robert (pub), D0009, E261, F0244, F0336, F0518, F0525, F0842–3, F0846, F0848
'Half a Life', F0563
Halifax, Edward F. L. Wood – 3rd Viscount, E094–5, E110, E112, F0184, F0465, G0398, H0360
'Halifax, Winston F. S. – 2nd Earl of Halifax', F0096
Hall, Melvin, F0466–7
Hall, William, F0468
Halliburton, Alastair, F0470
Halimi, André, H0626
Haltonian, G1647
Hambidge, Gore, F0131
Hambro, Carl, E317
Hamelin, Armand, E390
'ha-Mered ba-Midbar', A121
Hamilton, Alastair, F0470, G1217
Hamilton, Hamish (pub), E222, E367, F0029, F0109, F0460, F0754, F0756, F0783, F0908, F0965, F1009, F1111
Hamilton, Ian, G1267
Hamilton, James, G1623–4
Hamilton Journal News (Ohio), H1003
Hamizrah Hedadash, G1611
'Hamlet en Arabie', G0369
Hammerton, Sir John Alexander, F0471
Hamnett, Nina, F0472
Hamoudi, Sheikh, E110
Hancock, Percy S. P., F0473
'Hankey: Man of Secrets', F0907
Hanley, James, D0013–14, G0546
Hannoverishe Rundschau, H0875
Hanson, Thorkild, F0475
'Happy Years of Lawrence', H1152
Harcourt (pub), F0601

Harcourt Brace (pub), F0064, F0102, F0256, F0273, F0358, F0362, F0365, F0389, F0391, F0489, F0532, F0863, F0905, F0916, F1079, F1165–6
Harcourt Brace Jovanovich (pub), F0234, F0659–60
Harcourt Brace & World (pub), F0030, F0226, F0675, F0705, F0763
'The Hard Bright Flame', G1552
Harding, D.W., G1546
Harding, G. Lankester, F0476
Hardinge, Helen, F0477
Hardy, Florence Emily, F0480–81, F1046
Hardy, Thomas, F0282, F0296, F0401, F0480–82, F0744, F1045a, F1046, G1446, G1460
Hardwick, Michael, F0478–9
'Hargon's Pictures Lawrence of Arabia', G1702
Harper (pub), A096, F0237, F0243, F0350, F0408, F0459, F0706, F0755, F0919, F1112, F1187
Harper & Row (pub), E370, F0057, F0175, F0291, F0475, F0545, F0757, F0983, F0995, F1012, F1039
Harper's, G0526, G0783, G1012, G1109, G1165, G1653
Harrap, George G. (pub), E073–4, E398, F0145, F0171, F0257–9, F0290, F0589, F0928, F1017, F1100, F1102, F1005
Harrel-Courtès, Henry, G0651
Harriman, Florence Gaffray (Hurst), F0483
Harrisburg Patriot News, H1022
Harrison & Sons (pub), A009
Harrop, Dorothy A., F0484
Harrap (pub), F0622
Harry, Charles, F0573
Hart-Davis, Rupert (pub), E401, F0485, F0733, F0976
Harter, G.E., G0211
Hartford Times, H1189
Hartley, L.P., G0764
Hartman, Paul-Francis, G1585
Hartung, Philip T., G1064
Harvard University, E293–4, E0319, F0486, F0520–21, F1164
Harvey, Alan, H0878
'Hashemite Debt to Lawrence of Arabia', G1475
'The Hashemite Kings', F0759–60
Haskell House (pub), E082, E121, E127
Haskins, John, G1480
Hasluck, Eugene Lewis, F0487
Hassell, Christopher, F0488–9
Hastings, Max, H1201
Hatch, Robert (pub), A262, G1066
Halton, Frank Sydney, F0490
Hausmann, Walter, D0015
'Have You Read 100 Great Books?', F0491
Havelock, Francis, H0083
Haverstick, John, G0763
Le Havre Libre, H0695
Hawkes, Jacquetta, F0492
Hawkeye, H0958
Hawkins, Jack, E271
Hawthorne (pub), F0233, F0382
Hayakawa (pub), E316
Haycroft, Howard, F0613
Hayford, Elizabeth P., G1533, G1586
Hazard, Forrest E., G1378
Hazard, Harry W., F0493
Hazlitt, Henry, G0198
'He Gave A/C Shaw a Rocket', H0939
'He Knew Lawrence of Arabia Well', H0017

'He Staked Himself', H0269
'He Was With Lawrence in Arabia', F0131
'A Headlined Private', G0138
Headlines, G1514
Hearst, Lorna, F0113
'Heart-Beguiling Araby', F1062
Hecht, Yvon, H0578
'Le Hedjaz dans la Guerre Mondiale', F0140
'Hedjaz 1916–1918', G1284
'Hedjaz Railroad', H0776
'The Hedjaz Railroad: Its History', G1189
Heer, Friedrich, F0494
Heffer & Sons Ltd., E129, F0185
Hegener, Michael, H1261
Heibon-sha (pub), A082, E041
Heideman, Margaret, G1070
Heilbrun, Carolyn G., F0496–7
'Ein Heiliger Unseres Jahrhunderts? Zum 70 Geburtstag von T.E. Lawrence', G0910
Heimat und Gläube, G0599
Heinemann (pub), D0003, F0105, F0218, F0235, F0349, F0440, F0522, F0543, F0571, F0717, F0938, F0968, F0979, F0993, F1068
Heir-Davies, Harry, F0495
Heissenbüttel, Helmut, G0910
'Hejaz Stamps and Lawrence of Arabia', G1499
'Held und unfernalischer Lügner', H0915
'Hell in the Holy Land', G0393
Hellens, Franz, H0772
Hemingway, Ernest (ed), D0016
'Hemingway', F0730
Hemmer Gudme, Peter de, A068–9, A111
Henderson, Archibald, F0498
Henighan, T.J., G1443
Hennessy, Peter, H1237
Henroit, Émile, H0424, H0510, H0514
'Henry', F0332
Henry, William A., H1228
'Her Privates We', A140
Herald & Express, H0617
Herbert, Ernest, F0065
Herder (pub), A252
Hergenhan, L.T., B0052
The Heritage of Literature Series, E036
'Heritage of the Desert', F0304
Heritage Press, A025
'A Hermit in the Himalayas', F0160
'The Hermit of Peking', F1067
L'Herne, G1674
'Hero and Anti-Hero', G1070
'Hero as Rookie', G0746
'A Hero Challenged', G0834
'Hero Legend Troublesome to Lawrence', H1190
'The Hero of the Desert', H0652
'Hero or Mirage?', H1039
'Hero With a Secret', H0887
'Heroes of Modern Adventures', F0146
'Heroes of the Empty View', F0014
'Heroes of Tomorrow', H0756
Heron, Flodden W., G0458
'Les Héros désespérés ou le mal d'aujourd'hui', H0420
'Hero's Letters Shown', H0365
'Héros ou Imposteur?', H0777
'Hero's Pillars Crumble. Destroy Legend of Lawrence', H1291
'Un héros? Un aventurier?', H0685
Herre, Paul, G0876

Herwig, Holger H., F0499
'He's a Real Hero', G1703
'He's Roamed the Desert for a Century', H0781
Hesperides Editions, A151
Hesse, Eva, G1480
'Het Geheim Leven van Lawrence of Arabia', E311
Hete og Hjemme, G1258
Hewes, Henry, G0989, G1060
Hewick, Leah, G1183
Heyman, Neil M., F0499
Hii, J., G0980
Hibbard, Bill, H1132
Higgins, Trumbull, F0500
Higgs, A.S., G1567
High Point Enterprise, H1021
'High Relief', F1122
Higham, Thomas Farrant, D0017–18
Highet, Gilbert, F0500
'The Highway of the Three Kings', F1063
Hill, D., H1189
Hill, Edwin C., H0140
Hill, Margot, G0580
Hill, Roland, G0695
Hill & Wang (pub), F1025
Hillman & Curl (pub), F0376, F1080
Hillside Press, E388
Hirsch, Foster, F0502
Hirschorn, Clive, F0503
'His Brough is So Superior', H0803
'His Terrible Swift Sword', F0687
L'Histoire, G1638, G1644
Historama, G1333–4
Historia, G0686, G1157
Historiallinen Aikakuskirja, G0927
'Historic Houses: Lawrence of Arabia', G1668
Historische Zeitschrift, G0876
History, G1664
'History of Bodleian Library', F0240
History Book Club (pub), E368
'A History of English Literature', F0753
'A History of Exploration From the Earliest Times
    to the Present Day', F1018
'A History of Gregynog Press', F0484
'History of Israel', F0931
'A History of Our Time', F0540
'A History of Palestine', F0823
'History of Syria', F0504
'History of the Arabs', F0505
'A History of the British Secret Service', F0252
'History of the First World War', F0646, G1430
'A History of the Great War', F0164
'A History of the Royal Air Force College', F0261
'A History of Warfare', F0752
History Today, G1473, G1663
'Hitler und Lawrence', G0535
Hitti, Philip K., F0504–7
'Hittite Problems and the Excavation of
    Carchemish', F0511
'The Hittites', F0461
Hiwar, G1118
Hlutinn, Fyrri, A122
Hlutinn, Sídari, A122
HMSO, A012
Hoare, *see* Templewood, Lord
Hobby, G0909
Hobson, Harold, H0582, H1148
Hoch (pub), E366
Hochhuth, Rolf, F0508

Hochland, G0250, G0467
Hodder & Stoughton, F0161–2, F0167–8, F0170,
    F0182, F0220, F0249, F0354, F0402, F0405, F0407,
    F0409, F0411, F0455, F0718, F0944
Hodge, Alan, F0438
Hodgkins, E.C., H1195, H1216
Hodgson, Geraldine, F0509
Hodgson, H.J., G0276
Hodson, Gillman, F0189
Hoffman, Hermann, G0599
Hoffman, Hester R., F0510
Hoffmann und Campe (pub), E313
Hogarth, David G., A001, D0011, F0426,
    F0511–14, F0916–17, G0002, G0025, G0068,
    H0025
Hogarth Press, F0310, F0352
Hohenlobel, Urula zu, E201
Hohoff, Kurt, G0467
Holden, David, F0516–17
Hole, Edwyn, F0518
Holiday, G1108, G1336
Hollenbeck, Ralph, G1391
Hollis, Christopher, G1469
Hollis & Carter (pub), E232, F0998
Holloway, David, H0722
'The Hollywood Epic', F0502
'Hollywood Gold', F0855
Hollywood Independent, H1154
Hollywood Reporter, H0591, H0602
Holme, Nancy, E147
Holme (pub), F1174
Holmeboe, Knud, F0519
Holmes, Oliver Wendall, F0520–21
'Holmes-Einstein Letters', F0520
'Holmes-Laski Letters', F0521
Holroyd, Michael, F0522–3
Holt, Henry (pub), E212, F0007, F0483
Holt, Rinehart, Winston (pub), F0198, F0517,
    F0523, F0584, F0591, F0678, F0695, F0836, F0909,
    F0917, F0952, F1065
Holywell Press, F0815
'Homage', F0946
'The Home Letters of T.E. Lawrence and His
    Brothers', A245–7, G0665–9, G0672, G0674–8,
    G0680–81, H0436–40
Home News, H1020
'The Home of Lawrence of Arabia', G0649, H1299
Homer, A1410, A154, F0524, H0329
Homer, Frank X.J., G1537
'Homer. A Collection of Critical Essays', D0026
'Homer and His Translators', G0317
'Homer's Odyssey in Lawrence's Version', G0318
'L'Homme Qui A Perdu Son Ombre', H0540
Hommes et Mondes, E217, G0753, G0857, G0864
L'Homme le plus Mystérieux de l'Autre Guerre',
    H0451
'Homosexuals in History', F0921
Honolulu Star Bulletin, H0726
'Honours for Sale', F0451
Hope, Stanton, F0525
Hopkins, E.M., H0312
Hopkinson, Arthur Wells, F0526–26a
Hopkirk, Peter, H0746–7, H0775, H0872, H1153,
    H1161
'Horace Liveright', F0397
Horizon, G1004, G1278
Horizon Press, F0538
Horizon Picture, E271

Horn Book, G0238, G0345, G1011
Hornby, St. John, F0573
Horne, Alistair, F0527
Hornstein, Herbert, G0692
'Horoes con y sin Eseatandra', F0807
'Hortense', F0932a
Horowitz Publications, E282
Hoskins, Halford L., F0528
Hottinger, Arnold, F0529
Hotzat Saphim (pub), E242
Houghton (pub), F0231
Houghton Mifflin (pub), F0096, F0111, F0164,
    F0169, F0191, F0289, F0387, F0688, F0707, F0758,
    F0773, F0860, F0898, F0964, F1142, F1144
'The Houghton Library, 1842–1967', F0486
'The Hound and the Horn', G0145
Hourani, Albert, G1635, G1653
House, E. M., F0530, H0418
'A House Divided', E325
'The House of Saud', F0517
'The House Over the Hedge', H0429
Housewife, G0730
Houssemaine, Helène, E259, G1485
Houston, Guyla Bond, E298
'How Did They Die?', F0272
'How He Waited For Turks to Kill Him', H0053
'How History Gets Rewritten: Lawrence of Arabia
    in the Theater', G1148
'How Lawrence Cut the Pie', G1400, H1081
'How Lawrence Helped to Frame the Greatest
    Hoax Since the Trojan Horse', G0080
'How Lawrence Joined the R.A.F.', H0425
'How Lawrence of Arabia Died', H1284
'How Lawrence of Arabia Saw Him Off', H0324
'How Lawrence Organized Revolt in the Desert',
    H0231
'How Lawrence Taught Me to Spy', H0890
'How the Seven Pillars of Wisdom Was Published',
    G0276
'How the Turks Tortured Lawrence of Arabia',
    G0047
'How to Win a Scholarship: Advice From School
    Celebrities', B0004
'How to Write, Speak and Think More Effectively',
    F0350
'How Young English Archaeologist Captured
    Damascus', G0015
Howard, Edwin, H0701
Howard, G. Wren, B0033
Howard, Harry N., F0531
Howard, Leslie Ruth, F0532
Howard, Michael S., F0533
Howard, Philip, F0534
Howarth, David, F0535–6
Howarth, H., G0587
Howe, Irving, F0537–8, G1001, G1018
Howe, Lionel, F0539
Howe, Quincy, F0540
Howells, Roy, F0541
Hubert, Emmanuelle, G1218
Hudson Review, G0872–3, G0954, G0995, G1018,
    G1429
'Hugh Walpole', F0485
Hughes, Richard, G0311, G0493
Hughes, Robert, G1535
Hughes-Stanton, Blair, G1648
Hugo, Leon, G1242

'Huit Chapitres de Le Mint', G0048
Hulbert, Jerry, G1655
Hull, Keith N., E396, G1456, G1502, G1509
Hull Daily Mail, H0430, H0473
'The Human Face', F0153
'Human Hero in Lawrence of Arabia', H1186
'Human Side of the New "Aircraftsman Shaw"',
    H0140
Humanities Research Center; see University of
    Texas Humanities Research Center
'Humanizing a Legend', G0986
'A Humbug Exalted', G1594
Humes, James C., F0542
Humphrey, Derek, H0848
Humphries, Stewart, G1572
'A Hundred Different Lives', F0710
'A Hundred Years of War', F0327
Huntington Herald Advertiser, H1098
Huntington Library (pub), F0124, F1056
Husbands, Martin, H0857
Hussein, King of Jordan, F0192, F0543
'Hussein's Kingdom', F0192
Hutchins, W.T., E036
Hutchinson (pub), E012–17, E026, E280, F0062,
    F0126, F0136, F0149, F0159, F0173, F0188, F0260,
    F0312, F0372, F0425, F0443, F0490, F0561, F0699,
    F0785, F0814, F0942–3, F0975, F1040a, F1083,
    F1085, F1148, F1150, F1153, F1158
Hutin, Marcel, H0004
Huxley, Aldous, F0070
Huxley, Julian, F0544–5
Hyacinth Press, F0056
Hyde, H. Montgomery, E372a, E373–4, G1598,
    G1603, G1605, H1222, H1227
'Hygiene des Lettres', F0313–14
Hynes, Samuel, F0546
Hyperion (pub), A233a

'I, Claudius', F0436–7
I Contemporanei, E252
'I Did Not Die in 1935', H0289
'I Did the First TV News Program in History',
    G1547
'I Flew Lawrence in War Crazed Arabia', G0216
'I Have Loved England', F0739
'I Knew Lawrence Well', G0474
'I Knew the Real Lawrence', G1039
'I Married This World', H0717
'I Remember Lawrence of Arabia', G0546, G1463
'I Saw Damascus Fall', G1675
'I Seek My Prey in the Waters', F0285
'I Was With Lawrence of Arabia', G1677
Icon Books (pub), E125
'If I Forget Thee O Jerusalem', F0973
'If the Arabs Had Won', G1303
Igirisu to Rorensu to Arabia, E147a
'Il faut en finir avec l'affaire syrienne', H0006
'Il Leggendario Lawrence', G1688
Il Progresso Italo-Americana, H1138
'Il Vero Volto di Lawrence d'Arabia', G1166
'Il y a vingt-cinq ans mourait un roi sans royaume',
    H0578
'The Illicit Adventure', F1156
Illustrated, G0711, G0714, G0729
Illustrated Comics, E344
Illustrated London News, G0069, G0258, G0315,
    G0494, G0623, G0668, G0716, G0936, G0970,
    G1002–3, G1024, G1031, G1058, G1065, G1155,
    G1267

'An Illustrated Souvenir With a History of the Assembly Rooms', F0066
L'Illustration, G0005, G0279
'Un illustre inconnu: T.E. Lawrence', G0856
'L'Image de la France et des Français pour T.E. Lawrence', G1596
'Images Ethniques, et Concept de Race chez Lawrence d'Arabie', G1649
Impact, G1156
Impact International, G1672
'The Imperious Amateur Looks Back', F1116
Imperial Camel Corps, G1296
'Imperial Camel Corps', F0548
'Imperial Camel Corps With Colonel Lawrence', A139, F0792
'Imperial Sunset', F0079
'Imperialism and Nationalism in the Fertile Crescent', F0018
'The Imperialist Character', G0621
'Imported Sun Into the Desert', H0605
'Imposter or Imperialist?', G1359
'In Aleppo Once', F0022
'In Defense of Lawrence', G0107, H1207
'In Lawrence's Bodyguard', E050–53, E087–8
'In Memoriam', H0846
'In Memory of T.E. Lawrence', G0316, G0373
'In Modern Dress', G0194
'In Search of Lawrence of Arabia', G0959, G1035
'In Search of Lost Worlds', F0321
'In the Desert', H0172
'In the Desert Scots Driver's Tales of Lawrence's Exploits', H0174
'In the Margin of History', F0782
'In the Service of an Alien Race', G1542
'In the Steps of Lawrence of Arabia', E128
'In the Steps of Moses the Conqueror', D0012
'In the Steps of St. Francis', F0886
'In the Steps of St. Paul', F0765
'In the Steps of the Master', F0766
In Touch for Men, G1621
'In Wisdom's House: T.E. Lawrence in the Near East', G1606
Inchbold, Geoffrey, F0548
The Independent (Plymouth), H0825
'The Independent Arab', F1182
Independent Film News, G0966
'Un inépuisable sujet du nouveau sur le colonel Lawrence', H0554
Infantry, G1273
Infantry Journal, G0430
L'Information, H0516
'The Influence of T.E. Lawrence on British Foreign Policy in the Middle East 1918–1922', E298a
Inge, Rev. W.R., A162
Ingham, L.H., H0173
Ingrams, Doreen, F0549–50
Ingrams, Harold, F0551–2
'The Inner Conflict of T.E. Lawrence', G1343, H0866
'Inner Man', G1682
'Inquest on "Lawrence of Arabia"', H0265
'The Ins and Outs of Mesopotamia', F0676
'Inside Asia', F0459–60
'Inside Pan-Arabia', F0994
'Insist Lawrence Lives', H0306
'Inspired by Lawrence of Arabia', G1392
'Instant Lives', F0772
Instituto de Artes Gráficas (pub), E284

L'Insulaire, G0903
'The Intellectual History of Europe', F0494
'"L'Intelligence Service" anglais pendant la guerre', G0179
Interchurch Press, F0468
'L'Intermédiaire des Chercheurs et Curieux', G1386
'Internal Consistency and the Scope of Interpretation in Psychohistory', G1623
International Affairs, G0875
International Collector's Library (pub), A063–4
'International Drawing', G1660
International History, G1475
'International History is Novel', H0998
International Spectator, G1375
Inter-Profs E.S.E.U., G1601
'Intimate Friend the Lawrence Nobody Knows', H0212
'The Intimate Sex Lives of Famous People', F1089
'Introduction à "Un Livre, des voix" Présentation de Pierre Sipriot "Les Textes essentiels de T.E. Lawrence"', H1246
Invalide Liégeois, H0543
'An Investigation Into the Disturbing Facts of the Crash Which Killed Lawrence of Arabia', G1327
Iowa Bookshelf, H0973
'Iraq', F0693
Iran Tribune, H0868
Ireland, Philips W., G1186
Irish Press, H0895
Irish Times, H1209
'Ironside', G0550
Irvine, William, G1097
'Is the Cinema's Lawrence a Dramatic Disaster?', G1691
Isham, Ralph H., G0352, G0433
Isherwood, Christopher, F0052, F0553–5, F1008
Ishmael, Tarq Y., F0556
Isis, G0028, G1243
'Isis Idol: Mr. T.E. Lawrence (Arabia and All Souls)', G0028
Der Islam, G1315
'Islam Inflamed', F0761
'The Islamic East and North Africa', F0662
Islamic Review, G1189
'Isle of Purbeck', F0395
Islenzka (pub), A122
'Israel', F0875
'Israel Defense Forces, Education Officer', D0019
'Israel, the Arabs and the Middle East', F0537
'Israel Without Zionists', F0053
'It is Tough Being Lawrence', H0616
Itelliaander, Rolf, G1362
Itzkowitz, Norman, F0155
Iwanami-shinso (pub), E137
Izzeddin, Nejla, F0557

Jablonski, Edward, F0558
Jack, Peter Munro, G0376, G0548
Jackson, Esther, F0559
Jackson, Laura, G1479
Jackson Citizen Patriot, H1097
Jackson Sun, H1111
Jacobs, Jay, G1069
J'ai Lu, G0753
Jalabert, Louis, G0127, G0153
'Jan Smuts', F0239
Jannoud, Claude, H0703

Janus, Christopher, H1276
Jarche, James, F0560
Jarrolds, Norwich (pub), F0071
Jarry, E., G1063
Jarvis, C.S., F0561–5
'Jean Béraud-Villars, poète de l'histoire épique', G0651
Jeander, H0685
Jefferson, George, F0566
Jehanne (Theodora Duncan), E283, E300
Jenkins, Alan C., D0020
Jenkins, Thomas, H0777
Jenkins, Herbert (pub), F0016, F0954
Jennett, M., H1180
Jensen, Derrick, G1662
Jensen, Karin, E022
Jerablus, A001–3
Jerusalem Post, H1256
'Jesting Apostle', F1151
Jesty, Simon, A163–4
Jesus College Magazine, B0005, G0268–9
'Jesus College Record', F0568
Jewish Digest, G1147
Jewish Floridian, H1144
Jewish Frontier, G0597
Jewish Observer and Middle East Review, G1357
Jewish Publishing Society, F0087
Jewish Spectator, G1497
'Jimgrim and Allah's Peace', F0780
'J.M. Barrie, the Man Behind the Image', F0290
John, Augustus, A101a, E110, E133–4, E167, E251,
    E265, E309, E337, E353–5, E392, E401, F0299,
    F0522, F0569–70, G0554, G0572, G0644, G1103,
    H0063
John, Evan, F0571
John, Robert, F0572
'John Buchan', F0171, F0976–7
'John Buchan by His Wife and Friends', F0170
'John Bull Ungeschminkt', G0497
John O'London's, G0078, G0217, G0221, G0312,
    G0317, G0395, G0485, G0633, G0648, G0665,
    G1198, G1208, G1230
Johns, Richard, F0517
Johns, W.E., H0425
Johns Hopkins University Press (pub), F0317,
    F0599
Johnson. A.F., G0592
Johnson, C. (pub), F0548, F1055
Johnson, Chalmers A., G1007
Johnson, Donald B., H1198
Johnson, Foster Macy, F0573
Johnson, John, E117
Johnson, Mary, H0354
Johnson, Paul, G0865
'Jonathan Cape, Publisher', F0533
Jones, Alfred, E168
Jones, Basil, G0307
Jones, D.A.N., G1452
Jones, John, H0673
Jones, R., H0888
Jones, Thomas, F0574–5
Jordan, G1323
Jordan, Philip, H1258
'Jordan and the Holyland', F0881
'Jordan..Fra emirat Til Kongedømme', G0917
'Jorge Luis Borges', F0748
Joseph, Bernard, F0576
Joseph, Michael (pub), F0123, F0332, F0526, F0585

Jotterand, Franck, H0686
'Joue un Fils du Désert', H0588
'Jouera le personage le plus mystérieux de
    l'histoire moderne "Lawrence d'Arabie"', H1273
Jouin, Yves, G1284
Le Journal, G0263
Le Journal d'Alger, H0537
Le Journal de Genève, H0426, H0502, H0519,
    H0566, H0770
Journal de la Marine Marchande, G0845
Journal de la Société des Lecteurs, G0751
Journal de Débats, G0156
Le Journal des Lettres, G9882
Le Journal du Dimanche, H0596, H0783, H1273
Journal Herald, H1085
Journal of Contemporary History, G1606, G1655
Journal of Near Eastern Studies, G0653
Journal of the Society for Army Historical
    Research, G1632
Journal of the Society of Film and Television Arts
    Limited, G1032
'Journey to the End of an Era', F0466–7
'The Journey's Echo', F0990
'The Journals of Arnold Bennett', F0081
Joynson, H.C., G1209
Juin, Hubert, G0820
'Julius Caesar', F0165–6
Jürgen, E., G0603
Juterczenka, Manfred von, F0577
Juventud (pub), A136–7

Kadogawa (pub), A127, E042
Kael, Pauline, G1110
'The Kaer of Ibu Wardini', B0005
'Kalamazoo Boy In Startling Syrian Find', H0002
Kalamazoo Gazette, H0002, H1019
Kamm, Josephine, F0579
Kansas City Star, H1057
Kanters, Robert, G1255
Karen, Robert, F0906
Karl, Fredrick R., G1698
Karsten, O., H0397
Kashani, Jamal, H0868
Kashiwagura Toshizooyaku, A082
Katz, Samuel, F0580
Kausner, Carl L., H1057
Kavaler, Lucy, F0581
Kauffmann, Stanley, G1062
Kearny Hub, H1102
Kearsey, A., F0582
Kedourie, Elie, F0583, G0664, G1179, G1568,
    G1579, G1591, H0883
Keegan, John, F0584
Keen, Henry, A090, A092
Kegan, Paul, A003
Kehler, Henning, H0750
'Kein Helden Mit Lawrence', H1238
Keith, Agnes Newton, F0585, G1235
Keith, Sir Arthur, A155, A157
Keller, Helen Rex, D0021
Kellett, E.E., G0314
Kelly, Frederick, H0948
Kelly, J.B., F0586
Kemal, Mustafa, F0375–6, F0737, F1174–5
'Kemal Ataturk', F0375–6
Kemp, Robert, G0792, G0815, G0829, G0832
Kennedy, Arthur, E271
Kennedy, Eileen, G1399

Kennet, Baroness Kathleen (Bruce) Young, F0587
Kennett, John, E219
Kennington, Eric H., A032, A196, D004, E029–30, E033–4, E037, E170, E259, E400, F0588, G0064, G0392, G0427, G0575, G0708, H0654, H1168
Kennington, Mrs., G0730
Kent, Howard, E280, H0699
Kenyon, Sir Frederick G., A006–8, G0374
Kerényi, Cornelia, A252–3
Kerényi, Karl, A254
Kern, Edward, G1312
Keyhan Intern (Iran), H0780
Khayats (pub), F0531, F1184–5
Kiernan, Reginald Hugh, E073–6, F0589, G0359
Kiesel, Frédérick, H0743
Kilduff, Peter, G1337
Kilgour, Bayard L., E293–4
Kilner, Peter, E356–7 (uses pseudonym Peter Brent)
Kimche, Jon, F0590–94, H0873, H1256
'A Kind of Hero: Lawrence of Arabia', G1038
Kine Weekly, H0598
Kinematograph Weekly, G1061, G1151
King, Francis, F0595, G1583
King, R.F., G1250–51
King, Stephen H., E297, E320, F0596
'The King-Crane Commission', F0531
'King Faisal of Iraq', F0312
King Features (pub), E344
'King Hussein and His Arabian Nights', G0023
King, Littlewood and King (pub), F0604
'The Kingdom of Jordan', F0824
'Kings and Camels', F0178
'The King's Grace', F0167
Kinross, Lord, F0887, G0577, H0814
Kipling, Rudyard, G1081
Kirby, H.T., G0470
Kirjateollisuus (pub), A113
Kirkbride, Sir Alec S., E335–6, F0597–8, H0551, H0820
Kirsch, Robert, G1592, H0551, H0633, H0742, H1229
Kirstein, Lincoln, G0226, G0531
Kitabevi, Arkin (pub), E292
Klieman, Aaron S., E396, F0599
Das Kleine Blatt, H0926
'Der Kleine und der Grosse Aufstand', G0697
Klopenstein, Willi, H1168
Knickerbocker, Peine, H0630
Knight, G. Wilson, F0600
Knight, Ronald D., E399
Knightley, Phillip, E301–19, E348–50, F0100, F0601, F0816, G1359–60, G1363, G1370, G1373, G1380–82, G1386–7, G1391, G1394–7, G1399, G1405, G1407, G1411, G1416, G1418, G1423–4, G1426, G1440, G1483, G1543, G1564, G1580, G1582, G1685, G1692, H0853, H0856, H0877, H0888, H0891–3, H0897, H0899, H0901–3, H0907–9, H0914, H0918–20, H0922, H0928, H0936, H0941–7, H0949, H0954–7, H0959, H0969–70, H0973, H0978, H0982–5, H0987–90, H0993–5, H0999, H1001–3, H1006–9, H1013–14, H1024, H1035, H1044, H1052–6, H1060, H1066–7, H1071, H1074–5, H0179, H1084, H0187–8, H1090–91, H1094–6, H1102–4, H1106–7, H1110, H1112–H1113, H1115–19, H1124–5, H1127, H1129–32, H1135,
H1138, H1140, H1148, H1150, H1192, H1243, H1279, H1296
Knopf (pub), A093, F0014, F0070, F0079, F0110, F0158, F0202–3, F0205, F0282, F0316, F0442, F0492, F0931, F1048
Knowles, John, F0602, G1104
Koch, Werner, H0909
Koepper, Wolfgang, G0697
Koestler, Arthur, F0603
Kohlhammer, W., E246, F0796
Kokomo Tribune, H1131
Kolisko, Eugen, F0604, G0473
Kölnische Zeitung, H0397
Kommando, G1049
Komroff, Manuel, F0605
Konody, Paul George, F0606
Korda, Alexander, F0611–12
Korda, Michael, F0607
'"Korol' Feisal' i polkounik', F0009
Kosmos (pub), A089, E050
'Der Kranke Held', G0502
Kraus, Fritz, G0858
Kraus, René, F0608–9
Kress von Kressenstein, Col. Baron Friederich, G0032
Kubie, Nora, F0610
Kuhn, Ferdinand, H0178, H0185, H0216
Kulik, Karol, F0611–12
Kunitz, Stanley, F0613
'Kut', F0738
Kutay, Cemal, E291
Kuysman, Dan, F0614

L., A., G0909
L., A.J., H0304
L., H.L., G0559
L., J.D., G0807
L., M.P., G0738
Liii (*see also* Lawrence ii), B0001
L.A. Sky Writer, G1314
La Badie, Donald W., G1082
La Cour, Paul, G0420
'La Ligue Arabe', G0757
Lacoste, Raymond, G0715, G1376
Lacouture, Jean, H0585, H0691, H1146
Ladies' Home Journal, G1304
Ladrière, Jean, H0797
'Lady Astor Defends Col. T.E. Lawrence', H0116
'Lady Astor Rides Motorcycle Driven by Colonel Lawrence', H0114
'Lady Chatterley's Lover', F0623–4
'Lady Gregory's Journals, 1916–1930', F0450
Laffin, John, F0615
Laffont, Robert (pub), E312
Lahr, John, F0616
Laird, J.T., G0930
Lalou, René, G0684, G0750, G0810
Lam, J.B.L., G0216
Lambert, Elizabeth, G1668
Lamore, Pierre, H0444
Lamplugh, Lois, H1152
Lancashire, David, H0782
Lancashire Evening Post, H0612
'A Lance for the Arabs', F0699
Lancer Books (pub), F0208
Lancet, G0477
Lancken, H. de, H0757
'The Land of Midian', F0847

The Land of Three Faiths', F0426
Landau, Joseph, H1039
Landau, Rom, F0617
The Landmark, B0016
Landor, Walter Savage, A229
Lane, Arthur E., F0618
Lane, John (pub), F0930, F1051
Langdon, David, F0887
Langer, L., G0237
Langer, William L., G1344
Langford, Richard E., H1060
'Lapidation d'une idole', G0715
Laquer, Walter, F0619–21
Larès, Maurice, E377–8, E398, E394, E396, F0781,
    G1316, G1365, G1573, G1596, G1601–2, G1644,
    G1649–50, G1658
Larousse Mensuel Illustré, G0163, G0367, G0606,
    G0809
Las Vegas Sun, H0732
Las Vergnas, Raymond, G0753, G1227
Lask, Thomas, H0960
'Last Crusade', G0422
'Last Fight for Life: Lawrence of Arabia Secrets
    Revealed', H0229
The Last Gleanings', H1290
The Latest Great Cause', F1110
The Last Great Puritan', G0336
'Last Hours of Lawrence', H0265
The Last Inspection', F0638
The Last Lawrence Veil', H1100
'Last Mystery of Hero Lawrence', H1270
The Last Nomad', F1037
'Last of the Great Loners', G1336
'The Last Portrait of Aircraftsman Shaw', H0304
'Last Word on Lawrence', H1223
'A Late Beginning', F0783
'The Later Years of Thomas Hardy', F0480
The Latest From Colonel Lawrence', G0071
'Latin Castles in Syria', G0390
Lattes, Jean-Claude, G1257
'Laughing Torso', F0472
'Laughter in the Next Room', F0974
Lauras, A., G0793
'Laurence (sic) d'Arabia', G1367
'Laurens b'chayyim ub'agada', E104
'Laurens u'l'Acharav Hemered Bamidbar', E329
Laverne, Gaston, H0507
Le Vien, Jack, F0622
'Lavrens'e Karşi Kuşçubaşi', E291
Lawrence, Arnold Walter, A178–9, A181,
    A220–29, E070, E072, E083–4, E107–12, E134,
    E150, E1452, E250–51, E256–7, E259, E303,
    G0432, G0434, G0436, G0439–40, G0444,
    G0447, G0450–51, G0453, G0456, G0460,
    G0462, G0498, G0504–5, G0519, G0525, G0690,
    G1008–9, G1010, G1014–16, G1040, G1070,
    G1224, G1691, H0299, H0381–2, H0385–7,
    H0454, H0628, H0639, H0701, H0910, H1290
Lawrence, D.H., A124, A162, A229, F0623–4,
    F0983, F1189, G1227
'Lawrence, D.H.', B0024
Lawrence, E., B0004
Lawrence, Frank H., A246, G0665–9, G0672,
    G0674–8, G0680–81, H0436–40
Lawrence, Montague Robert, A246–7, H0436–40
Lawrence, Sarah, E138–40
Lawrence, William George, A246–7, G0665–9,
    G0672, G0674–8, G0680–81, H0436–40

Lawrence ii, B0002
'Lawrence', E083–4, E279, E334, G0248, G0251,
    G0333, G0345, G0349, G0353–5, G0359, G1104,
    G1145, G1191, G1196, G1372, G1694–5, H0368,
    G0460, H0642, H0731, H0937
'Lawrence à Britannia', G0173
'De Lawrence à Learoyd', G1658
'Lawrence – A Legend Unveiled', H0076
'Lawrence a Man or Myth?', G0721
'Lawrence a Nettle of Briers', H0815
'Lawrence Accused Himself of Deceit Held
    Pledges Worthless', H0403
'Lawrence af Arabien, Myten, Manden og
    Strategen', G0490
'Lawrence After Arabia', G0406
'Lawrence After the Mid East', H1072
'Lawrence, Aldington and Some Critics', G0862
'Lawrence, Aldington y le Verdad', G0804
'Lawrence: Alias Ross and Shaw', G0251
'Lawrence An Unofficial Portrait', G0427
'Lawrence and All Souls', E231
'Lawrence and Arab Nationalism', G1132
'Lawrence and Clive', G0379
'Lawrence and Faisal', H0144
'Lawrence and Generalship', G0357
'Lawrence and His Desert Raiders', E289–90,
    G1317
'Lawrence and His Epic', G0304
'Lawrence and His Legacy', E337
'Lawrence and His Legend', H0465
'Lawrence and King Hussein: The 1921
    Negotiations', G0479
'Lawrence and Lloyd George', F0647–8
'Lawrence and Mao Together', E337a
'Lawrence and the Arab Cause', G0520
'Lawrence and the Arab Revolt', F0792, G1663
'Lawrence and the Arabian Adventure', E037,
    G0139, G0143, G0146–8, G0150, G0425,
    H0065–6, H0069
'Lawrence and the Arabs', D0001, E029–42, E056,
    E098, G0068, G0112–15, G0121, G0123, G0139,
    G0143, G0145–8, G0218, G1430, G1689, H0029,
    H0048
'Lawrence and the Arabs of Iraq', F0693
'Lawrence and the Armenians', G1626
'Lawrence and the Demon of the Absolute', G0873
'Lawrence and the Hedjaz', G0043
'Lawrence, and the Legend that Misfired', H1249
'Lawrence and the Presumed Connection With
    Arabs', H1252
'Lawrence and the War', G1202
Lawrence & Wishart (pub), F0368
'Lawrence and Woolley', G0382
'Lawrence as a Crusader', G0312
'Lawrence as a Friend', G0299
'Lawrence as a Soldier', G0234
'Lawrence as a Strategist', G0237
'Lawrence as an Arab Saint', G0152
'Lawrence as Bureaucrat', E396
'Lawrence As Critic', H0412
'Lawrence as I Knew Him', F0782, G0257, H0223
'Lawrence As Spy, Not Savior', H1068
'Lawrence at Clouds Hill', G0541, G0598
'Lawrence at Rest', G1452
Lawrence av Arabien, E159–60, E319
'Lawrence Ban', H0729
'Lawrence, Bildnis Eines Forschers Politikers,
    Soldaten und Menschen', G0463

'Lawrence Bitter Over Fate of Arabs', H0058
'Lawrence Bobs Up to Confound Doubter', H0094
'Lawrence Book on Sale Next Year', H0863
'Lawrence Book Price Set at $500,000', H0334
'Lawrence Book Rips Lawrence', H0332
'Lawrence Boom', H0913
'Lawrence Buried With Simple Rites', H0267
'Lawrence By a Woman Who Never Met Him',
   H1288
'Lawrence Clew Seen', H0347
'Lawrence Clings to Life', H0197
'Lawrence Con Man of Desert Author Says',
   H1105
'Lawrence Confond ses Détracteurs', H0488
'Lawrence Copyright Seen in Danger', H0044
'Lawrence Cottage Kept as Memorial', H0351
'Lawrence D'Arabie', E214–15, E240, E245, E247,
   E252, E254, E278, E391, F0313, G1683
'Lawrence d'Arabie: Du Mythe à la Realtié', G1402
'Lawrence de Arabia', E102, E200, E202, E229,
   E244, E263–4, E281, E284
'Lawrence de Arabia y Otros essayos', E177
'Lawrence di Arabia', E243
'Lawrence d'Arabie', E380, G0604, G0896, G0901,
   G0964, G0968, G0977, G0980, G1019, G1051,
   G1056, G1063, G1103, G0627, H0629, H0631–2,
   H0679, H0699
'De Lawrence d'Arabie à Camp David', H1230
'Lawrence d'Arabie archéologue', G1218
'"Lawrence d'Arabie" au Coeur de la Révolte',
   H0669
'Lawrence d'Arabie Bourreau de soi-même', G1157
'Lawrence d'Arabie Contesté', H1235
'Lawrence d'Arabie de David Lean', H0683
'Lawrence d'Arabie de F. Armitage', H0565
'Lawrence d'Arabie, un imposteur?', H0456
'Lawrence d'Arabie et les Châteaux des Croisés',
   E389
'Lawrence d'Arabie et Son Secret', H0422
'"Lawrence d'Arabie" favori pour l'Oscar du
   Cinéma', H0670
'Lawrence d'Arabie fut-il un produit de la
   publicité?', H0435
'Lawrence d'Arabie. Grandeur et Misère des
   Héros', H1174
'Lawrence d'Arabie: L'Envers d'une Légende',
   G0799
'Lawrence d'Arabie ou Lawrence de Sion?', G1366
'Lawrence d'Arabie ou la recherche scrupuleuse
   de l'ascète', H1263
'Lawrence d'Arabie ou le rêve fracassé', H0626
'Lawrence d'Arabie. Qui était le motocycliste?',
   H1162
'Lawrence d'Arabie un Livre d'Images Pieuses',
   H0682
'Lawrence de David Lean', H0686
'Lawrence Dead', H0241
'Lawrence Dead: Britain Honors Hero of Arabia',
   H0218
'Lawrence Death of 1,000 Cuts', H1247
'Lawrence Death Probe 50 Years On', H1257
'Lawrence Death Will Set Free No...', H0247
'Lawrence Derides Reports of Spying', H0082
'Lawrence Détestait la France parce qu'il aimait
   Dahoum', H0481
'Lawrence Dies and a New Crop of Legends is
   Born', G0259

'Lawrence Dies of Crash Injuries After a Six Day
   Fight by Doctors', H0206
'Lawrence e os Arabes', E157–8
'Lawrence Emotional Struggle Examined', H1040
'The Lawrence Enigma', G1350, G1699
'Lawrence-Enthüllung in Paris Erscheinen', H0453
'Lawrence est de retour', G1644
'Lawrence et le RêveArabe', G1638
'Lawrence et Les Arabes', E039–40
'Lawrence et les Sept Piliers de la Sagesse', G0606
'Lawrence et l'Innocence de l'Action', F0856, G0602
'Lawrence et Son Corps', G0618
'Lawrence Exhibit At Whittier College', H0766
'Lawrence Exhibit Now on Display at USC
   Library', H0719
'Lawrence Exhibit on at Whittier', H0762
'Lawrence Exhibit on Display', H0760
'Lawrence Explains Fall of Kut-El-Amman', H0022
'Lawrence Faces the En-Dewrance Test', H1232
'Lawrence Facing the Crisis Today', H0195
'Lawrence Faisal and the Arabs' Cause at the Paris
   Peace Conference – a French Immorality Play',
   F0596
'The Lawrence Family', G0674
'"Lawrence" Film Opens With Fanfare', H0656
'Lawrence For Palestine', H0102
'Lawrence Fought for British Empire', H1010
'Lawrence, Friend of Arabs', H1057
'Lawrence Fund Left to Orphans', H0315
'Lawrence Gift Refused', H0840
'Lawrence: Grave Anxiety', H0198
'Lawrence: Grave Fears', H0200
'Lawrence Grave News Last Night', H0211
'Lawrence Has a New Dimension', H1049
'Lawrence Has New Hero Role', H0122
'"Lawrence" Has Tremendous Show Case', G1194
'Lawrence – Held oder Hochstapler', H0452
'Lawrence Hero of Arab Revolt to Quit', H0163
'Lawrence Hero of Fatal Air Disaster', G0124
'Lawrence: Hero or Imposter', G0702
'Lawrence Hero or Villain', H0885
'Lawrence: Herunter von den Säulen', G0673
'Lawrence Hides Identity Even When Near
   Death', H0238
'Lawrence, Homme Fasciste ou Athée Parfait',
   G0630
'Lawrence, His Life', G01612
'The Lawrence I Knew', H0242, H0461
Lawrence Il Re Senza Corona, E085
'Lawrence, imposteur?', H0509
'Lawrence in an Arab Context', G1267
'Lawrence in Full', G0076
'Lawrence in Medical Hands', H1209
'Lawrence in Obituaries Again', H1028
'Lawrence in Oxford', G0284
'Lawrence in the Balance', H0127
'Lawrence in the Blue', E087–8, G0405
'Lawrence in the Dock', G0712
'Lawrence in the R.A.F.', G0571
'Lawrence Inquest: Car Mystery', H0274
'Lawrence Into Ross', G0717
'Lawrence is Already a Legend', H0046
'Lawrence is Kept Closely Guarded', H0204
'Lawrence is Near Death', H0207
'Lawrence is Ordered to Britain From India',
   H0087
'Lawrence Isn't a Hero in Arabia', H1269

'Lawrence Issues His Arabian Book', H0023
'Lawrence Items at USC Library', H1141
'Lawrence l'Arabe', G0270, G0446
'Lawrence l'Arabe ou la Guerre au Désert', G0291
'Lawrence Lauds Thomas', H0134
'Lawrence Lawrencia', G0200
'Lawrence Leaves Air Force', H0167
'Lawrence Le Véridique', G0731
'Lawrence Led Fascinating Life – All of them', H1110
'Lawrence Left a MSS.', H0303
'The Lawrence Legend', G0117, G0704, G0944, H0459
'Lawrence Legend Furthered by Latest Co-op Efforts', H1034
'Lawrence Legend Shortened', H0968
'Lawrence le Raté', G0748
'The Lawrence Letters', G0493
'Lawrence Letters Sold for $3,800 Here', H0361
'Lawrence: Lies or Legends?', G0657
'Lawrence L'Imposteur', E190, H0468
'Lawrence L'Imposteur précédée d'une réponse de R. Aldington à de Fallois', G0786
'Lawrence Lingers But Hope is Faint', H0185
'"Lawrence" Location Getting Film Supply', H0591
'"Lawrence" Looms as an Attendance Big Box Office Grosser', G1115
'Lawrence Made Up Rape Story Says Author', H1213
'Lawrence Makes the Dole', H0831
'Lawrence, Man and Legend', H0466
'Lawrence Man of Mysteries', H0248
'Lawrence Manuscript Sold to Pay a Blackmailer', H0377
'Lawrence May Visit Arabia Again, Says London News', H0137
'Lawrence Memorial', H0356
'Lawrence Memorial Medal', G0338
'Lawrence Might-Have-Been', H0961
'Lawrence Minus the Legend', H1078
'Lawrence MS Bought by Wells', G0344
'Lawrence MSS', H0341
'Lawrence Mystery of Black Car', H0858
'Lawrence Mystery Remains Unsolved', H1101
'Lawrence na Arabia', H1261
'A Lawrence Needed to Lead Cubans', H0714
'Lawrence No Better But Hopes are Held', H0201
'Lawrence, notre frère', F0049, G0609
'Lawrence of Arabia', B0033, E073–6, E078, E100, E137, E160, E191–9, E226, E232–44, E249, E253, E260–4, E344, E317, E348–50, E381–2, F0210–16, F0419, F0447, F0464–5, F0640–41, F0723, F0772, F0809, F0888–9, G0060–61, G0145, G0175, G0246, G0254, G0286, G0298, G0306, G0310, G0321–2, G0325, G0359, G0489, G0539, G0652, G0656, G0658, G0673, G0682–3, G0694, G0700, G0704–10, G0713, G0716, G0718, G0720, G0726, G0733, G0735, G0738, G0784, G0826, G0834, G0844, G0846, G0851, G0861, G0863, G0867, G0869, G0872, G0875–6, G0926, G0969–71, G0974–5, G0978–9, G0981–2, G0985, G0998, G1000, G1011, G1013, G1025, G1034, G1049–1050, G1053, G0159, G1154, G1156, G1158, G1184, G1186, G1243, G1263–4, G1266, G1268, G1288, G1397, G1449, G1564, G1580, G1621, G1699, H0027, H0032, H0045, H0060, H0068, H0085, H0153, H0171, H0173,
H0177, H0228, H0246, H0251, H0279, H0297, H0310, H0314, H0336, H0342, H0360, H0392, H0443, H0446, H0457, H0462–3, H0469–71, H0484–6, H0544, H0546, H0549, H0576, H0622, H0624–5, H0630, H0640, H0651, H0655, H0660, H0814, H0929, H1024, H1042, H1154, H1211
'Lawrence of Arabia a Genius', H0427
'Lawrence of Arabia: A Legend in His Lifetime', H1262
'Lawrence of Arabia, a man of mystery', F0275
'Lawrence of Arabia A Mystification– An Impression– A Tribute', G0082
'Lawrence of Arabia: A Northampton Comrade's Memories', H0291
'Lawrence of Arabia: A Personal Impression of a Comrade in the Great War', F0998
'Lawrence of Arabia: a return', H1134
'Lawrence of Arabia: A Review', H1136
'Lawrence of Arabia – a whole new picture', H1064
'Lawrence of Arabia Again Some Secrets are Divulged', H1132
'"Lawrence of Arabia" Alive?', G0300
'Lawrence of Arabia an Analysis of a Man of Destiny', E123
'Lawrence of Arabia an Authentic Hero', G0223
'Lawrence of Arabia and Dorset', E295–6
'Lawrence of Arabia and H.H. Richardson', G1654
'Lawrence of Arabia and His Super Speed Boat', G0555
'Lawrence of Arabia and His World', E358–9, G1562, G1571, G1574, G1576
'Lawrence of Arabia and Mount Batten', H0825
'Lawrence of Arabia and Pole Hill', E361, G1517
'Lawrence of Arabia and Seven Pillars of Wisdom', G1022
'Lawrence of Arabia and Sex', H1151
'Lawrence of Arabia and the Brough Superior', G1295
'Lawrence of Arabia and the False Lawrence', H0419
'Lawrence of Arabia and Wareham', E287
'"Lawrence of Arabia" and Zionism', G1497
'Lawrence of Arabia Appreciations', H0157
'Lawrence of Arabia Arrest "Order" Unconfirmed', H0086
'Lawrence of Arabia Arrest "Ordered" by Afghan Authorities', H0084
'Lawrence of Arabia as a Buck Private', G0134
'Lawrence of Arabia as a Train Wrecker', G0065
'Lawrence of Arabia as Critic and Friend', G0395
'Lawrence of Arabia as I Knew Him', H0411
'Lawrence of Arabia As Revealed in His Own Words', G0513
'"Lawrence of Arabia" as Screen Biography', H0657
'Lawrence of Arabia: As Yet Unresolved', G0138
'Lawrence of Arabia as Yet Unexplained', H0067
'Lawrence of Arabia Back on Book Shelves', H1120
'Lawrence of Arabia Book Features New Facts', H1105
'Lawrence of Arabia – Brass Rubber!', G0470
'Lawrence of Arabia Buried', H0256
Lawrence of Arabia Committee, E068
'Lawrence of Arabia Company on Location in Morocco as They Recreate the Final Charge of the Arabs', G1024
'Lawrence of Arabia Cycles Into Seclusion', H0168

'Lawrence of Arabia Dies', H0166
'Lawrence of Arabia Dies of Injuries', H0245
'Lawrence of Arabia Dies of Motorcycle Injuries',
    H0209
'Lawrence of Arabia Discovered Again', H0166
'Lawrence of Arabia Draws a Map', F0338
'Lawrence of Arabia Dying After Crash on
    Motorcycle', H0178
'Lawrence of Arabia Estate', H0337
'Lawrence of Arabia Fights Soviet in India', H0074
'Lawrence of Arabia' (Film), E266–8, F0398, F0604,
    G0948, G0950, G0956, G0960–67, G0972,
    G0984, G1004–5, G1012, G1030–34, G1036–8,
    G1042, G1044, G1046–8, G1050, G1053–4,
    G1057, G1059–62, G1064–66, G1069, G1077,
    G1080, G1082, G1086, G1088, G1090, G1096,
    G1098–9, G1110, G1115, G1117, G1127, G1143,
    G1145, G1149, G1153, G1159, G1162, G1194,
    G1198, G1258, G1271, G1301, G1311, G1321,
    G1439, G1464, G1628, G1643, G1699, G1704,
    G1706, H0581, H0591–3, H0595, H0597–8,
    H0601–3, H0605–13, H0615, H0619–21, H0638,
    H0643–9, H0651, H0656–7, H0664–5,
    H0669–71, H0674, H0676, H0678–81, H0683–4,
    H0686–7, H0701, H0712, H0714, H0724–5,
    H0756, H0769, H0811, H1271
'Lawrence of Arabia First Edition for £11,100',
    H1176
'Lawrence of Arabia: From Camels to Target
    Boats', G1656
'Lawrence of Arabia Funeral Today', H0257
'"Lawrence of Arabia" Gets Italian "Oscar"', H0769
'Lawrence of Arabia, Great Britain', G0984
'Lawrence of Arabia Guard Over State Papers',
    H0192
'Lawrence of Arabia Guerrilla Warrior!', G1619
'Lawrence of Arabia Had Benefit of New Material',
    H1082
'Lawrence of Arabia Hides in London', H0090
'Lawrence of Arabia His Own Story', H0288
'Lawrence of Arabia. Home From India.
    Exclusive', H0091
'Lawrence of Arabia Hurt in Highway Crash',
    H0181
'Lawrence of Arabia, Illegitimate Son', G1379
'Lawrence of Arabia in a New Disguise', H0034
'Lawrence of Arabia in a New Light', H0974
'Lawrence of Arabia in Crash, Near Death', H0169
'Lawrence of Arabia is Given Fighting...', H0199
'Lawrence of Arabia in lichte Freunde', G0461
'Lawrence of Arabia in the R.A.F.', H0454
'Lawrence of Arabia Injured Seriously', H0184
'Lawrence of Arabia Inquest Tomorrow', H0227
'Lawrence of Arabia is Honored in London:
    Memorial Bust is Dedicated at St Paul's', H0358
'"Lawrence of Arabia" Led Colorful Life', H0225
'Lawrence of Arabia Leaves £7,400', H0159
'Lawrence of Arabia: Legend in His Lifetime',
    H1259
'Lawrence of Arabia Memorial', E068, H0317
'Lawrence of Arabia: Memories and a Tribute',
    G0265
The Lawrence of Arabia Myth', G1125
'Lawrence of Arabia New Material Shows His
    Own Side', H1050
'"Lawrence of Arabia" One More Appraisal',
    G1618

Lawrence of Arabia One of His Last Letters',
    H0156
'Lawrence of Arabia or Lawrence of England',
    G1375
'Lawrence of Arabia Papers', G1330
'Lawrence of Arabia Prize Picture', G1149
'Lawrence of Arabia Read Him', H0793
'Lawrence of Arabia Reply to A.T. Wilson', C0017
'Lawrence of Arabia Revealed', H1085
'Lawrence of Arabia "Secrets" Revealed', H1036
'Lawrence of Arabia Seeking Peace in Waziristan',
    H0079
'Lawrence of Arabia Seen in a New Light', H1108
'"Lawrence of Arabia" Seen in New Perspective',
    H0981
'Lawrence of Arabia Slain', H1215
'Lawrence of Arabia Slain, Author Claims', H1214
'Lawrence of Arabia Soldier-of-Fortune Who
    Became a Desert King', G0940
'Lawrence of Arabia Speaks', F1095
'Lawrence of Arabia – Startling Attack on
    Uncrowned King', H0050
'Lawrence of Arabia Still a Real Enigma', H1099
'Lawrence of Arabia Still Elusive Subject', H1012,
    H1017
'Lawrence of Arabia Still Unconscious', H0203
'The Lawrence of Arabia Story', E221
'Lawrence of Arabia Story of His Book', H0025
'Lawrence of Arabia Sweeps to the Right Flank',
    F1045
'Lawrence of Arabia Talks', H0150
'Lawrence of Arabia Target of Air Bombs', H0145
'Lawrence of Arabia the (Almost) Free Man', F0448
'Lawrence of Arabia, the Facts Without the
    Fiction', E322
'Lawrence of Arabia, the Literary Impulse',
    E346–7, G1525, G1529, G1558, G1561
'Lawrence of Arabia: the Man, the Myth, the
    Movie', G1643
'Lawrence of Arabia: the Master Illusionist', E397
'Lawrence of Arabia: the One-Man Monastery',
    H0382
'Lawrence of Arabia: the Portraits From
    Imagination 1922–1979', E396
'Lawrence of Arabia: the Work Behind the
    Legend', G0273
'Lawrence of Arabia, Thomas Hardy and the Four
    Black Tea Sets', F1045a
'Lawrence of Arabia Threw His Sheikh's Robes
    Into Thames', H0357
'"Lawrence of Arabia" to be Filmed', H0151
'"Lawrence of Arabia" to Quit British Army',
    H0161
'Lawrence of Arabia Translator to Homer', G0197
'"Lawrence of Arabia" Unconscious', H0179,
    H0183
'Lawrence of Arabia: Venture in Debunking',
    G0656
'Lawrence of Arabia Very Ill', H0180
'Lawrence of Arabia Walked Back Into History',
    G1554
'Lawrence of Arabia – War's Spiritual Toll', G0267
'Lawrence of Arabia Was a Man Not a Legend',
    H0160
'Lawrence of Arabia Was a Spy', H0953
'Lawrence of Arabia Was Elusive', H1056
'Lawrence of Arabia, Who He Was and What He
    Did', G0056

Lawrence of Arabia: Why Have They Never Thought of This Before?', G0956

'Lawrence of Arabia Without Allenby', G1208

'Lawrence of Arabia Writes From Beyond', H0749

'Lawrence of Arabia, Zionism and Palestine', E141

'Lawrence of Arabia's Bizarre Double Life', H1258

'Lawrence of Arabia's Crash Bike Sold for £1', H0747

'Lawrence of Arabia's Debt to Seapower', G1617

'Lawrence of Arabia's Hangup at War's End', H1296

'Lawrence of Arabia's Letters', G0648

'Lawrence of Arabia's Life Remains As Elusive as Ever', H1051

'Lawrence of Arabia's Life was a Tragedy' (in Italian), G1332

'Lawrence of Arabia's Secret', H0856

'Lawrence of Arabia's Secret Power', H0213

'Lawrence of England', G0354

'Lawrence of Enigma', H1080

'Lawrence of Leeds', G1028

'Lawrence of Paradox', H1204

'Lawrence of Princeton', G1300

'Lawrence of the Arabs', G0425

'Lawrence of the Hedjaz', G0044

'Lawrence of the House Next Door', H1260

'Lawrence of the Mint, Ross of the R.A.F.', G1503

'Lawrence of the Odeon', H0653

'Lawrence of What?', G1545, H1208

'Lawrence og hans Arabere', E099

'Lawrence on Arabia', G0540

'Lawrence Papers Sold for $24,000', H1157

'Lawrence, Prince of Mecca', E028

'Lawrence Quits Army', H0165

'Lawrence Remembered Mystery Roses Appear Again', H1266

'Lawrence Report On Revolt is Sold', H0340

'Lawrence Reported Writing a New Book on Middle East', H0077

'Lawrence: Review of His Book Scores News Beat by 14 Years', G0407

'Lawrence: R.I.P.', G0538

'Lawrence, roi secret de l'Arabie', G0904, G0909, G0912–14, H0567–70

'Lawrence/Ross/Shaw', G1020, G1075

'Un "Lawrence" Sans Passion', H0511

'Lawrence Saw Philby's Father as "Rather a Red"', H1254

'Lawrence, Scholar and Archaeologist in Early Life Freed Arabia From Turks', H1280

'Lawrence Secrets to be Revealed', H0879

'Lawrence, Soldat, Diplomate, Écrivain, demeure une figure attachante et étrange', H0515

'Lawrence Speaking', G0492

'Lawrence – Speaks From the Grave', G0371

'Lawrence Still a Man of Mystery', G0106

'Lawrence Still a Private', H0070

'Lawrence Still Elusive Figure', H1092

'Lawrence Story', H0889

'"Lawrence" Takes "Season" Record', G1704

'A Lawrence Talks About That Legend', H0734

'Lawrence, T.E.', F0306

'"Lawrence" Team Reunited', H0773

'Lawrence the Amazing', H0026

'Lawrence the Anti-Hero Hero', G1001

'Lawrence the Arabian Knight', E090

'Lawrence the Brough', G1669

'Lawrence the Chameleon', G0509

Lawrence the Engima', H0059

'Lawrence: the Enigmatic "Ablest Soldier"', H1184

'Lawrence the Last Crusade', E115–16, G0421–4, G0426, G0429, G0442, G0445

'Lawrence the Last Hours', H0236

'Lawrence: the Last Letter', H1293

'Lawrence the Man and the Legend', H1202

'Lawrence the Nation Maker', G0070

'Lawrence – the Pro-Arab Zionist', G1672

'Lawrence the Soldier', G0222

'Lawrence – the Twentieth-Century Hero', F0368

'Lawrence the Ubiquitous', H0081

'Lawrence the Uncrowned King of the Arabs', E054

'Lawrence, the Young Man', G0174

'Lawrence: 30 Years After', G1211

'Lawrence to Have a Simple Funeral', H0216

'Lawrence to Quit RAF', H0162

'Lawrence, Twentieth-Century Hero', G0292

'Lawrence, Twice a Hero', G1546

'Lawrence und der Freiheit der Araber', G0500

'Lawrence van Arabie', E239, E343

Lawrence ve Arap Ísyani, E292

'Lawrence Vindicated', G0745

'Lawrence von Arabia', G0245

'Lawrence von Arabien', E216, E246, E371, G0364, G0466, G0637, G0737, H0874

'Lawrence von Arabien auf Defektem', G1369

'Lawrence von Arabien auf Defektem Sockel', H0920

'Lawrence von Arabien – Auf den Spuren eines Abenteurers', E390

'Lawrence von Arabien Erregt Seit', G0467

'Lawrence von Arabien in Neuester Sicht', H0934

'Lawrence von Arabien und T.E. Shaw', G0625

'Lawrence wa al Arab', E255–9

'Lawrence, Was He a Double Dealer?', H0878

'Lawrence, Was He a Woman Hater?', G0730

'Lawrence Was Here or Was It Mr. O'Toole?', H1166

'Lawrence Was My Orderly', G1111

'Lawrence Won't Lecture', H0041

'Lawrence y el Libro de Aldington', G0803

'Lawrenciana', H1274

'Lawrence's Arabian Knights', G0078

'Lawrence's Book is Due in the Fall', H0319

'Lawrence's Book To Appear in Full', H0298

'Lawrence's Burden', G0633

'Lawrence's Campaigns Relived by Old Comrades', H1280

'Lawrence's Confession', H0623

'Lawrence's Death Denied', H0300

'Lawrence's Defenders', G0661

'Lawrence's Emotional Conflict', H1055

'Lawrence's Emotional Struggle', H1023, H1045

'Lawrence's Emotional Struggle After the Middle-East War Deal', H1037,, H1067, H1069, H0173, H1137

'Lawrence's Emotions After the Middle East War', H1047

'Lawrence's Epic of Arabia', G0334, H0346

'Lawrence's Essay', H0309

'Lawrence's Friend Refuses to Sell His Letters', H0501

'Lawrence's Great Book', H0322

'Lawrence's House Shaken Up', H0635

'Lawrence's Last Book', H0333

'Lawrence's Lat.', G0412

Lawrence's Letter for the War Museum', H0904
'Lawrence's Library', H0710
'Lawrence's Life Extolled by King', H0252
'Lawrence's Meadow Grave', H0275
'Lawrence's Medievalism', E396
'Lawrence's Own Epitaph', H0292
'Lawrence's Own Obituary', H0268
'Lawrence's Revolt in the Desert', G0281
'Lawrence's Royalties Finance Education Fund',
    H0315
'Lawrence's Secret Arabian "Slush Fund"', H1237
'Lawrence's Seven Pillars Exceeds Fondest Hopes',
    H0348
'Lawrence's Story of Arabia Assailed', H0152
'Lawrence's Struggle After Middle East War',
    H1048
'Lawrence's Struggle After War', H1111
'Lawrence's Struggle Told After Mid-East War',
    H1133
'Lawrence's Torse Saved for College', H0741, H0870
'Lawrence's Version of Odyssey Ready', H0119
'Lawrence's War Book $20,000 a Copy Here',
    H0035
'Lawrence's Writing', H0305
'Lawrenciana: Recuerdos de Lawrence de Arabia',
    G1256
Lawson, E.F., H0258
Lazare, Christopher, G0452
Le Clézio, J.M.G., H1240
Leckie, Robert, D0023
Leach, Sally, F0625
'Leachman O.C. Desert', F1157
Leader Magazine, G0620
Lean, David, E226, E266, E268, E271, F0972,
    G1054, H0587, H0683, H0686
Leavis, F.R., F0026
'Lebanon in History', F0506
'Leben Ohne Legende', A248
Leckie, R., D0023
Leclant, J., G0881
Le Corbeau, Adrien, A094-7
Lectures Françaises, G0883
'Led Air Raids For Lawrence, Killed', H0139
'Led By Lawrence', E052-3
Lee, Jasper (pub), F0491
Leed, Eric J., F0627
Leeds, E. Thurlow, E402
'A Leffrinekweke, un Jeune écrivain anglais,
    J.W. Wilson prépare la "biographie officielle' de
    son légendaire compatriote Lawrence d'Arabie',
    H1178
Left Review, G0292
Legate, David, H1223
'Legacy of the Desert', F0037
'Legend Among the Bedouin', G1146
'Legend of Arabia?', H1217
'The Legend of Lawrence of Arabia Proves to be
    Just a Legend', G1270
'The Legend of T.E. Lawrence', G1690
'The Legend of T.E. Lawrence an Astrological
    Profile', G1092
'A Legend Shaken', G1581
'A Legend That Dies Hard', G1357
'Le Légendaire Colonel Lawrence ne fut-il qu'un
    Mythomane', G0655
'Legendary Lawrence', G0151
'De La Légende à l'Histoire', H0516
'La Légende de Lawrence de Arabia Reulta una

egendá', G1706
'Le Légende du colonel Lawrence', H0529
'Legion of the Marching Madmen', F0099
Legman, G., F0628
Legrand, Edy, A024-5
Lehmann, John, F0629
Leibovici, Marcel, G0796
Leibson, Paul, H1075
Leicester Galleries, A032, A099
Leicester Mercury, H0179, H0255
Leiftur (pub), E021
Leitch, David, F0816, H1166
Lenczowski, George, G0630
Lengyel, Emil, F0631-3, G0590, G0822, G0846
Leonard, John, H1113
Leopold (pub), A112
Lepape, Pierce, H1241, H1246
Lesley, Cole, F0634
Leslie, Shane, F0635
Lessing, Erich, A252-4
'A Letter From England', G0185
'A Letter From T.E. Lawrence to His Mother', A192
'Letter of T.E. Lawrence in Bodleian', H0737
'Letter to Robert Graves', B0045
'Letter to "The Times"', C0009
'Lettere di Thomas Edward Lawrence', A209
'Letters From Limbo', F0894
'Letters From Syria', F0991
'Letters From T.E. Shaw to Bruce Rogers', A160
'Letters From T.E. Shaw to Viscount Cerlow', A193
'Letters May Be Fakes', H0417
'Letters of a Man of Legend', G0522
'The Letters of D'Arcy Cresswell', F0242
'The Letters of D.H. Lawrence', F1189
'The Letters of Ezra Pound', F0863
'The Letters of Gertrude Bell', F0073-5
'The Letters of J.E. Flecker to Frank Savery', F0348
'The Letters of Sean O'Casey', F0808
'Letters of T.E. Lawrence', A202-9, A249, B0008,
    B0023, B0037, C0013-14, E069-70, G0365,
    G0484-9, G0492-4, G0504-5, G0512-15,
    G0517-18, G0520, G0522, G0527, G0530-31,
    G0617, G1070, H0395, H0398, H0402, H0404,
    H0409, H0413, H0750
'Letters of T.E. Lawrence: Edited by David
    Garnett', G0559
'Letters of the Earl of Oxford and Asquith to A
    Friend', F0001
'Letters to Mother', D0030
'Letters to T.E. Lawrence', E250-1, G1008-9,
    G1010, G1014-16, H0628, H0639
'Lettres', B0044
'Lettres à Lionel Curtis', B0039
'Lettres Anglo-Américaines', G0753
'Lettres de T.E. Lawrence', A206-7, H0403
'Lettres et Spectacles', H0577
Les Lettres Françaises, H0416, H0420, H0505,
    H0518, H0668
Les Lettres Nouvelles, G0782
'Lettres Sur les Sept Piliers', B0041, H0416
Leurs Figures, E040
Levende Talen, G1319
Levi, G., G0172
Levin, Meyer, F0636, G1090
Lewin, Ronald, F0637
Lewis, Alun, F0638
Lewis, Cecil Day, A256-60, F0251, F0639, G0484
Lewis, Peter, F0622

Lewis, Wyndham, F0640–1, G0466, G0872
Lewis (pub), F0397
Lewiston Maine Journal, H1107
Lexington Herald-Leader, H1018
Lias, Godfrey, F0642
Libération, H0595, H0685
'Liberté de l'Esprit', G0605
Liberté Dimanche, H0643
Liberty, G0216, G0393, G0419, G0472
Library and Book News, G1423
'Library Features Exhibit of Lawrence of Arabia', H0767
Library Journal, G0353, G0798, G0919, G0974, G1013, G1071, G1106, G1126, G1150, G1154, G1181, G1292, G1317, G1331, G1370, G1428, G1500, G1529, G1533, G1564, G1571, G1583, G1605, G1695
Library of Book News, G1413
'A Library of Literary Criticism', F1027
La Libre Belgique (Brussels), H0456, H0491, H0533, H0584, H0759
Liddell Hart, Basil Henry, A203, A213, A215, A217–18, E058–62, E064–6, E100–101, E130–4, E178, E209–11, F0448, F0643–55, F0723, G0217–21, G0224–5, G0227–8, G0231–6, G0228–41, G0289, G0322, G0366, G0372, G0489, G0490, G0494, G0506–10, G0514, G0729, G0760, G0804, G0813, G0839, G0973, G1095, G1126, G1129–30, G1146, G1171, G1384–5, G1664, H0049, H0147, H0149, H0240, H0399, H0401, H0409, H0427, H0460, H0478, H0625, H0655, H0673, H0715, H0828
'The Liddell Hart Memoirs', F0647
Lidforss, F., E022
Lidstone, G.H., F0656
'Liebe zum Führer', G0950
Liebman, Seymour B., H1144
'The Life and Letters of Lady Wester Wemyss', F1120
'The Life and Letters of Lord Wester Wemyss', F1119
Life and Letters Series, E036
'Life and Work of Thomas Hardy', F0482
'Life for Life's Sake', F0011
'Life Histories and Psychobiology', F0924
Life Magazine, F0657, G0988, G0993, G1037, G1229, G1233, G1310, G1312, G1694
'The Life of Charles M. Doughty', F0512–14
'Life of Ezra Pound', F1000
'The Life of James Elroy Flecker', F0509
'Life of Lawrence of Arabia Filled With Mystery, Enigma', H1127
'Life of Lord Lloyd', F0004
'The Life of Noel Coward', F0634
'The Life of Sir Percy Cox', F0425
'The Life of Thomas Hardy', F0481
'The Life to Come and Other Stories', F0363
The Light, H0940
'Light on Britain's...', H0735
'The Lighted Window', F0185
Lilienthal, Alfred M., F0658
Lilico, Stuart, G0552
Limited Edition Club (pub), A024, A154
'Limited Edition of the Mint Disappears', G1329
Lincoln, Trebitsch, H0083
Lincoln Echo, H0027
Lincolns-Praeger (pub), E164

The Lincolnshire Yeomanry Goes Marching On', H0841
Lindau, Betsy, H1135
Lindbergh, Charles A., F0660
'Links Col. Lawrence to Kurdish Revolt', H0108
'The Lion and the Honeycomb', F0102
Lippincott (pub), F0030, F0325, F0608, F0896, F0927, F0982
Lipton, Dean, G1125
Lire, H0462
List (pub), A029, A072–3, A075, A077–8, A116–17, A185, A200, A208, A243, A248, E112, E216
'List of Items Presented to Harvard by Bayard L. Kilgour', E293
Listener, G0254–5, G0305, G0331, G0455, G0475, G0588, G0672, G0707, G0719, G0764, G0768–9, G0778, G0781, G0908, G1035, G1042, G1363, G1452, G1546
Listowel, Judith, G1254
Die Literärische Deutschland, G0637
'Literary Adventurer', G0142
'Literary Coup', G0409
Literary Digest, G0015, G0036, G0047, G0075, G0125, G0142, G0197, G0208, G0262, G0300, G0340–1, G0370, G0409
Literary Guide, G0705
Literary Guild, E302, F0609, F0966
'The Literary Life', F0839
'Literary Lifelines', F0012
'A Literary Lounger', G0970
Literary Review, G0038
Dië Literatur, G0462
'Literature and Sincerity', F0838
'Littérature du 20 siècle', F0661
'Littérature du Vingtième Siècle', F0918
'La Littérature d'un Lawrence', G0794
'The Literature of England', F0311
'The Literature of War', F0926
Literaturnia Gazeta, G0947
Lithgow, Adrian, H1270
Little, Margaret, H0857
Little, Brown & Company (pub), E352–4, F0037, F0146, F0194, F0324, F0401, F0414, F0605, F0619, F0649–50, F0708, F0710, F0883, F0969, F0974, F0977, F1026, F1059, F1133, F1175
'Little Night Music', G0990
'The Little Things That Meant a Lot', H1251
Littlefield, David W., F0662, G1370, G1695
Litvinoff, Barnet, F0663
'Live Letters', H0802
Liveright, Horace, F0397
Liveright (pub), F0076
Liverpool Post, H0900
Living Age, B0018, G0105, G0107, G0141, G0299, G0339
Livraria Classica (pub), E157–8
Le Livre de la Mort, G1206
Le Livre Français, G0895
'Le Livre de la Semaine: Le Matrice, de T.E. Lawrence', G0750
'La Livrée de la Mort', G0821
Les Livres, G0881, G1100
Livres Choisis, G0693, G0773
Livres de France, G0832, G1210
Livres et Lectures, G0788, G0913
Lloyd, Lord, F0004
Lloyd, Seton, F0664–5

Lloyd George, Earl David, F0069, F0575, F0647, F0666–7, F0995, G0327
'Lloyd George', F0575, F0995
'Lock, Stock and Barrel', F0896
Lockhart, Freda Bruce, G1703
Lockhart, Sir Robert Bruce, F0668
Loewel, Pierre, H0446
'London Alive With U.S. Film Workers', H0621
London Calling, G0549
London Express, H0842
London Illustrated News, G0623, G1155
'London Letter: Moral West End', G0954
'London Lights Are All Aglow', G0952
London Magazine, E209–10, G0760, G0787, G0797, G0813, G1527
London Mercury, G0090, G0489, H0409
London Mercury and Bookman, G0277
London Review, G1280
London Scottish Regimental Gazette, G0926
London Standard, H1260
London Studio, G0392
London Telegram, H0448, H0847
'Lonely Leader', G0346
Long, J. (pub), F0286
'Long Awaited Liberation of Arabic Syria', G0008
'A Long Row of Candles', F1107
'Long Week-End', F0438
Longacre Press (pub), F0398
Longanesi (pub), A209
Longford, Lady Elizabeth, E356–7
Longgood, William F., F0669
Longman, M.E., F0340
Longmans (pub), A001–2, F0097, F0488, F0947, F1109
Longmans Green (pub), E036, F0132, F0311, F0822, F1015, F1186
Longmont Times-Call, H1043
Longrigg, S.H. G0875
Lönnroth, Erik, E159–60, F0663, G0875
Look, G1195, G1303
'Look at Origins of Problems in Middle East', H1277
'Look What They've Done to "Lawrence of Arabia" Now', H1155
Lorain Journal, H0944
Lord, Louis, G0199
'Lord Allenby's Tribute', H0239
'Lord Lothian (Philip Kerr) 1882–1940', F0181
'Lord Wavell', F0220
'Lord of Arabia', F0041–2
'Lorence ish arav', E242
Los Angeles Examiner, H0225, H0597
Los Angeles Herald Examiner, H0606, H0833
Los Angeles Mirror, H1271
Los Angeles Times, H0122, H0209, H0224, H0334, H0336–7, H0347, H0365, H0373, H0375, H0405, H0408, H0419, H0550, H0552, H0579, H0633, H0656, H0712, H0724, H0742, H0765, H0769, H0773, H0782, H0822, H0826, H0838, H0849, H0921, H1126, H1141–2, H1147, H1165, H1212, H1219, H1224–5, H1229, H1247, H1268, H1271
Los Angeles Times Book Review, G1539, G1588, G1592
Los Angeles Times Calendar H0644, H1151, H1251
Los Angeles Times Sunday Magazine, G0371
Los Angeles T.V. Times, G1464
'Lost Cities', F0198

The Lost Heroes: T.E. Lawrence', G1289
'"Lost" Letters', H0740
'Lost? Stolen? Cancelled? Literary Properties', G0458
Lothian, Lord (Philip Kerr), F0181
Lothian Regional Council (pub), F0196
Louisiana State University (pub), E346–7
Louisville Times, H1039
'Le Loup et Le Léopard', F0084
Love, Kennet, F0671
'Love, Rage Campaign for "Arabia" Outlined', H0611
Lovelock, R.C.D., G0740
'The Lovely Land', F0700
'The Loves of George Bernard Shaw', F0283–4
Loveman, Amy, G0214, G0230
Lovett, Robert M., F0753
'Lowell Thomas, the Stranger Everyone Knows', F0131
Lowndes, Mrs. Belloc, G0185
'Loyal Enemy', F0372
'Loyalties Mesopotamia', F1138–9
Lucas, E.V., F0672
Lucas, Frank Laurence, F0673
Lucas-Duberton, J., G0295
Luce, Robert B., F0674
Lücke, Theodor, E066
Lunt, James D., F0675, G0755, G1288, G1430
Lunt, Ray, G0940
Lupis, Dom, E120–7
'Lurans Kama 'Ariftuh', E323
'The Lure of the Middle East', F1082
'Luirns al-Arab ala Khuta Hirtzil', E327
'Lus et jugés. Des ouvrages de Valeur', H0695
Lutterworth (pub), F1171
Lyautey, Pierre, G0897, G0901
Lyell, Thomas, F0676
Lyle, Rob, G0727, G0787, G0862
Lynch, Brian, H0895
Lynd, Robert, H0042
Lyons, Leonard, H0941–6, H0949, H0954–7, H0959, H0964
'Lytton Strachey', F0523

M., A., G1683
M., A.W.H., G0615
'Ma Première Rencontre avec Lawrence', G0457
Macaulay, T.B., H0106
McBey, James, F0445
McCall, J.G., H1077
McCall's, G1421
McCance, William, G0538
McConnell, Frank, F0677
McCormick, Donald, F0678–9
MacDonald, Charles J., G0250
MacDonald, D., G1090
MacDonald, D.B., G0151
MacDonald (pub), F0045, F0471, F1134
MacDonald Educational (pub), E381
MacDonnell, A.G., G0221
McDowell, Frederick P.W., F0680
McEntree, Girard Lindsley, F0681
MacEwen, Gwendolyn, E392, H1245
McGill University, E298a
McGraw-Hill (pub), E110, E309, E355, F0537, F0671, F1044
McGregor, Jack, G1301
McHandy, Archibald, H0470

Machen, Arthur, G0317
Mack, John, E352–5, F0155, G1343–5, G1409, G1418, G1436, G1521–3, G1530, G1533–41, G1549–50, G1557–8, G1561, G1577, G1624, G1626, H0866, H1179–80, H1188, H1191, H1193, H1206
McKay, David (pub), E075, F0344, F0394, F0541, F0853
McKay, John, H0174
'McKay's Guide to the Middle East', F0394
Mackenzie, Compton, F0682
McKinnon, Ian, F0683
McKnight, Gerald, F0684, G1107
Maclaren-Ross, J., G0797
MacLean, Alistair, E252–4, G0998, G1000, G1011, G1013, G1025, H0640
Maclean, Fitzroy, F0685–6
MacLean, Hugh, G1687
MacLean, James N.M., G0926
Maclean, Norman, F0687
MacLean's Magazine, G0564
MacLeish, Archibald, F0688
MacMillan, George, F0689
Macmillan (pub), A247, A253, D0021, F0004, F0017, F0027, F0043, F0053–4, F0113, F0120, F0143, F0181, F0215, F0247, F0267–8, F0392, F0424, F0449, F0480–1, F0485, F0497, F0500, F0504–5, F0528, F0578, F0688, F0782, F0787, F0797, F0801, F0808, F0852, F0868, F0893, F0914, F0920, F0926, F0962, F0970–1, F1007, F1033, F1069, F1106, F1113, F1127, F1147, F1160
MacMunn, Sir George, G0041, G0110, G0120
Macphail, Andrew, E047–8, G0159–62, G0167–70, G0477–8, H0100–1
'MAC-V Fort Bragg, Lawrence of Arabia', H1295
Mad, C., G0977
Mad Magazine, G1164, G1174
'Madame Tussaud's Exhibition', F0690
Mademoiselle, G1113
Maddocks, Melvin, H0657
'Mad's Dave Berg Looks at the U.S.A.', F0088
Madsen, Axel, F0691
Magazine Littéraire, G1277
The Magazine of the Wesleyan Methodist Church, G0612
Magill, Frank M., F0692
Maggs Bros. Ltd. (pub) E098, E400
'The Magic of a Name', F0798
'The Magus', F0367
Mahon, M., A259
Mail on Sunday, H1258
Main, Ernest, F0693
Main-Echo, H0925
Main-Post, H0914
Le Maine Libre, H0443, H0447
Mainstream, G1403
Major, André, H0801
'Makers of Modern Culture', F1161
'Makik', G0050
'The Making of a Conqueror', G0040
'The Making of the Auden Canon', F0068
'The Making of the Mint', H0455
Le Mal Pensants, G0630
Malagol, G., E243
Malin, Charles, A249
Mallet, Robert, A250
Malraux, André, E171–4, E340, F0112, F0234, F0383, F0691, F0694–8, F0828, G0584–5, G0594, G0605, G0614, G0628, G0873, G1240, G1498

Malraux', F0383, F0691
'Malraux and T.E. Lawrence', E363, G1240
'Malraux, History and Autobiography: Seven Pillars of Wisdom', G1498
'Malraux, Life and Work', F0234
Mam, Arthur F., H0074
'Man and Legend', H0960
'The Man Behind the Legend', H1077
'The Man Behind the Legend of Lawrence of Arabia', H1079
Man Magazine (Australia), G1192
'Man of Action, Man of Letters', G1477
'Man of Letters Sees Love Poetry Dying Out', H0822
'The Man of Many Devices', G0314
'A Man With a Hump on His Mind', H1185
'The Man Who Backed Into the Limelight', H1222
'Man Who Exercised a Remarkable Spell "Lawrence of Arabia"', H0173
'A Man Who Knew Lawrence', G1241
'The Man Who Lived Twice', F0061
'Man Who Might Have Conquered East', G0110
'The Man Who Served With Lawrence in the Desert', H0641
Manchester, F.B., H1127
Manchester Guardian , H0223, H0243, H0249, H0280, H0323, H0380–1, H0398, H0401, H0412, H0463, H0475, H0551, H0717, H0736, H0809, H1218, H1227
Manchester Herald, H0987
Manchester University Press, D0010a
Mandate, G1584–5
Mankato Free Press (Minn), H1050
'Männer und Machte des Britischen Weltreiches', G0516
Mannin, Ethel, F0699–700
Manning, Frederick, A140, F0701
Man's World, G1223
Mansfield, Peter, E337, F0702, G1363
Mansire, Paul, H0522
Manson, Anne, H0494
'Manuscripts Presented to Harvard by Bayard L. Kilgour', E294
'The Many Aspects of Lawrence of Arabia', H1086
'Mao Tse-Tung', F0827
Maracabru, Pierre, H0682
'The March of Archaeology', F0203
'The March to Tunis', F0755
'March to Wadi-Aish', G1291
Marchegay, Gilberte, E190
Marchés Coloniaux du Monde, H0545
Marchés Tropicaux du Monde, G0902
Marco Polo (Monte-Carlo), H0701, G0812
Marcossen, Isaac F., F0703
Mardersteig, Giovanni, A249
'Margaret est Tenace: elle veut voir "Lawrence d'Arabie" à Paris', H0671
'La Marie Stuart du Désert', G1207
Marine Corps Gazette, G0868
Marion, Denis, G0856
'The Mark of Merlin', F0678
'Mark Sykes', F0635
Marlowe, John, F0704
Le Maroc, G0777
'Married to Genius', F0731
Marriott, Paul J., E375
Marsh, Sir Edward, F0488–9, F0705–6, G0526
Marshall, K.W., G0560–61

Marshall, Kenneth, G1527
Marshall Town Times-Republican, H1104
Mariscovetére y durán, Miquel, E102
Martin, B.K., G1565
Martin, Bobby, H0980
Martin, Gilbert, F0707
Martin, Robert K., F0967
Martinsville Bulletin, H1056
Marty, Jacques, A028
Marwick, Arthur, F0708
Marzieh, Gail, H0829
Mason, Harold Andrew, F0709
'Massacre', B0017–8
Massey, Raymond, F0710
Massey, William Thomas, F0711, G1675
Massignon, Louis, F0712–13, G0617, G1652, G1674, H1253
'Master Guerrilla of Araby's Desert', G1306
'Masterplots', F0692
Mather, Bobby, H0936, H0965
Matignon, Renaud, H1174
Le Matin, H0012
L'Matin d'Anvers, H0583
La Matrice, A182–4, A250, F0314, H0488, H0491–2, H0495, H0498, H0505, H0525, H0530
'La Matrice, de T.E. Lawrence', H0495
'La Matrice (ou la Réponse d'un Imposteur)', G0849
'Le Matricule 338171, c'était le Colonel Lawrence', H0494
Matrix, G1648, G1665
Matte, Marcel, G1089
Maueeri, James, G1678
Maugham, Robin, F0714–16
Maulnier, Thierry, G0968
Mauriac, Claude, G1374, H0580, H0683
'Maurice Baring' , F0979
Maurois, André, A162, G0608
Mauron, Charles, A008, A070
Maxwell, Elsa, F0717
Mayer, Emile, G0360
Mayfair Books (pub), E234
Mayra, B., A114
Mazars, Pierre, H0487, H0511
MD, G0931
MD en Espanol, G1055
MD of Canada, G1175, G1416
'The Meaning of Fiction', F0229
'Mecca the Blessed; Medina the Radiant', F0315
'Mecca's Revolt Against the Turk', G0025
'Med Lawrence I Arabien', E019, E022
Medici Society, A013–15
'The Medievalism of T.E. Lawrence (of Arabia)', E395
'Mediterranean Front', F0756
Mee, Arthur, F0718
Mee, Charles L., F0719
'A Meeting With Lawrence', H0258
Meinertzhagen, Richard, F0720–22
Meisel, James H., G0593
Mélanges Malraux Miscellany, G1498
'Les Mémoires d'Outre-Tombe de Lawrence', H0492
'Memoirs', F0820–21, F0936, F1003
'Memoirs of King Abdullah, F0002–3
'Memoirs of a Public Servant', F0934
'Memoirs of a Publisher', F0278
'The Memoirs of Captain Liddell Hart', F0648

Memorial to Lawrence', H0301
'Memorial Unveiled at St Pauls', H0359
'Memories of Lawrence', H0286
'Memories of T.E.', H0763
'Memories of T.E. Lawrence', H0371
'Memory-Hold-the-Door', F0168
Memphis Press-Scimiter, H0701
'Men and Books – the Downward Urge', G0723
'Men and Memories', F0910–12, G0187
'The Men Around Churchill', F0608
'Men at war', D0016
'Men in Print', A229, B0024, B0028, E161, G0553
'Men of Turmoil', F0723
'Men Who Make Your World', F0812
'Men, Women and Thing', F0860
Mendelsohn, Peter de, G0637
Mendelson, Edward, F0724–5
Menominee Herald Leader, H0986
Mentor (pub), F0803
Mer et Outre-Mer, G0905
Mera, Jean, H0555
Mercure, H0525
Mercure de France, F0856, G0180, G0607, G0629, G0700, G0811, G0894
El Mercurio, G1256, H1274
Meredith Press (pub), E290
Merifeld, R.J., G0941
Merill Herald, H1102
Merkur (Baden-Baden), G0601
Merkur (Stuttgart), G0629–40
Merry, Bruce C., G1460
Merthyr Express, H0600
Merton, Wilfred (pub), A141
Merz, Charles, G0091
'Mes Rapports avec Lawrence en 1917', F0713
'Mesopotamia: the Truth About the Campaign', C0013
'Message to Damascus', G1701
'Mesure de Lawrence', F1019
'La métamorphose du colonel Lawrence "roi sans couronne" d'Arabie en simple soldat', G0765
Metcalfe, F.B., H0475
Methuen (pub), A230, F0274, F0342, F0554, F0560, F0616, F0672, F0750, F0767, F0811, F0851, F0858, F0948, F1092
Meulen, Daniel van der, F0726
Meulenijzer, Victor, E122
Meyer, Gerald, H0953
Meyers, Jeffrey, E335–6, E338, E396, F0727–31, G1389, G1408, G1424, G1454, G1481, G1500, G1519, G1550, G1556, G1560, G1576, G1604, H1106, H1169, H1172–3
Meynell, Francis, F0732
Meynell, Viola, F0733–4
Miami Beach Sun, H0943
Miami News, H1193
Michel, Albin (pub), E204, F0084, F0661
Michie, Allen A., F0735
Michigan Alumnus Quarterly Review, G0593
Michigan City News Dispatch, H0996
Michigan Quarterly Review, G1342, G1642–3
The Microbibliophile, G1633
Mid-East, G1351
'The Middle East', F0005, F0080, F0342, F0528, F0736, F0767–8, F0790, F0922, F0997
'The Middle East, an Anthropological Approach', F0301
'Middle East Diary', F0721–2

The Middle East Forum, G0976, G1112, G1285, G1341
'The Middle East. How we are losing prestige', C0008
'The Middle East in Transition', F0621
'The Middle East in World Affairs', F0630
'Middle East in Political System', F0925
Middle East Institute (pub), F0845
'The Middle East, Its Governments and Politicians', F0020
The Middle East Journal, G0733, G1186, G1199, G1226, G1409, G1418
Middle East Studies Association Bulletin, G1661
'The Middle East Today', F0836
'Middle East Treasure', G1215
'Middle East Window', F0132
'The Middle East Yesterday and Today', D0022
Middle Eastern Studies, G1179, G1568, G1618
Middleton Press, H1045
Midi Libre, H0500, H0538
Midway, G1408
Miquel, André, G1140, G1231
Mikusch, Dagobert von, A078, A116, F0737
Miles, Hamish, G0448
Milford, Humphrey, A001-2, A144-5
Military Affairs, G1440
'Military History of the World War', F0681
'Military Operations Egypt and Palestine', F0689
'Military Report on the Sinai Peninsula', A009
Military Review, B0049, G0679, G0867, G1142
'A Military View of T.E. Lawrence', G1397
Millar, Ronald, F0738
Millatt, Richard, G1158
Miller, Alice (Duer), F0739
Miller, David Hunter, F0740
Miller, David W., D0022
Miller, E., G1030
Miller, Edward, F0742
Miller, Judith, G1660
Miller, Wright Watts, F0743
Millgate, Michael, F0744
Mills, Gordon, G1023
Milne, James, G0654
Milton, George Fort, G0144
Milwaukee Journal, H0163, H0187-8, H0208, H0222, H0271, H0333, H0335, H1132, H1150
Milwaukee Review, H0793
Milwaukee Sentinel, H0162, H0186, H0197, H0204, H0207, H0221, H0315, H0343
Milwaukee State Journal, H0196, H0332
Minchir, Neville, F0745
'The Mind on the Wing', F1117
Minima (pub), E102
Ministerstwa Obrony Narodowej (pub), E207
'Minorities', A256-60, G1452, G1459
Minot North Dakota News, H1008
'The Mint', A166-85, A241, B0029, B0047, B042, C023, E329, F0411-2, G0685, G0689, G0693, G0717, G0719-20, G0722-3, G0728, G0736, G0740-44, G0746, G0750-52, G0754, G0756, G0762-4, G0772-3, G0783, G0793, G0797, G0802, G0809, G0817, G0855, G0859, G1465, G1470-72, G1490, G1502, H0376, H0448, H0455, H0472, H0474, H0476-7, H0479, H0488-91, H0493, H0496-8, H1167, H1240
'The Mint and the Metal', G0740
'The Mint is Bound to Shock', H0474
Minton, Balch & Co. (pub), F0723

inute, H0791
Miquel, Robert, G0739
'The Miracle', G1335
'Les mirages de Lawrence d'Arabie', H1241
Miroir de l'Histoire, G1625
'Le Miroir des Limbes', F0697
'The Mirror of Degradation', H0624
'Mirror to Damascus', F1059
'Misconception', H0449
'Misgivings Over Handcuffs', H0835
'Missing Pages of Lawrence's Manuscript Discovered', H0719
'The Mist Procession', F1083
'Mr. Churchill on T.E. Lawrence', G0408
'Mr. Levin and Mr. Lawrence', G1090
'Mr. T.E. Shaw', H0176
'Mrs. G.B.S.', F0290-F0291
Mitre Press (pub), F0978
'A Mixed Bag of Lawrenciana', G0552
'Mixed Biscuits', B0025
Mizpah (pub), A121
'Moby Dick and the Seven Pillars of Wisdom', G1491
'Modell T.E. Lawrence und Saint-Exupéry', G0601
'A Modern Ascetic', H0120
Modern Churchman, G0298
'Modern Guerrilla Warfare', F0810
Modern Language Journal, G1240
Modern Library (pub), F0437, F0959
'Modern Literary Manuscripts from King's College, Cambridge', F0746
Modern Maturity, F1476
'A Modern Monumental Effigy: Kennington's Lawrence of Arabia', G0623
'Modern Mystic', G0473
'The Modern Researcher', F0064
'The Modest Author of a $20,000 Book', H0036
Mohrt, Michel, G0765
Moinet, Pierre, G0589
Moirex, Maxine, H0631
Molnar, Thomas, F0747
Mon Programme, H0542
Monalef (pub), E255
Der Monat, G0759
Monatschrift für das Deutsche Geistesleben, G0500-501
Mondadori (pub), A123-6, E315
Le Monde, H0422, H0424, H0441, H0444, H0510, H0529, H0676, H0680, H0691, H0754-5, H0861, H1139, H1146, H1240, H1263
Monde Nouveau, G0732
Monegal, Emir Rodriquez, F0748
Monkhouse, Geoffrey, H0717
Monotype Recorder, G0276
Monroe, Elizabeth, F0749-51, G1359, G1425
Monten, A181
Montgomery, Bernard L., (Field Marshal Earl), F0206, F0752
'Montgomery of Alamein', F0206
Moniel, Vincent, E259, F0781
Mont-Louis (pub), E143
Montréal-Matin, H0794
Montréal Star, H1185, H1223
Moody, William Vaughn, F0753
Moon, A.R., F0822
Moore, A., G0261
Moore, Clark D., D0022
Moore, Gilbert, H1125

Moore, Harry Tatlock, G1084, G1133
Moorehead, Alan, F0754–7
Moorhouse, Geoffrey, H1218
Moran, Lord, F0758
'More About 338171', G1128
'More Lawrence, Less Legend', G0352
'More Letters From T.E. Shaw to Bruce Rogers', A165
'More Light on Lawrence of Arabia', G1539
'More on Lawrence', H0423
'More on Lawrence of Arabia', H1029
'More on the Life of T.E. Lawrence', H1228
'More to Say About Lawrence', H1033
Morin, Edgar, H0420
Morley, Christopher, G0281, G0386
Morley, F.V., G0278
Morning Advocate, H0949
Morning Herald, H0859
Morning Post, C0014, H0013, H0078, H0105, H0143–4, H0213, H0246, H0283–4, H0317, H0329, H0342, H0382
Morris, James, F0759–64
Morris, Jan, G1552
Morris, John, G1699
Morris, Richard M., G1119
Morris, Robert K., G1542
Morrow, William (pub), F0265, F0644, F0691, F0776, F0837, F0932, F1042, F1091
Morsey, Konrad, E365, E396, G1595, G1612
'Mort sous un faux nom en 1935 Lawrence d'Arabie avait refusé d'être vice-roi des Indes', H1242
Mortimer, Raymond, G0801, H0458
Morton, H.V., F0765–8
Mosaic Press (pub), E392
'Mosaik Meines Lebens', A243
Moser, Barry, A154
Mosley, Leonard, E145, F0768–71
Mospolografa (pub), A135
Moss, Howard, F0772
'The Most Famous Privates in Any Army', G0177, H0117
'Most Powerful Man in the World', F0900
'The Most Romantic Figure of the War', G0258
'The Mother of "T.E." Courageous Story of Mrs. Lawrence', H1282
Motion Picture Daily, H0611
Motion Picture Exhibitor, G1301
'Motor Cycle Maker Dies', H0932
Motor Cycle News, C0024
'The Motor Cycle That Killed Lawrence of Arabia', G1634
Motorcycle, G1136, G1204
'Mound Alone Marks Where Lawrence Lies', H0261
'Mounds of the Near East', F0664
Mountfort, Guy, F0773–4
Mousa, Suleiman, E255–9, F0019, G1680a, F0775, F0951a, G1043, G1264, G1266–7, G1270, G1282, G1285, G1290, G1297–8, G1309, G1315, G1485–G1486, G1638, G1670, G1689, H0814–17, H0826, H0829, H08360
'Movie Film Suit', H0821
Movies Illustrated, G1149
'Mozakerat Al Malek Abdullah', F0021
'Mozakrati an al Thawara Al Arabia', F0015
Mrazek, James L., G0325
'Mud on the White Robe', G0709

ueser, Anne, E344
Muggeridge, Malcolm, F0776–7, G0836, G0971, G1357, G1445
Mühlberger, Josef, G0696
Muir, Edwin, H0353
Muir, Ramsay, F0778
Mulder, Elisabeth, A136
Müller, Erich, G0464
Muller, Frederick (pub), E187, F0887
Mulligan, Hugh A., H1267
'The Multiple Personae of Lawrence of Arabia', H1128
Mumby, Frank Arthur, F0779
Muncie Press, H1007
Mundy, Talbot, F0780
'The Murder of Lawrence of Arabia', E384–5, G1615
Muret, M., G0156
Murray, A.T., G0210
Murray, Gilbert, G0194
Murray, H., G0203
Murray, John (pub), E047, F0023, F0280, F0333, F0337, F0478, F0550, F0552, F0562–4, F0587, F0598, F0987–8, F0990–91, F1063, F1182
Murry, John Middleton, A162
Murtough, Brian, H0764
Musfreesboro News Journal, H1110
'Mustaphal Kemal of Turkey', F1174–5
'My Brother, Evelyn and Other Profiles', F1099
'My Contacts With Lawrence in 1917', H1253
'My Darling Clementine', F0343–5
'My Diary at the Conference at Paris', F0740
'My Head! My Head!', F0439
'My Life and Times', F0682
'My Link With Lawrence of Arabia in Beyond', G1205
'My Lives', F0733
'My Naval Life', F0136
'My 77 Years', F0087
'Myself: by Lawrence', C0018
'Mysteries and Confusions Surrealistic Portrait of Lawrence', H0630
'Mystérieux colonel Lawrence', H0684
'The Mysterious A.C. 2', E136
'The Mysterious "Lawrence of Arabia"', G0164
'The Mysterious S.A.', G0874
'The Mystery and the Man', G0920
'Mystery Car', H0277
'The Mystery Colonel Lawrence', G0376
'Mystery Motorist', G1010
'Mystery of Black Car', H0272
'Mystery of Car', H0258
'The Mystery of Lawrence', G1068
'The Mystery of Lord Kitchener's Death', F0679
'Mystery Shrouded Lawrence Secret Told by Friend', H0254
'La Mystique de T.E. Lawrence', F0661, F0918
'Myth, Fact and T.E. Lawrence', G0987
'Le Mythe d'Étiemble', F0781

N., H.M.R., A261
N., M.H., G1657
NAAFI Review, G1111
Nabuys, Jhr. R.H.G., A112
Nadeau, Maurice, G0607, G0629
Nagy, Laszlo, H0626
'Nahoot am Mikrofon', F0577
Nakano, Yoshio, E137

Naldrett Press, F1106
'Namesake', G1076
Namier, L.B., E110, F0782, G0299, H0223, H0323, H0398
'Nancy', F1011–13
'Nancy Astor', F0221–2, F0453
Napa Register, H1006
Napier, Priscilla, F0783
'Napoleon in Burnous: The Lives of T.E. Lawrence', G1667
'Narrative', G1390
'Narrow Pass, Black Mountain', F0204
Nash, Paul, E043–6, F0092
Natan, Alex, H0886
Nathan, Fernand (pub), E254
Nation , G0118, G0144, G0198, G0231, G0288, G0354, G0429, G0451–2, G0531, G0835, G1066, G1542
La Nation, H0703
Nation and Atheneum, G0074, G0123
La Nation Belge, H0507
National and English Review, G0479
National Book League (pub), F0334
National Geographic, G0014, G0149, G0249, G0418, G0542, G0576, G0582, G1185, G1313
National Magazine, G0100
National Portrait Gallery, E387
National Review, B0051, G1077, G1401, G1412
National Review (England), G0327, G0372, G0505, G0566
National Travel Club (pub), F0253
National Trust, E130–34
'The National Trust', F0929
Nationalsozialistische Landpost, G0499, G0516
'Nations Mourn', H0222
Natur och Kultur (pub), A088, A236
'The Nature of War', F0584
'The Near East', F0468, F1180
Near East and India, G0087, G0158, G0256, G0316
'The Near East in History', F0507
'Near to Greatness', F0149
Neave, Daniel, F0784–5
'Ned', E379, G1610, G1611, H1234
La Nef, G0610–11
'The Negev', F0319
'Neglected Powers', F0600
The Neglected War: Mesopotamia', F0059
Nelson, Nina. F0786–7
Nelson, Thomas (pub), E038, E080, E301–3, E305–7, E350
'A Nest of Eagles', G0668
'N'était-ce donc que cela?', G0584–5
Neue Deutsche Hafte, G0879
Neue Osnabrücke Zeitung, H0896
Die Neue Rundschau, B0036, G0308
Neue Zuericher Zeitung, G0141, H0941
Neues Abendland, G0692
'Neues Über T.E. Lawrence', H0891
Neuphilologische Monatschrift, G0364
Die Neuren Sprachen, G0855
Nevakivi, Jukka, F0788, G0927
The Never Before Told Story of Lawrence of Arabia', H1059
New Adelphia, G0173–4
New American Library (pub), E238, E385, F0104, F0106, F0524, F0614, F1136
The New Arabia', H0264
'A New Battle of Petra', G0029

New Biography of Lawrence', H1191
'New Book at £4,000 a Copy', H0038–9
'New Book on Lawrence of Arabia', H1074
'New Book on Lawrence of Arabia Looks at Origins of Middle East', H1093
New Britain Herald, H1130
New Century (pub), F0271
New Coterie, G0064
'New Data on Lawrence of Arabia', H1018
'New Data On Times, Trials of the King "King of the Bedouins"', H0980
New Directions (pub), F0862
'New Evidence Effectively Shatters the Legend of a Gallant Liberator', H0938
'New Evidence Undercuts Hero', H0952
'New Faces of Lawrence', G1413
New Haven Register, H0948
'New Insights Offered', H1083
'New Judgements on Three of the War's Big Reputations', H0101
'A New Lawrence of Arabia', G0562
'New Lawrence of Arabia Letters', H0290
'New Lawrence Study Fails to Solve Enigma', H1089
'New Lawrence Volume Causes Concern in Britain', H0375
'New Legends Out of Old', G1360
'New Light on Lawrence', G0496, H0883
'New Light on Lawrence, His Middle East Dealing', H1026
'New Light Shed on Lawrence of Arabia's Feelings', H0971
The New Limerick', F0628
'New Material Aids Lawrence of Arabia Book', H1097
'New Material Available About Lawrence of Arabia', H1109
'A New Memorial to Lawrence of Arabia', H1233
New Middle East, G1340
'A New 1001 Nights in Arabia', G0036
New Outlook, G1132
New Republic, B0050, G0091, G0143, G0226, G0343, G0422, G0447, G0663, G0745, G0766, G0779–80, G0870, G0990, G1062, G1561
'New Screen News', G1143, G1145
'A New Side of Lawrence of Arabia and the Arabs', H1129
New Statesman, G0070, G0112, G0159, G0203, G0220, G0261, G0436, G0493, G0619, G0634, G0669–70, G0712, G0721–2, G0865, G0874, G0933, G0945, G0971, G1015, G1036, G1293, G1543, G1582
New Statesman and Nation, G0282, G0836
'New Tablet for the "Shrine" at the Bottom of the Garden', H1170
'New Tales About Lawrence of Arabia', G0132
'The New World of Islam', F1001
New World Press (pub), F0572
New York Evening Post, H0015, H0069
New York Geographic Society, F1077
New York Herald Tribune, H0075, H0218–20, H0270, H0368, H0402, H0490, H0590; Book Review, G0147, G0169, G0255, G0248, G0335, G0421, G0444, G0508, G0515, G0652, G0676, G0743, G0816, G0826, G0921, G0982, G1000, G1105, G1129
New York Post, H0344, H0603, H0941
New York Public Library (pub), F0013, F0992

New York Review of Books, G0513, G1171, G1532, G1590, G1599
New York Sun, H0001, H0062
New York Times, H0011, H0018, H0020–23, H0031, H0033–4, H0036–7, H0041–2, H0046–7, H0049, H0058–9, H0063–4, H0067–8, H0070, H0072, H0077, H0081–2, H0087–90, H0093, H0095–9, H0102–4, H0106–8, H0111–21, H0123–5, H0128, H0134, H0136–8, H0141–2, H0146, H0148, H0152, H0161, H0165–6, H0171, H0175, H0178, H0185, H0195, H0201, H0203, H0205–6, H0215–7, H0252, H0254, H0267, H0269, H0292–5, H0298, H0302–3, H0307, H0310, H0312–5, H0318–9, H0331, H0340, H0346, H0354–5, H0358, H0361, H0383–4, H0390, H0392–3, H0403, H0406, H0413–8, H0498, H0575, H0601, H0637, H0661, H0675, H0690, H0705, H0721, H0725, H0776, H0821, H0864, H0960, H1157; Book Review, G0138, G0170, G0186, G0196, G0224, G0290, G0334, G0355, G0388, G0397, G0424, G0440, G0507, G0548, G0658, G0675, G0726, G0742, G0823, G0834, G0920, G0981, G1017, G1097, G1130, G1139, G1394, G1594, G1608, G1611, G1640, G1693; Magazine, G0567, G0579, G0994, G1451, G1516, G1660
'The New York Times Chronicle of American Life', F0852
New York University, E340, F0626
New York World, H0056, H0065, H0074
New Yorker, G0332, G0511, G0643, G0680, G0851, G0923, G1043, G1247, G1511, G1513, G1589
New Zealand Woman's Weekly, G1183
Newark Sunday News, H1068
Newburgh News, H1017
Newby, Eric, H0819
Newby, Margaret, G1354
Newcombe, S.F., G0297
Newins, Edward, F0789
Newman, Edward W. P., F0790
Newman, Edwin, H1038
Newport News Press, H1082
The News, H0719
News, H0964
News and Observer, H1038
'News and Views of London', H0307
'News Broken to Mother', H0252
News Chronicle, H0150, H0177, H0247, H0250, H0280–82, H0285, H0461, H0474, H1299
News of the World, H0160, H0410, H0744
News Review, G0412
News Telegraph, H1001
Newsday, G1692
Newsfront G1420
Newsweek, G0215, G0251, G0260, G0333, G0384, G0407, G0486, G0656–7, G0661, G0744, G0986, G1044, G1076, G1135, G1384, G1534
Newton & Co. Ltd. (pub), A139, F0791–2
Nexus, G1125
Niagra Falls Gazette, H1067
Nice-Matin, H0528
Nicolson, Sir Harold, F0793–5, G0704
Nicholson & Watson (pub), F0108, F0617, F1004, F1179
Nickerson, Hoffman, G0357
Nicol, Eric, H0698
'Nietzsche and Lawrence', G1408
'Nietzsche in England', F1032

'Night Climber Mr. X', H0779
'Nile Mother and Mistress', G0626
'Nile to Aleppo', F0267–8
'The Nili Spies', F0310
Nine, B0045, G0862
'£950 a First Edition', H0844
'1914–1918: World War I', F1114
'1919 Colonel A.E. Lawrence', F0606
'923-Arm-L', G0877
'99 Lives of Peter O'Toole', G1107
Nitschke, August, F0796
'No Deterent', H0867
'No End of a Lesson', F0806
'No Golden Journey', F0968
'No Man's Land', F0627
'No Military Ceremony at Funeral', H0287
'No Nazi Revolt in the Desert', G0545
'No Way to Treat a Lady', G1680
Nobile, Phillip, F0797
Nockolds, Harold, F0798
Noir et Blanc, H0471
'Nomad', F0715–16
'The Nonesuch Century', F0800
Nonesuch Press, F0799–800
'Noon and Night (1916–1918)', D0025
Noor-Eesti Kirjastus Tartus (pub), A083
Noquères, Henri, G1006
Nord Bayerischer Kurier, H0919
Nord-Éclair, H0534, H0562, H0718
Nord See Zeitung, H0903
Nordstedt & Söners (pub), E319
Norman, Charles, F0801
Norman, Geraldine, H1176
North American Review, G0236
North Pennsylvania Reporter, H1000
'Northern Najd', F0454
Northampton Independent, H0291
Norton, John H., G0216
Norton, W.W. (pub), A170, E0080, F0135, F0148, F0346, F0410, F0438
Norwood Editions (pub), E046
'Not a Suitable Hobby for an Airman', E404
'Not in the Limelight', F1148
'Not Much Like Lawrence', H0662
'Not so Much a Hero…', G1551
'Note From T.E. Shaw to His Subscribers', A038
'A Note on James Elroy Flecker', A229
Notes Bibliographiques, G0912
'Notes de Lecture', G1650
'Notes on T.E. Lawrence', G1199
'Notes on the Middle East', A010a
'Notes on the Way', F0893
'Nothing but a Great Man', G1523
'Notice to Subscribers', A037
Notoloulus, James A., G1200
'Notre Action en Syrie', H0012
Notre Dame Press, F0348
Notre République, H0798
'Notre T.E. Lawrence', G0925
Nottingham Evening Post, H0932
Nouschi, André, G1406
La Nouveau Candide, H0667
'Un nouveau livre sur le colonel Lawrence', H0560
'Un Nouveau Portrait de T.E. Lawrence par Roger Stéphane et Quelques Autres', H0585
'Du Nouveau Sur Lawrence d'Arabie', H0861
Le Nouvel Observateur, G1206, G1415, G1488
Nouvelle Gazette, H0532

Nouvelle Revue Critique (pub), E065
La Nouvelle Revue de Lausanne, G0980
Nouvelle Revue d'Outre Mer, G0699, G0841
La Nouvelle Revue Française, G0557, G0570,
   G0796, G0886, G1220
Nouvelles Littéraires, G0608, G0684, G0750,
   G0789, G0792, G0991, G1087, G1227, G1236,
   G1248–9, G1503–4
'The Novels of Colin Wilson', F1066
'Nov. 1918', F0150
Now and Then, A162, B0023, B0030, B0034,
   G0063, G0171, G0274–5, G0278, G0365,
   G0374–5, G0385, G0408, G0448, G0488
'Les Noyers d'Altenburg', F0698
N.R.F. (pub), F0314
'A Number of People', F0706, G0526
'No. 2 Polstead Road', G0670
'Numen Inest', G0311
'Nuri-As-Said', F0095
Nutting, Anthony, E232–44, F0802–6, G0969,
   G0974–5, G0978–9, G0981–2, G0985, G1186,
   H0622, H0624–5, H0630, H0817
Nyberg, H.S., A031
Nye, Robert, H1197

Oakes, Philip, H0699
Oates, Quentin, G1544
'Oberst Lawrence', E066, E112, G0378, G0599
'Oberst Lawrence als Autor und Kritiker', G0459
'Oberst Lawrence und der Aufstand der Araber
   im Weltkreig', G0416
Obolonski, Robert, G1620
O'Brien, E., G0970
O'Brien, Philip M., E388, E396, G1633
Observateur, H0472
L'Observateur du Moyen-Orient, H0554
Observer, B0008, B0010, G0073, G0117, G0184,
   G0265, G0283, G0304, G0318, G0394, G0402,
   G0434, G0482–3, G0631, G0667, G0704, G0717,
   G1040–41, G1137, G1187, G1281, G1299, G1357,
   G1361, G1383, G1410, G1927, G1445, G1545,
   G1554, G1572, G1689–91, H0819, H1207–8
'Obstinate Mr. Doughty', G1353
Ocampo, Victoria, A179–80, B0043, E148–56,
   E177, F0807, G0573, G0581, G0800, G1102,
   G1122–3, G1128, G1134, G1139, G1146, G1150,
   H1287
O'Casey, Sean, F0808
O'Connell, Shaun, H1183
Occult Review, G0454
O'Conner, J.J., G0837
O.D.E.J. (pub), E278
Odeon Theatre, E268
Odhams (pub), F0187, F0340, F0667
O'Donnell, Thomas James, E326, E383, E396,
   G1548, G1578
'Odysseus Lawrence Private Shaw', H1283
'The Odyssey', A141–54, B0031, D0017, F0524,
   G0189–90, G0192–9, G0202–3, G0210–11,
   G0213, G0241, G0313–14, G0331, G1217, H0328,
   H0330, H1283
'The Odyssey as a Novel', G0313
'The Odyssey Lawrence's Unique Version', H0328
'The Odyssey of Col. Lawrence', G0196
'The Odyssey of Homer Newly Translated Into
   English Prose by T.E. Shaw', G0210
Les Oeuvres Libres, G0619
'Of Such is History', G0027

'Die Offenbarung Arabiens', A029
The "Office"', F0224
Officina Bodoni (pub), A244
'Offstage', G0972
O'Flaherty, Terence, H0732
Oggi, G1688
Ohio University Press, E383, F0742
Ohnesorge, Henk, H0920
Økonomig Politik, G0917
Olafsson, Bogi, A122
'O Lorens tis Aravias', E241
Olcina, Paule et Raymond, E312
'The Old Friendship of Two Men Named Shaw',
   H0668
'Old Mid East Telegraph to be Restored', H0838
Oldberg, Karl, H0994, H0998
'Older People', F0121–2
Oldham Evening Chronicle & Standard, H0618
Olinder, Gunnar, A236
Olinder, Vera, A236, E319
Oliver, Jocelyn, F0809
Oliver & Boyd (pub), F0036, F0720
Olivier, Laurence, H0597
Olson, Robert, G1595
Oltumwa Courier (Iowa), H0995
'Oman, A History', F0853–4
O'N., J., H0799
'On a Desert Railway – A Blue-Eyed Ghost',
   H0777
'On Books, and People', G0708
'On English Poetry', F0440
'On Guard! A History of the 10th (Torbay)
   Battalion', F0656
'On T.E. Lawrence', G1319
'On the Couch', H1195
'On the Eve of Allenby's Final Victory', G1676
'On the Lawrence Trail Again', H0673
'On the Prose of T.E. Lawrence', G1455
'On to Damascus', G1172
'On Translating Homer', G0198
'On Writing Well', F1187
'Once in Sinai', F0858
'Once There Was a Hero', G1130
'100 Great Modern Lives', F0187
'The £100,000 Book by T.E. Lawrence', H0376
'$1,150 For Lawrence Book', H0097
'One Shaw to Another', H0722
'One Thousand Vampires', G1193
'One-Way Correspondence', G1016
'One Who Served Under Him', H0213
'One Who Was There Remembers Derra', H0571
Opdika News, H1037
Opelousas World, H1036
'Opera Minora', F0713
Orangeburg Times and Democrat, H1072
'Oprøret I Ørkenen', A111, A131
Orbis (pub), A110
Orchard Books (pub), E404
'Orde Wingate', F1013–14
'Orders of the Day', F1159
The Oregonian, H0981
Orgill, Douglas, E334, G1695
'L'Orient des mythomanes', G1486
'Oriental Assembly', A220–25, B0009, B0011,
   G0498, G0519, G0525, G0581, G1693, H1290
'The Oriental Express', F0063
'Orientations', F1004–5
'The Origins of Totalitarianism', F0038

'Ornament of Honour', E113, G0436, G0438, G0443, G0445, G0452, H0380, H0388
Orpen, Sir William, F0606, G0293
'Orphans at No. 10', G1427
Osanka, Franklin Mark, F0810
O'Shea, Raymond, F0811
'Other Places, Other Times', H1286
'Other Things Than War', F0471
O'Toole, Peter, E126, E271, F0371, F0807, G0960, G1033, G1080, G1087, G1097, G1099, G1100, G1107, G1113, G1124, G1162, H0588, H0597, H0608, H0613, H0646–7, H1166
'O'Toole Interpretas un Guion de Robert Bolt', F0807
'O'Toole of Arabia', G1029, G1086–7, H0647
'O'Toole of the Oulde Sod', G1124
Otterden Press, E351
'Ottoman Empire and Its Successors', F0702
'Où Sont les Aventuriers', H0798
Ouest-France, G1365, H0523
Ouest Médical, G1056
'Our Gritty Love Affair With the Desert', H0813
'Our Lawrence', F1009
'Out of the Wilderness', G1024
Outlook, G0152, G0182, G0242
The Outsider', F1142
Overseas Press Club of America, F0812
Owen, David Lloyd, F0813
Owen, Frank, F0814
Owensboro Messenger-Inquirer, H1084
'Oxford', F0762–3
'The Oxford Book of Greek in Translation', D0018
An Oxford Friend, G0265
Oxford High School for Boys, E117–18
Oxford High School Magazine, B0001–4
'Oxford in 1907 (With a Glimpse of T.E. Lawrence), G1616
'Oxford Limited', F0144
Oxford Magazine, G0284, G1184, G1191, G1196, G1202
Oxford Mail, H0662, H0728, H0730–31, H0739, H0778–9, H1168, H1196
'Oxford "Peaks"', H0779
'Oxford Poetry 1948', F0133
Oxford Times, A034
Oxford University, Jesus College, F0815
Oxford University Press, A001–2, A144–51, D0017–18, E083, E094–5, E142, E256–8, F0018, F0060, F0129, F0183, F0240, F0300, F0320, F0457, F0465, F0501, F0512–13, F0534, F0574–5, F0588, F0655, F0677, F0924, F1024, F1047, F1064, F1101, F1103, F1138–9, F1168

P., M.-A., H0543
Paar, Jack, G1176–7
Packard Co. (pub), F0994
Page, Bruce, F0816
Page, L.C. (pub), E090
'Pageant of Life', F1043
Paideuma, G1480, G1565
'"Painting" With Smoke', G1183
Paints, Mack, H1186
Paladin/Granada Publishing, E369
'A Paladin of Arabia', F0138
'Palestine at the Cross-Roads', F0329
'The Palestine Campaigns', F1107
'The Palestine Diary', F0572
Palestine Exploration Fund, A004–5, F0817, G0297

Palestine Exploration Quarterly, G0001, G0003–4, G0009, G0130, G0176, G0399, G0417, G0504, G0893
'Palestine Mission', F0243
Palestine News, C0001
'Palestine on the Eve', F0330
'Palestine on Israel', F0590
'Palestine Papers 1917–1922', F0549–50
'Palestine: the Land of Three Faiths', F0426–7
'Palgrave of Arabia', F0017
Palo Alto News, H0963
Pan (pub), F0343, F0646
Panichas, George A., F0818–19
Państwowy Instytut Wydownczy (pub), A086
Pantheon Books (pub), F0759, F0761, F0764, F1000
Panther Books (pub), A175, E308
Papen, Franz von, F0820–21
La Papetier de France, G0819
Le Papetier-Libraire, G0885
Parade of Books, G1391
'Paradox of Arabia', G1555
Paragone, G0758
'Paragraphs on Printing', F0902
Paris-Casablanca, H0468
Paris-Jour, H0645, H0671
Paris Journal, H0588
Paris Match, G0948, G1095, G1099, G1512
Paris-Midi, G0252
Paris-Normandie, H0522, H0578
Paris-Presse, H0494, H0553
Paris-Presse l'Intransigéant, H0581, H0699
La Parisien, H0670
Parisien Libéré, H0649, H0693, H0785, H0800
Parker, Agnes Miller, A095, A097
Parker, E.W., F0822
Parkes, James, F0823
'Parlons un peu de mon épitaphe par le colonel Lawrence', G0263
'Parmi les livres du Côté des Montaigne et du Côté d'Augustin', G1255
Parnell, Charles L., G1617
'Parody of a Hero', G0835
'Parole Donnée', F0712
Parria, H0791
Parrish, Max (pub), E227, E289, F0065
Parrot, Jacques, H0672
Parsey (pub), F0556
Parsons, Louella, H0597
Partisan Review, G0650
Partridge, Eric (pub), E077, F0154
Pasadena Guardian, H1175
Pasadena Star News, H0129–33, H0167, H1179, H1298
'Pasadenan Shows Works on Lawrence', H1146
Pasauer Neue Presse, H0902
Pasca, Pia, H0442
'A Passion in the Desert', G1062
'Pastor's Progress', F0526–26a
Pasquior, Hélène, E240
'Passing of a Glamorous Figure', G0264
'The Passion for Words', G0553
'A Passionate Prodigality', F0013
Patai, Raphael, F0824
Patch, Blanche, F0825–6, G0714
Pateau, Jacques, H0579
Paternoster Lib. (pub), F0884
'The Patriot's Progress', F1134
Patton, Oliver B., G0679

Pattyn, X., G0913
'Paul Nash', F0092
Pavey, R.A., G0868
Pawtucket Valley Times, H1074
Payne, Robert, E260–64, F0827–8, G1186, G1264, G1266, G1268, G1455, H0814, H1286
Payot (pub), A008, A028, A070–71, A114, E020, E214–15, F0140
'Peacemaking 1919', F0795
Pearl, Jack, G1156
Pearman, D.G., A139
Pearson, Hesketh, F0829–33
'Peculiar Person', H1218
'A Peek at Lawrence's $500,000 Book', G0419
'Peer and Private Pay Tribute', H0282
'The Pen and the Sword Were Friends', G1097
'A Penetrating Rattigan Play', H0582
Peniakoff, Vladimir, F0834
Pennsylvania State University, E395
Pennsylvania State University Press, A255, F0378
Penguin (pub), A049, A178, A239, E141, F0042, F0461, F0634, F0875, F1035
Penzer, Norman Mosley, F0835
People, G1158, H0213, H0407
'People and Politics of the Middle East', F0248
'People are Talking About', G1033
'People I Have Shot', F0560
'The People's Chronology', F1065
Pepper, Dhiela, G1500
Perch, Eve, G1012
'Perdition in the Mediterranean', G0472
Perez, Don, F0836
The Periodical, G1025, G1575
Perkins, G., H0143
'Permissive Biography', G1608
'Perpetual Attraction', G1524
Perrin, Les, H0813
Perros, Georges, G0732
Perruchot, Henri, G0606
Perry, Herry, E029–30
'Persian Pictures', F0076–7
'The Personal Act', F1109
'Personal and Historical Memoirs of an East African Administration', F0036
'Personal Glimpses – Wrecking Turkish Trains With Lawrence of Arabia', G0075
'Personal History', F0964–5
'Personality and Power', F0263
'Perspectives of the Arab World', G0871
'Perspectives on Lawrence', G0872
Pertinax, H0005–6
'Peter O'Toole', F0371, G1099
'Peter O'Toole's Two Big Years', H0646
Peter, Laurence J., F0837
'Peter O'Toole Don Juan d'Arabie Affronte la Soif du Désert', H0613
Petit, D. Pastor, G1203
Petit, Henri, H0800
Le Petit Journal, H0801
Le Peuple, H0513, H0530
Peyre, Henri, F0838
Phelps, Robert, F0839
Philadelphia Daily News, H0942
Philadelphia Inquirer, H0980
Philby, Harry St. John Bridger, F0751, F0816, F0840–51, G0073, G117, G273, H0264, H0321
'Philby', F0816
'Philby of Arabia', F0751

Philharmonic Hall, E005
Philip, G. & Son (pub), F0778
Phillips, Cabell, F0852
Phillips, Jill M., E372
Phillips, Wendall, F0853–4
Philosophical Library (pub), F0003, F1172
'The Philosophy of the Guerrilla Fighter', G1325
Philpot, A.M. (pub), F0676, F0835
Phoenix House (pub), F0241, F0479
'The Phoenix Land', F0335
Phoenix Republic, H1136
Photoplay, G0956, G1005
Psychic News, H0749, H1297
'Pi', F0903
Picabia, Pancho, G0795
Picador (pub), F0603
Pickard, Roy, F0855
Picon, Gaëtan, F0856, G0602
Pictorial Knowledge, G1435
Pictorial Museum, Wareham (pub), E287, E295–6, E322
Picture Post, G0538, G0644
'Le Piège Sioniste sera brisé', G1358
'The Pier-Glass', F0441–2
'A Pilgrim in Arabia', F0848–9
'A Pilgrim in Palestine', F0341
'The Pilgrim Railway', G1275
Pilgrim Trust, London, F0857
'A Pilgrim's Script', F1051
'Pilgrim's Way', F0169
'Pilot to T.E. Lawrence', H0837
Pilot-Pines, H1135
'Pilsudski e Lawrence', G0296
Pine, Martin, H1115–17
Pirmasener Zeitung, H0876
Pitman (pub), F0743
Pitt, Barrie, H1287
Pittsburgh Monthly Bulletin, G0139
Planeta (pub), E202
'Plaque to "Lawrence of Arabia"', H0812
Playboy, G1308
Playground Cricket, B0002
'The Playwright in Films', G1047
Plaza & Janes (pub), E244
'Plenty Hot on "Arabia" Location', H0610
Plexus, G1402
Plomer, William, A162
Plon (pub), F0118, F1031
'Plot to Start War Against the Soviet Charged in Moscow', G0112
Plowden, Joan M. C., F0858
'Le Plus Musulman des Chrétiens', G1415
PMLA, G1481
Pocket Books (pub), F1090
Pocket Library, E139
'Poems', F0899
'Poet and Painter', F0129
'Poet of the Arab Sands', G0681
Poetry, G0445, G1243
Point de Vue, G0739
'Point Four and the Middle East', G0616
Poirtier, Lucien, G0939, G0943
'Pole Hill', G0030
Poliak, Abraham N., G1132
Police-Magazine, G0266
'Political Evolution of the Middle East', F0982
'Political Motivation Wrapped in a Personal Enigma', G0981

'Politics and Literature in Modern Britain', F1097
'Politik im Dienst der Abstraktion, Thomas Edward Lawrence', F0796
Poll, Bernhard, F0859
Poll, Flavio, H1138
'Poor Lawrence', G0971
'Poor worms', H0842
Poore, C.G., H0148
Le Populaire du Centre, H0586
Popular Aviation, G0551
Popular Flying, G0307
'Popular Gardening', G1274
Popular Library (pub), E010
Portland, Duke of, F0860
Portland Evening Post, H0100
'Portmadoc Urban and District Guide', F0861
'Portrait de l'Aventurier', E171–5, G0629, G1237–9, G1248–9, G1252, G1261, G1277, H0424, H0783–91, H0794–7
'Portrait de l'Aventurier, de Roger Stéphane', H0797
'Un portrait de l'aventurier selon Roger Stéphane', G1257
'Un Portrait Français du Colonel Lawrence', H0510
'Portrait of a Desert', F0773–4
'Portrait of a Hero', G1534
'A Portrait of André Malraux', F0828
'Portrait of Lawrence', G1531
'Portrait of Max', F0072
'Portrait of T.E. Lawrence', E076–97, F0872, G0389, H0353; (see also Richards T.E. Lawrence, E126–7)
'Portrait Plaque of T.E. Lawrence', E129
'Portrait Without Death', G1247
The Portraits of T.E. Lawrence', E351
Post, Keith, H1171
'Post-Bag Diversions', F0672
Post-Crescent, H1081
'Post-Mortem Journal', E285
'Post-Victorian Britain: 1900–1956', F0948
Potter, Clarkson N. (pub), E235–6, F0802, F0805
Poughkeepsie Journal, H1071
Pound, Ezra, B0045, F0801, F0862–3, F1000, G1565
'Pour Connaître Lawrence d'Arabie', H0770
'Pour Détruire la Légende de Lawrence', H0434
'Pour Enforcer un Culte Nécessaire', H0799
'Pour et Contre T.E. Lawrence', H0527
Powell, A., G0706
Powell, D., H0652
Powell, Edward Alexander, F0864–5
Powell, Lawrence Clark, F0866–7
'Power Paly', F0771
Practical Christianity, G0840
Praeger (pub), F0302, F0476, F0551, F0593, F0621, F0651–2, F0726
Pratt Institute Quarterly, G0150, G0326, G0520
'Pre Pillars', G1318, H0852
Prediction, G1092, G1354
'Prelude to War', G0465
'Première de Lawrence d'Arabie Devant la Reine d'Angleterre', H0648
Prentice-Hall (pub), D0026, F0125, F0153, F0301, F0403–4, F0828, F0925
'Presentation of the Lawrence Memorial Medal by the President', G0413
Presland, John, F0868
Presley, John W., F0869
Press-Register, H1055

Le Presse, H0482, H0672
Presse de la Cité, F0932a
Preston, Richard, F0870, G0741
Preuves, G0818
'Pre-War', F1160
Price, Clair, G0177
'Price of Greatness', G0591
Pridham, Llewellyn, F0275
Prigent, Simone, F0871
Prince, A.E., G0325
'Le Prince de la Mecque', H0547
'Prince Dynamite', E219, F0605, G0558
'A Prince of Arabia', F0999
'Prince of Mecca', G0710
'A Prince of Our Disorder', E352–5, G1409, G1521–3, G1530, G1533–41, G1549–50, G1557–8, G1561, G1577, H1177, H1179–80, H1188, H1191, H1193, H1206
'Prince Vaillant', E278
Princeton University Library Chronicle, G1081
Princeton University Press, F0824, F1073
'Principles and Persuasions', F1115
'Principles of Textual Criticism', F1056
'The Printer to the Post', F0086
Prinz, Lucie, H1255
Pritchett, V.S., F0872–4, G0634, G0722, G1532
Prittie, Terence, F0875
'Private Army', F0834
Private Eye, G1355
'Private Libraries Associates', F0484
The Private Library, G1458, G1468, G1479
'Private Shaw and Public Shaw', E275–7, G1071, G1076, G1078, G1083–4, G1091, G1094, G1097, G1105, G1109, G1138, H0668, H0677, H0705, H0707, H0709, H0722
'Private "Shaw" Working', H0098
'Le Prix Sainte-Beuve à Robert Raviniaux et Roger Stéphane', H0784
'Proceedings at the Unveiling of the Memorial to Lawrence of Arabia', E117–18
Proceedings of the American Philosophical Society, G0928
'Le Procès T.E. Lawrence', G0831
Procopio, Frank, G1273
'La prodigieuse histoire du colonel Lawrence', G0524
'Producer of the Long trek With "Lawrence of Arabia"', H0637
'Le Professeur Lawrence, frère de fameux "Lawrence d'Arabia"', H0645
'Professor on a Camel', H0935
Profils Anglais, Romances de Guerre', F0309
Progrès, H0515
'Progress of Nations', F0876
'Promise of Greatness', F0818–19
'Proof in Bronze', H1157
'Propagandist', H0828
Propes, Aileen W., G1428
'Prophesied Coup by Italy', H0021
'Prophet in Blue Blazer', H1287
'A Propos du Colonel Lawrence', G0864
'Propositos de Lawrence de Arabia', F0807
Prose, G1455
Prost, M., H0532
'Prototype E.T.L. (sic)', F0917
'Prototype T.E.L.', G0641
La Provençal, H0531, H0792
La Provençal Dimanche, H0632

Providence Journal, H1114
Pryce-Jones, Alan, H1059, H1085
'Psychoanalysis and Historical Biography', G1436
'Psychodynamics of T.E. Lawrence', H1019
Psychohistory Review, G1623
'Psychological Dimensions of Near Eastern Studies', F0155
PTV (pub), E397
Prys-Jones, A.G., G0918
Puaux, Gabriel, G0757
Public Affairs Press, F0576
Public Opinion, G0287
Publishers' prospectuses, A043–5, A055–8, A064, A073, A103, A106, A115, A124, A140, A142–3, A145, A164, A174, A212, A222, A227, A235, A245, E031, E044, E118, E120, E129, E155, E161–2, E178, E194, E196, E258, E286, E296, E303–6, E314, E333, E347
Publisher's Weekly (PW), A143, G0229, G0481, G1381, G1521, G1562, G1577, G1610, G1615
'Publishing and Bookselling', F0779
Pueblo Colorado Star and Journal and Chieftan, H1091
Pughe, J.M., H0150
Pulkownik, B., A132–3
'Pulkownik Lawrence', E207
Punch, G0115, G0492, G0706, G1014, G1128, G1153, G1266
Punkik, Herbert, G0917
'Pursuit of Bigness', H0725
Pustay, John S., F0877
Putnam's, G.P. (pub), E357, F0210, F0329–30, F0519, F0636, F0647, F0663, F0679, F0739, F1003, F1058, F1126, F1132, F1137
'Putting the Weight in Ancient Days', B0031
'Puzzle of Poems Lawrence Loved', H1153
'The Puzzle of T.E. Lawrence', H1255
Pyramid Books (pub), E260, F0973

'Quand un Arabe juge Lawrence', G1140
'Qantas Rising', F0380
Quaritch, Bernard, A001–2
'Quatre leaders de l'histoire (Jacques Bénoist-Mechin, Lawrence d'Arabie)', H1226
Quarterly Journal of the Library of Congress, G1462, G1492
Quarterly Review, G0381, G0498
Quartet Books, F0189, F1160a, F1155, F1157
'Quarto Club Papers, 1928/1929', F0878
Quayle, Anthony, E271
Queen's Hall, E002
Queen's Observer, H1116
Queen's Quarterly, G0325, G1484, G1687
Quennell, Peter, F0879, G0675, G1608
Quercus, P.E.G., G0241, G0301, G0433
'Queries for Biographers of T.E. Lawrence', G1518
'Quest For Lawrence', G0975
'La Questione dell' 'Ur Partigiano Johnny', G1636
'Qui Est-Ce?', F0871
'Qui était Lawrence d'Arabie?', G1277
'Qui Etait le Vrai Lawrence?', G1697
Quigly, Isabel, G1038
Quinn, Anthony, E271
Quinn, Paul, E090–91
'A Quite Remarkable Father', F0532

R., A., G0694, G0756, G0842

R., A.M., G027
R., L., G0900
R., R., H1162–3
Raban, Jonathan, F0880
Rabine, Henry, H0684
'Railway Cut by Lawrence of Arabia Still Crippled', H1165
'The Railway Magazine', G1214, G1219
Rains, Claude, E271
Raintree Publishers (pub), E382
'Ralph Fox, a Writer in Arms', F0368
Rambaud, Jacques, E190
'Ramping', B0029, B0035
Ramsay, William, H1267
Randall, Rona, F0881
Randell, William, E227–8
Random, Roderick, G0046
Random House (pub), A021–3, E224, E253, D0072, F0156, F1607, F0632, F0654, F0732, F0744, F0777, F0874, F0963
'Rank and File', G1632
'The Rape of Palestine', F1186
Rapid City Journal, H1129
Le Rappel, H0549
'Rare Lawrence First Edition Vanishes', H0848
'Rare T.E. Lawrence Work Gone From British Museum', G1331
La Rassegna Italiana, G0296
Raswan, Carl R., F0882–5
Rattigan, Col. Clive, G0222
Rattigan, Terence, E222–6, F0189, G0932,G0933, G0935–6, G0954–5, G0986, G0989–G0990, G0995–G0996, G1093, G1247, H0579, H0582
'Rattigan Explains Lawrence of Arabia', H0579
Rausch, Jürgen, G0747, G0879
Raviniaux, Robert, H0784
Raymond, Allen, H0064
Raymond, Ernest, F0886
Raymond, John, G1266
Raymond, Rene, F0887
Le Rayon d'Égypte, G0850
'R.D.B.'s Procession', F0108
Read, Herbert, A162, F0093–4, F0888–90, G1008
The Reader, H0979
'Reader in the History of Books and Printing', F1146
Reader's Digest, F0891, G0061, G0177, G0957, G1170, G1178, G1448
'The Reader's Digest of Books', D0021
'A Reader's Guide to W.H. Auden', F0377
Reader's Union (pub), A156, F0141, F0204, F0889, F1005, F1036
Reading Eagle, H1035
'The Real Colonel Lawrence', G0137
'The Real Lawrence', H0226, H0716, H0916
'The Real Lawrence of Arabia', G1170, G1173
'The Real T.E. Lawrence', G1579
'The Real War', F0649
Réalités, G0882, G1349, G1368
'Retreat: Clouds Hill', H0717
'Rebecca West and Peter O'Toole "A Dialogue"', G1162
'Rebelión en el Desierto', A129–30, A136–7
'Rebellion in Palestine', F0704
'Rebuilding the Hejaz Railroad', G1323
'A Recently Discovered Letter From T.E. Lawrence to My Father', G1494

'Recherche de descendants Corbel, Fécelier Martinet ayant connu famille Lawrence 1891–4; 1906–8', G1365
'La Recherche du Châtiment, T.E. Lawrence', F0118
Reclam (pub), A201, D0005
'Reclam Lesetoffe Lehrpraktische Analyses Folge 6', D0015
'Recollections of a Rebel', F0126
'Recollections of T.E.L.', E402
'Recording Britain', F0857
Red Cross Magazine, G0010
'Red Dust', F0098
Redbook, G1162
Reddick, Peter, E403
Redding Record-Searchlight, H1125
Redlands News, G1279
'The Reel Lawrence', G1082
Rees, Goronwy, G0480
Rees, R., G0173
'Reflections on Greatness', H0628
Reforme, G0748
Regnery, Henry (pub), E198, F0557
Register, H1180
Reid, Brian Holden, G1663–4
'Reincarnation and Other Essays', F0604
'Reincarnation: Lawrence of Arabia', G0473
Reinhardt (pub), F0047
Reinholds, P., A128
'Reisen in Arabia Deserta', A030
Reitlinger, H., A003
Relations Internationales, G1596, G1650
'Release of Damascus', C0001
'Relics of Lawrence', H0371
'Religion and Rebel', F1143–4
'Remembering Kut', F0784
'A Reminiscence of Lawrence', G1182
'Reminiscences of an Old Pro', H1210
Renaudin, André, H0643
Reno New Gazette, H1016
Rensburg, J.F.J. von, G1049
'Reopening Old Wounds', H1159
'A Reply to Captain Liddell Hart', G0813
'Report Lawrence Now a Moslem Saint Spying on the Bolshevist Agent in India', H0072
'Report on Middle East Conference', A033
'Reportage über Lawrence von Arabien', H0947
The Reporter, G0767, G1069
Reporter, H1070
Reprint Society (pub), A046, A232, F0211, F0298, F0804
République, H0555
'Reputations, Ten Years After', F0650
Research Studies, G1526, G1559
'Resignation of Colonel Lawrence as Advisor', H0013
'Resistance', F0355
'Retrato del Aventurero', E175
'Retreat to Victory', F0735
'Das Retrospective Gepack: Maurice Baring und T.E. Lawrence', G0622
Reutlinger General-Anzeiger, H0899
Revai (pub), A079
'Les Revendications Arabes. Le France et Syrie', H0005
Review of English Literature, G1244
'A Review of Novels by D.H. Lawrence', A229
Review of Politics, G0621

Review of Reviews, G0008, G0018, G0060, G0235, G0273, G0351
'A Review of Short Stories of H.G. Wells', A229
'A Review of the Works of Walter Savage Landor', A229
'Reviewer's Scoop', G0411
'The Revisions of Seven Pillars of Wisdom, G1481
'Revolt', G0094
'Revolt From the Desert', G1265
'Revolt in the Desert', A100–135, C0016, C0020, D0009, D0021, D0027–9, D0031, G0053–4, G0057–8, G0066–7, G0069–72, G0074, G0076, G0083, G0086–9, G0091–2, G0094–5, G0101, G0103, G0109, G0119, G0131, G0133, G0136, G0154–5, G0164, G0181, G0230, G0281, G0620, G1272, H0044–5, H0048, H0720
'"Revolt in the Desert" and Its Author', D0005, G0063
'Revolt to Revolution', D0010a
'Revolta in Deşert', A134
'La Révolte dans le Désert', A114, A250
'Révolte dans le désert ou l'étrange épopée du Colonel Lawrence', G0252
'Revolutionary War in World Strategy', F1053
Revue des Deux Mondes, G0099, G0295, G0391, G0532, G0808
Revue de France, G0272
Revue de la Défense Nationale, G0900
Revue de Littérature Comparée, G0537, G1658
La Revue de Paris, G0003, G0369, G0613, G0731, G0757, G0786, G0891, G0968, G1255
Revue des Etudes Islamiques, G0617
Revue Française de Science Politique, G0911
Revue Historique de l'Armée, G1284
La Revue Internationale, B0047
Revue Militaire Générale, G0929
Revue Militaire d'Information, G0825, G0939
La Revue Pour Tous, G0691
Rex (pub), E122
Reyer, Georges, G0630, G1697
Reynal & Co. (pub), F0370, F0854
Reynal & Hitchcock (pub), F0456
Reynaud, E.M., G0528
Reynolds, Quentin, D0023
Reynolds, T.S., F0892
Rheinische Post (Düsseldorf), H0931
Die Rheinpfalz (Ludwigshafen), H0908
Rhonda, Viscountess, F0893
Rhode, Eric, G1042
Rhys, Ernest, F0894
Rice, Howard, G1081
Rice, John, H1268–9
Rich, Barbara (pseudonym – see Robert Graves and Laura Riding), A159
Rich & Cowan (pub), D0012, E128, F0765–6, F0886
Richard, John, H1185
'Richard Aldington to Defend His Book', H0414
'Richard Aldington: il m'a convancu de la pureté de ses intentions', G0671
'Richard Aldington in His Last Years', G1133
Richards, Jeffrey, G1655
Richards, Vyvyan, E096–7, E124–7, E361, E403, G0389, G0769, H0353, H0371
Richards Press (pub), F0451
Richardson, Bill, H0738
Richardson, H.H., G1654
Richmond Independent, H1015
Richmond Times-Dispatch, H0970

Rick, Josef, G0535
'The Riddle of "S.A." of the Seven Pillars of Wisdom', H0854
'Riddle of the "Arch Spy"', H0658
'Riddle of the Sands', G1131
'Ride to Babylon', F0324
Rider (pub), F0955
Riding, Laura, G0244; *see also* Barbara Rich, A159
Ridley, Maurice Roy, F0895
Rigby, Douglas, F0896
Rigby, Elizabeth, F0896
Rigby, Graham, G1468
'Rigging the Lawrence Case', G1590
Right Book Club (pub), F1140
Rihani, Ameen, F0897–8
Riley, Mary Ann, H1001
Rinn, Hermann (pub), E201
Rio, Armand, G1210
'The Rise and Fall of the Well-Made Play', F1025
Le Risque, G0446, G0457
Rivarol, G0770
'River Niger', A163–4
'Rivers in the Desert', F0412–13
Rivington, Arabell, F0899
'La Rivolta nel Deserto', A123–6
'Road to a Legend', H0748
'Road to Damascus', G0343
'The Road to Mecca', F0046–7
'Road to Nineveh', F0610
'Robert Bridges 1844–1930', F1047
'Robert Graves', F0952, F0980
'Robert Graves, Lawrence Vindicated', F0674
'The Robert Graves Manuscripts and Letters at Southern Illinois University, An Introduction', F0869
Roberts, Chalmers, G0082
Roberts, Glenys, H1260
Roberts, Glyn, F0900
Roberts, Marguerite, F1046
Robertson, C.W., G1166
Robertson, Keith, H1196
Robertson, Wilmot, F0901
Robinson, Edward, E083–4, E164–5, F0809, G0248, G0345, G0349, G0353, G0355–6, G0359
'Robson', F0078
Robson, J. Michael, H1114
Rochester Post-Bulletin, H1005
Rockford Register-Republic, H1124
Rockford Register Star, H1034
Rockliff (pub), F0263
Rocky Mountain News, H1128
Rodman, Selden, E115–16, G0421–4, G0426, G0429, G0439, G0442, G0445, G0823, H0378–9
'Roger Stéphane a complété son portrait de l'aventurier', H0788
Rogers, Bruce (pub), A141, A145, A151, A160, A165, F0294, F0902–3, F0992
'Le Roi Feycal et le Colonel Lawrence', G0272
'The Role of Syrians and Iraqiis in the Arab Revolt', G1285
Rollins, Carl Purington, G0202
Rollo, Charles J., G0678, G0772
Rolls, Sam Cottingham, E114, G1677, H0291, H0382
'The Rolls Mystique', G1278
Romains, Jules, H0535–6
Romance Notes, G1460
'Romance of the Bosphorus', F0785

'The Romance of the Last Crusade', F0396, H0378–9
'The Romantic as a Man of Action', G0627
'Romantic Riddle', G0931, G1175
'The Romantic Riddle of Lawrence of Arabia', G0988
Rommel, Erwin, F0637, F0905
'Rommel as Military Commander', F0637
Ronald (pub), F0304
'Ronald Cartland', F0188
Roodes, B.H., E085
Roseler, David, E028
Rosenbaum, Ron, G1653
Rosenberg, Harold , G0445
Rosenberg, Howard, H1247, H1251
Rosenblum, Ralph, F0906
Rosenfelder, Karl, G0516
Rosenthal, Jean, E190
Roskill, Stephen, F0907
Ross, A/c; *see* 352087 A/c Ross, under 'Three'
Ross, J.H. (pseudonym of TEL), A094–5, A097
Ross, L.H., A096
'Ross', E222–6, F1033, G0932–3, G0935–6, G0954–5, G0986, G0989–90, G0995–6, G1093, G1247, H0579, H0582
'Ross at the Depot', G0722
Rosselli, John, G0767, H0463
Rosswell Record, H0982
Rostow, Eugene, E327
Rota, Bertram (pub), A257, E401, G1022
Rothe, Hans, A208
Rothenstein, John, F0908–9
Rothenstein, Sir William, F0910–16, F0981, G0178, G0187, G0201, G0578
Rougemont, Denis de, F0917, G0601, G0641
The Round Table, B0009, G1425
'Round Table and Middle Eastern Peace Settlement', G1425
Roundel, G0817
Rousseaux, André, F0918, G0604, H0403, H0527
Roussel, Jeanne, E039–40
Routledge (pub), F0223, F0888, F1018
Routledge & Kegan Paul (pub), F0463, F0600, F0730
'Row on Lawrence of Arabia Rages', H0550
Rowley, Peter, G1539
Rowan, Littlefield (pub), F1097
Rowse, A. L., F0919–21, G1139, H1200
Roy (pub), E025, E228
Royal Academy Illustrated, G0363
Royal Air Force Cadet College Journal, G0103, G0398
Royal Air Force Cadet Magazine, G0062
Royal Air Force College Journal, B0029, B0031, B0035, G0324, G0577, G0615
Royal Air Force Flying Review, G0906
Royal Air Force Review, G0592
Royal Albert Hall, E003
Royal Central Asian Society Journal, G0034, G0045, G0088, G0247, G0294, G0338, G0362, G0413, G0525, G1338
Royal Engineers' Journal, B0006
Royal Institute of British Architects Journal, G0358
Royal Institute of International Affairs, F0736, F0922
Royal Opera House, E001
'Royal Prince of "Lawrence of Arabia"', G1151
'Royal Soap Opera', G0836

Royal United Services Institute Journal, G0032, G1141, G1276
Royal World Première Performance (film), E268
Rudge, William Edwin, A160, F0902
Rukeyser, Muriel, G0422
'Rulers of Mecca', F0259
Rumbold, Richard, F0923
Runyan, William McKinley, F0924
Rusconi (pub), E391
Russell, Francis, G1401
Russell, Henry T., H0129–33, H0145
Russell, Ian, H0658
Russo, William, G1621
Rustow, Dan, F0925
Rutherford, Andrew, F0926
Rutter, Owen, F0927–8, G0304
Ryan, Peter, F0929
Rypins, Stanley, G1114

'S' (pseudonym of T.E.L.), B0031
S., K.S. (General Sir George MacMunn), G0041
S., W.K., G1487
'S.A.', G1607
'S.A. The Spy in T.E.'s Life', H0868
Saarbrucker Zeitung, H0901
'Sabuku no Hanran', A127
Saccone, Eduardo, G1636
'Sacelsanas Tuksnesi', A128
Sachar, Howard M., F0930–31, G0663
Sacramento Mirror, H1087
S.A.C.S.E. (pub), E085
Sadoul, Georges, H0688
'Safety Last', F0998
Sage (pub), F0130
Sagittaire, E171
Said, Edward, G1390, G1429
'Said and Done', F0241
Saint Catherine (pub), F0395
'Saint Joan, Major Barbara and Androcles and the Lion', F0959
St John Irvine, F0932
Saint-Laurent, Cecil, F0932a
Saint-Louis Globe-Democrat, H1296
St. Louis Library Bulletin, G0146
St. Louis Post-Despatch, H0953
St. Martin's (pub), F0224, F0371, F0520, F0702, F0728, F1147
St. Nicholas Magazine, G0098, G0106
St. Paul's Dispatch, H0184
St. Paul's Cathedral, E093
St. Petersburg Times, H1033
Saisons, G0585
'Saladin, nous voici!', H1139
Salanova, Cécile, G1402
'Salar the Salmon', F1135–6
Salisbury Times, H1032
Salmagundi, G1390
Salmon, Edmond, F0933
Salt Lake Tribune, H0957
Salter, Arthur, Baron, F0934
'Sam Spiegel Will Use 500 Camels for Background in "Lawrence of Arabia"', H0606
Samedi Soir, H0434
Sampson, George, F0935
Sampson, Low, Marston (pub), F0099, F1095
Samuel, Edwin, G1493
Samuel, Herbert L.S., Viscount, F0936

'Samuel Shepheard Cairo', F0123
San Antonio Express, H0237
San Diego Union, H1255
San Francisco Chronicle, H0389, H0496, H0630, H0636, H0715, H0732, H0738, H0771, H0972, H1269, H1295
San Francisco Examiner, H0244, H0668, H0712, H09716
San Francisco News Call Bulletin, H0714
San Francisco Sunday Examiner and Chronicle, H0856, H1080
San Mateo Times, H0956, H1096
San Raphael Independent, H1079
Sancla (pub), E208
'Sand on Our Eyes', H0817
'The Sand Kings of Oman', F0811
'The Sand of the Silence of T.E. Lawrence', G1420
Sandall, Roger, G1080
'The Sandcastle', G1582
Sander, Frederick, E123
Sands, William, G0922
Sanger, Richard H., F0937
Santa Barbara News-Press, H1127
Santa Monica Independent Journal (CA), H0994
Santana, Hubert de, H1188
Santilla (pub), E229
Sartre, Jean-Paul, E171–5, F0747
'Sartre, Ideologue of Our Times', F0747
Sassoon, Sir Philip, F0938–9
Sassoon, Siegfried, F0431, F0940–41
'The Saturday Book', F0942–3
Saturday Evening Post, G1086
Saturday Night, G0749
Saturday Review, G0042, G0046, G0049, G0057–8, G0066–7, G0072, G0076–7, G0084–6, G0108, G0114, G0160, G0166–8, G0181, G0185, G0188–9, G0194–5, G0202, G0211–14, G0222–3, G0230, G0241, G0264, G0280–81, G0289, G0301, G0329, G0336, G0386–7, G0396, G0401, G0406, G0410, G0423, G0433, G0439, G0443, G0506, G0512, G0552, G0645, G0681, G0762–3, G0822, G0846, G0898, G0922, G0979, G1027, G1046–8, G1060, G1084, G1116, G1119–21, G1146, G1169, G1246, G1482, G1523
'Sa'udi Arabia', F0850, F1073
'Saudi Arabia in the Nineteenth Century, F1147
Sauvigny, Bertier de, G0877
Savage, Raymond, F0944–5, G0049, H0034, H0305
'A Savage War of Peace', F0527
'Say Lawrence is in Area', H0103
Sayigh, Anis, G1118
'The Sayings and Doings of T.E.', E363
Scarfe, Muriel, G1232
Scene G1029, G1045
'Scenes and Portraits', F0701
Schaukroff, Xaver, G0164
Scheller, Rolf, G1371
Scheltens & Giltay (pub), E239
Schleswiger Nachrichten, H0894
Scheyer, Amram, E329
'Schillern des Spiel in Britische Gold', H0884
Schirrmacher, Wolf, G0497
Schlegel, Otto (pub), E066
Schliemann, Heinrich, A252–3
Schmidt, Albert-Marie, G0748
Schneider, Marcel, G1249
Schofield, Roy, E381–2

'The Scholar at Work', F0625
'Scholar Turned Fighter', H0238
'Scholar Warrior', G0190
Scholartis Press, E077
Scholastic Book Services (pub), E126
Schønberg (pub), A181
Die Schöne Literature, G0128
Schroers, Rolf, A201, E167
Schuman (pub), F0827
Schwaan (pub), F0577
Schwakopf, Jerzy, A086
Schwartz, William Carroll, G1584
Schweitzer Monatshefte für Politik und Kultur, G0246
'La science et l'art militaire de T.E. Lawrence', F0781
'Science of Guerrilla Warfare', B0011, D0011
'"SCOOP" Was Lawrence of Arabia a Contributor to Service Journal?', G1647
'Scorn for Honors Marked Romantic Career of Lawrence, Hero of Arabia', H0205, H0217
Scorpion (pub), F0951a
The Scotsman, H0174, H0328, H0635, H1197
Scott, Kathleen, F0946
Scott, Paul, G1551
Scott-James, R.A., F0947
'Scott, Lawrence and the Myth of British Decadence', G0566
Scottish Field, G0474
Scoville, Sheila Ann, G1661
Scranton Times, H1113
Scribner's, Charles (pub), A157, E358, F0048, F0061, F0230, F0281, F0341, F0467, F0530, F0595, F0681, F1001
Scroggs, B0004
'At Sea With T.E. Lawrence', G1572
Seaby's Coin and Medal Bulletin, G1404
Seaman, Lewis C. B., F0948
'Search for Tomorrow', F0617
Searight, Sarah, F0949–50
Sears, J.H. (pub), F0195
Secker, Martin (pub), F0439, F0441
Secker & Warburg (pub), F0590, F0592, F0602, F0738, F1057
'The Second Arab Awakening', F0591
'A Second Treasury of the World's Great Letters', D0002–3
'Secret Book of Lawrence of Arabia', H0158
'Le Secret de T.E. Lawrence', G0703
'Le Secret de Thomas Edward Lawrence', G1504
'Le Secret des Mille Visages de Lawrence l'Inconnu', G0701
'Secret Despatches From Arabia', A010, A226–8, E161, E327, G0533, G0540, G1316
'Le Secret du Colonel Lawrence', E143–4a
'Secret Lawrence Admirer Says It With Flowers', H1265
'Secret Lives', H0775
'The Secret Lives of Lawrence of Arabia', E193, E301–19, G1359–60, G1363, G1370, G1373, G1380–82, G1386–7, G1391, G1394–7, G1399, G1405, G1407, G1411, G1416, G1418, G1423–4, G1426, G1440, H1685, G1692, H0851, H0853, H0856, H0888, H0928, H0936, H0941–6, H0949, H0954–7, H0959, H0969–70, H0973, H0978, H0982–5, H0987–90, H0993–5, H0999, H1001–3, H1006–9, H1013–4, H1024, H1035,
H1044, H1052–6, H1060, H1066–7, H1071, H1074–5, H1079, H1084, H1087–8, H1090–91, H1094–6, H1102–4, H1106–7, H1110, H1112–3, H1115–9, H1124–5, H1127, H1129–32, H1135, H1138, H1140, H1144, H1148, H1150, H1279, H1296
'Secret Lives of Lawrence Well Detailed', H1061
'"Secret Lives" Tells More of T.E. Lawrence', H1006
'The Secret of the Hittites', F0205
'The Secret of the Knife', F0071
Secrétan, Philippe, H0634
'Secrets of the War on Mecca', C0006
'The Secret's Out', H1123
See Magazine, G0951
'See Saw in the Middle East', G1168
Seeley Service (pub), F0606
'Seitse Tarkuse Sammast', A083
Sejersted, Georg Wasmuth, E099
Selander, Sten, A138
'Selbstbildnis In Briefen', A208
'Selbstbildnis T.E. Lawrence', G0600
'Selbstbildnis von T.E. Lawrence', G0308
'Selected Letters of T.E. Lawrence', A232–3, A233a, E178
La Sélection des Libraires de France, G0889
'Selections From Seven Pillars of Wisdom', A230–31
'Self Made Legend', G1535
'Self Portrait of an Artist', F0587
'Self-Portrait of T.E. Lawrence', H0448
'Self-Portrait of the Author From Selected Writings', G0634
'A Selfconscious Genius Made and Broken by War', G0485
Seligo, Irene, F0951, G0428
Selma Times, H1140
La Semaine à Paris, H0795
Une Semaine de Paris, G1506
La Semaine Internationale, H0484, H0499
Sender Frei Berlin, E390
Senior Scholastic, G1068
'The Sensitive Arab', G0031
'Sense and Nonsense in the Biography of T.E. Lawrence', E363
Sentinel, H1123
'Les Sept Piliers de la Sagesse', A070–71, A250, G1100–101, G0660, G0795, G1163, G1386
'Les 7 piliers de la sagesse. La confession du Colonel Lawrence', G0153
'Les Sept Piliers de la Sagesse par T.E. Lawrence', G0468
Serez, Naci, E292
Serjeant, R.B., F0951a
'Service Life', B0032
'Services Set for W.J. Miller Ex-Aide to Lawrence of Arabia', H0871
'Servir sin ser Premiado', F0807
'A Set Piece: January 1918', B0012
'I Sette Pilastri della Saggezza', A080–81
Le Seuil (pub), F0049
'Seven Fallen Pillars', F0592–3
'Seven League Boots', F0469
'Seven Pillars of Mystery', G0614
'Seven Pillars of Wisdom', A034–89, A226, A230–31, A241, D0006–7, D0022–5, E086, E178, F0093–4, F0692, F0888–9, G0042, G0062, G0085, G0188, G0278, G0283, G0285, G0290, G0298, G0302, G0305, G0310–11, G0315,

G0323, G0326–7, G0330, G0333–4, G0337, G0339, G0341, G0347–8, G0350–51, G0354, G0368, G0381, G0403–4, G0418, G0437, G0441, G0468, G0503, G0536, G1072, G1100–1, G1477, G1481, G1487, G1491, G1498, G1509, G1519, G1679, G1685, H0028, H0078, H0135, H0299, H0311, H0321, H0323, H0325, H0327, H0338, H0344–5, H0348, H0663, H0667, H0692– 3, H0696–7, H0706, H0718

'Seven Pillars of Wisdom an anonymous note on the texts of Seven Pillars and Revolt in the Desert', B0023, B0034

'The Seven Pillars of Wisdom and Revolt in the Desert', A103

'Seven Pillars of Wisdom Sold for £5,500', G1614

'Seven Pillars of Wisdom T.E. Lawrence in Life and Death', E401

'Seven Pillars of Wisdom, T.E. Lawrence's Icon Book', G0725

'Seven Pillars of Wisdom: The Secret Contestable Documentary', E396

'Seven Poems Dedicated to T.E. Lawrence', E283

Seventeen, G1030

Sewannee Review, G1550

Seymour, William Kean, G1457, G1471

Seymour-Smith, Martin, F0952, G1089

Shaffer, Robert, F0953

Shah, Ikbal Ali Sidar, F0954

Shah, Sayed Idries, F0955

Shahani, R.K., G1263

Shahbander, Abdul, H0127

Shales, Tom, H1219

Shanks, Edward, G0072, H0371, H0400

Sharif, Omar, E271, F0956

Sharpley, Anne, G1158, H0733

'Shatten der T.E. Lawrence', H0898

Shavian, G1180, G1242

Shaw, Charlotte, F0290–91

Shaw, George Bernard, A099–110, A118–9, A121, A162, D004–5, E110, E352–E353, F0283–4, F0288, F0378, F0478, F0498, F0825–6, F0829–33, F0932, F0957–61, F1074, F1085, F1128, F1149, F1153, G0063, G0071, G0081, G1137, G1180, G1242, H0030, H0668, H0675, H0677, H0705, H0707, H0709

Shaw, T.E., A038–9, A143–4, A146, A150–54, A160, A162, A165, A193, A252–3, A259, B0035, E069–70

Shaw, William I., G1440

'Shaw', H0677

'Shaw Aircraftsman', H0030

'Shaw and Lawrence', G1094

'Shaw Exhibition', F1074

'Shaw, Formerly Lawrence of Arabia', G0307

'Shaw in Durban', G1242

'"Shaw" is Shaw's Guest', H0011

'Shaw Lauds Lawrence Conqueror of Arabia', H0033

Shaw Review, G1167

'Shaw-Ede T.E. Lawrence's Letters to H.S. Ede 1927–1935', A234–5, G0571, G0574

'Shaw's Corner', F1153

'Sheba's Daughters', F0851

Sheboygan Press, H0993

Sheean, Vincent, F0962–6, G0335, G0652, G0676, G0762

'The Sheep Had Three Necks', H0804

'Sheeref Lawrence's Book', H0031

Shelby Star, H0971

Shepard, Samuel, F0123

Shepard, William G., G0010

'Shepheard's Hotel', F0786–7

Sheridan House (pub), F0328

Sherer Herz, Judith, F0967

'Sherif Feisal: King of Irak', B0016

Sherwood, Jane, E285–6

Sherwood, John, F0968

Shiftah, Nasr A., E166

'Shifting Sands', F0139

'Shifting Sands of Legend', H1227

Shillito, E., G0286

Shirer, William, F0969

Shoe String Press (pub), E333

Sholl, Anna McClure, G0306

'A Short Guide to the Imperial War Museum', F0447

'A Short History of the Arab People's, F0406

'A Short History of World War I', F0300

Shotwell, James T., F0970

Show Magazine, G0960, G1082

Shreveport Times, H1119

Shuckburgh, Sir John, C0014

Shumway, Harry Irving, E090–92, G0388, H0317–8

Sichtermann, Helmut, A252–3

Sidebotham, Herbert, F0971

Sidgwick & Jackson (pub), E205, E348–9, F0361, F0453, F1050, F1183

'Sieben Säulen der Unweisheit', H0931

'Die Sieben Säulen der Weisheit', A072–8, H0397

'Siedem Filarów Madrości', A086

'The Siege', F0137

Siegel, Larry, G1164

Siegel, William, E050–51

'Siegfried's Journey', F0940–41

'Los Siete Pilares de la Sabiduria', A066

Sight and Sound, G0967

Sih mard-i ajib, E166

'Silence in Zikhorn', G0587

Silver, Alain, F0972

'The Silver Lady', F0745

Silverberg, Robert, F0973

Simmons, John S.G., E231

Simon, G0007

Simon, John, G0995, G0997, G0999

Simon & Schuster (pub), D0002, F0046, F0279, F0540, F0555, F0674

'The Simple Funeral of Lawrence of Arabia', H0293

Simpson, B.D. (pub), E144a

Simpson, Colin, E301–19, G1359–60, G1363, G1370, G1373, G1380–82, G1386–7, G1391, G1394–7, G1399, G1405, G1407, G1411, G1416, G1418, G1423–4, G1426, G1440, G1685, G1692, H0853, H0856, H0877, H0888, H0891–3, H0897, H0899, H0901–3, H0907–9, H0914, H0918–20, H0922, H0928, H0936, H0941–7, H0949, H0954–7, H0959, H0969–70, H0973, H0978, H0982–5, H0987–90, H0993–5, H0999, H1001–3, H1006–9, H1013–4, H1024, H1035, H1044, H1052–6, H1060, H1066–7, H1071, H1074–5, H1079, H1084, H1087–8, H1090–91, H1094–6, H1102–4, H1106–7, H1110, H1112–3, H1115–9, H1124–5, H1127, H1129–32, H1135, H1138, H1140, H1148, H1150, H1213, H1279, H1293, H1296

Sims, Reginald G., E106, E363
'Sinai', F0091
'Since Fifty', F0913–4
Sindbad (pub), E259
Singer, Kurt D., D0024
'Single Bed For Three', E280, H0699
Sioux City Journal, H1066
Sioux City Sunday Journal, H0978
'Sir Alec in "Lawrence of Arabia"', H0607
'Sir Harold Wernher's Copy of Seven Pillars of
   Wisdom to Quaritch', H0845
'Sir Hubert Wilkins', G1044
'Sir William Orpen', F0606
Sitwell, Sir Osbert, F0974
'Sixteen Portraits of People Whose Houses Have
   Been Preserved by the National Trust', F1006
'Sixty Minutes With Winston Churchill', F1055
Skaraveos (pub), E241
'Skilful Portrait of Enigmatic Hero', H1189
Skinner, W.W., H0842
Skokie Life, H1049
Skúlason, Páll, E021
Slade, Gurney (pseudonym for Stephen Bartlett),
   E050–53, E057, E087–8, G0405
'Slagen Tell Slant', A187
'Slipstream', F0887
Sloan, A., F0975
'Sluggish Lot', H0912
'A Small "Trek"', H0700
Smith, A.W., G0379, G0530
Smith, Burt, G1569, G1656
Smith, Clare Sydney, E138–40
Smith, Jack H0921, H1224–5
Smith, Janet Adam, F0976–7
Smith, Peter (pub), F0101
Smith, R. Skilbeek, F0978
Smith, Sydney, H0483
Smith & Haas (pub), F0428, F0436, F1131
Smithsonian, G1609, G1629
Smuts, Jan, F0239
Smyth, Ethel, F0979
Smythe, Colin (pub), F0197
Snipes, Katherine, F0980
'Snippets of a Hero', G0638
Snodgrass, W.P., G0859
'Snuggling With Lawrence', G1599
Snyder News, H1045
Societäts (pub), F0951
Société Belge d'Etudes et d'Expansion, G0888
Society for Promoting Christian Knowledge
   (pub), F0190
Le Soir, H0772
Le Soir de Bruxelles, H0509, H0557
'The Soldier of Mystery', G1122
'A Soldier With the Arabs', F0407–8
'Soldiers', F0508
'Soldiers and Soldiering', F1108
'A Soldier's Homer', G0870
'Solitary Hero', G1508
'Solitary in the Ranks', E372a, E373–4, G1598,
   G1603, G1605, H0476, H1222, H1227
'Solitary warrior', G0635
Soliogy, Hugo, H0833
'Some Eminent Post-Victorians', H0742
'Some Letters From Abroad', F0349
'Some Notes From the Golden Cockerel Press',
   F0418
'Some Notes on Lawrence of Arabia', G1161

'Some Notes on the Writing of the Seven Pillars of
   Wisdom', A039
'Some Reflections on the Life of T.E. Lawrence',
   F0185
'Some Unpublished Letters From T.E. Lawrence
   to Frederic Manning', B0052
Somerset American, H1120
'Sondages', F1019
'Songe et Mensonge de Lawrence', E259, G1486–7
'Songs and Slang of the British Soldier', F0154
Sonyel, S.R., G1672
Sorbonne (pub), E378
Sorgel, Henk Ohne, G1369
'The Soul of the Arabian Revolution', G0021
'Sound Sense on T.E. Lawrence', H1171
'A Sound Spanking For A Hero', H0976
'Sous un même Burnous deux Mondes
   s'entrechoquent', G1700
South Atlantic Quarterly, G1201, G1389, G1502
South Pasadena Review, H0761
Southerly, B0052
Southern Evening Echo, H1232
Southern Illinois University Press (pub), F0246,
   F0393
Southern Review, G0366
Southern Scene (Japan), G1127
Southfield Jewish News, H0974, H1095
'Souvenir Press', F0264
'Soviet Imperialism in Afghanistan', G0243
Spandau Volksblat, G1372
Sparks, Douglas, H1110
'Sparks From Lawrence's Pen', G0512
Spartenburg Journal, H1070
'Der Späte Lawrence', G0696
Speaight, Robert, F0981
Spearman, Neville (pub), E285–6
Spécial, G1221
'Special Forces For Desert Warfare', F0423
'Special Forces in the Desert: The Lawrence
   Legend and the Light Car Patrols', F0423
'Special Trailers on "Lawrence"', G1074
Les Spectacles de Monde, G1103, G1245
Spectator, B0024–8, G0071, G0113, G0124, G0162,
   G0219, G0257, G0311, G0314, G0382, G0436,
   G0480, G0484, G0510, G0571, G0632, G0666,
   G0710, G0728, G0807, G0932, G0975, G1010,
   G1038, G1089, G1172, G1188, G1272, G1469,
   G1552, G1583
'Speeches on Foreign Policy', F0465
'The Spell of Arabia: Charles Doughty and T.E.
   Lawrence', G0588
'Spelling Above to T.E. Lawrence', H0614
Spencer, William, F0982
Spender, Stephen, A162, E325, F0983
Sperber, Manès, F0984–6, G0818
The Sphere, G0011, G0041, G0157
Spiegel, Sam F., E266, E268, E271, H0606
Der Spiegel, G0673, G0949–50, G1346, G1382
'The Spiegel touch', G1048
'Spirit of Lawrence of Arabia', H0335
'Spirit of Place', F0293
'Spirit Return of Two Celebrities: Lawrence of
   Arabia and Dylan Thomas Speak at Seance',
   H1297
'Spoors of Spooks', F0316
Spring Books (pub), A203
Springfield Republican, H0048, H0055, H0311,
   H0366, H0385, H0438, H0497, H0573, H1031

Springfield State Journal-Register, H1030
Squire, Sir John, G0217, G0494, G0668, G0716
Staats, Fr. (pub), E218
Stacpole, Aleric, G1184, G1191
Stadelmeyer, Peter, G0687
Stallworthy, Jon, G1244
Stamp Collecting, G1499
'Stamps and the History of the Hijaz', G1620
'Standards of Greatness', G0480
'A Standing Civil War', G1429
Stanford today, G1001
Stanford University Press, F1002
Stanley, Arthur, D0025
Stanley, Donald, H0668, H0716
The Star, H0068, H0183, H0200, H0242, H0263–5,
   H0290, H0698
Star Bulletin & Advertisor, H0969
Stark, Freya, F0987–91
Stark, Lewis, F0992
Stars & Stripes, H0882
'Stars on Location', H0699
'A Start in Freedom', F0354
The State Columbus, H1090
State Times, H0985
Statesville Record, H0999
Statist, G1254
Stedell, Jonathan, H0748
Steed, Wickham Henry, F0993
'Steel Chariots in the Desert', E114, H0382
Stein & Day (pub), E398a, F0003, F0406, F0542
Steiner, George, D0026, G1130
Steiner, Morris Jacob, F0994
Stendhal, E143–4a
Stent, F.W., G0471
Stéphane, Roger, A250, E171–E5, E189,
   G0610–G11, G0618, G0629, G0938, G1237–9,
   G1248–9, G1252, G1261, G1277, H0492, H0583,
   H0585–6, H0783–91, H0794–7
'Stéphane en est resté roi', H0791
Stephens, Lincoln, G0182
Stephens, Robert, G1689
'The Steps of the Master are Hard to Find', H0764
'Sterbensmüde vom Freien Willen T.E. Lawrence
   – ein Leben ohne Auftrag', G0747
Steuben, Fritz, E056
Stevenson, Frances, F0995
Stewart, Desmond, E367–71, F0996–7, G1581,
   G1586–7, G1589, G1593–4, G1597–600,
   H1214–5, H1218, H1223, H1227, H1293
Stewart, Phillip, G1112
'Still Searching', H0850
Stimmen die Zeit, G0464, G0502
Stinehour Press (pub), F0294
Stirling, Walter Francis, F0998, G0205, H0228,
   H0478
Stitt, George, F0999
Stoch (pub), F0956
Stock, Noel, F1000
Stockton Record, H1065
Stoddard, Lothrop, F1001
Stöger, August K., E366
Stokes, Frederick A. (pub), E050–53
Stokes, Wallace, H0478
Stone, Wilfred, F1002
Storia Illustrata, G1166
'Storm Centers of the Near East', F0443
'The Storm Over Lawrence', G0729
Storr, Anthony G1557, H1199

Storrs, Sir Ronald, E101, E141, F1003–6, G0455,
   G0499, G0539, G0549, G0588, G0622, G0631,
   G0707, G0803, H0242, H0313, H0479
'Storrs and Lawrence', H0313
'The Story of Israel', F0636
'The Story of Plymouth', F1091
'The Story of the Arab Legion', F0409
'Story Telling and Myth Making', F0677
'Strains and Stresses in the Middle East', G0590
Strand Magazine, G0017
'The Strange Character, Colonel Lawrence', F0277
'Strange Encounter', G1645
'The Strange Relationship Between Thomas
   Hardy and Thomas Lawrence', G1442
'The Strange Self-Told Tales of T.E. Lawrence',
   G0491
'Stranger Than Fiction', G1588
'Strangest Adventures of the War', H0214
'Strategist of Desert Dies in Military Hospital',
   H0243
'Strategy', F0651
'Strategy and Tactics', G1426
Straus, Ralph H0029, H0045
Street Lives ,G1538
Stricker, Perry (pub), E078
'Stripped', G1543
'A Stripped Lawrence', H1156
Strong, L.A.G., F1006
'The Struggle For Arab Independence', F1185
'Struggle, 1914–1920', F1178
Stuart, Brian, H0478
'Studies and Further Studies in a Dying Cùlture',
   F0200
'Studies in a Dying Culture', F0199, F0201
Studies in American Fiction, G1491
Studies In the Twentieth Century, G1496
Studio, G0578
'Sturly', D0008
Stuttgarter Zeitung, H0453, H0915, H1236
'A Subaltern in Macedonia and Judea', F0978
'Sublimated Aladdin', F0111
Subscriber's Edition, A035–40
'The Subscriber's Seven Pillars of Wisdom: The
   Visual Aspect', E396
Sudamericana (pub), E200
Süddeutsche Zeitung, H0947
Sueffert, George, G0630
'Suez', F1039
'Suez Story', F0669
'Suez, The Twice Fought War', F0671
'Suez To Singapore', F0156
Sugarman, Sidney, G1356, G1441, G1475
'Suitors and Suppliants', F1025
'Suleiman Mousa T.E. Lawrence: An Arab View',
   G1315
Sullivan, Anthony T., G1351
Sulpher Springs News Telegram, H0984
'Sultan in Oman', F0764
Sulzberger, C.L., F1007
'A Summary of the Strategy and Tactics of the
   Egypt and Palestine Campaign With Details of
   the 1917–1918 Operations Illustrating the
   Principles of War', F0582
'The Summer of the Hero', G1421
Summers, Claude, F1008
'Summer's Lease', F0908–9
Sun, H0746–7, H0764, H0818, H0831, H0840
'The Sun Never Sets', F0777

'The Sunday Gentlemen', F1090
Sunday Chronicle, C0017, H0026, H0211–12, H0460, H0624, H0810, H0820
Sunday Dispatch, H0309, H0411
Sunday Express, H0164, H0210, H0694, H0777
Sunday Graphic and Sunday News, H0327
Sunday Mercury, H0616
Sunday News, H0621
Sunday Oklahoma, H1190
Sunday Pictorial, H0091
Sunday Record, H0977
Sunday Star, H1078
Sunday Telegraph, H0651, H0673, H0817, H1200, H1205
Sunday Times, C0008, C0013, C0023, E302–3, H0029, H0039–40, H0048, H0052–3, H0109, H0147, H0321, H0371, H0400, H0425, H0437, H0454–5, H0458, H0470, H0479, H0622, H0699, H0848, H0851, H0853–5, H0857–8, H0860, H0863, H0879, H0883, H0889, H0906, H0933, H1166–7, H1192, H1199, H1213, H1222, H1243–4, H1250, H1293, H1294
Sunday Times Magazine, G1289
'Sunny Intervals', F1118
'Super Trivia Encyclopedia', F1173
'Supplementary List of Lantern Slides', F0792
'The Suppressed Introductory Chapter', A262
Sur (periodical), B0038, B0042–3, G0573, G0775, G0800–805, G1102, G1134, G1286
Sur (pub), A066, A179–80, A205, E148–50, F0807
Surfin, M., G1223
'Surgeons Struggle to Save Lawrence', H0188
'The Surrender of Medina', G1568
Survey, G0122
Sutherland, L.W., F1009
Swaffer, Hannen, G0208
'Swifter then Eagles', F0315
Sydney Morning Herald, H0859
Sykes, Christopher, E193, E197, F1010–16, G1010, G1545, H1208
Sykes, Frederick, F1017
Sykes, Mark, F0635
Sykes, Sir Percy, F1018
Sylvestre, Guy, F1019
'Sylvia Beach and the Lost Generation', F0346
Symes, Sir Stewart, F1020
Symons, Julian, G1289, H0827, H1222
'Symons and Lawrence', G1293
Synergetic Press, F0338
Synthèses, G0586, G0799
Syria, F0336, G0014
'The Syrian Desert', F0424
'Syrian Harvest', F0518
'The Syrian Question', C0005
'Le Syrie et les droits du Hejaz', H0010

T., E.E. (Miss), Hardy's Parlour Maid, F0296
T., M.E., G0312
T., W., G1400
Tabachnick, Stephen E., E325, E328, E341, E376, E396, F1021, G1461, G1496, G1526, G1559, G1656, G1660, G1664
La Table Ronde, E189, G0641, G0683, G0820–21
The Tablet, G0724, G0934, G1131
Der Tagesspiegel, G0702, H0452
'Taking Time Off To Visit The Country Cottage of Lawrence of Arabia', G1279
Talbot, David, H1204

Talbot, Serge, G0925
'The Tale Bearers', F0873–4
'Tale of An Old Soldier', F0241
'Tale of Lawrence Amuses Commons', H0093
'Tales From Arabian Nights', H1250
'Tales of Lawrence of Arabia', G0205
Talese, Gay F1022, G1124
'Talks Today on Lawrence's Railway', H0806
'Tallulah, Darling', F0143
'Le Talon d'Achille Essais', F0986
Tammsaars, A.H., A083
'The Tanks', F0652
Tantivy Press (pub), F0502
Taplinger (pub), F0252, F0855, F1053
Targ, William, F1023
Taraud, Jean, G0524
Tarikh Alourdon Fi Alkarn Al Fishrin, F0019
'Tarka the Otter', A229, F1137
Tarouth, Ahmad, H0768
Die Tat. G0428
Tatler, G0963
Tauber, Herbert, G0759
Tauchnitz, B. (pub), F1016
Tavernier, René, H0515
Taylor, A.J.P., F1024
Taylor, Alan, G1182
Taylor, Alfred, H0428
Taylor, Doris N., H1190
Taylor, John Russell, F1025–6
Taylor, Lydia, G1182
Taylor, Thomas (pub), F0958
'T.E.', G0274, G0305, G0514, H0215
'T.E. – A Mere Myth', H1201
'T.E. , as Critic and Friend', G0380
'"T.E." By a Bookseller', G0561
'"T.E." By a Bookseller and News From Way Coppice', G0560
'T.E.L.', G0375
'T.E.L. Find', G1281
'T.E. Héros ou Imposteur?', H0503
'T.E. on Film', G1584
'T.E. Lawrence', A250, D0005, E064, E071–2, E079–82, E094–5, E124–7, E186, E205–6, E218, E356–7, E360, E367–71, E374, E376, E393, E398a, E400, F0133, F0290–91, F0306, F0334, F0358–60, F0600, F0873–4, F1006, F1106, F1115, G0163, G0212, G0226, G0269, G0275, G0332, G0335, G0359, G0367, G0381, G0383, G0397–8, G0484, G0511, G0529, G0613, G0758, G0805, G0834, G0938, G1171, G1244, G1424, G1501, G1508, G1515, G1581, G1586–7, G1589, G1593–4, G1597–1600, H0232, H0249, H0362, H0366, H0371, H0583, H0585–6, H0827, H0910, H1098, H1214–5, H1218, H1223, H1227
'T.E. Lawrence A Bibliographical Note', E086
'T.E. Lawrence, a Bibliography', E119–21, E338, G0495, G1454, G1500, G1604, H0396
'T.E. Lawrence, a Classic Case of Masochism', H0857
'T.E. Lawrence: A Hero More Complex Than Most', H1114
'T.E. Lawrence: A Legend Built on Exaggeration', H1220
'T.E. Lawrence: A Memory of the Hedjaz 1918', H0551
'T.E. Lawrence a New Myth', H1294
'T.E. Lawrence – A Pragmatic Study', G1276
'T.E. Lawrence, A Reader's Guide', E331–E333

'T.E. Lawrence: A Remoulding of the Legend', G1567

'T.E. Lawrence, A Study In Heroism', F0199–F0201

'T.E. Lawrence A Study of Heroism and Conflict', G1345

'T.E. Lawrence Agent of British Imperialism', H0948

'T.E. Lawrence, Aldington and the Truth', E209–E210, G0760

'T.E. Lawrence: an appreciation of his military leadership', E342

'T.E. Lawrence, an Arab View', E256–8, G1043, G1264, G1266–7, G1270, G1282, G1290, G1297–8, G1309, G1315, G1485–6, G1689, H0814–8, H0826, H0829

'T.E. Lawrence: An Effigy in Wareham Church, Dorset', G0544

'T.E. Lawrence and Anglo-American Diplomacy, 1914–1922', E186a

'T.E. Lawrence and Arab Nationalism', F0596

'T.E. Lawrence & Co. Slept Here', H1239

'T.E. Lawrence and Dollars and Sense', G0481

'T.E. Lawrence and Fine Printing', E388, G1633

'T.E. Lawrence and France: Friends or Foes?', E396

'T.E. Lawrence and His Arab Contemporaries', F0751a

'T.E. Lawrence and His Brothers', G0665

'T.E. Lawrence and His Critics', F0846

'T.E. Lawrence and His Letters', G0486

'T.E. Lawrence and Liddell Hart', G1664

'T.E. Lawrence and Lord Alfred Douglas', G0942

'T.E. Lawrence and Louis Massignon', G1652

'T.E. Lawrence and Moby Dick', G1526

'T.E. Lawrence and the British Museum', G1364

'T.E. Lawrence and the Confessional Tradition', G1548

'T.E. Lawrence and the Heroic Narrative Mode', E341

'T.E. Lawrence and "The Mint"', G1471

'T.E. Lawrence and the Printing of Seven Pillars of Wisdom', G1666

'T.E. Lawrence and the Riddle of S.A.', G1116

'T.E. Lawrence and the Seizin Press', G1468

'T.E. Lawrence and the Streets in the Tropics', G0358

'T.E. Lawrence and the Uses of Psychology in Biography of Figures', F0155

'T.E. Lawrence – Another Point of View', G0807

'T.E. Lawrence as a Writer', G1023

'T.E. Lawrence as I Knew Him', G0918

'T.E. Lawrence at Oxford', G0918

'T.E. Lawrence av Arabien', A236

'T.E. Lawrence Book Designer', E403

'T.E. Lawrence Book Is Missing', H0847

'T.E. Lawrence Book is Taken to Task', H0911

'T.E. Lawrence Books from the London Reference Collection of J.M. Wilson', G1684

'T.E. Lawrence By His Friends', E072, E107–12, E178, E226, G0400, G0422, G0432, G0434–6, G0439–40, G0444, G0447, G0450–51, G0453, G0455, G0890, H0381–2, H0385–7

'T.E. Lawrence by His Friends, edited by A.W. Lawrence', F0554

'T.E. Lawrence Collection at the University of Texas', G1021

'T.E. Lawrence: Contrast and Conflict', G0448

'T.E. Lawrence dans son pays', H0485

'T.E. Lawrence d'après sa correspondance', G0528

'T.E. Lawrence der Zweigeschtige', G0659

'T.E. Lawrence: Die Sieben Säulen der Weisheit' H0397

'T.E. Lawrence, 1888–', F0247

'T.E. Lawrence (1888–1935)', F0729, F1027

'T.E. Lawrence en guerre', G0589

'T.E. Lawrence: En Kritiserad Hjälte', G0688

'T.E. Lawrence en Proie aux Images', H0691

'T.E. Lawrence: Enigma Exposed', H0940

'T.E. Lawrence et le Métier d'Artiste', H0580

'T.E. Lawrence et Ses Deux Légendes', G0818

'T.E. Lawrence Evidence on Blackburn Iris Flying Boat Disaster', H0126

'T.E. Lawrence Exhibit at Whittier', H0761

'T.E. Lawrence Exhibit Here', H1142

'T.E. Lawrence – Fact and Legend', G0320

'T.E. Lawrence, Feisal, and Weizman', G1338, G1341

'T.E. Lawrence/Fifty Letters', E265, G1073

'T.E. Lawrence Funeral', H0352

'T.E. Lawrence héritier de Nietzsche', F1086, H0426

'T.E. Lawrence: Hero', G1687

'T.E. Lawrence, Héros modeste et orgueilleux', G0586

'T.E. Lawrence – Hinn Ókrýndi Konungur Arabíu', G0556

'The T.E. Lawrence His Family Knew', G0675

'T.E. Lawrence Impaled', G0105

'T.E. Lawrence Imperialist und Charackter', G0361

'T.E. Lawrence, imposteur ou mystificateur?', H0442

'T.E. Lawrence in a New Role', G0184, H0108

'T.E. Lawrence in Amman 1921', G1453

'"T.E. Lawrence" in Arabia and After', E058–62, E064–6, G0217–21, G0224–5, G0227–8, G0231–6, G0238–41, G0247, G0372, G0490, H0147, H0149

'T.E. Lawrence in Buchan: A Little Known Episode', G0654

'T.E. Lawrence in His Letters', H0394

'T.E. Lawrence in Life and Death', G0534

'T.E. Lawrence in Poetry', G0445

'T.E. Lawrence in Retreat', G0574

'T.E. Lawrence: Intelligence Officer', E396

'T.E. Lawrence, La France et Les Français', E377–E378

'T.E. Lawrence: La Matrice', G0751

'T.E. Lawrence Le Matricé', G0796

'T.E. Lawrence, le plus grand homme de notre temps', H0577

'T.E. Lawrence Leaves Book to Publish', H0155

'T.E. Lawrence – Legende und Wirklichkeit', G0858

'T.E. Lawrence Lettres', G0570, G0610

'T.E. Lawrence, l'Homme qui Réinventa le Guérilla', H0703

'T.E. Lawrence Man or Myth', G0839

'T.E. Lawrence Memorial Medal', G0362

'T.E. Lawrence mis à nu (sur la Matrice)', H1240

'T.E. Lawrence Mr. Aldington's Charges', H0458

'T.E. Lawrence: New Legends For Old', G0734

'T.E. Lawrence, 1919. Pencil on Paper', F0299

'T.E. Lawrence Notes Bring $500 in Auction', H0350, H0383

'T.E. Lawrence: Notes For Collectors', G1489

'T.E. Lawrence oder die Schrecken der Freiheit', G0879

'T.E. Lawrence of Arabia', G0568
'T.E. Lawrence of Arabia. A Collector's Booklist', E330
'T.E. Lawrence on Elgar', H0406
'T.E. Lawrence on Himself', G0482
'T.E. Lawrence on Self', H0400
'T.E. Lawrence ou l'Honneur de Soi', G1503
'The T.E. Lawrence Poems', E392, H1245
'T.E. Lawrence: Portrait of an Englishman', G0563
'The T.E. Lawrence Puzzle', E396, G1657, G1661, G1664
'T.E. Lawrence Reappears', H0111
'The T.E. Lawrence Revival in English Studies', G1559
'The T.E. Lawrence River Crew', E170
'T.E. Lawrence Schicksal und Gestalt', E167
'The T.E. Lawrence Silver Cup', E168
T.E. Lawrence Society, Newsletter, G1665
'T.E. Lawrence – Some New Light on the Face of a Hero', H0633
'T.E. Lawrence, Some Trivial Memories', G0580
'T.E. Lawrence: Strategist', E396
T.E. Lawrence Studies, E362–4, G1528, G1566
T.E. Lawrence Studies Newsletter, G1631
'T.E. Lawrence: Technical Writer', E396
'T.E. Lawrence: The End of the Legend', G1403
'T.E. Lawrence: The Inner Being', H1229
'T.E. Lawrence, the Legend and the Man', G0684
'T.E. Lawrence – The Man', G0549
'T.E. Lawrence: The Mechanical Monk', E396
'T.E. Lawrence, The Mint ein Psycholisches Problem', G0855
'T.E. Lawrence: The Problem of Heroism', F0538, G1018
'T.E. Lawrence: The Problem of Interpretation', G0930
'T.E. Lawrence: Through His Own Eyes and Another's', G0366
'T.E. Lawrence to His Biographer, Liddell Hart', A211, A215–6, G0496, G0506–10, G0514, H0398, H0401
'T.E. Lawrence to His Biographer, Robert Graves', A210, A214, A216, C0018, G0496, G0506–10, G0514, H0398, H0401
'T.E. Lawrence to His Biographers Robert Graves and Liddell Hart', A212–3, A217–8, G1095, G1126, G1129–30, G1146, G1171, H0673, H0715
'T.E. Lawrence to His Friends', C0022, H0391
'T.E. Lawrence: Torn Between Ideals and Sordid Reality', G1592
'T.E. Lawrence, un Tricheur qui a lu l'Ecclésiaste', H0581
'T.E. Lawrence und der arabische Aufstand 1916/18', E365, G1595, G1612
'T.E. Lawrence und die Ängst', G0639
'T.E. Lawrence Unreal Service', H0281
'T.E. Lawrence: Valet de Chambre de l'Idéal', G0607
'T.E. Lawrence's Amazing Career', H0244
'T.E. Lawrence's Arabic', H0836
'T.E. Lawrence's breve', H0750
'T.E. Lawrence's Death', H0280
'T.E. Lawrence's Emotional Tussle', H1000
'T.E. Lawrence's Expeditions', G0400
'T.E. Lawrence's Perilous Parodies', G1456
'T.E. Lawrence's Private Anthology', G1457
'T.E. Lawrence's Seven Pillars of Wisdom', G1443

'T.E. Lawrence's Seven Pillars of Wisdom As a Work of Art', E328
'T.E. Lawrence's Struggles Probed', H0992
'T.E. Lawrence's Tale of Arabia', H0135
'T.E. Shaw', F0392
'T.E. Shaw, the Odyssey of Homer', G0199
'A Teacher's Guide to Lawrence of Arabia' (film), E270
'Team Justifies Book on Lawrence', H1043
'Technique of Automatic Writing', G1354
Tehran Journal, H0768
Teitinen, Hikki, A113
Telegram, H0664–5
Telerama, H1162–3, H1241, H1246
Télé-Sept Jours, H1177, H1226, H1230, H1242
Television and Film Annual, G1053
'Tell Me the Truth About Lawrence', H0733
'Un Témoin dépose la vérité Sur Lawrence d'Arabie', G1087
Temple, Ruth Z., F1027
Temple University Press, F0620
Templeton, Colin, H0283
Templewood, Samuel J.G. Hoare, 1st Viscount, F1028
'Tempestuous Journey', F0814
Temps, H0008
Les Temps Modernes, B0044, B0048, G0597, G0618, G0907
'Ten Days Off', F0292
'Ten Poems More', E300
'£10,000 for Lawrence Letters', H1158
'£10,000 for Letter', H1160
'£10,000 for Service Papers of Lawrence', H1161
Tennessee Studies in Literature, G1378
'Tents and Towers of Arabia', F0953
'Terence Rattigan', F0189
'Terence Rattigan Talks to John Simon', G0999
'La Terrible Notte della Tortuna', H1272
Teschner, Gerhard, H0915
'Testimonials', G1015
'Testimonios', F0807
Texas Quarterly, G1020–23, G1134, G1456, G1483, G1509
Texte und Zeichen, G0697
'Les Textes Essentiels de T.E. Lawrence', A242, G1216, G1221, G1227, G1231, G1236, G1253, H0751–5, H0757, H0759, H0772, H1246
Thames & Hudson (pub), E359
Tharaud, Jérome, F1031, G0524
'That Noble Cabinet', F0742
Thatcher, David, F1032
'"That's The Way It Was" says a man who knows', H0665
Theatre Arts, G0952, G0972, G0997, G0999, G1093
'Theatre Chronicle', G0995
Théâtre de Destin, E189
Theater World, G0942
'Theatre World Annual', F1033
'Theft on MINT', H0849
Then and Now, A162, B0023, D0005
'Theodora Duncan Collection of T.E. Lawrence', E321
'Théorie de la Guérila', B0047
'There Could Have Been Peace', F0594
'There's Little Evidence of Lawrence in Arabia', H1268
'These Men, Thy Friends', F1048

'These Names Make News', H0308
'These Were the Hours', F0246
Thesiger, Wilfred, F1034–7, H1207
Thesing, William, F0157
Theses, E147, E186a, E297, E298a, E320, E326, E328, E339, E240–42, E377, E395
Thespis, G0955
'They Knew Lawrence', G0439
'They Rode Camels Into Battle', H0834
Thibauld, André, E288a
'Thief of Mint From British Museum', G1292
Thies, Henri, E065
'The Third Route', F0938–9
'The Thirteenth Tribe', F0603
'Thirty Books Later They're Still Dealing With Lawrence of Arabia', H1016
'$30,800 First Week for "Arabia" in Tokyo', G1088
'Thirty Years With G.B.S.', F0825–6
'This Expanding War', F0653
'This is a Triumph of Filmcraft', H0664
'This Man Lawrence', G0081
Thobie, J., G1650
Thomas, Bertram, A155–7, B0030, F1038, G0186
Thomas, Hugh, F1039
Thomas, John, E187–8, G1154
Thomas, Lowell, D0027–9, E001–27, F0131, F0140–45, G0011–12, G0017, G0021, G0023–7, G0037, G0040, G0056, G0061, G0065, G0080, G0093, G0098, G0104, G0106, G0108, G0110–12, G0116, G0122, G0124, G0129, G0242, G0287, G0393, G0472, G0733, G1039, G1108, G1170, G1173, G1176, G1305, G1463, G1476, G1547, G1570, G1627, G1642, G1681, H0016, H0055–7, H0419, H0636
Thomas, Ronald Wills (uses pseudonym of James Cadell), E227–9
Thomas, Sidney, H1101
'Thomas Edward Lawrence', E179, E181, E184–5, F0187, F0287, F0679, F0734
'Thomas Edward Lawrence and Classic Statesmanship', E297
'Thomas Edward Lawrence in the City of Artisans', E320
'Thomas Edward Lawrence: the Lessons of Arabia', F0620
'Thomas Hardy, a Biography', F0744
'Thomas Hardy and T.E. Lawrence: Two English Sources for Beppe', G1460
Thomas Hardy Yearbook, F1045a, F1046
'Thomas Hardy's Later Years', F0401
'Thomas Lawrence Incognito', G0037
'Thomas Lawrence, The Man', G0027
'Thomas Lawrence the Soul of the Arabian Revolt', G0059
'Thomas on Thomas', H1278
Thompson, E. Bigelow, G0259
Thompson, Edward, F1047
Thompson, Howard, H0637
Thompson, John, G1566
Thompson, Reginald Campbell, F1050–51
Thompson, Reginald Williams, F1052
Thompson, Sir Robert, F1053
Thompson, V.M., E404
Thompson, Walter, F1054–5
Thomson, John, F0333
Thornton Butterworth (pub), F0212
Thornton, J. & Sons (pub), E117–18
Thorpe, James, F1056

'Thought the Reputation of T.E. Lawrence...', H0905
'Thoughts and Talks, 1935–1937', F1140
Thoulouze, Michel, H1230
Thoumin, Richard, F1057–8
'Three Deserts', F0564–5
'352087 A/c Ross', A166–74, A177–82, A185
'3 Plotters Confess at Moscow Trial', H0115
'338171 T.E.', E148–56, G0573, G0581, G1122–3, G1128, G1139, G1146, G1150
'Three Persons', E047–8, G0159–62, G0164, G0169–70, G0477–8, H0100–101
'Three Shaw-Centered Books', G1114
'3 T.E. Lawrence Letters Come to Light', H0704
'Threnos for T.E. Lawrence', G0662
'Through the Fog of War', F0654
'Through Thirty Years', F0993
Thubron, Colin, F1059
Thurtle, Ernest, F1060
Tibawi, A.L., G1338, G1341
Tibble, Anne, F1061
Tidrick, Kathryn, F1062
Tilskueren, G0420, G0490
Tiltman, H. Hessell, F0145–6
Time & Tide, G0624, G0713, G0723, G0866, G1122, G1197, G1392
'Time in the East', F0571
Time-Life (pub), E337, F0996
Time Magazine, G0190, G0330, G0411, G0514, G0523, G0638, G0677, G0718, G0746, G0935, G0961, G0978, G0985, G1028, G1057, G1098, G1143, G1152, G1302, G1321, G1385, G1388, G1422, G1535
The Times, C0002–5, C0009, C0011, F0657, F0686, H0007, H0024–5, H0043, H0054, H0176–7, H0239–41, H0251, H0253, H0279, H0297, H0299, H0301, H0305, H0325, H0330, H0356, H0359–61, H0364, H0369–70, H0372, H0391, H0394, H0399, H0427, H0436, H0465, H0469, H0476, H0623, H0639, H0652, H0655, H0660, H0663, H0704, H0710, H0735, H0745, H0816, H0827–8, H0835–6, H0846, H0852, H0862, H0866, H0872–3, H0877, H0888, H0910, H0912–3, H1153, H1155, H1161, H1164, H1176, H1195, H1216, H1237, H1239, H1248–9
'The Times Diary Lost Lawrence', H1164
Times Herald Record, H0946
Times Literary Supplement, G0068, G0116, G0121, G0161, G0187, G0218, G0302, G0309–10, G0313, G0359, G0377, G0389–90, G0400, G0405, G0425, G0432, G0476, G0486, G0495, G0519, G0533, G0540, G0574, G0635–6, G0674, G0709, G0720, G0863, G0915, G0946, G0969, G0973, G1009, G1073, G1123, G1138, G1264, G1318, G1343, G1359, G1364, G1438, G1456, G1470, G1477, G1510, G1555–6, G1600, G1635, G1651
Times of Brazil, H0483
The Times Record, H1054
Times Union, H0968
'Time's Winged Chariot', F1060
'Tinned Soldier', F0269
TLS, see Times Literary Supplement
Tipp, Jack, H0771
'To Big For Wealth and Glory Lawrence the Soldier Dies to Live Forever', H0236
'To Film "Lawrence of Arabia"', H0096
'To Gain the Rear', G1142
'To Homer Through Pope', F0709

'To Print Parts of Lawrence Book', H0037
'To S.A.', A251, B0043
'To T.E. Lawrence', G0438
'To tell you in the future I shall write very few letters', A161
'To the Dear Memory of T.E. Lawrence', E230
Tod, M.N., A004–7
Toldenado, André D., H0524
Tomlinson, H.M., A162
'Ton-up Pilgrims', H0810
'Too True to Be Good, Village Wooing, & On the Rocks', F0960–61, H0675
Toronto Star, H1188, H1215, H1234, H1245
Toronto Telegram, H0238, H0267, H0878, H1292
'Torture', D0016
'Tortured Hero', G0978
Toucan Press (pub), F0296, F1045a, F1046
'Tour of Duty', F1020
Toureil, Jacqueline, H0648
Town and Country, G0352
Townshend, Edmund, H0806
Toy, Barbara, F1063
Toynbee, Arnold, E327, F1064, G0717
'Tracking the Train Lawrence Wrecked', H0745
'The Tragedy of Lawrence', G0329
Trager, James, F1065
'The Tragic and Epic in T.E. Lawrence', G1200
'Trial & Error', F1111–12
'Train Blown off the Rails for the Film Lawrence of Arabia', G1002
'The Train Lawrence Wrecked', H0746
'Transaction Books (pub), F0248
Transition (Paris), G0594
'Translator's Note', D0026
Travel, G1025
Travel Book Co, F0700
'Travellers in Ancient Lands', F1077
'Travels in Arabia Deserta', G0402, H0793
Traver, Linda J., G1606
Treasure (Australia), G1414
'Treasures of Time', F0264
Tredell, Nicolas, F1066
Trego, Karen, G1531
'Trelawny', F0043
'Trenchard', F0134–5
Trenton Review, G1241
Trewin, J.C., G0936
Trevelyan, Raleigh, A104
Trevor-Roper, Hugh (Lord Dacre), F1067, G1594
Triad Films, E397
La Tribune de Genève, H0560, H0570, H0634
La Tribune de Lausanne, H0754, H0788
La Tribune Sioniste de France, H0564
'Tribute to Lawrence Part I: In War', G0254; 'Part II: In Peace', G0255
'Triumphant Pilgrimage', F0927–8
'Trois Aventures', G0774
'The Trojan Horse Enters Damascus', G0024
'El Troquel', A179–80
'"El Troquel" de T.E. Lawrence', G0802
'Trouble in Arabia', G0141, H0015
Troy News, H1118
'True Adventures of Spies', F0605
'The True Book About Lawrence of Arabia', E187–8
'The True Story of Lawrence of Arabia', E188
Trust Books (pub), E233
Truth, G0708, G0727, G0735

'The Truth About T.E. Lawrence', G0110
'The Truth About the Peace Treaties', F0666
Tschiffely, Aime Felix, F1068
Tsunda, Waka, H0982, H0989–92, H1002, H1004–5, H1007–8, H1010–11, H1015, H1017, H1019–21, H1023, H1027, H1029–33, H1037, H1041, H1043, H1045–6, H1048, H1050–51, H1053–6, H1058, H1062, H1064, H1069, H1072, H1074, H1082–3, H1089, H1092–3, H1096, H1099, H1103, H1108–9, H1111–12, H1122, H1124, H1129–31, H1133, H1137, H1277, H1279
Tuck (pub), F1087
Tucker, Betty, G1274
Tucker, Martha, G0567, H0414
Tucker, Martin, F1027
Tucson Star-Citizen, H1112
Tudor, Herald, H0641
Tudor (pub), F0912
Tunbridge, P., G1647
Tuohy, Frank, F1069
'Turbulent Years', F0703
Türk Düşmani, E176
'Turkey', F0632
'Turkey Astir at News Lawrence is in Region', H0107
'Turkey Surrenders Absolutely', H0002
'Turkish Press Links Lawrence in Revolt', H0123
'Turkophil', G0157
Turner, W.J., G0571
TV Guide, G1176–G1177, G1271, G1311, G1463, G1547
TV Times, G0941
Twayne Publishers, E376, F0680, F1021
Tweedsmuir, Lady (Susan Buchan), F1071
'20e anniversaire: 1888–1935 T.E. Lawrence', H0507
Twentieth Century, G0734
'Twentieth Century Authors', F0613
'Twentieth Century Culture', F0175
'Twentieth Century English Literature', F1092
'20th Century Journal', F0969
'Twenty-Five Thousand Sunsets', F1125
'Twenty-Four Portraits', F0915–16
'20,863 Books Signed by Lawrence', H1231
'Twilight of the Gods', A090–93
'Twin Rivers', F0665
Twitchell, Karl Saben, F1073
'Two and a Half Pillars of Wisdom', G1045
Two "Arabian" Romantics Charles Doughty and T.E. Lawrence', G1461
'Two Arabic Folk Tales', A196
Two Calcolviphicians, B0003
'Two Cheers For Democracy', F0364–6
'Two Flamboyant Fathers', F0265
'Two Hundred Class Royal Air Force Seaplane Tender', A158
'Two Men Who Have a Century of Service', H0728
'Two Newsmen Probe Secrets of Lawrence of Arabia's Life', H1071
'Two Newsmen Write Book About Lawrence of Arabia', H1046
'The Two Sides of "Lawrence of Arabia": Aubrey and Meek', G1167
'Two Studies in Destiny', G1193
'Two Styles Combined', H0650
'Two Translations', G0207
'Two Unpublished Letters to Ezra Pound', B0046
'The Two Veils of T.E. Lawrence', G1496

Two Worlds, G1205
Tynan, Kenneth, H1289
'Typographical Partnership', F0904

Uellenberg, Gisela, G0640
'En Uhaandterlig Krystal', G0420
'Ulysses', G0268
'Un saint en salopette', F0313
Unan, Mustafa (pub), E291
'Den "Unbekante" Lawrence von Arabiens',
  G1371
Uncorrected Proofs, A147, A167, A171, A176,
  A220, A237, A256, E029, E096, E115, E145, E151,
  E191, E250, E277, E301, E335, E348
'"Uncrowned King" as Private Soldier', H0061
'The Uncrowned King of Arabia', G0041
'The Uncrowned King of Arabia, Colonel T.E.
  Lawrence', G0017
'"Uncrowned King's" Simple Burial', H0255
'Une Campagne au Hedjaz', G0007
'Une énigme qui bouleverse l'Angleterre Lawrence
  héros de légende ou imposteur?', G0739
'Une Figure de Grand Aventurier', H0535
'Unearthing Greatest Hittite Inscription World
  Has Seen for Three Thousand Years', H0002
'Uneasy Lies the Head', F0543
'Unexpected', F0159
'The Unforgettable Winston Churchill', F0657
Ungar (pub), F0980, F1008, F1027
'Der ungekrönte König von Arabien', G0128
'Unguarded Secret', G1469
Unicorn Press, F0138-9
'El Unicornio enuna Cabelleriza', F0807
'A Uniform Series of Great and Memorable
  Books', E161
Union Action, G0880
Union Generale d'Editions, F0712
United Empire, G0449
United Services Institution Journal, G1263
United States Naval Institute Proceedings, G1617
United States of India Journal, G1288
'United States Policy and the Partition of Turkey
  1914-1924', F0317
Universitaires (pub), F1086
Université de Lille (pub), E377
University Microfilm, F0423
University of California (pub), F0178, F0219,
  F0529, F1098
University of California, Los Angeles, A251
University of Centerburg (pub), F0242
University of Chicago (pub), F0214
University of Connecticut (pub), E328
University of Georgia (pub), E396, F0482
University of Illinois, E326
University of London (pub), F0788
University of Michigan (pub), F1180
University of Minnesota (pub), F0068
University of Mississippi Press, F0288
University of Pennsylvania, F0272
University of Southern California, E147
University of Texas. Humanities Research Center,
  E265, F0625, F1073a-74, G1073
University of Toronto (pub), F0287, F0967
University of Virginia, F0209
University Press of Arabia (pub), F0597
'The Unknown Lawrence', G1401
'Unmasking a False Hero', G0947

'An Unpublished Letter of Lawrence of Arabia',
  B0051
'The Unravelling of Ross', H1289
'An Unsolicited Tribute', G0755
'Unter Dem Prägestock', A185
'The Unveiling of Arabia', F0589
'An Unwanted Cycle', H0921
'Uppresinin Í Eydimörkinni', A122
'Uppror i Öknen', A138
Urbina, Pedro A., E284
Uris, Leon, F1075
Ursini, David, F0972
'A U.S. Lawrence of Arabia', H0552
'L'Usage de la Lecture', F0856
Ustanak U Pustinji, A089
'Utöpische und Apokalyptische Elemente der
  Englische Gegenwart', G0464

Vaczek, Louis, F1077
Valensin, G., G1417
Valeurs, B0041, G0581
Vallentine, Mitchell (pub), E160
Van Doren, Carl, F1078
Van Doren, Charles, D0030
Van Doren, Mark, G0354
Van Gelder, G.J.H., G1375
Van Loon, Hendrick Willem, F1079
Van Nostrand (pub), F0507
Van Paassen, Pierre, F1080-81
Van Sinderen, F1082
Van Vyve, Henry, G0586
Van Wert Times Bulletin, H1133
Vanderbilt University, E186a
'The Vanished Galahads', G0677
Vanguard (pub), F1149
'Vanity Fair', F0026
Vansittart, Robert Gilbert, baron, F1083, H0459
Varanini, Varo, G0296
Vaughan, Agnes Carr, F1084
'Veil is Lifted by Mystery Officer', G1032
Venaissin, G., H0498
'Verdict on Schweitzer', F0684
'La Véritable Histoire de Lawrence d'Arabia',
  G1334, H0672
'Le Véritable Lawrence', G0806
Vers L'Avenir, H0569
'Die Versuchung der Reinheit Über T.E.
  Lawrence', G0640
'The Very Image', G0483
'Very Superior', G1136
Verper, Will, G0128
'V'Hotsa'at Sheba', E329
Vickery, C.E., G0034
'A Victim of the Dream', H1198
'Victor Hugo, Julius Caesar, Stendhal, T.E.
  Lawrence, Virgil, Winston Churchill', D0019
Victoria Advocate, H0952
Victoria and Albert Museum (pub), F0817
'Victoria Ocampo The Hero's Inner Life Was a
  Nightmare', G1139
'La Vida Secreta de Lawrence de Arabia', E318
'La Vida y el Mito de T.E. Lawrence', G1203
'La Vie Aventureuse de Colonel Lawrence', G025
'La Vie des Métiers "Médicine"', G0938
'La Vie du Colonel Lawrence', E065
'Les Vies Secrètes de Lawrence d'Arabie', E312
View Points, G1400
Viewpoints, G1182, G1211, G1215, G1228

La Vigie, H0506
Viking (pub), A241, E115-6, F0011-12, F0026, F0091, F0137, F0527, F0715, F0724, F0906, F0941
Vilarroya, E281
'Village Funeral for Lawrence of Arabia', H0230
Villard, Oswald G., G0288
Vincennes Sun Commercial, H1047
Vinneuil, François, G1103
Vintage Books (pub), F0873
The Vintage M/C Club, G1669
Virginia Kirkus, G0685, G0791, G0953, G0998, G1380, G1522
Virginia Quarterly Review, G0522, G0580, G1114, G1298, G1560, G1576
'Viscount Halifax', F0184
'Visdommens Syu Søjler', A068-9, A084
'Vishetens Sju Pelare', A088
Vísir Sunnu-Dagsblad, G0556
'Visitors' Guide to the County of Dorset', F0262
'La Vite Segrete di Lawrence D'Arabia', E315
'Des Vivants et des Morts, Témoignages, 1948-1953', F1086
'Vive Che!', F0890
'Vocation in the Desert Lawrence of Arabia and Charles de Foucauld', G1446
Vocke, Harald, H0927, H1238
Le Voix du Nord, H0631, H1178
Vogue, G1033, G1300
Volgar, Lewis, G0681
Volk im Werden, G0463
de Volkskraat, H1261
Volpe (pub), E252
'Vom Unbekanten Colonel Lawrence', G0251
von Salomon, Ernest, E171-4
Voss, Wm. Erik, E402
Vosstanie v pustyne, A135
'En Vovehals', E027
'Voyage to a Beginning', F1145
The Voyages of Ulysses', A252-3
Vredenburg, E., F1087
Vroman, A.C., A023
Vulliamy, C.E., F1088

W., A.T.P., G0284
W., D., G0934
W., E.L., G0284
W., N.F., G1278
W Movies, G1570
Wachsmuth, Bruno, G0500-501
Wagner, Mary, H0962-3
'Wahrheit Über Lawrence', H0896
Wain, Noel, H0805
Wake Forest College Press, F0353
Wales, G0918
Walker, David, G1243
Walker, Sir Emery, A141, A145, F0904
Walker, Gil, E252-3
Walker (pub), F0516
Wall Street Journal, H1210
Wallace, Irving, F1089-90
Walling, R.A.J., F1091
Wallrof, Karlheinz, G0659
Walpole, Sir Hugh, A162, E401, F0485, G0534
Walsh, John, G1667
Walsh, Moira, G1059
'A Wanderer After Sensations', G1560
'Wanderings in the Middle East', F0975
Wagenheim, Sophie Freifrau von, G0416

'The Wanton Chase' F0879
'War in the Desert', E091-2, F0007, F0410-11, G0183, G0388, G1031, H0367-8
'War in the Land of Arabian Knights', G0012
'War in the Shadows', F0050
'War Lawrence ein Verater Arabiens?', H0875
'The War Lords', F0194
'War Memories', F0667
'The War of the Departments', C0007
'War Scenes for "Lawrence" Shot by 5 Cameras', H0724
War Stories, G0183
'Wara Moat Lawrence', G1672
Ward, A.C., F1092
Ward, Bernard T., E361, G1517
Ward Lock (pub), F0419
Wareham Borough Council, F1093
'Wareham Purbeck', F1094
Wareham, Purbeck Rural District Council, F1094
Wargrave Press (pub), F1094
Warne, Frederick Co. (pub), E052-3, E057, E088
Warner, M.H.C., F1045a
Warner, Oliver, G0566
Warner, Patricia Nell, G1607
Warner (pub), F0089
'The Warner Bros', F0503
Warren, C.H., G0568
'War's Most Romantic Figure', G0018
'The Wartime Journals of Charles A. Lindbergh', F0660
'Was Lawrence a Great Soldier?', G0414, G0430-31
'Was Lawrence a Red Herring?', H1244
'Was T.E. Lawrence a Fake?', G0767
'Was That All, Then?', G0594
Washburn (pub), F0184
Washington Daily News, H0976
Washington Post, H0967; Book World, G1395
'Wassmuss "The German Lawrence"', F1015-16
'Wassmuss and Lawrence', G0543
'The Waste Land in Seven Pillars of Wisdom', E396
Waterfront, G1656
Waterhouse, Francis A., F1095
Waters, Harold, F1162
Wathis, K.H., F1096
Watson, George, F1097
Watt, Ian, F1098
Waugh, Alec, F1099
Wausau Record-Herald, H1103
'Wavell', F0225-6
Wavell, Archibald P. (Earl), F0220, F1100-108
Wayne, Philip, F1109
Wayne State University Press, F0229, F0618
Waynesville Mountaineer, H1137
'The Way to Win Wars', F0655
'The Way West and the Wilderness', F0158
Weales, Gerald, G1094
'Weasel Words', F0534
'The Weekend Library', D0031
The Weekend Scotsman, H1169
Weeks, Donald, E393
Weeks, Edward, G1396
'Weh dem, der Wüsten birgt', G0692
Weidenfeld (pub), F0923
Weidenfeld & Nicolson (pub), E355-6, F0142, F0207, F0318, F0326, F0949, F1121
Weidmannsche (pub), F0859

Weintraub, Rodelle, A255, E346–7, E396, G1318, G1342, G1397, G1478, G1491, G1525, G1529, G1558, G1561
Weintraub, Stanley, A255, E275–7, E346, E396, F0306, F1110, G0981, G1076, G1078, G1084, G1091, G1094, G1097, G1105, G1109, G1138, G1146, G1148, G1159, G1167, G1180, G1201, G1241, G1280, G1318, G1342, G1394, G1397, G1478, G1491, G1525, G1529, G1558, G1561, G1598, H0668, H0677, H0705, H0707, H0709, H0722
Weisl, W., G1707
Weiss, Leopold ,G0140, H0015
Weiss (pub), F0160
Weizmann, Chaim, F0663, F0111–112, F1120, G1338, H0369
'Weizmann', F0663
Wells, H. G., A162, A229, F1096, F1113
Wells, Sam, G1295
'The Wells of Ibn Sa'ud', F0726
'The Wells Short Stories', B0028
Die Welt, H0920
Welt am Sonntag, G1362
Die Welt der Literatur, G1369
Welt und Wort, G0696
Weltbühne, G1707
Weltsch, R., G0771
'Wer War Oberst Lawrence?', G0501
'Were the Arabs Doublecrossed by Lawrence?', H0872
Werenth, William, H0601
Werner Laurie Ltd. (pub), F0468
Werstein, Irving, F1114
'Wesker's Mint', G1280
'Wessex, Dorset', F0295
West, Anthony, F1115, G0851, G1421
West, Herbert Faulkner, F0116–18
West, Rebecca, G1162
West Coast Review of Books, G1657
West Cumberland Times, H0017
West Palm Beach Post-Times, H1064
Westbane, Jean, G1053
Westbourne, Jean, F0398
Westdeutscher Rundfunk: Begleitheft, G1495
Wester Wemyss, Lady Victoria, F1119–20
Westermann, William, G0033
Westermanns Monatshefte, G0543
Western Gazette, H1264, H1266
Western Morning News, H1152
Western Morning News and Daily Gazette, H0173
'Western Review', G0859
Western Weekly News, H0126
'Westfälische Nachrichten, H0924
Westholm (pub), F1116, F1118
Westminster, Duke of, E114
Westview Press, F0421
Wetsgel, Meyer, F1121
Weybright & Talley, F1110
Wezarat Alalaalam (pub), E225a
'What do the Arabs Think of Lawrence of Arabia', G0647
'What do You Know About This Film?', G1005
'What if Lawrence Hadn't Learned Arabic?', G1135
'What Lawrence Wished for Thomas', G1681
'What Next in Europe?', F1126
'What Really Happened at Paris?', F0530
'What Was Lawrence's Secret?', G0536
'What Was T.E. Lawrence Really Like?', H1275

'What Would Lawrence Think?', H0768
'What's New', G0992
'W.H. Auden', F0191, F0463
'W.H. Auden as a Social Poet', F0172
Wheeler, Sir Charles, F1122, G0363
Wheeler, Keith, G0988
Wheeler, N., G1045
'When Its Time to Say "No More Ruins"', H0819
'When Lawrence Made a Quiet Exit', H1149
'When Lawrence Said "No" to King George', G0125
'When the Shooting Stops .. and the Cutting Begins', F0906
'The Whispering Gallery', F0629
White, T.H., F1123
White, William, G1075
'The White/Garnett Letters', F1123
'The White King of the Arabs', G0098
'The White Knight of the Desert', H1187
'The White Llama', F0384
White Lion Press (pub), F1104
'The White Nile', F0757
Whitelow, Guillermo, E200
Whitman Pub. Co., F0558
Whitmore, Betty, G1279
Whitney, Peter D., H0550
Whitson Pub. Co., F0869
Whitten, Benjamin Jr., A251
'Whittier College Exhibit of Duncan Collection', H0758
'Who Really Killed Lawrence of Arabia?', G1514
'Who Said Heroes Like Lawrence Had Vanished?', H0694
'Who Slapped Lawrence of Arabia?', H0859
'Who Was the Founder of "Greater Arabia"?', G0771
'Why I Debunked the Lawrence Legend', G0711
'Why I Decided to Debunk a Hero', H0483
'Why Lawrence of Arabia Lied', H1028
'Why Mr. O'Toole Is Sleeping on His Face', H0588
'Why Things Go Wrong', F0837
Whybrow, Stanley, F1124
'The Widow of the Jewels', F0190
Wightman, G.B.H., G1293
Wilgey, H. de Winton, H0285
Wilcox, D.A., G1619
Wilcox, Herbert, F1125
Wilde, Oscar, E191–3, E387
'The Wilderness of Zin', A004–8, G0002, G0213, G0374, G0376–7, G0382, G0387, H0364
Wilkins, Sir Hubert, F1044
Wilkinson, Clennell, G0090
Will, A., G0103
'Will "Real" Lawrence Please Stand Up?', H1076
'The Will to Power', H1169
Willert, Arthur, F1126
Williams & Norgate (pub), A220–24
'William Ramsay Knew Lawrence and His Arabia', H1267
'William Rothenstein', F0981
Williams, A., H0456
Williams, Ann, F1127
Williams, Kenneth, G0320, G0491
Williams, Owen Maynard, G0014, G0542, G0582, H0001–2
Williams, O., G0505
Williams, Piers, F0305
Williams, R.P., G0145

JWilliamson, Audrey, F1128
Williamson, E., H0799
Williamson, Henry, A162, A229, E145–6, F0399, F1129–37, G0662, G0665
Wilmington Morning News, H1086
Wilson, Andrew, G1383
Wilson, Sir Arnold Talbot, F1138–40, G0088, H0051–2, H0418
Wilson, Colin, F1141–5
Wilson, Jeremy M., A154, A178, A256–60, E360, G1452, G1459, G1489, G1510, G1666, G1684, H1294
Wilson (pub), F0613
'Wilson, House and the Arabs in 1919', H0418
Winchell, Walter, H0296
Winckler, Paul A., F1146
'Wind in the Sahara', F0114
Winder, Richard Bayley, F1147
Winegarten, Renée, G1403
Winer, Bart Keith, D0003
'Windfall Helped Pair With Lawrence Study', H0891
Wingate, Orde, F1013–14
Wingate, Sir Ronald, F1148, G1276
'The Winged Life', F0923
'Winged Victory', F1181
Wingfield-Stratford, E., G0223
Winkler, Eugen Gottlob, A244, G0378
Winona News, H1063
Winsten, Stephen, F1085, F1149–51, F1153
Winston (pub), F0464
'Winston Churchill', F0609, F1052
'Winston Churchill and the Dardanelles', F0500
'Winston S. Churchill', F0218, F0231, F0237
'Winston S. Churchill: His Complete Speeches', F0217
Winstone, Harry V. F., F1154–7, H1244, H1249
'A Winter Bouquet', F1071
The Winter Owl, B0017
Winters, Oscar, G1480
Winterton, Earl, F1158–60, H0478, H0571
Wintle, Justin, F1160a, F1161
Wisberg, Aubrey, F1162
Wisconsin Library Bulletin, G0111, G0442
Wisconsin News, H0202
Wisconsin State Journal, H0168, H0296
Wiseman, Thomas, F1163
'Wit and the Wages of Wisdom', G1084
Witchita Falls Times, H1077
'With Allenby in Palestine', E001–2
'With Allenby in Palestine and Lawrence in Arabia', E002–5
'With Allenby in the Holy Land', F1045
'With Feisal at Court and Afield', B0013
'With Fire and Sword', D0023
'With General Allenby at Covent Garden Theatre', G0011
'With Lawrence in Arabia', E006–23, F1042, G0040, G0112, G0242, G0287, G1305, H0016
'With Lawrence of Arabia in the Ranks: Personal Recollections of a Private in the Tank Corps', G0097
'With Lawrence in the Tank Corps', G0100
'With Lawrence to Damascus', E142
'With Lawrence's Guerrillas', B0021
'With the Imperial Camel Corps', G0843
Witherby (pub), F0193
Withers, F. Leslie, H0616

Wohl, Robert, F1164
'Woman Who Taught Lawrence Calls Him "Saint"', H0882
Woman's City Club Magazine, G0104
'Women's Federation Playing "Lawrence"', G1067
Women's Weekly, H0756
'The Wonder Book of Daring Deeds', F0419
Wood, Anthony, H0778, H1168
Wood, Jack, G1449
Woodbridge News Tribune, H1014
Woodcock, George, G1484
'The Woodcut An Annual', F0379
The Wooden Boat, G1569
Woodhouse, C.M., G0734
Woodings, R.B., G0175
Woolf, Leonard, G0074
Woolf, S.J., G0251
Woolf, Virginia, F1165–6
Woolfenden, John R., H0601
Woolley, Sir C. Leonard, A001–8, F1167–72
Worcester Sunday Telegram, H1198
'Work Attempts to Assess Lawrence's Worth', H1145
'Working With Lawrence', F0267–8
'Works of Burton, Lawrence Shown', H1271
World Books (pub), A046–67, A232, F0303, F0866, F0903, F1010, F1013, F1022
World Digest, G0562, G0565
World Landmark Books, E253
'A World More Attractive', F0538
'World of the Bible', F0817
'The World of the Past', F0492
World Politics, G1007
World Pub., F0321, F0323, F0494, F0752
World Review, B0045, G0614
The World Today, G0082–3, G0097, G0110, G0120
'World War I, An Outline History', F0057
World Wide Adventure', G1352
'World Without End', F0633
'World Without Time', F0789
World's Classics, A146
'The World's Greatest Spy Stories', D0024
World's Work, B0013–5, B0019–22, G0056, G0061, G0065, G0080–81, G0093, G0101, G0132, G0134, G0137, G0140, G0695
Worms, Roger (pseudonym Roger Stéphane), A250, E171–5, E189
Worsfold, James, F0933
Wort und Wahrheit, G0628, G0695
Worth, Fred L., F1173
Wortham, Hugh E., F1174–5
Worthington, Peter, H0665, H1292
Wouk, Herman, F1176
'The Wounded Spirit', E335–6, H1169, H1172–3
'A Wreath for Lawrence', G0451
Wrench, John Evelyn, F1178–9
Wright, T., F0789
'Writer on Lawrence Sentenced in Fraud', H0384
'Writer's Collection Keeps Lawrence Legend Alive', G1259
'A Writer's Diary', F1165
'Writers' Houses', F0479
'Wrongs of the Arabs', H0104
'W.S. Churchill', F0707
'Wüste in Flammen', E366
Wyatt, Woodrow, H1250
Wylie, Jeff, H1278

X., Major F.Q., G1351
'Xenophon and the Seven Pillars of Wisdom',
  G1519

Yale, William, F1180, G0521, G0869
Yale Review, G0096, G0151, G0239, G0376, G0521,
  G1200
Yale University Press, F0831
Yardley, Michael, E398, E398a, G1630
'The Yarn of the Yeoman', F0490
Yayinevi, Muallin Fuad Gücüyener (pub), E176
'Y.B. and T.E. Lawrence', F1178
'A Year to Remember', G1058
Yeates, Victor M., F1181
'Yeats', F1069
Yeats, William Butler, F1069
Yeats-Brown, Francis, F1178, G0257, G0380, G0395
Yeoman, G0843
'Yes, There is a Lowell Thomas', G0957
Yiddisher Kemfer, G0771
'Yon's Lawrence of Arabia', H0923
Yorkshire Daily News, H0151
Yorkshire Evening News, H0289
Yorkshire Evening Post, H0288, H0615, H0830,
  H0832, H0834, H0837
Yorkshire Post, H0620, H0763, H1149, H1203,
  H1280
Yoseloff (pub), F0722
Young, Sir Hubert, F1182, G0050
'The Young Lawrence of Arabia', E227-9, E375,
  G0945-6, G0953, H0590
Youngstown Vindicator, H1291
Youth's Companion, G0016, G0019, G0029, G0031,
  G0051

'"Yunost" Pavla Stroganovai Drugia
  Charaktoristiki', F0009

Z., E., H0898
Z Magazine, G1628
'Zarves', F0271
Zec, Donald, H0642, H0647
Zehren, Erich, F1183
Zeine, Zeine W., F1184-5
Die Zeit, H0886, H0909
Zeitschrift für Politik, G0416
Zeitschrift für Religions und Geistsgeschichte,
  G0603
'Zekriah an Althawara Al Arabia Al-Koubra
  Marshourat Malfteh', F0008
'Zenobia of Palmyra', F1084
'Zeugen Unserer Zeit: T.E. Lawrence und J.
  Ortega Y Gasset', G1035
Zhantieva, Dilyara, G0947
Ziff, William B., F1186
Ziman, H.D., H0477
Zinsser, William K., F1187, G0959
'The Zionist Connection', F0658
'Zionist Position Delimited in the Knightley and
  Simpson New Volume Describing "The Secret
  Lives of Lawrence of Arabia"', H1094-5, H1121
'The Zondervan Pictorial Bible Atlas', F0103
Zondervan Press, F0103
'Zuerischer Zeitung', H0015
zur Nedden, Otto C.A., E218
Zweig, Paul, F1188, G1530
'Zwischen Traum und Tat', F0951
Zytaruk, George J., F1189